PHILIP'S

STREET ATLAS
Derbyshire

Buxton, Chesterfield, Derby, Long Eaton, Matlock, Swadlincote

www.philips-maps.co.uk
First published in 1995 by Philip's,
Philip's, a division of
Octopus Publishing Group Ltd
www.octopusbooks.co.uk
Endeavour House
189 Shaftesbury Avenue
London WC2H 8JY
An Hachette UK Company
www.hachette.co.uk
Fourth colour edition 2010
Fourth impression 2014

DBYDA

978-1-84907-083-6 (spiral)

© Philip's 2010

 Ordnance Survey®

This product includes mapping data licensed
from Ordnance Survey® with the permission
of the Controller of Her Majesty's Stationery
Office. © Crown copyright 2010. All rights
reserved. Licence number 100011710.

Contents

II Mobile safety cameras

III Major administrative and Postcode boundaries

IV Key to map pages

VI Route planning

X Key to map symbols

1 **Street maps** at 3½ inches to 1 mile

266 **Street maps** of Chesterfield and Derby at 7 inches to 1 mile

268 **Index** of towns, villages, streets, hospitals, industrial estates, railway stations, schools, shopping centres, universities and places of interest

Mobile safety cameras

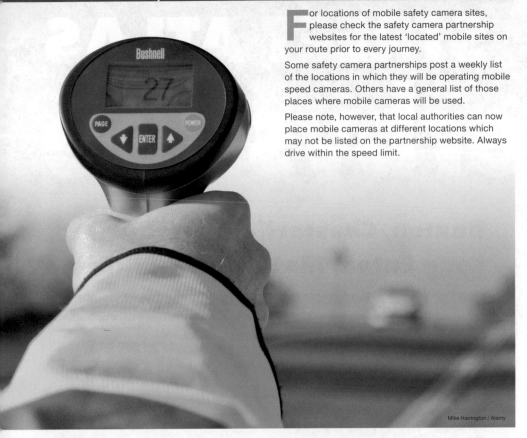

Mike Harrington / Alamy

For locations of mobile safety camera sites, please check the safety camera partnership websites for the latest 'located' mobile sites on your route prior to every journey.

Some safety camera partnerships post a weekly list of the locations in which they will be operating mobile speed cameras. Others have a general list of those places where mobile cameras will be used.

Please note, however, that local authorities can now place mobile cameras at different locations which may not be listed on the partnership website. Always drive within the speed limit.

Useful websites

Derby and Derbyshire Road Safety Partnership
http://www.slowitdown.co.uk

Cheshire Road Safety Group
www.mysaferroads.org.uk

Greater Manchester Casualty Reduction Partnership
www.drivesafe.org.uk

Leicester, Leicestershire & Rutland Safety Camera Scheme
www.speedorsafety.com

Nottinghamshire Safety Camera Partnership
www.nottspeed.com

South Yorkshire Safety Camera Partnership
www.safetycamera.org

Staffordshire Safer Roads Partnership
www.staffssaferroads.co.uk

West Yorkshire Casualty Reduction Partnership
www.safetycameraswestyorkshire.co.uk

Further information
www.dvla.gov.uk
http://think.direct.gov.uk/
www.dft.gov.uk
www.roadsafe.com

Major administrative and Postcode boundaries

County and unitary authority boundaries
Postcode boundaries
Area covered by this atlas

SD
Oldham
SE
Kirklees
Holme
HD9
Barnsley
SK15
Tameside
SJ
SK
SK13
Sheffield
SK14
Glossop
Compstall
90
Derwent
S6
Marple
SK6
Sheffield
Rotherham
SK22
Hayfield
High Peak
S33
S2
S13
S14
Sheffield
Stockport
New Mills
Edale
Bamford
S10
S12
Disley
Chinley
Hope
S8
S20
S26
S81
SK12
Bradwell
Hathersage
S11
S17
Killamarsh
Whaley
Bridge
Chapel-en-
le-Frith
S32
S21
Whitwell
SK23
Eyam
Dronfield
S80
Cheshire
East
SK10
Tideswell
S18
S41
Staveley
S43
Clowne
Buxton
DE45
Chesterfield
SK11
SK17
Taddington
Baslow
Chesterfield
Bolsover
70
Holymoorside
S40
Bolsover
Bakewell
S42
S44
NG20
North East
Derbyshire
Shirebrook
Longnor
Darley
Dale
NG19
Mansfield
Woodhouse
Youlgreave
S45
Clay Cross
Derbyshire
60
Hartington
Matlock
NG17
Derbyshire
Dales
DE4
Middleton
Tibshelf
DE55
Crich
Alfreton
Nottinghamshire
Parwich
Wirksworth
Pinxton
Ripley
50
Amber
Valley
DE5
NG16
Ashbourne
Belper
Heanor
Eastwood
DE56
DE75
Duffield
City of
Nottingham
Denstone
DE6
Little
Eaton
DE7
Ilkeston
40
ST14
Shirley
DE22
Erewash
NG9
DE1
Ockbrook
Stapleford
DE3
Derby
Long
Eaton
Sudbury
DE23
City of
DE72
NG10
Etwall
Derby
Shardlow
NG11
ST14
Hilton
DE65
DE24
Egginton
South
Weston-on-
Trent
DE74
Tutbury
Derbyshire
Castle
Donington
DE13
DE73
Ticknall
DE15
Staffordshire
DE13
DE14
Swadlincote
Leicestershire
DE11
LE65
Linton
DE12
Netherseal
B79
Leicestershire

Scale
0   5   10   15 km
0   5   10 miles

SJ
SK

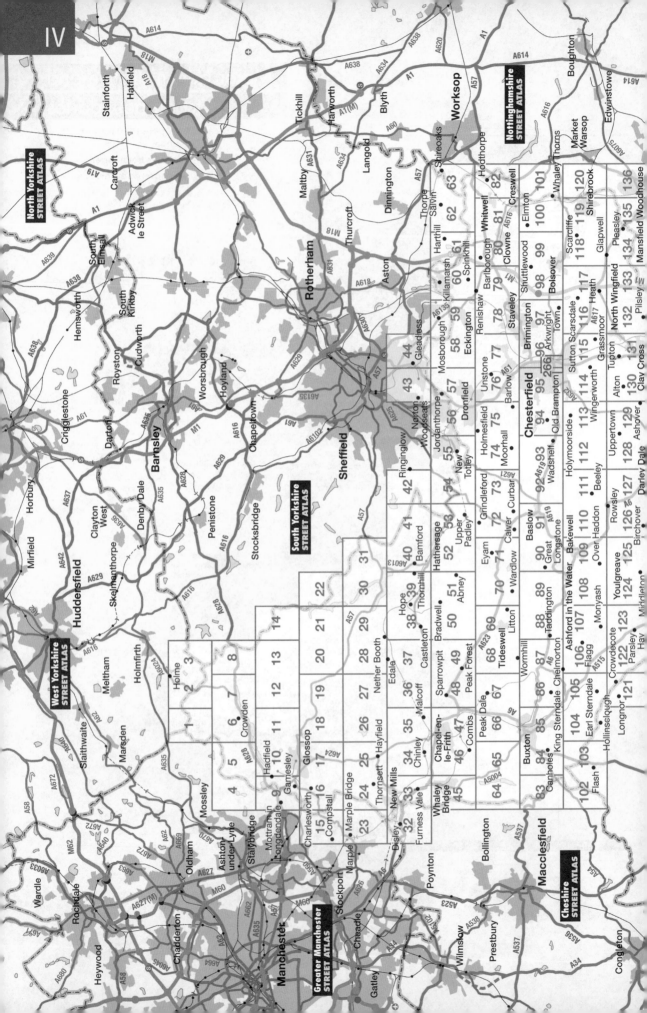

Key to map pages

123	Map pages at 3½ inches to 1 mile
266	Map pages at 7 inches to 1 mile

Leicestershire STREET ATLAS

Warwickshire STREET ATLAS

Staffordshire STREET ATLAS

Scale

20 km

10 miles

15

10

5

Route planning

Scale

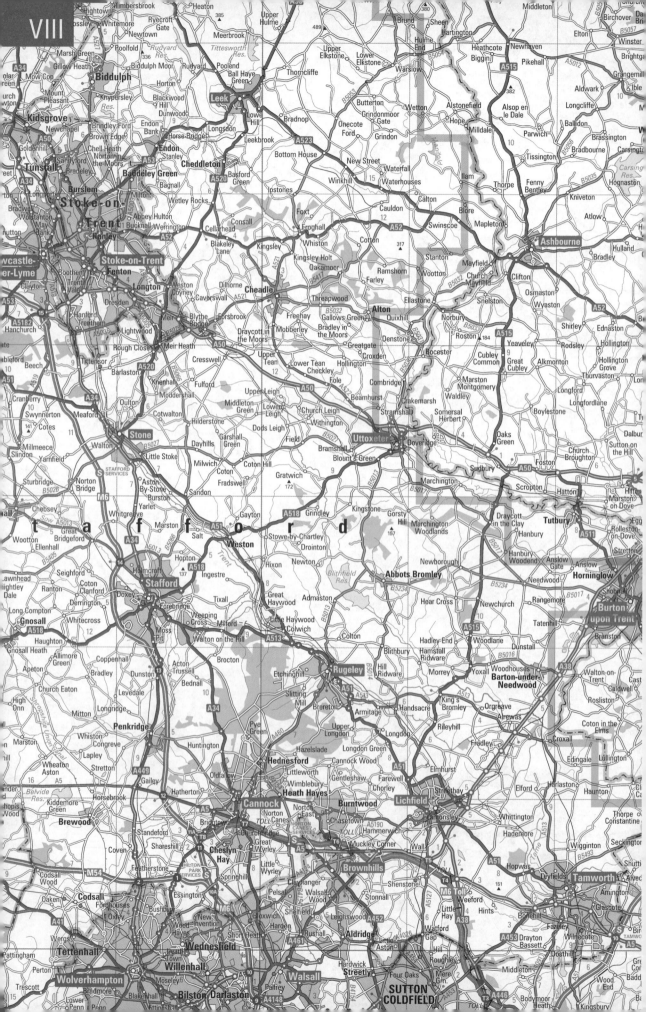

Key to map symbols

	Motorway with junction number (22)
	Primary route – dual/single carriageway
	A road – dual/single carriageway
	B road – dual/single carriageway
	Minor road – dual/single carriageway
	Other minor road – dual/single carriageway
	Road under construction
	Tunnel, covered road
	Speed cameras – single, multiple
	Rural track, private road or narrow road in urban area
	Gate or obstruction to traffic – restrictions may not apply at all times or to all vehicles
	Path, bridleway, byway open to all traffic, restricted byway
	Pedestrianised area
BS22	Postcode boundaries
	County or unitary authority boundaries
	Railway with station
	Tunnel
	Railway under construction
	Metro station
	Private railway station
	Miniature railway
	Tramway, tramway under construction
	Tram stop, tram stop under construction
	Bus, coach station

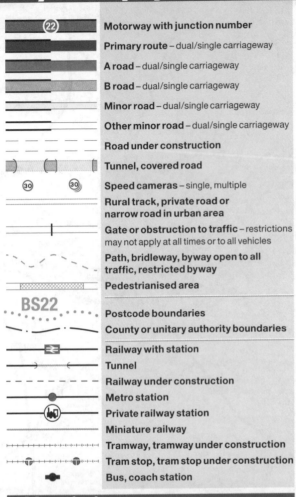

◆	Ambulance station
◆	Coastguard station
◆	Fire station
◆	Police station
✚	Accident and Emergency entrance to hospital
H	Hospital
+	Place of worship
i	Information centre – open all year
🛒 P	Shopping centre, parking
P&R PO	Park and Ride, Post Office
⚑ 🚐	Camping site, caravan site
▶ ✕	Golf course, picnic site
Church ROMAN FORT	Non-Roman antiquity, Roman antiquity
Univ	Important buildings, schools, colleges, universities and hospitals
	Woods, built-up area

River Medway	Water name
	River, weir
	Stream
	Canal, lock, tunnel
	Water
	Tidal water

58 ◀ **87**

246

Adjoining page indicators and overlap bands – the colour of the arrow and band indicates the scale of the adjoining or overlapping page (see scales below)

The dark grey border on the inside edge of some pages indicates that the mapping does not continue onto the adjacent page

The small numbers around the edges of the maps identify the 1-kilometre National Grid lines

Abbreviations

Abbreviation	Full	Abbreviation	Full
Acad	Academy	Meml	Memorial
Allot Gdns	Allotments	Mon	Monument
Cemy	Cemetery	Mus	Museum
C Ctr	Civic centre	Obsy	Observatory
CH	Club house	Pal	Royal palace
Coll	College	PH	Public house
Crem	Crematorium	Recn Gd	Recreation ground
Ent	Enterprise	Resr	Reservoir
Ex H	Exhibition hall	Ret Pk	Retail park
Ind Est	Industrial Estate	Sch	School
IRB Sta	Inshore rescue boat station	Sh Ctr	Shopping centre
Inst	Institute	TH	Town hall / house
Ct	Law court	Trad Est	Trading estate
L Ctr	Leisure centre	Univ	University
LC	Level crossing	W Twr	Water tower
Liby	Library	Wks	Works
Mkt	Market	YH	Youth hostel

Enlarged maps only

	Railway or bus station building
	Place of interest
	Parkland

The map scale on the pages numbered in blue is 3½ inches to 1 mile
5.52 cm to 1 km • 1 : 18 103

0	¼ mile	½ mile	¾ mile	1 mile
0	250m	500m	750m	1km

The map scale on the pages numbered in red is 7 inches to 1 mile
11.04 cm to 1 km • 1 : 9051

0	220yds	440yds	660yds	½ mile
0	125m	250m	375m	500m

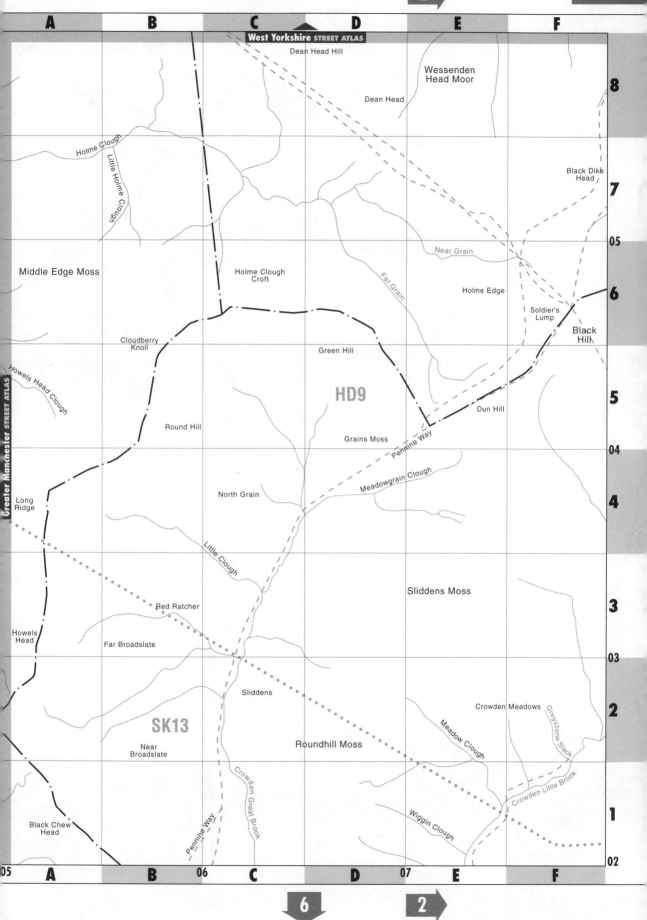

West Yorkshire STREET ATLAS

Greater Manchester STREET ATLAS

A   B   C   D   E   F

8
Wessenden
Head Moor

Dean Head Hill
Dean Head

7
Black Dike
Head

Holme Clough
Little Holme Clough

05

Middle Edge Moss
Holme Clough
Croft
Near Grain
Holme Edge

6
Far Grain
Soldier's
Lump
Black
Hill

Cloudberry
Knoll
Green Hill

Howels Head Clough
HD9

5
Round Hill
Dun Hill

Grains Moss
Pennine Way
04

Long
Ridge
North Grain
Meadowgrain Clough

4

Little Clough

Red Ratcher
Sliddens Moss
3

Howels
Head
Far Broadslate
03

SK13
Sliddens
Crowden Meadows
2

Greystone Slack

Near
Broadslate
Roundhill Moss
Meadow Clough

Crowden Little Brook

Pennine Way
Crowden Great Brook
Wiggin Clough

1

Black Chew
Head

02

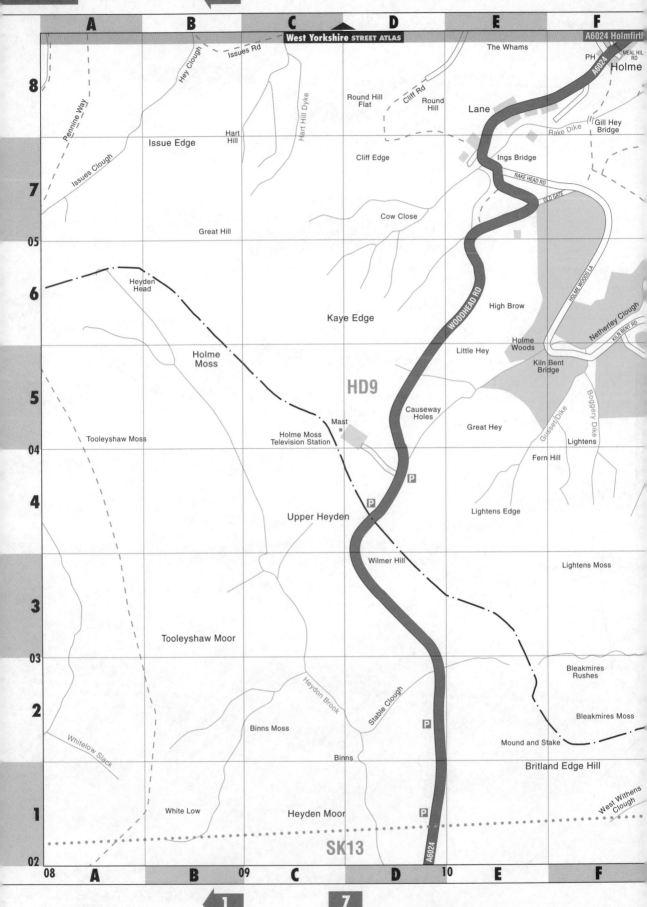

8

The Whams

PH

MEAL HIL RD

A6024

Holme

Round Hill Flat

Cliff Rd

Round Hill

Lane

Rake Dike

Gill Hey Bridge

Pennine Way

Hey Clough

Issues Rd

Hart Hill Dyke

Issue Edge

Hart Hill

Cliff Edge

Ings Bridge

RAKE HEAD RD

Issues Clough

7

OLD GATE

Great Hill

Cow Close

HOLME WOODS LA

05

Heyden Head

Netherley Clough

KILN BENT RD

6

Kaye Edge

High Brow

Holme Moss

Little Hey

Holme Woods

HD9

Kiln Bent Bridge

Boggery Dike

Gussel Dike

5

WOODHEAD RD

Causeway Holes

Great Hey

Lightens

Tooleyshaw Moss

Mast

Holme Moss Television Station

Fern Hill

04

P

P

4

Upper Heyden

Lightens Edge

Lightens Moss

Wilmer Hill

3

Tooleyshaw Moor

03

Bleakmires Rushes

Heyden Brook

Stable Clough

2

Binns Moss

P

Bleakmires Moss

Whitelow Slack

Binns

Mound and Stake

Britland Edge Hill

1

White Low

Heyden Moor

P

West Withens Clough

A6024

SK13

02

08

A B 09 C D 10 E F

1

7

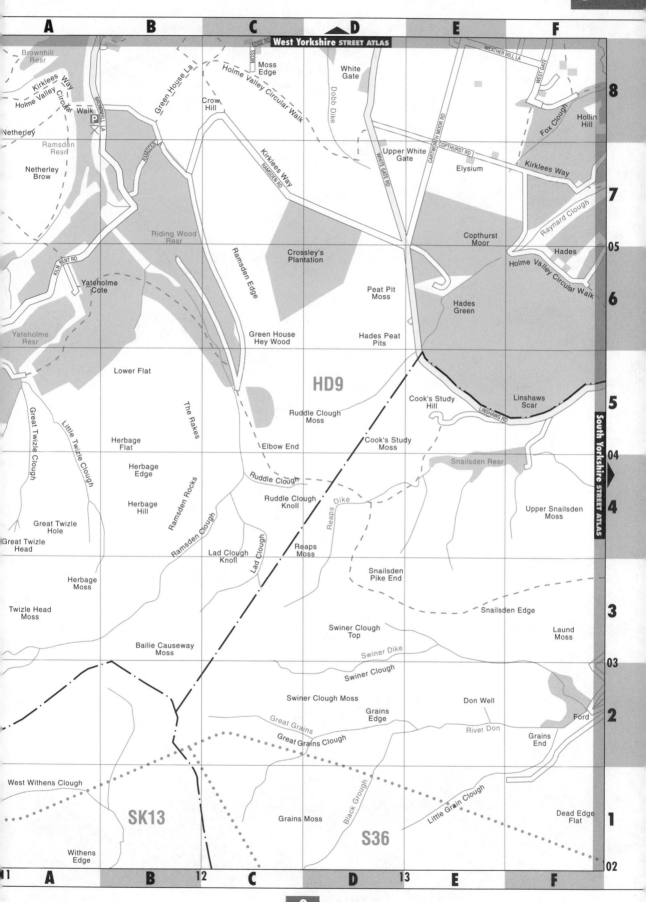

West Yorkshire STREET ATLAS

South Yorkshire STREET ATLAS

Brownhill Resr
Kirklees Way
Holme Valley Circular Walk
Netherley
Ramsden Resr
Netherley Brow
BROWNHILL LA
RAMSDEN
Green House La
Crow Hill
EDGE RD
MOSS
Moss Edge
Holme Valley Circular Walk
White Gate
Dobb Dike
Upper White Gate
WHITE GATE RD
CARTWORTH MOOR RD
COPTHURST RD
WEATHER HILL LA
WEST GATE
Fox Clough
Hollin Hill
Elysium
Kirklees Way
Raynard Clough
Hades
Copthurst Moor
Holme Valley Circular Walk
Riding Wood Resr
Ramsden Edge
Crossley's Plantation
Peat Pit Moss
Hades Green
KILN BENT RD
Yateholme Cote
RAMSDEN RD
KIRKLEES WAY
Green House Hey Wood
Hades Peat Pits
Yateholme Resr
Lower Flat
The Rakes
Ruddle Clough Moss
Cook's Study Hill
Linshaws Scar
LINSHAWS RD
HD9
Great Twizle Clough
Little Twizle Clough
Herbage Flat
Elbow End
Cook's Study Moss
Snailsden Resr
Great Twizle Hole
Great Twizle Head
Herbage Edge
Ramsden Rocks
Herbage Hill
Ruddle Clough
Ruddle Clough Knoll
Reaps Dike
Upper Snailsden Moss
Ramsden Clough
Lad Clough Knoll
Lad Clough
Reaps Moss
Snailsden Pike End
Herbage Moss
Twizle Head Moss
Snailsden Edge
Laund Moss
Bailie Causeway Moss
Swiner Clough Top
Swiner Dike
Swiner Clough
Swiner Clough Moss
Don Well
Grains Edge
River Don
Grains End
Ford
Great Grains
Great Grains Clough
West Withens Clough
Black Grough
Little Grain Clough
Dead Edge Flat
SK13
Grains Moss
S36
Withens Edge

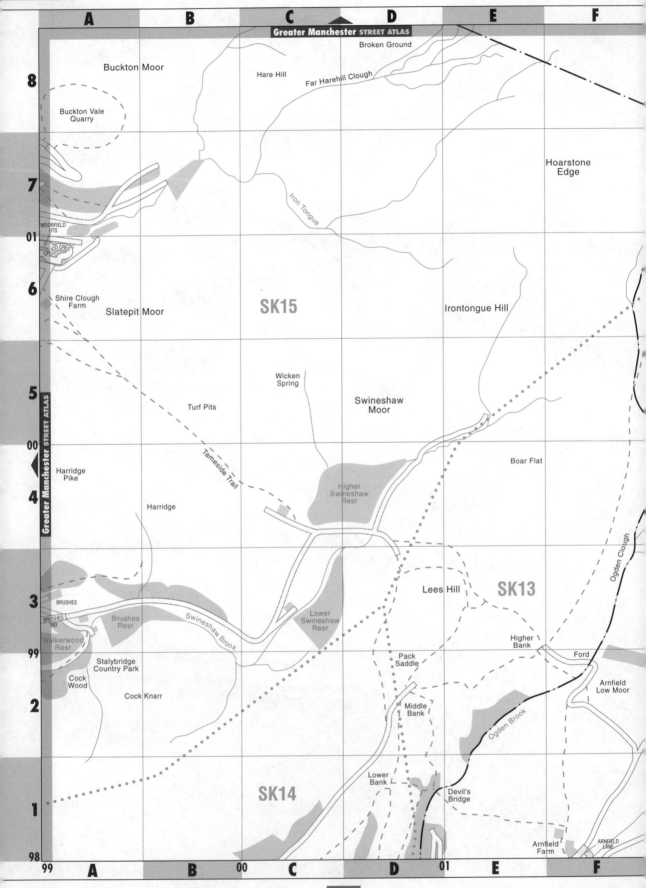

Broken Ground

Buckton Moor

Hare Hill

Far Harehill Clough

8

Buckton Vale
Quarry

Hoarstone
Edge

7

Iron Tongue

MOORFIELD
HTS

01

CALICO CRES

6

Shire Clough
Farm

Slatepit Moor

SK15

Irontongue Hill

Wicken
Spring

5

Turf Pits

Swineshaw
Moor

Boar Flat

Tameside Trail

00

Harridge
Pike

4

Harridge

Higher
Swineshaw
Resr

Ogden Clough

Lees Hill

SK13

3

BRUSHES

BRUSHES
RD

Brushes
Resr

Swineshaw Brook

Lower
Swineshaw
Resr

Higher
Bank

Ford

Walkerwood
Resr

Pack
Saddle

99

Stalybridge
Country Park

Arnfield
Low Moor

Cock
Wood

Cock Knarr

Middle
Bank

2

Ogden Brook

SK14

Lower
Bank

Devil's
Bridge

1

Arnfield
Farm

ARNFIELD
LANE

98

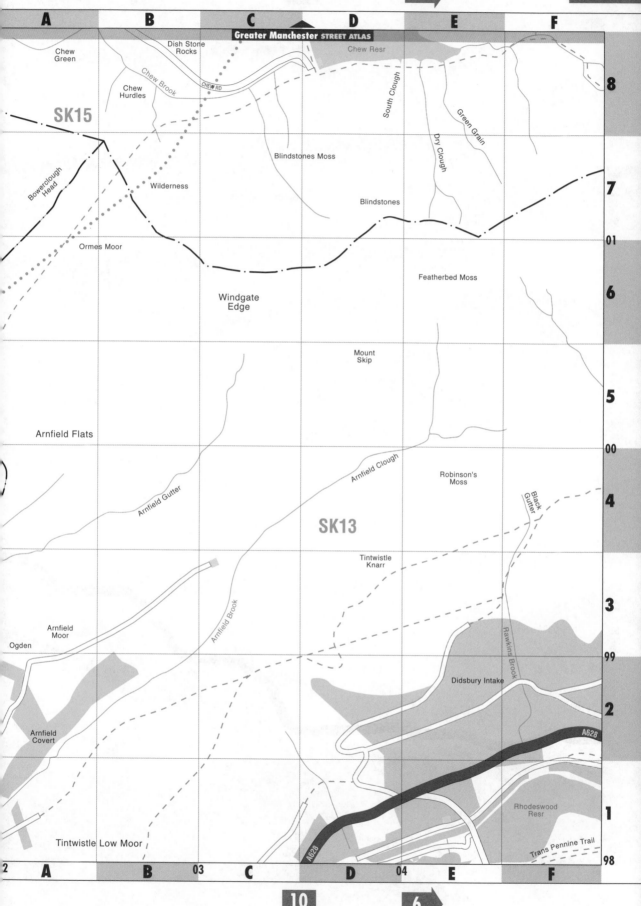

Chew Green

Dish Stone Rocks

Chew Resr

Chew Brook

CHEW RD

Chew Hurdles

SK15

South Clough

Green Grain

Blindstones Moss

Dry Clough

Bowerclough Head

Wilderness

Blindstones

8

7

01

Ormes Moor

Windgate Edge

Featherbed Moss

6

Mount Skip

5

Arnfield Flats

00

Arnfield Clough

Robinson's Moss

Black Gutter

Arnfield Gutter

SK13

4

Tintwistle Knarr

3

Arnfield Brook

Arnfield Moor

Ogden

99

Didsbury Intake

Rawkins Brook

2

Arnfield Covert

A628

Rhodeswood Resr

1

Tintwistle Low Moor

A628

Trans Pennine Trail

98

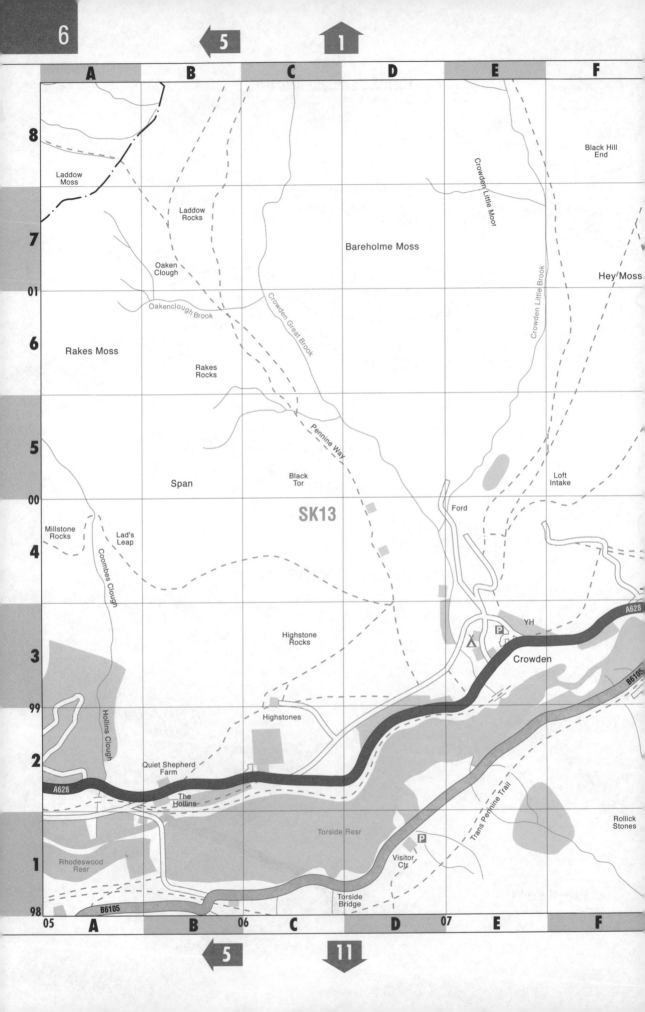

A B C D E F

8

Laddow
Moss

Laddow
Rocks

7

Oaken
Clough

Bareholme Moss

Crowden Little Moor

Black Hill
End

Hey Moss

01

Oakenclough Brook

Crowden Great Brook

Crowden Little Brook

6

Rakes Moss

Rakes
Rocks

5

Span

Black
Tor

Pennine Way

Loft
Intake

00

SK13

Ford

4

Millstone
Rocks

Lad's
Leap

Coombes Clough

3

Highstone
Rocks

Highstones

Crowden

YH

A628

B6105

99

Hollins Clough

Quiet Shepherd
Farm

2

The
Hollins

A628

Trans Pennine Trail

Rollick
Stones

1

Rhodeswood
Resr

Torside Resr

Visitor
Ctr

98

B6105

Torside
Bridge

05 A B 06 C D 07 E F

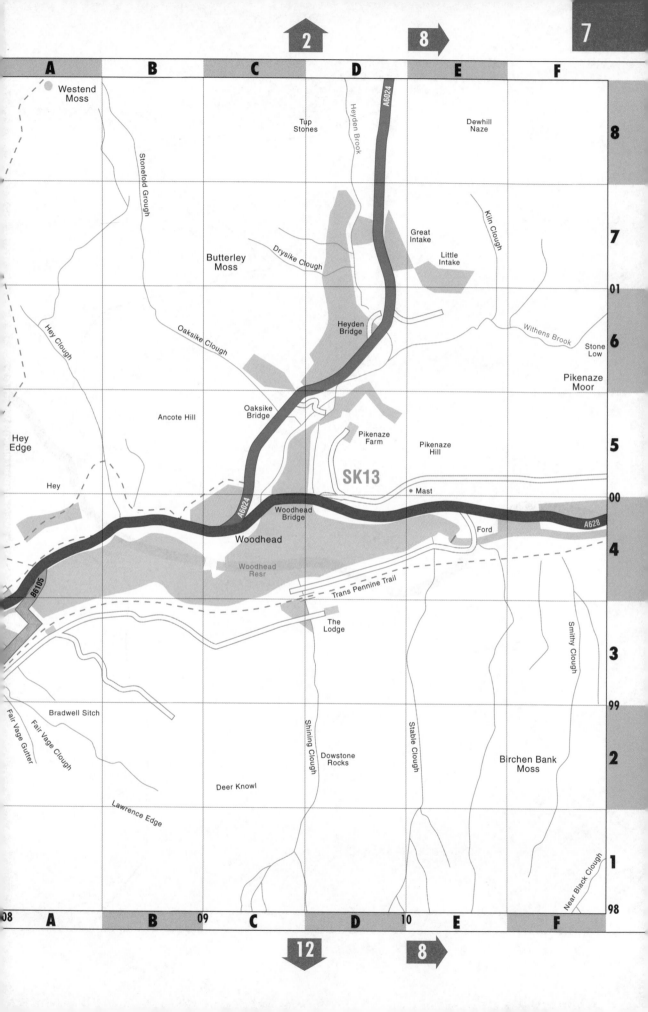

A B C D E F

8 Westend Moss

Tup Stones

Heyden Brook

A6024

Dewhill Naze

7 Stonefold Grough

Butterley Moss

Drysike Clough

Great Intake

Little Intake

Kiln Clough

01

6 Hey Clough

Oaksike Clough

Heyden Bridge

Withens Brook

Stone Low

Pikenaze Moor

5 Hey Edge

Hey

Ancote Hill

Oaksike Bridge

A6024

Pikenaze Farm

Pikenaze Hill

SK13

Mast

00

Woodhead Bridge

Woodhead

Ford

A628

4 B6105

Woodhead Resr

Trans Pennine Trail

The Lodge

Smithy Clough

3 Bradwell Sitch

99

Fair Vage Gutter

Fair Vage Clough

Shining Clough

Dowstone Rocks

Stable Clough

Birchen Bank Moss

2 Deer Knowl

Lawrence Edge

Near Black Clough

1

98

A   B   C   D   E   F

8

7

01

6

5

00

4

3

99

2

1

98

11   A   B   12   C   D   13   E   F

Withens Moor

Withens Brook

Cat Clough

Dead Edge End

Upper Dead Edge

Dead Edge Moss

Wike Head

Upper Head Moss

Upper Head

Pillar

Smallden Clough Head

Red Hole

Air Shaft

Wike

Wike Edge

Upper Head Dike

Round Hill

Air Shaft

Salter's Brook

Longside Moss

S36

Pikenaze Moor

Audernshaw Clough

Ford

Woodhead Tunnel (dis)

Hawthorn Clough

Netherhead Clough

Longside Edge

Salter's Brook Bridge

P

Salter's Brook Moss

Salter's Brook

A628

Ironbower Moss

SK13

Longdendale Trail

Long Side

Longside End

Round Hill Nick

P

A628

River Etherow

Ford

Birchen Bank Wood

Shooting Cabins

Swan Clough

Rose Clough

Far Small Clough

Near Small Clough

Middle Small Clough

Near Black Clough

Middle Black Clough

Far Black Clough

Middle Small Clough Head

Far Small Clough Head

Featherbed Moss

Swains Head

Dean Head

River Derwent

A-Z Barnsley   South Yorkshire STREET ATLAS

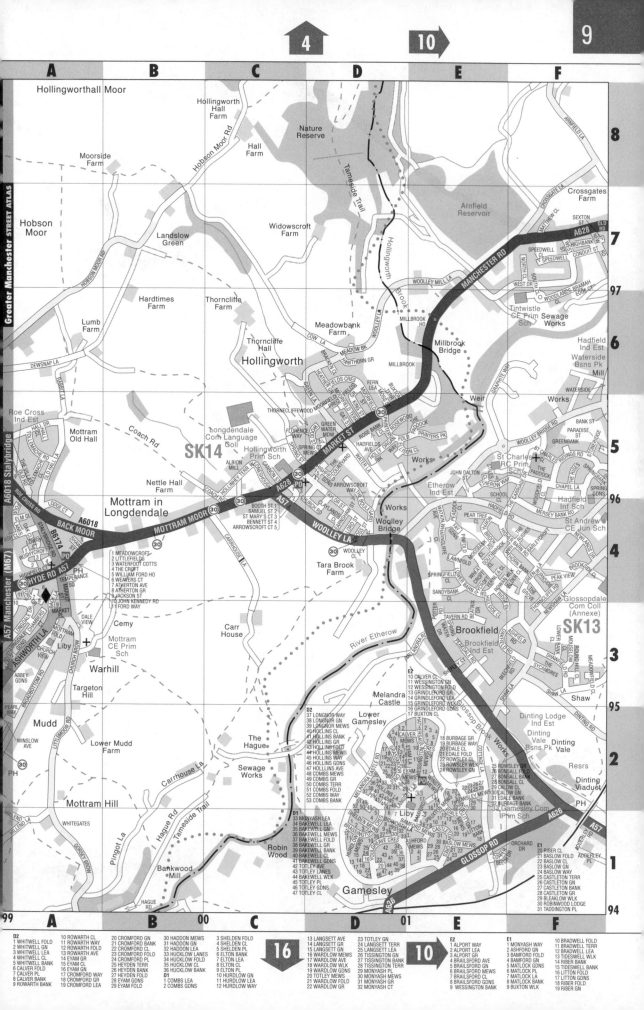

Greater Manchester STREET ATLAS

A57 Manchester (M67)   A6018 Stalybridge

D2
1 WHITWELL FOLD
2 WHITWELL GN
3 WHITWELL LEA
4 WHITWELL CL
5 WHITWELL BANK
6 CALVER FOLD
7 CALVER PL
8 CALVER BANK
9 ROWARTH BANK

10 ROWARTH CL
11 ROWARTH WAY
12 ROWARTH FOLD
13 ROWARTH AVE
14 EYAM GR
15 EYAM CL
16 EYAM GN
17 CROMFORD WAY
18 EYAM GDNS
19 CROMFORD LEA

20 CROMFORD GN
21 CROMFORD BANK
22 CROMFORD CL
23 CROMFORD FOLD
24 CROMFORD PL
25 HEYDEN TERR
26 HEYDEN MEWS
27 HEYDEN FOLD
28 EYAM GDNS
29 EYAM FOLD

30 HADDON MEWS
31 HADDON BANK
32 HADDON LEA
33 HUCKLOW CL
34 HUCKLOW LANES
35 HUCKLOW
36 HUCKLOW MEWS
D1
1 COMBS LEA
2 COMBS GDNS

3 SHELDEN FOLD
4 SHELDEN CL
5 SHELDEN PL
6 ELTON BANK
7 ELTON GR
8 ELTON CL
9 ELTON PL
10 HURDLOW GN
11 HURDLOW LEA
12 HURDLOW WAY

13 LANGSETT AVE
14 LANGSETT GR
15 LANGSETT GN
16 TISSINGTON CL
17 WARDLOW GR
18 WARDLOW WLK
19 WARDLOW GDNS
20 TOTLEY MEWS
21 WARDLOW FOLD
22 WARDLOW GR

23 TOTLEY GN
24 LANGSETT TERR
25 LANGSETT LEA
26 TISSINGTON CL
27 TISSINGTON BANK
28 TISSINGTON TERR
29 MONYASH PL
30 MONYASH MEWS
31 MONYASH GR
32 MONYASH CT

E2
1 ALPORT WAY
2 ALPORT LEA
3 ALPORT GR
4 BRAILSFORD AVE
5 BRAILSFORD GN
6 BRAILSFORD TERR
7 BRAILSFORD CL
8 BRAILSFORD GDNS
9 WESSINGTON BANK

E1
1 MONYASH WAY
2 ASHFORD GN
3 BAMFORD FOLD
4 BAMFORD GN
5 MATLOCK GDNS
6 MATLOCK CL
7 MATLOCK LA
8 MATLOCK BANK
9 BUXTON WLK

10 BRADWELL FOLD
11 BRADWELL TERR
12 BRADWELL LEA
13 TIDESWELL WLK
14 RIBER BANK
15 TIDESWELL GR
16 LITTON FOLD
17 LITTON GDNS
18 RIBER FOLD
19 RIBER GN

D2
37 LONGNOR WAY
38 LONGNOR GN
39 LONGNOR MEWS
40 HOLLINS CL
41 HOLLINS BANK
42 HOLLINS GR
43 HOLLINS FOLD
44 HOLLINS MEWS
45 ROWSLEY WAY
46 HOLLINS GDNS
47 HOLLINS AVE
48 COMBS MEWS
49 COMBS GR
50 COMBS TERR
51 COMBS FOLD
52 COMBS WAY
53 COMBS BANK

D1
33 MONYASH LEA
34 BAKEWELL LEA
35 BAKEWELL GN
36 BAKEWELL MEWS
37 BAKEWELL FOLD
38 BAKEWELL BANK
39 BAKEWELL BANK
40 BAKEWELL CL
41 BAKEWELL GDNS
42 TOTLEY AVE
43 TOTLEY FOLD
44 BAKEWELL WLK
45 TOTLEY GDNS
46 TOTLEY GDNS
47 TOTLEY CL

E2
10 CALVER CL
11 WESSINGTON GN
12 WESSINGTON FOLD
13 GRINDLEFORD GR
14 GRINDLEFORD LEA
15 GRINDLEFORD WLK
16 GRINDLEFORD GDNS
17 BUXTON CL
18 BURBAGE GR
19 BURBAGE WAY
20 EDALE CL
21 EDALE FOLD
22 ROWSLEY WLK
24 ROWSLEY GN
25 ROWSLEY GR
26 BONSALL FOLD
27 BONSALL CL
28 BONSALL GN
29 EDALE BANK
30 CALDW GN
31 EDALE BANK
32 BURBAGE BANK

E1
20 RIBER CL
21 BASLOW FOLD
22 BASLOW GN
23 BASLOW GN
24 BASLOW WAY
25 CASTLETON TERR
26 CASTLETON GN
27 CASTLETON BANK
28 CASTLETON GR
29 BLEAKLOW WLK
30 ROBINWOOD LODGE
31 TADDINGTON PL

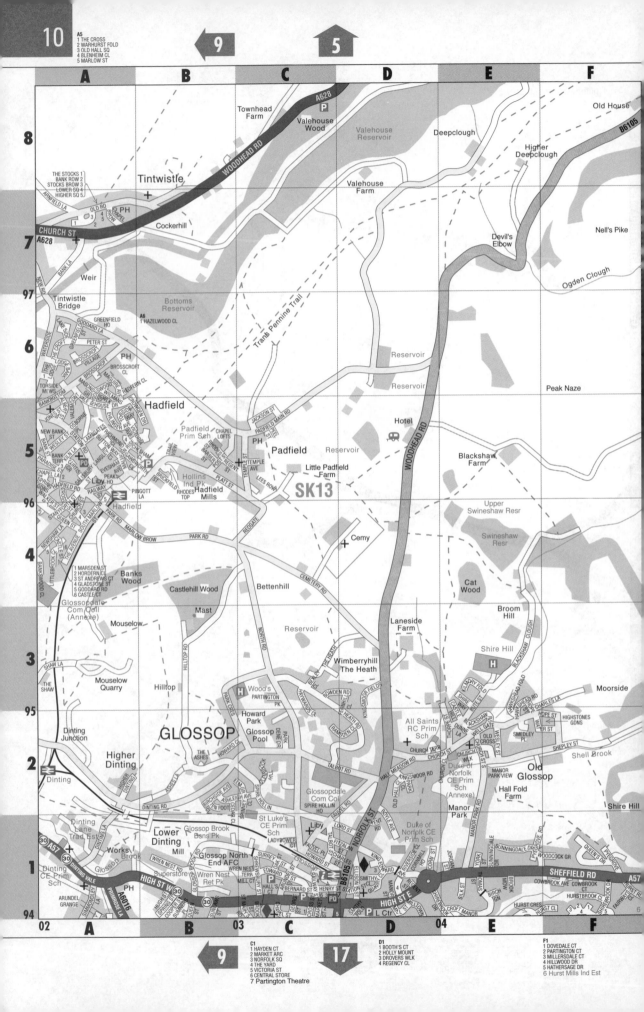

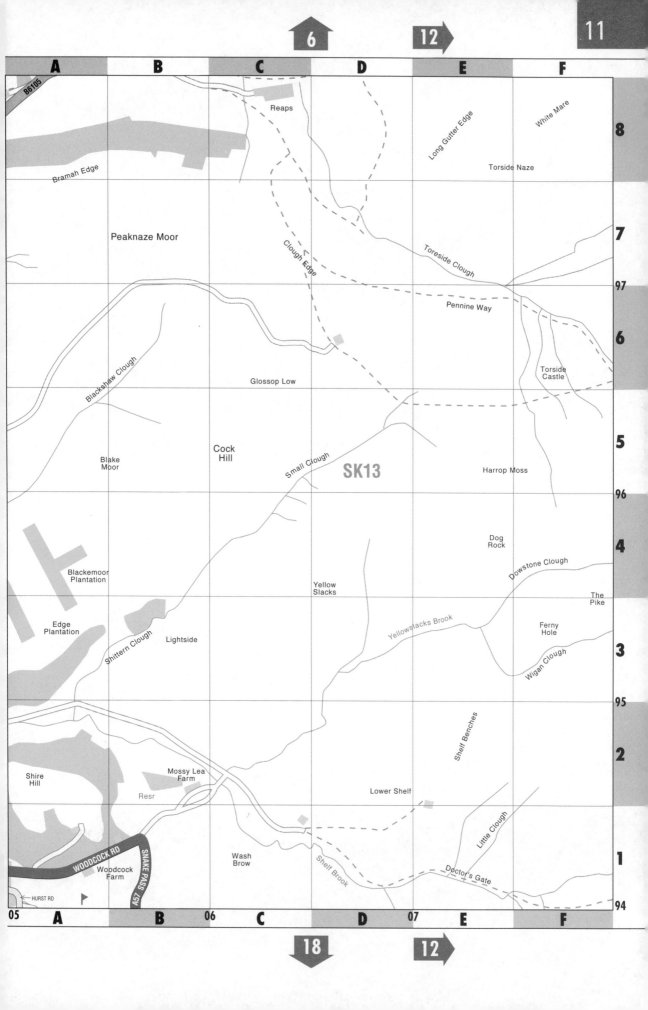

A   B   C   D   E   F

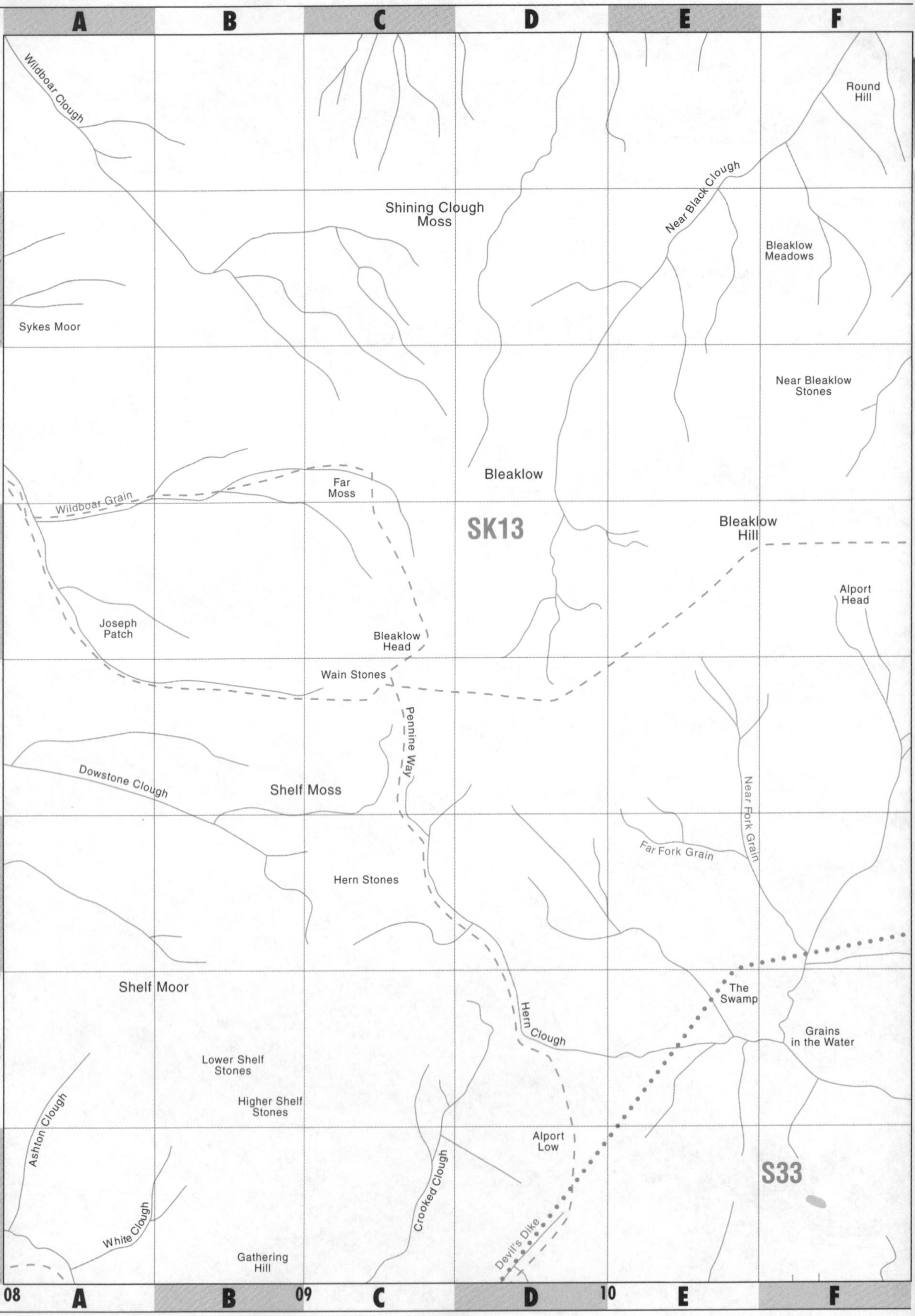

8

Wildboar Clough

Round
Hill

Shining Clough
Moss

Near Black Clough

Bleaklow
Meadows

7

Sykes Moor

97

Near Bleaklow
Stones

6

Bleaklow

Far
Moss

Wildboar Grain

SK13

Bleaklow
Hill

Alport
Head

5

Joseph
Patch

Bleaklow
Head

96

Wain Stones

Pennine Way

4

Dowstone Clough

Shelf Moss

Near Fork Grain

Far Fork Grain

Hern Stones

3

95

Shelf Moor

The
Swamp

Grains
in the Water

2

Lower Shelf
Stones

Hern Clough

Higher Shelf
Stones

Alport
Low

S33

1

Ashton Clough

Crooked Clough

White Clough

Devil's Dike

Gathering
Hill

94

08   A   B   09   C   D   10   E   F

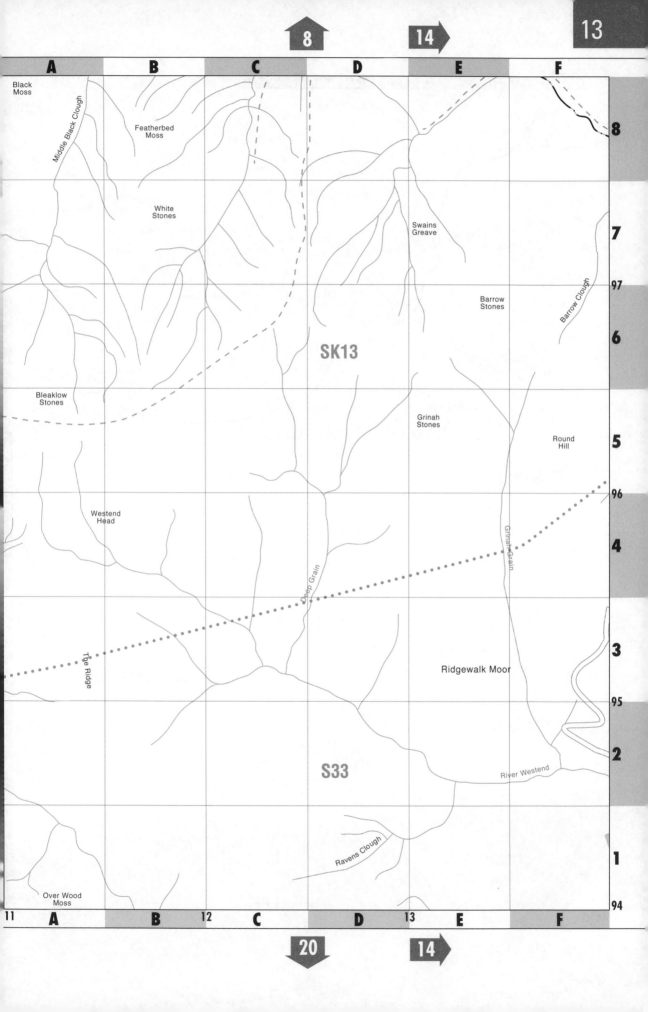

Black
Moss

Middle Black Clough

Featherbed
Moss

White
Stones

Swains
Greave

8

7

Barrow
Stones

Barrow Clough

97

6

SK13

Bleaklow
Stones

Grinah
Stones

Round
Hill

5

96

Westend
Head

Grinah Grain

4

Deep Grain

The Ridge

Ridgewalk Moor

3

95

2

S33

River Westend

Ravens Clough

1

Over Wood
Moss

94

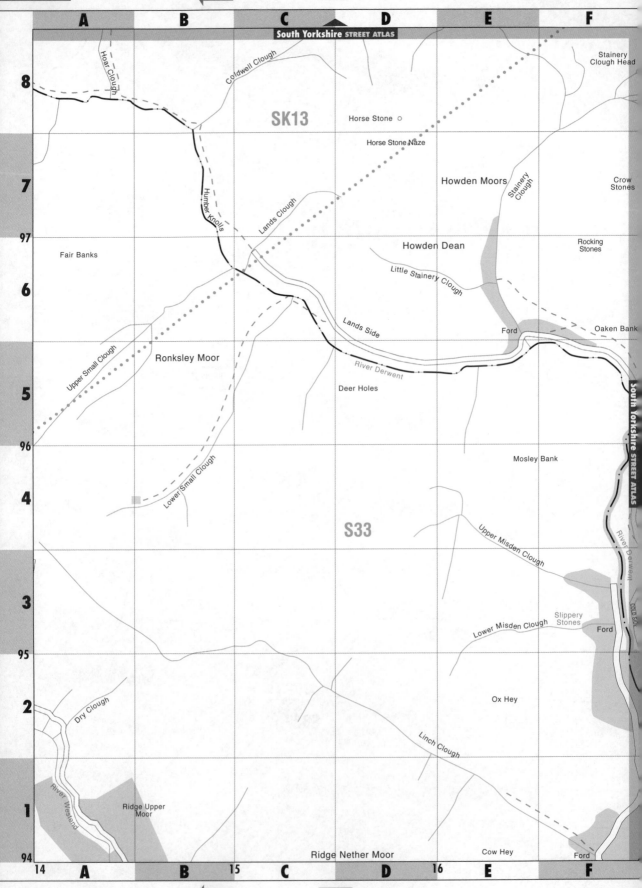

South Yorkshire STREET ATLAS

A **B** **C** **D** **E** **F**

Hoar Clough

Coldwell Clough

Stainery Clough Head

8

SK13

Horse Stone ○

Horse Stone Naze

7

Howden Moors

Stainery Clough

Crow Stones

Humber Knolls

Lands Clough

97

Fair Banks

Howden Dean

Rocking Stones

Little Stainery Clough

6

Upper Small Clough

Ronksley Moor

Lands Side

Ford

Oaken Bank

River Derwent

5

Deer Holes

96

Mosley Bank

Lower Small Clough

4

S33

Upper Misden Clough

River Derwent

3

Slippery Stones

Cold Side

Lower Misden Clough

Ford

95

Dry Clough

Ox Hey

2

Linch Clough

River Westend

1

Ridge Upper Moor

94

Ridge Nether Moor

Cow Hey

Ford

14 **A** **B** **15** **C** **D** **16** **E** **F**

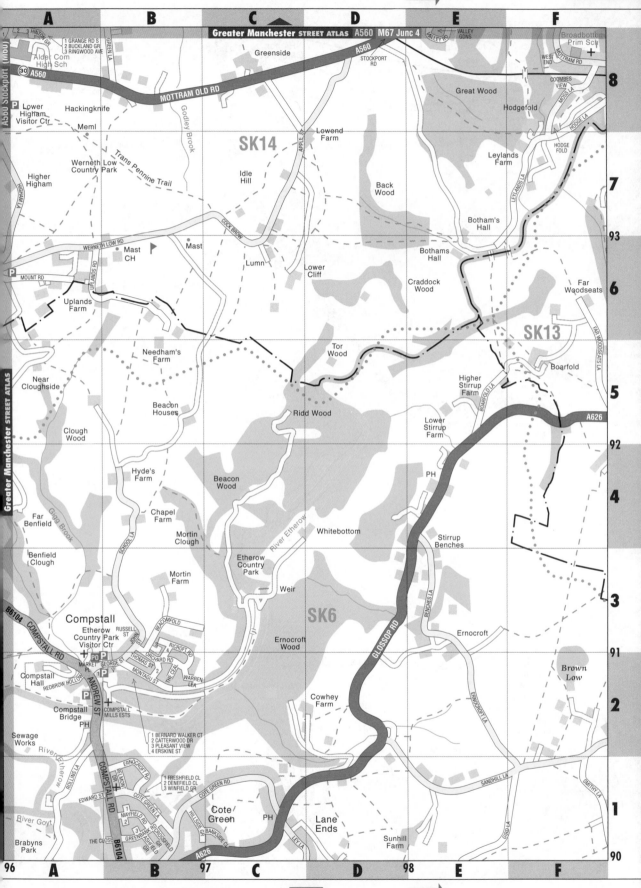

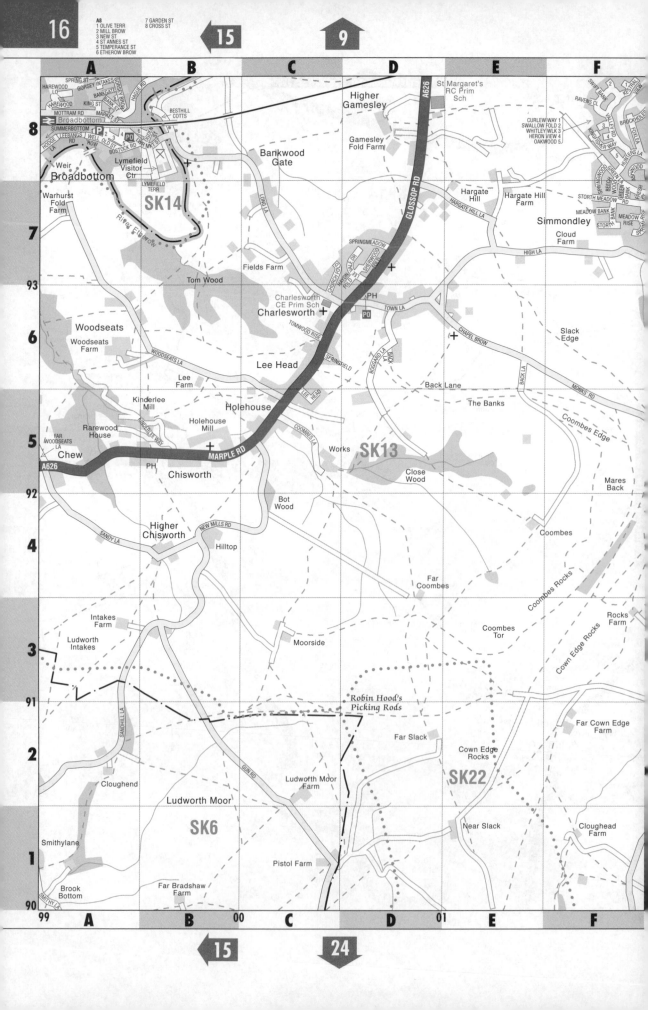

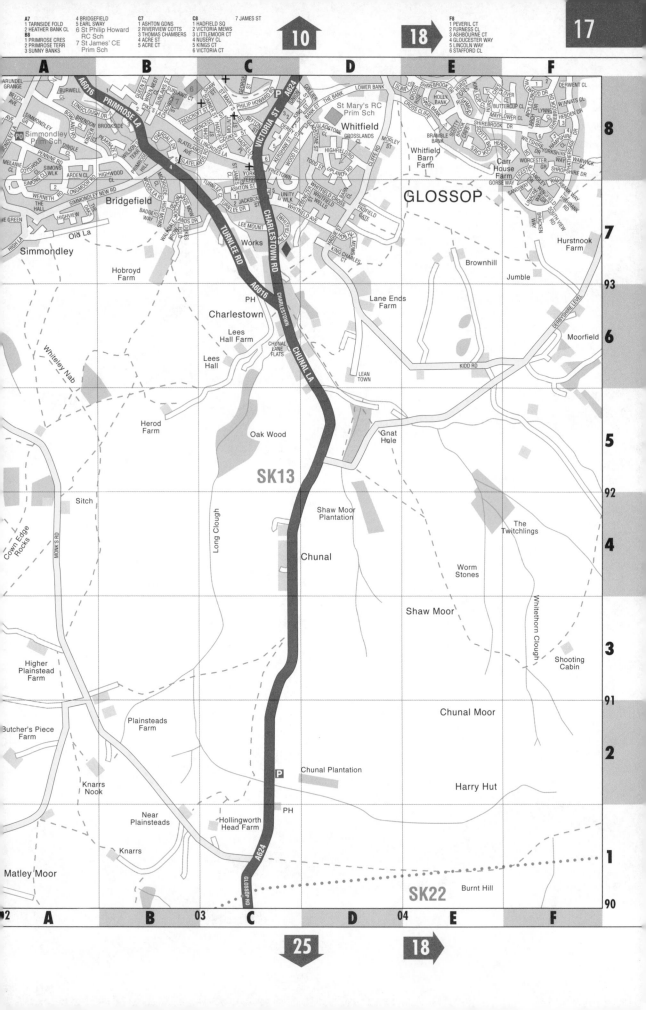

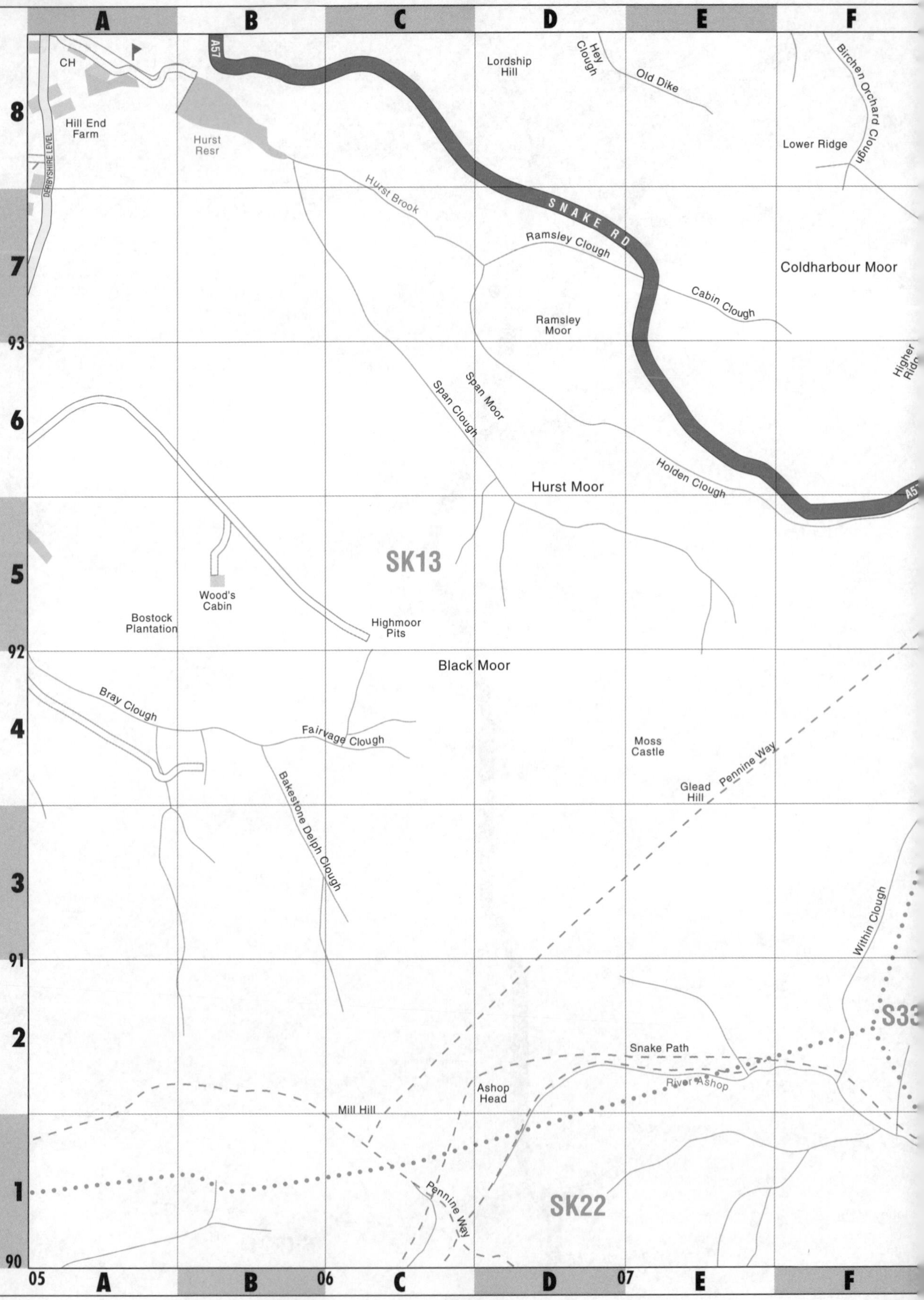

A B C D E F

8 CH Hill End Farm Hurst Resr Lordship Hill Hey Clough Old Dike Birchen Orchard Clough Lower Ridge

Hurst Brook SNAKE RD Ramsley Clough Cabin Clough Coldharbour Moor

7

93 Ramsley Moor Higher Ridge

6 Span Clough Span Moor Holden Clough A57

Hurst Moor

5 Wood's Cabin Highmoor Pits SK13

Bostock Plantation

92 Black Moor

4 Bray Clough Fairvage Clough Moss Castle Pennine Way

Bakestone Delph Clough Glead Hill

3 Within Clough

91 S33

2 Snake Path River Ashop

Ashop Head

Mill Hill

1 Pennine Way SK22

90

05 A B 06 C D 07 E F

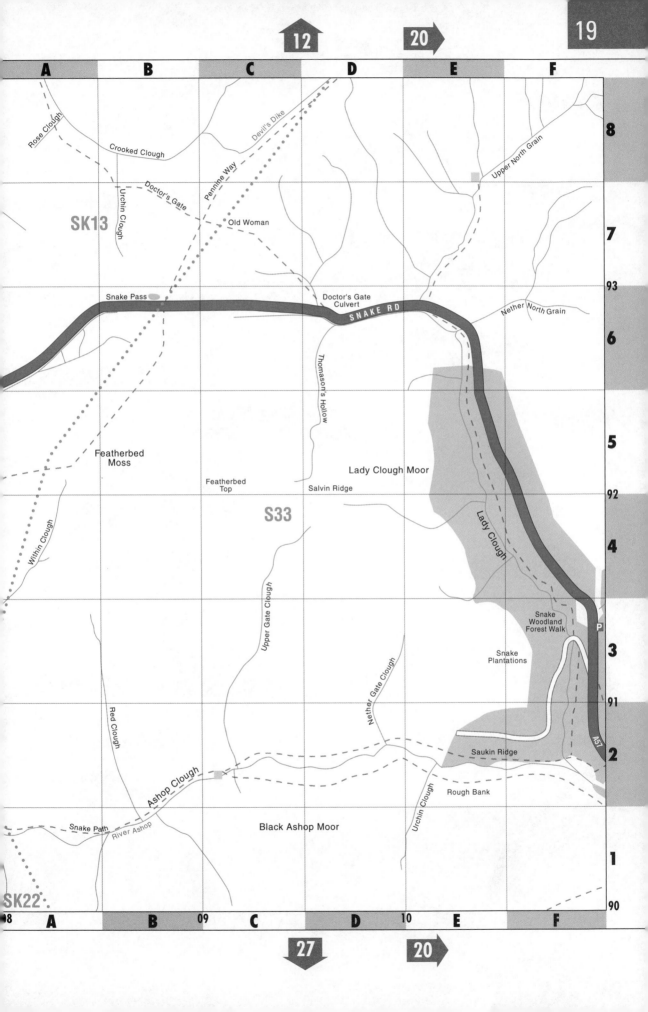

19
13

| | **A** | **B** | **C** | **D** | **E** | **F** |

8 Over Wood Moss

Alport Moor

Miry Clough

Glethering Clough

Black Clough

Westend Moor

7 Upper Reddale Clough

Nether Reddale Clough

Grindlesgrain Tor

River Alport

93

6

Alport Dale

S33

5 Hope Forest

92

Birchin Clough

4 Ferny Side

Shooting Cabin

3 Alport Valley Plantations

Dinas Sitch Tor

Oyster Clough

Swint Clough

Alport Farm

Alport Castles Farm

91 Ford

2 A57

PH

SNAKE RD

Cowberry Tor

Cowms Rocks

Hey Ridge

Ashton Tor

Woodlands Valley

1

Knots

Cowms Moor

A57

90

| 11 | **A** | **B** | 12 | **C** | **D** | 13 | **E** | **F** |

19
28

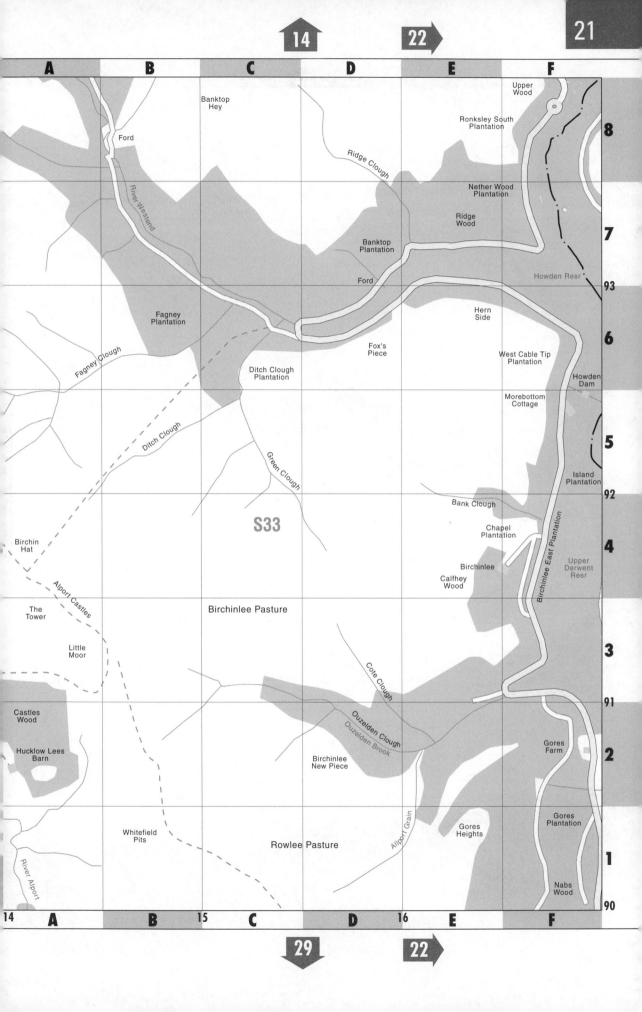

A | B | C | D | E | F

Upper Wood

Ronksley South Plantation

8

Banktop Hey

Ford

Ridge Clough

Nether Wood Plantation

River Westend

Ridge Wood

7

Banktop Plantation

Ford

93

Fagney Plantation

Hern Side

6

Fagney Clough

Fox's Piece

West Cable Tip Plantation

Ditch Clough Plantation

Howden Dam

Morebottom Cottage

5

Ditch Clough

Green Clough

Island Plantation

92

Bank Clough

S33

Birchin Hat

Chapel Plantation

4

Birchinlee

Calfhey Wood

Birchinlee East Plantation

Upper Derwent Resr

The Tower

Alport Castles

Birchinlee Pasture

Little Moor

3

Castles Wood

Cote Clough

91

Ouzelden Clough

Ouzelden Brook

Gores Farm

2

Hucklow Lees Barn

Birchinlee New Piece

Whitefield Pits

Rowlee Pasture

Alport Grain

Gores Heights

Gores Plantation

1

River Alport

Nabs Wood

90

Howden Resr

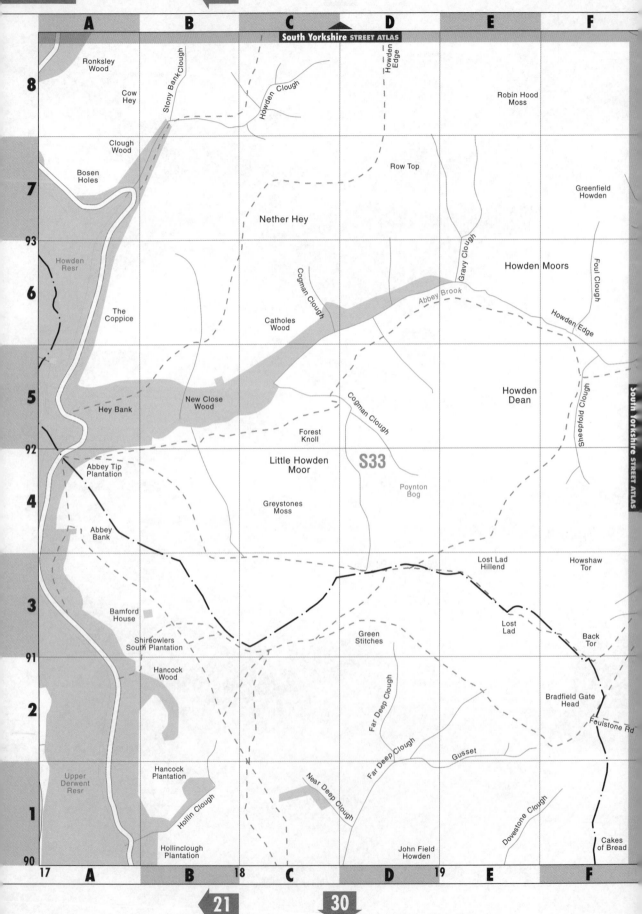

South Yorkshire STREET ATLAS

South Yorkshire STREET ATLAS

A **B** **C** **D** **E** **F**

8

Ronksley
Wood

Cow Hey

Stony Bank Clough

Howden Clough

Howden Edge

Robin Hood
Moss

Clough
Wood

7

Bosen
Holes

Row Top

Greenfield
Howden

93

Howden Resr

Nether Hey

Howden Moors

Foul Clough

6

The Coppice

Cogman Clough

Catholes
Wood

Abbey Brook

Gravy Clough

Howden Edge

5

Hey Bank

New Close
Wood

Cogman Clough

Howden
Dean

Sheepfold Clough

Forest
Knoll

92

Abbey Tip
Plantation

Little Howden
Moor

S33

Poynton
Bog

4

Abbey
Bank

Greystones
Moss

Lost Lad
Hillend

Howshaw
Tor

3

Bamford
House

Green
Stitches

Lost
Lad

Back
Tor

Shireowlers
South Plantation

91

Hancock
Wood

Bradfield Gate
Head

2

Far Deep Clough

Foulstone Rd

Hancock
Plantation

Far Deep Clough

Gusset

Upper
Derwent
Resr

Near Deep Clough

Dovestone Clough

1

Hollin Clough

John Field
Howden

Cakes
of Bread

90

Hollinclough
Plantation

17 **A** **B** **18** **C** **D** **19** **E** **F**

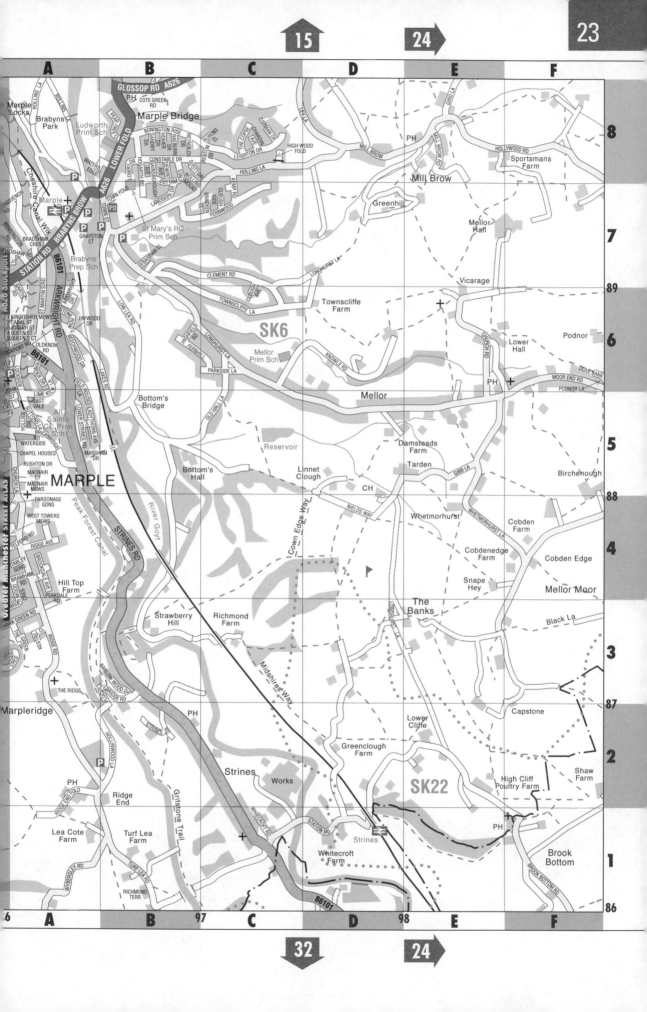

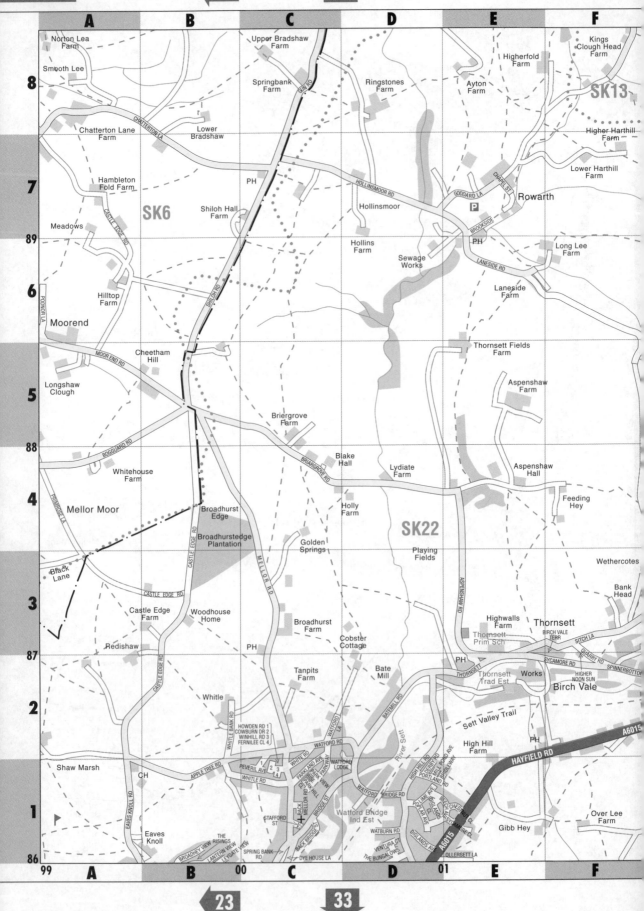

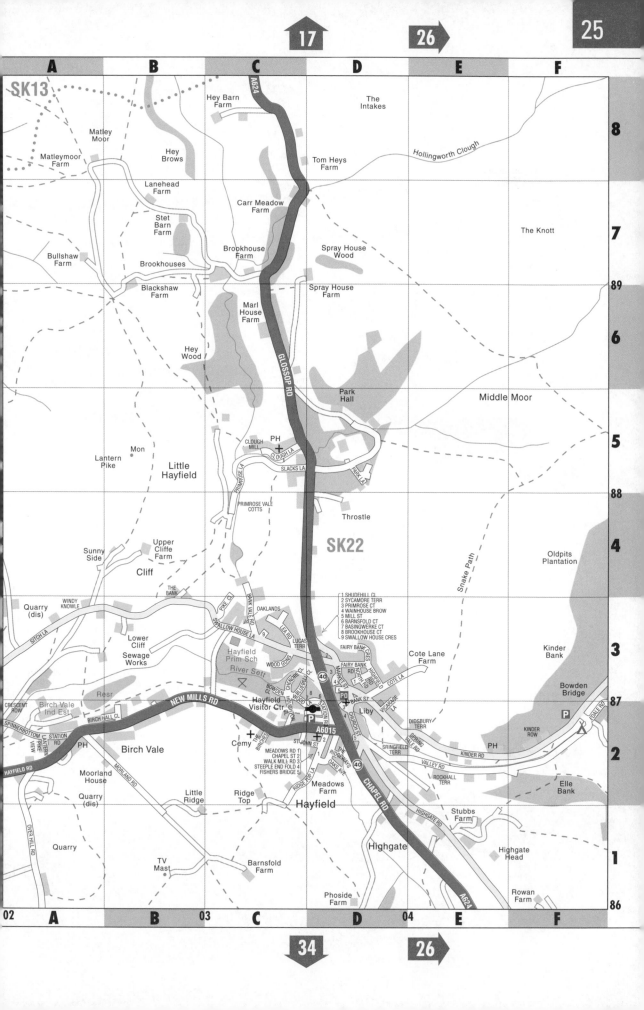

25
18

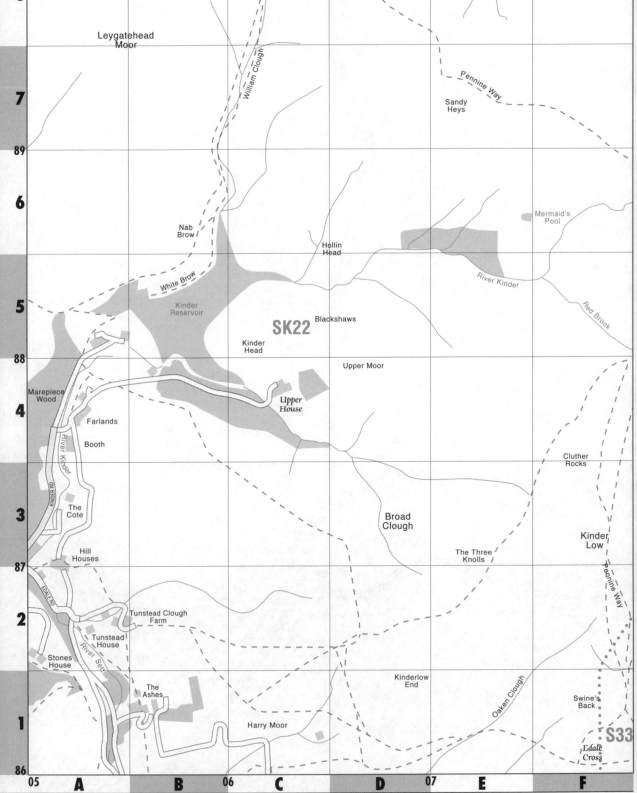

25
35

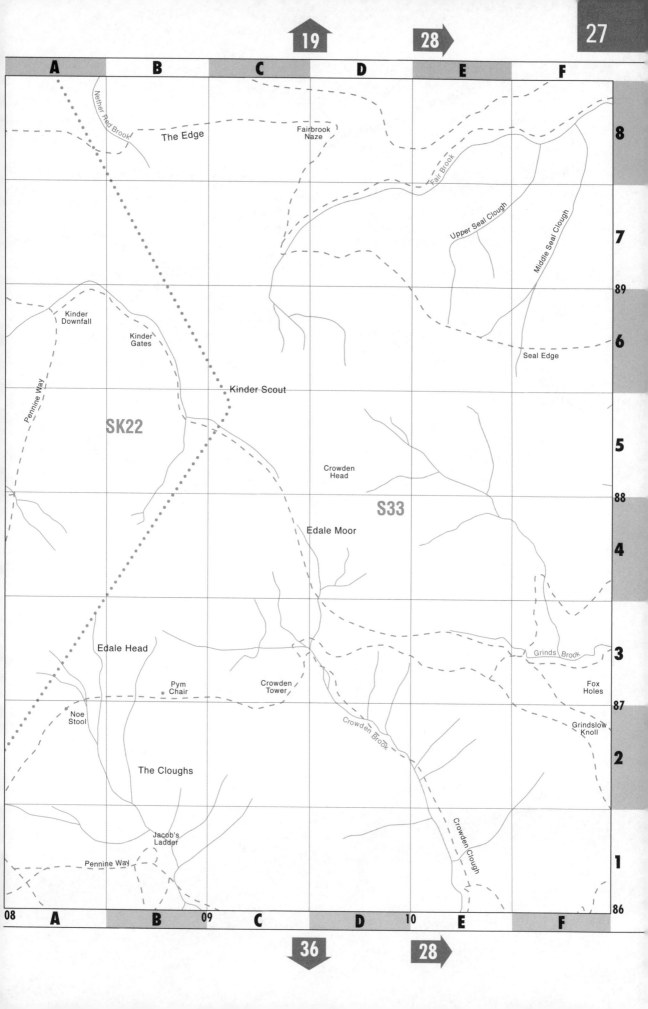

A   B   C   D   E   F

8

Nether Red Brook

The Edge

Fairbrook Naze

Fair Brook

7

Upper Seal Clough

Middle Seal Clough

89

Kinder Downfall

Kinder Gates

6

Seal Edge

Pennine Way

Kinder Scout

SK22

5

Crowden Head

S33

88

Edale Moor

4

Edale Head

Grinds Brook

3

Pym Chair

Crowden Tower

Fox Holes

87

Noe Stool

Crowden Brook

Grindslow Knoll

2

The Cloughs

Jacob's Ladder

Crowden Clough

1

Pennine Way

86

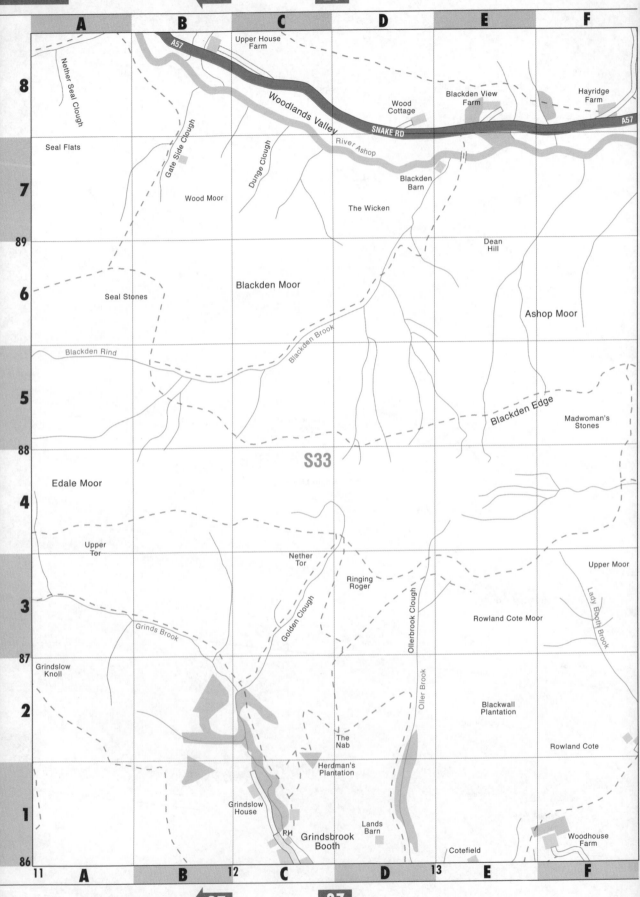

A B C D E F

8

Nether Seal Clough

A57

Upper House Farm

Woodlands Valley

Blackden View Farm

Wood Cottage

Hayridge Farm

SNAKE RD

A57

Seal Flats

Gate Side Clough

River Ashop

7

Dunge Clough

Wood Moor

Blackden Barn

The Wicken

Blackden Moor

Dean Hill

89

6

Seal Stones

Blackden Brook

Ashop Moor

Blackden Rind

5

Blackden Edge

Madwoman's Stones

88

S33

Edale Moor

4

Upper Tor

Nether Tor

Upper Moor

Ringing Roger

Ollerbrook Clough

Lady Booth Brook

3

Grinds Brook

Golden Clough

Rowland Cote Moor

87

Grindslow Knoll

Oller Brook

Blackwall Plantation

2

The Nab

Rowland Cote

Herdman's Plantation

Grindslow House

Lands Barn

Woodhouse Farm

1

PH

Grindsbrook Booth

Cotefield

86

11 A B 12 C D 13 E F

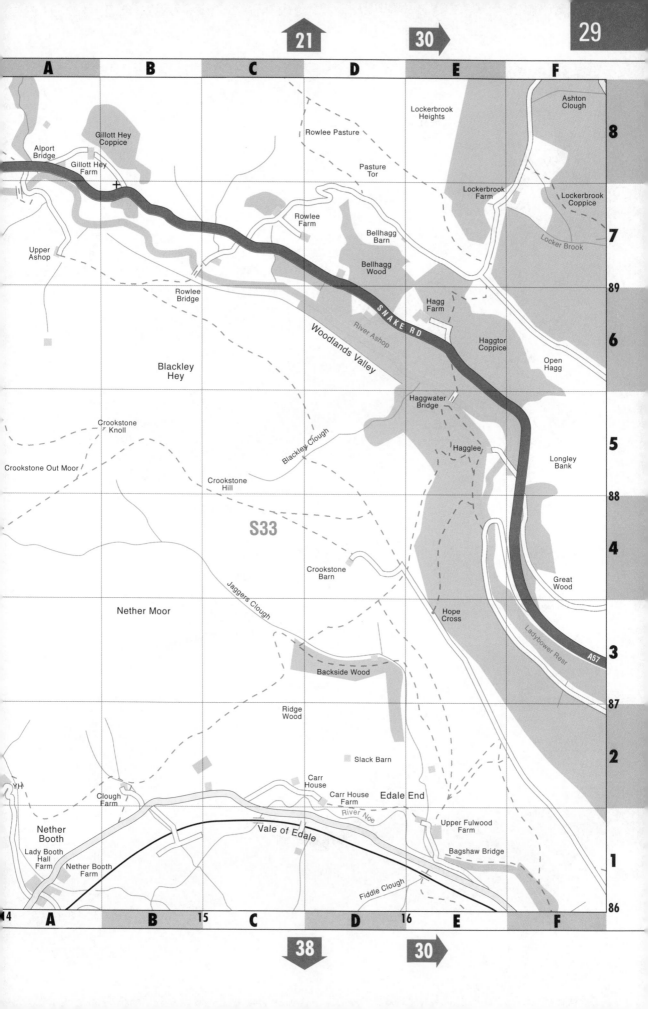

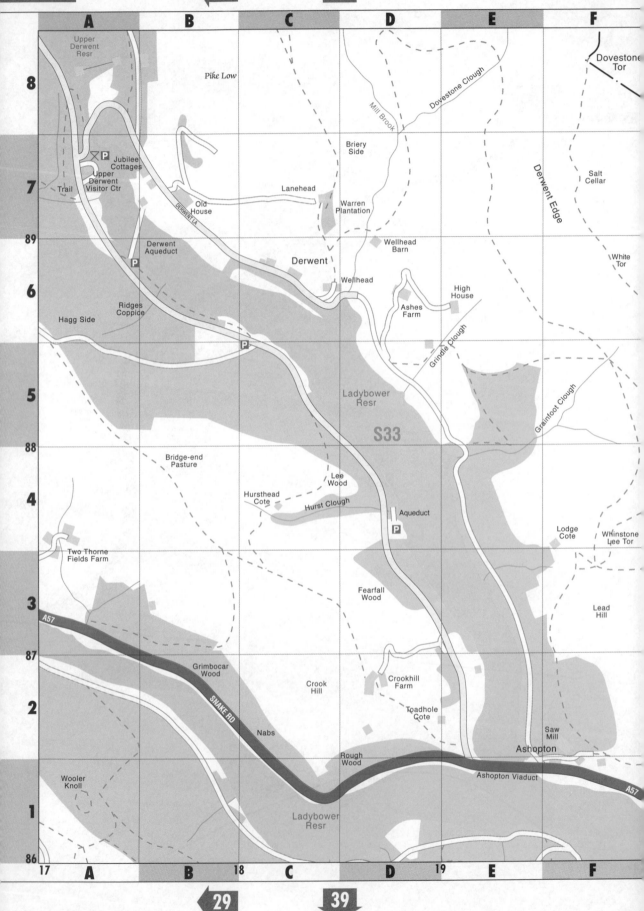

8

Upper Derwent Resr

Pike Low

Dovestone Clough

Mill Brook

Dovestone Tor

Briery Side

Salt Cellar

Jubilee Cottages
P
Upper Derwent Visitor Ctr
Trail

7

Derwent Edge

Lanehead

Old House

DERWENT LA

Warren Plantation

White Tor

89

Derwent Aqueduct
P

Wellhead Barn

Derwent

6

Ridges Coppice

Wellhead

Ashes Farm

High House

Hagg Side

P

Grindle Clough

Ladybower Resr

5

Grainfoot Clough

88

S33

Bridge-end Pasture

Lee Wood

4

Hursthead Cote

Hurst Clough

Aqueduct
P

Lodge Cote

Whinstone Lee Tor

Two Thorne Fields Farm

Fearfall Wood

3

A57

Lead Hill

87

Grimbocar Wood

Crook Hill

Crookhill Farm

SNAKE RD

2

Nabs

Toadhole Cote

Saw Mill

Ashopton

Rough Wood

Ashopton Viaduct

A57

1

Wooler Knoll

Ladybower Resr

86

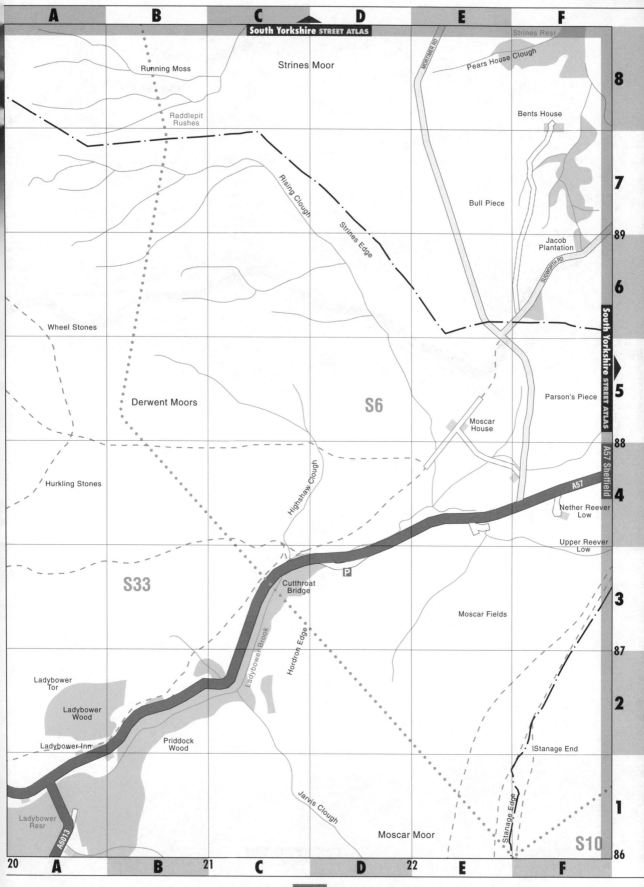

South Yorkshire STREET ATLAS

Strines Resr

Pears House Clough

Running Moss

Strines Moor

8

Raddlepit
Rushes

Bents House

Rising Clough

Strines Edge

Bull Piece

7

89

Jacob
Plantation

Wheel Stones

6

Derwent Moors

S6

Parson's Piece

5

Moscar
House

88

Hurkling Stones

Highshaw Clough

A57

4

Nether Reever
Low

Upper Reever
Low

S33

P

Cutthroat
Bridge

3

Moscar Fields

87

Ladybower
Tor

Ladybower Brook

Hordron Edge

2

Ladybower
Wood

Priddock
Wood

Stanage End

Ladybower Inn

Jarvis Clough

1

Ladybower
Resr

A6013

Moscar Moor

Stanage Edge

S10

86

20   A   21   B   C   22   D   E   F

40

South Yorkshire STREET ATLAS   A57 Sheffield

MORTIMER RD

SUGWORTH RD

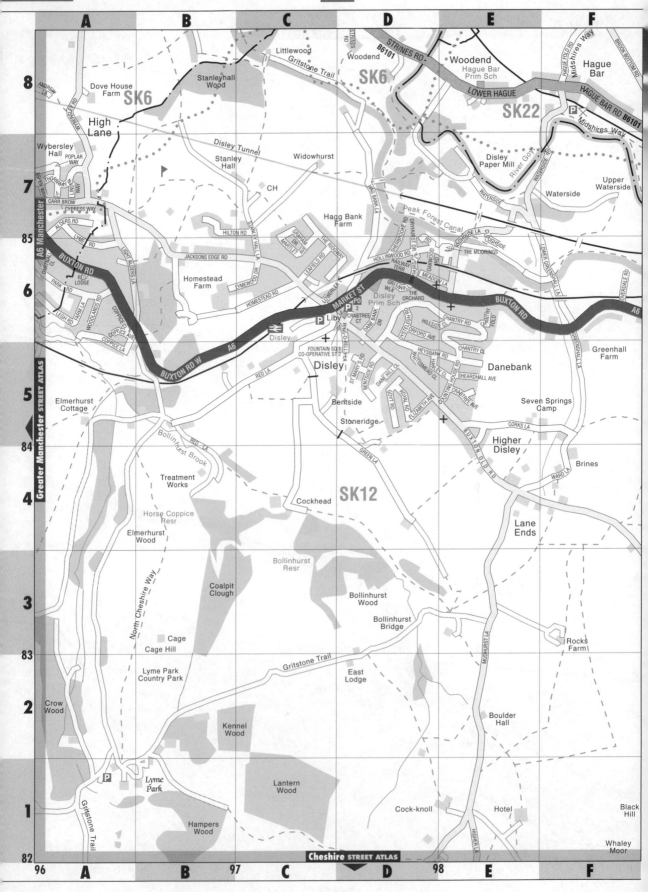

Greater Manchester STREET ATLAS

Cheshire STREET ATLAS

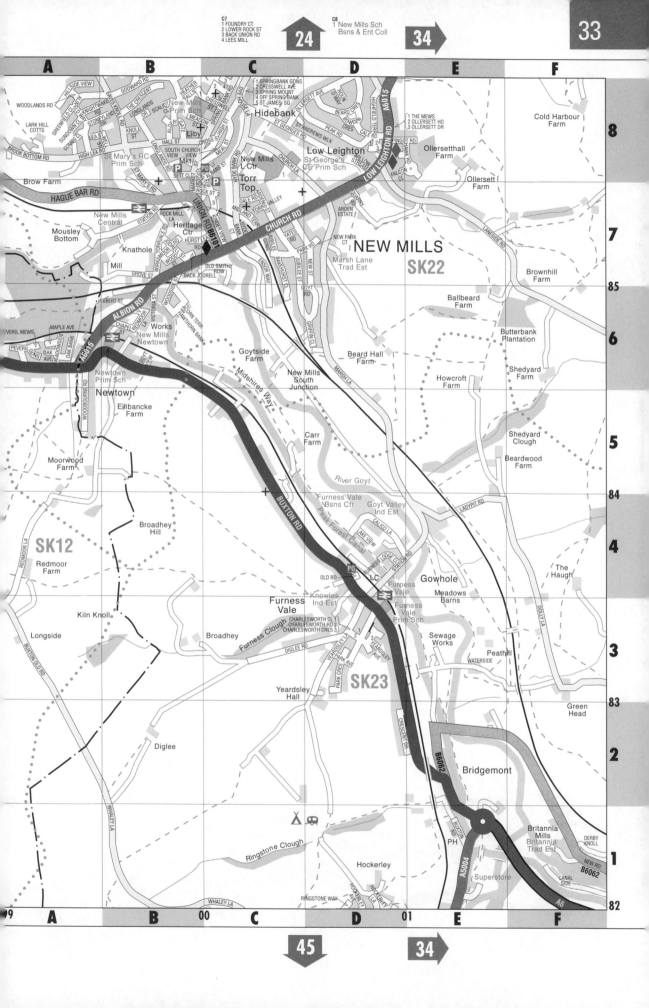

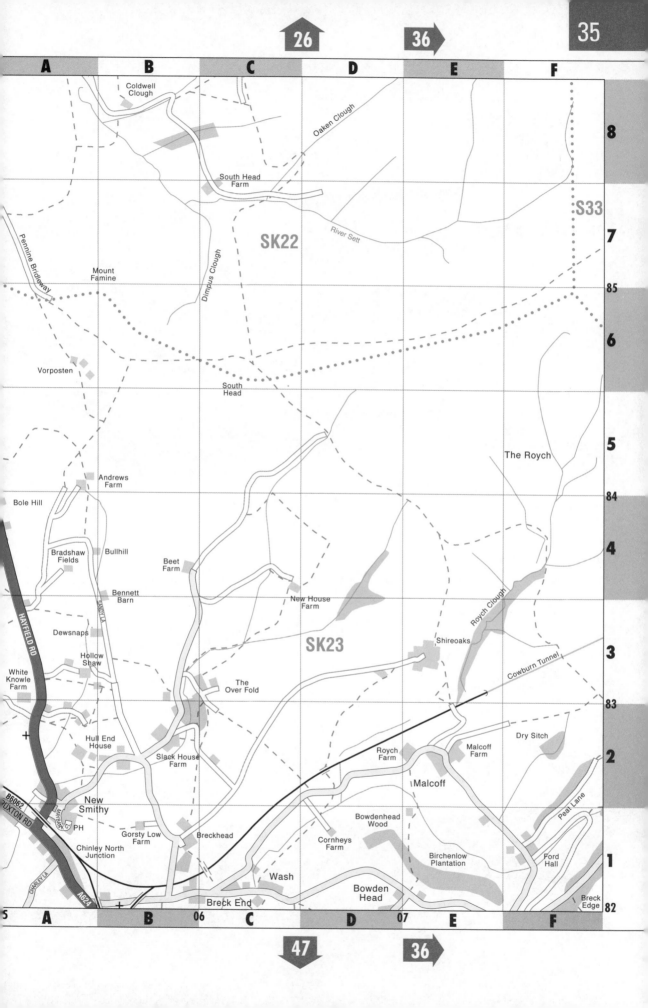

A B C D E F

8

S33

7

85

6

SK22

Coldwell Clough

Oaken Clough

South Head Farm

River Sett

Pennine Bridleway

Mount Famine

Dimpus Clough

Vorposten

South Head

The Roych

5

84

Andrews Farm

Bole Hill

Bradshaw Fields

Bullhill

Beet Farm

New House Farm

Roych Clough

4

Bennett Barn

SANDY LA

Dewsnaps

SK23

Shireoaks

Cowburn Tunnel

3

83

Hollow Shaw

White Knowle Farm

The Over Fold

HAYFIELD RD

Hull End House

Slack House Farm

Roych Farm

Malcoff Farm

Dry Sitch

2

Malcoff

B6062

BUXTON RD

New Smithy

MYBANK

PH

Gorsty Low Farm

Breckhead

Cornheys Farm

Bowdenhead Wood

Peat Lane

Chinley North Junction

Wash

Birchenlow Plantation

Ford Hall

1

CHARLEY LA

A624

Breck End

Bowden Head

Breck Edge

82

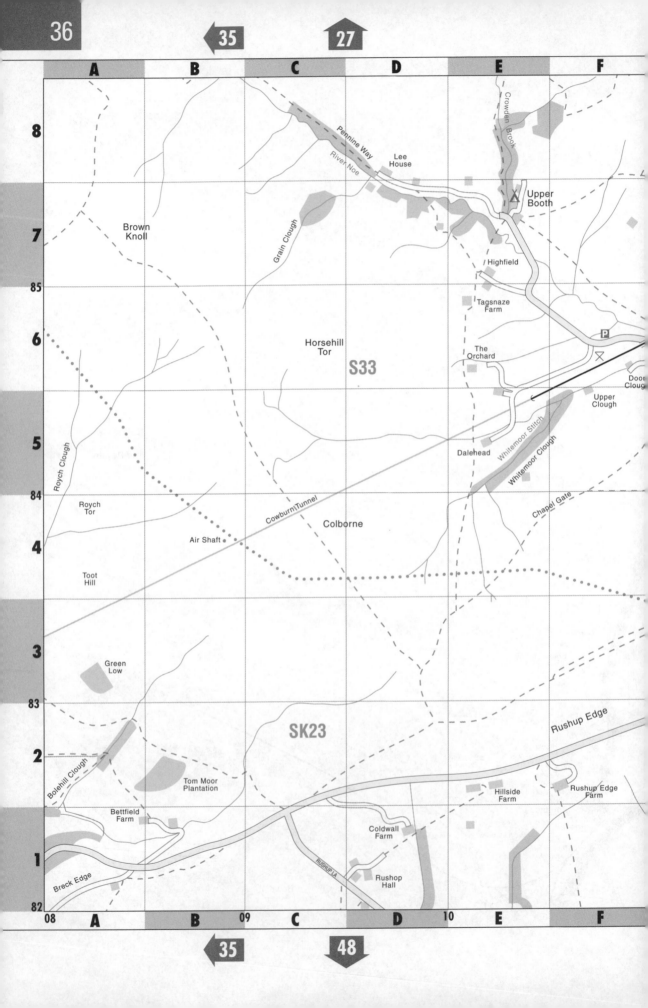

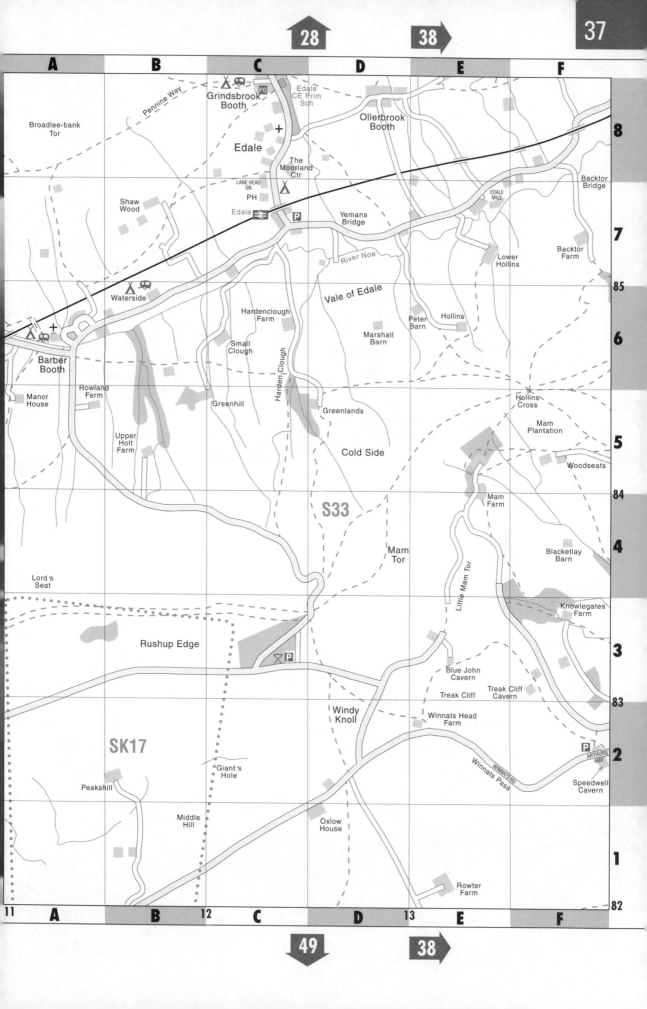

37 29

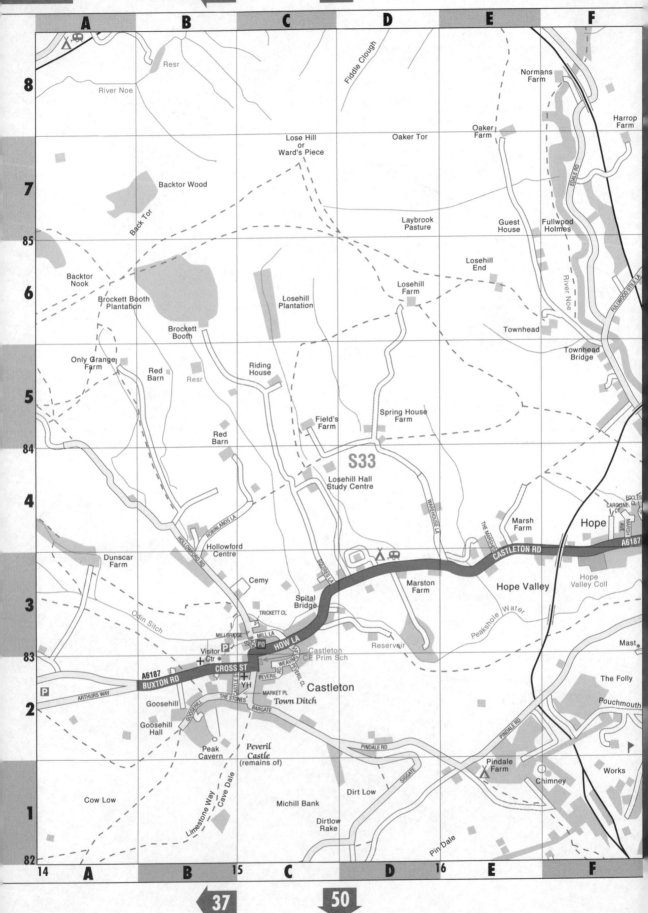

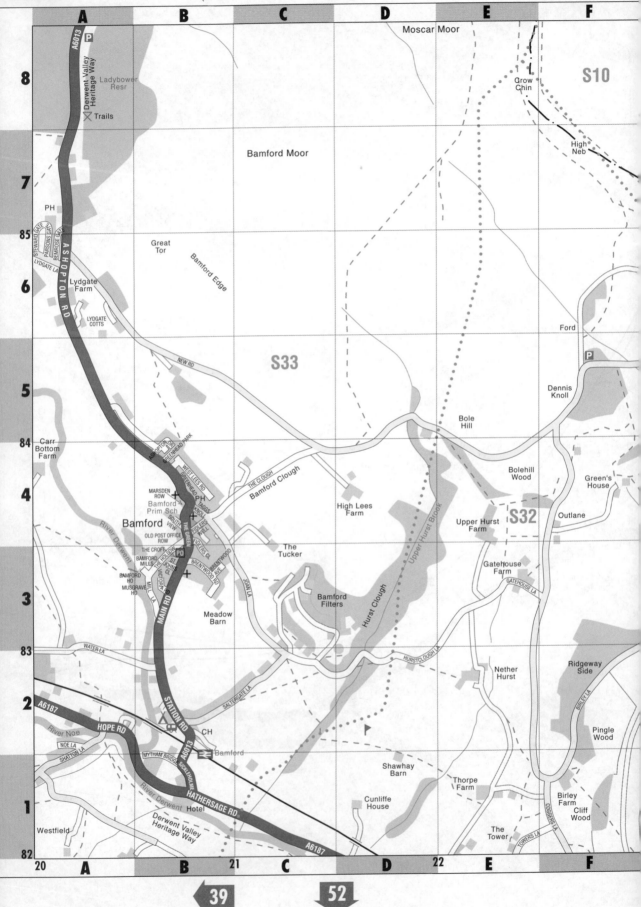

39
31

A B C D E F

8

S10

Moscar Moor

Crow Chin

High Neb

A6013

P

Derwent Valley Heritage Way

Ladybower Resr

Trails

Bamford Moor

7

85

PH

STEWARD GATE

PARSONS LAW

BELMIRDGE CATE

LYDGATE LA

ASHOPTON RD

Great Tor

Bamford Edge

Ford

6

Lydgate Farm

LYDGATE COTTS

P

NEW RD

S33

Dennis Knoll

5

Bole Hill

Bolehill Wood

84

Carr Bottom Farm

ASHOPTON RD

WEST LEES RD

GREENHEAD

GREENHEAD PARK

THE CLOUGH

Bamford Clough

Green's House

4

MARSDEN ROW

Bamford Prim Sch

PH

TAGGS

KNOLL

Bamford

High Lees Farm

Upper Hurst Farm

S32

Outlane

River Derwent

SOUTH VIEW

THE GREEN

LOVERS CL

WELL

OLD POST OFFICE ROW

The Tucker

Upper Hurst Brook

Gatehouse Farm

GATEHOUSE LA

THE CROFT

PO

BAMFORD MILLS

THE HOLLIN

ST JOHN'S CL

VICTORIA

BRENTWOOD RD

BRENTWOOD AVE.

BAMFORD HO

MUSGRAVE HO

MILL LA

MAIN RD

JOAN LA

Bamford Filters

Hurst Clough

3

Meadow Barn

83

WATER LA

HURSTCLOUGH LA

Nether Hurst

Ridgeway Side

2

A6187

HOPE RD

STATION RD

SALTERGATE LA

BIRLEY LA

River Noe

NOE LA

CH

A6013

Pingle Wood

SHATTON LA

MYTHAM BRIDGE

SICKLEHOLME

Bamford

Shawhay Barn

Thorpe Farm

Birley Farm

River Derwent

HATHERSAGE RD

Hotel

Cunliffe House

Cliff Wood

1

Westfield

Derwent Valley Heritage Way

A6187

The Tower

TOWERS LA

COGGERS LA

82

20 A B 21 C 22 D E F

39
52

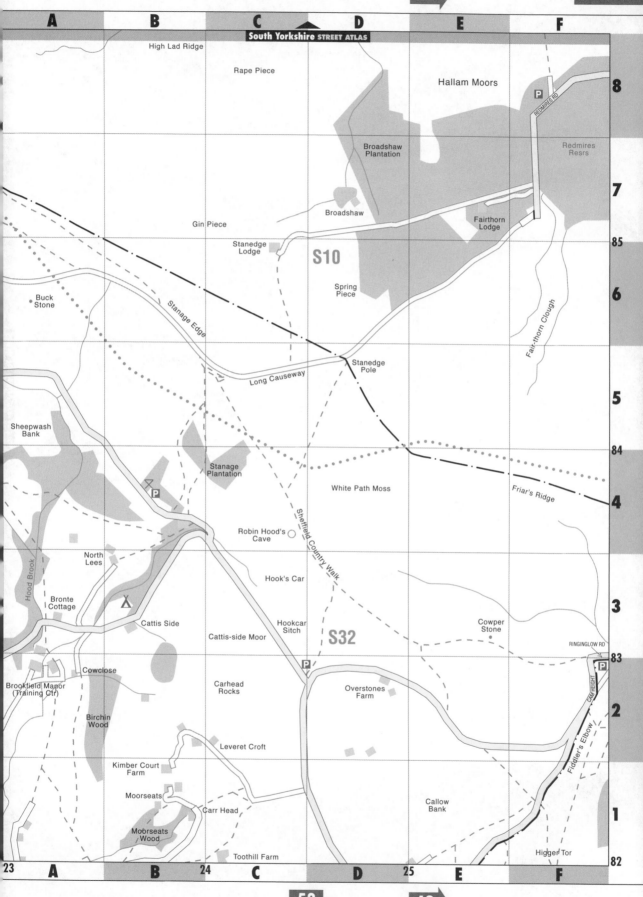

A **B** **C** **D** **E** **F**

High Lad Ridge

Rape Piece

Hallam Moors

8

Broadshaw
Plantation

Redmires
Resrs

7

Broadshaw

Gin Piece

Fairthorn
Lodge

Stanedge
Lodge

85

S10

Spring
Piece

6

Buck
Stone

Stanage Edge

Fair-thorn Clough

Stanedge
Pole

5

Long Causeway

Sheepwash
Bank

84

Stanage
Plantation

White Path Moss

Friar's Ridge

4

Robin Hood's
Cave

Sheffield Country Walk

North
Lees

Hook's Car

Cowper
Stone

RINGINGLOW RD

Bronte
Cottage

Hookcar
Sitch

S32

83

Cattis Side

Cattis-side Moor

Cowclose

Carhead
Rocks

Overstones
Farm

2

Brookfield Manor
(Training Ctr)

Birchin
Wood

Leveret Croft

Fiddler's Elbow

Kimber Court
Farm

Moorseats

Callow
Bank

1

Moorseats
Wood

Carr Head

Toothill Farm

Higger Tor

82

Hood Brook

41

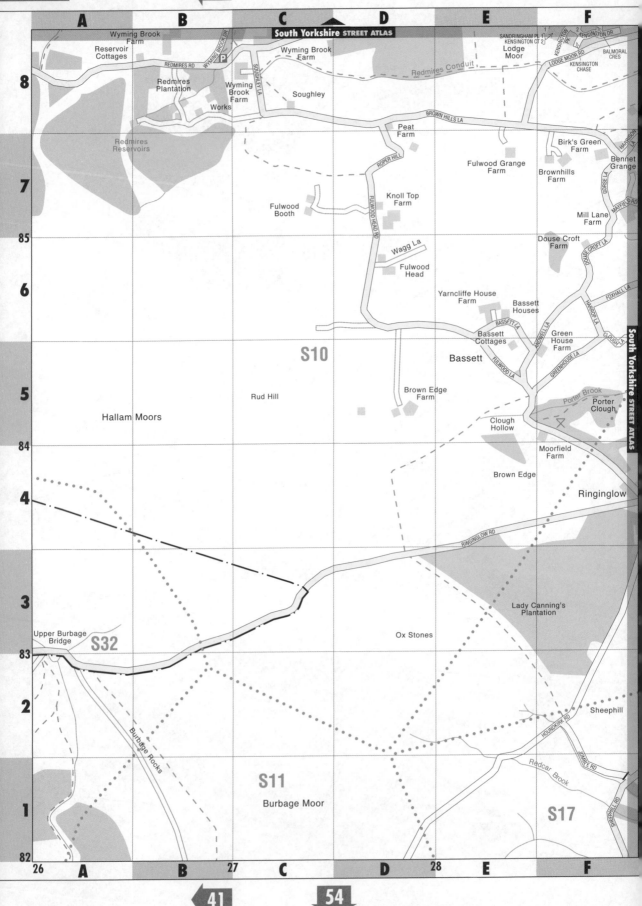

A B C D E F

Wyming Brook Farm
Reservoir Cottages
REDMIRES RD
WYMING BROOK DR
P
Wyming Brook Farm
Redmires Conduit
SANDRINGHAM PL
KENSINGTON CT
KENSINGTON PK
KENSINGTON DR
Lodge Moor
LODGE MOOR RD
KENSINGTON CHASE
BALMORAL CRES

8

Redmires Plantation
Wyming Brook Farm
Works
Soughley
SOUGHLEY LA
Peat Farm
BROWN HILLS LA
HARRISON LA
Birk's Green Farm
Bennet Grange

Redmires Reservoirs
ROPER HILL
Fulwood Grange Farm
Brownhills Farm
GORSE LA
MAYFIELD RD

7

Fulwood Booth
Knoll Top Farm
FULWOOD HEAD RD
Mill Lane Farm

85

Wagg La
Fulwood Head
Douse Croft Farm
DOUSE CROFT LA

6

Yarncliffe House Farm
Bassett Houses
FOXHALL LA
HOWELL LA
HARROP LA
CLOUGH LA

S10
BASSETT LA
Bassett Cottages
Bassett
Green House Farm
GREENHOUSE LA

Rud Hill
Brown Edge Farm
FULWOOD LA
Porter Brook
Porter Clough

5

Hallam Moors
Clough Hollow

84

Moorfield Farm

Brown Edge
Ringinglow

4

RINGINGLOW RD

Lady Canning's Plantation

3

Upper Burbage Bridge
S32
Ox Stones

83

Sheephill
HOUNDKIRK RD

2

Burbage Rocks
Redcar Brook
JUNIPER RD

S11
Burbage Moor
S17
SHEEPHILL RD

1

82

26 A B 27 C D 28 E F

41
54

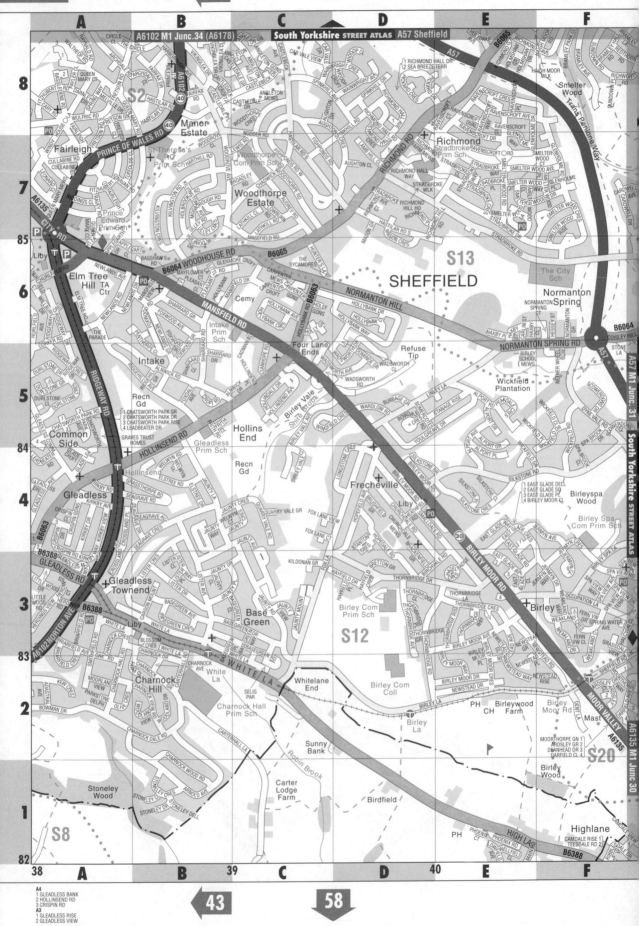

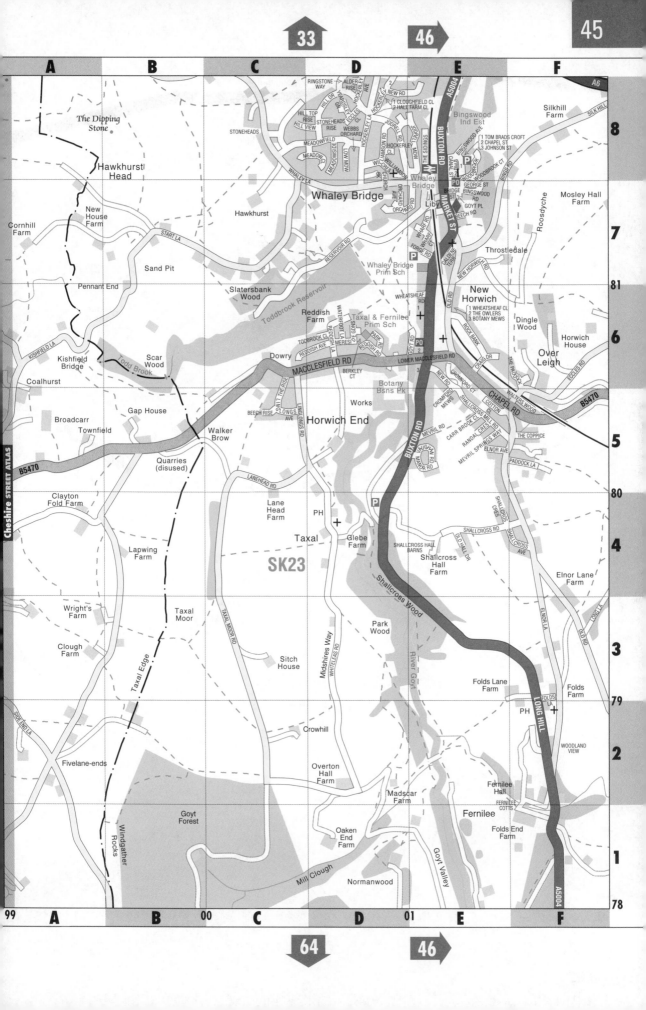

A · B · C · D · E · F

The Dipping Stone

Hawkhurst Head

Cornhill Farm

New House Farm

Hawkhurst

STONEHEADS

RINGSTONE WAY
ALDERLEY RISE
HOCKERLEY AVE
NEW RD
1 CLOUGHFIELD CL
2 HALF FARM CL

HILL TOP RISE
HILL DR
HILL VIEW
STONEHEADS RISE
HOCKERLEY LA
ECCLES
WEBBS ORCHARD
LOW MDW
MEADOWSIDE
MEADOW
HOCKERLEY CL
WILLIAMSON
WHALEY LA
WILLIAMSON RD

Whaley Bridge

Whaley Bridge

Bingswood Ind Est

Silkhill Farm
SILK HILL

TOM BRADS CROFT
2 CHAPEL ST
3 JOHNSON ST

Mosley Hall Farm

Roosdyche

A5004 · A6 · BUXTON RD

CANAL ST
BINGSWOOD AVE
NOR WOODBROOK CT
GEORGE ST
BINGSWOOD RD
GOYT PL
BRIDGE ST
BEECH RD

Pennant End

Sand Pit

START LA

RESERVOIR RD

Slatersbank Wood

Reddish Farm

Toddbrook Reservoir

WATERPOOL
Taxal & Fernilee Prim Sch

Whaley Bridge Prim Sch

FORGE RD

WHEATSHEAF RD
OLD RD
NEW HORWICH RD

New Horwich
1 WHEATSHEAF CL
2 THE OWLERS
3 BOTANY MEWS

Throstledale

Dingle Wood

Horwich House

Over Leigh
EGGLES RD

Kishfield Bridge
KISHFIELD LA
Todd Brook

Scar Wood

Coalhurst

Broadcarr

Gap House

Townfield

Walker Brow

Quarries (disused)

Dowry
TODDBROOK CL
REDDISH AVE
MERES CL
REDDISH LA
PARK RD
REDDISH RD
Macclesfield Rd
LOWER MACCLESFIELD RD
BERKLEY CT

SWN'T TH RISE
BEECH RISE
LONGS AVE
LINGLONGS RD

Botany Bsns Pk

Works

Horwich End

BUXTON RD

GOYT RD
ROCK BANK
CROMFORD CT
CRAIG DR
CROMFORD MEWS
NEW RD
CARR BROOK CL
SHALLCROSS MILL RD
RANDAL CRES
MEVRIL SPRINGS WAY
ELNOR AVE
PADDOCK LA
MEVRIL RD
VAUGHAN WAY
MANOR RD

Chapel Rd
COTTON
WALTERS WOOD
THE PADDOCK
THE COPPICE

B5470

B5470

Clayton Fold Farm

Lapwing Farm

Lane Head Farm

PH
Taxal
Glebe Farm

LANEHEAD RD

SHALLCROSS RD
SHALLCROSS HALL BARNS
Shallcross Hall Farm

SHALLCROSS CRES
SHALLCROSS AVE
OLD HALL DR

Elnor Lane Farm

Wright's Farm

Clough Farm

TAXAL MOOR RD

Taxal Moor

TAXAL EDGE

Sitch House

WHITE LEAS RD
MIDSHIRES WAY

SK23

Park Wood

Shallcross Wood

River Goyt

ELNOR LA

Folds Lane Farm

PH

Folds Farm

LONG HILL
FOLDS LA

WOODLAND VIEW

OLD RD
LONG LA

Fivelane-ends

SIDE END LA

Crowhill

Overton Hall Farm

Madscar Farm

Fernilee Hall

Fernilee
FERNILEE COTTS

Ferilee

Goyt Forest

Windgather Rocks

Mill Clough

Oaken End Farm

Normanwood

Goyt Valley

Folds End Farm

A5004

8 · 7 · 81 · 6 · 5 · 80 · 4 · 3 · 79 · 2 · 1 · 78

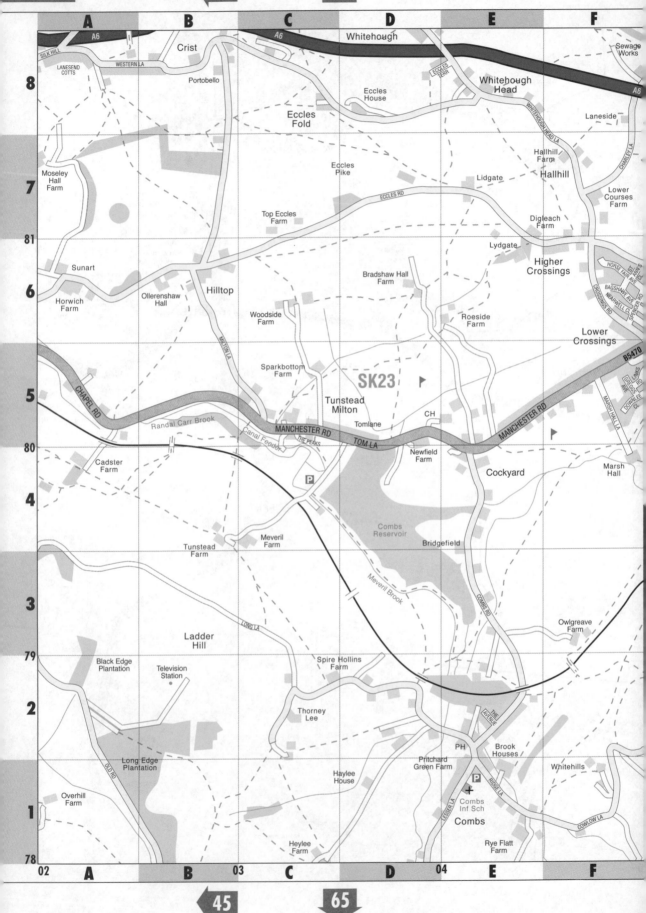

A6
Silk Hill
LANESEND COTTS
WESTERN LA
Crist
Portobello
Whitehough
A6
Eccles House
Sewage Works
ECCLES TERR
Whitehough Head
Laneside
8
Eccles Fold
WHITENOUGHHEAD LA
CHARLEY LA
Eccles Pike
Hallhill Farm
Hallhill
7
Moseley Hall Farm
ECCLES RD
Lidgate
Lower Courses Farm
Top Eccles Farm
Digleach Farm
81
Lydgate
Sunart
Bradshaw Hall Farm
Higher Crossings
HORSE FAIR AVE
6
Horwich Farm
Hilltop
Woodside Farm
Roeside Farm
SWIFTS
BAGSHAVE AVE
NEARWELL
SPENCER CL
CROSSINGS RD
Ollerenshaw Hall
Lower Crossings
MILTON LA
Sparkbottom Farm
SK23
B5470
CHAPEL RD
Tunstead Milton
CH
MANCHESTER RD
DOWNLEE CL
GREGS RD
CROSS LINKS
MARSH HALL LA
5
Randal Carr Brook
Tomlane
Canal Feeder
MANCHESTER RD
TOM LA
80
THE PEAKS
Newfield Farm
Marsh Hall
Cadster Farm
P
Cockyard
4
Combs Reservoir
Meveril Farm
Bridgefield
Tunstead Farm
COMBS RD
Meveril Brook
3
Owlgreave Farm
LONG LA
Ladder Hill
79
Black Edge Plantation
Spire Hollins Farm
Television Station
THE AVENUE
2
Thorney Lee
Brook Houses
OLD RD
Long Edge Plantation
PH
Whitehills
Pritchard Green Farm
P
RIDGE LA
Haylee House
Overhill Farm
LESSER LA
Combs Inf Sch
1
Combs
COWLOW LA
Heylee Farm
Rye Flatt Farm
78

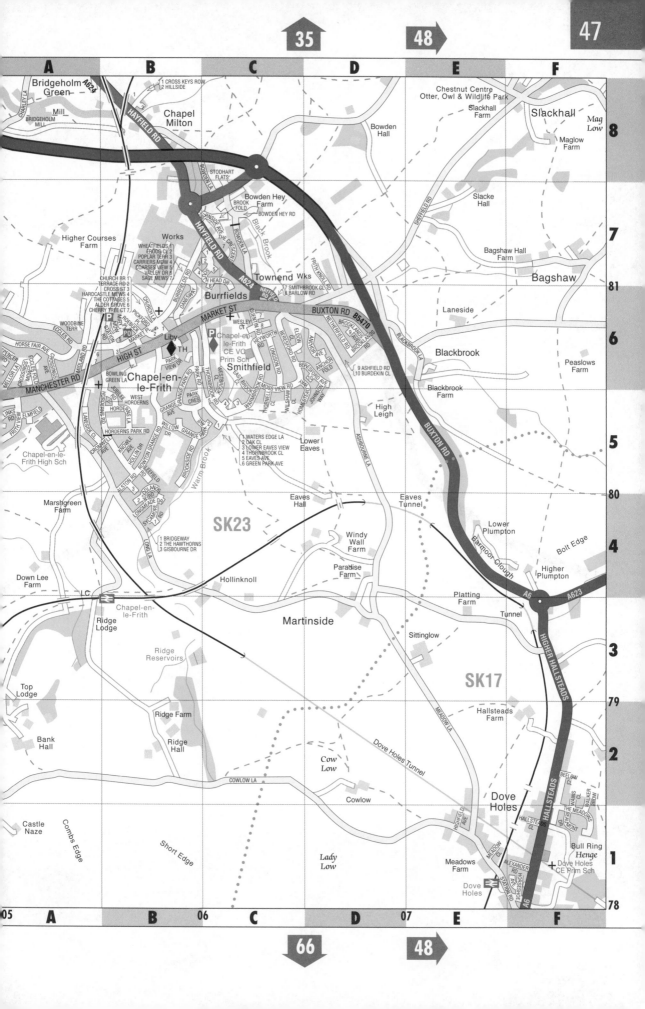

A B C D E F

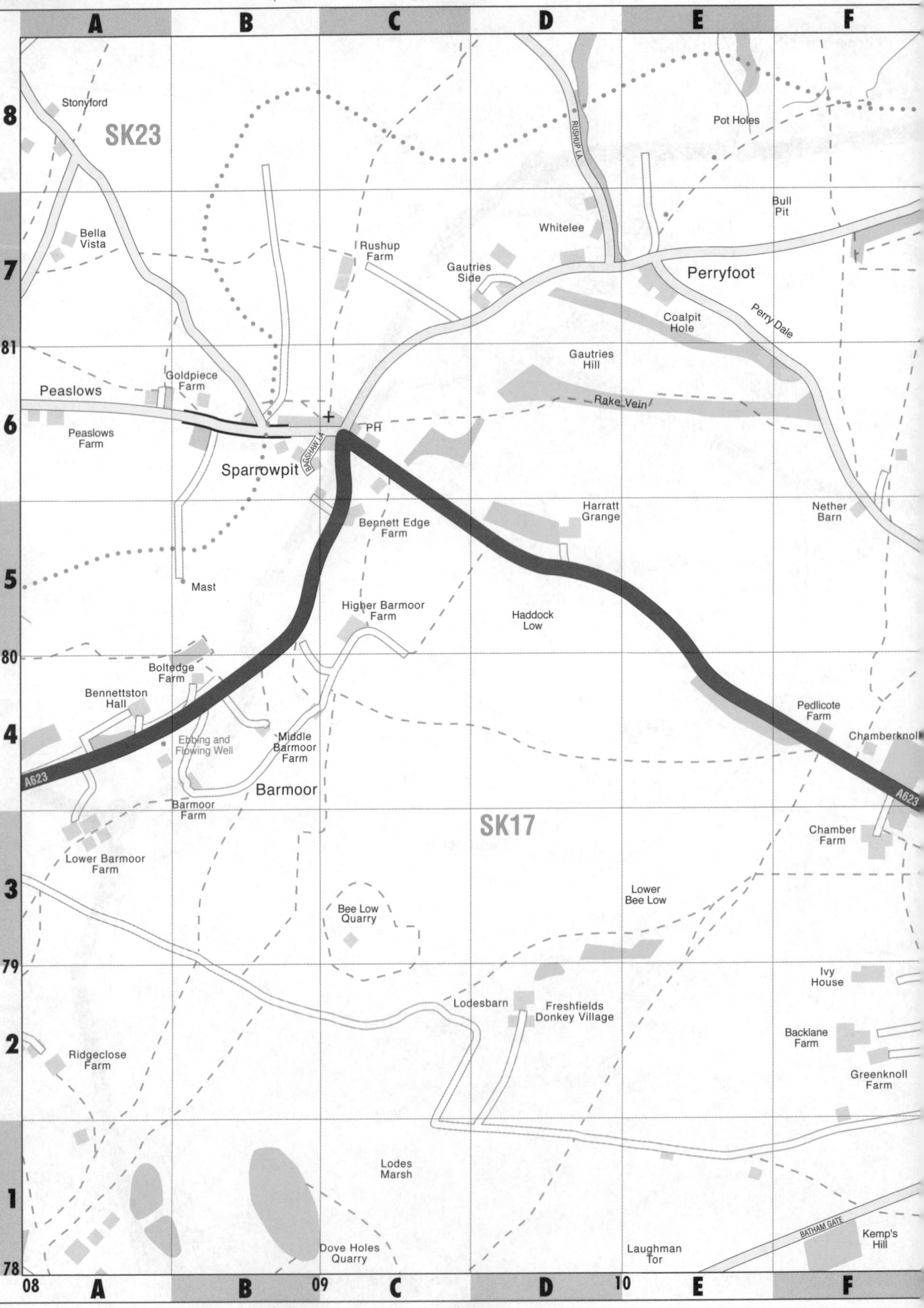

8 Stonyford

SK23

Pot Holes

Bull Pit

7 Bella Vista

Rushup Farm

Gautries Side

Whitelee

Perryfoot

Perry Dale

81

Coalpit Hole

Gautries Hill

Peaslows

Goldpiece Farm

Rake Vein

Nether Barn

6 Peaslows Farm

BAGSHAW LA

PH

Sparrowpit

Harratt Grange

Bennett Edge Farm

5 Mast

Higher Barmoor Farm

Haddock Low

80 Boltedge Farm

Bennettston Hall

Ebbing and Flowing Well

Middle Barmoor Farm

Pedlicote Farm

Chamberknoll

4 A623 Barmoor Farm

Barmoor

SK17

Chamber Farm

A623

3 Lower Barmoor Farm

Bee Low Quarry

Lower Bee Low

79 Ivy House

Lodesbarn

Freshfields Donkey Village

Backlane Farm

2 Ridgeclose Farm

Greenknoll Farm

1 Lodes Marsh

BATHAM GATE

Kemp's Hill

Dove Holes Quarry

Laughman Tor

78

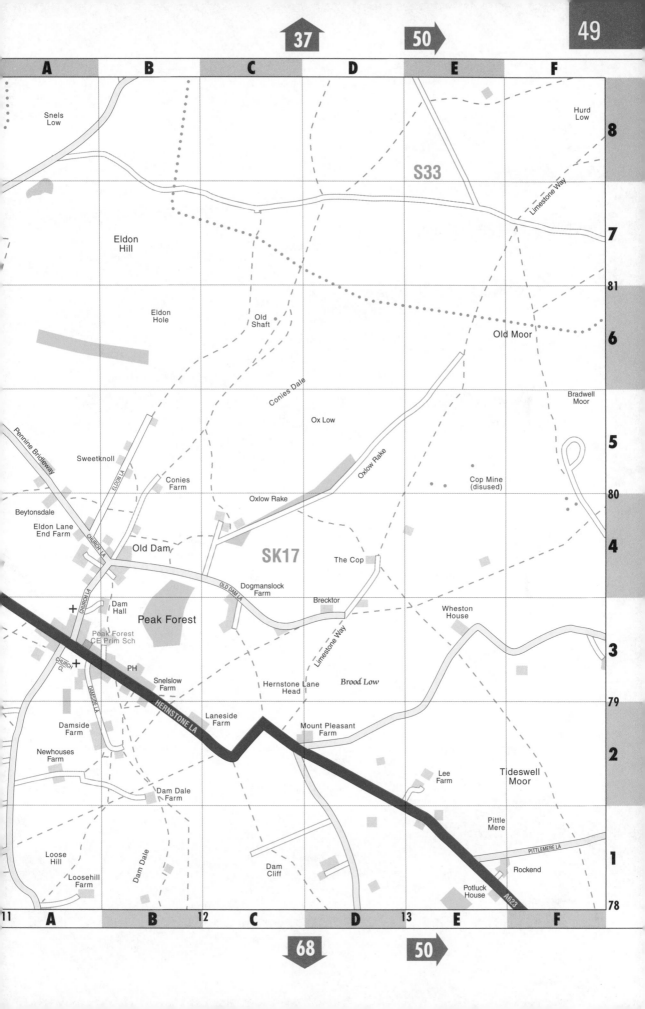

A B C D E F

8

Limestone Way

Dirtlow Rake

S33

Smalldale

Michlow
Low

MICHLOW L

7

CRESSWELLPART LA

Within
House

GRANBY RD

Smalldale
Head

Paradise
Farm

SMALLDALE HEAD RD

MOORBROOK LA

OUTLANDS RD

81

Outlands
Head

6

Potter
Barn

CLEMENT LA

Green
Dale

NEW LA

Newall
Nook

Bradwell Moor

Moss Rake

Hartlemoor
Farm

Mines
(dis)

Hartle
Dale

JEFFREY LA

5

Old Shafts

LAMBPART LA

Mines
(dis)

Earl Rake

Jennings
Dale

80

TOPHOLE RD

Green Dale

4

Berrystall
Lodge

Intake Dale

NEW RD B6049

Stanlow Dale

Intake
Farm

3

Shuttle Rake

SK17

Coplow
Dale

Lower
Farm

The
Holmes

79

Hucklow
Moor

Little Hucklow

2

Tideswell
Moor

Home
Farm

Bushy Heath
Farm

Forest Lane
Farm

FOREST LA

+

1

PITTLEMERE LA

New
Farm

Tideslow
Farm

78

Whiterake

TV Mast

14 A B 15 C D 16 E F

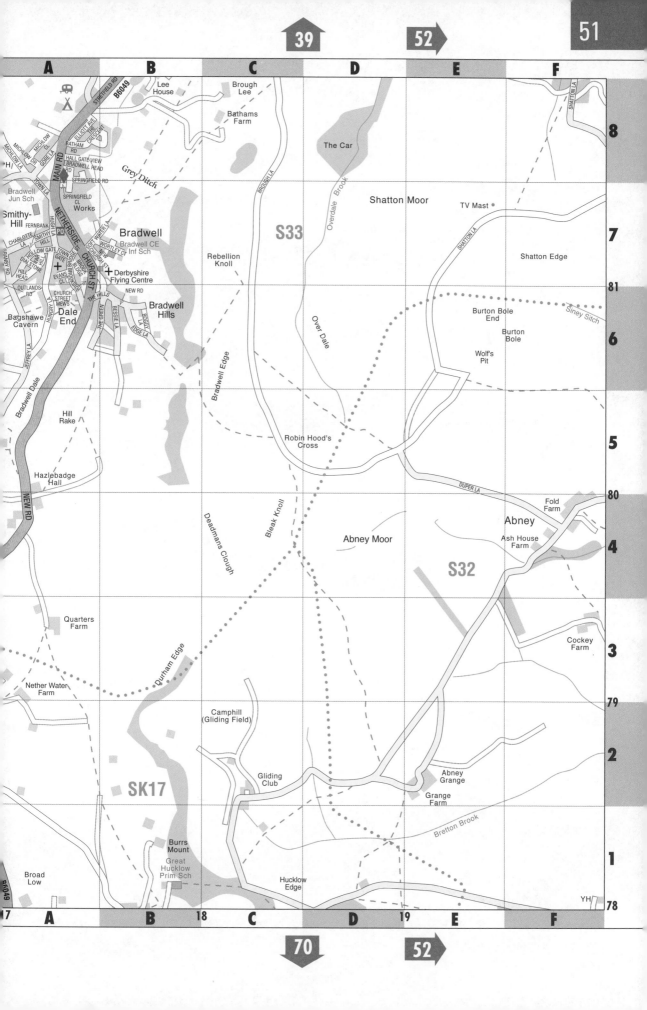

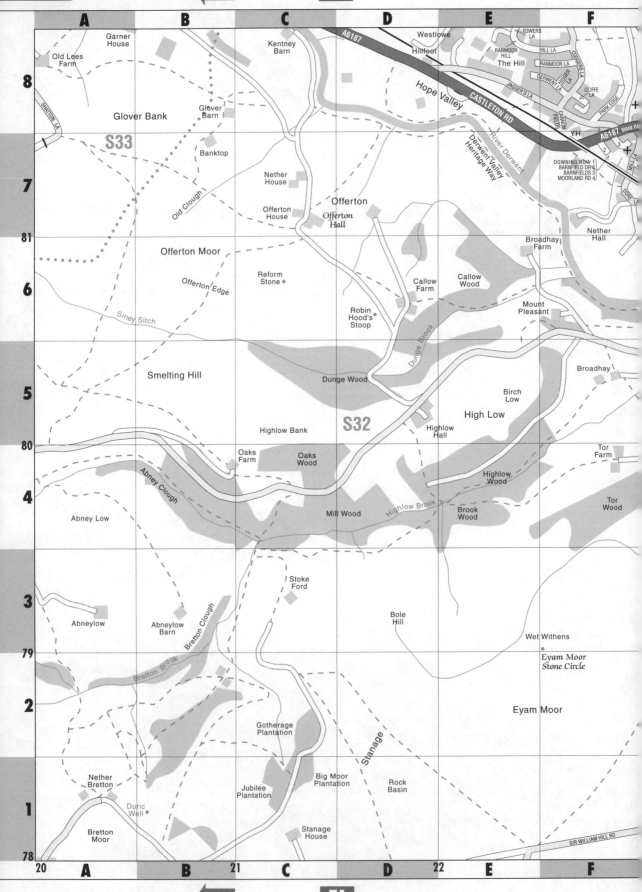

A6187

CASTLETON RD

Hope Valley

Westlowe

Hillfeet

TOWERS LA

RANMOOR HILL LA

HILL LA

COPPERS LA

The Hill

RANMOOR LA

DERWENT LA

HIGGER LA

JAGGER'S LA

CANYON FIELDS

CLIFFE LA

PARK EDGE

YH

A6187 MAIN RD

Garner House

Old Lees Farm

8

Glover Bank

S33

Glover Barn

Banktop

Kentney Barn

River Derwent

Derwent Valley Heritage Way

DOWNING ROW 1
BARNFIELD DR 2
BARNFIELDS 3
MOORLAND RD 4

MILL LA

DORE LA

Nether House

7

Old Clough

Nether House

Offerton House

Offerton

Offerton Hall

Broadhay Farm

Nether Hall

81

Offerton Moor

Offerton Edge

Reform Stone

Callow Farm

Callow Wood

Broadhay Farm

6

Siney Sitch

Robin Hood's Stoop

Dunge Brook

Mount Pleasant

Smelting Hill

Dunge Wood

Broadhay

5

Highlow Bank

S32

Birch Low

High Low

Highlow Hall

Oaks Farm

Oaks Wood

Tor Farm

80

Abney Clough

Highlow Wood

4

Abney Low

Mill Wood

Highlow Brook

Brook Wood

Tor Wood

Abneylow

Abneylow Barn

Bretton Clough

Stoke Ford

Bole Hill

Wet Withens

3

Eyam Moor Stone Circle

Bretton Brook

79

2

Gotherage Plantation

Stanage

Eyam Moor

Nether Bretton

Duric Well

Jubilee Plantation

Big Moor Plantation

Rock Basin

1

Bretton Moor

Stanage House

SIR WILLIAM HILL RD

78

20   A   B   21   C   D   22   E   F

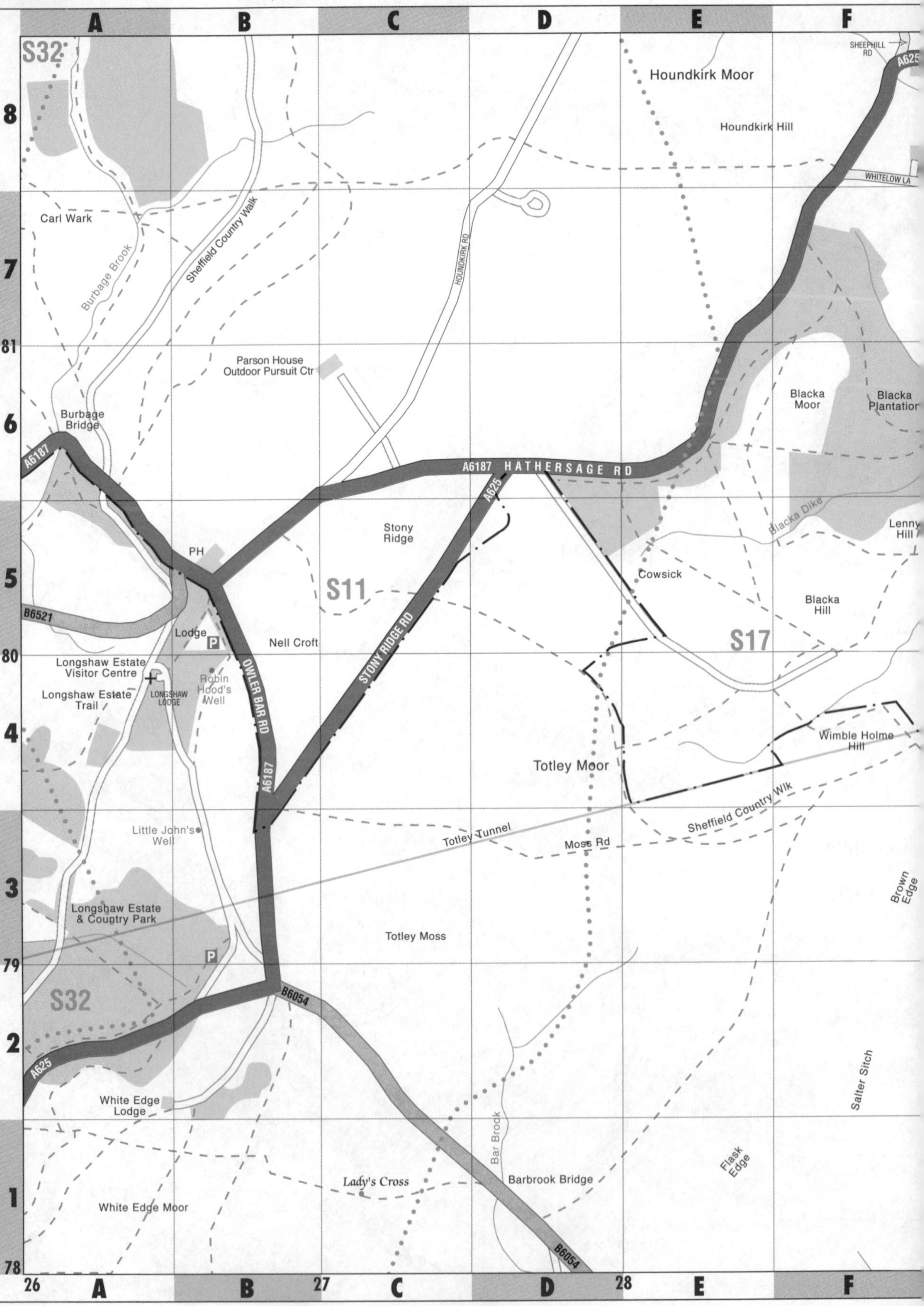

53
42

A | B | C | D | E | F

S32

Houndkirk Moor

Houndkirk Hill

SHEEPHILL RD

A625

8

WHITELOW LA

Carl Wark

Burbage Brook

Sheffield Country Walk

HOUNDKIRK RD

7

81

Parson House Outdoor Pursuit Ctr

Blacka Moor

Blacka Plantation

Burbage Bridge

A6187

A6187 HATHERSAGE RD

6

A625

Blacka Dike

PH

Stony Ridge

Cowsick

Lenny Hill

5

S11

Blacka Hill

B6521

STONY RIDGE RD

Lodge

P

Nell Croft

S17

80

Longshaw Estate Visitor Centre

Robin Hood's Well

OWLER BAR RD

A6191

Wimble Holme Hill

Longshaw Estate Trail

LONGSHAW LODGE

Totley Moor

4

Little John's Well

Totley Tunnel

Moss Rd

Sheffield Country Wlk

3

Longshaw Estate & Country Park

Totley Moss

P

Brown Edge

79

S32

B6054

2

A625

White Edge Lodge

Bar Brook

Salter Sitch

Flask Edge

Lady's Cross

Barbrook Bridge

1

White Edge Moor

B6054

78

26 | A | B | 27 | C | D | 28 | E | F

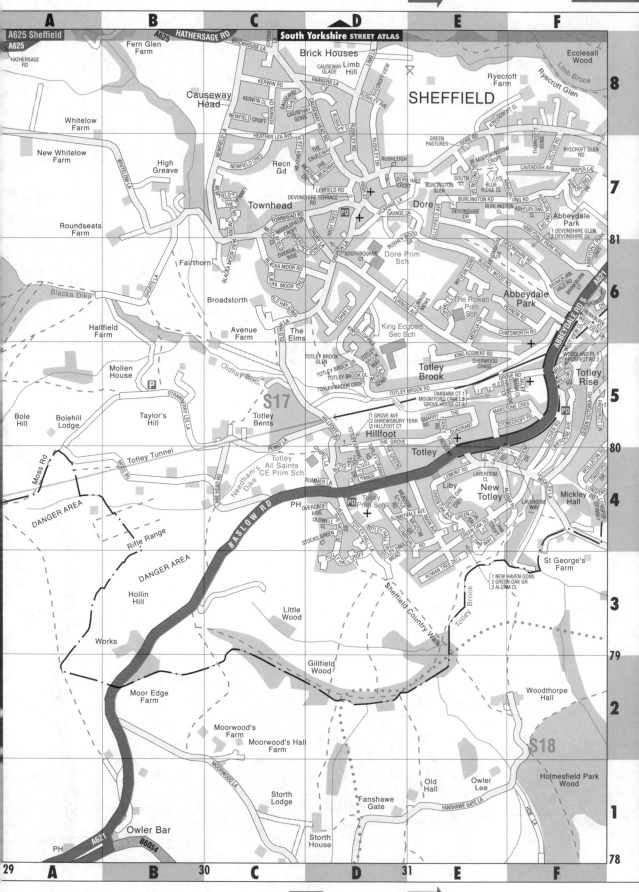

South Yorkshire STREET ATLAS

A625 Sheffield
A625
HATHERSAGE RD A625

HATHERSAGE RD

Brick Houses
Fern Glen Farm
Causeway Head
Whitelow Farm
New Whitelow Farm
High Greave
Townhead
Recn Gd
SHEFFIELD
Ryecroft Farm
Ryecroft Glen
Ecclesall Wood
Limb Brook

8

Roundseats Farm

Fairthorn
Broadstorth
Dore
Abbeydale Park
7

Blacka Dike
Hallfield Farm
Avenue Farm
The Elms
Dore Prim Sch
Southbourne Ct
The Rowan Prim Sch
Abbeydale Park
81

6

Mollen House
Taylor's Hill
Oldhay Brook
Totley Brook
King Egbert Sec Sch
King Egbert Rd
Sherwood Chase
Woodland Pl
Prospect Rd
Totley Rise

Bole Hill
Bolehill Lodge
S17
Totley Bents
Hillfoot
Totley Brook
Totley
The Quadrant
5

Moss Rd
Totley Tunnel
Needham's Dike
Totley All Saints CE Prim Sch
Liby
New Totley
Mickley Hall
80

DANGER AREA
Rifle Range
Totley Prim Sch
PH
4

DANGER AREA
Hollin Hill
St George's Farm

Works
Little Wood
Sheffield Country Walk
Totley Brook
3

Moor Edge Farm
Gillfield Wood
Woodthorpe Hall
79

BASLOW RD
Moorwood's Farm
Moorwood's Hall Farm
S18
2

Storth Lodge
Fanshawe Gate
Old Hall
Owler Lee
Holmesfield Park Wood

Storth House
FANSHAWE GATE LA
1

Owler Bar
PH A621 B6054

78

A B C D E F

8
7
81
6
5
80
4
3
79
2
1
78

35 36 37

A1
1 GOSFORTH LA
2 HILLSIDE AVE
3 NETHERDENE RD
4 PEMBROKE RD
5 UPPER SCHOOL LA
6 HIGHDALE FOLD

B1
1 SCARSDALE CROSS
2 SCARSDALE RD
3 PALMER CRES

Graves Park
Little Norton
CHARLES ASHMORE RD
Serpentine Wlk
GRAVES TRUST HOMES
Norton
LITTLE NORTON LA
BIRCH FARM AVE
GREENFIELD RD
LITTLE NORTON DR
LITTLE NORTON WAY
HUNSTONE AVE
NORTON PARK VIEW
NORTON PARK AVE
NORTON PARK RD
NORTON PARK DR
NORTON PARK CRES
CINDERHILL LA
B6057
Graves Tennis & L Ctr
The Sheffield Coll (Norton Coll)
Jordanthorpe
1 LITTLE NORTON WAY
2 HAIGH MEMORIAL HOMES
3 GREENHILL MAIN RD
4 GREENHILL PARKWAY
Meadowhead Sch Hotel
Sports Gd
LUPTON DR
LUPTON WLK
OWEDGES DR
OWEDGES RD
Lowedges
LOWEDGES PL
MEADOWHEAD
A61
CHESTERFIELD RD S
A6102
ROBERT RD
PO
Batemoor
BATEMOOR PL
BATEMOOR WLK
BATEMOOR RD
BATEMOOR CL
WHINACRE WLK
BOWSHAW VIEW
BOWSHAW RD
Lower Meadows Prim Sch
ORMOND RD
ORMOND CL
DYCHE LA
DYCHE CL
DYCHE RD
WHITE THORNS VIEW
WHITE THORNS DR
WHITE THORNS CL
Jordanthorpe Ctr
Liby
HAZLEBARROW RD
HAZLEBARROW CT
HAZLEBARROW CRES
HAZLEBARROW DR
JORDANTHORPE VIEW
JORDANTHORPE DR
LINGFOOT AVE
LINGFOOT WLK
SELLY OAK RD
SELLY OAK GR
JORDANTHORPE PARKWAY
BOCHUM PARKWAY
Mossbrook Sch
Jordanthorpe Plantation
CLOONMORE DR
HENLEY AVE
BROCKLEHURST AVE
SCHOOL LA
NORTON LA
THE MEADS
Oakes Park
A6102
Broomfield Wood
Lightwood Farm
Lightwood
LIGHTWOOD LA
HAZLEHURST LA
Hazlebarrow Farm
Newfield Spring Wood
S8
Coalpit Wood
Long Wood
The Moss
Nor Wood
Bridle Road Wood
Owler Car Wood
OWLER CAR LA
Whinacre Wood
Hillside Nurseries
Sicklebrook Farm
SICKLEBROOK LA
B6158
Ockley Farm
CROSS LA
DYCHE LA
Ppg Sta
Birchitt
Sheffield Country Walk
SHEFFIELD RD
Henpepper Farm
Holmefield Farm
PIGHILLS LA
Coal Aston
THORPE AVE
FARM WALK
WESTBANK CL
CUNLIFFE ST
WILSON RD
MEADOW CL
Birches Fold
RAWLINS CT
Cross and Birches Farm
ECKINGTON RD
Woodcock Farm
Bentley Hall
B6056
Nursery
Bentley Farm
Bentleyhall Farm
ASH LA
Holmley Common
HOLMLEY LA
BROOK LA
HOLMLEY BANK
BIRCHITT VIEW
FAIRVIEW RD
HILL CRES
SYCAMORE AVE
HAWTHORNE AVE
ELM TREE RD
LENTHAL RD
MARSH AVE
AVON CL
TRENT GR
DERWENT CL
DERWENT RD
SUMMERFIELD RD
GREEN LA
S18
KILN HILL
CROSS LA
BROWN LA
DRURY LA
WESTBANK FORRESTER'S CL
STONE CL
ASTON CL
LANGDALE DR
BENTS LA
BEATS CRES
FALCON RD
WARREN RISE
FALCON CL
RIDGEWAY
ECKINGTON RD
PROSPECT RD
BARNARD AVE
FERNDALE CL
FERNDALE RD
FERNDALE RISE
FRITHWOOD
FRITHWOOD CL
WOOD CL
Bentleyhall Farm
Ibbotson's Farm
Northfield Jun Sch
HOLMESDALE RD
HOLMESDALE CL
OAKHILL RD
THE KNOLL
OAKDELL
Holmesdale Inf Sch
Frith Wood
Summerley Farm
SUMMERLEY RD
Air strip
Snape Hill
LAIDEN AVE
OWLTHORNE AVE
ELM TREE AVE
SNAPE HILL LA
CONVERGLY CL
PERCIL ST
HARTINGTON RD
FANSHAW RD
ALEXANDRA RD
GLADYS BUXTON COM ED CTR
HADDON CL
HASSOP CL
PADDOCK WAY
HARDWICK
THE LAWN
The Avenue
Holmesdale
Greendale Sh Ctr
1 HARTINGTON CT
2 GREENDALE CT
3 STONELOW GN
STONELOW RD
SHIREOAKS RD
SHIREOAKS RD
FRITHWOOD DR
Summerley
ELM TREE FARM
SUMMERLEY LOWER RD
Snape Hill
THIRLMERE DR
SNAPE HILL CL
Lucas Works
Stonelow Jun Sch
Park Ave
GREEN CROSS
PRINCESS RD
HOLBURN CL
EGERTON RD
The Dronfield Henry Fanshawe Sch
Liby
Sp Ctr
WARDS YD
C Ctr
Dronfield Inf Sch
FAIRWATER
FAIRWINDS CL
GLEDHILL CL
Dronfield Jun Sch
GOMERSAL LA
MOONPENNY WAY
ARCHER AVE
NETHERDENE RD
HALLOWES
CROSS LA
The Forge
Dronfield
PO
COLLINS YD
STONE BANK CT
MILL LA
Quoit Green
CHESTERFIELD RD
B6158
Cliffe Park
Riverside Studios
Hunter Pk
Traso Bsns Pk
CALL WHITE LA
BIRCHL HOUSE WAY
STONELOW RD
FRITHWOOD PARKGATE
Bridgefield Wood
BACK LA
TOWN END
B6057

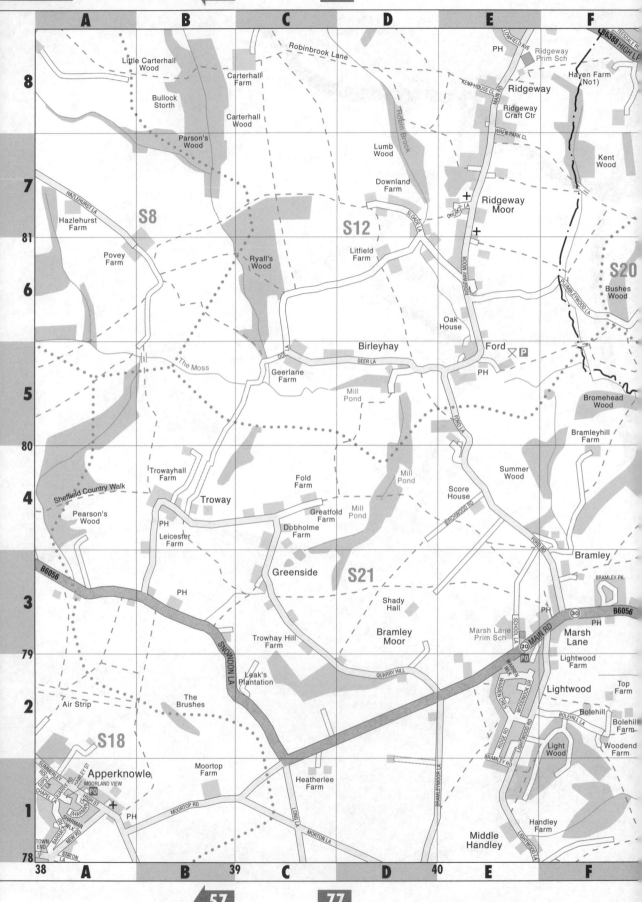

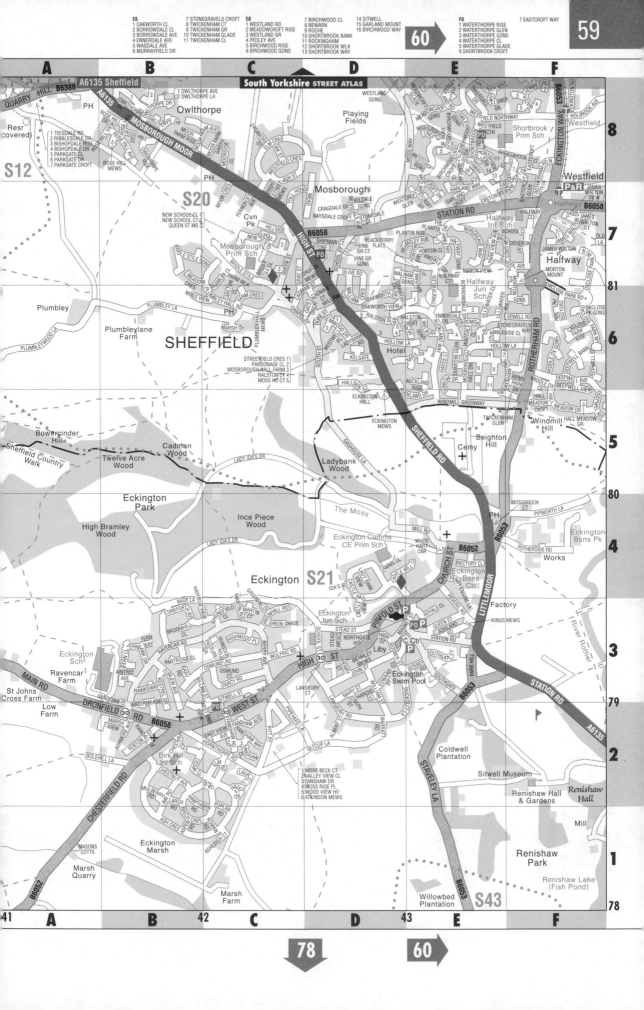

M1 Leeds

Nor Wood

Spoil Heap

Hard Field

Baugy Hill

Top Farm

Poplar Farm

North Farm

North Farm Cl

Beehive Farm

Woodall

KILLAMARSH LA

Killamarsh Pond

Woodall Pond

S21

Low Plantation

Sewage Wks

Woodall House Farm

Broad Bridge

WOODALL LA

Harthill

Chapel Yd

Rectory Gdns

Jackys La

Orchard Lee

PH

Kye La

Street Farm Cl

Woodall Bottoms

Stone Hill

S26

Harthill Resr

Harthill Prim Sch

Priory Ct

Crescent

Hewitt Pl

Firvale

Common Rd

Woodall Service Area

Woodall Common

Woodall Rd

DONCOR LA

Motel

Fir Hill

Mansfield Rd

Woodall Common

Birkenhead Wood

Carr Farm Cottage

Carr Farm

Pebleygrove Farm

PH

Pebley Oaks

Pebley Resr

Harthill Field

WARD LA

S43

ROTHERHAM RD

Crabtree Wood

Car Plantation

S80

Hawke Wood

Garden Plantation

Nitticarhill Wood

Butcherlawn Pond

Nitticarhill Rd

Nitticarhill

Barlborough Hall Sch

Longrybank Wood

A618

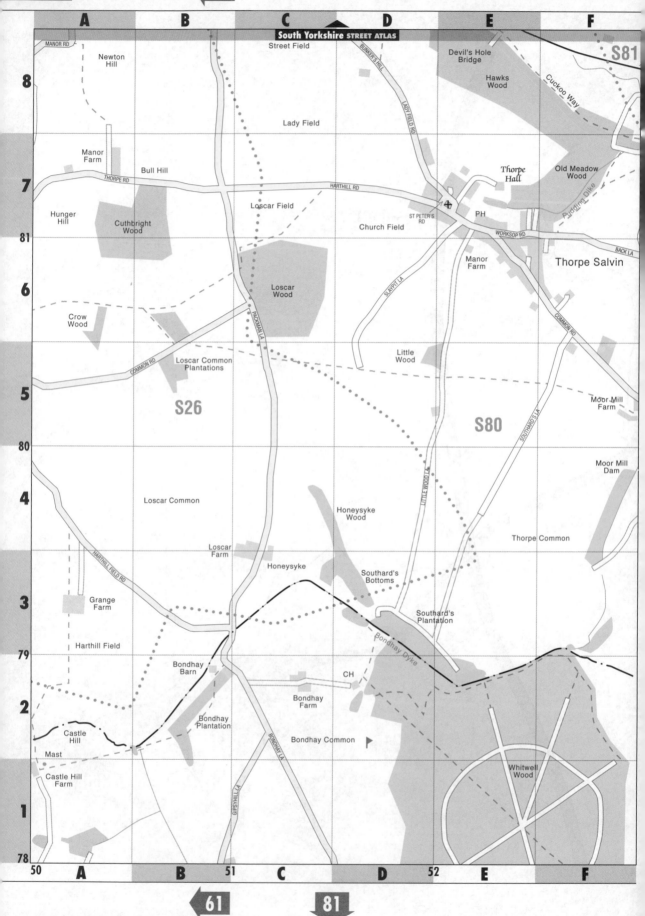

South Yorkshire STREET ATLAS

S81

MANOR RD

Newton Hill

Street Field

BUNKER'S HILL

Devil's Hole Bridge

Hawks Wood

Cuckoo Way

8

Lady Field

LADY FIELD RD

Manor Farm

Bull Hill

THORPE RD

Harthill RD

Thorpe Hall

Old Meadow Wood

Pudding Dike

7

Hunger Hill

Cuthbright Wood

Loscar Field

Church Field

ST PETER'S RD

PH

Manor Farm

Thorpe Salvin

WORKSOP RD

BACK LA

81

Crow Wood

Loscar Wood

PACKMAN LA

SLAYPIT LA

Little Wood

COMMON RD

6

Loscar Common Plantations

COMMON RD

S26

S80

Moor Mill Farm

5

SOUTHARD'S LA

80

Loscar Common

Honeysyke Wood

LITTLE WOOD LA

Thorpe Common

Moor Mill Dam

4

HARTHILL FIELD RD

Loscar Farm

Honeysyke

Southard's Bottoms

Southard's Plantation

3

Grange Farm

Harthill Field

Bondhay Dyke

79

Bondhay Barn

CH

Bondhay Farm

2

Castle Hill

Mast

Bondhay Plantation

GIPSY HILL LA

BONDHAY LA

Bondhay Common

Whitwell Wood

Castle Hill Farm

1

78

50   A   B   51   C   D   52   E   F

Fan Field

Fan Field Farm

Low Spring Wood

Brancliffe Grange

Potters Nook Bridge

Pilgrim Ct

St Luke's CE Prim Sch

S81

Old Spring Wood

Turnerwood Bridge

Broad Wood

Low Mdw Row

Branclffe La

Monks Cl

Cartwright St

Woodside Rd

Elmtree Cl

PO

Turnerwood

Chesterfield Canal

Cinder Hill

Glenthorn Cl

Middle Mdw

Leeds Cl

Cornwall Rd

Cherry Tree Ave

Shireoaks

LC

Walnut Ave

PH

Bethel Terr

St Lukes View

Shireoaks Row

Marina

Common Rd

81

Back La

Bondhay Dyke

Hatfield Farm

+ Shireoaks

River Ryton

Bottom Farm

Little La

Thorpe La

PH

Shireoaks Rd

6

Netherthorpe

The Hall

Sp Gd

Lob Wells Wood

Top Farm

Oak Wood

Spring La

Netherthorpe Airfield

Shireoaks Park Wood

Top Hall

Thorpe Rd

Nether

Common Rd

River Ryton

80

Whittwell Rd

S80

Scratta Wood

Holme Carr

Spring La

Dumb Hall La

Steetley La

Darfoulds Dike

Silver Birches

3

79

Whittwell Rd

Works

Dumb Hall

Scratta La

Steetley Farm Cottages

Armstrong Quarry

Firbeck Common

Firbeck Farm

Firbeck House

Steetley Holme +

Firbeck Cla

Firbeck Cottage

A619

Darfoulds

Featherbed La

A619 Worksop

Arrow Farm

A619

78

Nottinghamshire STREET ATLAS

Browtop
Farm

Hodgel Brook

Ladbitch
Wood

Oldfield

Works

River Goyt

LONG HILL

A5004

A5004

P

Hoo Moor

SK23

Goyt Forest

Pymchair
Farm

P

Pym Chair

EMBRIDGE S.WY

Midshires Way

Goyt Valley

Fernilee Reservoir

Calfhay
Wood

Cheshire STREET ATLAS

Oldgate
Nick

Jep Clough

THE STREET

The Street

Goyt Valley
Walks

Cats Tor

Withinleach
Moor

SK10

P

P

Bunsal
Cob

Sailing
Club

Foxlow Edge

The Tors

Errwood Reservoir

SK17

Errwood Hall

P

Errwood
Forest Walks

GOYT'S LA

SK11

Shooter's Clough

River Goyt

Stake
Side

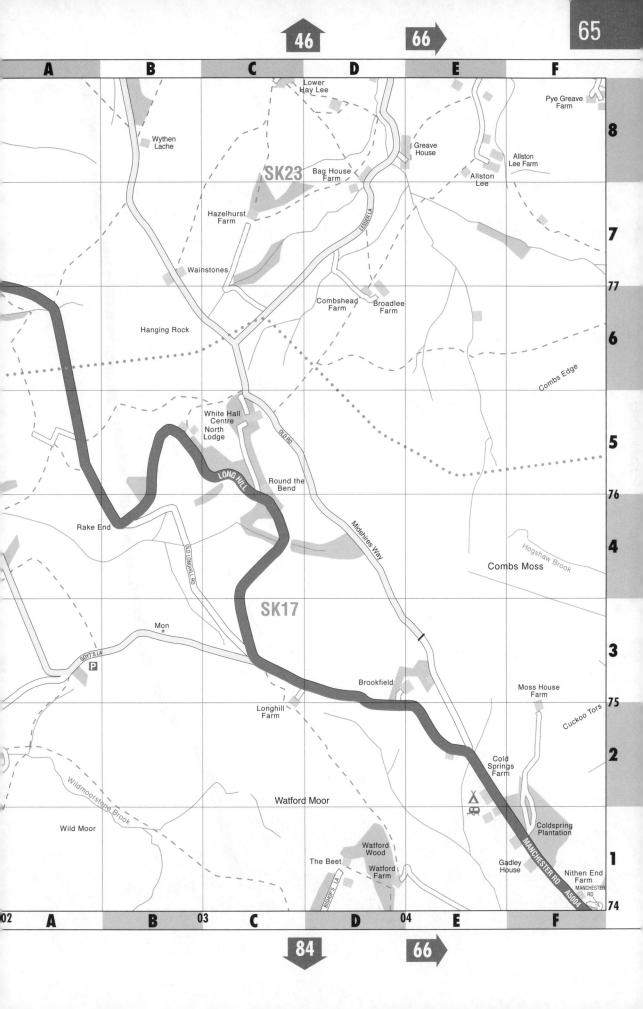

65
47

| | A | B | C | D | E | F |

8

7

77

6

5

76

4

3

75

2

1

74

Pyegreaye Brook

SK23

Hob Tor

Resrs

The Meadows Sch

Ashpiece Farm

1 STATION RD
2 HALLSTEADS

DALE RD

PH

BUXTON RD

P

Bibbington

LONGRIDGE LA

Combs Moss

Black Edge

Blackedge Resr

Blackedge Farm

Tom Thorn Farm

Field Farm

BATHAM GATE

SK17

Thorn Head Farm

Batham Gate

Tomthorn

WATERSWALLOWS LA

High Peak Nurseries

Hogshaw Brook

Television Station

Mast

Resr

Turner Lodge

Brook House

Breezemount Farm

Waterswallows Green

Brownedge Plantation

Lightwood Resr

Frome Lodge

Brookhouse Farm

Light Wood

Works

Hogshaw Brook

NURSERY DR

BROWN EDGE RD

The Barms Farm

DAISYMERE LA

WATERSWALLOWS RD

BUXTON

Nunsfield Farm

Fairfield Common

A6

Corbar Hill

LIGHTWOOD RD

WILLIAMSON AVE

BIRCH CL

LADYCROFT

CROSSHAW DR

Corbar Woods

WYE HO

CORBAR RD

SYCAMORE CL

SHERATON RD

ASPEN CL

CHESTNUT CL

LANSDOWNE RD

LASCELLES RD

St Anne's RC Prim Sch

30

BARMS WAY

NUNSFIELD RD

GLENMOOR RD

ST PETER'S RD

FAIRFIELD RD

LINKS VIEW

MOORFIELD

CHERRY TREE DR

MOON PL

SCROL TERR

GOLF TERR

CLEER PL

CROSS ST

ASHWOOD RD

DAKIN CT

TOWN END

PH

CH

WATERSWALLOWS MS

TESSERA

Townend Farm

| 05 | A | | B | 06 | C | | D | 07 | E | | F |

65
85

A B C D E F

8

Sewage Works

Dove Holes Quarry

Lodes La

Smalldale

Batham Gate

Heath Farm

7

SMALLDALE COTTS

Works

Smalldale Rd

Middle Hill

77

PH

SMALL KNOWLE END

6

Higher Bibbington

Batham Gate Rd

Gorsey Nook

Withered Low

Wormhill Moor

Church Ave

Peak Dale

School Rd

Highfields

PO

Ppg Sta

5

Peak Dale Prim Sch

Meadow Ave

Memorial Pl

Sewage Works

SK17

Thornheyes Farm

Upper End

New St

Ferndale Ave

Ferndale Rd

76

Longbridge La

Broadlow Farm

Spring Bank

Upper End Rd

Buxton Bridge

4

Bole Hill

Waterswallows Ind Pk

Great Rocks Lees

3

WATERSWALLOWS LA

Waterswallows La

Hardybarn

Taylor Farm

WATERSWALLOWS LA

Water Swallows

75

Tunstead

Waterswallows Green

Green La

2

Daisymere La

Waterswallows Quarry

Hardybarn La

Great Rocks Tunnel

Green La

Green Fairfield

Greenfairfield Farm

Redgap La

Daisymere Farm

1

Tunstead Works

74

08 A 09 B C D 10 E F

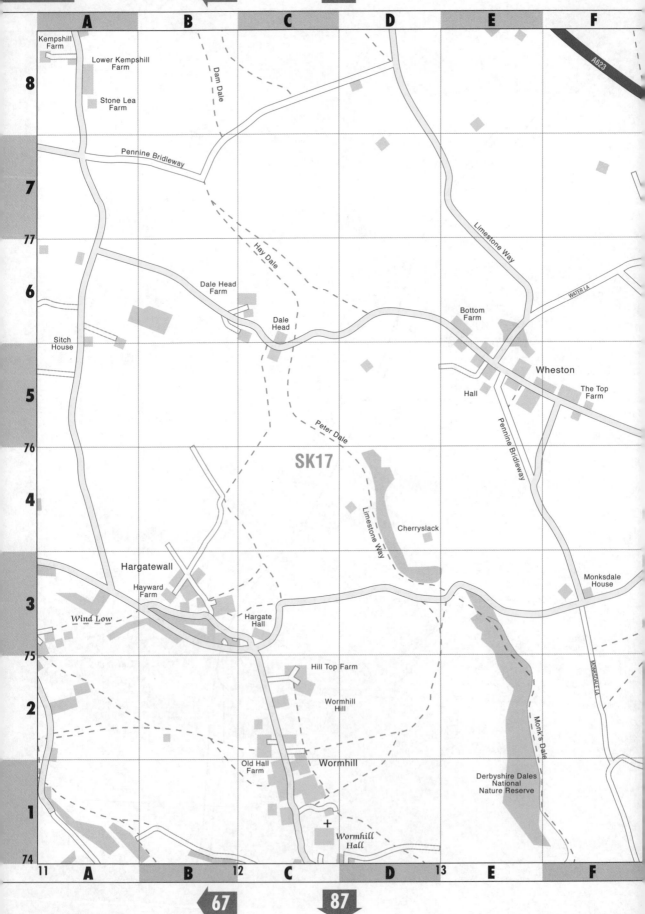

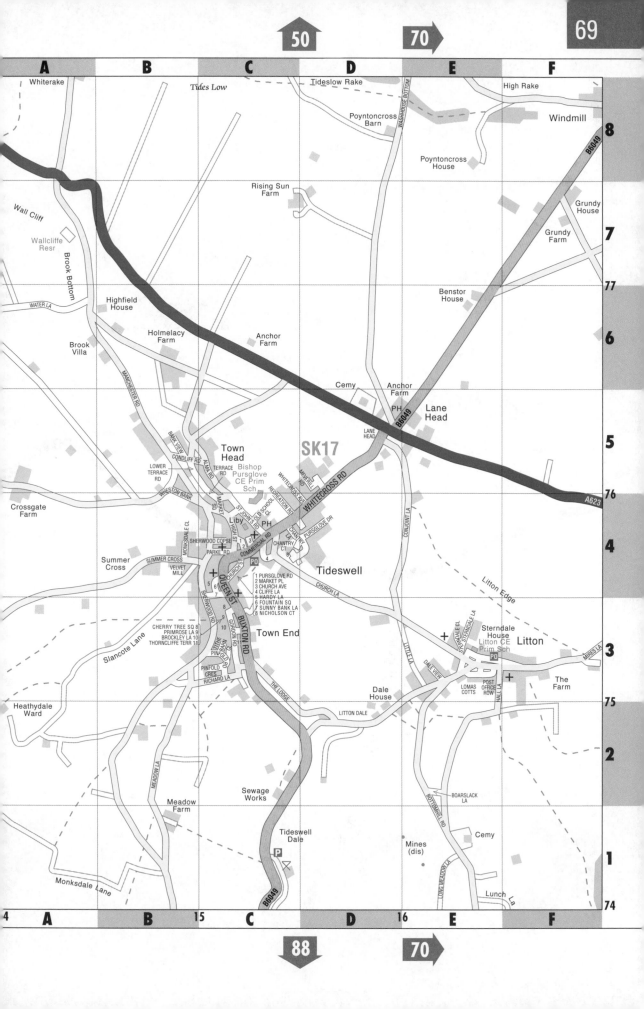

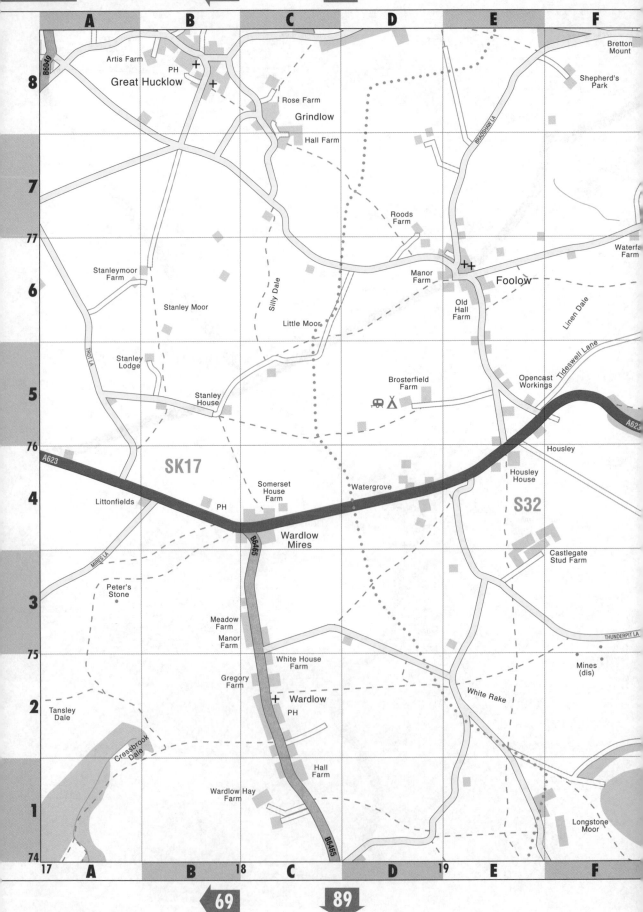

A B C D E F

8

Artis Farm
Great Hucklow
PH
Rose Farm
Grindlow
Hall Farm

Bretton Mount
Shepherd's Park

7

Roods Farm

77

Stanleymoor Farm

Manor Farm
Foolow

Waterfa
Farm

6

Stanley Moor

Silly Dale

Little Moor

Old Hall Farm

Linen Dale

Stanley Lodge

Brosterfield Farm

Opencast Workings

5

Stanley House

Housley

76

SK17
A623

Housley House

Littonfields
PH

Somerset House Farm

Watergrove

S32

4

Wardlow Mires
B6465

Castlegate Stud Farm

MIRES LA

THUNDERPIT LA

Peter's Stone

3

Meadow Farm
Manor Farm

75

Mines (dis)

White House Farm

2

Tansley Dale

Gregory Farm

Wardlow
PH

White Rake

Cressbrook Dale

Hall Farm

1

Wardlow Hay Farm

Longstone Moor

B6465

74

17 A B 18 C D 19 E F

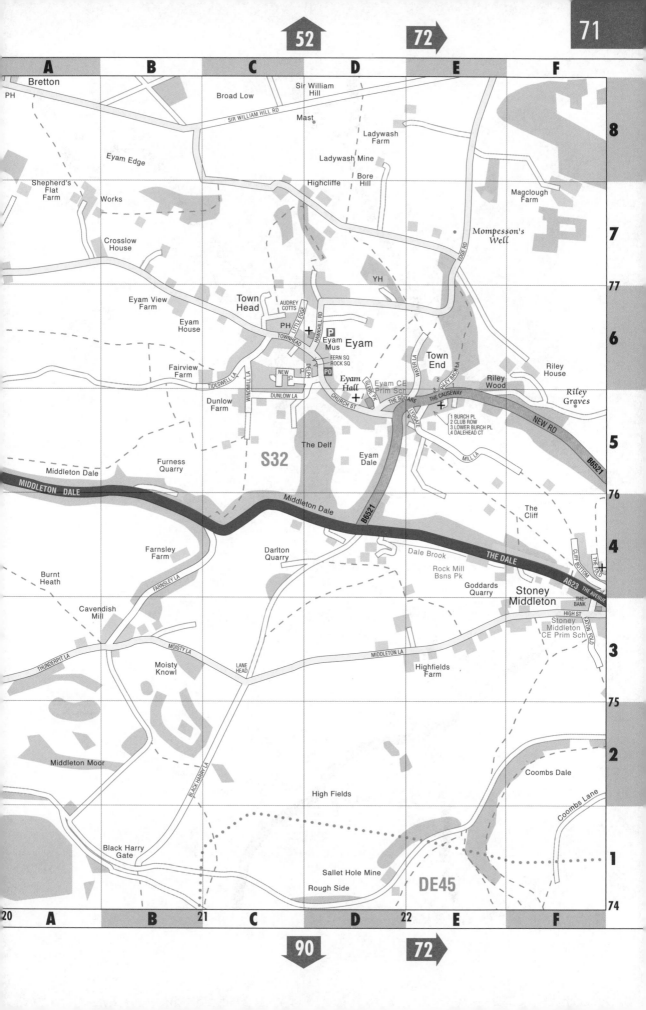

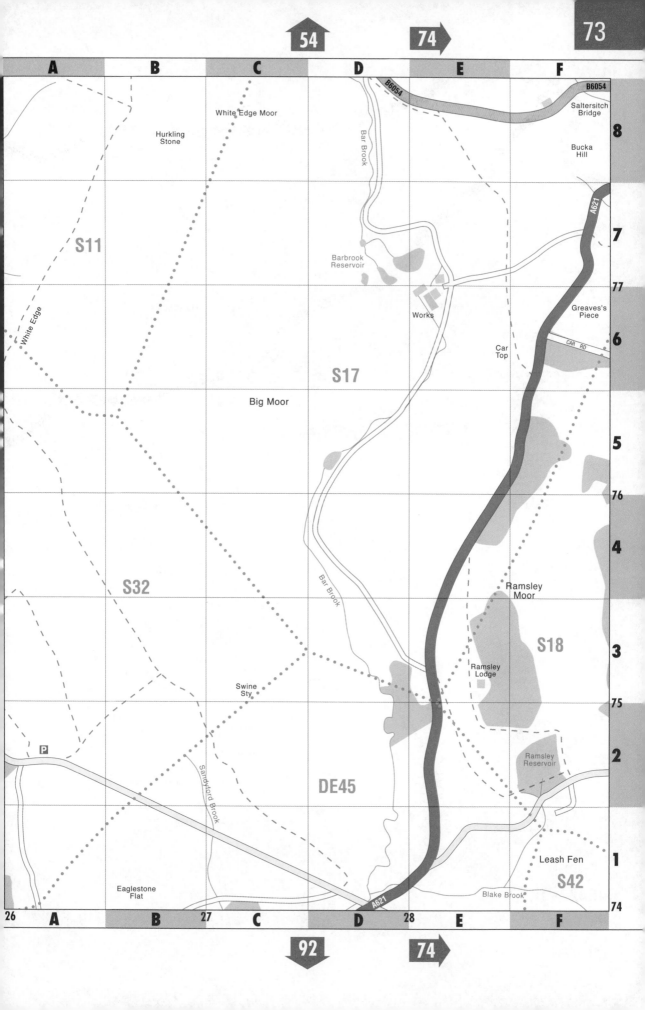

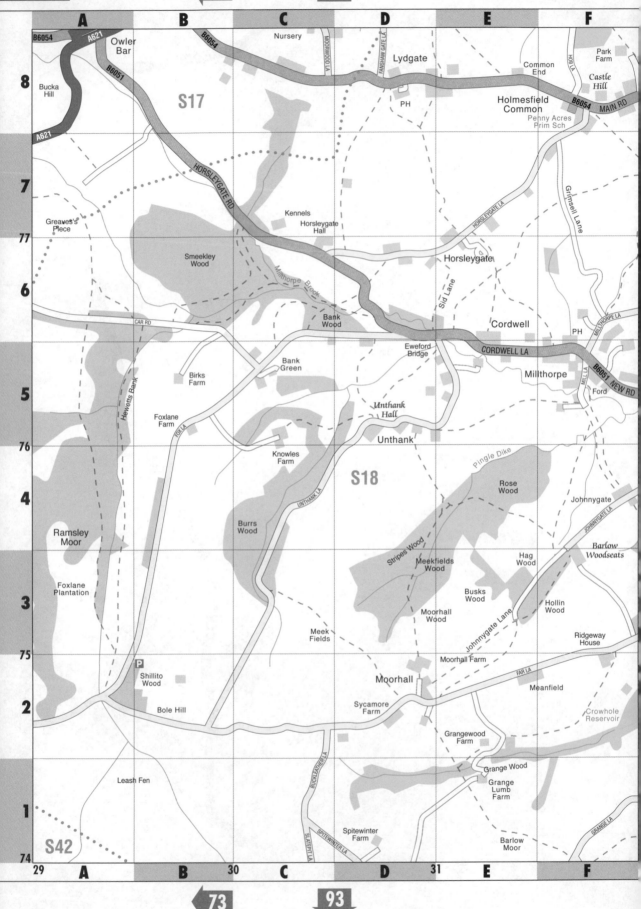

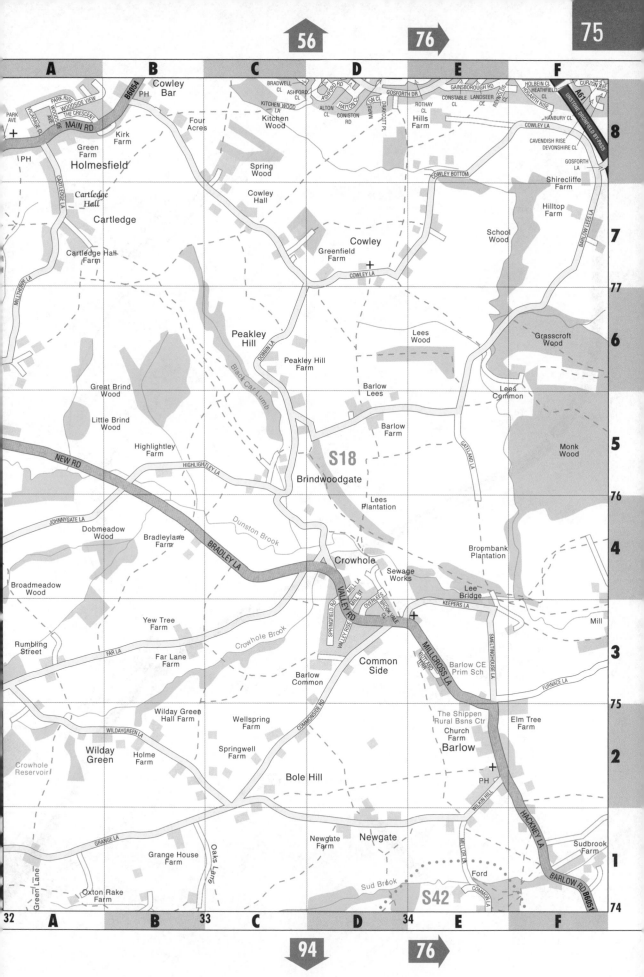

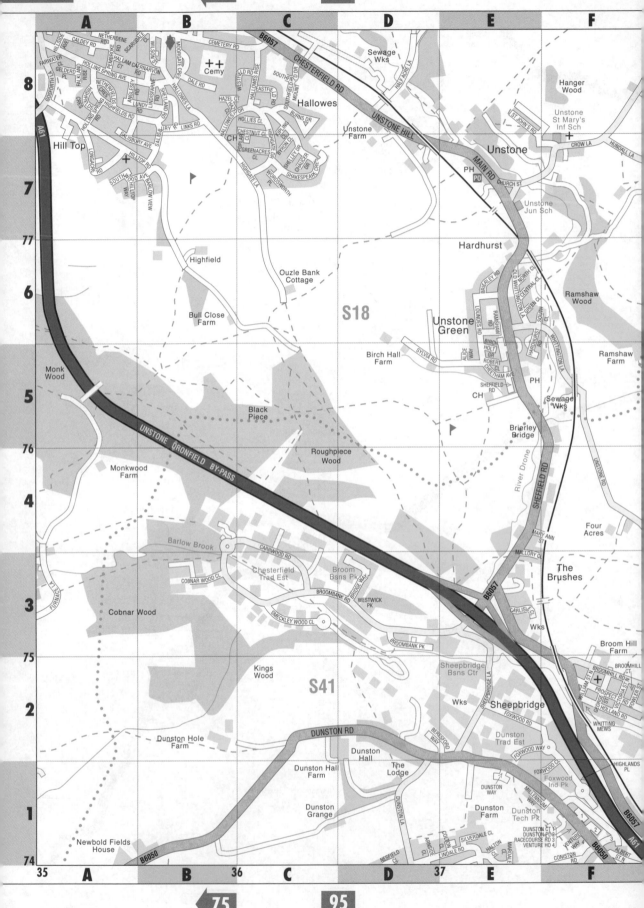

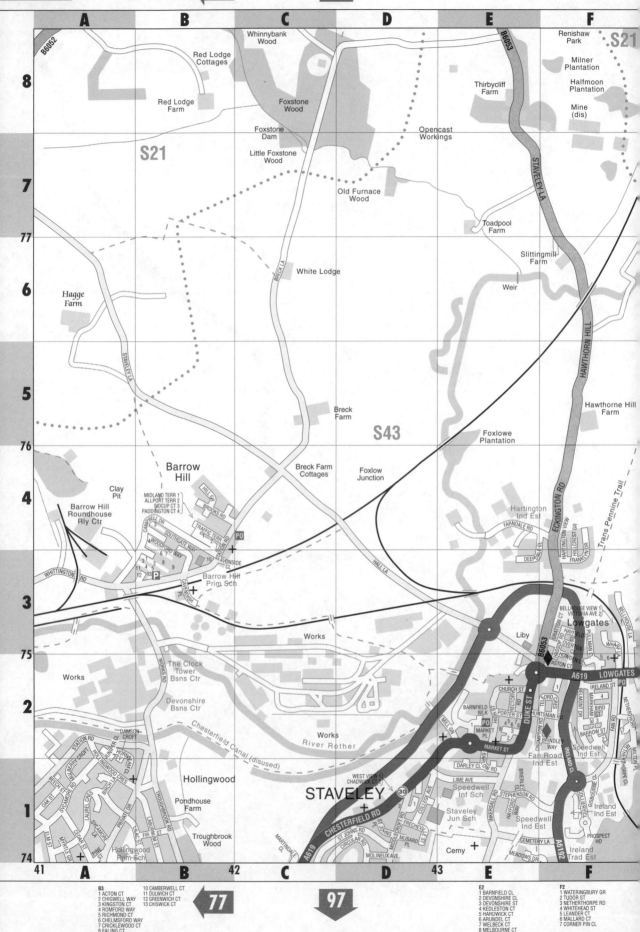

B3
1 ACTON CT
2 CHIGWELL WAY
3 KINGSTON CT
4 ROMFORD WAY
5 RICHMOND CT
6 CHELMSFORD WAY
7 CRICKLEWOOD CT
8 EALING CT
9 DUEWELL CT

10 CAMBERWELL CT
11 DULWICH CT
12 GREENWICH CT
13 CHISWICK CT

E2
1 BARNFIELD CL
2 DEVONSHIRE CL
3 DEVONSHIRE ST
4 KEDLESTON CT
5 HARDWICK CT
6 ARUNDEL CT
7 WELBECK CT
8 MELBOURNE CT
9 PORTER HO

F2
1 WATERINGBURY GR
2 TUDOR ST
3 NETHERTHORPE RD
4 WHITEHEAD ST
5 LEANDER CT
6 MALLARD CT
7 CORNER PIN CL

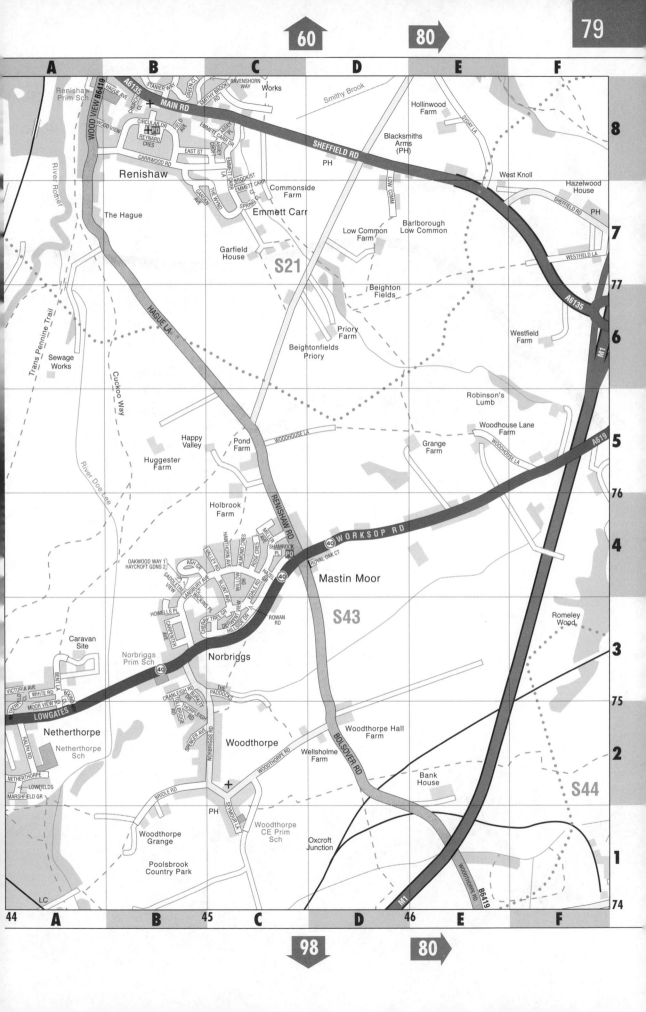

A B C D E F

8

Arrow Farm

Burnt Leys
Cottages

Steetley
Corner

Firbeck La

PH

Burnt Leys
Farm

Red Hill

7

CLINTHILL LA A619

Darfoulds Dike

Ratcliffe
Grange
Farm

WORKSOP RD B6043

Ratcliffe
Cottages

77

SUNNYSIDE

Birks
Farms

Birks
Cottages

6

LONGCROFT
VIEW

Hodthorpe

Sewage
Works

New
Farm

Whitwell

KINGS WAY

ST MARTIN'S WLK

GREENFIELD AVE

BIRCH RD

BIRKS GL

BROAD LA

KING ST

QUEENS RD

BROAD PL

Hall Leys
Farm

Hodthorpe
Prim Sch

1 SPRING ST
2 LONGHURST VIEW

5

Whitwell
Prim Sch

Whitwell

WHITWELL

GREEN LA

S80

Ox Pastures
Farm

Wallingbrook
Wood

Walling Brook

76

Southfield
Ind Site

New
Cottages

Depot

Penny
Green

Belph

Belph
Grange

Bismark
Plantation

Millwood Brook

4

MILLASH LA

Penny Green
Cottages

Springfield
Farm

Millwood
Lodge

3

Chy

Works

Mill
Wood

Ganabrig
Wood

West Park

Burial Ground
Plantation

75

HENNYMOOR LA

B6042

Ladycroft
Wood

2

CRAGS RD

Henneymoor
Farm

Fishpond
Lodge

Robin Hood Way

Oaksetts
Lodge

Cowclose
Wood

1

B6042

Caves Cresswell Crags

Craggs
Cottages

Pin
Hole

CRAGS RD

Creswell
Crags
Visitor Ctr

Crags
Pond

Craft
Ctr

74

Church
Hole

A60

53 A B 54 C D 55 E F

MANSFIELD RD

A60 WORKSOP

Nottinghamshire STREET ATLAS

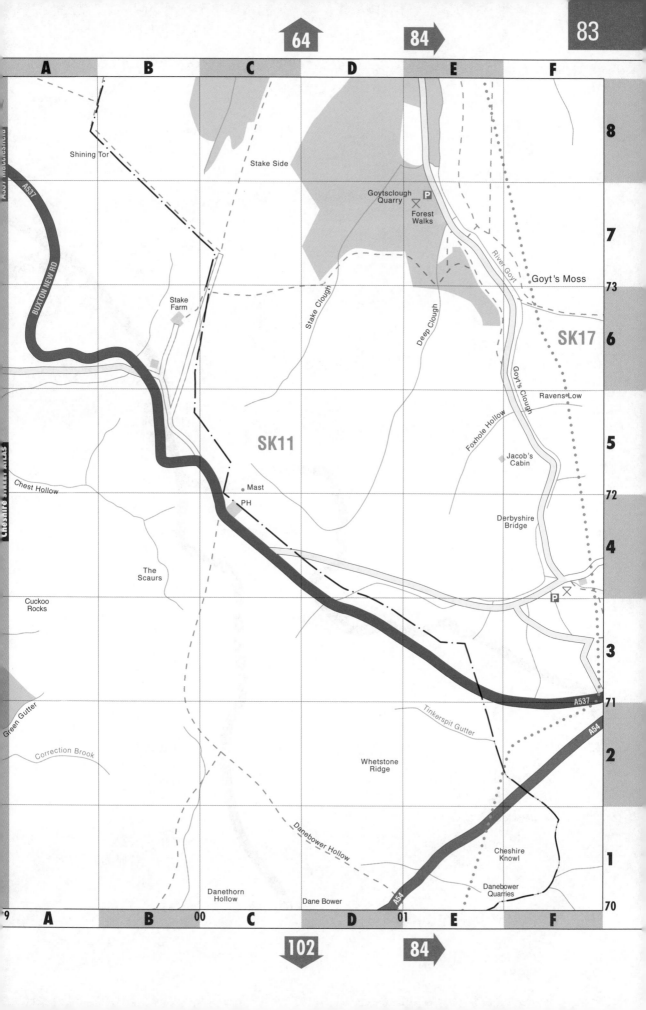

A B C D E F

8

A537 Macclesfield

Shining Tor

Stake Side

Goytsclough
Quarry

P
Forest
Walks

7

River Goyt

Goyt's Moss

73

BUXTON NEW RD

A537

Stake Clough

Stake Farm

Deep Clough

SK17

6

Goyt's Clough

Ravens Low

Chest Hollow

SK11

Foxhole Hollow

Jacob's
Cabin

5

72

Mast

PH

Derbyshire
Bridge

4

The
Scaurs

Cuckoo
Rocks

P

3

A537

71

Green Gutter

Tinkerspit Gutter

A54

Correction Brook

Whetstone
Ridge

2

Danebower Hollow

Cheshire
Knowl

1

A54

Danethorn
Hollow

Dane Bower

Danebower
Quarries

70

'9 A B 00 C D 01 E F

Cheshire STREET ATLAS

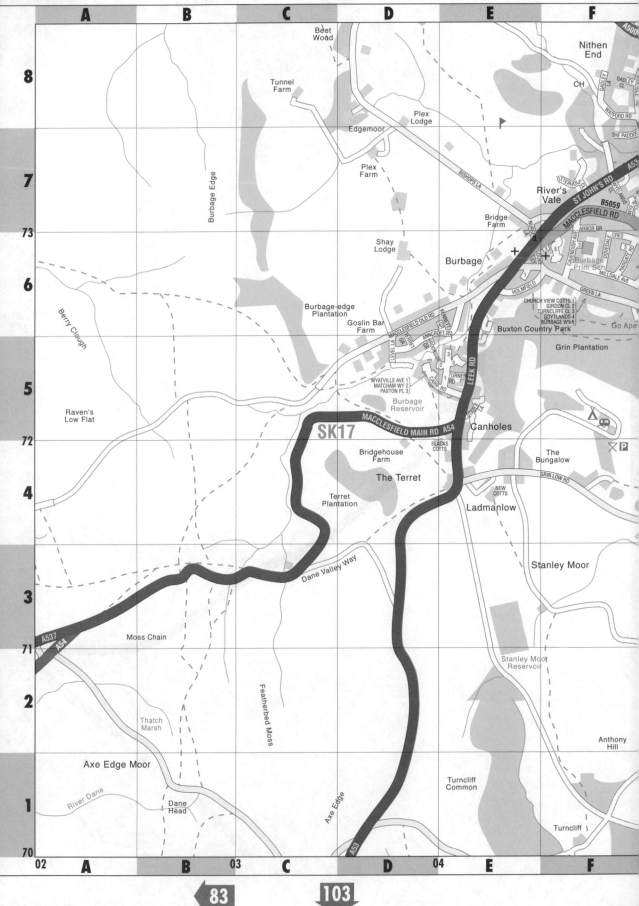

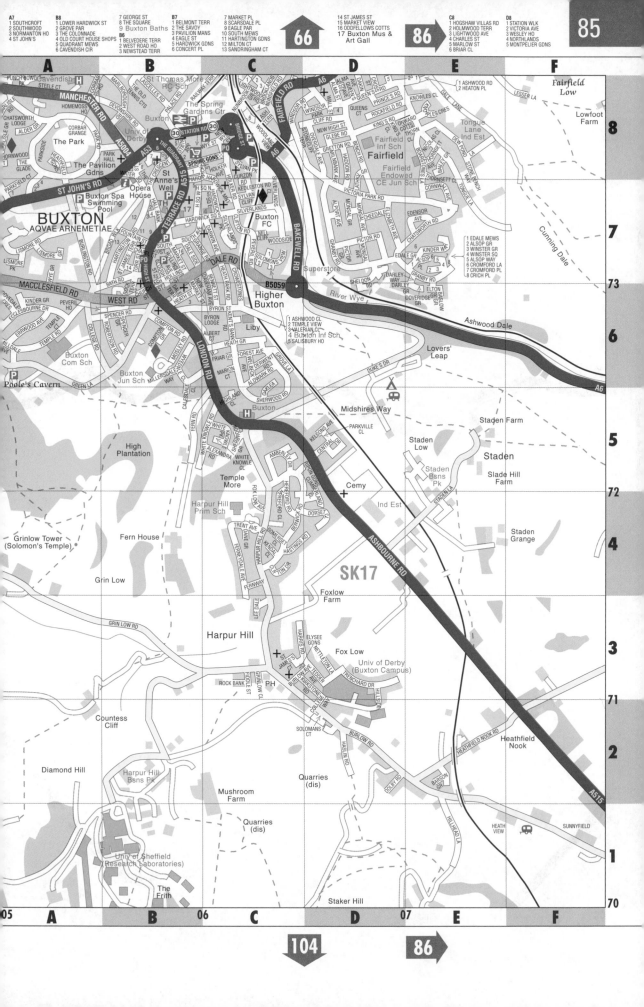

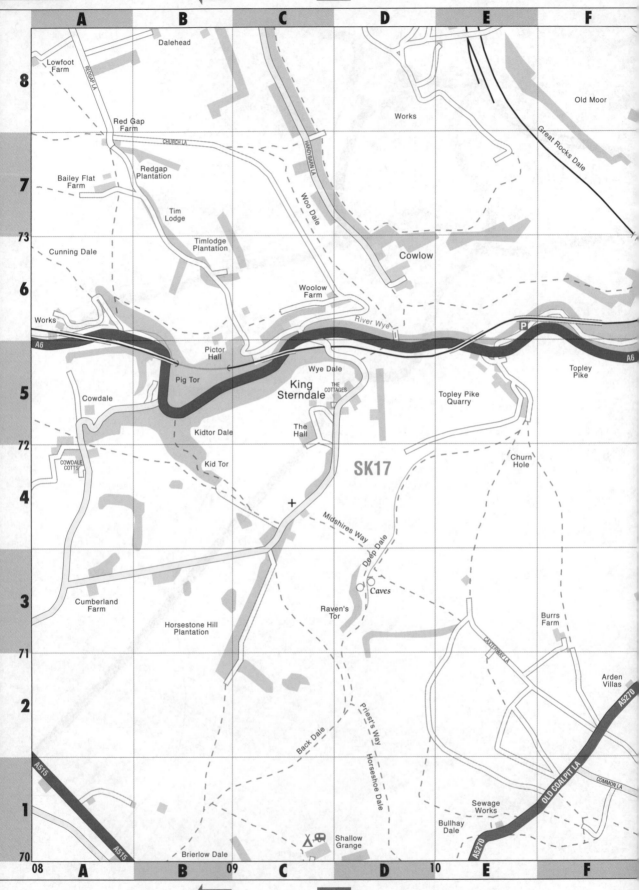

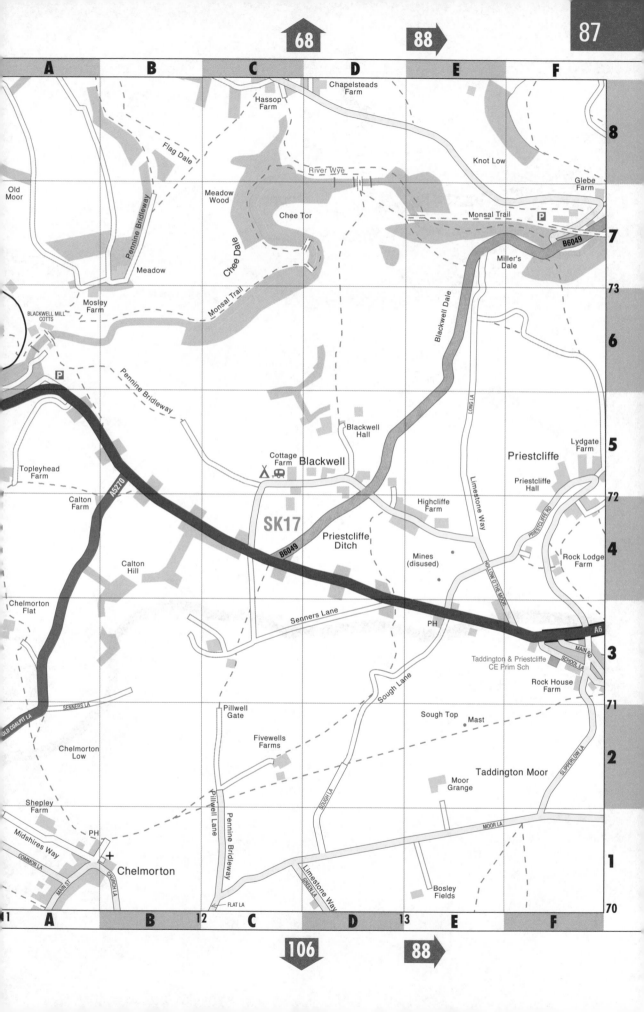

87
69

A **B** **C** **D** **E** **F**

8

Limestone Way

Monksdale Farm

MEADOW LA

B6049

Beltonville

Tideswell Dale

NEW HOUSES

LUNCH LA

ROCK VIEW

B6049

PH

Ravenstor YH

Hammerton Hill

Miller's Dale

Field Study Centre

Slack Side

LITTONSLACK

BOTTOMHILL RD

TOP COTTS

7

Miller's Dale

CURZON TERR

RIVER VIEW

Litton Mill

73

Priestcliffe Lees (Nature Reserve)

River Wye

Monsal Trail

Cressbrook Hall

Moorhigh Mine (dis)

Burfoot

6

Mines (dis)

Bull Tor

BULLTOR LANE

BROADWAY LANE

High Field

5

72

SK17

High Dale

Brushfield

4

Top Farm

Middle Farm

Lower Farm

Brushfield Hough

Horse Stead

A6

Taddington Dale

New Plantation

3

LOWER SMITHY LA

Waterlees Road

SCHOOL LA

CHAPEL LA

Taddington

HADES LA

THE CROFT

MAIN RD

Water Lees

71

SMITHY LA

PH

WESLEYAN CHAPEL LA

Sewage Works

Lodley View

A6

2

Taddington Field

MOOR LA

Taddington Wood

1

THE JARNETT

BARE JARNETT RD

Coombe Farm

70

14 **A** **B** **15** **C** **D** **16** **E** **F**

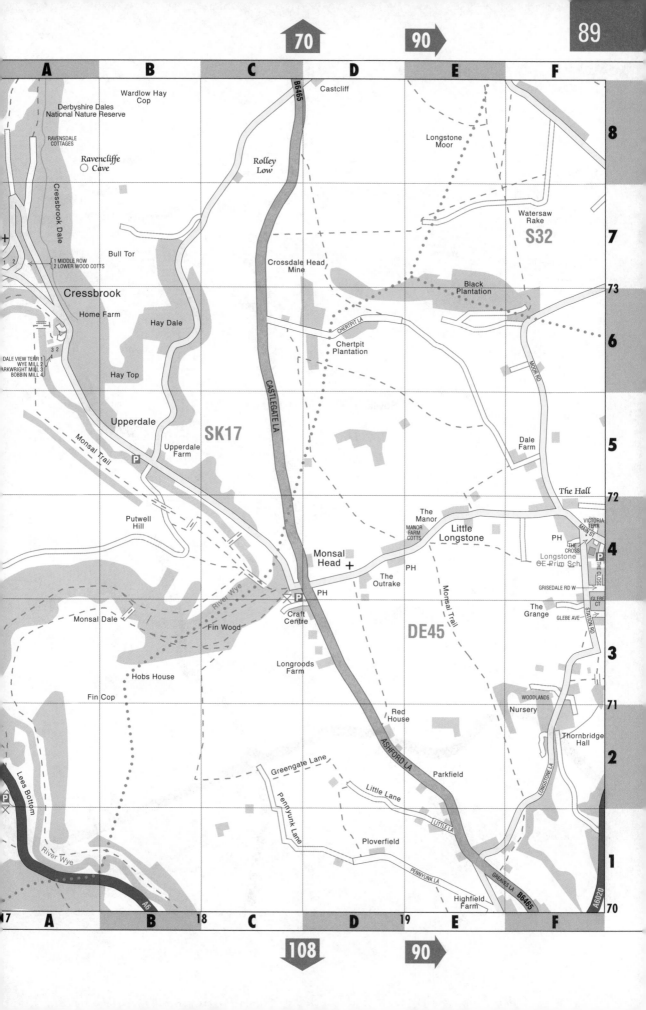

A   B   C   D   E   F

8

Mines (disused)

Deep Rake

Opencast Workings

Longstone Moor Farm

Opencast Workings

BRAMLEY LA

S32

High Rake

Bleaklow

Opencast Workings

7

Beacon Rod

Longstone Edge

Opencast Workings

Opencast Workings

Hassop Common

B6001

73

Opencast Workings

6

Top Farm

Hardrake Lane

Rowland

Torrs Farm

PH

Dog Kennel Wood

5

Underedge

Hassop Hall

Home Farm

Hassop

BEGGARWAY LA

Hermitage Pond

72

LONGREAVE LA

Long Rake Plantation

Bowling Green Wood

+

Standhill Farm

Longstone Bsns Pk

BARN FURLONG

CHURCH LA

The Mires

Great Longstone

DE45

Hassop Park

Flatts Farm

Birchill Bank Wood

4

MAIN ST

CROFT RD

EDGE VIEW DR

ORISEDALE RD W

ORISEDALE RD E

1 2 3 4

MIRES LA

GRISEDALE RD W
FIRHILL RD
GLEBE AVE
GLEBE CT

1 SUNNY BANK
2 SPRING BANK
3 WESTERN VIEW
4 THE MEADOWS

Buskey Cottage

Oak Wood

Park Farm

Birchills Farm

3

71

Toll Bar House

Rowdale House

Monsal Trail

2

A6020

Churchdale Farm

Cracknowl Wood

Station Farm

HASSOP RD

Nether Wood

A619

B6048

Churchdale Hall

Flatt Plantation

A6020

Old Hollow Plantation

1

BASLOW RD   A619

B6001

Cracknowl House

70

20   A   21   B   C   22   D   E   F

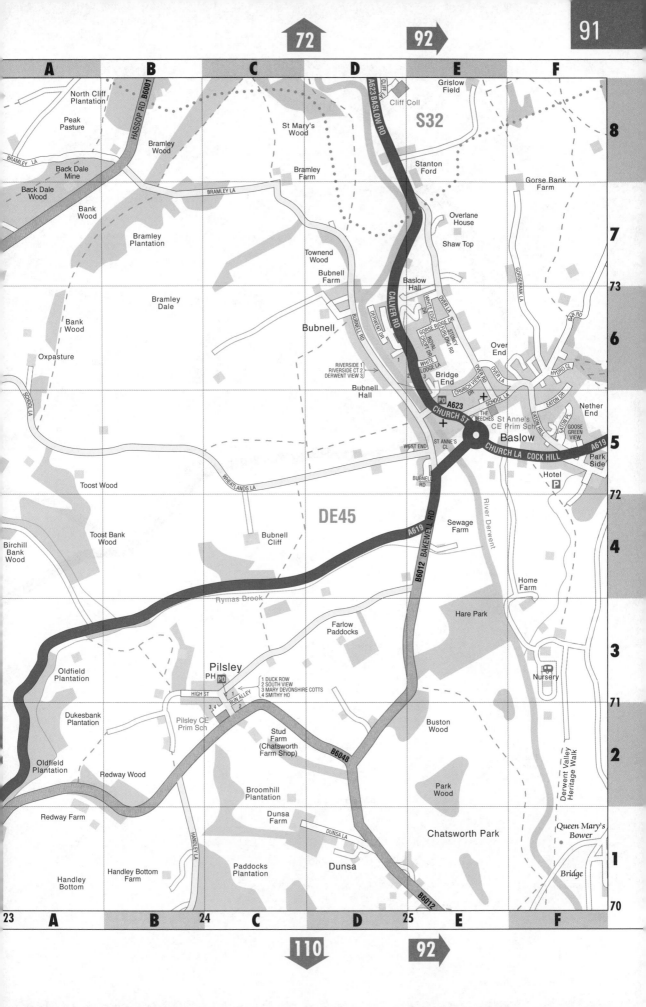

A **B** **C** **D** **E** **F**

8

Bar Brook

A621

Wellington's Monument

Jack Flat

7

Baslow Bar

BAR RD

SHEFFIELD RD

Raddowhole Plantation

Gardom's Edge

73

Bar Brook

Yeld Wood

Nelson's Monument

6

Yeldwood Farm

A621

Far End

Yeld Farm

Moorside Farm

Birchen Edge

East Moor

DE45

5

A619

Robin Hood

PH

P

Robin Hood Farm

Newbridge Farm

Park Lodge

Jumble Coppice

Saw Mill

Heathy Lea Brook

B6050

B6050

72

Chatsworth Park

Robin Hood Plantations

Stone Low

4

Dobb Edge

Emperor Stream

A619

S42

Umberley Brook

71

Parkgate

Gibbet Wood

3

The Hunting Tower

Gibbet Moor

2

Bunker's Hill Wood

Emperor Lake

P

Stand Wood

Swiss Cottage

1

Chatsworth House

Swiss Lake

70

26

A 27 **B** **C** 28 **D** **E** **F**

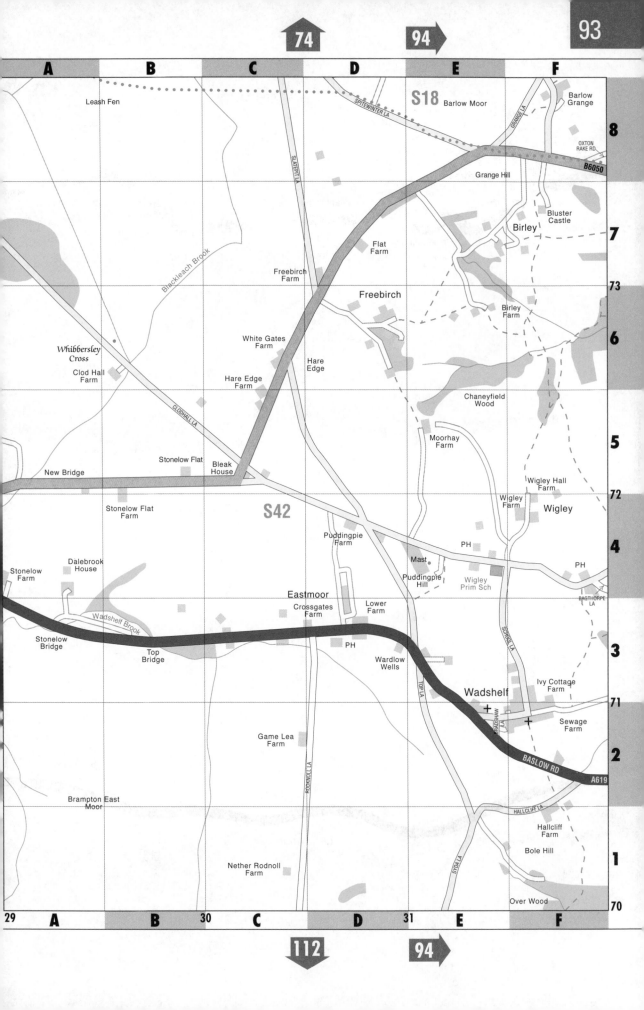

A B C D E F

Leash Fen

SPITEWINTER LA

S18 Barlow Moor

GRANGE LA

Barlow Grange

OXTON RAKE RD

B6050

Grange Hill

Bluster Castle

Birley

Flat Farm

Freebirch Farm

Freebirch

73

Birley Farm

White Gates Farm

Hare Edge

Chaneyfield Wood

6

Whibbersley Cross

Clod Hall Farm

Hare Edge Farm

Moorhay Farm

Wigley Hall Farm

CLODHALL LA

SLATEPIT LA

BLACKLEACH BROOK

Stonelow Flat

Bleak House

Wigley Farm

Wigley

72

New Bridge

S42

Puddingpie Farm

PH

PH

Stonelow Flat Farm

Mast

Puddingpie Hill

Wigley Prim Sch

BAGTHORPE LA

4

Dalebrook House

Eastmoor

Crossgates Farm

Lower Farm

Stonelow Farm

Wadshelf Brook

PH

Wardlow Wells

Wadshelf

SCROLL LA

Ivy Cottage Farm

71

Stonelow Bridge

Top Bridge

Sewage Farm

BRADSHAW LA

TOP LA

Game Lea Farm

BASLOW RD

A619

RODNOLL LA

Brampton East Moor

HALLCLIFF LA

Hallcliff Farm

SYDA LA

Bole Hill

Nether Rodnoll Farm

Over Wood

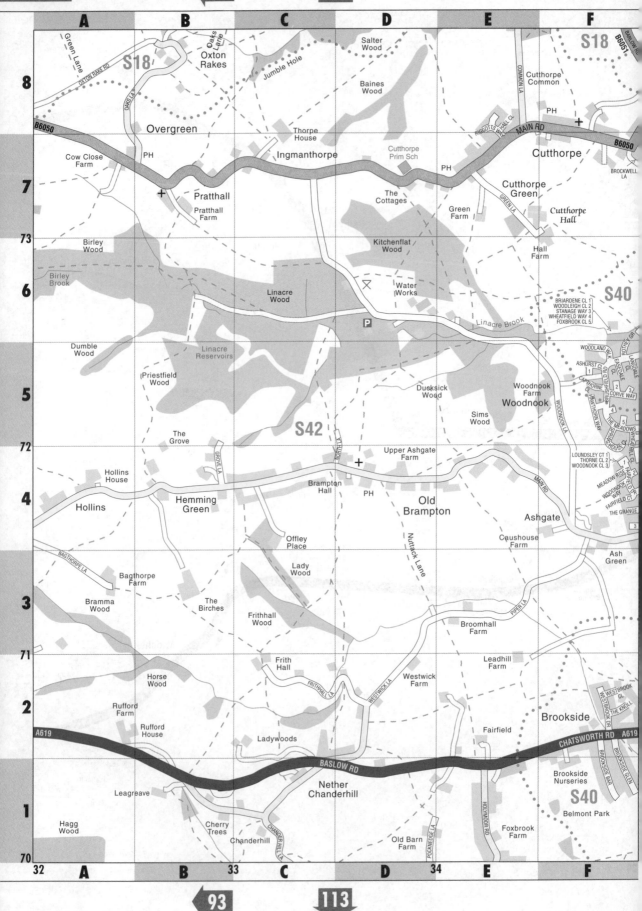

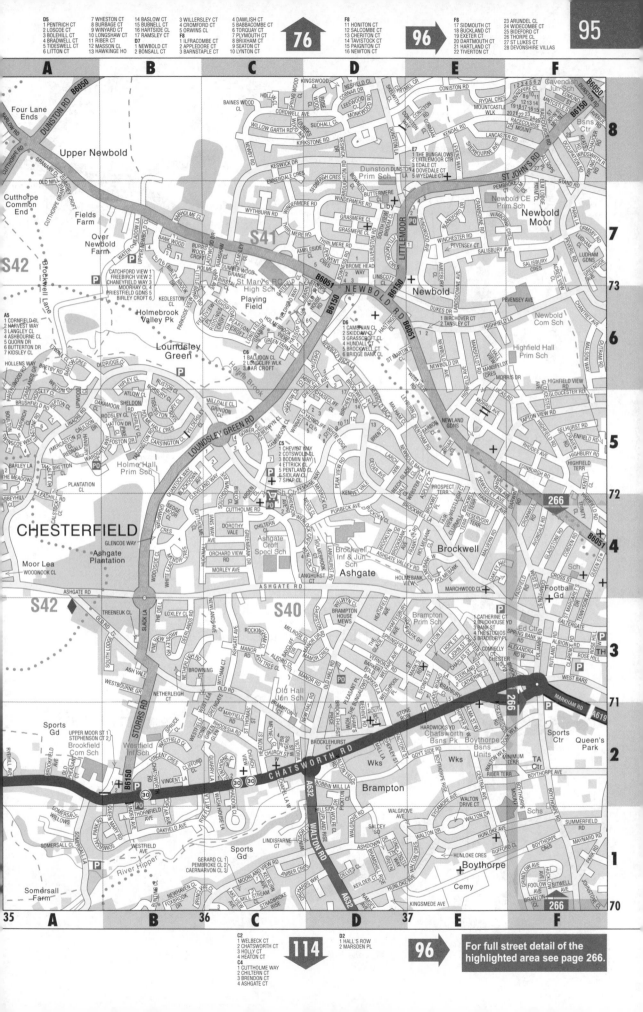

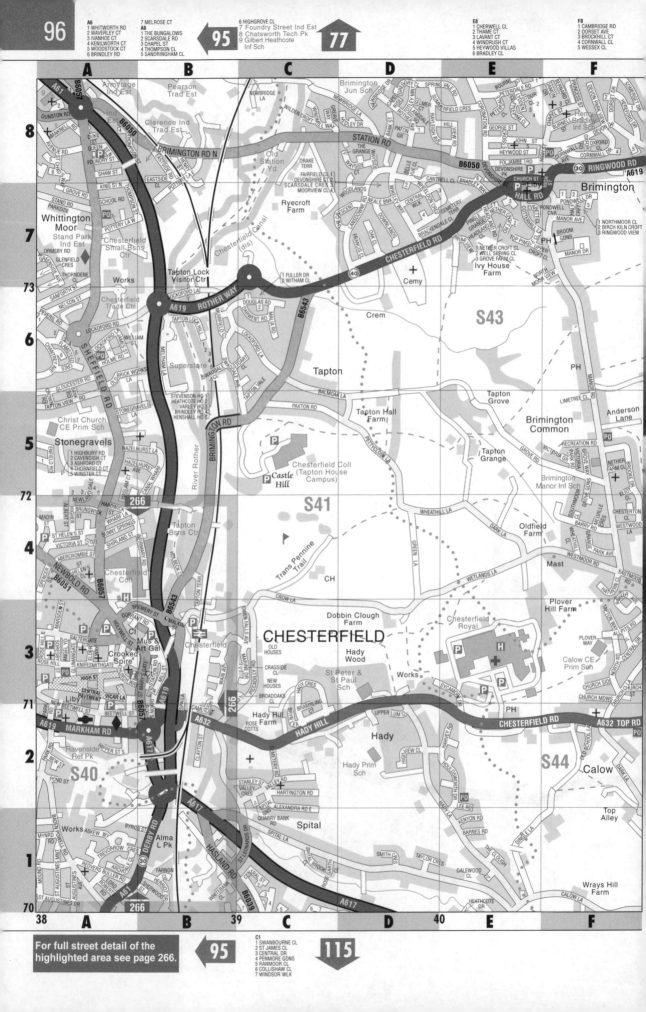

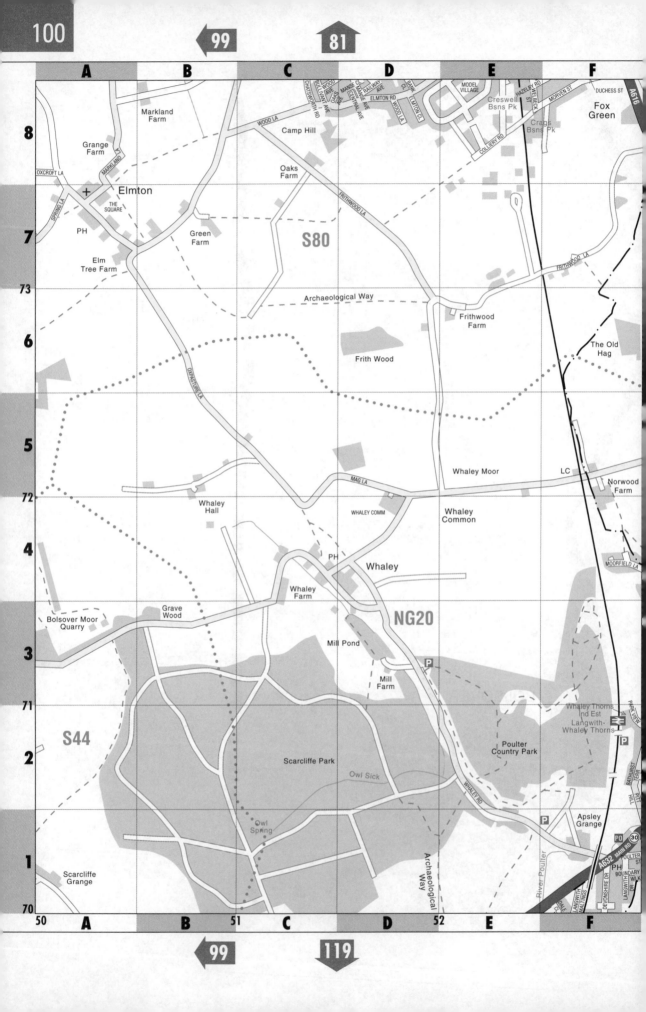

A B C D E F

8

Markland
Farm

Grange
Farm

Camp Hill

WOOD LA

MODEL
VILLAGE

Creswell
Bsns Pk

Crags
Bsns Pk

DUCHESS ST

Fox
Green

A616

OXCROFT LA

+ Elmton

THE
SQUARE

PH

7

Green
Farm

Oaks
Farm

FRITHWOOD LA

S80

Frithwood
Farm

FRITHWOOD LA

Elm
Tree Farm

73

Archaeological Way

6

OXPASTURE LA

Frith Wood

The Old
Hag

5

Whaley Moor

LC

Norwood
Farm

72

Whaley
Hall

MAG LA

WHALEY COMM

Whaley
Common

4

PH

Whaley

MOORFIELD LA

Whaley
Farm

Grave
Wood

NG20

Bolsover Moor
Quarry

Mill Pond

3

Mill
Farm

P

Whaley Thorns
Ind Est
Langwith-
Whaley Thorns

PARK VIEW

71

S44

Scarcliffe Park

Owl Sick

Poulter
Country Park

P

BATHURST

2

Owl
Spring

WHALEY RD

P

Apsley
Grange

PITT
HILL

1

Scarcliffe
Grange

Archaeological
Way

River Poulter

A632 MAIN RD

PO
30

PH

BOUNDARY
WLK

POULTER
ST

DEVONSHIRE DR

LANGWITH
MALTINGS

70

50 A 51 B C 52 D E F

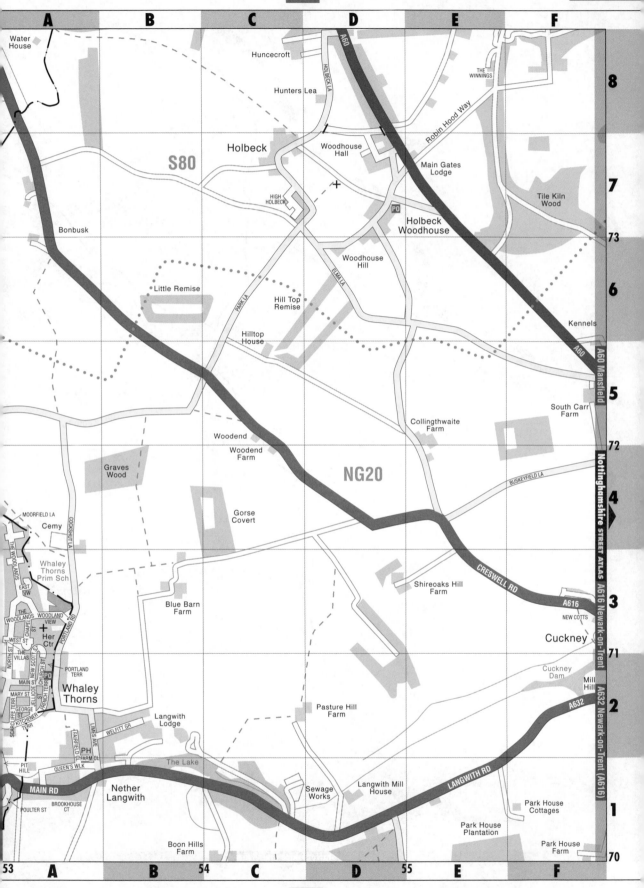

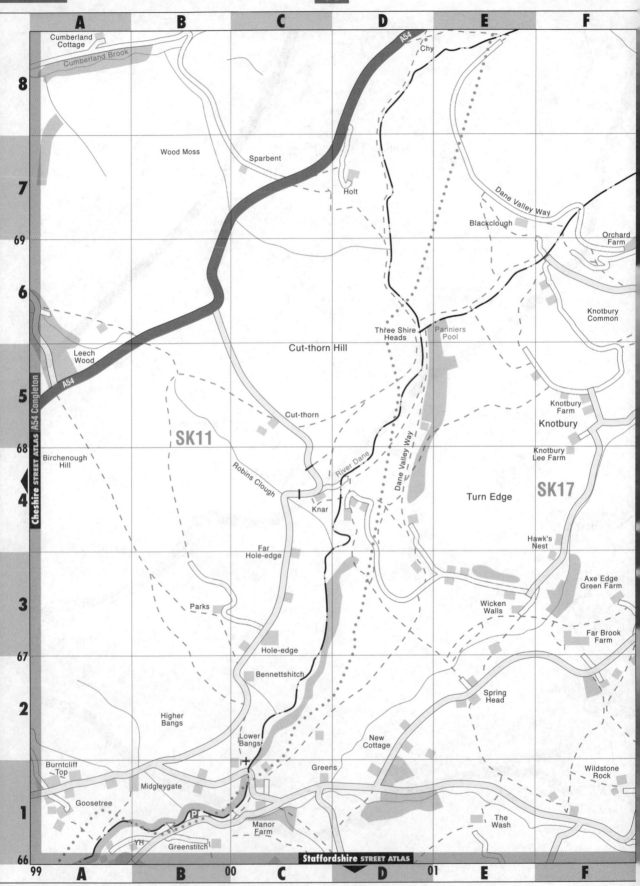

83

Cumberland Cottage

Cumberland Brook

Wood Moss

Sparbent

Holt

Chy

A54

Dane Valley Way

Blackclough

Orchard Farm

8

7

69

6

Leech Wood

A54

Three Shire Heads

Panniers Pool

Knotbury Common

Cut-thorn Hill

Cheshire STREET ATLAS A54 Congleton

5

Cut-thorn

SK11

Knotbury Farm

Knotbury

68

Robins Clough

River Dane

Dane Valley Way

Knotbury Lee Farm

SK17

4

Birchenough Hill

Knar

Turn Edge

Hawk's Nest

Far Hole-edge

Axe Edge Green Farm

Parks

Wicken Walls

3

67

Hole-edge

Bennettshitch

Far Brook Farm

Spring Head

2

Higher Bangs

Lower Bangs

New Cottage

Wildstone Rock

Burntcliff Top

Greens

The Wash

1

Goosetree

Midgleygate

P

Manor Farm

YH

Greenstitch

66

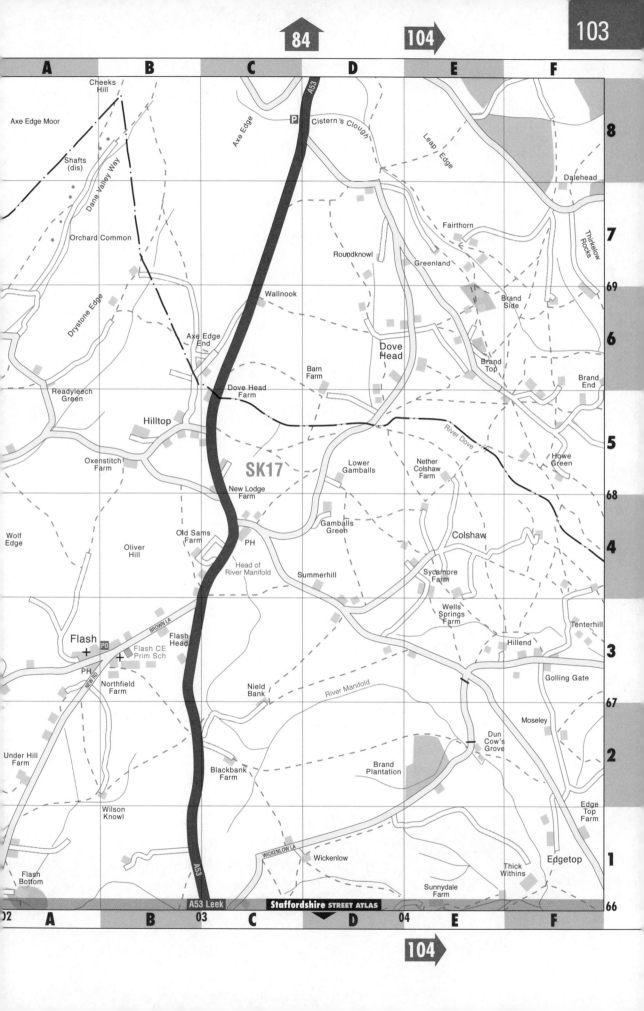

A B C D E F

8

7

69

6

5

68

4

3

67

2

1

66

Cheeks Hill

Axe Edge Moor

Shafts (dis)

Dane Valley Way

Orchard Common

Cistern's Clough

Leap Edge

Daleheim

Fairthorn

Thirkelow Rocks

Roundknowl

Greenland

Wallnook

Brand Side

Drystone Edge

Axe Edge

Axe Edge End

Dove Head

Brand Top

Brand End

Readyleech Green

Dove Head Farm

Barn Farm

River Dove

Hilltop

Oxenstitch Farm

SK17

Lower Gamballs

Nether Colshaw Farm

Howe Green

New Lodge Farm

Wolf Edge

Oliver Hill

Old Sams Farm

PH

Gamballs Green

Colshaw

Head of River Manifold

Summerhill

Sycamore Farm

Wells Springs Farm

Tenterhill

Flash

PO

Flash Head

BROWN LA

Hillend

Golling Gate

PH

NEW RD

Flash CE Prim Sch

Northfield Farm

Nield Bank

River Manifold

67

Moseley

Under Hill Farm

Dun Cow's Grove

Blackbank Farm

Brand Plantation

Edge Top Farm

Wilson Knowl

A53

Edgetop

Flash Bottom

WICKENLOW LA

Wickenlow

Thick Withins

Sunnydale Farm

02 A B 03 C D 04 E F

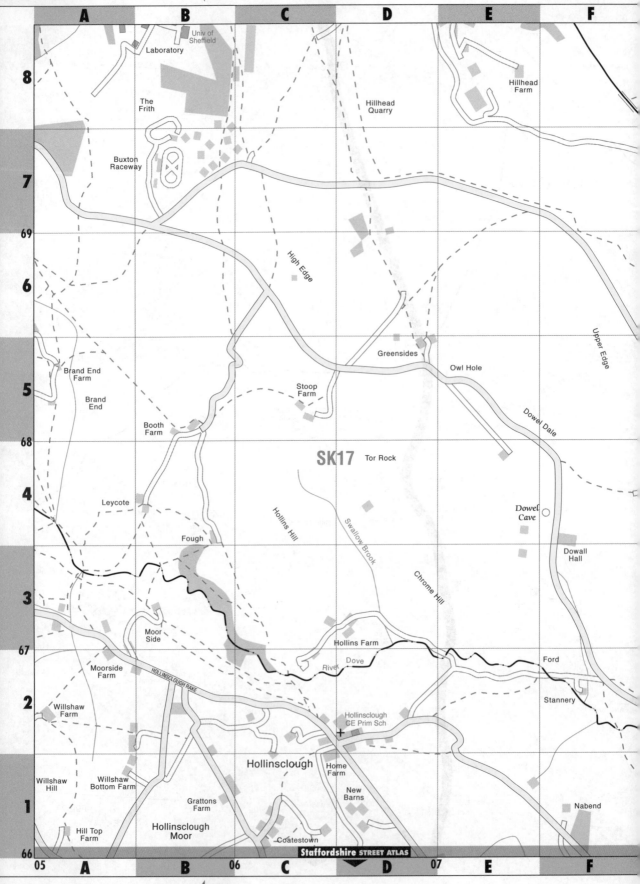

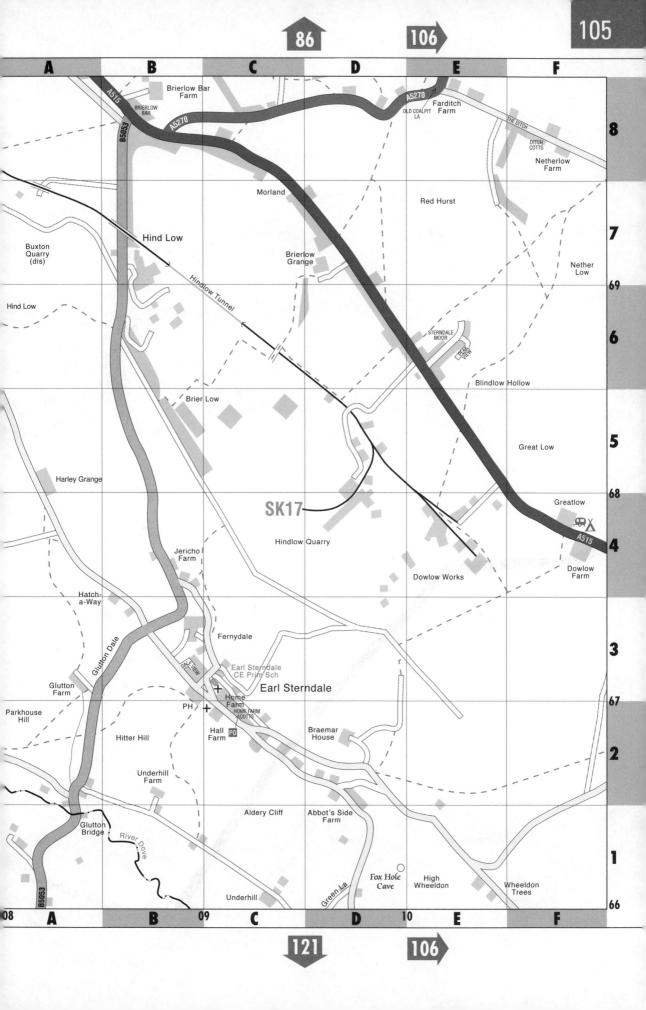

A B C D E F

8 Chelmorton

Townend Farm

The Paddock

7 Town Head

Mines (disused)

Town Head Farm

69 New Buildings Farm

Ash Tree Farm

6 Flagg

Back o' th' Hill Farm

Flagg Hall

Hobson Farm

PH

Blinder House

Mines (disused)

5

68

SK17

4 A515 Hall Pomeroy

PH

Street House Farm

Pomeroy Cotts

Street Farm

Stonebench La

Flagg Moor Farm

Flagg Moor

Mines (disused)

3

67

Hurdlow Hall

Hurdlow Grange

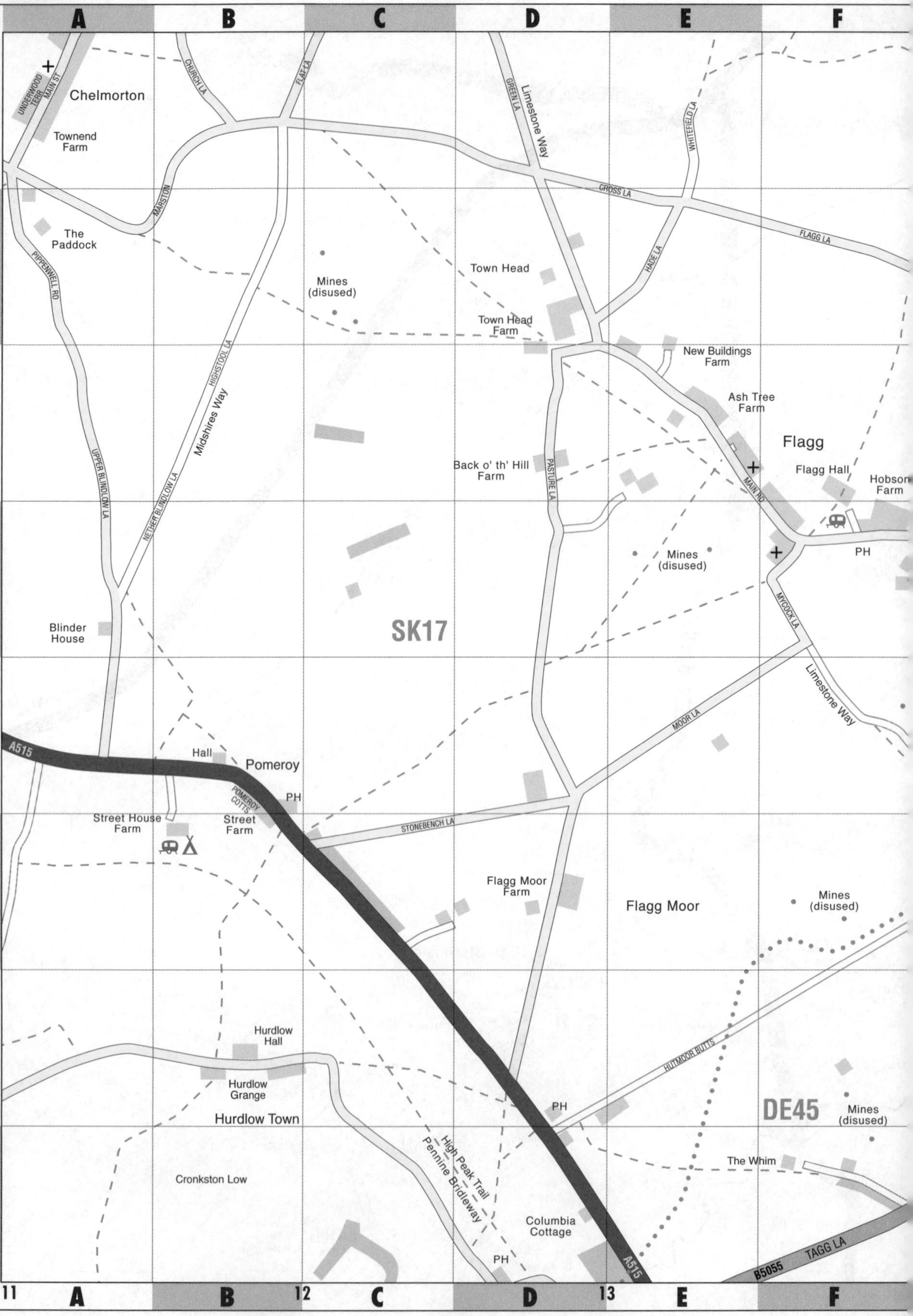

Hurdlow Town

PH

DE45

Mines (disused)

2

Cronkston Low

High Peak Trail Pennine Bridleway

The Whim

1

Columbia Cottage

PH

A515

66 PH

TAGG LA

B5055

11 A 12 B C 13 D E F

UNDERWOOD TERR
MAIN ST
CHURCH LA
FLAT LA
MARSTON
GREEN LA
LIMESTONE WAY
CROSS LA
HADE LA
WHITEFIELD LA
FLAGG LA
PIPPENWELL RD
HIGHSTOOL LA
Midshires Way
NETHER BLINDLOW LA
UPPER BLINDLOW LA
PASTURE LA
MAIN RD
MYCOCK LA
MOOR LA
Limestone Way
HILTMOOR BUTTS

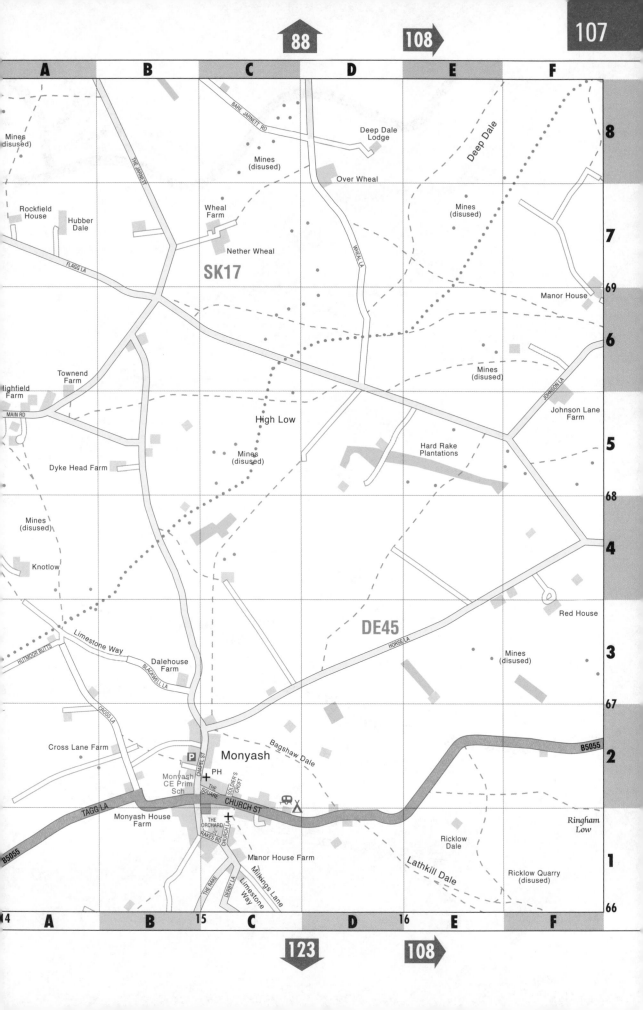

A B C D E F

Mines
(disused)

BARE JARNETT RD

Deep Dale
Lodge

Deep Dale

8

Over Wheal

Mines
(disused)

Rockfield
House

Hubber
Dale

Wheal
Farm

THE JARNETT

7

Nether Wheal

WHEAL LA

69

FLAGG LA

SK17

Manor House

6

Townend
Farm

Highfield
Farm

MAIN RD

High Low

Mines
(disused)

JOHNSON LA

Johnson Lane
Farm

5

Hard Rake
Plantations

Dyke Head Farm

Mines
(disused)

68

Mines
(disused)

4

Knotlow

Red House

Limestone Way

HUTMOOR BUTTS

DE45

HORSE LA

Mines
(disused)

3

Dalehouse
Farm

BLACKWELL LA

67

CROSS LA

B5055

2

Cross Lane Farm

Monyash

Bagshaw Dale

P

CHAPEL ST

Monyash
CE Prim
Sch

PH

SOLDIER'S CROFT

THE SQUARE

TAGG LA

CHURCH ST

Ricklow
Dale

Ringham
Low

B5055

Monyash House
Farm

THE ORCHARD

HAKES RD

CHURCH LA

Manor House Farm

Lathkill Dale

Ricklow Quarry
(disused)

1

THE RAKE

DERBY LA

Milkings Lane

Limestone Way

66

A 14 B 15 C D 16 E F

107
89

A B C D E F

8

Great Shacklow Wood

Weir

River Wye

Little Shacklow Wood

Ashford in the Water

HIGHFIELD
VICARAGE LA
HILL CROSS
GREAVES LA
HALL END LA
A6020
TRINITY CL
COURT LA
FENNEL ST
CHURCH ST
WATTS
BUXTON RD
CHERRY CL
BETTY LA
MOUNT PLEASANT
NEW RD (BASLOW RD)
PO
B6465
Mill

THE DUKE S DR

A6 BUXTON RD

CORNBROOK 1
HILLMORTON 2
MILLSTONE LA
JOHN BANK LA

7

Mast

Arrock Plantation

Rose Farm

JOHNSON LA
Top Farm
PH
Sheldon

Lower Farm

Opencast Workings

Opencast Workings

Dirtlow Farm

69

6

Woodbine Farm

Dirtlow Plantations

Kirk Dale

Cowden Plantations

Magpie Mine (disused)

5

Truebell Lane

DE45

Opencast Workings

Green Cowden Farm

68

4

Shafts (dis)

Bole Hill

Bole Hill Farm

B5055

3

Blores Barn Farm

GREEN LA

Melbourne Farm

67

Haddon Grove Farm

2

B5055

Organ Ground

Opencast Workings

Mandale Rake

Haddon Grove

Mines (dis)

Twin Dales

1

Haddon Grove Farm

Weir
River Lathkill

66

17 A 18 B C 19 D E F

107
124

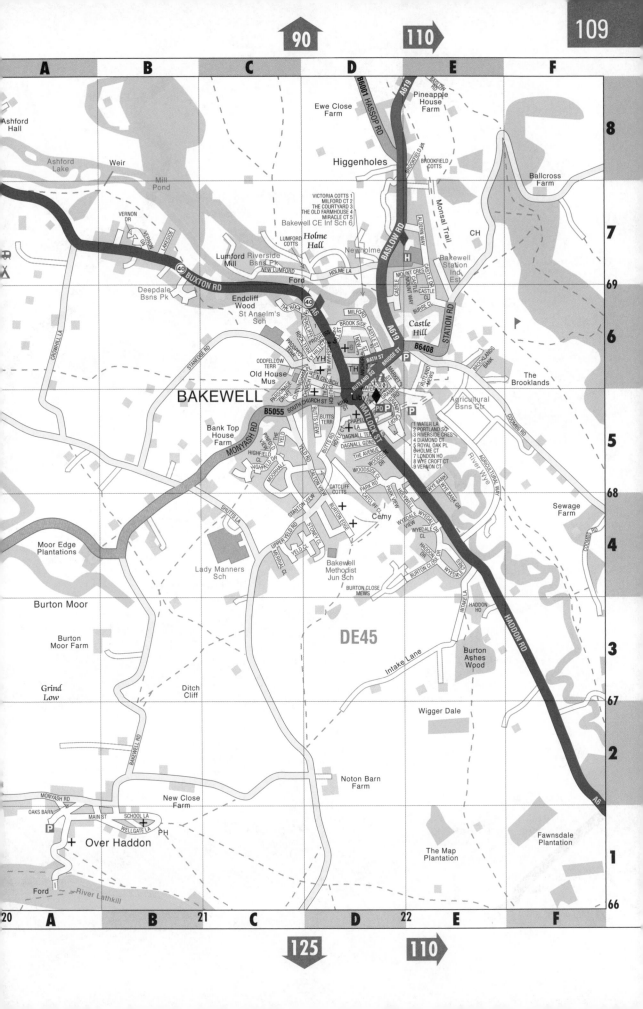

109
91

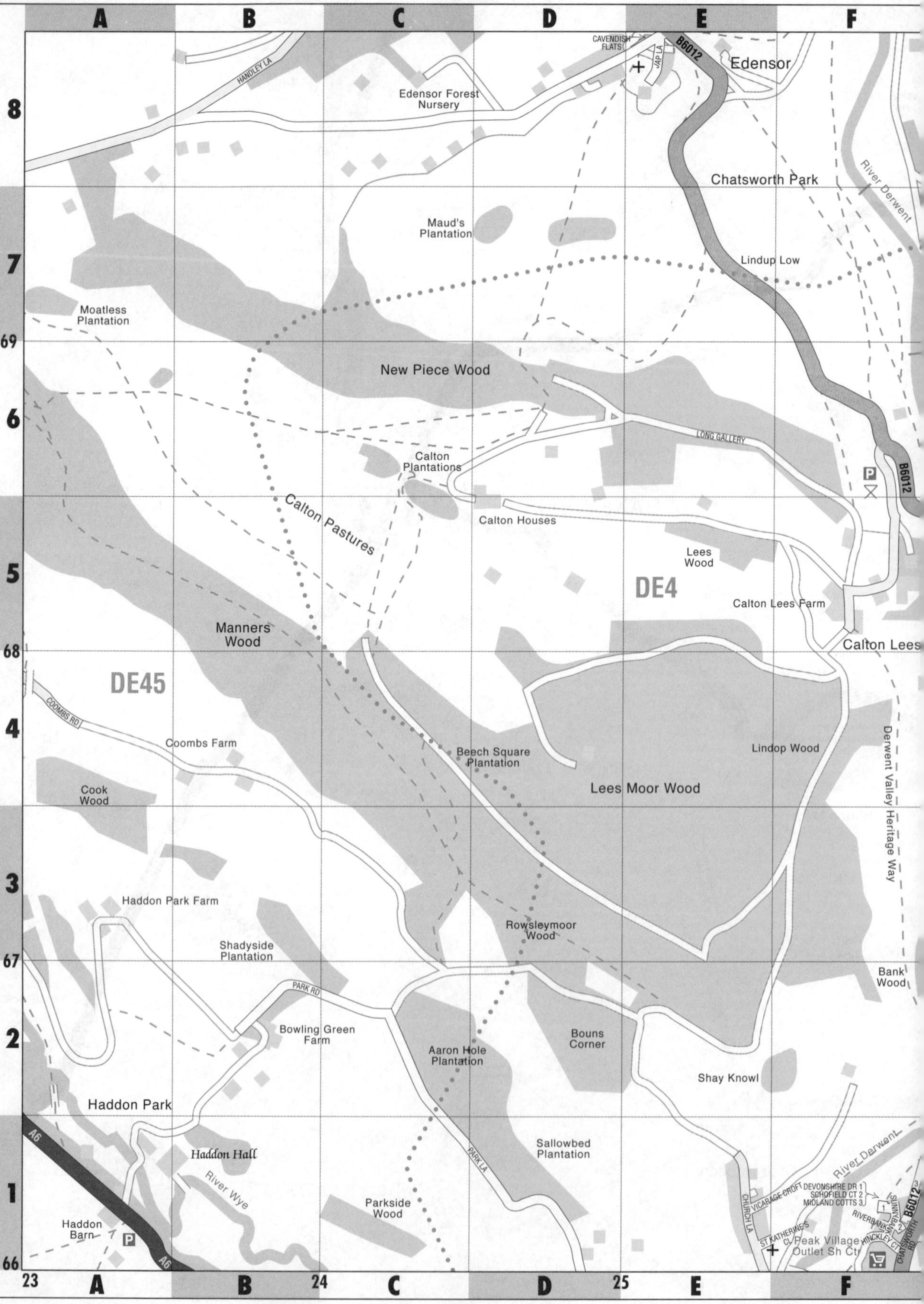

A
B
C
D
E
F
8
7
69
6
5
68
4
3
67
2
1
66
23
24
25
CAVENDISH FLATS
JAP LA
B6012
Edensor
HANDLEY LA
Edensor Forest
Nursery
Chatsworth Park
River Derwent
Maud's
Plantation
Lindup Low
Moatless
Plantation
New Piece Wood
LONG GALLERY
Calton
Plantations
B6012
Calton Pastures
Calton Houses
Lees
Wood
DE4
Calton Lees Farm
Manners
Wood
Calton Lees
DE45
COOMBS RD
Coombs Farm
Beech Square
Plantation
Lindop Wood
Derwent Valley Heritage Way
Lees Moor Wood
Cook
Wood
Haddon Park Farm
Rowsleymoor
Wood
Shadyside
Plantation
Bank
Wood
PARK RD
Bowling Green
Farm
Bouns
Corner
Aaron Hole
Plantation
Shay Knowl
Haddon Park
A6
Haddon Hall
Sallowbed
Plantation
PARK LA
River Derwent
River Wye
Parkside
Wood
CHURCH LA
VICARAGE CROFT
DEVONSHIRE DR 1
SCHOFIELD CT 2
MIDLAND COTTS 3
Haddon
Barn
P
A6
ST KATHERINE'S CL
RIVERBANK
Peak Village
Outlet Sh Ctr
HINCKLEY CT
CHATSWORTH RD
B6012
A
B
C
D
E
F

109
126

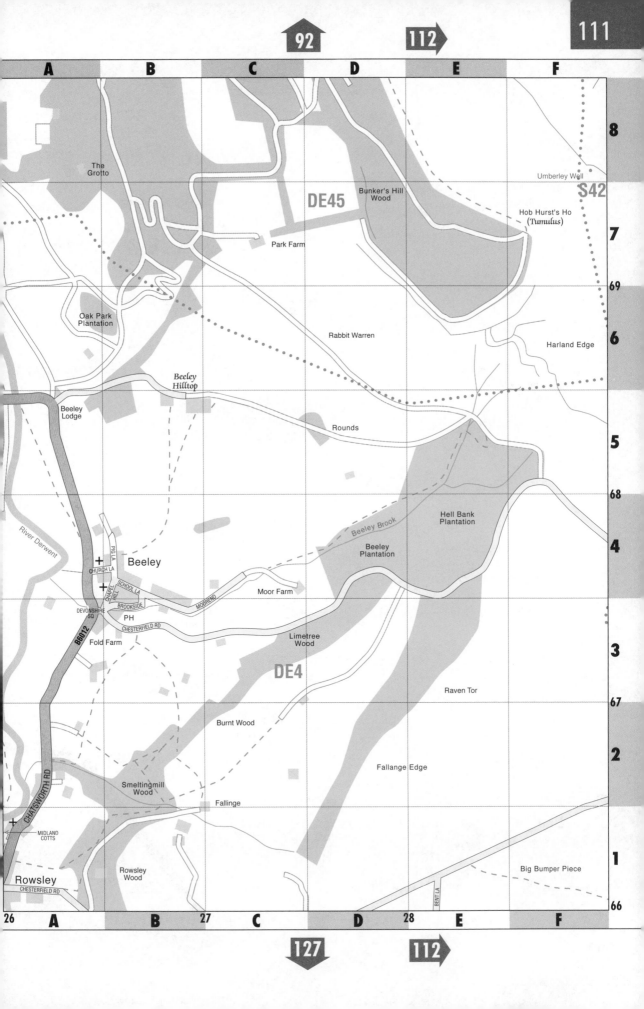

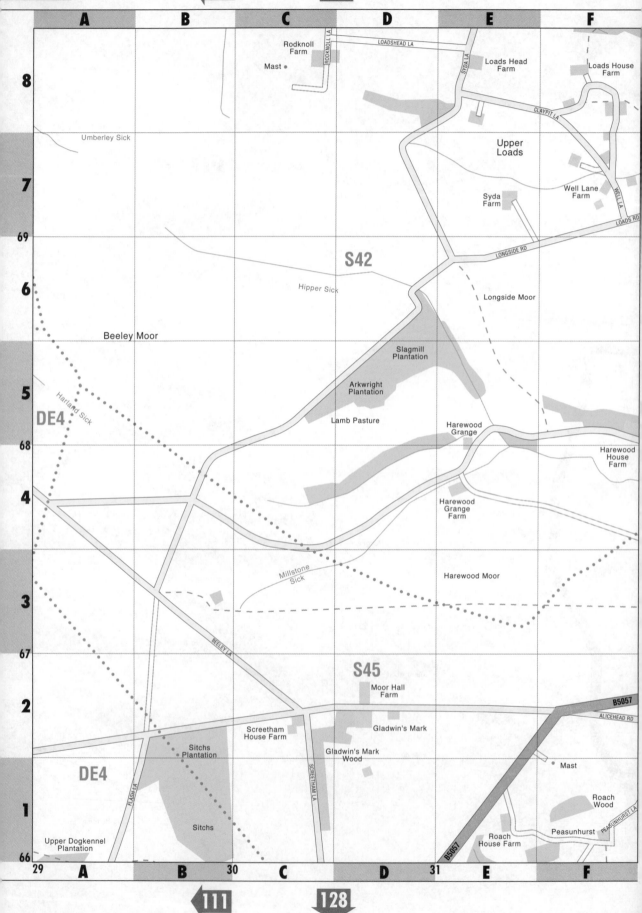

A B C D E F

8

Rodknoll Farm

LOADSHEAD LA

RODKNOLL LA

Mast

SYDA LA

Loads Head Farm

Loads House Farm

CLAYPIT LA

Upper Loads

Umberley Sick

7

Well Lane Farm

WELL LA

Syda Farm

LOADS RD

69

S42

LONGSIDE RD

Hipper Sick

Longside Moor

6

Beeley Moor

Slagmill Plantation

5

Harland Sick

Arkwright Plantation

DE4

Lamb Pasture

Harewood Grange

Harewood House Farm

68

4

Harewood Grange Farm

Millstone Sick

Harewood Moor

3

BEELEY LA

67

S45

2

Moor Hall Farm

B5057

ALICEHEAD RD

Screetham House Farm

Gladwin's Mark

Sitchs Plantation

Gladwin's Mark Wood

SCREETHAM LA

DE4

FLASH LA

Mast

Roach Wood

1

PEASUNHURST LA

Sitchs

Roach House Farm

Peasunhurst

B5057

Upper Dogkennel Plantation

66

29 A B 30 C D 31 E F

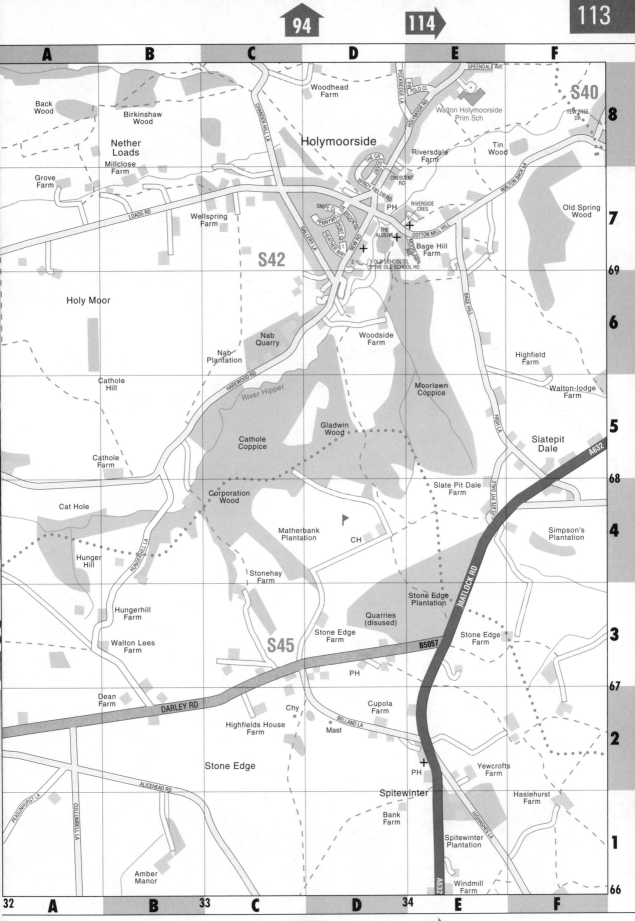

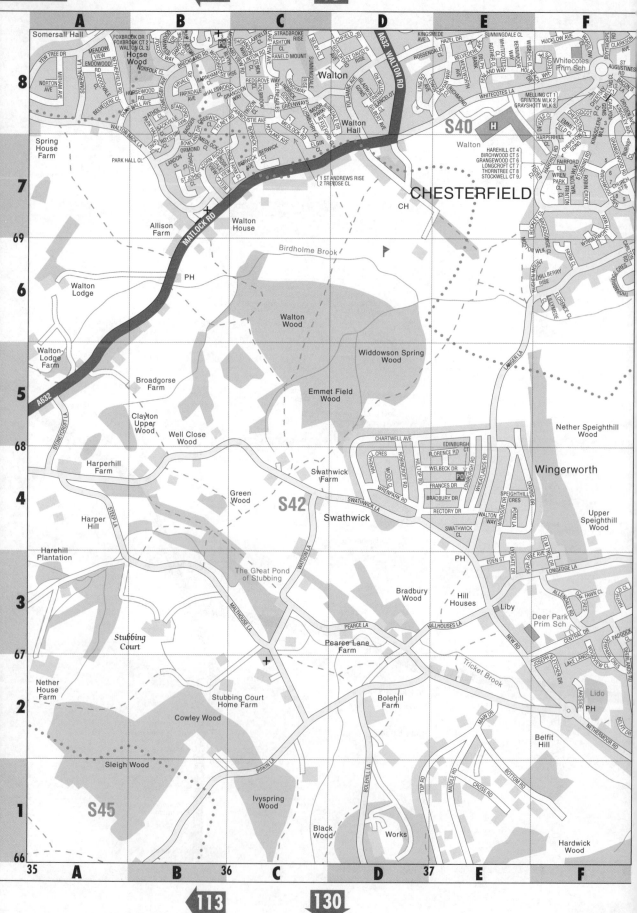

115
97

A B C D E F

8

Nether House Farm

CALOW LA

HALF FLASH LA

Calow Green

Calowgreen Farm

BACK LA

MOOR LA

Spoil Heap

Sutton Lane Farm

7

Woodnook Farm

S44

Bull Paddock Farm

SUTTON LA

69

Hall Farm

6

HASSOCKY LA

Calow Brook

Sutton Springs Wood

ROCK LA

Springwood Farm

Yewtree Farm

SHIRE LA

5

S41

A617

RAILWAY COTTS

Hill Farm

B6425

Muster Brook

High House Farm

68

B6039

Temple Normanton Bsns Pk

Bond's Main

SPRINGWOOD ST

Temple Normanton Prim Sch

POSTMANS LA

4

Grassmoor Country Park

MILL LA

CHURCH LA

SUTTON VIEW

S42

A617

Musterbrook Bridge

3

Cemy

Temple Normanton

CHURCH FARM MEWS

BIRKIN LA

MANSFIELD RD

67

Philadelphia

High Top Poultry Farm

Holmewood Bsns Pk

CHESTERFIELD RD

Five Pits Trail

Williamthorpe Ponds

Williamthorpe Ind Pk

MOORLAND DR

LILAC CL

GORSE BANK

SLACK LA

Heath Prim Sch

2

Lings Farm

Enterprise Dr

SUTTON WAY

MAYFIELD

WOODSOME PK

Sewage Works

BRAMBLE CL

BRICKYARD

HEATHER AVE

FERN CL

A6175

CHESTERFIELD RD

B6038

Holmewood Ind Pk

PARK RD

Works

QUEENS WLK

WOOD ST

HEATH RD

Holmewoods

HARDWICK VIEW RD

Holmewood Ind Est

1

B6039

SCHELTER

FRESH WATERS

Pavilion Workshops

DICKENS DR

LAWRENCE AVE

SHAKESPEARE ST

TENNYSON ST

SHAW ST

MASEFIELD AVE

COMPTON ST

HUNLOKE RD

DUKES CL

QUEENSWAY

DEVONSHIRE TERR

MALKIN COTTS

ASTWITH CL

STAINSBY CL

66

41 A 42 B C 43 D E F

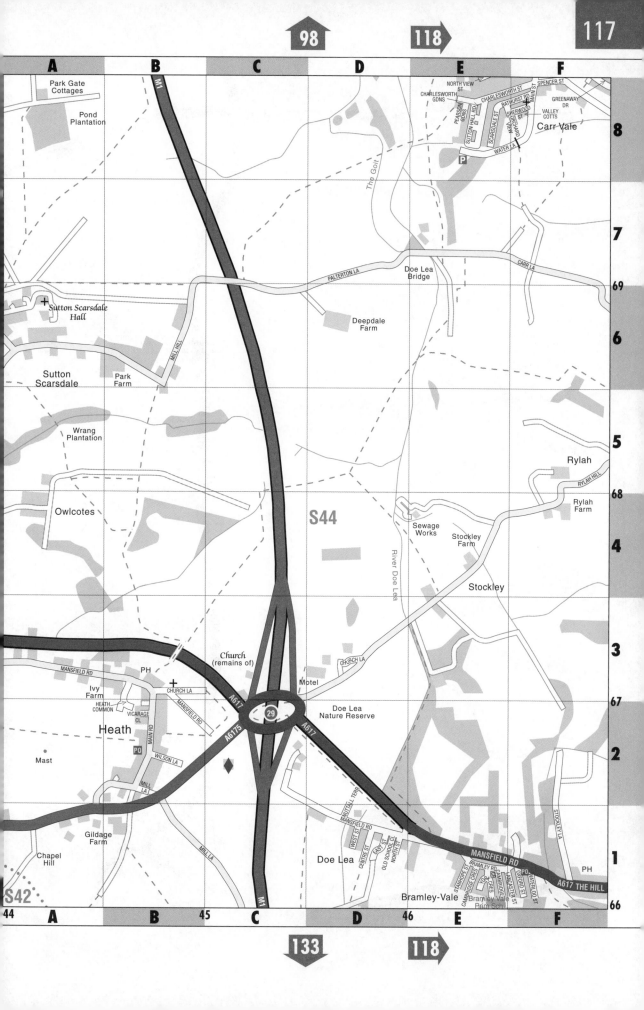

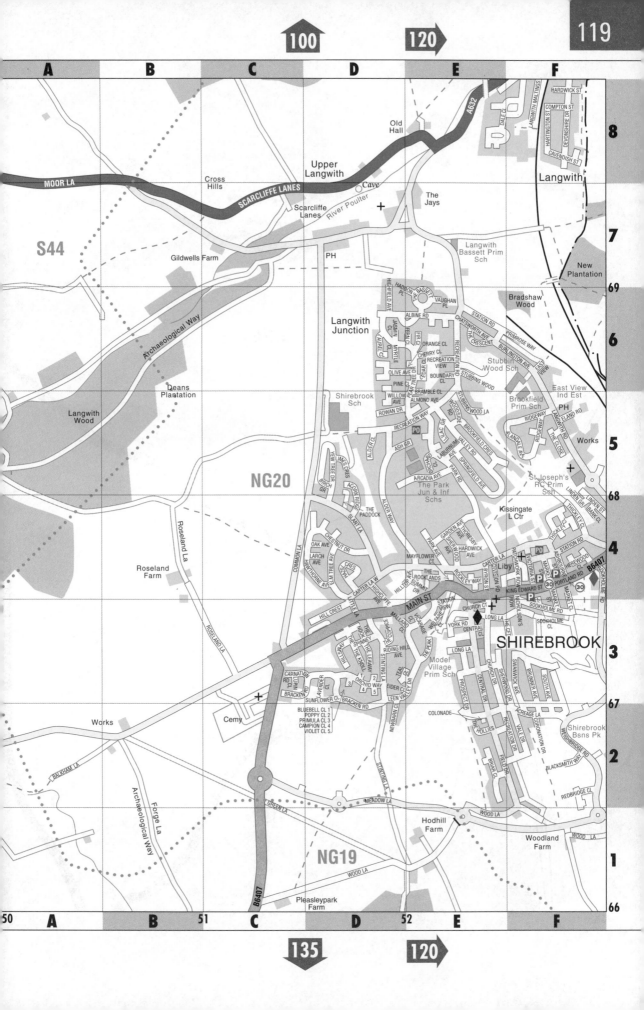

A   B   C   D   E   F

8

Park House Farm

Boon Hills Wood

Top Farm

Cuckney Hay Wood

7

Lady's Grove

Warsop Wood

Minster Wood

Collier Spring

WOOD LA

LIME CRES

BRICK ST

SYCAMORE ST

69

Lord Stubbins Wood

NG20

6

B6031

Warsop Cottage Farm

William Wood Farm

5

Parson's Wood

WILLIAM WOOD LA

RHEIN O' THORNS

Hills and Holes

Askew Spa

STONEBRIDGE LA

ARGYLE CL

68

1 MUSTERS ST
2 NEW LINDEN ST
3 MANVERS ST
4 MANVERS CT

EAST ST

GRAVELSHANK RD

NORTH ST

KING ST

HEWETT ST

AMCOTT PL

WEST ST

HAMILTON DR

LANGWITH RD

FLETCH ST

4

STATION RD

SHIREBROOK

Sookholme Lodge Farm

PH

Warsop Vale

Sookholme Moor

VERNON CT

VERNON ST

HARDWICK ST

Shirebrook

MERCHANT ST

William Wood Bridge

Bolly Lane

Hammerwater Bridge

SOOKHOLME LA

River Meden

Works

Vernon Street Ind Est

Spring Lane

SOOKHOLME RD

3

Shirebrook Bsns Pk

LONGSTER LA

B6407

B6031

CARTER LA

Mill Farm

WEIGHBRIDGE RD

67

Spring Farm

Sookholme

2

BATH LA

Bath Lane Farm

Sookholme Bath

Spion Kop

MOSSDALE CL

MANSFIELD RD

WOOD LA

NG19

Rough Wood

A60

1

Ox Pasture Wood

SOOKHOLME RD

Nettleworth Farm

B6407

66

Spring Wood

53   A   B   54   C   D   55   E   F

Nottinghamshire STREET ATLAS

A60 Worksop

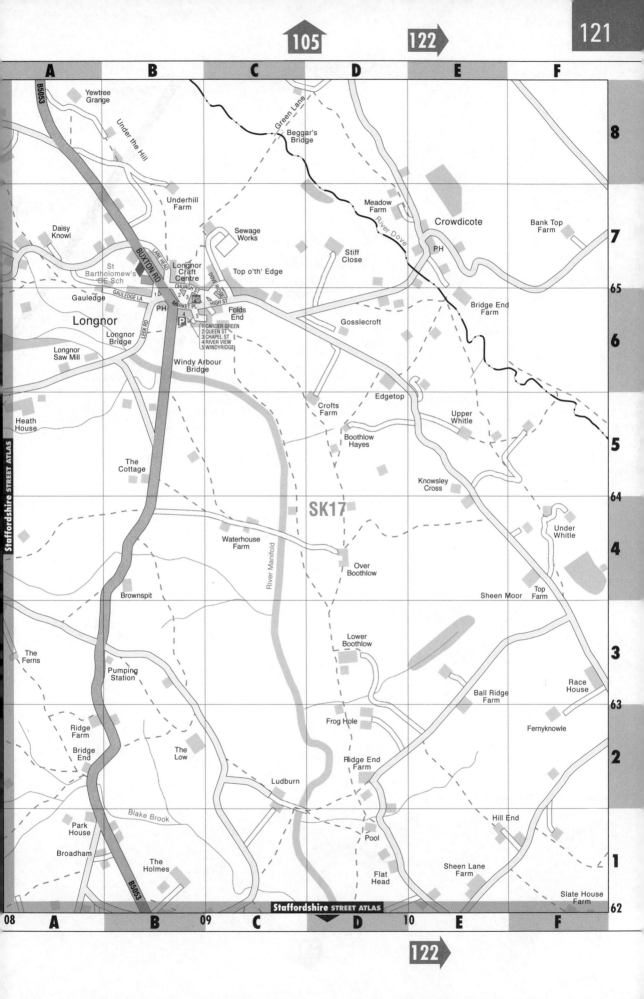

A   B   C   D   E   F

8

7

65

6

5

64

4

3

63

2

1

62

B5053

Yewtree Grange

Under the Hill

Green Lane

Beggar's Bridge

Underhill Farm

Meadow Farm

River Dove

Crowdicote

Bank Top Farm

PH

Daisy Knowl

Sewage Works

St Bartholomew's CE Sch

BUXTON RD

LANE HEAD

Longnor Craft Centre

CHURCH ST

DOVE RIDGE

Top o'th' Edge

Stiff Close

Gauledge

GAULEDGE LA

MARKET PL

HIGH ST

Folds End

Bridge End Farm

Longnor

PH

LEEK RD

P

Gosslecroft

1   2   3
4   5

1 CARDER GREEN
2 QUEEN ST
3 CHAPEL ST
4 RIVER VIEW
5 WINDYRIDGE

Longnor Bridge

Longnor Saw Mill

Windy Arbour Bridge

Crofts Farm

Edgetop

Upper Whitle

Heath House

Boothlow Hayes

The Cottage

Knowsley Cross

SK17

Under Whitle

Waterhouse Farm

River Manifold

Over Boothlow

Sheen Moor

Top Farm

Brownspit

Lower Boothlow

Ball Ridge Farm

Race House

The Ferns

Fernyknowle

Pumping Station

Frog Hole

Ridge Farm

Bridge End

The Low

Ridge End Farm

Ludburn

Blake Brook

Hill End

Park House

Pool

Broadham

The Holmes

Flat Head

Sheen Lane Farm

Slate House Farm

B5053

Staffordshire STREET ATLAS

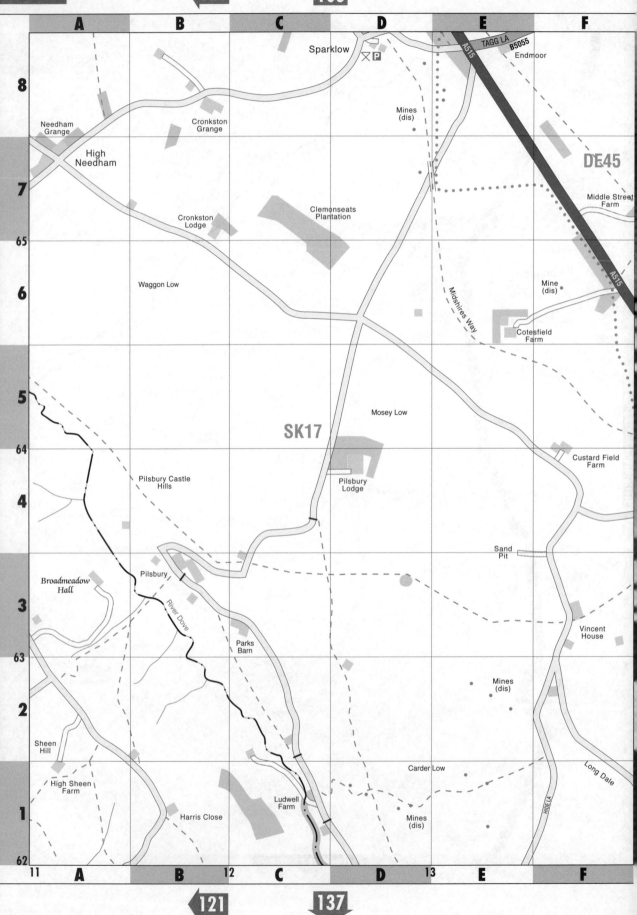

Sparklow

Endmoor

TAGG LA

B5055

A515

DE45

Needham Grange

High Needham

Cronkston Grange

Middle Street Farm

Cronkston Lodge

Clemonseats Plantation

Waggon Low

Midshires Way

Mine (dis)

Mines (dis)

Cotesfield Farm

Mosey Low

SK17

Pilsbury Castle Hills

Pilsbury Lodge

Custard Field Farm

Sand Pit

Broadmeadow Hall

Pilsbury

River Dove

Parks Barn

Vincent House

Mines (dis)

Sheen Hill

High Sheen Farm

Harris Close

Ludwell Farm

Carder Low

Long Dale

HIDE LA

Mines (dis)

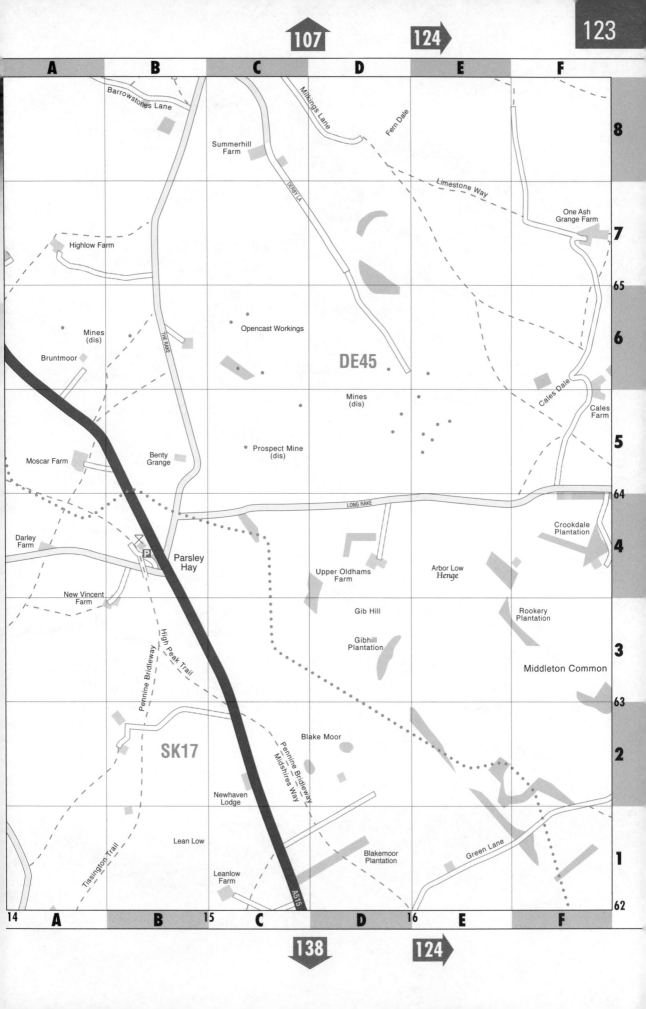

123
108

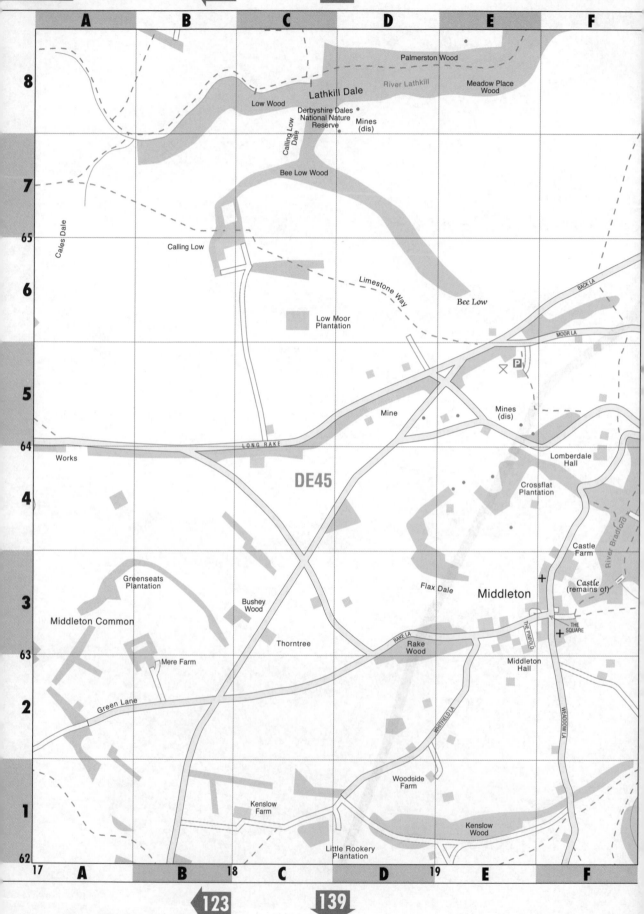

Palmerston Wood

River Lathkill

Meadow Place Wood

Lathkill Dale

Low Wood

Derbyshire Dales National Nature Reserve

Mines (dis)

Calling Low Dale

Bee Low Wood

Cales Dale

Calling Low

Limestone Way

Bee Low

Low Moor Plantation

BACK LA

MOOR LA

P

Works

LONG RAKE

Mine

Mines (dis)

DE45

Lomberdale Hall

Crossflat Plantation

Greenseats Plantation

Castle Farm

River Bradford

Flax Dale

Middleton

Castle (remains of)

Bushey Wood

Middleton Common

THE SQUARE

Thorntree

RAKE LA

Rake Wood

THE PINFOLD

Mere Farm

Middleton Hall

Green Lane

WHITFIELD LA

WEADOW LA

Woodside Farm

Kenslow Farm

Kenslow Wood

Little Rookery Plantation

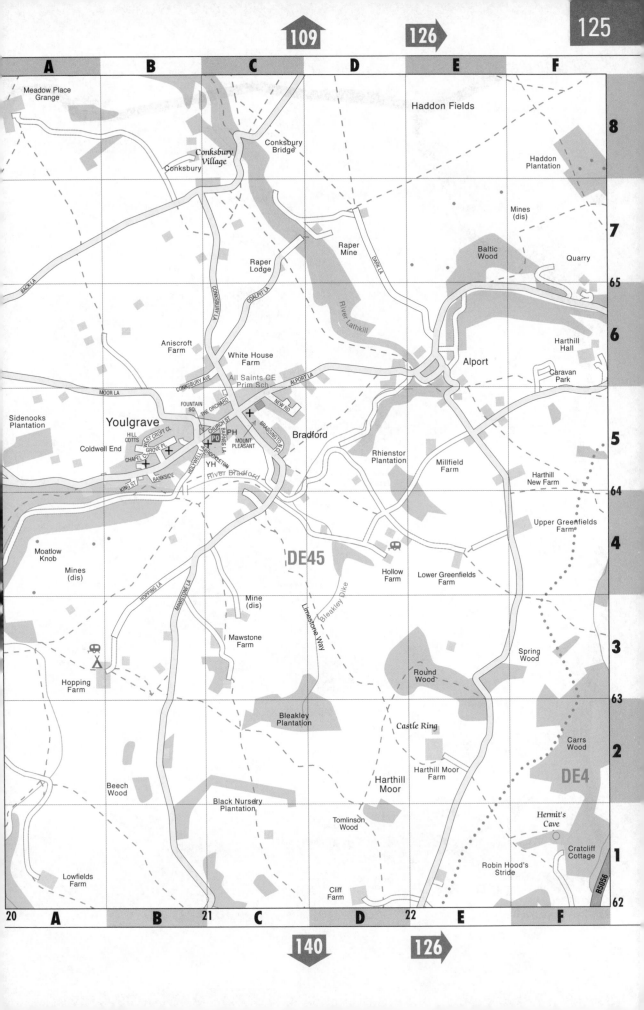

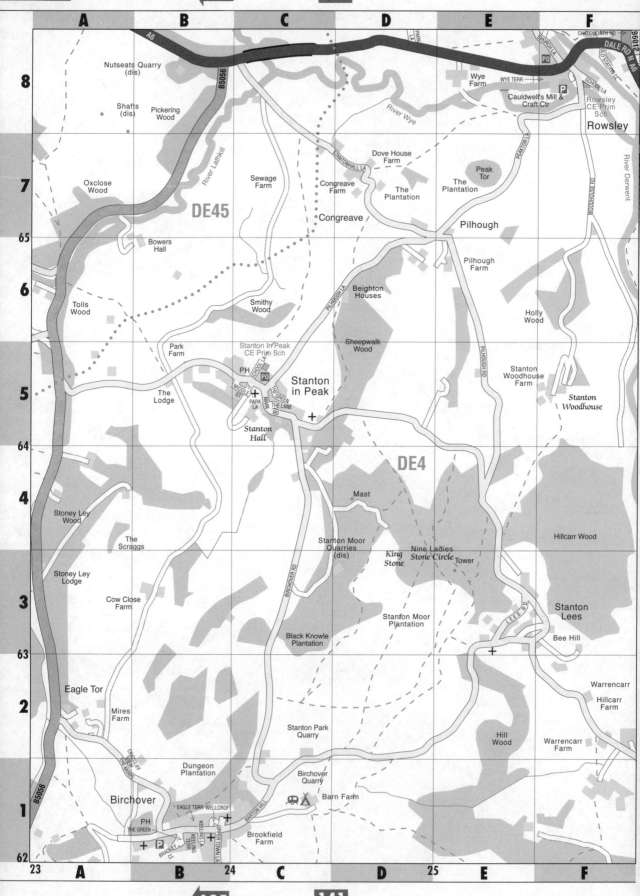

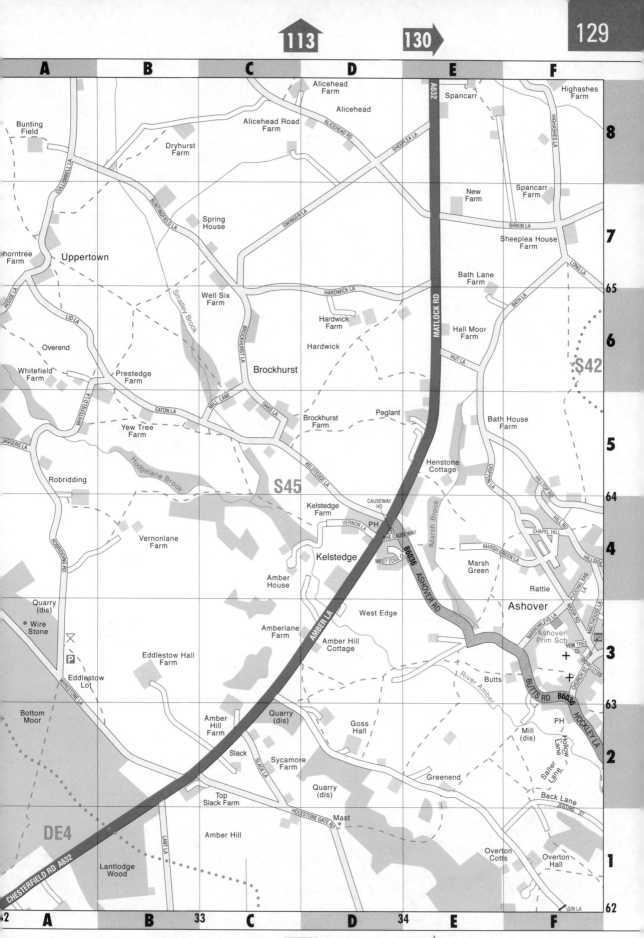

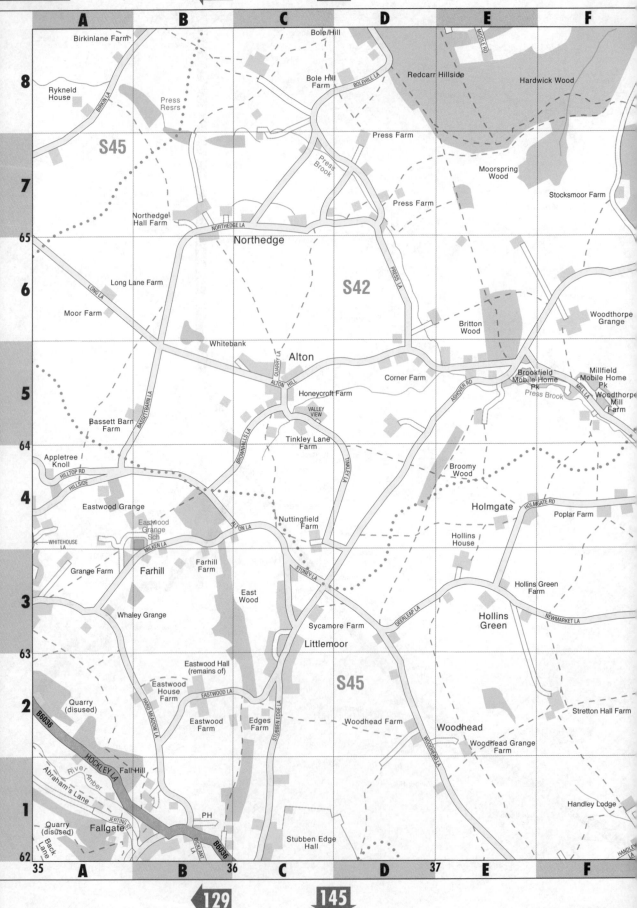

Birkinlane Farm

Bole Hill

8

Rykneld
House

Press
Resrs

Bole Hill
Farm

BOLEHILL LA

Redcarr Hillside

Hardwick Wood

MIDDLE RD

S45

Press Farm

Press
Brook

7

Moorspring
Wood

Stocksmoor Farm

Northedge
Hall Farm

NORTHEDGE LA

Press Farm

65

Northedge

Long Lane Farm

LONG LA

S42

6

Woodthorpe
Grange

Moor Farm

Britton
Wood

PRESS LA

Whitebank

Alton

QUARRY LA

Corner Farm

Brookfield
Mobile Home
Pk

Millfield
Mobile Home
Pk

5

Honeycroft Farm

ALTON HILL

ASHOVER RD

Press Brook

Woodthorpe
Mill
Farm

MILL LA

Bassett Barn
Farm

BASSETTBARN LA

VALLEY
VIEW

64

Tinkley Lane
Farm

Appletree
Knoll

BROOMHILLS LA

Broomy
Wood

HILLTOP RD

TINKLEY LA

4

HILLSIDE

Eastwood Grange

Nuttingfield
Farm

Holmgate

Poplar Farm

HOLMGATE RD

WHITEHOUSE
LA

Eastwood
Grange
Sch

ALTON LA

Hollins
House

MILKEN LA

Grange Farm

Farhill
Farm

Hollins Green
Farm

Farhill

STONEY LA

3

Whaley Grange

East
Wood

Sycamore Farm

DEER LEAP LA

Hollins
Green

NEWMARKET LA

63

Littlemoor

Eastwood Hall
(remains of)

HARD MEADOW LA

S45

2

Quarry
(disused)

Eastwood
House
Farm

EASTWOOD LA

Stretton Hall Farm

B6036

Eastwood
Farm

STUBBEN EDGE LA

Edges
Farm

Woodhead Farm

Woodhead

WOODHEAD LA

Woodhead Grange
Farm

HOCKLEY LA

River Amber

Fall Hill

Abraham's Lane

1

Quarry
(disused)

Fallgate

JERTING LA

PH

BUCKLAHT
LA

B6036

Stubben Edge
Hall

Handley Lodge

HANDLEY

Back
Lane

62

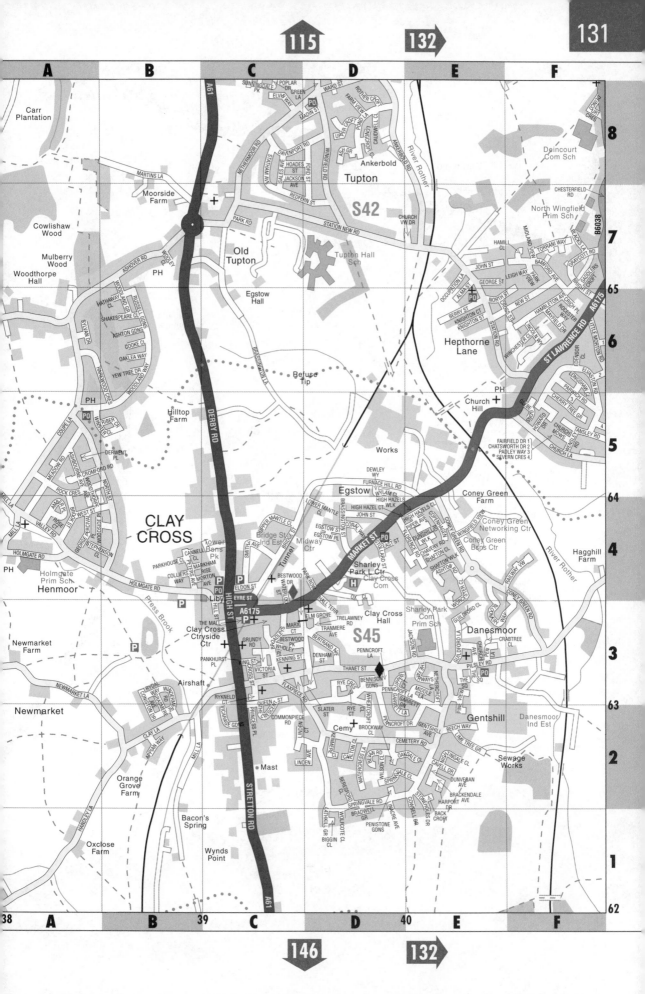

131 116

A B C D E F

8

7

65

6

5

64

4

3

63

2

1

62

Williamthorpe

North Wingfield

Hillyfields

WILLIAMTHORPE RD

Highfields

HIGHFIELDS WAY 1
MEADOW CROFT 2
HIGHFIELDS DR 3
FABRIC VIEW 4
PEWIT CL 5

S42

Cemy

1 WAIN WAY
2 HOLBROOK WAY
3 DARLEY WAY
4 DETHICK WAY

B6039

CHESTERFIELD RD
CHURCHLAND RD

MASEFIELD AVE
SEARSTON AVE
RALLEY CL
HALL FARM
MEADON
MORNINGTON RD
HUNLOKE RD
CENTRAL ST
SPRINGFIELD CL
BARNFIELD CL

HEATH RD
Liby
OLD COLLIERY
A6175

HARDWICK
PO
1 ST ALBANS CL
2 QUEENSWAY
STAINSBY CL
HARDWICK CT
HARDWICK VIEW RD
Holmewood Ind Est

TIBSHELF RD

Common End

S44

Holme Farm

Stainsby Common

High House Farm

BRANCH LA

Park View Farm

Hardstoft Common

LITTLE MORTON RD
SEVERN CRES
TANSLEY RD
CHURCH CL
CHURCH LA

PARKHOUSE RD

Seanor Farm

SEANOR LA

Bridle Path Farm

Timber Lane Farm

TIMBER LA

Broomridding Wood

Five Pits Trail

Hagg Hill

Parkhouse Green

Park House Farm

Poplar Farm
Park House Prim Sch
DALE VIEW CL

Headland Farm

LOCKO RD

Moorhouse Farm

Pear Tree Farm

Locko Lane Farm

LOCKO LA

Lower Pilsley

Waterloo

S45

VALLEY CL
DALE VIEW RD
THE ACRES
ACACIA RD
RUPERT ST
ACRES RD
HAZEL AVE

PH

GREEN LA

The Herb Garden at Hardstoft

DEEP LA

PH

EVELYN DEVONSHIRE COTTS

B6039

Bushypark Farm

Hallgate Farm

Tenacres

HALLGATE LA

LONSDALE CL
BROOM AVE
PADLEY WOOD RD
GRANGE RD
SLACK'S LA
CROM CROFT RD
THE PADDOCKS
BACK LA
GRANBY CL
Old Hall CL
ROTHER ST
Upper Pilsley

DARK LA
DARK LA
WARREN LA

Pilsley

1 WILLOW CL
2 BRUNSWICK ST
3 PROSPECT RD

NEW ST
STATION RD
SOUTH ST

DE55

PEAR TREE AVE
SREEVES AVE
DIMMON ...
QUEENSWAY
LANSBURY AVE
PH
CHURCH ST
GREEN CL
PO
SEANOR LA
MANOR ..
ROUSE ST
Pilsley Prim Sch

MORTON RD
ELM RD
Nether Pilsley

River Rother

131 147

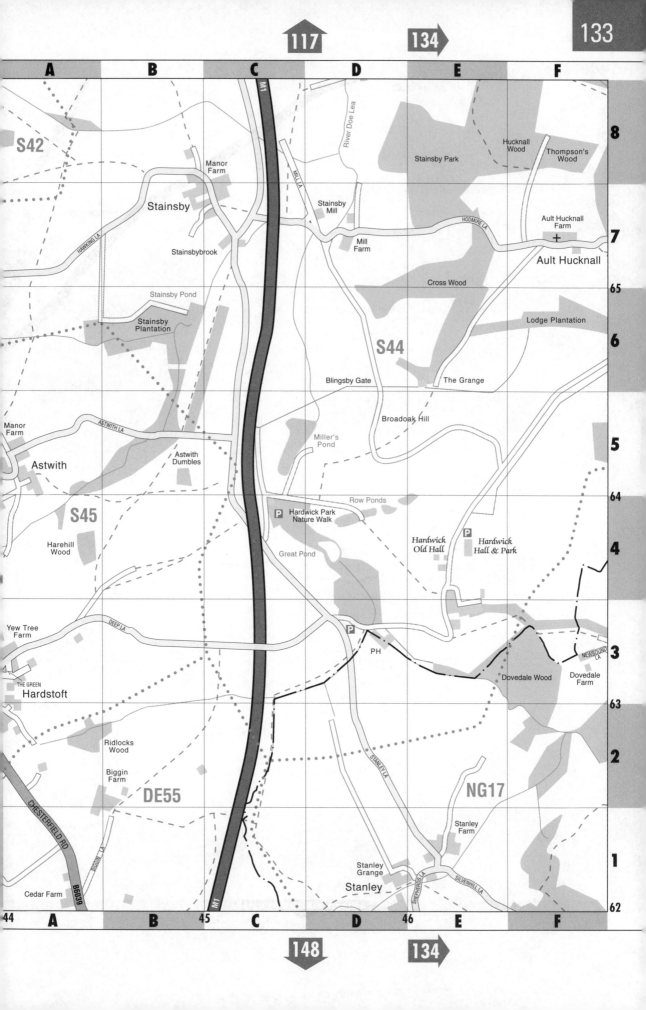

Glapwell

Griff
Wood

S44

Top Farm

Rowthorne

Hall Farm

Car
Plantation

Car Ponds

Park Piece

Longman
Nook

Field La

Farfield Lane

Merril Sick

Norcliff
Wood

NG19

Batley Farm

Pleasley Pit
Country Park

Hill Top
Farm

New
Houghton

Works

Anthony Bek
Com Prim Sch

Pleasley Colliery
Mus

Hardwick Park
Farm

Norwood

Norwood
Lodge

NG17

Crossley
Plantation

Hare
Plantation

Rowthorne Trail
Nature Reserve

Newbound
Farm

Newboundmill
Farm

Baxterhill

Hill Farm

River Meden

Little Dawgates
Wood

Longdge Lane

Batley La

Newbound La

Newbound La

Longhedge La

Moorhaigh La

Baxter Hill

Dale La

Green Green La

Mansfield Rd

Chesterfield Rd

A617

A617

B6417

B6417

Rotherham Rd

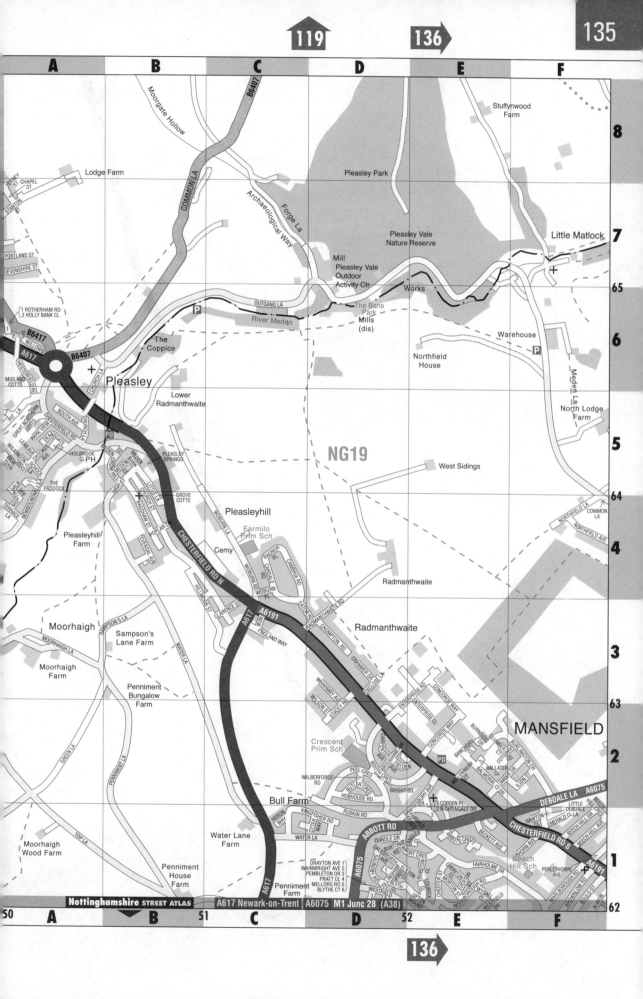

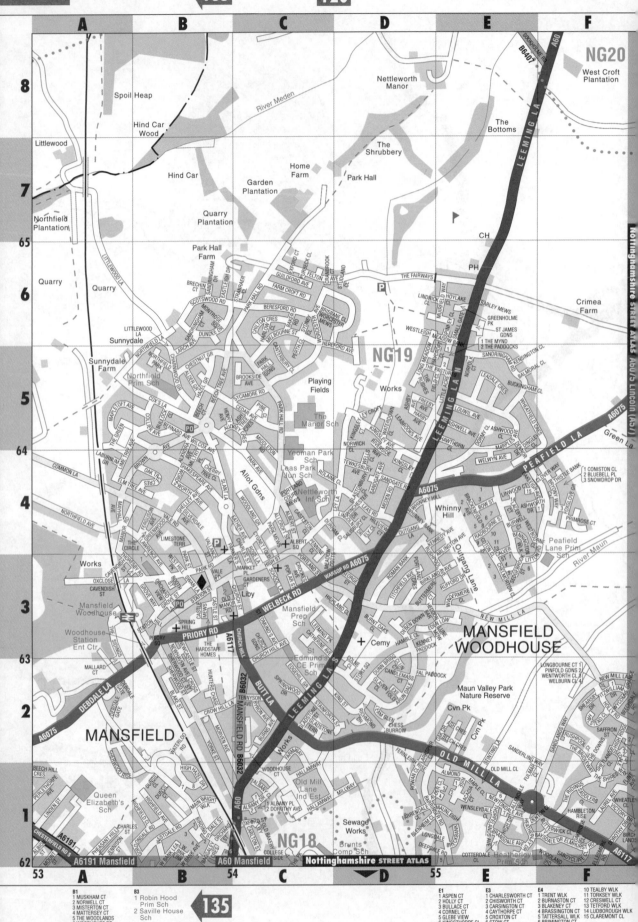

B1	**B3**	**E1**	**E3**	**E4**	
1 MUSKHAM CT	1 Robin Hood	1 ASPEN CT	1 CHARLESWORTH CT	1 TRENT WLK	10 TEALBY WLK
2 NORWELL CT	Prim Sch	2 HOLLY CT	2 CHISWORTH CT	2 BURNASTON CT	11 TORKSEY WLK
3 MISTERTON CT	2 Saville House	3 BULLACE CT	3 CARSINGTON CT	3 BLAKENEY CT	12 CRESWELL CT
4 MATTERSEY CT	Sch	4 CORNEL CT	4 CAYTHORPE CT	4 BRASSINGTON CT	13 TETFORD WLK
5 THE WOODLANDS		5 GLEBE VIEW	5 CROXTON CT	5 TATTERSALL WLK	14 LUDBOROUGH WLK
6 WOODHOUSE RD		6 KINGSTHORPE CL	6 STOW CT	6 BRIMINGTON CT	15 CLAREMONT CL
7 DUNSIL RD		7 BRACKMILLS CL		7 TRUSLEY WLK	
8 MAIN BRIGHT RD				8 REPTON CT	
				9 THURLBY CT	

A **B** **C** **D** **E** **F**

8

7

61

6

5

60

4

59

3

2

1

58

Manor Farm

The Palace Farm

PO

Lower House

Sheen

PH

POWN ST

Townend

Newfield

Crakelow

Bridge-end

Factory

Hartington

SK17

Mast

Scaldersitch

Banktop

The Raikes

Raikes Farm

Hartington Bridge

River Dove

Lower Hurst Farm

Upper Hurst

Harecops

Archford Moor Farm

Archford Moor

Beresford Lane

Beresford Lane Farm

Field House Farm

Barracks Farm

BERESFORD LA

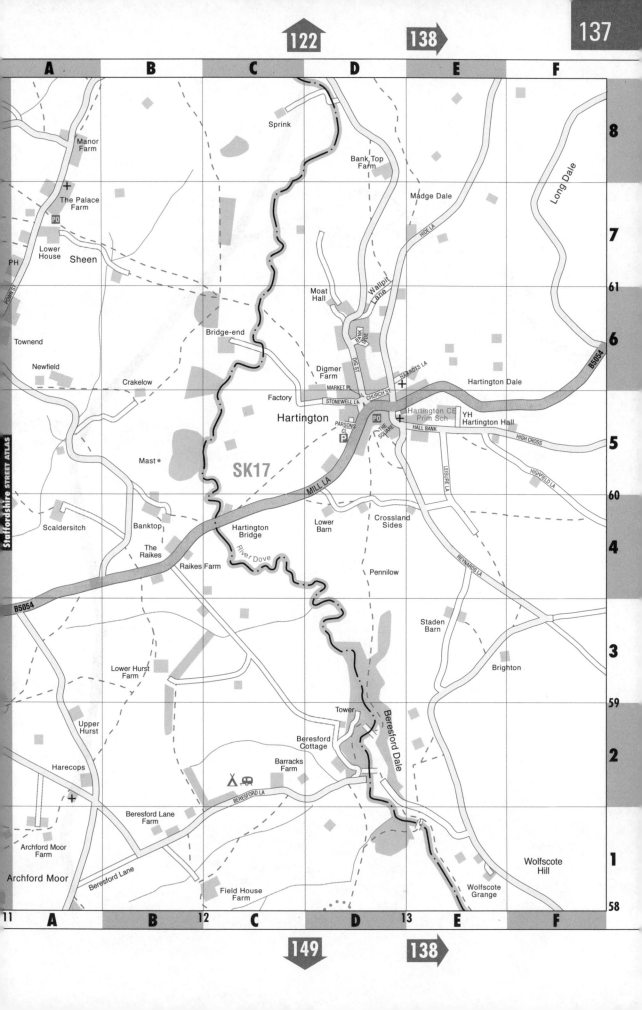

Beresford Cottage

Tower

Beresford Dale

Pennilow

Lower Barn

Crossland Sides

Staden Barn

Brighton

Wolfscote Grange

Wolfscote Hill

Sprink

Bank Top Farm

Madge Dale

HIDE LA

Wallpit Lane

Moat Hall

BANK SIDE

Digmer Farm

MARKET PL

DIG ST

STONEWELL LA

CHURCH ST

HARROTS LA

Hartington Dale

PARSONS CL

P

PO

THE SQUARE

Hartington CE Prim Sch

YH
Hartington Hall

HALL BANK

HIGH CROSS

LEISURE LA

HIGHFIELD LA

MILL LA

REYNARDS LA

B5054

B5054

Long Dale

Staffordshire STREET ATLAS

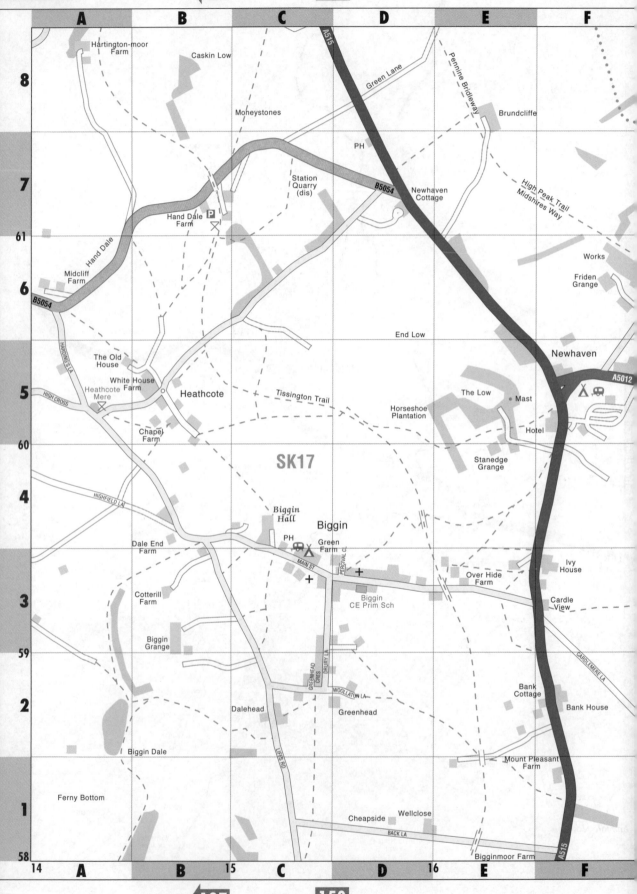

Hartington-moor Farm

Caskin Low

Moneystones

Green Lane

Pennine Bridleway

Brundcliffe

PH

Station Quarry (dis)

B5054

Newhaven Cottage

High Peak Trail
Midshires Way

Works

Hand Dale Farm

P

Friden Grange

Hand Dale

Midcliff Farm

B5054

End Low

Newhaven

A5012

The Old House

White House Farm

Heathcote Mere

Heathcote

Tissington Trail

The Low

Mast

Horseshoe Plantation

Hotel

HARDINGS LA

HIGH CROSS

Chapel Farm

SK17

Stanedge Grange

HIGHFIELD LA

Biggin Hall

Biggin

Dale End Farm

PH

Green Farm

Over Hide Farm

Ivy House

Cotterill Farm

Biggin CE Prim Sch

PERCIVAL CL

Cardle View

Biggin Grange

DRURY LA

GREENHEAD CRES

WOOLLATON LA

Bank Cottage

Bank House

CARDLEMERE LA

Dalehead

Greenhead

LIFFS RD

Biggin Dale

Mount Pleasant Farm

Ferny Bottom

Cheapside

Wellclose

BACK LA

Bigginmoor Farm

A515

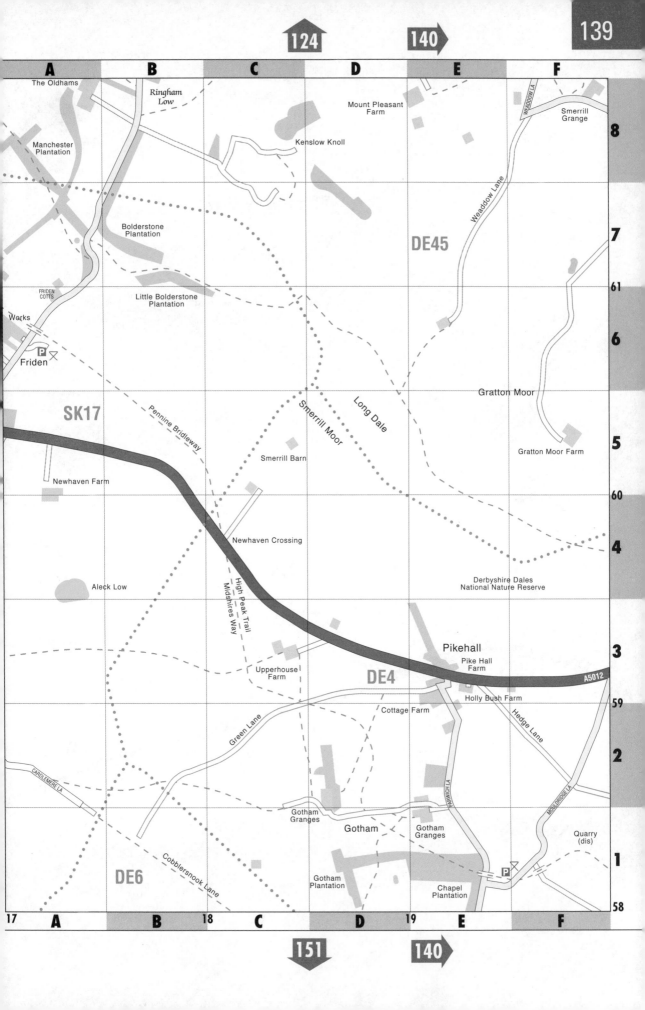

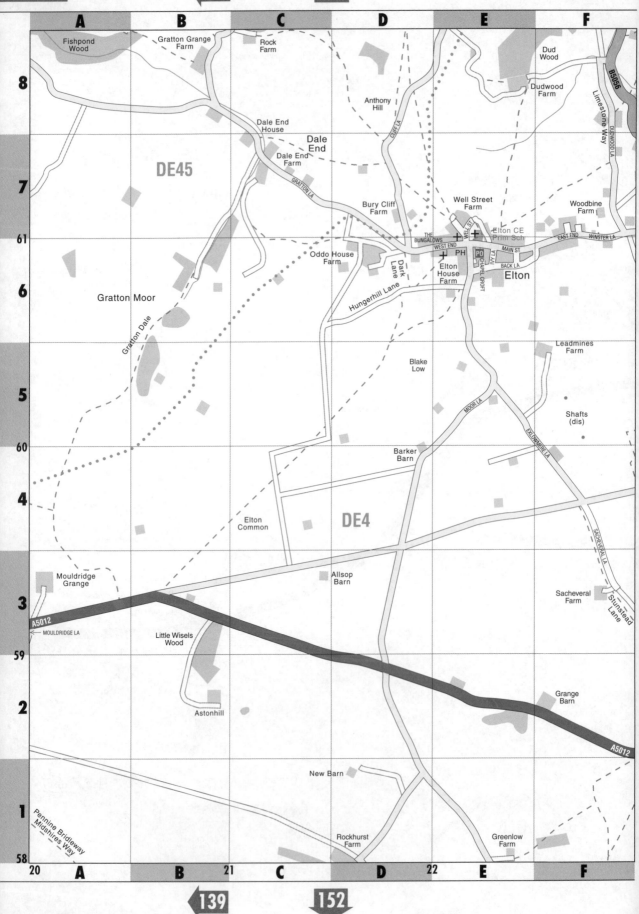

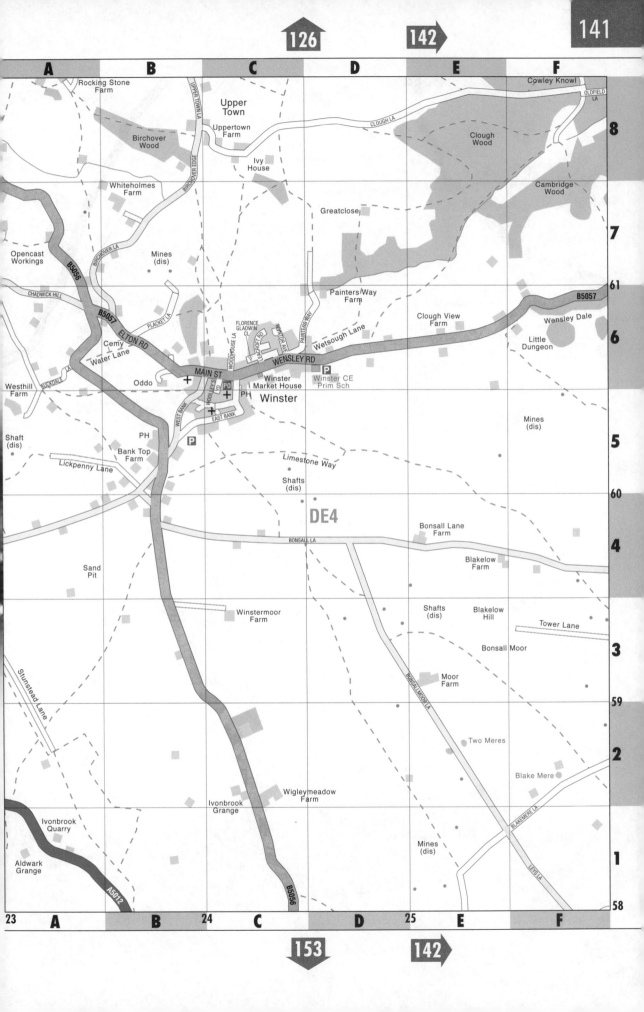

A B C D E F

8
7
61
6
5
60
4
3
59
2
1
58

23 A B 24 C D 25 E F

Rocking Stone Farm

Upper Town

Uppertown Farm

Birchover Wood

Ivy House

UPPER TOWN LA

BIRCHOVER EDGE

CLOUGH LA

Clough Wood

Cowley Knowl

OLDFIELD LA

Cambridge Wood

Whiteholmes Farm

Greatclose

Opencast Workings

B5056

BIRCHOVER LA

Mines (dis)

Painters Way Farm

Clough View Farm

B5057

Wensley Dale

Little Dungeon

CHADWICK HILL

B5057

PLACKET LA

ELTON RD

Water Lane

Cemy

BUCKDALE LA

WOODHOUSE LA

FLORENCE GLADWIN CL

SEACRUFT RD

NEWTON AVE

PAINTERS WAY

Wetsough Lane

WENSLEY RD

Westhill Farm

Oddo

MAIN ST

WOOLLEYS

PO

PH

Winster Market House

Winster

Winster CE Prim Sch

P

Mines (dis)

Shaft (dis)

PH

Bank Top Farm

WEST BANK

EAST BANK

P

Limestone Way

Shafts (dis)

Bonsall Lane Farm

Blakelow Farm

Lickpenny Lane

DE4

BONSALL LA

Sand Pit

Winstermoor Farm

Shafts (dis)

Blakelow Hill

Tower Lane

Bonsall Moor

BONSALL MOOR LA

Moor Farm

Stunstead Lane

Two Meres

Blake Mere

Wigleymeadow Farm

BLAKEMERE LA

Ivonbrook Grange

B5056

Mines (dis)

LEYS LA

Ivonbrook Quarry

Aldwark Grange

A5012

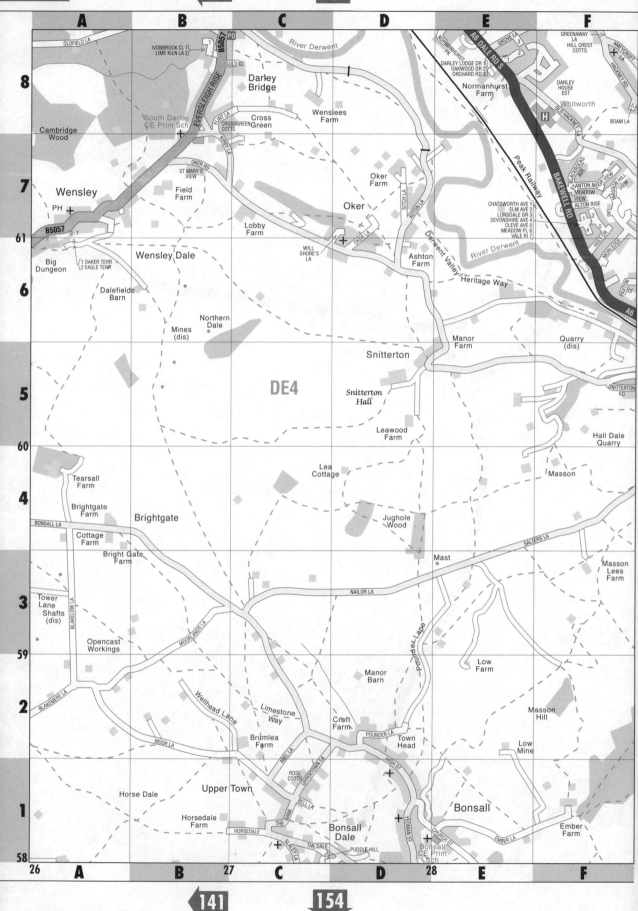

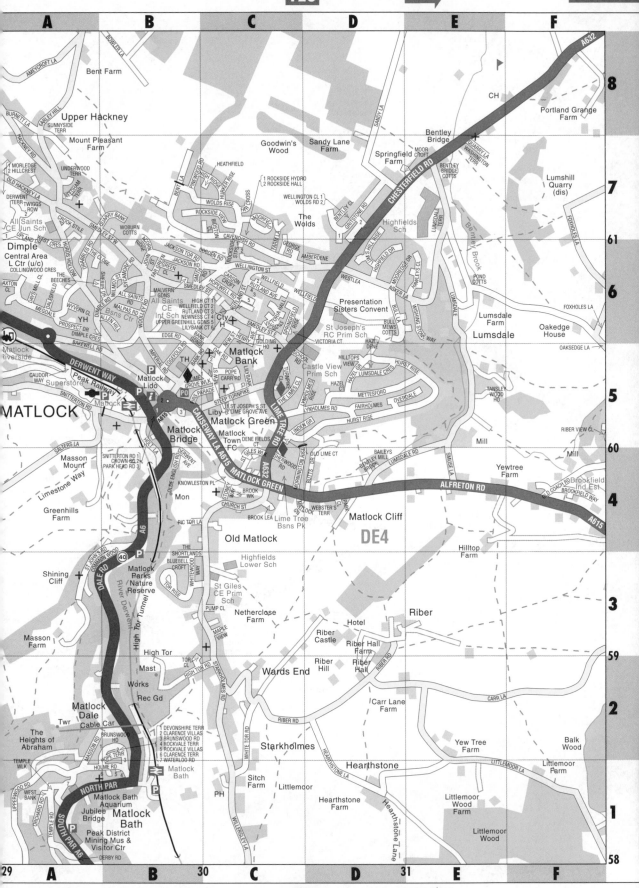

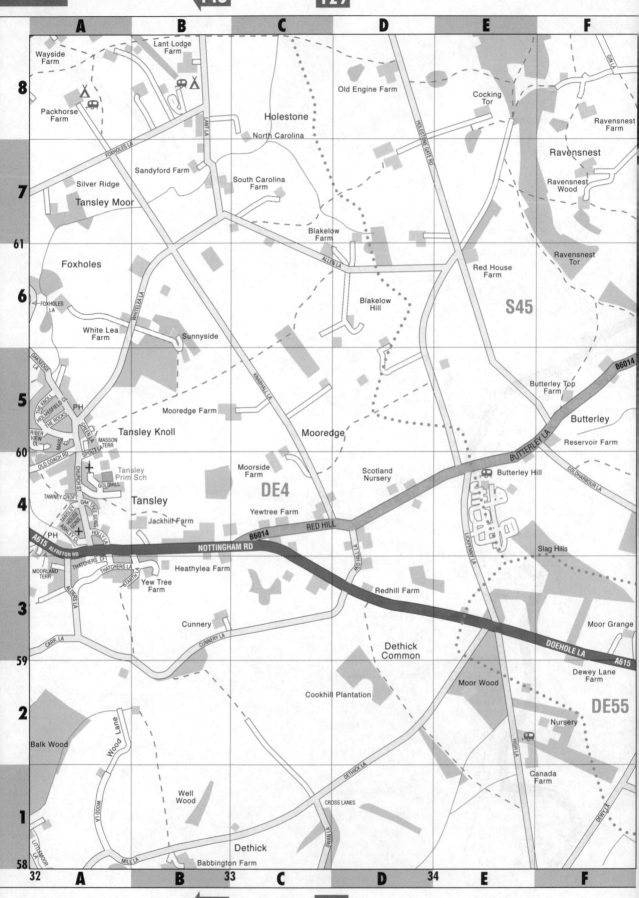

Wayside
Farm

Lant Lodge
Farm

Packhorse
Farm

Holestone

Old Engine Farm

Cocking
Tor

Ravensnest
Farm

Ravensnest

North Carolina

Silver Ridge

Sandyford Farm

South Carolina
Farm

Tansley Moor

Ravensnest
Wood

Blakelow
Farm

Foxholes

ALLEN LA

Red House
Farm

Ravensnest
Tor

S45

FOXHOLES LA

Blakelow
Hill

White Lea
Farm

Sunnyside

Butterley Top
Farm

B6014

WHITE LEA LA

KNABHALL LA

Mooredge Farm

Mooredge

Butterley

BUTTERLEY LA

Reservoir Farm

COLDHARBOUR LA

OAKSEDGE LA

THE KNOLL
HOLMESFIELD CL
THE ROCKS

PH

Tansley Knoll

RIBER
VIEW
CL

MASSON
LA TERR

Moorside
Farm

Scotland
Nursery

Butterley Hill

Old Coach Rd

SPORT LA

GREEN

Tansley
Prim Sch

DE4

Butterley Hill

Slag Hills

MASI CL

GOLDHILL

CHURCH ST

Tansley

Yewtree Farm

LOCKPENNY LA

TAWNEY CROFT

OAK TREE GDNS

Jackhill Farm

RED HILL

PH

HOLLY LA

RED HILL LA

Yew Tree
Farm

B6014

RED HILL

A615

ALFRETON RD

NOTTINGHAM RD

MOORLAND
TERR

THATCHERS CFT

THATCHERS LA

Heathylea Farm

Redhill Farm

Moor Grange

ALDERS LA

STARTH LA

DOEHOLE LA

A615

CARR LA

Cunnery

CUNNERY LA

Dethick
Common

Moor Wood

Dewey Lane
Farm

DE55

Cookhill Plantation

Moor Wood

Nursery

Wood Lane

Balk Wood

HIGH LA

WOOD LA

Well
Wood

Canada
Farm

LITTLEMOOR LA

Dethick

CROSS LANES

DEWY LA

MILL LA

Babbington Farm

SWAN LA

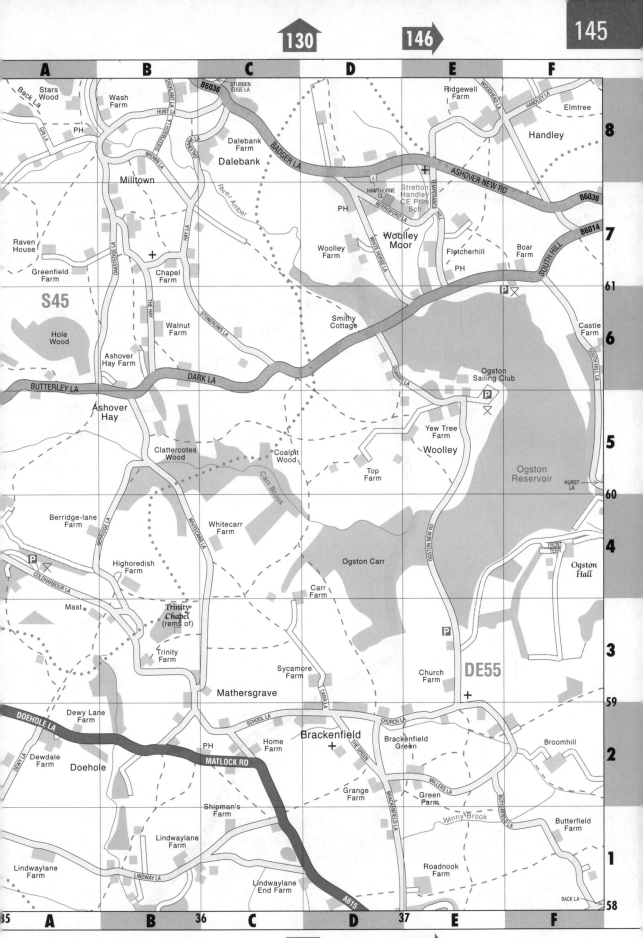

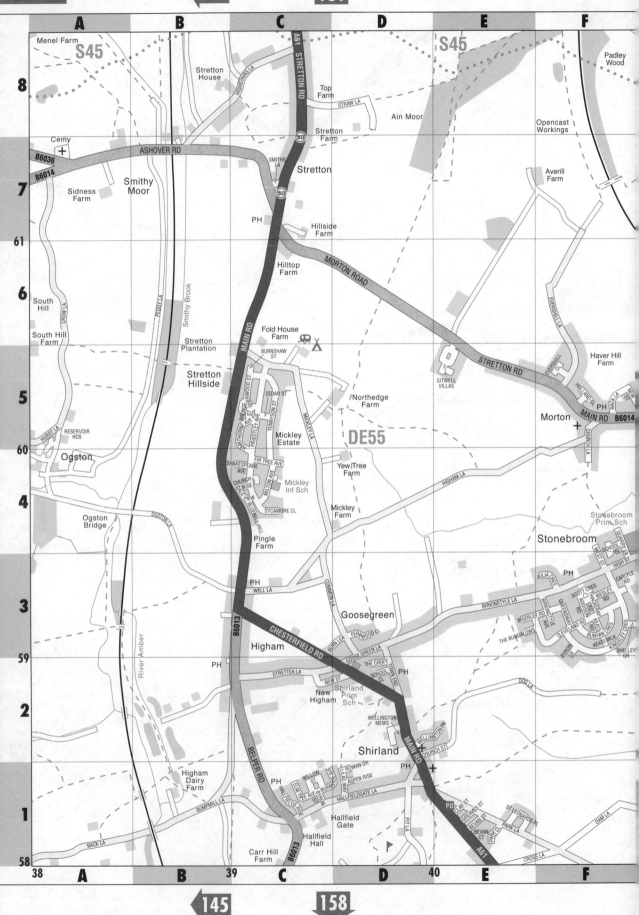

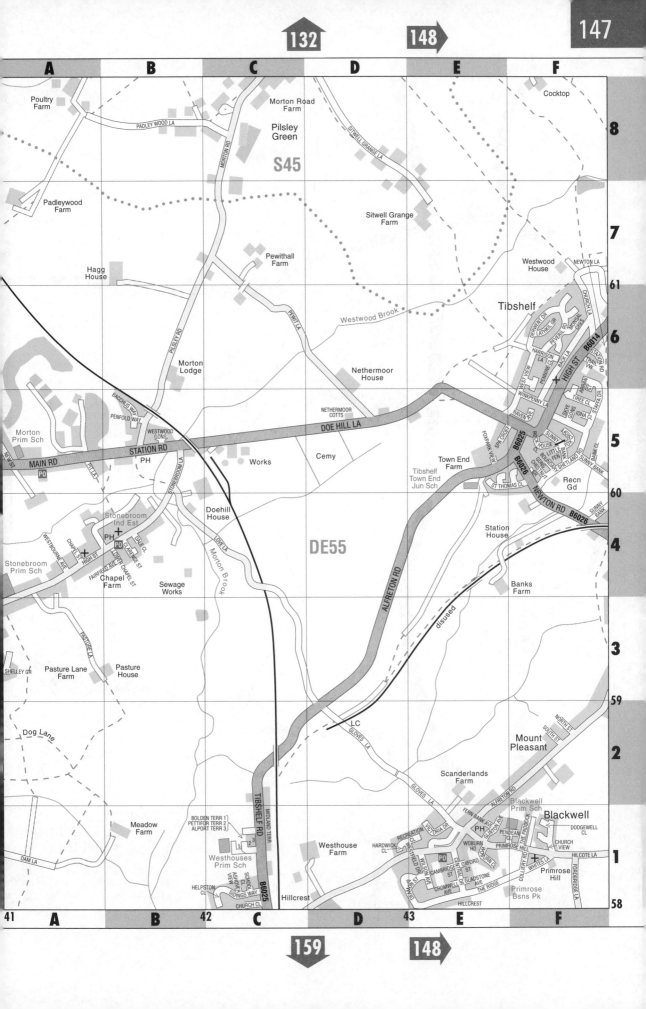

A B C D E F

Poultry Farm

Morton Road Farm

Pilsley Green

Cocktop

PADLEY WOOD LA

MORTON RD

S45

SITWELL GRANGE LA

8

Padleywood Farm

Sitwell Grange Farm

7

Hagg House

Pewithall Farm

PILSLEY RD

PENNIT LA

Westwood Brook

Westwood House

NEWTON LA

61

Tibshelf

CHURCH LA

6

Morton Lodge

Nethermoor House

DERWENT DR
ATHWL GR
PEVERIL RD
WEST VIEW
HARRISON LA
PENNINE CL
BACK LA
HIGH ST
STATION RD
TRAIN VW
B6014
MORGAN GDNS

Morton Prim Sch

BACCHUS WAY

PENFOLD WAY

WESTWOOD GDNS

STONEBROOM LA

DOE HILL LA

NETHERMOOR COTTS

WINKPENNY LA

RAVEN AVE

TIREE CL
SKYE CL
IONA CL
STAFFA DR

SPA CROFT
FOXPARK VIEW
ROCK CL
LITTLE FEN
CHESTNUT
BOUNDARY CL
SUNNY HOUSE
SHETLAND
SUNNY BANK
B6025
B6026

5

NEW ST

MAIN RD

STATION RD

PH

PITT LA

PO

Works

Cemy

Town End Farm

Tibshelf Town End Jun Sch

ST THOMAS CL

Recn Gd

SUNNY BANK

60

Stonebroom Ind Est

Doehill House

DE55

NEWTON RD

B6026

4

Stonebroom Prim Sch

WESTBOURNE AVE

CHAPEL ST
HIGH ST
PH
PO
DALE CL
CLARENCE ST
FAIRFIELD AVE
LOWER CHAPEL ST

Chapel Farm

Sewage Works

MORTON BROOK

LOVE LA

ALFRETON RD

disused

Station House

Banks Farm

SHELLEY GR

Pasture Lane Farm

PASTURE LA

Pasture House

3

59

Dog Lane

LC

GLOVES LA

Mount Pleasant

NORTH ST

SOUTH ST

2

Meadow Farm

DAM LA

BOLDEN TERR 1
PETTIFOR TERR 2
ALPORT TERR 3

TIBSHELF RD

MIDLAND TERR

Westhouse Farm

Scanderlands Farm

RECREATION RD
VICTORIA DR
WOBURN HO
HARDWICK CL
WESTFIELD DR
WILSON AVE
PRIMROSE HILL
WOBURN CL
FERN BANK AVE
ALFRETON RD

Blackwell Prim Sch

Blackwell

PENDEAN CL
THE PADDOCK
DODGEWELL CL
CHURCH VIEW
PH

1

Westhouses Prim Sch

HELPSTON CL

SCHOOL CL
ASHOVER VIEW
SIDINGS WAY

B6025

CHURCH CL

Hillcrest

CAMBRIDGE ST
OXFORD ST
CENTRAL DR
CROMWELL AVE
GLADSTONE AVE
HILLCREST
THE RIDGE
DOWELL ST
PO
COLLIERY RD
WHITES LA
HILCOTE LA
FORBRIDGE LA

Primrose Hill

Primrose Bsns Pk

58

41 42 43

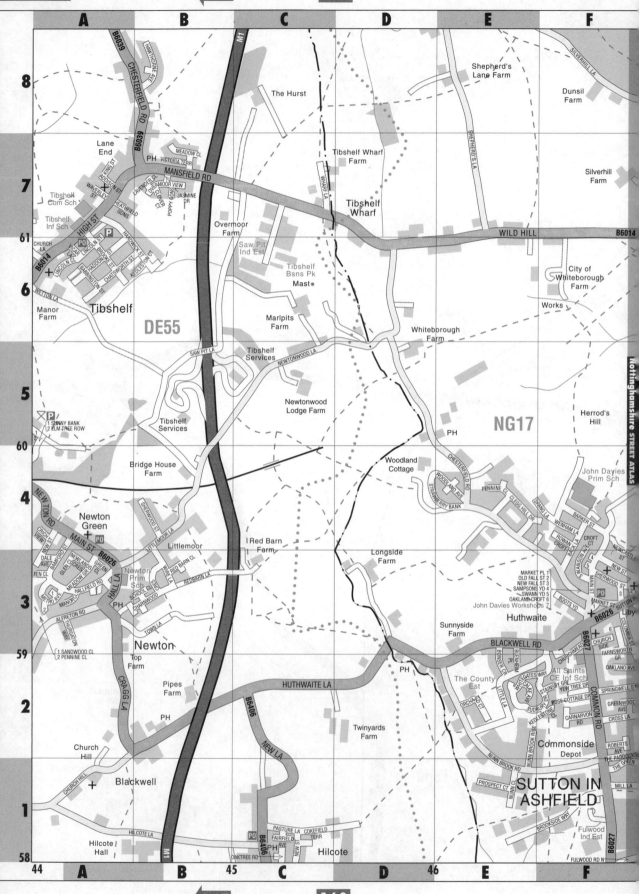

Nottinghamshire STREET ATLAS

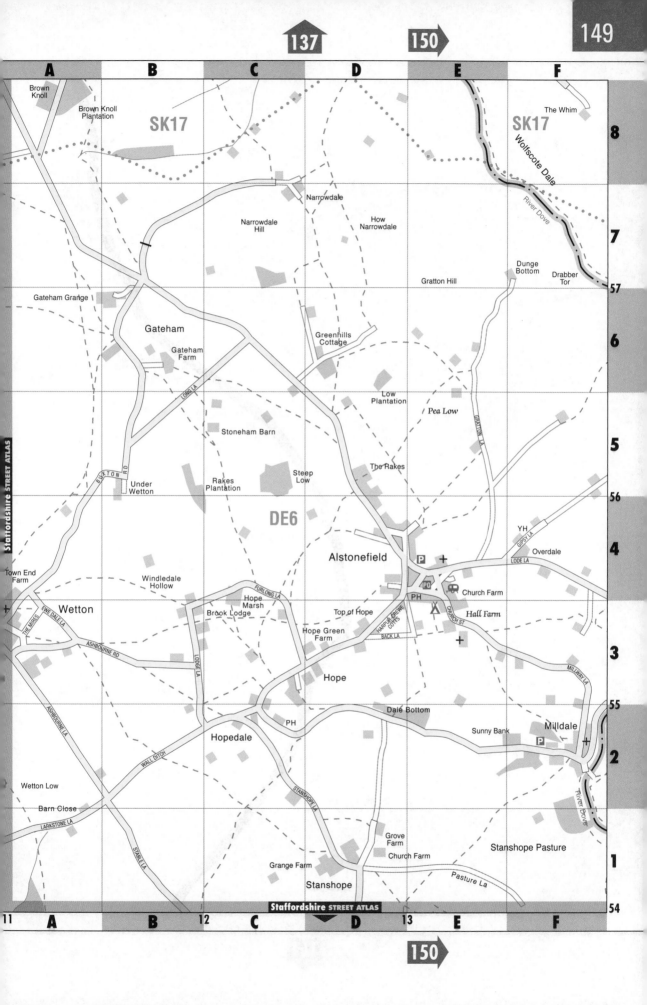

SK17

8

Brown
Knoll

Brown Knoll
Plantation

The Whim

SK17

Wolfscote Dale

River Dove

Narrowdale

Narrowdale
Hill

How
Narrowdale

7

57

Gratton Hill

Dunge
Bottom

Drabber
Tor

Gateham Grange

Gateham

Greenhills
Cottage

6

Gateham
Farm

LONG LA

Low
Plantation

Pea Low

GRATTON LA

Stoneham Barn

Steep
Low

The Rakes

5

56

BUXTON RD

Under
Wetton

Rakes
Plantation

DE6

YH

GIPSY LA

Overdale

LODE LA

4

Alstonefield

P

Church Farm

PO

Town End
Farm

Windledale
Hollow

Hope
Marsh

FURLONG LA

Top of Hope

PH

Hall Farm

THE MIRES

EWE DALE LA

Wetton

Brook Lodge

HARPUR CREWE
COTTS

CHURCH ST

MILLWAY LA

LODGE LA

Hope Green
Farm

BACK LA

3

55

ASHBOURNE RD

Hope

Dale Bottom

Milldale

Sunny Bank

ASHBOURNE LA

PH

P

Hopedale

WALL DITCH

2

Wetton Low

STANSHOPE LA

Barn Close

Grove
Farm

LARKSTONE LA

Stanshope Pasture

STABLE LA

Church Farm

1

Grange Farm

Stanshope

Pasture La

54

149
138

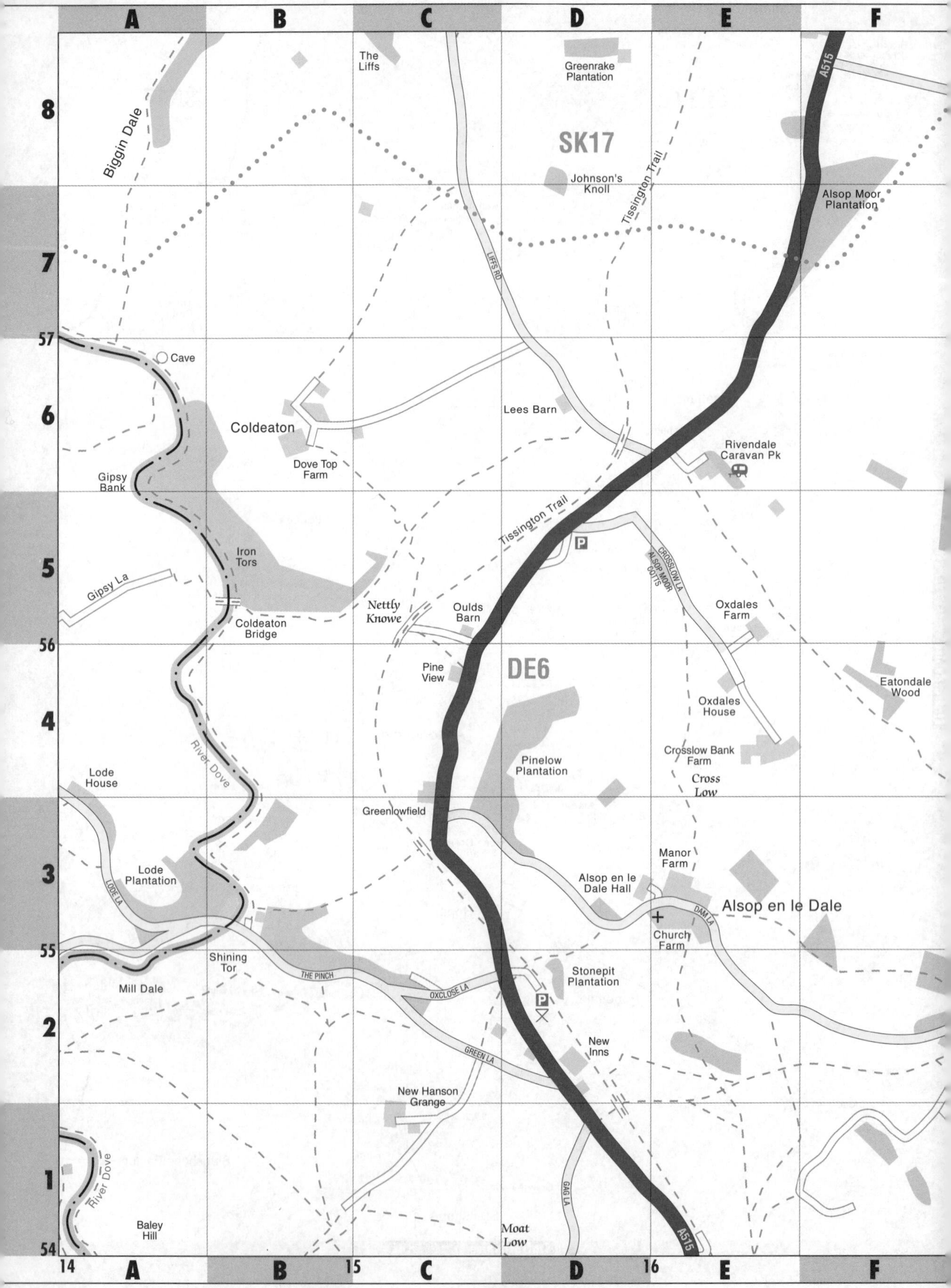

A **B** **C** **D** **E** **F**

8

Biggin Dale

The Liffs

Greenrake Plantation

SK17

Johnson's Knoll

Alsop Moor Plantation

A515

7

Cave

57

Coldeaton

Lees Barn

6

Dove Top Farm

Rivendale Caravan Pk

Gipsy Bank

Iron Tors

Tissington Trail

5

Gipsy La

Nettly Knowe

Oulds Barn

P

ALSOP MOOR COTTS

CROSSLOW LA

Oxdales Farm

Coldeaton Bridge

56

Pine View

DE6

Eatondale Wood

River Dove

Oxdales House

4

Lode House

Pinelow Plantation

Crosslow Bank Farm

Cross Low

Lode La

Greenlowfield

Manor Farm

3

Lode Plantation

Alsop en le Dale Hall

Alsop en le Dale

DAM LA

Church Farm

55

Shining Tor

THE PINCH

Mill Dale

OXCLOSE LA

Stonepit Plantation

P

New Inns

2

GREEN LA

New Hanson Grange

1

River Dove

G46 LA

Moat Low

A515

Baley Hill

54

14 **A** **B** **15** **C** **D** **16** **E** **F**

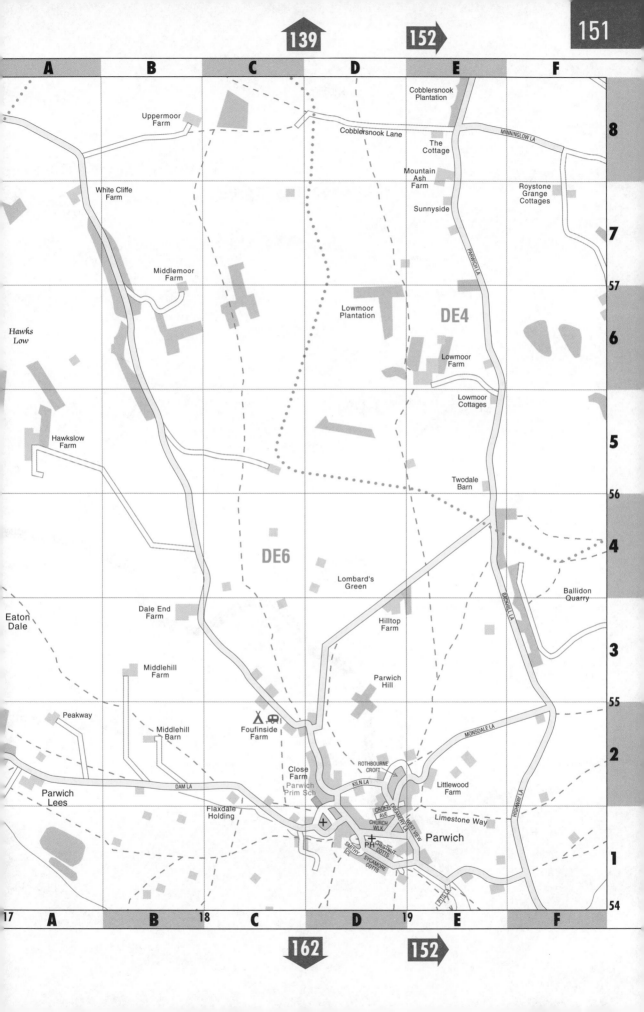

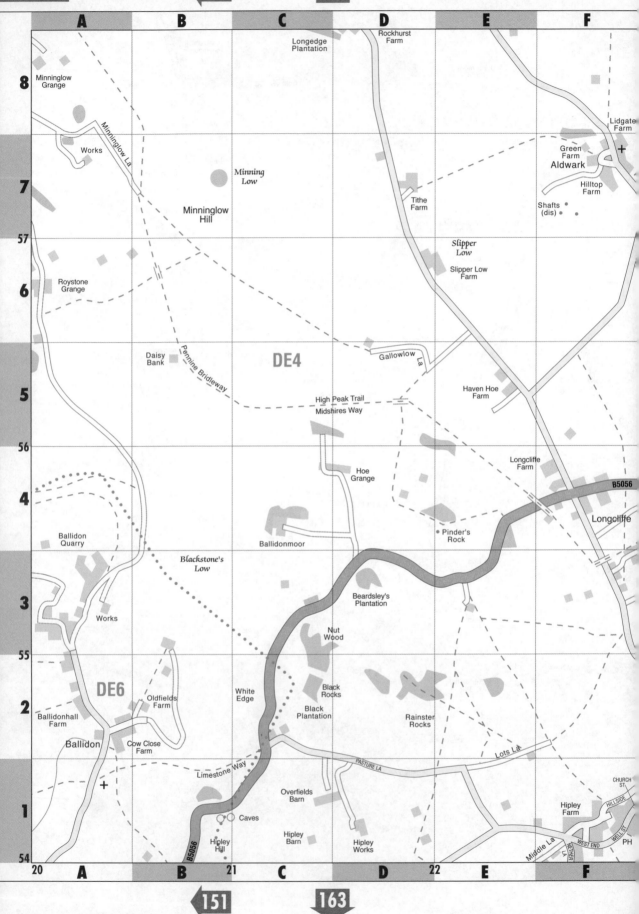

151
140

A B C D E F

8 Minninglow
Grange

Works

Minninglow La

Longedge
Plantation

Rockhurst
Farm

Lidgate
Farm

Green
Farm
Aldwark

7 Minning
Low

Minninglow
Hill

Tithe
Farm

Hilltop
Farm

Shafts
(dis)

57

6 Royston
Grange

*Slipper
Low*

Slipper Low
Farm

Daisy
Bank

DE4

Gallowlow La

Haven Hoe
Farm

5 High Peak Trail
Midshires Way

56 Longcliffe
Farm

B5056

4 Ballidon
Quarry

Hoe
Grange

Longcliffe

*Blackstone's
Low*

Ballidonmoor

Pinder's
Rock

3 Works

Beardsley's
Plantation

Nut
Wood

55

2 Ballidonhall
Farm

DE6

Oldfields
Farm

White
Edge

Black
Rocks

Black
Plantation

Rainster
Rocks

Lots La

Ballidon

Cow Close
Farm

Limestone Way

PASTURE LA

CHURCH
ST.

Overfields
Barn

Hipley
Farm

HILLSIDE

1 Caves

Hipley
Hill

B5056

Hipley
Barn

Hipley
Works

Middle La

NETHER LA

WEST END

WELL ST.

PH

54

20 A B 21 C D 22 E F

151
163

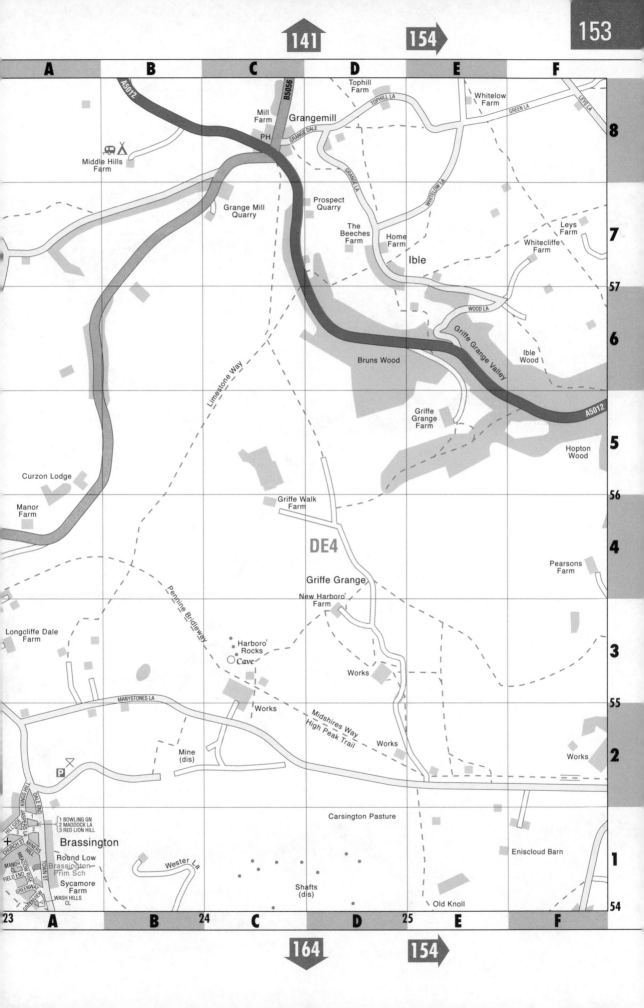

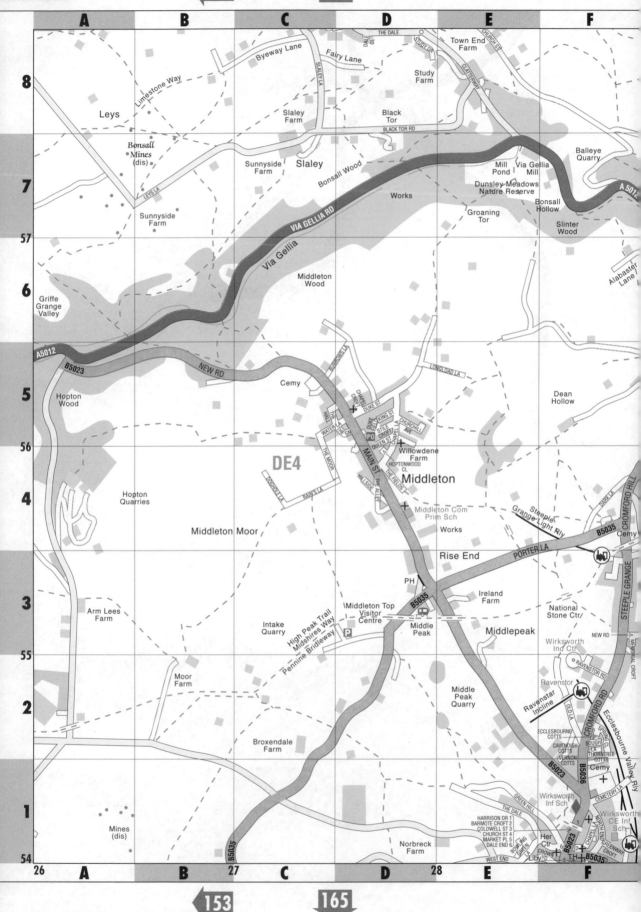

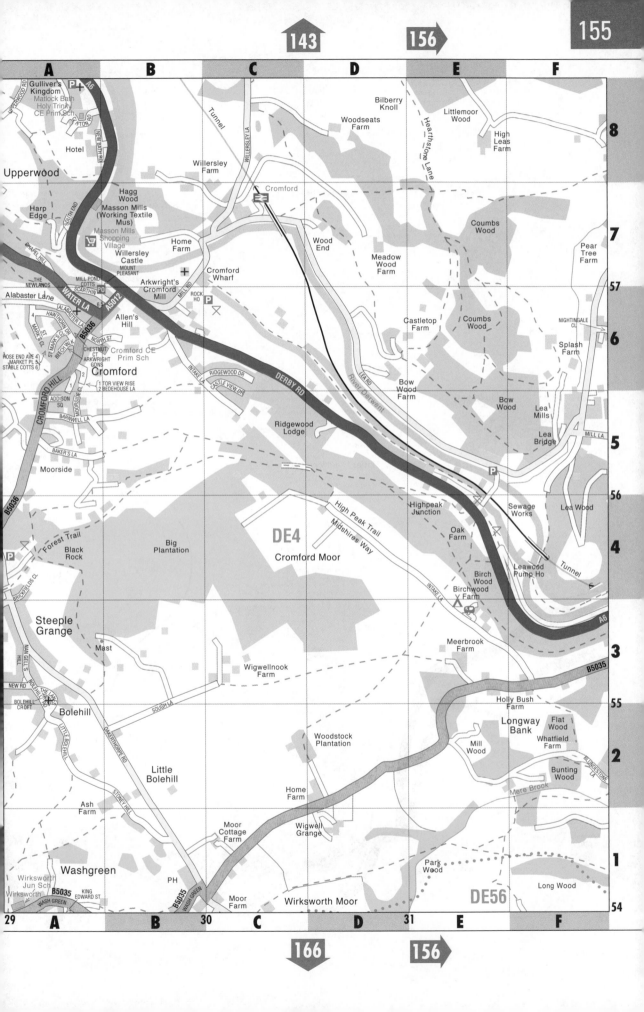

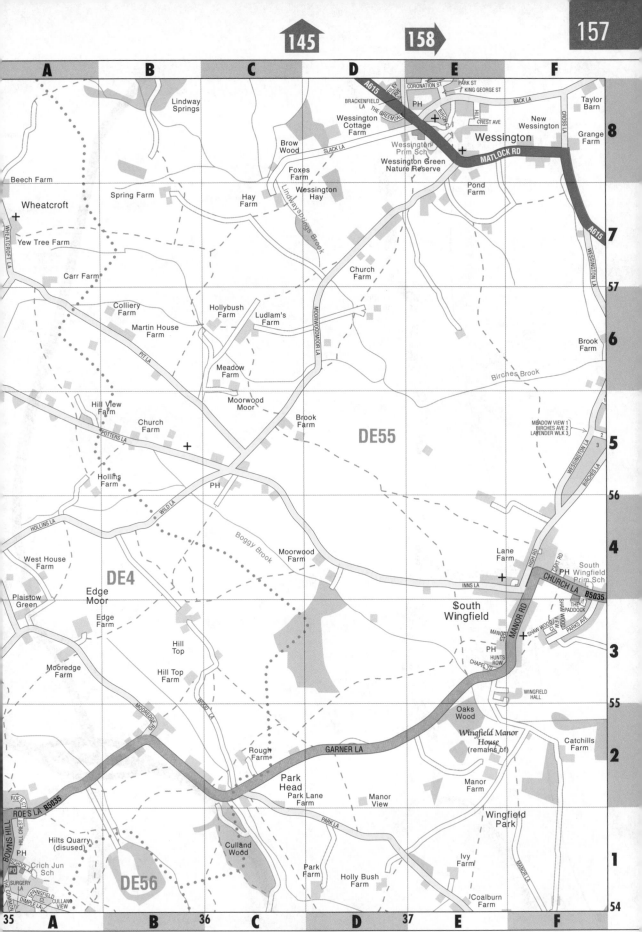

157
146

157
169

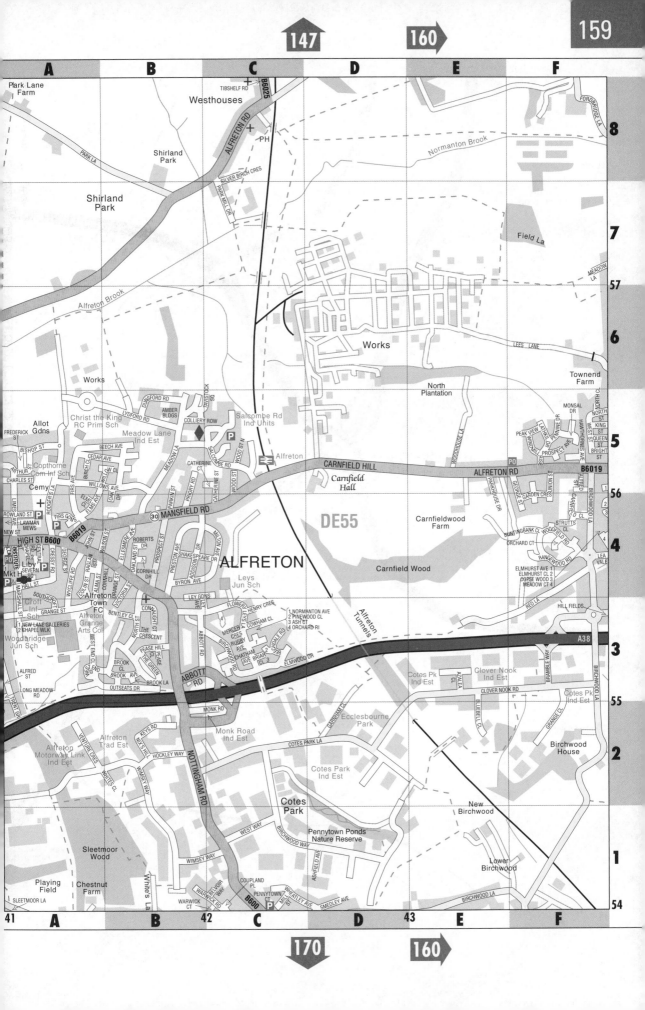

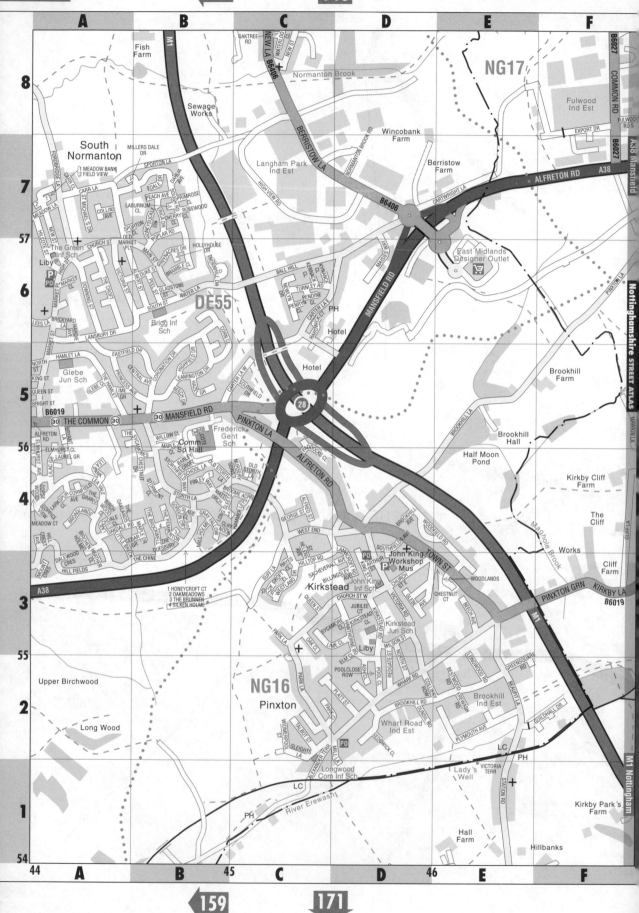

159
148

NG17

B6027

COMMON RD

A38 Mansfield

Fish Farm

Fulwood Ind Est

EXPORT DR

FULWO OD'S

B6027

Sewage Works

South Normanton

MILLERS DALE DR

1 MEADOW BANK
2 FIELD VIEW

SPORTON LA

CARR LA

Langham Park Ind Est

BERRISTOW LA

NORMANTON BROOK RD

Normanton Brook

OAKTREE RD

NEW LA B6406

NEW ST

Wincobank Farm

ALFRETON RD A38

Berristow Farm

CARTWRIGHT LA

B6406

MANSFIELD RD

East Midlands Designer Outlet

PINXTON LA

Nottinghamshire STREET ATLAS

DE55

Brookhill Farm

Brookhill Hall

Brookhill LA

Half Moon Pond

Kirkby Cliff Farm

The Cliff

Works

Cliff Farm

B6019

THE COMMON

MANSFIELD RD

PINXTON LA

ALFRETON RD

28

Frederick Gent Sch

Comm Sp Hall

Magpie Brook

Upper Birchwood

Long Wood

NG16

Pinxton

1 HONEYCROFT CT
2 OAKMEADOWS
3 THE BRUNNEN
4 SILKEN HOLME

Kirkstead

John King Workshop Mus

John King Inf Sch

Kirkstead Jun Sch

TOWN ST

WOODFIELD RD

Woodlands

PINXTON GRN

KIRKBY LA

M1

B6019

Brookhill Ind Est

Wharf Road Ind Est

Longwood Com Inf Sch

LC

River Erewash

PH

Lady's Well

VICTORIA TERR

STATION RD

Hall Farm

Kirkby Park's Farm

Hillbanks

M1 Nottingham

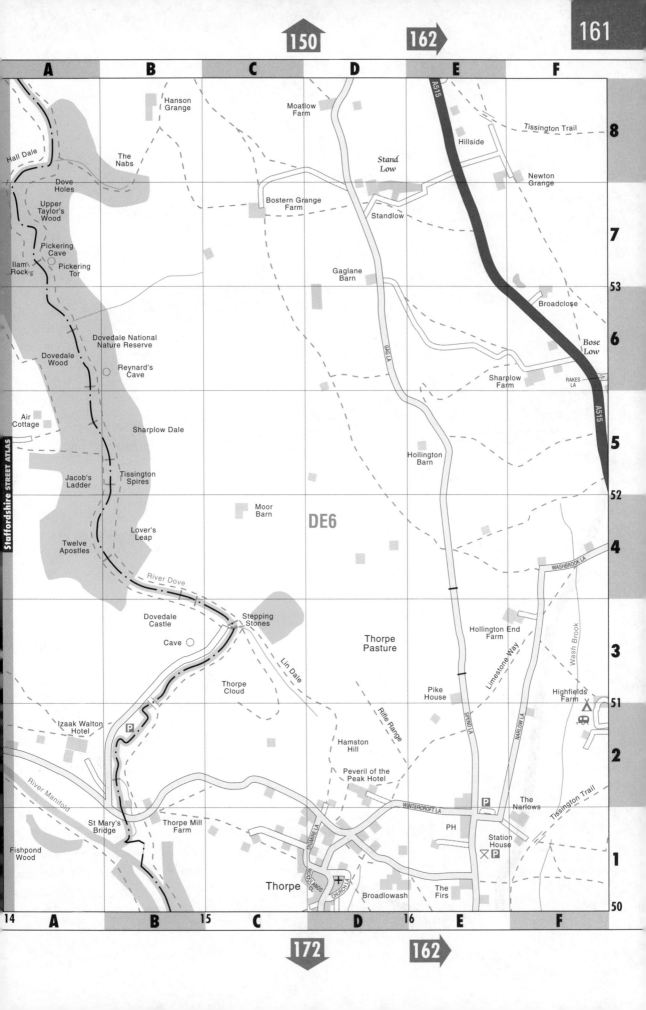

A B C D E F

8
7
53
6
5
52
4
51
2
1
50

14 A B 15 C D 16 E F

Hall Dale
The Nabs
Hanson Grange
Moatlow Farm
Stand Low
A515
Hillside
Tissington Trail
Newton Grange
Dove Holes
Upper Taylor's Wood
Bostern Grange Farm
Standlow
Pickering Cave
Ilam Rock
Pickering Tor
Gaglane Barn
Broadclose
Dovedale National Nature Reserve
Reynard's Cave
Bose Low
Dovedale Wood
Sharplow Farm
RAKES LA
A515
Air Cottage
Sharplow Dale
GAG LA
Hollington Barn
Jacob's Ladder
Tissington Spires
Moor Barn
DE6
Twelve Apostles
Lover's Leap
River Dove
WASHBROOK LA
Dovedale Castle
Stepping Stones
Thorpe Pasture
Hollington End Farm
Limestone Way
Wash Brook
Cave
Lin Dale
Thorpe Cloud
Pike House
Highfields Farm
Izaak Walton Hotel
P
Rifle Range
Hamston Hill
SPEND LA
NARLOW LA
Peveril of the Peak Hotel
The Narlows
Tissington Trail
River Manifold
St Mary's Bridge
Thorpe Mill Farm
WINTERCROFT LA
P
PH
Station House
P
Fishpond Wood
DIGMIRE LA
WOZLANDS CL
CHURCH LA
Thorpe
Broadlowash
The Firs

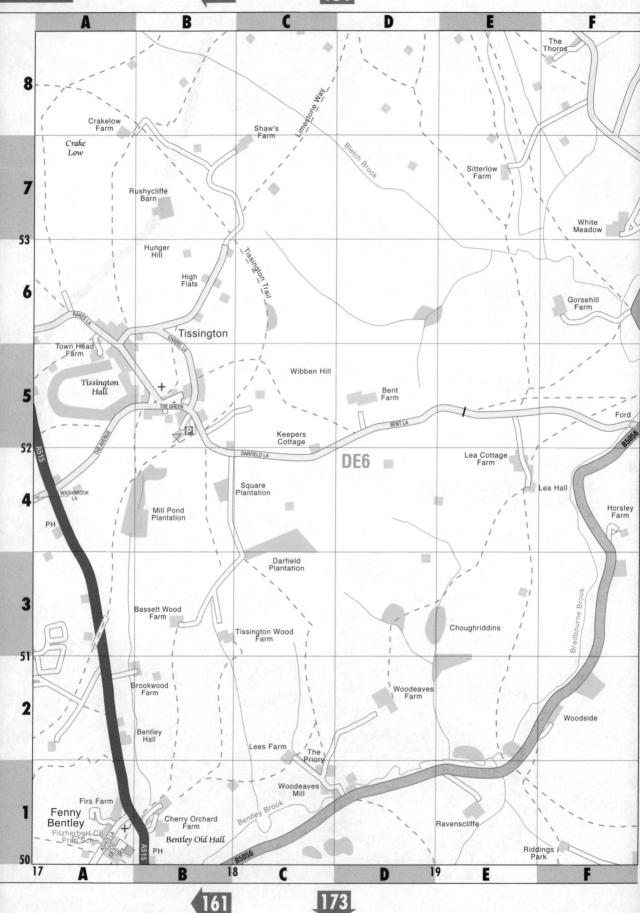

A B C D E F

8

The Thorns

Crakelow Farm

Crake Low

Shaw's Farm

Limestone Way

Bletch Brook

Sitterlow Farm

7

Rushycliffe Barn

White Meadow

53

Hunger Hill

High Flats

Tissington Trail

Gorsehill Farm

6

RAKES LA

Town Head Farm

Tissington

CHAPEL LA

Tissington Hall

Wibben Hill

Bent Farm

5

THE GREEN

THE AVENUE

Keepers Cottage

BENT LA

Ford

B5056

52

A515

P

DARFIELD LA

DE6

Lea Cottage Farm

WASHBROOK LA

Square Plantation

Lea Hall

4

PH

Mill Pond Plantation

Horsley Farm

Darfield Plantation

3

Bassett Wood Farm

Tissington Wood Farm

Choughriddins

Bradbourne Brook

51

Brookwood Farm

Woodeaves Farm

2

Woodside

Bentley Hall

Lees Farm

The Priory

Woodeaves Mill

1

Firs Farm

Fenny Bentley

Cherry Orchard Farm

Ravenscliffe

Fitzherbert CE Prim Sch

ASHES LA

SCHOOL CL

A515

PH

Bentley Old Hall

Bentley Brook

Riddings Park

50

B5056

17 A B 18 C D 19 E F

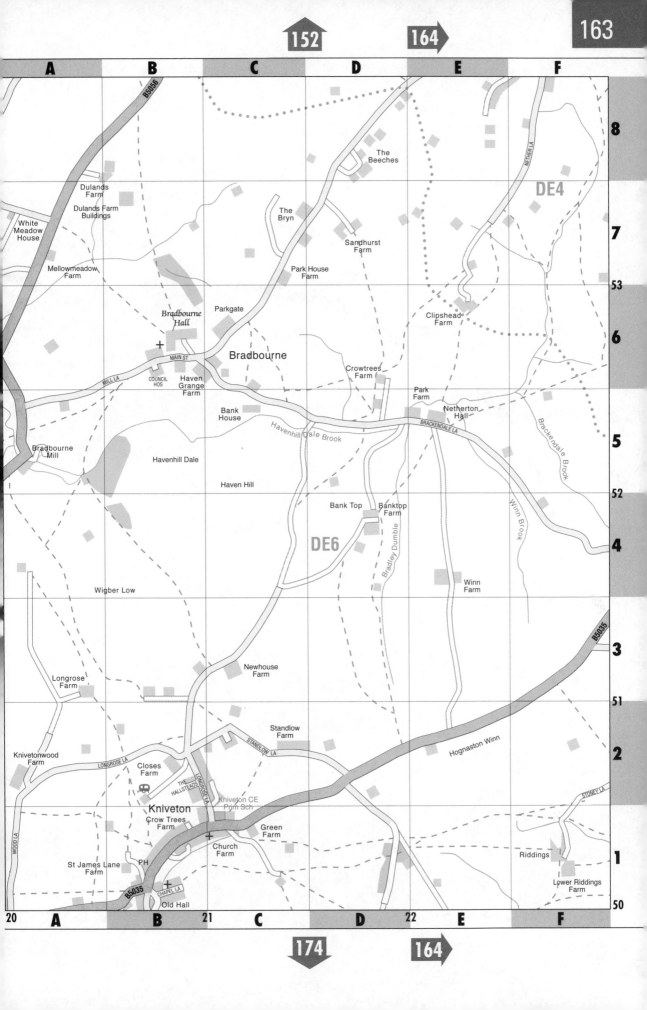

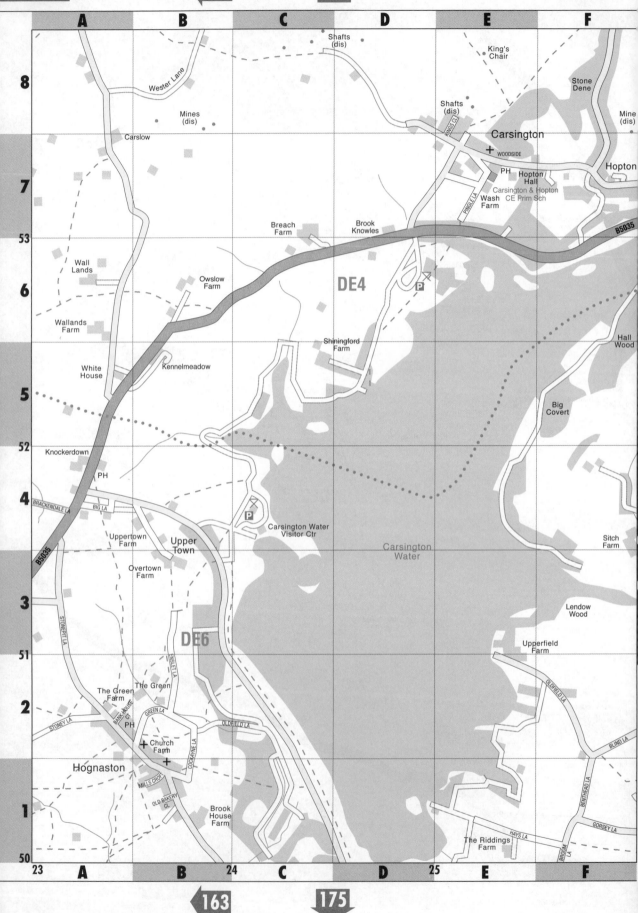

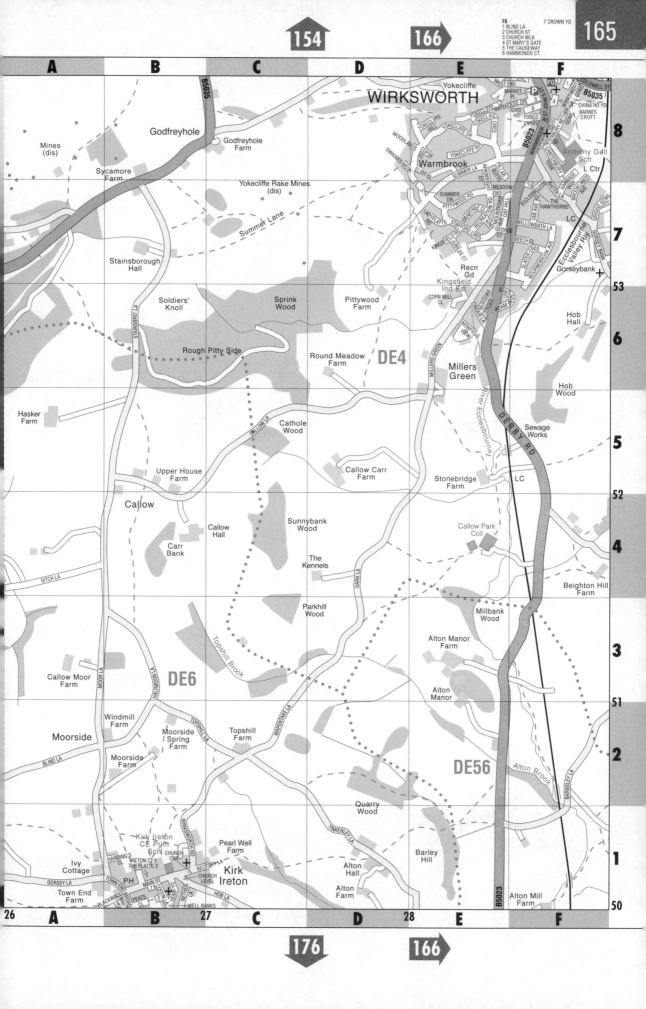

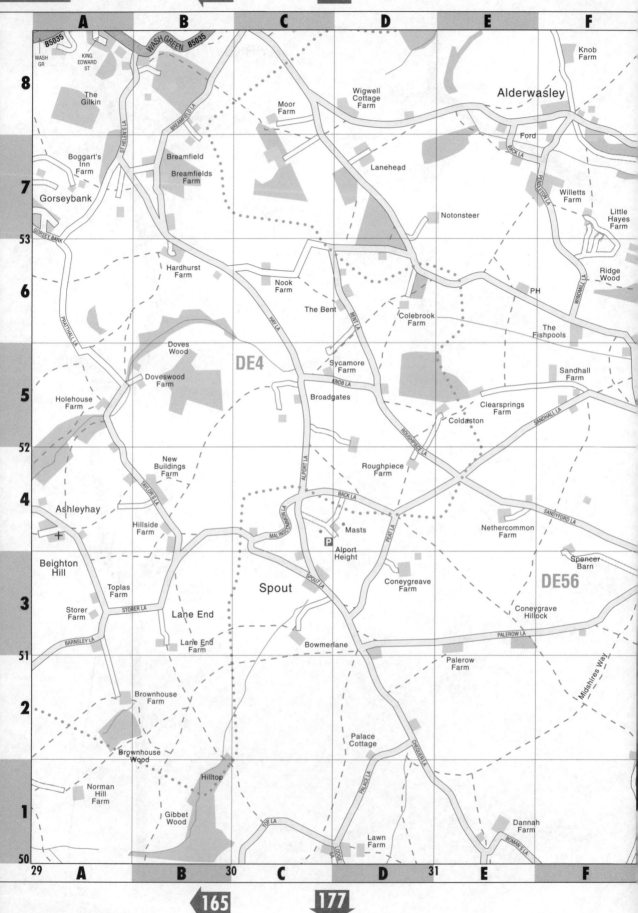

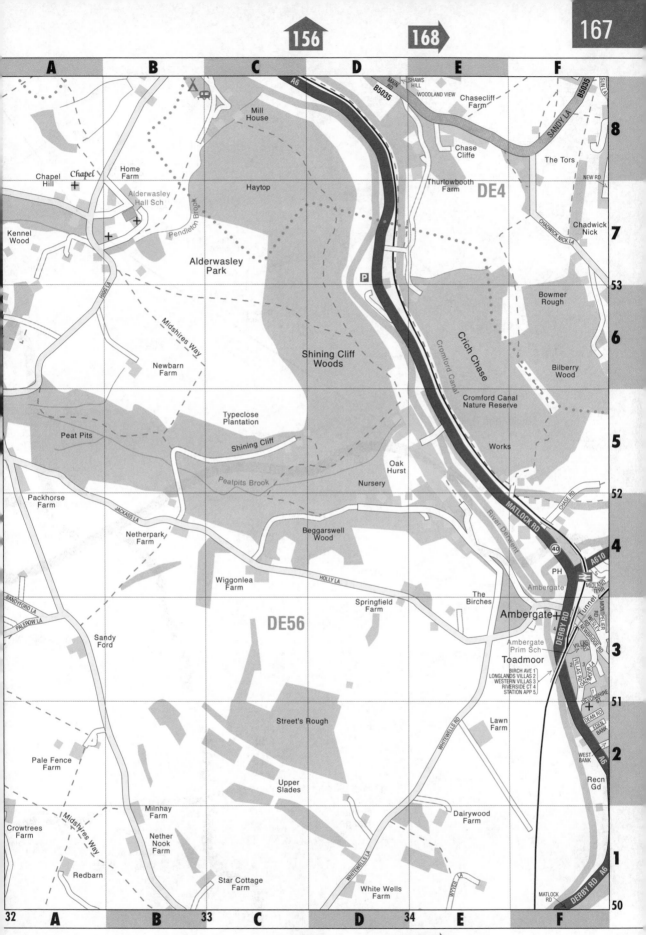

A   B   C   D   E   F

8
7
53
6
5
52
4
3
51
2
1
50

A6
B5035
MAIN RD
SHAWS HILL
WOODLAND VIEW
Chasecliff Farm
SANDY LA
B5035
SUN LA

Mill House

Chapel Hill
Chapel
Home Farm
Chase Cliffe
Thurlowbooth Farm
DE4
The Tors
NEW RD
Chadwick Nick
CHADWICK NICK LA

Alderwasley Hall Sch
Haytop

Kennel Wood
Pendleton Brook

Bowmer Rough

Alderwasley Park

HIGG LA
Midshires Way

Shining Cliff Woods
Crich Chase
Cromford Canal
Bilberry Wood

Newbarn Farm
Cromford Canal Nature Reserve

Typeclose Plantation
Works

Peat Pits
Shining Cliff
Peatpits Brook
Oak Hurst
Nursery

Packhorse Farm
JACKASS LA
MATLOCK RD
CHASE RD

Netherpark Farm
Beggarswell Wood
River Derwent
40
A610
Ambergate
PH
MIDLAND
TERR

Wiggonlea Farm
HOLLY LA
The Birches
Ambergate
Tunnel
MONTPELIER RD
WEST

SANDYFORD LA
Springfield Farm
Ambergate Prim Sch
Toadmoor
DERBY RD
RIVERSIDE
VILLAS
VILLAS RD

DE56
PALEROW LA
BIRCH AVE 1
LONGLANDS VILLAS 2
WESTERN VILLAS 3
RIVERSIDE CT 4
STATION APP 5
DEVONSHIRE ST
DEAN RD

Sandy Ford
Street's Rough
Lawn Farm
EDEN BANK

Pale Fence Farm
WEST BANK
A6
Recn Gd

Upper Slades

Crowtrees Farm
Midshires Way
Milnhay Farm
Dairywood Farm

Nether Nook Farm
WHITEWELLS RD

Redbarn
Star Cottage Farm
WHITEWELLS LA
White Wells Farm
WYVER LA
MATLOCK RD
DERBY RD A6

32   A   B   33   C   D   34   E   F

167 157

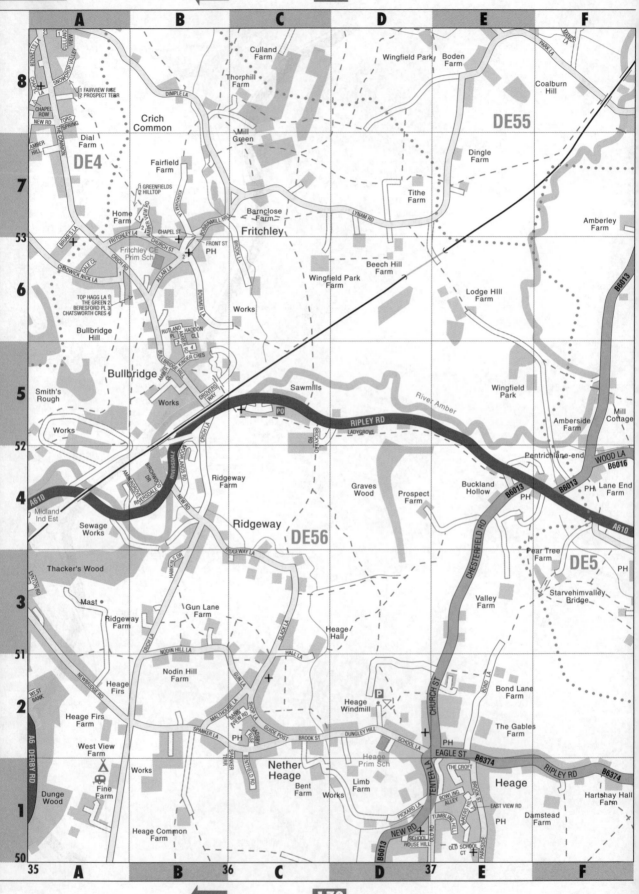

167 179

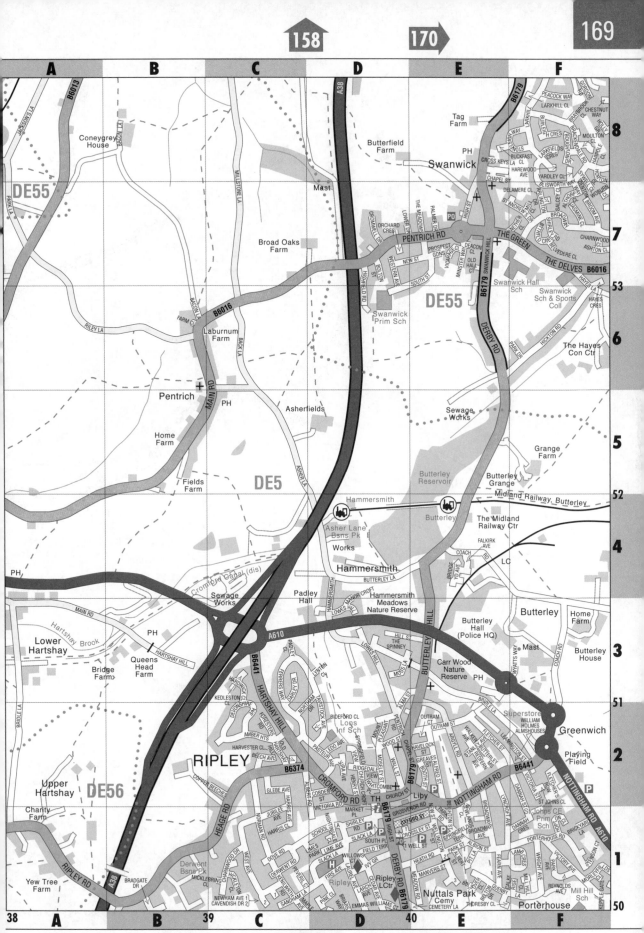

E1
1 LOWER MILL
2 MANVERS AVE
3 CLUMBER CL

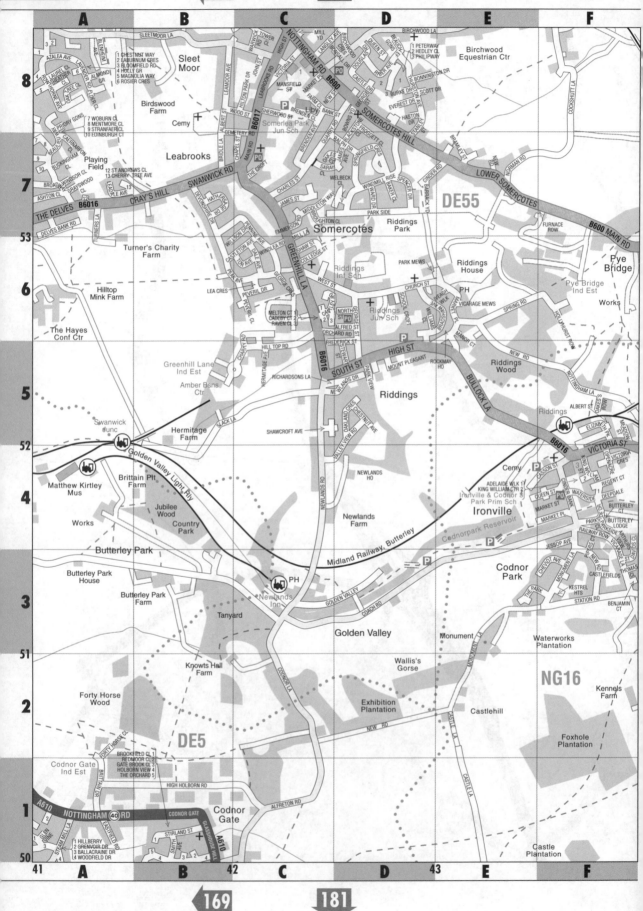

169

C8
1 Somercotes
Inf Sch

159

A   **B**   **C**   **D**   **E**   **F**

8

1 AZALEA AVE
2 LAUREL CL
3 ALMOND
   GR
4 MAGNOLIA WAY
5 ROSIER CRES

1 CHESTNUT WAY
2 LABURNUM CRES
3 BLOOMFIELD RD
4 HOLLY GR
5 MAGNOLIA WAY
6 ROSIER CRES

Sleet
Moor

Birchwood
Equestrian Ctr

1 PETERWAY
2 HEDLEY CL
3 PHILIPWAY

Birdswood
Farm

Cemy

7 WOBURN CL
8 MENTMORE CL
9 STRANRAER CL
10 EDINBURGH CT

Leabrooks

Playing
Field

DE55

7

12 ST ANDREWS CL
13 CHERRY TREE AVE

SWANWICK RD

CRAY'S HILL

THE DELVES

B6016

LOWER SOMERCOTES

Somercotes

B600 MAIN RD

FURNACE
ROW

53

Turner's Charity
Farm

Riddings
Park

Pye
Bridge

6

Hilltop
Mink Farm

Riddings
Inf Sch

Park Mews

Riddings
House

PH

Pye Bridge
Ind Est

Works

LEA CRES

The Hayes
Conf Ctr

1 MELTON CT
2 CADEBY CT
3 RAVEN CL

NORTHGATE
PO

Riddings
Jun Sch

Vicarage Mews

SPRING RD

Greenhill Lane
Ind Est

B6016

SOUTH ST

HIGH ST

Riddings
Wood

NEW RD

5

Amber Bsns
Ctr

RICHARDSONS LA

Riddings

BULLOCK LA

Riddings

B6016

VICTORIA ST

52

Swanwick
Junc

SHAWCROFT AVE

Cemy

Hermitage
Farm

NEWLANDS
HO

ADELAIDE WLK
KING WILLIAM CTR
Ironville & Codnor
Park Prim Sch

4

Matthew Kirtley
Mus

Golden Valley Light Rly

Brittain Pit
Farm

Newlands
Farm

Ironville

DEEPDALE

BUTTERLEY
CT

Works

Jubilee
Wood

Country
Park

Codnorpark Reservoir

BUTTERLEY
LODGE

Butterley Park

Codnor
Park

3

Butterley Park
House

Butterley Park
Farm

Newlands
Inn

PH

Midland Railway, Butterley

KESTREL
HTS

Tanyard

GOLDEN VALLEY

Golden Valley

Monument

Waterworks
Plantation

51

Knowts Hall
Farm

Wallis's
Gorse

NG16

Kennels
Farm

2

Forty Horse
Wood

Exhibition
Plantation

Castlehill

Foxhole
Plantation

DE5

BROOKFIELD CL 1
REDMOOR CL 2
GATE BROOK CL 3
HOLBORN VIEW 4
THE ORCHARD 5

NEW RD

1

Codnor Gate
Ind Est

HIGH HOLBORN RD

A610

NOTTINGHAM RD

ALFRETON RD

Codnor
Gate

Codnor Gate

A610

Castle
Plantation

50

1 HILLBERRY
2 GRENVOIR DR
3 BALLACRAINE DR
4 WOODFIELD DR

A   41   **B**   42   **C**   **D**   43   **E**   **F**

169

181

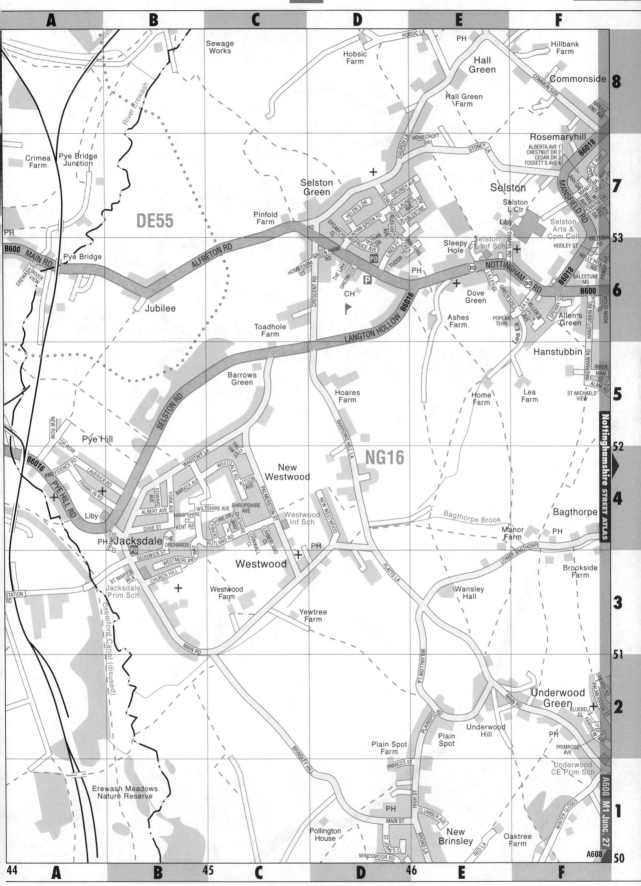

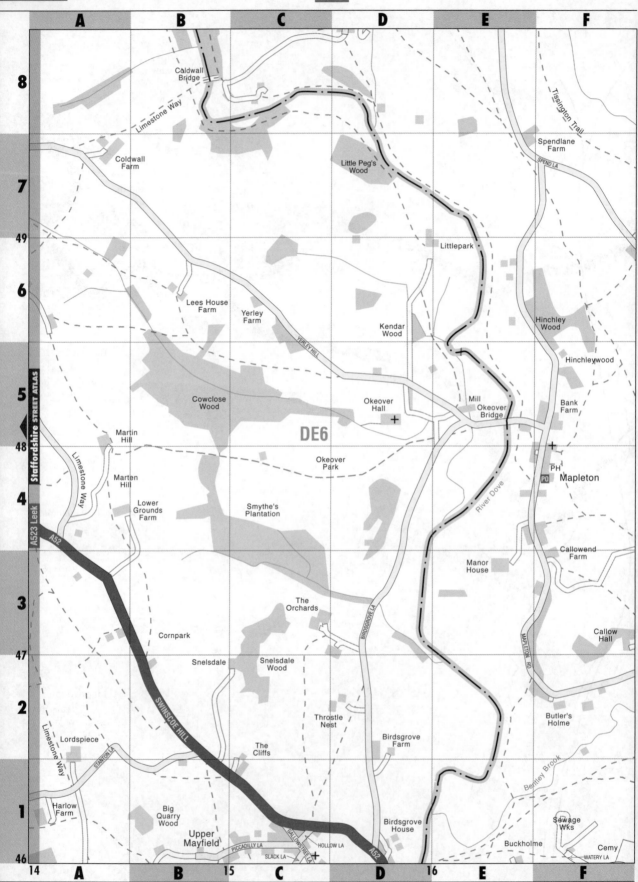

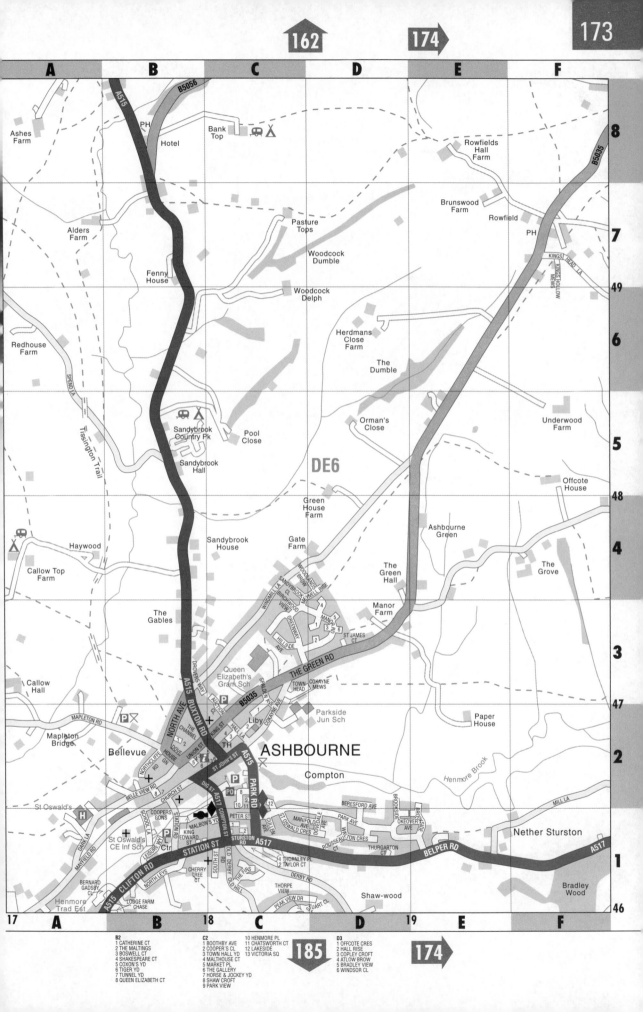

A B C D E F

8
7
49
6
5
48
4
3
47
2
1
46

Ashes Farm

B5056

A515

PH

Hotel

Bank Top

Rowfields Hall Farm

Brunswood Farm

Rowfield

PH

B5035

KINGS HEAD LA

KINGS HOLLOW MEWS

Alders Farm

Pasture Tops

Woodcock Dumble

Fenny House

Woodcock Delph

Herdmans Close Farm

Redhouse Farm

The Dumble

SPEND LA

Tissington Trail

Sandybrook Country Pk

Pool Close

Orman's Close

Underwood Farm

Sandybrook Hall

DE6

Offcote House

Haywood

Sandybrook House

Green House Farm

Ashbourne Green

The Grove

Callow Top Farm

Gate Farm

The Green Hall

The Gables

WINDMILL LA

SANDYBROOK CL

WOODCOCK BROW

HEMFELL RISE

BIRCHWOOD VIEW

GREENWAY

Manor Farm

Callow Hall

HILLSIDE AVE

MANOR RD

St James Ct

MAPLETON RD

Queen Elizabeth's Gram Sch

THE GREEN RD

TOWN HEAD

COKAYNE MEWS

Paper House

Bellevue

NORTH AVE

BUXTON RD

AUCTION

B5035

KING ST

HALL LA

COKAYNE AVE

Liby

Parkside Jun Sch

DROVERS WAY

THE CHANNEL

UNION ST

ALCOVE

NORTHCLIFFE RD

BELLE VIEW RD

CHURCH ST

ST JOHN'S ST

TH

ASHBOURNE

Compton

Henmore Brook

Mapleton Bridge

St Oswald's

H

St Oswald's CE Inf Sch

SCHOOL LA

LEISURE

KING EDWARD ST

MALBON'S YD

DIG ST

COMPTON ST

PARK RD

PO

Beresford Ave

Park Ave

MANIFOLDDALE AVE

DOVEDALE AVE

ST OSWALD CRES

BROOKSIDE

OKEOVER AVE

BROOKSIDE AVE

MILL LA

Nether Sturston

A517

DARK LA

MAYFIELD RD

COOPERS GDNS

Ctr

STATION ST

A515

CLIFTON RD

A517

COMPTON ST

STURSTON RD

Peter St

CULLEN AVE

WALKTON CRES

ROUSSEAU CT

THURGARTON CT

A517

BELPER RD

Bernard Gadsby CL

NORTH LEYS

LODGE FARM CHASE

CHERRY TREE CT

ST HUGHS

OLD DERBY RD

OLD HILL

THE FIRS

THORPE VIEW

DERBY RD

THORNLEY PL

TAYLOR CT

Shaw-wood

Bradley Wood

Henmore Trad Est

PEAK VIEW DR

STUART CL

17 A 18 B C 19 D E F

B2
1 CATHERINE CT
2 THE MALTINGS
3 BOSWELL CT
4 SHAKESPEARE CT
5 COXON'S YD
6 TIGER YD
7 TUNNEL YD
8 QUEEN ELIZABETH CT

C2
1 BOOTHBY AVE
2 COOPER'S CL
3 TOWN HALL YD
4 MALTHOUSE CT
5 MARKET PL
6 THE GALLERY
7 HORSE & JOCKEY YD
8 SHAW CROFT
9 PARK VIEW
10 HENMORE PL
11 CHATSWORTH CT
12 LAKESIDE
13 VICTORIA SQ

D3
1 OFFCOTE CRES
2 HALL RISE
3 COPLEY CROFT
4 ATLOW BROW
5 BRADLEY VIEW
6 WINDSOR CL

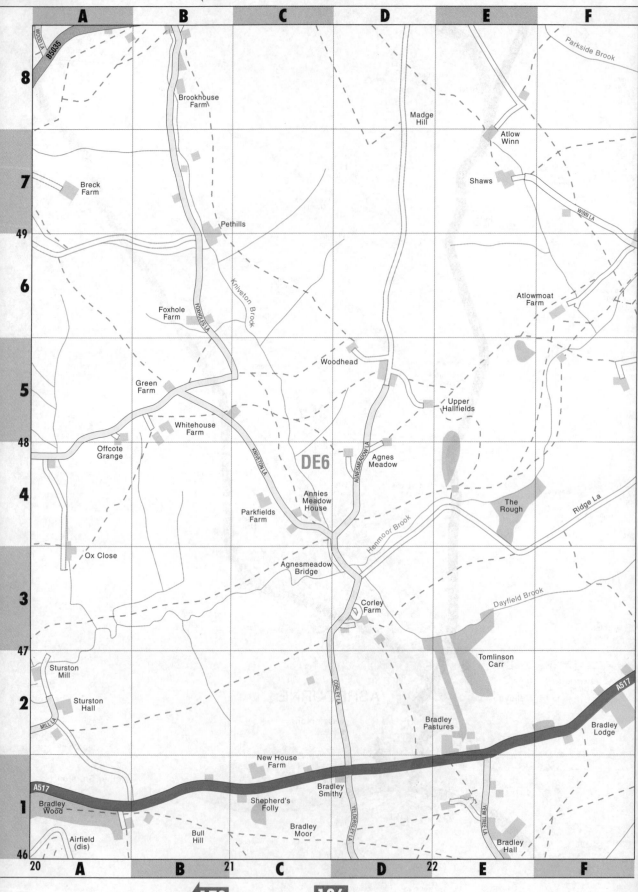

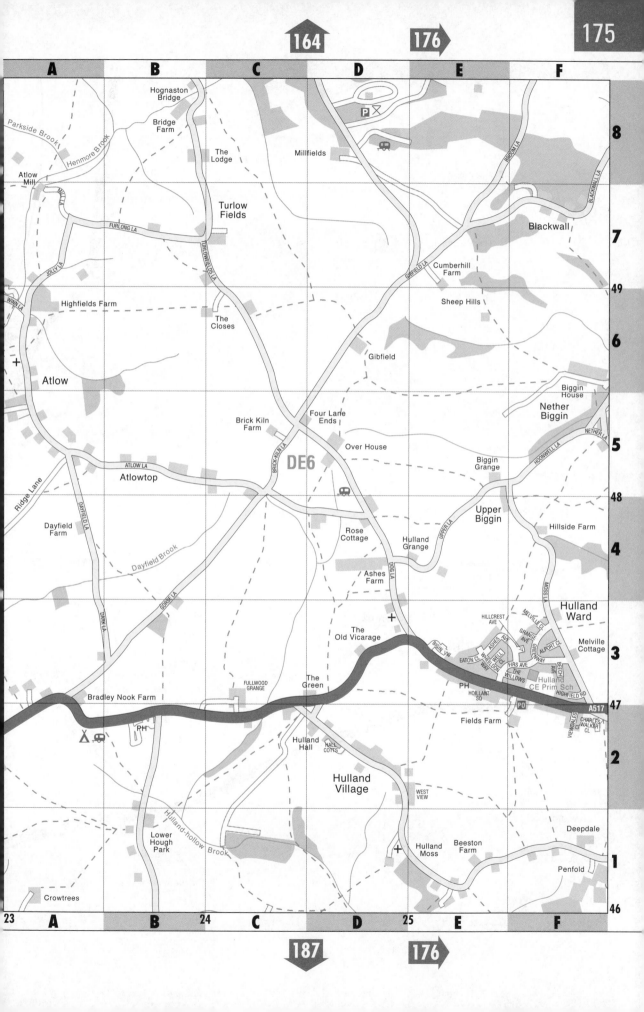

← 175
165

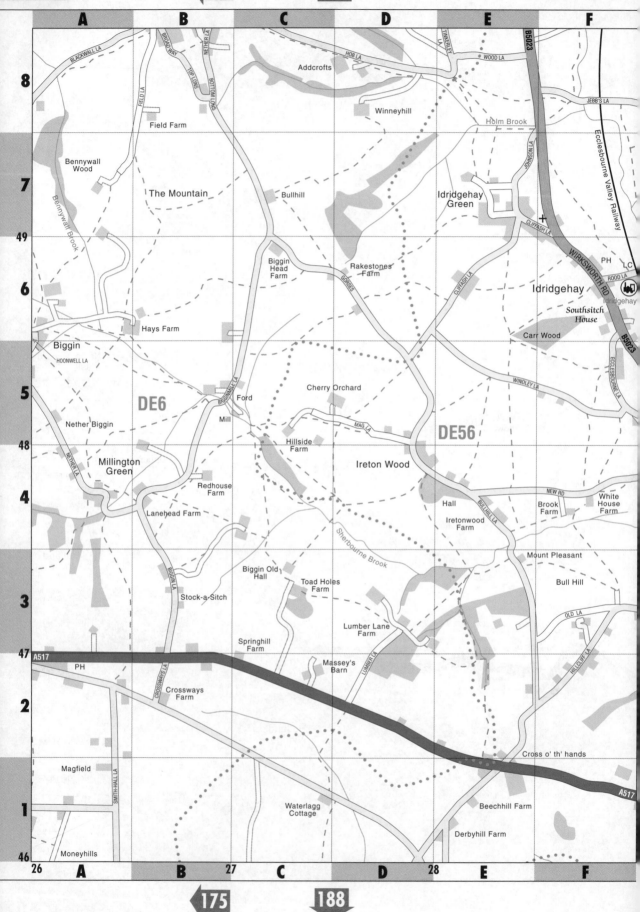

← 175
188

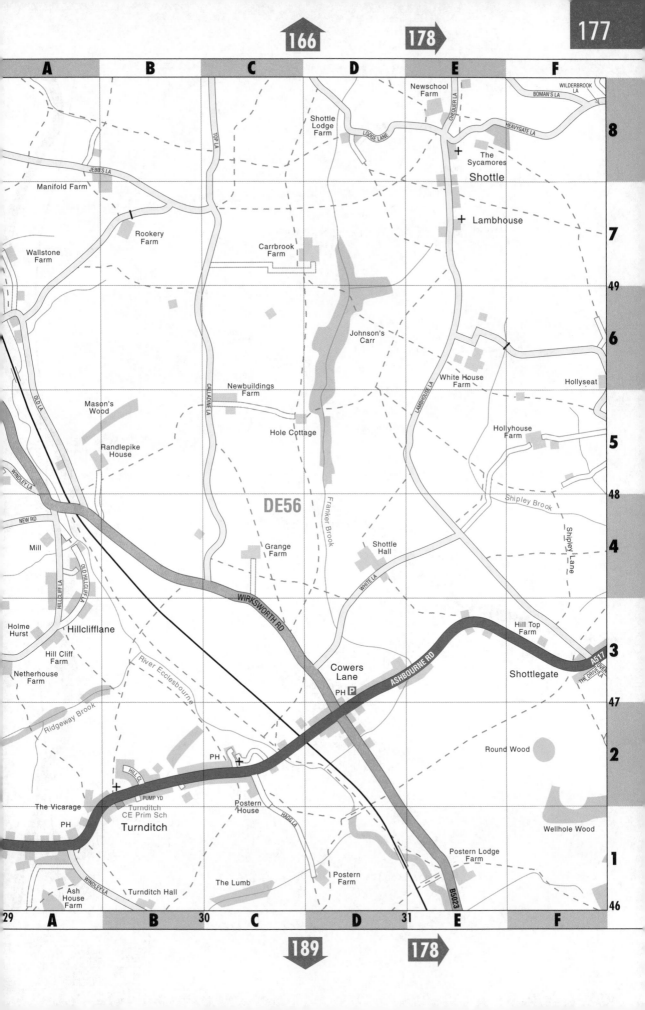

A B C D E F

8
7
49
6
5
48
4
3
47
2
1
46

Newschool Farm
WILDERBROOK LA
BOMAN'S LA
CHEQUER LA
HEAVYGATE LA
Shottle Lodge Farm
LODGE LANE
The Sycamores
Shottle
Lambhouse
TOP LA
JEBB'S LA
Manifold Farm
Rookery Farm
Carrbrook Farm
Wallstone Farm
White House Farm
Hollyseat
CALLADINE LA
Newbuildings Farm
Johnson's Carr
LAMBHOUSE LA
Mason's Wood
Hole Cottage
Hollyhouse Farm
Randlepike House
Shipley Brook
DE56
Franker Brook
Shipley Lane
OLD LA
WINDLEY LA
Grange Farm
Shottle Hall
NEW RD
Mill
WHITE LA
Hill Top Farm
WIRKSWORTH RD
HILLCLIFF LA
OLD HILLCLIFF LA
Holme Hurst
Hillclifflane
Cowers Lane
Shottlegate
A517
THE DRIVE
SPENCE LA
Hill Cliff Farm
ASHBOURNE RD
Netherhouse Farm
PH P
River Ecclesbourne
Ridgeway Brook
Round Wood
PH
HILL CL
PUMP YD
The Vicarage
Turnditch CE Prim Sch
Postern House
HAGG LA
Postern Lodge Farm
Wellhole Wood
PH
Turnditch
WINDLEY LA
Turnditch Hall
The Lumb
Postern Farm
B5023
Ash House Farm

F3
1 WELLINGTON CT
2 CHEAPSIDE
3 BELLE ACRE CL
4 HERITAGE CT
5 BROOK CL
6 LEIGHTON WAY
7 MIDLAND VIEW

F4
1 ST GEORGE'S PL
2 CROWN TERR
3 CLUSTERS CT
4 SHORT ROW
5 FIELD ROW
6 THE ORCHARD
7 CHURCH WLK
8 ST PETER'S CL
9 CHURCH LA

10 ST LAURENCE GDNS
11 BRIDGEFIELD CT

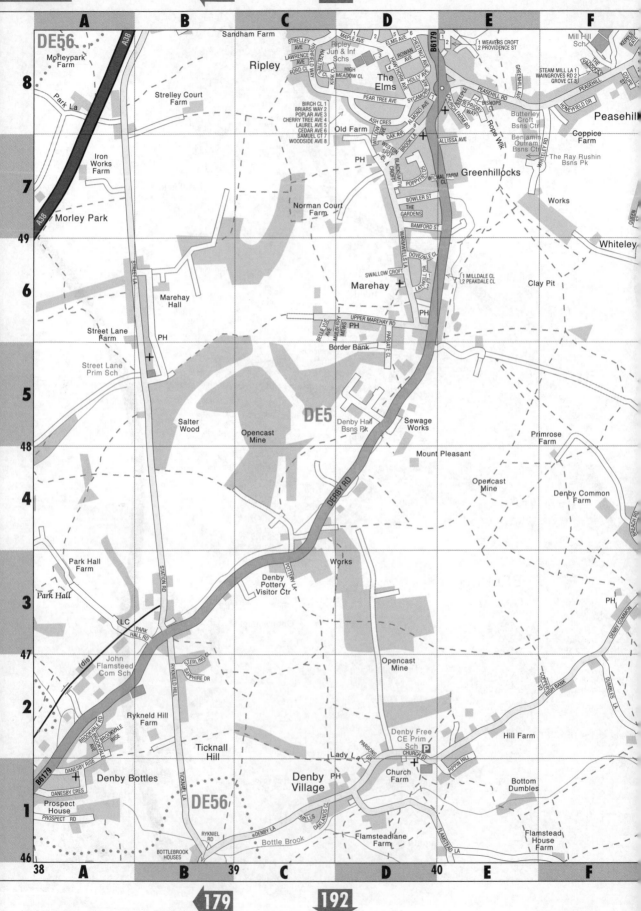

DE56

A38

A38

Morleypark Farm

Park La

Strelley Court Farm

Sandham Farm

Ripley

STRELLEY AVE
LAWRENCE AVE
FORD CL
HIGHFIELD WAY
HAZEL CL
KIRK CL
HIGH MEADOW CL

MAPLE AVE
Ripley Jun & Inf Schs
ROWAN AVE
HAWTHORN AVE
HOLLY CL
SYCAMORE CL

ELMS AVE
CHESTNUT AVE
ALMOND AVE
The Elms

B6179

1 WEAVERS CROFT
2 PROVIDENCE ST

BISHOPS

Mill Hill Sch

KEPPLE GATE

THE PADDOCKS

1 STEAM MILL LA
WAINGROVES RD 2
GROVE CT 3

GREENHILL AVE

Peasehill

COUPE SDR

8

Iron Works Farm

BIRCH CL 1
BRIARS WAY 2
POPLAR AVE 3
CHERRY TREE AVE 4
LAUREL AVE 5
CEDAR AVE 6
SAMUEL CT 7
WOODSIDE AVE 8

PEAR TREE AVE

ASH CRES
OAK AVE

Old Farm

WESTON SPOT CL
BROOK LA

ALLISSA AVE

PEASEHILL RD

DRE PRIORY WAY

CHURCH FARM CL

Rope Wlk

Butterley Croft Bsns Ctr

Benjamin Outram Bsns Ctr

HONEYFIELD DR

WHITELEY RD

The Ray Rushin Bsns Pk

Coppice Farm

Peasehill

Morley Park

PH

BLACKSMITH CROFT

POPPY CL

WICHAL FARM CL

Greenhillocks

Works

Whiteley

7

49

Norman Court Farm

Marehay Hall

SWALLOW CROFT

Marehay

BOWLER ST
THE GARDENS
BAMFORD ST

WARWICK LA

DOVEDALE CL

LARK HILL DR

1 MILLDALE CL
2 PEAKDALE CL

Clay Pit

6

Street Lane Farm

PH

Street Lane Prim Sch

STREET LA

BELLE VUE AVE
MULBERRY MEWS

UPPER MAREHAY RD

PH

Border Bank

PARGATE CL

PH

DE5

Salter Wood

Opencast Mine

Denby Hall Bsns Pk

Sewage Works

Primrose Farm

5

48

Mount Pleasant

Opencast Mine

Denby Common Farm

BREACH RD

4

Park Hall Farm

Park Hall

STATION RD

DERBY RD

Denby Pottery Visitor Ctr

POTTERY LA

Works

Opencast Mine

PH

DENBY COMMON

COPPICE VIEW

HIGH BANK

DUMBLES LA

3

LC

PARK HALL RD

(dis)

John Flamsteed Com Sch

STERLING CL
SAPPHIRE DR
RYKNELD HILL

47

2

Park Hall Farm

BROOKVALE RD
BROOKVALE AVE
BROOKVALE RISE

Rykneld Hill Farm

Ticknall Hill

TICKNALL LA

PARSONS CL

Denby Free CE Prim Sch

LADY LA

CHURCH ST
PIPPIN HILL

Church Farm

Hill Farm

Bottom Dumbles

B6179

DANESBY RISE
DANESBY CRES

Denby Bottles

Prospect House

PROSPECT RD

DE56

RYKNIEL RD

DENBY LA

Bottle Brook

BOTTLEBROOK HOUSES

CAPELLS CL
OAKLANDS CL

Denby Village

PH

FLAMSTEAD LA

Flamsteadlane Farm

Flamstead House Farm

1

46

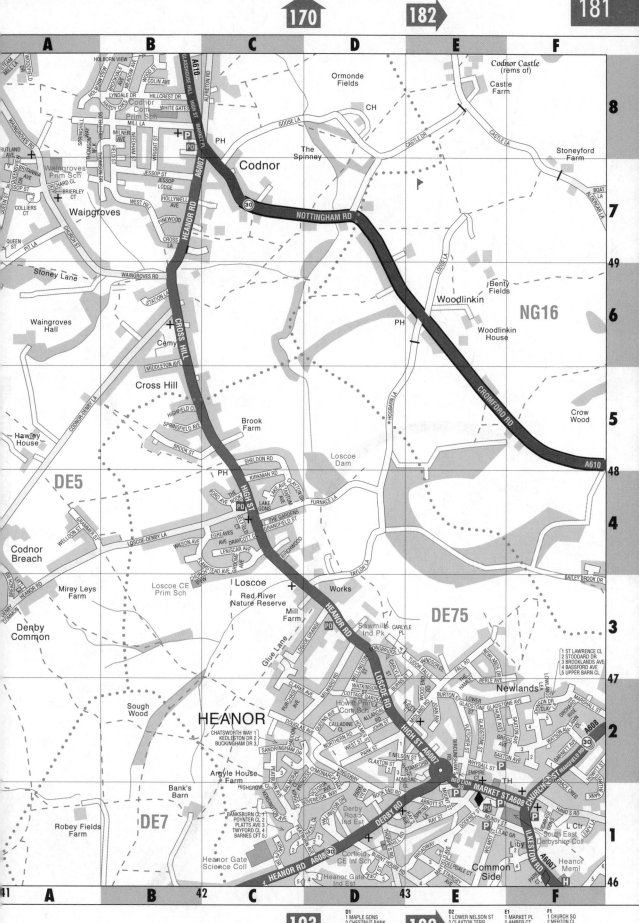

D1
1 MAPLE GDNS
2 CHESTNUT BANK
3 HEANOR GATE
4 HEANOR GATE RD
5 KIRKHAM CL

D2
1 LOWER NELSON ST
2 CLAXTON TERR
3 UPPER NELSON ST
4 HAMPTON CT
5 STAMFORD CT

E1
1 MARKET PL
2 AMBER CT
3 THE MEADOWS
4 LOCTON AVE

F1
1 CHURCH SQ
2 MERTON CL
3 TRINITY WAY
4 GREYFRIARS CL
5 WESTFIELD AVE
6 ELLA BANK RD

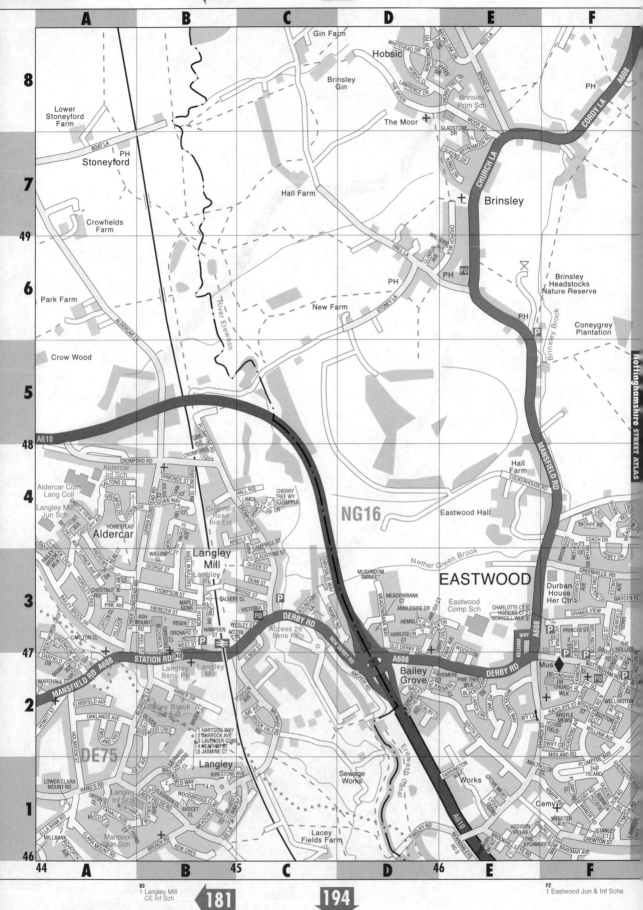

← 181
171

Nottinghamshire STREET ATLAS

Gin Farm

Hobsic

Whitehead Dr

Brinsley Gin

Brinsley Prim Sch

The Moor

Gladstone Dr

Brynsmoor Rd

Queens Dr

Kings Dr

Church La

Brinsley

Cordy La

A608

PH

Lower Stoneyford Farm

Boat La

PH

Stoneyford

Hall Farm

Hall La

Church Wlk

PH

P.O

Brinsley Headstocks Nature Reserve

Crowfields Farm

River Erewash

New Farm

Stoney La

PH

PH

Brinsley Brook

Coneygrey Plantation

Park Farm

Aldercar La

PH

P

Crow Wood

A610

Mansfield Rd

Cromford Rd

Cromford Rd

Aldercar Inf Sch

Caltons Cl

Ormonde Terr

Hall Rd

Hall Farm

Cockerhouse Rd

Cherry Tree Wy

Crabapple Dr

NG16

Eastwood Hall

Aldercar Com Lang Coll

Langley Mill Jun Sch

Crown Way

Limes Cl

Aldercar

Homestead Rd

Argyle St

Campbell St

Langley Mill

Gladstone St

Langley Pk

Queen St

Dean St

Mushroom Farm Ct

Nether Green Brook

EASTWOOD

Durban House Her Ctr

George St

Thompson St

Bridge St

Calvert Cl

Victoria St

Christmas Way

Linkmel Rd

Meadowbank Ct

Ambleside Dr

Eastwood Comp Sch

Park Cres

Thorpe Rd

Coach Dr

Brookside

Greenhills Rd

P

Derby Rd

P.O

Wesley St

Boundary Rd

Hemsley Ct

Harlequin Ct

Charlotte Ct

Hopkins Ct

Scargill Wlk

Grange View

Atherfield

Princes St

Wellington St

Elmor St

Access 26 Bsns Pk

Old Derby Rd

Kelham Way

A608

The Hollies

47

Station Rd

30

Langley Mill

Langley Bsns Pk

Hampden St

Acorn Ctr

West St

Orchard St

P

A608

New Derby Rd

Derby Rd

A608

Mus

Bailey Grove

Devonshire Dr

Church Wlk

P.O

P

Mansfield Rd A608

Langley Mill

Amber Dr

Elnor St

Tomson Ave

Midland Ave

Scalby Cl

South St

Oak Dr

Ryemere

Pine Tree Wlk

Blackthorn

Ratcliffe St

Bishops Ct

Wellington St

Howitt St

Elmsfield Ave

Oaklands Ave

Bailey Brook Ind Est

Rosewood Cres

Lime Ave

Brook Vale Rd

1 Hartside Way
2 Garrock Ave
3 Lavender Gdns
4 Heather St
5 Jasmine Ct

Hoggs Field

Argyle Mews

William Ave

Swift Cl

Midland Rd

DE75

Langley

Leonard Ave

Cheshire Ave

Julie Ave

Brookland Dr

Lacey Fields Rd

Woodbridge Cl

Avocet Cl

Erewash Canal

Sewage Works

Works

Farrington Wy

Grove Mews

A610

Malthouse Cl

Plumptre Way

Queens Rd

Lower Clara Mount Rd

Hand's Rd

Langley Inf Sch

Kirkstone Ave

Newham

Meadow Rise

Gisborne St

Lee La

Knapp Ave

Lyda Gdns

Addison Villas

The Sycamores

Stanley Ct

Chewton St

Ella Bank Rd

Millbank

Clara Mount Rd

Marlpool Jun Sch

Breach Rd

Kew Cres

Lacey Fields Farm

Brookhill Leys Rd

Braemar Ave

Seymour Rd

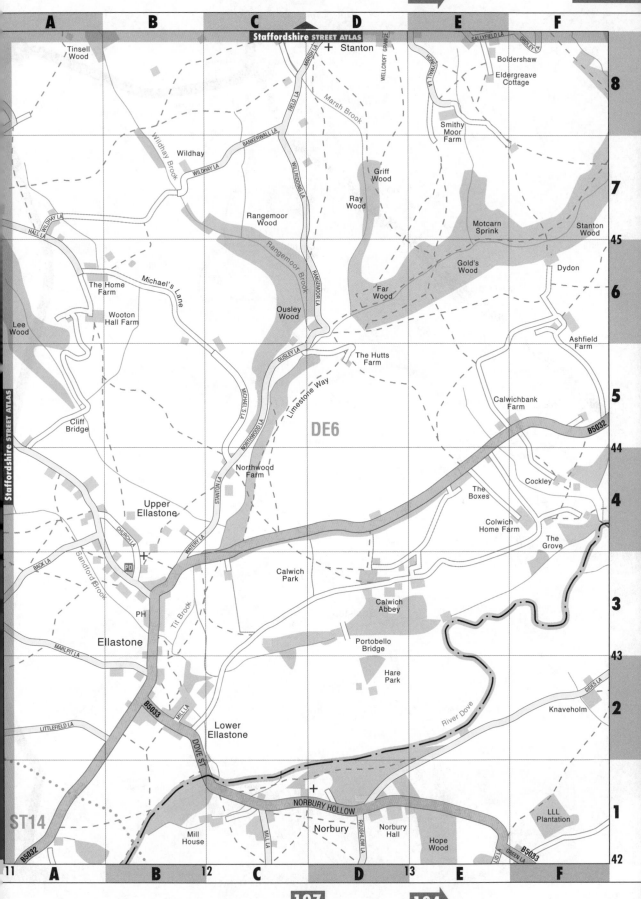

Staffordshire STREET ATLAS

+ Stanton

Tinsell Wood

Wellcroft Grange

Boldershaw

Sallyfield La

Eldergreave Cottage

Marsh Brook

Smithy Moor Farm

Wildhay Brook

Wildhay

Bankerwall La

Wildhay La

Griff Wood

Ray Wood

Motcarn Sprink

Stanton Wood

45

Hall La

Wildhay La

Rangemoor Wood

Rangemoor Brook

Gold's Wood

Dydon

7

The Home Farm

Michael's Lane

Far Wood

6

Lee Wood

Wooton Hall Farm

Ousley Wood

Ashfield Farm

Ousley La

The Hutts Farm

Calwichbank Farm

5

Limestone Way

Cliff Bridge

DE6

B5032

44

Northwood Farm

Cockley

Upper Ellastone

The Boxes

4

Church La

Water La

Colwich Home Farm

The Grove

Back La

Sandford Brook

PO

Stanton La

Northwood La

Calwich Park

3

PH

Tit Brook

Calwich Abbey

Ellastone

Marlpit La

Portobello Bridge

43

Hare Park

River Dove

Sides La

Knaveholm

2

Littlefield La

B5033

Mill La

Lower Ellastone

Dove St

Mill La

Rough Low La

LLL Plantation

1

ST14

B5032

Mill House

Norbury Hollow

Norbury

Norbury Hall

Hope Wood

Lll La

Green La

B5033

42

Staffordshire STREET ATLAS

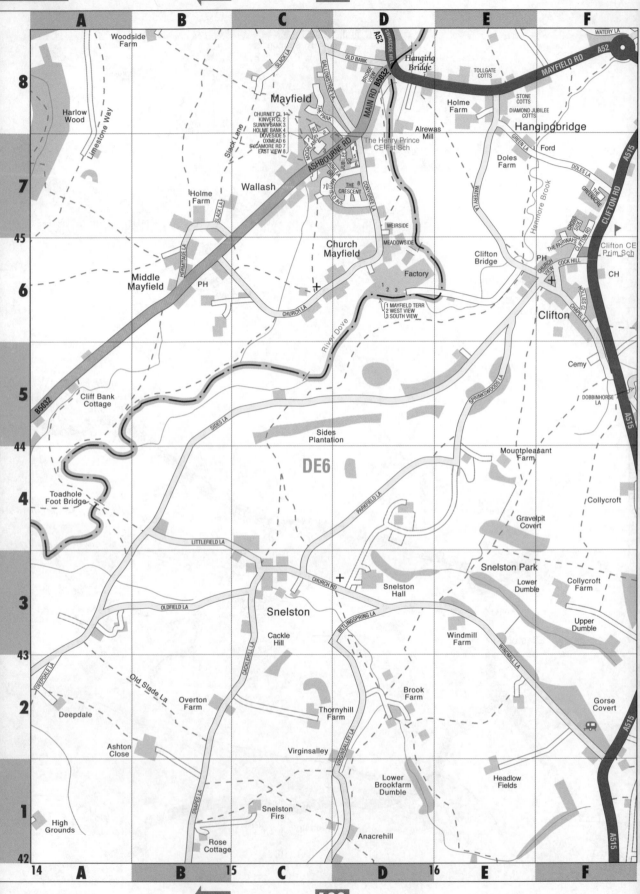

185
174

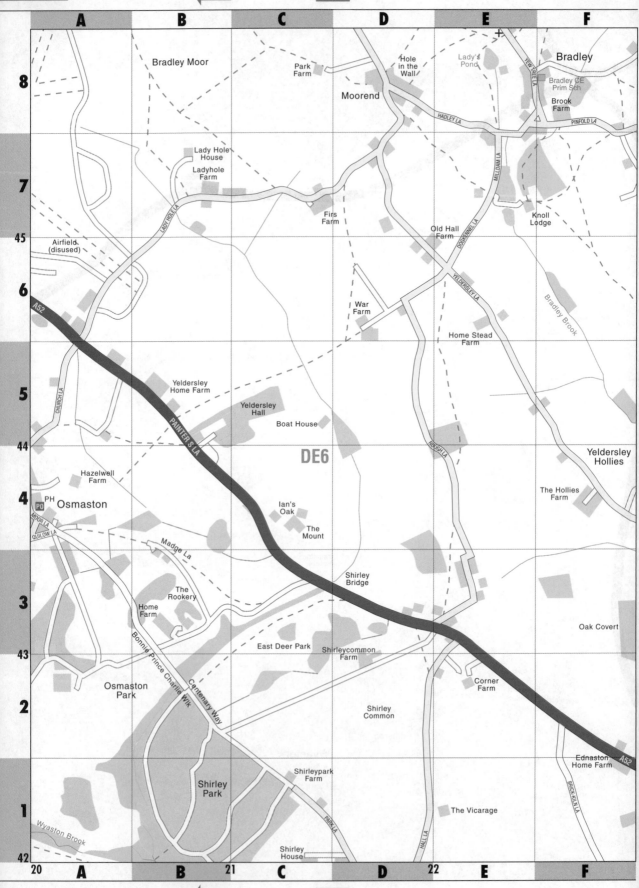

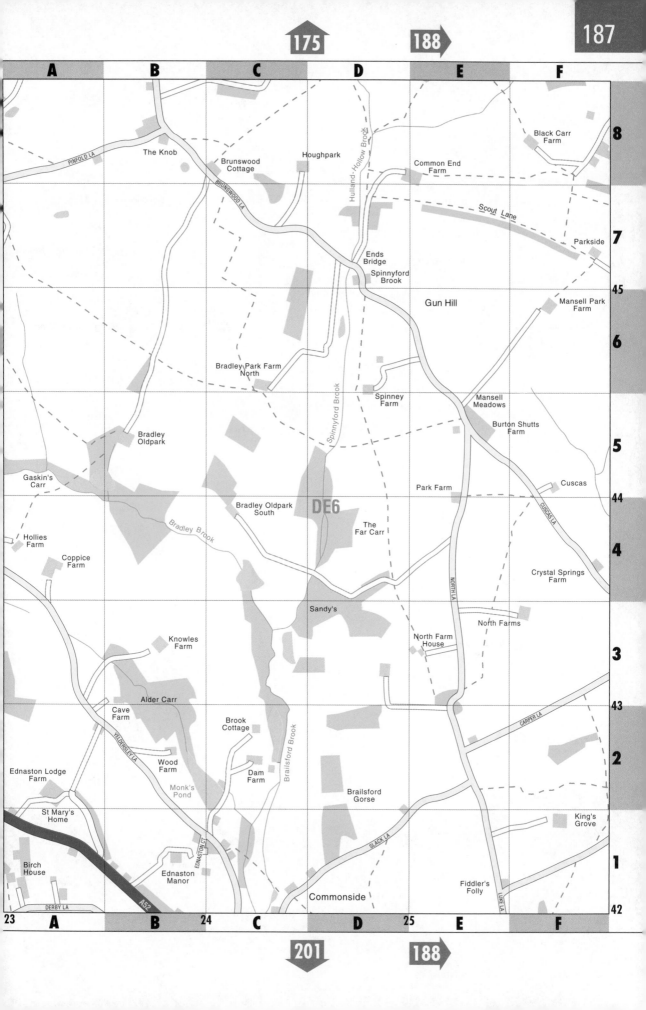

A   B   C   D   E   F

8

The Knob

Brunswood Cottage

Houghpark

Black Carr Farm

Common End Farm

Scout Lane

PINFOLD LA

BRUNSWOOD LA

Hulland-Hollow Brook

Parkside

7

45

Ends Bridge

Spinnyford Brook

Gun Hill

Mansell Park Farm

6

Bradley Park Farm North

Spinney Farm

Mansell Meadows

Burton Shutts Farm

Spinnyford Brook

Bradley Oldpark

5

Gaskin's Carr

Park Farm

Cuscas

CUSCAS LA

44

Bradley Oldpark South

DE6

The Far Carr

Hollies Farm

Bradley Brook

4

Coppice Farm

Crystal Springs Farm

NORTH LA

Sandy's

North Farms

Knowles Farm

North Farm House

3

Alder Carr

43

Cave Farm

Brook Cottage

CARPER LA

YELDERSLEY LA

Wood Farm

Dam Farm

Brailsford Brook

2

Ednaston Lodge Farm

Monk's Pond

Brailsford Gorse

King's Grove

St Mary's Home

SLACK LA

1

LUKE LA

Birch House

EDNASTON CT

Ednaston Manor

Fiddler's Folly

Commonside

A52

DERBY LA

42

23   A   B   24   C   D   25   E   F

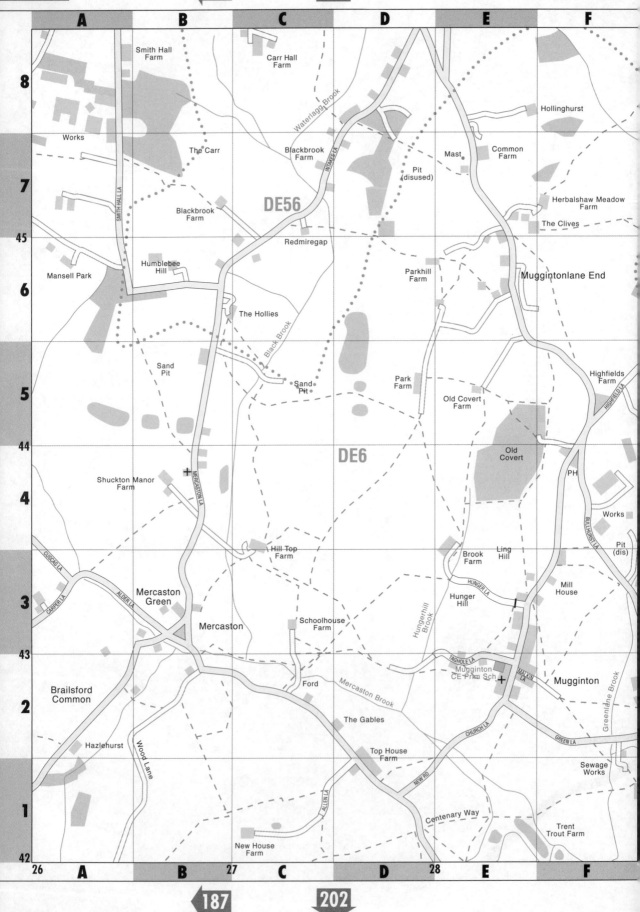

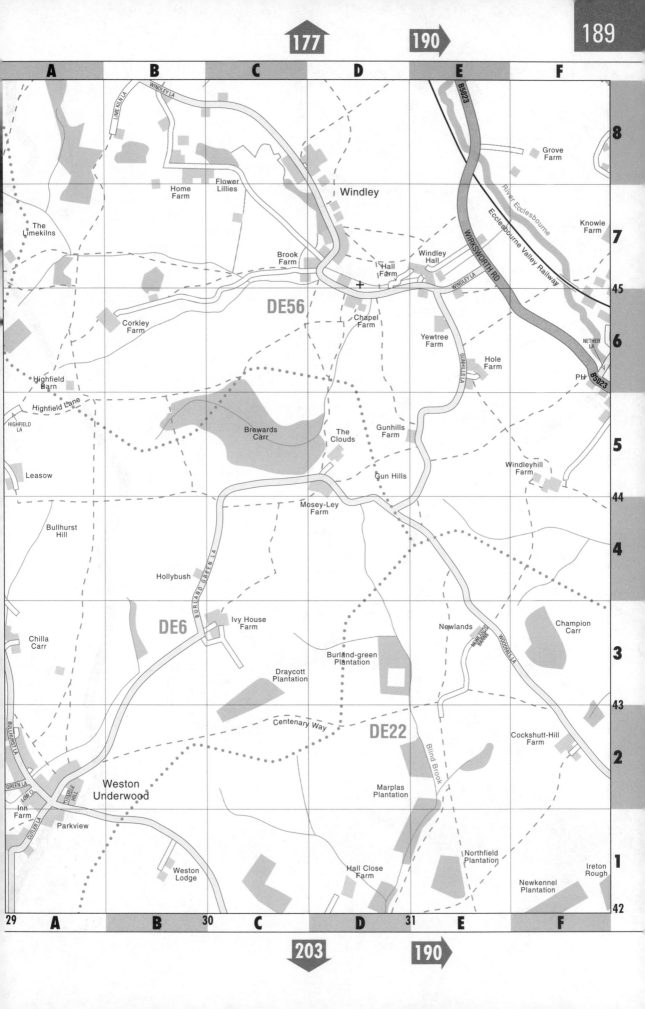

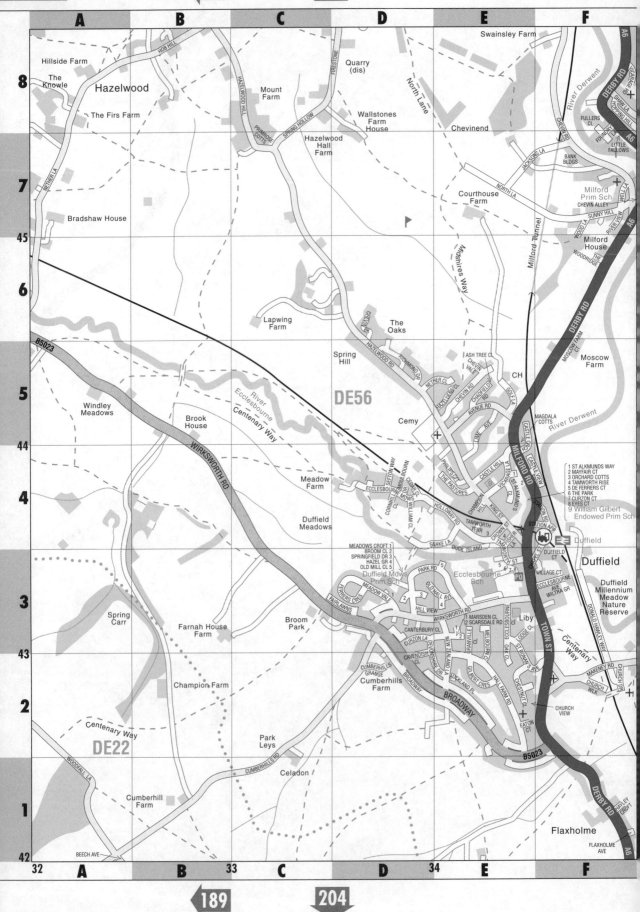

189 178

A B C D E F

8
7
45
6
5
44
4
3
43
2
1
42

Hillside Farm
The Knowle
Hazelwood
The Firs Farm
HOB HILL
HAZELWOOD HILL
Mount Farm
PRIMROSE COTTS
SPRING HOLLOW
FIRESTONE
Quarry (dis)
Wallstones Farm House
North Lane
Swainsley Farm
Chevinend
DERBY RD
SHAW LA
HOPPING HILL
FULLERS CL
FOUNDRY LA
LITTLE FALLOWS
A6

NETHER LA
Bradshaw House
Hazelwood Hall Farm
Courthouse Farm
NORTH LA
JACKSONS LA
BANK BLDGS
CHEVIN RD
Milford Prim Sch
CHEVIN ALLEY
WOOD LA
SUNNY HILL
RIVER VIEW
WELL LA
Milford House
THE WOODRIDGE
A6

B5023
Windley Meadows
Brook House
River Ecclesbourne
Centenary Way
Lapwing Farm
Spring Hill
The Oaks
CHEVIN BK
HAZELWOOD RD
RICHMOND DR
NETHER CL
ASH TREE CL
CHEVIN VALE
CHOPEFIELD RD
GOLF LA
CH
Magdala Cotts
Moscow Farm
MOSCOW FARM CT
River Derwent
DE56
HAZELCRAIG CL
CHEVIN RD
AVENUE RD
CASTLE CROFT
MILFORD RD
CASTLE VIEW
Milford Tunnel
WIRKSWORTH RD
Meadow Farm
ECCLESBOURNE MDWS
Duffield Meadows
CORNHILLS
SEFTON WAY
CEDARS CL
MOWBOURN
WILLIAM CL
CHAMPION CL
THE PASTURES
PHILIPS CROFT
HOLLOWAY RD
CASTLE HILL
KING ST
TAMWORTH TERR
VICARAGE LA
ST ALKMUND'S
CROWN ST
STATION APR
STATION RD
CASTLE VIEW
MILFORD RD
1 ST ALKMUNDS WAY
2 MAYFAIR CT
3 ORCHARD COTTS
4 TAMWORTH RISE
5 DE FERRERS CT
6 THE PARK
7 CURZON CT
8 EYES CT
9 WILLIAM GILBERT Endowed Prim Sch

Cemy
LIME AVE
Duffield CT
Duffield
Duffield
PO
VILLAGE CT
Duffield Millennium Meadow Nature Reserve

Spring Carr
Farnah House Farm
Broom Park
FAIRLAWNS
FERRERS CRES
MEADOW VALE
OLD HALL AVE
PARK RD
HILL VIEW
WIRKSWORTH RD
Ecclesbourne Sch
Duffield Mdws Prim Sch
MEADOWS CROFT 1
BROOM CL 2
SPRINGFIELD DR 3
HAZEL GR 4
OLD MILL CL 5
SNAKE LA
DUCK ISLAND
ECCLESBOURNE AVE
WILTRA GR
Liby
TOWN ST
Centenary Way
MAKENEY RD
CHURCH RD
CHURCH WLK

Champion Farm
CUMBERHILLS RD
Cumberhills Grange
Cumberhills Farm
CANTERBURY CL
CURZON LA
CAVENDISH CL
DEVONSHIRE DR
NEW ZEALAND LA
GRANVILLE
BROADWAY
ROCKLAND PL
GILBERT CRES
1 MARSDEN CL
2 SCARSDALE RD
MELBOURY RD
OAK CL
LODGE CL
ST RONAN'S AVE
CHESTNUT CL
DONALD HAWLEY WAY
Church View

Centenary Way
DE22
WOODFALL LA
Park Leys
CUMBERHILLS RD
Celadon
EATON CT
B5023
BROADWAY
CHURCH VIEW
B5023

Cumberhill Farm
DERBY RD
Flaxholme
FLAXHOLME AVE
BAYLEY CROFT
A6

BEECH AVE

32 A 33 B C 34 D E F

189 204

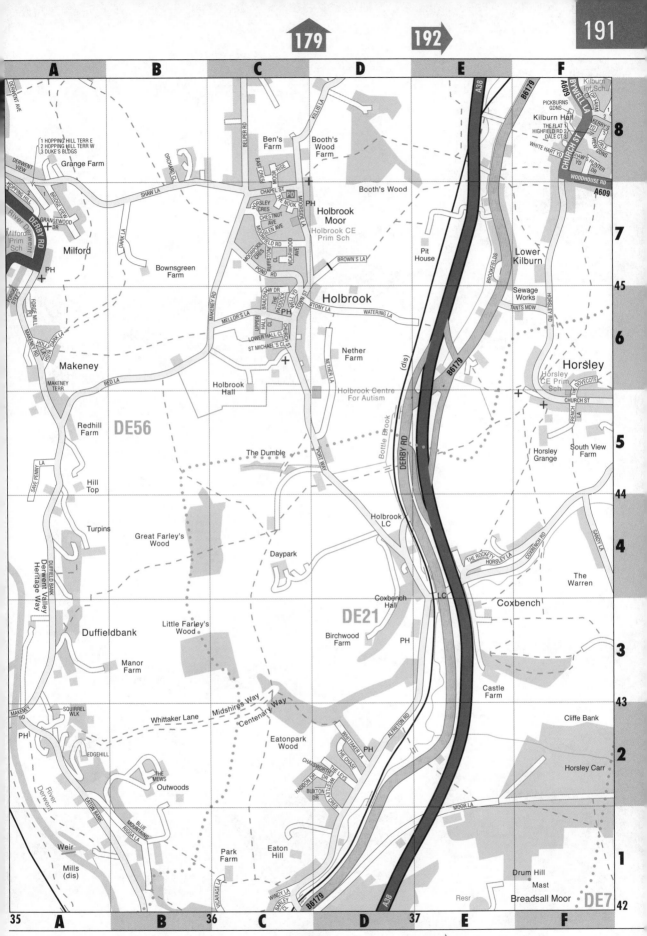

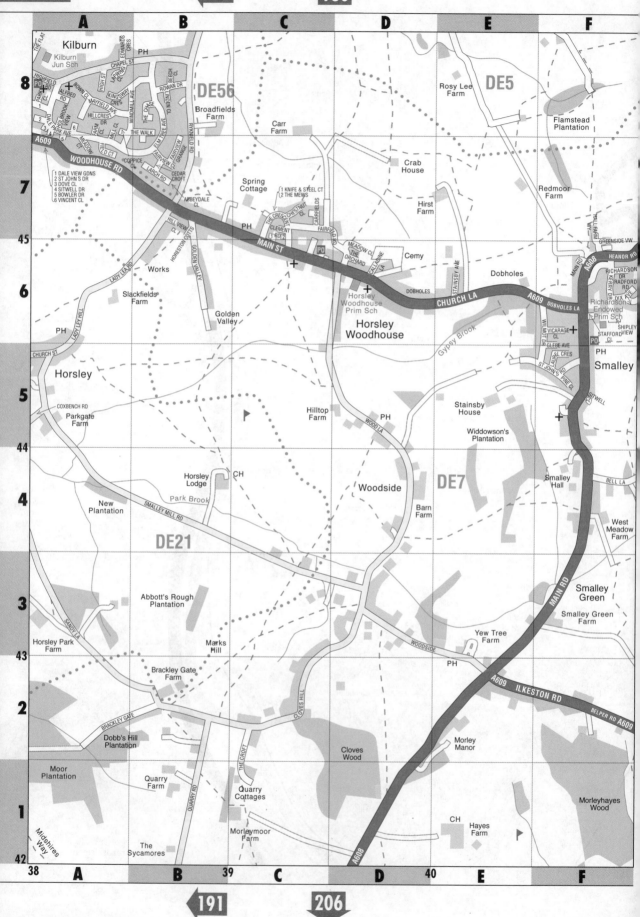

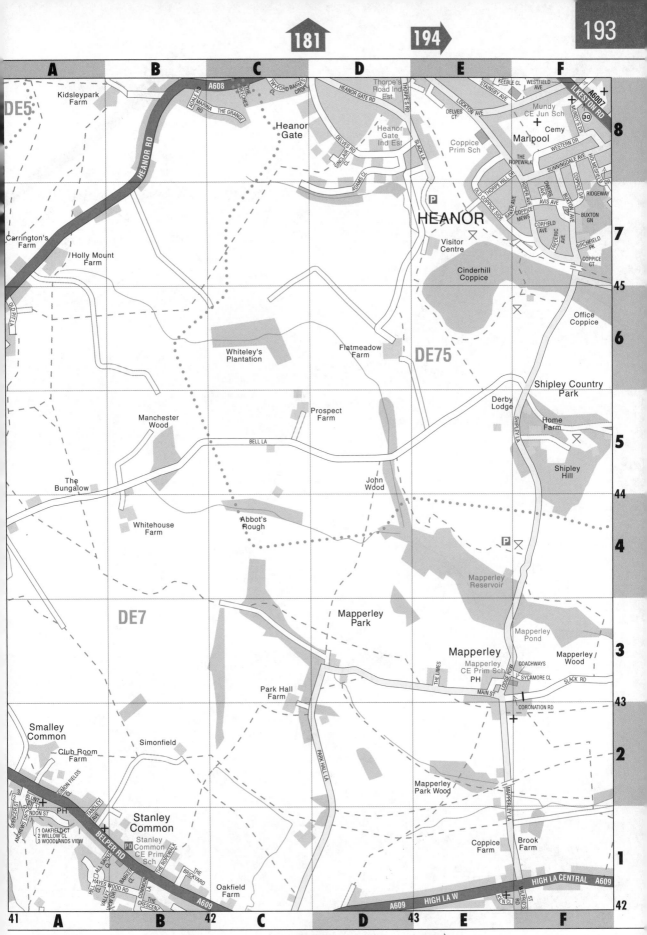

A B C D E F

8

1 SUNNINGDALE AVE
2 HUFTON'S DR

Marlpool Inf Sch

ILKESTON RD A6007 HARDY BARN

Hufton's Coppice

7

HASSOCK LA N

Algrave Hall Farm

Purdy House Farm

NG16

Shipley Gate

Canal (dis)

PH

45

DE75

The Field

Lakeside Bsns Ctr

Shipley

Michael House Sch

Poplars Farm

6

HASSOCK LA S

Cotmanhay Wood

THATCHMARSH

Erewash Canal

5

Shipley Lake

HARTINGTON PL 1
MILLERSDALE AVE 2
BIRCHOVER PL 3
CASTLETON AVE 4
DEVONSHIRE CL 5
LONGCROFT AVE 6

THE COPSE

Chapel Hill Farm

BEAUVALE DR

Cotmanhay Inf & Jun Sch

1 LANGWITH CL
2 BUTTERLEY CL
3 BLACKWELL AVE
4 HARTSHAY CL
5 RYEFIELD AVE
6 NORWOOD CL
7 BRANDS CL
8 LINGS CL
9 SEYMOUR CL

44

WOODSIDE CRES

BEAUVALE DR

FOXLEY CT

1 WALLSEND CL
2 BRAMPTON CL

Shipley Wood

CHURCH ST

Cotmanhay

Bennerley Fields Specl Sch

Bennerley Sch

4

Shipley Country Park

Ilkeston Com

DE7

MOUNT PLEASANT

RICHMOND AVE

BENNERLEY AVE

VERNON ST

Lodge Farm

Shipley Common

VICARAGE AVE

LITTON CL STAPLETON RD

PORTLAND RD

3

SHIPLEY COMMON LA

HEANOR RD

NORMAN CRES

PRIMROSE ST

Granby Jun Sch

Head House Farm

WAKEFIELD CROFT

HARLECH CL

MILLBANK

NEWSTEAD RD S

HADDON ST

Charlotte Inf Sch

REDLAND

43

CHERITON DR

EMSWORTH CL

SUMMERFIELDS WAY

BROUGHTON CL

Boatmans Cl

2

Mapperley Brook

The Brook

SANDERS CL TURNBERRY

MASON RD

ILKESTON

Mast

Allotment Gardens

Ind Est

Booth Trad Est

Lower Bloomsgrove RD

1

West Hallam

PH

Manners Ind Est

FALCON CT

Orchard Bsns Pk

Mercian Ave

RUTLAND ST A6096

MANNERS RD

Victoria Park L Ctr

42

HIGH LA CENTRAL A609

HEDINGHAM CL

BRISTOL RD

B6007

A6007

44 A 45 B C 45 D 46 E F

E1
1 BRUSSELLS TERR
2 STAMFORD ST
3 STATION CT
4 FULLWOOD AVE
5 PROVIDENCE PL
6 FULLWOOD ST
7 WHARNCLIFFE RD
8 JACKSON AVE
9 GREGORY ST

F1
1 BURLEIGH ST
2 ESSEX ST
3 DURHAM ST
4 NORTHGATE ST
5 WILTON ST
6 WEST TERR
7 NORTH ST
8 CHAPEL ST
9 UPPER CHAPEL ST

10 RIGLEY AVE
11 Chaucer Jun Sch

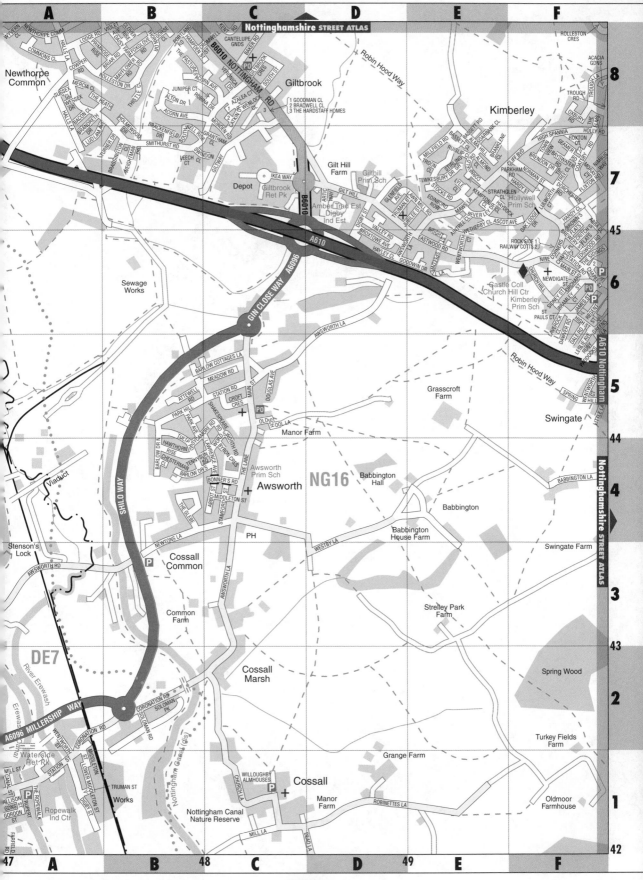

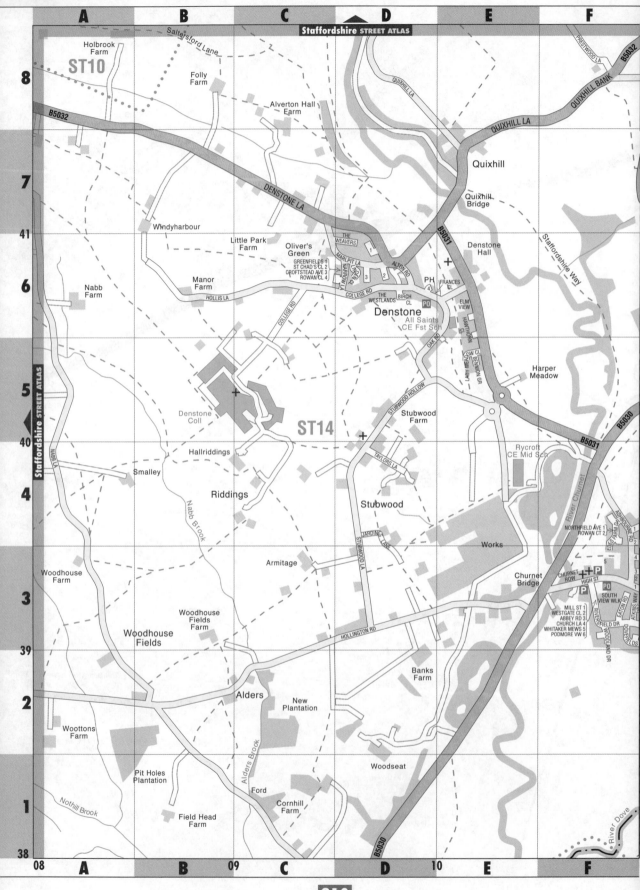

ST10

ST14

Holbrook Farm

Saltersford Lane

Folly Farm

Alverton Hall Farm

B5032

Quixhill La

Quixhill

Quixhill Bank

QUIXHILL LA

DENSTONE LA

Quixhill Bridge

Windyharbour

Little Park Farm

Oliver's Green

THE WEAVERS

Denstone Hall

B5031

Staffordshire Way

Nabb Farm

Manor Farm

HOLLIS LA

GREENFIELDS 1
ST CHAD'S CL 2
CROFTSTEAD AVE 3
ROWAN CL 4

MARL PIT LA

NARROW LA

LINDEN CL

ALTON RD

COLLEGE RD

THE WESTLANDS

BIRCH CL

FRANCES CL

PH

PO

ELM VIEW

Denstone
All Saints
CE Fst Sch

COLLEGE RD

OAK RD

LOW CL

VERNON GR

HAWTHORN CL

Harper Meadow

Denstone Coll

STUBWOOD HOLLOW

Stubwood Farm

Hallriddings

ST14

B5031

B5030

Smalley

NABB LA

Riddings

Nabb Brook

TAYLORS LA

Stubwood

Rycroft CE Mid Sch

Woodhouse Farm

STUBWOOD LA

Armitage

Works

NORTHFIELD AVE 1
ROWAN CT 2

ASHBOURNE RD

JARDINE LA

Churnet Bridge

CHURNET ROW

HIGH ST

River Churnet

Woodhouse Fields Farm

HOLLINGTON RD

Banks Farm

SOUTH VIEW WLK

PO

MILL ST 1
WESTGATE CL 2
ABBEY RD 3
CHURCH LA 4
WHITAKER MEWS 5
PODMORE VW 6

EATON RD

FIELD DR

ATKINS WAY

DOVE

WOODLAND DR

Woodhouse Fields

Alders

New Plantation

Woodseat

Woottons Farm

Alders Brook

Pit Holes Plantation

Ford

Cornhill Farm

Nothill Brook

Field Head Farm

B5030

River Dove

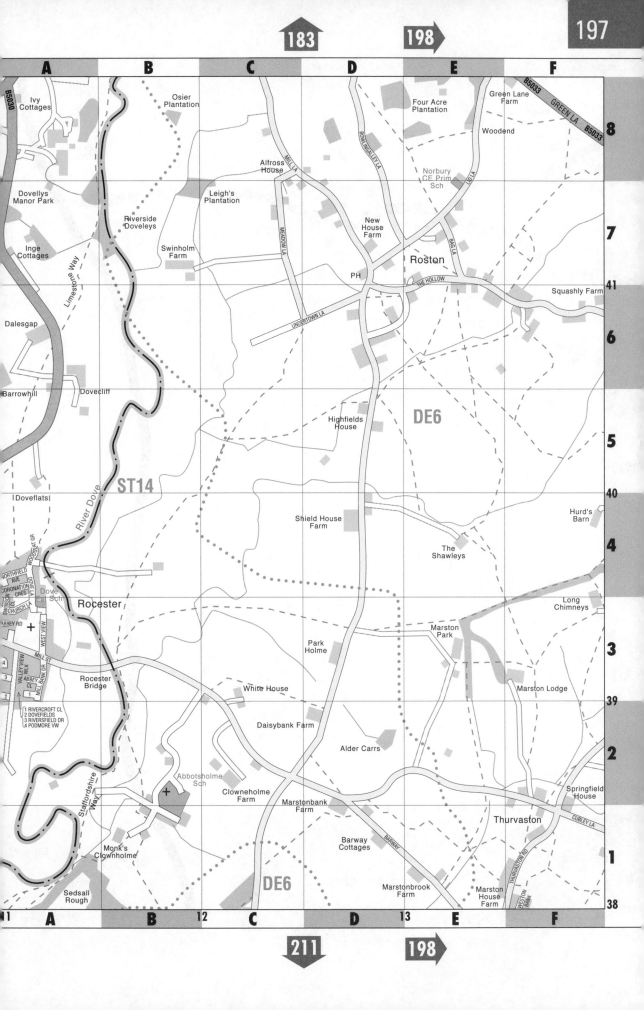

197
184

A **B** **C** **D** **E** **F**

8

Shepherdswood

Chapel House

Cindershills Wood

Darley Moor

B5033

GREEN LA

Snelston Common

Old Queen Farm

Flat Covert

SNAPES LA

VIRGINSALLEY LA

COCKSHEAD LA

B5033

7

Common Farm

John Roe's Covert

Grange Cottage

41

Quarry (dis)

Grange Farm

Manor House

Top Stydd

6

Birchwood Park

Roston Common

Cubley Brook

Birchwoodmoor

5

Cubley Wood Farm

Marstoncommon Farm

40

Woodhay Farm

DE6

Accession Wood

HOLLIES LA

The Hollies

Side Gate

4

Broad Lane

Sandhills Farm

Cubley Covert

Sammy's Wood

Whiterley

Cubley Common

3

Holme Lea

Cubley Cottage Farm

39

Gorse Covert

Common Farm

2

Mountpleasant Farm

Rough Grounds

THE ROW

Great Cubley

1

Birch Field Farm

The Spinney

Brookside Farm

CUBLEY LA

SHAW LA

Cubley Fields Farm

DERBY LA

A515

LONG MDW

38

14 **A** **B** **15** **C** **D** **16** **E** **F**

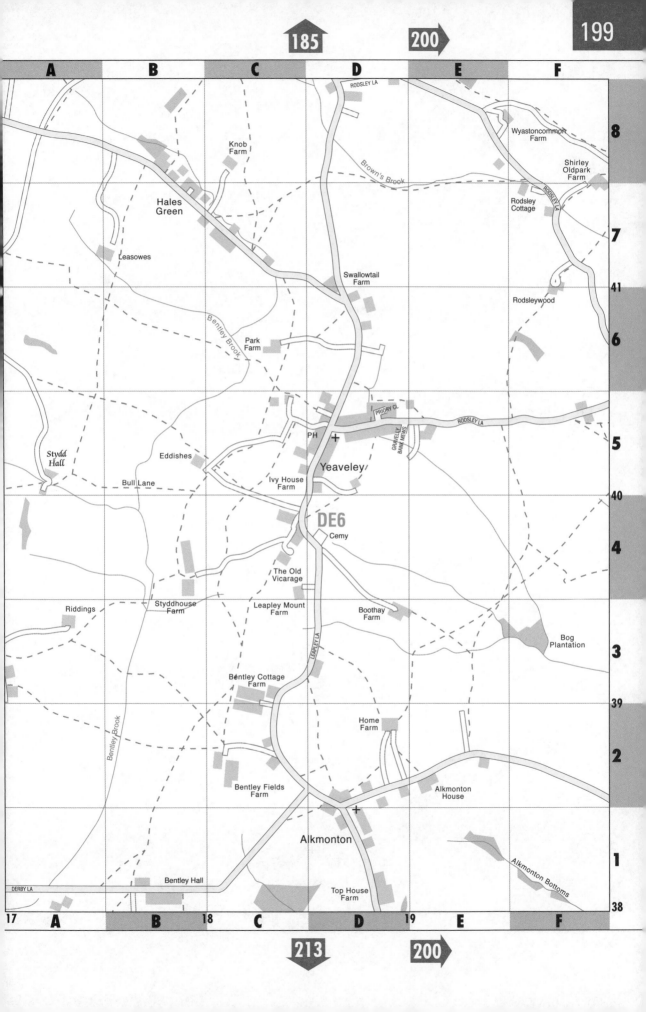

A   B   C   D   E   F

8
Wyastoncommon Farm
Shirley Oldpark Farm
7
41
6
5
40
4
3
39
2
1
38

RODSLEY LA
Brown's Brook
Knob Farm
Hales Green
Leasowes
Swallowtail Farm
Rodsleywood
Rodsley Cottage
RODSLEY LA
Park Farm
Bentley Brook
PRIORY CL
RODSLEY LA
PH
Yeaveley
GRAVELLY BANK MEWS
Eddishes
Stydd Hall
Bull Lane
Ivy House Farm
DE6
Cemy
The Old Vicarage
Styddhouse Farm
Leapley Mount Farm
Boothay Farm
Bog Plantation
Riddings
LEAPLEY LA
Bentley Cottage Farm
Home Farm
Bentley Brook
Bentley Fields Farm
Alkmonton House
Alkmonton
Bentley Hall
Top House Farm
Alkmonton Bottoms
DERBY LA

17 A   B   18 C   D   19 E   F   38

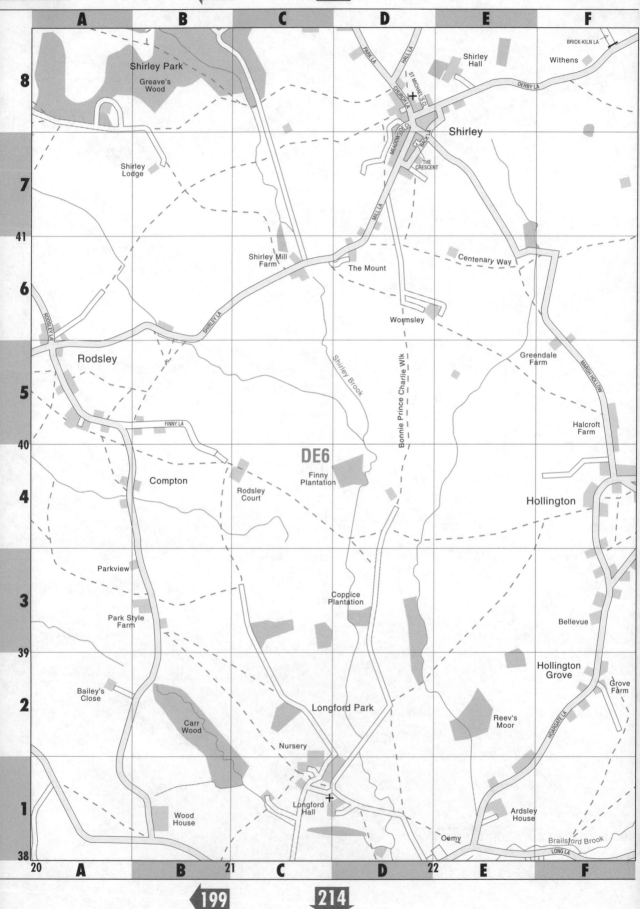

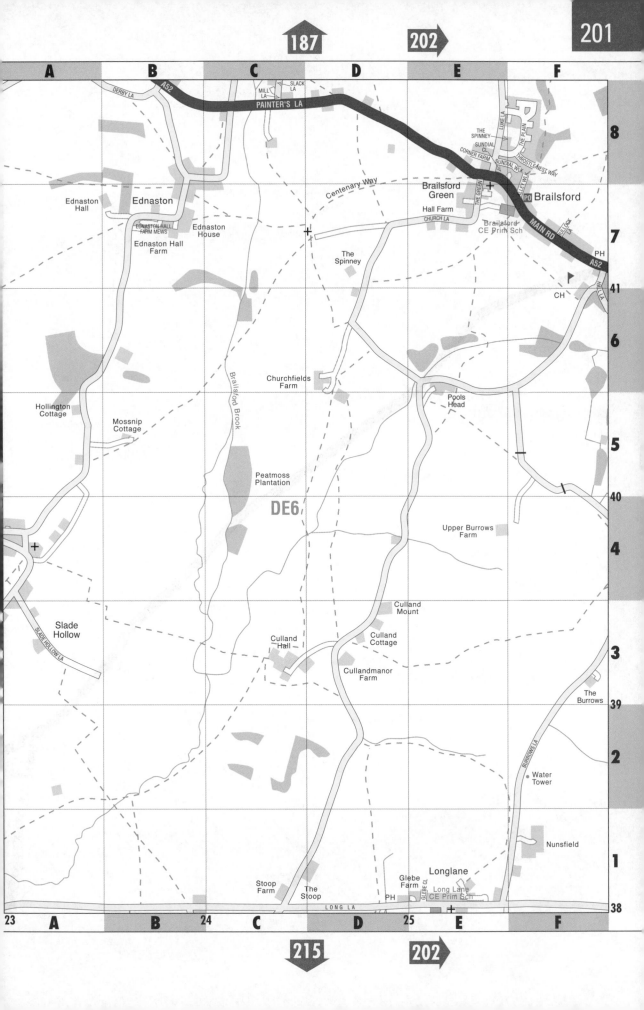

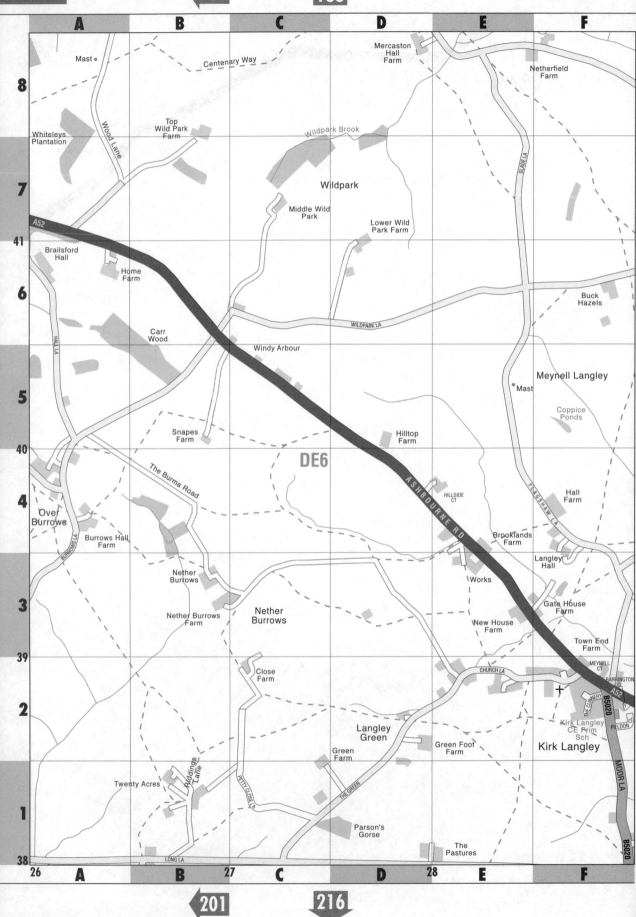

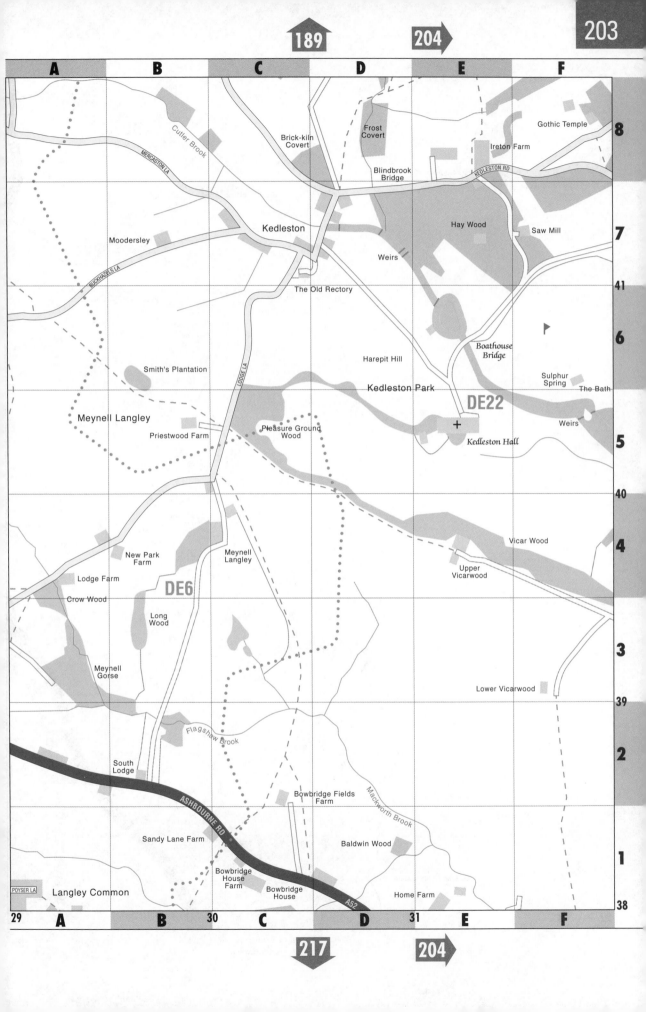

189
204

A B C D E F

8 Gothic Temple
Brick-kiln Covert
Frost Covert
Cutler Brook
MERCASTON LA
Ireton Farm
Blindbrook Bridge
KEDLESTON RD

7 Kedleston
Moodersley
Hay Wood
Saw Mill
Weirs
BUCKHAZELS LA

41 The Old Rectory

6 Harepit Hill
Boathouse Bridge

Smith's Plantation
LODGE LA
Kedleston Park
Sulphur Spring
The Bath

5 Meynell Langley
Priestwood Farm
Pleasure Ground Wood
DE22
Kedleston Hall
Weirs

40

4 New Park Farm
Meynell Langley
Vicar Wood
Upper Vicarwood

Lodge Farm
DE6
Crow Wood
Long Wood

3 Meynell Gorse
Lower Vicarwood

39

2 Flagshaw Brook
South Lodge
ASHBOURNE RD
Bowbridge Fields Farm
Mackworth Brook

1 Sandy Lane Farm
Baldwin Wood
Bowbridge House Farm
Bowbridge House
A52
Home Farm

POYSER LA
Langley Common

38

29 **A** **B** 30 **C** **D** 31 **E** **F**

A B C D E F

8

Mast
Park Nook Farm
Park Nook
Quarndon Hill
Burley Meadows
BEECH AVE
INN LA
THE COMMON
Park Nook Wood
Burley Wood
Burleywood Farmhouse
DE56
DERBY RD
A6

7

Park Nook Wood
Quarndon Common
Burley Hill
Bunker's Hill
Burley Grange
COACH DR
MONTPELIER
SIXEY'S HILL
BURLEY DR
BURLEY LA

41

The Curzon Prim Sch
Quarndon
CH
WOODLANDS LA

6

CH
Hotel
Water Tower
Big Wood
CH
Allestree Hall
Allestree Park Nature Reserve
P
P
BARN CL
CHURCH RD

5

Bottom Covert
Cannon Hill
PH
KEDLESTON RD

40

DE22
OLD VICARAGE LA
OLD CHURCH CL
BROOK CL
Woodlands Sch
ACRESVIEW FIELD
LABURNUM CRES
MIDD
CHARLESTOWN DR
TAMAR AVE
ELM GR
MAPLE GR
IMPERIAL
WOODLANDS RD
WEST BANK RD
FIRS CRES
ST MAWES CL
LISKEARD DR
ST AGNES AVE
CHARTERSTONE LA
PINGLE
RIDINGS
LADYCROFT PADDOCK
CORNHILL

4

CRABTREE CL
CURZON CL
BANCROFT DR
SHEROSIDE CL
BLENHEIM DR
WOODSTOCK CL
KINGSLEY RD
THORN
ASH
LOCKWOOD RD
OAK CL
BLENHEIM PAR
CHANDRES CT
FOXES WLK
Portway Inf & Jun Schs
ROBIN CROFT RD
M'LBERRIES
PARK VIEW CL
RYDAL CL
CHURCH WLK
ST EDMUND'S
GISBORNE CRES
KINGS CROFT
P
Allestree

3

ASKERFIELD AVE
RAVENSDALE RD
ASHBROOK CL
CRABTREE HILL
CORBTHORN DR
HARDWICK AVE
BIRCHES RD
LARCH AVE
HOLLIES RD
HAREWOOD RD
ALTON CL
WELWYN AVE
SYCAMORE AVE
ALLESTREE LA
BEAURPER AVE
THIRLMERE AVE
NESS WLK
LEA CL
BUTTERMERE DR
WINDERMERE CRES
PORTREATH DR
TAY CL
CALDER CL
CAVENDISH AVE
DEVONSHIRE AVE
ST GEORGE'S HO
DRUM CL
A38

39

SOMME RD
NETHERWOOD CT
ROSEMOUNT CL
MEMORIAL RD
QUARNDON VIEW
SCARSDALE AVE
ST NICHOLAS
The Orchards
ABBEY HILL RD
BRIARSGATE
FAIRWAY
CLIFTON RD
JOHN'S CL
PENTEWEN CL
FERRERS WAY
CADGWITH DR
FONLANDS
CHISWICK
ORTH CRES
BARDEN DR
FRIARS CL
THATCH CL
THE CLOSE
Walter Evans CE Prim Sch
DUFFIELD RD

2

Markeaton Brook
MENIN RD
LENS RD
YPRES RD
BELLINGHAM DR
OTTERBURN DR
AMBLECOTE
LAWN AVE
FAIRWAY CRES
BEELEY CL
LILAC WLK
LAWN Liby
PO
BIRCHOVER WAY
BANK SIDE
THE RISE
CAUSEWAY
HARPSWELL
TRESILL
EVE
BINNINGTON
FINNWELL
MISTERTON
THE CREST
SLACK LA
QUEENSWAY
St Benedict RC Sch & Performing Arts Coll
SONGBIRD
LAVENDER ROW
PLOUGH GATE
WILLOW
COPPICE CL

1

Markeaton Stones
STOODLEY PIKE GDNS
WIDDYBANK CL
RIBBLESDALE CL
NETHER PARK DR
HASKEYS
CYPRESS CL
OSIERS CL
KEDLESTON RD
AMBER RD
MELBOURNE CL
NORBURY CL
WHITEWAY
Lawn Prim Sch
LANSCOMBE PARK RD
BERRY PARK CL
FARNWAY
WEST CL
ALSTONFIELD DR
MARCHINGTON
WYASTON
CARSINGTON
SLACK LA
High
MILE ASH LA
WINDLEY CRES
VICARWOOD AVE
DARLEY PARK RD
DARLEY GROVE
St Mary's RC Prim Sch
A6

38

Osierbed Wood
Markeaton House
DOEDALE RISE
KEDLESTON CL
JACKSDALE
EDALE CL
FINDERN CL
HOLLAND VIEW
CARSINGTON CL
THORPELANDS DR
CARSINGTON MEWS
Univ of Derby
CATHERINE McAULEY HO
HIGHFIELD
BENDALL GDNS
BEECHWOOD PK
DARLEY PARK DR
A38

32 A 33 B C 34 D E F

D2
1 CARSINGTON HO
2 NORBURY CT
3 KEDLESTON CT

F2
1 WICKERSLEY CL
2 MALTBY CL
3 ST HUGH'S CL
4 ST MATTHEW'S WLK

F3
1 BIRCHOVER HO
2 CHURCH LA N
3 TUDOR CT

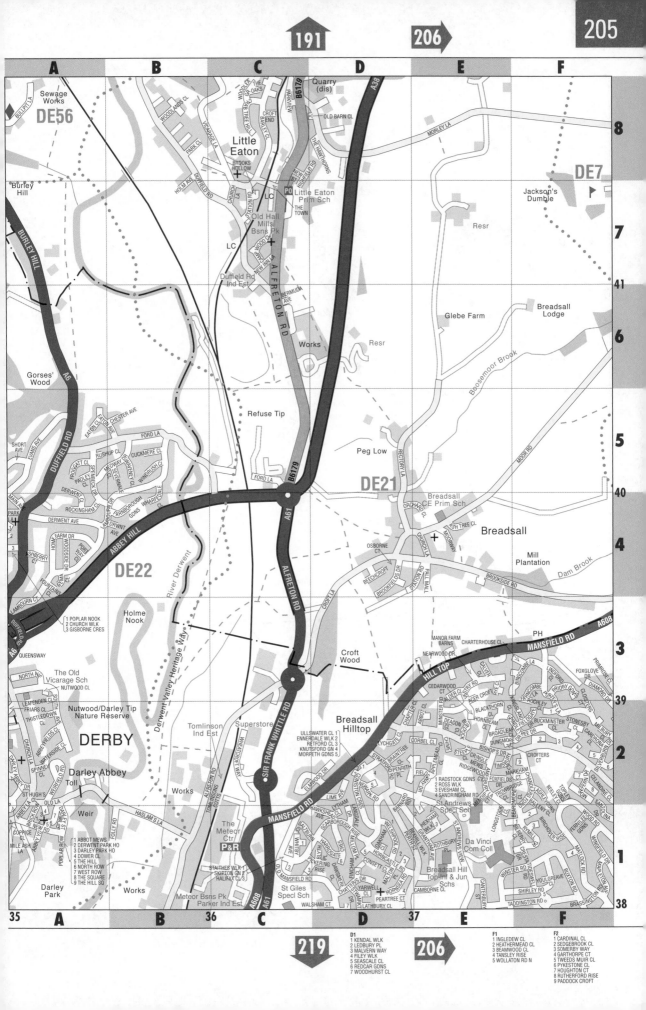

D1
1 KENDAL WLK
2 LEDBURY PL
3 MALVERN WAY
4 FILEY WLK
5 SEASCALE CL
6 REDCAR GDNS
7 WOODHURST CL

F1
1 INGLEDEW CL
2 HEATHERMEAD CL
3 BEAMWOOD CL
4 TANSLEY RISE
5 WOLLATON RD N

F2
1 CARDINAL CL
2 SEDGEBROOK CL
3 SOMERBY WAY
4 GARTHORPE CT
5 TWEEDS MUIR CL
6 PYKESTONE CL
7 HOUGHTON CT
8 RUTHERFORD RISE
9 PADDOCK CROFT

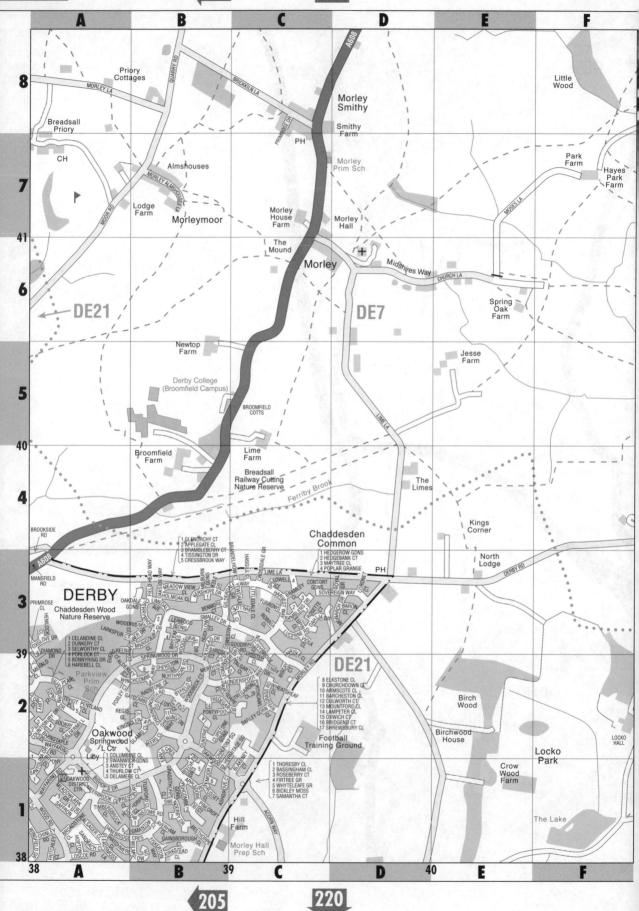

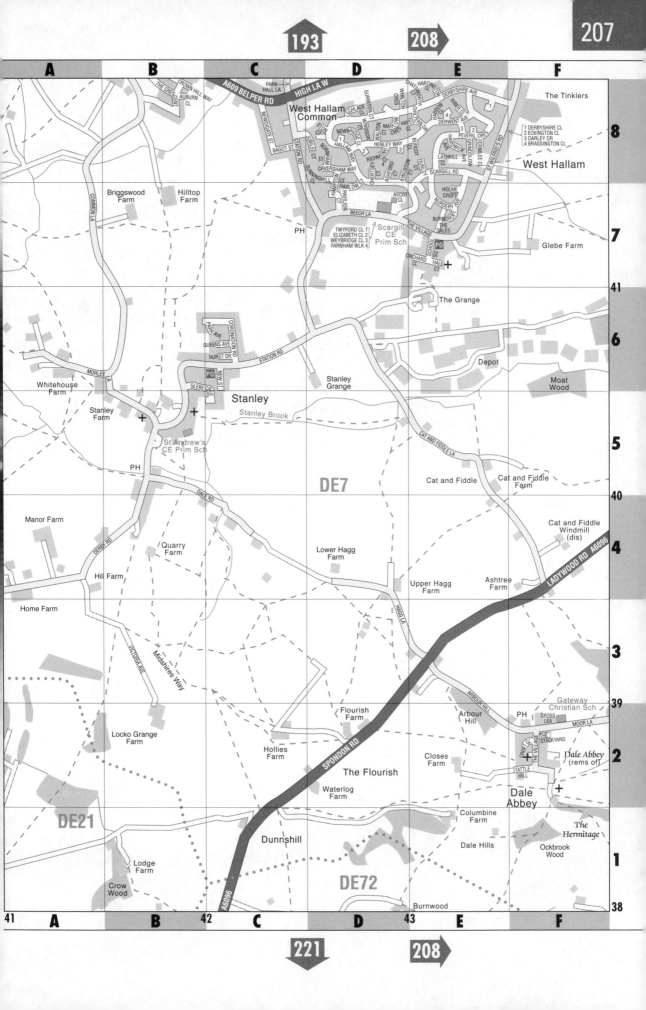

A   B   C   D   E   F

8

7

41

6

40

5

4

39

3

2

1

38

West Hallam Common

The Tinklers

1 DERBYSHIRE CL
2 ECKINGTON CL
3 DARLEY DR
4 BRASSINGTON CL

West Hallam

CROWN HILL WAY
THE CRES
AUBURN CL

A609 BELPER RD   HIGH LA W
PARK
HALL LA

CHATSWORTH ST
HARTINGTON ST
DERBYSHIRE AVE
HILTON CL
WHITTON
LEDBURY
RIBERS CL

NEWGATE ST
STATION RD
BAGOT ST

LECHLADE CL
ETON
WINDSOR
SURBITON CT
CHILSON DR

HADDON
DERWENT AVE
PEVERIL CRES

NEWBRIDGE CT
HALLAM WAY
JUBILEE CT
BURNHAM CT
SUNNINGHILL CT
HUMPHREY
RD
CAVERSHAM WAY
HARLOW CT
PAVILION
ST
PH

MAP
CRES
MARLOW
HENLEY WAY
RICHMOND
HERTFORD
ASHFORD
KINGSTON
ASCOT
CL

HARDWICK AVE
FERNILEE CL
GRINDSLOW
HURLEY
SCARGILL RD
LATHKILL CL

Briggswood
Farm

Hilltop
Farm

TWYFORD CL 1
ELIZABETH CL 2
WEYBRIDGE CL 3
FARNHAM WLK 4

Scargill
CE
Prim Sch

BEECH LA

HOLME
CROFT
NURSERY AVE

HICKTON
RD

BURNCROFT
THE DALES
THE VILLAGE

Glebe Farm

ORCHARD
CL
HALL
CT
PO

COMMON LA

The Grange

Whitehouse
Farm

MORLEY
LA

PARK AVE
QUEENS AVE
CORONATION RD
HURST DR
STATION RD
PO
GLEBE CRES
NEW ST

Stanley

Stanley
Grange

Depot

Moat
Wood

Stanley
Farm
St Andrew's
CE Prim Sch
PH
DALE RD

Stanley Brook

DE7

Cat and Fiddle

CAT AND FIDDLE LA

Cat and Fiddle
Farm

Manor Farm

Quarry
Farm

Lower Hagg
Farm

Cat and Fiddle
Windmill
(dis)

LADYWOOD RD A6096

DERBY RD
Hill Farm

Upper Hagg
Farm

Ashtree
Farm

Home Farm

VICTORIA AVE
Midshires Way

HAGG LA

Gateway
Christian Sch

Locko Grange
Farm

Flourish
Farm

Arbour
Hill

ARBOUR HILL
PH
CROSS
LEA
MOOR LA

Hollies
Farm

SPONDON RD

The Flourish

Closes
Farm

PROFT CL
THE VILLAGE
THE STACKYARD

Dale Abbey
(rems of)

DE21

Waterlog
Farm

TATTLE
HILL

Dale
Abbey

A6096

Dunnshill

Columbine
Farm

The
Hermitage

Lodge
Farm

Dale Hills

Ockbrook
Wood

Crow
Wood

DE72

Burnwood

41   A   B   C   42   D   E   43   F   F

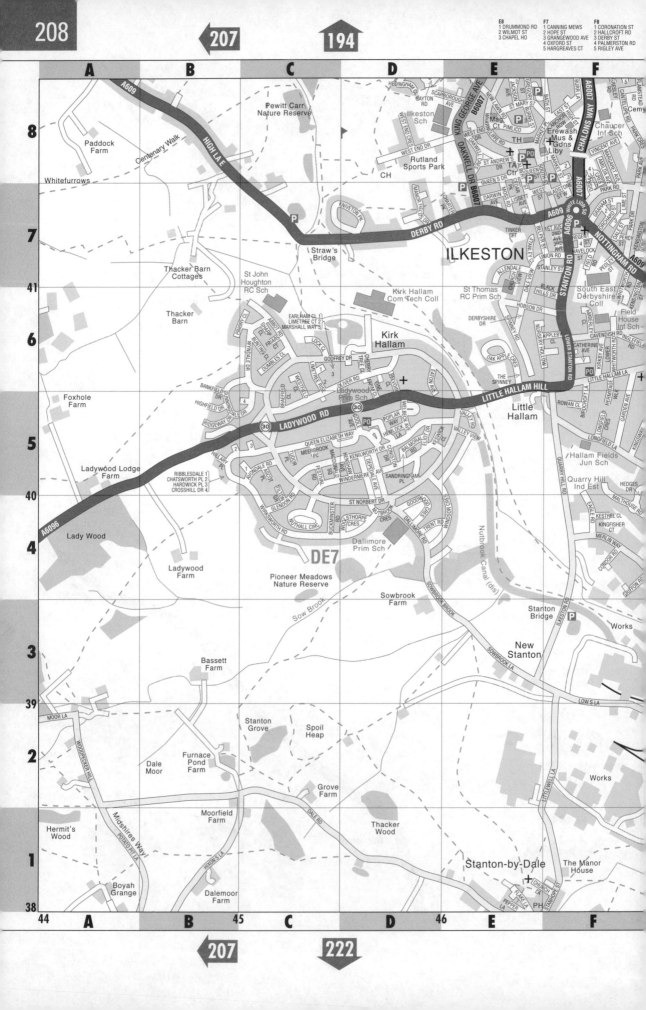

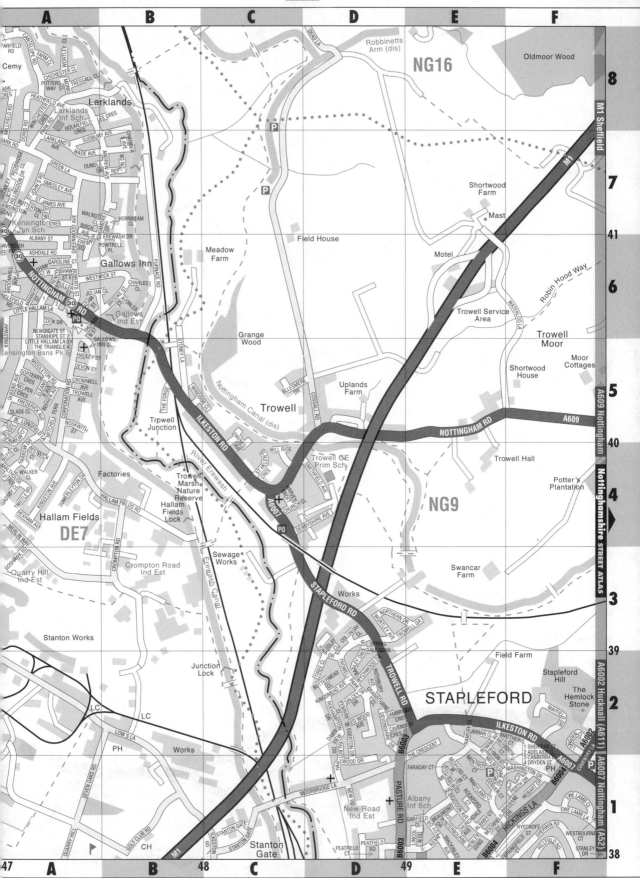

A B C D E F

8

7

37

6

5

36

4

3

35

2

1

34

08 A B 09 C D 10 E F

Nothill Brook
Combridge Farm
Combridge
Lowfields
Alders Brook
Brookend House
Limecrofts
Eaton Dovedale
River Churnet
The Riddings
HOOK LA
Longacre Farm
Crakemarsh Hall
Crakemarsh
ST14
Eaton Hall Farm
DE6
Creighton Farm
Creighton
CREIGHTON LA
Crakemarsh Farm
River Dove
BARNWELL CL
BROOM CLOSE LA
THE ORCHARD
1 CEDAR DR
2 CHURCH FARM
VICARAGE DR
Stramshall
Bridge Farm
Riversmede
River Tean
Sidford Wood
Staffordshire Way
Spath
B5030
Spath Cottage Farm
Cottonmill Farm
Leasows Farm
River Tean
ASHBOURNE RD
A518
A50 Stoke-on-Trent
A522 Cheadle
A50
A518
THE DOVE WAY
Sewage Works
Noah's Ark
A50
Dove Bridge
Motel
Park Ave
New Rd
The Heath
A522
BADGERY
NLEY CRES
WEAVER RD
NORFIELD
GREENACRES DR
THE LAWNS
B5030
ASHBOURNE RD
CHEADLE RD
JOHNSON RD
PARK AVE
UTTOXETER
The Wharf
DERBY RD
A4518
Bentley Rd
Gardner Rd
Redfern Rd
School Rd
Mosley Dr
Grange Rd
Windsor Dr
Old Lodge Cl
Applewood Cl
Princess Rd
St Mary's Cres
Heathlands Dr
Holly Rd
Westward Cl
Heath Rd
Mellor Dr
Slater Fields
Croft Gr
Pennycroft La
Gas St
Eaton St
Lightfoot Rd
Jones Way
PO
A522 Uttoxeter
A518 Stafford

A1
1 HERMITAGE GDNS
2 THE HORNBEAMS
3 HEATH CROSS
4 Tynsel Parkes CE Fst Sch

B1
1 ORCHARD CL
2 BOWLING GREEN RD
3 WINDMILL CL
4 St Mary's CE Fst Sch
5 THE LIMES

A B C D E F

8 7 37 6 5 36 4 36 3 35 2 1 34

Morry House Farm

ST14

Marston Montgomery Prim School
Manor House

1 WESTON BANK
2 THURVASTON RD

PEARL BANK

Marston Montgomery

PH

Eaton Barn

Sedsall Farm

Havenhouse Farm

WALDLEY LA

Beggarsbutts

Banktop

The Beeches

Waldley

Waldley Farm

Marston Woodhouse

Marston Brook

Eaton Wood

Old Woodhouse Farm

Upper Eaton Farm

Upwoods Farm

DE6

Lady Coppice

Hill Farm

MARSTON LA

Holmlea Farm

Somersal Farm

Mount Pleasant

Victory Farm

Woodhouse Farm

Somersal Herbert

The Hall

North Lodge

Grove Cottages

Eaton Lodge

Brocksford Brook

Oaklea

DERBY RD
UPWOODS RD

Field Farm

Mill Cottage

GROVE LA

MARSTON LA
PH
MARSTON LA

BABBS LA
DERBY RD

Mill Farm

River Dove

Doveridge

HALL DR
MILL LA

DAK DR
WEST DR
PARK CRES
EAST DR
COOK LA
MAPLE CL
HAWTHORN CL
LAKE SIDE
ORCHARD CT
HIGH ST
CHURCH LA
SAND LA
FLORENCE DR
CAVENDISH CL
ALMS RD
BAKER'S LA

PO

A50

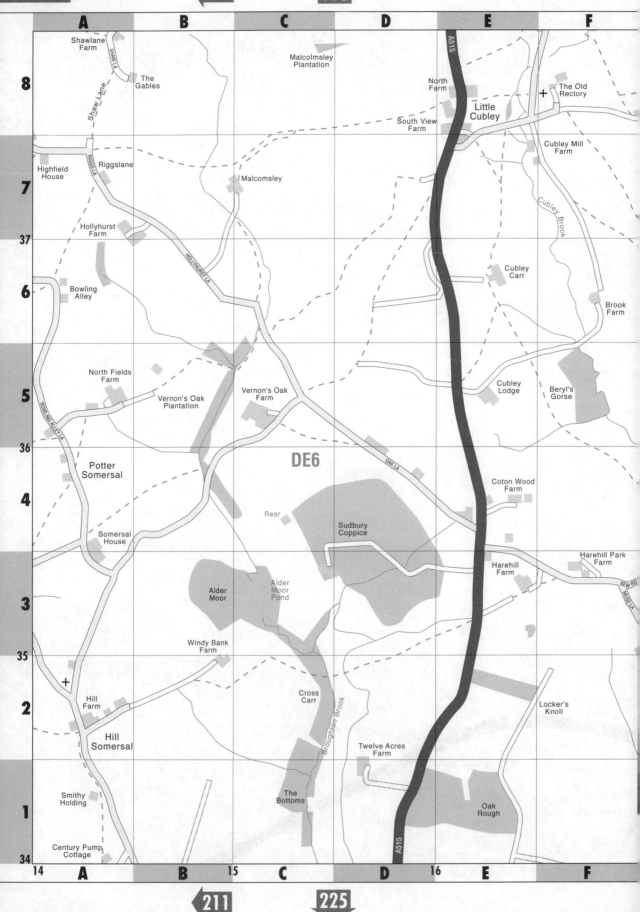

A B C D E F

8

North Farm
Little Cubley
The Old Rectory
South View Farm
Cubley Mill Farm

Shawlane Farm
The Gables
Shaw Lane

7

Highfield House
Riggslane
Malcomsley
Cubley Brook

37

Hollyhurst Farm
HOLLYHURST LA

Cubley Carr

6

Bowling Alley
Brook Farm

RIGGS LA

5

North Fields Farm
Vernon's Oak Plantation
Vernon's Oak Farm
Cubley Lodge
Beryl's Gorse

36

Potter Somersal
BOWLING ALLEY LA
OAK LA
DE6
Coton Wood Farm

4

Somersal House
Resr
Sudbury Coppice
Harehill Farm
Harehill Park Farm
NEW RD
MUSE LA

3

Alder Moor
Alder Moor Pond

35

Windy Bank Farm
Cross Carr
Locker's Knoll

2

Hill Farm
Hill Somersal
Boughton Brook
Twelve Acres Farm

1

Smithy Holding
The Bottoms
Oak Rough

34

Century Pump Cottage
A515

14 A 15 B C 15 D 16 E F

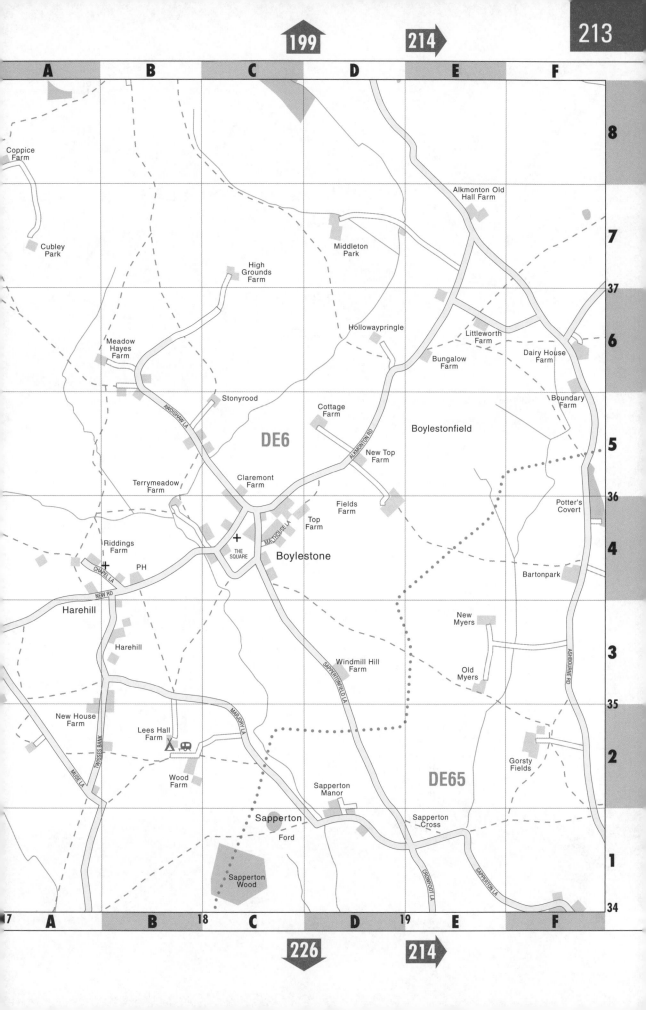

213
200

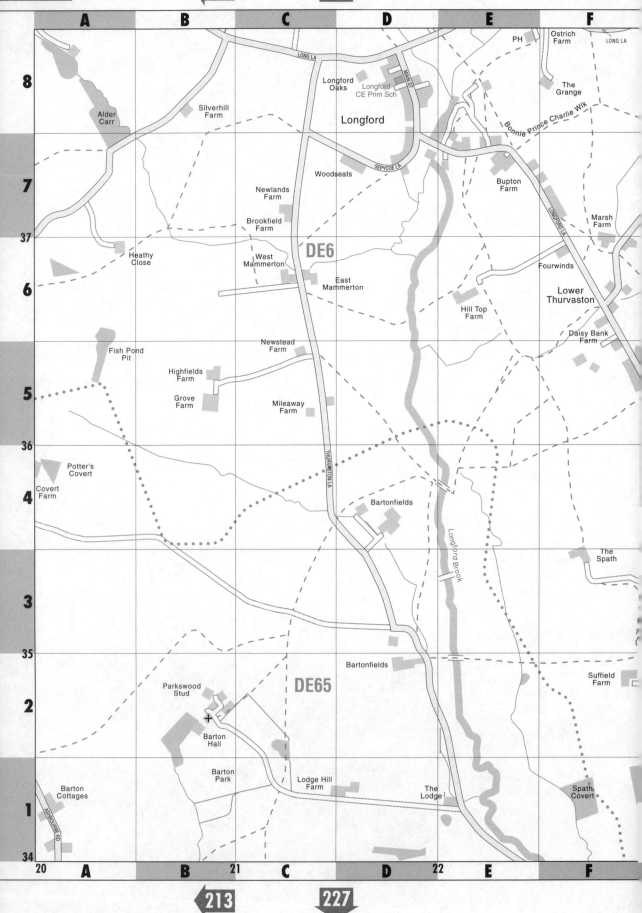

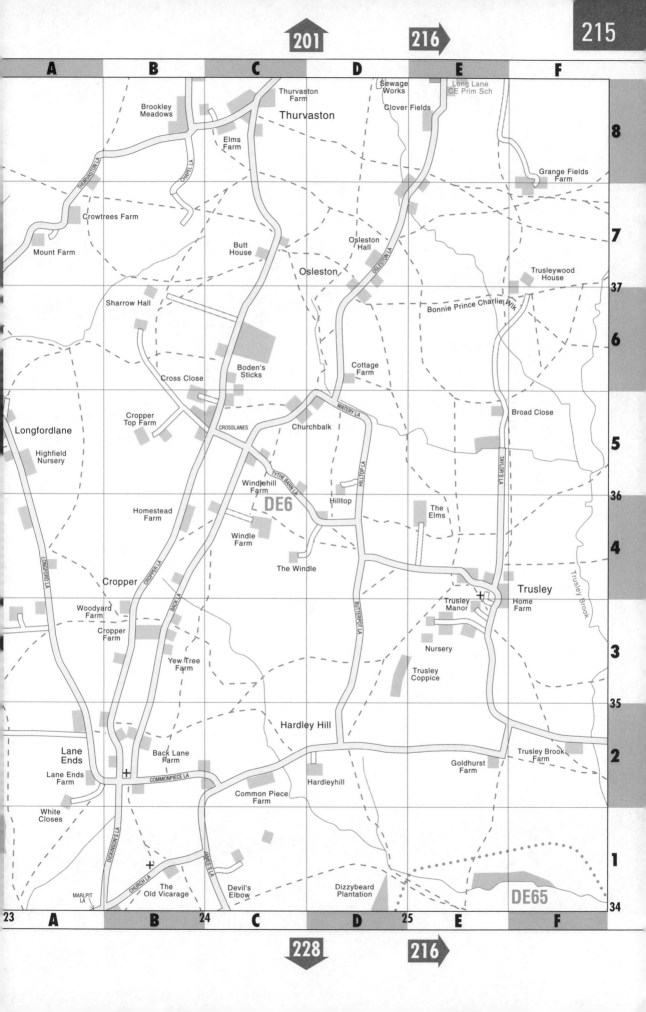

A   B   C   D   E   F

Thurvaston Farm
Brookley Meadows
Thurvaston
Elms Farm
Sewage Works
Clover Fields
Long Lane CE Prim Sch
Grange Fields Farm

8

Crowtrees Farm
Mount Farm
Butt House
Osleston
Osleston Hall
Trusleywood House

7

37

Sharrow Hall
Bonnie Prince Charlie Wlk

6

Longfordlane
Highfield Nursery
Cross Close
Cropper Top Farm
Boden's Sticks
CROSSLANES
Churchbalk
WATERY LA
Cottage Farm
Broad Close

5

Homestead Farm
Windlehill Farm
DE6
TYTHE BARN LA
Hilltop
HILLTOP LA
The Elms
TAYLOR'S LA

36

4

Windle Farm
The Windle
BUTTERPOT LA

CROPPER LA
Cropper
Woodyard Farm
Cropper Farm
Yew Tree Farm
BACK LA
Trusley Manor
Trusley
Home Farm
Nursery
Trusley Brook
Trusley Coppice

3

35

Lane Ends
Back Lane Farm
Lane Ends Farm
COMMONPIECE LA
Hardley Hill
Common Piece Farm
Hardleyhill
Goldhurst Farm
Trusley Brook Farm

2

White Closes
DICKINSON'S LA
CHURCH LA
JAMES'S LA
The Old Vicarage
Devil's Elbow
Dizzybeard Plantation
DE65

1

MARLPIT LA

LONGFORD LA

THURVASTON LA

CHAPEL LA

OSLESTON LA

23   A   B   24   C   D   25   E   F   34

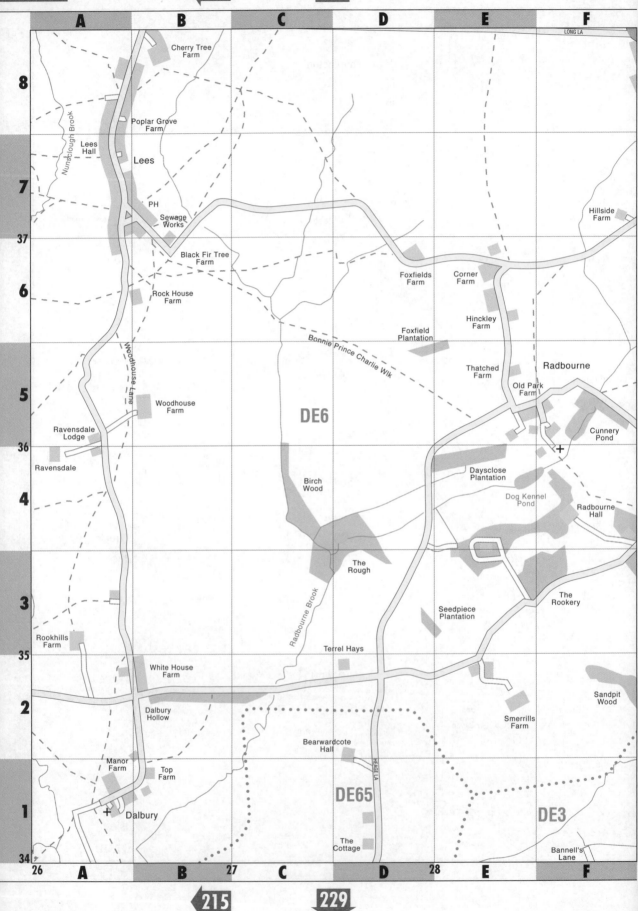

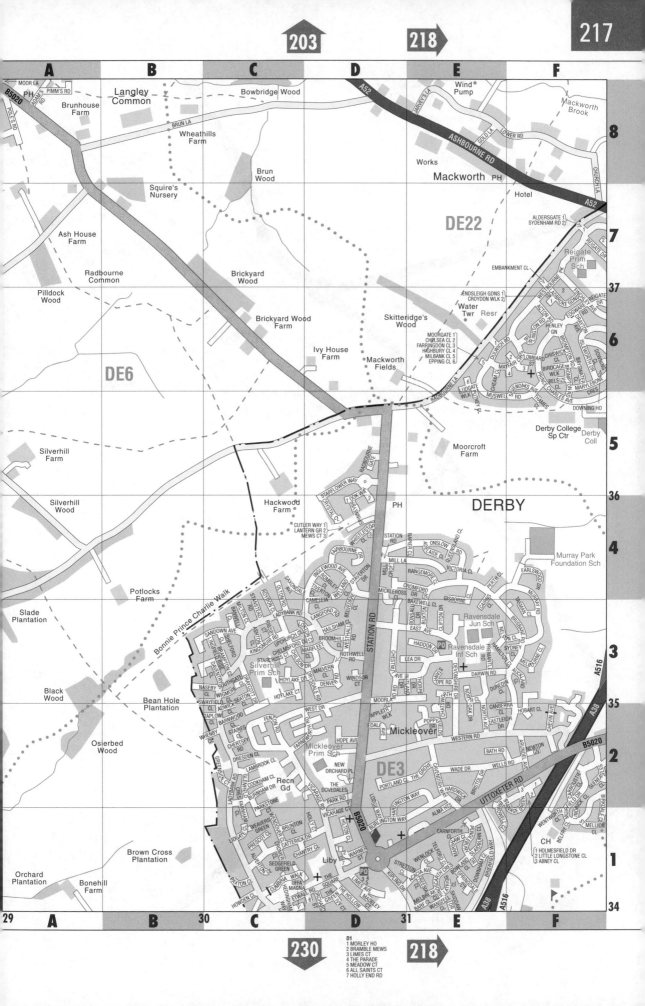

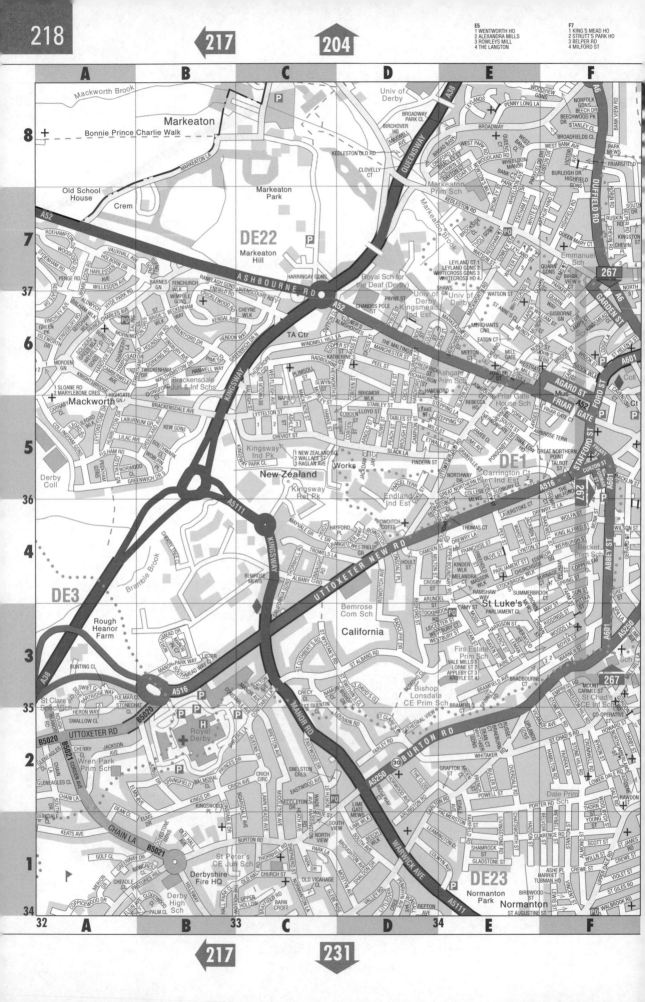

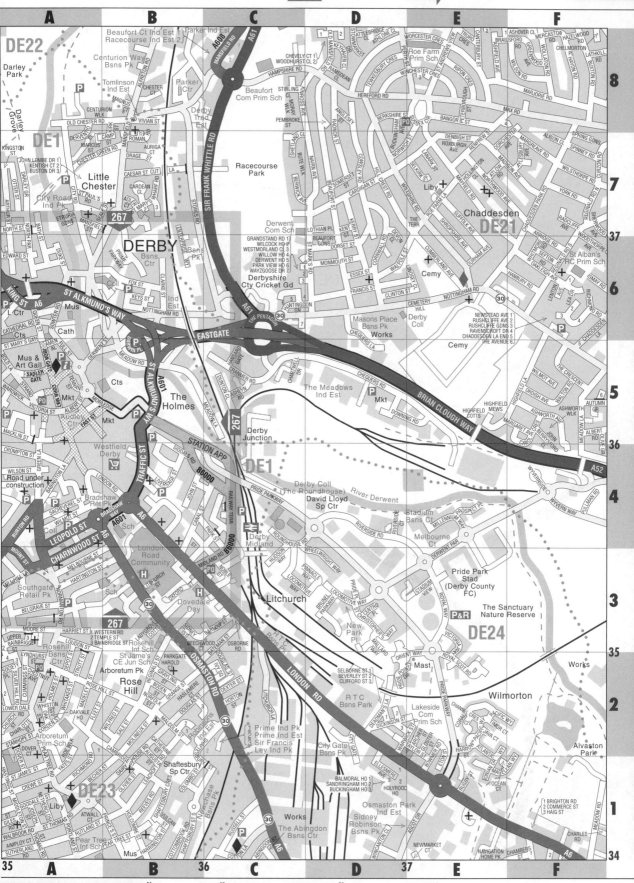

E8
1 ASHOVER RD
2 TADDINGTON CL
3 RINGWOOD CL
4 LIVERPOOL ST

A1
1 Hardwick Prim Sch

A2
1 PETERHOUSE TERR
2 CO-OPERATIVE ST
3 INDUSTRIAL ST
4 PROVIDENT ST

B2
1 ARTHUR CT
2 TINTAGEL CL
3 ALEXANDRA GDNS

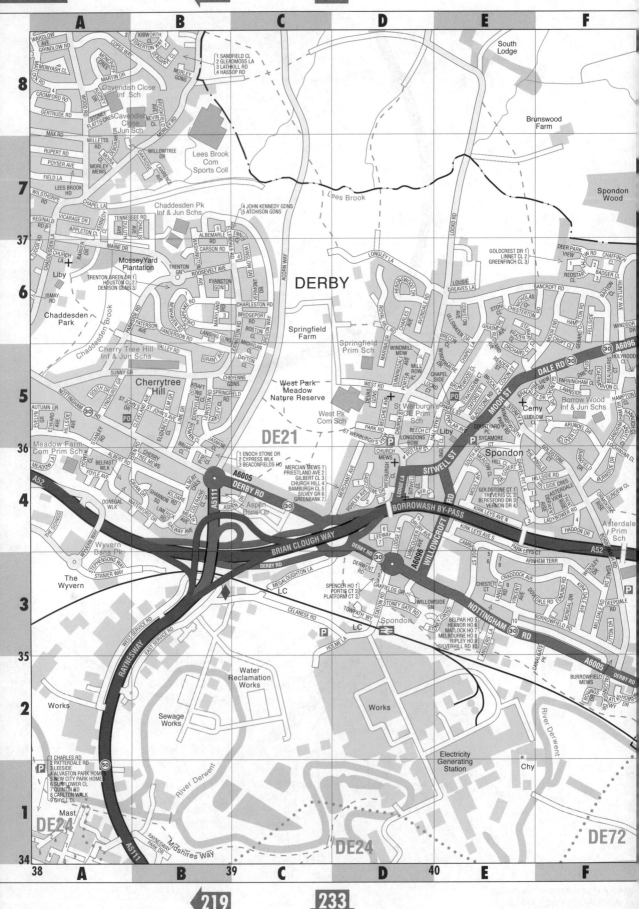

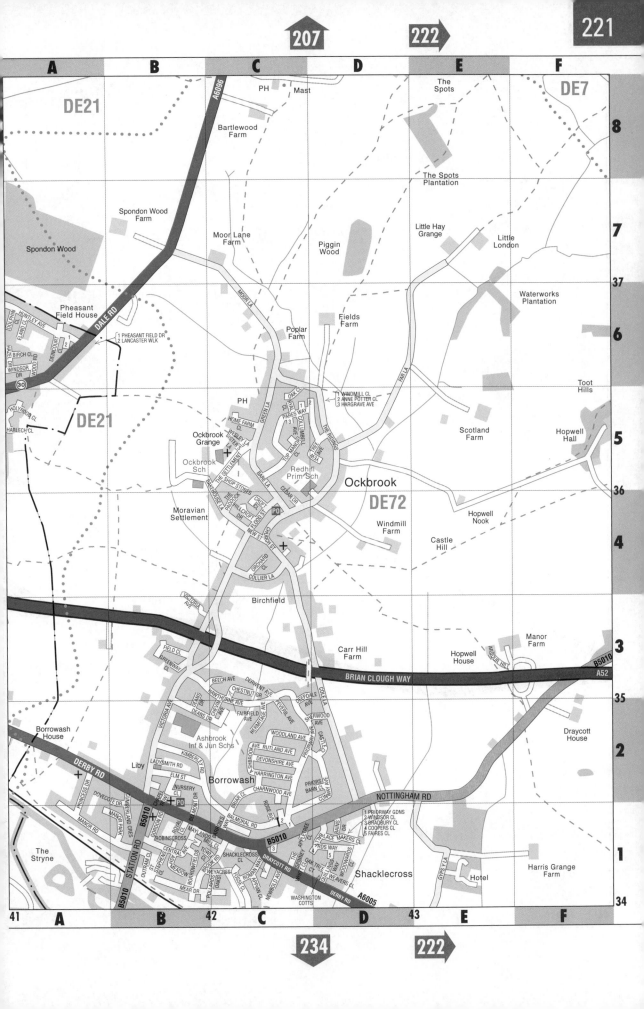

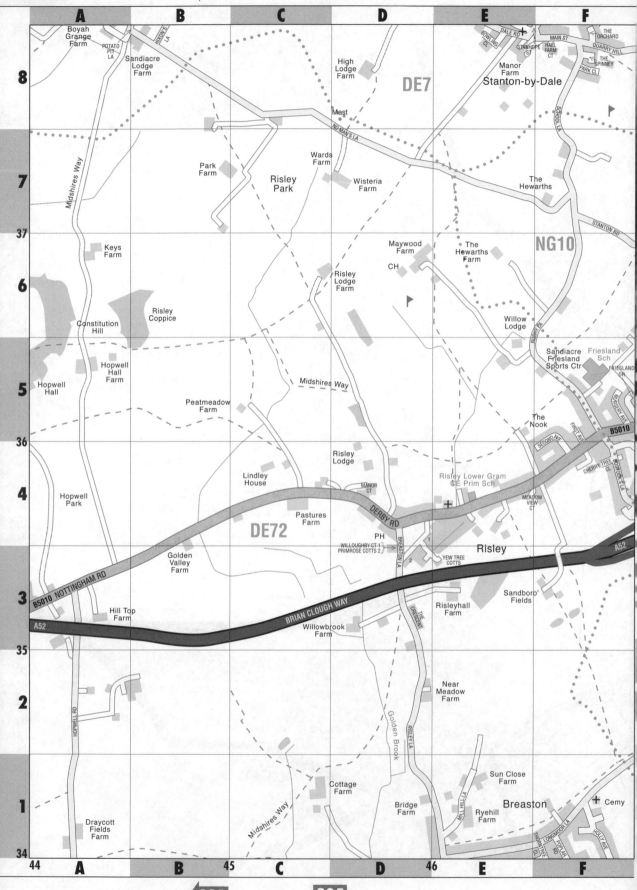

221
208

A   B   C   D   E   F

8

Boyah
Grange
Farm

POTATO
PITT LA

Sandiacre
Lodge
Farm

HIXON'S LA

DE7

DALE RD

BOWLING CL

STANHOPE ST

MAIN ST

HALL
FARM
CT

THE
ORCHARD

QUARRY HILL

THE
SPINNEY

PARK CL

Manor
Farm

Stanton-by-Dale

High
Lodge
Farm

SCHOOL LA

Midshires Way

Park
Farm

Risley
Park

Wards
Farm

Wisteria
Farm

Mast

NO MAN'S LA

The
Hewarths

7

STANTON RD

37

Keys
Farm

Risley
Lodge
Farm

Maywood
Farm

CH

The
Hewarths
Farm

NG10

RUSHY LA

6

Risley
Coppice

Constitution
Hill

Willow
Lodge

Hopwell
Hall
Farm

Midshires Way

Sandiacre
Friesland
Sports Ctr

Friesland
Sch

FRIESLAND
DR

NURSERY AVE

Hopwell
Hall

Peatmeadow
Farm

The
Nook

FIRST AVE

SECOND AVE

B5010

5

36

Hopwell
Park

Lindley
House

Risley
Lodge

MANOR
CT

Risley Lower Gram
CE Prim Sch

MEADOW
VIEW
CT

CHERRY TREE CL

BUXTON CL

Pastures
Farm

DERBY RD

A52

DE72

Golden
Valley
Farm

BREASTON LA

WILLOUGHBY CT 1
PRIMROSE COTTS 2

PH

1

2

YEW TREE
COTTS

Risley

4

Sandboro'
Fields

B5010 NOTTINGHAM RD

A52

Hill Top
Farm

BRIAN CLOUGH WAY

Willowbrook
Farm

THE CRESCENT

Risleyhall
Farm

3

35

HOPWELL RD

Near
Meadow
Farm

RISLEY LA

2

Golden Brook

Cottage
Farm

Bridge
Farm

MILL HILL LA

Sun Close
Farm

Ryehill
Farm

Breaston

Cemy

1

Draycott
Fields
Farm

Midshires Way

LONGMOOR RD

THORNTREE CL

HOLLY AVE

44   A   B   45   C   D   46   E   F   34

221
235

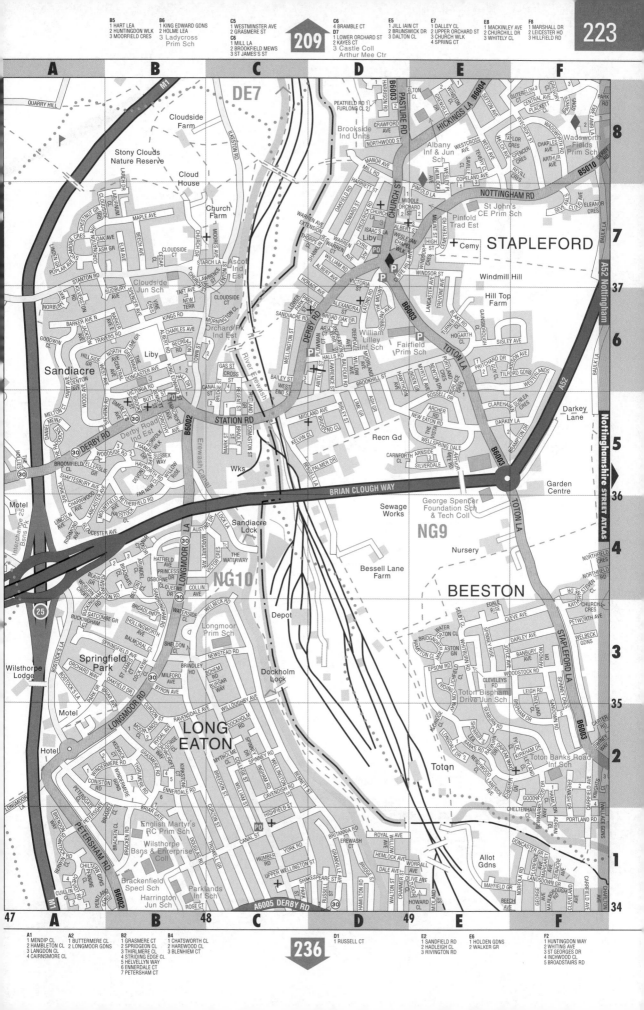

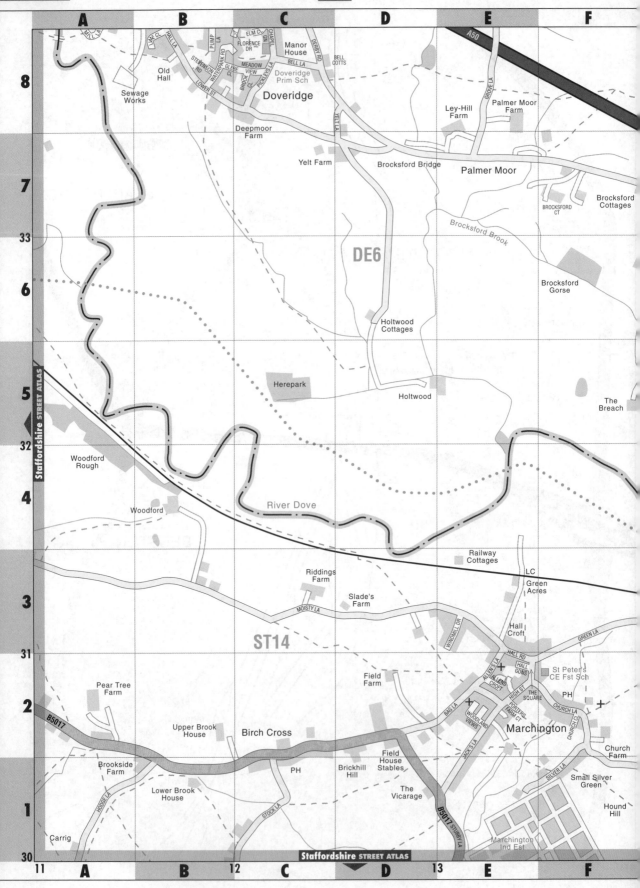

A B C D E F

8

7

33

6

5

32

4

3

31

2

1

30

11 A B 12 C D 13 E F

A50

Sewage Works

Old Hall

LYNE CL
HALL LA
PUMP LA
STEVENSON RD
WATERPARK RD
GLEBE CL
LOWER ST
BROOK CL
PORTLEY LA
CHAPEL LA
ELM CT
FLORENCE DR
MEADOW VIEW

Manor House

BELL LA
DERBY RD

BELL COTTS

Doveridge Prim Sch

Doveridge

Deepmoor Farm

YELT LA

Yelt Farm

Brocksford Bridge

Ley-Hill Farm

GROVE LA

Palmer Moor Farm

Palmer Moor

DE6

Brocksford Brook

BROCKSFORD CT

Brocksford Cottages

Brocksford Gorse

Holtwood Cottages

Herepark

Holtwood

The Breach

Woodford Rough

Woodford

River Dove

Railway Cottages

LC

Green Acres

Riddings Farm

Slade's Farm

MOISTY LA

ST14

Hall Croft

WINDMILL DR

HALL RD

GREEN LA

St Peter's CE Fst Sch

Field Farm

Pear Tree Farm

ALLEN'S LA
HALL GDNS
ALLENS CROFT
HIGH ST
BAG LA
THE SQUARE
PORTERS FARM CT
CHURCH LA
PH
Marchington
CHURCH CL

B5017

Upper Brook House

Birch Cross

PH

WOODLAND VIEWS

JACK'S LA

Field House Stables

Brickhill Hill

Brookside Farm

HODGE LA

Lower Brook House

STOCK LA

The Vicarage

B5017 STUBBY LA

Church Farm

SILVER LA

Small Silver Green

Hound Hill

Carrig

Marchington Ind Est

Staffordshire STREET ATLAS

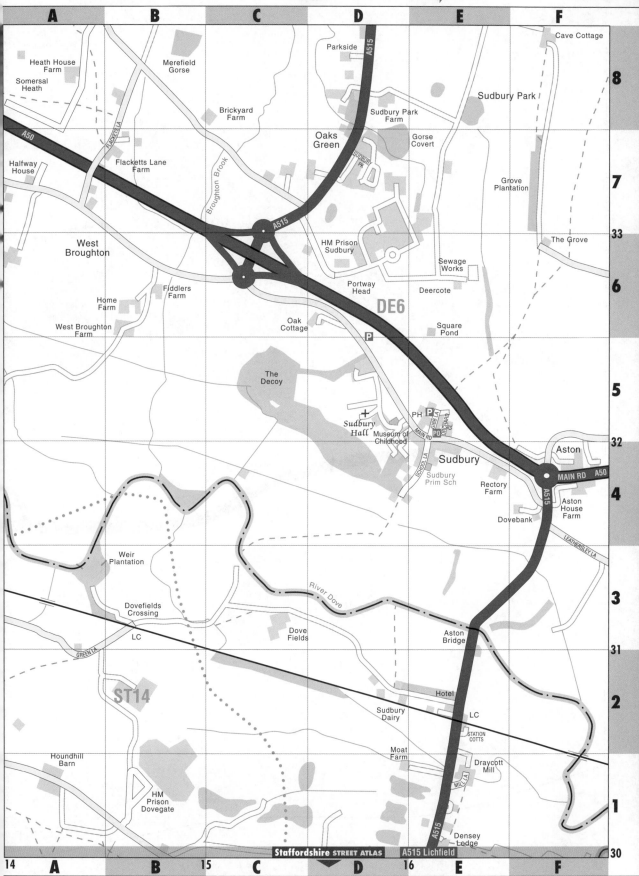

225
213

A B C D E F

8

The Homestead

Mackley House

Fox Hole

Sapperton Brook

Foston Mill Farm

Crowfoot Farm

CROWFOOT LA

Dale Brook

MUSE LA

7

Muselane Farm

Cotefield Farm

33

WOODHOUSE LA

Dalebrook

Ford

6

Aston Heath

Broomhill Farm

Conygree Wood

Aston Heath Farm

Foston Brook

Haylane Farm

HAY LA

Rough Wood

WOODYARD LA

Breach Gorse

BREACH LA

Sailor's Holme

COPLOW LA

5

DE6

Home Farm

DE65

Lawn House

ASTON LA

32

MAIN RD

Foston

Roundhouse Gall

Tomlinson Bsns Pk

A50

UTTOXETER RD

UTTOXETER RD

A50

4

Maidensley Farm

WOODLAND DR

HM Detention Centre

Lemon's Holme

Cote House

UTTOXETER RD

Dale Brook

Puddingbag Covert

Roundabout Covert

Fishpond Plantation

The Churchleys

3

Leathersley Farm

31

LEATHERSLEY LA

WATERY LA

2

BROOM'S LA

Sweet Holme

Scropton

1

River Dove

Ivy House Farm

SCROPTON RD

+ PH

Brookside Farm

LC

MILL

30

River Dove

Brookhouse Farm

LC

17 A B 18 C D 19 E F

214
228

A **B** **C** **D** **E** **F**

8

Church
Broughton

SAPPERTON LA

ASHBOURNE RD

CHURCH RD

CHAPEL LA

MAIN ST

ALDEN CL

PH

1 FEARN CL
2 MEADOW RISE
3 THE ETCHELLS

Church
Broughton
CE Prim Sch

Badder
Green
Farm

Badder
Green

Bent Brook

Bent
House

Sutton
Heath

Longford Brook

COMMON LA

Mount
Pleasant

SCHOOL PIECE LA

TIPPER'S LA

OLD HALL LA

BADWAY LA

LITTLEFIELD RD

SUTTON RD

7

COTE BOTTOM LA

BROUGHTON LA

BOGGY LA

Broughton
House
Farm

The Bent

33

Limbersitch Brook

WOODYARD LA

BOGGY LA

Littlemeadow La

Heath Top
Farm

Heathtop

DARK LA

BENT LA

Claypit
Hill

Limbersitch
Farm

LIMBERSITCH LA

6

Airfield
(dis)

Birchill's
Farm

5

Dove
Valley
Pk

PARK AVE

CHURCH BROUGHTON RD

Heath
House

CH

Hatton Fields
Farm

Hatton
Fields

Hoon Drive
Farm

32

PACKENHAM BVD

A511

PARK AVE

Pennywaste
Wood

Heath
Cottage
Farm

MARY LA

DE65

SUTTON LA

Newlands
Farm

4

Works

Hoon Mount
Farm

A50

UTTOXETER RD

Heath
Farm

Sycamore
Farm

CHURCH BROUGHTON RD

BREACH LA

Hockley
Farm

Hatton
House

Hoon Hall
Farm

3

31

Guinea
Farm

BROOK LA

MALTHOUSE LA

DERBY RD

UTTOXETER RD

NETHERCLOSE LA

SAWPIT LA

PH

STATION RD

PH

Birch Gr

LIME GR

The
Fields

2

YEW TREE CT

THE HAYS

BROOK CL

GRANVILLE CL

RYE FLATTS LA

THE SHIELING

BRADSHAW MDW

YEW TREE RD

Rogers

PETERS

The Firs
Farm

COOPERS CROFT

LEY CROFT

EATON CL

CHURCH MEWS

Cherry
Cottage

1

FLAX CROFT

WOODMANS
CROFT

HEATH WAY

HANBURY AVE

CLEY CL

BLOSSOM
WLK

HASSALL LA

SCROPTON RD

RUSSET CL

BRAMLEY CT

HOLM

FIELD AVE

A511

Heath Fields
Prim Sch

30

239
228

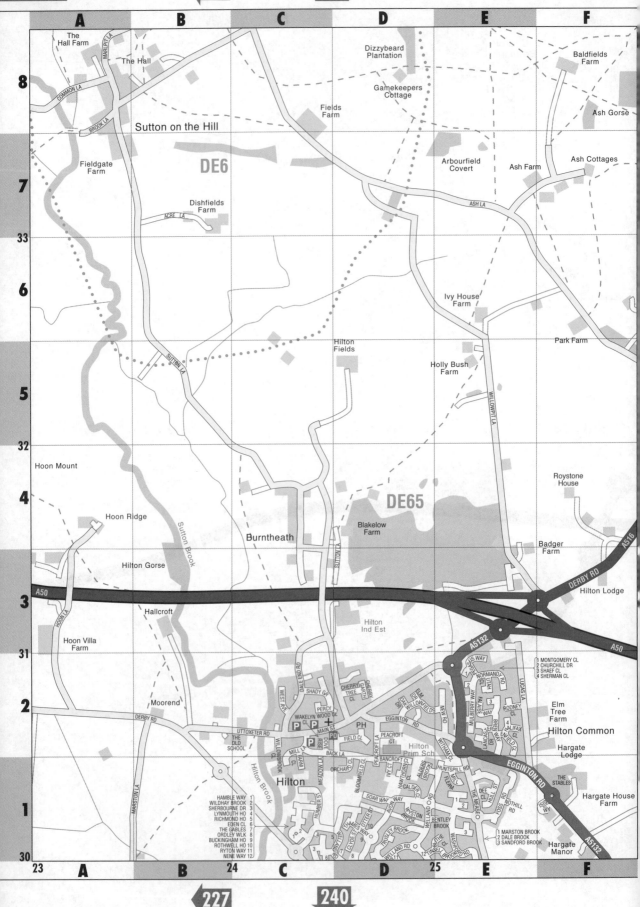

A B C D E F

8

7

33

6

5

32

4

3

31

2

1

30

The Hall Farm
The Hall
Sutton on the Hill
DE6
Fieldgate Farm
Dishfields Farm
ACRE LA
MARLPIT LA
COMMON LA
BROOK LA

Dizzybeard Plantation
Gamekeepers Cottage
Fields Farm
Arbourfield Covert
ASH LA
Ash Farm
Ash Gorse
Baldfields Farm
Ash Cottages

Ivy House Farm
Park Farm
Holly Bush Farm
WILLOWPIT LA
SUTTON LA

Hilton Fields

Hoon Mount
Hoon Ridge
Hilton Gorse
SUTTON LA
Sutton Brook
Burntheath
Blakelow Farm
DE65
Badger Farm
Roystone House
DERBY RD
A516
Hilton Lodge

A50
HOON LA
Hallcroft
Hilton Ind Est
A5132
A50

Hoon Villa Farm
Moorend
DERBY RD
UTTOXETER RD
The Old School
WILLOWBROOK
Hilton Brook
Hilton
MARSTON LA

1 Montgomery Cl
2 Churchill Dr
3 Shaef Cl
4 Sherman Cl
Elm Tree Farm
Hilton Common
Hargate Lodge
THE STABLES
Hargate House Farm
EGGINTON RD
A5132
Hargate Manor

Hilton Prim Sch
PH
WAKELYN WOOD CL
DALE END RD
WEST AVE
PERCY
SHADY GR
CHERRY TREE CL
MAIN ST
PEACROFT CT
EGGINTON RD
NEW RD

1 Hamble Way
2 Wildhay Brook
3 Sherbourne Dr
4 Lynmouth Ho
5 Richmond Ho
6 Eden Cl
7 The Gables
8 Ordley Wlk
9 Buckingham Ho
10 Rothwell Ho
11 Ryton Way
12 Nene Way

1 Marston Brook
2 Dale Brook
3 Sandford Brook

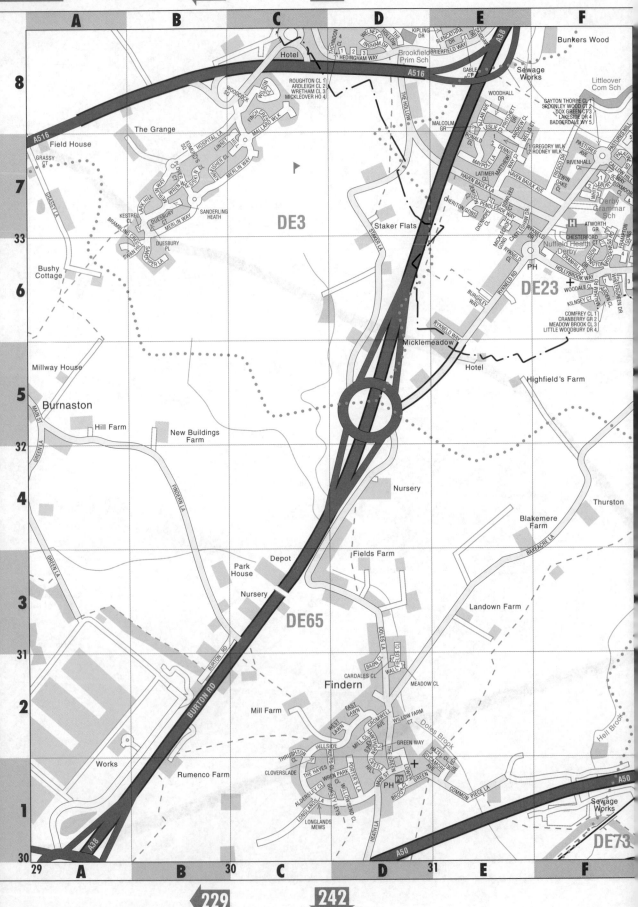

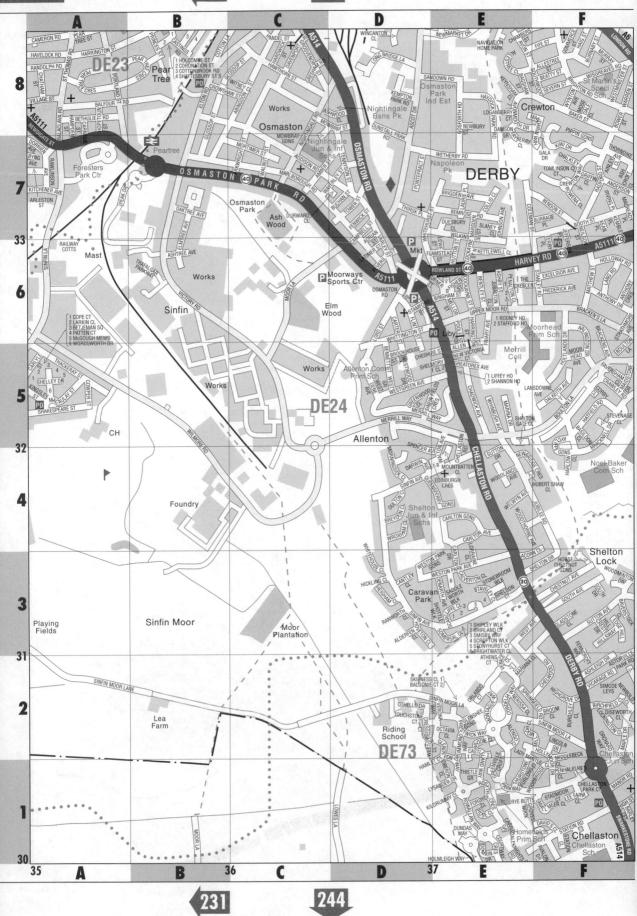

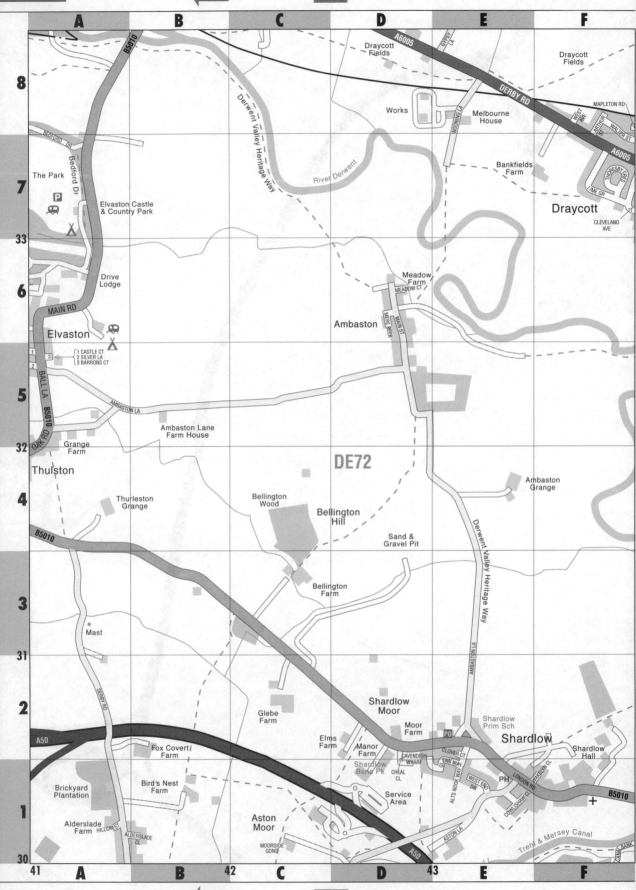

A8
1 HARTSIDE GDNS
2 PORLOCK CL
3 MICKLEDON CL
4 COTSWOLD CL
5 MALVERN GDNS
6 BRECON CL

7 BREDON CL
8 INGLEBOROUGH GDNS
9 THE PLANTATIONS
10 COPSESIDE CL

235

223

B5
1 HICKLING CL
2 WIDDOWSON RD
3 BARN CL
4 BRAMLEY RD

DE72

DERBY RD

WILSTHORPE RD
A6005

Trent Coll

Cemy

THE PINGLE 1
BENNETT ST 2
HAMILTON RD 3
ALEXANDRA RD 4
PARKLAND MEWS 6

Wilsthorpe

West Park

LONG EATON

West Park L Ctr

Golden Brook

CLUMBER ST 1
ST JOHN S ST 2
KIRKEWHITE AVE 3
KIRKEWHITE HO 4
MILTON TERR 5
KIRTON AVE 6
KILBY HO 7
WEST PARK CT 8

Stanton Vale Sch

1 HATTON CROFTS
2 SAWMAND CL
3 CLARENCE RD
4 COCKLEYS
5 OZIER HOLT

The Long Eaton Sch

Erewash Canal

Dovedale Prim Sch

Derwent Street Ind Est

New Sawley

Brooklands Prim Sch

St Laurence CE Prim Sch

Acton Road Ind Est

Works

Forbes Hole Nature Reserve

Factory

Breydon Ind Ctr

Long Eaton

Sawley Jun & Inf Schs

Sawley

1 WILNE AVE
2 CHURCH AVE
3 TRENT HO

TAMWORTH RD

PORTLAND RD

Allot Gdns

NG10

Sheets Stores Ind Est

Trent Farm

Sheetstores Junction

Narrow Bridge

Trent Rifle Lodge

South Junction

Cranfleet Farm

Trent Valley Way

Cranfleet Canal

Grounds Farm

CH

PH

Trent Junction

Trentlock

Harrington Bridge

River Trent

Club

Sailing Club

Sawley Cut

Derwent Valley Heritage Way

Sawley Bridge Marina

River Soar

Red Hill

Wood Hill

NG11

Ratcliffe on Soar Power Station

Redhill Lock

Redhill Farm

DE74

Lockington Grounds Farm

Ratcliffe Junction

235

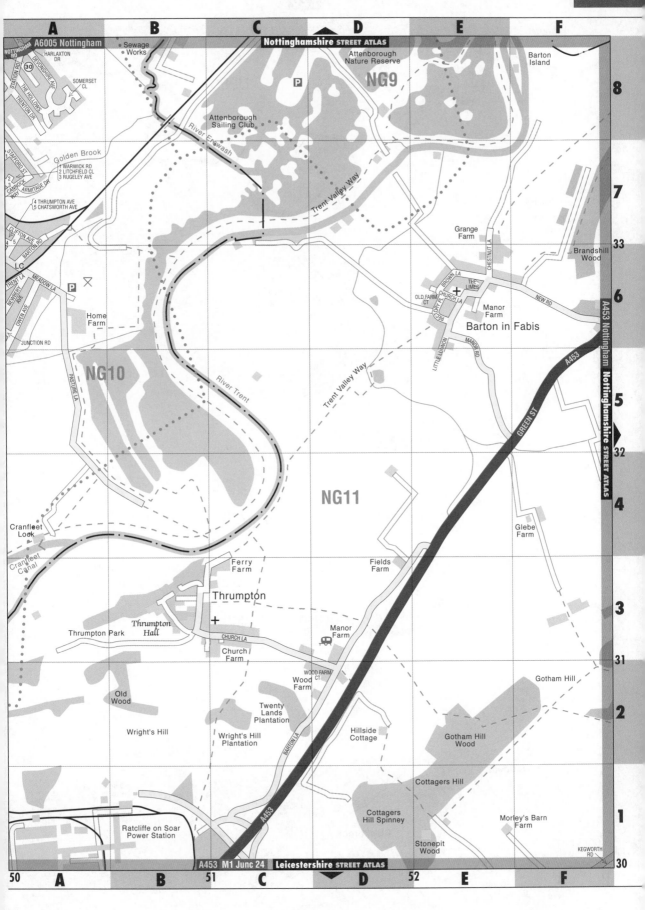

NG9

A6005 Nottingham

NOTTINGHAM RD

HARLAXTON DR

DEVONSHIRE AVE

SOMERSET CL

THE HOLLOWS

TRENTON DR

Sewage Works

Attenborough Nature Reserve

Barton Island

Golden Brook

STAFFORD ST

CANNOCK WAY

ARMITAGE DR

1 WARWICK RD
2 LITCHFIELD CL
3 RUGELEY AVE

4 THRUMPTON AVE
5 CHATSWORTH AVE

Attenborough Sailing Club

River Erewash

Trent Valley Way

Grange Farm

Brandshill Wood

CLIFTON AVE

BARTON RD

LC

NEWBERY AVE

OWEN AVE

TRENT LA

MEADOW LA

Home Farm

JUNCTION RD

PASTURE LA

NG10

River Trent

Trent Valley Way

CHESTNUT LA

BROWN LA

THE LIMES

OLD FARM CT

CHURCH LA

Manor Farm

NEW RD

Barton in Fabis

LITTLE LINDON

MANOR RD

A453 Nottingham

GREEN ST

A453

Trent Valley Way

NG11

Glebe Farm

Cranfleet Lock

Cranfleet Canal

Ferry Farm

Thrumpton

Fields Farm

Thrumpton Park

Thrumpton Hall

CHURCH LA

Manor Farm

Gotham Hill

Church Farm

WOOD FARM CT

Wood Farm

Old Wood

Twenty Lands Plantation

BARTON LA

Hillside Cottage

Gotham Hill Wood

Wright's Hill

Wright's Hill Plantation

Cottagers Hill

Cottagers Hill Spinney

Morley's Barn Farm

A453

Ratcliffe on Soar Power Station

Stonepit Wood

KEGWORTH RD

50 A B 51 C D 52 E F

8 7 33 6 5 32 4 3 31 2 1 30

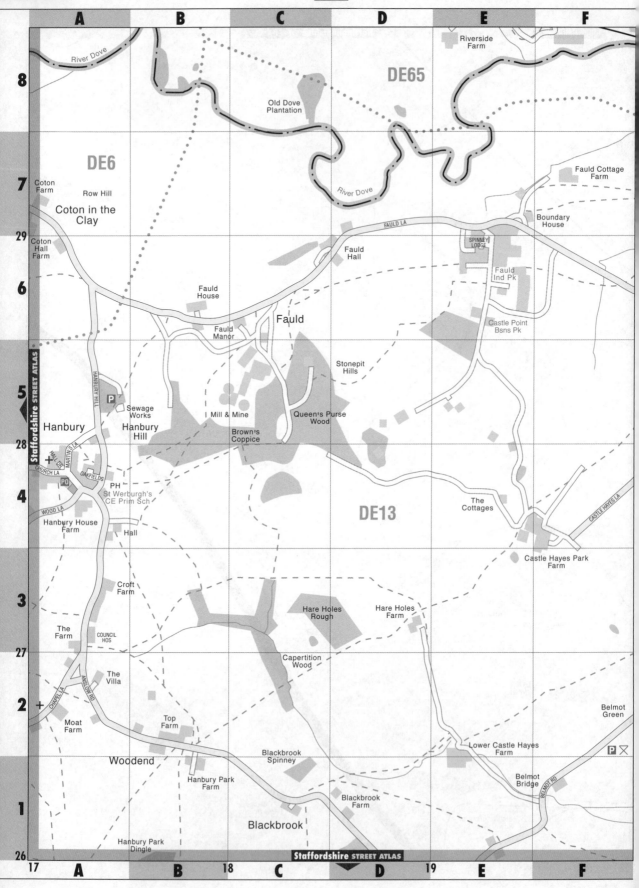

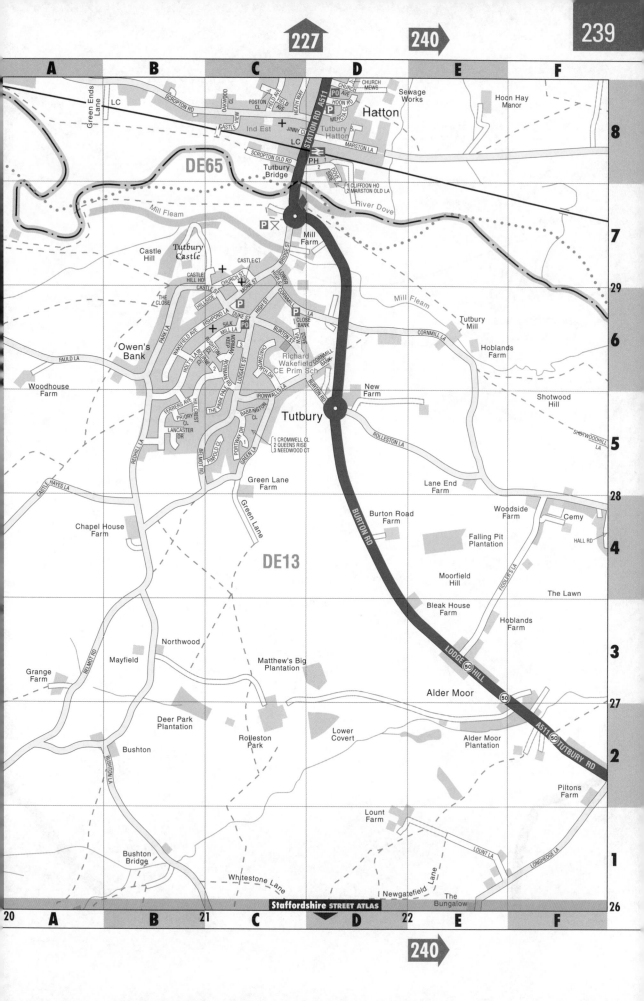

DE65

Hilton

Marston on Dove

Ivy House Farm

The Hall

Dove Bank Farm

Marston LC

SHERBOURNE DR

WINDRUSH RD 1
RIBBLE CL 2
SEVERN DR 3
WYE CL 4
CHURNET RD 5

Depot

Birch-trees Farm

PH

Egginton Junction

Derby Airfield

Hilton Brook

Dove Bridge

Old River Dove

River Dove

Mill Fleam

Works

Home Farm Park Homes

1 BLADON'S YD
2 BLACKSMITHS YD

Ford

Netherfield Grange

PH

Rolleston

1 THE PADDOCK
2 MOSLEY MEWS

John of Rolleston Prim Sch

NEEDWOOD AVE 1
GARRATT SQ 2
FOREST SCHOOL ST 3

STATION RD

MEADOW VIEW

TWENTYLANDS

Sunnymead Farm

Rolleston on Dove

DE13

Dove Cliff

PH

CH

Cross Farm

Beacon Hill

Cross La

Field Grove Farm

Nature Trail

Sunnymead Farm

Darfoulde House

Craythorne Farm

Craythorne

LOHENGRIN CT 1
CAMELOT CL 2
KNIGHTS CT 3
TARQUIN CL 4

William Shrewsbury Prim Sch

Beam Hill

LONGHEDGE LA

TUTBURY RD
A511

1 BARRINGTON CL
2 DEVERON CL

RENE CL

SEVERN CL

GLENEAGLES DR

ATHELSTAN WAY

FARADAY AVE 1
SPENCER CL 2

Stretton

Station Walk

Fountains High Sch

Fountains Prim Sch

HAREHEDGE LA

BITHAM LA

Works

E1
1 PRINCESS WAY
2 CARISBROOKE DR
3 BRIDGE FARM
4 CHILTON CT

F1
1 ALDERHOLME DR
2 MANTON CL

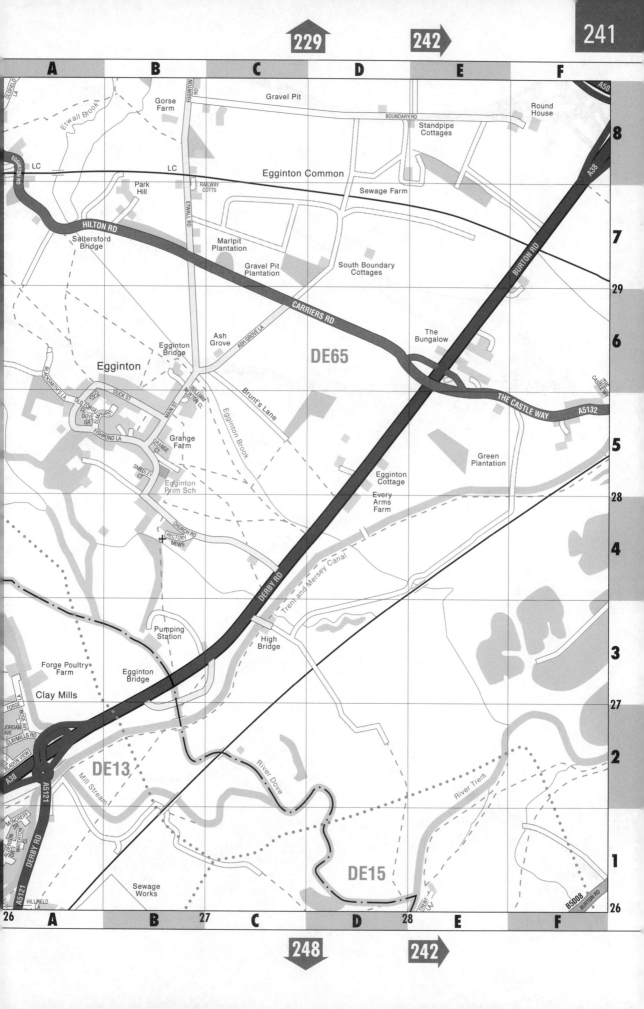

241
230

241
249

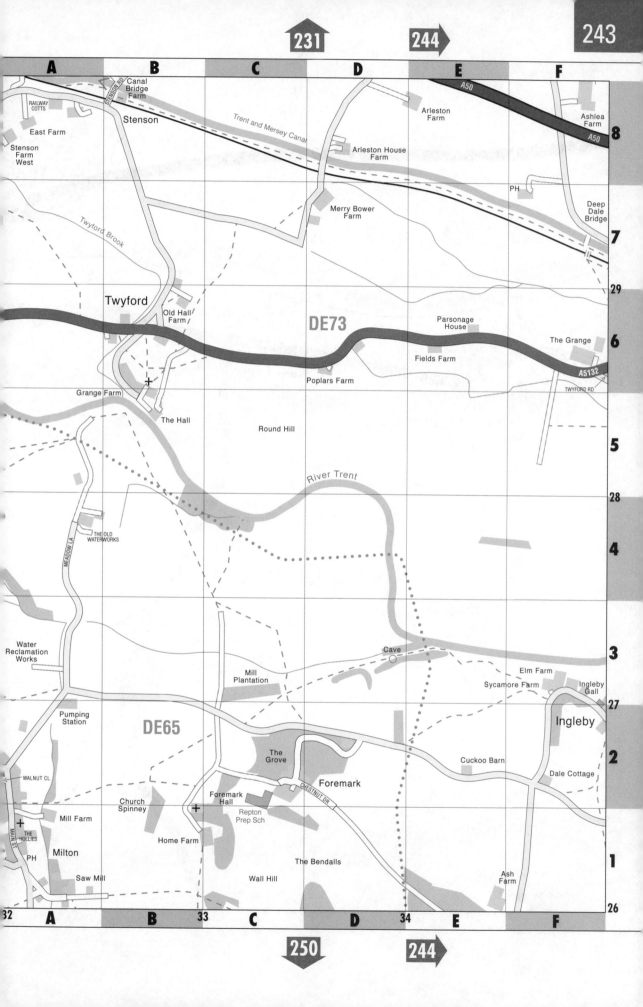

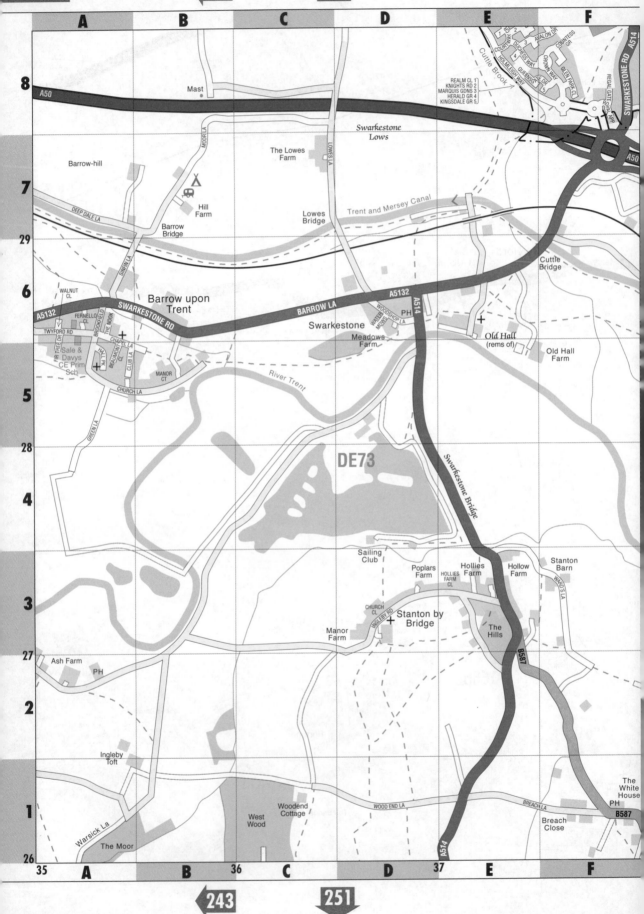

A50

Mast

Barrow-hill

The Lowes
Farm

LOWES LA

Swarkestone
Lows

Cuttle Brook

SWARKESTONE RD

A514

COUNTRY DR
DUCHESS WAY
HOLMLEIGH WAY
QUEENS GR
AVALON DR
CROWN WAY
GLEN PARK CL
COUNTESS GR
REGAL GATEWAY APP

REALM CL 1
KNIGHTS RD 2
MARQUIS GDNS 3
HERALD GR 4
KINGSDALE GR 5

A50

8

DEEP DALE LA

Hill
Farm

Barrow
Bridge

Lowes
Bridge

Trent and Mersey Canal

Cuttle
Bridge

7

29

SINFIN LA

MOOR LA

WALNUT
CL

Barrow upon
Trent

A5132

BARROW LA

A5132

WOODSHOP LA
WATER
MDWS LA

PH

Meadows
Farm

Swarkestone

A514

Old Hall
(rems of)

Old Hall
Farm

6

TWYFORD RD
FERNELLO
CL
BROOKFIELD
THE NOOK
FIR TREE DR
Sale &
Davys
CE Prim
Sch
CHAPEL LA
HALL LA
BEAUMONT
CL
CLUB LA
MANOR
CT

CHURCH LA

River Trent

5

GREEN LA

28

DE73

4

Swarkestone Bridge

Sailing
Club

Poplars
Farm

HOLLIES
FARM
CL

Hollies
Farm

Hollow
Farm

Stanton
Barn

WARD'S LA

3

27

Ash Farm

PH

CHURCH
CL

INGLEBY RD

Manor
Farm

Stanton by
Bridge

The
Hills

B587

2

Ingleby
Toft

1

Warsick La

The Moor

West
Wood

Woodend
Cottage

WOOD END LA

BREACH LA

A514

B587

Breach
Close

The
White
House
PH

B587

26

35

A B 36 C D 37 E F

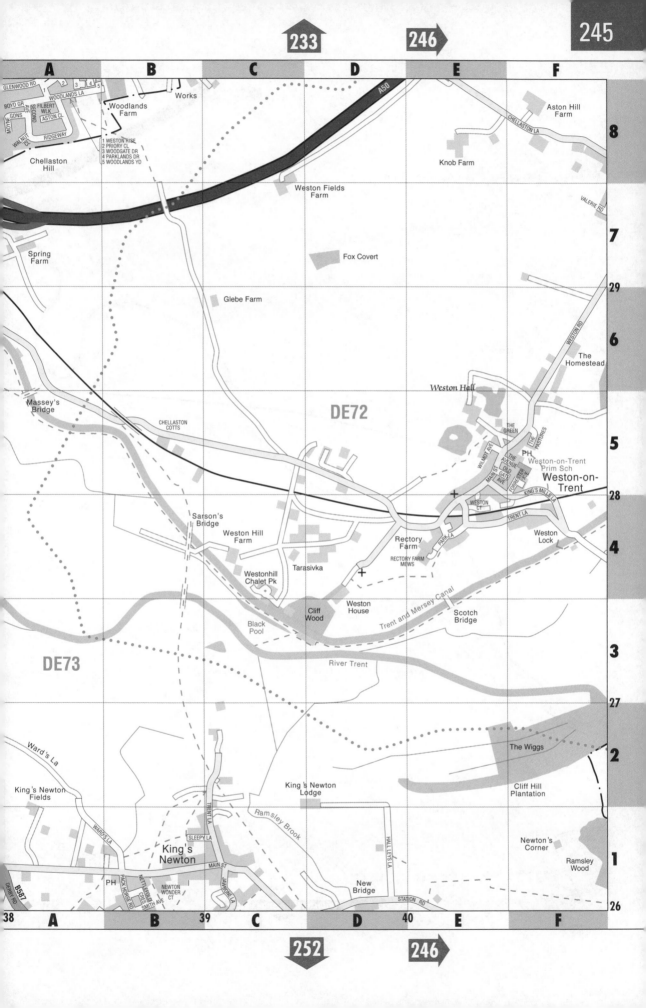

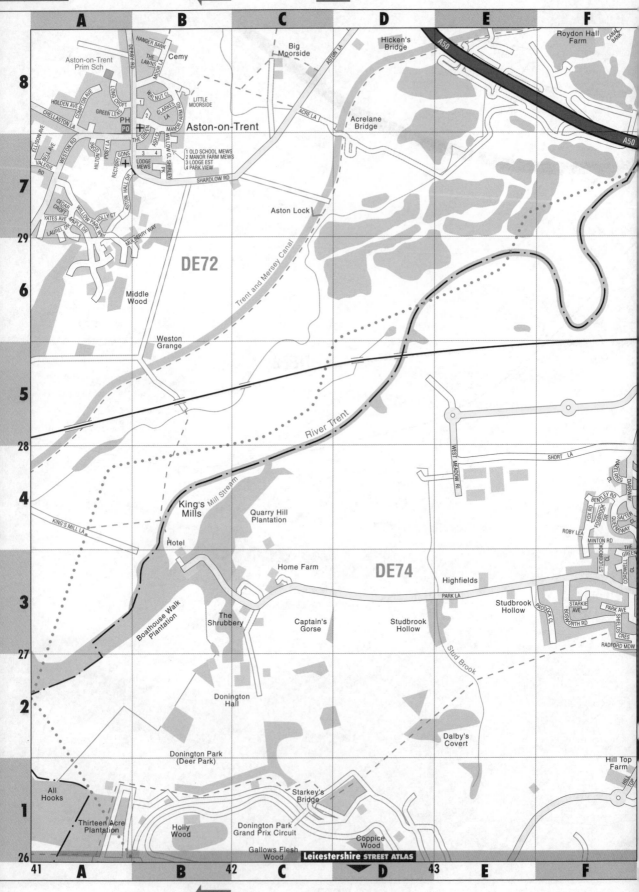

Leicestershire STREET ATLAS

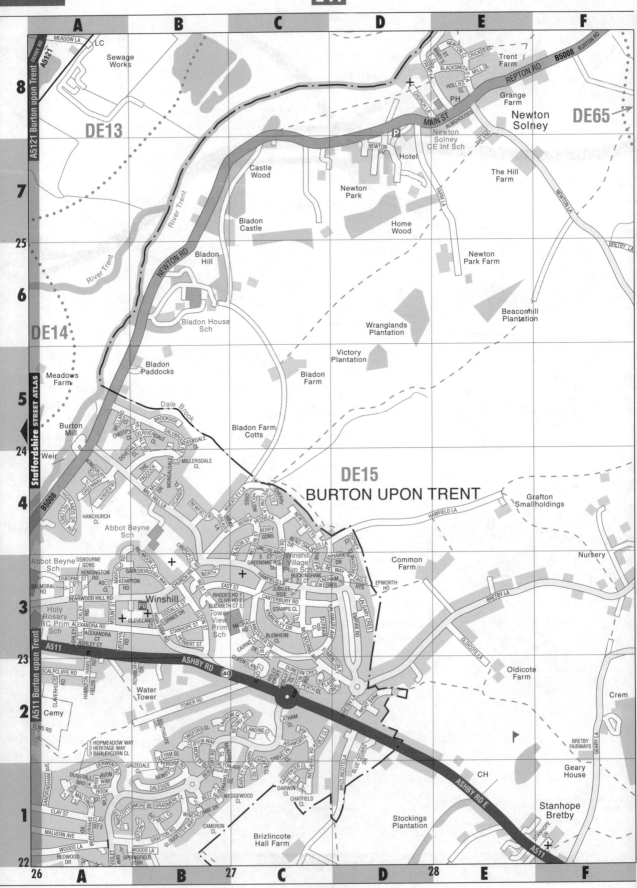

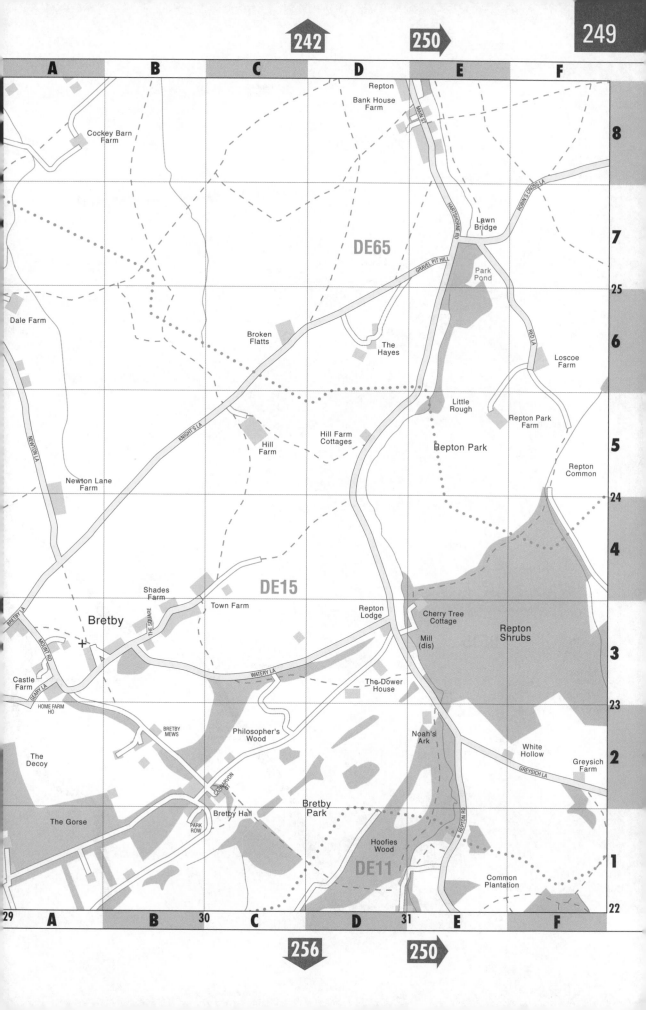

249
243

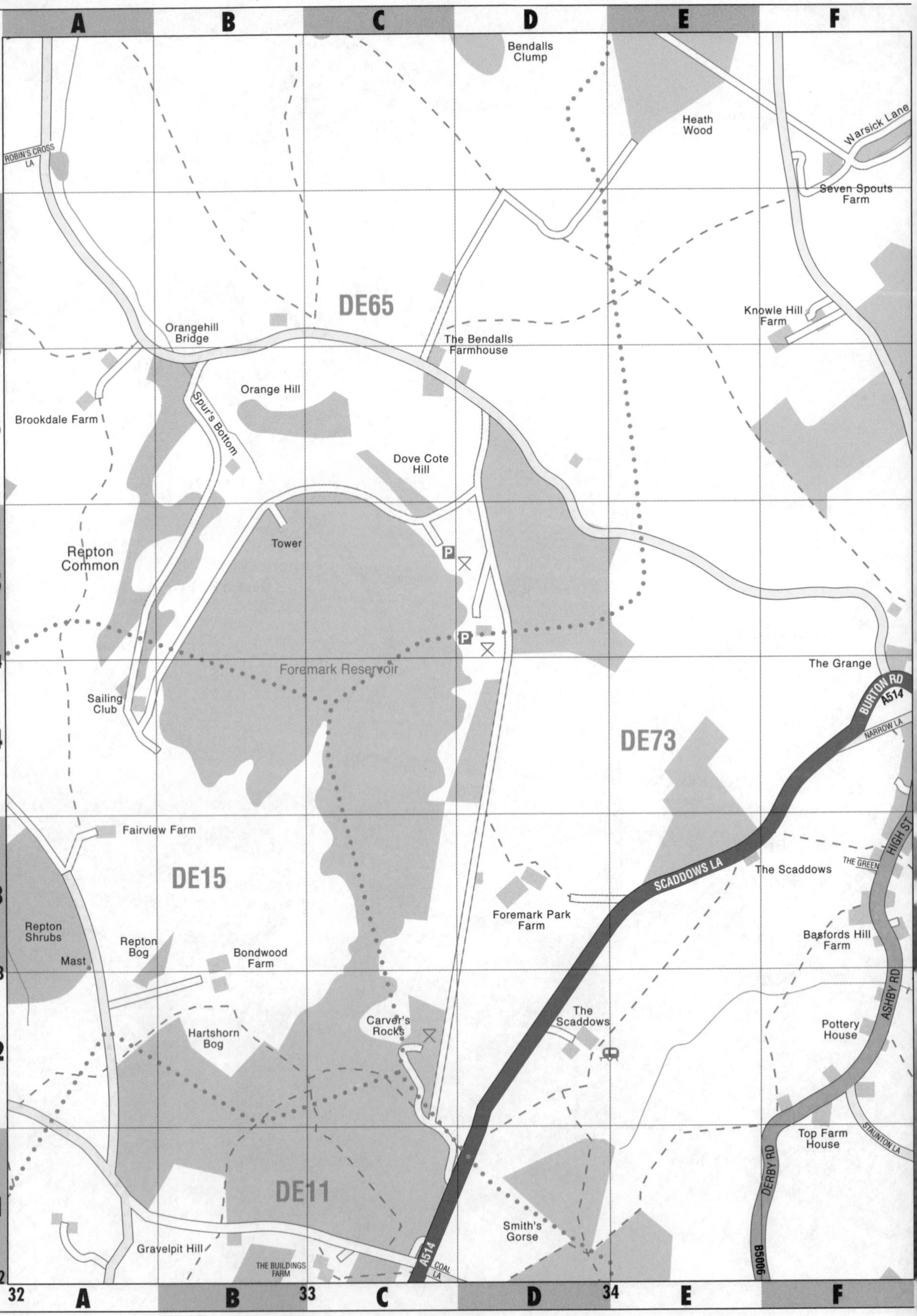

A **B** **C** **D** **E** **F**

8

ROBIN'S CROSS LA

Warsick Lane

Bendalls Clump

Heath Wood

Seven Spouts Farm

7

DE65

Knowle Hill Farm

Orangehill Bridge

25

The Bendalls Farmhouse

Orange Hill

Brookdale Farm

Spur's Bottom

6

Dove Cote Hill

Repton Common

Tower

P

5

P

24

Foremark Reservoir

The Grange

BURTON RD A514

NARROW LA

Sailing Club

DE73

4

DE15

Fairview Farm

HIGH ST

THE GREEN

The Scaddows

SCADDOWS LA

ASHBY RD

3

Foremark Park Farm

Basfords Hill Farm

Repton Shrubs

Mast

Repton Bog

Bondwood Farm

23

The Scaddows

Pottery House

Hartshorn Bog

Carver's Rocks

2

DERBY RD

Top Farm House

STAUNTON LA

1

DE11

Smith's Gorse

B5006

Gravelpit Hill

A514

COAL LA

22

THE BUILDINGS FARM

32 **A** **B** **33** **C** **D** **34** **E** **F**

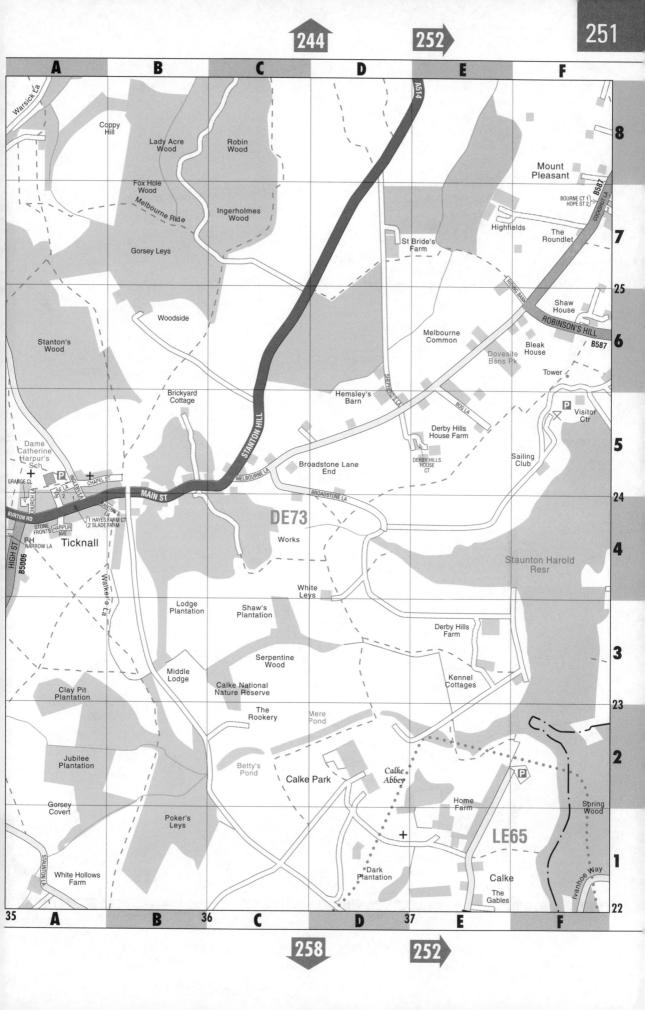

A8
1 LOAKE CT
2 THE CROFT
3 REDWAY CROFT
4 LAMPAD CL

251 245

A B C D E F

Leicestershire STREET ATLAS

WOODLANDS CL
MELTON AVE
WINDSOR AVE
SMITH AVE
Cemy
NOTTINGDON WAY
JAWBONE LA
STATION RD
MAIN ST
Station Rd
PH
Station Yd
Carr Brook
Melbourne View
Station Rd

8

B587
COCKSHUT LA
ACACIA DR
BENBOW AVE
DRAKE CL
HARDACRE
BLACKTHORN
DERBY RD
OAKLANDS WAY
GRANGE CL
QUEENSWAY
BLACKMORE AVE
Melbourne Inf Sch
Melbourne Jun Sch
Melbourne
Ramsley Brook

Cockshut La Bsns Ctr
Lilypool
THE LILYPOOLS
HOPE CT
COMMERCE ST
UNION ST
VICTORIA ST
NORTH ST
SOUTH ST
KINGS ST
GEORGE ST
THOMAS
MOIRA ST
QUICK CL
DUNNICLIFFE LA
BEECH AVE
CHAPEL ST
JUBILEE CL
PALMERSTON ST
CASTLE LA
CASTLE ST
P
PH THE MEWS
FORTY FOOT LA

7
New York
ORCHARD CL
THE PINGLE
HATTON CT
WASHINGTON CL
SELINA ST
HIGH ST
THOMAS COOK
MARKET ST
PENN LA
POTTER ST
CHURCH ST
BISHOP
P
Liby
Melbourne L Ctr
CASTLE MILLS
BLACKWELL LA
CASTLE MEWS
1 CHURCH MEWS
2 POTTERS YD
3 CHANTRY CL
4 SALISBURY LA

25
ASHBY RD
PENISTON ST
RISE
CHURCH SQ
Melbourne Hall & Gardens
WILSON RISE
SHORT HILL
SLADE LA

6
B587
ROBINSON'S HILL
The Pool
POOL RD
Nurseries
MAIN ST
PH
BULL'S HEAD ROW
DOB LA
Wilson

The Intake
CALKE RD
Pool Farm
Chestnut Park
GREEN LA
CH

5
Woodhouses
Woodhouse Farm
DE73
Park Farm
Quarry Wood

24
Staunton Harold Reservoir
Works
Melbourne Parks

4
High Wood
The Common Farm
Square Plantation
Paddock Pool
Hobbes' Hole
P
The Bulwarks Fort
TONGE LA

3
Melbourne Plantation
The Coppice
Gorse Covert
Breedon Hill
SOURRELL LA
MANOR CT

23
Coppice Nook
GREEN LA
HOLLOW LA
RECTORY RD
THE DELPH
PO
HILLSIDE
CHURCH ST
MAIN ST
TATWIN CL
THE DOVECOTE CL
FRAIN GDNS
St Hardulphs CE Prim Sch
DOCTORS LA

2
BURNEY LA
THE CRESCENT
HASTINGS
LOVEYS CROFT
STUDFARM CL
THE LIME KILNS
SAXON CL
Breedon on the Hill

1
Spring Wood
Scotland
ASHBY RD
SOUTHWORTH RD
NOTTINGHAM RD
WORTHINGTON LA
Charity Farm

Springwood Farm
Ivanhoe Way
Scotlands Farm
LE65
LE65
A42 Ashby-de-la-Zouch
A42 M1 Junc 23A

22
B587

38 A B 39 C D 40 E F

251

Tatenhill

DARK LA →

PH Manor Farm

MANOR CROFT

CORONATION COTTS

Yews Bridge

Robinson's Plantation

Brookfields Farm

Lawns Farm Cottage

Branston Lock

EIGHTH AVE Superstore

Bean's Covert

Branston

Centrum East Ret Pk

CROWN SQ

FARADAY CT

Ryknield Prim Sch

Branston Bridge

Branston Water Park

DE14

Hotel

F7
1 BLENHEIM HO
2 CHATSWORTH HO
3 REGENTS HO

Drakelow Nature Reserve

Black Meadow Wood

Tatenhill Lock

Works

Gallow Bridge

Works

Ppg Sta

Works

The Way for the Millennium

Trent & Mersey Canal

Works

LICHFIELD RD

Gorsehall Plantation

DE13

Drakelow Power Station

DE15

River Trent

Newbold Manor Farm

Sewage Works

Warren Hill

Warren Farm

DE12

Graycar Bsns Pk

Motel

Rylance Farm

B5016

STATION RD B5016

WHARF HOS

PH

BARTON TURN

A38

Barton Turn

Walton Bridge

STATION LA

RIVERSIDE

Barr Hall

Walton-on-Trent

MEWIES CL

PH

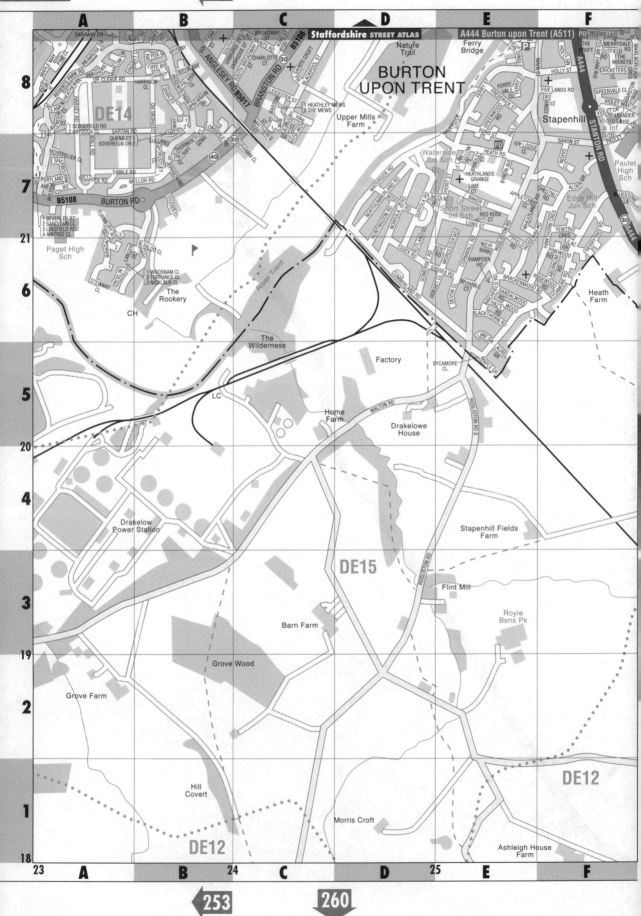

253

Staffordshire STREET ATLAS

A444 Burton upon Trent (A511)

BURTON UPON TRENT

Stapenhill

DE14

DE15

DE12

DE12

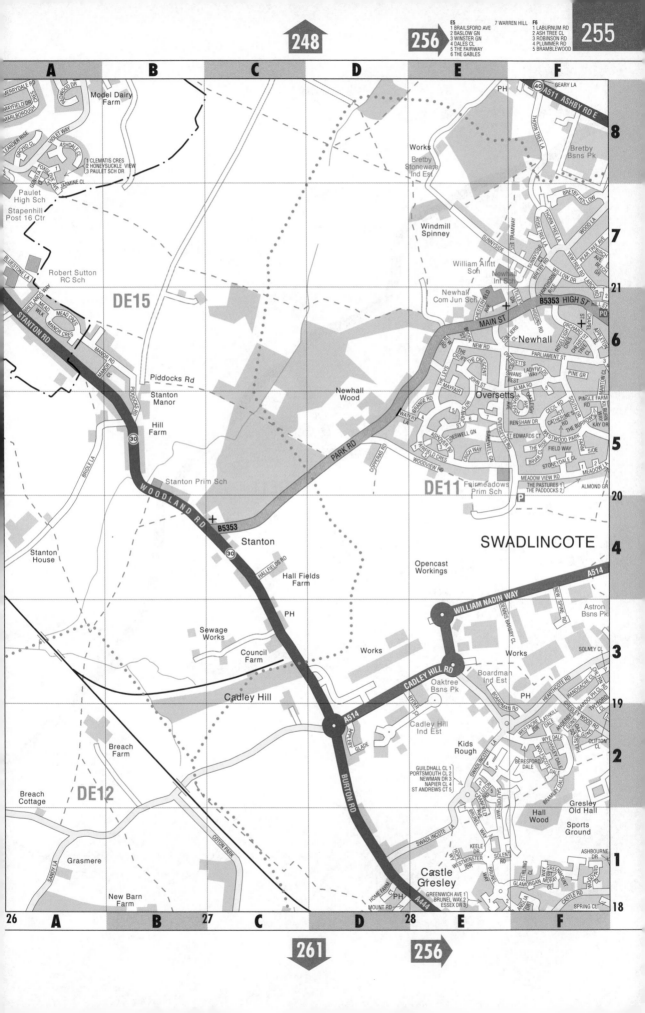

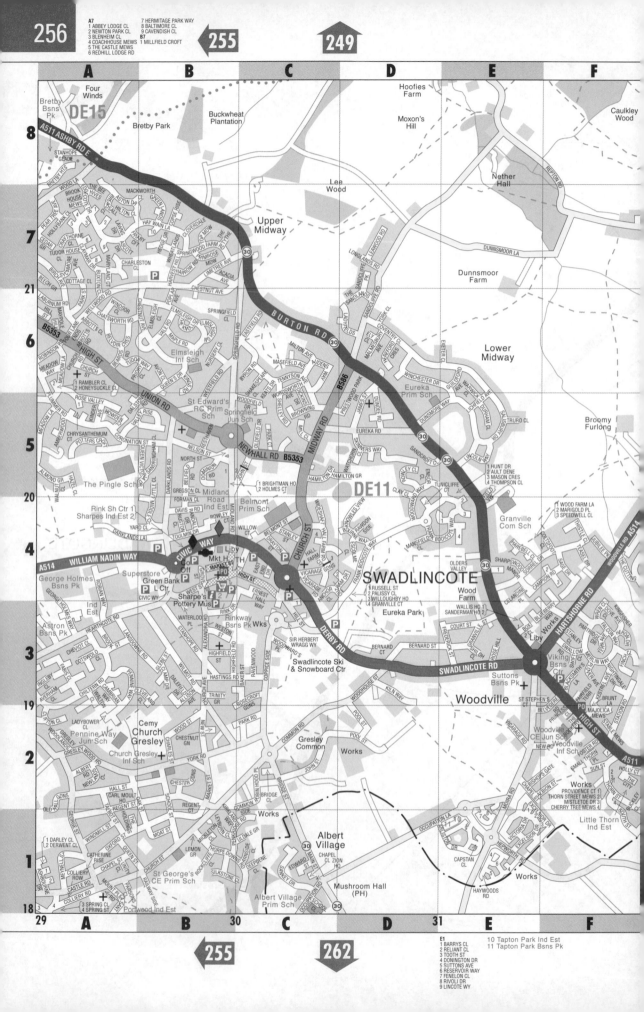

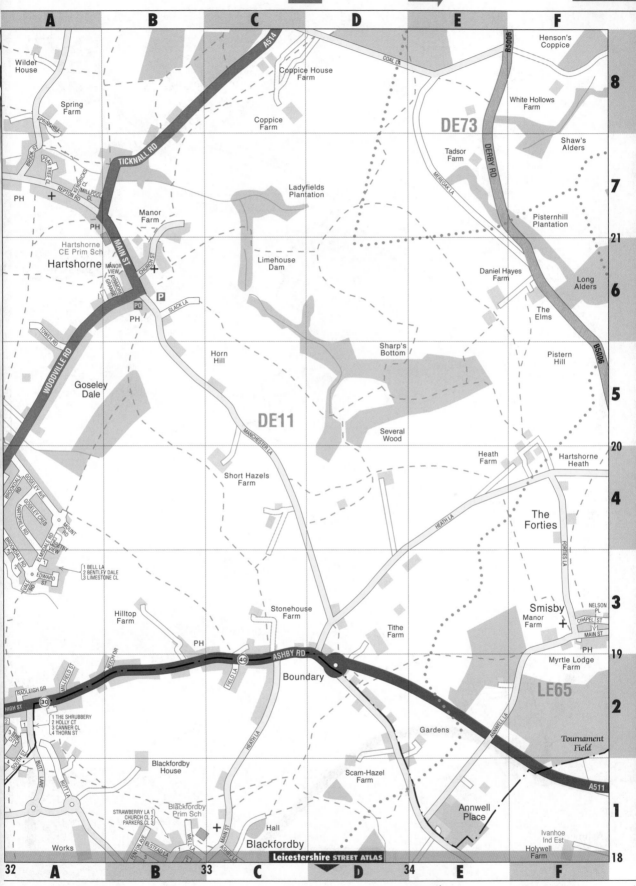

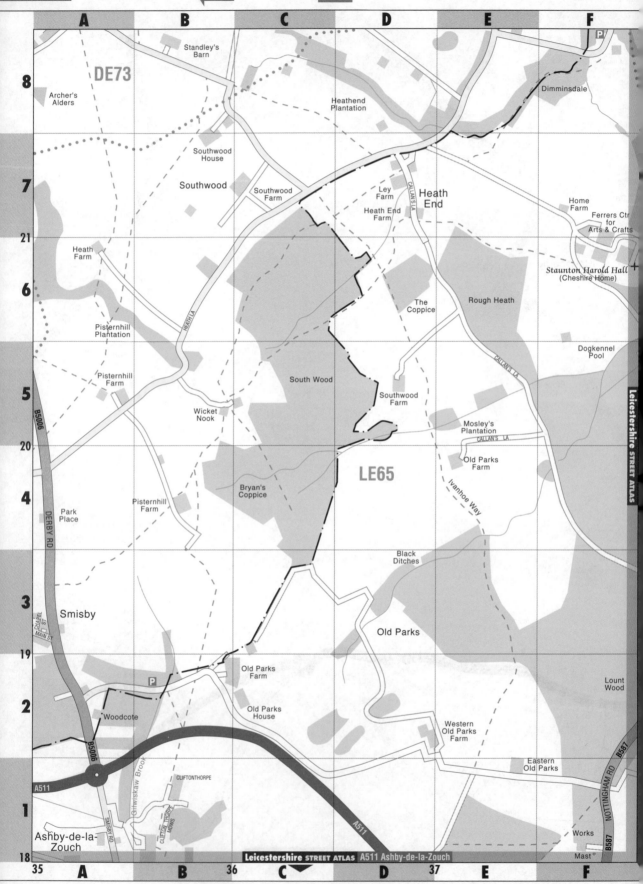

DE73

Archer's
Alders

Standley's
Barn

Heathend
Plantation

Dimminsdale

8

Southwood
House

Southwood

Southwood
Farm

Ley
Farm

Heath
End

Heath End
Farm

Home
Farm

Ferrers Ctr
for
Arts & Crafts

7

21

Heath
Farm

Staunton Harold Hall
(Cheshire Home)

6

Pisternhill
Plantation

HEATH LA

The Coppice

Rough Heath

Dogkennel
Pool

Pisternhill
Farm

South Wood

Southwood
Farm

CALLAN'S LA

5

B5006

Wicket
Nook

Mosley's
Plantation

CALLAN'S LA

20

LE65

Old Parks
Farm

4

Park
Place

Pisternhill
Farm

Bryan's
Coppice

Ivanhoe Way

DERBY RD

Black
Ditches

3

Smisby

Old Parks

19

Old Parks
Farm

Lount
Wood

B5006

2

P

Woodcote

Old Parks
House

Western
Old Parks
Farm

NOTTINGHAM RD

B587

A511

Gilwiskaw Brook

CLIFTONTHORPE

CLIFTON THORPE MDWS

SMISBY RD

Eastern
Old Parks

B587

1

Ashby-de-la-
Zouch

A511

Works

Mast

18

35   A   B   36   C   D   37   E   F

Leicestershire STREET ATLAS

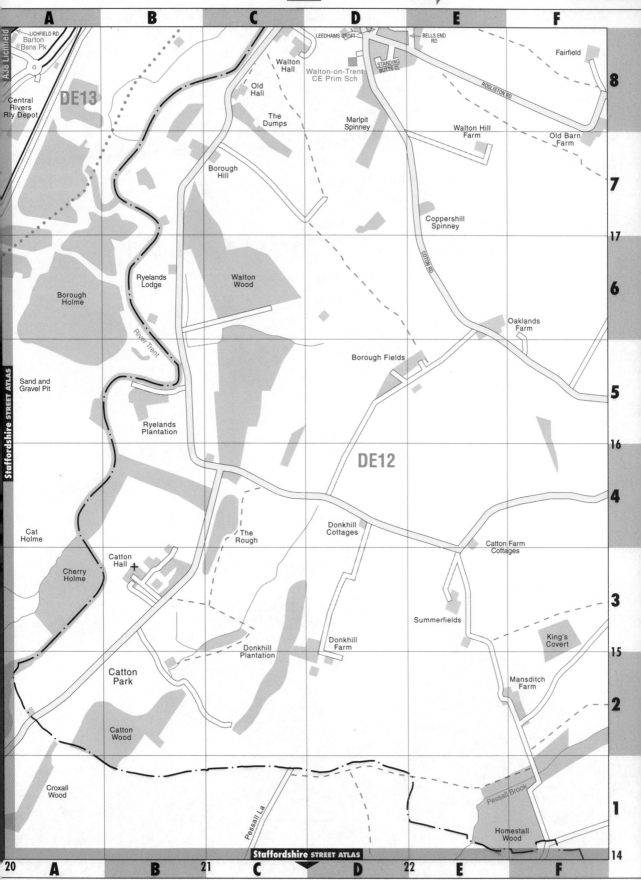

259
254

A **B** **C** **D** **E** **F**

DE15

8

ROSLISTON RD

Corner Farm

Nursery

Rosliston Forestry Ctr

Priory Farm

SANDY LA

Walton Lane Farm

Fox Covert

Caldwell

MAIN ST

Manor Farm

7

Calves Croft Farm

CHURCH LA

Pegasus Sch

17

Moonraker

THE CHASE

BURTON RD

Rosliston CE Prim Sch

Rosliston

Caldwell Covert

CAULDWELL RD

PH

6

HOLDON CROFT

PO

THE GLEBE

GARAGE WLK

YEW TREE RD

MAIN ST

YEW TREE GDNS

NEW ST

STRAWBERRY LA

LINTON RD

Blakenhall Farm

CATTON LA

5

COTON RD

Field House Farm

Beehive Farm

P

16

DE12

Longfurlong Farm

P

Lads Grave

4

Coton in the Elms

BURTON RD

Pessall Brook

P

Overfields Farm

Church Croft

Coton in the Elms CE Prim Sch

COTON LA

Church Farm

ELMS RD

CHAPMANS CROFT

COTON LA

3

GREENACRE PK

GLEBE CL

ELMS LA

MAIN ST

CHAPEL ST

COALPIT LA

CROFT FLATS LA

Church Flatts Farm

15

CHURCH ST

NEW RD

MILL ST

PH

HILL GREEN CL

Malt House Farm

Pessall Brook

2

Raddle Farm Wood

LITTLE LIVERPOOL

Pessall Brook

1

The Crosses

Grafton House

14

23 **A** **B** 24 **C** **D** 25 **E** **F**

255 262

A B C D E F

8

7

17

6

5

16

4

3

15

2

1

14

DE11

High Cross
Bank

Mount
Pleasant

DE12

Hill Crest
Farm

Badger
Wood

Coton
Park

Sewage
Works

Grange
Farm

Manor
Farm

Linton

Foxley
Wood

Greenfields

Waterfallows
Farm

Linton
Heath

Grangewood
Gdns

Linton
Prim Sch

Longlands

Cauldwell Rd

PH

Green Field Dr

Pear Tree Dr

Chesterfield Dr

The Crest

Seal View

Cedar Gr

The Close

Princess Ave

Charlton Cl

Warren Dr

High St

Park Cl

Hillside Rd

Sycamore Dr

Windsor Rd

Patrick Cl

Emery Cl

Helston Cl

Main St

Weathern Field

Colliery La

Woodside
Farm

Sealwood La

Sealwood La

Sealwood
Farm

Middle
Hayes
Farm

Green La

Sealwood La

Green La

Lullington Rd

Top Wood

Botany Bay
Farm

Park Farm

Potter's
Wood

Grange
Wood

Gunby Hill

Green La

Gunby
Lea

Grangewood
Zoo

Craft Ctr

Grangewood
Hall

Gunby
Farm

Lodge Rd

Woodfields
Farm

Grangewood
Lodge

Grangewood

Woodside
Farm

Grenvue

Mount Rd

The Scotts

Coton Pk

Burton Rd

Burton Rd

Mount Pleasant Rd

Linton Rd

Arnold Cl

Castle Croft

Bridge Cross St

Chapel St

Arthur St

Cedar Rd

Bass's Cres

Pine Wlk

Oak Cl

High Cross

Fields La

Burton Rd A444

A444 Burton Rd

Knob Fields

Essex Dr

Buckingham Dr

Brunel Wlk

Castle Rd

Princess St

Anglia Dr

Station St

Fox Field

The Linnet
Independent
Learning Ctr

PO

PH

PH

PO

P

P

P

Sandy La

26 A B 27 C D 28 E F

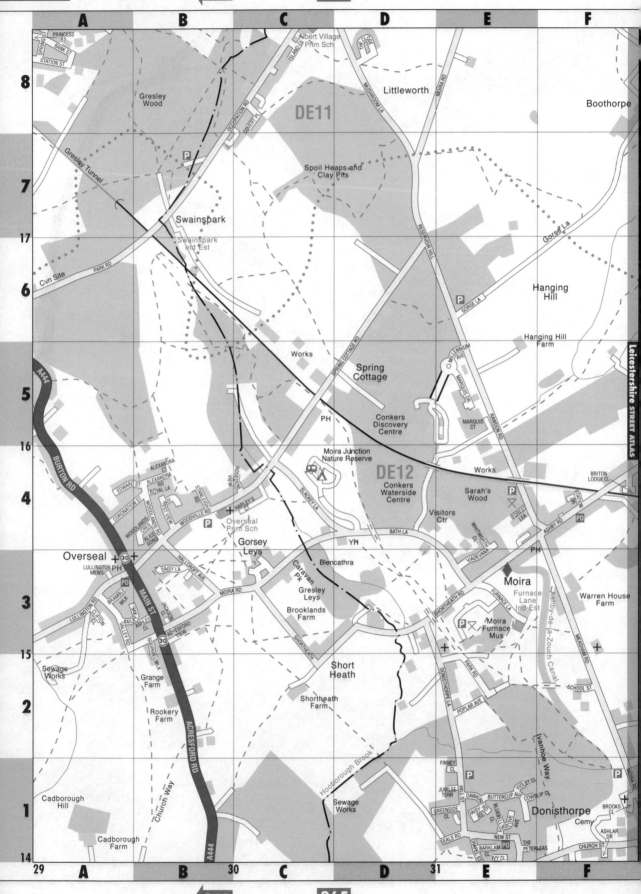

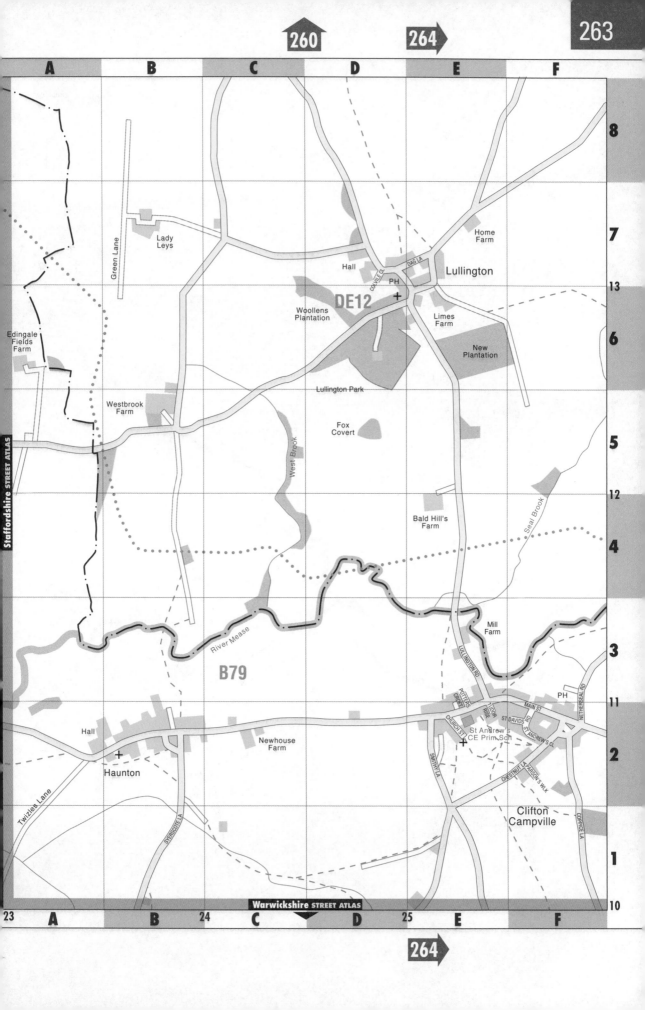

A B C D E F

8
7
13
6
5
12
4
3
11
2
1
10

Staffordshire STREET ATLAS

Green Lane
Lady Leys
Home Farm
Hall
DAG LA
Lullington
DA VILE CL
PH
DE12
Woollens Plantation
Limes Farm
New Plantation
Edingale Fields Farm
Westbrook Farm
Lullington Park
Fox Covert
West Brook
Bald Hill's Farm
Seal Brook
River Mease
B79
Mill Farm
LULLINGTON RD
Hall
Newhouse Farm
POTTERS CROFT
TUDOR RISE
MAIN ST
PH
ST DAVIDS RD
NETHERSEAL RD
CHURCH ST
St Andrew's CE Prim Sch
ST ANDREW'S CL
Haunton
SMITHY LA
CHESTNUT LA
PARSON'S WLK
Twizles Lane
SYERSCOTE LA
Clifton Campville
COPPICE LA

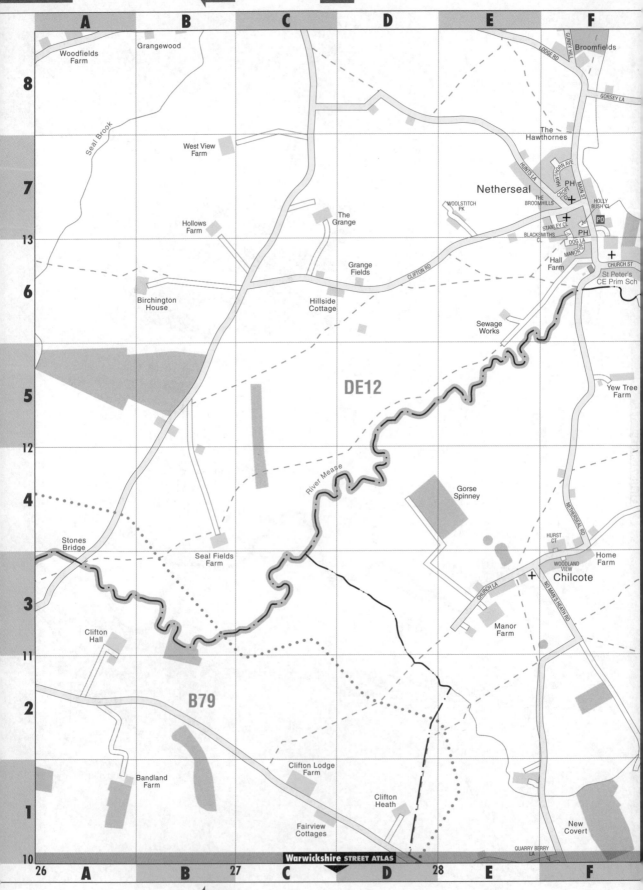

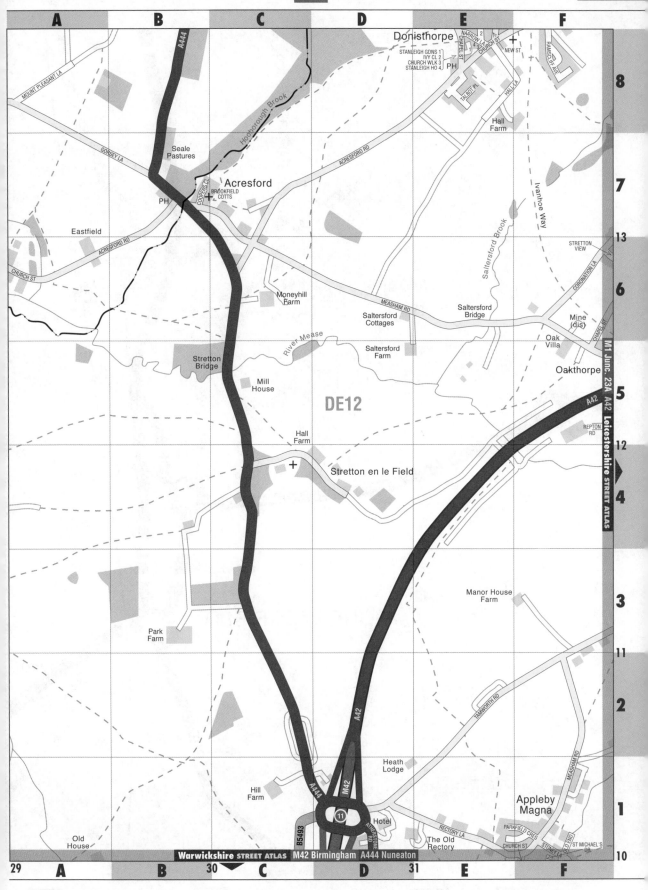

Donisthorpe

STANLEIGH GDNS 1
IVY CL 2
CHURCH WLK 3
STANLEIGH HO 4

NEW ST

Hall Farm

Acresford

Seale Pastures

BROOKFIELD COTTS

PH

Eastfield

Church St

Mount Pleasant La

Gorsey La

Acresford Rd

Coopers Cl

Ivanhoe Way

Saltersford Brook

Stretton View

Coronation La

Chapel St

Mine (dis)

Oak Villa

Oakthorpe

M1 Junc. 23A   A42   Leicestershire STREET ATLAS

Moneyhill Farm

Saltersford Cottages

Measham Rd

Saltersford Bridge

River Mease

Stretton Bridge

Saltersford Farm

Mill House

DE12

Hall Farm

Stretton en le Field

A42

Repton Rd

Park Farm

Manor House Farm

Tamworth Rd

A42

A444

Hill Farm

Heath Lodge

Appleby Magna

Measham Rd

M42

Parkfield Cres

Hotel

The Old Rectory

Rectory La

Church St

St Michael's Dr

Stoney La

B5493

Old House

11

Atherstone Rd

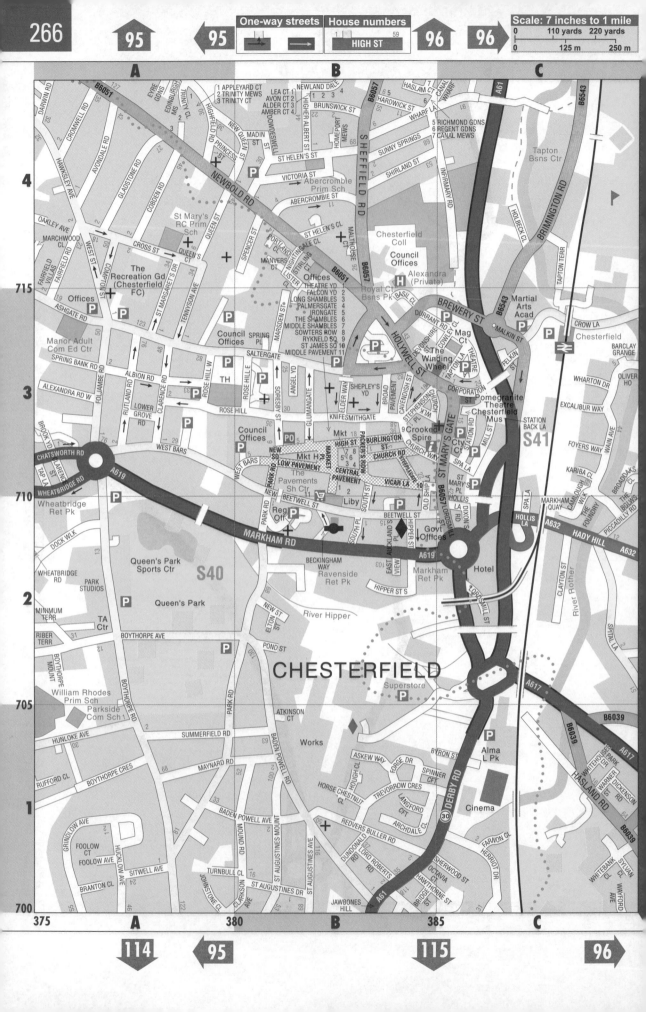

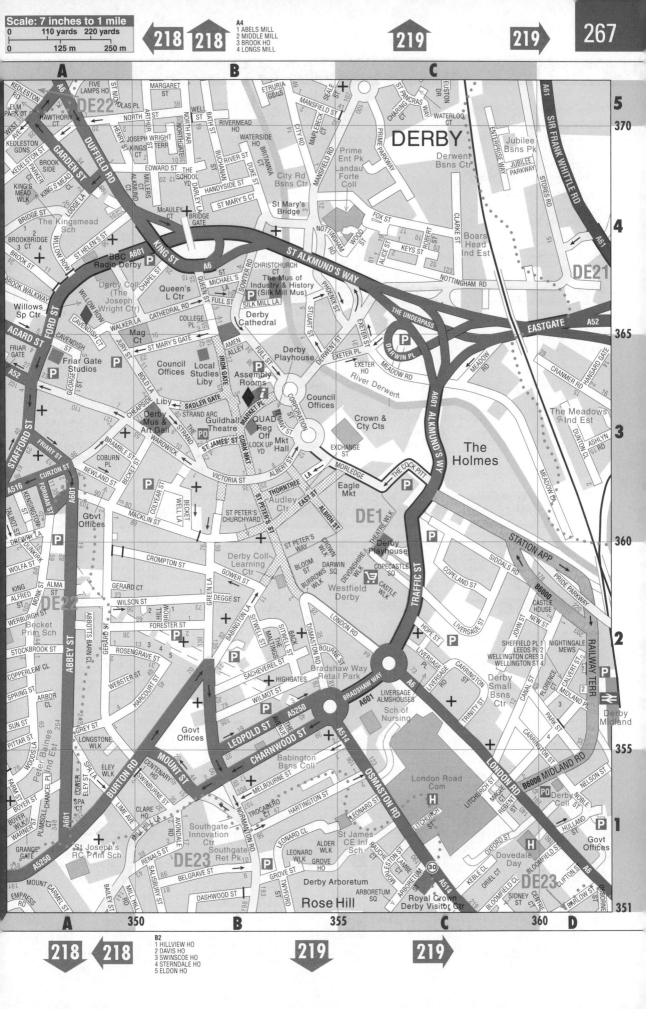

Index

Place name May be abbreviated on the map

Church Rd 6 Beckenham BR2.........**53** C6

Location number Present when a number indicates the place's position in a crowded area of mapping

Locality, town or village Shown when more than one place has the same name

Postcode district District for the indexed place

Page and grid square Page number and grid reference for the standard mapping

Cities, towns and villages are listed in CAPITAL LETTERS

Public and commercial buildings are highlighted in magenta   **Places of interest** are highlighted in blue with a star★

Abbreviations used in the index

Acad	Academy	Comm	Common	Gd	Ground	L	Leisure	Prom	Promenade
App	Approach	Cott	Cottage	Gdn	Garden	La	Lane	Rd	Road
Arc	Arcade	Cres	Crescent	Gn	Green	Liby	Library	Recn	Recreation
Ave	Avenue	Cswy	Causeway	Gr	Grove	Mdw	Meadow	Ret	Retail
Bglw	Bungalow	Ct	Court	H	Hall	Meml	Memorial	Sh	Shopping
Bldg	Building	Ctr	Centre	Ho	House	Mkt	Market	Sq	Square
Bsns, Bus	Business	Ctry	Country	Hospl	Hospital	Mus	Museum	St	Street
Bvd	Boulevard	Cty	County	HQ	Headquarters	Orch	Orchard	Sta	Station
Cath	Cathedral	Dr	Drive	Hts	Heights	Pal	Palace	Terr	Terrace
Cir	Circus	Dro	Drove	Ind	Industrial	Par	Parade	TH	Town Hall
Cl	Close	Ed	Education	Inst	Institute	Pas	Passage	Univ	University
Cnr	Corner	Emb	Embankment	Int	International	Pk	Park	Wk, Wlk	Walk
Coll	College	Est	Estate	Intc	Interchange	Pl	Place	Wr	Water
Com	Community	Ex	Exhibition	Junc	Junction	Prec	Precinct	Yd	Yard

Index of towns, villages, streets, hospitals, industrial estates, railway stations, schools, shopping centres, universities and places of interest

1st–Ald

1st Ave DE7 . . . . 208 F7
2nd Ave DE7 . . . . 208 F7
3rd Ave DE7 . . . . 208 F7

A

Abba Cl NG16 . . . . 195 F7
Abbey Brook Ct 1 S8 . . 56 E8
Abbey Brook Dr S8 . . . . . 56 E8
Abbey Cl ST14 . . . . 197 A3
Abbey Croft
  Chesterfield S40 . . . . 95 A7
  Renishaw S21 . . . . 79 C8
Abbeydale Cl DE56 . . . . 192 B7
Abbeydale Ct S17 . . . . 56 A7
Abbeydale Industrial
  Hamlet★ S7 . . . . 56 B8
ABBEYDALE PARK 55 F6
Abbeydale Park Cres S17. 55 F6
Abbeydale Park Rise S17. 55 F6
Abbeydale Rd S7 . . . . 43 A8
Abbeydale Road S S17 . . 56 A7
Abbeyfields Cl DE22 . . . . 205 A2
Abbey Gdns 9 A3
Abbey Hill DE21, DE22 . . 205 B4
Abbeyhill Cl S42 . . . . 95 A4
Abbey Hill Rd DE22 . . . . 204 D2
Abbey La DE22 . . . . 205 A1
Abbey Lodge Cl 1 DE11. 256 A7
Abbey Pl S21 . . . . 79 C8
Abbey St
  Derby DE1, DE22 . . . . 267 A2
  Ilkeston DE7 . . . . 194 F2
Abbey View Dr S8. . . . . 43 A3
Abbey View Hts 3 S8. . . . 43 A3
Abbey View Rd S8 . . . . 43 A3
Abbey Yd DE22 . . . . 205 A1
Abbot Beyne Sch DE15 . . 248 A3
Abbot Cl DE21 . . . . 205 E2
Abbot Mews DE22. . . . . . 205 A1
Abbot Rd DE7. . . . . 208 C6
Abbots Croft NG19 . . . . 135 E1
Abbotsford Mews DE7. . 194 D3
Abbots Gr DE56 . . . . 179 A5
Abbotsholme Sch ST14. . 197 B7
Abbot St NG16. . . . . 195 C4
Abbott Rd
  Alfreton DE55 . . . . 159 B3
  Mansfield NG19. . . . . 135 D1

Abbotts Barn Cl DE22 . . 267 A2
Abbotts Cl DE11 . . . . 256 A6
Abbotts Rd DE11. . . . . . . 256 A6
Abbott St
  Heanor DE75 . . . . 181 E1
  Long Eaton NG10. . . . . 236 D6
Abel La DE4 . . . . 142 C2
Abells DE5 . . . . 180 C1
Abels Mill 1 DE1 . . . . . . 267 A4
Abercrombie Prim Sch
  S41. . . . . 266 B4
Abercrombie St S41 . . . . 266 B4
Aberdare Cl DE21 . . . . . . 206 B2
Abingdon Bsns Ctr The
  DE24. . . . . 219 C1
Abingdon St DE24. . . . . . 232 C8
ABNEY 51 F4
Abney Cl
  Chesterfield S40 . . . . 95 D6
  Derby DE3 . . . . 217 C2
  Sheffield S14 . . . . 43 C6
Abney Dr S14. . . . . 43 C6
Abney Rd S14. . . . . 43 C6
Acacia Ave
  Brimington S43 . . . . 97 A8
  Derby DE3 . . . . 217 E1
  Swadlincote DE11 . . . . 256 B7
Acacia Cres S21 . . . . 60 B5
Acacia Croft DE56. . . . . . 179 B2
Acacia Ct NG19 . . . . 136 E1
Acacia Dr
  Melbourne DE73 . . . . 252 A8
  Pilsley S45. . . . . 132 B3
Acacia Gdns NG16 . . . . . 195 F8
Access 26 Bsns Pk NG16 182 C3
Acer Cl
  Killamarsh S21 . . . . 60 C5
  Pinxton NG16. . . . . 160 C3
Acer Croft DE21. . . . . 205 E3
Acorn Ave NG16 . . . . 195 C8
Acorn Ctr NG16 . . . . 182 C3
Acorn Dr DE56. . . . . 179 A5
Acorn Ridge
  Chesterfield S40 . . . . 114 B7
  Matlock DE4. . . . . 143 B6
  Shirebrook NG20 . . . . 119 D5
Acorn Terr SK22 . . . . 33 B6
Acorn Way
  Belper DE56. . . . . 179 A5
  Derby DE21 . . . . 220 C6
Acreage La NG20 . . . . . . 119 F2
Acre Ct 5 SK13. . . . . 17 C7

Acrefield Way DE73 . . . . 233 B2
Acre La
  Aston-on-Trent DE72 . . . . 246 D7
  Sutton on the Hill DE6 . . . 228 B7
ACRESFORD 265 C7
Acresford Rd
  Donisthorpe DE12 . . . . 265 D7
  Netherseal DE12 . . . . 265 B6
  Overseal DE12. . . . . 262 B2
Acresford View DE12. . . . 262 B3
Acres Rd S45 . . . . 132 B3
Acre St 4 SK13 . . . . 17 C7
Acres The S45 . . . . 132 B4
Acresview Cl DE22 . . . . . 204 D4
Acres View Cl S41 . . . . 95 F7
Acton Ave NG10. . . . . 236 E6
Acton Cl NG10 . . . . 236 E6
Acton Ct 1 S43. . . . . 78 B3
Acton Gr NG10. . . . . 236 E6
Acton Rd
  Derby DE22 . . . . 217 F6
  Long Eaton NG10. . . . . 236 E6
Acton Road Ind Est
  NG10. . . . . 236 E6
Acton St NG10 . . . . 236 E6
Adale Rd DE7. . . . . 193 B8
Adam Bede Cres DE4. . . 165 F6
Adams Cl DE75 . . . . 193 D7
Adams Ct DE7 . . . . 194 E3
Adam's Rd DE6 . . . . 217 A8
Adam St DE7 . . . . 209 A6
Adastral Ave S12. . . . . 44 A2
Adderley Pl SK13 . . . . 9 F1
Adderley Rd SK13 . . . . 9 F1
Addison Dr DE55. . . . . . . 159 B4
Addison Rd
  Derby DE24 . . . . 232 C7
  Stonebroom DE55 . . . . 146 F3
Addison Sq DE4. . . . . 155 A5
Addison St DE55 . . . . 148 A4
Addison Villas NG16. . . . 182 E1
Adelaide Cl
  Derby DE3 . . . . 217 E4
  Stapleford NG9 . . . . 209 F1
Adelaide Cres DE15 . . . . 248 C2
Adelaide Wlk NG16. . . . . 170 F4
Adelphi Cl DE23. . . . . 231 A6
Adelphi Way S43. . . . . 97 E8
Adin Ave S44. . . . . 98 F6
Adler Ct DE1. . . . . 219 B7
Adlington Ave S42 . . . . . 115 C2
Adlington La S32 . . . . 72 C8
Admiral Cl DE75 . . . . 181 D2

Adrian Cl NG9 . . . . 223 F1
Adrian St DE24. . . . . 232 D6
Adwick Cl DE3 . . . . 217 C2
Agard St DE1 . . . . 267 A4
Agnesmeadow La DE6. . 174 D4
Agricultural Bsns Ctr
  DE45. . . . . 109 E5
Agricultural Way DE45 . . 109 E5
Aimploy Ct DE23 . . . . . . 219 A1
Ainley Cl DE24 . . . . 232 F7
Ainsworth Dr DE23. . . . . 231 E7
Aintree Ave S21 . . . . 59 B3
Aintree Cl
  Burton upon Trent DE14 . . 254 A4
  Kimberley NG16. . . . . 195 E7
Airedale Cl NG10. . . . . . . 236 A6
Airedale Wlk 3 DE24 . . 233 C6
Akley Bank Cl S17 . . . . . . 55 F5
Alabaster La DE4 . . . . . . 155 A6
Alandale Ave NG20. . . . . 119 F3
Albany Cl NG19 . . . . 136 C1
Albany Ct NG9 . . . . 209 E1
Albany Dr NG19 . . . . 136 C1
Albany Inf & Jun Schs
  NG9. . . . . 223 E8
Albany Inf Sch NG9 . . . . 209 E1
Albany Jun Sch NG9 . . . . 209 E1
Albany Pl NG19 . . . . 136 C1
Albany Rd DE22 . . . . 218 C4
Albany St DE7 . . . . 209 A6
Albemarle Rd DE21 . . . . 220 B7
Alberta Ave NG16 . . . . . . 171 F7
Albert Ave
  Chesterfield S43 . . . . 77 D3
  Jacksdale NG16. . . . . 171 B4
  Stapleford NG9 . . . . 223 D7
Albert Cres DE21. . . . . . . 220 B4
Albert Ct SK17 . . . . 85 C6
Albert Rd
  Breaston DE72. . . . . 235 B7
  Chesterfield S43 . . . . 77 D3
  Derby DE21 . . . . 220 A4
  Long Eaton NG10. . . . . 236 D8
  Ripley DE5. . . . . 169 C2
  Sandiacre NG10. . . . . 223 B6
  Sheffield, Heeley S8 . . . . . . 43 A6
  Swadlincote DE11 . . . . 256 A2
Albert Sq NG19 . . . . 136 C4
Albert St
  Belper DE56. . . . . 178 F4
  Derby DE1. . . . . 267 B3
  Eastwood NG16 . . . . 182 F3
  Eckington S21 . . . . 59 D2
  Glossop SK13. . . . . 10 A5

Albert St continued
  Ilkeston DE7 . . . . 208 E8
  Ironville NG16. . . . . 170 F5
  Mansfield Woodhouse
    NG19. . . . . 136 C4
  Ripley DE5. . . . . 169 E1
  Somercotes DE55 . . . . 170 B8
  South Normanton DE55. . . 160 B6
  Stapleford NG9 . . . . 223 D7
Albert Street N S41 . . . . . 76 F1
ALBERT VILLAGE 256 C1
Albert Village Prim Sch
  DE11. . . . . 256 C1
Albine Rd NG20 . . . . 119 E6
Albion Cl S17 . . . . 55 F5
Albion Mill SK14 . . . . 9 C1
Albion Rd
  Chesterfield S40 . . . . 266 A3
  Long Eaton NG10. . . . . 236 F8
  New Mills SK22 . . . . 33 B6
Albion St
  Derby DE1. . . . . 267 B3
  Ilkeston DE7 . . . . 194 F1
  Mansfield NG19. . . . . 135 F1
  Ripley DE5. . . . . 169 E1
  Woodville DE11 . . . . 256 F2
Albrighton Ave DE24 . . . 231 D2
Aldam Cl S17 . . . . 55 E4
Aldam Croft S17. . . . . 55 E4
Aldam Rd S17. . . . . 55 F4
Aldam Way S17. . . . . 55 E4
Alder Brook S23 . . . . 34 E2
Alderbrook Cl DE13 . . . . 240 B4
ALDERCAR 182 A4
Aldercar Com Language Coll
  NG16. . . . . 182 A4
Aldercar Inf Sch NG16. . . 182 A4
Aldercar La NG16. . . . . . . 182 A6
Alder Cl
  Derby DE21 . . . . 205 E3
  Glossop SK13. . . . . 9 F4
  Mansfield NG19. . . . . 136 C1
  Shirebrook NG20 . . . . 119 D5
Alder Com High Sch SK14 15 A8
Alder Ct S41. . . . . 266 B4
Alderfen Ct DE24. . . . . . . 232 D3
Alder Gr
  Burton upon Trent DE15 . . 254 F7
  Buxton SK17 . . . . 85 A8
  Mansfield Woodhouse
    NG19. . . . . 136 B5
Alder Grove SK23 . . . . 47 A6
Alderholme Dr 1 DE13. 240 F1
Alder La DE6 . . . . 188 A3

Alderley Ct DE21 . . . . 206 A2
Alderney Rd **3** S8 . . . . . . 43 A7
Aldern Way DE45 . . . . 109 E7
Alder Rd DE56 . . . . 179 A3
Alder Rise SK23 . . . . 45 D8
ALDERS 196 C2
Alders Ave SK23 . . . . 34 E1
Alders Brook DE65 . . . . . . 228 D1
Aldersgate
  Derby DE22 . . . . 217 F7
  New Mills SK22 . . . . 33 B8
Alders La
  Chinley SK23 . . . . 34 E2
  Tansley DE4 . . . . 144 A3
Alderslade Cl DE72 . . . . . . 234 B1
Aldersley Cl DE65 . . . . 230 C1
Alderson Dr DE13 . . . . 240 F1
Alderson Pl S2 . . . . 43 A8
Alderson Rd S2 . . . . 43 A8
Alderson Road N S2 . . . . . . 43 A8
Alders Rd SK12 . . . . 32 A7
Alders Reach DE13 . . . . . . 240 B4
Alders The S42 . . . . 113 D7
ALDERWASLEY 166 E8
Alderwasley Hall Sch
  DE56 . . . . 167 B7
Alder Way NG20 . . . . 119 D4
Alder Wlk DE23 . . . . 267 B1
Aldred Cl S21 . . . . 60 E8
Aldred's La DE75, NG16 . . . 182 B2
Aldridge Cl NG9 . . . . 223 E2
ALDWARK 152 F7
Aldwark Rd SK17 . . . . 85 C6
Aldwych DE22 . . . . 218 A6
Alexander Ave NG16 . . . . . 171 D7
Alexander Rd SK17 . . . . 47 F1
Alexander Terr DE12 . . . . . 160 C1
Alexandra Ave NG19 . . . . . 136 B5
Alexandra Ct
  Burton upon Trent DE15 . . 248 A3
  Overseal DE12 . . . . 262 B4
Alexandra Gdns **3** DE23 . . 219 B2
Alexandra Mills **2** DE1. . . 218 E5
Alexandra Private Hospl
  S41 . . . . 266 B4
Alexandra Rd
  Burton upon Trent DE15 . . 248 A3
  Buxton SK17 . . . . 85 C5
  Dronfield S18 . . . . 57 B2
  Long Eaton NG10 . . . . . . 236 D8
  Overseal DE12 . . . . 262 B4
  Sheffield S2 . . . . 43 B7
  Swadlincote DE11 . . . . . . 256 B3
Alexandra Road E S41 . . . . . 96 C1
Alexandra Road W S40 . . . . 266 A3
Alexandra St
  Eastwood NG16 . . . . 182 F2
  Stapleford NG9 . . . . 223 D6
Alexandre Cl DE23 . . . . . . 231 D6
Alford Cl S40 . . . . 95 C3
Alfred Rd DE23 . . . . 192 A8
Alfred St
  Alfreton DE55 . . . . 158 F3
  Pinxton NG16 . . . . 160 C4
  Ripley DE5 . . . . 169 E2
  Somercotes DE55 . . . . . . 170 D6
  South Normanton DE55 . . 159 F5
ALFRETON 159 C4
Alfreton Grange Arts Coll
  DE55 . . . . 159 A3
Alfreton L Ctr DE55 . . . . . . 158 F4
Alfreton Motorway Link Ind
  Est DE55 . . . . 159 A4
Alfreton Rd
  Blackwell DE55 . . . . 147 E2
  Breadsall DE21 . . . . 205 B2
  Codnor DE5 . . . . 170 C1
  Holbrook DE21 . . . . 191 D2
  Little Eaton DE21 . . . . . . 205 C6
  Matlock DE4 . . . . 143 E4
  Pinxton NG16 . . . . 160 C4
  Selston DE55, NG16 . . . . 171 C6
  Tibshelf DE55 . . . . 147 D4
Alfreton Sta DE55 . . . . 159 C5
Alfreton Trad Est DE55 . . . . 159 B2
Algar Cl S2 . . . . 43 E7
Algar Cres S2 . . . . 43 F7
Algar Dr S2 . . . . 43 E7
Algar Pl S2 . . . . 43 E7
Algar Rd S2 . . . . 43 E7
Alice Gdns DE12 . . . . 262 B4
Alicehead Rd S45 . . . . 113 B2
Alice St DE1 . . . . 267 C4
Alice's View S42 . . . . 132 A8
Alice Way S18 . . . . 76 E5
Alison Cl DE21 . . . . 219 F7
ALKMONTON 199 D1
Alkmonton Rd DE6 . . . . . . 213 D5
Alkmund Ct DE1 . . . . 267 B4
Allan Ave DE23 . . . . 230 E8
Allandale Rd DE75 . . . . . . 181 D2
Allan La DE56 . . . . 168 B6
Allcroft St NG19 . . . . 136 C4
Allenby Cl S8 . . . . 56 E7
Allenby Dr S8 . . . . 56 E7
Allendale DE7 . . . . 208 E7
Allendale Rd S42 . . . . 114 F3
Allendale Way NG19 . . . . . 136 E1
Allen Hill DE4 . . . . 143 B6
Allen La
  Ashover DE4 . . . . 144 C6
  Weston Underwood DE6 . . 188 C1
Allens Croft ST14 . . . . 224 E2
Allen's Green Ave NG16 . . . 171 F6
Allen's La ST14 . . . . 224 E2
ALLENTON DE24 . . . . 232 E5
ALLENTON 232 D5

Allenton Com Prim Sch
  DE24 . . . . 232 D5
ALLESTREE 204 F3
Allestree Cl DE24 . . . . 232 E8
Allestree Dr S18 . . . . 56 C1
Allestree La DE22 . . . . 204 D3
Allestree Park Nature
  Reserve★ DE22 . . . . . . 204 F5
Allestree St DE24 . . . . 232 F8
Alley The DE4 . . . . 154 D4
Alley Wlk DE6 . . . . 201 F7
Allison Ave DE11 . . . . 256 B3
Allison Gdns DE7 . . . . 195 A1
Alissa Ave DE5 . . . . 180 E7
Allpits Rd S44 . . . . 96 F1
Allport Terr S43 . . . . 78 B4
All Saints CE Fst Sch
  ST14 . . . . 196 E6
All Saints CE Inf Sch
  DE4 . . . . 143 B6
All Saints CE Jun Sch
  DE4 . . . . 143 A7
All Saints CE Prim Sch
  Marple SK6 . . . . 23 A5
  Youlgreave DE45 . . . . . . 125 C5
All Saints Cl DE7 . . . . 193 B1
All Saints Croft DE14 . . . . 254 C8
All Saints **6** DE3 . . . . . . 217 D1
All Saints RC Prim Sch
  SK13 . . . . 10 D2
All Saints Rd DE14 . . . . . . 254 C8
All Saints' Rd DE4 . . . . 143 B6
Allsops Pl S41 . . . . 95 F8
Allstone Lee DE56 . . . . . . 178 F5
Alma CI NE7 . . . . 194 E5
Alma Cres S18 . . . . 57 A3
Alma Hill NG16 . . . . 195 E7
Alma Hts DE3 . . . . 217 C1
Alma L Pk★ S40 . . . . 266 C1
Alma Rd
  North Wingfield S42 . . . . 132 A8
  Selston NG16 . . . . 171 F5
  Swadlincote DE11 . . . . . . 255 F6
  Tideswell SK17 . . . . 69 C5
Alma Sq SK17 . . . . 85 D8
Alma St
  Alfreton DE55 . . . . 159 A4
  Buxton SK17 . . . . 85 D8
  Derby DE22 . . . . 267 A2
  Melbourne DE73 . . . . . . 252 A7
  North Wingfield S42 . . . . 131 E6
  Ripley DE5 . . . . 169 D3
Alma Street W S40 . . . . 95 E2
Almond Ave
  Ripley DE5 . . . . 180 D8
  Shirebrook NG20 . . . . . . 119 E5
Almond Cl
  Calow S44 . . . . 97 A3
  Kimberley NG16 . . . . 195 E7
Almond Cres S43 . . . . 79 C4
Almond Ct DE13 . . . . 240 E1
Almond Dr S21 . . . . 60 C5
Almond Gr
  Swadlincote DE11 . . . . . . 256 A5
  Swanwick DE55 . . . . 170 A8
Almond Rise NG19 . . . . . . 136 E1
Almond St DE23 . . . . 218 F1
Almshouses
  Etwall DE65 . . . . 229 B5
  Newton Solney DE15 . . . . 248 E8
Alms Rd DE7 . . . . 211 C1
Alnwick Dr S12 . . . . 44 C5
Alnwick Rd S12 . . . . 44 B5
Alonso Cl DE73 . . . . 232 E2
Alpha Rd SK23 . . . . 34 E2
Alpine Gr S43 . . . . 97 A8
Alport Ave
  Buxton SK17 . . . . 85 D7
  Sheffield S12 . . . . 44 E5
Alport Cl
  Belper DE56 . . . . 179 B5
  Hulland Ward DE6 . . . . . 175 F3
Alport Dr S12 . . . . 44 E5
Alport Gr
  3 Gamesley SK13 . . . . . 9 E2
  Sheffield S12 . . . . 44 E5
Alport La
  Spout DE4, DE56 . . . . . . 166 C4
  Youlgreave DE45 . . . . . . 125 C6
Alport Lea **2** SK13 . . . . . . 9 E2
Alport Pl S12 . . . . 44 E4
Alport Rd S12 . . . . 44 E5
Alport Rise S18 . . . . 56 D2
Alport Terr DE55 . . . . 147 C1
Alport Way **1** SK13 . . . . . 9 E2
Alsager Cl DE21 . . . . 206 A1
Alsfeld Way SK22 . . . . 33 A8
ALSOP EN LE DALE 150 E3
Alsop La DE4 . . . . 156 C2
Alsop Moor Cotts DE6 . . . . 150 E5
Alsop Pl SK17 . . . . 85 E7
Alsop Way SK17 . . . . 85 E7
ALSTONEFIELD 149 D4
Alstonfield Dr DE22 . . . . . 204 E1
Alston Rd SK23 . . . . 47 B5
Althorp Cl DE55 . . . . 169 F7
ALTON 130 C5
Alton Cl
  Chesterfield S40 . . . . . . 114 B8
  Derby DE22 . . . . 204 D3
  Dronfield S18 . . . . 75 D8
Alton Dr NG16 . . . . 195 B8
Alton Hill S42 . . . . 130 C5
Alton La S45 . . . . 130 C4
Alton Rd
  Belper DE56 . . . . 179 C4
  Denstone ST14 . . . . 196 D6
Alton Rise DE4 . . . . 142 F7

Alts Nook Way DE72. . . . . 234 E1
Alum Chine Cl S41 . . . . . . 115 C8
Alum Cl S41 . . . . 233 C7
ALVASTON 233 B8
Alvaston Inf Sch DE24 . . . . 233 C7
Alvaston Jun Com Sch
  DE24 . . . . 233 C7
Alvaston Park Homes
  DE24 . . . . 220 A1
Alvaston Pk★ DE24 . . . . . 219 F2
Alvaston St DE24. . . . . . . 233 B8
Alvenor St DE7 . . . . 194 F1
Alverton Cl DE3 . . . . 217 C1
Alveston Pk Homes
  DE24 . . . . 233 A8
Alward's Cl DE24. . . . . . . 233 A6
AMBASTON 234 D6
Ambaston La
  Elvaston DE72 . . . . 234 A5
  Shardlow DE72 . . . . 234 E2
Amber Bldgs DE55 . . . . . . 159 B5
Amber Bsns Ctr DE55 . . . . 170 B5
Amber Cl DE56 . . . . 168 B5
Amber Cres S40 . . . . 95 C1
Amber Croft S43 . . . . 97 C7
Amber Ct
  Belper DE56 . . . . 179 A6
  Chesterfield S41 . . . . . . 266 B4
  2 Heanor DE75 . . . . . . 181 E1
Amberdene DE4 . . . . 143 D6
Amber Dr NG16 . . . . 182 B2
AMBERGATE 167 F3
Ambergate Prim Sch
  DE56 . . . . 167 F3
Ambergate Sta DE56 . . . . 167 F4
Amber Gr S18 . . . . 158 F2
Ambergrove DE56 . . . . . . 168 B4
Amber Hill DE4 . . . . 168 A7
Amber Hts DE5 . . . . 169 C2
Amber La S45 . . . . 129 D3
Amberley Cl DE7 . . . . 208 F6
Amberley Dr
  Buxton SK17 . . . . 85 C5
  Derby DE22 . . . . 204 F7
Amber Pl S45 . . . . 131 A4
Amber Rd
  Bullbridge DE56 . . . . 168 B6
  Derby DE22 . . . . 204 D1
Amber St DE24 . . . . 232 C7
Amber Terr DE55 . . . . 158 B6
Amber Trad Est NG16 . . . . 195 D7
Ambervale DE23 . . . . 231 A6
Amber View Rd DE56. . . . . 168 B7
Amberwood DE11 . . . . . . 256 A5
Ambleside Cl
  Chesterfield S41 . . . . 95 C7
  Sheffield S20 . . . . 59 E6
Ambleside Dr
  Bolsover S44 . . . . 98 F1
  Eastwood NG16 . . . . 182 D3
Ambrose Terr DE1 . . . . . . 218 E5
Amen Alley DE1 . . . . 267 B3
Amesbury Cl S41 . . . . 95 E7
Amesbury La DE21 . . . . . . 205 E2
Ameycroft La DE4 . . . . . . 143 A8
Amilda Ave DE7 . . . . 208 F8
Amy St DE22 . . . . 218 E4
Anchor Ave SK23 . . . . 47 C6
Anchor Cl DE11 . . . . 256 C4
Anchor Fold SK23 . . . . 47 D6
Anchor Rd NG16 . . . . 182 D2
Anchor Row DE7 . . . . 208 F8
Anchor Sq DE45 . . . . 109 D6
Anderby Gdns DE11 . . . . . 255 F2
Anderson Cl S43 . . . . 77 E3
Anderson St DE24 . . . . . . 232 F7
Andrew Ave DE7 . . . . 209 B7
Andrew Cl DE23 . . . . 230 E8
Andrew La SK6 . . . . 32 A8
Andrews Dr
  Langley Mill NG16 . . . . . 182 A3
  Stanley Common DE7 . . . 193 A1
Andrew St S6 . . . . 15 A2
Andwell La S10 . . . . 42 F6
Angelica Cl DE23. . . . . . . 231 D5
Angel Yd S40 . . . . 266 B3
Angerford Ave S8 . . . . 43 A4
Anglers' La DE21 . . . . 220 E3
Anglesey Rd
  Burton upon Trent DE14 . . 254 B8
  Dronfield S18. . . . . 76 A8
Anglesey St
  Burton upon Trent DE14 . . 253 C8
  Derby DE21 . . . . 219 D8
Angleton Ave S2 . . . . 44 C8
Angleton Cl S2 . . . . 44 C8
Angleton Gdns S2 . . . . . . 44 C8
Angleton Gn S2 . . . . 44 C8
Angleton Mews S2 . . . . . . 44 C8
Anglia Dr DE11 . . . . 255 F1
Ankerbold Rd S42 . . . . . . 131 D8
Anncroft Rd SK17 . . . . 84 D5
Anne Potter Cl DE72 . . . . . 221 D5
Annesley Cl
  Chesterfield S41 . . . . . . 115 C8
  Sheffield S8 . . . . 56 F7
Annesley Rd S8 . . . . 56 F7
Anns Grove Prim Sch **7**
  S2 . . . . 43 A7
Anns Rd S2. . . . . 43 A7
Anns Road N S2 . . . . 43 B7
Ann St S80 . . . . 81 E1
Annwell La LE65 . . . . 257 E2
ANNWELL PLACE 257 E1
Anslow La DE13 . . . . 240 A2
Anslow Rd DE13 . . . . 238 B2
Anson Wlk DE7 . . . . 194 F3

Anstee Rd NG10 . . . . 236 C5
Anstey Ct S21 . . . . 266 A1
Anthony Bek Com Prim Sch
  NG19. . . . . 134 F6
Anthony Cres DE24. . . . . . 232 F6
Anthony Dr DE24. . . . . . . 232 F6
Anthony Gell Sch DE4 . . . . 165 F8
Antill St NG9 . . . . 223 D6
Apiary Gate DE74 . . . . . . 247 B3
APPERKNOWLE 58 A1
Appian Cl DE72 . . . . 221 C1
Appian Way
  Clay Cross S45 . . . . 131 B2
  Derby DE24 . . . . 233 D5
Appleby Cl DE7 . . . . 208 F6
Appleby Glade DE11. . . . . 255 D2
APPLEBY MAGNA 265 F1
Appleby Rd NG19 . . . . . . 134 F6
Applecroft Cl S44 . . . . 118 B1
Applecross Ct DE24 . . . . . 231 E3
Appledore Ct **2** S41 . . . . . 95 F8
Appledore Dr DE21. . . . . . 206 B3
Appledown Way DE23 . . . . 231 A6
Applegarth Cl S12 . . . . 44 A6
Applegarth Dr S12 . . . . 44 A6
Applegate Cl DE21. . . . . . 206 B3
Applemead Cl DE21 . . . . . 205 E2
Apple St SK14 . . . . 15 C7
Appleton Cl
  Burton upon Trent DE15 . . 254 E7
  Derby DE21 . . . . 220 A7
  Swadlincote DE11 . . . . . . 255 F6
Appleton Dr
  Belper DE56 . . . . 179 B6
  Glossop SK13. . . . . 17 F8
Appletree Cl DE72 . . . . . . 221 C1
Appletree Dr S18 . . . . 57 A1
Appletree Rd
  Bolsover S44 . . . . 80 B1
  Hatton DE65 . . . . 227 C1
Appletree Wlk DE3 . . . . . . 217 D2
Applewood Cl
  Belper DE56 . . . . 179 B5
  Uttoxeter ST14 . . . . 210 A1
Appleyard Ct S41 . . . . 266 A4
Arbor Cl DE22 . . . . 267 A2
Arboretum Prim Sch
  DE23 . . . . 219 A2
Arboretum Sq DE23 . . . . . 267 C1
Arboretum St DE23 . . . . . 267 C1
Arbor Gr SK17 . . . . 84 F7
Arbor Low (Henge)★
  DE45 . . . . 123 E4
Arbour Cl S41 . . . . 115 D6
Arbour Hill
  Borrowash DE72 . . . . . . 221 E3
  Dale Abbey DE7 . . . . . . 207 E3
ARBOURTHORNE 43 E8
Arbourthorne Com Prim Sch
  S2 . . . . 43 D6
Arbourthorne Cotts S2. . . . 43 D8
ARBOURTHORNE
  ESTATE 43 E6
Arbourthorne Rd S2 . . . . . 43 E6
Arcadia Ave NG20 . . . . . . 119 E5
Archdale Cl
  Chesterfield S40 . . . . . . 266 B1
  Sheffield S2 . . . . 44 B8
Archdale Rd S2 . . . . 44 A8
Archer Rd NG9 . . . . 223 E5
Archer St
  Derby DE24 . . . . 219 E2
  Ilkeston DE7 . . . . 194 E3
Arden Cl
  Chesterfield S40 . . . . 95 C5
  Derby DE23 . . . . 218 E2
  Glossop SK13 . . . . 17 A8
Arden St SK22 . . . . 33 C7
Ardleigh Cl DE3 . . . . 230 D8
Ardsley Cl
  Heanor DE75 . . . . 182 A2
  Sheffield S20 . . . . 44 F2
Ardsley Dr S20 . . . . 44 F2
Ardsley Gr S20. . . . . 44 F2
Ardsley Rd S40 . . . . 95 B3
Argyle Cl
  Market Warsop NG20 . . . 120 F4
  Sheffield S8 . . . . 43 B5
Argyle Mews NG16 . . . . . 182 F2
Argyle Rd S8 . . . . 43 B5
Argyle St
  Derby DE22 . . . . 218 F3
  Langley Mill NG16 . . . . . 182 C4
Argyll Cl DE21 . . . . 220 F5
Argyll Rd DE5 . . . . 169 E2
Aria Ct NG9. . . . . 223 D6
Arkendale Wlk **4** DE24. . . 233 C6
Arkle Gn DE24 . . . . 231 E4
Arklow Cl S41 . . . . 115 B8
Arkwright Ave DE56 . . . . . 179 C6
Arkwright Cl DE4 . . . . 127 C3
Arkwright Dr SK6 . . . . 23 A6
Arkwright Gdns DE4 . . . . . 155 A6
Arkwright Prim Sch S44. . . 97 D3
Arkwright Rd SK6 . . . . 23 A6
Arkwright's Cromford Mill★
  DE4. . . . . 155 C2
Arkwright St
  Derby DE24 . . . . 232 C7
  Wirksworth DE4 . . . . . . 165 E8
ARKWRIGHT TOWN 97 D3
Arleston La DE24 . . . . 231 D2
Arleston St DE23 . . . . 231 F7
Arlington Ave NG19 . . . . . 136 E4

Arlington Dr
  Derby DE24 . . . . 232 F6
  Swanwick DE55 . . . . 169 F7
Arlington Rd DE23 . . . . . . 218 D2
Arliston Dr DE11 . . . . 256 E1
Armitage Rd DE7 . . . . 237 A7
Armscote Cl DE21 . . . . . . 206 B2
Arms Park Dr S20 . . . . 59 F6
Armytage Ind Est S41 . . . . . 77 A1
Arnfield La SK13 . . . . 9 F8
Arnhem Terr DE21 . . . . . . 220 F3
Arnold Ave
  Long Eaton NG10 . . . . . . 236 A4
  Sheffield S12 . . . . 44 B1
Arnold Cl DE11 . . . . 261 E7
Arnold Cres NG10 . . . . . . 236 A4
Arnold St DE22 . . . . 218 D5
Arnside NG9 . . . . 223 E5
Arnside Cl
  Chesterfield S41 . . . . 76 D1
  Swadlincote DE11 . . . . . 256 C1
Arran Cl
  Derby DE24 . . . . 231 E3
  Stapleford NG9 . . . . 209 E2
Arran Ct DE55 . . . . 147 F6
Arreton Ct DE24 . . . . 233 C5
Arridge Rd DE21 . . . . 219 F6
Arrowscroft Ct SK14 . . . . . . 9 D5
Arrowscroft Way SK14 . . . . 9 D4
Arthington Blgs S2 . . . . . . 43 A6
Arthington St S8 . . . . 43 A6
Arthur Ave NG9 . . . . 223 F8
Arthur Ct **1** DE23 . . . . . 219 B2
Arthur Hind Cl DE22. . . . . 218 F7
Arthur Mee Rd NG9 . . . . . 223 E5
Arthurs Ct DE13 . . . . 240 E2
Arthur Short Cl S80 . . . . . . 82 A6
Arthur St
  Alfreton DE55 . . . . 159 A5
  Derby DE1 . . . . 267 B5
  Draycott DE72 . . . . 234 F8
  Linton DE11 . . . . 261 E7
  Pinxton NG16. . . . . 160 D3
Arthurs View NG16 . . . . . 170 F4
Arthurs Way S33 . . . . 38 A2
Artic Way NG16 . . . . 195 D2
Artisan View S8 . . . . 43 A6
Arun Dale NG19 . . . . 136 D2
Arundel Ave DE3 . . . . 217 F2
Arundel Cl
  23 Chesterfield S41. . . . . 95 F8
  Dronfield S18. . . . . 56 D1
  Sandiacre NG10 . . . . . . 223 B4
Arundel Ct **6** S43 . . . . . . 78 E2
Arundel Dr DE7 . . . . 220 F5
Arundel Grange SK13 . . . . 17 A8
Arundel St
  Derby DE22 . . . . 218 D4
  Glossop SK13. . . . . 10 C1
Asbourne Ct DE7. . . . . . . 194 D1
Ascot Ave NG16 . . . . 195 E7
Ascot Cl
  Burton upon Trent DE15 . . 248 A3
  West Hallam DE7. . . . . . 207 D7
Ascot Dr DE24 . . . . 232 D8
Ascot Ind Est NG10. . . . . . 223 C7
Ascot Pl DE7. . . . . 208 C5
Ascott Dr DE11 . . . . 256 A5
Ash Acre DE56 . . . . 179 D4
Ashberry Ct DE22 . . . . . . 205 A4
ASHBOURNE 173 C2
Ashbourne Ave S45 . . . . . 131 A5
Ashbourne Cl **4** S40 . . . . 95 A5
Ashbourne Ct
  Derby DE22 . . . . 218 E6
  3 Glossop SK13 . . . . . . 17 F8
Ashbourne Dr DE11 . . . . . 256 A5
Ashbourne La
  Chapel-en-le-Frith SK23 . . . 47 D5
  Wetton DE6 . . . . 149 A2
Ashbourne L Ctr DE6. . . . . 173 B1
Ashbourne Rd
  Alstonefield DE6 . . . . . . 149 B3
  Belper DE56. . . . . 178 C4
  Buxton SK17 . . . . 85 D4
  Church Broughton DE65 . . 213 F3
  Derby DE22 . . . . 218 C2
  Kirk Langley DE6 . . . . . . 202 D4
  Mackworth DE22 . . . . . . 217 E8
  Mayfield DE6 . . . . 184 C7
  Rocester ST14 . . . . 196 F4
  Shottle DE56 . . . . 177 D3
  Uttoxeter ST14 . . . . 210 B1
Ashbourne St NG20 . . . . . 119 F4
Ashbrook DE7. . . . . 248 A1
Ashbrook Ave DE72 . . . . . 221 C2
Ashbrook Cl DE22 . . . . . . 204 C3
Ashbrook Inf Sch DE72. . . . 221 B2
Ashbrook Jun Sch DE72. . . 221 B2
Ashbury Dr S8 . . . . 43 C2
Ashbury La S8 . . . . 43 C2
Ashby Ave NG19 . . . . 136 D5
ASHBY-DE-LA-ZOUCH . . . 258 A1
Ashby La DE11 . . . . 257 C1
Ashby Rd
  Blackfordby DE11, LE65. . . 257 D2
  Breedon on the Hill DE73 . . 252 E2
  Burton upon Trent DE15 . . 248 B2
  Melbourne DE73 . . . . . . 252 A6
  Moira DE12 . . . . 262 F4
Ashby Road E DE15 . . . . . 248 E1
Ashby St DE24 . . . . 232 E6
Ash Cl
  Aston-on-Trent DE72 . . . . 246 B7
  Barlborough S43 . . . . . . 80 B6

Ash Cl continued
Derby DE22 . . . .**204** D4
Killamarsh S21 . . . . **60** C5
Mottram in Longdendale
SK14 . . . . **9** A4
Pinxton NG16 . . . .**160** D2
Ashcombe Gdns DE21 . .**206** B1
Ash Cres
Eckington S21 . . . . **59** B1
Mansfield Woodhouse
NG19 . . . .**136** E2
Ripley DE5 . . . .**180** D8
Ashcroft Cl DE24 . . . .**232** F7
Ashcroft Ct S41 . . . . **77** B3
Ashcroft Dr S41 . . . . **77** B2
Ash Croft Prim Sch
DE24 . . . .**231** E2
Ash Ct DE55 . . . .**159** C3
Ashdale Cl DE15 . . . .**255** A8
Ashdale Rd DE7 . . . .**209** A6
Ashdene Gdns DE56 . . . .**179** C5
Ashdown Dr S40 . . . . **95** D1
Ashe La DE65 . . . .**229** A5
Ashe Pl DE23 . . . .**218** F1
Asher La DE5 . . . .**169** C5
Asher Lane Bsns Pk DE5 **169** D4
Ashes Ave DE6 . . . .**175** F3
Ashes La
Fenny Bentley DE6 . . . .**162** A1
Glossop SK13 . . . . **10** B2
Ashes The SK13 . . . . **10** B2
Ashfield Ave
Derby DE21 . . . .**219** E8
Somercotes DE55 . . . .**159** D1
Ashfield Cl S12 . . . . **43** F4
Ashfield Dr S12 . . . . **43** F4
Ashfield Gr SK6 . . . . **15** B1
Ashfield Rd
Chapel-en-le-Frith SK23 . . **47** D6
Chesterfield S41 . . . .**115** D8
Glossop SK13 . . . .**9** F3
Ash Fields DE56 . . . .**179** A2
Ashford Ave S42 . . . .**132** A7
Ashford Cl S18 . . . . **75** D8
Ashford Ct
Chesterfield S41 . . . . **96** A5
West Hallam DE7 . . . .**207** D8
Ashford Gn S13 . . . .**9** E1
ASHFORD IN THE
WATER **108** E7
Ashford La DE45 . . . . **89** D2
Ashford Mews SK13 . . . .**9** E1
Ashford Pl DE7 . . . .**194** E5
Ashford Rd S18 . . . . **75** D8
Ashford Rise DE56 . . . . . .**179** C6
Ashforth Ave DE75 . . . . .**194** A8
Ashfurlong Cl S17 . . . . **55** F7
Ashfurlong Dr S17 . . . . **55** F7
Ashfurlong Pk S17 . . . . **55** F7
Ashfurlong Rd S17 . . . . **55** F7
ASHGATE
Chesterfield **95** C4
Old Brampton **94** F4
Ashgate Ave S40 . . . . **95** C3
Ashgate Croft Specl Sch
S40 . . . . **95** C4
Ashgate Ct S40 . . . . **95** C4
Ashgate Prim Sch DE22 .**218** D6
Ashgate Rd S40 . . . . **95** C3
Ashgate Valley Rd S40 . . **95** D4
Ash Gr
Brinsley NG16 . . . .**182** D8
Chinley SK23 . . . . **34** E1
Long Eaton NG10 . . . .**236** C6
Mastin Moor S43 . . . . **79** B4
Sandiacre NG10 . . . .**223** A7
Selston NG16 . . . .**171** F7
Shirebrook NG20 . . . .**119** E5
Stapleford NG9 . . . .**223** D5
Tupton S42 . . . .**131** D8
Ashgrove Ct DE21 . . . . . .**206** B1
Ash Grove La DE65 . . . . .**241** C6
Ash La
Chesterfield S21 . . . . **77** D8
Sutton on the Hill DE6,
DE65 . . . .**228** E7
Unstone S18 . . . . **57** F3
Ashland Rd S21 . . . . **59** E3
Ashlar Dr DE12 . . . .**262** F1
Ashlea Dr DE6 . . . .**184** D7
Ashlea Wlk S43 . . . . **81** A5
Ashleigh Ave
Glossop SK13 . . . . **10** B2
Sheffield S12 . . . . **43** F5
Swadlincote DE11 . . . .**255** F6
Ashleigh Cl S41 . . . . **77** B3
Ashleigh Croft S12 . . . . . . **43** F5
Ashleigh Ct S21 . . . . **59** C1
Ashleigh Dr
Chellaston DE73 . . . .**232** F2
Sheffield S12 . . . . **43** F5
Ashleigh Pl S12 . . . . **43** F5
Ashleigh Rd S43 . . . . **80** B7
Ashley Cl
Killamarsh S21 . . . . **60** D6
Overseal DE12 . . . .**262** B3
Tansley DE4 . . . .**144** A4
Ashley Ct DE15 . . . .**248** A3
ASHLEYHAY **166** A4
Ashley La S21 . . . . **60** D6
Ashley St DE22 . . . .**218** C5
Ashlyn Rd DE21 . . . .**219** C5
Ashmeadow DE7 . . . .**221** B1
Ashmeadow Ct DE6 . . . . .**185** D8
Ashmore Ave S21 . . . . **59** B2

Ash Mount Rd NG16 . . . . .**182** B3
Ashop Rd DE56 . . . .**179** D5
ASHOPTON **30** E2
Ashopton Ave DE23 . . . .**231** F8
Ashopton Dr S33 . . . . **40** B4
Ashopton Rd
Bamford S33 . . . . **40** A6
Chesterfield S41 . . . . **95** C6
ASHOVER **129** F3
Ashover Cl DE21 . . . .**219** F8
ASHOVER HAY **145** B5
Ashover New Rd DE55,
S45 . . . .**145** E8
Ashover Prim Sch S45 . .**129** F3
Ashover Rd
Alton S45 . . . .**130** C5
Ashover S45 . . . .**129** E4
Brackenfield DE55 . . . .**146** B7
Derby, Chaddesden
DE21 . . . .**219** E8
Derby DE22 . . . .**204** D2
Staveley S43 . . . . **97** C6
Swadlincote DE11 . . . .**255** E5
Tupton S42 . . . .**131** B7
Ashover View DE55 . . . . .**147** C1
Ash St
Buxton SK17 . . . . **85** B6
Ilkeston DE7 . . . .**194** E4
Sheffield, Mosborough S20 . **59** C8
Ash Terr SK17 . . . . **85** C8
Ashton Cl
Chesterfield S40 . . . .**114** C8
Derby DE23 . . . .**217** C3
Killamarsh S21 . . . . **60** C6
Swanwick DE55 . . . .**170** A7
Ashton Gdns
Clay Cross S42 . . . .**131** B6
Glossop SK13 . . . . **17** C7
Ashton Rd S45 . . . .**131** E4
Ashton St SK13 . . . . **17** C7
Ashton Way DE56 . . . . . .**179** D4
Ashtree Ave DE24 . . . . . .**232** B6
Ash Tree Cl
Breadsall DE21 . . . .**205** E4
Chesterfield S40 . . . . **95** C3
Duffield DE56 . . . .**190** E5
Swadlincote DE11 . . . .**255** F6
Ash Tree Cres NG19 . . . .**136** C5
Ash Tree Rd S43 . . . . **80** E2
Ashurst Cl S40 . . . . **94** F5
Ash Vale S40 . . . . **95** B3
Ashview Cl NG10 . . . .**236** A8
Ash View Cl DE65 . . . . . .**229** B3
Ashwater Cl DE24 . . . . . .**231** F2
Ashwell Ave NG19 . . . . . .**136** E5
Ashwood SK13 . . . . **16** F8
Ashwood Cl
Buxton SK17 . . . . **85** C7
Derby DE24 . . . .**232** D8
Mansfield Woodhouse
NG19 . . . .**136** E5
Ashwood Rd
Buxton SK17 . . . . **66** E1
Disley SK12 . . . . **32** D6
Ashworth Ave
Burton upon Trent DE15 . .**248** A1
Derby DE21 . . . .**219** F5
Ashworth Dr NG19 . . . . .**136** E4
Ashworth La SK14 . . . .**9** A3
Ashworth Wlk DE21 . . . . .**219** F5
Askerfield Ave DE22 . . . .**204** C4
Asker La DE4 . . . .**143** D6
Askew Gr DE65 . . . .**242** D2
Askew Way S40 . . . .**266** B1
Asline Rd S2 . . . . **43** A8
Aspen Bsns Ctr DE21 . . .**220** B4
Aspen Cl
Buxton SK17 . . . . **66** B1
Killamarsh S21 . . . . **60** C6
Aspen Ct NG19 . . . .**136** E1
Aspen Dr DE21 . . . .**220** C4
Aspen Rd S21 . . . . **59** B1
Aspen Rise DE55 . . . .**146** D1
Aspenshaw Rd SK22 . . . . **24** E3
Aspen Way SK6 . . . . **32** A7
Aspley Cl S40 . . . . **95** E5
Astcote Cl DE75 . . . .**182** A1
Asterdale Prim Sch
DE21 . . . .**220** F3
Asterdale View DE21 . . . .**220** F3
Aster Gdns DE23 . . . .**231** B6
Astil St DE15 . . . .**254** F8
Astlow Dr DE56 . . . .**179** B6
ASTON
Hope **39** C4
Sudbury **225** F4
Aston Cl
Chellaston DE73 . . . .**245** A8
Dronfield S18 . . . . **57** C3
Aston Ct S43 . . . . **78** F2
Aston Dr DE11 . . . .**256** A7
Aston Gn NG9 . . . .**223** E3
Aston Hall DE72 . . . .**246** A7
ASTON HEATH **226** B6
Aston La
Chellaston DE73 . . . .**233** B1
Hope S33 . . . . **39** C4
Shardlow DE72 . . . .**234** E1
Sudbury DE6 . . . .**226** A5
Wensley DE4 . . . .**142** D7
ASTON-ON-TRENT **246** B8
Aston-on-Trent Prim Sch
DE72 . . . .**246** A8
Aston Rd DE23 . . . .**231** C5
Astorville Park Rd DE73 .**232** F2
Astron Bsns Pk DE11 . . . .**256** A3
ASTWITH **133** A5
Astwith Cl S44 . . . .**116** F1

Astwith La S44, S45 . . . . .**133** B5
Atchison Gdns DE21 . . . .**220** B7
Athens Ct DE73 . . . .**232** E2
Atherfield Gdns NG16 . . .**182** F3
Atherfield Wlk DE24 . . . .**233** C5
Atherstone Rd DE12 . . . .**265** D1
Atherton Ave SK14 . . . .**9** A4
Atherton Cl S2 . . . . **43** F6
Atherton Gr SK14 . . . . **9** A4
Atherton Rd
Ilkeston DE7 . . . .**194** C3
Sheffield S2 . . . . **43** F6
Athlestan Way DE13 . . . .**240** C1
Athlone Cl DE21 . . . .**219** D8
Athol Cl
Chesterfield S40 . . . .**114** B8
Derby DE24 . . . .**231** E4
Atkin Pl S2 . . . . **43** A8
Atkinson Ct S40 . . . .**266** B1
Atkinson Mews S21 . . . . . **59** C3
Atkins Way ST14 . . . .**196** F3
Atlantic Cres S8 . . . . **56** E6
Atlantic Dr S8 . . . . **56** E6
Atlantic Way
Derby DE24 . . . .**219** E2
Sheffield S8 . . . . **56** E6
Atlantic Wlk S8 . . . . **56** E6
Atlas Way DE21 . . . .**220** F2
ATLOW **175** A6
Atlow Brow DE6 . . . .**173** D3
Atlow Cl S40 . . . . **95** B5
Atlow La DE6 . . . .**175** A5
Atlow Rd DE21 . . . .**219** E2
ATLOWTOP **175** B5
Attenborough Nature
Reserve★ NG9 . . . .**237** D8
Attewell Cl DE72 . . . .**235** B7
Attewell Rd NG16 . . . . . .**195** B5
Attlebridge Cl DE21 . . . .**219** D8
Attlee Rd S43 . . . . **97** B7
Atwall Ct DE23 . . . .**219** A1
Atworth Gr DE23 . . . .**230** F7
Auburn Cl DE7 . . . .**207** B8
Auckland Cl DE3 . . . .**217** F3
Auckland Dr S20 . . . . **59** E5
Auckland Pl DE56 . . . . . .**190** E2
Auckland Rise S20 . . . . . . **59** E6
Auckland's Pl S40 . . . . . .**266** B2
Auckland Way S20 . . . . . . **59** E6
Auction Cl DE6 . . . .**173** C2
Auden Cl DE65 . . . .**227** A8
Audens Way DE11 . . . . . .**256** C6
Audley Cl DE7 . . . .**194** D3
Audley Ctr DE1 . . . .**267** B3
Audrey Cotts S32 . . . . **71** C6
Audrey Cres NG19 . . . . . .**136** C5
Audrey Dr DE21 . . . .**220** A8
Audrey Rd S13 . . . . **44** C7
Aughton Cl S13 . . . . **44** D7
Aughton Cres S13 . . . . **44** D7
Aughton Dr S13 . . . . **44** C8
Augusta St DE23 . . . .**219** B2
Ault Dene DE11 . . . .**256** E4
AULT HUCKNALL **133** F7
Ault Hucknall La S44 . . . .**134** A7
Aults Cl DE65 . . . .**230** C1
Auriga Ct DE1 . . . .**219** B7
Austen Ave
Derby DE23 . . . .**231** B8
Long Eaton NG10 . . . .**236** C5
Austins Dr NG10 . . . .**223** B4
Austin Sq DE23 . . . .**231** F7
Austin St NG20 . . . .**120** A4
Autumn Gr DE21 . . . .**219** F5
Avalon Dr DE73 . . . .**244** F8
Avenue 1 S41 . . . .**115** B8
Avenue 2 S41 . . . .**115** B8
Avenue 3 S41 . . . .**115** B8
Avenue 4 S41 . . . .**115** B8
Avenue 5 S41 . . . .**115** B8
Avenue 6 S41 . . . .**115** B8
Avenue 7 S41 . . . .**115** B8
Avenue 8 S41 . . . .**115** B8
Avenue Cl S32 . . . . **72** A3
Avenue Rd
Chesterfield S41 . . . . **96** A8
Duffield DE56 . . . .**190** E5
Avenue The
Bakewell DE45 . . . .**109** D5
Belper DE56 . . . .**178** F2
Chapel-en-le-Frith SK23 . . **46** E2
Derby, Chaddesden DE21. .**219** F5
Derby DE1 . . . .**267** B2
Dronfield S18 . . . . **57** B2
Glossop SK13 . . . . **10** A4
Northwood DE4 . . . .**127** B6
Spinkhill S21 . . . . **60** D2
Stoney Middleton S32 . . . . **72** A3
Tissington DE6 . . . .**162** A5
Weston-on-Trent DE72 . . .**245** E5
Averham Cl
Derby DE21 . . . .**206** B1
Swadlincote DE11 . . . .**256** A3
Aviemore Cl S43 . . . . **77** E4
Aviemore Way DE24 . . . .**231** E4
Avis Ave DE75 . . . .**193** F7
Avocet Cl DE65 . . . .**182** B1
Avocet Ct DE24 . . . .**231** D4
Avocet Pl NG20 . . . .**120** D5
Avon Cl
Derby DE24 . . . .**231** D2
Dronfield S18 . . . . **57** B3
Swadlincote DE11 . . . .**256** B6
Avon Ct S41 . . . .**266** B4
Avondale Cl NG10 . . . . . .**236** A6
Avondale Rd
Bolsover S44 . . . .**118** A8
Chesterfield S40 . . . .**266** A4

Avondale Rd continued
Derby DE23 . . . .**267** B1
Derby, Spondon DE21 . . . .**220** D6
Ilkeston DE7 . . . .**208** C5
Staveley S43 . . . . **97** D7
Avonlea Cl DE7 . . . .**209** B6
Avonmouth Dr DE24 . . . .**232** E8
Avonside Cl S43 . . . . **78** B3
Avon St DE24 . . . .**232** E8
Avon Way
Burton upon Trent DE15 . .**248** A1
Hilton DE65 . . . .**228** D1
Awdishaw La DE6 . . . . . .**213** B5
AWSWORTH **195** C4
Awsworth La
Cossall S16 . . . .**195** C3
Kimberley NG16 . . . .**195** D6
Awsworth Prim Sch
NG16 . . . .**195** C4
Awsworth Rd DE7 . . . . . .**194** F2
Aycliffe Gdns DE24 . . . . .**232** F4
Aylesbury Ave DE21 . . . .**219** F7
Aylward Cl S2 . . . . **43** F7
Aylward Rd S2 . . . . **43** F7
Ayncourt Rd S42 . . . .**132** B7
Ayr Cl DE21 . . . .**220** D4
Ayre St DE55 . . . .**170** D7
Azalea Ave DE55 . . . .**170** A8
Azalea Cl DE55 . . . .**159** E3
Azalea Ct NG16 . . . .**195** C3

B

Babbacombe Cl DE24 . . .**233** C7
Babbacombe Ct S41 . . . . **95** F8
Babbington Cl DE13 . . . .**239** C5
Babbington La NG16 . . . .**195** F4
Babbington St DE55 . . . .**148** A6
Babbs La DE6 . . . .**211** C1
Babington Bsns Coll
DE1 . . . .**267** B1
Babington Cl S2 . . . . **43** F7
Babington Ct S2 . . . . **43** F7
Babington Hospl DE56 . .**178** F2
Babington La DE1 . . . . . .**267** B2
Bacchus Way DE55 . . . . .**147** B5
Back Bridge St SK22 . . . . **24** C1
Back Croft S45 . . . .**131** E2
Backhill La DE55 . . . .**151** F3
Back Jodrell St SK22 . . . . **33** B7
Back La
Alderwasley DE56 . . . .**166** E7
Alstonefield DE6 . . . .**149** E3
Biggin SK17 . . . .**138** D1
Brackenfield DE55 . . . .**146** A1
Calow S44 . . . .**116** B8
Castle Donington DE74 . . .**247** A6
Chellaston DE73 . . . .**233** A2
Darley Dale DE4 . . . .**127** F4
Eckington S21 . . . . **59** B3
Ellastone DE6 . . . .**183** A3
Elton DE4 . . . .**140** E6
Glapwell S44 . . . .**118** B1
Glossop SK13 . . . . **16** D6
Hathersage S32 . . . . **53** A7
Hilton DE65 . . . .**228** D2
Ilkeston DE7 . . . .**194** E2
Mottram in Longdendale
SK14 . . . . **9** A4
Palterton S44 . . . .**118** B5
Pilsley S45 . . . .**132** C2
Ripley DE5 . . . .**169** C6
Shirley DE6 . . . .**200** D7
Spout DE4 . . . .**166** D4
Stonebroom DE55 . . . .**146** F5
Sutton in Ashfield NG17 . .**148** F4
Thorpe Salvin S80 . . . . **63** B6
Thurvaston DE6 . . . .**215** B3
Tibshelf DE55 . . . .**147** F6
Unstone S18 . . . . **57** F1
Wessington DE55 . . . .**157** F8
Youlgreave DE45 . . . .**125** A6
Back Mellor Rd SK22 . . . . **24** C1
BACKMOOR **43** C2
Back Moor SK14 . . . .**9** A4
Backmoor Cres S8 . . . . . . **43** C2
Backmoor Rd S8 . . . . **43** D2
Back Rd S18 . . . . **57** F1
Back School La DE4 . . . . .**127** E2
Back Sitwell St DE1 . . . . .**267** B2
Back South St S43 . . . . . . **77** D3
Back St S33 . . . . **38** C3
Back Union Rd SK22 . . . . **33** C7
Back Wyver La DE56 . . . .**178** F5
Bacon Cl NG16 . . . .**195** A8
Bacon La DE5 . . . .**169** B6
Bacons La S40 . . . .**115** A8
Baden Powell Ave S40 . .**266** B1
Baden Powell Rd S40 . . .**266** B2
Badger Cl
Chesterfield S40 . . . .**114** B7
Derby DE21 . . . .**220** F6
Badgerdale Way DE23 . . .**231** A7
Badger La S45 . . . .**145** C8
Badgers Way SK13 . . . . . . **17** B7
Badgery Cl ST14 . . . .**210** A2
Badway La DE65 . . . .**227** C8
Bage Hill S42 . . . .**113** C6
Baggaley Cres NG19 . . . .**136** B1
Bag La
Marchington ST14 . . . .**224** E2
Roston DE6 . . . .**197** E2
Bagot St DE7 . . . .**207** C8
BAGSHAW **47** F7
Bagshaw Hill DE45 . . . . .**109** D6
Bagshaw La SK17 . . . . **48** B6
Bagshaw's Rd S12 . . . . . . **44** B6

Bagshaw St
Derby DE24 . . . .**232** E8
Pleasley NG19 . . . .**135** B4
BAGTHORPE **171** F4
Bagthorpe La S42 . . . . **94** A3
Bailey Ave DE12 . . . .**262** A3
Bailey Brook Cres
Aldercar NG16 . . . .**182** A4
Langley Mill NG16 . . . .**182** A3
Bailey Brook Dr NG16 . . .**182** A3
Bailey Brook Ind Est
NG16 . . . .**182** B2
Bailey Brook Rd NE7 . . . .**194** F5
Bailey Brook Wlk NG16 . .**182** A3
Bailey Dr S21 . . . . **60** C8
Bailey Gr SK17 . . . . **85** E8
BAILEY GROVE **182** D2
Bailey Grove Rd NG16 . . .**182** D2
Baileys Mill DE4 . . . .**143** D4
Bailey St
Derby DE23 . . . .**267** A1
Stapleford NG9 . . . .**223** C6
Bainbridge Rd S44 . . . . . . **98** F1
Bainbridge St DE23 . . . . .**219** A3
Baines Wood Cl S41 . . . . . **95** C8
Bains Dr DE72 . . . .**221** D1
Bakeacre La DE65 . . . . . .**230** E3
Bakehouse La DE72 . . . . .**221** C5
Bakehurst Cl SK22 . . . . . . **33** C7
Baker Ave DE75 . . . .**193** F7
Baker Cl DE55 . . . .**170** D7
Baker Dr S21 . . . . **60** C6
Baker Rd
Eastwood NG16 . . . .**195** C8
Mansfield Woodhouse
NG19 . . . .**136** C6
Bakers Hill DE56 . . . .**168** E1
Bakers La DE4 . . . .**156** A8
Baker's La
Cromford DE4 . . . .**155** A5
Doveridge DE6 . . . .**211** C1
Baker St
Burton upon Trent DE15 . .**254** E7
Creswell S80 . . . . **81** E2
Derby DE24 . . . .**232** F8
Ilkeston DE7 . . . .**194** F1
Swadlincote DE11 . . . .**256** C3
BAKESTONE MOOR **81** E5
Bakestone Moor S80 . . . . **81** F5
BAKEWELL **109** C5
Bakewell Bank SK13 . . . . . .**9** D1
Bakewell CE Inf Sch
DE45 . . . .**109** D6
Bakewell Cl
Derby DE3 . . . .**217** E3
Gamesley SK13 . . . .**9** D1
Bakewell Dr DE74 . . . . . .**247** A2
Bakewell Fold SK13 . . . . . .**9** D1
Bakewell Gdns SK13 . . . . . .**9** D1
Bakewell Gn
Gamesley SK13 . . . .**9** D1
Swadlincote DE11 . . . .**255** E5
Bakewell Gr SK13 . . . .**9** D1
Bakewell Lea SK13 . . . .**9** D1
Bakewell Meth Jun Sch
DE45 . . . .**109** D4
Bakewell Mews SK13 . . . . .**9** D1
Bakewell Rd
Baslow DE45 . . . . **91** E4
Buxton SK17 . . . . **85** C7
Darley Dale DE4 . . . .**142** F7
Long Eaton NG10 . . . .**236** E5
Matlock DE4 . . . .**143** A5
Over Haddon DE45 . . . . . .**109** B2
Staveley S43 . . . . **97** C5
Bakewell St DE22 . . . .**218** F4
Bakewell Station Ind Est
DE45 . . . .**109** C7
Bakewell Wlk SK13 . . . .**9** D1
Balaclava Rd DE23 . . . . . .**232** A8
Balfour Rd
Derby DE23 . . . .**232** A8
Stapleford NG9 . . . .**223** D6
Balgonie Ct DE73 . . . .**232** E2
Balham Wlk DE22 . . . .**218** A6
Balkham La NG20 . . . .**119** A2
Ballacraine Dr DE5 . . . . .**170** A1
Ballards Way DE72 . . . . . .**221** D1
Ballater Cl
Derby DE24 . . . .**231** E4
Mansfield NG19 . . . .**135** E2
Balleny Cl DE21 . . . .**205** F2
Ball Hill DE55 . . . .**160** C6
BALLIDON **152** A2
Ballidon Cl S41 . . . . **95** C6
Ball La DE72 . . . .**234** A5
Balmoak La S41 . . . . **96** C5
Balmoral Cl
Derby DE23 . . . .**218** B2
Heanor DE75 . . . .**181** C1
Mansfield Woodhouse
NG19 . . . .**136** E5
Sandiacre NG10 . . . .**223** B3
Balmoral Cres
Dronfield S18 . . . . **56** D2
Sheffield S10 . . . . **42** F8
Balmoral Ct DE74 . . . . . .**247** D5
Balmoral Dr NG19 . . . . . .**135** E2
Balmoral Rd
Borrowash DE72 . . . .**221** C1
Burton upon Trent DE15 . .**248** A3
Ilkeston DE7 . . . .**208** D5
Balmoral Way S43 . . . . . . **77** E4
Baltimore Cl DE11 . . . . . .**256** A7
Bamburgh Cl DE22 . . . . . .**204** D4
BAMFORD **40** B4
Bamford Ave
Derby DE23 . . . .**231** F8

Bamford Ave *continued*
North Wingfield S42 . . . . **131** F7
Bamford Fold 🟥 SK13 . . . . . .**9** E1
Bamford Gn 🟥 SK13 . . . .**9** E1
Bamford Ho S33 . . . . **40** B3
Bamford La SK13 . . . .**9** E1
Bamford Mews SK13 . . . .**9** E1
Bamford Mills S33 . . . . **40** B3
Bamford Prim Sch S33 . . . **40** B4
Bamford Rd S43 . . . . **97** C5
Bamford St
Chesterfield S43 . . . . **77** D4
Newton DE55 . . . . **148** A3
Ripley DE5 . . . . **180** D7
Bamford Sta S33 . . . . **40** B1
Banbury Ave NG9 . . . . **223** F3
Banchory Cl NG19 . . . . **135** E2
Bancroft Cl NG19 . . . . **135** E2
Bancroft Dr DE22 . . . . **204** C4
Bancroft The DE65 . . . . . . **229** B3
Bangor St DE21 . . . . **219** E8
Bank Bldgs SK13 . . . . **10** A5
Bankbottom SK13 . . . . **10** A5
Bank Cl
Bolsover S44 . . . . **99** A3
Creswell S80 . . . . **100** D8
Shirebrook NG20 . . . . **119** F4
Tibshelf DE55 . . . . **147** F5
Bank Ct DE22 . . . . **218** E8
Bankerwall La DE6 . . . . . . **183** C7
Bankfield Dr
Derby DE21 . . . . **220** F4
Ilkeston DE7 . . . . **208** B6
Bankgate SK14 . . . . **16** A8
Bank Gdns S43 . . . . **143** B6
Bankholmes Cl DE24 . . . . . **231** E2
Bank House Ct DE6 . . . . . **164** A2
Bank La SK13 . . . . **10** A7
Bank Rd
Chesterfield S41 . . . . **96** A6
Matlock DE4 . . . . **143** C5
Bank Row S33 . . . . **10** A7
Banksburn Cl DE75 . . . . . . **181** C1
Bankside DE45 . . . . **125** B5
Bank Side
Derby DE22 . . . . **204** E2
Hartington SK17 . . . . **137** D6
Bankside Cl SK6 . . . . **15** C1
Banks Rd NG9 . . . . **223** E2
Bank St
Brimington S43 . . . . **96** D8
Broadbottom SK14 . . . . **16** A8
Chesterfield S40 . . . . **95** E3
Glossop SK13 . . . . **17** D8
Hadfield SK13 . . . . **10** A5
Hayfield SK22 . . . . **25** D3
Langley Mill NG16 . . . . . . **182** C3
Long Eaton NG10 . . . . **236** E7
Somercotes DE55 . . . . **170** C8
Swadlincote DE11 . . . . **262** A8
BANKS THE **23** E3
Bankswood Cl SK13 . . . . . . **10** A4
Bank Terr SK13 . . . . **10** A5
Bank The
Bonsall DE4 . . . . **142** C1
Glossop SK13 . . . . **17** D8
Hayfield SK22 . . . . **25** B4
Stoney Middleton S32 . . . . **71** F4
BANK TOP **53** A8
Bank Top La S30 . . . . **72** C8
Bank Vale Rd SK22 . . . . . . **25** C3
Bank View SK17 . . . . **69** B5
Bank View Rd
Derby DE22 . . . . **218** F8
Nether Heage DE56 . . . . . . **168** C2
Bankwood Cl S14 . . . . **43** D5
Bank Wood Cl S40 . . . . **95** B7
BANKWOOD GATE **16** C8
Bankwood Prim Sch S14 . **43** D5
Bankwood Rd S14 . . . . **43** D5
Bannels Ave DE23 . . . . **231** B7
Banton's La DE73 . . . . **251** A4
Banwell Cl DE3 . . . . **217** C3
BARBER BOOTH **37** A6
Barber Cl DE7 . . . . **194** E3
Barber's La S21 . . . . **60** D7
Barber St SK13 . . . . **10** B5
Barbon Cl S40 . . . . **95** E5
Barcheston Cl DE21 . . . . . **206** B2
Barclay Ct DE7 . . . . **194** D3
Barclay Grange S41 . . . . . **266** C3
Bar Croft 🟥 S40 . . . . **95** C6
Barden Dr DE22 . . . . **204** F3
Bardolph Cl DE11 . . . . **255** F3
Bardsey Ct DE21 . . . . **206** B2
Bare Jarnett Road SK17 . **88** B1
Bare La DE72 . . . . **221** C5
Barf Cl DE3 . . . . **217** C1
BARGATE **179** C1
Bargate S33 . . . . **38** C2
Bargate Cl DE56 . . . . **179** C1
Bargate La DE65 . . . . **242** B5
Bargate Rd DE56 . . . . **179** B1
Barholme Cl S41 . . . . **95** B7
Barker Avenue E NG10 . . **223** B6
Barker Avenue N NG10 . . **223** A6
Barker Cl DE7 . . . . **193** B1
Barker Fold S40 . . . . **95** D3
Barker Gate DE7 . . . . **194** F2
Barker La S40 . . . . **95** D3
Barker St NG17 . . . . **148** F4
Barklam Cl DE12 . . . . **262** E1
BARLBOROUGH **80** B7
BARLBOROUGH COMMON **80** B5
Barlborough Hall Sch S43 **61** B1

Barlborough Prim Sch SK43 . . . . **80** B7
Barlborough Rd
Clowne S43 . . . . **80** D5
Ilkeston DE7 . . . . **194** F5
Barley Cft DE73 . . . . **232** F1
Barley Cl DE21 . . . . **205** C8
Barleycorn Cl DE15 . . . . . **248** A1
Barley Corn Cl DE21 . . . . . **206** C2
Barleycroft SK13 . . . . **9** F4
Barley Croft
Belper DE56 . . . . **179** B2
South Normanton DE55 . . **160** B4
Barley Dale Dr NG9 . . . . . **209** D2
Barley La S42 . . . . **95** A5
Barley Mews
Dronfield S18 . . . . **56** B2
Mansfield Woodhouse NG19 . . . . **136** E6
Barling Dr DE7 . . . . **194** C2
BARLOW **75** E2
Barlow CE Prim Sch S18 . **75** E3
Barlow Cottages La NG16 . . . . **195** C5
Barlow Drive N NG16 . . . . **195** B4
Barlow Drive S NG16 . . . . **195** B4
Barlow Lees La S18 . . . . . . **75** F7
Barlow Rd
Chapel-en-le-Frith SK23 . . **47** C6
Cutthorpe S18, S42 . . . . . . **94** F8
Staveley S43 . . . . **78** E1
Barlow St DE1, DE23 . . . . . **267** D1
Barlow View S18 . . . . **76** B7
Barlow Wood Dr SK6 . . . . . **23** B3
Barmote Croft DE4 . . . . . . **154** F1
Barms Way SK17 . . . . **66** D1
Barnard Ave S18 . . . . **57** D3
Barnard Rd DE21 . . . . **205** D2
Barn Cl
Castle Donington DE74 . . **247** B3
Chesterfield S41 . . . . **95** D6
Findern DE65 . . . . **230** D2
Glossop SK13 . . . . **17** D7
🟥 Nottingham NG10 . . . **236** C5
Quarndon DE22 . . . . **204** C6
Barn Croft DE23 . . . . **218** C1
Barnes Ave S18 . . . . **56** E2
Barnes Croft
Heanor DE75 . . . . **181** C1
Wirksworth DE4 . . . . **165** F8
Barnes Gn DE22 . . . . **218** B7
Barnes La
Dronfield S18 . . . . **56** C3
Youlgreave DE45 . . . . **125** C5
Barnes Rd S41 . . . . **96** E1
Barnfield Cl
Holmewood S42 . . . . **132** E8
🟥 Staveley S43 . . . . **78** E2
Barnfield Dr S32 . . . . **52** F7
Barnfields S32 . . . . **52** F7
Barnfield Wlk S43 . . . . **78** E2
Barn Furlong DE45 . . . . . . **90** A4
Barnham Cl S40 . . . . **114** B8
Barnsfold Ct SK22 . . . . **25** D3
Barnsley La DE4, DE56 . . . **165** F2
Barnstaple Cl DE21 . . . . . **206** A2
Barnstaple Ct 🟥 S41 . . . . **95** F4
Barns The S42 . . . . **115** B4
Barnwell Cl ST14 . . . . **210** A4
Barnwell La DE4 . . . . **155** A5
Barnwood Cl DE3 . . . . **217** C2
Baron Cl DE21 . . . . **206** D3
Barrack Rd S18 . . . . **58** A1
Barrack Yd DE55 . . . . **170** D7
Barratt Rd S21 . . . . **59** D2
Bar Rd
Baslow DE45 . . . . **91** F4
Curbar S32 . . . . **72** F2
Barrett St DE24 . . . . **233** A7
Barrie Dr DE24 . . . . **231** F5
Barringer Rd NG19 . . . . . . **136** D1
Barrington Cl
Burton upon Trent DE13 . **240** C1
Kirk Langley DE6 . . . . **202** F2
Barrons Ct DE72 . . . . **234** A5
Barron's Way DE72 . . . . . . **221** C1
Barroon DE74 . . . . **247** B3
Barry Rd S43 . . . . **96** F4
Barrys Cl 🟥 DE11 . . . . . . **256** E1
Barson Gr SK17 . . . . **85** E2
Bartle Ave S12 . . . . **43** F4
Bartle Dr S12 . . . . **43** F4
Bartle Rd S12 . . . . **43** F4
Bartle Way S12 . . . . **43** F4
Barton Bsns Pk DE13 . . . . **259** A8
Barton Cl DE21 . . . . **220** F6
Barton Cres S40 . . . . **95** A6
Barton Hill DE4 . . . . **126** C1
BARTON IN FABIS **237** E6
Barton Knowle DE56 . . . . **179** D4
Barton La NG11 . . . . **237** C2
Barton Rd
Long Eaton NG10 . . . . **237** A6
Sheffield S8 . . . . **43** A6
Barton St
Burton upon Trent DE14 . **254** C8
Clowne S43 . . . . **80** F4
BARTON TURN **253** B1
Barton Turn DE13 . . . . **253** A1

Barway DE6 . . . . **211** E8
Basegreen Ave S12 . . . . . . **44** B3
Basegreen Cl S12 . . . . **44** B3
Basegreen Cres S12 . . . . . . **44** B3
Basegreen Dr S12 . . . . **44** C3
Basegreen Pl S12 . . . . **44** C3
Basegreen Rd S12 . . . . **44** C3
Basegreen Way S12 . . . . . . **44** C3
Basil St S41 . . . . **266** B3
Basildon Cl DE24 . . . . **232** F5
Basingwerke Ct SK22 . . . . . **25** D3
BASLOW **91** F5
Baslow Cl
🟥 Gamesley SK13 . . . . **9** E1
Long Eaton NG10 . . . . **236** A5
Baslow Ct 🟥 S40 . . . . **95** D5
Baslow Dr DE22 . . . . **204** F3
Baslow Fold 🟥 SK13 . . . . . . **9** E1
Baslow Gn
🟥 Gamesley SK13 . . . . **9** E1
🟥 Swadlincote DE11 . . . . **255** E5
Baslow Gr SK17 . . . . **85** A6
Baslow Mews SK13 . . . .**9** E1
Baslow Rd
Bakewell DE45 . . . . **109** D7
Curbar S32 . . . . **72** D1
Holymoorside S42 . . . . **94** C1
Sheffield S17 . . . . **55** C4
Baslow Way 🟥 SK13 . . . .**9** E1
BASSETT **42** E5
Bassettbarn La S42 . . . . . **130** B5
Bassett Cl
Ilkeston DE7 . . . . **194** C3
Kimberley NG16 . . . . **195** E7
Bassett La S10 . . . . **42** E6
Bassett Rd NG16 . . . . **195** E7
Bassett The NG20 . . . . . . **119** E6
Bassford Ave DE75 . . . . . . **181** F2
Bassingham Ct DE21 . . . . **206** B1
Bassledene Ct 🟥 S2 . . . . . . **44** A8
Bassledene Rd S2 . . . . **44** A8
Bass's Cres DE11 . . . . **261** E7
Bass St DE22 . . . . **218** D6
Bateman Cl S43 . . . . **77** D4
Bateman St DE23 . . . . **219** C3
Batemill Rd SK22 . . . . **24** D2
BATEMOOR **57** A5
Batemoor Cl S8 . . . . **57** A6
Batemoor Dr S8 . . . . **57** A6
Batemoor Pl S8 . . . . **57** A6
Batemoor Rd S8 . . . . **57** A5
Batemoor Wlk S8 . . . . **57** A6
Bate Wood Ave S43 . . . . . . **97** B5
BATHAM GATE **66** F4
Batham Gate SK17 . . . . **48** F1
Batham Gate Rd SK17 . . . . **67** B6
Batham Rd S33 . . . . **51** A8
Bath La
Ashover S45 . . . . **129** F6
Moira DE12 . . . . **262** D4
Shirebrook NG19 . . . . **120** C2
Bath Rd
Buxton SK17 . . . . **85** B6
Derby DE3 . . . . **217** E2
Bath St
Bakewell DE45 . . . . **109** D6
Derby DE1 . . . . **267** B5
Ilkeston DE7 . . . . **194** E1
Bathurst Rd S44 . . . . **117** F8
Batholme Terr NG20 . . . . **100** F2
Batley La NG19 . . . . **134** E4
Batt St S8 . . . . **43** A8
Baulk La
Beeston NG9 . . . . **223** F7
Hathersage S32 . . . . **53** A8
Baverstock Cl DE73 . . . . . **232** F3
Baxter Hill NG19 . . . . **134** F3
Baxter Sq DE23 . . . . **231** A5
Baycliff Dr S40 . . . . **95** C3
Bay Ct S21 . . . . **60** C5
Bayleaf Cres DE21 . . . . . . **206** B3
Baysdale Croft S20 . . . . **59** D7
Baysdale Dr NG19 . . . . . . **136** F1
Bayswater Cl DE21 . . . . . . **217** F6
Bayswater Rd NG16 . . . . . **195** F7
Bazley Rd S2 . . . . **43** F6
Long Eaton NG10 . . . . **236** E7
Beackden Cl DE56 . . . . . . **179** E4
Beacomfold SK6 . . . . **15** B3
Beacon Dr DE13 . . . . **240** B3
Beaconfields Ho DE21 . . . **220** B4
Beacon Rd DE13 . . . . **240** B3
Beaconsfield St NG10 . . . . **236** E7
Beam Cl DE23 . . . . **240** A1
Beamwood Cl 🟥 DE21 . . . **205** F1
Beard Cres SK22 . . . . **33** D8
Beardmore Cl DE21 . . . . . **205** F2
Beards Rd DE11 . . . . **256** A6
Bearwood Hill Rd DE15 . . **248** A3
Beatrix Dr DE13 . . . . **9** E3
Beatty St DE24 . . . . **232** F8
Beatty Wlk DE7 . . . . **194** F3
BEAUCHIEF **56** D8
Beauchief Abbey La S8 . . . **56** C8
Beauchief Abbey (rems of)*
S8 . . . . **56** C8
Beauchief Dr S17 . . . . **56** C7
Beauchief Gdns DE55 . . . **170** D8
Beaufit La NG16 . . . . **160** D2
Beaufort Com Prim Sch
DE21 . . . . **219** C8
Beaufort Court Ind Est
DE21 . . . . **219** C8
Beaufort Rd
Burton upon Trent DE15 . **248** B1
Derby DE24 . . . . **231** B2
Beaufort St DE21 . . . . **219** D7
Beaulieu Way DE55 . . . . . **170** A7
Beaumaris Ct DE21 . . . . . **220** F5

Beaumont Cl
Barrow upon Trent DE73 . **244** A5
Belper DE56 . . . . **179** D4
Stapleford NG9 . . . . **209** E1
Beaumont Dr SK17 . . . . **47** F1
Beaumont Wlk DE23 . . . . . **231** E6
Beaurepaire Cres DE56 . . **179** B5
Beaureper Ave DE22 . . . . **204** E3
Beauvale Dr DE7 . . . . **194** C5
Becher St DE23 . . . . **219** A1
Beck Cl S44 . . . . **99** C2
Beckenham Way DE22 . . . **218** B6
Becket Ave S8 . . . . **56** D6
Becket Cres S8 . . . . **56** E6
Becket Prim Sch DE22 . . . **218** F4
Becket Rd S8 . . . . **56** E6
Becket St DE1 . . . . **267** A3
Becket Well La DE1 . . . . . . **267** B3
Becket Wlk S8 . . . . **56** E6
Beckett Ave NG19 . . . . . . **135** E1
Beckitt Cl DE24 . . . . **233** A8
Becksitch La DE56 . . . . . . **178** F2
Beckstich Ct DE56 . . . . . . **178** F1
Bedehouse La DE4 . . . . . . **155** A6
Bedford Cl DE22 . . . . **218** D3
Bedford Ct NG9 . . . . **209** E1
Bedford Rd DE15 . . . . **254** D7
Bedford St DE22 . . . . **218** D3
Bedgrave Cl S21 . . . . **60** F8
Bedgrave Gdns NG10 . . . . **236** E7
Belfield Rd
Etwall DE65 . . . . **229** C3
Swadlincote DE11 . . . . . . **256** B5
Belfield St DE7 . . . . **194** F2
Belfield Terr DE65 . . . . . . **229** B3
Belfit Dr S42 . . . . **114** F2
Belf Moor Cl S80 . . . . **82** A5
Belfry Cl DE3 . . . . **217** F1
Belfry The DE13 . . . . **240** C1
Belgrade Ave SK23 . . . . . . **34** E1
Belgrave Cl DE56 . . . . **179** C5
Belgrave Sq 🟥 S2 . . . . **43** A8
Belgrave St DE23 . . . . **267** B1
Belklane Dr S21 . . . . **60** E7
Bella Cl NG16 . . . . **182** B4
Belland La S45 . . . . **113** D2
Bell Ave DE72 . . . . **246** A7
Bell Cotts DE6 . . . . **224** C8
Belle Acre Cl 🟥 DE56 . . . **178** F3
Belle View Rd DE6 . . . . . . **173** B2
BELLEVUE **173** B2
Belle Vue Ave DE5 . . . . . . **180** C6
Belle Vue Cl S43 . . . . **96** D8
Bellhouse La S43 . . . . **78** F3
Bell House La S43 . . . . **78** F3
Bellhouse View S43 . . . . . . **78** F3
Bellingham Ct DE22 . . . . . **204** C2
Bell La
Bonsall DE4 . . . . **142** C1
Doveridge DE6 . . . . **224** C8
Hartshorne DE11 . . . . **257** A3
Heanor DE7, DE75 . . . . . . **193** C5
Bellrope Acre DE56 . . . . . **179** B2
Bells End Rd DE12 . . . . . . **253** D1
Bellsfield Cl S80 . . . . **82** A5
Belmont Ave DE72 . . . . . . **235** E8
Belmont Dr
Borrowash DE72 . . . . **221** B1
Marple SK6 . . . . **15** B1
Staveley S43 . . . . **78** F2
Belmont Prim Sch DE11 . **256** C4
Belmont St DE11 . . . . **256** C4
Belmont Terr 🟥 SK17 . . . . **85** B7
Belmot Rd DE13 . . . . **239** B4
Belpar Ho DE21 . . . . **220** E3
BELPER **179** B3
Belper La DE56 . . . . **178** E6
BELPER LANE END **178** C7
Belper L Ctr DE56 . . . . . . **179** D4
Belper Parks Nature Reserve* DE56 . . . . **179** A3
Belper Rd
Ashbourne DE6 . . . . **173** E1
🟥 Derby DE22 . . . . **218** F7
Holbrook DE56 . . . . **191** C8
Kilburn DE56 . . . . **179** E2
Morley DE7 . . . . **192** F2
Shirland DE55 . . . . **146** C2
Stanley Common DE7 . . . **193** B1
West Hallam DE7 . . . . . . **207** C8
Belper Sch DE56 . . . . **179** D4
Belper St DE7 . . . . **208** F7
Belper Sta DE56 . . . . **178** F4
BELPH **82** C4
Belsize Cl DE22 . . . . **217** F6
Belton Cl
Dronfield S18 . . . . **56** C1
Sandiacre NG10 . . . . **223** B4
Belton Dr DE5 . . . . **169** C1
Belvedere Ave S40 . . . . . . **114** E8
Belvedere Cl
Chesterfield S40 . . . . **114** A8
Derby DE3 . . . . **217** D3
Swanwick DE55 . . . . **169** F7
Belvedere Rd DE11 . . . . . **256** F2
Belvedere Terr 🟥 SK17 . . . **85** B6
Belvoir Cl
Breaston DE72 . . . . **235** D7
Ilkeston DE7 . . . . **208** D6
Long Eaton NG10 . . . . . . **236** E5
Belvoir Cres DE11 . . . . . . **256** A6
Belvoir St DE23 . . . . **218** F1
Belvoir Way DE55 . . . . . . **159** C1
Bembridge Dr DE24 . . . . . **233** C5
Bemrose Com Sch DE22 . **218** D4
Bemrose Gate S33 . . . . **40** A6
Bemrose Mews DE22 . . . . **218** C4

BEELEY **111** B4
Beeley Cl
Belper DE56 . . . . **179** C6
Creswell S80 . . . . **81** D1
Derby DE22 . . . . **204** D2
Derby, Oakwood DE21 . . . **205** F2
North Wingfield S42 . . . . **132** A7
Staveley S43 . . . . **97** C6
Beeley La DE4 . . . . **112** B3
Beeley View S40 . . . . **114** B7
Beeley Way S43 . . . . **97** C5
Beelow Cl SK17 . . . . **47** C7
BEESTON **223** E4
Beeston Cl S18 . . . . **56** C2
Beetroot Tree The*
DE72 . . . . **235** A7
Beetwell St S40 . . . . **266** B2
Beggarway La DE45 . . . . . . **90** B5
Beighton Dr DE5 . . . . **169** E1
Bek Cl NG19 . . . . **134** F7
Beldon Cl S2 . . . . **43** D7
Beldon Pl S2 . . . . **43** D7
Beldon Rd S2 . . . . **43** D7
Belfast Wlk DE21 . . . . **220** A4
Belfield Ct
Etwall DE65 . . . . **229** B3
Heanor DE75 . . . . **181** C4
Belfield Gdns NG10 . . . . . **236** E7

Bemrose Rd DE24......232 E7
Benbow Ave DE73......252 A8
Benches La SK6........15 E3
Bench Rd SK17.........85 D8
Bendall Gn DE23.......231 C5
Bendan Gdns DE22.....204 E1
Bend Oak Dr DE15.....248 C4
Benjamin Ct NG16......170 F3
Benjamin Outram Bsns Ctr
  DE5................180 E2
Benmore St DE21......206 B3
Benner Ave DE7.......209 A5
Bennerley Ave DE7.....194 F4
Bennerley Fields Specl Sch
  DE7................194 F4
Bennerley Sch DE7.....194 F4
Bennetts La DE6.......168 A8
Bennett St
  Buxton SK17.........85 C6
  Derby DE24..........232 D5
  Hollingworth SK14.....9 D5
  Long Eaton NG10....223 C2
  Sandiacre NG10.....223 B5
Bennimoor Way S40...114 E8
Bennington Wlk NG19..136 E4
Bennion Gr S41.......196 E5
Bennison Gdns S45....131 D3
Bensley Cl DE73......233 A1
Benson St DE24.......232 F7
Bentfield Rd DE56....168 C1
Bentham Rd S40........95 E5
Benthead La DE4......164 F1
Bentinck Dr S43........81 A4
Bentinck Rd S44........98 F7
Bentink Cl S81........81 C1
Bent La
  Church Broughton DE65..227 C6
  Darley Dale DE4.....127 D6
  Matlock DE4.........143 B7
  Spout DE4, DE56....166 C2
  Staveley S43.........79 A3
  Tissington DE6......162 D5
Bentley Bridge Cotts
  DE4................143 E7
Bentley Brook
  Hilton DE65.........228 D1
  Matlock DE4.........143 D4
Bentley Cl
  Alfreton DE55.......159 B3
  Matlock DE4.........143 D7
Bentley Dale DE11....257 A3
Bentley Rd
  Castle Donington DE74..246 F4
  Uttoxeter ST14......210 A2
Bentley St DE24......232 E6
Benton Dr SK6.........23 C8
Bents Cres S18........57 C3
Bentside Rd SK12......32 D5
Bents La S18..........57 C3
Bent The S32..........72 E3
Beowulf Covert DE13..240 B1
Beresford Ave
  Ashbourne DE6......173 D2
  Chapel-en-le-Frith SK23..47 C6
Beresford Cl S45......131 D2
Beresford Dale DE11..255 F2
Beresford Dr
  Derby DE21.........220 E4
  Ilkeston DE7........194 E5
Beresford La SK17....137 C2
Beresford Pl DE56....168 B6
Beresford Rd
  Chapel-en-le-Frith SK23..47 C6
  Long Eaton NG10....236 A5
  Mansfield Woodhouse
  NG19...............136 C6
Beresford Way S41.....76 D2
Berkeley Ave NG10...236 C6
Berkeley Ct DE23.....231 D7
Berkley Ct SK23.......45 D6
Berkshire St DE21....219 D8
Berle Ave DE75......181 E2
Bermuda Ave DE21....205 C6
Bernard Ave NG19....136 B5
Bernard Cl S43........96 F8
Bernard Ct DE11.....256 D3
Bernard Gadsby Cl DE6..173 A1
Bernard St
  Glossop SK13.........10 C1
  Swadlincote DE11....256 D3
Bernard Walker Ct SK6..15 B2
Berners Cl S2.........43 E6
Berners Dr S2.........43 E6
Berners Pl S2.........43 E6
Berners Rd S2.........43 E6
Berridge La S45......145 B4
Berrisford La DE55...145 D7
Berristow La DE55....160 C7
Berry Ave S21.........59 C3
Berry Gdns DE15.....248 C4
Berry Hedge La DE15..248 C4
Berry Park Cl DE22...204 E1
Berry St S42.........131 E6
Bertrand Ave S45.....131 D3
Berwick Ave
  Chesterfield S40.....114 C7
  Derby DE21..........219 C7
Berwick Cl DE24.....233 B5
Berwick Ct S40......114 C7
Berwick Dr DE24.....231 D3
Berwick Rd SK17......85 C4
Berwin Cl NG10......223 A1
Berwyn Cl S40.........95 C5
Besom La S32.........53 A8
Bessalone Dr DE56...179 A6

Bessell La NG9.......223 D5
Bessie La S33.........51 B6
Best Ave DE15........248 B1
Besthill Cotts SK14...16 B8
Besthorpe Cl DE21....206 B1
Bestwick Ave DE75...182 B1
Bestwick Cl DE7......209 A4
Bestwood Dr S45.....131 D3
Bestwood Pk S45.....131 C3
Bestwood Rd NG16...160 E2
Bethel Terr S81........63 E7
Bethulie Rd DE23....232 A8
Betjeman Sq DE24....232 A5
Betlingspring La DE6..184 D3
Betony Cl S21.........60 B5
Betony Rd DE15......248 C2
Betty La DE45........108 F8
Bevan Ct DE55.......146 E1
Bevan Dr S43..........97 B7
Bevan Rd S45........131 D2
Bevan St DE55.......146 E1
Beverley Dr NG16....195 E7
Beverley Rd DE14....254 A7
Beverleys Rd S8.......43 A4
Beverley St DE24....219 D2
Bevin Pl S42.........132 A7
Bewdley Cl DE73.....233 A3
Bexhill Wlk DE21.....205 E1
Bexley Cl SK13........10 C3
BIBBINGTON........66 F7
Bicester Ave DE24....231 C2
Bickley Moss DE21...206 B1
Bideford Cl DE5......169 D2
Bideford Ct S41.......95 F8
Bideford Dr DE23....231 D6
Bidston Cl DE4......143 C7
Bidworth La SK13......9 D1
BIGGIN
  Hartington.........138 C4
  Hulland Ward.......176 A5
Biggin CE Prim Sch
  SK17..............138 D3
Biggin Cl S45........131 D1
Biggin La
  Alfreton DE55.......133 A1
  Hulland Ward DE6...176 B3
Bigginmill La DE6....176 C5
Biggin The DE74.....247 B3
Bigin View DE6......175 E3
Big La DE6...........164 A4
Bilberry Cl DE21.....205 F1
Bilby La S43..........77 C1
Billam St S21..........59 B3
Billingsley Ave NG16..160 D3
Bingham St DE24....232 E6
Bings Rd SK23........45 F8
Bingswood Ave SK23..45 E8
Bingswood Ind Est SK23..45 E8
Bingswood Rd SK23...45 E8
Binscombe La DE21...205 F3
Birch Ave
  Ambergate DE56....167 F3
  Ilkeston DE7.........209 A4
  Swadlincote DE11...256 A7
Birch Cl
  Alfreton DE55.......159 A5
  Burton upon Trent DE14..254 A8
  Buxton SK17..........66 B1
  Denstone ST14......196 D6
  Derby DE21.........221 A6
  Grassmoor S42......115 F3
  Killamarsh S21.......60 C5
  Ripley DE5..........180 D8
  Wessington DE55...157 E8
BIRCH CROSS........224 C2
Birchen Cl
  Chesterfield S40......95 D5
  Dronfield S18.........56 D1
Birchen Holme DE55..160 A4
Birches Ave DE55....157 F5
Birches Fold S18......57 C4
Birches La
  Dronfield S18........57 C4
  South Wingfield DE55..158 A5
Birches Rd DE22.....204 D4
Birches The SK22......25 C2
Birch Farm Ave S8....57 A8
Birchfield Cl DE73....232 F2
Birchfield Pk DE75...193 F7
Birchfield Rd DE15...254 E6
Birch Gn SK13.........10 E1
Birch Gr
  Hatton DE65........227 D2
  Shirebrook NG20....119 D5
Birch Hall Cl SK22.....25 B2
Birch Holt Gr S18.....76 E5
Birch House Way S18..57 C1
Birchills The S80......81 C1
Birchitt Cl S17........56 C5
Birchitt Ct S17........56 C5
Birchitt Pl S17........56 C5
Birchitt Rd S17.......56 C5
Birchitt View S18......57 A3
Birch Kiln Croft S43...96 F7
Birch La S43...........78 A1
Birchlands NG19.....136 F1
Birchlands Dr S21.....60 D5
BIRCHOVER.........126 B1
Birchover Ct S41......95 E6
Birchover Edge DE4..141 B8
Birchover Ho
  1 Derby, Allestree
  DE22..............204 F3
  Derby, Markeaton DE22..218 D8
Birchover La DE4....141 B7
Birchover Pl DE7.....194 E5
Birchover Rd DE4....126 C3
Birchover Rise DE21..205 F1

Birchover Way DE22..204 E2
Birch Rd S80..........82 C6
Birchside Ave SK13....10 B2
Birch St NG20........120 F6
BIRCH VALE...........25 B2
Birch Vale Ind Est SK22..25 A2
Birchvale Rd S12......44 D3
Birch Vale Terr SK22...24 F3
Birchview Cl DE56....179 B2
Birch View Ct DE1....218 F7
Birchway Gr DE23....231 A6
Birchwood DE75......181 C4
Birchwood Ave
  Derby DE23.........231 D6
  Long Eaton, Breaston
  NG10...............236 A7
  Long Eaton, New Sawley
  NG10...............236 A5
Birchwood Cl
  7 Sheffield S20.....59 E8
  South Normanton DE55..160 A4
Birchwood Cres
  Chesterfield S40.....114 F7
  Somercotes DE55...170 D8
Birchwood Croft S20..59 E8
Birchwood Ct S40....114 F7
Birchwood Dr DE56..168 B4
Birchwood Gdns **6** S20..59 E8
Birchwood Gr S20.....59 E8
Birchwood La DE55..159 E3
Birchwood Rd
  Alfreton DE55.......159 C3
  Eckington S21........58 D4
Birchwood Rise **5** S20..59 E8
Birchwood View
  Ashbourne DE6......173 C3
  Sheffield S20.........59 E8
Birchwood Way
  16 Sheffield S20....59 E8
  Somercotes DE55...159 C1
Bircumshaw's Rd DE75..181 E2
Birdcage Wlk DE22...217 F6
Birdcroft La DE7.....208 F5
BIRDHOLME.........115 A7
Birdholme Cres S40..115 A8
Birding St NG19.....136 B1
Birdsgrove La
  Ashbourne DE6......172 D3
  Mayfield DE6........172 D4
Bird St S43...........78 F2
Birdwood St DE23...218 F1
Birkdale Ave DE14...254 A6
Birkdale Cl
  Derby DE3..........218 A2
  Ilkeston DE7........194 D1
Birkdale Dr S40.....114 D8
Birk Hill Inf Sch S21..59 B2
Birkin Ave S42.......115 C1
Birkin La
  Grassmoor S42......115 F2
  Holmewood S42.....116 A3
  Wingerworth S40, S42..114 C1
Birkin Lane W S42....115 F2
Birkinstyle Ave DE55..146 F3
Birkinstyle La DE55..146 E3
Birkland Ave NG19...136 D3
Birks Cl S80..........82 D6
Birley Brook Dr S40...95 B7
Birley Com Coll S12...44 D3
Birley Com Prim Sch S12..44 D3
Birley Croft S41.......95 B7
BIRLEYHAY...........58 D5
Birley La
  Bamford S32.........40 F2
  Sheffield S12.........44 D2
Birley Moor Ave S12...44 E3
Birley Moor Cl S12....44 E3
Birley Moor Cres S12..44 E2
Birley Moor Dr S12....44 E2
Birley Moor Pl S12.....44 E2
Birley Moor Rd S12....44 E4
Birley Moor Way S12..44 E2
Birley School Mews S13..44 E5
Birley Spa Com Prim Sch
  S12...............44 F4
Birley Spa La S12......44 F3
Birley St NG9........223 D6
Birley Vale Ave S12...44 C5
Birley Vale Cl S12.....44 C4
Birstall Cl S41........95 C7
Biscay Ct DE21......206 C2
Bishopdale Cl NG10..236 A6
Bishopdale Dr S20.....59 A8
Bishopdale Rise S20...59 A8
Bishop Lonsdale CE Prim Sch
  DE22..............218 E3
Bishop Purslove CE Pirmary
  Sch SK17............69 C4
Bishops Cl DE5......180 E8
Bishopscourt Rd S8...43 A5
Bishops Ct
  Melbourne DE73....252 B7
  Sheffield S8..........43 B5
Bishop's Dr DE73....252 B7
Bishop's Dr DE21....205 E2
Bishops Gate DE11..256 E2
Bishop's Gn DE22....218 D3
Bishop's House (Mus)*
  S8................43 A4
Bishop's La SK17......84 E7
Bishop St
  Alfreton DE55.......159 A5
  Eastwood NG16.....182 F2
Bispham Dr NG9.....223 F2
Bitham Ct DE13.....240 C1
Bitham La DE13.....240 D1

Blaby Cl DE23........231 E6
Blacka Moor Cres S17..55 C6
Blacka Moor Rd S17...55 C6
Blacka Moor View S17..55 C6
Blackbanks S44.......80 A1
Blackberry Ct S43.....80 D4
Blackberry Flats S20...59 E7
Blackberry Way S56..179 F2
Blackbird Row DE56..179 C1
BLACKBROOK
  Belper.............178 B4
  Chapel-en-le-Frith....47 E6
  Tutbury............238 C1
Blackbrook La S43.....47 E6
Blackburn Pl DE7.....194 E3
Blackcliff Field Cl S80..82 A5
Blackdown Ave S40....95 B5
BLACKFORDBY.......257 C1
Blackfordby Prim Sch
  DE11..............257 B1
Black Harry La S32....71 B2
Black Hills Dr DE7....208 F6
Blackmore St DE23...231 F7
Blackmount Ct **5** DE24..231 D3
Blackpool St DE14...254 C8
Black Rock* DE4....155 A4
Blackrocks Ave DE4..142 F7
Blackshaw Clough SK13..10 E3
Blackshaw Rd SK13...10 E2
Blacks La S42........131 D7
Blacksmith Croft DE5..180 D7
Blacksmith La S44....97 A3
Blacksmiths Cl
  Glapwell S44.......118 C1
  Nethersole DE12....264 F7
Blacksmith's La
  Egginton DE65......241 A6
  Newton Solney DE15..248 E8
  Woodville DE11.....256 F3
Blacksmiths Yd
  Darley Dale DE4.....127 E2
  Rolleston DE13......240 B4
Blacksmith Way NG20..119 F2
Blackstock Cl S14.....43 D2
Blackstock Cres S14...43 D2
Blackstock Dr S14.....43 D2
Blackstock Rd S14.....43 D4
Blackstone Cl DE55..170 D7
Blackthorn Cl
  Chesterfield S41.....115 D8
  Derby DE21.........205 E2
  Melbourne DE73....252 A8
Blackthorn Dr NG16..182 E2
Blackthorne Cl DE56..179 F2
Blackthorn Rd DE15..254 E6
Black Tor Rd DE4....154 D8
BLACKWALL.........175 F7
Blackwall La DE6....176 A8
BLACKWELL
  Sutton in Ashfield...147 F1
  Taddington..........87 D5
Blackwell Ave DE7...194 F5
Blackwell La
  Melbourne DE73....252 B7
  Monyash S45........107 B3
Blackwell Mill Cotts SK17..87 A6
Blackwell Prim Sch
  DE55..............147 F1
Blackwell Rd NG17...148 E3
Bladon House Sch DE15..248 B6
Bladon St DE15......248 C4
Bladon View DE13...241 A2
Blagdon Cl DE4......127 C3
Blagreaves Ave DE23..231 C5
Blagreaves La DE23..231 C6
Blair Gr NG10.......223 C4
Blair Ho DE23........231 C5
Blakebrook Dr DE73..233 A3
Blake Cl NG10.......236 B5
Blakeley La DE65....229 B2
Blakelow Dr DE65...229 B3
Blakelow La DE4.....142 A3
Blakemere La DE4...141 F1
Blakemore Ave DE73..252 B8
Blakeney Ct
  Derby DE21.........206 C1
  3 Mansfield Woodhouse
  NG19...............136 E4
Blake Rd NG9........223 E6
Blake St
  Ilkeston DE7........194 F1
  Mansfield Woodhouse
  NG19...............136 B2
Blanch Croft DE73...252 B7
Blandford Ave NG10..236 B6
Blandford Cl DE24...233 D6
Blandford Dr S41......95 E7
Blankney Cl DE24....231 D2
Blay Ct S43...........77 D4
Bleaklow Wlk **29** SK13..9 E1
Blencathra Dr DE3...230 E8
Blenheim Ave DE55..170 A8
Blenheim Cl
  Burton upon Trent DE15..248 C3
  4 Glossop SK13....10 A5
  Mansfield NG19.....136 D1
  3 Swadlincote DE11..256 A7
Blenheim Ct DE56...179 D5
Blenheim Dr DE22...204 D4
Blenheim Ho **1** DE14..253 F7
Blenheim Mews S20..229 C4
Blenheim Par DE22..204 D4
Blenheim Pl NG17...148 E3
Blenheim Rd DE6.....185 E7
Blenhiem Ct **3** NG10..223 B4
Blind La
  Bolsover S44........98 F3
  Breaston DE72......235 D8

Blind La continued
  Darley Dale DE4.....127 F1
  Kirk Ireton DE6.....165 A2
  1 Wirksworth DE4..165 F8
Blisworth Way DE55..169 F8
Blithe Cl DE65......228 E1
Blithfield Gdns DE73..233 A2
Bloomery Way S45...131 E3
Bloomfield Cl
  Derby DE1..........267 C4
  Hilton DE65.........228 D1
Bloomfield Rd DE55..170 A8
Bloomfield St DE1...267 C4
Bloomsgrove Rd DE7..194 F2
Bloom St DE1........267 B2
Blore Cl DE6........185 D8
Blossom Cres S12.....44 B3
Blossom Wlk DE65...227 C1
Bluebank View S43...77 D3
Bluebell Cl
  Barlborough S43.....80 B6
  Derby DE24.........231 D2
  Donisthorpe DE12..262 E1
  Hayfield SK22........25 C3
  Shirebrook NG20...119 D3
  Somercotes DE55...159 E2
  Underwood Green NG16..171 F2
Blue Bell Cl S43......97 B5
Bluebell Croft DE4...143 B3
Bluebell Hill DE55...146 C4
Bluebell Pl NG19....136 F4
Bluebell Way DE75..182 B3
Bluebell Wlk S80.....81 E3
Blueberry Cl S43......97 B5
Blueberry Way DE11..256 F3
Bluebird Ct DE24....231 D4
Blue Cedars Dr DE15..248 D2
Blue John Cavern* S33..37 E3
Blue Lodge Cl S43....97 B5
Blue Mountains DE56..191 B1
Blue Ridge Cl S17.....55 E7
Bluestone La DE15...255 A7
Blundestone La DE4..156 A2
Blunt Ave S43.........79 C4
Blunt St DE7.........193 A2
Blyth Cl
  Chesterfield S40....114 B8
  Mansfield NG19.....135 D1
Blyth Ct DE74.......247 B4
Blythe Ct NG19......135 D1
Blyth Pl DE21........205 D1
Boam La DE4.........142 F8
Boardman Ind Est DE11..255 B4
Boardman Rd DE11..255 E2
Boarfold La SK6.......15 E5
Boars Head Ind Est DE1..267 C4
Boarslack La SK17.....69 E2
Boarstones La SK17...85 E8
Boat La NG16........182 A7
Boatmans Cl DE7....194 F5
Bobbin Mill SK17.....89 A6
Bobbinmill Hill DE56..168 B7
Bobbin Mill La S40....95 D2
Bobbin Way DE56...179 C5
Bochum Parkway S8...57 C8
Bocking La S8........56 E8
Bocking Rise S8......56 E8
Boden St DE23......219 B2
Bodmin Cl DE24.....231 D3
Bodmin Way **3** S40...95 C5
Boggard La SK13......16 D6
Bogguard Rd SK6.....24 A4
Boggy La
  Bradwell S33.........51 B6
  Church Broughton, Heathtop
  DE65..............227 A6
Bog La DE73.........251 E5
Bohem Rd NG10.....223 C3
Boiley La S21.........60 C4
Boland Rd S8.........56 D5
Bolden Terr DE55...147 C1
Bold La DE1.........267 B3
BOLEHILL
  Calow.............97 B1
  Sheffield...........43 A2
  Wirksworth.........155 A2
BOLE HILL...........75 C2
Bole Hill S8..........43 A2
Bole Hill Cotts S44....97 A1
Bolehill Croft DE4...155 A3
Bolehill Ct **3** S40....95 D5
Bolehill La
  Eckington S21........58 F2
  Northedge S42......130 C3
  Wingerworth S42...114 D1
Bolehill Rd DE4......155 A3
BOLSOVER............99 B3
Bolsover Bsns Pk S44..98 E2
Bolsover Castle* S44...99 A2
Bolsover CE Jun Sch S44..99 B2
Bolsover Cl DE5......169 E1
Bolsover Hill S44......99 A2
Bolsover Hospl S44....99 C2
Bolsover Inf Sch S44...99 B2
Bolsover Rd
  Mastin Moor S43.....79 D2
  Shuttlewood S44.....98 F6
Bolsover Sch S44.....99 C1
Bolton St DE55......169 D7
Boman's La DE56....177 F8
Bonchurch Cl DE24..233 C5
Bondfield Rd S43......97 C7
Bondgate DE74......247 B3
Bondhay La S80.......62 C2
Bond La DE56.......168 E2
Bonds Cl DE7........194 F5
Bond St S43..........97 C8
Bonington Rise SK6...23 B8

Bonner's Rd NG16 . . . . . . 195 C4
Bonnington Dr DE55 . . . . 170 D8
Bonnyrigg Dr DE21 . . . . . 206 A2
BONSALL 142 E1
Bonsall Ave DE23 . . . . . . 231 D8
Bonsall Bank SK13 . . . . .9 E2
Bonsall CE Prim Sch
 DE4 . . . . 142 E1
Bonsall Cl SK13 . . . . .9 E2
Bonsall Ct
 2 Chesterfield S41 . . . . . 95 D7
 Long Eaton NG10 . . . . . . 236 F8
BONSALL DALE 142 D1
Bonsall Dr
 Derby DE3 . . . . 217 E3
 Somercotes DE55 . . . . . . 170 D8
Bonsall Fold SK13 . . . . .9 E2
Bonsall La
 Alfreton DE55 . . . . 158 F4
 Winster DE4 . . . . 141 C4
Bonsallmoor La DE4 . . . . 141 E3
Bonsall St NG10 . . . . 236 E8
Bonser Cres NG17 . . . . . . 148 E2
Booker Cl S43 . . . . 97 C6
Boothby Ave **1** DE6 . . . 173 C2
Booth Cres NG19 . . . . 135 D2
Booth Dr DE6 . . . . 185 C8
BOOTHGATE 179 E7
Boothgate DE56 . . . . 179 E7
Boot Hill DE65 . . . . 242 C3
BOOTHORPE 262 F8
Booth's Ct **1** SK13 . . . . 10 D1
Booth St
 Derby DE24 . . . . 232 F7
 Hollingworth SK14 . . . . 9 C5
 Mansfield Woodhouse
  NG19 . . . . 136 B3
 Ripley DE5 . . . . 169 E2
Booth Trad Est NE7 . . . . 194 F2
Boots Yd NG17 . . . . 148 F3
Border Cl S43 . . . . 80 F3
Border Cres DE24 . . . . . . 233 B5
Border La S80 . . . . 80 F2
Borlace Cres NG9 . . . . . . 223 E6
Borough St DE74 . . . . 247 B3
BORROWASH 221 C2
Borrowash By-pass
 DE72 . . . . 221 C3
Borrowash Rd DE21 . . . . 220 F4
Borrowdale Ave **3** S20 . . 59 E6
Borrowdale Cl **2** S20 . . . 59 E6
Borrowdale Dr
 Long Eaton NG10 . . . . . . 236 A6
 Sheffield S20 . . . . 59 E6
Borrowdale Rd S20 . . . . . 59 E6
Borrowfield Rd DE21 . . . 220 F3
Borrowfields DE72 . . . . . 221 B1
Borrow Wood Inf Sch
 DE21 . . . . 220 F5
Borrow Wood Jun Sch
 DE21 . . . . 220 F5
Boscastle Rd DE24 . . . . . 233 B6
Boscawen Ct NE7 . . . . . . 194 F4
Boscowan Ct DE7 . . . . . . 194 F4
Bosley Mews DE56 . . . . . 178 F5
Bostock Rd SK14 . . . . 16 A8
Bostock's La
 Long Eaton NG10 . . . . . . 223 A3
 Risley NG10, NG72 . . . . . 222 F4
Boston Cl DE21 . . . . 220 C6
Boswell Cl **3** DE6 . . . . . 173 B2
Boswell Sq DE23 . . . . 231 F7
Bosworth Ave DE23 . . . . 231 E6
Bosworth Rd DE74 . . . . . 246 F3
Bosworth Way NG10 . . . 236 E5
Botany Bsns Pk S45 . . . . . 45 D6
Botany Mews SK23 . . . . . . 45 E6
Bothe Cl NG10 . . . . 236 C6
Bottlebrook Houses DE5 180 B1
Bottomhill Rd SK17 . . . . . . 69 E1
Bottom Lons DE6 . . . . . . 176 B8
Bottom Rd S42 . . . . 114 E1
Boughton Dr DE55 . . . . . 169 F8
Boughton La S43 . . . . 80 D4
Bould St NG19 . . . . 135 F1
Boulevard The SK14 . . . . . . 9 D4
BOULTON 233 B6
Boulton Cl S40 . . . . 95 A5
Boulton Dr DE24 . . . . 233 A6
Boulton La
 Derby, Allenton DE24 . . . 232 F5
 Derby DE24 . . . . 233 A6
Boulton Prim Sch DE24 . 233 A6
BOUNDARY 257 C2
Boundary Cl
 Shirebrook NG20 . . . . . . 119 E6
 Staveley S43 . . . . 79 A3
Boundary Gdns DE55 . . . 147 F5
Boundary La NG16 . . . . . 182 C3
Boundary Rd
 Derby DE22 . . . . 218 E4
 Egginton DE65 . . . . 241 D8
Boundary Wlk NG20 . . . . 100 F1
Bournebrook Ave DE4 . . 165 F7
Bourne Cl
 Brimington S43 . . . . 96 E8
 Tutbury DE13 . . . . 239 B6
Bourne Dr NG16 . . . . 182 B3
Bourne Mill Cl S43 . . . . . . 80 B6
Bourne Sq DE72 . . . . 235 E7
Bourne St DE1 . . . . 267 B2
Bourne Way DE11 . . . . . . 256 D4
Bowbank Cl DE23 . . . . . . 231 A6
Bowbridge Ave DE23 . . . 231 C5
Bowden Cl SK22 . . . . 25 C3
Bowden Cres SK22 . . . . . . 33 D8
BOWDEN HEAD 35 D1

Bowden Hey Rd SK23 . . . . 47 C7
Bowden La
 Chapel-en-le-Frith SK23 . . 47 C7
 Hope S33 . . . . 39 A4
Bowden Rd SK13 . . . . 10 C3
Bowdon Ave S43 . . . . 80 A6
Bower Dr DE4 . . . . 156 F1
Bower Farm Rd S41 . . . . . 77 B2
Bower St DE24 . . . . 232 F8
Boweswell Rd DE7 . . . . . 194 E2
Bowland Cl DE3 . . . . 217 E1
Bowland Dr S40 . . . . 114 B7
Bowland Rd SK13 . . . . 17 A8
Bowlees Ct DE23 . . . . 230 E7
Bowler La
 Darley Dale DE4 . . . . 143 B8
 Matlock DE4 . . . . 143 B8
Bowler Rd DE4 . . . . 127 C3
Bowler St DE5 . . . . 180 D7
Bowling Alley La DE6 . . . 168 E1
Bowlingalley La DE6 . . . 197 D8
Bowling Alley La DE6 . . . 212 A5
Bowling Cl DE7 . . . . 222 E8
Bowling Gn DE4 . . . . 153 A1
Bowling Green La
 Chapel-en-le-Frith SK23 . . 47 B6
 Wirksworth DE4 . . . . 154 L1
Bowling Green Rd **2**
 ST14 . . . . 210 B1
Bowman Cl S12 . . . . 43 F2
Bowmer La DE56 . . . . 168 B6
Bowmer Rd DE24 . . . . . . 219 E1
Bown Cl DE56 . . . . 192 A8
Bowness Cl
 Chesterfield S41 . . . . 95 D7
 Dronfield S18 . . . . 56 E1
Bowness Rd S41 . . . . 95 D7
Bowns Hill DE4 . . . . 157 A1
Bowns Yd DE55 . . . . 170 D8
BOWSHAW 56 F4
Bowshaw S18 . . . . 56 F4
Bowshaw Ave S8 . . . . 57 A5
Bowshaw Cl S8 . . . . 57 A5
Bowshaw View S8 . . . . . . 57 A5
Bow St NG19 . . . . 136 E4
Box Cl DE11 . . . . 256 E3
Boxmoor Cl DE23 . . . . . . 230 F7
Boyd Gr DE73 . . . . 245 A8
Boyer St DE22 . . . . 267 A1
Boyer Wlk DE22 . . . . 267 A1
BOYLESTONE 213 C4
Boylestone Rd DE23 . . . . 231 C5
BOYLESTONFIELD 213 E5
BOYTHORPE 95 E1
Boythorpe Ave S40 . . . . . 266 A2
Boythorpe Bsns Units S40 95 E2
Boythorpe Cl DE7 . . . . . . 194 F5
Boythorpe Cres S40 . . . . 266 A1
Boythorpe Mount S40 . . 266 A2
Boythorpe Rd S40 . . . . . . 266 A2
Boythorpe Rise S40 . . . . . 95 E2
Brabyns Brow SK6 . . . . . . 23 A7
Brabyns Prep Sch SK6 . . . 23 A7
Bracken Ave S44 . . . . 116 F1
Bracken Cl
 Hollingworth SK14 . . . . 9 D6
 Long Eaton NG10 . . . . . . 223 B1
 Marple SK6 . . . . 23 C7
Brackendale Ave S45 . . . 131 E2
Brackendale Cl S43 . . . . . . 96 D7
Brackendale La DE6 . . . . 163 E5
Brackendale Rd DE55 . . . 169 F8
BRACKENFIELD 145 D2
Brackenfield Ave NG19 . 136 E4
Brackenfield Dr NG16 . . 195 B7
Brackenfield Gr S12 . . . . . 44 D3
Brackenfield La
 Brackenfield DE55 . . . . . 145 D1
 Wessington DE55 . . . . . . 157 D8
Brackenfield Specl Sch
 NG10 . . . . 223 B1
Bracken La DE4 . . . . 156 B5
Bracken Rd
 Long Eaton NG10 . . . . . . 223 B1
 Shirebrook NG20 . . . . . . 119 D3
Brackens Ave DE24 . . . . . 232 F5
Brackensdale Ave DE22 . 218 B5
Brackensdale Inf Sch
 DE22 . . . . 218 B6
Brackensdale Jun Sch
 DE22 . . . . 218 B6
Brackens La S43 . . . . 80 B6
Bracken's La DE24 . . . . . 232 F6
Bracken Way SK13 . . . . . . 17 F7
Brackenwood Rd DE15 . 254 E6
Brackley Dr DE21 . . . . . . 220 E5
Brackley Gate DE7 . . . . . 192 A2
Brackmills Cl **7** NG19 . 136 E1
Bracknell Dr DE24 . . . . . 232 F5
BRADBOURNE 163 C6
Bradbourne Cl S43 . . . . . . 97 C8
Bradbourne Ct DE22 . . . . 218 E3
Bradbury Cl
 Borrowash DE72 . . . . . . 221 C1
 Chesterfield S40 . . . . 95 E3
Bradbury Dr S42 . . . . 114 E4
Bradbury Pl S40 . . . . 95 E3
Bradbury St S8 . . . . 43 A6
Braddon Ave NG9 . . . . . . 209 E1
Bradgate Cl NG10 . . . . . . 223 B4
Bradgate Croft S41 . . . . . 115 C7
Bradgate Ct DE23 . . . . . . 231 E6
Bradgate Dr DE5 . . . . 169 B1
Brading Cl DE24 . . . . 233 D5
BRADLEY 186 F8
Bradley CE Prim Sch
 DE6 . . . . 186 F8

Bradley Cl
 Birchover DE4 . . . . 126 B1
 6 Brimington S43 . . . . . . 96 E8
Bradley Dr DE56 . . . . 179 B4
Bradley La S18 . . . . 75 C4
Bradley St
 Burton upon Trent DE15 . 254 E7
 Derby DE22 . . . . 218 E8
 Sandiacre NG10 . . . . 223 C5
Bradley View **5** DE6 . . 173 D3
Bradley Way S43 . . . . 96 E7
Bradmoor Gr DE73 . . . . . 233 B2
Bradshaw Ave DE55 . . . . 170 E6
Bradshaw Cres SK6 . . . . . 23 A7
Bradshaw Croft DE56 . . . 178 E6
Bradshaw Dr DE56 . . . . . 191 C6
Bradshaw La
 Old Brampton S42 . . . . . . 93 E2
 Stoney Middleton S32 . . . 70 E8
Bradshaw Mdw DE65 . . . 227 C1
Bradshaw Rd
 Marple SK6 . . . . 23 A7
 Staveley S43 . . . . 97 B6
Bradshaw St NG10 . . . . . 236 B5
Bradshaw Way DE1 . . . . 267 C2
Bradshaw Way Ret Pk
 DE1 . . . . 267 B2
BRADWAY 56 C5
BRADWAY BANK 56 A6
Bradway Cl S17 . . . . 56 B5
Bradway Dr S17 . . . . 56 B5
Bradway Grange Rd S17 . 56 C5
Bradway Rd
 Sheffield, Bradway S17 . . 56 B5
 Sheffield, Lower Bradway
  S17 . . . . 56 C6
BRADWELL 51 B7
Bradwell CE Inf Sch S33 . 51 B7
Bradwell Cl
 Derby DE3 . . . . 217 E1
 Dronfield S18 . . . . 56 C1
 Eastwood NG16 . . . . 195 C8
Bradwell Ct **4** S40 . . . . 95 D5
Bradwell Fold **10** SK13 . . 9 E1
Bradwell Gr S45 . . . . 131 D2
Bradwell Head Rd S33 . . 51 A8
BRADWELL HILLS 51 A7
Bradwell Jun Sch S33 . . . 51 A7
Bradwell Lea **12** SK13 . . 9 E1
Bradwell Pl S43 . . . . 97 C7
Bradwell St **1** S2 . . . . . . 43 B6
Bradwell Terr **11** SK13 . . . 9 E1
Bradwell Way DE56 . . . . 179 B5
Braeburn Ct S43 . . . . 218 E2
Braefield Cl DE7 . . . . 208 C5
Braemar Ave NG16 . . . . . 182 F1
Braemar Cl
 Chesterfield S43 . . . . 77 C4
 11 Derby DE24 . . . . 231 D3
Brafield Cl DE56 . . . . 179 D4
BRAILSFORD 201 F7
Brailsford Ave
 4 Gamesley SK13 . . . . . . 9 E2
 1 Swadlincote DE11 . . . 255 E5
Brailsford CE Prim Sch
 DE6 . . . . 201 E7
Brailsford Cl **7** SK13 . . . .9 E2
Brailsford Gdns **8** SK13 . .9 E2
Brailsford Gn **5** SK13 . . . .9 E2
Brailsford Mews **6** SK13 . .9 E2
Brailsford Rd DE21 . . . . . 219 F8
Braintree Cl DE11 . . . . . . 205 D2
Braithwell Cl DE22 . . . . . 204 F2
Bramah Edge Ct SK13 . . . .9 F7
Bramall Ct S2 . . . . 43 A8
Bramall La S2 . . . . 43 A8
Bramble Bank SK13 . . . . 17 E8
Brambleberry Ct DE21 . . 206 B3
Bramble Cl
 Holmewood S44 . . . . 116 F1
 Long Eaton NG10 . . . . . . 223 B2
 Shirebrook NG20 . . . . . . 119 E6
 South Normanton DE55 . 160 B6
Bramble Ct
 Burton upon Trent DE15 . 254 E6
 4 Nottingham NG10 . . . 223 C6
Bramble Mews **2** DE3 . 217 D1
Bramble St DE1 . . . . 267 A3
Bramble Way
 Kilburn DE56 . . . . 179 F2
 South Normanton DE55 . 159 F3
Bramblewick Dr DE23 . . 231 A6
Bramble Wlk DE12 . . . . . 262 A3
Bramblewood **5** DE55 . 255 F6
Brambling Cres DE3 . . . . 230 B6
Brambling Ct S41 . . . . 96 C2
Bramell Cl DE14 . . . . 253 F7
Bramfield Ave DE23 . . . . 218 E3
Bramfield Ct DE22 . . . . . 218 E4
Bramham Rd SK6 . . . . 23 A4
BRAMLEY 58 F3
Bramley Ave S13 . . . . 44 F8
Bramley Cl
 Derby DE21 . . . . 206 C3
 Sheffield S20 . . . . 59 C7
 Staveley S43 . . . . 97 B5
Bramley Ct
 Hatton DE65 . . . . 227 C1
 Kimberley NG16 . . . . 195 F6
Bramley Dale DE11 . . . . . 255 F2
Bramley Hall Rd S13 . . . . 44 F8
Bramley La
 Baslow DE45 . . . . 91 C7
 Sheffield S13 . . . . 44 F8
Bramley Mews S21 . . . . . . 59 D3
Bramleymoor La S21 . . . . 58 E1
Bramley Park Cl S21 . . . . . 44 F8
Bramley Pk S21 . . . . 58 F3

Bramley Rd
 Bramley-Vale S44 . . . . . . 117 E1
 Eckington S21 . . . . 58 E1
 4 Nottingham NG10 . . . 236 B5
Bramley St DE55 . . . . 170 E7
BRAMLEY-VALE 117 E1
Bramley Vale Prim Sch
 S44 . . . . 117 E1
Bramlyn Cl S43 . . . . 80 D5
Bramlyn Ct S43 . . . . 80 D5
BRAMPTON 95 D2
Brampton Ave DE75 . . . . 182 A2
Brampton Cl
 Derby DE21 . . . . 217 C3
 Ilkeston DE7 . . . . 194 F4
Brampton Ct
 Belper DE56 . . . . 179 D4
 Chesterfield S40 . . . . 95 C2
Brampton Dr **9** DE21 . . 223 F5
Brampton House Mews
 S40 . . . . 95 D3
Brampton Prim Sch S40 . 95 D1
Bramshill Rise S40 . . . . . . 95 D1
Branch La S45 . . . . 132 F5
Brancliffe La S81 . . . . 63 F8
Brandelhow Ct DE21 . . . 206 C3
Brandene Cl S44 . . . . 97 A3
Brandreth Dr NG16 . . . . 195 A8
Brands Cl DE7 . . . . 194 F5
Branklene Cl NG16 . . . . . 195 E2
Branksome Ave DE24 . . . 233 C7
Branksome Chine Ave
 S41 . . . . 115 C8
Bransdale Ave NG19 . . . 136 E1
Bransdale Cl NG10 . . . . . 236 B6
BRANSTON 253 F7
Branston Rd
 Burton upon Trent DE14 . 254 C8
 Tatenhill DE13, DE14 . . . 253 C8
Branton Cl S40 . . . . 266 A1
BRASSINGTON 153 A1
Brassington Cl
 Eastwood NG16 . . . . 195 B7
 West Hallam DE7 . . . . . . 207 E8
 Youlgreave DE45 . . . . . . 125 C5
Brassington Cres SK13 . . . 9 D1
Brassington Ct **4** NG19 . 136 E4
Brassington La S42, S45 . 131 C6
Brassington Prim Sch
 DE4 . . . . 153 A1
Brassington Rd DE21 . . . 205 F1
Brassington St S45 . . . . . 131 D4
Braybrook Cl DE55 . . . . . 169 F8
Brayfield Ave DE23 . . . . . 231 D8
Brayfield Rd DE23 . . . . . . 231 C8
Breach La
 Barrow upon Trent DE73 . 244 E1
 Hatton DE65 . . . . 227 C3
 Scropton DE6 . . . . 226 C5
Breach Rd
 Denby DE75 . . . . 181 A4
 Heanor DE75 . . . . 194 A8
BREADSALL 205 E4
Breadsall CE Prim Sch
 DE21 . . . . 205 E4
Breadsall Cl DE11 . . . . . . 256 A7
Breadsall Ct DE7 . . . . 194 F3
BREADSALL HILLTOP . . . 205 D2
Breadsall Hill Top Inf Sch
 DE21 . . . . 205 E4
Breadsall Hill Top Jun Sch
 DE21 . . . . 205 E4
Breadsall Rly Cutting Nature
 Reserve★ DE7 . . . . 206 C4
Breamfield La DE4 . . . . . 166 B8
Brearley Ave S43 . . . . 77 D3
Brearley Cl S41 . . . . 77 B3
Brearley Hall S41 . . . . 77 C4
Brearley St S41 . . . . 77 C3
Brearley Wetland Nature
 Reserve★ S41 . . . . 77 C2
BREASTON 235 D7
Breaston Ind Est DE72 . . 235 C7
Breaston La DE72 . . . . . . 222 D3
Brechin Ct NG19 . . . . 136 B6
Breckbank NG19 . . . . 136 E1
BRECK END 35 C1
Breck La S21, S43 . . . . . . 78 C6
Breckland Rd S40, S42 . . 114 B8
Brecknock Dr NG10 . . . . 236 A7
Brecon Cl
 Chesterfield S40 . . . . 95 C5
 Derby DE21 . . . . 220 E6
 6 Long Eaton NG10 . . . 236 A8
Bredon Cl **7** NG10 . . . . 236 A8
Breedon Ave DE23 . . . . . 231 D5
Breedon Hill Rd DE23 . . 218 F3
BREEDON ON THE HILL . . 252 E2
Breedon St NG10 . . . . . . 223 C2
Brenden Ave DE55 . . . . . 170 C7
Brenden Cl DE55 . . . . 170 C8
Brendon Ave S40 . . . . 95 C4
Brendon Cl SK13 . . . . 17 A8
Brendon Ct **3** S40 . . . . . 95 C4
Brendon Dr NG16 . . . . . . 195 F7
Brendon Way NG10 . . . . 223 A1
Brent Cl S40 . . . . 95 D5
Brentford Dr DE22 . . . . . 218 B6
Brentnall Cl NG10 . . . . . . 236 B7
Brentwood Ave S33 . . . . . 40 B3
Brentwood Rd S33 . . . . . . 40 B3
Bren Way DE65 . . . . 228 E2
BRETBY 249 A3
Bretby Bsns Pk DE15 . . . 255 F8
Bretby Fairways DE15 . . 248 F2
Bretby Hollow DE11 . . . . 255 F7
Bretby Hts DE11 . . . . 256 A8

Bretby La
 Bretby DE15 . . . . 248 E3
 Burton upon Trent DE15 . 248 D2
 Burton upon Trent DE15 . 248 F6
Bretby Rd
 Chesterfield S40 . . . . 95 A6
 Swadlincote DE11 . . . . . 255 F7
Bretby Sq DE23 . . . . 231 C5
Bretby Stoneware Ind Est
 DE11 . . . . 255 E8
Bretby View DE15 . . . . . . 257 A4
Bretlands Way DE15 . . . . 255 A6
BRETTON 71 A8
Bretton Ave
 Bolsover S44 . . . . 99 C2
 Derby DE23 . . . . 218 C2
Bretton Cl S40 . . . . 95 A5
Bretton Gr S12 . . . . 44 D3
Bretton Rd DE56 . . . . 179 E5
Brewery St
 Chesterfield S41 . . . . 266 C3
 Kimberley NG16 . . . . 195 F6
Breydon Cl DE24 . . . . 232 D4
Breydon Ind Ctr NG10 . . 236 F7
Brian Clough Way
 Derby DE21 . . . . 220 C4
 Risley DE72 . . . . 222 C3
 Stapleford NG9 . . . . 223 D5
Briar Ave NG10 . . . . 223 A3
Briar Briggs Rd S44 . . . . . 98 C3
Briar Cl
 Alfreton DE55 . . . . 159 C3
 Borrowash DE72 . . . . . . 221 C3
 6 Buxton SK17 . . . . 85 C8
 Chesterfield S41 . . . . 95 C5
 Derby DE21 . . . . 220 B5
 Shirebrook NG20 . . . . . . 119 E2
 Swadlincote DE11 . . . . . 255 F5
Briardene Cl S40 . . . . 94 F5
Briarfield Ave S12 . . . . . . 44 A3
Briarfield Cres S12 . . . . . 44 A2
Briarfield Rd S12 . . . . 44 A3
Briar Gate NG10 . . . . 223 B1
Briargrove Rd S22 . . . . . . 24 C4
Briar Lea Cl DE24 . . . . . . 231 F4
Briar Rd NG16 . . . . 195 B8
Briars Cl S21 . . . . 60 D5
Briarsgate DE22 . . . . 204 D2
Briar's La DE4 . . . . 168 A2
Briars Way DE5 . . . . 180 D8
Briar View S43 . . . . 96 F7
Briarwood Cres SK6 . . . . . 23 A3
Briarwood Way DE23 . . . 231 C6
Brickbridge Rd SK6 . . . . . 23 A5
Brickfields Cl DE4 . . . . . . 155 A4
Brickfield St SK13 . . . . . . 10 B5
Brickhouse La S17 . . . . . . 55 C8
BRICK HOUSES 55 D8
Brickhouse Yd S40 . . . . . . 95 E3
Brickkiln La DE7 . . . . 206 C8
Brick-kiln La
 Brailsford DE6 . . . . 186 F1
 Hulland Ward DE6 . . . . . 175 D3
Brick Kiln La DE13 . . . . . 240 A3
Brick Row DE22 . . . . 205 A1
Brick St DE1 . . . . 218 E4
Brickyard Cotts DE6 . . . . 185 D8
Brickyard La
 Kilburn DE56 . . . . 179 F2
 Ripley DE5 . . . . 169 E5
 South Normanton DE55 . 160 A6
Brickyard Rd DE56 . . . . . 168 C5
Brickyard The DE7 . . . . . 193 B1
Bricky Cl S43 . . . . 80 D5
Bridge Bank Cl **6** S40 . . 95 D6
Bridge Cl
 Swadlincote DE11 . . . . . 256 C2
 Whitwell S80 . . . . 82 A5
Bridge End Ave NG16 . . 171 F8
Bridge Farm **3** DE13 . . 240 E1
BRIDGEFIELD 17 B7
Bridgefield **4** SK13 . . . . 17 B8
Bridge Field DE72 . . . . . . 235 C7
Bridgefield Ct **11** DE56 . 178 F4
Bridge Foot DE56 . . . . . . 178 F5
Bridge Gate DE1 . . . . 267 B4
Bridge Hill DE56 . . . . 178 E5
BRIDGEHOLM GREEN 47 A8
Bridgeholm Mill SK23 . . . 47 A8
BRIDGEMONT 33 E2
Bridgend Cl NG9 . . . . 223 D5
Bridgend Ct DE21 . . . . . . 206 C2
Bridgeness Rd DE23 . . . . 230 D4
Bridgeport Rd DE21 . . . . 220 C6
Bridge St Ind Est S45 . . . 131 C4
Bridgeside DE11 . . . . 240 E1
Bridge St
 Bakewell DE45 . . . . 109 D6
 Belper DE56 . . . . 178 F4
 Bradwell S33 . . . . 51 A7
 Burton upon Trent, Stretton
  DE13 . . . . 240 E1
 Buxton SK17 . . . . 85 C8
 Chesterfield S40 . . . . 266 B1
 Clay Cross S45 . . . . 131 C3
 Derby DE1 . . . . 267 A4
 Ilkeston DE7 . . . . 194 F4
 Killamarsh S21 . . . . 60 D6
 Langley Mill NG16 . . . . . 182 C3
 Linton DE12 . . . . 261 E8
 Long Eaton NG10 . . . . . . 223 D1
 New Mills SK22 . . . . 24 C1
 Pilsley S45 . . . . 132 C2
 Sandiacre NG10 . . . . 223 C5
 Swadlincote DE11 . . . . . 256 C2

Bridge St *continued*
Tupton S42 115 D1
Tutbury DE13 239 C7
Whaley Bridge SK23 45 E7
Bridge View
Belper DE56 191 A7
Mayfield DE6 184 D8
Bridgewater St S42 115 C1
Bridgeway SK23 47 B4
Bridge Way S41 76 D3
Bridge Yd Ave DE5 169 E4
Bridgford Ave DE14 253 F7
Bridgnorth Way NG9 223 E3
Bridgwater Cl DE24 233 C7
Bridle Cl DE73 233 A1
Bridlegate La DE24 233 D7
Bridle La
Ripley, Greenwich DE5 169 E2
Ripley, Lower Hartshay DE5, DE56 169 A2
Somercotes DE55 170 B7
Swadlincote DE15 255 A5
Bridle Rd
Bolsover S44 80 B1
Staveley S43 79 B2
Bridle Stile S20 59 C7
Bridle Stile Cl S20 59 C7
Bridle Stile Gdns S20 59 B7
Bridleway SK22 24 D1
Bridleway The NG19 136 F1
Brierfield Way DE3 230 E8
Brierley Cl S43 78 E1
BRIERLEY GREEN 34 B2
Brierley Pk SK23 34 B1
Brierley Rd
Stonebroom DE55 146 F3
Unstone Green S18 76 E6
Brierlow Bar SK17 105 B8
Brigden Ave DE24 232 E7
Brigg Inf Sch DE55 160 B6
Brighstone Cl DE24 233 C5
BRIGHTGATE 142 B4
Brightman Ho DE11 256 B5
Bright Mdw S20 60 A5
Brighton Rd DE24 232 F8
Bright Sq NG19 135 D2
Bright St
Derby DE22 218 D5
Ilkeston DE7 194 E3
Kimberley NG16 195 E6
North Wingfield S42 131 F6
South Normanton DE55 159 F5
Brightwater Cl DE24 232 E3
Brigmor Wlk DE22 218 C5
BRIMINGTON 96 F7
Brimington Cl NE7 194 F6
BRIMINGTON COMMON 96 F5
Brimington Ct 6 NG19 136 E4
Brimington Jun Sch S43 96 D8
Brimington Manor Inf Sch S43 96 F5
Brimington Rd S41 96 B5
Brimington Road N S41 96 B8
Brimmesfield Cl S2 43 F7
Brimmesfield Dr S2 43 E8
Brimmesfield Rd S2 43 E7
Brincliffe Cl S40 95 B1
Brindle Way DE23 231 A5
Brindley Cl S8 43 A4
Brindley Cres S8 43 A4
Brindley Ct S21 60 C6
Brindley Ho
Chesterfield S41 96 B6
Long Eaton NG10 223 B3
Brindley Rd 6 S41 96 A6
Brindley Way S43 78 F2
Brindley Wlk DE24 231 E2
BRINDWOODGATE 75 D5
Brinkburn Cl S17 55 F6
Brinkburn Ct S17 55 F6
Brinkburn Dr S17 55 F6
Brinkburn Vale Rd S17 55 F6
BRINSLEY 182 E7
Brinsley Headstocks Nature Reserve* NG16 182 F6
Brinsley Hill NG16 171 C2
Brinsley Prim Sch NG16 182 E8
Brisbane Cl NG19 136 C6
Brisbane Dr NG9 209 F1
Brisbane Rd DE3 217 F3
Briset Cl DE24 231 E2
Bristol Dr DE3 217 E2
Bristol Rd DE7 194 E1
Britannia Ave DE5 181 A7
Britannia Ct DE1 267 B4
Britannia Dr DE13 240 D1
Britannia Rd
Chesterfield S40 115 B7
Long Eaton NG10 223 D1
Britannia Trad Est SK23 33 F1
Briton Lodge Cl DE12 262 F4
Brittain Dr DE5 170 A1
Brittain Pit Farm* DE5 170 A4
Brixham Ct 8 S41 95 F8
Brizlincote La DE15 248 D1
Broad Bank DE22 218 E8
BROADBOTTOM 16 A8
Broadbottom Prim Sch SK14 15 F8
Broadbottom Rd SK14 9 A3
Broadbottom Sta SK14 16 A8
Broadfield Rd S2 43 A7
Broadfields Cl DE22 218 F8
Broadgorse Cl S40 114 F7
Broadhey View SK22 24 B1
BROADHOLM 179 A7
Broadholme La DE56 179 A8
Broad La
Brinsley NG16 182 E8
Creswell S80 82 D6
Elvaston DE72 233 F4
Broadlands
Sandiacre NG10 223 B3
South Normanton DE55 160 A4
Broadleaf Cl DE21 205 E2
Broadley Rd S13 44 C7
Broadleys S45 131 C3
Broadmeadow DE4 127 C3
Broad Oak Dr
Brinsley NG16 182 E8
Stapleford NG9 223 D6
Broadoaks Cl S41 266 C3
Broad Pavement S40 266 B3
Broad Pl S80 82 C6
Broad Rushes DE74 247 B6
Broad St NG10 236 D7
Broadstairs Rd 5 NG9 223 F2
Broadstone Cl DE21 206 A1
Broadstone La DE73 251 D4
Broadway
Derby DE22 218 E8
Duffield DE56 190 E2
Heanor DE75 181 E1
Ilkeston DE7 194 E3
Ripley DE5 169 E1
Swanwick DE55 169 F7
Broad Way DE6 176 B8
Broadway Ave DE5 169 E1
Broadway Lane SK17 88 A5
Broadway Park Cl DE22 218 E8
Broadway St DE14 254 C8
Broad Wlk
Buxton SK17 85 B7
Darley Dale DE4 127 C3
Brockhall Rise DE75 182 A1
Brockhill Ct 3 S43 96 F8
Brockholes SK13 16 F8
BROCKHURST 129 C6
Brockhurst La S45 129 C6
Brocklehurst Ave S8 57 C8
Brocklehurst Ct S40 95 D2
Brocklehurst Piece S40 95 D2
Brockley DE21 220 E5
Brockley Ave S44 98 F6
Brockley La SK17 69 C3
Brockley Prim Sch S44 98 F7
Brocksford Ct DE6 224 F7
Brockway Cl S45 131 D2
BROCKWELL 95 E4
Brockwell Ct 5 S41 95 D6
Brockwell Inf & Jun Sch S40 95 D4
Brockwell La
Chesterfield S40 95 E4
Cutthorpe S42 94 F7
Brockwell Pl S40 95 E4
Brockwell Terr S40 95 E4
Brockwell The DE55 160 B4
Brodie Cl DE73 232 E2
Brome Head Way S41 95 D7
Bromley Ct DE7 209 A7
Bromley St DE22 218 E7
Brompton Rd DE22 217 F6
Bromyard Dr DE73 233 A3
Bronte Cl NG10 236 A7
Bronte Pl DE23 231 B8
Bronte St DE55 146 C5
Brook Ave DE55 159 B3
Brookbank Ave S40 95 D4
Brookbank Rd S43 80 F4
Brook Bldgs S33 51 A7
BROOK BOTTOM 23 F1
Brook Bottom Rd SK22 33 A8
Brookbridge Ct DE1 267 A4
Brook Cl
Alfreton DE55 159 B3
5 Belper DE56 178 F3
Doveridge DE6 224 C8
Findern DE65 230 D1
Hatton DE65 227 D2
Holymoorside S42 113 D7
Long Eaton NG10 236 E5
Quarndon DE22 204 C4
Brook Cotts DE7 194 F3
Brook Ct
Elvaston DE72 233 F4
Heanor NG16 182 B2
Brookdale Ave SK6 23 A4
Brookdale Dr DE23 231 A5
Brookdale Rd DE11 257 A4
Brooke Dr S43 96 F5
Brook End DE65 242 D3
Brooke St
Ilkeston DE7 209 B6
Sandiacre NG10 223 B5
Tibshelf DE55 148 A6
BROOKFIELD 9 E3
Brookfield DE73 244 A6
Brookfield Ave
Chesterfield S40 95 A2
Derby, Chaddesden DE21 220 B8
Derby, Littleover DE23 231 D6
Brookfield Cl DE5 170 B1
Brookfield Com Sch S40 95 A2
Brookfield Cotts
Acresford DE12 265 C7
Bakewell DE45 109 E8
Brookfield Cres NG20 119 E5
Brookfield Ind Est
Glossop SK13 9 E3
Tansley DE4 143 F4
Brookfield La DE45 109 E8
Brookfield Mews 2 NG10 223 C6
Brookfield Mobile Home Pk S42 130 F5
Brookfield Prim Sch
Derby DE3 230 D8
Shirebrook NG20 119 F5
Brookfield Rd S44 118 A8
Brookfields
Calver S32 72 C1
Horsley DE56 191 E7
Brookfields Bsns Pk DE65 229 D6
Brookfields Dr DE21 205 D4
Brookfield Way
Heanor DE75 182 B1
Tansley DE4 143 F4
Brook Fold SK23 47 C7
Brookhill S43 80 F4
Brookhill Ave NG16 160 D4
Brookhill Ind Est NG16 160 E2
Brookhill La NG16 160 E5
Brookhill Leys Rd NG16 182 E1
Brookhill Rd NG16 160 D2
Brookhill St NG9 223 D6
Brook Ho 3 DE1 267 A4
Brookhouse Ct
Hayfield SK22 25 D3
Whaley Thorns NG20 101 A1
Brook House Mews
Repton DE65 242 D2
Swadlincote DE11 256 A7
Brookhouse St DE24 232 D5
Brook La
Alfreton DE55 159 B3
Clowne S43 80 F4
Crich DE56 168 C6
Hatton DE65 227 C3
Ripley DE5 180 D7
Sutton on the Hill DE6 228 A8
Brooklands SK17 85 C8
Brooklands Ave
Chapel-en-le-Frith SK23 47 D6
Heanor DE75 181 F2
Wirksworth DE4 165 F7
Brooklands Bank DE45 109 E6
Brooklands Dr
Derby DE23 231 C8
Glossop SK13 17 B7
Brooklands Prim Sch NG10 236 D6
Brooklands Rd SK23 47 D6
Brook Lea DE4 143 C4
Brookleton DE45 125 C5
Brooklyn Dr S40 95 D4
Brooklyn Pl 2 S8 43 A5
Brooklyn Rd 5 S8 43 A5
Brook Mdw SK13 10 E1
Brook Rd
Borrowash DE72 221 B1
Elvaston DE72 233 F4
Sheffield S8 43 A5
Brooks Cl DE12 262 F1
Brooks Hollow DE21 205 C7
BROOKSIDE 94 F2
Brookside
Ashbourne DE6 173 D1
Beeley DE4 111 B3
Bradwell S33 51 A7
Burton upon Trent DE15 248 B5
Derby DE1 267 A4
Eastwood NG16 182 F4
Glossop SK13 17 B8
New Mills SK22 24 F7
Whaley Bridge SK23 34 A1
Brook Side
Bakewell DE45 109 D6
Belper DE56 178 F3
Rolleston DE13 240 B4
Brookside Ave NG19 136 C5
Brookside Bar S40 94 F1
Brookside Cl
Derby DE1 218 E7
Glossop SK13 9 F4
Long Eaton NG10 236 B8
Repton DE65 242 D2
Brookside Glen S40 94 F1
Brookside Gr SK17 84 D5
Brookside Ind Units NG9 223 D8
Brookside Rd
Breadsall DE21 205 E4
Chapel-en-le-Frith SK23 47 B5
Brookside Way NG17 148 F1
Brooks Rd S43 78 B4
Brook St
Clay Cross S45 131 A4
Derby DE1 267 A4
Glossop SK13 10 C1
Hartshorne DE11 257 A7
Heage DE56 168 E1
Heanor DE75 181 B5
Nether Heage DE56 168 C2
Renishaw S21 79 C8
Swadlincote DE11 256 A3
Swadlincote, Newhall DE11 255 E6
Brookvale Ave
Codnor DE5 181 B8
Denby Village DE5 180 A2
Brook Vale Cl S18 75 D3
Brookvale Rd DE5 180 A2
Brook Vale Rd NG16 182 C2
Brookvale Rise DE5 180 A2
Brookview Ct S18 57 A3
Brook Walkway DE1 267 A4
Brook Wlk DE4 143 C4
Brook Yd S40 266 A3
Broom Ave
Pilsley S45 132 C2
Swanwick DE55 169 F7
Broombank Pk S41 76 D3
Broombank Rd S41 76 C3
Broom Bsns Pk S41 76 D3
Broom Cl
Belper DE56 178 E6
Chellaston DE73 232 F2
Chesterfield S41 95 D7
Derby, Sinfin DE73 231 E2
Duffield DE56 190 D3
Broom Dr S42 115 E2
Broome Acre DE55 160 C4
Broomfield Ave S41 115 D7
Broomfield Cl NG10 223 A5
Broomfield Cotts DE7 206 C5
Broom Gdns S43 96 F7
Broomhill Ave DE7 209 A6
Broomhill Cl
Derby DE3 217 D3
Eckington S21 59 B3
Broomhill Cotts DE65 229 C2
Broomhill Ct S41 76 F2
Broomhill Rd S41 76 F2
Broomhills La DE65 242 D1
Broomhills The DE12 264 F7
Broom La DE6 175 E7
Broom's La DE6 226 B2
Broomyclose La ST14 210 A4
Brosscroft SK13 10 A6
Brosscroft Cl
Glossop SK13 10 A6
Hadfield SK13 10 A6
Brosscroft Village SK13 10 A6
BROUGH 39 D2
Brougham Ave NG19 135 D2
Brough La S33 51 C7
Brough Rd DE15 248 C3
Brough St DE22 218 D5
Broughton Ave DE23 218 D1
Broughton Cl
Church Broughton DE65 227 A8
Ilkeston DE7 194 D2
Somercotes DE55 170 C7
Broughton Rd S41 95 D7
Brow Cres S20 59 F7
Brown Ave NG19 136 B4
Brown Edge Rd SK17 66 C2
Brownhill La HD9 3 B8
Brownhills La S42 130 C4
Brown Hills La S10 42 E8
Browning Cir DE23 231 F7
Browning Ct S40 95 B3
Browning Rd DE11 256 C5
Browning St DE23 231 F7
Brown La
Ashover S45 145 B8
Barton in Fabis NG11 237 E6
Dronfield S18 57 C3
Flash SK17 103 B3
Brownlow Rd NG19 135 F1
Brown's Flats NG16 195 F6
Brown's La DE56 191 D7
Brown's Rd NG10 236 E8
Broxtowe Ave NG16 195 D6
Brunel Parkway DE24 219 D3
Brunel Way
Castle Gresley DE11 255 E1
Church Gresley DE11 261 F8
Brun La DE6, DE22 217 B8
Brunnen The DE55 160 B4
Brunner Ave NG20 119 F3
Brunswick Dr 2 NG9 223 E5
Brunswick St
Chesterfield S41 266 B4
Derby DE23 231 F8
Pilsley S45 132 C1
Brunswood Cl DE21 220 E5
Brunswood Ho DE4 143 B2
Brunswood La DE6 187 C7
Brunswood Rd DE4 143 B1
Brunt La DE11 256 F3
Brunton Cl DE3 217 C1
Brunts Comp Sch NG19 136 C1
Brushes SK15 4 A3
Brushes Rd SK15 4 A3
BRUSHES THE 76 F3
BRUSHFIELD 88 D4
Brushfield Gr S12 44 D4
Brushfield Rd S40 94 F5
Brussells Terr 1 DE7 194 E1
Bryant La DE55 160 A5
Bryn Lea S41 96 C2
Brynsmoor Rd NG16 182 E7
Bryony DE14 254 B8
Bryony Cl
Derby DE21 206 A1
Killamarsh S21 60 B6
Bryony Way NG19 136 F4
BUBNELL 91 D6
Bubnell Ct 15 S40 95 D5
Bubnell Rd
Baslow DE45 91 D6
Dronfield S18 56 E2
Buchanan St DE1 267 B4
Buchan St DE24 232 D7
Buckdale La DE4 141 A6
Buckden Cl S40 95 D4
Buckfast Cl DE55 169 E8
Buckford La DE65, DE73 242 E8
Buckhazels La DE6, DE22 203 B7
Buckingham Ave DE21 219 D8
Buckingham Cl
2 Dronfield S18 56 D2
Mansfield Woodhouse NG19 136 E5
Swanwick DE55 170 A7
Buckingham Ct
Burton upon Trent DE15 248 C3
Sandiacre NG10 223 A3
Buckingham Dr
Church Gresley DE11 261 F8
Heanor DE75 181 C2
Buckingham Ho DE65 228 D1
Buckingham Rd NG10 223 A4
Buckland Cl DE1 218 E6
Buckland Ct 18 S41 95 F8
Buckland Gr SK14 15 A8
Buckleather La S18 74 C1
Buckley Cl DE11 256 F2
Buckminster Cl DE21 205 F2
Buckminster Rd DE7 208 C4
Buck Wood View S14 43 D5
Bullace Ct 3 NG19 136 E1
BULLBRIDGE 168 B5
Bullbridge Hill DE56 168 B5
Buller St
Derby DE23 218 E2
Ilkeston DE7 209 A6
BULL FARM 135 C2
Bullfinch Cl DE56 179 B2
Bullhill La DE56 176 E3
Bullhurst La DE6 188 F4
Bulling La DE4 156 F1
Bullivant Ave S80 100 C8
Bull La DE4 143 D6
Bull Mews Cotts DE4 143 C5
Bullock Cl NG19 136 B5
Bullock La
Brailsford DE6 201 F7
Ironville NG16, DE55 170 E5
Bullpit La DE56 205 A8
Bull's Head Row DE73 252 E6
Bullsmoor DE56 179 C4
Bulltor Lane SK17 88 B5
Bumpmill La DE55 146 B1
Bun Alley DE45 91 C3
Bungalows The
Chesterfield, Brampton S40 95 D3
Chesterfield, Hady S41 266 C2
1 Chesterfield, Newbold S41 95 E7
1 Chesterfield, Whittington Moor S41 96 A8
Clowne S43 81 A4
Elton DE4 140 D6
Killamarsh S21 60 C6
New Mills SK22 24 D1
Stonebroom DE55 146 E3
Bunkers Hill S21 60 E6
Bunker's Hill S80 62 D8
Buntingbank Cl DE55 159 F4
Bunting Cl
Chesterfield S42 95 B1
Derby DE3 218 A3
Ilkeston DE7 208 C6
Sheffield S8 43 B2
Buntingfield La S45 129 B7
Bunting Ho S41 77 A3
Bunting Nook S8 43 B1
Bunyan Cres DE55 146 F3
Bunyan Green Rd NG16 171 D7
BURBAGE 84 E6
Burbage Bank SK13 9 E2
Burbage Cl
Belper DE56 179 D5
Dronfield S18 56 D2
Burbage Ct 8 S40 95 D5
Burbage Gr
Gamesley SK13 9 E2
Sheffield S12 44 D5
Burbage Pl DE24 232 F7
Burbage Prim Sch SK17 84 F6
Burbage Rd S43 97 D8
Burbage Way
Buxton SK17 84 F6
Gamesley SK13 9 E2
Burch Pl S32 71 E6
Burcot Cl DE7 207 E8
Burdekin Cl SK23 47 C6
Burdett Way DE65 242 D3
Burdock Cl DE21 205 E2
Burgess Cl S41 115 D7
Burghley Cl DE73 232 F2
Burghley Way DE23 230 E6
Burke Dr DE55 170 D8
Burkitt Dr S43 79 B3
Burland Green La DE6 189 B4
Burleigh Cres DE55 169 F8
Burleigh Dr DE22 218 F8
Burleigh St 1 DE7 194 F1
Burley Cl S40 115 A7
Burley Dr DE22 204 E7
Burley Hill DE22 205 A7
Burley La DE22 204 E7
Burlington Ave NG20 119 F6
Burlington Cl
Breaston DE72 235 D8
Sheffield S17 55 E7
Burlington Dr NG19 135 F2
Burlington Glen S17 55 E7
Burlington Gr S17 55 E7
Burlington Rd
Buxton SK17 85 A7
Derby DE22 217 F6
Sheffield S17 55 E7
Burlington St S40 266 B3
Burlington Way DE3 217 D1
Burlow Ave SK17 85 C3
Burlow Rd SK17 85 D2
Burnaby St DE24 232 F8
Burnage Ct DE22 218 F4
BURNASTON 229 F5
Burnaston Cl S18 56 C1

Burnaston Ct 2 NG19 . . . 136 E4
Burnaston La DE65 . . . . . 229 D5
Burnbridge Rd S41 . . . . . . 77 C3
Burncroft DE7 . . . . 207 E7
Burnell St S43 . . . . 96 F8
Burnett La DE4 . . . . 143 A8
Burney La DE73 . . . . 252 C2
Burnham Cl DE7 . . . . 207 D8
Burnham Dr DE3 . . . . 217 C2
Burns Ave NG19 . . . . 136 C2
Burns Cl
Chesterfield S40 . . . . 114 F7
Derby DE23 . . . . 231 B8
Burns Dr
Dronfield S18 . . . . 76 C8
Grassmoor S42 . . . . 115 E3
Burnshaw St DE55 . . . . . 146 C5
Burnside
Glossop SK13 . . . . 9 F4
Rolleston DE13 . . . . 240 B4
Burnside Ave
Chapel-en-le-Frith SK23 . . . 47 C7
Sheffield S8 . . . . 43 A5
Shirland DE55 . . . . 146 D1
Burnside Cl DE24 . . . . 231 D3
Burnside Ct DE24 . . . . 233 A8
Burnside Dr
Derby DE21 . . . . 220 F4
Mansfield NG19 . . . . 135 E2
Burnside St DE24 . . . . 233 A8
Burns St
Heanor DE75 . . . . 181 D2
Ilkeston DE7 . . . . 208 E8
BURNTHEATH 228 C4
Burnt House Rd DE75 . . . 181 D1
Burnt Oaks Cl NG19 . . . . 136 D3
Burre Cl DE45 . . . . 109 E6
BURRFIELDS 47 C6
Burrfields Rd SK23 . . . . 47 B6
Burr La DE7 . . . . 194 F1
Burrowfield Mews DE21 . 220 F2
Burrows La
Brailsford DE6 . . . . 201 F2
Middleton DE4 . . . . 154 D5
Burrows The DE11 . . . . . . 255 F5
Burrows Wlk DE1 . . . . 267 B2
Burrs Wood Croft S41 . . . . 95 B7
Bursar Way NG10 . . . . 223 C3
Bursdon Cl S41 . . . . 77 A1
Burton Close Dr DE45 . . . 109 E4
Burton Close Mews
DE45 . . . . 109 D4
Burton Edge DE45 . . . . . . 109 D4
Burton Rd
Burnaston DE65 . . . . 230 B2
Burton upon Trent DE14 . . 254 B7
Castle Gresley DE11 . . . . . 255 D2
Coton in the Elms DE12 . . . 260 D3
Derby DE23 . . . . 218 C1
Findern DE65 . . . . 230 B2
Overseal DE12 . . . . 262 A4
Repton DE15, DE65 . . . . . . 242 B2
Rosliston DE12 . . . . 260 C6
Swadlincote DE11 . . . . 256 D6
Ticknall DE73 . . . . 250 F4
Tutbury DE13 . . . . 239 D4
Willington DE65 . . . . 241 F7
Burton St
Heanor DE75 . . . . 181 E2
Tutbury DE13 . . . . 239 C6
BURTON UPON TRENT . . . 254 D8
Burwell Cl SK13 . . . . 17 A8
Burwell Ct NG19 . . . . 136 E4
Buscott Dr DE6 . . . . 185 B8
Bushey Wood Gr S17 . . . . . 55 D7
Bushey Wood Rd S17 . . . . 55 E6
Bushton La DE13 . . . . 239 B2
Bushy Cl NG10 . . . . 236 B6
Business Pk The NG19 . . . 135 D6
Buskeyfield La NG20 . . . . 101 F4
Butcher's La DE4 . . . . 127 F4
Bute St SK13 . . . . 10 E3
Bute Wlk DE21 . . . . 219 C7
Butler Cres NG19 . . . . 135 D2
Butler Way S21 . . . . 60 C6
Buttercup Ave DE12 . . . . . 262 E1
Buttercup Cl SK13 . . . . 17 E8
Butterfield Cres DE55 . . . 169 F7
Butterfield La DE55 . . . . . 145 E1
Butterhall Cl S80 . . . . 82 A5
BUTTERLEY
Ripley 169 F3
Tansley 144 F5
Butterley Cl NE7 . . . . 194 F6
Butterley Croft Bsns Ctr
DE5 . . . . 180 E8
Butterley Ct NG16 . . . . 170 F4
Butterley Hill DE5 . . . . 169 E3
Butterley La
Ashover DE4, S45 . . . . 144 E5
Ripley DE5 . . . . 169 D4
Butterley Lodge NG16 . . . 170 F4
Butterley Mews DE5 . . . . 169 E2
Butterley Sta★ DE5 . . . . . 169 E4
Buttermead Cl NG9 . . . . . 209 D2
Buttermere Cl
Chesterfield S41 . . . . 95 D7
1 Long Eaton NG10 . . . . . 223 A2
Buttermere Ct NG19 . . . . . 136 D3
Buttermere Dr
Derby DE22 . . . . 204 E3
Dronfield S18 . . . . 56 E1
Buttermilk La S44 . . . . 98 D4
Butterpot La DE6 . . . . 215 D3
Butterton Cl DE7 . . . . 209 A7
Butterton Dr 6 S40 . . . . . . 95 A5
Butterwick Cl
Derby DE23 . . . . 231 E5
Butterwick Cl *continued*
Forest Town NG19 . . . . 136 F1
Butt Hill S80 . . . . 81 F6
Butt Hill Cl S80 . . . . 81 F6
Butt La
Blackfordby DE11 . . . . 257 A1
Mansfield Woodhouse
NG19 . . . . 136 C2
Buttonoak Dr DE73 . . . . . . 233 A3
Butts Cl DE7 . . . . 209 A4
Butts Dr DE4 . . . . 143 D4
Butts Hill S17 . . . . 55 D4
Butts Rd
Ashover S45 . . . . 129 F3
Bakewell DE45 . . . . 109 D5
Darley Dale DE4 . . . . 127 B3
Butt St NG10 . . . . 223 B5
Butts Terr DE45 . . . . 109 D5
Butts The DE56 . . . . 179 A3
Butts View DE45 . . . . 109 D5
BUXTON 85 A7
Buxton Ave DE75 . . . . 193 F7
Buxton Baths 9 SK17 . . . . 85 B8
Buxton Cl
17 Gamesley SK13 . . . . 9 E2
Swadlincote DE11 . . . . 256 A7
Buxton Com Sch SK17 . . . . 85 A6
Buxton Ct DE7 . . . . 194 D1
Buxton Ctry Pk★ SK17 . . . 84 E6
Buxton Dr
Derby DE3 . . . . 217 E3
Little Eaton DE21 . . . . 191 D2
Buxton Gn DE75 . . . . 193 F7
Buxton Hospl SK17 . . . . 85 C5
Buxton Inf Sch SK17 . . . . . 85 C7
Buxton Jun Sch SK17 . . . . . 85 B6
Buxton Mews SK13 . . . . 9 E2
Buxton Mus & Art Gall★ 17
SK17 . . . . 85 B7
Buxton New Rd SK11 . . . . . 83 A6
Buxton Old Rd SK12 . . . . . . 32 E4
Buxton Raceway★ SK17 . 104 B7
Buxton Rd
Alstonefield DE6 . . . . 149 B5
Ashbourne DE6 . . . . 173 B2
Ashford in the Water DE45 108 E8
Bakewell DE45 . . . . 109 B7
Castleton S33 . . . . 38 B2
Chapel-en-le-Frith SK17,
SK23 . . . . 47 E5
Chinley SK23 . . . . 34 F2
Derby DE21 . . . . 219 F8
Dove Holes SK17 . . . . 66 F8
High Lane SK12 . . . . 32 A6
Horwich End, New Horwich
SK23 . . . . 45 E6
Longnor SK17 . . . . 121 B7
Mansfield NG19 . . . . 135 D1
New Mills SK22, SK23 . . . . . 33 C4
Tideswell SK17 . . . . 69 C3
Whaley Bridge SK23 . . . . . . 33 E1
Buxton Road W SK12 . . . . . 32 B5
Buxton Spa Swimming Pool
SK17 . . . . 85 A7
Buxton Sta SK17 . . . . 85 B8
Buxton Terr SK14 . . . . 9 D5
Buxton Wlk 9 SK13 . . . . 9 E1
BUXWORTH 34 A1
Buxworth Prim Sch SK23 . 34 A1
Byfield Cl DE21 . . . . 206 B2
Byng Ave 2 DE23 . . . . 231 F7
Byron Ave
Alfreton DE55 . . . . 159 B4
Burton upon Trent DE15 . . 254 E7
Long Eaton NG10 . . . . 223 B3
Mansfield Woodhouse
NG19 . . . . 136 C2
Byron Cl
Dronfield S18 . . . . 76 C7
Grassmoor S42 . . . . 115 E3
Byron Cres NG16 . . . . 195 C4
Byron Ct NG9 . . . . 209 E2
Byron Gr DE55 . . . . 146 F3
Byron Lodge SK17 . . . . 85 C6
Byron Rd
Chesterfield S40 . . . . 115 A8
Swadlincote DE11 . . . . 256 C6
Byron St
Buxton SK17 . . . . 85 C6
Chesterfield S40 . . . . 266 C1
Derby DE23 . . . . 218 F2
Ilkeston DE7 . . . . 194 F1
Shirebrook NG20 . . . . 119 E4
Shirland DE55 . . . . 146 C1
Bywell La DE56 . . . . 179 F1

C

Cabot Cl DE56 . . . . 179 E5
Cacklehill La DE6 . . . . 184 C2
Cadeby Ct DE55 . . . . 170 C6
Cadgwith Dr DE22 . . . . . . 204 E3
Cadley Hill Ind Est DE11 . 255 E2
Cadley Hill Rd DE11 . . . . . 255 E3
Cadman Ct S20 . . . . 59 D6
Cadman Rd S12 . . . . 44 C6
Cadman St S20 . . . . 59 D6
Cadwell Cl DE24 . . . . 233 D6
Caerhays Ct DE24 . . . . 231 D3
Caernarfon Cl DE55 . . . . . 170 A7
Caernarvon Cl
Chesterfield S40 . . . . 95 C1
Derby DE21 . . . . 220 F5
Caernarvon Rd S18 . . . . . . 76 B8
Caesar St DE1 . . . . 219 B7
Cairn Dr S43 . . . . 77 D4
Cairngorm Cl S43 . . . . 77 D4
Cairngorm Dr DE24 . . . . . 231 D3
Cairns Cl
Burton upon Trent DE15 . . 248 C3
Derby DE3 . . . . 217 E3
Cairnsmore Cl 4 NG10 . . 223 A1
Caldene Terr SK23 . . . . 45 E7
Calder Cl
Derby DE22 . . . . 204 E3
Hilton DE65 . . . . 228 D1
Calderdale Dr NG10 . . . . . 236 A6
Caldermill Dr DE21 . . . . . . 206 A2
Caldey Rd S18 . . . . 76 A8
CALDWELL 260 E7
Cale Rd SK22 . . . . 33 D8
Calesdale Cl SK17 . . . . 85 B5
Calf Croft S80 . . . . 82 A5
Calgary Cres DE15 . . . . . . 248 D3
Calico Cres SK15 . . . . 4 A6
Calico La SK23 . . . . 33 D4
CALIFORNIA 218 D3
California Gdns DE22 . . . 218 C4
California La S43 . . . . 80 A7
CALKE 251 E1
Calke Abbey★ LE65 . . . . . 251 D2
Calke Ave NG17 . . . . 148 E2
Calke National Nature
Reserve★ DE73 . . . . 251 C3
Calke Rd DE73 . . . . 252 A6
Calke Rise DE5 . . . . 169 F1
Calladine Cl DE75 . . . . 181 D2
Calladine La
Horsley Woodhouse DE7 . . 192 D6
Shottle DE56 . . . . 177 C5
Callan's La
Ashby-de-la-Zouch LE65 . . 258 E5
Heath End LE65 . . . . 258 D7
Calley Ave NE7 . . . . 194 F6
CALLOW 165 B4
Callow Dr S14 . . . . 43 D5
Callow Hill Way DE23 . . . 231 A7
Callow La DE4, DE6 . . . . . . 165 C5
Callow Mount S14 . . . . 43 D5
Callow Park Coll DE4 . . . . 165 E4
Callow Pl S14 . . . . 43 D5
Callow Rd S14 . . . . 43 C5
Callywhite La S18 . . . . 57 C1
CALOW 96 F1
Calow Brook Dr S41 . . . . 115 E8
Calow CE Prim Sch S44 . . 96 F3
Calow Cl SK13 . . . . 9 E2
Calow Gn SK13 . . . . 9 E2
CALOW GREEN 116 A8
Calow La
Calow S41, S44 . . . . 96 F1
Chesterfield S41 . . . . 115 E8
Calow Lane Ind Est S41 . 115 E8
Calstock Cl S40 . . . . 95 A4
CALTON LEES 110 F5
Calton View DE45 . . . . 109 D5
CALVER 72 C2
Calver Ave S42 . . . . 132 A7
Calver Bank 8 SK13 . . . . . . 9 D2
Calver Cl
Belper DE56 . . . . 179 B6
Derby DE21 . . . . 205 E3
10 Gamesley SK13 . . . . 9 E2
Calver Cres S43 . . . . 97 D8
Calver Fold 6 SK13 . . . . 9 D2
Calver Mews SK13 . . . . 9 E2
Calver Mill S32 . . . . 72 D2
Calver Pl 7 SK13 . . . . 9 D2
Calver Rd DE45 . . . . 91 D6
CALVER SOUGH 72 C2
Calver St NG19 . . . . 136 E4
Calvert Cl NG16 . . . . 182 B3
Calverton Cl DE24 . . . . 232 E3
Calvert St DE1 . . . . 267 D2
Calvin Cl DE24 . . . . 233 A5
Camberwell Ave DE22 . . . 218 A6
Camberwell Ct 10 S43 . . . . 78 B3
Camborne Cl DE21 . . . . . . 205 E1
Cambrian Cl 1 S40 . . . . 95 D6
Cambrian Way DE11 . . . . . 256 A3
Cambria Rd NG19 . . . . 135 C4
Cambridge Cres
Bramley-Vale S44 . . . . 117 E1
Stapleford NG9 . . . . 209 D2
Cambridge Ct 13 S8 . . . . . . 43 B6
Cambridge Lodge 14 S8 . . 43 B6
Cambridge Rd
1 Brimington S43 . . . . 96 F8
Sheffield S8 . . . . 43 B6
Cambridge St
Blackwell DE55 . . . . 147 E1
Derby, Rose Hill DE23 . . . . 219 B2
Derby, Spondon DE21 . . . . 220 E3
Camdale Rise S12 . . . . 44 F1
Camdale View S12 . . . . 44 F1
Camden St DE22 . . . . 218 D4
Camellia Cl DE3 . . . . 217 D3
Camelot Cl DE13 . . . . 240 E2
Cameron Cl DE15 . . . . 248 B1
Cameron Rd DE23 . . . . 231 F8
Camerory Way S43 . . . . 77 D5
Cam Height S32 . . . . 41 F2
Camlough Wlk S41 . . . . . . 266 C2
Camms Cl S21 . . . . 59 D4
Campbell Ct S43 . . . . 77 D4
Campbell Dr S43 . . . . 78 B4
Campbell St
Belper DE56 . . . . 178 F3
Derby DE24 . . . . 232 D7
Langley Mill NG16 . . . . 182 C4
Campion Cl NG20 . . . . 119 D3
Campion Dr S21 . . . . 60 C6
Campion Hill DE74 . . . . . . 247 A4
Campion Rd DE11 . . . . 256 F4
Campion St DE22 . . . . 218 D5
Campsie Ct 8 DE24 . . . . . 231 D3
Camp St DE1 . . . . 219 B7
Camp Wood Cl DE21 . . . . 205 C7
Canada St DE56 . . . . 179 A2
Canal Bank DE72 . . . . 235 A1
Canal Bridge
Killamarsh S21 . . . . 60 D6
Willington DE65 . . . . 242 A6
Canalgate Pk DE21 . . . . . . 220 F3
Canal Mews S41 . . . . 266 B4
Canalside S21 . . . . 60 B1
Canal Side SK23 . . . . 33 F1
Canal St
Derby DE1 . . . . 267 C2
Ilkeston DE7 . . . . 195 A1
Long Eaton NG10 . . . . 223 C1
Marple SK6 . . . . 23 A6
Sandiacre NG10 . . . . 223 C6
Whaley Bridge SK23 . . . . . . 45 E8
Canal Wharf S41 . . . . 96 B5
Canberra Cl
Derby DE3 . . . . 217 E2
Stapleford NG9 . . . . 209 F1
Candlemass Ct NG19 . . . . 136 D2
CANHOLES 84 E5
Cannell Cl S45 . . . . 131 B4
Canner Cl DE11 . . . . 257 A2
Canning Mews 1 DE7 . . . 208 F7
Cannock Way NG10 . . . . . 237 A7
Cannon Fields S32 . . . . 52 F8
Cannon St SK14 . . . . 9 C5
Canon's Wlk DE22 . . . . . . 204 F2
Cantelupe Gdns NG16 . . . 195 C7
Cantelupe Rd DE7 . . . . 209 A8
Canterbury Cl
Chesterfield S40 . . . . 115 A8
Duffield DE56 . . . . 190 E3
Mansfield Woodhouse
NG19 . . . . 136 C5
Canterbury Rd
Burton upon Trent DE15 . . 248 C3
Sheffield S8 . . . . 43 B5
Wirksworth DE4 . . . . 165 F8
Canterbury St DE21 . . . . . 219 E8
Canterbury Terr DE4 . . . . 165 F8
Cantley Cl DE24 . . . . 232 D3
Cantley Rd DE55 . . . . 170 C6
Cantrell Cl S43 . . . . 96 D8
Capel Rise S43 . . . . 96 D8
Capstan Cl DE11 . . . . 256 E1
Capthorne Cl S40 . . . . 94 F5
Caraway Dr DE14 . . . . 254 A8
Cardale Rd NG19 . . . . 135 C4
Cardales Cl DE65 . . . . 230 D2
Cardean Cl DE1 . . . . 219 B7
Carder Gn SK17 . . . . 121 B6
Cardigan St DE21 . . . . 219 D7
Cardinal Cl 1 DE21 . . . . . 205 F2
Cardlemere La SK17 . . . . 138 F2
Cardrona Cl DE21 . . . . 205 F2
Cardwell Ave S13 . . . . 44 F7
Cardwell Dr S13 . . . . 44 F7
Carfield Ave S8 . . . . 43 B5
Carfield La S8 . . . . 43 C5
Carfield Pl S8 . . . . 43 B5
Carfield Prim Sch S8 . . . . 43 B5
Carisbrooke Dr 2 DE13 . 240 E1
Carisbrooke Gdns DE23 . 231 C6
Carlin Cl DE72 . . . . 235 E8
Carlin St S13 . . . . 44 E6
Carlisle Ave DE23 . . . . 231 B8
Carlisle Cl S41 . . . . 76 E3
Carlisle Gr SK17 . . . . 85 A8
Carlisle Rd SK17 . . . . 84 F8
Carl Moult Ho DE11 . . . . . 256 A2
Carlton Ave
Derby DE24 . . . . 232 E4
Northwood DE4 . . . . 127 A6
Carlton Cl
Clay Cross S45 . . . . 131 D2
Heanor DE75 . . . . 182 A3
Sheffield S20 . . . . 59 C6
Carlton Dr DE24 . . . . 232 E3
Carlton Gdns DE24 . . . . . . 232 E4
Carlton Mews S2 . . . . 43 E7
Carlton Rd
Chesterfield S40 . . . . 115 A6
Derby DE23 . . . . 218 E2
Long Eaton NG10 . . . . 236 B5
Carlton St NG19 . . . . 136 C1
Carlton Walk DE24 . . . . . . 220 A1
Carlton Wlk DE24 . . . . 233 A8
Carlyle Inf Sch DE23 . . . . 231 B8
Carlyle Pl DE75 . . . . 181 D3
Carlyle Rd DE55 . . . . 146 F3
Carlyle St
Derby DE24 . . . . 231 F5
Heanor DE75 . . . . 181 D3
Carlyon Gdns S40 . . . . 114 F8
Carnaby Cl DE22 . . . . 218 A5
Carnarvon Ct DE15 . . . . . . 249 C2
Carnarvon Rd NG17 . . . . . 148 F2
Carnation Rd NG20 . . . . . . 119 C3
Carnegie St DE23 . . . . 232 A8
Carnfield Cl DE55 . . . . 159 F4
Carnfield Hall★ DE55 . . . . 159 D5
Carnfield Hill DE55 . . . . . . 159 D5
Carnforth Cl
Derby DE3 . . . . 217 E1
Stapleford NG9 . . . . 223 D5
Carnival Way DE74 . . . . . . 247 B4
Carnoustie Ave S40 . . . . . 114 C8
Carnoustie Cl DE3 . . . . 217 F2
Carol Cres DE21 . . . . 219 F5
Caroline Cl DE24 . . . . 233 D7
Caroline Ct
Hope S33 . . . . 38 F4
Ilkeston DE7 . . . . 209 A6
Carpenter Ave
Mansfield NG19 . . . . 135 D2
Mastin Moor S43 . . . . 79 B3
Carpenter Cl DE15 . . . . . . 248 C2
Carpenter Croft S12 . . . . . 44 C6
Carpenter Gdns S12 . . . . . 44 C6
Carpenter Mews S12 . . . . . 44 C6
Carper La DE6 . . . . 187 F2
Carradale Gr DE73 . . . . . . 232 E1
Carr Bank SK13 . . . . 17 E8
Carr Brook Cl SK23 . . . . 45 E5
Carr Brow SK6 . . . . 32 A7
Carr Cl DE55 . . . . 160 A7
Car Rd S18 . . . . 74 B6
Carrfield Ave
Beeston NG9 . . . . 223 F2
Long Eaton NG10 . . . . 223 F1
Carrfield Ct 8 S8 . . . . 43 B6
Carrfield Dr S8 . . . . 43 B6
Carrfield La S8 . . . . 43 B6
Carrfield Rd S8 . . . . 43 B6
Carrfields DE7 . . . . 192 C7
Carrfield St S8 . . . . 43 B6
Carrhouse La SK14 . . . . 9 C4
Carriage Dr The SK13 . . . . . 9 F5
Carriers Mdw SK23 . . . . 47 B7
Carriers Rd DE65 . . . . 241 D6
Carrington Court Ind Est
DE1 . . . . 218 E5
Carrington St DE1 . . . . . . 267 C2
Carr La
Brackenfield DE55 . . . . 145 D3
Dronfield S18 . . . . 56 C2
Matlock DE4 . . . . 143 E2
Scarcliffe S44 . . . . 117 F7
South Normanton DE55 . . . 160 A7
Thornhill S33 . . . . 39 F5
Carr Lane Mews S18 . . . . . 56 D2
Carrock Ave DE75 . . . . 182 B1
Carron Cl DE24 . . . . 231 E4
Carr Rd SK17 . . . . 84 D5
Carrs Cl DE74 . . . . 247 A3
CARR VALE 117 F8
Carr Vale Rd S44 . . . . 98 F1
Carr Wood Nature Reserve★
DE5 . . . . 169 E3
Carrwood Rd
Chesterfield S41 . . . . 76 C4
Renishaw S21 . . . . 79 B8
CARSINGTON 164 E7
Carsington Cl S40 . . . . 95 B5
Carsington Cres DE22 . . . 204 D1
Carsington Ct 3 NG19 . . . 136 E3
Carsington Ho 1 DE22 . . 204 D2
Carsington & Hopton CE
Prim Sch DE4 . . . . 164 E7
Carsington Mews DE22 . . 204 E1
Carsington Water Visitor
Ctr★ DE6 . . . . 164 C4
Carson Croft DE4 . . . . 143 C6
Carson Mount S12 . . . . 44 B3
Carson Rd DE21 . . . . 220 B6
Carter Cl NG10 . . . . 236 B6
Carter Grange 11 S8 . . . . . 43 B6
Carterhall La S12 . . . . 44 C2
Carterhall Rd S12 . . . . 44 B2
Carter La
Shirebrook NG20 . . . . 119 E4
Shirebrook, Warsop Vale
NG20 . . . . 120 C4
Carter Lane E DE55 . . . . . 160 C6
Carter Lane W
Shirebrook NG20 . . . . 119 D4
South Normanton DE55 . . . 160 C5
Carter Pl S8 . . . . 43 B6
Carter Rd
Beeston NG9 . . . . 223 F2
Sheffield S8 . . . . 43 A6
Carter St DE24 . . . . 232 D6
CARTLEDGE 75 B7
Cartledge La S18 . . . . 75 A7
Cartmel Cl S18 . . . . 56 E1
Cartmel Cres S41 . . . . 95 E8
Cart Rd DE55 . . . . 157 F4
Cartworth Moor Rd HD9 . . . . 3 E8
Cartwright La DE55 . . . . . 160 E7
Cartwright St S81 . . . . 63 F7
Car Vale Dr S13 . . . . 44 C8
Car Vale View S13 . . . . 44 C8
Carver Cl S26 . . . . 61 E6
Carver Way S26 . . . . 61 E6
Cary Gr S2 . . . . 43 F8
Cary Rd
Eckington S21 . . . . 59 B3
Sheffield S2 . . . . 44 A8
Cascade Gr DE23 . . . . 231 A7
Casson Ave DE24 . . . . 233 A6
Casson Dr S26 . . . . 61 E7
Casson St NG16 . . . . 170 F4
Castings Rd DE23 . . . . 232 B8
Castlebeck Ave S2 . . . . 44 C8
Castlebeck Dr S2 . . . . 44 C8
Castle Cl
Bakewell DE45 . . . . 109 E6
Borrowash DE72 . . . . 221 D2
Castle Coll Arthur Mee Ctr 3
NG9 . . . . 223 D7
Castle Coll Church Hill Ctr
NG16 . . . . 195 F6
Castlecraig Ct DE24 . . . . . 231 E2
Castle Croft
Derby DE24 . . . . 233 D5
Linton DE11 . . . . 261 E8
Castle Ct
Elvaston DE72 . . . . 234 A5

Castle Ct continued
Glossop SK13............. **10** A4
Tutbury DE13........... **239** C7
Castledale Croft S2.... **44** B8
Castledale Gr S2....... **44** C8
Castledale Pl S2....... **44** B8
CASTLE DONINGTON... **247** C3
Castle Donington Com Coll
DE74................... **247** B3
Castle Dr
Bakewell DE45........... **109** E7
Codnor NG16........... **181** E8
Somercotes DE55....... **170** D8
Castle Edge Rd
New Mills SK22.......... **24** B2
Stockport SK6.......... **24** A7
Castlefields NG16....... **170** F3
Castlegate La SK17, DE45 . **89** C5
Castle Gn S44.......... **118** B7
CASTLE GRESLEY....... **255** E1
Castle Hayes La DE13 . . **239** A5
Castle Hill
Castle Donington DE74 . . . **247** B4
Duffield DE56............ **190** E4
Eckington S21............ **59** D4
Findern DE65............ **230** D1
Glossop SK13............. **10** E2
Castle Hill Cl S21........ **59** D4
Castle Hill Ho DE13..... **239** B7
Castle Ho DE1.......... **267** D2
Castle Ind Est S44....... **98** E2
Castle La
Bolsover S44............. **99** A1
Ironville NG16.......... **170** E1
Melbourne DE73........ **252** B7
Castleland Way DE73.... **232** E2
Castle Mews
Mansfield Woodhouse
NG19................. **136** B3
Melbourne DE73........ **252** B7
Castle Mews The 🖪
DE11................. **256** A7
Castle Mills DE73....... **252** B7
Castle Mount Cres DE45 . **109** D7
Castle Mount Way DE45 . **109** D7
Castle Orch DE56........ **190** E4
Castle Point Bsns Pk
DE13................. **238** E6
Castle Rd DE11......... **255** F1
Castlerigg Way 🖪 S18... **56** E1
Castle Row S17.......... **56** B6
Castlerow Cl S17........ **56** B6
Castlerow Dr S17........ **56** B6
Castlerow View S17...... **56** B6
Castleshaw Dr DE23..... **230** E7
Castle St
Bakewell DE45........... **109** D6
Bolsover S44............. **99** A1
Castleton S33........... **38** B2
Glossop SK13............. **10** A4
Mansfield Woodhouse
NG19................. **136** B3
Melbourne DE73........ **252** B7
Tutbury DE13........... **239** C6
CASTLETON............ **38** C2
Castleton Ave
Derby DE23.............. **231** F8
Ilkeston DE7............ **194** E5
Somercotes DE55....... **170** C6
Castleton Bank 27 SK13.. **9** E1
Castleton CE Prim Sch
S33.................. **38** C2
Castleton Cl NG19....... **136** C4
Castleton Cres SK13......**9** E1
Castleton Gn 28 SK13... **9** E1
Castleton Gr
22 Gamesley SK13....... **9** E1
Staveley S43............. **97** B5
Castleton Rd
Hathersage S32.......... **52** E8
Hope S33................ **38** E3
Castleton Terr 25 SK13....**9** E1
Castleton Visitor Ctr★
S33.................. **38** B2
Castle View
Aldercar NG16.......... **182** A4
Duffield DE56............ **190** E4
Eckington S21............ **59** D3
Hatton DE65............ **239** C7
Palterton S44........... **118** B6
Castle View Dr DE4...... **155** C6
Castle View Prim Sch
DE4.................. **143** D5
Castle Way The DE65.... **241** F5
Castle Wlk DE1......... **267** C2
Cat And Fiddle La DE7.. **207** E5
Catchford View S40...... **95** B7
Catcliff Cl DE45......... **109** D4
Catcliff Cotts DE45...... **109** D5
Cat & Fiddle Windmill The★
DE7.................. **207** F4
Cathedral Rd DE1....... **267** B4
Cathedral View DE22.... **218** D2
Catherine Ave
Ilkeston DE7............ **208** F6
Mansfield Woodhouse
NG19................. **136** C3
Catherine Ct
Alfreton DE55........... **159** C5
🖪 Ashbourne DE6....... **173** B2
Chesterfield S40......... **95** E3
Catherine McAuley Ho
DE22................. **204** E1
Catherine Rise DE11.... **256** A1

Catherine St
Alfreton DE55........... **159** C4
Chesterfield S40......... **95** E3
Derby DE23............. **219** B2
Cath of All Saints, Derby★
DE1.................. **267** B4
Catkin Dr NG16......... **195** C8
Cat La S2, S8........... **43** C5
Cator Rd NG19......... **135** D3
Catterick Dr DE3........ **217** C1
Catterwood Dr SK6..... **15** B2
Catton La DE12........ **260** B5
Caudor Way DE4....... **143** A5
Caudwell Cl S42........ **131** D8
Caudwell's Mill & Craft Ctr★
DE4.................. **126** F8
Cauldon Dr S40......... **95** A5
Cauldwell Rd DE12...... **261** B6
Causeway DE22......... **204** E2
Causeway Gdns S17...... **55** D8
Causeway Glade
Sheffield S17............ **55** C8
Sheffield S17............ **55** D8
CAUSEWAY HEAD...... **55** C8
Causeway Head Rd S17... **55** D8
Causeway Ho S45....... **129** D4
Causeway La
Crich DE4............... **156** F5
Matlock DE4............ **143** C5
Causeway The
Ashover S45............ **129** D4
Eyam S32............... **71** E5
Sheffield S17............ **55** D7
🖪 Wirksworth DE4....... **165** F8
Cavan Dr DE21......... **220** B4
Cavell Dr S45........... **131** E2
Cavendish Ave
Buxton SK17............ **84** F6
Derby DE22............. **204** F3
Sheffield, Abbeydale Park
S17.................. **55** F7
Cavendish Cir 6 SK17... **85** B8
Cavendish Cl
Castle Donington DE74 . . . **247** A2
Creswell S80............ **81** D1
Doveridge DE6.......... **211** C1
Duffield DE56........... **190** D2
Holmewood S42......... **116** E1
Shardlow DE72......... **235** B2
🟡 Swadlincote DE11...... **256** A7
Cavendish Close Inf Sch
DE21................. **220** A8
Cavendish Close Jun Sch
DE21................. **220** B8
Cavendish Cotts DE4.... **154** F2
Cavendish Cres NG9..... **209** D2
Cavendish Ct
Chesterfield S41........ **96** A5
Derby DE1.............. **267** A4
Shardlow DE72......... **235** A1
Cavendish Dr
Ashbourne DE6.......... **185** D8
Clowne S43............. **81** A4
Ripley DE5.............. **169** C1
Cavendish Flats DE45 . . . **110** E8
Cavendish Hospl The
SK17................. **85** A8
Cavendish Jun Sch S41 . . **95** F8
Cavendish Pl S43........ **78** B3
Cavendish Rd
Bolsover S44............. **99** B1
Ilkeston DE7............ **208** F6
Long Eaton NG10........ **223** C2
Matlock DE4............ **143** C7
Cavendish Rise S18...... **75** F8
Cavendish Sq S21....... **77** D8
Cavendish St
Chesterfield S40........ **266** B3
Derby DE1.............. **267** A3
Langwith NG20.......... **119** F8
Mansfield Woodhouse
NG19................. **136** A3
Staveley S43............. **97** D8
Cavendish Street N S41 . . **77** A2
Cavendish Way DE3..... **217** C2
Cavendish Wharf DE72... **234** D2
Cavendish Wlk S44...... **99** A2
Caversfield Cl DE23...... **231** A8
Caversham Way DE7..... **207** D8
Cavill Rd S8............ **43** A3
Cawdor Rd S2.......... **43** F6
Caxterway La SK17...... **86** E3
Caxton Cl S43.......... **77** D3
Caxton Ct DE23........ **231** E6
Caxton St DE23........ **231** E7
Caythorpe Ct 4 NG19... **136** E3
Ceal The SK6........... **15** B2
Cecil Ave S18.......... **57** A2
Cecil Rd
Dronfield S18............ **57** A2
Swadlincote DE11....... **255** F5
Cecil St DE22.......... **218** D6
Cedar Ave
Alfreton DE55........... **159** A5
Chesterfield S40......... **95** D5
Long Eaton NG10........ **236** C5
Mansfield Woodhouse
NG19................. **136** C5
Ripley DE5.............. **169** D1
Cedar Cl
Ashbourne DE6.......... **185** D7
Duffield DE56........... **190** D4
Eckington S21............ **59** B2
Glapwell S44............ **118** B1
Glossop SK13............. **10** B2
Killamarsh S21........... **60** C5
Sandiacre NG10......... **223** B7
Shirebrook NG20........ **119** E6

Cedar Croft
Aston-on-Trent DE72..... **246** A7
Kilburn DE56........... **192** B7
Cedar Dr
Ockbrook DE72.......... **221** C4
Selston NG16........... **171** F7
Uttoxeter ST14......... **210** A4
Cedar Gr
Belper DE56............. **179** B2
Linton DE12............ **261** C6
South Normanton DE55. . . **160** B4
Swadlincote DE11....... **256** A7
Cedar Park Dr S44...... **99** C2
Cedar Pk DE7.......... **208** E7
Cedar Rd
Castle Donington DE74 . . . **247** B2
Linton DE11............ **261** E7
Cedar St
Brimington S43.......... **78** A1
Derby DE22............. **218** E8
Shirland DE55.......... **146** C5
Cedarwood Ct DE21..... **205** E2
Celandine Cl
Burton upon Trent DE15 . . **248** C2
Derby DE21............. **206** A2
Celandine Ct S17........ **56** A5
Celandine Gdns S17...... **56** A5
Celandine Pl DE11...... **256** E4
Celanese Rd DE21....... **220** C3
Cemetery Hill DE21...... **219** E6
Cemetery La
Ripley DE5.............. **169** E1
Staveley S43............. **78** E1
Wirksworth DE4......... **154** F1
Cemetery Rd
Belper DE56............. **179** A5
Chesterfield S41........ **96** C2
Clay Cross S45.......... **131** E2
Dronfield S18............ **76** B8
Glossop SK13............. **10** C4
Somercotes DE55....... **170** C7
Stapleford NG9......... **223** E7
Cemetery Terr S43....... **96** E7
Centenary Ho DE1...... **267** B1
Central Area L Ctr DE4 . **143** A6
Central Ave
Borrowash DE72......... **221** B1
Chesterfield S40......... **95** E2
Creswell S80............ **100** D8
Sandiacre NG10......... **223** B6
South Normanton DE55. . . **160** B5
Stapleford NG9......... **223** F8
Central Dr
Blackwell DE55.......... **147** E1
Buxton SK17............ **85** D5
Calow S44............... **96** F3
🖪 Chesterfield S41....... **96** C1
Shirebrook NG20........ **119** E3
Wingerworth S42........ **114** F3
Central Pavement S40 . . **266** B3
Central Rd DE55........ **159** A4
Central St
Chesterfield S41........ **96** C1
Holmewood S42......... **132** E8
Central Store 6 SK13.... **10** C1
Central Wlk S43......... **96** D7
Centre Ct DE1.......... **267** C1
Centre St S44.......... **117** D1
Centro Pl DE24......... **219** D3
Centurion Way Bsns Pk
DE14................. **253** F8
CHADDESDEN.......... **219** E7
Chaddesden Cl S18...... **56** C1
Chaddesden La DE21..... **220** A6
Chaddesden Lane End
DE21................. **219** F6
Chaddesden Park Inf Sch
DE21................. **220** B6
Chaddesden Park Jun Sch
DE21................. **220** B7
Chaddesden Park Rd
DE21................. **219** F7
Chaddesden Wood Nature
Reserve★ DE21........ **206** A3
Chadfield Rd DE56...... **190** E5
Chadwell Cl S41........ **115** C7
Chadwick Ave DE24..... **232** E5
Chadwick Ct S43........ **78** D1
Chadwick Hill DE4...... **141** A6
Chadwick Nick La
Crich DE4............... **167** F7
Fritchley DE4............ **168** A6
Chadwick Rd S13....... **44** C7
Chadwick St SK13....... **17** B8
Chaffinch Cl DE21...... **220** F6
Chain La DE3.......... **218** A2
Chalfont Sq DE21....... **206** B2
Chalkley Cl DE24........ **232** F7
Challands Cl S41....... **115** C8
Challands Way S41...... **115** C8
Challis Ave DE21....... **220** B7
Challoner Gn S20....... **59** E8
Challoner Way S20...... **59** E8
Chalons Cl DE7......... **194** F1
Chalons Way DE7....... **208** F8
Chambers Ave DE7...... **209** B7
Chambers Ct SK14...... **9** A3
Chambers St DE24...... **219** F1
Champion Ave DE7...... **194** C3
Champion Hill DE56..... **190** E4
Chancel Pl DE22........ **267** A1
Chancery La DE22....... **218** A6
Chancet Wood Cl S8.... **56** F8

Chancet Wood Dr S8.... **56** F8
Chancet Wood Rd 🖪 S8.. **56** F8
Chancet Wood Rise S8... **56** F8
Chancet Wood View S8... **56** F8
Chander Hill La S42..... **113** C8
Chandlers Ford DE21.... **205** F2
Chandos Cres S21....... **60** D6
Chandos Pole St DE22.... **218** D6
Chandres Ct DE24....... **204** E4
Chaneyfield Way S40..... **95** B7
Channel Cres DE24...... **219** E2
Channel The DE6....... **173** B2
Chantrey Ave S41....... **96** A6
Chantrey Rd S8......... **43** A3
Chantry Cl
Derby DE3.............. **217** C1
Disley SK12............. **32** E5
Long Eaton NG10........ **236** A4
Melbourne DE73........ **252** B7
Chantry Ct SK17........ **69** C4
Chantry Fold SK12...... **32** E6
Chantry La SK17........ **69** D4
Chantry Rd SK12........ **32** E6
Chapel Brow
Broadbottom SK13........ **16** E6
Glossop SK13............. **10** A7
Chapel Cl
Clowne S43............. **80** E4
Moira DE11............. **256** C1
Willington DE65........ **242** B6
Youlgreave DE45........ **125** B5
Chapel Croft
Elton DE4.............. **140** E6
Middleton DE4.......... **154** D5
Chapel Ct DE7.......... **194** F4
CHAPEL-EN-LE-FRITH... **47** B6
Chapel-en-le-Frith CE VC
Prim Sch SK23......... **47** C6
Chapel-en-le-Frith High Sch
SK23................. **47** A5
Chapel-en-le-Frith Sta
SK23................. **47** B3
Chapel Gn DE6.......... **224** C8
Chapel Hill
Ashover S45............ **129** F4
Beeley DE4.............. **111** B4
Cromford DE4........... **155** A7
Chapel Ho 🖪 DE7....... **208** E8
Chapel Houses SK6...... **23** A5
Chapel La
Apperknowle S18......... **58** A1
Bakewell DE45.......... **109** D5
Barrow upon Trent DE73 . . **244** A6
Boylestone DE6.......... **213** B4
Chellaston DE73......... **233** A1
Church Broughton DE65 . . **227** B8
Clifton DE6............. **184** F6
Crich DE4............... **168** A8
Derby, Chaddesden DE21. . **220** A7
Derby, Spondon DE21..... **220** E5
Glossop SK13.............**9** F5
Hanbury DE13........... **238** A2
Holloway DE4........... **156** B5
Kniveton DE6........... **163** B1
Middleton DE4.......... **154** D5
Rolleston DE13.......... **240** B4
Sheffield, Hillfoot S17...... **55** D4
Taddington SK17......... **88** B3
Thurvaston DE6......... **215** B8
Tissington DE6.......... **162** B6
Wirksworth DE4......... **154** F1
Chapel Lane E S41....... **115** D7
Chapel Lane W S40...... **95** C2
Chapel Lofts SK13....... **10** B5
CHAPEL MILTON........ **47** B8
Chapel Pl NG16......... **195** F6
Chapel Rd
Bolsover S44............. **98** F1
Grassmoor S42.......... **115** F3
Hayfield SK22........... **25** D2
Horwich End SK23........ **45** E5
Selston NG16........... **171** E6
Chapel Row
Borrowash DE72......... **221** B2
Crich DE4............... **168** A8
Chapel Side DE21....... **220** E5
Chapel St
Alfreton DE55........... **159** A4
Belper DE56............. **178** F3
Brimington S43.......... **96** F8
Buxton SK17............ **85** B7
🖪 Chesterfield S41....... **96** A8
Coton in the Elms DE12... **260** D3
Derby DE1.............. **267** B4
Derby, Spondon DE21..... **220** E5
Donisthorpe DE12....... **265** E8
Donisthorpe, Oakthorpe
DE12................. **265** F6
Duffield DE56........... **190** F3
Eastwood NG16......... **182** F1
Fritchley DE56.......... **168** B6
Glossop SK13............. **10** C1
Hayfield SK22........... **25** D2
Heanor DE75............ **194** A8
Holbrook DE56.......... **191** C7
🟡 Ilkeston DE7.......... **194** F1
Kilburn DE56........... **192** A8
Kimberley NG16......... **195** F6
Linton DE11............ **261** E8
Long Eaton NG10........ **236** E7
Longnor SK17........... **121** B6
Melbourne DE73........ **252** B6
Monyash DE45.......... **107** B2
New Houghton NG19..... **135** A2
New Mills, Rowarth SK22 . . **24** E7
New Mills SK22......... **33** B6
Ripley DE5.............. **169** D2
Sheffield S20............ **59** C6

Chapel St continued
Smisby LE65............ **257** F3
Somercotes DE55....... **170** C7
Stonebroom DE55....... **147** A4
Swadlincote, Church Gresley
DE11................. **256** A1
Swadlincote, Newhall
DE11................. **255** F6
Swanwick DE55......... **169** E8
Ticknall DE73.......... **251** A6
Whaley Bridge SK23...... **45** E8
Whaley Thorns NG20..... **101** A3
Woodville DE11........ **256** F2
Chapel Way S42........ **115** D1
Chapel Wlk
Alfreton DE55........... **159** A4
Curbar S32.............. **72** E2
Chapel Yd
Dronfield S18............ **57** A2
Harthill S26............. **61** E6
South Wingfield DE55.... **157** E3
Chapman Ave DE24..... **233** B6
Chapman La S42........ **115** F3
Chapmans Croft DE12... **260** D3
Chapter Cl DE21........ **205** D2
Chardin Ave SK6........ **23** C8
Charing Ct DE1......... **267** C5
Charingworth Rd DE21.. **206** B2
Chariot Cl DE24........ **233** D5
Charity Rd DE55........ **170** C5
Charlbury Cl DE23...... **231** A8
Charles Ashmore Rd S8.. **57** A8
Charles Ave
Derby DE21............. **220** D6
Sandiacre NG10......... **223** B6
Stapleford NG9......... **223** F8
Charles Cl DE7.......... **209** B6
Charles La SK13......... **10** E3
Charles Rd DE24........ **220** A1
Charles St
Alfreton DE55........... **159** A5
🖪 Buxton SK17.......... **85** C8
Chesterfield S40......... **95** E3
Glossop SK13............. **10** C1
Long Eaton NG10........ **236** D6
Mansfield NG19.......... **136** A1
Somercotes DE55....... **170** C7
Swadlincote DE11....... **256** B2
Charleston Cl DE11..... **256** A7
Charleston Rd DE21..... **220** C6
CHARLESTOWN......... **17** C6
Charlestown SK13....... **17** C6
Charlestown Dr DE22.... **204** D4
Charlestown Rd SK13.... **17** C7
Charles Walker Cl DE6.. **175** F2
CHARLESWORTH........ **16** C6
Charlesworth CE Prim Sch
SK13................. **16** C6
Charlesworth Cl SK23... **33** D3
Charlesworth Cres SK23.. **33** D3
Charlesworth Ct 🖪
NG19................. **136** E3
Charlesworth Gdns S44 . **117** E8
Charlesworth Rd SK23 . . **33** D3
Charlesworth St S44..... **117** E8
Charley La SK23........ **47** A8
Charlotte Ct
Burton upon Trent DE14 . . **254** C8
Eastwood NG16......... **182** F3
Sheffield S2............. **43** B8
Charlotte Inf Sch DE7... **194** E2
Charlotte La S33........ **51** A7
Charlotte Rd S2........ **43** B8
Charlotte St
Derby DE23............. **219** A2
Ilkeston DE7............ **194** E3
Charlton Ave NG10...... **223** F1
Charlton Cl DE12........ **261** D5
Charnock Ave S12....... **44** B2
Charnock Cres S12...... **44** A3
Charnock Dale Rd S12... **44** B2
Charnock Dr S12........ **44** B3
Charnock Gr S12........ **44** B2
Charnock Hall Prim Sch
S12.................. **44** B2
Charnock Hall Rd S12... **44** A2
Charnock View Rd S12... **44** B2
Charnock Wood Rd S12.. **44** B1
Charnwood Ave
Belper DE56............. **179** A4
Borrowash DE72......... **221** C2
Castle Donington DE74.... **247** C3
Derby DE23............. **231** D5
Long Eaton NG10........ **236** B4
Sandiacre NG10......... **223** A4
Charnwood Cl DE55..... **169** D2
Charnwood Cres DE55... **148** B3
Charnwood Dr DE5...... **169** C1
Charnwood Gr NG19..... **136** B5
Charnwood St DE1...... **267** B2
Charter Cl S44.......... **134** B8
Charterhouse Cl DE21... **205** F3
Charter Pk DE7......... **208** E7
Charterstone La DE22.... **204** E4
Chartwell Ave S42...... **114** D5
Chartwell Dr DE21...... **219** C5
Chase Cl DE73.......... **233** B2
Chasecliff Cl S40....... **95** D5
Chase Rd DE56.......... **167** F4
Chase The
Derby DE21............. **231** F4
Kilburn DE56........... **192** B8
Little Eaton DE21....... **191** D2
Rosliston DE12.......... **260** C6
Chase View DE4........ **156** F1
Chatfield Cl DE15....... **248** C1
Chatham Ave DE55...... **159** C3
Chatham Ct DE56....... **179** D4

Chatham St DE23 . . . . . . **232** A8
Chatsworth Ave
　Clowne S43 . . . . **80** F4
　Crich DE4 . . . . **156** F1
　Darley Dale DE4 . . . . . . **142** F7
　Long Eaton NG10 . . . . . . **237** A6
　Shireoaks NG20 . . . . **119** E6
Chatsworth Bsns Pk S40 . **95** E2
Chatsworth Cl
　Alfreton DE55 . . . . **158** F3
　Bolsover S44 . . . . **99** C2
　1 Sandiacre NG10 . . . . . **223** B4
Chatsworth Cres
　Bullbridge DE56 . . . . . . **168** B5
　Derby DE22 . . . . **204** F3
Chatsworth Ct
　11 Ashbourne DE6 . . . . . **173** C2
　2 Chesterfield S40 . . . . . **95** C2
　Derby DE24 . . . . **231** F4
　Staveley S43 . . . . **97** D8
　West Hallam DE7 . . . . . . **207** E8
Chatsworth Dr
　Derby DE3 . . . . **217** E3
　Little Eaton DE21 . . . . . . **191** D2
　North Wingfield S42 . . . . **131** F6
　Tutbury DE13 . . . . **239** C6
Chatsworth Farm Shop★
　DE45 . . . . **91** C2
Chatsworth Ho★ DE45 . . . **92** A1
Chatsworth Ho 2 DE14 . . **253** F7
Chatsworth Lodge SK17 . . **85** A8
Chatsworth Park Ave S12 . **44** A5
Chatsworth Park Dr S12 . . **44** A5
Chatsworth Park Gr S12 . . **44** A5
Chatsworth Park Rd S12 . . **44** A5
Chatsworth Park Rise
　S12 . . . . **44** A5
Chatsworth Pl
　Dronfield S18 . . . . **56** D2
　Ilkeston DE7 . . . . **208** B5
Chatsworth Rd
　Buxton SK17 . . . . **85** E7
　Chesterfield S40 . . . . **95** C2
　Creswell S80 . . . . **81** C1
　Rowsley DE4 . . . . **111** A3
　Sheffield S17 . . . . **55** F6
　Swadlincote DE11 . . . . . **256** A6
Chatsworth St
　Derby DE23 . . . . **218** E1
　Tibshelf DE55 . . . . **148** A6
Chatsworth Tech Pk 8
　S41 . . . . **96** A8
Chatsworth View S32 . . . . **72** E1
Chatsworth Way DE75 . . . **181** C2
Chatteris Dr DE21 . . . . . . **205** D1
Chatterton La
　Marple SK6 . . . . **24** A8
　Mellor SK6 . . . . **24** B8
Chaucer Dr S18 . . . . **76** C7
Chaucer Inf Sch DE7 . . . . **208** F8
Chaucer Jun Sch 11 DE7 **194** F1
Chaucer Rd S41 . . . . **95** F8
Chaucer St DE7 . . . . **194** F1
Chaucer Terr DE23 . . . . . . **231** F7
Chavery Rd S45 . . . . **131** E4
Cheadle Cl DE23 . . . . **218** E1
Cheadle Rd ST14 . . . . **210** B1
Cheal Cl DE72 . . . . **234** D2
Cheam Cl DE22 . . . . **217** E6
Cheapside
　2 Belper DE56 . . . . **178** F3
　Derby DE1 . . . . **267** B3
Chedworth Dr DE24 . . . . **233** D6
Cheedale SK17 . . . . **85** D7
Cheedale Ave S40 . . . . **95** D6
Cheedale Cl
　Burton upon Trent DE15 . **248** B5
　Chesterfield S40 . . . . **95** D6
Cheetham Ave S18 . . . . . . **76** E5
CHELLASTON **233** A1
Chellaston Brickworks
　Nature Reserve★ DE73 **233** A1
Chellaston Cotts DE7 . . . **245** B5
Chellaston Inf Sch DE73 . **233** A2
Chellaston Jun Sch
　DE73 . . . . **232** F1
Chellaston La DE72, DE73 **233** D1
Chellaston Park Ct DE73 . **232** F1
Chellaston Rd DE24 . . . . **232** E4
Chellaston Sch DE73 . . . . **232** F1
Chelmarsh Cl DE73 . . . . . **233** A3
CHELMORTON **87** B1
Chelmorton Cl NG19 . . . . **136** E3
Chelmorton Pl DE21 . . . . **219** F8
Chelmsford Cl DE3 . . . . . **217** C3
Chelmsford Way 6 S43 . . **78** B3
Chelsea Cl DE22 . . . . **217** F6
Cheltenham Cl NG9 . . . . . **223** F2
Chelwood Rd DE73 . . . . . **232** F2
Chendre Cl SK22 . . . . **25** C3
Chepstow Cl S40 . . . . **114** F8
Chepstow Gdns S40 . . . . **114** F7
Chequer La DE56 . . . . . . **166** D2
Chequers La DE21 . . . . . **219** D6
Chequers Rd DE21 . . . . . **219** D5
Cheribough Rd DE74 . . . **247** A3
Cheriton Cl NG19 . . . . . . **135** E1
Cheriton Ct 13 S41 . . . . . **95** F8
Cheriton Dr DE7 . . . . **194** C3
Cheriton Gdns DE23 . . . **230** E7
Cherry Bank Rd S8 . . . . . **43** A3
Cherry Cl
　Ashford in the Water
　　DE45 . . . . **108** F8
　Breaston DE72 . . . . **235** E8
　Derby DE3 . . . . **218** A2
　Shirebrook NG20 . . . . . . **119** E6

Cherry Cl continued
　South Normanton DE55 . . **160** B7
Cherry Cl DE14 . . . . **253** F8
Cherrydale Ct DE23 . . . . **231** A6
Cherry Garth DE65 . . . . . **228** D2
Cherry Leys DE15 . . . . . . **248** C4
Cherry St S2 . . . . **43** A8
Cherry Street S S2 . . . . . **43** A8
Cherry Tree Ave
　Belper DE56 . . . . **179** B6
　Ripley DE5 . . . . **180** D8
　Shireoaks S81 . . . . **63** F7
　Swanwick DE55 . . . . . . **170** A7
Cherry Tree Cl
　Bolsover S44 . . . . **99** C1
　Brinsley NG16 . . . . **182** E8
　Clowne S43 . . . . **80** E3
　Derby DE22 . . . . **218** B4
　Hilton DE65 . . . . **228** D2
　Ilkeston DE7 . . . . **208** D6
　Mansfield Woodhouse
　　NG19 . . . . **136** B4
　Risley DE72 . . . . **222** F4
　Swadlincote DE11 . . . . . **255** F6
Cherry Tree Ct
　Ashbourne DE6 . . . . **173** B1
　Chapel-en-le-Frith SK23 . . **47** A6
Cherry Tree Dr
　Buxton SK17 . . . . **66** D1
　Creswell S80 . . . . **81** D2
　Killamarsh S21 . . . . **60** D5
　Long Duckmanton S44 . . . **98** A4
Cherry Tree Gr
　Mastin Moor S43 . . . . **79** C3
　North Wingfield S42 . . . **131** F5
CHERRYTREE HILL **220** B5
Cherry Tree Hill Inf Sch
　DE21 . . . . **220** B5
Cherry Tree Hill Jun Sch
　DE21 . . . . **220** B5
Cherry Tree Mews
　Derby DE21 . . . . **220** B4
　Woodville DE11 . . . . **256** F2
Cherrytree Rd DE15 . . . . **254** F6
Cherry Tree Sq SK17 . . . . **69** C3
Cherry Tree Way NG16 . . **182** C4
Chertpit La SK17, DE45 . . . **89** D6
Chertsey Cl S40 . . . . **114** F8
Chertsey Ct DE7 . . . . **207** D8
Chertsey Rd DE3 . . . . . . **217** C2
Cherwell Cl 1 S43 . . . . . . **96** E8
Chesapeake Rd DE21 . . . **220** B6
Chesham Cl
　Glossop SK13 . . . . **10** B5
　Hadfield SK13 . . . . **10** B5
Cheshire St DE24 . . . . . . **232** E5
Cheshire Way NG16 . . . . **171** C4
Chess Burrow NG19 . . . . **136** D2
Chessel Cl S8 . . . . **43** A4
Chester Ave DE22 . . . . . . **205** B5
Chester Ct
　Derby, Little Chester
　　DE21 . . . . **219** B8
　Derby, Spondon DE21 . . . **220** E3
　Eckington S21 . . . . **59** B2
CHESTERFIELD **266** B2
Chesterfield Ave
　Chesterfield S43 . . . . **77** A3
　Long Eaton NG10 . . . . . **236** F7
　Swadlincote DE11 . . . . . **255** E6
Chesterfield Coll S41 . . . **266** B4
**Chesterfield Coll (Clowne
　Campus)** S43 . . . . **80** E4
**Chesterfield Coll (Tapton
　House Campus)** S41 . . . **96** C5
Chesterfield Dr DE21 . . . **261** C6
Chesterfield Mus★ S41 . . **266** C3
Chesterfield Rd
　Alfreton DE55 . . . . **158** F5
　Barlborough S43 . . . . **80** A5
　Beeley DE4 . . . . **111** B3
　Belper DE56 . . . . **179** B4
　Brimington, Middlecroft S43 **97** B8
　Brimington, Tapton S41,
　　S43 . . . . **96** D7
　Calow S41, S44 . . . . **96** E2
　Darley Dale DE4 . . . . . . **127** C2
　Dronfield S18 . . . . **57** B1
　Eckington S21 . . . . **59** B2
　Farley DE4 . . . . **128** F1
　Grassmoor S42 . . . . **115** F1
　Heage DE56 . . . . **168** E3
　Holmewood S42 . . . . . . **116** C2
　Long Duckmanton S44 . . . **98** C3
　New Houghton NG19 . . . **134** F7
　North Wingfield S42 . . . **132** A8
　Pilsley DE55, S45 . . . . . . **133** A1
　Pleasley NG19 . . . . **135** A6
　Rowsley DE4 . . . . **111** A1
　5 Sheffield S8 . . . . **43** A6
　Shirland DE55 . . . . **146** C3
　Shuttlewood S44 . . . . **98** E5
　Sutton in Ashfield NG17 . **148** E4
Chesterfield Road N
　NG19 . . . . **135** D3
Chesterfield Road S S8 . . **57** A4
Chesterfield Royal Hospl
　S44 . . . . **96** A4
Chesterfield Small Bsns Ctr
　S41 . . . . **96** A6
Chesterfield Sta S41 . . . . **266** C3
Chesterfield Trade Ctr
　S41 . . . . **96** A6
Chesterfield Trad Est S41 . **76** C3
Chesterford Ct DE23 . . . **230** F6
Chester Gdns DE11 . . . . **256** B2
Chester Gn NG9 . . . . **223** F2

Chester Green Rd DE1 . . **219** A7
Chester Ho S40 . . . . **95** E3
Chesterman Cl NG16 . . . . **195** B4
Chester St
　Chesterfield S40 . . . . **95** E3
　Mansfield NG19 . . . . **135** E1
Chesterton Ave DE23 . . . **231** E7
Chesterton Cl S43 . . . . . . **96** F4
Chesterton Rd DE21 . . . . **220** E6
Chestnut Ave
　Belper DE56 . . . . **179** A2
　Chellaston DE73 . . . . . . **232** F3
　Derby DE3 . . . . **217** D3
　Derby, Rose Hill DE23 . . **219** A2
　Eckington S21 . . . . **59** B2
　Holbrook DE56 . . . . **191** C7
　Killamarsh S21 . . . . **60** C5
　Ripley DE5 . . . . **180** D8
　Somercotes DE55 . . . . . **170** D5
　Swadlincote DE11 . . . . . **256** B6
Chestnut Bank 2 DE75 . . **181** D1
**Chestnut Centre Otter, Owl &
　Wildlife Pk★** SK23 . . . . **47** E8
Chestnut Cl
　Buxton SK17 . . . . **66** B1
　Dronfield S18 . . . . **76** C8
　Duffield DE56 . . . . **190** E2
　Horsley Woodhouse DE7 . **192** C7
　New Mills SK22 . . . . **24** C1
Chestnut Cotts DE6 . . . . **151** D1
Chestnut Ct
　Cromford DE4 . . . . **155** A6
　Pinxton NG16 . . . . **160** E3
Chestnut Dr
　Ashbourne DE6 . . . . **185** D7
　Clowne S43 . . . . **80** D4
　Creswell S80 . . . . **81** D2
　Repton DE65 . . . . **243** D2
　Selston NG16 . . . . **171** F7
　Shirebrook NG20 . . . . . **119** C6
　South Normanton DE55 . **160** B4
Chestnut Gn DE11 . . . . . **256** B2
Chestnut Gr
　Borrowash DE72 . . . . . . **221** C3
　Etwall DE65 . . . . **229** B3
　Mansfield Woodhouse
　　NG19 . . . . **136** B5
　Sandiacre NG10 . . . . . . **223** A7
　Tibshelf DE55 . . . . **147** F5
Chestnut La
　Barton in Fabis NG11 . . . **237** E6
　Clifton Campville B79 . . . **263** F2
Chestnut Rd
　Burton upon Trent DE15 . **254** F7
　Langley Mill NG16 . . . . . **182** A3
Chestnuts The NG10 . . . **236** A8
Chestnut Way
　Repton DE65 . . . . **242** C2
　Swanwick DE55 . . . . . . **170** A8
Chevely Ct DE21 . . . . **219** D8
Cheverton Cl DE24 . . . . . **233** D5
Chevin Alley DE56 . . . . . **190** F7
Chevin Ave
　Borrowash DE72 . . . . . . **221** C2
　Derby DE3 . . . . **217** F2
Chevin Bank DE56 . . . . . **190** D6
Chevin Mews DE56 . . . . **178** F2
Chevin Pl DE1 . . . . **218** F7
Chevin Rd
　Belper, Chevinside DE56 . **178** E2
　Belper, Milford DE56 . . . **190** F8
　Derby DE1 . . . . **218** F7
　Duffield DE56 . . . . **190** E5
CHEVINSIDE **178** E2
Chevin The DE13 . . . . . . **240** C1
Chevin Vale DE56 . . . . . . **190** E5
Chevin View DE56 . . . . . **178** E4
Cheviot Ave NG16 . . . . . **170** F3
Cheviot Cl DE11 . . . . **256** A3
Cheviot Rd NG10 . . . . . . **223** A1
Cheviot St DE22 . . . . **218** C5
Cheviot Way 1 S40 . . . . . **95** C5
CHEW **16** A5
Chew Rd SK15 . . . . **5** C8
Chewton St NG16 . . . . . . **182** F1
Cheyenne Gdns DE21 . . . **220** C5
Cheyne Wlk DE22 . . . . . . **218** C6
Chichester Cl DE7 . . . . . **209** A8
Chigwell Way 2 S43 . . . . . **78** B3
CHILCOTE **264** F3
Chilson Dr DE3 . . . . **217** C3
Chiltern Cl
　Chesterfield S40 . . . . **95** C4
　Grassmoor S42 . . . . **115** F3
Chiltern Ct 2 S40 . . . . **95** C4
Chiltern Dr DE7 . . . . **207** E8
Chiltern Gdns NG10 . . . . **223** A1
Chiltern Rd DE11 . . . . . . **256** A3
Chilton Cres NG19 . . . . . **136** C6
Chilton Ct 4 DE13 . . . . . **240** E1
Chime Cl DE21 . . . . **205** E2
China House Yd DE4 . . . . **165** F8
Chine The DE55 . . . . **160** B3
Chingford Ct DE22 . . . . . **218** B6
CHINLEY **34** F1
CHINLEY HEAD **34** F5
Chinley Lodge SK23 . . . . . **34** E2
Chinley Prim Sch SK23 . . **34** F1
Chinley Rd DE21 . . . . **206** A1
Chinley Sta SK23 . . . . **34** D2
Chippinghouse Rd S2 . . . **43** A7
Chiswick Cl DE22 . . . . . . **217** F6
Chiswick Ct 13 S43 . . . . . . **78** B3
CHISWORTH **16** B5
Chisworth Ct 2 NG19 . . . **136** E3
Chiverton Cl S18 . . . . **57** A2
Chorlton Terr ST14 . . . . . **210** H1

Christ Church CE Prim Sch
　S41 . . . . **96** A5
Christchurch Ct DE1 . . . **267** B4
Christ the King RC Prim Sch
　DE55 . . . . **159** A5
Chrysalis Way NG16 . . . . **182** D3
Chrysanthemum Ct
　DE11 . . . . **256** A5
CHUNAL **17** D4
Chunal La SK13 . . . . **17** D5
Chunal Lane Flats SK13 . . **17** C6
Church Al DE45 . . . . **109** D5
Church Alley DE45 . . . . . **109** D5
Church Ave
　Buxton SK17 . . . . **67** B5
　Clay Cross S45 . . . . **131** E3
　Hatton DE65 . . . . **239** D8
　Long Eaton NG10 . . . . . **236** A4
　Swadlincote DE11 . . . . . **256** B3
　Tideswell SK17 . . . . **69** C4
Church Bank
　Hathersage S32 . . . . **53** A8
　Whaley Bridge SK23 . . . . **45** D7
CHURCH BROUGHTON . . **227** B8
**Church Broughton CE Prim
　Sch** DE65 . . . . **227** B8
**CHURCH BROUGHTON,
　HEATHTOP** **227** A6
Church Broughton Rd
　DE65 . . . . **227** C3
Church Brow
　Chapel-en-le-Frith SK23 . . **47** B6
　Mottram in Longdendale
　　SK14 . . . . **9** A3
Church Cl
　Barrow upon Trent DE73 . **244** C3
　Blackfordby DE11 . . . . . **257** B1
　Blackwell DE55 . . . . **147** C1
　Burton upon Trent DE15 . **248** B3
　Chellaston DE73 . . . . . . **233** A1
　Clowne S43 . . . . **80** F3
　Glossop SK13 . . . . **10** E2
　Marchington ST14 . . . . . **224** F2
　North Wingfield S45 . . . **132** A5
　Peak Forest SK17 . . . . . . **49** A3
　Renishaw S21 . . . . **79** B8
　Staveley S43 . . . . **97** C7
　Trowell NG9 . . . . **209** C4
　Willington DE65 . . . . . . **242** B5
　Wingerworth S42 . . . . . . **115** A4
Church Cnr DE55 . . . . . . **165** B1
Church Cres NG9 . . . . . . **223** F3
Church Croft
　Coton in the Elms DE12 . **260** C3
　Ripley DE5 . . . . **169** D2
Churchdale Ave NG9 . . . **209** E1
Churchdale Mews S12 . . . **44** D4
Churchdale Rd S12 . . . . . . **44** D4
Churchdown Cl DE21 . . . **206** B2
Church Dr
　Duffield DE56 . . . . **190** F2
　Ilkeston DE7 . . . . **194** D4
　Sandiacre NG10 . . . . . . **223** B7
　Shirebrook NG20 . . . . . **119** C3
Church Farm ST14 . . . . . **210** A4
Church Farm Mews S42 . **116** B3
Church Farm Rd DE5 . . . **180** E8
Churchfields S80 . . . . **81** E1
Church Fold SK13 . . . . . . **16** C7
Church Gdns NG19 . . . . . **136** C3
CHURCH GRESLEY **256** B2
Church Gresley Inf Sch
　DE11 . . . . **256** B2
Church Hill
　Derby DE21 . . . . **220** D4
　Etwall DE65 . . . . **229** B3
　Jacksdale NG16 . . . . **171** B3
　Kimberley NG16 . . . . . . **195** F6
　Mansfield Woodhouse
　　NG19 . . . . **136** C3
　Newton DE55 . . . . **148** A1
Church Hill Ave NG19 . . . **136** C3
Church Hill St DE15 . . . . **248** B3
Churchill Ave DE4 . . . . . **154** D5
Churchill Cl DE72 . . . . . . **235** D8
Churchill Dr
　Hilton DE65 . . . . **228** E2
　2 Stapleford NG9 . . . . . **223** E8
Church La
　Bakewell DE45 . . . . **109** D6
　Barrow upon Trent DE73 . **244** A5
　Barton in Fabis NG11 . . . **237** E6
　Baslow DE45 . . . . **91** E5
　Beeley DE4 . . . . **111** A4
　Belper DE56 . . . . **179** A4
　Brackenfield DE55 . . . . . **145** D2
　Brailsford DE6 . . . . **201** E7
　Breadsall DE21 . . . . **205** E4
　Brinsley NG16 . . . . **182** E7
　Buxton SK17 . . . . **86** B7
　Caldwell DE12 . . . . **260** E2
　Calow S44 . . . . **97** A3
　Castle Donington DE74 . **247** B3
　Chapel-en-le-Frith SK23 . . **47** B6
　Chelmorton SK17 . . . . . **106** B8
　Chilcote DE12 . . . . **264** E3
　Clowne S43 . . . . **80** F3
　Cossall NG16 . . . . **195** C1
　Derby, Chaddesden DE21 . **220** A6
　Derby, Darley Abbey DE22 **205** A2
　Doveridge DE6 . . . . **211** B1
　Eckington S12 . . . . **58** E7
　Ellastone DE6 . . . . **183** B4
　Great Longstone DE45 . . . **90** A4
　Hanbury DE13 . . . . **238** A4
　Heath S44 . . . . **117** A3
　Heath, Stockley S44 . . . . **117** D3

Church La continued
　Hemington DE74 . . . . . . **247** E4
　Holmewood S42 . . . . . . **116** B3
　Horsley Woodhouse DE7 . **192** E6
　Killamarsh S21 . . . . **60** E6
　Kirk Langley DE6 . . . . . . **202** E2
　Little Eaton DE21 . . . . . . **205** C7
　Mackworth DE22 . . . . . . **217** F7
　Marchington ST14 . . . . . **224** F2
　Marple SK6 . . . . **23** A5
　Mayfield DE6 . . . . **184** C6
　Monyash DE45 . . . . **107** C1
　Morley DE7 . . . . **206** E6
　New Mills SK22 . . . . **33** C8
　Newton Solney DE15 . . . **248** D8
　North Wingfield S42 . . . **131** F5
　Osmaston DE6 . . . . **186** A5
　Peak Forest SK17 . . . . . . **49** A3
　Pleasley NG19 . . . . **135** A5
　Rocester ST14 . . . . **197** A3
　Rowsley DE4 . . . . **110** E1
　Selston NG16 . . . . **171** D7
　Sheffield, Townhead S17 . . **55** D6
　Shirley DE6 . . . . **200** D8
　South Wingfield DE55 . . . **157** F4
　Stanton-by-Dale DE7 . . . **208** F1
　Stapleford NG9 . . . . **223** D7
　Stonebroom DE55 . . . . . **146** F5
　Sutton on the Hill DE6 . . **215** B1
　Thorpe DE6 . . . . **161** D1
　Thrumpton NG11 . . . . . . **237** C3
　Tibshelf DE55 . . . . **147** F6
　Ticknall DE73 . . . . **251** A4
　Tideswell SK17 . . . . **69** C4
　Weston Underwood DE6 . **188** E2
Churchland Ave S42 . . . . **132** D8
Church Lane N
　Chesterfield S41 . . . . **77** A3
　2 Chesterfield S41 . . . . **204** F3
Church Level DE6 . . . . . . **165** B1
CHURCH MAYFIELD **184** D6
Church Mdws
　Calow S44 . . . . **96** F3
　North Wingfield S42 . . . **131** F5
Churchmead NG17 . . . . . **148** F3
Church Mews
　Derby DE21 . . . . **220** D4
　Hatton DE65 . . . . **227** D1
　Killamarsh S21 . . . . **60** E2
　Melbourne DE73 . . . . . . **252** B7
　Sheffield S20 . . . . **59** D7
Church Rd
　Branston DE14 . . . . **253** E7
　Burton upon Trent DE13 . **240** F2
　Chesterfield S40 . . . . . . **266** B3
　Church Broughton DE65 . **227** C8
　Darley Dale DE4 . . . . . . **127** B2
　Egginton DE65 . . . . **241** B3
　Hollingworth SK14 . . . . . . **9** D4
　Marple SK6 . . . . **23** E6
　New Mills SK22 . . . . **33** C7
　Quarndon DE22 . . . . . . **204** C5
　Rolleston DE13 . . . . **240** A4
　Shuttlewood S44 . . . . **99** A6
　Shuttlewood, Stanfree S44 . **99** B8
　Snelston DE6 . . . . **184** C3
　Swadlincote DE11 . . . . . **256** A6
Church Rise DE55 . . . . . . **146** C4
Churchside
　Grassmoor S41 . . . . **115** D5
　Willington DE65 . . . . . . **242** A5
Church Side
　Calow S44 . . . . **96** F3
　Sutton in Ashfield NG17 . **148** F3
Churchside La S41 . . . . . **115** D6
Churchside Wlk DE22 . . . **218** E4
Church Sq
　1 Heanor DE75 . . . . **181** F1
　Melbourne DE73 . . . . . . **252** B6
Church St
　Alfreton DE55 . . . . **158** F4
　Alstonefield DE6 . . . . . . **149** E3
　Appleby Magna DE12 . . **265** F1
　Ashbourne DE6 . . . . **173** B2
　Ashford in the Water DE45 **108** F8
　Ashover S45 . . . . **129** F3
　Barlborough S43 . . . . **80** B7
　Baslow DE45 . . . . **91** E5
　Belper DE56 . . . . **179** A3
　Bolsover S44 . . . . **99** A1
　Bonsall DE4 . . . . **142** E1
　Bradwell S33 . . . . **51** A7
　Brassington DE4 . . . . . . **153** A1
　Brimington S43 . . . . **96** E8
　Buxton SK17 . . . . **85** B6
　Calow S44 . . . . **96** F3
　Clifton Campville B79 . . . **263** E2
　Clowne S43 . . . . **80** E3
　Coton in the Elms DE12 . **260** C3
　Creswell S80 . . . . **81** D1
　Denby Village DE5 . . . . . **180** D1
　Derby, Alvaston DE24 . . . **233** C7
　Derby DE23 . . . . **218** A1
　Derby, Rose Hill DE23 . . **219** A2
　Derby, Spondon DE21 . . . **220** D5
　Donisthorpe DE12 . . . . . **262** F1
　Dronfield S18 . . . . **57** A1
　Eastwood NG16 . . . . . . **182** F2
　Eckington S21 . . . . **59** E4
　Eyam S32 . . . . **71** D5
　Fritchley DE56 . . . . **168** B6
　Glossop SK13 . . . . **10** D2
　Hadfield SK13 . . . . **10** A4
　Hartington SK17 . . . . . . **137** D5
　Hartshorne DE11 . . . . . . **257** B6

Church St continued
Hayfield SK22 . . . . 25 D2
Heage DE56 . . . . 168 E2
Holbrook DE56 . . . . 191 C6
Holloway DE4 . . . . 156 A6
Horsley DE21 . . . . 191 F5
Ilkeston DE7 . . . . 194 E4
Kilburn DE56 . . . . 191 F8
Lockington DE74 . . . . 247 F4
Longnor SK17 . . . . 121 B6
Mansfield Woodhouse
   NG19 . . . . 136 C3
Marple SK6 . . . . 23 A5
Matlock DE4 . . . . 143 C4
Melbourne DE73 . . . . 252 B7
Monyash SK45 . . . . 107 C2
Netherseal DE12 . . . . 264 F6
Ockbrook DE72 . . . . 221 C4
Pilsley S45 . . . . 132 C1
Pleasley NG19 . . . . 135 B4
Ripley DE5 . . . . 169 D2
Ripley, Waingroves DE5 . . . 181 A7
Sandiacre NG10 . . . . 223 B7
Shirland DE55 . . . . 146 D2
Somercotes DE55 . . . . 170 D6
South Normanton DE55 . . . 160 A6
Stapleford NG9 . . . . 223 D7
Staveley S43 . . . . 78 E2
Swadlincote DE11 . . . . 256 B1
Swadlincote, Lower Medway
   DE11 . . . . 256 C4
Swadlincote, Newhall
   DE11 . . . . 256 A6
Tansley DE4 . . . . 144 A4
Tideswell SK17 . . . . 69 C4
Tintwistle SK13 . . . . 10 A7
Tutbury DE13 . . . . 239 C7
Unstone S18 . . . . 76 E7
Whaley Thorns NG20 . . . . . 101 A2
2 Wirksworth DE4 . . . . . . 165 F8
Youlgreave DE45 . . . . 125 C5
Church Street E NG16 . . . . 160 D3
Church Street Mews S33 . 51 A7
Church Street N S41 . . . . . 77 A3
Church Street S
Chesterfield S40 . . . . 115 A7
Glossop SK13 . . . . 10 E2
Church Street W
Chesterfield S40 . . . . 95 C2
Pinxton NG16 . . . . 160 D3
Church Terr SK13 . . . . 10 D2
CHURCHTOWN 127 B2
CHURCH TOWN 60 E6
Church View
Alfreton DE55 . . . . 147 F1
Barlborough S43 . . . . 80 A7
Belper DE56 . . . . 179 A4
Blackwell DE55 . . . . 147 F1
Breaston DE72 . . . . 235 D7
Chesterfield S40 . . . . 95 C2
Clifton DE6 . . . . 184 F6
Clowne S43 . . . . 80 F3
Duffield DE56 . . . . 190 E2
Glapwell S44 . . . . 134 B8
Heanor DE75 . . . . 181 B4
Ilkeston DE7 . . . . 208 E7
Killamarsh S21 . . . . 60 E7
Mottram in Longdendale
   SK14 . . . . 9 A3
New Houghton NG19 . . . . . 134 F7
New Mills SK22 . . . . 33 C8
Church View Cotts SK17 . . 84 E6
Church View Dr
Baslow DE45 . . . . 91 E6
Tupton S42 . . . . 131 E7
Churchward Dr DE13 . . . . 240 F1
Church Way S40 . . . . 266 B3
Church Wlk
7 Belper DE56 . . . . 178 F4
Brinsley NG16 . . . . 182 E6
Chesterfield, Glasshouse
   Common S43 . . . . 77 D4
Chesterfield S40 . . . . 266 B3
Derby DE22 . . . . 204 A4
Donisthorpe DE12 . . . . 265 E8
Duffield DE56 . . . . 190 F2
Eastwood NG16 . . . . 182 F2
Glossop SK13 . . . . 10 E2
Parwich DE6 . . . . 151 D1
3 Stapleford NG9 . . . . 223 E7
3 Wirksworth DE4 . . . . . . 165 F8
Churnet Cl DE6 . . . . 184 C7
Churnet Rd DE65 . . . . 240 D8
Churnet Row ST14 . . . . . . 196 F3
Churston Rd S40 . . . . 95 D3
Cinder Bank NG16 . . . . . . 170 F4
CINDERHILL 179 E1
Cinder Hill S81 . . . . 63 D7
Cinderhill La S8 . . . . 57 C8
Circle Cl S2 . . . . 44 B8
Circle The
Derby DE24 . . . . 231 E5
Mansfield Woodhouse
   NG19 . . . . 136 B4
Sheffield S2 . . . . 44 A8
Circular Dr S21 . . . . 79 B8
Circular Rd
Chesterfield S40 . . . . 115 B8
Staveley S43 . . . . 78 D1
City Gate DE24 . . . . 219 D2
City Gate Bsns Pk DE24 . 219 D2

City Rd
Derby DE1 . . . . 219 A2
Sheffield S12, S2 . . . . 43 F8
City Rd Bsns Ctr DE1 . . . . 267 B4
City Road Ind Pk DE1 . . . 219 A7
City Sch The S13 . . . . 44 F6
City The
Blackfordby DE11 . . . . 257 A2
Woodville DE11 . . . . 256 F2
Civic Ctr S18 . . . . 57 A1
Civic Way DE11 . . . . 256 B4
Clamp Dr DE11 . . . . 256 B3
Clapgun St DE74 . . . . 247 B3
Clara Mount Rd DE75 . . . 182 A1
Clarehaven NG9 . . . . 223 E5
Clare Ho DE1 . . . . 267 B1
Claremont Cl **15** NG19 . . 136 E4
Clarence Ind Trad Est
   S41 . . . . 96 B8
Clarence Rd
Chesterfield S40 . . . . 266 A3
Derby DE23 . . . . 218 F1
Long Eaton NG10 . . . . 236 C6
Clarence St
Chesterfield S40 . . . . 266 A3
Pleasley NG19 . . . . 135 C3
Stonebroom DE55 . . . . 147 B4
Clarence Terr DE4 . . . . . . 143 A1
Clarence Villas DE4 . . . . . 143 B2
Clarendon Rd S43 . . . . 97 C7
Clarke Ave DE75 . . . . 181 C2
Clarke Dr NG10 . . . . 236 A4
Clarkes Cl ST14 . . . . 210 B1
Clarkes La DE72 . . . . 246 B8
Clarke St DE1 . . . . 267 C4
Clarkson Ave S40 . . . . 266 B1
Claterway DE4 . . . . 154 E8
Claverhouse Rd DE15 . . . 248 A2
Claxton St DE75 . . . . 181 D2
Claxton Terr **2** DE75 . . . 181 D2
Clay Cl DE11 . . . . 256 D5
CLAY CROSS 131 B4
Clay Cross Com Hospl
   S45 . . . . 131 D4
Clay Cross Countryside Ctr★
   . . . . 131 C3
Claye St NG10 . . . . 236 E7
Clay La
Clay Cross S45 . . . . 131 B2
Heanor DE75 . . . . 181 D2
Claylands Cl SK14 . . . . 9 D4
Claylands Gr S80 . . . . 81 E5
Claylands Pl S80 . . . . 81 E5
Claylands Rd S80 . . . . 81 E5
Claymar Dr DE11 . . . . 256 A6
CLAY MILLS 241 A3
Claymills Rd DE13 . . . . 241 A2
Claypit La S42 . . . . 112 F8
Clay Pit Way S43 . . . . 80 C6
Clay's La DE14 . . . . 253 F8
Clay St
Burton upon Trent DE15 . . 248 A1
Draycott DE72 . . . . 235 A4
Shirland DE55 . . . . 146 E1
Clay Street E DE15 . . . . . . 248 A1
Clayton Gr DE75 . . . . 181 C4
Clayton St S41 . . . . 266 C2
Cleave Rd DE14 . . . . 254 A8
Clegg Hill Dr NG17 . . . . . 148 E4
Clematis Cres DE15 . . . . . 255 A8
Clement La SK17/S33 . . . . 50 C6
Clement Rd
Horsley Woodhouse DE7 . . 192 D1
Marple SK6 . . . . 23 C7
Cleve Ave
Beeston NG9 . . . . 223 F3
Darley Dale DE4 . . . . 142 F7
Cleveland Ave
Derby DE21 . . . . 220 B5
Draycott DE72 . . . . 235 A4
Long Eaton NG10 . . . . 223 F1
Cleveland Cl DE11 . . . . 256 B3
Cleveland Dr DE15 . . . . . . 248 B3
Cleveland Rd DE55 . . . . . . 146 F3
Cleveland Way S40 . . . . . . 95 C5
Cleveleys Rd NG9 . . . . 223 E3
Clewley Rd DE14 . . . . 253 F8
Cliffash La DE56 . . . . 176 E6
Cliff Bottom S32 . . . . 71 F4
Cliff Bvd NG16 . . . . 195 F7
Cliff Coll S32 . . . . 91 D8
Cliffdon Ho DE65 . . . . 239 D8
Cliffefield Rd S8 . . . . 43 A5
Cliffe Field Rd S8 . . . . 43 A4
Cliffe Hill Ave NG9 . . . . . . 223 D7
Cliffe La
Hathersage S32 . . . . 52 F8
Tideswell SK17 . . . . 69 C4
Cliffe Rd SK13 . . . . 17 D8
Cliffe View Rd S8 . . . . 43 A5
Cliff Hill S43 . . . . 80 D3
Cliff La
Curbar S32 . . . . 72 E1
Elton DE45 . . . . 140 D8
Kirby-in-A NG16 . . . . 160 F4
Cliff Nook DE55 . . . . 160 B4
Clifford Cl
Chesterfield S40 . . . . 95 B2
Long Eaton NG10 . . . . 236 A4
Clifford St
Derby DE24 . . . . 219 D2
Long Eaton NG10 . . . . 236 E7
Cliff Rd SK17 . . . . 85 D8
CLIFTON 184 F6
Clifton Ave
Barlborough S43 . . . . 80 A7
Long Eaton NG10 . . . . 237 A7
CLIFTON CAMPVILLE . . . 263 F1

Clifton CE Prim Sch DE6 184 F6
Clifton Cl
Overseal DE12 . . . . 262 A3
Swadlincote DE11 . . . . 256 A2
Clifton Dr
Buxton SK17 . . . . 85 C4
Derby DE3 . . . . 217 E3
Clifton Rd
Ashbourne DE6 . . . . 185 A8
Buxton SK17 . . . . 85 C7
Derby DE22 . . . . 204 D3
Matlock Bath DE4 . . . . 155 A8
Netherseal DE12 . . . . 264 D6
Clifton St
Chesterfield S40 . . . . 95 E3
Derby DE1 . . . . 267 D1
Cliftonthorpe LE65 . . . . . . 258 B1
Clifton Thorpe Mdws
   LE65 . . . . 258 B1
Clifton Way DE15 . . . . 248 B2
Clinthill La S80 . . . . 81 E7
Clinton Ave NG16 . . . . 182 D6
Clinton St DE21 . . . . 219 D6
Clipstone Gdns DE21 . . . . 206 B2
Clive Ho DE15 . . . . 248 C3
Clock Tower Bsns Ctr The
   S43 . . . . 78 B2
Clodhall La
Curbar S32 . . . . 72 F2
Old Brampton S42 . . . . 93 B5
Cloisters Ct DE21 . . . . 205 F2
Cloonmore Croft S8 . . . . . 43 C1
Cloonmore Dr S8 . . . . 43 C1
Close Bank DE13 . . . . 239 C6
Close The
Derby, Allestree DE22 . . . . . 204 F2
Derby, Normanton Park
   DE23 . . . . 218 D2
Great Longstone DE45 . . . . 89 F4
Linton DE12 . . . . 261 C5
Marple SK6 . . . . 15 B1
Matlock DE4 . . . . 143 B6
Moira DE11 . . . . 262 D8
Shirebrook NG20 . . . . 119 F5
Tutbury DE13 . . . . 239 B6
Cloud Ave NG9 . . . . 223 F7
Cloudside Ct NG10 . . . . . . 223 B7
Cloudside Jun Sch NG10 . 223 B7
Cloudside Rd NG10 . . . . . . 223 A7
Cloudwood Cl DE23 . . . . . 218 B1
Clough Ave SK6 . . . . 23 C6
Clough Bank S2 . . . . 43 B8
Cloughfield Cl SK23 . . . . . 45 D8
Clough La
Hayfield SK22 . . . . 25 C5
Sheffield S10 . . . . 42 F5
Wensley DE4 . . . . 141 D8
Clough Mill SK22 . . . . 25 C5
Cloughside SK12 . . . . 32 E6
Clough Side SK6 . . . . 23 C7
Clough St SK17 . . . . 85 B7
Clough The
Bamford S33 . . . . 40 C4
Chesterfield S41 . . . . 96 E1
Clovelly Ct DE22 . . . . 218 D8
Clover Cl DE21 . . . . 220 F5
Clover Ct
Branston DE14 . . . . 253 E6
Shardlow DE72 . . . . 234 E2
Sheffield S8 . . . . 43 C2
Tibshelf DE55 . . . . 148 B7
Cloverdale DE11 . . . . 256 B7
Cloverdale Dr DE24 . . . . . . 231 F2
Clover Nook Ind Est
   DE55 . . . . 159 E3
Clover Nook Rd DE55 . . . . 159 E3
Clover Rise NG16 . . . . 195 B8
Cloverslade DE65 . . . . 230 C1
Clover Way NG19 . . . . 136 F4
Cloves Hill DE7 . . . . 192 C2
CLOWNE 80 D3
Clowne Jun & Inf Schs
   S43 . . . . 80 E3
Clowne Rd
Barlborough S43 . . . . 80 C6
Shuttlewood S44 . . . . 99 A8
Club La DE73 . . . . 244 A5
Clubmill Terr S40 . . . . 95 E4
Club Row S32 . . . . 71 E6
Clumber Ave NG16 . . . . . . 171 E1
Clumber Cl
Ashbourne DE6 . . . . 185 B8
Clowne S43 . . . . 80 F4
3 Ripley DE5 . . . . 169 E1
Clumber Ct NG19 . . . . 135 E2
Clumber Dr NG19 . . . . 135 E2
Clumber Pl S43 . . . . 97 C6
Clumber St NG10 . . . . 236 D7
Clun Ct NG19 . . . . 136 D2
Clune St S43 . . . . 81 A5
Cluster Rd DE56 . . . . 178 F4
Clusters Ct **3** DE56 . . . . . 178 F4
Clyde St DE65 . . . . 228 D1
Coach Dr
Eastwood NG16 . . . . 182 F4
Quarndon DE22 . . . . 204 D7
Coachhouse Mews **4**
   DE11 . . . . 256 A7
Coach Rd
Hollingworth SK14 . . . . 9 C5
Ironville DE55 . . . . 170 D3
Ripley DE5 . . . . 169 E4
Shireoaks S81 . . . . 63 F6
Coach Way DE65 . . . . 242 C5
Coachways DE7 . . . . 193 F3
COAL ASTON 57 B4
Coal La DE11, DE73 . . . . . 257 D8

Coalpit La
Coton in the Elms DE12 . . . 260 E3
Youlgreave DE45 . . . . 125 C6
Coarses View SK23 . . . . . . 47 C7
Coasthill DE4 . . . . 156 F1
Coatsby Rd NG16 . . . . 195 F7
Cobden Pl NG19 . . . . 135 E2
Cobden Rd
Chesterfield S40 . . . . 266 A4
Matlock DE4 . . . . 143 C6
Cobden St
Derby DE22 . . . . 218 D5
Long Eaton NG10 . . . . 236 E7
Ripley DE5 . . . . 169 D2
Cobham Cl DE24 . . . . 231 D3
Cobnar Ave S8 . . . . 43 A2
Cobnar Dr
Chesterfield S41 . . . . 95 D8
Sheffield S8 . . . . 43 A2
Cobnar Rd S8 . . . . 43 A2
Cobnar Wood Cl S18 . . . . . 76 B3
Cobthorn Dr DE22 . . . . . . 204 C3
Coburn Pl DE1 . . . . 267 A3
COCK ALLEY 97 A1
Cock Ayne Cl NG10 . . . . . . 223 B3
Cockayne La S17 . . . . 55 A2
Cockayne Street N DE24 . 232 E6
Cockayne Street S DE24 . 232 E6
Cock Brow SK14 . . . . 15 C7
Cockcharme Gapp DE74 . 247 B6
Cockerhouse Rd NG16 . . . 182 E4
Cock Hill
Baslow DE45 . . . . 91 F5
Clifton DE6 . . . . 184 F6
Cockleys NG10 . . . . 236 C6
Cock Pitt The DE1 . . . . 267 C3
Cockshead La DE6 . . . . . . 198 D7
Cockshut La
Melbourne DE73 . . . . 251 F7
Whaley Thorns NG20 . . . . . 101 A4
Cockshut Lane Bsns Ctr
   DE73 . . . . 252 A7
Cockshutt Ave S8 . . . . 56 D8
Cockshutt Dr S8 . . . . 56 D8
Cockshutt La DE55 . . . . . . 170 F8
Cockshutt Rd S8 . . . . 56 D8
COCKYARD 46 E4
Cod Beck Cl DE24 . . . . 233 D6
Coddington La DE4 . . . . . . 156 E2
CODNOR 181 C7
CODNOR BREACH 181 A4
Codnor Com Prim Sch
   DE5 . . . . 181 B8
Codnor-Denby La DE5 . . . 181 A5
CODNOR GATE 170 B1
Codnor Gate DE5 . . . . 170 B1
Codnor Gate Ind Est
   DE5 . . . . 170 A1
Codnor La DE5 . . . . 170 C2
CODNOR PARK 170 E3
Coffin La DE6 . . . . 165 B1
Coggers La S32 . . . . 52 F8
Coisley Hill S13 . . . . 44 F6
Cokayne Ave DE6 . . . . 173 C2
Cokayne Mews DE6 . . . . . 173 C3
Cokefield Terr DE55 . . . . . 148 C1
Coke St DE22 . . . . 218 D5
COLDEATON 150 B4
Coldharbour La S45 . . . . . 145 A4
Cold Side S33 . . . . 14 F3
Coldstream Wlk DE24 . . . 231 E4
Coldwell St DE4 . . . . 165 F8
Cole La DE72 . . . . 221 D3
Coleman St DE24 . . . . 232 E7
Coleraine Cl DE21 . . . . 220 B4
Coleridge St
Derby, Littleover DE23 . . . . 231 E6
Derby, Normanton DE23 . . 231 F7
Colin Ave DE5 . . . . 181 B8
Colin St DE55 . . . . 159 A4
Collage Rd S21 . . . . 60 D2
Colledge St DE55 . . . . 170 C6
College Ave S43 . . . . 78 D1
College Mews DE1 . . . . . . 218 E5
College Rd
Buxton SK17 . . . . 85 A6
Denstone ST14 . . . . 196 C6
Spinkhill S21 . . . . 60 D2
College Side NG18 . . . . . . 136 C1
College St NG10 . . . . 223 C2
College View S43 . . . . 80 E3
College Way SK17 . . . . 85 D2
Collier Ave NG19 . . . . 136 B5
Collier La DE72 . . . . 221 C4
Colliers Cl DE11 . . . . 255 E6
Colliers Ct DE5 . . . . 181 A7
Collier St SK13 . . . . 17 C8
Colliers Trek S43 . . . . 80 C5
Colliers Way S45 . . . . 131 B4
Colliery Cl S43 . . . . 78 F1
Colliery La DE12 . . . . 261 D2
Colliery Rd
Blackwell DE55 . . . . 147 F1
Creswell S80 . . . . 100 E8
Swadlincote DE11 . . . . 256 A1
Colliery Row
Alfreton DE55 . . . . 159 B5
Pinxton NG16 . . . . 160 D4
Swadlincote DE11 . . . . 256 A1
Collin Ave NG10 . . . . 223 B4
Collingham Gdns DE22 . . 218 A5
Collingham Rd NG19 . . . . 135 D1
Collingwood Cres DE4 . . . 143 A6
Collingwood Rd NG10 . . . 236 E6
Collins Ave DE55 . . . . 160 A7
Collins Yd S18 . . . . 57 B1
Collis Cl DE24 . . . . 232 E7
Collishaw Cl **6** S41 . . . . . . 96 C1

Columbell Ave DE72 . . . . . 221 C5
Colne Cl NG19 . . . . 136 D2
Colombo St DE23 . . . . 219 B1
Colonade NG20 . . . . 119 E2
Colonnade The **3** SK17 . . 85 B8
Colonsay Cl NG9 . . . . 209 D3
COLSHAW 103 E4
Colton Cl S41 . . . . 76 E1
Coltsfoot Cl DE11 . . . . 256 F4
Coltsfoot Dr DE24 . . . . 231 F2
Coltsworth La S43 . . . . 80 E8
Columbell Way DE4 . . . . . 127 D2
Columbia St NG17 . . . . . . 148 F3
Columbine Cl DE21 . . . . . . 206 A1
Colver Rd S2 . . . . 43 A8
Colvile Cl DE12 . . . . 263 D7
Colvile St DE22 . . . . 218 D6
Colwell Dr DE24 . . . . 233 D5
Colwick Cl NG19 . . . . 135 E1
Colwyn Ave DE23 . . . . 218 D5
Colyear St DE1 . . . . 267 B3
COMBRIDGE 210 C8
COMBS 46 E1
Combs Bank **53** SK13 . . . . 9 D1
Combs Cl SK22 . . . . 33 A8
Combs Fold **51** SK13 . . . . . 9 D2
Combs Gdns **2** SK13 . . . . . 9 D1
Combs Gr **49** SK13 . . . . . . 9 D2
Combs Inf Sch SK23 . . . . . 46 E1
Combs Lea **1** SK13 . . . . . . 9 D1
Combs Mews **48** SK13 . . . . 9 D2
Combs Rd SK23 . . . . 46 E3
Combs Terr **50** SK13 . . . . . 9 D2
Combs Way **52** SK13 . . . . . 9 D2
Comfrey Cl DE23 . . . . 230 F6
Commerce St
Derby DE24 . . . . 232 F8
Melbourne DE73 . . . . 252 A7
Commercial Rd SK17 . . . . 69 C4
COMMON END 132 F7
Common End DE65 . . . . . . 229 B7
Common La
Chelmorton SK17 . . . . 87 A1
Cutthorpe S42 . . . . 94 E8
Mansfield Woodhouse
   NG19 . . . . 136 A4
Shirebrook NG20 . . . . 119 C4
Shirland DE55 . . . . 146 D3
Stanley DE7 . . . . 207 A7
Sutton on the Hill DE6 . . . . 228 A8
Commonpiece La DE6 . . . 215 B2
Common Piece La DE65 . . 230 E1
Commonpiece Rd S45 . . . . 131 C3
Common Rd
Harthill S26 . . . . 62 B5
Sutton in Ashfield NG17 . . . 148 F2
Swadlincote DE11 . . . . 256 C2
Thorpe Salvin S80 . . . . 62 F6
Commons Cl NG16 . . . . . . 195 A8
COMMONSIDE
Brailsford 187 D1
Selston 171 F8
Sutton in Ashfield 148 F2
COMMON SIDE
Barlow 75 D3
Heanor 181 D1
Common Side
Selston NG16 . . . . 171 F8
Swadlincote DE11 . . . . 256 C2
Commonside Rd S18 . . . . . 75 D2
Commonside The
Crich DE4 . . . . 168 A7
Quarndon DE22 . . . . 204 C8
South Normanton DE55 . . . 160 A5
Common Wood DE4 . . . . . 143 B3
Compass Cres S41 . . . . 77 C3
COMPSTALL 15 A3
Compstall Mills Ests SK6 . 15 B2
Compstall Rd
Compstall SK6 . . . . 15 A3
Marple SK6 . . . . 15 A2
COMPTON 173 D2
Compton Ave DE72 . . . . . . 246 A8
Compton Cl **6** DE24 . . . . . 233 C6
Compton Dr S80 . . . . 81 D1
Compton Gr SK17 . . . . 85 B6
Compton Rd SK17 . . . . 85 B6
Compton St
Ashbourne DE6 . . . . 173 C2
Chesterfield S40 . . . . 266 A4
Holmewood S42 . . . . 116 E1
Langwith NG20 . . . . 119 F8
Conalan Ave S17 . . . . 56 B5
Concert Pl **6** SK17 . . . . . . 85 B7
Concorde Way NG19 . . . . . 135 E3
Condliff Rd SK17 . . . . 69 B5
Condor Rd DE7 . . . . 208 F4
Conduit Rd S44 . . . . 118 B8
Conduit St
Glossop SK13 . . . . 9 F7
Tintwistle SK13 . . . . 9 F7
Coney Green Bsns Ctr
   S45 . . . . 131 E4
Coney Green Networking Ctr
   S45 . . . . 131 E4
Coney Green Rd S45 . . . . . 131 E4
CONGREAVE 126 D7
Coniston Ave DE21 . . . . . . 220 E6
Coniston Cl NG19 . . . . 136 F4
Coniston Cres DE21 . . . . . . 205 D2
Coniston Dr
Clay Cross S45 . . . . 131 B2
Ilkeston DE7 . . . . 208 D5
Coniston Rd
Chesterfield S41 . . . . 95 E8
Dronfield S18 . . . . 56 E1
Long Eaton NG10 . . . . 223 A2
Coniston Way S41 . . . . 95 E8

Conjoint La SK17. . . . . . . 69 E4
Conkers Discovery Ctr★
  DE12. . . . . 262 D5
Conkers Waterside Ctr★
  DE12. . . . . 262 D4
Conksbury Ave DE45 . . . . 125 C6
Conksbury La DE45 . . . . . 125 C6
Connaught Ct DE55 . . . . . 159 B3
Connaught Rd DE22. . . . . 218 C4
Connelly Ct S40. . . . . 95 C3
Consett Cl DE21. . . . . 205 D1
Consort Gdns DE21. . . . . 206 C3
Constable Cl
  8 Dronfield S18. . . . . . . 56 E1
  Sheffield S14. . . . . 43 E2
Constable Dr
  Derby DE23 . . . . 218 B1
  Marple SK6. . . . . 23 B8
  Sheffield S14. . . . . 43 D2
Constable La DE23 . . . . . 218 C3
Constable Pl S14. . . . . 43 D2
Constable Rd S14. . . . . . . 43 D2
Constable Way S14. . . . . . 43 D2
Convent Cl DE55 . . . . 254 F8
Conway Ave DE72. . . . . . 221 D6
Conway Rd NG10. . . . . . . 236 F8
Conway St NG10. . . . . . . 236 F8
Conygree La DE6 . . . . 184 D7
Cook Cl DE56 . . . . 179 E5
Cook Dr DE7. . . . . 209 A6
Cooke & Beard Homes S8 43 B5
Cooke Cl
  Clay Cross S42. . . . . 131 B6
  Long Eaton NG10. . . . . . 236 B7
Cookfield DE56. . . . . 179 E8
Cookham Cl DE3 . . . . 217 C2
Cook La DE6 . . . . 211 B1
Cooks Dr DE74. . . . . 247 A3
Coole Well Cl S43. . . . . . . 97 D8
Coombes Cl SK13. . . . . . . 16 C5
Coombes View SK14 . . . . . 15 F8
Coombs Rd DE45. . . . . . . 109 F5
Co-operative St
  Derby DE23 . . . . 218 F2
  Disley SK12. . . . . 32 D6
  Long Eaton NG10. . . . . . 236 E6
Coopers Cl
  Acresford DE12. . . . . . . 265 B7
  Borrowash DE72. . . . . . 221 D1
Cooper's Cl 2 DE6. . . . . . 173 C2
Coopers Croft DE65 . . . . 227 C1
Coopers Gdns DE6 . . . . . 173 B1
Cooper St
  Derby DE22 . . . . 218 D6
  Glossop SK13. . . . . 10 B1
Copecastle Sq DE1. . . . . 267 C2
Cope Ct DE24. . . . . 232 A5
Copeland Ave NG9 . . . . . 223 E8
Copeland St DE1. . . . . . . 267 C2
Copenhagen Rd S45 . . . . 131 E4
Copestake Cl NG10. . . . . 236 A7
Copes Way
  Derby DE21. . . . . 220 A8
  Uttoxeter ST14 . . . . 210 A1
Copley Croft 3 DE6. . . . . 173 D3
COPLOW DALE 50 E3
Coplow La DE65 . . . . 226 D5
Copperas Rd DE55 . . . . . 255 D5
Copper Beech Dr SK13. . . . 9 E1
Copper Beeches DE5. . . . 169 C2
Copperleaf Cl DE22 . . . . 267 A2
Copper Yd DE5 . . . . 180 F2
Coppice Ave
  High Lane SK12. . . . . 32 A6
  Ilkeston DE7 . . . . 194 D5
Coppice Cl
  Chesterfield S41 . . . . . . 115 D6
  Derby DE22 . . . . 204 F1
  High Lane SK12. . . . . 32 A6
  Kilburn DE56 . . . . 192 A4
Coppice Ct DE75. . . . . . . 193 F7
Coppice Dr
  Eastwood NG16. . . . . . . 182 D3
  Heanor DE75 . . . . 193 F7
Coppice End Rd DE22 . . . 204 C1
Coppice La
  Clifton Campville B79 . . . 263 F1
  High Lane SK12. . . . . 32 A5
Coppice Mews DE75 . . . . 193 F7
Coppice Prim Sch DE75 . 193 E8
Coppice Side DE11. . . . . 256 C3
Coppice The
  Horwich End SK23. . . . . . 45 F5
  Shirebrook NG20. . . . . . 119 D3
Coppice View DE55 . . . . 160 A4
Coppicewood Dr DE23 . . 218 A1
Copse Cl DE4. . . . . 165 E8
Copse Gr DE23. . . . . 231 A7
Copse Rise DE11. . . . . . . 256 B7
Copseside Cl 10 NG10. . . 236 A8
Copse The
  Ilkeston DE7 . . . . 194 D5
  Marple SK6. . . . . 23 C8
Copsewood DE55 . . . . . . 160 A4
Copsey Croft Ct NG10 . . 236 F7
Copthorne Com Inf Sch
  DE55. . . . . 159 A5
Copthurst Rd HD9. . . . . 3 E7
Coral Ct DE24. . . . . 219 E2
Coral Way S45. . . . . 131 D4
Corbar Grange SK17. . . . . 85 A8
Corbar Rd SK17. . . . . 66 B1
Corbar Woods La SK17. . . 66 A1
Corbel Cl DE21. . . . . 205 E2
Corbridge Gr DE23 . . . . . 231 A7
CORBRIGGS 115 F5
Corby Cl DE24 . . . . 232 F5

Cordelia Way DE73. . . . . 232 E2
Corden Ave DE3 . . . . 218 A2
Corden St DE23 . . . . 219 A2
Cordville Cl DE21 . . . . . . 220 B5
CORDWELL 74 E6
Cordwell Ave S41. . . . . . . 95 C8
Cordwell Cl
  Castle Donington DE74. . 246 F3
  Staveley S43 . . . . 97 D8
Cordwell La S18. . . . . 74 E5
Cordy La
  Brinsley NG16 . . . . 182 F8
  Selston NG16. . . . . 182 F8
Corfe Cl DE23. . . . . 231 D6
Corfield Ave DE75. . . . . . 193 F7
Corfield CE Inf Sch
  DE75. . . . . 181 D1
Coriander Gdns DE23 . . . 231 D4
Corinium Cl DE24 . . . . . . 233 D5
Corker Rd S12. . . . . 44 A6
Corks La SK12 . . . . 32 E5
Corley La DE6 . . . . 174 D2
Cornbrook DE45 . . . . 108 F7
Cornel Ct 4 NG19 . . . . . . 136 E1
Corner Farm DE6 . . . . . . 201 E8
Corner Pin Cl 7 S43 . . . . . 78 F2
Cornfield Ave S44. . . . . . 160 A4
Cornfield Cl 1 S42. . . . . . 95 A5
Cornfield Rd NG16 . . . . . 195 E7
Cornhill DE22. . . . . 204 F4
Cornhill Cl DE56. . . . . . . 190 D4
Cornhill Dr DE55 . . . . . . 159 B4
Cornmill Bank DE13. . . . . 239 D6
Cornmill Cl
  Bolsover S44. . . . . 99 B2
  Calver S32. . . . . 72 C1
  Derby DE22 . . . . 233 D5
Corn Mill Cl DE4 . . . . 165 E6
Cornmill Ho SK13 . . . . 10 D1
Cornmill La DE13 . . . . . . 239 E6
Corn Mkt DE1. . . . . 267 B3
Corn St SK13 . . . . 10 D1
Cornwall Ave
  Brimington S43 . . . . 96 F8
  Buxton SK17 . . . . 85 E7
Cornwall Cl
  4 Brimington S43 . . . . . . 96 F8
  Westwood NG16 . . . . . . 171 C4
Cornwall Dr
  Brimington S43 . . . . 96 F8
  Grassmoor S42 . . . . 115 F3
Cornwallis Cl NG10 . . . . . 236 D6
Cornwall Rd
  Burton upon Trent DE15 . 254 E6
  Derby DE21. . . . . 219 D6
  Shireoaks S81 . . . . 63 F7
Coronation Ave
  Belper DE56. . . . . 179 A5
  Derby DE23 . . . . 233 C5
  New Houghton NG19. . . . 134 F7
  Sandiacre NG10. . . . . . . 223 A7
Coronation Cl DE73. . . . . 252 B8
Coronation Cotts DE13 . . 253 A8
Coronation Cres ST14. . . 197 A4
Coronation Dr
  Shirebrook NG20. . . . . . 119 F2
  South Normanton DE55. . 160 B5
Coronation La DE12. . . . . 265 F6
Coronation Rd
  Brimington S43 . . . . 96 E8
  Cossall DE7, NG16. . . . . 195 A4
  Mapperley DE7 . . . . 193 F3
  Stanley DE7 . . . . 207 C6
Coronation St
  Derby DE23 . . . . 232 B8
  1 Ilkeston DE7. . . . . . . 208 F8
  Overseal DE12 . . . . 262 A4
  Swadlincote DE11 . . . . . 256 A5
  Whitwell S80 . . . . 82 A6
Coronet Ct DE21 . . . . 206 D3
Corporation Rd DE7. . . . . 209 A5
Corporation St
  Chesterfield S41 . . . . . . 266 C3
  Derby DE1. . . . . 267 B3
Corve Way S40 . . . . 94 F5
COSSALL 195 C1
COSSALL COMMON 195 B3
COSSALL MARSH 195 C2
Cossall Rd NG9 . . . . 209 D5
Cote Bottom La DE65. . . . 227 A7
COTE GREEN. 15 C1
Cote Green La SK6. . . . . . 15 B1
Cote Green Rd SK6. . . . . . 15 C1
Cote Hilloc DE4. . . . . 127 A6
Cote La SK22 . . . . 25 D3
COTES PARK 159 C4
Cotes Park Ind Est DE55 159 D2
Cotes Park La DE55 . . . . . 159 C2
Cotgrave Rd NG19 . . . . . 135 F2
Cotman Dr SK6. . . . . 23 C8
COTMANHAY. 194 E4
Cotmanhay Inf & Jun Sch
  DE7. . . . . 194 E5
Cotmanhay Rd DE7 . . . . . 194 F3
Coton Cl NG19 . . . . 136 E4
COTON IN THE CLAY 238 A7
COTON IN THE ELMS 260 C4
Coton in the Elms CE Prim
  Sch DE12. . . . . 260 D3
Coton La
  Coton in the Elms DE12. . 260 F3
  Rosliston DE12 . . . . 260 D5
COTON PARK 261 C8
Coton Pk DE12. . . . . 255 C1
Coton Rd DE12 . . . . 259 E6

Cotswold Cl
  2 Chesterfield S40. . . . . 95 C5
  Derby DE23 . . . . 231 C8
Cotswold Dr
  Glossop SK13. . . . . 17 A8
  3 Long Eaton NG10 . . . 236 B8
  Swadlincote DE11 . . . . . 256 A3
Cotswold Dr S42. . . . . . . 115 E3
Cotswold Rd DE14 . . . . . 253 F8
Cottage Cl
  Heage DE56. . . . . 179 E8
  Ilkeston DE7 . . . . 194 D3
  Poolsbrook S43. . . . . 98 A7
  Swadlincote DE11 . . . . . 256 A7
Cottage Ct DE56 . . . . 179 E3
Cottage Garden La DE75 181 D2
Cottages The SK23. . . . . . 47 B6
Cottam Cres SK6. . . . . 23 B7
Cottam Dr S43. . . . . 80 C6
Cotterdale Cl NG19. . . . . 136 E1
Cotterhill La S43. . . . . 96 F7
Cottesmore Cl DE15 . . . . 248 B1
Cottesmore Rd DE15 . . . . 248 A1
Cottisford Cl DE23 . . . . . 231 A8
Cottonbrook Rd DE23 . . . 232 B8
Cotton Cl S23. . . . . 45 E5
Cotton La S42. . . . . 214 C1
Cotton Mill Hill S42. . . . . 113 C7
Cotton St S44. . . . . 99 A1
Cotts The SK17 . . . . 86 D5
Council Hos
  Bradbourne DE6 . . . . . . 163 B6
  Hanbury DE13 . . . . 238 A3
Countess Gr DE73. . . . . . 244 F8
Counting House Rd SK12. 32 E5
Countisbury Dr DE21. . . . 206 A2
County Est The NG17. . . . 148 E2
Coupe La S42, S45. . . . . . 131 A5
Coupe Dr DE5 . . . . 180 F8
Coupland Cl S41. . . . . 77 C4
Coupland Pl DE55. . . . . . 159 C1
Court Farm La DE14. . . . . 253 E7
Courtland Dr DE24. . . . . 233 B6
Courtland Gdns DE24 . . . 233 B7
Courtland Rd DE65. . . . . 229 C3
Courtney Way DE56. . . . . 179 D5
Court Pl S43. . . . . 97 C8
Court St DE11. . . . . 256 C1
Courtway Cres DE73. . . . 244 E8
Courtyard Mews DE24. . . 233 A6
Courtyard Pl DE21 . . . . . 220 E5
Courtyard The
  Bakewell DE45. . . . . 109 D6
  Belper DE56. . . . . 179 A4
  Darley Dale DE4 . . . . . . 127 C3
  Hollingworth SK14. . . . . . 9 D5
Coventry Cl DE11 . . . . . . 256 D6
Coventry La NG9 . . . . . . 209 F2
Coverdale Wlk DE24 . . . . 233 C7
Covert Pl DE21. . . . . 262 C8
Covert The DE21. . . . . . . 220 E4
Cowbrook Ave SK13. . . . . 10 F1
Cowbrook Cl SK13. . . . . . 10 F1
Cowburn Dr S42. . . . . . . 24 C1
Cowdale Cotts SK17. . . . . 86 A4
Cowdray Cl DE24. . . . . . . 231 D2
COWERS LANE 177 D3
Cowham Cl DE55. . . . . . . 159 C3
COWHILL. 179 A2
Cow La
  Brimington S43 . . . . 77 E1
  Hyde SK14. . . . . 9 D6
COWLEY 75 D7
COWLEY BAR 75 B8
Cowley Bottom S18. . . . . 75 E8
Cowley Cl
  Chesterfield S41 . . . . . . 266 C3
  Ilkeston DE7 . . . . 194 F5
Cowley Gdns S20. . . . . . . 59 E8
Cowley La S18. . . . . 75 D7
Cowley St DE22 . . . . 218 E7
Cowlishaw Cl DE72. . . . . 234 E1
Cowper Rd NG16. . . . . . . 195 A8
Cowper St DE24. . . . . . . 232 A5
Cowpingle La S43. . . . . . . 77 E1
Cowsell Dr S45 . . . . 131 E2
Cowsley Rd DE21 . . . . . . 219 D7
Cowslip Cl DE12 . . . . 262 E1
Cowslip Mdw DE72. . . . . 235 B7
COXBENCH. 191 F3
Coxbench Rd DE21. . . . . 191 F4
Cox Green Ct DE23 . . . . . 230 F7
Coxon St DE21 . . . . 220 E5
Coxon's Yd 5 DE6 . . . . . . 173 B2
Cox's La NG19 . . . . 136 B5
Crabapple Dr NG16 . . . . 182 C4
Crabtree Ave SK12 . . . . . . 32 E5
Crabtree Cl
  Castle Donington DE74. . 247 A2
  Clay Cross S45. . . . . 131 E3
  Derby DE22 . . . . 204 C4
  Wirksworth DE4. . . . . . . 165 E7
Crabtree Cl SK12 . . . . 32 E5
Crabtree Hill DE22. . . . . 204 C3
Crab Tree Hill DE21. . . . . 205 C8
Cracken Cl SK23 . . . . 34 D2
Craddock Ave DE21 . . . . 220 E3
Cradock Mews S2 . . . . 43 F7
Cradock Rd S2 . . . . 43 F7
Crafty Flats La DE12. . . . 260 F3
Cragdale Gr S20. . . . . 59 D7
Cragg La DE55 . . . . 148 A2
Craggon Dr S43. . . . . 77 D4
Craggs Dr S43. . . . . 80 E3

Craggs Rd S44. . . . . 99 A2
Craglands Gr S40 . . . . . . 95 A5
Crags Bsns Pk S80. . . . . . 100 E8
Cragside Cl S41. . . . . 96 C3
Crags Rd S80. . . . . 82 A1
Crags View S80. . . . . 81 F1
Craig St NG10. . . . . 236 E7
Craig Dr SK23. . . . . 45 E6
Craiglee Dr 1 DE24 . . . . 231 D3
Craig St NG10. . . . . 236 E7
CRAKEMARSH. 210 D5
Cranberry Gr DE23 . . . . . 230 F6
Cranborne Rd S41 . . . . . . 95 F6
Cranbourne Cl NG9 . . . . 209 D2
Cranbrook Ct NG19. . . . . 136 C5
Cranfield Ave DE11 . . . . . 255 E2
Cranfleet Way NG10. . . . 236 B7
Cranhill Cl DE23 . . . . 230 F6
Cranleigh Rd S43 . . . . 79 B3
Cranmer Gr NG19 . . . . . . 135 C3
Cranmer Rd DE21. . . . . . 267 D3
Cranmer St
  Ilkeston DE7 . . . . 194 F1
  Long Eaton NG10. . . . . . 223 D1
Cratcliff View DE4 . . . . . . 126 A1
Craven Rd S41. . . . . 95 F5
Crawford Ave NG9 . . . . . 223 D8
Crawford Rd S8. . . . . 43 A4
Crawley Rd DE24. . . . . . . 232 F5
Crawshaw Ave S8. . . . . . . 56 D8
Crawshaw Gr S8. . . . . 56 D8
Crawshaw Mews S18. . . . 56 C1
Crayford Rd DE24 . . . . . . 233 A5
Cray's Hill DE55. . . . . . . 170 B7
CRAYTHORNE 240 D2
Craythorne Cl DE11 . . . . 256 A7
Craythorne Rd DE13. . . . 240 D3
Creamery La DE6 . . . . . . 151 D1
Crecy Cl DE22 . . . . 218 C3
CREIGHTON 210 A5
Creighton La ST14 . . . . . 210 A5
Crescent
  Breaston DE72. . . . . 235 C7
  Ilkeston DE7 . . . . 61 E5
Crescent Dr SK23 . . . . . . 33 D2
Crescent Prim Sch
  NG19. . . . . 135 D2
Crescent Rd
  Ashover S42 . . . . 113 D7
  Selston NG16. . . . . 171 D6
Crescent Row S22 . . . . . . 25 A2
Crescent The
  Alfreton DE55 . . . . 159 B3
  Barlborough S43 . . . . 80 C6
  Bradwell S33 . . . . 51 A8
  Breaston DE72. . . . . 235 C7
  Breedon on the Hill DE73 252 E2
  Brimington S43 . . . . 96 C7
  Buxton SK17 . . . . 85 B8
  Chapel-en-le-Frith SK23 . 47 C7
  Clay Cross S45. . . . . 131 C2
  Derby, Boulton DE24 . . . 232 E6
  Derby, Chaddesden DE21. 219 F5
  Holmesfield S18. . . . . 75 A8
  Holymoorside S42. . . . . . 113 D8
  Hope S33 . . . . 39 A4
  Horsley Woodhouse DE7. 192 C7
  Mayfield DE6 . . . . 184 D7
  New Mills SK22 . . . . 33 B8
  Repton DE65. . . . . 242 D2
  Risley DE72. . . . . 222 D3
  Sheffield S17 . . . . 55 E5
  Shirebrook NG20 . . . . . . 119 E6
  Shirley DE6 . . . . 200 D7
  Stanley DE7 . . . . 207 B8
  Stapleford NG9 . . . . 209 E2
  Swadlincote DE11 . . . . . 255 E6
CRESSBROOK 89 A6
Cressbrook Ave S42. . . . . 132 B7
Cressbrook Way DE56. . . 206 B3
Cressida Ct DE73. . . . . . . 232 D2
Cresswell Ave SK22 . . . . . 33 C8
Cresswellpart La S33. . . . 50 E7
Cresswell St S22. . . . . 33 C8
Cressy Rd DE55 . . . . 159 A4
Cresta Gr DE21 . . . . 205 F1
Crest Cl DE13 . . . . 240 E1
Crest The
  Derby DE22 . . . . 204 E2
  Linton DE12. . . . . 261 C6
CRESWELL 81 F2
Creswell Bsns Pk S80. . . . 100 E8
Creswell CE Inf Sch S80. . 81 E1
Creswell Crags★ S80. . . . . 82 A1
Creswell Ct 12 NG19. . . . 136 E4
Creswell Jun Sch S80. . . . 81 E1
Creswell L Ctr S80. . . . . . 81 F1
Creswell Rd
  Clowne S43 . . . . 80 F4
  Cuckney NG20. . . . . 101 E3
Creswell Sta S80. . . . . 81 E1
Creswick Cl S40 . . . . 114 B8
Crewe St DE23. . . . . 218 F1
CREWTON 232 F8
Crewton Way DE24. . . . . 232 F7
CRICH 156 F1
Crich Ave DE23 . . . . 218 C2
Crich Carr CE Prim Sch
  DE4. . . . . 156 C1
Crich CE Inf Sch DE4. . . . 156 F1
Crich Cir DE23 . . . . 218 C2
CRICH COMMON 168 B8
Crich Jun Sch DE4. . . . . . 157 A1
Crich La
  Belper DE56. . . . . 179 A7
  Ridgeway DE56 . . . . 168 B3
Crich Pl
  Buxton SK17 . . . . 85 E7
  North Wingfield S42 . . . . 131 F6
Crich Rd
  Fritchley DE56. . . . . 168 A6

Crich Rd continued
  Staveley S43 . . . . 97 C7
Crich Tramway Village★
  DE4. . . . . 156 E2
Crich View
  Bolsover S44. . . . . 118 B8
  Heage DE56. . . . . 179 E3
  Newton DE55. . . . . 148 A4
Crich Way DE11. . . . . . . 255 F5
Cricket Cl DE15 . . . . 248 E8
Cricketers Cl DE15 . . . . . 254 F8
Cricketers Ct DE23 . . . . . 231 D8
Cricket View S43 . . . . 80 E2
Cricklewood Ct 7 S43. . . 78 B3
Cricklewood Rd DE22 . . . 218 B6
Cringle Mews DE21 . . . . 205 E2
Cripton La S45. . . . . 129 E5
Crispin Cl S12. . . . . 44 A4
Crispin Dr S12. . . . . 44 A4
Crispin Gdns S12 . . . . 44 A4
Crispin Rd 3 S12. . . . . . . 44 A4
CRIST. 46 B8
Critchley St DE7 . . . . 194 F1
Critch's Flats NG16. . . . . 195 F6
Croft Ave DE55 . . . . 151 D1
Croft Cl
  Dale Abbey DE7 . . . . . . 207 F2
  Derby DE21. . . . . 220 F5
  Nethersea DE12 . . . . . . 264 F7
  Ockbrook DE72. . . . . . . 221 C4
  Pinxton NG16 . . . . 160 C3
  Rolleston DE13 . . . . 240 B4
Croft Cres NG16 . . . . 195 C5
Croft Ct NG17. . . . . 148 F4
Croft End DE21 . . . . 205 D3
Crofters Cl S21. . . . . 60 C4
Crofters Ct DE21. . . . . . . 205 E2
Croft Gr ST14 . . . . 210 C1
Croft Inf Sch DE55 . . . . . 159 A3
Croft La DE21. . . . . 205 D3
Croft Lea S18. . . . . 56 C2
Croft Manor SK13 . . . . . . 10 E1
Crofton Cl S18. . . . . 56 F1
Crofton Rise S18. . . . . . . 56 F1
Croft Rd
  Great Longstone DE45. . . 90 A4
  Sheffield, Intake S12. . . . 44 B5
Croftstead Ave ST14 . . . . 196 D6
Crofts The S32. . . . . 53 A8
Croft The
  Bamford S33 . . . . 40 B3
  Belper DE56. . . . . 179 C1
  Burton upon Trent DE15 . 254 F8
  Derby DE23 . . . . 231 D8
  Draycott DE72 . . . . 235 A6
  Glossop SK13. . . . . 10 A6
  Heage DE56. . . . . 168 E1
  2 Melbourne DE73. . . . 252 A8
  Morley DE7 . . . . 192 C2
  Mottram in Longdendale
   SK14. . . . . 9 A4
  Shirebrook NG20. . . . . . 119 F3
  Shirland DE55 . . . . 146 D2
  Somercotes DE55 . . . . . 170 C7
  South Normanton DE55. . 160 A6
  Swadlincote DE11 . . . . . 255 E6
  Taddington SK17. . . . . . . 88 A3
Croft View
  Clowne S43 . . . . 80 F3
  Staveley S43 . . . . 97 C6
Croft Wlk S80 . . . . 82 A6
Cromarty Cl DE24 . . . . . . 231 E4
Cromarty Rise S18. . . . . . 56 D2
Cromdale Ave S43 . . . . . . 77 D4
Cromer Cl DE3. . . . . 217 C1
CROMFORD. 155 A6
Cromford Bank 21 SK13. . . 9 D2
Cromford Canal Nature
  Reserve★ DE4 . . . . 167 E5
Cromford CE Prim Sch
  DE4. . . . . 155 B6
Cromford Cl
  Aldercar NG16. . . . . 182 B4
  22 Gamesley SK13. . . . . . 9 D2
  Long Eaton NG10. . . . . . 236 A5
  North Wingfield S42 . . . . 132 B7
Cromford Ct
  4 Chesterfield S41. . . . . 95 D7
  Horwich End SK23. . . . . . 45 E6
Cromford Dr
  Derby DE3 . . . . 217 E4
  Staveley S43 . . . . 97 C8
Cromford Fold 23 SK13. . . 9 D2
Cromford Gn 20 SK13 . . . . 9 D2
Cromford Gr 18 SK13. . . . . 9 D2
Cromford Hill DE4. . . . . . 155 A5
Cromford La SK17. . . . . . . 85 E7
Cromford Lea 19 SK13. . . . 9 D2
Cromford Mews SK23. . . . 45 E5
Cromford Pl
  Buxton SK17 . . . . 85 E7
  24 Gamesley SK13. . . . . . 9 D2
Cromford Rd
  Aldercar NG16. . . . . 182 B4
  Clay Cross S45. . . . . 131 A5
  Crich DE4. . . . . 156 F2
  Derby DE21. . . . . 220 A8
  Heanor NG16. . . . . 181 E5
  Ripley DE5 . . . . 169 C2
  Wirksworth DE4. . . . . . . 154 F1
Cromford Road Ind Est
  NG16. . . . . 182 B4
Cromford Sta DE4. . . . . . 155 C7
Cromford Way 17 SK13. . . . 9 D2
Cromford Wharf★ DE4. . . 155 C7

Crompton Cl DE4 . . . . . . **127** E1
Crompton Rd
　Ilkeston DE7 . . . . **209** B4
　Mansfield NG19 . . . . **135** D3
　Staveley S43 . . . . **78** F2
Crompton Road Ind Est
DE7 . . . . **209** B3
Crompton St
　Derby DE1 . . . . **267** B2
　New Houghton NG19 . . . . . **134** F8
Cromwell Ave
　Blackwell DE55 . . . . **147** E1
　Chapel-en-le-Frith SK23 . . **47** A5
　Findern DE65 . . . . **230** D2
　Ilkeston DE7 . . . . **209** A5
Cromwell Cl DE13 . . . . . . **239** C5
Cromwell Dr DE55 . . . . . . **169** D7
Cromwell Rd
　Bolsover S44 . . . . **118** B8
　Chesterfield S40 . . . . **266** A4
　Derby DE23 . . . . **218** F2
Cromwell St NG16 . . . . . . **195** C8
**Crooked Spire (St Mary & All
　Saints Church)**★ S40 . . . **266** B3
Crookes Ave
　Mansfield Woodhouse
　NG19 . . . . **136** C3
　Pleasley NG19 . . . . **135** A5
Crook Stile DE4 . . . . **143** A7
CROPPER **215** B4
Cropper La DE6 . . . . **215** B4
Cropston Cl S41 . . . . **115** C7
Cropton Cl DE24 . . . . **233** C6
Crosby St DE22 . . . . **218** D4
Cross Chantrey Rd S8 . . . . **43** A3
Cross Cl DE23 . . . . **231** C8
Cross Cliffe SK13 . . . . **17** E8
Crossdale Gr DE21 . . . . . . **206** C3
Crossfield Gr SK6 . . . . **15** B1
Crossgate La SK13 . . . . **9** F7
Crossgreen Cotts DE4 . . . **142** B8
CROSS HILL **181** B5
Crosshill DE5 . . . . **181** B6
Crosshill Dr DE7 . . . . **208** C5
Crossings Ave SK23 . . . . . **47** A6
Crossings Mdw SK23 . . . . **47** A6
Crossings Rd SK23 . . . . . . **46** F6
Cross Keys La DE55 . . . . . **169** E7
Cross Keys Row SK23 . . . . **47** B8
Cross La
　Calver S32 . . . . **72** B2
　Codnor DE5 . . . . **181** B7
　Dronfield, Coal Aston S18 . **57** C3
　Dronfield, Quoit Green S18 . **57** B1
　Dronfield S18 . . . . **57** C5
　Flagg SK17 . . . . **106** E7
　Monyash DE45 . . . . **107** B2
　Rolleston DE13 . . . . **240** B2
　Sheffield S17 . . . . **55** C8
　Shirland DE55 . . . . **158** E8
　Sutton in Ashfield NG17 . . **148** F2
　Wessington DE55 . . . . **157** F8
Crossland Dr S12 . . . . **44** A3
Crossland Pl S12 . . . . **44** A4
Crossland Rd S32 . . . . **53** A7
Crosslands Cl SK13 . . . . . . **17** D8
Crossland Villas S32 . . . . **53** A7
Crosslanes DE6 . . . . **215** C5
Cross Lanes DE4 . . . . **144** C1
Cross Lea DE7 . . . . **207** F2
Crossley St DE5 . . . . **169** E2
Cross London St S43 . . . . . **77** D3
Crosslow La DE6 . . . . **150** E5
Cross Myrtle Rd S2 . . . . . . **43** B7
Cross Park Rd ■ S8 . . . . . **43** A5
Cross Rd ST14 . . . . **210** B1
Cross Rise SK13 . . . . **17** E8
Cross Side DE6 . . . . **184** F7
Cross St
　Bolsover S44 . . . . **118** C8
　Breedon on the Hill DE73 . **252** F2
　Brimington S43 . . . . **96** E8
　■ Broadbottom SK14 . . . **16** A8
　Buxton SK17 . . . . **85** D8
　Castleton S33 . . . . **38** B2
　Chapel-en-le-Frith SK23 . . **47** B6
　Chesterfield S40 . . . . **266** A4
　Clay Cross S45 . . . . **131** C3
　Derby DE22 . . . . **218** D6
　Glossop SK13 . . . . **10** C1
　Grassmoor S42 . . . . **115** F3
　Hadfield SK13 . . . . **10** A5
　Hollingworth SK14 . . . . **9** D4
　Killamarsh S21 . . . . **60** F7
　Linton DE11 . . . . **261** E8
　Long Eaton NG10 . . . . **236** E8
　Mansfield Woodhouse
　NG19 . . . . **136** B2
　New Mills SK22 . . . . **33** C8
　North Wingfield S42 . . . . . **131** E6
　Sandiacre NG10 . . . . **223** C6
Cross The
　■ Glossop SK13 . . . . **10** A5
　Great Longstone DE45 . . . . **89** F4
Crossways La DE6 . . . . . . **176** B2
Cross Wellington St S43 . . **77** D3
Crow Croft Rd S45 . . . . . . **132** C2
Crowcroft Way NG10 . . . . . **223** B2
CROWDEN **6** E3
Crowden Dr SK13 . . . . **10** B5
CROWDICOTE **121** E7
Crowestones SK17 . . . . **85** C6
Crowfoot La DE65 . . . . **226** E8
Crow Hill NG19 . . . . **135** B5
Crowhill La DE45 . . . . **109** A6

Crow Hill La NG19 . . . . . . **136** B2
CROWHOLE **75** D4
Crow La
　Brackenfield DE55 . . . . . . **146** A6
　Chesterfield S41 . . . . **96** C3
　Unstone S18 . . . . **76** F7
Crown Cl
　Chesterfield S43 . . . . **77** D3
　Long Eaton NG10 . . . . **236** A7
Crown Hill Way DE7 . . . . . **207** B8
Crownland Dr DE73 . . . . . **233** A2
Crown Mews DE22 . . . . . . **218** E3
Crown Rd S41 . . . . **96** A5
Crown Sq
　Branston DE14 . . . . **253** E8
　Matlock DE4 . . . . **143** B5
Crown St
　Clowne S43 . . . . **80** E3
　Derby DE22 . . . . **218** E3
　Duffield DE56 . . . . **190** E4
Crown Terr ■ DE56 . . . . . **178** F4
Crown Way
　Aldercar NG16 . . . . **182** B4
　Chellaston DE73 . . . . **244** F8
Crown Wlk DE1 . . . . **267** B2
Crown Yd DE4 . . . . **154** F1
Crowshaw St DE24 . . . . . . **232** B8
Crowther Pl ■ S7 . . . . **43** A8
Croxton Ct ■ NG19 . . . . . **136** E3
Croydon Wlk DE22 . . . . . . **217** F6
Cruck Cl S18 . . . . **56** E2
Crystal Cl DE3 . . . . **217** D4
Cubley La DE6 . . . . **198** B1
Cuckmere Cl DE22 . . . . . . **205** B5
Cuckoostone La DE4 . . . . . **128** F2
Cuillin Cl NG10 . . . . **223** A4
Cullabine Ct S2 . . . . **44** A7
Cullabine Rd S2 . . . . **44** A7
Culland Rd DE14 . . . . **254** B7
Culland View DE4 . . . . . . **168** A8
Cullen Ave DE6 . . . . **173** C1
Cullumbell La S45 . . . . . . **129** A7
Culworth Cl DE56 . . . . . . **179** D4
Culworth Ct DE21 . . . . . . **206** B2
Cumberhills Grange
DE56 . . . . **190** D2
Cumberhills Rd DE22,
DE56 . . . . **190** C1
Cumberland Ave DE21 . . . **219** E6
Cumberland Cl
　Buxton SK17 . . . . **85** D4
　Westwood NG16 . . . . **171** C4
Cumberland Cres DE72 . . **221** B2
Cumberland Rd DE15 . . . . **254** D6
Cumbria Wlk DE3 . . . . . . **217** C1
Cummings St DE23 . . . . . **219** A2
Cundy Rd S44 . . . . **99** A3
Cunliffe St S18 . . . . **57** C4
Cunnery La DE4 . . . . **144** B3
Cunnery The DE6 . . . . **202** F2
Cunningham Pl DE45 . . . . **109** D6
CURBAR **72** E2
Curbar Cl S42 . . . . **132** A7
Curbar Curve S43 . . . . **97** C6
Curbar Hill S32 . . . . **72** D2
Curbar Prim Sch S32 . . . . **72** D1
Curborough Dr DE24 . . . . **233** D6
Curlew Ave S21 . . . . **59** B3
Curlew Cl DE24 . . . . **231** D4
Curlew Way SK13 . . . . **16** F8
Curtis Gr SK13 . . . . **10** A5
Curzon Ave S18 . . . . **75** F8
Curzon Cl
　Derby DE22 . . . . **204** C4
　Killamarsh S21 . . . . **60** D6
Curzon Ct DE56 . . . . **190** E3
Curzon La
　Derby DE24 . . . . **233** A8
　Duffield DE56 . . . . **190** D3
Curzon Prim Sch The
DE22 . . . . **204** D6
Curzon Rd
　Buxton SK17 . . . . **85** C7
　Derby DE21 . . . . **219** F7
Curzon St
　Derby DE1 . . . . **267** A3
　Long Eaton NG10 . . . . **223** B2
Curzon Terr SK17 . . . . **88** D7
Cuscas La DE6 . . . . **187** F4
Cut La DE1, DE21 . . . . **219** B7
Cutler Cl S21 . . . . **60** B7
Cutler La DE6 . . . . **189** A1
Cutler Way DE3 . . . . **217** D4
Cuttholme Cl S40 . . . . **95** B4
Cuttholme Rd S40 . . . . . . **95** C4
Cuttholme Way ■ S40 . . . **95** C4
CUTTHORPE **94** F7
Cutthorpe Grange S40 . . . **95** A7
CUTTHORPE GREEN **94** E7
Cutthorpe Prim Sch S42 . **94** D7
Cutthorpe Rd S40 . . . . **95** A8
Cutting The DE11 . . . . . . **256** F4
Cuttlebrook Cl DE23 . . . . **231** E6
Cyclamen Cl DE14 . . . . . . **254** A8
Cygnet Fold NG19 . . . . . . **136** C4
Cypress Ave S8 . . . . **43** C1
Cypress Cl S21 . . . . **60** C5
Cypress Way SK6 . . . . **32** A7
Cypress Wlk DE21 . . . . . . **220** B5
Cyprus Rd S8 . . . . **43** A5
Cyril Ave NG9 . . . . **223** D7

D

Dade Ave S43 . . . . **97** C6
Dag La DE12 . . . . **263** E7
Dagnall Gdns DE45 . . . . . **109** D5
Dagnall Terr DE45 . . . . . . **109** D5
Dagnam Cl S2 . . . . **43** F6
Dagnam Cres S2 . . . . **43** F6
Dagnam Dr S2 . . . . **43** F7
Dagnam Pl S2 . . . . **43** F6
Dagnam Rd S2 . . . . **43** F7
Dahlia Ave DE55 . . . . **160** B7
Dahlia Dr DE21 . . . . **206** C3
Dairy House Rd DE23 . . . . **219** B1
Daisy Cl DE12 . . . . **262** E1
Daisy Farm Rd NG16 . . . . **195** B8
Daisy La DE12 . . . . **262** B3
Daisymere La SK17 . . . . . . **67** A2
Dakeyne Cl DE4 . . . . **127** F1
Dakin Ave SK17 . . . . **85** D8
Dakin Ct SK17 . . . . **66** E1
DALBURY **216** B1
Dalbury Rd S18 . . . . **56** C1
Dalbury Wlk DE23 . . . . . . **231** C5
DALE ABBEY **207** F2
Daleacre Ave DE74 . . . . . . **247** F5
Dale Ave
　Long Eaton NG10 . . . . **223** D1
　Newton DE55 . . . . **148** A3
　Somercotes DE55 . . . . . . **170** C6
DALEBANK **145** C8
Dale Bank Cres S43 . . . . . . **77** D3
Dalebank La S45 . . . . **145** B8
Dale Brook DE55 . . . . **228** E1
Dalebrook Rd DE15 . . . . . **248** B5
Dale Cl
　Breaston DE72 . . . . **235** D8
　Fritchley DE56 . . . . **168** A6
　Langwith NG20 . . . . **119** E8
　Matlock DE4 . . . . **154** D8
　Staveley S43 . . . . **97** C8
　Stonebroom DE55 . . . . . . **147** B4
　Whaley Thorns NG20 . . . . **100** F1
Dale Cres
　Hathersage S32 . . . . **53** B8
　Tupton S42 . . . . **115** C1
Dale Ct DE56 . . . . **191** F8
DALE END
　Bradwell **51** A6
　Elton **140** C7
Dale End
　Brassington DE4 . . . . **153** A1
　Wirksworth DE4 . . . . **154** F1
Dale End Rd DE65 . . . . . . **228** C2
Dalefield Dr DE11 . . . . . . **256** B3
Dalehead Ct S32 . . . . **71** E5
Dale Hill DE55 . . . . **158** B5
Dale La
　Buxton SK17 . . . . **85** E8
　Glapwell S44 . . . . **134** D7
Dale Park Ave DE56 . . . . . **192** A8
Dale Prim Sch DE23 . . . . **218** F2
Dale Rd
　Buxton, Higher Buxton
　SK17 . . . . **85** C7
　Buxton, Peak Dale SK17 . . **67** B7
　Derby, Alvaston DE24 . . . **233** B7
　Derby, Normanton DE23 . . **218** F2
　Dronfield S18 . . . . **76** B8
　Killamarsh S21 . . . . **60** E6
　Kimberley NG16 . . . . **195** F6
　Matlock Bath DE4 . . . . . . **143** B3
　New Mills SK22 . . . . **33** C7
　Stanley DE7 . . . . **207** C4
　Stanton-by-Dale DE7 . . . . **208** C1
　Tupton S42 . . . . **115** C1
Dale Road N DE4 . . . . **127** A5
Dale Road S DE4 . . . . **127** D1
Dales Cl ■ DE11 . . . . **255** E5
Dalesfield DE4 . . . . **143** A6
Dalesgate Cl DE23 . . . . . . **231** C5
Daleside DE15 . . . . **248** B1
Dale Side SK17 . . . . **85** B7
Dale St
　Ilkeston DE7 . . . . **208** F7
　Mansfield NG19 . . . . **136** B1
Dales The DE7 . . . . **207** E7
Dalestorth Ave NG19 . . . . **135** D1
Dale Terr SK17 . . . . **85** B6
Dale The
　Bonsall DE4 . . . . **142** D1
　Hathersage S32 . . . . **53** B8
　Stoney Middleton S32 . . . . **71** E4
　Wirksworth DE4 . . . . **154** E1
Dale View
　Earl Sterndale SK17 . . . . **105** B3
　Ilkeston DE7 . . . . **208** E7
　Litton SK17 . . . . **69** E3
　Mottram in Longdendale
　SK14 . . . . **9** A3
　Shirland DE55 . . . . **146** C4
Dale View Cl S45 . . . . **132** B3
Dale View Gdns DE56 . . . **191** F8
Dale View Rd S45 . . . . . . **132** B4
Dale View Terr SK17 . . . . . **89** A6
Dalewood Cl S41 . . . . **96** E1
Dalewood Cres DE55 . . . . **160** A3
Dalkeith Ave DE24 . . . . . . **232** F5
Dalley Cl ■ NG9 . . . . **223** E7
Dalley La DE56 . . . . **178** C6
Dallimore Prim Sch DE7 . **208** D4
Dallimore Rd DE7 . . . . . . **208** D4
Dalness Ct ■ DE24 . . . . . **231** D3
Dalston Rd DE11 . . . . **256** A5
Dalton Ave
　Burton upon Trent DE15 . . **248** B1

Dalton Ave continued
　Derby DE22 . . . . **218** C3
Dalton Cl ■ NG9 . . . . **223** E5
Dalton Dr DE56 . . . . **179** A4
Daltons Cl NG16 . . . . **182** A4
Dalvey Way S43 . . . . **77** D5
**Dame Catherine Harpur's
　Sch** DE73 . . . . **251** A5
Dam La
　Alsop en le Dale DE6 . . . . **150** E3
　Shirland DE55 . . . . **146** F1
Damon Cl S45 . . . . **132** C1
Damon Dr S43 . . . . **96** F8
Damsbrook Dr S43 . . . . . . **80** E3
Damsbrook La
　Bolsover S80 . . . . **99** D8
　Clowne S43 . . . . **80** D1
Dam Side DE56 . . . . **179** A4
Damside La SK17 . . . . **49** A3
Damson Croft S43 . . . . **78** A2
Damson Gr DE24 . . . . **232** E8
Danbury Cl S42 . . . . **115** E3
Danby Ave S41 . . . . **77** B2
DANEBANK **32** E5
Dane Bank Dr SK12 . . . . . . **32** D6
Danebridge Cres DE21 . . **206** A1
Dane Gr SK17 . . . . **85** C4
Dane Hill Cl SK12 . . . . **32** D5
Danesby Cres DE5 . . . . . . **180** A1
Danesby Rise DE5 . . . . . . **180** A1
DANESMOOR **131** E3
Danesmoor Ind Est S45 . **131** F2
Danesway SK23 . . . . **47** B6
Daniel Mews NG10 . . . . . **223** A5
Dannah Cres DE5 . . . . **169** F1
Dannah St DE5 . . . . **169** F2
Darby St DE23 . . . . **218** F2
Darcy Rd S21 . . . . **59** C3
Daresbury Cl S2 . . . . **43** D6
Daresbury Dr S2 . . . . **43** D6
Daresbury Pl S2 . . . . **43** D6
Daresbury Rd S2 . . . . **43** D6
Daresbury View S2 . . . . . . **43** D6
Darfield Ave S20 . . . . **44** F2
Darfield Cl S20 . . . . **44** F2
Darfield Dr DE75 . . . . **182** A2
Darfield La DE6 . . . . **162** C4
DARFOULDS **63** F1
Darkey La NG9 . . . . **223** E5
Dark La
　Ashbourne DE6 . . . . **173** A1
　Ashover DE55 . . . . **145** C6
　Bradley DE6 . . . . **175** B3
　Calow S44 . . . . **96** F2
　Chesterfield S44 . . . . **96** E4
　Church Broughton DE65 . . **227** B6
　Crich DE4 . . . . **156** F5
　Cromford DE4 . . . . **154** F4
　Holbrook DE56 . . . . **191** B7
　North Wingfield S42 . . . . . **132** B7
　Tatenhill DE13 . . . . **253** A8
　Wirksworth DE4, DE56 . . **165** D3
　Youlgreave DE45 . . . . **125** D7
Darklands La DE11 . . . . . . **256** A4
Darklands Rd DE11 . . . . . . **256** B5
DARLEY ABBEY **205** A2
Darley Abbey Dr DE22 . . . **204** F2
Darley Ave
　Beeston NG9 . . . . **223** F3
　Darley Dale DE4 . . . . **127** C3
　North Wingfield S42 . . . . . **132** B7
DARLEY BRIDGE **142** C8
**Darley Churchtown CE Prim
　Sch** DE4 . . . . **127** B3
Darley Cl
　Burton upon Trent DE15 . . **248** C1
　Harthill S26 . . . . **61** E6
　Staveley S43 . . . . **78** E1
　Swadlincote DE11 . . . . . . **256** A1
DARLEY DALE **127** C2
Darley Dale DE11 . . . . **255** F2
Darley Dale Prim Sch
DE4 . . . . **127** E2
Darley Dale Sta★ DE4 . . . **127** C2
Darley Dr
　Long Eaton NG10 . . . . **236** A5
　Ripley DE5 . . . . **169** C3
　West Hallam DE7 . . . . . . **207** E8
Darley Gr
　Buxton SK17 . . . . **85** D6
　Derby DE1 . . . . **219** A7
DARLEY HILLSIDE **127** D4
Darley House Est DE4 . . . **142** E8
Darley La DE1 . . . . **267** B4
Darley Lodge Dr DE4 . . . . **142** E8
**Darley Moor Motor Cycle
　Racing Circuit** DE6 . . . **185** A1
Darley Park★ DE22 . . . . . **205** A1
Darley Park Dr DE22 . . . . **204** F1
Darley Park Ho DE22 . . . . **205** A1
Darley Park Rd DE22 . . . . **204** F1
Darley Rd S45 . . . . **113** B2
Darley Sq DE7 . . . . **194** E5
Darley St DE22 . . . . **205** A1
Darley Way
　Buxton SK17 . . . . **85** E7
　North Wingfield S42 . . . . . **132** B7
Darnley Dr S2 . . . . **44** A8
Darsway DE74 . . . . **246** F4
Dartford Pl DE24 . . . . **233** A5
Dartmouth Ct ■ S41 . . . . . **95** F8
Dartnall Cl SK12 . . . . **32** A6
Darwent Rd S41 . . . . **96** C6
Darwin Ave
　Buxton SK17 . . . . **85** C7
　Chesterfield S40 . . . . **95** E5
　Derby DE24 . . . . **232** D4
　Ilkeston DE7 . . . . **208** E7

Darwin Cl DE15 . . . . **248** C1
Darwin Forest Ctry Patk★
DE4 . . . . **128** C7
Darwin Pl DE1 . . . . **267** C3
Darwin Rd
　Chesterfield S40 . . . . **266** A4
　Derby DE3 . . . . **217** E3
　Long Eaton NG10 . . . . **236** B5
Darwin Sq DE1 . . . . **267** B2
Darwood La S44 . . . . **118** B4
Dashwood St DE73 . . . . . . **267** B1
Datchet Cl DE23 . . . . **231** A8
Daveham Ave SK17 . . . . **85** C3
Davenport Rd
　Derby DE24 . . . . **232** C8
　Tupton S42 . . . . **131** C8
Daventry Cl DE3 . . . . **217** C3
Davey Ct S44 . . . . **98** F3
Davian Way S40 . . . . **114** E8
David Lloyd Sp Ctr DE24 . **219** D4
David's Cl DE73 . . . . **232** F1
Davids Dr S42 . . . . **114** E4
Da Vinci Com Coll DE21 . . **205** E1
Davis Ho ■ DE1 . . . . **267** B2
Davis Rd DE11 . . . . **256** B4
Dawber La S21 . . . . **60** F7
Dawgates La NG19 . . . . . . **134** F2
Dawkins Rd DE12 . . . . **262** E1
Dawlish Ct
　■ Chesterfield S41 . . . . . . **95** F8
　Derby DE24 . . . . **233** C7
　Eastwood NG16 . . . . **182** D3
Dawn View NG9 . . . . **209** D2
Dawsmere Cl DE21 . . . . . . **205** D1
Dawver Rd NG16 . . . . **195** F6
Dayfield La DE6 . . . . **175** A4
Day Gr SK14 . . . . **9** A3
Daylesford Cl DE23 . . . . . **231** A8
Days La DE56 . . . . **178** F3
Days Mill Cl DE4 . . . . **143** A6
Dayton Cl DE21 . . . . **220** C5
Dayton Ct DE22 . . . . **218** E8
Deacon Cl
　Derby DE21 . . . . **205** E2
　Swanwick DE55 . . . . **169** E7
Dead La NG16 . . . . **195** D1
Deadman's La DE24 . . . . . **219** D2
Deamon St DE55 . . . . **147** E1
Dean Ct DE23 . . . . **218** A2
Dean Ct DE23 . . . . **218** E2
Deanhead Dr S20 . . . . **44** F2
Dean Rd DE56 . . . . **167** F2
Deans Dr DE72 . . . . **221** B2
Deansgate NG19 . . . . **135** A5
Dean St
　Derby DE22 . . . . **218** E3
　Langley Mill NG16 . . . . . . **182** C3
Debdale La NG19 . . . . **136** A2
Deben Cl S40 . . . . **114** C8
Deben Down NG19 . . . . . . **136** D3
Deborah Dr DE21 . . . . **220** A7
Dee Cl
　Derby DE24 . . . . **231** E3
　Derby DE65 . . . . **228** E1
Dee La DE65 . . . . **229** F6
Deepdale NG16 . . . . **170** F4
Deepdale Ave
　Borrowash DE72 . . . . **221** C3
　Stapleford NG9 . . . . **223** D6
Deepdale Bsns Pk DE45 . **109** B6
Deepdale Cl
　Burton upon Trent DE15 . . **248** B5
　Staveley S43 . . . . **78** E3
Deepdale Ct DE75 . . . . . . **181** E1
Deepdale La DE6 . . . . **184** A2
Deep Dale La
　Barrow upon Trent DE73 . . **244** A7
　Derby DE24, DE73 . . . . . . **231** F1
Deepdale Rd
　Belper DE56 . . . . **179** B5
　Bolsover S44 . . . . **98** F3
　Derby DE21 . . . . **220** F3
　Long Eaton NG10 . . . . **236** A5
　Mansfield NG19 . . . . **136** E1
Deepdene Cl DE11 . . . . . . **256** C1
Deep La S44, S45 . . . . **133** B3
DEEP PIT **43** F8
Deepsick La S44 . . . . **97** C1
Deepwell Ave S20 . . . . **59** F6
Deepwell Bank S20 . . . . . . **59** F6
Deepwell Ct S20 . . . . **59** F6
Deepwell View S20 . . . . . . **59** F6
Deerlands Rd
　Chesterfield S40 . . . . **95** B3
　Wingerworth S42 . . . . . . **114** F2
Deerleap La S42 . . . . **130** D3
Deerpark Cres S42 . . . . . . **114** F3
Deer Park Prim Sch S42 . **114** F3
Deer Park View DE21 . . . . **220** F6
De Ferrers Ct DE56 . . . . . **190** E3
Degge St DE1 . . . . **267** B2
Deincourt Cl DE21 . . . . . . **221** A6
Deincourt Com Sch S42 . **131** F8
Deincourt Cres S42 . . . . . **131** F8
Delamere Cl
　Breaston DE72 . . . . **235** D8
　Derby DE21 . . . . **206** A1
　Swanwick DE55 . . . . **169** F7
Delf St S2 . . . . **43** B7
Delhi Cl DE15 . . . . **248** C3
Dell The S40 . . . . **95** B3
Delph Bank S40 . . . . **114** E8
Delph Cl S32 . . . . **71** D6
Delph The DE73 . . . . **252** F2
Delven La DE74 . . . . **247** B3
Delves Bank Rd DE55 . . . **170** A7
Delves Cl S40 . . . . **95** D1
Delves Ct DE75 . . . . **193** E8

Delves Rd
Heanor DE75 . . . . .193 D8
Killamarsh S21 . . . . 60 C6
Delves The DE55 . . . . .169 F7
Denacre Ave NG10 . . . . . .223 F1
Denacre La DE4 . . . . .127 F3
Denarth Ave DE24 . . . . . . .232 E3
Denbigh St DE21 . . . . .219 E7
DENBY BOTTLES 180 A1
Denby Comm DE5 . . . . . . .180 B3
DENBY COMMON 181 A3
Denby Free CE Prim Sch
DE5 . . . . .180 C1
Denby Hall Bsns Pk DE5 180 D5
Denby Hall Rd NE7 . . . . . .194 F6
Denby La DE5, DE8 . . . . . .180 C1
Denby Pottery Visitor Ctr★
DE5 . . . . .180 C3
Denby Rd S43 . . . . 97 C7
DENBY VILLAGE 180 C1
Denefield Cl SK6 . . . . 15 B1
Dene Fields Ct DE4 . . . . . .143 C5
Denham St S45 . . . . .131 D3
Denison Gdns DE21 . . . . . .220 B6
Denman Cres S32 . . . . 72 A3
Denmark Rd S2 . . . . 43 B6
Dennis Barsby Cl DE11 . . .255 E3
Dennis Cl DE23 . . . . .230 E7
Dennor Dr NG19 . . . . .136 E5
Denson Cl 4 S2 . . . . 43 B6
DENSTONE 196 D6
Denstone Coll ST14 . . . . . .196 B5
Denstone Dr DE24 . . . . . . .233 A4
Denstone La ST14 . . . . . . .196 C7
Dentdale Ct DE23 . . . . . . .233 C7
Dent La S12 . . . . 44 F2
Denton Ave NG10 . . . . .223 A6
Denton Cl NG19 . . . . .136 E1
Denton Way DE55 . . . . . . .169 F7
Denver Ct NG9 . . . . .209 E4
Denver Rd DE3 . . . . .217 D3
Depedale Ave DE7 . . . . . . .208 D5
Depot St DE23 . . . . .219 A2
DERBY 267 C4
Derby Arboretum★
DE23 . . . . .267 B1
Derby Assembly Rooms★
DE1 . . . . .267 B3
Derby Cath★ DE1 . . . . . . .267 B3
Derby Coll (Broomfield
Campus) DE7 . . . . .206 B5
Derby Coll Learning Ctr
DE1 . . . . .267 B2
Derby Coll (Masons Pl)
DE21 . . . . .219 E6
Derby Coll (Prince Charlies
Ave) DE22 . . . . .218 A5
Derby Coll Sp Ctr DE22 . . .217 F5
Derby Coll (The Joseph
Wright Ctr) DE1. . . . . . .267 A4
Derby Coll (The Quantum
Ctr) DE1. . . . . .267 D1
Derby Coll (The
Roundhouse) DE24 . . . . .219 C4
Derby Gram Sch DE23. . . . .230 F7
Derby High Sch DE23 . . . . .218 B1
Derby Hills House Ct
DE73 . . . . .251 E5
Derby Knoll SK23 . . . . 33 F1
Derby La
Brailsford DE6 . . . . .201 B8
Derby DE23 . . . . .231 F8
Great Cubley DE6 . . . . . . .198 F1
Monyash DE45 . . . . .123 C7
Shirley DE6 . . . . .200 E8
Derby Midland Sta DE1 . . .219 C4
Derby Moor Com Sports Coll
DE23. . . . . .231 B7
Derby Mus & Art Gall★
DE1 . . . . .267 B3
Derby Pl S2 . . . . 43 C6
Derby Playhouse★ DE1. . . .267 B2
Derby Rd
Alfreton DE55 . . . . .158 F3
Ambergate DE56 . . . . .167 F3
Ashbourne DE6 . . . . .185 E7
Aston-on-Trent DE72 . . . . .234 A2
Borrowash DE21, DE72 . . . .221 A2
Burton upon Trent DE13 . . .241 A1
Chellaston DE73 . . . . .232 F2
Clay Cross S45, S42 . . . . . .131 C5
Cromford DE4 . . . . .155 C6
Dale Abbey DE7, DE21. . . . .206 E3
Derby, Spondon DE21 . . . . .220 C3
Doveridge DE6 . . . . .211 B1
Draycott DE72 . . . . .234 E8
Duffield DE56 . . . . .190 F6
Eastwood NG16 . . . . .182 E2
Egginton DE65 . . . . .241 C4
Etwall DE65 . . . . .229 A4
Hatton DE65 . . . . .227 E2
Heanor DE75 . . . . .181 D1
Hilton DE65 . . . . .228 F3
Hilton DE65 . . . . .240 C8
Horsley DE21, DE56, ...191 D5
Ilkeston DE7 . . . . .208 D7
Kilburn DE56 . . . . .179 F1
Langley Mill NG16 . . . . . . .182 C3
Long Eaton NG10. . . . . . . .236 B8
Marston on Dove DE65 . . . .228 B2
Melbourne DE73 . . . . .252 A8
New Mills SK22 . . . . 24 D1
Ripley DE5 . . . . .180 C3
Risley DE72 . . . . .222 D4
Sandiacre NG10. . . . . .223 A5
Smisby LE65. . . . . .258 A4
Stanley DE7 . . . . .207 B4

Derby Rd continued
Stapleford NG9 . . . . .223 D6
Swadlincote DE11 . . . . . . .256 C3
Swanwick DE55, DE55 . . . . .169 E5
Ticknall DE11, DE73. . . . . . .257 F7
Uttoxeter ST14 . . . . .210 D1
Wingerworth S42 . . . . .115 A6
Wirksworth DE4 . . . . .165 E6
Derby Road Ind Est
Heanor DE75 . . . . .181 D1
Sandiacre NG10. . . . . .223 B5
Derbyshire Ave
Trowell NG9 . . . . .209 D4
West Hallam DE7. . . . . . . .207 E8
Derbyshire Cl DE7 . . . . . . .207 E8
Derbyshire Craft Ctr★
S32. . . . . 72 D2
Derbyshire Cty Cricket Gd
DE21. . . . . .219 C6
Derbyshire Dr
Castle Donington DE74 . . . .247 B4
Ilkeston DE7 . . . . .208 E6
Westwood NG16 . . . . .171 C4
Derbyshire Flying Ctr★
S33 . . . . 51 A7
Derbyshire La S8 . . . . 43 A3
Derbyshire Level SK13 . . . . 17 F6
Derbyshire Dales National
Nature Reserve★ SK17 . . 89 A8
Derby Small Bsns Ctr
Derby DE1 . . . . .267 C2
Derby, Pear Tree DE23 . . . . .219 B1
Derby's Mus of Industry &
History (Silk Mill Mus)★
DE1 . . . . .267 B3
Derby St
Glossop SK13 . . . . 17 C8
3 Ilkeston DE7 . . . . .208 F8
Sheffield S2 . . . . 43 C6
Derby Terr S2 . . . . 43 C6
Derby Trad Est DE21 . . . . .219 B8
Derrington Leys DE24 . . . . .233 D6
Derventio Cl DE1 . . . . .219 A7
DERWENT 30 C6
Derwent Ave
Belper DE56. . . . . .179 A1
Borrowash DE72 . . . . .221 C3
Darley Dale DE4 . . . . .127 C4
Derby DE72 . . . . .205 A4
Grindleford S32. . . . . 72 C8
Ilkeston DE7 . . . . .194 D2
West Hallam DE7. . . . . . . .207 E8
Derwent Bsns Ctr DE1 . . . .267 C4
Derwent Bsns Pk DE5 . . . . .169 B1
Derwent Cl
Derby DE22 . . . . .205 A4
Dronfield S18. . . . . 57 B3
Glossop SK13. . . . . 17 F8
Grindleford S32. . . . . 72 C8
Swadlincote DE11 . . . . . . .256 A1
Derwent Com Sch DE21 . . .219 C7
Derwent Cres S41 . . . . 95 D7
Derwent Ct
Belper DE56 . . . . .179 B4
5 Sheffield S17 . . . . 56 A5
Willington DE65 . . . . .242 B6
Derwent Dr
Baslow DE45 . . . . 91 D6
Chinley SK23 . . . . 34 E1
Derby DE24 . . . . .231 D2
Tibshelf DE55. . . . . .147 F6
Derwent Gdns DE6 . . . . . . .185 D8
Derwent Gr DE55 . . . . .158 F2
Derwent Ho DE21 . . . . .219 C6
Derwent La
Derwent S33 . . . . 30 B7
Hathersage S32. . . . . 52 F8
Northwood DE4. . . . . .127 A6
Derwent Par DE21, DE24 . . .219 E3
Derwent Park Ho DE22 . . . .205 A1
Derwent Pl S45 . . . . .131 A5
Derwent Rd
Burton upon Trent DE15 . . .248 A2
Buxton SK17 . . . . 85 C6
Derby DE21 . . . . .220 D3
Dronfield S18. . . . . 57 B3
Ripley DE5 . . . . .169 C1
Derwent Rise DE21. . . . . . .220 F4
Derwentside Ind Pk
DE56 . . . . .178 F1
Derwent Sq SK23 . . . . 34 E1
Derwent St
Belper DE56. . . . . .178 F5
Derby DE1 . . . . .267 C4
Draycott DE72 . . . . .235 A7
Long Eaton NG10. . . . . . . .236 C6
Derwent Street Ind Est
NG10. . . . . .236 C6
Derwent Terr DE21. . . . . . .143 A7
Derwent Vale DE56 . . . . . . .178 F2
Derwent Valley Visitor Ctr★
DE56 . . . . .178 F5
Derwent View
Baslow DE45 . . . . 91 E6
Belper, Milford DE56. . . . . .191 A8
Belper, Mount Pleasant
DE56. . . . . .178 F5
Darley Dale DE4 . . . . .127 B3
Mastin Moor S43. . . . . 79 C3
Derwent Way DE4. . . . . . . .143 A5
Desborough Rd NG16 . . . . .171 D7
De Sutton Pl S26. . . . . 61 E5
DETHICK 156 B8
Dethick La DE4 . . . . .144 D1
Dethick Way S42. . . . . .132 B7
Devas Gdns DE21 . . . . .220 D5
Deveron Cl DE13 . . . . .240 C1
Deveron Rd S20 . . . . 59 F7

Devizes Cl S40. . . . . .114 F8
Devon Cl
Burton upon Trent DE15 . . .254 E6
Grassmoor S42 . . . . .115 F2
Sandiacre NG10. . . . . .223 B5
Devon Dr S43. . . . . 96 F8
Devon Park View S43 . . . . . 96 F8
Devonshire Ave
Borrowash DE72 . . . . .221 C2
Darley Dale DE4 . . . . .142 F7
Derby DE22 . . . . .204 F3
Long Eaton NG10. . . . . . . .237 A8
Ripley DE5 . . . . .169 C2
Devonshire Avenue E
S41. . . . . .115 C8
Devonshire Avenue N S43 77 D3
Devonshire Bsns Ctr S43 . 78 B2
Devonshire Cl
Chesterfield S41 . . . . 95 F8
Dronfield S18. . . . . 57 B8
Ilkeston DE7 . . . . .194 E5
Sheffield S17 . . . . 55 F6
2 Staveley S43. . . . . 78 C7
Devonshire Cotts S44 . . . . .118 E6
Devonshire Ct S43 . . . . 96 D7
Devonshire Dr
Chinley SK23 . . . . 34 E2
Creswell S80 . . . . 81 C1
Derby DE3 . . . . .217 E3
Duffield DE56 . . . . .190 D2
Eastwood NG16 . . . . .182 F2
Langwith NG20 . . . . .119 F8
Rowsley DE4 . . . . .110 F1
Sheffield S17 . . . . 55 E7
Somercotes DE55 . . . . . . .170 B7
Stapleford NG9 . . . . .209 D2
Devonshire Glen S17. . . . . . 55 F6
Devonshire Gr S17. . . . . 55 E6
Chesterfield S41 . . . . .266 B3
New Houghton NG19. . . . . .135 A7
3 Staveley S43. . . . . 78 C2
Devonshire Pk S43. . . . . 96 E8
Devonshire Rd
Buxton SK17 . . . . 85 B8
Sheffield S17 . . . . 55 F6
Devonshire Road E S41 . . .115 C8
Devonshire Road N S43 . . 77 D3
Devonshire Sq S42. . . . . . . .111 A3
Devonshire St
Ambergate DE56 . . . . .167 F3
Brimington S43 . . . . 96 E8
Chesterfield S41 . . . . .266 B3
New Houghton NG19. . . . . .135 A7
3 Staveley S43. . . . . 78 C2
Devonshire Terr
Holmewood S42. . . . . .116 E1
Matlock Bath DE4 . . . . .143 A2
Devonshire Terrace Rd
S17. . . . . 55 D7
Devonshire Villas 28 S41 . 95 F8
Devonshire Way S43 . . . . . . 81 A4
Devonshire Wlk DE1 . . . . . .267 C2
Devon St DE7 . . . . .209 A5
De Warren Pl S26. . . . . 61 F5
Dewchurch Dr DE23. . . . . . .231 E5
Dewint Ave SK6. . . . . 23 B8
Dewley Way S45 . . . . .131 D5
Dew Pond La SK17 . . . . 85 E8
Dewsnap La SK14. . . . . 9 A6
Dewy La DE4, DE55 . . . . . . .144 F1
Dexter St DE23. . . . . .219 C2
DH Lawrence Birthplace
Mus★ NG16 . . . . .182 F2
Dialstone S33. . . . . 51 A7
Diamond Ct DE45 . . . . .109 D5
Diamond Dr DE21 . . . . .205 F3
Diamond Jubilee Cotts
DE6 . . . . .184 E8
Dibble Rd DE14 . . . . .254 A7
Dickens Dr
Holmewood S42. . . . . .116 D1
Swadlincote DE11 . . . . . . .256 C5
Dickens Sq DE23. . . . . .231 F7
Dickenson Rd S41 . . . . .266 C1
Dickenson St DE24 . . . . . . .219 D2
Dickinson's La DE6 . . . . . . .215 B1
Dickinson St DE24 . . . . . . .219 D2
Dicklant La S45 . . . . .145 B8
Didcot Cl S40. . . . . .114 F8
Didsbury Terr SK22 . . . . 25 E2
Dig St
Ashbourne DE6 . . . . .173 B2
Hartington SK17 . . . . .137 D6
DIMPLE 143 A6
Dimple Cres DE4. . . . . .143 B5
Dimple La DE56. . . . . .168 B8
Dimple Rd DE4 . . . . .143 A6
Dimple Road Bsns Ctr
DE4. . . . . .143 B6
Dingle Cl S13. . . . . 17 A8
Dingle La S41, S44. . . . . 96 E1
Dingle The DE15 . . . . .254 E8
Dingley Cl NG19 . . . . .136 E5
Dinmore Grange DE11. . . . .257 B6
Dinting CE Prim Sch
SK13 . . . . 10 A1
Dinting La SK13 . . . . 10 A1
Dinting Lane Trad Est
SK13. . . . . 10 A1
Dinting Lodge Ind Est SK13 9 F2
Dinting Rd SK13. . . . . 10 B2
Dinting Sta SK13. . . . . 10 A1
Dinting Vale SK13. . . . . 10 A1
Dinting Vale Bsns Pk SK13. .9 F2

Discovery Way S41. . . . . 77 A1
Diseworth CE DE73 . . . . . . .232 F2
Diseworth Rd DE74 . . . . . . .247 A1
Dishwell La S26. . . . . 61 E6
DISLEY 32 C5
Disley Prim Sch SK12 . . . . . 32 C6
Disley Sta SK12 . . . . 32 C6
Disraeli Cres DE7 . . . . .208 F8
Ditch Cotts SK17 . . . . .105 E8
Ditch The SK17 . . . . .105 E8
Division Dr NG20 . . . . .119 E4
Division St S43 . . . . 97 C8
Dix Ave DE7 . . . . .192 F6
Dixie St NG16 . . . . .171 B4
Dixon Croft S43. . . . . 77 D4
Dixon Ct S41 . . . . 77 B3
Dixon's Rd S41 . . . . .266 C2
Dobbinhorse La DE6 . . . . . .185 B5
Dobbin La S18. . . . . 75 C6
Dobbs St S21 . . . . 60 C6
Dobholes DE7 . . . . .192 D6
Dobholes La DE7. . . . . .192 F6
Dobson Pl S43. . . . . 97 B6
Dockholm Rd NG10 . . . . . . .223 C2
Dock Wlk S40 . . . . .266 A2
Doctor La S26. . . . . 61 F5
Doctor's La DE73 . . . . .252 F2
Dodburn Ct DE24 . . . . .231 D4
Dodgewell Cl DE55 . . . . . . .147 F1
Dodslow Ave DE13 . . . . . . .240 B3
Doe Hill La DE55 . . . . .147 D5
DOEHOLE 145 A2
Doehole La
Ashover DE55 . . . . .144 F3
Brackenfield DE55 . . . . . . .145 A2
Doe La S12. . . . . 58 C5
DOE LEA 117 D1
Doe Lea Nature Reserve★
S44. . . . . .117 D2
Doghole La DE4. . . . . .154 C4
Dogkennel La DE6 . . . . .186 E7
Dog La
Hulland Ward DE6 . . . . . . .175 D4
Netherseal DE12 . . . . .264 F6
Stonebroom DE55 . . . . . . .146 E2
Wilson DE73 . . . . .252 E6
Dolby Rd SK17 . . . . 85 D2
Doles La
Clifton DE6 . . . . .184 F7
Findern DE65 . . . . .230 D3
Whitwell S80 . . . . 82 B7
Dolly La
Chinley SK23 . . . . 34 A2
Furness Vale SK23. . . . . 33 F3
Dolly Wood Cl SK23 . . . . . . 34 B1
Dolphin Cl DE21 . . . . .221 A6
Domain Dr DE73 . . . . .232 E1
Dominion Rd DE11 . . . . . . .256 B5
Dominoe Gr S12 . . . . 44 D5
Donald Hawley Way
DE56 . . . . .190 F3
Doncaster Ave NG10 . . . . . .223 B6
Doncaster Gr NG10. . . . . . . .223 F5
Donegal Wlk DE21 . . . . . . .220 A4
Donington Cl DE23 . . . . . . .231 E5
Donington Dr
Derby DE23 . . . . .231 E5
4 Woodville DE11 . . . . . . .256 E1
Donington Grand Prix
Circuit★ DE74 . . . . .246 C1
Donington La DE72, DE74 247 C7
DONISTHORPE 262 F1
Donisthorpe La DE12. . . . . .262 E2
Donkey La S32. . . . . 72 C2
Donner Cres DE7 . . . . .194 E5
Dorchester Ave DE21. . . . . .219 F7
Dorchester Rd NG16 . . . . . .195 F7
DORE 55 E7
Dore Cl S17 . . . . 56 A7
Dore Ct S17 . . . . 56 A7
Dore Hall Croft S17 . . . . 55 D7
Dore La S32 . . . . 53 A7
Dore Prim Sch S17 . . . . 55 D6
Dore Rd S17. . . . . 55 E8
Dore & Totley Sta S17. . . . . 56 A7
Doris Rd DE7 . . . . .209 A7
Dorking Rd DE22. . . . . .218 B6
Dormy Cl NG19 . . . . .136 E5
Dorothy Ave
Mansfield Woodhouse
NG19. . . . . .136 C1
Sandiacre NG10. . . . . .223 B5
Dorothy Dr NG19. . . . . .136 F1
Dorothy Vale S40 . . . . 95 C4
Dorrien Ave DE23 . . . . .232 A7
Dorset Ave 2 S43 . . . . 96 F8
Dorset Cl
Brimington S43 . . . . 77 F1
Burton upon Trent DE15 . . .254 E6
Buxton SK17 . . . . 85 D4
Dorset Dr S43. . . . . 96 F8
Dorset St DE21 . . . . .219 D6
Dorterry Cres DE7 . . . . .209 A5
Douglas Ave
Awsworth NG16. . . . . .195 C5
Heanor DE75 . . . . .181 C4
Douglas Rd
Chesterfield S41 . . . . 96 C6
Long Eaton NG10. . . . . . . .223 B1
Somercotes DE55 . . . . . . .170 D8
Douglas St
Derby DE23 . . . . .219 B2
Derby DE23 . . . . .219 C2
Douse Croft La S10. . . . . 42 F6
Dove Bk SK6. . . . . 23 F6
Dove Cl
Derby DE3 . . . . .218 A3
Kilburn DE56 . . . . .192 A8

Dove Cl continued
Woodville DE11 . . . . .256 F3
Dovecliff Cres DE13 . . . . . .240 F2
Dovecliff Rd DE13. . . . . . . .240 E3
Dovecote DE74 . . . . .247 B4
Dovecote Dr DE72. . . . . . . .221 B2
Dovecotes S45. . . . . .129 C5
Dovecote The
Breedon on the Hill DE73 . .252 F2
Horsley DE21. . . . . .191 F6
Dovedale Ave
Ashbourne DE6 . . . . .173 D1
Derby DE24 . . . . .233 C2
Long Eaton NG10. . . . . . . .236 B6
Staveley S43. . . . . 97 B5
Dovedale Circ DE7 . . . . . . .194 E5
Dovedale Cl
Burton upon Trent DE15 . . .248 B5
Ripley DE5 . . . . .180 D6
Dovedale Cres
Belper DE56. . . . . .179 B5
Buxton SK17 . . . . 84 F6
Dovedale Ct DE6 . . . . .185 E8
Dovedale Ct
4 Chesterfield S41. . . . . . . 95 E7
1 Glossop SK13 . . . . 10 F1
Long Eaton NG10. . . . . . . .236 B6
Dovedale Day Hospl
DE1 . . . . .267 C1
Dovedale National Nature
Reserve★ DE6 . . . . .161 A6
Dovedale Prim Sch
NG10. . . . . .236 B6
Dovedale Rd DE21 . . . . .220 F3
Dovedale Rise DE22 . . . . . .204 D1
Dovedales The DE7 . . . . . . .217 D2
Dovefields ST14 . . . . .196 F3
Dove Fst Sch ST14 . . . . . . .197 A3
Dove Gr DE65. . . . . .241 A5
DOVE HEAD 103 D6
DOVE HOLES. 47 E2
Dove Holes CE Prim Sch
SK17. . . . . 47 F1
Dove Holes Sta SK17. . . . . . 47 E1
Dove House Gn DE6. . . . . . .173 B2
Dove La
Long Eaton NG10. . . . . . . .236 C8
Rocester ST14 . . . . .197 A4
Dove Lea DE13 . . . . .240 B4
Dover Ct DE23 . . . . .219 A2
Dove Rd DE5 . . . . .169 C1
DOVERIDGE 211 A1
Dove Ridge SK17. . . . . .121 C6
Doveridge Cl S41 . . . . 77 A2
Doveridge Gr SK17. . . . . 85 E6
Doveridge Prim Sch
DE6. . . . . .224 C8
Doveridge Rd DE15 . . . . . . .248 B1
Doveridge Wlk DE23 . . . . . .231 C5
Dove Rise DE22 . . . . .228 C2
Dover St
Creswell S80 . . . . 81 E1
Derby DE23 . . . . .219 A1
Doveside DE65. . . . . .184 D7
Dove Side DE65. . . . . .239 D8
Dovesite Bsns Pk DE73 . . . .251 E6
Dove St DE11 . . . . .183 B2
Dovestone Gdns DE23 . . . . .218 B1
Dove Valley Pk DE65. . . . . .227 A5
Dove View DE13 . . . . .239 C6
Dove Way The ST14 . . . . . . .210 C2
Dovewood Ct DE23 . . . . . . .231 A7
Dowcarr La S26. . . . . 61 C5
Dowdeswell St S41. . . . . . . .266 B4
Dower Cl DE22. . . . . .205 A1
Dowie Way DE4. . . . . .156 F2
Downham Cl DE3 . . . . .217 E1
Downing Cl DE22 . . . . .217 F6
Downing Ho DE22 . . . . .217 F6
Downing Rd
Derby DE21 . . . . .219 D5
Sheffield S8 . . . . 56 E8
Downing Row S32 . . . . 52 F8
Downing St DE55 . . . . .160 A6
Downings The S26 . . . . 61 F5
Downlands S43. . . . . 96 D7
Downlee Cl SK23. . . . . 46 F5
Downmeadow DE56 . . . . . . .179 E8
Downs The NG19. . . . . .136 F1
Drabbles Rd DE4. . . . . .143 A6
Drage St DE1 . . . . .219 B7
Drakelow Nature Reserve★
1 DE14 . . . . .253 F6
Drake Terr S43 . . . . 96 C8
DRAYCOTT 234 E7
Draycott Cl DE75. . . . . .181 C4
Draycott Ct DE3. . . . . .194 F3
Draycott Dr DE3 . . . . .217 C3
Draycott Mills DE72 . . . . . .235 A7
Draycott Pl S18. . . . . 75 D8
Draycott Prim Sch DE72 235 A7
Draycott Rd
Borrowash DE72 . . . . .221 C4
Breaston DE72. . . . . .235 C7
Long Eaton NG10. . . . . . . .236 A4
North Wingfield S42 . . . . . .131 F7
Drayton Ave
Derby DE22 . . . . .217 F6
Mansfield NG19 . . . . .135 D1
Drayton St DE11 . . . . .256 C4
Dresden Cl DE3 . . . . .217 C2
Drewry Ct DE1 . . . . .218 F5
Drewry La DE22. . . . . .218 F4
Dreyfus Cl DE1. . . . . .220 F5
Drive The DE56 . . . . .177 F3

DRONFIELD........................56 E2
Dronfield Henry Fanshawe
Sch The S18.............57 B2
Dronfield Inf Sch S18....57 A1
Dronfield Jun Sch S18....57 A1
Dronfield Pl DE7.........194 E5
Dronfield Rd S21.........59 B2
Dronfield Sp Ctr S18.....57 A1
Dronfield Sta S18........57 A1
Drovers Way
Ashbourne DE6.........173 B3
Bullbridge DE56........168 B5
Drovers Wlk **3** SK13....10 D1
Drum Cl DE22............204 F3
Drummond Rd DE7........194 E1
Drummond Way DE73......232 E2
Drury Ave DE21..........220 D4
Drury La
Biggin SK17...........138 C2
Dronfield S18.........57 C3
Sheffield S17..........55 D7
Dryden Ave S40.........115 A8
Dryden Ct NG9..........209 E1
Dryden St DE23.........231 F7
Dryhurst Rd DE3........32 D6
Dryhurst La SK12.......32 D6
Drysdale Rd DE3........217 D3
Duchess St
Creswell S80...........81 F1
Whitwell S80..........82 A6
Duchess Way DE73.......244 E8
Duck Island DE56.......190 E4
DUCKMANTON.............98 A5
Duckmanton Prim Sch
S44...................98 A5
Duckmanton Rd S44......98 A5
Duck Row DE45..........91 C3
Ducksett La S21........59 E2
Duck St DE65...........241 B5
Dudwood La DE4.........140 F7
Duesbury Cl DE24.......232 E2
Duesbury Ct DE3........230 B7
Duesbury Pl DE3........230 B7
Duesbury The DE55......160 B4
Duewell Ct **9** S43....78 B3
DUFFIELD...............190 F3
DUFFIELDBANK...........191 A3
Duffield Bank DE56.....191 A4
Duffield Cl NG10.......236 A5
Duffield Ct DE56.......190 F3
Duffield Meadows Prim Sch
DE56.................190 D3
Duffield Millennium Mdw
Nature Reserve★ DE56..190 F3
Duffield Rd DE22.......205 A5
Duffield Rd Ind Est DE21 205 C7
Duffield Sta★ DE56.....170 F4
Duffield Sta DE56......190 F4
Duke Field DE4.........154 D5
Duke of Norfolk CE Prim Sch
SK13.................10 D1
Duke of Norfolk CE Prim Sch
(Annexe) SK13........10 E2
Dukeries Ct S43........80 F3
Dukeries La DE21.......206 B2
Duke's Bldgs DE56......191 A7
Dukes Cl S42...........116 E1
Dukes Dr
Chesterfield S41......95 E6
Curbar S32............72 D2
Duke's Dr
Buxton SK17...........85 C5
Glapwell S44..........134 A7
Dukes Fold SK13........17 B7
Dukes Pl DE7...........194 E4
Dukes St SK13..........17 C8
Duke St
Buxton SK17...........84 E6
Chesterfield S41......96 A8
Clowne S43............81 A4
Creswell S80..........81 F1
Derby DE1.............267 B4
Ilkeston DE7..........194 E4
Middleton DE4.........154 D5
Sheffield S20.........59 D6
South Normanton DE55..160 B6
Staveley S43..........78 E2
Tutbury DE13..........239 C6
Whitwell S80..........82 A6
Duluth Ave DE21........220 A4
Dulverton Ave DE24.....231 C2
Dulwich Ct **11** S43....78 B3
Dulwich Rd DE22........217 E6
Dumb Hall La S80.......63 B4
Dumbles Cl DE7.........208 C6
Dumbles La DE5.........180 F2
Dumbles Rd S44.........98 F1
Dumbleton Rd S21.......60 E5
Dumble Wood Grange
S41..................95 C7
Dunbar Cl
Derby DE24............231 E2
Nottingham NG10.......236 E4
Duncan Cl DE56.........179 B6
Duncan Rd DE23.........231 F8
Duncombe Dr DE6........185 C8
Dundas Way DE73........232 E1
Dundee Dr NG19.........136 B6
Dundee Rd DE11.........256 D5
Dundonald Rd S40.......266 B1
Dunedin Cl DE3.........217 E3
Dunedin Cres DE15......248 C2
Dunedin Glen S20.......59 E6
Dunedin Gr S20.........59 E6

Dungley Hill DE56......168 D2
Dungreave Ave DE4......127 A5
Dunkery Ct DE21........206 A2
Dunkirk DE22...........267 A2
Dunlow La S32..........71 C5
Dunn Brigg NG19........136 D2
Dunn Dr NG10...........236 B7
Dunne La SK13..........10 E2
Dunnicliffe La DE73....252 A7
DUNNSHILL.............207 C1
Dunsford Rd DE55.......159 B5
Dunshill Wlk S45.......131 E4
Dunsil Cl NG19.........136 B1
Dunsil Ct NG19.........136 B1
Dunsil Rd
7 Mansfield NG19....136 B1
Pinxton NG16..........160 D2
Dunsley Mdws Nature
Reserve★ DE4..........154 E7
Dunsmore Dr DE21.......205 F2
Dunsmore Way DE11......256 D5
Dunstall Brook DE15....248 A1
Dunstall Park Rd DE24..232 D8
Dunstall Rd DE13.......253 A7
Dunston Cl NG10........236 F7
Dunston Ct S41.........76 F1
Dunston La S41.........95 D8
Dunston Pl S41.........76 F1
Dunston Prim Sch S41...95 D8
Dunston Rd S41.........76 D2
Dunston Tech Pk S41....76 E1
Dunston Trad Est S41...76 E2
Dunston Way S41........76 E1
Dunton Cl DE21.........267 D3
Dunvegan Ave S45.......131 E2
Dunvegan Cl DE24.......231 D2
Duper La S32...........51 E5
Durban Cl DE15.........248 C3
Durban House Her Ctr★
NG16.................182 F3
Durham Ave
Chesterfield S43......77 D3
Derby DE21............219 E6
Grassmoor S42.........115 F2
Durham Cl
Chesterfield S43......77 D3
Mansfield Woodhouse
NG19................136 D4
Swadlincote DE11......256 E5
Durham St **3** DE7....194 F1
Durley Chine Dr S41....115 C8
Durlstone Cl S12.......44 A5
Durlstone Cres S12.....44 A5
Durlstone Dr S12.......44 A5
Durlstone Gr S12.......44 A5
Durrant Rd S41.........266 B3
Durvale Ct S17.........55 E6
Durward Cl DE24........232 C7
Dyche Cl S8............57 B6
Dyche Dr S8............57 B6
Dyche La S8, S18.......57 B5
Dyche Pl S8............57 B6
Dyche Rd S8............57 B6
Dye House La SK22......33 C8
Dykes Cl S44...........99 A2
Dyke Vale Rd S12.......44 F5
Dymond Gr S42..........115 F3
Dystelegh Rd SK12......32 D6

E

Each Well La DE55......158 F3
Eagle Cl DE56..........178 F2
Eagle Hts DE15.........248 D3
Eagle Par **9** SK17....85 B7
Eagle Rd DE7...........208 F4
Eagle St
4 Buxton SK17......85 B7
Heage DE56............168 E2
Eagle Terr
Birchover DE4.........126 B1
Wensley DE4...........142 A4
EAGLE TOR.............126 A2
Ealand St DE13.........240 D4
Ealing Cl DE22.........218 B6
Ealing Ct **8** S43....78 B3
Eardley Cl DE21........220 B5
Earlham Cl DE7.........208 C6
Earls Cres DE21........206 B2
EARL STERNDALE........105 C3
Earl Sterndale CE Prim Sch
SK17.................105 C3
Earl Sway **5** SK13....17 B8
Earlswood Cl DE72......235 D8
Earlswood Dr DE3.......217 F4
Earnshaw St SK14.......9 D4
Easedale Cl S40........94 F5
East Ave
Derby DE3.............217 E3
Stanfree S44..........80 B1
East Bank DE4..........141 C5
East Bank Pl S2........43 B6
East Bank Rd S2........43 B6
East Bank Way S2.......43 B6
Eastbrae Rd DE23.......231 D7
East Brook Cl SK23.....47 C6
East Cl DE22...........204 E2
Eastcliffe Ct S2.......43 C8
East Cres
Holbrook DE56.........191 C8
Long Duckmanton S44...98 A6
East Croft Ave DE23....231 D5
Eastcroft Cl S20.......59 F8

Eastcroft Dr S20.......59 F8
Eastcroft Glen S20.....59 F8
Eastcroft View S20.....59 F7
Eastcroft Way **7** S20..59 F8
East Dr DE6............211 B1
East End DE4...........140 F7
East End Dr DE11.......256 C4
Eastern Ave
Bolsover S44..........118 B8
Sheffield S2..........43 E7
Eastern Cres S2........43 D6
Eastern Dr S2..........43 D7
Eastern Wlk S2.........43 D7
Eastfield Rd
Dronfield S18.........76 C8
Ripley DE5............170 A1
Swadlincote DE11......256 C6
Eastgate DE1, DE21.....267 C4
East Glade Ave S12.....44 E3
East Glade Cl S12......44 E3
East Glade Cres S12....44 E4
East Glade Dell S12....44 E4
East Glade Pl S12......44 E3
East Glade Rd S12......44 E3
East Glade Sq S12......44 E3
East Glade Way S12.....44 E4
East Lawn DE65.........230 D2
Eastleigh Ct S41.......115 D8
Eastleigh Dr
Derby DE3.............217 E2
Mansfield Woodhouse
NG19................136 B6
East Midlands Aeropark★
DE74.................247 A1
East Midlands Airport
DE74.................247 C1
East Midlands Designer
Outlet (Sh Ctr) DE55..159 C5
EASTMOOR.............93 D4
Eastmoor Rd S43.......96 F4
East Nelson St DE75....181 D2
East Par S80...........82 A5
East Rd S2.............43 B7
East Service Rd DE21...220 B3
Eastside Cl S41........96 B8
Eastside Rd S41........96 B8
East St
Bramley-Vale S44......117 D1
Burton upon Trent DE15..248 C3
Clay Cross S45........131 D4
Clowne S43............81 A5
Creswell S80..........81 D1
Derby DE1.............267 B3
Heanor DE75...........194 A8
Ilkeston DE7..........208 F8
Long Eaton NG10.......236 F8
Renishaw S21..........79 B8
Scarcliffe S44........118 E6
Warsop Vale NG20......120 D5
East Vale SK6..........23 A5
East View
Chesterfield S40......266 B2
Mayfield DE6..........184 D7
Shirebrook NG20.......119 F6
Whaley Thorns NG20....101 A3
East View Ave S21......59 C2
East View Ind Est NG20..119 F6
East View Rd DE56......168 E1
Eastview Terr NG16.....182 B3
Eastway DE74...........247 B3
EASTWOOD.............182 E3
Eastwood Ave DE23.....218 C2
Eastwood Cl S41........115 D8
Eastwood Comp Sch
NG16.................182 E3
Eastwood Cotts S32....53 B8
Eastwood Dr
Calow S44.............97 B2
Derby DE23............218 C2
Eastwood Grange Sch
S45.................130 B4
Eastwood Jun & Inf Schs **1**
NG16................182 F2
Eastwood La S45........130 B2
Eastwood Park Apartments
S41.................115 C7
Eastwood Park Dr S41...115 D8
Eastwood Rd NG16......195 E6
Eather Ave NG19.......136 C4
Eaton Ave
Derby DE22............205 B5
Ilkeston DE7..........208 D6
Eaton Bank DE56.......191 A1
Eaton Cl
Derby DE22............205 A5
Hatton DE65...........227 D1
Hulland Ward DE6......175 E3
Eaton Ct
Derby DE1.............218 E6
Duffield DE56.........190 D4
Eaton Dr DE45.........91 F5
Eaton Fold S32........71 F3
Eaton Grange Dr NG10..236 A8
Eaton Hill DE45.......91 F5
Eaton La S45..........129 B5
Eaton Pl DE45.........91 F5
Eaton Rd
Castle Donington DE74..247 B3
Rocester ST14.........196 F3
Eatons Rd NG9.........223 D6
Eaton St SK14.........210 C1
Eaves Ave SK23........47 C5
Eaves Knoll Rd SK22....33 B8
Ebenezer St
Glossop SK13..........17 D7
Ilkeston DE7..........194 F3
Langley Mill NG16.....182 B3

Ecclesbourne Ave DE56..190 F3
Ecclesbourne Cl
Duffield DE56.........190 E3
Wirksworth DE4........165 F7
Ecclesbourne Cotts DE4..154 F2
Ecclesbourne Dr SK17...85 A6
Ecclesbourne La DE6....176 F5
Ecclesbourne Mdws
DE56.................190 D4
Ecclesbourne Pk DE55..159 D2
Ecclesbourne Sch DE56..190 E3
Ecclesbourne Valley Rly★
DE4..................154 F2
Eccles Cl
Hope S33..............39 A4
Whaley Bridge SK23....45 D8
ECCLES FOLD...........46 C8
Eccles Fold SK23.......47 A6
Eccles Rd
Chapel-en-le-Frith, Higher
Crossings S33........47 A6
Chapel-en-le-Frith, Hilltop
SK23...............46 C7
Eccles Terr SK23.......46 D8
ECKINGTON............59 C4
Eckington Bsns Ctr S21..59 E4
Eckington Camms CE Prim
Sch S21..............59 D4
Eckington Cl DE7.......207 E8
Eckington Hall S20.....59 D5
Eckington Jun Sch S21..59 D3
Eckington Mews S20....59 D5
Eckington Rd
Chesterfield S43......77 D5
Dronfield S18.........57 D4
Sheffield S20.........59 F8
Staveley S43..........78 F4
Eckington Sch S21.....59 A3
Eckington Swimming Pool
S21.................59 D4
Eckington Way S20.....59 F8
EDALE.................37 C8
Edale Ave
Derby, Alvaston DE24..233 B7
Derby DE23............218 E2
Derby, Markeaton DE3..217 D2
Edale Bank SK13........9 A1
Edale CE Prim Sch S33..37 C8
Edale Cl
Derby DE22............204 D1
Gamesley SK13.........9 E2
Long Eaton NG10.......236 B6
Edale Cres SK13........9 E1
Edale Ct **3** S41.....95 E7
Edale Dr
Derby DE21............220 F3
South Normanton DE55..160 B7
EDALE END.............29 D2
Edale Fold SK13........9 E1
Edale Gr SK17..........85 E7
Edale Mews SK17.......85 E7
Edale Mill S33.........37 E7
Edale Rd
Hayfield SK22.........26 A2
Hope S33..............38 F7
Mastin Moor S43.......79 C6
Edale Rise NG9.........223 E3
Edale Sq DE7..........194 E5
Edale Sta S33.........37 C7
Edale Way DE56.........179 A5
Eden Bank DE56........167 F2
Eden Cl DE65..........240 C8
Edenhall Rd S2........43 F7
Eden Low NG19.........136 E3
Eden Rd DE21..........220 B4
EDENSOR..............110 E8
Edensor Ave SK17......85 E7
Edensor Cl S42........131 F6
Edensor Ct S43........97 C8
Edensor Dr DE56.......179 C6
Edensor Sq DE22.......218 F4
Eden St
Derby DE24............233 A8
Wingerworth S42.......114 E3
Edes Farm Dr ST14.....196 F4
Edgbaston Ct DE23.....231 C8
Edgecote Dr DE11......256 A7
Edgefold Rd DE4.......143 B5
Edgehill DE56.........191 A2
Edgehill Gr NG19......136 C2
Edge Hill Jun Sch DE15..254 F7
Edge La S33...........51 B6
Edgelaw Ct **2** DE24..231 D3
Edge Mount View S32...72 E2
Edge Rd
Eyam S32..............71 E7
Matlock DE4...........143 B6
EDGETOP..............103 F1
Edge View S32.........72 B3
Edge View S32.........72 C7
Edge View Dr DE45.....90 A4
Edgware Rd DE22.......217 F6
Edgwood Rd NG16......195 F6
Edinboro Row NG16.....195 E6
Edinburgh Cres DE24...232 E4
Edinburgh Ct
Chesterfield S42......114 E4
Swanwick DE55........170 A7
Edinburgh Mews S41....266 A4
Edinburgh Rd
Chesterfield S41......95 F5
Wingerworth S42......114 E4
Edith Wood Cl DE24....233 B5
EDLASTON.............185 C2
Edlaston La DE6.......185 B2
Edmonton Pl DE15.....248 D2

Edmund Ave S17........56 D6
Edmund Cl S17.........56 D6
Edmund Dr S17.........56 D6
Edmund Rd
Derby DE21............220 F3
Sheffield S2..........43 B8
Edmund's Sq DE3.......230 B7
Edmund St S41.........95 B8
Ednaston Ave DE23.....231 D5
Ednaston Hall Farm Mews
DE6..................201 B7
Edward Ave
Derby DE21............220 A5
Jacksdale NG16........171 B4
Edward Rd NG10.......236 D8
Edwards Cres DE56.....192 A8
Edward St
Aldercar NG16.........182 B4
Belper DE56...........179 A4
Derby DE1.............267 B4
Eckington S21.........59 D3
Glossop SK13..........10 C1
Hartshorne DE11.......257 A3
Marple SK6...........15 B1
Moira DE11............256 C1
Overseal DE12.........262 A4
Stapleford NG9........223 D7
Staveley S43..........97 C8
Edward Wlk S42........115 D1
Edwin Ave S40.........114 D8
Edwin Rd S2..........43 C6
Edwinstowe Rd DE21....206 B1
Egerton Dr NG9........209 D2
Egerton Rd S18........57 B2
Eggesford Rd DE24.....231 D2
Eggington Rd DE65.....240 F3
EGGINTON..............241 B6
Egginton Prim Sch DE65..241 B5
Egginton Rd
Etwall DE65...........229 B2
Hilton DE65...........228 D2
Egmanton Cl DE21......206 B1
Egreaves Ave DE75.....181 C4
EGSTOW...............131 D5
Egstow Pl S45.........131 D4
Egstow St S45.........131 D4
Ehlinger Ave SK13.....10 A5
Eider Cl NG20.........119 D3
Eighth Ave DE14.......253 F8
Eland Cl DE21.........221 A5
Eland Rd NG20.........119 F5
Elder Cl DE55.........170 A4
Elder Ct S21..........60 C5
Elder Way S40.........266 B3
Eldon Cl SK23.........47 C6
Eldon Ho **5** DE1....267 B2
Eldon St
Burton upon Trent DE15..248 A6
Clay Cross S45........131 C4
Eleanor Ave DE7.......209 A5
Eleanor Cres NG9......223 F7
Elesmere Ct DE7.......194 D1
Eley Cl DE7...........194 C2
Eley Wlk DE1..........267 A1
Elgar Dr NG10.........236 B5
Elgin Ave DE23........218 A1
Elgin Cl S40..........114 C7
Eliot Cl
Calow S43.............96 F5
Long Eaton NG10......236 B5
Wirksworth DE4........165 E8
Eliot Dr DE7..........208 C5
Eliot Rd DE23.........231 B8
Elizabeth Ave
Buxton SK17...........85 D7
Disley SK12...........32 D5
Rolleston DE13........240 B3
Elizabeth Cl
Derby DE21............220 B5
West Hallam DE7.......207 D8
Elizabeth Ct
Burton upon Trent DE15..248 C3
Ilkeston DE7..........194 D1
Elizabeth Pk NG16.....170 F5
Elizabeth Villas DE6...185 C8
Elkstone Cl DE21......206 B2
Elkstone Rd S40.......95 A5
Ella Bank Rd DE75.....182 A1
ELLASTONE.............183 B3
Ellastone Gdns DE24...233 B7
Ellendale Rd DE21.....220 B7
Ellerslie Gr NG10.....223 A5
Ellesmere Ave
Alfreton DE55.........159 B4
Derby DE24............219 C5
Ellesmere Dr NG9......209 C5
Ellesmere Rd NG19.....136 F1
Elliott Ave S33.......51 A8
Elliott Dr S43........97 C6
Ellis Cl NG10.........236 C6
Ellison Ave DE72......246 A7
Ellison Cl SK14.......9 D5
Ellisons Rd S21.......60 F8
Ellison St SK13.......10 D1
Elma La S80...........101 C6
Elm Ave
Belper DE56...........179 B2
Darley Dale DE4.......142 F7
Long Eaton NG10.......236 D8
Sandiacre NG10.......223 B7
Elm Cl
Bolsover S44..........99 C1
Branston DE14.........253 F8
Chesterfield S41......95 F8
Doveridge DE6.........224 C8
Killamarsh S21........60 C5

Elm Cl *continued*
Mottram in Longdendale SK14 . . . 9 A4
Pinxton NG16 . . . 160 D3
Elm Cres S20 . . . 59 C8
Elm Dr
Hilton DE65 . . . 228 D2
Killamarsh S21 . . . 60 C5
Elmfield SK23 . . . 47 A5
Elm Gr
Clay Cross S45 . . . 131 D3
Derby, Cherrytree Hill DE21 . . . 220 B5
Derby DE22 . . . 204 D5
Glossop SK13 . . . 10 C2
Elmhurst DE65 . . . 241 A5
Elmhurst Ave DE55 . . . 160 A4
Elmhurst Cl DE55 . . . 160 A4
Elmhurst Rd NG19 . . . 136 F1
Elm Lodge Farm Cl S41 . . 95 F7
Elm Park Ct DE1 . . . 267 A5
Elm Rd
Eckington S21 . . . 59 C2
Pilsley S45 . . . 132 C1
Elms Ave
Alfreton DE55 . . . 159 A4
Derby DE23 . . . 218 B2
Ripley DE5 . . . 180 D8
Elms Cl DE55 . . . 159 A4
Elmsdale Rd DE11 . . . 257 A4
Elms Dr DE23 . . . 218 B1
Elms Farm Way DE23 . . . 231 A8
Elmsfield Ave DE75 . . . 182 A2
Elms Gr DE65 . . . 229 C3
Elmslea Ave DE12 . . . 260 D3
Elmsleigh Cl DE11 . . . 256 B6
Elmsleigh Dr DE11 . . . 256 B6
Elmsleigh Gr DE11 . . . 256 B6
Elmsleigh Inf Sch DE11 . . 256 B6
Elms Rd
Burton upon Trent DE15 . . 248 A1
Coton in the Elms DE12 . . . 260 D3
Elms St DE1 . . . 218 F7
Elm St
Borrowash DE72 . . . 221 B2
Brimington S43 . . . 97 A8
Holmewood S42 . . . 116 B4
ELMS THE . . . 180 D8
Elms The NG16 . . . 195 F7
ELMTON . . . 100 A7
Elmton Cl
Clowne S43 . . . 80 F3
Creswell S80 . . . 100 D8
Elmton La S44 . . . 99 C3
Elmton Park Mews S80 . . . 99 E5
Elmton Rd S80 . . . 81 E1
Elmton View S80 . . . 81 D2
Elmtree Ave
Derby DE24 . . . 232 B7
Selston NG16 . . . 171 F7
Elm Tree Ave
Kilburn DE56 . . . 192 B7
Mansfield Woodhouse NG19 . . . 136 A4
Shirebrook NG20 . . . 119 D4
Shirland DE55 . . . 146 C1
Elmtree Cl S81 . . . 63 F7
Elm Tree Cres S18 . . . 57 A3
Elm Tree Dr S42 . . . 114 F4
Elm Tree Ho S12 . . . 44 A6
Elm Tree Row DE55 . . . 148 A5
Elm View ST14 . . . 196 E6
Elm Wlk S45 . . . 132 C1
Elmwood Dr
Alfreton DE55 . . . 159 C3
Derby DE21 . . . 205 D2
Sheffield S20 . . . 59 D6
Elnor Ave SK23 . . . 45 E5
Elnor La SK23 . . . 45 F4
Elnor St NG16 . . . 182 C3
Elsecar Cl DE56 . . . 179 D5
Elstead La DE11 . . . 257 B1
Elston Cl NG19 . . . 135 D1
Elstree Dr S12 . . . 44 B4
Elstree Rd S12 . . . 44 B4
ELTON . . . 140 E6
Elton Bank 6 SK13 . . . 9 D1
Elton CE Prim Sch DE4 . . 140 E6
Elton Cl
8 Gamesley SK13 . . . 9 D1
North Wingfield S42 . . . 132 A5
Stapleford NG9 . . . 223 D8
Elton Gr SK17 . . . 85 E6
Elton Lea 7 SK13 . . . 9 D1
Elton Pl 9 SK13 . . . 9 D1
Elton Rd
Derby DE24 . . . 232 B8
Winster DE4 . . . 141 B6
Elton St S40 . . . 266 B1
Elton View S43 . . . 97 D8
ELVASTON . . . 234 A6
Elvaston Castle & Ctry Pk★ DE21 . . . 233 F6
Elvaston Cl S18 . . . 56 B1
Elvaston Dr NG10 . . . 236 A4
Elvaston La DE24 . . . 233 C7
Elvaston Nature Reserve★ DE24 . . . 233 E7
Elvaston Rd S42 . . . 131 F6
Elvaston St DE72 . . . 235 B7
Elveden Dr DE7 . . . 194 C3
Elvin Way S42 . . . 131 C8
Elwood Rd S17 . . . 56 C6
Elwyn Cl DE13 . . . 240 D1
Ely Cl
Mansfield Woodhouse NG19 . . . 136 D4
Swadlincote DE11 . . . 256 D6
Elyn Ave S42 . . . 132 B7
Elysee Gdns SK17 . . . 85 C3
Embankment Cl DE22 . . . 217 F7
Ember La DE4 . . . 142 E1
Embridge Cswy SK10 . . . 64 B5
Emerald Cl
Derby DE21 . . . 206 A2
Mansfield NG19 . . . 135 F1
Emerson Sq DE23 . . . 231 F6
Emery Cl DE12 . . . 261 D5
Emmanuel Sch DE22 . . . 218 F7
Emmas Williams Ct DE5 169 D1
Emmerson Rd DE55 . . . 170 C7
Emmet Field Cl S40 . . . 114 F8
EMMETT CARR . . . 79 C7
Emmett Carr Cl S21 . . . 79 C7
Emmett Carr Dr S21 . . . 79 C8
Emmett Carr La S21 . . . 79 C8
Empire Ct DE75 . . . 181 E2
Empire Rd DE15 . . . 248 D3
Empress Rd DE23 . . . 267 A1
Emsworth Cl DE7 . . . 194 D3
Endland Ind Est DE1 . . . 218 D5
Endowood Rd S40 . . . 114 A8
Endsleigh Gdns DE22 . . . 217 F6
End The DE15 . . . 248 E8
Enfield Cl DE65 . . . 228 E2
Enfield Rd
Chesterfield S41 . . . 96 A5
Derby DE22 . . . 218 B6
England Cres DE75 . . . 182 A2
English Martyrs RC Prim Sch NG10 . . . 223 B1
Ennerdale Ave 4 S20 . . . 59 E6
Ennerdale Cl S18 . . . 56 E1
Ennerdale Cres S41 . . . 95 C8
Ennerdale Ct 6 NG10 . . . 223 B2
Ennerdale Dr S20 . . . 59 E6
Ennerdale Rd NG10 . . . 223 B2
Ennerdale Wlk DE21 . . . 205 D2
Ennis Cl DE21 . . . 220 C7
Enoch Stone Dr DE21 . . . 220 B4
Enslet La DE6 . . . 164 B2
Ensor Cl DE11 . . . 256 D5
Ensor Way SK22 . . . 33 C7
Enterprise Cl NG19 . . . 135 E2
Enterprise Ct S80 . . . 81 E1
Enterprise Ct DE7 . . . 194 D1
Enterprise Dr S42 . . . 116 D1
Enterprise Rd NG19 . . . 135 E3
Enterprise Way
Derby DE21 . . . 267 C4
Sheffield S20 . . . 60 B8
Epping Cl DE22 . . . 217 E6
Epsom Cl DE14 . . . 253 F7
Epsom Rd NG9 . . . 223 E3
Epworth Dr DE24 . . . 233 A4
Epworth Ho DE15 . . . 248 D3
Erdington Way NG9 . . . 223 E3
Erewash Ct
Ilkeston DE7 . . . 194 D1
Long Eaton NG10 . . . 223 D1
Erewash Dr DE7 . . . 209 B6
Erewash Gr NG9 . . . 223 F2
Erewash Mus & Gdns★ DE7 . . . 208 F8
Erewash Rd NG16 . . . 160 E2
Erewash Sq DE7 . . . 209 A6
Erewash St DE55 . . . 171 A6
Erica Dr DE55 . . . 160 B7
Erin Rd S43, S44 . . . 98 B7
Ernest Hall Way DE11 . . . 256 C4
Ernocroft La SK6 . . . 15 E2
Ernocroft Rd SK6 . . . 15 B1
Errington Ave S2 . . . 43 E6
Errington Cl S2 . . . 43 E6
Errington Cres S2 . . . 43 E6
Errington Rd
Chesterfield S40 . . . 114 D8
Sheffield S2 . . . 43 E6
Errington Way S2 . . . 43 E7
Errwood Ave SK17 . . . 85 A6
Errwood Forest Walks★ SK17 . . . 64 E2
Erskine Cres S2 . . . 43 C7
Erskine Rd S2 . . . 43 C7
Erskine St SK6 . . . 15 B3
Erskine View S2 . . . 43 C7
Escolme Cl DE11 . . . 256 D4
Eskdale Cl
Bolsover S44 . . . 98 F1
Dronfield S18 . . . 56 E1
Long Eaton NG10 . . . 236 B5
Eskdale Wlk DE24 . . . 233 D6
Essendine Cres S8 . . . 43 B3
Essex Dr DE11 . . . 255 E1
Essex Rd DE15 . . . 254 D6
Essex St
Derby DE21 . . . 219 D6
2 Ilkeston DE7 . . . 194 F1
Estwic Ave NG16 . . . 182 F3
Etchells The DE65 . . . 227 A8
Etherow Brow 6 SK14 . . . 16 A8
Etherow Ctry Pk★ SK6 . . . 15 C3
Etherow Ctry Pk Visitor Ctr★ SK6 . . . 15 B2
Etherow Way SK13 . . . 9 E5
Eton Ct DE7 . . . 207 D8
Eton St DE24 . . . 219 E1
Etruria Gdns DE1 . . . 267 B5
Etta's Way DE65 . . . 229 B4
Ettrick Cl 4 S40 . . . 95 C5
Ettrick Dr DE24 . . . 231 E2
ETWALL . . . 229 C3
Etwall Cl S40 . . . 95 A6
ETWALL COMMON . . . 229 D2
Etwall La DE65 . . . 229 F5
Etwall L Ctr DE65 . . . 229 B4
Etwall Prim Sch DE65 . . . 229 B4
Etwall Rd
Derby DE3 . . . 217 C1
Egginton DE65 . . . 241 B7
Willington DE65 . . . 242 A7
Etwall St DE22 . . . 218 E5
Eureka Prim Sch DE11 . . 256 D5
Eureka Rd DE11 . . . 256 D5
Euston Dr DE1 . . . 219 B7
Evans Ave DE22 . . . 205 A5
Evans Cl S33 . . . 51 A7
Evanston Gdns DE21 . . . 220 B6
Evelyn Devonshire Cotts S45 . . . 132 F2
Evelyn Gr DE21 . . . 220 A5
Everard Ave S17 . . . 56 A5
Everard Dr S17 . . . 56 A5
Everard Glade 3 S17 . . . 56 A5
Everest Dr DE55 . . . 170 D8
Everett Cl S43 . . . 96 E7
Evergreen Cl DE21 . . . 206 A3
Evershill Cl DE55 . . . 146 F5
Evershill La DE55 . . . 146 F6
Eversleigh Rise DE4 . . . 142 B8
Everton St NG19 . . . 135 E1
Evesham Ave SK13 . . . 10 A5
Evesham Cl DE21 . . . 205 E1
Ewart La DE55 . . . 158 F3
Ewe Dale La DE6 . . . 149 A3
Ewe Lamb Cl NG9 . . . 209 F1
Ewe Lamb La NG9 . . . 209 F1
Excalibur Way S41 . . . 266 C3
Excelsior Ave DE24 . . . 232 F6
Excelsior Dr DE11 . . . 256 E1
Exchange St DE1 . . . 267 B3
Exe Fold NG19 . . . 136 D2
Exeter Cl DE11 . . . 256 E6
Exeter Ct 19 S41 . . . 95 F8
Exeter Ho DE1 . . . 267 C3
Exeter Pl DE1 . . . 267 C3
Exeter St DE1 . . . 267 C4
Exford Ct NG19 . . . 136 C6
Exlowmere La DE4 . . . 140 F5
Export Dr NG17 . . . 160 F8
EYAM . . . 71 D6
Eyam CE Prim Sch S32 . . . 71 D5
Eyam Cl
Burton upon Trent DE15 . . 248 B2
15 Gamesley SK13 . . . 9 D2
North Wingfield S42 . . . 132 A8
Eyam Fold 29 SK13 . . . 9 D2
Eyam Gdns 28 SK13 . . . 9 D2
Eyam Gn 16 SK13 . . . 9 D2
Eyam Gr 14 SK13 . . . 9 D2
Eyam Hall★ S32 . . . 71 D5
Eyam La SK13 . . . 9 E2
Eyam Lea SK13 . . . 9 E2
Eyam Mews SK13 . . . 9 E2
Eyam Moor Stone Circle★ S32 . . . 52 F3
Eyam Mus★ S32 . . . 71 D6
Eyam Wlk DE56 . . . 179 A5
Eyes Ct DE56 . . . 190 E3
Eyre Gdns S40 . . . 266 A4
Eyre's Gdns DE7 . . . 194 F2
Eyre St
Clay Cross S45 . . . 131 C3
Creswell S80 . . . 81 D1
Eyre Street E S41 . . . 115 C8
Eyrie The
Burton upon Trent DE15 . . 248 C3
Derby DE24 . . . 231 E3

F

Fabis Cl DE11 . . . 256 A3
Fabric View S42 . . . 132 D8
Factory La DE7 . . . 194 E2
Factory St S40 . . . 95 D2
Fairbourne Dr DE3 . . . 217 D4
Fairburn Croft Cres S43 . . 80 B6
Faircroft Ave NG10 . . . 223 B5
Fairdene DE23 . . . 218 F2
Faires Cl DE72 . . . 221 D1
Faire St DE22 . . . 218 E3
Fairfax Dr S2 . . . 44 B8
Fairfax Rd
Derby DE23 . . . 218 F2
Sheffield S2 . . . 44 B8
Fairfax Rise S2 . . . 44 B8
FAIRFIELD . . . 85 D8
Fairfield Ave
Borrowash DE72 . . . 221 C3
Hilcote DE55 . . . 148 C1
Rolleston DE13 . . . 240 D4
Stonebroom DE55 . . . 147 B4
Fairfield Cl
Brimington S43 . . . 96 D8
Whaley Thorns NG20 . . . 101 A2
Fairfield Cres
Long Eaton NG10 . . . 236 B4
Swadlincote DE11 . . . 255 E5
Fairfield Ct S42 . . . 94 F4
Fairfield Dr S42 . . . 94 F4
Fairfield Endowed CE Jun Sch SK17 . . . 85 E7
Fairfield Inf Sch SK17 . . . 85 E8
Fairfield Prim Sch NG9 . . 223 D6
Fairfield Rd
Bolsover S44 . . . 118 A8
Buxton SK17 . . . 85 C8
Chesterfield S40 . . . 266 A4
Derby DE23 . . . 218 E1
Horsley Woodhouse DE7 . . 192 C7
Fairfield Terr DE11 . . . 256 F3
Fairfield Villas S40 . . . 266 A4
Fairford Cl S40 . . . 114 F7
Fairford Gdns DE23 . . . 231 A6
Fairham Rd DE13 . . . 240 F1
Fairholme Dr NG19 . . . 135 E1
Fairholmes DE4 . . . 143 D5
Fairisle Cl DE21 . . . 206 C3
Fairlawns DE56 . . . 190 D3
Fair Lea Cl NG10 . . . 236 D6
Fairleigh S2 . . . 44 A8
Fairmeadows Prim Sch DE11 . . . 255 E5
Fair View S40 . . . 95 E4
Fairview Ave NG16 . . . 171 F2
Fairview Cl
Derby DE23 . . . 231 A8
Kilburn DE56 . . . 192 B7
Fairview Grange DE56 . . . 192 B7
Fairview Rd S18 . . . 57 A3
Fairview Rise DE4 . . . 168 A8
Fairway DE14 . . . 254 B6
Fairway Cl DE22 . . . 204 D2
Fairway Cres DE22 . . . 204 D2
Fairways Cl SK13 . . . 10 F1
Fairways The
Clay Cross S45 . . . 131 E3
Clifton DE6 . . . 184 F6
Mansfield Woodhouse NG19 . . . 136 D6
Fairway The 5 DE11 . . . 255 E5
Fairwinds Cl S18 . . . 57 A1
Fairwood Dr DE24 . . . 233 D6
Fairy Bank Cres SK22 . . . 25 D3
Fairy Bank Rd SK22 . . . 25 D3
Falaise Way DE65 . . . 228 E2
Falcon Cl SK22 . . . 33 D8
Falcon Ct DE7 . . . 194 D1
Falcon Rd S18 . . . 57 C3
Falcon Rise S18 . . . 57 D3
Falconside Dr DE21 . . . 220 F2
Falcons Rise DE56 . . . 179 C5
Falcon Way
Derby DE24 . . . 231 E2
Woodville DE11 . . . 256 F3
Falcon Yd S40 . . . 266 B3
Faldo Cl DE14 . . . 254 B6
Falkirk Ave DE5 . . . 169 E4
Falkland Rise S18 . . . 76 A8
Fallowfield Rd S43 . . . 77 D3
Fallow Rd DE21 . . . 220 F6
Fall Rd DE75 . . . 181 E3
Falmouth Rd DE24 . . . 233 C5
Fal Paddock NG19 . . . 136 D2
Fanny Ave S21 . . . 60 E5
Fan Rd S43 . . . 78 F1
Fan Road Ind Est S43 . . . 78 F2
Fanshaw Ave S21 . . . 59 C2
Fanshaw Bank S18 . . . 57 A1
Fanshaw Cl S21 . . . 59 C2
Fanshaw Dr S21 . . . 59 C2
Fanshawe Gate La S17, S18 . . . 55 E1
Fanshaw Rd
Dronfield S18 . . . 57 B2
Eckington S21 . . . 59 C2
Fanshaw Way S21 . . . 59 C2
Faraday Ave DE13 . . . 240 D1
Faraday Ct
Branston DE14 . . . 253 E7
Stapleford NG9 . . . 209 E1
Far Clay Gr S81 . . . 63 F7
Far Croft DE72 . . . 235 D8
Far Cross DE4 . . . 143 C7
Farfield Rd DE7 . . . 209 A8
Far Green DE4 . . . 143 B6
Far Hill S33 . . . 51 A7
Farish Pl 5 S2 . . . 43 B6
Far La
Barlow S18 . . . 75 B3
Ockbrook DE72 . . . 221 D6
FAR LAUND . . . 179 C6
Far Laund DE56 . . . 179 B6
FARLEY . . . 128 B1
Farley Hill DE4 . . . 143 A8
Farley La DE4 . . . 128 B3
Farley Rd DE23 . . . 218 D2
Farlow Rd S18 . . . 56 E2
Farm Cl
Belper DE56 . . . 179 C4
Chesterfield S40 . . . 114 F6
Dronfield S18 . . . 57 B4
Hilton DE65 . . . 228 C1
Ilkeston DE7 . . . 209 A8
Kilburn DE56 . . . 192 A8
Long Eaton NG10 . . . 236 E5
Ripley DE5 . . . 169 B6
Sheffield S12 . . . 44 A2
Somercotes DE55 . . . 170 C8
Whaley Thorns NG20 . . . 101 A2
Farm Cres S20 . . . 59 C6
Farm Croft Rd NG19 . . . 136 C6
Farm Dr DE24 . . . 233 A5
Farmfields Cl S44 . . . 98 E3
Farmhouse Rd DE24 . . . 231 E2
Farmilo Cres NG19 . . . 135 E1
Farmilo Prim Sch NG19 . 135 C4
Farm La
High Lane SK12 . . . 32 A6
Matlock DE4 . . . 143 C7
Newton Solney DE15 . . . 248 E7
Farmlands La DE23 . . . 231 B6
Farm Side DE11 . . . 255 F5
Farm St DE22 . . . 267 A1
Farmstead Cl S14 . . . 43 D5
Farm View S42 . . . 131 D8
Farmway NG19 . . . 136 C2
Farm Wlk S20 . . . 59 C7
FARNAH GREEN . . . 178 C3
Farnah Green Rd DE56 . . 178 D3
Farnborough Gdns DE22 205 B4
Farncombe La DE21 . . . 205 F3
Farndale Ave S40 . . . 114 B8
Farndale Cl NG10 . . . 236 A5
Farndale Ct 5 DE24 . . . 233 C6
Farndale Rd
Chesterfield S43 . . . 78 E4
Staveley S43 . . . 78 E4
Farndon Dr NG9 . . . 223 F3
Far New Cl NG10 . . . 223 B5
Farneworth Rd DE3 . . . 217 D2
Farnham Cl DE3 . . . 217 C1
Farnham Wlk DE7 . . . 207 D8
Farningham Cl DE21 . . . 220 F5
Farnon Cl S40 . . . 266 C1
Farnsley La S32 . . . 71 B4
Farnsworth Gr NG17 . . . 148 F3
Farnsworth St S41 . . . 115 C8
Farnway DE22 . . . 204 E1
Farrendale Cl NG19 . . . 136 D1
Farrier Gdns DE23 . . . 231 A7
Farriers Croft DE7 . . . 194 C3
Farriers Way S21 . . . 60 D5
Farringdon Cl DE22 . . . 217 F6
Farrington Way NG16 . . . 182 E1
Farthing Ct NG10 . . . 236 B7
Farwater Cl S18 . . . 76 A8
Farwater La S18 . . . 56 F1
Far Woodseats La SK13 . . 15 F5
FAULD . . . 238 C6
Fauld Ind Pk DE13 . . . 238 E6
Fauld La
Tutbury DE13 . . . 239 A6
Tutbury, Fauld DE13 . . . 238 D7
Fauvel Pl SK13 . . . 10 C1
Fauvel Rd SK13 . . . 10 C2
Faversham Cl DE24 . . . 232 F5
Fawn Cl S42 . . . 114 F3
Fay Gdns SK13 . . . 9 E4
Faywood Dr SK6 . . . 23 A6
Fearn Ave DE5 . . . 169 E1
Fearn Cl
Church Broughton DE65 . . 227 B8
Long Eaton DE72 . . . 236 A7
Featherbed La
Bolsover S44 . . . 99 A5
Darfoulds S80 . . . 63 F1
Felkin St S41 . . . 266 C3
Fellbrigg Rd S2 . . . 43 D7
Fellow Lands Way DE73 . 233 A2
Fellside
Belper DE56 . . . 179 A4
Derby DE21 . . . 220 F6
Fellview Cl S32 . . . 53 A7
Felton Ave NG19 . . . 136 C6
Fenchurch Wlk DE22 . . . 218 B7
Fen Cl DE55 . . . 148 A3
Fenelon Cl 7 DE11 . . . 256 E1
Fenland Way S40 . . . 114 E8
Fennel St DE45 . . . 108 E8
FENNY BENTLEY . . . 162 A1
Fenton Ave DE11 . . . 257 B1
Fenton Rd DE3 . . . 217 C2
Fenton St S21 . . . 59 B2
Fenwick St DE24 . . . 232 D7
Ferguson Ave NG19 . . . 136 B4
Fern Ave
Staveley S43 . . . 97 D8
Willington DE65 . . . 242 C6
Fernbank S33 . . . 51 A7
Fern Bank Ave DE55 . . . 147 E1
Fernbank Dr S21 . . . 59 B3
Fern Cl
Eckington S21 . . . 59 B3
Holmewood S44 . . . 116 F1
Shirebrook NG20 . . . 119 E6
Willington DE65 . . . 242 C6
Fern Cres NG16 . . . 182 D3
Ferncroft Ave S20 . . . 59 C7
Ferncroft Wlk DE73 . . . 232 F2
Ferndale Ave SK17 . . . 67 C4
Ferndale Cl S18 . . . 57 D3
Ferndale Rd
Buxton SK17 . . . 67 C4
Dronfield S18 . . . 57 D3
Ferndale Rise S18 . . . 57 D3
Ferndene Dr NG10 . . . 236 A7
Fernello Cl DE73 . . . 244 A6
Ferneydale Ave SK17 . . . 85 C4
Fernhill SK6 . . . 23 B6
Fernhill Cl SK13 . . . 10 D3
Fernhill Ct DE73 . . . 233 A3
FERNILEE . . . 45 E1
Fernilee Cl
New Mills SK22 . . . 24 C1
West Hallam DE7 . . . 207 E8
Fernilee Cotts SK23 . . . 45 E1
Fernilee Gdns DE21 . . . 205 F1
Fern Lea
Hollingworth SK14 . . . 9 D6
Shirland DE55 . . . 146 D3
Fernlea Cl SK13 . . . 9 E4
Fernleigh Rise NG19 . . . 136 D1
Fern Rd SK17 . . . 85 B5
Fern Royd S32 . . . 53 A7
Fern Sq S32 . . . 71 D6
Fern View Cl S12 . . . 44 F3
Fern View Gr S12 . . . 44 F3
Fernway SK17 . . . 85 C4
Fern Way S21 . . . 59 B3
Fernwood SK6 . . . 23 C7
Fernwood Cl
Chesterfield S41 . . . 115 E7
Derby DE23 . . . 231 C8
Shirland DE55 . . . 146 D3
Ferrers Ave DE13 . . . 239 B5

Ferrers Cl DE74......247 A3
Ferrers Cres DE56......190 D3
Ferrers Ctr for Arts &
Crafts★ LE65......258 F7
Ferrers Way
　Derby DE22......204 E2
　Ripley DE5......169 C3
Ferry Gn DE65......242 B5
Ferry St DE15......254 E8
Ferry Vale Cl DE15......254 E8
Festival Ave DE72......235 C7
Festival Rd
　Branston DE14......253 E7
　Ilkeston DE7......208 C5
Fiddler's La DE13......239 F4
Fiddle St SK17......85 C3
Fidlers Cl S33......40 B3
Fidlers Well S33......40 B4
Field Ave
　Hatton DE65......239 C8
　Renishaw S21......79 B8
Field Cl
　Borrowash DE72......221 B3
　Breaston DE72......235 F7
　Dronfield S18......56 C2
　Hilton DE65......228 D2
　Mansfield Woodhouse
　NG19......136 D5
Field Cres DE24......233 A5
Field Ct
　Chesterfield S43......77 D4
　Kilburn DE56......192 A7
Field Dr
　Derby DE24......233 A5
　Rolleston DE13......240 A3
　Shirebrook NG20......119 E2
Fielden Ave NG19......135 D2
Field End DE4......153 A1
Fieldfare Ct DE13......231 A6
Fieldfare Ho S41......77 B3
Fieldgate Dr DE21......205 F2
Fieldhead Rd S8......43 A7
Field Head Way S41......95 C6
Field Head Way DE21......206 B3
Field House La SK6......23 A6
Fielding's Rd S80......81 F1
Field La
　Belper DE56......178 F4
　Blackfordby DE11......257 C2
　Derby, Boulton DE24......233 B5
　Derby, Chaddesden DE21......220 A7
　Glapwell NG19, S44......134 C6
　Killamarsh S21......60 B5
　Kirk Ireton DE6......176 B8
　Mayfield DE6......183 C8
Fieldon Cl DE6......202 F2
Field Rd DE7......208 F7
Field Rise DE23......231 C7
Field Row **5** DE56......178 F4
Fields Cres SK14......9 D6
Fields Farm Rd NG10......236 E5
Fields Gr SK14......9 D5
Fields La DE11......261 F6
Field St DE5......181 B8
Fields The DE4......154 D4
Fieldsway Dr DE21......205 E2
Field Terr DE5......169 D1
Field The DE75......194 A6
Field View
　Chesterfield S40......115 A7
　Clowne S80......80 F3
　Shuttlewood S44......98 F6
　South Normanton DE55......160 A7
　Swadlincote DE11......256 E5
Field View Cl
　Derby DE24......233 B5
　Westwood NG16......171 C4
Fieldview Pl S41......95 C6
Field Way DE11......255 F5
Fife St DE24......232 F8
Filbert Wlk DE73......245 A8
Filey Wlk **4** DE21......205 D1
Fincham Cl DE21......205 D1
Finch Cl DE11......256 F3
Finch Cres DE3......230 C8
Finchley Ave DE22......217 F6
FINDERN......230 D2
Findern Cl
　Belper DE56......179 B6
　Derby DE22......204 D1
Findern Cty Prim Sch
DE65......242 E8
Findern La
　Burnaston DE65......230 B4
　Willington DE65......242 B6
Findern St DE22......218 D5
Finley Way DE55......160 B4
Finmere Cl DE23......231 A8
Finney Cl DE12......262 E1
Finningley Dr DE22......204 F2
Finny La DE6......200 B5
Finsbury Ave DE22......218 B6
Finsley Wlk DE23......231 E6
Firbeck La S80......63 A1
Firestone DE4......178 D1
Firfield Ave DE72......235 E8
Firfield Prim Sch DE72......235 E7
Fir Pl S21......60 C5
Fir Rd S21......59 C2
Firs Ave
　Alfreton DE55......159 A5
　Hulland Ward DE6......175 F3
　Ripley DE5......169 D1

Firs Cres DE22......204 E4
Firs Estate Prim Sch
DE22......218 E3
Firs Gdns DE55......159 A4
Firs Par DE4......143 C5
Firs St NG10......236 A4
Fir St S43......78 B1
First Ave
　Branston DE14......253 E7
　Risley NG10......222 F5
Firs The DE6......173 C1
Firth Ct S43......77 D4
Firthwood Ave S18......57 D3
Firthwood Cl S18......57 D3
Firthwood Rd S18......57 D3
Fir Tree Ave DE55......146 C4
Fir Tree Dr DE73......244 A6
Firtree Gr DE21......206 B2
Firvale S26......61 E5
Firvale Rd S40......114 B8
Fisher Cl
　Chesterfield S40......114 F7
　Repton DE65......242 D2
Fisher Ct DE7......194 F4
Fisher La DE56......190 E4
Fishers Bridge SK22......25 D2
Fisher St DE24......232 E6
Fishpond La
　Egginton DE65......241 A5
　Tutbury DE13......239 C6
Fishponds Cl S42......115 A3
Fishponds Rd S13......44 C7
Fishponds Road W S13......44 C7
Fiskerton Way DE21......206 B1
Fitzalan St SK13......10 C1
Fitzherbert CE Prim Sch
DE6......162 A1
Fitzhubert Rd S2......44 A8
Fitzroy Rd S2......43 B6
Fitzwilliam Dr NG19......136 F2
Five Lamps Ct DE1......218 F6
Five Lamps Ho DE1......267 A5
Five Lands Rd DE15......254 F8
Five Trees Ave S17......56 A6
Five Trees Cl S17......56 A6
Five Trees Dr S17......56 A6
Flackets La DE6......225 B7
FLAGG......106 F6
Flagg La SK17......106 F7
Flagshaw La DE6......202 F4
Flake La DE7......208 L1
Flamstead Ave DE75......181 C4
Flamstead La DE5......180 E1
Flamstead Rd DE7......194 F1
Flamstead St DE24......232 E6
Flamsteed Cres S41......96 A6
FLASH......103 A3
Flash CE Prim Sch SK17......103 B3
Flash La DE4......128 A7
Flat La SK17......106 B8
Flat The DE56......191 F8
Flatts La NG16......171 D3
Flatts The DE6......165 B1
Flax Croft DE65......227 C1
FLAXHOLME......190 F1
Flaxholme Ave DE56......190 F1
Flaxpiece Rd S45......131 D3
Fleet Cres DE56......178 F3
Fleet Pk DE56......179 A3
Fleet St DE23......219 A2
Fleet The DE56......178 F2
Fletcher Ave S18......57 A1
Fletcher's Row DE5......169 F2
Fletcher St
　Heanor DE75......181 E2
　Long Eaton NG10......236 D8
　Ripley DE5......169 E2
Fletches The DE13......240 B1
Fleury Cl S14......43 E4
Fleury Cres S14......43 E4
Fleury Pl S14......43 E4
Fleury Rd S14......43 E4
Fleury Rise S14......43 E4
Flint Ave NG19......136 F1
Flint La DE4......142 B8
Flintson Ave S43......77 D4
Flint St DE24......232 E6
Flixton Rd NG16......195 F7
Flood St DE72......221 C4
Florence Ave NG10......223 F1
Florence Cl
　Chesterfield S40......114 F6
　Pleasley NG19......134 F4
Florence Ct
　Derby DE1......267 D2
　Ilkeston DE7......194 F1
Florence Dr DE6......224 C8
Florence Gladwin Cl
DE4......141 C6
Florence Rd
　Clay Cross S45......131 E4
　Wingerworth S42......114 E4
Florence Way SK14......9 D5
Florin Gdns NG10......236 B7
FLOURISH THE......207 D2
Flowery Leys La DE55......159 C3
Fly Hill DE45......109 D6
Foggs Entry DE4......165 F8
Foggs Hill DE4......127 C4
Folds La S43......45 F3
Folds Yd DE4......156 F2
Fold The S32......71 F4
Foljambe Ave S40......114 D8
Foljambe Rd
　Brimington S43......96 D4
　Chesterfield S40......266 A3
Folkestone Dr DE24......233 A5
Folly Rd DE22......205 B1

Fontwell Rd DE14......253 F7
FOOLOW......70 E6
Foolow Ave S40......266 A1
Foolow Ct S40......266 A1
Forbes Cl NG10......236 E5
Forbes Hole Nature
Reserve★ NG10......236 F5
FORD......58 E5
Ford Ave DE75......181 C4
Fordbridge La DE55......160 A7
Ford Cl
　Dronfield S18......56 F1
　Ripley DE5......180 C8
Ford Gr SK14......9 A4
Ford La
　Breadsall DE21......205 C5
　Derby DE22......205 B5
　Eckington S12, S21......58 E5
　Willington DE65......242 C5
Ford Rd S21......58 E4
Ford St
　Belper DE56......178 F4
　Burton upon Trent DE15......254 E7
　Derby DE1......267 A4
　Tupton S42......131 D8
Ford Way SK14......9 A4
Fordwells Cl DE23......231 A8
Fordyce Cl DE73......232 E1
FOREMARK......243 D2
Foremark Ave DE23......231 E8
Forest Ave SK17......85 C6
Forest Cl DE56......179 B5
Forest Ct S43......80 B6
Forest Dr S45......132 C2
Foresters Rd DE5......169 C2
Forester St DE1......267 B2
Forest La SK17......50 C2
Forest Lea DE12......262 A4
Forest School St DE13......240 C4
Forest View DE12......262 B4
Forge Cl DE65......242 D2
Forge Dr S40......266 B1
Forge La
　Burton upon Trent DE13......241 A2
　Killamarsh S21......60 B7
Forge Mill Pl DE56......191 A6
Forge Rd SK23......45 E7
Forge Steps DE56......191 A6
Forge Terr SK23......34 E1
Forge The
　Dronfield S18......57 A1
　Trowell NG9......209 B5
Forman Cl DE11......256 B4
Forman St DE22......267 A3
Forrester Ave DE72......245 F5
Forrester's La S18......57 C4
Forshaw Cl DE6......185 C8
Forth Ave S18......56 D2
Forties La LE65......257 F3
Forty Foot La DE73......252 F7
Forty Horse Cl DE5......170 A2
Forum Cl DE24......233 D5
Fosbrook Dr DE74......246 F4
Fosbrooke Dr NG10......236 D5
Fosse Cl DE72......221 C1
Fossett's Ave NG16......171 F7
Foss Rd DE55......228 E1
Foster Rd DE11......256 F2
FOSTON......226 D4
Foston Cl DE65......239 C8
Foston Dr S40......95 B5
Foundry Ct **1** SK22......33 C7
Foundry La DE56......190 F8
Foundry Street Ind Est **7**
S41......96 A8
Foundry The S41......266 C2
Fountains Cl DE22......205 A4
Fountains High Sch
DE13......240 C1
Fountains Prim Sch
DE13......240 D1
Fountain Sq
　Disley SK12......32 D6
　Tideswell SK17......69 C4
　Youlgreave DE45......125 B5
Fountain St SK17......85 B7
FOURLANE ENDS......158 C4
Four Lane Ends
　Darley Dale DE4......127 C1
　Swadlincote DE11......256 A6
Four Lanes SK14......9 A4
Fowler Ave DE21......220 D4
Fowler St
　Chesterfield S41......76 F2
　Derby DE22......218 E6
　Draycott DE72......235 B7
Foxbrook Cl
　Chesterfield S42......94 F5
　Derby DE23......231 A8
Foxbrook Ct S40......114 B8
Foxbrook Dr S40......114 B8
Fox Cl
　Burton upon Trent DE14......254 B8
　Derby DE24......231 D2
　Long Eaton NG10......236 D5
Foxcote Way S40......114 B8
Foxcroft Chase S21......60 C6
Foxcroft Dr S21......60 C5
Foxcroft Gr S21......60 C6
Foxdale Ave S12......44 B5
Foxdell Way DE73......233 A2
Foxes Wlk DE22......204 E4
Foxes Yd SK17......66 D1
Fox Field DE11......261 F8
Foxfields Dr DE21......205 E2

Foxglove Ave
　Burton upon Trent DE15......255 A8
　Donisthorpe DE12......262 E1
Foxglove Cl S44......97 A3
Foxglove Dr DE21......206 A3
Foxglove Gr NG19......136 F4
Foxglove Rd NG16......195 B8
FOX GREEN......100 F8
Foxhall La S10......42 F6
Foxholes La
　Kniveton DE6......174 B6
　Tansley DE4......144 A7
Fox La
　Holmesfield S18......74 B5
　Sheffield, Base Green S12......44 C3
　Sheffield, Lower Bradway
　S17......56 D6
Foxlands Ave DE22......204 F2
Fox Lane Ct S12......44 C4
Fox Lane View S12......44 C4
Foxlea SK13......16 F8
Foxley Ct DE21......206 A2
Foxley Oaks S41......77 B1
Foxley Rd DE7......194 F5
Fox Low Ave SK17......85 C4
Foxpark View DE55......147 E5
Fox Rd
　Castle Donington DE74......246 F4
　Whitwell S80......82 A6
Fox St DE1......267 C4
Foxstone Cl S43......97 D8
Foxton Cl DE7......194 C3
Foxwood Ave S12......44 B6
Foxwood Cl
　Chesterfield S41......115 D6
　Chesterfield, Sheepbridge
　S41......76 F1
Foxwood Dr S12......44 B6
Foxwood Gr S12......44 B5
Foxwood Ind Pk S41......76 F1
Foxwood Rd
　Chesterfield S41......76 F2
　Sheffield S12......44 B6
Foxwood Way S41......76 E2
Foyers Way S41......266 C3
Foyle Ave DE21......220 A4
Frain Gdns DE7......252 F2
Framingham Pl S2......43 D7
Framlingham Rd S2......43 D7
Frampton Gdns DE23......230 F6
Frances Ct ST14......196 A6
Frances Dr S42......114 E4
Frances St NG16......171 D1
Franchise St DE22......218 E4
Francis Cl S43......96 D7
Francis Ct NG16......171 B4
Francis St DE21......219 D6
Frank Bodicote Way
DE11......256 D4
Franklin Ave S80......81 F5
Franklin Cl DE15......248 B1
Franklin Cres S80......81 F5
Franklin Rd NG16......171 A4
Franklyn Dr
　Derby DE24......233 A6
　Staveley S43......78 F3
Franklyn Rd S40......95 E4
Frazer Cl DE21......220 E6
Frecheville St S43......78 D1
Frederic Ave DE75......193 F7
Frederick Ave
　Derby DE24......232 F6
　Ilkeston DE7......209 A5
Frederick Gent Sch
DE55......160 B5
Frederick Rd NG9......223 D7
Frederick St
　Alfreton DE55......159 A5
　Burton upon Trent DE15......254 E8
　Derby DE22......218 D6
　Grassmoor S42......115 E3
　Long Eaton NG10......236 F7
　Somercotes DE55......170 D5
　Woodville DE11......256 E3
FREEBIRCH......93 D6
Freebirch View S40......95 B7
Freeby Ave NG19......136 D5
Freehold St DE22......218 E4
Freeland Cl NG9......223 F3
Freeman Ave DE23......231 E6
Freesia Cl DE3......217 E1
Freetown SK13......17 C8
Fremantle Rd DE3......217 E3
French La DE21......191 F5
French St
　Derby DE23......218 E2
　Ilkeston DE7......209 A6
French Terr NG20......101 A2
Fresco Dr DE23......230 F7
Fresh Ct SK13......16 F7
Freshfield Cl SK6......15 B1
Freshfields Donkey Village★
SK17......48 D2
Freshwater Ho DE24......233 C7
Freshwaters S42......116 D1
Fretson Cl S2......44 D1
Fretson Gn S2......44 A8
Fretson Rd S2......44 A8
Fretson Rd S S2......44 A8
Freydon Way S44......97 A3
Friar Gate DE1......218 F5
Friar Gate Ct DE1......218 F5
Friar Gate House Sch
DE1......218 E6
Friar Gate Studios DE1......267 A3
Friar Gr SK17......85 C6
Friars Cl DE22......205 A2
Friars Ct DE7......208 C6

Friarsfield DE22......218 F8
Friar St NG10......236 D7
Friary Ave DE24......232 E6
Friary Croft DE11......256 A7
Friary St DE1......267 A3
FRIDEN......139 A6
Friden Cl SK17......139 A6
Friesland Dr NG10......222 F5
Friesland Sch NG10......222 F5
Frinton Cl S40......114 F7
Frisby Ave NG10......236 E6
FRITCHLEY......168 C7
Fritchley CE Prim Sch
DE56......168 B6
Fritchley Cl DE21......206 A1
Fritchley La DE56......168 A7
Frith Cl S12......44 B5
Frithhall La S42......94 C2
Frith Knoll Rd SK23......47 D7
Frith Rd S12......44 B5
Frith View SK23......47 A5
Frithwood Dr S18......57 C2
Frithwood La
　Creswell S80......100 F7
　Elmton S80......100 D7
Frizams La DE73......242 F7
FROGGATT......72 C5
Froggatt Cl
　Derby DE22......205 A5
　Staveley S43......97 C6
Froggett Cl DE55......170 D7
Front St DE56......168 B6
Front Terr DE55......145 F4
Frood Cl SK23......47 C7
Frost Ave NG16......182 A4
Frost Fields DE74......247 B4
Fryar Rd NG16......182 F4
Fulbrook Rd DE23......231 A8
Fulford Cl S40......114 C8
Fulham Rd DE22......218 A5
Fuller Dr S41......96 C6
Fullers Cl DE56......190 F8
Fulleylove Ct S44......99 B1
Full St DE1......267 B3
Fullwood Ave **4** DE7......194 E1
Fullwood Grange DE6......175 C3
Fullwood Ind Est NG17......148 F1
Fullwood St **6** DE7......194 E1
Fullwood Stile La S33......38 F6
Fulmar Cl
　Derby DE3......218 A3
　Mansfield NG19......136 F4
Fulwood Dr NG10......236 A7
Fulwood Head Rd S10......42 D7
Fulwood Ind Est NG17......160 F8
Fulwood La S10, S11......42 E5
Fulwood Road N NG17......148 F1
Fulwood Road S NG17......160 F8
Furlong Cl NG9......223 D8
Furlong La
　Alstonefield DE6......149 C4
　Atlow DE6......175 B7
Furnace Cl S42......115 E2
Furnace Hillock Way
S41......115 C5
Furnace Hill Rd S45......131 D5
Furnace La
　Barlow S18......75 F3
　Heanor DE75......181 D4
　Moira DE12......262 E3
Furnace Lane Ind Est
DE12......262 E3
Furnace Rd DE7......209 B6
Furnace Row DE55......170 F7
Furnall Ave DE45......90 A3
Furness Cl **2** SK13......17 F8
Furness Lodge Cl SK23......33 D4
FURNESS VALE......33 C3
Furness Vale Bsns Ctr
SK23......33 D4
Furness Vale Prim Sch
SK23......33 D3
Furness Vale Sta SK23......33 D4
Furniss Ave S17......55 D6
Furniss Mews S17......55 E6
Furrows Cl DE21......206 C3
Fyfield Rd DE15......254 E6
Fylde Cl NG9......223 F2

G

Gable Ct DE3......230 E8
Gables Cl S42......132 D8
Gables The
　Hilton DE65......228 D1
　6 Swadlincote DE11......255 E5
Gadley Cl SK17......84 F8
Gadley La SK17......84 F8
Gadsby Cl DE7......209 A4
Gadsby Rise DE56......168 C2
Gag La DE6......161 D6
Gainsborough Ave SK6......23 B8
Gainsborough Cl
　Derby DE21......206 B1
　Long Eaton NG10......236 E6
　Stapleford NG9......223 E6
Gainsborough Rd S18......75 C3
Gainsborough Way DE15......248 B3
Gairloch Cl DE24......231 D2
Gala Dr DE24......232 F2
Galahad Dr DE13......240 E2
Gallery La S42......113 D7
Gallery The **6** DE5......173 C2
Gallows Ind Est DE7......209 B6
GALLOWS INN......209 B6
Gallows Inn Cl DE7......209 A6
Gallowstree La DE6......184 C8

Galway Ave DE21 .... 220 B4
GAMESLEY 9 D1
Gamesley Com Prim Sch
SK13 .... 9 E2
Gander La S43 .... 80 B5
Gang La S44 .... 118 E5
Gannow Cl S21 .... 60 F7
Gapsick La S43, S80 ...... 81 B5
Garden Ave
Ilkeston DE7 .... 208 F5
New Houghton NG19 ...... 134 F7
Renishaw S21 .... 79 B7
Shirebrook NG20 .... 119 E4
Garden Cl S43 .... 77 D3
Garden Cres
Castle Donington DE74 ... 247 B3
South Normanton DE55 ... 159 F4
Gardeners Ct
Bolsover S44 .... 99 A2
Mansfield Woodhouse
NG19 .... 136 C3
Garden Rd NG16 .... 182 F3
Garden St
7 Broadbottom SK14 ..... 16 A8
Derby DE1 .... 267 A4
Gardens The
Heanor DE75 .... 181 C4
Ripley DE5 .... 180 D7
Gardner Pl ST14 .... 210 A1
Gardom Cl S18 .... 56 D1
Garfield Ave DE72 .... 235 A7
Garfield Cl
Derby DE23 .... 231 C6
Stapleford NG9 .... 209 E1
Garland Cl S20 .... 59 E7
Garland Croft S20 .... 59 E7
Garland Mount 15 S20 .... 59 E8
Garland Way S20 .... 59 E7
Garner La DE4, DE55 ..... 157 D2
Garnett Ave DE75 .... 181 F2
Garnham Cl DE55 .... 159 D2
Garrett Gn S45 .... 131 E3
Garrett La S45 .... 131 D2
Garrett Sq DE13 .... 240 C4
Garrick St DE24 .... 233 A7
Garry Cl DE24 .... 231 D2
Garsdale Ct DE24 .... 233 D6
Gartan Rd DE14 .... 254 A8
Garth Cres DE24 .... 233 B6
Garthorpe Ct 4 DE21 ... 205 F2
Garth Rd SK6 .... 23 A6
Garth Way S18 .... 56 F1
Garth Way Cl S18 .... 56 F1
Gartrice Gdns S20 .... 60 A5
Gartrice Gr S20 .... 60 A5
Gary Cl DE23 .... 231 D5
Gascoigne Dr DE21 ...... 220 D4
Gashouse La S20, S21 ..... 59 D5
Gaskell Ave DE23 .... 231 E7
Gasny Ave DE74 .... 247 B5
Gas St
Hollingworth SK14 .... 9 D5
Sandiacre NG10 .... 223 C6
Uttoxeter ST14 .... 210 C1
Gatcombe Cl
Burton upon Trent DE13 .. 240 D1
Derby DE21 .... 206 B2
Gatcombe Gr NG10 ...... 223 A3
Gate Brook Cl DE5 ...... 170 B1
Gatefield Cl S41 .... 95 C7
Gate Ho DE4 .... 165 F8
Gate Ho The S32 .... 72 D2
Gatehouse Dr DE4 ...... 165 F8
Gatehouse La S32 .... 40 E3
Gateland La S18 .... 75 E5
Gateway Christian Sch
DE7 .... 207 F2
Gauledge La SK17 .... 121 B6
Gaunt Cl
Killamarsh S21 .... 60 C6
Sheffield S14 .... 43 D3
Gaunt Dr S14 .... 43 D3
Gaunt Pl S14 .... 43 D4
Gaunt Rd S14 .... 43 D3
Gaunt Way S14 .... 43 D3
Gawain Gr DE13 .... 240 E2
Gawsworth Cl SK13 ...... 10 A5
Gayton Ave DE23 .... 231 D6
Gayton Com Jun Sch
DE23 .... 231 D6
Gayton Rd NE7 .... 194 D1
Gayton Thorpe Cl DE23 .. 230 F7
Geary La DE15 .... 248 F2
Geer La S12 .... 58 D5
Gelderd Pl S18 .... 76 A8
Gema Cl DE22 .... 205 A4
Genista Cl DE15 .... 255 A8
GENTSHILL 131 E2
Gentshill Ave S45 .... 131 E2
George Ave NG10 .... 223 F1
George Cres DE55 .... 170 C6
George Dutton Ind Pk
DE6 .... 185 E8
George Holmes Bsns Pk
DE11 .... 256 A4
George Holmes Way
DE11 .... 256 A3
George Inn Ct S80 .... 81 F6
George Percival Pl S45 .. 131 A4
George Rd DE4 .... 143 C6
George Spencer Foundation
Sch & Tech Coll NG9 ... 223 E5
George St
Alfreton DE55 .... 159 A4
Ashbourne DE6 .... 185 B8
Belper DE56 .... 178 F4
Brimington S43 .... 96 E8
7 Buxton SK17 .... 85 B8
George St *continued*
Chesterfield S41 .... 76 F2
Compstall SK6 .... 15 B2
Derby DE1 .... 267 A3
Glossop SK13 .... 17 C8
Langley Mill NG16 ...... 182 B3
Mansfield Woodhouse
NG19 .... 136 D3
Melbourne DE73 .... 252 A7
North Wingfield S42 .... 131 E7
Pinxton NG16 .... 160 C4
Somercotes DE55 .... 170 D8
Somercotes, Riddings
DE55 .... 170 D6
South Normanton DE55 .. 159 F5
Swadlincote DE11 ...... 256 A1
Whaley Bridge SK23 ..... 45 E7
Whaley Thorns NG20 .... 101 A2
Georgina Ct DE74 .... 247 B4
Gerard Cl
Chesterfield S40 .... 95 C1
Derby DE21 .... 220 F6
15 Sheffield S8 .... 43 B6
Gerard Ct DE1 .... 267 A2
Gerard Gr DE65 .... 229 C4
Gerard St
Derby DE1 .... 267 A2
Sheffield S8 .... 43 B6
Gertrude Rd
Derby DE21 .... 220 A8
Draycott DE72 .... 235 A7
Gervase Ave S8 .... 56 E6
Gervase Dr S8 .... 56 E6
Gervase Pl S8 .... 56 E6
Gervase Rd S8 .... 56 E6
Gervase Wlk 2 S8 .... 56 E6
Ghyll Cl DE24 .... 220 A1
Gibb Ct S43 .... 77 D4
Gibb La
Marple SK6 .... 23 E5
Sudbury DE6 .... 225 E5
Gibbons Ave NG9 ...... 223 D6
Gibbons Dr S14 .... 43 E2
Gibbons Way S14 .... 43 E2
Gibbons Wlk S14 .... 43 E2
Gibb St NG10 .... 236 E7
Gibfield La
Belper DE56 .... 178 F2
Kirk Ireton DE6 .... 175 F7
Gifford Rd S8 .... 43 A7
Gilbert Ave S40 .... 114 D8
Gilbert Cl DE21 .... 220 D4
Gilbert Cres DE56 .... 190 E2
Gilbert Heathcote Inf Sch 9
S41 .... 96 A8
Gilbert St DE24 .... 233 B6
Gilderdale Way DE21 .... 206 B3
Gillamoor Ct DE24 ...... 233 D6
Gilleyfield Ave S17 ...... 55 E7
Gilliver Gdns DE72 ...... 235 A7
Gill La DE4 .... 127 C4
Gillott St DE75 .... 194 A8
Gill's La S42 .... 115 E2
GILTBROOK 195 C8
Giltbrook Cres NG16 .... 195 C8
Giltbrook Ret Pk NG16 .. 195 C7
Gilt Hill NG16 .... 195 D7
Gilthill Prim Sch NG16 .. 195 D7
Giltway NG16 .... 195 C7
Gimson Cl DE7 .... 194 C3
Gin Close Way NG16 .... 195 C6
Gin La S45 .... 144 F8
Gipsyhill La S80 .... 81 B8
Gipsy La
Alstonefield DE6 .... 149 F4
Apperknowle S18 .... 58 A1
Chesterfield S41 .... 77 B1
Gird La SK6 .... 15 E1
Girdon Cl SK17 .... 84 F6
Gisborne Cl DE3 .... 217 E3
Gisborne Cres DE22 ..... 204 F4
Gisborne Gn DE1 .... 218 E6
Gisbourne Cl S43 .... 78 F1
Gisbourne Dr SK23 ...... 47 B5
Glade Cl S40 .... 95 E5
Glade Croft S12 .... 44 A4
Glade Lea S12 .... 44 A4
Glade The
Buxton SK17 .... 85 A8
Chesterfield S40 .... 95 D3
Gladstone Ave
Blackwell DE55 .... 147 E1
Heanor DE75 .... 181 F2
Gladstone Cl
Chellaston DE73 .... 232 F3
Glossop SK13 .... 17 D8
Gladstone Dr NG16 ..... 182 E7
Gladstone Rd
Alfreton DE55 .... 158 F3
Chesterfield S40 .... 266 A4
Derby DE21 .... 220 E5
Gladstone St W DE7 ..... 208 F7
Gladstone St
Derby DE23 .... 218 E1
Glossop SK13 .... 17 D8
Hadfield SK13 .... 10 A4
Heanor DE75 .... 181 E2
Langley Mill NG16 ..... 182 C3
Long Eaton NG10 ...... 236 D6
Mansfield Woodhouse
NG19 .... 136 C2
South Normanton DE55 .. 160 B6
Gladstone Terr NG19 .... 136 C2
Gladwin Gdns S40 ...... 114 D8
Gladys Buxton Com Ed Ctr
S18 .... 57 C2
Glaisdale Nook DE24 .... 233 D6
Glamis Cl DE21 .... 206 B2
Glamorgan Way DE11 ... 255 F1
GLAPWELL 134 C8
Glapwell La S44 .... 118 B2
GLASSHOUSE COMMON ... 77 D5
Glasshouse Hill DE5 .... 181 B8
Glasshouse La S43 .... 77 D4
Glastonbury Cl NG19 ... 136 D4
Glastonbury Rd DE24 ... 233 C7
Glaven Cl NG19 .... 136 D2
Gleadless Ave S12 .... 44 A4
Gleadless Bank S12 ...... 43 F4
Gleadless Comm S12 ..... 44 A5
Gleadless Ct S2 .... 43 B6
Gleadless Dr S12 .... 43 F4
Gleadless Mount S12 .... 44 A3
Gleadless Prim Sch S12 .. 44 B5
Gleadless Rd S12, S14, S2 . 43 D5
Gleadless Rise
1 Sheffield, Gleadless
Townend S12 .... 44 A3
Sheffield S12 .... 43 F5
GLEADLESS VALLEY 43 E3
Gleadless Valley Nature
Reserve★ S8 .... 43 C4
Gleadless View
2 Sheffield, Gleadless
Townend S12 .... 44 A3
Sheffield S12 .... 43 F5
Gleadsmoss La DE21 .... 206 A1
Glebe Ave
Great Longstone DE45 .... 90 A3
Harthill S26 .... 61 E7
Pinxton NG16 .... 160 D3
Ripley DE5 .... 169 C2
Smalley DE7 .... 192 F6
Glebe Cl
Coton in the Elms DE12 .. 260 C3
Doveridge DE6 .... 224 B8
Holmewood S42 .... 132 D8
Rolleston DE13 .... 240 A4
South Normanton DE55 .. 160 A5
Thurvaston DE6 .... 201 E1
Glebe Cres
Ilkeston DE7 .... 209 A7
Stanley DE7 .... 207 B6
Glebe Ct DE45 .... 90 A3
Glebe Farm Cl S26 .... 61 E7
Glebe Field Cl DE4 ..... 156 F1
Glebe Gdns S42 .... 131 F5
Glebe Jun Sch DE55 .... 160 A5
Glebe Pk S32 .... 71 D5
Glebe Rd SK17 .... 85 D8
Glebe Rise DE23 .... 218 D1
Glebe St DE11 .... 256 B3
Glebe The
Awsworth NG16 .... 195 B4
Chesterfield S41 .... 77 A2
Rosliston DE12 .... 260 C6
Glebe View
Barlborough S43 .... 80 B6
5 Forest Town NG19 .... 136 E1
Glebe Way The S41 ...... 77 A2
Gledhill Cl S18 .... 57 A1
Glen Ave DE56 .... 191 C7
Glenavon Cl S43 .... 77 D5
Glenbrook Hill SK13 ..... 10 C2
Glen Cl DE55 .... 148 A3
Glencoe Way S40 .... 95 B4
Glencroft Cl DE14 ...... 254 B7
Glencroft Dr DE24 ...... 231 D3
Glendale Dr DE21 ...... 220 F5
Glendevon Way DE73 .... 232 E2
Glendon Rd
Derby DE24 .... 231 D3
Ilkeston DE7 .... 208 C4
Glendon St DE7 .... 193 A1
Gleneagles Cl
Chesterfield S40 .... 114 C8
Derby DE3 .... 217 F2
Gleneagles Dr DE13 .... 240 C1
Glenfield Ave NG16 ..... 195 D7
Glenfield Cres
Chesterfield S41 .... 96 A7
Derby DE3 .... 217 C2
Glenfield Rd NG10 ..... 236 D5
Glengarry Way DE24 .... 231 E4
Glenholme Dr S13 .... 44 E7
Glenholme Pl S13 .... 44 F7
Glenholme Rd S13 .... 44 F7
Glenholme Way S13 ..... 44 E7
Glenmoor Rd SK17 ...... 66 D1
Glenmore Cl S43 .... 97 B5
Glenmore Croft S12 ..... 44 C6
Glenmore Dr DE24 ..... 231 D3
Glenmoy Cl DE23 ...... 231 D7
Glenn Way DE72 .... 234 E1
Glenorchy Ct DE21 ..... 206 B3
Glen Park Cl DE73 ..... 244 F8
Glen Rd DE4 .... 156 D1
Glenshee Gdns DE73 .... 232 E2
Glenthorn Cl S81 .... 63 F7
Glenthorne Cl S40 .... 95 C2
Glen Vale S18 .... 56 D1
Glen View DE56 .... 178 F2
Glen View Rd S8 .... 56 E8
Glen Vine DE5 .... 170 A1
Glenwood Rd DE73 ..... 245 A8
Glinton Ave DE55 ...... 147 E1
GLOSSOP 10 B2
Glossop Brook Bsns Pk
SK13 .... 10 B1
Glossop Brook Rd SK13 .. 10 B1
Glossop Central Sta SK13 10 C1
Glossopdale Com Coll
SK13 .... 10 C2
Glossopdale Com Coll
(Annexe) SK13 .... 10 A4
Glossop L Ctr SK13 ...... 10 D1
Glossop Pool SK13 .... 10 C2
Glossop Rd
Broadbottom SK13 .... 16 D7
Gamesley SK13 .... 9 E1
Hayfield SK22 .... 25 C6
Marple SK6 .... 15 D3
Glossop's Croft S41 ...... 77 B2
Glossop St DE24 .... 232 B8
Gloster St DE24 .... 219 E2
Gloucester Ave
Chesterfield S41 .... 95 F5
Sandiacre NG10 .... 223 A4
Gloucester Rd S41 .... 95 F5
Gloucester Way
Burton upon Trent DE15 .. 248 B1
4 Glossop SK13 .... 17 F8
Glover Rd
Castle Donington DE74 ... 247 B4
Sheffield, Highfield S8 .... 43 A7
Sheffield, Totley Rise S17 .. 55 F5
Gloves La
Alfreton DE55 .... 147 E2
Blackwell DE55 .... 147 D2
Glumangate S40 .... 266 B3
Go Ape!★ SK17 .... 84 F6
Goathland Rd DE24 ..... 231 D2
Goatscliffe Cotts S32 ..... 72 C7
Goatscliff Farm La S32 ... 72 B7
Goddard La
Glossop SK13 .... 10 A6
New Mills SK22 .... 24 E7
Goddard Rd SK13 .... 10 A4
Godfrey Dr DE7 .... 208 D6
GODFREYHOLE 165 B8
Godfrey St DE75 .... 181 E1
Godkin Dr NG16 .... 182 A4
Godward Rd SK22 .... 33 B8
Gold Cl DE4 .... 142 B8
Goldcrest Dr DE21 ..... 220 F6
Goldcrest Ho S41 .... 77 B3
GOLDEN VALLEY 170 D3
Golden Valley
Horsley Woodhouse DE7 .. 192 B6
Somercotes DE55 ...... 170 D3
Golden Valley Light Rly★
DE5 .... 170 B4
Golders Green Wlk DE22 218 A6
Goldhill DE4 .... 144 A4
Golding Ho DE4 .... 143 C6
Gold La DE22 .... 217 E8
Goldstone Ct DE21 ..... 220 E4
Golf Cl DE23 .... 218 A1
Golf Club Rd DE7 ...... 209 B1
Golf La DE56 .... 190 E5
Golf Terr SK17 .... 66 D1
Gomersal La S18 .... 57 A1
Goodale St DE23 .... 219 A1
Goodman Cl NG16 ..... 195 C8
Goodman Ct S44 .... 97 A3
Goodrington Rd DE21 ... 206 C3
Goodsmoor Rd DE23,
DE24 .... 231 E5
Goodsmoor Rd Ind Est
DE24 .... 231 E5
Goods Rd DE56 .... 178 F2
Goods Yd DE56 .... 178 F1
Goodwin Cl NG10 ...... 223 A6
Goodwin Dr NG16 ...... 195 E6
Goodwin Rd 6 S8 .... 43 A6
Goodwin's La DE56 ..... 178 C1
Goodwood Cl DE13 ..... 240 C1
Goodwood Cres DE7 .... 208 D4
Goodwood Dr
Beeston NG9 .... 223 F2
Derby DE24 .... 233 C6
Gooker La DE55 .... 158 F3
Goole Ave DE7 .... 208 D5
GOOSEGREEN 146 D3
Goose Green La DE55 .. 146 D3
Goose Green View DE45 .. 91 F5
Goosehill S33 .... 38 B2
Goose La DE5 .... 181 C8
Gordon Ave S8 .... 43 A2
Gordon Cres DE55 ..... 160 B4
Gordondale Rd NG19 ... 136 B1
Gordon Rd
Borrowash DE72 .... 221 B1
Derby DE23 .... 218 F3
Swanwick DE55 .... 169 F8
Tideswell SK17 .... 69 C3
Gordon St DE7 .... 195 A1
Gordon Works 12 S2 ..... 43 A6
Gore La S33 .... 51 A8
Gorman Cl S41 .... 95 E8
Gorse Bank S44 .... 116 F2
Gorsebank La DE45 ...... 91 F7
Gorse Cl
Derby DE23 .... 231 B6
Eastwood NG16 .... 195 B8
Long Eaton NG10 ...... 223 B2
Gorse Dr S21 .... 60 D5
Gorsehill Gr DE23 ..... 231 A7
Gorse La
Bradley DE6 .... 175 B3
Moira DE12 .... 262 E6
Sheffield S10 .... 42 F7
Gorse Ridge Dr DE45 .... 91 E6
Gorses
Alderwasley DE56 ..... 178 C8
Idridgehay DE6 .... 176 D5
Gorse Valley Rd S41 .... 115 E7
Gorse Valley Way S41 ... 115 E7
Gorse Way SK13 .... 17 F7
GORSEYBANK 166 A7
Gorsey Bank DE4 ...... 165 F7
Gorsey Brigg S18 .... 56 D1
Gorseybrigg Prim Sch
S18 .... 56 D1
Gorsey Brow SK14 .... 9 A1
Gorsey Cl DE56 .... 178 E6
Gorsey Intakes SK14 ..... 16 A8
Gorsey La
Kirk Ireton DE6 .... 165 A1
Netherseal DE12 .... 265 A7
GORSEY LEYS 262 C4
Gorsty Leys DE65 ...... 230 D1
Gosber Rd S21 .... 59 E3
Gosber St S21 .... 59 D3
Goseley Ave DE11 ..... 257 A4
Goseley Cres DE11 ..... 257 A4
Gosforth Ave NE7 ...... 194 E6
Gosforth Cl S18 .... 56 F1
Gosforth Cres 3 S18 ..... 56 F1
Gosforth Dr S18 .... 75 D8
Gosforth Gn S18 .... 56 F1
Gosforth La S18 .... 56 F1
Gosforth Rd DE24 ...... 232 E8
GOSFORTH VALLEY 56 E2
Goshawk Rd DE7 .... 209 A3
GOTHAM 139 D1
Gower Cres S40 .... 95 C5
Gower St DE1 .... 267 B2
GOWHOLE 33 E4
Goyt Forest Walks★ SK11. 83 E7
Goytlands SK17 .... 84 F6
Goyt Pl SK23 .... 45 E7
Goyt Rd
Disley SK12 .... 32 D5
Horwich End SK23 ...... 45 E6
New Mills SK22 .... 33 D6
Goyt Side Rd S40 .... 95 E2
Goyt's La SK17 .... 65 A3
Goyt Valley Ind Est SK23 .. 33 D4
Goyt Valley Walks★ SK17 . 64 E4
Goyt View SK22 .... 33 B6
Grace Cres DE75 ...... 181 F2
Grafham Cl DE73 ...... 233 A2
Grafton Rd DE15 ...... 248 B1
Grafton St DE23 .... 218 E2
Grafton Terr DE4 ...... 127 A5
Graham Cl DE14 ...... 254 C7
Graham Dr SK12 .... 32 C6
Graham St DE7 .... 208 F7
Grammer St DE5 ...... 181 A4
Grampian Cres S40 ...... 95 B4
Grampian Prim Sch
DE24 .... 231 D4
Grampian Way
Derby DE24 .... 231 E4
Long Eaton NG10 ...... 236 A8
Granary Cl S40 .... 95 A8
Granby Ave SK23 .... 34 E1
Granby Cl S45 .... 132 C2
Granby Croft DE45 ..... 109 D5
Granby Jun Sch DE7 .... 194 E3
Granby Rd
Bakewell DE45 .... 109 D5
Bradwell S33 .... 50 F7
Buxton SK17 .... 85 D7
Granby St DE7 .... 194 E2
Grandfield St DE75 .... 181 C4
Grandstand Rd DE21 ... 219 C6
Grange Ave
Breaston DE72 .... 235 D8
Chapel-en-le-Frith SK23 ... 47 B5
Derby DE23 .... 231 E7
Dronfield S18 .... 56 E1
Hulland Ward DE6 ..... 175 F3
Grange Cl
Melbourne DE73 ...... 252 B8
Somercotes DE55 ...... 159 F2
Ticknall DE73 .... 251 A4
Grange Ct DE65 .... 241 B5
Grange Dale DE4 ...... 153 C8
Grange Dr
Castle Donington DE74 ... 247 A3
Long Eaton NG10 ...... 236 F8
Grange Farm Cl DE74 ... 247 D5
Grange Gate DE22 ..... 267 A1
Grange La
Barlow S18 .... 75 B1
Darley Dale DE4 .... 127 F1
Ible DE4 .... 153 D7
GRANGEMILL 153 D8
Grangemill Pl S43 .... 97 C8
Grangeover Way DE22 .. 218 D4
Grange Park Ave
Calow S43 .... 96 F4
Chapel-en-le-Frith SK23 ... 47 B5
Grange Park Rd SK23 .... 47 B5
Grange Pk NG10 .... 236 F8
Grange Prim Sch NG10 .. 236 F8
Grange Rd
Buxton SK17 .... 85 C7
Derby DE24 .... 233 B6
Long Eaton NG10 ...... 236 F8
Pilsley S45 .... 132 C2
Swadlincote DE11 ..... 255 E5
Uttoxeter ST14 .... 210 A1
Grange Road S SK14 ..... 15 A8
Grange St
Alfreton DE55 .... 159 A3
Derby DE23 .... 219 B2
Grange The
Brimington S43 .... 96 D8
Chesterfield S42 .... 94 F4
Smalley DE75 .... 193 C8
South Normanton DE55 .. 160 A4
Grange View NG16 ..... 182 F3
Grange Wlk S42 .... 115 E2
Grangewood Ave 3 DE7 208 F7
Grangewood Ct S40 .... 114 F7
Grangewood Dr DE56 ... 191 A7

Grangewood Gdns DE12 . 261 D6
Grangewood Rd S40 . . . . . 114 F7
Grangewood Zoo★ DE12 261 E2
Gransden Way S40. . . . . . . 114 C8
Grant Ave DE21 . . . . 220 B5
Grantham Ave DE21 . . . . . 205 E1
Grantham Cl NG16 . . . . . . 195 C7
Granville Ave NG10 . . . . . . 223 D1
Granville Cl
  Chesterfield S41 . . . . 115 D8
  Duffield DE56. . . . . 190 E3
  Hatton DE65 . . . . 227 D1
Granville Com Sch DE11. 256 E4
Granville Ct DE11 . . . . 256 C4
Granville St
  Derby DE1 . . . . 218 E5
  Woodville DE11 . . . . 256 E3
Graphite Way
  Glossop SK13. . . . . .9 F6
  Hollingworth SK13. . . . . . . .9 F6
Grasmere Ave
  Clay Cross S45. . . . . 131 B3
  Derby DE21 . . . . 220 E6
Grasmere Cl
  Burton upon Trent DE15 . 248 B1
  Chesterfield S41 . . . . 95 D7
Grasmere Cres DE24 . . . . 231 E4
Grasmere Ct **1** NG10 . . . 223 B2
Grasmere Rd
  Dronfield S18. . . . . 56 D1
  Long Eaton NG10. . . . . . . 223 B4
Grasmere St **2** NG10 . . . 223 C5
Grasscroft Cl **3** S40. . . . . 95 D6
Grasscroft Mobile Home Pk
  S43. . . . . 77 D5
Grassdale View S12. . . . . . 44 F3
GRASSHILL 115 E4
GRASSMOOR 115 F3
Grassmoor Cl S12. . . . . . . 43 F5
Grassmoor Cres SK13 . . . . . 9 D2
Grassmoor Ctry Pk★ S42,
  S41. . . . . 116 A4
Grassmoor Prim Sch
  S42. . . . . 115 F2
Grass St DE7. . . . . 194 E3
Grassthorpe Cl DE21 . . . . 206 B1
Grassthorpe Rd S12. . . . . . 44 B4
Grassy Ct DE3 . . . . 230 A7
Grassy La DE65 . . . . 230 A7
Gratton Ct S43. . . . . 78 F3
Gratton La
  Ashbourne DE6 . . . . 149 E5
  Elton DE45 . . . . 140 C7
Gravelly Bank Mews
  DE6 . . . . 199 D5
Gravel Pit Cotts DE65 . . . 229 B1
Gravel Pit Hill DE65 . . . . . 249 E7
Gravel Pit La DE21 . . . . . . 220 E4
Graves Park Animal Farm★
  S8 . . . . 43 B1
Graves Tennis & L Ctr S8 . 57 B7
Graves Trust Homes
  Sheffield, Common Side
    S12. . . . . 44 A5
  Sheffield, Greenhill S8. . . . 56 F8
  Sheffield, Little Norton S8. . 57 A8
Graycar Bsns Pk DE13. . . 253 B2
Gray Fallow DE55 . . . . . . 160 B4
Grayling St DE23 . . . . 219 B2
Grays Cl DE74. . . . . 247 B3
Grayshott Wlk S40 . . . . . . 114 F8
Gray St
  Clowne S43 . . . . 80 F4
  Sheffield, Mosborough S20 . 59 C7
Grayston Ct S43. . . . . 23 B7
Grayswood Cl DE55 . . . . . 170 A7
Great Common Cl S43. . . . 80 B6
Great Croft S18. . . . . 56 D2
GREAT CUBLEY 198 F1
GREAT HUCKLOW 70 B8
Great Hucklow Prim Sch
  SK17. . . . . 51 B1
GREAT LONGSTONE 90 B4
Great Northern Cl DE7 . 194 E2
Great Northern Cotts
  NG19 . . . . 135 A5
Great Northern Point
  DE22 . . . . 218 F4
Great Northern Rd
  Derby DE1 . . . . 218 F5
  Eastwood NG16. . . . . 182 D2
Greatorex Ave DE24 . . . . 232 E5
GREAT WILNE. 235 C2
Greaves La DE45 . . . . 108 F8
Greaves St
  Ripley DE5 . . . . 169 E2
  Shirland DE55 . . . . 146 E1
Greave Way S43 . . . . 96 C8
Greenacre Ave DE75 . . . . 182 A3
Greenacre Pk DE12 . . . . . 260 C3
Greenacres DE23 . . . . 231 B8
Greenacres Cl S18 . . . . 76 C7
Greenacres Dr
  South Normanton DE55. . 160 B6
  Uttoxeter ST14 . . . . 210 A2
Greenacre The DE6 . . . . . 184 F7
Green Ave DE73. . . . . 233 A1
Greenaway Dr S44 . . . . . . 118 A3
Greenaway La DE4 . . . . . . 127 E1
Greenbank
  Derby DE21 . . . . 220 D4
  Hollingworth SK13. . . . . . . .9 F5
Green Bank SK13 . . . . 16 F7
Greenbank Dr S40 . . . . 95 C4
Green Bank L Ctr DE11. . 256 B4

Greenbank Rd SK6 . . . . . . 15 B1
Greenburn Cl DE23. . . . . 231 C6
Green Chase S21 . . . . 59 C3
Green Cl
  Curbar S32. . . . . 72 E2
  Matlock DE4. . . . . 143 B6
  Newton DE55. . . . . 148 A3
  Renishaw S21 . . . . 79 B8
  Staveley S43 . . . . 97 C6
  Unstone Green S18 . . . . . . 76 E6
  Willington DE65 . . . . 242 A6
Green Cres NG16 . . . . 171 E6
Green Cross S18. . . . . 57 B2
Greendale Ave S42. . . . . . 113 E8
Greendale Ct S18 . . . . 57 B2
Greendale Sh Ctr S18. . . . . 57 B2
Greendale The DE55 . . . . 157 D8
GREEN FAIRFIELD 67 C2
Green Farm Cl S40. . . . . . . 95 C6
Green Farm Rd NG16. . . . 171 D6
Greenfield Ave S80 . . . . . . 82 C6
Greenfield Cl
  New Mills SK22 . . . . 33 A8
  Sheffield S8 . . . . 56 F7
Greenfield Dr
  Linton DE12 . . . . 261 C6
  Sheffield S8 . . . . 56 F7
Greenfield Ho SK13 . . . . . 10 A6
Greenfield Rd S8 . . . . 56 F7
Greenfields
  Aldercar NG16. . . . . 182 A4
  Denstone ST14 . . . . 196 D6
  Eckington S21 . . . . 59 C3
  Fritchley DE56. . . . . 168 B7
Greenfields Ave DE23 . . . 231 B8
Greenfield St SK13 . . . . . . 10 A6
Greenfinch Cl DE21 . . . . . 220 F6
Greengate Cl S40 . . . . 95 C2
Green Glen S40. . . . . 95 C2
Greenhall Rd S21 . . . . 59 C3
Greenhead S33 . . . . 40 B4
Greenhead Cres SK17 . . . 138 C2
Greenhead Pk S33 . . . . 40 B4
GREENHILL 56 F7
Green Hill DE4 . . . . 154 E1
Greenhill Ave
  Ripley DE5 . . . . 180 E8
  Sheffield S8 . . . . 56 F8
Greenhill La S8 . . . . 170 C6
Greenhill Lane Ind Est
  DE55. . . . . 170 B5
Greenhill Main Rd S8 . . . . 56 F7
GREENHILLOCKS 180 E7
Greenhill Parkway S8 . . . . 56 D6
Greenhill Prim Sch S8 . . . . 56 F7
Greenhills Rd NG16 . . . . . 182 F3
Greenhill Wlk S12 . . . . 32 E6
Greenholme Pk NG19 . . . 136 E6
Greenhouse La S10 . . . . . . 42 F5
Green Inf Sch The DE55 . 160 A6
Green La
  Alsop en le Dale DE6. . . . 150 C2
  Bakewell DE45. . . . . 108 C3
  Barrow upon Trent DE73 . 244 A5
  Belper DE56. . . . . 178 F4
  Bonsall DE4 . . . . 153 F8
  Breedon on the Hill DE73 . 252 C2
  Burnaston DE65. . . . . 230 A4
  Buxton SK17 . . . . 85 A6
  Buxton, Water Swallows
    SK17. . . . . 67 C2
  Chelmorton SK17. . . . . . . 106 D8
  Chesterfield S41 . . . . 96 D4
  Chinley SK23 . . . . 34 E2
  Clifton DE6. . . . . 184 E7
  Compstall SK14 . . . . 15 B8
  Creswell S80 . . . . 82 C5
  Cutthorpe S42 . . . . 94 E7
  Darley Dale DE4 . . . . 127 B3
  Derby, Alvaston DE24 . . . 233 C8
  Derby DE1 . . . . 267 B2
  Disley SK12 . . . . 32 D4
  Dronfield S18. . . . . 57 B2
  Glossop, Brookfield SK13 . . .9 F4
  Glossop SK13. . . . . 16 F8
  Hognaston DE6 . . . . 164 B2
  Hollingworth SK14. . . . . . . .9 D6
  Ilkeston DE7 . . . . 209 A7
  Killamarsh S21 . . . . 60 C3
  Mansfield NG19. . . . . 135 A2
  Marchington ST14 . . . . . . 225 A2
  Ockbrook DE72 . . . . 221 C5
  Overseal DE12. . . . . 261 F4
  Pilsley S45. . . . . 132 C3
  Pleasley S44 . . . . 134 D8
  Roston DE6 . . . . 197 F8
  Shirebrook NG19, NG20 . . 119 C2
  Tansley DE4 . . . . 144 A5
  Tupton S42. . . . . 115 D1
  Tutbury DE13 . . . . 239 C5
  Weston Underwood DE6 . . 188 F2
  Wilson DE73 . . . . 252 E5
Greenland Ave DE22 . . . . 218 B5
Greenland Cl S42. . . . . 132 A7
Green Lands DE11 . . . . . . 256 B7
Green Lea S18. . . . . 56 C2
Green Leas DE72. . . . . 246 A8
Greenmount Cl DE23 . . . . 231 A6
Greenmount St DE11. . . . 255 C7
Green Oak Ave S17 . . . . . . 55 E4
Green Oak Cres S17. . . . . . 55 E4
Green Oak Dr S17. . . . . 55 E4
Green Oak Gr S17. . . . . 55 E4
Green Oak Rd S17 . . . . 55 E4
Green Park Ave SK23. . . . . 47 C6
Green Pastures S17. . . . . . 55 E7
Green Pk DE22. . . . . 218 A6
Green Rd The DE6 . . . . . . 173 C3

Greens Ct DE7 . . . . 194 D1
Greenshall La SK12 . . . . . . 32 F5
Greenshank Rd NG20. . . . 120 D4
GREENSIDE. 58 C3
Greenside NG16 . . . . 171 D6
Greenside Ave S41. . . . . . . 96 A7
Greenside Cl
  Barlborough S43 . . . . 80 C4
  Donisthorpe DE12 . . . . . . 262 E1
  Long Eaton NG10. . . . . . . 236 E7
Greenside Ct DE3 . . . . 217 C2
Greenside View DE7 . . . . . 192 F6
Greens La NG16. . . . . 195 F6
Greensmith Cl S18. . . . . . . 248 C3
Greensquare Rd NG16. . . 160 E2
Green St
  Barton in Fabis NG11 . . . . 237 F5
  Chesterfield S41 . . . . 77 A2
Green The
  Alfreton DE55 . . . . 159 B3
  Aston-on-Trent DE72 . . . . 246 B8
  Bamford S33 . . . . 40 B4
  Belper DE56. . . . . 179 A5
  Birchover DE4 . . . . 126 B1
  Brackenfield DE55 . . . . . . 145 D2
  Bradwell S33 . . . . 51 B6
  Brailsford DE6 . . . . 201 E7
  Breedon on the Hill DE73 . 252 E2
  Burton upon Trent DE13 . . 240 E1
  Castle Donington DE74. . . 247 A3
  Chesterfield S41 . . . . 115 D7
  Clowne S43 . . . . 80 E4
  Crich DE4. . . . . 156 D1
  Curbar S32. . . . . 72 D1
  Derby DE22 . . . . 204 D1
  Derby, Markeaton DE3. . . . 217 D1
  Draycott DE72 . . . . 235 A7
  Findern DE65 . . . . 230 D1
  Fritchley DE56. . . . . 168 B6
  Froggatt S32 . . . . 72 D5
  Glapwell S44 . . . . 134 B8
  Glossop SK13. . . . . 17 A7
  Hardstoft S45 . . . . 133 A3
  Kirk Langley DE6 . . . . 202 C1
  Mansfield Woodhouse
    NG19. . . . . 136 A5
  Marple SK6 . . . . 23 A3
  Matlock DE4. . . . . 154 D5
  Middleton DE4 . . . . 154 D5
  North Wingfield S42 . . . . . 132 A7
  Sheffield S17. . . . . 55 D4
  Stanton in Peak DE4 . . . . . 126 C5
  Sutton in Ashfield NG17 . . 148 F1
  Swanwick DE55. . . . . 169 E7
  Ticknall DE73 . . . . 250 F7
  Tissington DE6 . . . . 162 B5
  Weston-on-Trent DE72 . . . 245 F5
  Willington DE65 . . . . 242 A6
Greenvale Cl DE15 . . . . . . 254 F8
Greenview DE4 . . . . 153 A1
Greenville Croft DE73 . . . 232 E1
Green Water Mdw SK14 . . . 9 D5
Greenway
  Ashbourne DE6 . . . . 173 C3
  Brassington DE4 . . . . 153 A1
  Burton upon Trent DE15 . . 248 A4
  Hulland Ward DE6 . . . . . . 175 F3
  Whitwell S80 . . . . 81 F6
  Wingerworth S42. . . . . . . 115 C2
Green Way DE65 . . . . 230 D2
Greenway Cl
  Borrowash DE72 . . . . 221 B3
  Derby DE72 . . . . 221 B3
Greenway Croft DE4 . . . . 154 F1
Greenway Dr DE23 . . . . . . 218 A1
Greenways S40 . . . . 114 C8
Greenway The
  Derby DE72 . . . . 233 D5
  Sandiacre NG10. . . . . 223 B6
  Sheffield S8 . . . . 56 F8
GREENWICH 169 F2
Greenwich Ave DE11 . . . . 255 E1
Greenwich Ct **12** S43 . . . . . 78 B3
Greenwich Drive N DE22 218 C6
Greenwich Drive S DE22. 218 B5
Greenwood Ave
  Derby DE21 . . . . 219 F8
  Ilkeston DE7 . . . . 209 A7
  Mansfield Woodhouse
    NG19. . . . . 136 B4
  Sutton in Ashfield NG17 . . 148 F2
Greenwood Cl DE24. . . . . 232 D5
Greenwood Rd DE15 . . . . 254 E8
Greer La S44 . . . . 118 D1
Gregg Ave DE75. . . . . 181 F2
Greggs Ave SK23. . . . . 46 F5
Gregory Ave
  Aldercar NG16. . . . . 182 A4
  Breaston DE72. . . . . 235 C8
Gregory Cl
  Brimington S43 . . . . 96 D8
  Stapleford NG9 . . . . 223 F8
Gregory Ct **10** S8 . . . . 43 B6
Gregory La S43 . . . . 77 D1
Gregory Rd S8. . . . . 43 A6
Gregory St DE7 . . . . 208 E8
Gregorys Way DE56 . . . . . 179 C5
Gregory Wlk DE23 . . . . . . 230 E7
Gregson Cl DE11. . . . . 256 B5
Grendon Cl DE56. . . . . . . 179 B6
Grenfell Ave DE23. . . . . . . 231 E6
Grenville Dr
  Ilkeston DE7 . . . . 194 F3
  Stapleford NG9 . . . . 223 E8
Grenvoir Dr DE5 . . . . 170 A1
Gresham Rd DE24 . . . . . . 232 C8
Gresley Rd
  Ilkeston DE7 . . . . 194 F1

Gresley Rd continued
  Sheffield S8. . . . . 56 E5
Gresley Wlk S8 . . . . 56 E5
Gresley Woodlands
  DE11 . . . . 256 A2
Gresley Wood Rd
  Swadlincote DE11 . . . . . . 255 F2
  Woodville DE11 . . . . 256 A2
Gretton Ave DE13 . . . . . . 240 E1
Gretton Rd SK17 . . . . 85 D8
Greyfriars Cl **4** DE75. . . . 181 F1
Greysich La DE65 . . . . 249 F2
Grey St DE22 . . . . 267 A2
Greystones St S26 . . . . . . 61 D6
Griffe Field Prim Sch
  DE23. . . . . 231 A6
GRIFFE GRANGE. 153 D4
Griffin Cl
  Derby DE24 . . . . 232 F7
  New Mills SK22 . . . . 33 D6
  Staveley S43 . . . . 97 E8
Griffon Rd DE7 . . . . 208 F4
Griggs Gdns DE4. . . . . . . 165 F7
Grimshaw Ave DE24. . . . . 233 B7
GRINDLEFORD 72 C7
Grindleford Gdns **16** SK13 . .9 E2
Grindleford Gr **13** SK13. . . . .9 E2
Grindleford Lea **14** SK13 . . . .9 E2
Grindleford Prim Sch S32 72 C8
Grindleford Sta S32 . . . . . . 53 D2
Grindleford Wlk **15** SK13 . . . .9 E2
GRINDLOW 70 C8
Grindlow Ave S40. . . . . . . 266 A1
Grindlow Cl S14 . . . . 43 C6
Grindlow Dr S14 . . . . 43 C6
Grindlow Rd DE21 . . . . . . 220 A8
Grindon Cl S40 . . . . 95 C5
GRINDSBROOK BOOTH . . 37 C8
Grindslow Ave DE7 . . . . . 207 E8
Grinlow Cl SK17 . . . . 85 C3
Grin Low Rd SK17. . . . . . . 85 B3
Grinton Wlk S40 . . . . 114 F8
Grisedale Road E DE45 . . . 90 A4
Grisedale Road W DE45 . . 90 A4
Grisedale Wlk S18 . . . . 56 E1
Gritstone Rd DE4 . . . . . . 143 D7
Grizedale Cl DE15. . . . . . . 248 B1
Groombridge Cres DE23. 231 A6
Groome Ave DE75. . . . . . . 181 C4
Grosvenor Ave
  Breaston DE72. . . . . 235 F8
  Long Eaton NG10. . . . . . . 236 A4
Grosvenor Dr DE23. . . . . . 231 A6
Grosvenor Rd
  Eastwood NG16. . . . . 182 F2
  Marple SK6. . . . . 23 A7
  Ripley DE5 . . . . 169 D2
Grosvenor St DE24 . . . . . 232 C8
Grove Ave S17. . . . . 55 D5
Grovebury Dr DE23. . . . . . 231 C5
Grove Cl DE72 . . . . 233 F4
Grove Cotts NG19. . . . . . . 135 A4
Grove Ct
  Elvaston DE72 . . . . 233 F1
  Ripley DE5 . . . . 180 F8
Grove Gdns S43. . . . . 96 F5
Grove Ho DE23. . . . . 267 B1
Grove House Ct S17. . . . . . 55 E5
Grove La
  Buxton SK17 . . . . 85 C6
  Darley Dale DE4 . . . . 127 E1
  Old Brampton S42. . . . . . . 94 B4
  Somersal Herbert DE6. . . . 211 F2
Grove Mews NG16 . . . . . . 182 E1
Grove Par **2** SK17 . . . . 85 B8
Grove Pk DE65. . . . . 229 B2
Grove Pl DE45 . . . . 125 B5
Grove Rd
  Calow S43 . . . . 96 E5
  Chesterfield S41 . . . . 96 A7
  Sheffield, Totley Brook S17 . 55 F5
Groves Nook DE73 . . . . . . 232 E1
Grove St
  Chesterfield S41 . . . . 115 C8
  Derby DE23 . . . . 267 B1
  Mansfield Woodhouse
    NG19. . . . . 136 B3
  New Mills SK22 . . . . 33 B7
  Swadlincote DE11 . . . . . . 256 B4
Grove The
  Breaston DE72. . . . . 235 F8
  Derby DE3 . . . . 217 E2
  Glossop SK13. . . . . .9 F4
  Poolsbrook S43 . . . . 98 A8
  Sheffield, Hillfoot S17 . . . . 55 D5
  Tatenhill S43 . . . . 253 A8
Grove Way
  Calow S43 . . . . 96 F5
  Mansfield Woodhouse
    NG19. . . . . 136 B3
Grundy Ave NG16 . . . . . . 171 D7
Grundy Nook S80 . . . . 82 A5
Grundy Rd S45. . . . . 131 C3
Grunmore Dr DE13. . . . . . 240 E2
Guernsey Rd S2. . . . . 43 A7
Guide Post DE56. . . . . 168 C2
Guildford Ave
  Chesterfield S40 . . . . 114 D8
  Mansfield Woodhouse
    NG19. . . . . 136 C6
  Sheffield S2 . . . . 43 D8
  Swadlincote DE11 . . . . . . 256 E6
Guildford Cl S45 . . . . 131 C3
Guildford La S45. . . . . 131 C3
Guildford Rise S2. . . . . 43 E8
Guildford View S2 . . . . 43 E7
Guildford Wlk S2 . . . . 43 E8

Guildhall Cl DE11 . . . . . . 255 E2
Guildhall Dr NG16. . . . . . . 160 F2
Guildhall Theatre★ DE1 . 267 B3
Guinea Cl NG10. . . . . 236 A7
Guinevere Ave DE13. . . . . 240 E2
Gulliver's Kingdom★
  DE4. . . . . 155 A8
Gunby Hill DE12 . . . . 261 F2
Gunhills La DE56. . . . . 189 C6
Gun La DE56. . . . . 168 C2
Gun Rd SK6. . . . . 16 C2
Gurney Ave DE23 . . . . 231 D6
Gutersloh Ct NG9 . . . . . . 223 F8
GUTTER THE 179 C4
Guy Cl NG9 . . . . 223 E6
Gypsy La
  Creswell S80 . . . . 81 C5
  Draycott DE72 . . . . 221 E1

H

Hackney La S18. . . . . 75 F1
Hackney Rd DE4 . . . . 143 A7
Hackthorn Rd **4** S8. . . . . . 43 A3
Haddon Ave S43 . . . . 81 A4
Haddon Cl
  Alfreton DE55 . . . . 158 F3
  Bullbridge DE56. . . . . 168 B6
  Chesterfield S40 . . . . 95 C1
  Derby DE22 . . . . 204 D3
  Dronfield S18. . . . . 57 B2
  Heanor DE75 . . . . 181 C2
  West Hallam DE7. . . . . . . 207 E8
Haddon Ct DE6 . . . . 185 D8
Haddon Dr
  Bakewell DE45. . . . . 109 E4
  Derby DE22 . . . . 204 D3
  Derby, Markeaton DE3. . . . 217 D3
  Derby, Spondon DE21 . . . 220 F4
  Little Eaton DE21. . . . . . . 191 C2
Haddon Gn **31** SK13 . . . . . . 9 D2
Haddon Hall★ DE45. . . . . 110 B1
Haddon Ho DE45. . . . . . . 109 E3
Haddon Lea **32** SK13 . . . . . 9 D2
Haddon Mews **30** SK13. . . . 9 D2
Haddon Nurseries DE7 . . 194 E3
Haddon Pl
  Shirebrook NG20. . . . . . . 119 E6
  Staveley S43 . . . . 97 D8
Haddon Rd
  Bakewell DE45. . . . . 109 F3
  Buxton SK17 . . . . 85 D8
  North Wingfield S42 . . . . . 132 A8
Haddon St
  Derby DE23 . . . . 218 E1
  Ilkeston DE7 . . . . 194 E3
  Tibshelf DE55. . . . . 148 A6
Haddon Way NG10 . . . . . 235 F4
Hade La SK17. . . . . 106 E7
Hades La SK17 . . . . 88 B3
HADFIELD 10 A5
Hadfield Etherow Ind Est
  SK13. . . . . .9 F4
Hadfield Ind Est SK13 . . . . .9 F5
Hadfield Inf Sch SK13 . . . . .9 F5
Hadfield Pl SK13 . . . . 17 C8
Hadfield Rd
  Glossop SK13. . . . . .9 F4
  Hadfield SK13 . . . . 10 A5
Hadfields Ave SK14 . . . . . . .9 D5
Hadfield Sq **1** SK13. . . . . . 17 C8
Hadfield St SK13 . . . . 17 C8
Hadfield Sta SK13. . . . . . . 10 A5
Hadleigh Cl **2** NG9 . . . . . 223 E2
Hadley La DE56. . . . . 186 E8
Hadley St DE7 . . . . 209 A5
Hadstock Cl NG10. . . . . . . 223 B4
HADY 96 D2
Hady Cres S41. . . . . 96 C3
Hady Hill S41 . . . . 96 C2
Hady La S41 . . . . 96 E1
Hady Prim Sch S41 . . . . . . 96 D2
Hag Bank La SK12. . . . . . . 32 D7
Hagg La
  Dale Abbey DE7 . . . . 207 A4
  Turnditch DE56 . . . . 177 C1
Hague Ave S21. . . . . 79 B8
HAGUE BAR. 32 F8
Hague Bar Prim Sch SK22 32 E8
Hague Bar Rd SK22 . . . . . 33 A7
Hague Fold Rd SK22 . . . . . 32 F8
Hague La S21, S43. . . . . . . 79 B6
Hague Rd SK14 . . . . 16 A8
Hague St SK13. . . . . 17 D7
Haig Hill Farm Hamlet
  S42. . . . . 115 E1
Haigh Memorial Homes
  S8. . . . . 57 A7
Haigh Moor Rd S13 . . . . . . 44 F8
Haigh Moor Wlk S13 . . . . . 44 F8
Haig St DE24 . . . . 232 F8
Hailsham Cl DE3. . . . . 217 D3
Haines Cl DE24 . . . . 231 F4
Halcyon App S42. . . . . 115 C2
Halcyon Cl S12 . . . . 44 F3
Haldane Cl S80 . . . . 81 E2
Haldane Cres S44. . . . . 98 F2
HALES GREEN 199 B7
Halesworth Cl S40 . . . . . . 114 B8
Half Acre La S18. . . . . 76 D8
Half Croft S43 . . . . 96 F7
Halfmoon La DE6. . . . . . . 165 B3
HALFWAY 59 F7
Halfway Cl S20. . . . . 59 E7
Halfway Ctr S20. . . . . 59 E7
Halfway Dr S20. . . . . 59 E7
Halfway Gdns S20. . . . . . . 59 E7

Halfway Inf Sch S20 ..... 59 F7
Halfway Jun Sch S20 .. 59 E6
Halifax Cl
  Derby DE21 ....205 C1
  Hilton DE65 ....228 E2
Hallam Ct
  Dronfield S18...........76 A8
  Ilkeston DE7 ....194 F3
HALLAM FIELDS.........209 A4
Hallam Fields DE74 ....247 B2
Hallam Fields Jun Sch
  DE7..................208 F5
Hallam Fields Rd DE7 ..209 B4
HALLAM MOORS........41 E8
Hallamway NG19.......136 C1
Hallam Way DE7 ....207 D8
Hall Bank
  Buxton SK17 ....85 B7
  Hartington SK17 ......137 E5
Hall Cl
  Cutthorpe S42 ....94 E8
  Dronfield S18..........56 C2
  Mottram in Longdendale
   SK14.................9 A5
Hallcliff La S42 ....93 F1
Hall Cotts DE6 ....175 D2
Hallcroft Ave S18 ......56 C2
Hallcroft Rd 2 DE7 ...208 F8
Hall Ct DE7............207 E7
Halldale La DE4........127 E3
Hall Dale View DE4 ....127 D3
Hall Dr
  Doveridge DE6........211 A1
  Hanbury DE13 ....238 A4
  Mottram in Longdendale
   SK14.................9 A5
  Sandiacre NG10.......223 B6
Hall Dyke DE21 ....220 D5
Hall End La DE45......108 F8
Hall Farm S42 ....132 D8
Hall Farm Cl
  Castle Donington DE74 ..247 B3
  Chesterfield S41 ......115 D7
  Swadlincote DE11 .....256 C4
  Whaley Bridge SK23 ...45 D8
Hall Farm Ct DE7 .....222 F8
Hall Farm Gdns S42...132 D8
Hall Farm Rd
  Duffield DE56.........190 E2
  Swadlincote DE11 .....256 C4
Hall Farm Way DE7 ...192 F6
Hallfield Cl S42........115 A4
Hallfieldgate La DE55..146 D1
Hallfield Rd DE55......148 A3
Hallfields Rd DE15.....255 C4
Hallfields Rise DE55...146 C1
Hallflash La S44.......116 A8
Hallgate DE21 ....206 C3
Hallgate La S45........132 B2
Hall Gate View S33......51 A8
Hall Gdns
  Hemington DE74 ......247 D4
  Marchington ST14.....224 E2
HALL GREEN...........171 E8
Hall Green Ave DE7 ...240 F2
Hall Grounds DE13 ....240 A4
HALLHILL..............46 F7
Hallington Dr DE75....181 D1
Hall La
  Ashbourne DE6 ....173 C2
  Brailsford DE6.........202 A6
  Brinsley NG16.........182 D6
  Donisthorpe DE12 ....265 E8
  Doveridge DE6........224 B8
  Litton SK17 ....69 E3
  Mayfield DE6 ....183 A7
  Nether Heage DE56....168 C3
  Newton DE55.........148 A3
  Shirley DE6 ....200 D8
  Staveley S43 ....78 D3
  Willington DE65.......242 B5
Hall Leys La DE73 .....245 D1
Hall Meadow Croft S20..59 F5
Hall Meadow Dr S20 ....59 F5
Hall Meadow Gr S20 ....59 F5
Hall Meadow Rd SK13...10 D2
Hallmoor Rd DE4 ......127 C4
HALLOWES.............76 C8
Hallowes Ct S18 ....57 B1
Hallowes Dr S18........76 B8
Hallowes La S18 ....76 B8
Hallowes Rise S18......76 C8
Hall Park DE23 ....218 B1
Hall Pk DE73..........244 A5
Hall Rd
  Aldercar NG16........182 C4
  Brimington S43 ....96 E7
  Marchington ST14.....224 E2
  Rolleston DE13 ....239 F4
Hall Rise
  2 Ashbourne DE6 ....173 D3
  Darley Dale DE4.......127 D3
Hall's Ct SK13 ....10 C1
Hallside Ct S20 ....59 D6
Halls La NG16..........195 A8
Halls Rd NG9..........223 D6
Hall's Row 1 S40......95 D2
Hall St
  Alfreton DE55 ....159 A4
  Derby DE24 ....233 A7
  New Mills SK22 ....33 B8
  Swadlincote DE11 .....256 A2
Hallsteads SK17........47 F1
Hallsteads Cl SK17.....47 F1
Hallsteads The DE6....163 B2
Hall Terr S45 ....131 D3
Hall The
  Glossop SK13...........17 A7

Hall The continued
  Middleton DE4........154 D5
Hall View S41...........95 E6
Hall Wlk S42 ....115 D1
Hallworth Wlk S21.......58 E2
Hallyburton Cl S2.......43 C6
Hallyburton Dr S2 ......43 C6
Hallyburton Rd S2 .....43 C6
Halstead Cl NG19 .....136 F2
Halstock Dr DE24 .....233 C8
Halton Cl S41...........76 E1
Hamble Cl NG19 ......136 D3
Hambledon Cl S40 .....95 C5
Hambledon Dr DE24...231 D2
Hambleton Ave S42 ...131 F6
Hambleton Ct
  Ashbourne DE6 ....185 C8
  2 Long Eaton NG10 ..223 A1
Hambleton Rise NG19 ..136 F1
Hamble Way DE65 ....228 C1
Hamblin Cres DE24 ...231 F4
Hamill Cl S42..........131 F7
Hamilton Cl
  Beeston NG9 ....223 F2
  Derby DE3 ....217 F3
Hamilton Dr
  Market Warsop NG20 ..120 F4
  Swadlincote DE11 .....256 C5
Hamilton Fields DE15 ..248 A3
Hamilton Gr DE11......256 D5
Hamilton Rd
  Burton upon Trent DE15 ..248 A2
  Derby DE23 ....218 F2
  Derby, Spondon DE21 ..220 F6
  Long Eaton NG10 .....223 D1
Hamilton Terr DE65 ...242 B6
Hamlet Ct DE73........232 E1
Hamlet La DE55........160 A5
Hamlet The
  Heanor DE75 ....181 E3
  South Normanton DE55..160 A4
Hammer Leys DE55 ...160 C4
HAMMERSMITH.......169 D4
Hammersmith S43 ....169 D4
Hammersmith Meadows
  Nature Reserve★ DE5..169 D3
Hammersmith Sta★ S43 169 D4
Hammonds Ct 6 DE4 ..165 F8
Hampden Ho DE15.....254 E6
Hampden St
  Derby DE23 ....232 A8
  Eastwood NG16.......195 B8
  Langley Mill NG16.....182 B3
Hampshire Cl SK13......17 F8
Hampshire Ct NG16 ...171 B4
Hampshire Dr NG10....223 B5
Hampshire Rd DE21....219 C8
Hampstead Dr DE22...218 A6
Hampton Cl
  Beeston NG9 ....223 E3
  Derby DE21 ....220 F5
  West Hallam DE7......207 D8
Hampton Ct 4 DE75 ..181 D2
Hampton St S41 ....115 D7
HANBURY.............238 A5
Hanbury Ave DE65 ....227 D1
Hanbury Cl
  Chesterfield S40 ......95 A5
  Dronfield S18..........56 F1
Hanbury Hill DE13 ....238 A5
Hanbury Rd DE21 .....219 F6
Hanchurch Cl DE15 ...248 A4
Handby Ct S41.........115 D8
Handby St S41.........115 D8
Handel Mews DE6......185 D8
Handel St DE24 ....232 C8
Handford Cl DE22 .....218 D6
Handford St DE22 .....218 D5
HANDLEY.............145 F8
Handley Ct S43 ....77 D4
Handley La
  Ashover S45 ....145 F8
  Clay Cross S45........131 A1
  Pilsley DE45...........91 B1
Handley Rd S43.........77 D5
Handsacre Cl DE11....255 F3
Hand's Rd DE75........182 A1
Handyside St DE1......267 B4
Hangar Hill S80........82 A6
Hanger Bank DE72 ....246 B8
HANGINGBRIDGE.....184 F8
Hanley Cl SK12 ....32 D5
Hannage Way DE4 ....165 F7
Hanover Sq DE22 .....218 A6
Hansard Gate DE21 ...267 D3
Hanslynn DE72.........233 F4
Hanston Ct S43........77 D4
HANSTUBBIN..........171 F5
Hanstubbin Rd NG16..171 F5
Hanwell Way DE22 ....218 B6
Harbin Rd DE12.......253 D1
Harboro Cl DE6........185 B8
Harby Ave NG19 ......136 D5
Harcourt Cl
  Chesterfield S41 ......115 C7
  Ilkeston DE7 ....194 D1
Harcourt Pl DE74......247 B4
Harcourt Rd DE14.....253 D8
Harcourt St S41 ....267 B2
Hardacre Cl DE73......252 A8
Hardcastle Mews SK23 ..47 B6
HARDHURST..........76 C6
Hardhurst Rd
  Derby DE24 ....233 B5
  Unstone Green S18....76 B6
Hardie Ave DE55 ......160 A6
Hardie Pl S43..........97 D8
Hardie St S21..........59 D3

Harding's Cl DE6.......165 B1
Harding's La SK17 ....138 A5
Hard La S26............61 E8
Hard Meadow La S45 ..130 B2
HARDLEY HILL 215 C2
Hardstaff Homes The
  Eastwood NG16.......195 C8
  Mansfield Woodhouse
   NG19................136 B3
HARDSTOFT..........133 A3
Hardstoft Rd S45......132 E2
Hardwick Ave
  Chesterfield S43 ......77 D3
  Derby DE22 ....204 D3
  Glapwell S44 ....134 B8
  Shirebrook NG20......119 E4
  West Hallam DE7......207 E8
Hardwick Cl
  Blackwell DE55 ....147 D1
  Clowne S43 ....81 A4
  Dronfield S18..........57 C2
  Holmewood S42.......132 E8
  Ripley DE5...........169 C3
Hardwick Ct
  Holmewood S42.......132 E8
  Long Eaton NG10.....235 F4
  South Normanton DE55..160 C6
  5 Staveley S43........78 E2
Hardwick Dr
  Arkwright Town S44....97 D3
  Derby DE3 ....217 F2
Hardwick Gdns 5 SK17..85 B7
Hardwick Hall & Park★
  S44 ....133 E4
Hardwick La S45.......129 C6
Hardwick Mount SK17...85 C7
Hardwick Old Hall★ S44.133 E4
Hardwick Park Farm★
  NG17.................134 A3
Hardwick Pl DE7.......208 C5
Hardwick Prim Sch 1
  DE23.................219 A1
Hardwick Square E SK17.85 C7
Hardwick Square N SK17.85 C7
Hardwick Square S SK17.85 B7
Hardwick Square W SK17.85 B7
Hardwick St
  Buxton SK17 ....85 B8
  Chesterfield S41 ......266 B4
  Derby DE24 ....232 C8
  Langwith NG20 ....119 F8
  Shirebrook NG20......120 A4
  Tibshelf DE55.........148 A7
Hardwick's Yd S41......95 E2
Hardwick View Rd S42..132 F8
Hardy Barn DE75.......194 A7
Hardy Cl
  Kimberley NG16.......195 F7
  Long Eaton NG10.....236 D6
Hardy Cres DE5 ....181 B8
Hardy La SK17 ....69 C4
Hardy St
  Alfreton DE55 ....158 F5
  Kimberley NG16.......195 F7
Harebell Cl
  Derby DE21 ....206 A3
  Swadlincote DE11 .....256 E4
HAREHILL.............213 A3
Harehill Cres S42 .....114 D4
Harehill Cl S40 ....114 F7
Harehill Rd S40 ....114 F7
Harepit Cl DE24.......233 A5
Harewood Ave DE55...169 F8
Harewood Cl
  Belper DE56..........179 D5
  2 Sandiacre NG10....223 B4
Harewood Cres S42 ...131 B6
Harewood Lo SK14.....16 A8
Harewood Rd
  Derby DE22 ....204 D3
  Holymoorside S42.....114 F8
Hargate Hill La SK13...16 E7
Hargate Rd
  Burton upon Trent DE15..248 C1
  Buxton SK17 ....84 F6
HARGATEWALL........68 B3
Hargrave Ave DE72....221 C5
Hargreaves Cl DE23 ..231 A6
Hargreaves Ct 5 DE7..208 F7
Harlaxton Dr NG10....237 A8
Harlech Cl
  Derby DE21 ....221 A5
  Ilkeston DE7 ....194 C3
Harlequin Ct NG16 ...182 D3
Harlesden Ave DE22...218 A7
HARLESTHORPE.......80 E5
Harlesthorpe Ave S43..80 F5
Harlesthorpe La S43...80 E5
Harley's Ct DE12......262 C4
Harlow Cl
  Derby DE24 ....232 F4
  Mansfield Woodhouse
   NG19................136 C6
Harlow Ct DE7........207 D7
Harold Ave NG16......182 B4
Harold Ct DE23 ....219 B2
Harperhill Cl S40 .....114 F7
Harpole Cl DE55 ......169 F8
Harport Dr S45 ....131 E2
Harpswell Cl DE22 ....204 C2
Harpur Ave
  Derby DE23 ....231 B8
  Ticknall DE73.........251 A4
Harpur Crewe Cotts DE6 ..149 D3
HARPUR HILL.........85 C3

Harpur Hill Bsns Pk SK17..85 B2
Harpur Hill Prim Sch
  SK17.................85 C4
Harpur Hill Rd SK17....85 C4
Harrier Rd DE56 ......179 C5
Harrier Way DE24 ....231 E3
Harriet St DE23 ....219 A3
Harriett St NG9 ....223 D7
Harriet Tubman Ho
  DE23.................218 F1
Harrimans Dr DE72....235 F8
Harringay Gdns DE22..218 C6
Harrington Ave DE72..221 C2
Harrington Jun Sch
  NG10.................223 B8
Harrington Rd
  Derby DE23 ....218 C1
  10 Sheffield S2 ....43 A8
Harrington St
  Derby, Allenton DE24...232 E6
  Derby, Normanton DE23 ..232 A8
  Draycott DE72........235 B7
  Long Eaton NG10.....236 B5
Harris Ave DE5 ....169 C2
Harris Cl DE5 ....169 C1
Harrison Cl DE14......254 B8
Harrison Dr DE4 ......154 F1
Harrison La
  Sheffield S10 ....42 F7
  Tibshelf DE55.........147 F6
Harrison Rd NG9......223 D8
Harrison St DE22......218 E3
Harrison Way DE4 ....127 A6
Harris Rd SK17........85 C3
Harrogate Cres DE21..205 C1
Harrop La S10.........42 F6
Harrots La SK17.......137 D6
Harrow Dr
  Burton upon Trent DE14..254 C8
  Ilkeston DE7 ....209 A4
Harrow Rd DE11.......256 B7
Harrow St DE24.......219 E2
Hart Ave NG10........223 A6
Hartfield Cl S41........115 B7
Hartford Cl S8.........43 A3
Hartford Rd S8 ....43 A3
HARTHILL.............61 F6
Harthill Field Rd S26...62 A3
Harthill La S45 ....61 E1
Harthill Prim Sch S26..61 E5
Harthill Rd
  Sheffield S13 ....44 B7
  Thorpe Salvin S80.....62 D7
HARTINGTON.........137 D5
Hartington CE Prim Sch
  SK17.................137 D5
Hartington Cl DE7 ....207 E8
Hartington Ct
  Clowne S43 ....81 A4
  Dronfield S18..........57 B2
Hartington Dr
  Chinley SK23 ....34 E1
  Creswell S80 ....81 C1
Hartington Gdns 11 SK17..85 B7
Hartington Ind Est S43..78 E4
Hartington Pl DE7 ....194 E5
Hartington Rd
  Buxton SK17 ....85 B7
  Chesterfield S41 ......96 C2
  Dronfield S18..........57 B2
Hartington St
  Derby DE1, DE23 .....267 B1
  Langwith NG20 ....119 F8
Hartington View S43...78 F4
Hartington Way DE7 ..217 D2
Hartland Ct 21 S41....95 F8
Hartland Dr DE23 .....231 E6
Hartland Way S41......77 A1
Hart Lea 1 NG10 .....223 B5
Hartley St S2..........43 A7
Hartopp Ave S2........43 C6
Hartopp Cl S2..........43 C6
Hartopp Dr S2.........43 D6
Hartopp Rd S2........43 D6
Hartshay Cl DE7 ......194 F5
Hartshay Hill DE5.....169 C2
Hartshill Rd DE11.....257 A6
HARTSHORNE.........257 A6
Hartshorne CE Prim Sch
  DE11.................257 B6
Hartshorne Rd
  Derby DE23 ....231 C5
  Repton DE65 ....249 E2
  Woodville DE11.......256 F3
Hartside Cl 16 S40 .....95 D5
Hartside Gdns 1 NG10..236 A8
Hartside Way DE75....182 B1
Hartwood Dr NG9.....209 D1
Harvester Cl DE5......169 C2
Harvest Hill DE11 .....256 B7
Harvest Way
  2 Chesterfield S42....95 A5
  Derby DE21 ....206 C2
Harvey Clough Mews S8..43 B3
Harvey Clough Rd S8...43 B3
Harvey Croft NG9 .....209 C4
Harvey Ct S44 ....98 F2
Harvey Pl ST14 ....210 B1
Harvey Rd
  Burton upon Trent DE14..254 A8
  Castle Donington DE74..247 B2
  Chesterfield S41 ......96 C2
  Derby DE24 ....232 E6
Harwich Rd S2 ....43 F8
Harwood Ave DE14....253 F8
Harwood Cl S2 ....43 A8
Harwood St 2 S2......43 A8
Hasgill Cl DE21 ....206 C3

Haskeys Cl DE22 ......204 C2
Haslam Cres S8........56 E6
Haslam Ct
  Bolsover S44 ....98 F2
  Chesterfield S41 ......266 B4
Haslam Pl DE56.......179 C1
Haslam's La DE21, DE22..205 B1
HASLAND.............115 D7
HASLAND GREEN.....115 C7
Hasland Hall Com Sch
  S41 ....115 D7
Hasland Inf Sch S41...115 C8
Hasland Jun Sch S41..115 D7
Hasland Rd S41.......115 C8
Haslemere Ct DE23 ...219 B2
Haslemere Rd NG10 ..236 B8
Haslin Rd SK17........85 D2
Hassall Rd DE55 ......227 D1
Hassock Lane N DE75..194 B3
Hassock Lane S DE7,
  DE75.................194 C6
Hassocky La S44, S42...116 B6
HASSOP..............90 F5
Hassop Cl
  Chesterfield S41 ......95 C6
  Dronfield S18..........57 C2
Hassop Rd
  Calver S32 ....72 B1
  Derby DE21 ....220 A8
  Hassop DE45 ....90 D1
  Staveley S43 ....78 F3
Hastilar Cl S2..........44 B8
Hastilar Cl S2..........44 B8
Hastilar Road S S13....44 C7
Hastings Cl
  Breedon on the Hill
   DE73................252 E2
  Chesterfield S41 ......95 D6
Hastings Rd
  Buxton SK17 ....85 C4
  Swadlincote DE11 .....256 B3
Hastings St DE23......219 A1
Hasting St DE74.......247 B2
Haston Dr DE15.......170 D8
Hatchmere Cl DE21 ...206 A1
Hatfield Ave NG10 ....223 B4
Hatfield Rd DE24......232 F5
Hathaway Cl S42......131 B6
Hathern Cl
  Calow S43 ....96 F4
  Derby DE23 ....231 E5
  Long Eaton NG10.....236 D5
HATHERSAGE........53 B7
Hathersage Ave
  Derby DE23 ....231 E8
  Long Eaton NG10.....235 D5
Hathersage Cres SK13...9 E2
Hathersage Dr
  Glossop SK13..........17 F8
  Somercotes DE55.....170 B7
Hathersage Pk S32 ....53 A7
Hathersage Rd
  Bamford S32, S33......40 B1
  Sheffield S11, S17.....54 D6
Hathersage Sta S32....53 A7
HATTON..............239 D8
Hatton Cl S18..........75 D8
Hatton Crofts NG10 ...236 C5
Hatton Ct DE73 ....252 A7
Hatton Dr S40 ....95 B5
Haulton Dr DE74......247 A4
HAUNTON.............263 B2
Havelock Rd DE23.....232 A8
Havelock St
  Ilkeston DE7 ....208 F7
  Ripley DE5...........169 E2
Haven Baulk Ave DE23..230 E2
Haven Baulk La DE23...230 E7
Haven Ct DE24........233 D6
Havenwood Gr DE23...231 C5
Havercroft Terr S21....60 B7
Hawfield La DE15......248 E4
Hawke St DE22 ....218 C5
Hawk Green Rd SK6....23 A3
Hawkhill Rd S32 ....71 D6
Hawkinge Ho 13 S41...95 D5
Hawking La S44 ....133 A7
Hawkins Ct DE7........194 F4
Hawkins Dr DE56......168 B3
Hawk Rd S42 ....33 E8
Hawksdale Cl DE73....233 A2
Hawk's Dr DE15.......248 D3
Hawkshead Ave
  Derby DE21 ....205 D1
  Dronfield S18..........56 E1
Hawkshead Fold SK13...10 E3
Hawkshead Rd SK13 ...10 E3
Hawksley Ave S40 .....95 E4
Hawksley Dr
  Darley Dale DE4.......127 C4
  Rolleston DE13 ....240 B4
Hawksway S21.........59 B3
Hawkswood Cl DE4....143 C6
Hawley St S18 ....58 A1
Hawthorn Ave
  Breaston DE72........235 F8
  Derby DE24 ....233 A7
  Mastin Moor S43......79 C4
  Nethersael DE12......264 F7
  Ripley DE5...........180 D5
  Stapleford NG9 ......223 D6
Hawthorn Bank
  Glossop SK13..........9 F4
  New Mills SK22 ....33 B6

Hawthorn Cl
Ashbourne DE6 . . . . 185 D8
Chinley SK23 . . . . 34 E1
Clowne S43 . . . . 80 D4
Denstone ST14 . . . . 196 E6
Doveridge DE6 . . . . 211 B1
Hilton DE65 . . . . 228 D1
Hope S33 . . . . 39 A4
Mansfield Woodhouse
NG19 . . . . 136 E5
Hawthorn Cres
Burton upon Trent DE15 . . 254 F7
Findern DE65 . . . . 230 D2
Hawthorn Ct DE1 . . . . 267 A5
Hawthorn Dr DE4 . . . . 155 A6
Hawthorne Ave
Borrowash DE72 . . . . 221 C2
Creswell S80 . . . . 81 E2
Dronfield S18 . . . . 57 A3
Glapwell S44 . . . . 134 B8
Long Eaton NG10 . . . . 236 C6
Shirebrook NG20 . . . . 119 D4
Shirland DE55 . . . . 146 C5
Tibshelf DE55 . . . . 148 B8
Hawthorne Cl
Ashover DE55 . . . . 145 D8
Barlborough S43 . . . . 80 A6
Kilburn DE56 . . . . 179 F2
Killamarsh S21 . . . . 60 D5
Hawthorne Rd NG16 . . . . 160 D3
Hawthornes Ave DE55 . . . 159 F5
Hawthorne St S40 . . . . . . 266 C1
Hawthorn Gr SK14 . . . . . . 9 D6
Hawthorn Hill S43 . . . . . . 78 F6
Hawthorn Rd
Castle Donington DE74 . . . 247 B5
Eckington S21 . . . . 59 B2
Hawthorn Rise
Awsworth NG16 . . . . 195 B4
Swadlincote DE11 . . . . 255 F7
Hawthorn St DE24 . . . . . . 232 C8
Hawthorns The
Belper DE56 . . . . 179 D5
Chapel-en-le-Frith SK23 . . 47 B4
Little Eaton DE21 . . . . 205 D8
Wirksworth DE4 . . . . 165 F7
Hawthorn Way S42 . . . . . 94 F5
Hawton Cl DE13 . . . . 135 F1
Hawtrey Gdns DE24 . . . . . 233 A7
Haxby Cl S13 . . . . 44 E6
Haxby Pl S13 . . . . 44 E6
Haxby St S13 . . . . 44 E6
Haybrook Ct S17 . . . . 55 E5
Haycroft Cl DE23 . . . . 231 A7
Haycroft Gdns S43 . . . . . . 79 B4
Hayden Ct ⬛1 SK13 . . . . . . 10 C1
Haydn Fold SK13 . . . . 16 D7
Haydn Rd DE21 . . . . 219 F8
Haydock Cl
Burton upon Trent DE14 . . 254 A7
Kimberley NG16 . . . . 195 E7
Haydock Park Rd DE24 . . 232 E8
Hayes Ave
Breaston DE72 . . . . 235 B7
Derby DE23 . . . . 231 D8
Hayes Cl
Pinxton NG16 . . . . 160 C3
West Hallam DE7 . . . . 207 E8
Hayes Conf Ctr The
DE55 . . . . 170 A6
Hayes Cres DE55 . . . . 169 F7
Hayes Ct S20 . . . . 59 E6
Hayes Dr S20 . . . . 59 E6
Hayes Farm Ct DE73 . . . . . 251 A4
Hayes La DE55 . . . . 169 F7
Hayes The DE65 . . . . 230 C1
Hayes Wood Rd DE7 . . . . 193 A1
HAYFIELD 25 C2
Hayfield Cl
Belper DE56 . . . . 179 B5
Dronfield S18 . . . . 56 D1
Staveley S43 . . . . 78 F3
Wingerworth S42 . . . . 114 F3
Hayfield Cres S12 . . . . 44 D3
Hayfield Dr S12 . . . . 44 D3
Hayfield Gdns DE23 . . . . . 231 B6
Hayfield Pl S12 . . . . 44 D3
Hayfield Prim Sch SK22 . . 25 C3
Hayfield Rd
Chapel-en-le-Frith SK23 . . 47 B8
Chinley SK23 . . . . 35 A3
New Mills SK22 . . . . 24 E1
Hayfield Road E SK23 . . . 47 C6
Hayfield View S21 . . . . . . 59 C3
Hayfield Visitor Ctr ★
SK22 . . . . 25 C2
Hayford Pl DE22 . . . . 218 D4
Hayford Way S43 . . . . 78 E1
Hay La
Ashover S45 . . . . 145 B7
Scropton DE65 . . . . 226 E5
Spout DE4 . . . . 166 C5
Hayley Cl NG16 . . . . 195 D6
Hayley Croft DE56 . . . . . . 190 F1
Hayling Cl DE7 . . . . 194 C3
Haynes Ave NG9 . . . . 209 C5
Hays Cl DE7 . . . . 194 D2
Hays La DE6 . . . . 164 E1
Hays The DE65 . . . . 227 C2
Hay The S45 . . . . 145 B6
Hay Wain La DE11 . . . . . . 256 B7
Haywards Cl SK13 . . . . . . 10 C3
Haywood Cl DE24 . . . . . . 233 A5
Haywoods Rd DE11 . . . . . 256 E1

Hayworth Rd NG10 . . . . . 223 B5
Hazel Ave
Derby DE23 . . . . 231 D6
Killamarsh S21 . . . . 60 C5
Pilsley S45 . . . . 132 B3
Hazelbadge Cres S12 . . . 44 E3
Hazelby Rd S80 . . . . 100 F8
Hazel Cl
Ashbourne DE6 . . . . 185 D8
Dronfield S18 . . . . 76 B8
Findern DE65 . . . . 230 E2
Heanor DE75 . . . . 181 D1
Swadlincote DE11 . . . . 256 A5
Hazel Cres NG20 . . . . 119 D4
Hazel Ct
Dronfield S18 . . . . 76 B8
Matlock DE4 . . . . 143 D5
Hazel Dene DE4 . . . . 143 D5
Hazeldene CI DE56 . . . . . 190 E5
Hazeldene Cotts DE56 . . 178 D2
Hazel Dr
Chesterfield S40 . . . . 114 E8
Derby DE21 . . . . 221 A6
Wingerworth S42 . . . . 115 B3
HAZELFORD 53 A5
Hazel Gr
Calver S32 . . . . 72 C2
Duffield DE56 . . . . 190 E3
Mansfield Woodhouse
NG19 . . . . 136 B5
Mastin Moor S43 . . . . 79 C4
Matlock DE4 . . . . 143 D5
South Normanton DE55 . . 160 B5
Hazelhurst S41 . . . . 115 D6
Hazelhurst Ave S41 . . . . . 96 A5
Hazelhurst La S41 . . . . . . 96 A5
Hazelmere Rd S80 . . . . . . 81 D2
Hazel Rd S21 . . . . 59 C2
Hazelrigg Cl DE74 . . . . . . 246 F4
Hazeltree Cl DE5 . . . . 180 C8
HAZELWOOD 190 A8
Hazelwood Cl
⬛5 Dronfield S18 . . . . 56 C1
⬛1 Glossop SK13 . . . . 10 A6
Hazelwood Hill DE56 . . . 190 C8
Hazelwood Rd
Burton upon Trent DE15 . . 254 E6
Derby DE21 . . . . 219 F8
Duffield DE56 . . . . 190 D5
Hazlebarrow Cl S8 . . . . . . 57 C6
Hazlebarrow Cres S8 . . . 57 C7
Hazlebarrow Ct S8 . . . . . . 57 B7
Hazlebarrow Dr S8 . . . . . . 57 B7
Hazlebarrow Gr S8 . . . . . . 57 C7
Hazlebarrow Rd S8 . . . . . 57 B7
Hazlehurst Ave S41 . . . . . 96 B5
Hazlehurst La
Chesterfield S41 . . . . 96 B5
Eckington S8 . . . . 57 B8
Hazlewood Dr S43 . . . . . . 80 B6
Headingley Ct DE23 . . . . . 231 C8
Headland Cl S43 . . . . 96 E7
Headland Rd S43 . . . . 96 E7
HEAGE 168 E1
Heage La DE56 . . . . 229 D8
Heage Prim Sch DE56 . . . 168 D2
Heage Rd DE5 . . . . 169 C5
Heage Windmill ★ DE56 . 168 D2
Healaugh Way S40 . . . . . . 115 B8
Heale St S43 . . . . 80 E3
HEANOR 181 C2
HEANOR GATE 193 C8
Heanor Gate ⬛3 DE75 . . . 181 D1
Heanor Gate Ind Est
DE75 . . . . 193 D8
Heanor Gate Rd DE75 . . . 193 D8
Heanor Gate Science Coll
DE75 . . . . 181 C1
Heanor Ho DE21 . . . . 220 E3
Heanor Meml Hospl
DE75 . . . . 181 F1
Heanor Rd
Denby DE5 . . . . 181 A3
Heanor, Heanor Gate
DE75 . . . . 181 D1
Ilkeston DE7 . . . . 194 D3
Smalley DE7, DE75 . . . . . 193 B7
Hearthcote Rd DE11 . . . . 256 A3
HEARTHSTONE 143 D1
Hearthstone La DE4 . . . . 143 D1
HEATH 117 B2
Heath Ave
Derby DE23 . . . . 218 C1
Killamarsh S21 . . . . 60 D5
Heath Common S44 . . . . . 117 B2
HEATHCOTE 138 B5
Heathcote Cl DE24 . . . . . 233 C5
Heathcote Dr S41 . . . . . . 115 E8
Heathcote Ho S41 . . . . . . 96 B6
Heath Cross ⬛3 ST14 . . . 210 A1
Heath Ct
Chesterfield S40 . . . . 115 A8
Derby DE24 . . . . 231 E3
HEATH END 258 D7
Heather Ave S44 . . . . 116 F1
Heather Bank Cl ⬛2 SK13 . 17 A7
Heather Cl
Burton upon Trent DE14 . . 254 A8
Calow S44 . . . . 97 A3
Derby DE24 . . . . 231 D2
South Normanton DE55 . . 160 A3
Swanwick DE55 . . . . 170 A8
Heather Cres
Breaston DE72 . . . . 235 F7
Derby DE23 . . . . 231 C6
Heather Ct DE75 . . . . 182 B1
Heather Falls SK22 . . . . . . 33 B8
Heather Gdns S41 . . . . . . 115 E7

Heather Gr SK14 . . . . 9 D6
Heather La S32 . . . . 53 A6
Heather Lea Ave S17 . . . . 55 C7
Heather Lea Pl S17 . . . . . . 55 C7
Heatherley Dr NG19 . . . . 136 E1
Heatherley Prim Sch
NG19 . . . . 136 E1
Heathermead Cl ⬛2 DE21 205 F1
Heathers Edge S32 . . . . . 53 A6
Heather Vale S41 . . . . 115 E7
Heather Vale Cl S41 . . . . . 115 E7
Heather Vale Rd S41 . . . . 115 D7
Heather Way S42 . . . . 113 D7
Heathfield DE4 . . . . 143 C7
Heathfield Ave
Chesterfield S40 . . . . 95 D3
Ilkeston DE7 . . . . 209 A6
Heathfield Cl
Dronfield S18 . . . . 75 F8
Wingerworth S42 . . . . 115 B4
Heathfield Gdns
Buxton SK17 . . . . 85 A8
Tibshelf DE55 . . . . 148 A7
Heathfield Nook Rd SK17 . 85 C2
Heathfield Rd S12 . . . . 44 D4
Heath Fields Prim Sch
DE65 . . . . 227 C1
Heath Gdns DE72 . . . . . . 236 A8
Heath Gr SK17 . . . . 85 C6
Heath La
Blackfordby DE11 . . . . 257 C2
Findern DE65 . . . . 242 D8
Hartshorne DE11 . . . . 257 E4
Smisby LE65 . . . . 258 B6
Heathlands Dr ST14 . . . . . 210 B1
Heathlands Grange
DE15 . . . . 254 E7
Heathley Mews DE14 . . . 254 C8
Heath Park Rd SK17 . . . . . 85 C6
Heath Prim Sch S44 . . . . . 116 F1
Heath Rd
Burton upon Trent DE15 . . 254 E7
Glossop SK13 . . . . 10 D2
Holmewood S44 . . . . 116 E1
Holmewood, Williamthorpe
S42 . . . . 132 E8
Ripley S45 . . . . 169 E1
Uttoxeter ST14 . . . . 210 B1
Heath St SK17 . . . . 85 B6
HEATH THE 210 A1
Heath The
Eastwood NG16 . . . . 195 A8
Glossop SK13 . . . . 10 C3
HEATHTOP 227 A6
Heath View SK17 . . . . 85 E1
Heath Way DE65 . . . . 227 D1
Heaton Cl S18 . . . . 56 D1
Heaton Ct ⬛4 S40 . . . . 95 C2
Heaton Pl SK17 . . . . 85 E8
Heaton St S40 . . . . 95 C2
Heavygate La DE56 . . . . . 177 F8
Hebden Cl DE23 . . . . 230 F6
Hebden Dr SK13 . . . . 17 F8
Hebrides Cl DE24 . . . . 231 D3
Heddon Bar NG19 . . . . . . 136 E3
Hedgebank Ct DE21 . . . . 206 C3
Hedge Gr DE11 . . . . 256 B7
Hedgerow Gdns DE21 . . . 206 C3
Hedges Dr DE7 . . . . 209 A5
Hedgevale Cl DE23 . . . . . 231 A7
Hedingham Cl NE7 . . . . . . 194 D1
Hedingham Way DE3 . . . . 230 D8
Hedley Cl DE55 . . . . 170 D8
Hedley Dr S43 . . . . 96 D8
HEELEY 43 B6
Heeley Arches S2 . . . . 43 B6
Heeley Bank Rd S2 . . . . . . 43 B7
Heeley City Farm ★ S2 . . . 43 B7
Heeley Gn S2 . . . . 43 B6
Heigham Cl DE24 . . . . 232 D3
Heights of Abraham The ★
DE4 . . . . 143 A2
Helmsley Ave S20 . . . . 59 E7
Helmsley Cl S41 . . . . 95 C7
Helmton Dr S8 . . . . 43 A2
Helmton Rd S8 . . . . 43 A2
Helpston Cl DE55 . . . . 147 C1
Helston Cl
Chesterfield S41 . . . . 115 B8
Derby DE24 . . . . 233 B6
Linton DE12 . . . . 261 D5
Helvellyn Way ⬛5 NG10 . 223 B2
Heming Ave S45 . . . . 132 C2
HEMINGTON 247 D5
Hemington Ct DE74 . . . . . 247 C5
Hemington Hill DE74 . . . . 247 C4
Hemington La DE74 . . . . . 247 C5
Hemington Prim Sch
DE74 . . . . 247 D5
Hemlock Ave
Long Eaton NG10 . . . . 223 D1
Stapleford NG9 . . . . 223 E8
Hemlock Cl DE21 . . . . 206 A3
Hemlock La DE7 . . . . 208 D5
Hemlock Stone The ★
NG9 . . . . 209 F2
HEMMING GREEN 94 B4
Hemper Gr S8 . . . . 56 D7
Hemper La S8 . . . . 56 D7
Hemp Yd DE6 . . . . 165 B1
Hemsley Dr NG16 . . . . . . 182 D3
HEMSWORTH 43 D3
Hemsworth Rd S8, S14 . . 43 C2
Hendon Way DE22 . . . . . 218 B6
Henley Ave S8 . . . . 57 C8
Henley Gdns NG9 . . . . . . 209 E1
Henley Gn DE22 . . . . 217 F6
Henley Way DE7 . . . . 207 D8

HENMOOR 131 A4
Henmore ⬛10 DE6 . . . . . . 173 C2
Henmore Trad Est DE6 . . 173 A1
Hennymoor Cl S80 . . . . . . 82 A5
Hennymoor La S80 . . . . . . 82 C2
Henry Ave
Mansfield Woodhouse
NG19 . . . . 136 B5
Matlock DE4 . . . . 143 C6
Henry Bradley Inf Sch
S43 . . . . 96 F8
Henry Cres DE55 . . . . 159 C3
Henry Prince CE Fst Sch The
DE6 . . . . 184 D7
Henry St
Chesterfield S41 . . . . 96 B8
Derby DE1 . . . . 267 A4
Eckington S21 . . . . 59 D3
Glossop SK13 . . . . 10 C1
Grassmoor S42 . . . . 115 E3
Ripley DE5 . . . . 169 D2
Henshall Ho S41 . . . . 96 B6
Henshaw Ave DE7 . . . . . . 208 D5
Henshaw Pl DE7 . . . . 194 E4
HEPTHORNE LANE 131 E6
Hepworth Rd DE11 . . . . . 256 E1
Herald Gr DE73 . . . . 244 E8
Herbert St DE15 . . . . 248 B3
Herbert Strutt Prim Sch
DE56 . . . . 179 B2
Herb Garden at Hardstoft
The ★ S45 . . . . 132 E3
HERDINGS 43 F3
Herdings Ct S12 . . . . 44 A3
Herdings Rd S12 . . . . 44 A3
Herdings View S12 . . . . . . 44 A3
Hereford Ave NG19 . . . . . 136 D5
Hereford Cl SK17 . . . . 85 C4
Hereford Cres DE11 . . . . . 256 D6
Hereford Dr S43 . . . . 96 F8
Hereford Rd
Buxton SK17 . . . . 85 C4
Derby DE21 . . . . 219 D8
Hereward's Rd S14 . . . . . . 43 D1
Herewood Cl NG20 . . . . . 119 F4
Heritage Com Sch S43 . . . 80 D4
Heritage Ct ⬛4 DE56 . . . . 178 F3
Heritage Dr S43 . . . . 80 D5
Heritage Way DE15 . . . . . 248 A1
Hermitage Ave
Borrowash DE72 . . . . 221 C2
Somercotes DE55 . . . . 170 C5
Hermitage Ct DE21 . . . . . 206 B1
Hermitage Gdns ⬛1 ST14 210 A1
Hermitage La DE6 . . . . . . 184 B6
Hermitage Park Way ⬛7
DE11 . . . . 256 A7
Hermitage Wlk DE7 . . . . . 208 F6
Hernstone La SK17 . . . . . . 49 B2
Heron Cl SK13 . . . . 17 F8
Heron Dr DE11 . . . . 256 F3
Heronswood Dr DE21 . . . 220 D6
Heron View SK13 . . . . 16 F8
Heron Way
Derby DE3 . . . . 218 A2
Mansfield NG19 . . . . 135 C1
Herriot Dr S40 . . . . 266 C1
Hessey St S13 . . . . 44 F6
Hewers Holt S43 . . . . 80 B6
Hewett St NG20 . . . . 120 D5
Hewitt Pl S26 . . . . 61 E5
Hexham Ave DE7 . . . . 209 A4
Hexham Wlk DE21 . . . . . . 205 E1
Heyden Bank ⬛26 SK13 . . . 9 D2
Heyden Fold ⬛27 SK13 . . . . 9 D2
Heyden Terr ⬛25 SK13 . . . . 9 D2
Heydon Cl DE56 . . . . 179 B6
Heyford Ct DE75 . . . . 182 A1
Heysbank Rd SK12 . . . . . . 32 D5
Hey St NG10 . . . . 236 C4
Heywood St S43 . . . . 96 E8
Heywood View S43 . . . . . . 80 C6
Heywood Villas ⬛5 S43 . . 96 E8
Heyworth Rd SK23 . . . . . . 47 C6
Heyworth St DE22 . . . . . . 218 D6
Hibbert St S42 . . . . 33 B6
Hickings La NG9 . . . . 223 E8
Hickingwood La S43 . . . . . 81 A5
Hickinwood Cres S43 . . . . 80 F5
Hickleton Cl DE5 . . . . 169 C1
Hickling Cl
Derby DE24 . . . . 232 D3
⬛1 Nottingham NG10 . . . . 236 B5
Hickton Rd DE55 . . . . 169 F6
HIDEBANK 33 C8
Hide La SK17 . . . . 137 E7
Hides Gn S44 . . . . 99 A2
HIGGENHOLES 109 D8
Higger La S32 . . . . 52 F8
Higgins Rd DE11 . . . . 255 F6
Higg La DE56 . . . . 167 A6
Higgott Cl DE14 . . . . 254 B8
HIGHAM 146 C3
Higham La
Compstall SK14 . . . . 15 A7
Stonebroom DE55 . . . . . . 146 E4
Highashes La S45 . . . . 113 E1
Highbank SK13 . . . . 9 F7
High Bank DE5 . . . . 180 F2
Highbank Rd SK13 . . . . . . 17 F7
High Bank Rd DE15 . . . . . 248 B3
Highbury Cl DE22 . . . . . . 217 F6
Highbury Rd S41 . . . . 95 F5
Highcliffe Ave NG20 . . . . 119 D4
Highcroft Cl NG10 . . . . . . 236 E5
High Cross
Hartington SK17 . . . . 137 F5
Linton DE11 . . . . 261 F7

HIGH CROSS BANK 261 E8
High Ct DE4 . . . . 143 C6
Highdale Fold ⬛6 S18 . . . . 57 A1
High Edge Dr DE56 . . . . . 179 E8
High Edge Mews DE56 . . 179 A5
Higher Albert St S41 . . . . 266 B4
Higher Barn Rd SK13 . . . . 9 F4
HIGHER BIBBINGTON . . . 67 A6
HIGHER BUXTON 85 C6
HIGHER CHISWORTH . . . 16 B4
HIGHER CROSSINGS 46 F6
HIGHER DINTING 10 A2
Higher Dinting SK13 . . . . 10 A2
HIGHER DISLEY 32 E5
HIGHER GAMESLEY 16 D8
Higher Hallsteads SK17 . . 47 F3
Higher La SK12 . . . . 32 E5
Higher Noon Sun SK22 . . 24 F2
Higher Sq SK13 . . . . 10 A7
HIGHFIELD 43 A8
Highfield DE45 . . . . 108 E8
Highfield Ave
Chesterfield S41 . . . . 95 E6
Dove Holes SK17 . . . . 47 E1
Mansfield NG19 . . . . 136 E1
Shirebrook NG20 . . . . 119 D6
Highfield Cl
Bakewell DE45 . . . . 109 C5
Heanor DE75 . . . . 181 B5
Mansfield NG19 . . . . 136 B1
Highfield Cotts
Alfreton DE55 . . . . 158 D3
Derby DE21 . . . . 219 E5
Highfield Ct SK14 . . . . 9 A4
Highfield Dr
Bakewell DE45 . . . . 109 C5
Ilkeston DE7 . . . . 208 B5
Matlock DE4 . . . . 143 D6
South Normanton DE55 . . 160 B5
Highfield Gdns
Derby DE22 . . . . 218 F7
Hollingworth SK14 . . . . . . 9 D5
Highfield Hall Prim Sch
S41 . . . . 95 F6
Highfield La
Chesterfield S41 . . . . 95 E6
Derby DE21 . . . . 219 F5
Hartington SK17 . . . . 137 F5
Weston Underwood DE6 . . 188 F5
Highfield Mews DE21 . . . 219 E5
Highfield Pl S2 . . . . 43 A8
Highfield Rd
Ashbourne DE6 . . . . 185 B8
Belper DE56 . . . . 178 F2
Bolsover S44 . . . . 99 A1
Chesterfield S41 . . . . 266 A4
Derby DE22 . . . . 218 F7
Derby, Littleover DE23 . . . 231 C7
Glossop SK13 . . . . 17 D8
Hayfield SK22 . . . . 25 D3
Hulland Ward DE6 . . . . . . 175 F3
Kilburn DE56 . . . . 191 F8
Little Eaton DE21 . . . . 205 C8
Marple SK6 . . . . 23 B6
Swadlincote DE11 . . . . 256 B3
Swanwick DE55 . . . . 169 D7
HIGHFIELDS 132 C7
Highfields
Buxton SK17 . . . . 67 B5
Codnor DE5 . . . . 181 B8
Highfields Cres S18 . . . . . 76 A8
Highfields Dr
Holmewood S42 . . . . 132 D8
Linton DE12 . . . . 261 C6
Highfields Lower Sch
DE4 . . . . 143 C3
Highfields Park Dr DE22 . 204 E1
Highfields Rd S18 . . . . 76 A8
Highfields Sch DE4 . . . . . 143 E7
Highfield St
Long Eaton NG10 . . . . 223 C2
Swadlincote DE11 . . . . 256 B3
Highfields Way S42 . . . . . 132 D8
Highfield Terr
Chesterfield S41 . . . . 95 F5
New Mills SK22 . . . . 33 D8
Highfield View Rd S41 . . . 95 F5
Highfield Way DE5 . . . . . . 180 C8
HIGHGATE 25 D1
Highgate Cl S43 . . . . 77 D3
Highgate Dr
Dronfield S18 . . . . 76 C7
Ilkeston DE7 . . . . 194 D3
Highgate Gn DE22 . . . . . . 218 A5
Highgate La S18 . . . . 76 C7
Highgate Rd SK22 . . . . . . 25 E1
Highgates DE1 . . . . 267 B2
High Gr
Belper DE56 . . . . 179 D4
Mansfield NG19 . . . . 136 E1
Highgrove Cl
Burton upon Trent DE13 . . 240 C1
⬛6 Chesterfield S41 . . . . . 96 A8
Heanor DE75 . . . . 181 C1
Highgrove Dr DE73 . . . . . 232 F2
High Hazel Ct S45 . . . . . . 131 D4
High Hazel Dr NG19 . . . . 136 B1
High Hazels Cl S45 . . . . . . 131 E4
High Hazels Rd S43 . . . . . 80 B5
High Hazels Wlk S45 . . . . 131 E4
High Hill Rd SK22 . . . . . . 24 D1
High Holbeck S80 . . . . . . 101 C7
High Holborn DE7 . . . . . . 194 E3
High Holborn Rd DE5 . . . 170 B1
High La
Broadbottom SK13 . . . . . . 16 E7
Eckington S12 . . . . 44 E1

High La continued
Holloway, Dethick Common
DE4 . . . . **144** E2
Holloway, Upper Holloway
DE4 . . . . **156** D6
Holymoorside S42 . . . . . . **113** E5
Sheffield S12 . . . . **58** F8
Highland Cl
Buxton SK17 . . . . **85** C5
Mansfield Woodhouse
NG19 . . . . **136** D3
Highland Rd S43 . . . . **77** D4
Highlands Dr DE15 . . . . . **248** A4
Highlands Pl S41 . . . . **76** F1
HIGH LANE **32** A8
High Lane Central DE7 . . **193** F1
High Lane E DE7 . . . . **208** B8
High Lane W DE7 . . . . . . **193** E1
High Lea Rd SK22 . . . . **33** A8
High Leys Rd S43 . . . . **80** E2
Highlightley La S18 . . . . . **75** C5
HIGH LOW **52** E5
Highlow Cl S40 . . . . **95** C5
High Mdws SK13 . . . . **17** B7
High Meadow Cl DE5 . . . **180** D8
High Pavement DE56 . . . **179** A3
High Rd DE55 . . . . **157** F4
High Ridge
Mansfield NG19 . . . . **136** F2
Matlock DE4 . . . . **143** C7
High Spannia NG16 . . . . . **195** F7
High St
Alfreton DE55 . . . . **159** A4
Apperknowle S18 . . . . **58** A1
Barlborough S43 . . . . **80** A7
Belper DE56 . . . . **179** A4
Bolsover S44 . . . . **99** A1
Bonsall DE4 . . . . **142** D1
Brimington S43 . . . . **96** F7
Brinsley NG16 . . . . **171** E1
Buxton SK17 . . . . **85** B7
Calver S32 . . . . **72** B2
Castle Donington DE74 . . **247** A2
Chapel-en-le-Frith SK23 . . **47** B6
Chellaston DE73 . . . . **233** A1
Chesterfield S41, S43 . . . . **77** D4
Chesterfield, Stonegravels
S40 . . . . **266** B3
Clay Cross S45 . . . . **131** C3
Clowne S43 . . . . **80** D3
Codnor DE5 . . . . **181** B8
Doveridge DE6 . . . . **211** B1
Dronfield S18 . . . . **57** A1
Eckington S21 . . . . **59** D3
Ilkeston DE7 . . . . **208** F8
Kilburn DE56 . . . . **192** A8
Killamarsh S21 . . . . **60** D6
Kimberley NG16 . . . . **195** F6
Linton DE12 . . . . **261** C6
Long Eaton NG10 . . . . . . **236** E8
Longnor SK17 . . . . **121** C6
Mansfield Woodhouse
NG19 . . . . **136** C3
Marchington ST14 . . . . . . **224** E2
Melbourne DE73 . . . . **252** A7
New Mills SK22 . . . . **33** C8
Pilsley DE55 . . . . **91** C3
Pleasley NG19 . . . . **135** B5
Repton DE65 . . . . **242** D2
Ripley DE5 . . . . **169** D1
Rocester ST14 . . . . **196** F3
Sheffield, Dore S17 . . . . . . **55** D7
Sheffield, Mosborough S20 . **59** D7
Somercotes DE55 . . . . . . **170** C8
Somercotes, Riddings
DE55 . . . . **170** D5
South Normanton DE55 . . **160** A6
Stapleford NG9 . . . . **223** E7
Staveley S43 . . . . **78** E2
Stonebroom DE55 . . . . . . **147** A4
Stoney Middleton S32 . . . . **71** F3
Swadlincote, Church Gresley
DE11 . . . . **256** C3
Swadlincote, Newhall
DE11 . . . . **256** A6
Swanwick DE55 . . . . **169** F7
Tibshelf DE55 . . . . **148** A7
Ticknall DE73 . . . . **251** A4
Tideswell SK17 . . . . **69** C4
Tutbury DE13 . . . . **239** C6
Whitwell S80 . . . . **81** F6
Woodville DE11 . . . . **256** F2
Highstairs La DE55 . . . . . **146** C8
Highstones Gdns SK13 . . . **10** C2
Highstool La SK17 . . . . . **106** B6
High Street E SK13 . . . . . **10** D1
High Street Mews S20 . . . **59** C7
High Street W SK13 . . . . . **10** B1
High Tor ★ DE4 . . . . **143** B3
High Tor Rd DE4 . . . . . . **143** B2
High Trees S17 . . . . **55** D7
Highview SK13 . . . . **17** A7
High View Cl S41 . . . . **96** C3
High View Rd DE55 . . . . **160** C7
Highway La DE6 . . . . **151** F2
Highwood Ave DE56 . . . . **179** C1
High Wood Bank DE56 . . **179** C1
Highwood Cl SK13 . . . . . . **17** B8
High Wood Fold DE56 . . . **23** C8
Highwood La S80 . . . . **81** D5
Highwood Pl S21 . . . . **59** C3
High Wood Way S43 . . . . . **80** C5
Hilary Cl DE56 . . . . **179** E5
HILCOTE **148** C1
Hilcote La DE55 . . . . **148** B1
Hilcote St DE55 . . . . **160** A6
Hilderstone Cl DE24 . . . . **233** D6
Hillary Pl DE7 . . . . **208** B5

Hillberry DE5 . . . . **170** A1
Hillberry Rise S40 . . . . . . **114** F6
Hill Brow DE1 . . . . **267** B2
Hill Cl
Derby DE21 . . . . **220** E4
Stanley Common DE7 . . . **193** A1
Turnditch DE56 . . . . **177** B2
Hillcliff La
Hulland Ward DE56 . . . . **176** F2
Turnditch DE56 . . . . **177** A3
HILLCLIFFLANE **177** A3
Hill Cotts DE45 . . . . **125** B5
Hillcrest
Aston-on-Trent DE72 . . . **234** A1
Belper DE56 . . . . **179** E4
Blackwell DE55 . . . . **147** E1
Matlock DE4 . . . . **143** A7
Tutbury DE13 . . . . **239** B5
Hill Crest
Crich DE4 . . . . **157** A1
Shirebrook NG20 . . . . . . **119** D3
Hillcrest Ave
Burton upon Trent DE15 . **248** A4
Hulland Ward DE6 . . . . . **175** F3
South Normanton DE55 . . **160** A4
Hill Crest Cres S41 . . . . . **157** E8
Hill Crest Cotts DE4 . . . . **142** F8
Hillcrest Dr
Codnor DE5 . . . . **181** B8
Kilburn DE56 . . . . **192** A8
Hillcreste Dr DE73 . . . . . **232** F3
Hillcrest Gr S43 . . . . **78** F4
Hillcrest Rd S41 . . . . **115** D7
Hillcroft Dr DE72 . . . . . . **221** C4
HILLCROSS **231** C7
Hill Cross DE45 . . . . **108** F8
Hill Cross Ave DE23 . . . . **231** C7
Hill Cross Dr DE23 . . . . . **231** B7
Hill Dr SK23 . . . . **45** D8
Hilend SK14 . . . . **9** A1
Hillend La SK14 . . . . **9** A1
Hillfield La DE13 . . . . . . **240** F1
Hillfield Rd NG9 . . . . **209** F1
Hill Fields DE55 . . . . **160** A3
HILLFOOT **55** D5
Hillfoot La S17 . . . . **55** D4
Hillfoot Rd S17 . . . . **55** D5
Hill Gr S43 . . . . **78** B4
Hill Head S32 . . . . **51** A7
Hillhouses La S42 . . . . . . **114** E3
Hillingdon Dr DE7 . . . . . **209** A7
Hill La S32 . . . . **52** F8
Hillman Dr S43 . . . . **97** C7
Hillmoor St NG19 . . . . . . **135** C3
Hillmorton DE45 . . . . . . **108** F7
Hill Nook Cl DE73 . . . . . **233** A1
Hillock The S32 . . . . **72** E2
Hill Pond Ave SK22 . . . . . **24** D1
Hill Rd
Ashover S45 . . . . **129** F4
Heanor DE75 . . . . **181** D1
Hill Rise NG9 . . . . **209** C4
Hill Rise Cl DE23 . . . . . . **231** D8
HILLS AND HOLES **120** E5
Hillsdale Rd DE15 . . . . . . **248** B5
Hillside
Ashover S45 . . . . **130** A4
Brassington DE4 . . . . **152** F1
Buxton SK17 . . . . **85** D3
Castle Donington DE74 . . **247** B4
Chinley SK23 . . . . **47** B8
Curbar S32 . . . . **72** C2
Findern DE65 . . . . **230** C2
Holloway DE4 . . . . **156** A6
Langley Mill NG16 . . . . . **182** A3
Middleton DE4 . . . . **154** D4
Sheffield S20 . . . . **59** C7
Tutbury DE13 . . . . **239** C6
Whitwell S80 . . . . **81** F5
Hillside Ave
Ashbourne DE6 . . . . **173** C5
Derby DE21 . . . . **220** A5
Dronfield S18 . . . . **76** A8
Hillside Cl
Disley SK12 . . . . **32** E6
Glossop SK13 . . . . **9** E3
Whitwell S80 . . . . **81** F5
Hillside Cotts S32 . . . . **53** B7
Hillside Cres DE21 . . . . . **220** F4
Hillside Ct
Breedon on the Hill DE73 . **252** F2
Kirk Langley DE6 . . . . . . **202** E4
Hillside Dr
Chesterfield S40 . . . . **95** D1
Long Eaton NG10 . . . . . . **236** B8
Mastin Moor S43 . . . . **79** C3
Hillside Gdns DE11 . . . . . **255** F7
Hillside Gr
Marple SK6 . . . . **15** B1
Sandiacre NG10 . . . . **223** A6
Hillside Pk
Alfreton DE55 . . . . **158** B4
South Wingfield DE55 . . . **158** B4
Hillside Rd
Derby DE21 . . . . **220** F4
Linton DE12 . . . . **261** D7
Hillside Rise DE56 . . . . . **178** F2
Hillside View SK22 . . . . . . **33** A8
HILL SOMERSAL **212** A2
Hill Sq The DE22 . . . . . . **205** A1
Hills Rd DE72 . . . . **235** C7
Hill St
Burton upon Trent DE15 . **254** E8
Clay Cross S45 . . . . **131** C3
Donisthorpe DE12 . . . . . **262** E1

Hill St continued
Ripley DE5 . . . . **169** D3
Sheffield S2 . . . . **43** A8
Swadlincote, Church Gresley
DE11 . . . . **256** C3
Swadlincote DE11 . . . . . . **255** F6
Hills The S33 . . . . **51** A6
HILLSTOWN **118** C8
Hillstown Bsns Ctr S44 . . **118** B7
Hillsway
Chellaston DE73 . . . . **232** F3
Derby DE23 . . . . **218** B1
Shirebrook NG20 . . . . . . **119** D3
Hill The
Derby DE22 . . . . **205** A1
Glapwell S44 . . . . **118** A1
HILLTOP
Chapel-en-le-Frith **46** B6
Flash **103** B5
HILL TOP **76** A7
Hilltop DE56 . . . . **168** B7
Hill Top
Bolsover S44 . . . . **99** A2
Castle Donington DE74 . . **247** A1
Derby DE21 . . . . **205** E3
Hilltop Ave NG20 . . . . . . **119** E4
Hilltop Cl S44 . . . . **118** B1
Hilltop Inf Sch DE6 . . . . . **185** C8
Hilltop La
Belper DE56 . . . . **179** E2
Thurvaston DE6 . . . . **215** D5
Hilltop Rd
Ashover S45 . . . . **129** F5
Chesterfield S41 . . . . **77** B2
Dronfield S18 . . . . **76** B7
Glossop SK13 . . . . **10** B3
Pinxton NG16 . . . . **160** C3
Wingerworth S42 . . . . . . **114** D4
Hill Top Rd DE55 . . . . . . **170** C5
Hilltop Rise S43 . . . . **45** D8
Hilltops View DE4 . . . . . **143** D5
Hilltop Way S18 . . . . **76** A7
Hill View
Duffield DE56 . . . . **190** D3
Repton DE65 . . . . **242** F2
Whaley Bridge SK23 . . . . . **45** C8
Hill View Cl DE7 . . . . **192** B7
Hill View Ct NG19 . . . . . **136** D4
Hill View Gr DE21 . . . . . **220** E5
Hillview Ho [1] DE1 . . . . . **267** B2
Hill View Rd S43 . . . . **96** E8
Hillwood Dr SK13 . . . . **17** E8
HILLYFIELDS **132** B7
Hilton **228** C1
Hilton Cl
Derby DE73 . . . . **217** D1
Long Eaton NG10 . . . . . . **235** F4
Swadlincote DE11 . . . . . . **256** A7
HILTON COMMON **228** F2
Hilton Gdns DE72 . . . . . . **246** A7
Hilton Ind Est DE65 . . . . **228** D3
Hilton Park Dr DE55 . . . . **170** C8
Hilton Prim Sch DE65 . . . **228** D2
Hilton Rd
Disley SK12 . . . . **32** B7
Egginton DE65 . . . . **241** B7
Etwall DE65 . . . . **229** B4
Hinckley Ct DE4 . . . . **110** F1
Hind Ave DE72 . . . . **235** C4
Hindersitch La DE4 . . . . . **156** D2
HIND LOW **105** B7
Hindscarth Cres DE3 . . . . **217** E1
Hinton Gr SK14 . . . . **15** A4
Hipley S40 . . . . **95** B6
Hipper St S40 . . . . **266** B2
Hipper Street S S40 . . . . . **266** B2
Hipper Street W S40 . . . . . **95** C2
Hixon's La DE7 . . . . **208** B1
Hoades St S42 . . . . **131** C8
Hoargate La DE6 . . . . . . **200** F2
Hobart Cl
Burton upon Trent DE15 . **248** C4
Derby DE3 . . . . **217** F2
Hobart Dr NG9 . . . . **209** F1
Hob Hill DE56 . . . . **190** B8
Hob Hill Mdws SK13 . . . . . **17** D7
Hobhouse Rd NG19 . . . . . **135** D2
Hobkirk Dr DE24 . . . . . . **231** E2
Hob La DE6 . . . . **176** D8
HOBSIC **182** B8
Hobsic Cl NG16 . . . . **182** B8
Hobsic La NG16 . . . . **171** E8
Hobson Dr
Derby DE21 . . . . **220** F2
Ilkeston DE7 . . . . **208** E6
Hobson Moor Rd SK14 . . . . **9** A7
Hockerley Ave SK23 . . . . . **45** D8
Hockerley Cl SK23 . . . . . . **45** D8
Hockerley La SK23 . . . . . . **45** D8
Hockerley New Rd SK23 . . **45** D8
HOCKLEY **115** A2
Hockley La
Ashover S45 . . . . **130** A1
Wingerworth S42 . . . . . . **115** A3
Hockley Way DE55 . . . . . **159** B2
Hodder Cl DE4 . . . . **156** F2
Hodge Beck Cl DE24 . . . . **233** C6
Hodge Fold SK14 . . . . **15** F8
Hodge La
Ashover S45 . . . . **128** E7
Broadbottom SK14 . . . . . . **15** F8
Marchington ST14 . . . . . **224** A1
Hodmire La S44 . . . . **133** E7
HODTHORPE **82** C6
Hodthorpe Cl DE21 . . . . . **206** B1
Hodthorpe Prim Sch S80 . **82** C5
Hogarth Cl NG9 . . . . **223** E6

Hogarth Rd SK6 . . . . **23** B8
Hogarth Rise S18 . . . . **75** F8
Hogbarn La DE75, NG16 . . **181** D5
Hoggs Field NG16 . . . . . . **182** F2
HOGNASTON **164** A1
Hogshaw Dr SK17 . . . . **66** C1
Hogshaw Villas Rd [1]
SK17 . . . . **85** C8
Hoillant Sq DE6 . . . . **175** E3
Holbeach Dr S40 . . . . **114** E8
HOLBECK **101** C7
Holbeck Ave S44 . . . . **99** C2
Holbeck Cl S41 . . . . **266** C4
Holbeck La S80 . . . . **101** D8
Holbeck St S80 . . . . **81** D1
HOLBECK WOODHOUSE **101** E7
Holbein Cl S18 . . . . **75** F8
Holborn Dr DE22 . . . . . . **218** A7
Holborn View DE5 . . . . . **170** B1
HOLBROOK
Belper **191** D6
Sheffield **60** A8
Holbrook Ave
North Wingfield S42 . . . . **132** A7
Sheffield S20 . . . . **60** A8
Holbrook Centre For Autism
DE56 . . . . **191** D5
Holbrook CE Prim Sch
DE56 . . . . **191** C7
Holbrook Cl
Chesterfield S40 . . . . **114** C8
Pleasley NG19 . . . . **135** A5
Holbrook Gn S20 . . . . **60** A8
Holbrook Ind Est S20 . . . . **60** A8
HOLBROOK MOOR **191** D7
Holbrook Pl S43 . . . . **97** C6
Holbrook Rd
Belper DE56 . . . . **178** F2
Derby DE24 . . . . **233** B6
Sheffield S13 . . . . **44** B7
Holbrook St DE75 . . . . . . **182** A2
Holbrook View DE56 . . . . **192** A8
Holbrook Way S42 . . . . . . **132** A7
Holburn Ave S18 . . . . **57** A2
Holcombe St DE23 . . . . . **219** B1
Holden Ave DE72 . . . . . . **246** A8
Holden Ct DE24 . . . . **233** A8
Holden Gdns [1] NG9 . . . **223** E6
Holderness Cl DE24 . . . . . **231** D7
Holdings The DE11 . . . . . **256** A1
Holdon Croft DE12 . . . . . **260** C6
HOLEHOUSE **16** C5
HOLESTONE **144** C8
Holestone Gate Rd S45 . . **129** D1
Holker Ave SK17 . . . . **85** C8
Holker Rd SK17 . . . . **85** C7
Holkham Cl DE7 . . . . **194** C3
Holland Cl DE55 . . . . **146** F5
Holland Mdw NG10 . . . . . **236** D5
Holland Pl [8] S2 . . . . **43** A8
Holland Rd
Chesterfield S41 . . . . **76** F2
Sheffield S2 . . . . **43** A8
Hollbank Cotts DE55 . . . . **158** B3
Hollens Way S40 . . . . **95** A5
Hollies Cl
Clifton DE6 . . . . **184** F6
Dronfield S18 . . . . **76** C8
Newton Solney DE15 . . . . **248** E8
Hollies Dr SK6 . . . . **23** A5
Hollies Farm Cl DE73 . . . **244** E3
Hollies La S42 . . . . **198** C4
Hollies Rd DE22 . . . . **204** D3
Hollies The
Eastwood NG16 . . . . **182** F2
Repton DE65 . . . . **243** A1
Sandiacre NG10 . . . . **223** A5
Shirebrook NG20 . . . . . . **119** E2
Hollin Cl S41 . . . . **95** C8
Hollincross La SK13 . . . . . **17** C8
Hollindale Dr S12 . . . . **44** C5
Hollin Dr SK23 . . . . **47** B5
HOLLINGTON **200** F4
Hollington Cl DE21 . . . . . **219** C7
Hollington Rd ST14 . . . . . **196** F3
Hollingwood Cres S43 . . . . **78** A1
Hollingwood Prim Sch
S43 . . . . **78** A1
HOLLINGWORTH **9** C6
Hollingworth Ave NG10 . . **223** B3
Hollingworth Prim Sch
SK14 . . . . **9** C5
Hollinhey Terr SK14 . . . . . **9** C5
Hollin Hill Rd S43 . . . . . . **81** A3
HOLLINS **94** A4
Hollins Ave SK17 . . . . **85** B7
Hollins Bank [41] SK13 . . . . **9** D2
Hollins Cl [40] SK13 . . . . . . **9** D2
HOLLINSCLOUGH **104** B2
Hollinsclough CE Prim Sch
SK17 . . . . **104** B2
Hollinsclough Rake
SK17 . . . . **104** B2
Hollinsend Ave S12 . . . . . . **44** C5
Hollinsend Pl S12 . . . . **44** C5
Hollinsend Rd S12 . . . . . . **44** B5
Hollins Fold [43] SK13 . . . . **9** D2
Hollins Gdns [46] SK13 . . . . **9** D2
Hollins Gr [42] SK13 . . . . . . **9** D2
HOLLINS GREEN **130** E3
Hollins Ind Pk SK13 . . . . . **10** B5
Hollins La
Crich DE4 . . . . **157** A4
Marple SK6 . . . . **23** C8
Hollins Mews [44] SK13 . . . . **9** D2
Hollinsmoor Rd SK6, SK22 . **24** D7
Hollins Mount SK6 . . . . . . **23** B8

Hollins Spring Ave S18 . . . **76** A8
Hollins Spring Rd S18 . . . . **76** A8
Hollins St SK17 . . . . **85** B7
Hollins The DE4 . . . . **156** A6
Hollins Way [45] SK13 . . . . . **9** D2
Hollins Wood Cl DE4 . . . **156** A5
HOLLIN WOOD **34** B1
Hollinwood La SK6 . . . . . . **23** B2
Hollinwood Rd SK12 . . . . . **32** D6
Hollis La
Chesterfield S41 . . . . **266** C2
Denstone ST14 . . . . **196** B6
Hollis St DE24 . . . . **233** A8
Holllins Ave [47] SK13 . . . . . **9** D2
HOLLOWAY **156** B5
Holloway Rd
Derby DE24 . . . . **232** F6
Duffield DE56 . . . . **190** E4
Hollow Cres DE15 . . . . . . **248** C4
Hollowford Ctr S33 . . . . . . **38** C4
Hollowford Rd S33 . . . . . . **38** B4
Hollow Gate S33 . . . . **51** A7
Hollow La
Burton upon Trent DE15 . . **248** C4
Mayfield DE6 . . . . **172** C1
Sheffield, Mosborough S20 . **59** D6
Hollowood Ave DE23 . . . . **231** C8
Hollow O'the Moor SK17 . . **87** E4
Hollow Rd DE73 . . . . **252** E2
Hollows The NG10 . . . . . **237** A8
Hollow The
Bamford S33 . . . . **40** B3
Castle Donington DE74 . . **247** B4
Derby, Littleover DE23 . . **231** C8
Derby, Markeaton DE3 . . **230** D8
Holloway DE4 . . . . **156** B5
Roston DE6 . . . . **197** E7
Holly Ave
Breaston DE72 . . . . **222** F1
Creswell S80 . . . . **81** D2
Ripley DE5 . . . . **180** D8
Hollybank S12 . . . . **44** B6
Holly Bank
Glossop SK13 . . . . **17** E8
Hollingworth SK14 . . . . . . **9** D5
Hollybank Ave S12 . . . . . . **44** C6
Hollybank Cl
Sheffield S12 . . . . **44** D6
Swadlincote DE11 . . . . . . **256** A7
Holly Bank Cl
New Houghton NG19 . . . . **135** A6
South Wingfield DE55 . . . **158** B3
Hollybank Cres S12 . . . . . . **44** C6
Holly Bank Cl DE4 . . . . . **156** F1
Hollybank Dr S12 . . . . **44** D6
Hollybank Rd S12 . . . . **44** C6
Hollybank Way S12 . . . . . . **44** D6
Hollybrook Way DE23 . . . **230** F6
Holly Brook Way DE23 . . . **230** F6
Holly Bush Cl DE12 . . . . . **264** F7
Holly Bush La DE56 . . . . . **191** A6
Holly Cl
Ashbourne DE6 . . . . **185** D8
Chesterfield S41 . . . . **77** A3
Draycott DE72 . . . . **235** A7
Killamarsh S21 . . . . **60** C5
Holly Croft DE15 . . . . **248** C2
Holly Ct
Aston-on-Trent DE72 . . . **246** A4
[3] Chesterfield S40 . . . . . **95** C2
Derby DE3 . . . . **217** D1
[2] Mansfield NG19 . . . . **136** E1
Woodville DE11 . . . . **256** F2
Holly End Rd [7] DE3 . . . . **217** D1
Holly Gdns S12 . . . . **44** C6
Holly Gn DE15 . . . . **254** F8
Holly Gr
Sheffield S12 . . . . **44** C6
Swanwick DE55 . . . . **169** F8
Holly Hill Rd NG16 . . . . . **171** F6
Hollyhock Way DE14 . . . . **253** E6
Hollyhouse Dr DE55 . . . . **160** B6
Holly House La DE56 . . . . **178** C4
Holly House Specl Sch
S41 . . . . **77** A3
Hollyhurst La DE6 . . . . . . **212** B6
Hollyhurst Row DE55 . . . **170** F6
Holly La
Alderwasley DE56 . . . . . . **167** D4
Tansley DE4 . . . . **144** A4
Hollymoor Dr DE73 . . . . **232** F2
Holly Mount [2] SK13 . . . . **10** D1
Holly Rd
Kimberley NG16 . . . . **195** F7
Mansfield NG19 . . . . **136** F2
Uttoxeter ST14 . . . . **210** B1
Holly St DE15 . . . . **254** F8
Hollythorpe Cl S41 . . . . . **115** D8
Hollythorpe Cres S8 . . . . . **43** A4
Hollythorpe Rd S8 . . . . . . **43** B4
Hollywell Ave DE5 . . . . . **181** B3
Hollywell Prim Sch
NG16 . . . . **195** F7
Hollywood Rd SK6 . . . . . . **23** F8
Holm Ave DE21 . . . . **205** B2
Holm Cl S18 . . . . **56** D2
HOLME **2** F8
Holme Bank DE6 . . . . . . **184** D7
Holmebank Cl S40 . . . . . . **95** E4
Holmebank E S40 . . . . **95** E4
Holmebank View S40 . . . . **95** E4
Holmebank W S40 . . . . . . **95** E4
Holmebrook Ct S40 . . . . . **95** D4
Holmebrook View S41 . . . . **95** C6

Holme Cl
  Hatton DE65 .... 227 C1
  Holloway DE4 .... 156 A5
  Ilkeston DE7 .... 194 D2
Holme Croft DE7 ...... 207 E7
Holme Ct DE45 .... 109 D5
Holme Farm Ave DE15.. 254 F8
Holmefield Cres DE7.... 209 A8
Holmefield Rd S80...... 82 A6
Holme Hall Cres S40.... 95 B5
Holme Hall Prim Sch S40 95 B5
Holme La
  Bakewell DE45.......... 109 D7
  Derby DE21 .... 220 C3
Holme Lea 2 NG10 ...... 223 B6
Holme Park Ave S41 .... 95 C7
Holme Rd
  Chesterfield S41 ...... 96 A6
  Matlock Bath DE4 ...... 143 B1
Holmes Cl NG16.......... 182 A3
Holmes Ct DE11.......... 256 B5
HOLMESDALE 57 C2
Holmesdale Cl S18...... 57 C3
Holmesdale Inf Sch S18.. 57 C2
Holmesdale Rd S18 ...... 57 C2
HOLMESFIELD 75 A8
Holmesfield Cl DE4 ...... 144 A5
HOLMESFIELD COMMON .. 74 E8
Holmesfield Dr
  Derby DE3 .... 217 F2
  Shipley DE75 .... 194 A8
Holmesfield Rd S18...... 56 B1
Holmes Rd DE72 ...... 235 D8
Holmes St
  Derby DE23 .... 219 A2
  Heanor DE75 .... 181 D2
HOLMEWOOD 116 E1
Holmewood Ave NE7.... 194 F5
Holmewood Bsns Pk
  S42.......... 116 C2
Holmewood Dr NG16.... 195 B8
Holmewood Ind Est S42 132 F8
Holmewood Ind Pk S42.. 116 D1
Holme Woods La HD9 ....2 F6
Holmfield
  Buxton SK17 .... 84 E6
  Derby DE23 .... 231 E7
HOLMGATE 130 E4
Holmgate Prim Sch S45 131 A4
Holmgate Rd S45 ...... 131 A4
Holm La DE55.......... 158 A4
Holmleigh Way DE73.... 244 E8
Holmley Bank S18 ...... 57 A3
HOLMLEY COMMON 57 A3
Holmley La S18.......... 57 A3
Holmoak Cl DE21 ...... 206 B3
Holmshaw Dr S13...... 44 E8
Holmshaw Gr S13...... 44 E8
Holmwood Terr 2 SK17.. 85 C8
Holt Ave DE24 .... 233 C6
Holt Dr DE4.......... 142 F7
Holt La
  Lea DE4.......... 156 B7
  Matlock DE4.......... 143 B5
Holtlands Dr DE24 ...... 232 F5
Holt Rd DE4 .... 127 F1
Holt's La DE13 .... 239 B6
Holyhead Dr DE21...... 206 B3
HOLYMOORSIDE 113 D8
Holymoor Rd S42 ...... 113 E8
Holyoake Ave S13...... 44 E8
Holyoake Dr NG10 ...... 236 F7
Holyrood Cl DE21 ...... 221 A5
Holyrood Ho DE24 ...... 219 D1
Holy Rosary RC Prim Sch
  DE15.......... 248 A3
Holywell DE45 .... 109 D4
Holywell La DE45 ...... 125 B5
Holywell Rd DE7 ...... 194 C3
Holywell St S41.......... 266 B3
Homecroft Dr NG16 .... 171 E7
Home Farm Cl DE72.... 221 C5
Home Farm Cotts SK17.. 105 C2
Home Farm Ct
  Castle Gresley DE11 .... 255 D1
  Selston NG16.......... 171 C6
Home Farm Dr DE22 .... 205 A4
Home Farm Ho DE15 .... 249 A3
Home Farm Park Homes
  DE13 .... 240 A5
Homefields Prim Sch
  DE73.......... 232 E1
Homemoss Ho SK17.... 85 A8
Homeport Mews S41.... 266 B4
Homer Dr SK6.......... 23 B8
Homestead NG16.......... 182 A4
Homestead Rd SK12.... 32 C6
Homestead Way SK23 .. 47 C5
Honeycroft Cl DE56 .... 179 B2
Honeycroft Ct DE55 .... 160 B4
Honeyfield Dr DE5 ...... 180 F8
Honeysuckle Cl DE11.... 256 A6
Honeysuckle Dr DE55 .. 160 B7
Honeysuckle View DE15.. 255 A8
Honeywall La DE6........ 183 E8
Honingham Rd DE7.... 194 C3
Honiton Ct 11 S41...... 95 F8
Hook La ST14.......... 210 B6
Hoole St S41.......... 115 D8
Hooley Cl NG10.......... 236 B6
Hooley St NG16 ...... 171 F6
Hoon La DE65.......... 228 A3
Hoon Rd DE65.......... 239 D8
Hoonwell La DE6.......... 175 F5

HOPE
  Alstonefield 149 D3
  Castleton.......... 38 F4
Hope Ave DE3 .... 217 D2
HOPEDALE 149 C2
Hopedale Rd S12.......... 44 D4
Hopefield Ave S12...... 44 D4
Hope Prim Sch S33 ...... 39 A4
Hope Rd S33 .... 39 D2
Hope St
  Chesterfield S40 ...... 95 E3
  Derby DE1 .... 267 C2
  Glossop SK13.......... 10 E2
  2 Ilkeston DE7.......... 208 F7
  Melbourne DE73.......... 252 A7
Hope Sta S33.......... 39 C3
Hope Terr 143 B2
Hopetoun St DE23 ...... 232 A8
Hope Valley Coll S33 .... 38 F3
Hope Way DE11.......... 255 E1
Hopewell Rd DE4 ...... 143 C6
Hop Inge The S26.......... 61 F5
Hopkins Ct NG16.......... 182 F3
Hopmeadow Way DE15.. 248 A1
Hopping Hill S56.......... 190 F8
Hopping Hill Terrace E
  DE56.......... 191 A7
Hopping Hill Terrace W
  DE56.......... 191 A7
Hopping La DE45.......... 125 B3
HOPTON 164 F7
Hopton Cl
  Derby DE21 .... 206 A1
  Ripley DE5.......... 169 F1
Hoptonwood Cl DE4.... 154 D4
Hopwell Rd DE72 ...... 222 A2
Horace Ave NG9 ...... 223 D6
Hordern Cl S13.......... 10 A4
Horderns La SK23 ...... 47 B5
Horderns Park Rd SK23 .. 47 B5
Horderns La SK23 ...... 47 A5
Horeston Cotts DE7 .... 192 B7
Hornbeam Cl
  Brimington S43.......... 78 A2
  Derby DE21 .... 205 E2
  Ilkeston DE7.......... 209 B7
Hornbeams The 2 ST14.. 210 A1
Horncastle Rd DE21.... 205 D1
Horner Rd 1 S7.......... 43 A7
Hornscroft Rd S44...... 99 A1
Hornsea Rd DE21 ...... 205 D1
Hornthorpe Rd S21 .... 59 C2
Horridge St DE7 ...... 194 F4
Horse Chestnut Cl S40 .. 266 B1
Horse Chestnut Gdns
  DE73.......... 232 F3
Horsecroft Cl DE7.... 194 C2
Horsedale DE4.......... 142 C1
Horse Fair Ave DE4.... 47 A6
Horsehead La S44 ...... 99 C2
Horse & Jockey Yd 7
  DE6.......... 173 C2
Horseshoe Ave SK17 .... 47 F1
Horse Shoes The DE74.. 247 A6
Horsewood Rd S40...... 114 B8
HORSLEY 191 F6
Horsley CE Prim Sch
  DE21.......... 191 F5
Horsley Cl S40.......... 95 A5
Horsley Cres
  Holbrook DE56.......... 191 C7
  Langley Mill NG16...... 182 A3
HORSLEYGATE 74 E6
Horsleygate La S18 .... 74 E7
Horsleygate Rd S17, S18 .. 74 B7
Horsley La DE21...... 191 E4
Horsley Rd DE21, DE56.. 191 F6
HORSLEY
  WOODHOUSE 192 D6
Horsley Woodhouse Prim
  Sch DE7.......... 192 D6
Horton Cl
  Sheffield S20.......... 59 E7
  Swanwick DE55.......... 169 F8
Horton Dr S20.......... 59 E7
Horton St DE23 ...... 219 C2
HORWICH END 45 D5
Horwood Ave DE23.... 218 D2
Hoselett Field Rd NG10.. 236 E5
Hospital La DE3.......... 230 B7
Houfton Cres S44 ...... 98 F3
Houfton Rd S44.......... 98 F3
Hough Cl S40.......... 266 B1
Houghton Ave DE7 .... 194 C3
Houghton Cl SK22.......... 25 C2
Houghton Ct 7 DE21.. 205 F2
Houldsworth Cres S44 .. 98 F2
Houldsworth Dr S41 .... 96 E2
Hoult St DE22.......... 218 D4
Houndkirk Rd S11, S17.. 42 F2
Hounslow Rd DE22...... 218 B6
Houston Cl DE21.......... 220 B6
Hoveton Cl DE24 ...... 232 D3
Howard Cl
  Glossop SK13.......... 10 B2
  11 Long Eaton NG10.... 223 E1
Howard Dr
  Chesterfield S41 ...... 77 A2
  North Wingfield S42.... 131 F5
Howards Mdw SK13...... 17 B7
Howard St
  Derby DE23 .... 218 F2
  Glossop SK13.......... 10 C1
Howarth Cl NG10...... 236 A7
Howden Cl
  Derby DE3.......... 217 C1
  Staveley S43.......... 78 F2
  Swadlincote DE11...... 256 A5

Howden Rd SK22.......... 24 C1
Howells Pl S43.......... 79 B3
Howe St S22.......... 218 D5
Howitt Cres ST14 ...... 210 B2
Howitt Prim Com Sch
  DE75.......... 181 D2
Howitt St
  Heanor DE75.......... 181 F2
  Long Eaton NG10...... 236 E7
How La S33.......... 38 C3
Howth Cl DE21.......... 220 A4
Hoylake Ave S40.......... 114 C7
Hoylake Cl NG19 ...... 136 E6
Hoylake Ct DE3 .... 217 C3
Hoylake Dr DE3.......... 217 C3
Hoyland Ct DE56 ...... 179 E5
Hoyle Ct DE45.......... 109 D5
Hubert Shaw Cl DE24.. 232 E4
Huckerby Rd DE7 ...... 194 C2
Hucklow Ave
  Chesterfield S40 ...... 266 A1
  North Wingfield S42 .. 132 A8
  Staveley S43 .... 97 D7
Hucklow Bank 36 SK13 .. 9 D2
Hucklow Cl 35 SK13 .. 9 D2
Hucklow Ct DE21 ...... 206 B3
Hucklow Fold 34 SK13.. 9 D2
Hucklow Lanes 33 SK13 .. 9 D2
Hucknall Ave S40...... 95 C4
Hudson Cl S26.......... 61 E7
Hudson Mount S44...... 118 B8
Hudson Way DE24...... 219 C3
Hufton's Ct DE75.......... 194 A7
Hufton's Dr DE75 ...... 194 A7
Hugh La S33.......... 51 A7
Hugh St SK13.......... 10 B1
Hulland CE Prim Sch
  DE6.......... 175 F3
Hulland St DE1.......... 267 C4
Hulland View DE22...... 204 D1
HULLAND VILLAGE.......... 175 D2
HULLAND WARD 175 F3
Hull St DE65.......... 228 E1
Humber Cl DE24 ...... 233 C6
Humber Rd NG10 ...... 223 C1
Humber St DE65.......... 228 C1
Humbleton Dr DE22 .... 218 A5
Humphrey Rd S8.......... 56 E8
Humphrey St S8.......... 56 E8
HUNDALL 77 B7
Hundall Ct 4 S40.......... 95 D6
Hundall La
  Chesterfield S41 ...... 77 A4
  Unstone S18.......... 77 A7
Hungerhill La S42, S45.. 113 A7
Hunger La DE6.......... 188 E3
Hungry La
  Bradwell S33.......... 51 A6
  Hathersage S32.......... 53 B8
Hunloke Ave S40.......... 95 E1
Hunloke Cres S40.......... 95 E1
HUNLOKE ESTATE 115 C2
Hunloke Park Prim Sch
  S42.......... 115 A4
Hunloke Rd S42 ...... 132 E8
Hunloke View S42 ...... 115 B4
Hunsdon Rd S21...... 59 C3
Hunstone Ave S8.......... 57 A7
Hunt Ave DE75.......... 181 E2
Hunt Dr DE11.......... 256 E4
Hunter Dr DE56.......... 191 F8
Hunter Pk S18.......... 57 C1
Hunter Rd DE56.......... 179 D5
Hunters Chase NG19 .. 136 B2
Hunters Croft DE24 .... 231 E2
Hunters Green SK23.... 34 E1
Hunters La SK13.......... 16 F8
Hunter's La S13.......... 44 C6
Huntingdon Ave S44 .. 99 B1
Huntingdon Ct DE73.... 252 B8
Huntingdon Dr DE74.... 247 A4
Huntingdon Gn DE21.. 219 C6
Huntingdon Rd DE15.. 254 D7
Huntingdon Way 1 NG9 223 F2
Huntingdon Wlk 2
  NG10.......... 223 B5
Hunt La S45.......... 145 B8
Huntley Ave DE21 ...... 220 F5
Huntley Cl S43.......... 97 B8
Hunts La DE12.......... 264 E8
Huntsman Rd S43........ 78 F2
Huntspill Rd DE65...... 228 E1
Hunts Row S43.......... 157 E3
Hunt Way DE11.......... 256 E4
Hurdlow Gn 10 SK13 .. 9 D1
Hurdlow Lea 11 SK13.. 9 D1
Hurdlow Mews SK13.... 9 D1
Hurdlow Way 12 SK13.. 9 D1
Hurds Hollow DE4 ...... 143 A6
Hurker Rise DE4.......... 143 C7
Hurl Dr S12.......... 43 F5
Hurley Ct DE7 .... 207 E8
HURL FIELD.......... 43 E5
Hurlfield Ct S12.......... 44 A6
Hurlfield Dr S12.......... 43 F6
Hurlfield Rd S12.......... 43 F6
Hurstbrook Cl SK13...... 10 F1
Hurst Cl SK13.......... 10 E1
Hurstclough La S32, S33.. 40 D2
Hurst Cres SK13.......... 17 E8
Hurst Ct DE12.......... 264 F4
Hurst Dr
  Burton upon Trent DE13 .. 240 E1
  Stanley DE7.......... 207 C6
Hurst La DE55.......... 146 A5
Hurst Lea Rd SK22...... 33 C7
Hurst Mills Ind Est 6
  SK13.......... 10 F1
Hurst Rd SK13.......... 10 F1

Hurst Rise DE4.......... 143 D5
Huss's La NG10.......... 236 F7
Hutchings Cres S43...... 80 D5
HUTHWAITE 148 E3
Huthwaite All Saints CE Inf
  Sch NG17.......... 148 E2
Huthwaite La DE55...... 148 C2
Hut La
  Ashover S45.......... 129 E6
  Killamarsh S21 ...... 60 F4
Hutmoor Butts SK17 .... 107 A3
Hutton St DE24 ...... 232 E6
Huxley Cl DE23.......... 231 F7
Hyde Bank Ct SK22...... 33 C7
Hyde Bank Rd SK22...... 33 C8
Hyde Park Rd DE22 .... 218 A6
Hyde Rd SK14.......... 9 A4
Hydro Cl DE45.......... 91 F6
Hylton Cl DE14.......... 254 A7
Hyndley Rd S44.......... 98 F3

I

Ian Ave DE4 .... 165 F7
Ians Way S40.......... 95 C4
Ibbotsons Croft S32.... 53 A8
Ibbotsons Farm Cotts S32 53 A8
IBLE 153 E7
Ibsley Cl DE24 .... 233 C6
Ida's Rd S21.......... 59 D4
IDRIDGEHAY 176 F6
IDRIDGEHAY GREEN 176 E7
Idridgehay Sta * DE56.. 176 F6
Ikea Way NG16.......... 195 C7
Ilam Cl S43.......... 97 C6
Ilam Ct DE6.......... 185 D8
Ilam Sq DE7 .... 194 E5
Ilford Cl DE7.......... 194 D3
Ilford Ct S43.......... 77 D4
Ilford Rd DE22 ...... 218 A5
Ilford Wlk DE22 ...... 218 A5
Ilfracombe Ct 1 S41...... 95 F8
Ilion St NG19 ...... 135 F2
ILKESTON 208 E7
Ilkeston Com Hospl DE7 194 D4
Ilkeston Rd
  Heanor DE75.......... 193 F8
  Sandiacre DE7, NG10.... 223 C8
  Smalley DE7.......... 192 F2
  Stanton-by-Dale DE7.... 208 F3
  Stapleford NG9 ...... 209 F2
  Trowell NG9.......... 209 C5
Ilkeston Sch DE7.......... 208 D8
Imperial Ct DE22.......... 204 D5
Imperial Rd DE4 ...... 143 B5
Inchwood Cl 4 NG9.... 223 F7
Independent Hill DE55.. 158 F3
Industrial St 3 DE23 .. 219 A2
Infirmary Rd S41.......... 266 C4
Ingham Dr DE3 ...... 230 D8
Ingham Rd NG10 ...... 223 C2
Ingleborough Gdns 8
  NG10.......... 236 A8
INGLEBY 243 F2
Ingleby Ave DE23 ...... 231 F7
Ingleby Cl
  Dronfield S18.......... 56 C1
  Swadlincote DE11...... 256 A3
Ingleby Gall * DE73 .... 243 F3
Ingleby La S33.......... 251 A5
Ingleby Rd
  Barrow upon Trent DE73 .. 244 D3
  Long Eaton NG10...... 235 F4
Ingle Ct DE21.......... 220 E5
Ingledew Cl DE22...... 217 D4
Inglefield Rd DE7 ...... 209 A6
Ingleton Rd S41.......... 115 B7
Inglewood Ave DE3 .... 217 D4
Ingliston Cl DE24 ...... 233 D6
INGMANTHORPE 94 C7
Inkerman Cl NE7.......... 194 E5
Inkerman Rd NG16 .... 171 F5
Inkerman St NG16...... 171 F5
INKERSALL 97 D7
Inkersall Dr S20 ...... 59 E8
INKERSALL GREEN....... 97 D6
Inkersall Green Rd S43.. 97 C7
Inkersall Prim Sch S43.. 97 C7
Inkersall Rd S43.......... 97 E7
Inn La DE22.......... 204 B7
Inns La DE55.......... 157 E4
Institute La DE55.......... 159 A4
Instow Dr DE23.......... 231 D6
Intake La
  Bakewell DE45.......... 109 D8
  Cromford DE4.......... 155 B6
  Holloway DE4 .... 155 E4
Intake Prim Sch S12.... 44 C6
Intake Rd S44.......... 98 E3
Intakes La DE56.......... 188 C2
Interchange 25 Bsns Pk
  NG10.......... 223 A4
Inveraray Cl DE24...... 231 D3
Invernia Cl DE23 ...... 231 E5
Iona Cl
  Derby DE24 .... 231 E4
  Tibshelf DE55.......... 147 F5
Iona Dr NG9.......... 209 D2
Ionian Dr DE24.......... 219 E1
Ireland Cl S43.......... 78 F1
Ireland Ind Est S43...... 78 F1
Ireland St S43.......... 78 F2
Ireton Cl DE56.......... 179 E3
Ireton Ct DE6.......... 165 B1
IRETON WOOD 176 D4
Iron Cliff Rd S44.......... 98 F3

Irongate S40.......... 266 B3
Iron Gate DE1.......... 267 B3
Ironside Cl S14.......... 43 D3
Ironside Pl S14.......... 43 E3
Ironside Rd S14.......... 43 E3
Ironside Wlk S14 ...... 43 D3
IRONVILLE.......... 170 E4
Ironville & Codnor Park Prim
  Sch S16.......... 170 F4
Ironwalls La DE13...... 239 C5
Irvine Cl DE24 ...... 231 D3
Irving Pl DE24.......... 232 F7
Isaac's La NG9.......... 223 D7
Isis Way DE65.......... 228 F1
Island Cl DE11.......... 262 C6
Island The NG16.......... 182 F1
Islay Cl NG9.......... 209 D3
Islay Rd DE24.......... 231 E4
Isleworth Dr DE22.......... 217 F6
Ismay Rd DE21.......... 219 F6
Ivan Brook Cl 4 S18.... 56 C1
Ivanhoe Cl S42.......... 115 C1
Ivanhoe Ct 3 S41...... 96 A6
Ivanhoe Ind Est LE65.. 257 F1
Iveagh Wlk DE55.......... 170 E5
Ivonbrook Cl DE4 ...... 142 B8
Ivybridge Cl DE21...... 206 C3
Ivy Cl
  Chesterfield S41 ...... 77 A2
  Donisthorpe DE12...... 262 E1
  Willington DE65.......... 242 A5
Ivycroft SK13.......... 9 E4
Ivy Ct
  Derby DE3.......... 217 D1
  Egginton DE65.......... 241 A5
  Hilton DE65.......... 228 C1
  Sheffield S8.......... 43 C2
Ivy Farm Cl S43.......... 80 E3
Ivy Gr DE5.......... 169 D1
Ivy House Sch DE23.... 231 B7
Ivy La
  Eastwood NG16.......... 182 E2
  Elton DE4.......... 140 E6
Ivyleaf Way DE23.......... 231 B5
Ivy Lodge Cl DE15 ...... 254 E7
Ivy Side Cl S21.......... 60 D6
Ivy Side Gdns S21...... 60 D6
Ivy Spring Cl S42.......... 115 A4
Ivy Sq DE23 .... 219 C2
Ivywood Gdns S44 ...... 98 A5

J

Jackass La DE56 ...... 167 B4
Jackdaw Cl DE22 ...... 218 D5
Jacklin Cl DE14...... 254 A7
JACKSDALE 171 B4
Jacksdale DE22 ...... 204 D1
Jacksdale Prim Sch
  NG16.......... 171 B3
Jack's La ST14.......... 224 E2
Jackson Ave
  Derby DE3.......... 218 A4
  Ilkeston DE7.......... 208 E8
  Sandiacre NG10.......... 223 A6
  Tupton S42.......... 131 C3
Jackson Cl DE12 ...... 262 B3
Jackson Rd
  Clay Cross S45.......... 131 E3
  Matlock DE4.......... 143 B6
Jacksons Edge Rd SK12.. 32 B4
Jacksons La
  Belper DE56.......... 190 E7
  Etwall DE65.......... 229 C2
Jackson's La
  Heage DE56.......... 179 D7
  Ripley DE5.......... 169 A4
Jackson St
  Derby DE22 .... 218 A4
  Glossop, Padfield SK13 .... 10 C1
  Glossop SK13.......... 17 C7
  Mottram in Longdendale
    SK14.......... 9 A3
Jackson Tor Rd DE4.... 143 B6
Jackys La S26.......... 61 E6
Jacobean Ct DE15.......... 248 C4
Jaggers La DE4.......... 128 C5
Jagger's La S32.......... 52 E8
Jago Ave S43.......... 81 A4
James Andrew Cl S8.... 56 F7
James Andrew Cres S8.. 56 F7
James Andrew Croft S8.. 56 F7
James Ave DE55.......... 170 D7
James Brindley Way
  DE13.......... 240 F1
James Cl DE1.......... 218 E5
James's La DE6.......... 215 C1
James St
  Chesterfield S41 ...... 96 A4
  7 Glossop SK13.......... 17 C8
  Kimberley NG16.......... 195 E5
  Somercotes DE55 ...... 170 C7
  Swadlincote DE11...... 256 E5
James Walton Ct S20 .. 59 F7
James Walton Dr S20.. 59 F7
James Walton Pl S20.. 59 F7
James Walton View S20.. 59 F7
Jane La SK23 .... 34 B1
Jap La DE45.......... 110 E8
Jardine Ct DE72.......... 235 B7
Jardines La ST14.......... 196 D4
Jarnett The SK17.......... 107 B8
Jarvey's La DE22.......... 217 E8
Jarvis Ct DE24.......... 231 E2
Jarvis Rd DE24.......... 231 E2
Jasmin Cl NG20.......... 119 D6

Jasmine Cl
Burton upon Trent DE15 . . 255 A8
Derby DE21 . . . . 220 B5
Swanwick DE55 . . . . 169 F7
Jasmine Ct DE75 . . . . 182 B1
Jasmine Dr DE55 . . . . 148 B7
Jaspers La DE4 . . . . 153 A1
Jaunty Ave S12 . . . . 44 C4
Jaunty Cl S12 . . . . 44 B3
Jaunty Cres S12 . . . . 44 C4
Jaunty Dr S12 . . . . 44 B3
Jaunty La S12 . . . . 44 B4
Jaunty Mount S12 . . . . 44 C3
Jaunty Pl S12 . . . . 44 B3
Jaunty Rd S12 . . . . 44 C3
Jaunty View S12 . . . . 44 C3
Jaunty Way S12 . . . . 44 B4
Java Ct DE24 . . . . 219 E2
Jawbone La DE73 . . . . 252 C8
Jaw Bones Hill S40 . . . . 115 A8
Jay Ct DE22 . . . . 218 D5
Jebb Gdns S40 . . . . 95 C2
Jebb's La
Idridgehay DE56 . . . . 176 F8
Shottle DE56 . . . . 177 B8
Jedburgh Cl DE24 . . . . 231 E2
Jefferson Pl DE24 . . . . 232 F7
Jeffery St 6 S2 . . . . 43 B6
Jeffrey La S33 . . . . 51 A6
Jeffries Ave DE4 . . . . 156 F1
Jeffries La DE4 . . . . 156 F1
Jellicoe St NG20 . . . . 101 A2
Jemison Cl DE23 . . . . 230 E7
Jennison St NG19 . . . . 136 A1
Jenny's Ct DE56 . . . . 179 C5
Jephson Rd DE14 . . . . 254 B7
Jepson Rd S41 . . . . 115 C7
Jermyn Ave S12 . . . . 44 F4
Jermyn Cl S12 . . . . 44 F3
Jermyn Cres S12 . . . . 44 F4
Jermyn Dr S12 . . . . 44 F3
Jermyn Way S12 . . . . 44 F3
Jersey Rd S2 . . . . 43 A7
Jerting St S45 . . . . 130 A1
Jervis Ct DE7 . . . . 194 F3
Jervis Pl S43 . . . . 97 B6
Jesop Dr DE24 . . . . 231 E2
Jesses La DE56 . . . . 178 C7
Jessop Ave NG16 . . . . 170 F4
Jessop Lodge DE5 . . . . 181 B7
Jessop St DE5 . . . . 181 B7
Jill Iain Ct 1 NG9 . . . . 223 E5
Jinny Cl DE65 . . . . 239 C8
Joan Ave DE75 . . . . 181 E2
Joan La S33 . . . . 40 C3
Jodrell Ave DE56 . . . . 179 D3
Jodrell Mdw SK23 . . . . 45 E8
Jodrell Rd SK23 . . . . 45 D8
Jodrell St SK22 . . . . 33 B7
John Bank La DE45 . . . . 108 F7
John Berrysford Cl DE21 219 F5
John Dalton St SK13 . . . . 9 E5
John Davies Prim Sch
NG17 . . . . 148 F4
John Davies Workshops
S8 . . . . 43 B2
John Eaton's Almshouses
S8 . . . . 43 B2
John F Kennedy Gdns
DE21 . . . . 220 C6
John Flamsteed Com Sch
DE5 . . . . 180 B2
John Kennedy Rd SK14 . . . 9 A3
John King Inf Sch NG16 160 D3
John King Workshop Mus★
NG16 . . . . 160 D3
John Lombe Dr DE1 . . . . . . 219 A4
Johnnygate La S18 . . . . 75 A4
John of Rolleston Prim Sch
DE13 . . . . 240 B4
John O'Gaunts Way
DE56 . . . . 179 D4
John Port Cl DE65 . . . . 229 C4
John Port Sch DE65 . . . . . . 229 B4
Johnson Ave DE24 . . . . 232 E7
Johnson Dr DE75 . . . . 181 F2
Johnson La
Idridgehay DE56 . . . . 176 E7
Monyash DE45 . . . . 107 F6
Johnson Rd ST14 . . . . 210 B1
Johnson St SK23 . . . . 45 E8
Johnson Way SK23 . . . . 47 D6
John St
Alfreton DE55 . . . . 159 A4
Brimington S43 . . . . 96 E8
Chesterfield S40 . . . . 95 A4
Clay Cross S45 . . . . 131 D4
Clowne S43 . . . . 80 D3
Compstall SK6 . . . . 15 B3
Creswell S80 . . . . 81 E1
Derby DE1 . . . . 267 C2
Eckington S21 . . . . 59 D3
Glossop SK13 . . . . 17 C8
Heanor DE75 . . . . 181 D2
Ilkeston DE7 . . . . 194 F1
Marple SK6 . . . . 23 A5
Matlock DE4 . . . . 143 B6
North Wingfield S42 . . . . . 131 E7
Somercotes DE55 . . . . 170 C8
Swadlincote, Albert Village
DE11 . . . . 256 C2
Swadlincote DE11 . . . . 255 E6
Swadlincote, Lower Medway
DE11 . . . . 256 C5
Johnstone Cl S40 . . . . 266 A1
John Turner Rd DE4 . . . . . . 127 C3
Jolly La DE6 . . . . 175 A4
Jones St SK13 . . . . 10 A5

Jordan Ave DE13 . . . . 240 F2
Jordan St SK13 . . . . 10 E1
JORDANTHORPE 57 B7
Jordanthorpe Ctr S8 . . . . 57 B6
Jordanthorpe Gn S8 . . . . 57 C6
Jordanthorpe Parkway
S8 . . . . 57 C6
Jordanthorpe View S8 . . . . . . 57 C7
Joseph Fletcher Dr S42 . 114 F2
Joseph St
Belper DE56 . . . . 178 F4
Derby DE23 . . . . 219 A1
Eckington S21 . . . . 59 D3
Marple SK6 . . . . 23 A6
Joseph Wright Terr DE1 . 267 B4
Joyce Ave NG9 . . . . 223 F3
Jubalton Cl DE24 . . . . 232 E6
JUBILEE 171 B6
Jubilee Ave DE5 . . . . 169 C1
Jubilee Bsns Pk DE21 . . . . 267 C4
Jubilee Cotts S44 . . . . 97 A1
Jubilee Cres
Clowne S43 . . . . 81 A4
Killamarsh S21 . . . . 60 E7
Whitwell S80 . . . . 81 E5
Jubilee Ct
Belper DE56 . . . . 179 A2
Pinxton NG16 . . . . 160 D3
West Hallam DE7 . . . . 207 D8
Wirksworth DE4 . . . . 165 E7
Jubilee Gdns
New Mills SK22 . . . . 33 C7
Whitwell S80 . . . . 81 F5
Jubilee Pk DE11 . . . . 256 F4
Jubilee Pl S80 . . . . 81 F5
Jubilee Rd
Chapel-en-le-Frith SK23 . . . 47 B5
Derby DE24 . . . . 232 F4
Whitwell S80 . . . . 81 F5
Jubilee Rise DE15 . . . . 248 C3
Jubilee Sq DE6 . . . . 184 D7
Jubilee St
Kimberley NG16 . . . . 195 E7
New Mills SK22 . . . . 33 C7
Jubilee Terr DE12 . . . . 262 E1
Judson Ave NG9 . . . . 223 F6
Judy Hill DE4 . . . . 127 F1
Julia Cres DE55 . . . . 146 F3
Julian Cl DE7 . . . . 209 B6
Julie Ave DE75 . . . . 182 B1
Julius Cl S41 . . . . 182 B4
Jumble Rd S17 . . . . 42 F1
Junction Rd NG10 . . . . 237 A6
Junction St DE1 . . . . 218 E4
Juniper Cl S43 . . . . 78 A2
Juniper Ct NG16 . . . . 195 C8
Juniper Rise S21 . . . . 60 C5
Jura Ave DE5 . . . . 169 D2
Jury St DE1 . . . . 267 A3

K

Kariba Cl S41 . . . . 266 C3
Katherine Dr NG9 . . . . 223 F4
Katrine Wlk DE24 . . . . 231 E1
Kay Dr DE11 . . . . 255 F5
Kayes Ct 2 NG9 . . . . 223 D7
Kean Pl DE24 . . . . 232 F7
Kearsley Rd S2 . . . . 43 A8
Keats Ave DE23 . . . . 218 A1
Keats Cl NG10 . . . . 236 B5
Keats Dr DE11 . . . . 256 C6
Keats Rd
Chesterfield S41 . . . . 95 F8
Stonebroom DE55 . . . . . . 146 F3
Keats Way S42 . . . . 115 E4
Keats Wlk DE55 . . . . 146 F3
Keble Cl
Burton upon Trent DE15 . . 248 C2
Derby DE1 . . . . 267 C1
Kedleston st DE1 . . . . 267 A4
KEDLESTON 203 C7
Kedleston Cl
Burton upon Trent DE13 . . 240 C1
Chesterfield S41 . . . . 95 C6
Derby DE22 . . . . 204 D1
Long Eaton NG10 . . . . 236 A5
Ripley DE5 . . . . 169 C3
Kedleston Ct
3 Derby DE22 . . . . 204 D2
4 Staveley S43 . . . . 78 E2
Tibshelf DE55 . . . . 148 B6
Kedleston Dr
Heanor DE75 . . . . 181 C2
Ilkeston DE7 . . . . 194 D3
Kedlestone Cl NG17 . . . . . . 148 F2
Kedleston Gdns DE1 . . . . . 267 A4
Kedleston Hall★ DE22 . . . 203 E5
Kedleston Old Rd DE22 . . 218 D8
Kedleston Rd
Buxton SK17 . . . . 85 C7
Derby DE22 . . . . 218 E2
Quarndon DE22 . . . . 204 B5
Weston Underwood DE22 . 203 E8
Kedleston St DE1 . . . . 267 A4
Keeble Cl DE75 . . . . 193 E8
Keele Dr DE11 . . . . 255 E1
Keeling La DE4 . . . . 126 B1
Keeling Terr DE4 . . . . 126 B1
Keepers La S18 . . . . 75 E3
Kegworth Ave DE23 . . . . . . 231 C6
Kegworth Rd NG11 . . . . 237 F1
Keilder Ct S40 . . . . 95 D1
Kelburn Ave S40 . . . . 95 C1
Keldeston Cl S41 . . . . 95 C6

Keldholme La DE24 . . . . . . 233 D6
Kelgate S20 . . . . 59 D6
Kelham Way NG16 . . . . 182 E3
Kelmoor Rd DE24 . . . . 233 B7
Kelsons Ave SK17 . . . . 85 D5
Kelso Wlk DE24 . . . . 231 E2
KELSTEDGE 129 D4
Kelstedge La S45 . . . . 129 D5
Kelvedon Dr DE23 . . . . 231 A6
Kelvin Cl NG9 . . . . 223 C5
Kemble Pl DE24 . . . . 232 F7
Kemp Cl S21 . . . . 60 C6
Kemp Rd SK6 . . . . 23 C7
Kempton Cl NG16 . . . . 195 E7
Kempton Park Rd DE24 . . 232 D8
Kempton Rd DE15 . . . . 248 A3
Kendal Dr S18 . . . . 56 E1
Kendal Rd S41 . . . . 95 E8
Kendal Wlk 1 DE21 . . . . . . 205 D1
Kendon Ave DE23 . . . . 231 E6
Kendray Cl DE56 . . . . 179 D5
Kendricks Cl DE1 . . . . 257 A7
Kenilworth Ave DE23 . . . . 231 F8
Kenilworth Ct 4 S41 . . . . . 96 A6
Kenilworth Dr DE7 . . . . 208 D5
Kenilworth Rd DE5 . . . . 169 C1
Kenmere Cl S45 . . . . 131 D2
Kennack Cl DE55 . . . . 160 C6
Kennedy Ave
Long Eaton NG10 . . . . 236 C5
Mansfield Woodhouse
NG19 . . . . 136 D4
Kennedy Cl DE21 . . . . 220 A7
Kennedy Dr NG9 . . . . 209 E1
Kennet Paddock NG19 . . . 136 D3
Kennett Gr SK17 . . . . 84 E6
Kennet Vale S40 . . . . 95 D5
Kenninghall Cl S2 . . . . 43 D7
Kenninghall Dr S2 . . . . 43 D7
Kenninghall Mount S2 . . . . 43 D7
Kenninghall Rd S2 . . . . 43 D7
Kenning St S45 . . . . 131 C3
Kensal Rise DE22 . . . . 218 B6
Kensington Ave DE75 . . . . 181 C1
Kensington Bsns Pk DE7 . 194 F8
Kensington Chase S10 . . . . 42 F8
Kensington Cl NG19 . . . . . . 136 E5
Kensington Ct S10 . . . . 42 F8
Kensington Dr S10 . . . . 42 F8
Kensington Gdns DE7 . . . . 208 F7
Kensington Jun Sch
DE7 . . . . 209 A7
Kensington Pk S10 . . . . 42 F8
Kensington Rd
Burton upon Trent DE15 . . 248 A3
Sandiacre NG10 . . . . 223 A4
Kensington St
Derby DE1 . . . . 267 A3
Ilkeston DE7 . . . . 208 F6
Kent Ave NG16 . . . . 171 B4
Kent Cl S41 . . . . 95 F5
Kent Grange 12 S8 . . . . 43 B6
Kent House Cl S12 . . . . 58 E8
Kentish Ct DE7 . . . . 219 B7
Kentmere Cl S18 . . . . 56 E1
Kentmere Way S43 . . . . 97 C8
Kent Rd
Burton upon Trent DE15 . . 254 E6
Eastwood NG16 . . . . 195 C8
Glossop SK13 . . . . 10 D1
Sheffield S8 . . . . 43 B6
Kent's Bank Rd SK17 . . . . . 85 C6
Kent St
Chesterfield S41 . . . . 115 C8
Derby DE21 . . . . 219 D7
Kenwell Dr S17 . . . . 56 B5
Kenyon Rd S41 . . . . 96 E1
Keppel Ct DE7 . . . . 194 F3
Kepple Gate DE5 . . . . 180 F8
Kernel Cl DE7 . . . . 231 A8
Kerry Dr DE7 . . . . 192 F6
Kerry St DE21 . . . . 219 D7
Kerry's Yd DE7 . . . . 191 F8
Kershaw St SK13 . . . . 17 C8
Kershope Dr DE21 . . . . 206 B3
Kerwin Cl S17 . . . . 55 C8
Kerwin Dr S17 . . . . 55 C8
Kerwin Rd S17 . . . . 55 C8
Kestrel Cl
Bolsover S44 . . . . 98 F3
Burnaston DE3 . . . . 230 B7
Ilkeston DE7 . . . . 208 F4
Killamarsh S21 . . . . 60 B7
Marple SK6 . . . . 23 A3
Kestrel Dr S21 . . . . 59 B3
Kestrel Ho S41 . . . . 231 E2
Kestrel Hts NG16 . . . . 170 F4
Kestrels Croft DE24 . . . . . . 231 E3
Kestrel View SK13 . . . . 16 F8
Kestrel Way DE15 . . . . 248 D3
Keswick Ave DE23 . . . . 231 E6
Keswick Cl
Bolsover S44 . . . . 98 F1
Ilkeston DE7 . . . . 208 D5
Keswick Ct NG10 . . . . 223 B2
Keswick Dr
Chesterfield S41 . . . . 95 C8
Chesterfield S41 . . . . 95 D8
Keswick Pl S18 . . . . 56 D1
Kettlewell Cl DE24 . . . . 232 E6
Ketton Ave S8 . . . . 43 B3
Kevin Cl DE21 . . . . 220 B8
Kew Cres
Heanor DE75 . . . . 182 B1
Sheffield S12 . . . . 44 A2
Kew Gdns DE22 . . . . 218 B5

Keyhaven Cl DE21 . . . . 219 D8
Keynsham Cl DE24 . . . . . . 232 E8
Keys Rd DE55 . . . . 159 B2
Keys St DE1 . . . . 267 C4
Kibworth Cl
Chesterfield S41 . . . . 115 C7
Derby DE21 . . . . 220 B8
Kidd Rd SK13 . . . . 17 E6
Kidsley Cl 7 S40 . . . . 95 A5
Kilbourne Rd DE56 . . . . . . 179 C4
KILBURN 192 A8
Kilburn Dr DE7 . . . . 194 D3
Kilburn Inf Sch DE56 . . . . 191 F8
Kilburn Jun Sch DE56 . . . 192 A8
Kilburn La DE56 . . . . 179 C3
Kilburn Rd S18 . . . . 56 C1
Kilburn Toll Bar DE56 . . . . 179 F1
Kilburn Way DE11 . . . . 255 F5
Kilby Ho DE21 . . . . 236 F7
Kildale Gdns S20 . . . . 59 D7
Kildare Rd DE21 . . . . 220 B4
Kildonan Gr S12 . . . . 44 C3
Kildrummy Cl DE73 . . . . . . 232 E1
Killamarsh Inf Sch S21 . . . 60 E7
Killamarsh Jun Sch S21 . . 60 E7
Killamarsh La S21, S26 . . . 61 B6
Killamarsh Sp Ctr S21 . . . 60 D7
Killingworth Ave DE24 . . . 231 F4
Killis La
Belper DE56 . . . . 179 D1
Holbrook DE56 . . . . 191 D8
Kilmory Fold SK13 . . . . 10 E3
Kiln Bent Rd HD9 . . . . 3 A6
Kiln Cl DE7 . . . . 193 E1
Kiln Croft DE65 . . . . 229 C4
Kiln Hill S18 . . . . 57 C3
Kiln La
Glossop SK13 . . . . 10 A5
Parwich DE6 . . . . 151 D2
Kilnsey Ct DE23 . . . . 230 F6
Kiln Way NG11 . . . . 256 D3
Kilverston Rd NG10 . . . . . . 223 A6
Kilvington Ave S13 . . . . 44 B7
Kilvington Cres S13 . . . . . . 44 B7
Kilvington Rd S13 . . . . 44 B7
KIMBERLEY 195 F8
Kimberley Dr DE15 . . . . . . 248 C3
Kimberley Prim Sch
NG16 . . . . 195 F6
Kimberley Rd NG72 . . . . . . 221 B2
Kinder Ave DE11 . . . . 256 A5
Kinder Cl S13 . . . . 17 A8
Kinder Cres DE56 . . . . 168 B5
Kinder Dr SK6 . . . . 23 A6
Kinder Gr SK17 . . . . 85 A6
Kinderlee Way SK13 . . . . . . 16 B5
Kinder Rd
Hayfield SK22 . . . . 25 E2
Staveley S43 . . . . 97 B6
Kinder Row SK22 . . . . 25 F2
Kinder View SK22 . . . . 33 C7
Kinder Way SK17 . . . . 85 E7
Kinder Wlk DE22 . . . . 218 E4
King Alfred St DE22 . . . . . . 267 A2
King Charles Ct SK13 . . . . 17 D7
King Cup Cl S13 . . . . 17 E8
King Ecgbert Rd S17 . . . . . 55 E5
King Ecgbert Sec Sch
S17 . . . . 55 D6
King Edward Ave SK13 . . . 10 D1
King Edward Gdns 1
NG10 . . . . 223 B6
King Edward St
Ashbourne DE6 . . . . 173 B1
Sandiacre NG10 . . . . 223 B6
Shirebrook NG20 . . . . 119 F4
Wirksworth DE4 . . . . 166 A8
Kingfisher Ave DE11 . . . . . 256 F3
Kingfisher Cl DE3 . . . . 230 B7
Kingfisher Ct
Bolsover S44 . . . . 98 F3
Ilkeston DE7 . . . . 208 F4
Kingfisher Mews SK6 . . . . . 23 A6
Kingfisher Rd NG19 . . . . . . 135 D1
Kingfisher Way SK13 . . . . . 16 F8
Kingfisher Wlk DE24 . . . . . 231 E2
King George Ave DE7 . . . . 208 E8
King George St
Wessington DE55 . . . . 157 E8
Wirksworth DE4 . . . . 165 F1
Kingsbury Cl DE15 . . . . . . 248 A4
Kingsbury Rd DE22 . . . . . . 218 A6
Kings Cl
Carsington DE4 . . . . 164 E8
Clowne S43 . . . . 80 D3
Creswell S80 . . . . 81 F1
Heanor DE75 . . . . 181 C1
King's Cl SK17 . . . . 85 D8
Kingsclere Ave DE21 . . . . . 206 B2
Kingsclere Wlk S40 . . . . . . 114 F8
Kings Coppice S17 . . . . 55 E8
Kings Croft DE22 . . . . 204 F4
Kingscroft Cl S17 . . . . 55 E8
Kings Ct
Derby DE1 . . . . 267 B4
5 Glossop SK13 . . . . 17 C8
Kingsdale Cl NG10 . . . . . . 236 A5
Kingsdale Gr DE73 . . . . . . 244 F8
Kings Dr
Brinsley NG16 . . . . 182 E7
Derby DE3, DE23 . . . . 218 B2
Kingsfield Ind Est DE4 . . . 165 E6
Kingsfield Rd DE4 . . . . 165 E6
Kingsgate S32 . . . . 72 C2
Kings Gate DE74 . . . . 247 F4
Kings Head La DE6 . . . . . . 173 F7

Jas–Kir 291

Kings Hill DE4 . . . . 153 A2
Kings Hollow Mews DE6 . 173 F7
Kingsland Cl DE21 . . . . 205 F2
Kingsley Ave
Chesterfield S40 . . . . 114 F8
Mansfield Woodhouse
NG19 . . . . 136 D5
Kingsley Cl NG19 . . . . 136 D4
Kingsley Cres
Long Eaton NG10 . . . . 236 B4
Stonebroom DE55 . . . . . . 146 F3
Kingsley Ct NG19 . . . . 136 D5
Kingsley Rd DE22 . . . . 204 D4
Kingsley St DE24 . . . . 231 F5
Kingsmead Ave NG9 . . . . . 209 D2
King's Mead Cl DE1 . . . . . . 267 A4
King's Mead Ho 1 DE22 . 218 F7
Kingsmead Ind Est DE22 218 D6
Kingsmead Sch The DE1 . 267 A4
King's Mead Wlk DE1 . . . . 267 A4
Kingsmede Ave S40 . . . . . . 95 D1
Kings Mews S21 . . . . 59 E3
King's Mill La DE72 . . . . . . 245 F5
King's Mills La DE72 . . . . . 245 F5
Kingsmoor Fields SK13 . . . 10 D3
Kingsmoor Rd SK13 . . . . . . 10 D2
Kingsmuir Rd DE3 . . . . 217 C3
KING'S NEWTON 245 B1
Kings Rd
Sandiacre NG10 . . . . 223 B4
Swadlincote DE11 . . . . 256 B6
King's Rd SK17 . . . . 85 D8
King St
Alfreton DE55 . . . . 158 F4
Ashbourne DE6 . . . . 173 C2
Bakewell DE45 . . . . 109 D5
Belper DE56 . . . . 178 F3
Brimington S43 . . . . 77 F1
Broadbottom SK14 . . . . . . 16 A8
Burton upon Trent DE14 . . 254 C4
Clay Cross S45 . . . . 131 C3
Clowne S43 . . . . 80 E3
Creswell, Hodthorpe S80 . 82 C6
Creswell S80 . . . . 81 F1
Derby DE1 . . . . 267 B4
Duffield DE56 . . . . 190 E4
Eastwood NG16 . . . . 182 F2
Glossop SK13 . . . . 17 C8
Hollingworth SK14 . . . . . . 9 D5
Ilkeston DE7 . . . . 194 F1
Long Eaton NG10 . . . . 236 D8
Mansfield Woodhouse
NG19 . . . . 136 D2
Middleton DE4 . . . . 154 D5
Pinxton NG16 . . . . 160 D3
Shirebrook NG20 . . . . 120 D5
South Normanton DE55 . . 159 F5
Tibshelf DE55 . . . . 148 A7
Youlgreave DE45 . . . . 125 B5
KING STERNDALE 86 C5
Kingsthorpe Cl 6 NG19 . 136 E1
Kingston Ave DE7 . . . . 209 A4
Kingston Ct
3 Barrow Hill S43 . . . . . . 78 B3
West Hallam DE7 . . . . 207 D8
Kingston Rd DE15 . . . . 248 C2
Kingston St DE1 . . . . 218 F7
Kingston Way
Burton upon Trent DE14 . . 254 B8
Derby DE22 . . . . 218 B5
Heanor DE75 . . . . 181 D2
Ilkeston DE7 . . . . 209 A5
Kings Way S80 . . . . 82 C6
Kingsway
Burton upon Trent DE14 . . 254 B8
Derby DE22 . . . . 218 B5
Heanor DE75 . . . . 181 D2
Ilkeston DE7 . . . . 209 A5
Kingsway Cres DE22 . . . . . 192 A8
Kingsway Ind Pk DE22 . . . 218 C5
Kingsway Park Cl DE22 . . 218 C5
Kingsway Ret Pk DE22 . . . 218 C5
Kingswood Ave DE56 . . . . 179 C6
Kingswood Cl S41 . . . . 95 D8
Kingswood Pl DE23 . . . . . . 218 B2
King William Ctr NG16 . . . 170 F4
King William St NG16 . . . . 170 F4
Kinross Ave DE21 . . . . 219 C8
Kintyre Dr DE24 . . . . 231 D3
Kinver Cl DE6 . . . . 184 C8
Kinver Rd DE15 . . . . 248 A4
Kipling Cl S18 . . . . 76 C8
Kipling Dr DE3 . . . . 217 D1
Kipling Rd S41 . . . . 95 F8
Kirby Cl S41 . . . . 115 C7
Kirby La DE4 . . . . 142 B7
Kirkby Ave
Ilkeston DE7 . . . . 208 F6
Sheffield S12 . . . . 44 A4
Kirkby Dr S12 . . . . 44 A4
Kirkby La NG16 . . . . 160 F3
Kirkby Rd S12 . . . . 44 A4
Kirkby View S12 . . . . 44 A4
Kirkby Way S12 . . . . 44 A3
Kirk Cl DE55 . . . . 180 C8
Kirkcroft Ave S21 . . . . 60 D7
Kirkcroft Dr S21 . . . . 60 D6
Kirkcroft La S21 . . . . 60 D6
Kirk Dale Ave DE21 . . . . . . 220 F3
Kirkdale Cl S40 . . . . 115 B8
Kirkdale Gdns NG10 . . . . . 236 B6
Kirkdale Rd NG10 . . . . 236 B6
Kirkewhite Ave NG10 . . . . 236 D7
Kirkewhite Ho NG10 . . . . . 236 D7
Kirkfield Dr DE72 . . . . 235 D8
KIRK HALLAM 208 C5
Kirk Hallam Com Tech Coll
DE7 . . . . 208 D6

Kirkham Cl **5** DE75 . . . . .181 D1
Kirkham Dr NG9 . . . . .223 F2
Kirkham La DE56. . . . . . . .168 B7
KIRK IRETON 165 C1
Kirk Ireton CE Prim Sch
DE6. . . . . .165 B1
Kirkistown Cl DE24. . . . . .233 C6
Kirkland Cl DE74. . . . . . . .247 A3
Kirkland Way
12 Derby DE24. . . . . . . .231 D3
Swadlincote DE11 . . . . . .256 B1
KIRK LANGLEY 202 F2
Kirk Langley CE Prim Sch
DE6. . . . . .202 F2
Kirkley Dr DE75. . . . . .181 C1
Kirk Leys Avenue N
DE21. . . . . .220 E4
Kirk Leys Avenue S DE21 220 E4
Kirkman Rd DE75. . . . . . . .181 C4
Kirk's La DE56. . . . . .179 B3
Kirk St DE1. . . . . .219 B8
KIRKSTEAD 160 D3
Kirkstead Cl
Derby DE21 . . . . .206 B1
Pinxton NG16. . . . . .160 D3
Kirkstead Jun Sch NG16 160 D3
Kirkstead Rd NG16. . . . . . .160 D3
Kirkstone Ave DE75 . . . . . .182 B1
Kirkstone Ct NG10 . . . . . . .223 B2
Kirkstone Rd
Buxton SK17. . . . . .85 D3
Chesterfield S41 . . . . .95 D8
Kirton Ave NG10 . . . . .236 D7
Kishfield La SK23 . . . . .45 A6
Kissingate L Ctr NG20. . . .119 E4
Kitchener Ave DE23 . . . . . .231 F7
Kitchener Terr NG20 . . . . . .101 A2
Kitchen Wood La S18 . . . . .75 C8
Kitson Ave NG16. . . . . . . .171 C4
Kiwi Dr DE24. . . . . .232 F7
Knabb Rd DE4 . . . . .127 F3
Knabhall La DE4 . . . . .144 C5
Knapp Ave NG16. . . . . . . .182 F1
Knifesmithgate S40. . . . . .266 B3
Knife & Steel Ct DE7. . . . .192 C7
Knighton Cl S41. . . . . .115 B7
Knighton Ct S42 . . . . .131 E6
Knighton St S42 . . . . .131 E6
Knightsbridge DE22 . . . . . .218 A6
Knights Cl
Beeston NG9. . . . . .223 F2
Derby DE24 . . . . .231 E2
Knights Ct DE13 . . . . .240 E2
Knight's La DE15. . . . . . . .249 B5
Knights Rd DE73 . . . . .244 E8
Knightsyard Ct NG10 . . . . .236 C5
Knightwake Rd SK22. . . . . .33 A8
KNIVETON 163 B1
Kniveton CE Prim Sch
DE6. . . . . .163 C1
Kniveton La DE6 . . . . .174 C4
Kniveton Pk DE7 . . . . .208 C7
Knob Fields DE11 . . . . . . .261 E8
Knob La DE4. . . . . .166 D5
Knoll Cl DE23 . . . . .231 A8
Knoll St SK22. . . . . .33 B8
Knoll The
Chesterfield S40 . . . . .94 F2
Dronfield S18. . . . . .57 D3
Shirebrook NG20. . . . . . .119 D3
Swadlincote DE11 . . . . . .256 B6
Tansley S42. . . . . .144 A5
KNOTBURY 102 F5
Knowl Ave DE56 . . . . .178 E5
Knowle Ave SK23 . . . . .47 B5
Knowle Gn S17 . . . . .55 C7
Knowle Rd SK6. . . . . .23 C6
Knowles Cl SK17. . . . . .85 E8
Knowles Cres SK17. . . . . . .85 E8
Knowles Hill DE13 . . . . . . .240 B3
Knowles Ind Est SK23 . . . . .33 D3
Knowles View DE11 . . . . . .256 D4
Knowle Top S20. . . . . .59 E7
Knutsford Gn DE21. . . . . . .205 D2
Kraft Gdns DE21 . . . . .220 B5
Kye La S26. . . . . .61 E6
Kyle Cl S21. . . . . .60 B1
Kyle Gr DE21 . . . . .206 B3
Kyle Rd DE65 . . . . .240 D8
Kynance Cl
Derby DE24 . . . . .233 C5
South Normanton DE55. . .160 C6
Kynnersley Croft ST14. . . .210 B1

L

Laburnum Ave NG20 . . . .119 E5
Laburnum Cl
Bolsover S44. . . . . .99 C1
Creswell S80 . . . . .81 F1
Darley Dale DE4. . . . . . . .127 B3
Sandiacre NG10. . . . . . . .223 B7
South Normanton DE55. . .160 B7
Laburnum Cres
Derby DE22 . . . . .204 D4
Swanwick DE55. . . . . . . .170 A8
Laburnum Ct S44 . . . . .97 A3
Laburnum Gr
Derby DE22 . . . . .218 B5
Killamarsh S21. . . . . .60 C5
Mansfield Woodhouse
NG19. . . . . .136 A4

Laburnum Rd
Burton upon Trent DE15 . .254 F6
Swadlincote DE11 . . . . . .256 A6
Laburnum St S43 . . . . .78 B1
Laburnum Way DE65 . . . . .229 C3
Laceby Ct NG19. . . . . .136 E4
Lace Makers Cl DE72. . . . .221 D1
Lacey Cl DE7 . . . . .194 C3
Lacey Fields Rd DE75 . . . . .182 B1
Ladbroke Gdns DE22 . . . . .217 F6
Ladies Spring Ct S17. . . . . .56 A7
Ladies Spring Dr S17. . . . . .56 A7
Ladies Spring Gr S17. . . . . .56 A7
Ladle End La DE12 . . . . . .253 D1
LADMANLOW 84 E4
Ladybank Rd
Derby DE3. . . . . .217 C2
Sheffield S20. . . . . .59 D6
Lady Bank View S21. . . . . .59 D4
Ladybower Cl DE11 . . . . . .256 A2
Ladybower Ct
Glossop SK13. . . . . .10 C1
4 Sheffield S17. . . . . .56 A5
Ladybower Dr S32 . . . . . . .53 A7
Ladybower La S43 . . . . .97 D8
Ladybower Rd DE21. . . . . .220 F4
Ladycroft SK17. . . . . .66 C1
Ladycroft Paddock DE2 204 E4
Ladycross Inf Sch **3**
NG10. . . . . .223 B6
Lady Field Rd S80. . . . . . . .62 D8
Ladyfields DE11. . . . . .256 D6
Ladyfields Way DE11 . . . . .255 F6
Ladyflatts Rd DE4. . . . . . . .165 E7
Ladygrove DE56. . . . . .168 D5
Ladygrove Cotts DE23 . . . .219 B3
Ladygrove Rd DE4 . . . . . . .127 E2
Lady Hole La DE6 . . . . . . .186 B7
Lady Ida's Dr
Eckington S21. . . . . .59 C4
Sheffield S20, S21. . . . . . .59 C5
Ladylea Rd NG16. . . . . . . .236 A4
Lady Lea Rd DE21, DE7. . . .192 A6
Lady Ley Hill DE21 . . . . . . .192 A6
Lady Manners Sch DE45 109 C4
Lady Mantle Cl DE73 . . . . .232 E2
Lady Meadow Cl ST14. . . .196 E5
Ladypit Rd SK23. . . . . .33 E4
Ladysmith Rd DE72. . . . . .221 B2
Ladythorn Ave SK6. . . . . . .23 A5
Ladywell Cl DE13 . . . . .240 E1
Ladywell Ct DE56 . . . . . . .179 A3
Ladywood Ave DE56. . . . . .179 B5
Ladywood Dr S41 . . . . .95 C7
Ladywood Prim Sch DE7 208 D5
Ladywood Rd DE7. . . . . . . .208 C5
Lake Ave DE75 . . . . .181 C4
Lake Dr
Derby DE23 . . . . .231 F8
Doveridge DE6. . . . . .211 B1
Lake Gdns DE75. . . . . .181 C4
Lake Lands S42. . . . . .114 F2
Lakeside
12 Ashbourne DE6 . . . . .173 C2
Bakewell DE45. . . . . .109 B7
Wingerworth S42. . . . . . .114 F2
Lake Side
Doveridge DE6. . . . . .211 A1
Glossop SK13. . . . . .10 A6
Lakeside Bsns Ctr DE75 .194 A6
Lakeside Cl S41. . . . . .77 C4
Lakeside Com Prim Sch
DE24. . . . . .219 E2
Lakeside Cres NG10 . . . . .236 D5
Lakeside Dr DE23 . . . . . . .231 A7
Lakeside Inf Sch NG10 . . .236 C5
Lakes Rd SK6. . . . . .23 B6
Lake View SK23. . . . . .33 D4
Lake View Ave S40. . . . . . .95 C1
Lamb Cres DE5 . . . . .169 F1
Lambcroft Rd NG16 . . . . . .160 D3
Lambe Ct DE23 . . . . .267 C1
Lambgates SK13. . . . . .10 A5
Lamb Hill Cl S13. . . . . .44 D7
LAMBHOUSE 177 E7
Lambhouse La DE56. . . . . .177 E5
Lambley Dr DE22. . . . . . . .204 C2
Lambourn Ct DE22 . . . . . .205 A3
Lambourn Dr DE22 . . . . . .205 B4
Lambourne Ave DE6 . . . . .185 D8
Lambpart La SK17/S33. . . . .50 D5
Lambrook Cl DE3 . . . . .217 C2
Lambton Cl DE7 . . . . .194 E3
Lampad Cl **4** DE73. . . . . .252 A8
Lampeter Cl DE21 . . . . . . .206 B2
Lanark St DE21 . . . . .219 E7
Lancaster Ave
Sandiacre NG10. . . . . . . .223 A4
Stapleford NG9 . . . . .223 E7
Lancaster Dr
Hilton DE65 . . . . .228 E2
Tutbury DE13 . . . . .239 B5
Lancaster Rd S41. . . . . . . .95 E8
Lancaster Rise DE56 . . . . .179 A6
Lancaster St S44. . . . . . . .117 F1
Lancaster Wlk DE21. . . . . .221 A6
Lancelot Cl S40. . . . . .114 D8
Lancelot Dr DE13 . . . . . . .240 E2
Lancing Rd S2. . . . . .43 A8
Landau Forte Coll DE1 . .267 C4
Lander La DE56 . . . . .179 A4
Landmere DE24. . . . . .231 E3
Landmere Cl DE7. . . . . . . .194 C3
Landon Cl S40 . . . . .114 B7
Landsdowne Ave S41 . . . . .95 C5
Landsdown Gr NG10 . . . . .223 F1
Landseer Cl
4 Dronfield S18. . . . . . . .56 E1

Landseer Cl continued
Sheffield S14. . . . . .43 D2
Landseer Dr
Marple SK6. . . . . .23 B7
Sheffield S14. . . . . .43 E2
Landseer Pl S14 . . . . .43 E2
Landseer Wlk S14. . . . . . . .43 E2
LANE. 2 E8
LANE ENDS
Disley. 32 E4
Marple. 15 D1
Sutton on the Hill. 215 A2
LANE HEAD 69 E5
Lane Head
Longnor SK17. . . . . .121 B7
Stoney Middleton S32 . . . .71 C3
Tideswell SK17. . . . . .69 D5
Lane Head Gn S33 . . . . . . .37 C7
Lanehead Rd SK23 . . . . . . .45 C5
Lane Head Rd S17. . . . . . . .55 C4
Lanesend Cotts SK17. . . . . .46 A8
Laneside Ave NG9. . . . . . .223 E2
Laneside Cl SK23 . . . . .47 A5
Laneside Rd
New Mills, Rowarth SK22 . .24 E6
New Mills SK22. . . . . .33 E7
Lanes The DE4. . . . . .155 A3
Lane The
Awsworth NG16. . . . . . . .195 C4
Spinkhill S21 . . . . .60 D1
Stanton in Peak DE4 . . . .126 C5
Laneward Cl DE7 . . . . .194 D4
Langdale Cl S40. . . . . .94 F5
Langdale Dr
Derby DE21 . . . . .205 D1
Dronfield S18. . . . . .57 C3
Long Eaton NG10. . . . . . .236 A6
Langdale Sq S43 . . . . .96 D8
Langdon Cl **3** NG10. . . . .223 A1
Langen Cl DE14. . . . . .254 B6
Langer Cl DE14 . . . . .254 B6
Langerfield Ave S40. . . . . .115 A7
Langer La S40, S42 . . . . . .114 E5
Langford Croft S40 . . . . . .266 B1
Langford Rd DE3. . . . . .217 D3
Langham Park Ind Est
DE55. . . . . .160 C7
Langhurst Ct S40 . . . . .95 D4
Langhurst Rd S40. . . . . . . .95 D4
LANGLEY. 182 B1
Langley Ave
Ilkeston DE7 . . . . .194 D5
Somercotes DE55 . . . . . .170 C8
Langley Cl
3 Chesterfield S40. . . . . .95 A5
Mansfield NG19. . . . . . . .135 E1
LANGLEY COMMON 217 B8
Langley Ct SK13. . . . . .10 A5
Langley Dr SK13. . . . . .17 F8
LANGLEY GREEN 202 D2
Langley Inf Sch DE75. . . . .182 A1
LANGLEY MILL. 182 B3
Langley Mill CE Inf Sch **1**
NG16. . . . . .182 B3
Langley Mill Jun Sch
NG16. . . . . .182 A4
Langley Mill Sta NG16. . . .182 A3
Langley Pk NG16. . . . . . . .182 B3
Langley Rd DE21. . . . . . . .220 E3
Langley St DE22 . . . . .218 D6
Lang Rd DE24. . . . . .232 F6
Langsett Ave **13** SK13. . . . . .9 D1
Langsett Gn **15** SK13. . . . . . .9 D1
Langsett La SK13 . . . . .9 D2
Langsett Lea **25** SK13. . . . . .9 D1
Langsett Terr **14** SK13. . . . . .9 D1
Langstone Ave S44. . . . . . .99 C1
Langton Hollow NG16. . . . .171 D6
Langton The **4** DE22. . . . .218 E5
Langtree Ave S41 . . . . .77 A1
LANGWITH 119 F6
Langwith Bassett Prim Sch
NG20. . . . . .119 E7
Langwith Cl NE7 . . . . .194 F5
Langwith Dr NG20 . . . . . . .100 F1
LANGWITH JUNCTION. 119 D6
Langwith Maltings NG20 119 F8
Langwith Rd
Bolsover S44. . . . . .118 C8
Cuckney NG20 . . . . .101 E1
Scarcliffe S44. . . . . .118 F7
Shirebrook NG20. . . . . . .119 F5
Langwith-Whaley Thorns Sta
NG20. . . . . .100 F2
Lansbury Ave
Mastin Moor S43 . . . . .79 B4
Pilsley S45. . . . . .132 C1
Lansbury Ct S21 . . . . .59 D3
Lansbury Dr DE55 . . . . . . .160 A6
Lansbury Rd S21. . . . . . . .59 D2
Lanscombe Park Rd
DE22. . . . . .204 E1
Lansdowne Ave DE24. . . . .232 F5
Lansdowne Rd
Branston DE14. . . . . .253 F7
Brimington S43 . . . . .96 D7
Buxton SK17. . . . . .66 B1
Swadlincote DE11 . . . . . .256 A3
Lansing Gdns DE21. . . . . .220 B6
Lantern Gr DE3. . . . . .217 D4
Lantern Pike View SK22 . . .25 A2
Lantern View SK22. . . . . . .24 B1
Lant La DE4 . . . . .144 B8
Lapwing Cl
Belper DE56. . . . . .192 A8

Lapwing Cl continued
Derby DE24 . . . . .231 E2
Larch Ave
Killamarsh S21. . . . . .60 C5
Mansfield Woodhouse
NG19. . . . . .136 B5
Ripley DE5. . . . . .169 D1
Shirebrook NG20. . . . . . .119 D4
Larch Cl DE22. . . . . .204 D3
Larch Cres NG16 . . . . .182 E2
Larchdale Cl DE55 . . . . . . .160 A4
Larch Dr NG10 . . . . .223 B7
Larch Rd
Eckington S21. . . . . .59 B2
Kilburn DE56 . . . . .192 B7
Swadlincote DE11 . . . . . .255 F6
Larch Way
Chesterfield S40 . . . . .95 D5
Glossop SK13. . . . . .17 F8
Larges St DE23 . . . . .218 E5
Lark Cl DE23. . . . . .231 C6
Larkfields Cres DE55 . . . . .169 F8
Larkhill DE55 . . . . .169 F8
Larkhill Cl S43. . . . . .97 D8
Larkhill Cl DE55 . . . . .169 F8
Lark Hill DE3 . . . . .230 B7
Larkhill Cl DE55. . . . . .169 F8
Lark Hill Cotts SK22. . . . . .33 A8
Larkhill Cres DE24 . . . . . .231 F4
Larkin Cl DE24. . . . . .232 A5
LARKLANDS 209 B8
Larkland's Ave DE7 . . . . . .209 A7
Larklands Inf Sch DE7. . . .209 A8
Larkspur Cl
Mansfield NG19. . . . . . . .136 D2
South Normanton DE55. . .160 A4
Larkspur Ct DE21 . . . . . . .206 A3
Larkstone La DE6 . . . . . . .149 A1
Larpit Gn S80. . . . . .82 A5
Lascelles Rd SK17. . . . . . . .85 B8
Lashley Gdns DE21 . . . . . .205 F2
Latham Cl DE15. . . . . .248 C2
Lathbury Cl DE21 . . . . . . .205 D1
Lathkil Dr DE55 . . . . .159 F5
Lathkil Gr
Buxton SK17. . . . . .85 D7
Tibshelf DE55. . . . . .147 F6
Lathkill Ave
Derby DE24 . . . . .233 C7
Ilkeston DE7 . . . . .194 E5
Staveley S43. . . . . .97 C6
Lathkill Cl
Sheffield S13. . . . . .44 C7
West Hallam DE7. . . . . . .207 E8
Lathkill Dale DE11 . . . . . .255 F2
Lathkilldale Cres NG10 . . .236 A5
Lathkill Dr
Ashbourne DE6 . . . . .185 E8
Ripley DE5. . . . . .180 D6
Selston NG16. . . . . .171 F7
Lathkill Gr S45. . . . . .131 D1
Lathkill La DE4 . . . . .156 C2
Lathkill Rd
Derby DE21 . . . . .219 F8
Sheffield S13. . . . . .44 C7
Latimer Cl DE23. . . . . .230 E7
Latimer St DE24 . . . . .232 D6
Latrigg Cl DE3 . . . . .217 E1
Lauder Cl DE24 . . . . .231 E2
Launceston Rd DE24. . . . .233 B5
Laund Ave DE56 . . . . .179 B6
Laund Cl DE56 . . . . .179 A6
Laund Farm DE56 . . . . . . .179 C6
Laund Farm Mews DE56 .179 C6
Laund Hill DE56 . . . . .179 A5
Laund Nook DE56 . . . . . . .179 A5
Launds Ave NG16 . . . . . . .171 D7
Laurel Ave
Arkwright Town S44. . . . . .97 D3
Mansfield Woodhouse
NG19. . . . . .136 F1
Ripley DE5. . . . . .169 D1
Laurel Cl
Eckington S21. . . . . .59 C2
Shirebrook NG20. . . . . . .119 D6
Swanwick DE55. . . . . . . .170 A8
Laurel Cres
Brimington S43 . . . . .78 A1
Long Eaton NG10. . . . . . .236 C6
Smalley DE7. . . . . .192 F5
Laurel Dr
Aston-on-Trent DE72. . . . .246 A7
Killamarsh S21. . . . . .60 C5
Laurel Garth Cl S41 . . . . . .77 B3
Laurel Gr
Burton upon Trent DE15 . .254 E5
South Normanton DE55. . .160 A4
Laurence Cl S41. . . . . .77 A2
Laurie Pl DE24 . . . . .232 E2
Lavant Ct **3** S43 . . . . .96 E8
Lavender Cl
Burton upon Trent DE14 . .254 A8
Shirebrook NG20. . . . . . .119 D3
Tibshelf DE55. . . . . .148 B7
Lavender Gdns DE75. . . . .182 B1
Lavender Rd DE55 . . . . . . .170 A8
Lavender Row DE22. . . . . .204 F1
Lavender Wlk DE55 . . . . . .157 F5
Laverdene Ave S17. . . . . . .55 F5
Laverdene Cl S17. . . . . . . .55 E4
Laverdene Dr S17. . . . . . . .55 F4
Laverdene Rd S17. . . . . . . .55 E4
Laverdene Way S17. . . . . . .55 F4
Laverick Rd NG16. . . . . . . .171 A4
Laverock Cl NG16. . . . . . . .195 F6
Laverstoke Ct DE22 . . . . . .218 E4
Lawman Gdns DE55. . . . . .158 F4
Lawman Mews DE55 . . . . .159 A4
Lawn Ave
Derby DE22 . . . . .204 D2

Lawn Ave continued
Etwall DE65 . . . . .229 C5
Lawn Cl DE75 . . . . .181 E2
Lawnfold SK13. . . . . .9 E4
Lawn Heads Ave DE23. . . .218 C2
Lawnlea Cl DE23 . . . . .231 E5
Lawn Mill Rd NG16. . . . . . .195 E7
Lawn Prim Sch DE22. . . . .204 D1
Lawnside DE21 . . . . .220 F5
Lawns The
Aston-on-Trent DE72. . . . .246 B8
Rolleston DE13 . . . . .240 A4
Uttoxeter ST14 . . . . .210 A2
Lawnswood Cl DE23. . . . . .231 C8
Lawn The S18 . . . . .57 B2
Lawn Villas S44. . . . . .97 A2
Lawrence Ave
Awsworth NG16. . . . . . . .195 C4
Breaston DE72. . . . . .235 D8
Derby DE21 . . . . .220 B7
Eastwood NG16. . . . . . . .182 F2
Holmewood S42. . . . . . . .116 D1
Mansfield Woodhouse
NG19. . . . . .136 B4
Ripley DE5. . . . . .180 D8
Lawrence Dr NG16 . . . . . . .182 D8
Lawrence St
Derby DE23 . . . . .231 F8
Long Eaton NG10. . . . . . .236 D8
Sandiacre NG10. . . . . . . .223 B7
Stapleford NG9 . . . . .223 D6
Lawson Ave NG10. . . . . . .236 E7
Laxfield Cl S40. . . . . .114 C8
Layton Dr S41 . . . . .77 B1
LEA. 156 B7
Lea Bank DE55. . . . . .160 A4
LEA BRIDGE 156 A6
Leabrook Rd S18 . . . . .56 C1
LEABROOKS. 170 B7
Leabrooks Ave NG19 . . . . .136 D5
Leabrooks Rd DE55 . . . . . .170 C8
Lea Cl DE22. . . . . .204 E3
Lea Cres DE55 . . . . .170 C6
Leacroft Rd
Derby DE23 . . . . .219 B1
Winster DE4 . . . . .141 C4
Lea Ct S41. . . . . .266 B4
Leadale Ave DE55 . . . . . . .170 A7
Leadale Cres NG19. . . . . .136 E5
Leadbeater Dr S12. . . . . . . .44 A5
Leadbeater Rd S12. . . . . . .44 A4
Leaden Knowle SK23. . . . . .34 C1
Leadhill Rd S40. . . . . .95 A4
LEADMILL 53 B5
Lea Dr
Derby, Chaddesden
DE21. . . . . .219 F6
Derby, Markeaton DE3. . . .217 E3
Leafenden Cl DE22. . . . . . .205 A3
Leafgreen La DE23. . . . . . .231 C6
Leafield Rd SK12. . . . . .32 C6
Leafy La DE75. . . . . .181 C7
Lea Gardens★ DE4. . . . . . .156 A7
Leaholme Est S44. . . . . . . .98 D2
Leake St DE22 . . . . .218 D5
Lea La
Matlock DE4. . . . . .156 C2
Selston NG16. . . . . .171 F6
LEAM 53 A3
Lea Main Rd DE4. . . . . . . .156 B8
Leam Glen NG19 . . . . .136 D2
Leamington Cl DE23 . . . . .218 D1
Leamington Dr DE55 . . . . .160 B5
Leamington Rd DE14. . . . .253 F7
Leamington St DE5 . . . . . .169 F2
Leamoor Ave DE55. . . . . . .170 B8
Lea Moor Rd DE4 . . . . . . .156 E8
Leander Cl DE23. . . . . .231 D7
Leander Ct **5** S43 . . . . .78 F2
Leander Rise DE55 . . . . . .255 A8
Lean Town SK13. . . . . .17 D7
Leaper St DE1 . . . . .218 E6
Leapley La DE6 . . . . .199 D3
Lea Prim Sch DE4. . . . . . .156 A7
Lea Rd
Cromford DE4. . . . . .155 D6
Dronfield S18. . . . . .57 A1
Hayfield SK22. . . . . .25 C3
Lea DE4. . . . . .156 A7
Leas Ave NG19. . . . . .135 A5
Leashaw DE4. . . . . .156 C4
Leashaw Rd DE4 . . . . .156 C3
Leas Park Jun Sch NG19 136 C4
Leas Rd NG19. . . . . .136 D4
Lea St SK22. . . . . .33 B8
Leathersley La DE6, DE65 226 C2
Lea Vale DE55 . . . . .160 A4
Leaway The NG20. . . . . . .119 D3
Lea Wood Croft DE4 . . . . .156 A5
Leawood Gdns DE21. . . . .206 B3
Leawood Pump Ho★
DE4. . . . . .155 F4
Leawood Rd DE11. . . . . . .256 D7
Leche Croft DE56. . . . . . . .179 D4
Lechlade Cl DE7 . . . . .207 D8
Ledbury Chase DE24 . . . . .231 D2
Ledbury Pl **2** DE21 . . . . . .205 D1
Ledo Ave DE5. . . . . .169 D2
Leebangs Rd SK14. . . . . . .16 A8
Leech Ct NG16. . . . . .195 B7
Lee Cres DE7 . . . . .209 B8
Lee Dale SK17. . . . . .85 C3
Leedhams Croft DE12 . . . .259 D8
Leeds Pl DE1 . . . . .267 D2
Leeds Rd S81. . . . . .63 F7
Lee Farm Cl DE73. . . . . . .232 F1
Leefield Rd SK23. . . . . .47 B5

LEE HEAD 16 C6
Lee Head SK13 16 C5
Leek Rd
Buxton SK17 84 E5
Longnor SK17 121 B6
Lee La DE75 182 B1
Leeming La NG19, NG20 136 E7
Leeming Lane N NG19 136 E5
Leeming Lane S NG19 136 C2
Leeming Pk NG19 136 C3
Lee Mount SK13 17 C7
Leen Valley Dr NG20 119 D3
Lee Rd S41 96 E2
LEES 216 B7
Lees Brook Com Sports Coll DE21 220 B8
Lees Brook Ho DE21 220 A7
Lees Hall Ave S8 43 B5
Lees Hall Pl S8 43 B5
Lees Hall Rd S8 43 B4
Lees House Ct S8 43 A4
Leeside DE24 220 A1
Lees La DE55 159 F6
Lees Mill 4 SK22 33 C7
Lees Nook S8 43 A4
Lees Rd DE4 126 E3
Lees Row SK13 10 C5
Lees The DE72 233 D5
Leeswood Cl S41 95 D8
Lee Vale Dr SK13 16 D7
Leeway DE21 220 D4
Legh Rd SK12 32 A6
Leicester Dr SK13 17 F8
Leicester Ho 2 NG9 223 F8
Leicester St
Burton upon Trent DE14 254 C8
Derby DE22 218 E3
Long Eaton NG10 236 E6
Leigh Rd NG9 223 F3
Leighton Dr
Marple SK6 23 C8
Sheffield S14 43 F3
Leighton Pl S14 43 F3
Leighton Rd S14 43 E4
Leighton View S14 43 E5
Leighton Way 6 DE56 178 F3
Leigh Way S42 131 F7
Leisure La SK17 137 E5
Leisure Way DE6 173 B1
Leman St DE22 218 E3
Lemon Gr DE11 256 B1
Lemont Rd S17 55 E4
Leniscar Ave DE75 181 C4
Lens Rd DE22 204 C2
Lenthall Inf Sch S18 57 B3
Lenton Ave DE21 219 F6
Lenton St NG10 223 C7
Leominster Dr DE21 206 B2
Leonard Cheshire Cl DE75 182 B1
Leonard Cl
Derby DE23 267 B1
Sheffield S2 44 A7
Leonard St DE1 267 C1
Leonard Wlk DE23 267 B1
Leopold St
Derby DE1 267 B2
Long Eaton NG10 236 D8
Leslie Ave NG16 195 F6
Leslie Cl DE23 230 E8
Lesser La
Buxton SK17 85 F8
Chapel-en-le-Frith SK23 65 D7
Level La SK17 84 D5
Leven Cl DE24 231 F2
Levens Way S41 95 E8
Leveret Cl DE73 233 B2
Lewcote La DE7 194 A1
Lewis Rd S13 44 C7
Lewis St DE23 218 F1
Lewiston Rd DE21 220 B5
Lexington Rd DE21 220 C6
Ley Ave DE55 159 B3
Leyburn Cl
Chesterfield S40 95 E5
Swadlincote DE11 256 B1
Leycote Way DE56 178 F5
Ley Croft
Hatton DE65 227 C1
Mansfield Woodhouse NG19 136 D5
Leyfield Rd S17 55 D7
Leygate View SK22 33 B8
Ley Gdns DE55 159 B4
Ley La
Mansfield Woodhouse NG19 136 D4
Marple SK6 23 D8
Leyland Cl NG9 223 F2
Leyland Ct DE1 218 E7
Leyland Gdns DE1 218 E7
Leylands DE22 218 E8
Leylands La SK14 15 F7
Leyland St DE1 218 E7
LEYS 154 A8
Leys Ct DE56 179 D4
Leys Field Gdns DE73 233 A2
Leys Jun Sch DE55 159 C4
Leys La DE4 154 B7
Leys The
Little Eaton DE21 191 D2
Swadlincote DE11 255 E6
Leyton Ct S43 77 D4
Leytonstone Dr DE22 218 A5
Lichfield Ave DE11 256 E5
Lichfield Cl NG9 223 E3
Lichfield Dr DE24 233 A7
Lichfield Rd
Branston DE13, DE14 253 C4
Chesterfield S40 114 D8
Lichford Rd S2 43 C6
Lickpenny La DE4 144 E4
Lidgate Cl DE3 217 C1
Lid La
Ashover S45 129 A6
Roston DE6 197 E7
Liffey Ho DE24 232 E5
Liffs Rd DE6, SK17 150 C7
Light Alders La SK12 32 A6
Lightfoot Rd ST14 210 A1
LIGHTWOOD
Eckington 58 F2
Sheffield 57 F8
Lightwood Ave 3 SK17 85 C8
Lightwood La
Chesterfield S21 77 E8
Eckington, Middle Handley S21 58 E1
Eckington S8 43 F1
Lightwood Rd
Buxton SK17 66 B1
Eckington S21 58 E2
Lilac Ave DE22 218 A5
Lilac Cl
Derby DE24 233 A6
Holmewood S44 116 F2
Lilac Ct DE24 233 A6
Lilac Gr
Bolsover S44 99 C1
Burton upon Trent DE15 254 F6
Church Warsop NG20 120 F7
Glapwell S44 134 B8
Heanor DE75 181 E1
Shirebrook NG20 119 E5
South Normanton DE55 160 A4
Lilac Mews DE7 194 D3
Lilac St
Brimington S43 78 B1
Staveley S43 97 A8
Lilac Way
Derby DE22 204 D2
Shirland DE55 146 D1
Lilian Prime Cl DE24 233 B8
Lilley Cl NG16 171 E6
Lilley St DE24 233 B6
Lillymede Cl S40 114 F6
Lilybank Cl DE4 143 C5
Lilybank Ct DE4 143 C6
LILYPOOL 252 B7
Lilypools The DE73 252 B7
Limbersitch La DE65 227 F6
Limb La S17 55 D8
Lime Ave
Derby, Breadsall Hilltop DE21 205 D2
Derby DE1 267 A1
Duffield DE56 190 E5
Langley Mill NG16 182 C2
New Mills SK22 24 D1
Ripley DE5 169 D1
Staveley S43 78 E1
Lime Cl
Calow S44 97 A3
Doveridge DE6 224 B8
Pinxton NG16 160 D3
Lime Cres
Belper DE56 179 B2
Church Warsop NG20 120 F7
Lime Croft DE22 204 F4
Limecroft View S42 115 B3
Lime Ct DE15 254 E7
Limedale Ave DE21 206 B3
Lime Gate Mews DE23 218 D2
Lime Gr
Ashbourne DE6 185 C8
Burton upon Trent DE15 254 E5
Darley Dale DE4 127 C3
Derby DE21 220 B5
Draycott DE72 234 F7
Hatton DE65 227 D1
Long Eaton NG10 236 D8
Sandiacre NG10 223 B6
South Normanton DE55 160 A5
Stapleford NG9 223 D5
Lime Grove Ave DE4 143 C5
Lime Grove Wlk DE4 143 B5
LIMEKILN FIELD 99 A3
Limekiln Fields Rd S44 99 A3
Lime Kiln La
Marple SK6 23 A5
Turnditch DE56 189 B8
Wensley DE4 142 B8
Lime Kilns The DE73 252 F2
Limekiln Way
Barlborough S43 80 C6
Shireoaks S81 63 E7
Lime La
Derby DE21 206 C3
Morley DE7, DE21 206 D5
Lime Rd S21 59 B2
Limerick Rd DE21 220 B4
Limes Ave
Derby DE3 217 D1
Whaley Thorns NG20 101 A2
Limes Cl NG16 182 C4
Limes Cl The DE4 143 C5
Limes Cres NG20 119 D5
Limes Ct 3 DE3 217 D1
Limes Pk DE5 169 C1
Lime St DE7 208 F7
Limes The
Barton in Fabis NG11 237 E6
Mapperley DE7 193 E3
5 Uttoxeter ST14 210 B1
Limestone Cl DE11 257 A4
Limestone Terr NG19 136 B4
Lime Terr NG10 236 D8
Limetree Ave DE11 256 B7
Lime Tree Ave
Darley Dale DE4 127 B3
Glapwell S44 134 B8
Killamarsh S21 60 C5
Mansfield Woodhouse NG19 136 A5
Lime Tree Bsns Pk DE4 143 C4
Limetree Cl S43 96 F5
Limetree Ct DE7 208 C6
Lime Tree Gr
Arkwright Town S44 97 D3
Clay Cross S45 131 E2
Lime Tree Pk SK17 85 D6
Lime Tree Rd DE4 143 C5
Limetree Rise DE7 208 C6
Lime Wlk DE23 218 D1
Linacre Ave S45 131 D2
Linacre Rd S40, S42 95 A5
Linacre Reservoirs* S42 94 B5
Linacres Dr DE73 233 A2
Linacre Way SK13 17 F7
Linbery Cl DE55 158 B4
Lincoln Ave
Derby DE24 233 A8
Sandiacre NG10 223 A4
Lincoln Cl
Stapleford NG9 209 E1
Tibshelf DE55 148 A6
Lincoln Dr NG19 136 D4
Lincoln Gn DE73 232 F2
Lincoln Rd DE15 254 D7
Lincoln St
Alfreton DE55 158 F3
Chesterfield S40 115 A8
Tibshelf DE55 148 A6
Lincoln Way
5 Glossop SK13 17 F8
North Wingfield S42 131 F6
Swadlincote DE11 256 E5
Lincote Way 9 DE11 256 E1
Lindale Rd S41 76 E1
Lindale Way DE73 233 A2
Linden Ave
Chesterfield S40 95 B1
Clay Cross S45 131 D2
Dronfield S18 57 B3
Linden Cl
Denstone ST14 196 D6
Kilburn DE56 192 B8
Linden Ct S45 131 D2
Linden Dr S41 115 D6
Linden Gr
Matlock DE4 143 C5
Sandiacre NG10 223 A7
Shirebrook NG20 119 F4
Stapleford NG9 223 E6
Linden Park Gr S40 95 D3
Linden Rd S80 81 E2
Linden St
Mansfield NG19 136 A1
Shirebrook NG20 119 F4
Linden Way SK6 32 A7
Lindford Cl DE21 205 F3
Lindisfarne Cl 4 DE24 231 D3
Lindisfarne Ct S40 95 D1
Lindisfarne Rd S18 76 B8
Lindley St NG16 171 D6
Lindon Dr DE24 233 C6
Lindrick Cl
Derby DE3 217 F1
Mansfield Woodhouse NG19 136 D6
Lindrick Gdns S40 114 C8
Lindrick Way S43 80 B5
Lindsey Cl DE21 219 E6
Lindway La DE55 145 B1
Lingfield Rd DE14 253 F7
Lingfield Rise DE3 217 C3
Lingfoot Ave S8 57 B6
Lingfoot Cl S8 57 B6
Lingfoot Cres S8 57 C6
Lingfoot Dr S8 57 C6
Lingfoot Pl S8 57 B6
Lingfoot Wlk S8 57 C6
Ling La S44 118 C4
Linglongs Ave SK23 45 C5
Linglongs Rd SK23 45 C5
Ling Rd S40 114 D8
Lings Cl DE7 194 F5
Lings Cres S42 132 A8
Linkmel Rd NG16 182 C3
Links Cl DE24 231 F4
Links Rd
Chapel-en-le-Frith SK23 46 F5
Dronfield S18 76 B8
Links The NG16 171 D6
Links View SK17 66 D1
Linley La S12, S13 44 E5
Linnet Cl DE21 220 F6
Linnet Hill DE3 230 C7
Linnet Ho S41 77 A3
Linnet Ind Learning Ctr The DE11 261 F7
Linscott Cl S41 95 D7
Linshaws Rd HD9 3 E5
LINTON 261 D6
Linton Heath DE12 261 E6
Linton Prim Sch DE12 261 D5
Linton Rd
Chesterfield S40 114 C8
Linton DE11 261 E7
Rosliston DE12 260 E5
Linwood Cres NG16 182 F1
Linwood Ct NG19 136 E4
Lipp Ave S21 60 C7
Liskeard Dr DE22 204 D4
Lismore Ct 6 DE24 231 D3
Lismore Gr SK17 85 A7
Lismore Pk SK17 85 A7
Lismore Rd
Buxton SK17 85 A7
Sheffield S8 43 B5
Lissett Ave DE7 208 E7
Lister Ave S12 44 B3
Lister Cl
Chesterfield S41 266 B4
Derby DE3 218 B3
Sheffield S12 44 B3
Lister Cres S12 44 B3
Lister Dr S12 44 B3
Lister Pl S12 44 B3
Lister Way S12 44 B3
Liston Dr DE22 218 F8
Litchen Cl DE7 194 F2
Litchfield Cl NG10 237 A7
LITCHURCH 219 C3
Litchurch La DE24 219 C2
Litchurch St DE1 267 C1
Little Acre NG19 136 E5
LITTLE BOLEHILL 155 B2
Little Bolehill DE4 155 A2
Little Breck DE55 160 A4
Little Brind Rd S40 95 B7
Littlebrook Cl SK13 10 A4
LITTLE CHESTER 219 A7
Little Cl DE11 256 B5
LITTLE CUBLEY 212 E8
Littledale Cl DE21 206 C3
Little Debdale La NG19 135 F1
LITTLE EATON 205 C8
Little Eaton Prim Sch DE21 205 C7
Little Edge S32 71 C6
Little Fallows DE56 190 F7
Little Fen DE55 147 F5
Littlefield La
Ellastone DE6 183 A2
Snelston DE6 184 B4
Littlefield Rd DE65 227 C7
Littlefields SK14 9 A4
LITTLE HALLAM 208 E5
Little Hallam Hill DE7 208 E6
Little Hallam La DE7 209 A6
LITTLE HAYFIELD 25 B5
LITTLE HUCKLOW 50 E2
Little La
Ashford in the Water DE45 89 E1
Heanor DE5 181 A3
Kimberley NG16 195 F5
Litton SK17 69 E3
Pleasley NG19 135 B5
Sheffield, Woodthorpe Estate S12 44 B6
Shirebrook NG20 119 D3
Sutton in Ashfield NG17 148 E2
Thorpe Salvin S80 63 B6
Little Liverpool DE12 260 C1
Little London DE4 156 A6
LITTLE LONGSTONE 89 E4
Little Longstone Cl DE3 217 F2
Little Lunnon NG11 237 E6
LITTLE MATLOCK 135 F7
Little Meadow Rd DE73 233 A2
LITTLEMOOR 130 C3
Littlemoor
Chesterfield S41 95 D7
Eckington S21 59 E4
Littlemoor Bsns Ctr S21 59 E4
Littlemoor Cres S41 95 D7
Littlemoor Ct 3 SK13 17 C8
Littlemoor Ctr 2 S41 95 E7
Littlemoor La
Matlock Bath DE4 143 F1
Newton DE55 148 B4
Littlemoor Rd SK14 9 A2
Little Moorside DE72 246 B8
Little Morton Rd S42, S45 132 A5
LITTLE NORTON 57 A8
Little Norton Ave S8 57 A8
Little Norton Dr S8 57 A8
Little Norton La S8 57 A8
Little Norton Way S8 57 A7
LITTLEOVER 231 B8
Littleover Com Sch DE23 230 F8
Littleover Cres DE23 218 D1
Littleover La DE23 231 E8
Little Thorn Ind Est DE11 256 F2
Littlewell La DE7 208 F2
Little Woodbury Dr DE23 230 F6
Little Wood Dr S12 44 A3
Littlewood La NG19 136 A6
Little Wood La S26, S80 62 D4
Little Wood Rd S12 44 A3
LITTLEWORTH 262 D8
LITTON 69 F3
Litton Bank SK13 9 E1
Litton CE Prim Sch SK17 69 E3
Litton Cl
Belper DE56 179 B5
Ilkeston DE7 194 E4
Staveley S43 97 C8
Litton Ct 6 S40 95 D5
Litton Dale SK17 69 D2
Litton Dr DE21 220 F3
Litton Fold 16 SK13 9 E1
Litton Gdns 17 SK13 9 E1
Litton Mews SK13 9 E1
LITTON MILL 88 E7
Litton Rd NG19 136 E4
Littonslack SK17 88 E7
Liverpool St 4 DE21 219 E8
Liversage Almshouses DE1 267 C2
Liversage Pl DE1 267 C2
Liversage Rd DE1 267 C2
Liversage St DE1 267 C2
Livingstone Rd DE23 218 E1
Lloyd St DE22 218 D5
Loadshead La S42 112 D8
Loads Rd S42 113 B7
Loake Ct 1 DE73 252 A8
Lochinvar Cl DE21 220 F4
Lock Cl DE7 208 C6
LOCKINGTON 247 F5
Lockington Cl DE73 232 F2
Lockington Rd DE74 247 D5
Lock La
Long Eaton NG10 236 C4
Sandiacre NG10 223 C4
Locko Ct DE21 220 D5
Lockoford La
Chesterfield, Stonegravels S41 96 A6
Chesterfield, Tapton S41 96 C6
Lockoford Rd S41 96 A5
Locko Hall DE7 206 F2
Locko La S45 132 E3
Locko Rd
Derby DE21 220 E7
Pilsley S45 132 C4
Lockside SK6 23 A6
Lockton Ave DE75 193 E8
Lock Up Yd DE1 267 B3
Lockwood Rd DE22 204 D4
Locomotive Way DE24 219 C3
Lode La DE6 149 F4
Lodes La SK17 67 C7
Lodge Ave DE6 185 B8
Lodge Bank SK13 10 A6
Lodge Cl
Calow S43 97 A4
Duffield DE56 190 E3
Etwall DE65 229 C4
Lodge Ct SK14 9 A4
Lodge Dr
Belper DE56 178 E5
Wingerworth S42 115 A4
Lodge Est DE72 246 B7
Lodge Farm Chase DE6 185 B8
Lodge Farm Cl S40 114 C7
Lodge Hill DE13 239 E3
Lodge La
Alstonefield DE6 149 B3
Derby DE1 267 A4
Derby, Spondon DE21 220 D4
Heanor NG16 181 E6
Mackworth DE6, DE22 203 C5
Shottle DE56 177 D8
Lodge Mews DE72 246 B7
Lodge Moor Rd S10 42 F8
Lodge Pl S43 97 C6
Lodge Rd
Eastwood NG16 195 A8
Long Eaton NG10 236 D5
Netherseal DE12 261 D1
Lodge Row DE7 193 E3
Lodge St DE72 235 A7
Lodge The
Glossop SK13 10 A6
Tideswell SK17 69 C3
Lodge Way DE3 217 D1
Lodge Wlk S43 97 C6
Loganberry Ct DE24 232 E8
Lohengrin Ct DE13 240 E2
Lomas Cotts SK17 69 E3
Lombard St DE22 217 F6
Lomond Ave DE24 231 F2
London Ho DE45 109 D5
London Rd
Buxton SK17 85 C6
Castle Donington DE72 247 B8
Derby DE23, DE24 219 D2
Shardlow DE72 234 E1
Sheffield, Heeley S2 43 A6
Sheffield, Highfield S2 43 A8
London Road Com Hospl DE1 267 C1
London Road S S2 43 A7
London St S43 77 D3
Longacre Rd S18 76 A7
Long Acre View S20 60 A8
Long Acre Way S20 60 A8
Longbourne Ct NG19 136 F2
Longbow Cl DE13 240 C1
Longbow Gr DE13 240 C1
Longbridge La
Buxton SK17 67 B4
Heanor DE75 181 D3
Long Bridge La DE24 232 D8
LONGCLIFFE 152 F4
Longcliff Wlk 2 S41 95 C6
Longclough Dr SK13 17 A8
Longcourse La S44 98 A2
Long Croft DE72 246 A8
Longcroft Ave
Dronfield S18 56 C2
Ilkeston NE7 194 E5
Longcroft Cl S42 131 D8
Longcroft Cres S18 56 C2
Longcroft Ct S40 114 F7
Longcroft Rd S18 56 C2
Longcroft View S80 82 A6
Longdale NG19 136 E1
Longdale Dr SK14 9 A3
Longdale Gdns SK14 9 A3

Longden Cl NG9 . . . . **209** F2
Longdendale Com Language
Coll SK14. . . . . **9** C5
Longdons Row DE21 . . . . **220** D5
LONG DUCKMANTON . . . **98** A3
LONG EATON **236** C7
Long Eaton Sch The
NG10. . . . . **236** C6
Long Eaton Sta NG10. . . **236** C5
Long Eaton Trade Ctr
NG10. . . . . **236** F8
Longedge Gr S42 . . . . **115** B3
Longedge La S42 . . . . **114** F3
Longedge Rise S42 . . . . . . **115** A3
Longfield Cres DE7 . . . . . **208** F5
Long Field Grange S41 . . . **95** C6
Longfield La DE7. . . . . . . **208** F5
LONGFORD **214** D8
Longford CE Prim Sch
DE6 . . . . **214** D8
Longford Cl
Burton upon Trent DE15 . . **248** B2
Derby DE22 . . . . **204** D1
Sheffield S17. . . . . **56** A5
Longford Cres S17 . . . . . . **56** A5
Longford Dr S17 . . . . **55** F4
Longford La
Longford DE6. . . . . **214** F7
Sutton on the Hill DE6. . . . **215** A4
LONGFORDLANE **215** A5
Longford Rd S17. . . . . **56** A4
Longford Spinney S17. . . . **55** F4
Longford St DE22 . . . . . . **218** E8
Long Gallery DE4 . . . . **110** E6
Longhedge La
Burton upon Trent DE13 . . **239** F1
Pleasley NG19 . . . . **134** E5
Long Hill
Darley Dale DE4 . . . . **127** C4
Whaley Bridge SK17, SK23 . **65** C5
Longhurst La
Marple Bridge SK6 . . . . **23** D7
 1 Marple SK7. . . . . **24** C7
Stockport SK6 . . . . **23** D3
Longhurst View S80. . . . . . **81** F5
Long La
Alstonefield DE6 . . . . **149** B5
Ashover S42 . . . . **130** A6
Broadbottom SK13. . . . . . . **16** C7
Chapel-en-le-Frith, Combs
SK23. . . . . **46** C3
Chapel-en-le-Frith SK23 . . . **47** B4
Chesterfield S21 . . . . **77** C7
Holloway DE4 . . . . **156** B6
Killamarsh S21 . . . . **60** F6
Kirk Langley DE6 . . . . **202** B1
Longford DE6 . . . . **214** C8
Shipley DE75 . . . . **194** E7
Shirebrook NG20. . . . . **119** E3
Taddington SK17. . . . . **87** E5
Thurvaston DE6. . . . . **201** D1
Longlands S44. . . . . **99** B2
Longlands Dr SK22 . . . . **33** B8
Longlands La DE65. . . . . . **230** C1
Longlands Mews DE65 . . . **230** C1
Longlands Rd
New Mills SK22 . . . . **33** B8
Swadlincote DE11 . . . . **256** D7
Longlands Villas DE56. . . **167** F3
Long Lane CE Prim Sch
DE6 . . . . **201** E1
Longley La DE21 . . . . **220** D6
Longload La DE4. . . . . **154** E5
Long Mdw
Great Cubley DE6 . . . . **198** F1
Mansfield Woodhouse
NG19. . . . . **136** D5
Longmeade Dr SK23 . . . . . . **17** A7
Long Meadow La SK17 . . . . **69** E1
Long Meadow Rd DE55. . . **158** F3
Longmoor Gdns **2**
NG10. . . . . **223** A2
Longmoor La
Breaston DE72. . . . . **222** E1
Sandiacre NG10. . . . . **223** B4
Longmoor Prim Sch
NG10. . . . . **223** C3
Longmoor Rd
Glossop SK13. . . . . **17** A7
Long Eaton NG10. . . . . . . **223** B2
LONGNOR **121** A6
Longnor Craft Ctr ★
SK17. . . . . **121** B7
Longnor Gn **38** SK13. . . . . . **9** D2
Longnor Mews **39** SK13. . . . **9** D2
Longnor Way **37** SK13. . . . . **9** D2
Long Rake DE45 . . . . **123** D4
Longreave La DE45. . . . . . . **90** C4
Longridge La SK17 . . . . **66** F7
Longrose La DE6 . . . . **163** B2
Long Row
Belper DE56. . . . . **178** F4
Shardlow DE72 . . . . **235** B2
Long Row Prim Sch
DE56. . . . . **178** F4
Long Shambles S40 . . . . . **266** B3
Longshaw Cl
North Wingfield S42 . . . . . **131** F6
Staveley S43 . . . . **97** D8
Longshaw Ct **10** S40. . . . . . **95** D5
Longshaw Estate & Ctry Pk ★
S11 . . . . **54** A3
Longshaw Estate Trail ★
S11 . . . . **54** A4

Longshaw Estate Visitor
Ctr ★ S11. . . . . **54** A4
Longshaw Gdns DE24 . . . **233** A6
Longshaw Lodge S11 . . . . . **54** A4
Longside Rd S42. . . . . **112** E6
Long Sleets DE55 . . . . **160** B4
Longs Mill **4** DE1. . . . . . **267** A4
Longson Rd SK23 . . . . **47** C6
Long St DE15 . . . . **254** E7
Longster La NG20, NG19. . **120** C3
Longstock Cl DE21 . . . . . . **205** E1
Longstone Bsns Pk DE45 . . **90** A4
Longstone CE Prim Sch
DE45. . . . . **89** F4
Longstone Cres S12. . . . . . . **44** D4
Longstone La DE45. . . . . . . **89** F2
Longstone Rise DE56. . . . . **179** B6
Longstone Wlk DE1. . . . . . **267** A2
Longthorpe Ct DE23 . . . . . **231** A7
Longwalls La DE56 . . . . . . **178** C5
Longwood Com Inf Sch
NG16. . . . . **160** C2
Longwood Rd NG16. . . . . **160** C2
Lonsdale Dr NG9. . . . . **223** E5
Lonsdale Gr DE4 . . . . **142** F7
Lonsdale Pl DE22 . . . . **218** D4
Lonsdale Rd
Burton upon Trent DE14 . . **254** B8
Pilsley S45. . . . . **132** B2
Lons Inf Sch DE5 . . . . **169** D2
Loom Cl DE56. . . . . **179** C5
Loosemore Dr S12 . . . . **43** F5
Lord Haddon Rd DE7. . . . . **194** E1
Lord Roberts Rd S40 . . . . **266** B1
Lords Cl S44. . . . . **99** A1
Lordsmill St S41 . . . . **266** C2
Lord St
Derby DE24 . . . . **232** D6
Glossop SK13 . . . . **10** D1
Hollingworth SK14. . . . . **9** D4
Lorne Cl S18. . . . . **56** D2
Lornes Dr DE15 . . . . **248** B3
Lorne St DE22 . . . . **218** F3
Lorraine Cl DE24. . . . . **232** E3
LOSCOE **181** C3
Loscoe CE Prim Sch
DE75. . . . . **181** B3
Loscoe Ct **2** S40. . . . . **95** D5
Loscoe-Denby La DE5,
DE75. . . . . **181** B3
Loscoe Grange DE75 . . . . **181** D3
Loscoe Rd
Derby DE21 . . . . **206** A1
Heanor DE75. . . . . **181** D2
Losehill Hall Study Centre ★
S33 . . . . **38** C4
Losk Cnr S44. . . . . **118** D2
Losk La S44, NG19 . . . . . . **118** C3
Lothian Pl
Castle Donington DE74 . . . **247** A3
Derby DE21 . . . . **219** D7
Lothorien Cl DE23 . . . . . . **231** B7
Loudon St DE23 . . . . **219** A3
Loudoun Pl DE74. . . . . **247** A4
Loundes Rd S18 . . . . **76** E6
Loundes Wood Ave S41 . . . **95** C8
Loundsley Ct S42 . . . . **94** F4
LOUNDSLEY GREEN. **95** B6
Loundsley Green Rd S40 . . **95** C5
Lount La DE13 . . . . **239** E1
Lousie Greaves La DE21 . . **220** E6
Louvain Rd DE22, DE23. . . **218** D2
Louwil Ave NG19. . . . . **136** E5
Lovatt Cl DE13 . . . . **240** F2
Love La DE55 . . . . **147** C4
Loveys Croft DE73. . . . . . . **252** E2
Lowburn Rd S13. . . . . **44** C7
Low Cl DE6 . . . . **189** A2
Low Comm S21. . . . . **79** D7
LOWEDGES **57** A6
Lowedges Cl S8 . . . . **56** E6
Lowedges Cres S8 . . . . **56** F6
Lowedges Dr S8 . . . . **56** F6
Lowedges Pl S8 . . . . **57** A6
Lowedges Prim Sch S8 . . . . **56** E6
Lowedges Rd S8 . . . . **56** E6
Lower Bagthorpe NG16. . . **171** F3
Lower Bank SK13. . . . . **17** D8
Lower Bank Cl SK13. . . . . **9** F3
Lower Barn Rd SK13 . . . . **9** E4
Lower Bloomsgrove Rd
DE7 . . . . **194** F2
LOWER BRADWAY **56** C6
Lower Brook St NG10 . . . . **236** E7
Lower Burch Pl S32. . . . . . . **71** E5
Lower Chapel St
 9 Ilkeston DE7. . . . . **194** F1
Stonebroom DE55 . . . . **147** B4
Lower Clara Mount Rd
DE75. . . . . **182** A1
LOWER CROSSINGS. **46** F6
Lower Dale Rd DE23 . . . . . **218** F2
LOWER DINTING **10** B1
Lower Dr DE55. . . . . **169** D7
Lower Dunstead Rd
Aldercar NG16. . . . . **182** B3
Langley Mill NG16 . . . . **182** A3
Lower Eaves View SK23 . . . **47** C5
Lower Eley St DE1. . . . . . . **267** A1
LOWER ELLASTONE. **183** C2
Lower Fold SK6. . . . . **23** B8
Lower Gladstone St
DE75. . . . . **181** E2
Lower Gn DE55 . . . . **230** D1
Lower Granby St DE7. . . . . **194** F2
Lower Greenshall La SK12 . **32** E6
Lower Grove Rd S40 . . . . . **266** A3
Lower Hague SK22. . . . . **32** E8

Lower Hall Cl DE56. . . . . . **191** C6
Lower Hardwick St **1**
SK17. . . . . **85** B8
LOWER HARTSHAY. **169** A3
Lower Higham Visitor Ctr ★
SK14. . . . . **15** A8
Lower High St DE13 . . . . . **239** C7
LOWER KILBURN **191** F7
Lower La SK23 . . . . **34** D1
Lowerlea SK12. . . . . **32** C6
Lower Macclesfield Rd
SK23. . . . . **45** E6
Lower Mantle Cl S45. . . . . **131** D4
Lower Maples DE75. . . . . . **194** A8
Lower Market St SK14. . . . . **16** B8
Lower Meadows Prim Sch
S8 . . . . **57** A5
Lower Middleton St DE7. . **195** A1
LOWER MIDWAY **256** E6
Lower Mill **1** DE5. . . . . . . **169** E1
Lower Nelson St **1**
DE75. . . . . **181** D2
Lower Orchard St **1**
NG9 . . . . **223** D7
Lower Park St NG9. . . . . . **223** C6
LOWER PILSLEY. **132** B3
Lower Rd DE22 . . . . **217** F8
Lower Rock St **2** SK22 . . . . **33** C7
Lower Smithy La SK17. . . . . **88** A3
Lower Somercotes DE55 . . **170** E7
Lower Sq SK13. . . . . **10** A7
Lower St DE6 . . . . **224** B8
Lower Stanton Rd DE7 . . . **208** F6
Lower Strines Rd SK6 . . . . . **23** A5
Lower Terrace Rd SK17 . . . . **69** B5
LOWER THURVASTON . . . **214** F6
Lower Whitworth Rd
DE7 . . . . **208** F6
Lower Wood Cotts SK17. . . **89** A7
Lowes Hill DE5 . . . . **169** D3
Lowes La DE73. . . . . **244** C7
Lowe St DE24. . . . . **232** E6
LOWFIELD **43** B8
Lowfield Ave S12 . . . . **58** E8
Lowfield Ct **4** S2. . . . . **43** A7
Lowfield Prim Sch **8** S2. . . **43** A7
Lowfields S43 . . . . **79** A2
LOWGATES **78** F3
Lowgates S43 . . . . **79** A2
Lowlands Lea DE75 . . . . . . **181** F2
Lowlands Rd DE56. . . . . . . **179** B4
Low Lea Rd SK6. . . . . **23** B6
LOW LEIGHTON **33** D8
Low Leighton Rd SK22 . . . . **33** D8
Low Mdw SK23. . . . . **45** D8
Low Mdw Row S81. . . . . **63** E7
Low Pavement S40. . . . . . **266** B3
Lowry Ct SK14 . . . . **9** A4
Low's La DE7 . . . . **209** B2
Lowry Dr
Dronfield S18. . . . . **56** F1
Marple SK6. . . . . **23** F1
Lows Ct DE73 . . . . **233** B2
Lowside S32. . . . . **72** B2
Lowside Cl S32. . . . . **72** B2
Low St DE7 . . . . **209** B2
Loxley Cl
Chesterfield S40 . . . . **95** B3
Derby DE21 . . . . **206** B2
Loxley La S80. . . . . **82** A5
Loxton Ct DE3 . . . . **217** D3
Loyne Cl DE24 . . . . **231** F2
Lucas La DE65 . . . . **228** E2
Lucas Rd S41 . . . . **95** E5
Lucas Terr SK22 . . . . **25** C3
Lucas Works S18. . . . . **57** A2
Luccombe Dr DE24. . . . . . **233** D5
Lucerne Rd DE21. . . . . **206** C3
Ludborough Wlk **14**
NG19 . . . . **136** E4
Ludford Cl NG10 . . . . **236** E4
Ludgate St DE13 . . . . **239** C6
Ludgate Wlk DE22 . . . . . . **217** E6
Ludham Cl S41 . . . . **95** F7
Ludham Gdns S41. . . . . **95** F7
Ludlam Ave NG16 . . . . **195** A8
Ludlam Ho S2 . . . . **43** E6
Ludlow Cl DE21 . . . . **220** F5
Ludworth Prim Sch SK6. . . **23** B8
Luke La DE6 . . . . **201** E8
LULLINGTON **263** E7
Lullington Mews DE12. . . **262** A3
Lullington Rd
Clifton Campville B79 . . . . **263** E3
Overseal DE12. . . . . **262** A3
Lulworth Cl DE23 . . . . **231** D6
Lulworth Ct NG16 . . . . **195** F7
Lumber La DE6 . . . . **176** D2
Lumb La
Belper DE56. . . . . **178** C4
Hazelwood DE56 . . . . **178** B2
Northwood DE4 . . . . **127** B6
Lumford Cotts DE45. . . . . **109** D7
LUMSDALE **143** E6
Lumsdale DE4 . . . . **143** E6
Lumsdale Cres DE4 . . . . . **143** D5
Lumsdale Rd
Matlock DE4. . . . . **143** D4
Staveley S43 . . . . **97** C8
Lumsdale Terr DE4. . . . . . **143** E7
Lum's Hill Rise DE4 . . . . . **143** D6
Luna Croft S12 . . . . **43** F2
Lunch Lane SK17. . . . . **88** F8
Lundie Cl DE24 . . . . **231** D2
Lundy Rd S18. . . . . **76** B8
Lune Mdw NG19 . . . . **136** E3
Lupin Cl
Derby DE21 . . . . **206** C3
Shirebrook NG20. . . . . **119** D3

Lupin Way S44. . . . . **97** A3
Lupton Cres S8 . . . . **56** F6
Lupton Dr S8 . . . . **56** F6
Lupton Rd S8. . . . . **56** F6
Lupton Wlk S8. . . . . **57** A6
Luton Rd DE11 . . . . **255** E2
Lychgate Cl DE21 . . . . **205** D2
Lydden Cl S43 . . . . **96** E8
Lydford Ave S41 . . . . **77** B1
Lydford Rd DE55 . . . . **159** B5
LYDGATE **74** D8
Lydgate S32. . . . . **71** E5
Lydgate Cotts S33 . . . . **40** A6
Lydgate Dr S42 . . . . **114** E3
Lydgate La S33 . . . . **40** A6
Lydia Gdns NG16. . . . . **182** E1
Lydiate Cl DE21. . . . . **206** C2
Lyle Cl NG16 . . . . **195** F7
Lymefield Terr SK14 . . . . . . **16** B7
Lymefield Visitor Ctr ★
SK14 . . . . **16** B8
Lyme Park ★ SK12. . . . . **32** B1
Lyme Park Ctry Pk ★ SK12 **32** B2
Lyme Pk S43 . . . . **34** E2
Lyme Rd SK12 . . . . **32** A6
Lymewood Dr SK12. . . . . . . **32** C6
Lynam Rd DE55, DE56. . . . **168** D7
Lyncroft Ave DE5 . . . . **169** E1
Lyndale Dr DE5 . . . . **181** B8
Lynden Ave NG10 . . . . **236** D5
Lyndhurst Gr DE21 . . . . . . **220** A5
Lyndhurst St DE23 . . . . . . **219** A2
Lyne Ave SK13 . . . . **17** A8
Lynholmes Rd DE4 . . . . . . **143** D5
Lynholmes Rise DE4 . . . . . **143** D5
Lynmouth Dr DE7 . . . . **194** D3
Lynmouth Ho DE65. . . . . . **228** C1
Lynne Cl SK13 . . . . **17** E8
Lynton Cl DE5 . . . . **169** D3
Lynton Ct **10** S41. . . . . **95** F8
Lynton Rd DE56. . . . . **168** A3
Lynton St DE22 . . . . **218** E4
Lynwood Cl
Branston DE14. . . . . **253** F7
 1 Dronfield S18. . . . . **56** D1
Lynwood Rd
Branston DE14. . . . . **253** E8
Derby DE24 . . . . **231** F4
Lysander Dr DE73. . . . . . . **232** E1
Lytham Cl DE21 . . . . **205** D1
Lyttelton St DE22 . . . . **218** C5

M

M1 Commerce Pk S44 . . . **98** B4
McAdam Cl DE15. . . . . **248** B2
MacAulay St DE24. . . . . . . **232** A5
McAuley Ct DE1. . . . . **267** B4
Macclesfield Main Rd
SK17 . . . . **84** D5
Macclesfield Old Rd SK17 **84** D6
Macclesfield Rd
Buxton SK17 . . . . **85** A6
Horwich End SK23 . . . . **45** D6
MacDonald Cl S42 . . . . . . **115** F3
MacDonald Sq DE7 . . . . . **208** D5
McGough Mews DE24 . . . **232** A5
McGregor's Way S40. . . . . **115** B7
Machins Ct S18. . . . . **57** A2
Mackenzie St DE22. . . . . . **218** C5
Mackinley Ave NG9 . . . . . **209** E1
Macklin St DE1 . . . . **267** B3
MACKWORTH **217** E8
Mackworth Cl DE11 . . . . . **256** B7
Mackworth Rd DE1, DE22 **218** E6
McMahon Ave S43 . . . . **97** B6
Macnair Ct SK6. . . . . **23** A5
Macnair Mews SK6. . . . . . . **23** A5
McNeil Gr DE72. . . . . **235** A7
Macready Pl DE24. . . . . . . **232** F7
Maddock La DE4. . . . . **153** A1
Madehurst Gdns S2. . . . . . **43** B7
Madehurst Rd S2. . . . . **43** B7
Madehurst Rise S2. . . . . . . **43** B7
Madehurst View S2. . . . . . . **43** B7
Madeley Ct DE3. . . . . **217** D1
Madeley St DE23 . . . . **219** A2
Madin Dr S43. . . . . **97** B6
Madin St
Chesterfield S41 . . . . **266** B4
Tupton S42. . . . . **131** D8
Madison Ave DE21 . . . . . . **219** F7
Madras Rd DE15 . . . . **248** C3
Magdala Cotts DE56. . . . . **190** E5
Magee Cl DE1 . . . . **267** C1
Magellan Way DE24 . . . . . **219** E1
Mag La
Creswell NG20. . . . . **100** D5
Idridgehay DE56 . . . . **176** D5
Magnolia Way DE55. . . . . **170** A8
Magnus Ct DE21 . . . . **219** B8
Maguire Ave SK13 . . . . **10** A6
Maidstone Dr DE24 . . . . . **232** F5
Maidwell Cl DE56 . . . . **179** C6
Main Ave
Derby DE22 . . . . **204** F5
Sheffield S17. . . . . **55** E4
Main Bright Rd **8** NG19 . **136** B1
Main Bright Wlk NG19. . . **136** B1
Main Dr S42 . . . . **114** E2
Maine Dr DE21. . . . . **220** A6
Main Rd
Bamford S33 . . . . **40** B3
Bradwell S33. . . . . **51** A8
Brailsford DE6 . . . . **201** F7
Chesterfield, Ashgate S42. . **94** F4

Main Rd continued
Chesterfield, West Handley
S21. . . . . **77** D7
Crich DE4. . . . . **156** D1
Cutthorpe S42. . . . . **94** E8
Eckington, Lightwood S21. . **58** F3
Eckington, Ridgeway S12. . . **58** E8
Elvaston DE72. . . . . **234** A6
Flagg SK17. . . . . **106** E6
Grindleford S32. . . . . **72** C7
Hathersage S32. . . . . **53** A8
Heath S44 . . . . **117** B2
Holmesfield S18. . . . . **75** A8
Jacksdale NG16. . . . . **171** B3
Mayfield DE6 . . . . **184** D8
Renishaw S21 . . . . **79** B8
Ripley DE5 . . . . **169** A3
Ripley, Pentrich DE5 . . . . . **169** C5
Shirland DE55 . . . . **146** D1
Smalley DE7. . . . . **192** F3
Somercotes, Leabrooks
DE55 . . . . **170** C7
Somercotes, Pye Bridge
DE55 . . . . **170** F6
Stanton in Dale DE4. . . . . **126** C5
Stonebroom DE55 . . . . . . **147** A5
Sudbury, Aston DE6 . . . . . **226** A4
Sudbury DE6 . . . . **225** F4
Taddington SK17. . . . . **88** A3
Underwood Green NG16. . **171** F2
Unstone S18 . . . . **76** E7
Wensley DE4 . . . . **127** C1
Whaley Thorns NG20. . . . **101** A1
Main St
Awsworth NG16. . . . . **195** C5
Biggin SK17 . . . . **138** C3
Blackfordby DE11 . . . . **257** C1
Bolsover S44. . . . . **117** B8
Bradbourne DE6 . . . . **163** B6
Branston DE14. . . . . **253** F7
Breaston DE72. . . . . **235** D8
Breedon on the Hill DE73. **252** F2
Brinsley NG16. . . . . **171** D1
Burnaston DE65. . . . . **229** F5
Burton upon Trent, Stapenhill
DE15. . . . . **254** E8
Burton upon Trent, Stretton
DE13. . . . . **240** E1
Caldwell DE12 . . . . **260** F7
Calver S32. . . . . **72** C1
Chelmorton SK17. . . . . . . **106** A8
Church Broughton DE65 . . **227** B3
Clifton Campville B79 . . . . **263** F2
Coton in the Elms DE12. . . **260** D3
Eastwood NG16. . . . . **182** F1
Egginton DE65. . . . . **241** B5
Elton DE4. . . . . **140** E6
Elvaston DE72 . . . . **234** D6
Etwall DE65 . . . . **229** B4
Findern DE65. . . . . **230** D1
Great Longstone DE45. . . . **90** A4
Hartshorne DE11. . . . . . . **257** B6
Hemington DE74 . . . . **247** D5
Hilton DE65 . . . . **228** C2
Horsley Woodhouse DE7 . . **192** C6
Kimberley NG16. . . . . **195** F6
King's Newton DE73 . . . . **245** C1
Kirk Ireton DE6 . . . . **165** B1
Linton DE12 . . . . **261** D6
Lockington DE74 . . . . **247** F5
Long Eaton NG10. . . . . . . **236** E7
Longford DE6 . . . . **214** D8
Mapperley DE7 . . . . **193** E3
Middleton DE4 . . . . **154** D4
Moira DE11. . . . . **256** C1
Netherseal DE12 . . . . **264** F7
Newton DE55. . . . . **148** A4
Newton Solney DE15. . . . **248** E8
Over Haddon DE45 . . . . . **109** A1
Overseal DE12. . . . . **262** B3
Palterton S44. . . . . **118** A5
Repton DE65 . . . . **242** D1
Rosliston DE12 . . . . **260** D6
Scarcliffe S44. . . . . **118** C6
Shirebrook NG20. . . . . . . **119** E3
Smisby LE65. . . . . **257** F3
South Normanton DE55. . . **160** B8
Stanton-by-Dale DE7. . . . **222** F8
Sutton in Ashfield NG17 . . **148** F3
Swadlincote DE11 . . . . . . **255** E6
Tatenhill DE13 . . . . **253** A8
Ticknall, Milton DE65. . . . **243** A1
Ticknall DE73. . . . . **251** B4
Walton-on-Trent DE12. . . **253** D1
Weston-on-Trent DE72 . . **245** E5
Whaley Thorns NG20. . . . **101** A1
Wilson DE73 . . . . **252** E6
Winster DE4 . . . . **141** D2
Mais Cl DE4 . . . . **144** A5
Maisies Way DE55. . . . . . . **160** D6
Maize Cl DE23 . . . . **231** B6
Majolica Mews DE11. . . . . **256** F2
MAKENEY **191** A6
Makeney Rd
Belper DE56. . . . . **191** A5
Duffield DE56. . . . . **190** F2
Holbrook DE56. . . . . **191** C6
Makeney Terr DE56 . . . . . **191** A6
Malbon's Yd DE6. . . . . **173** C1
MALCOFF. **35** E2
Malcolm Gr DE23 . . . . **230** E8
Malcolm St DE23. . . . . **219** B2
Malham Cl S40 . . . . **95** D5
Malham Gdns S20 . . . . **59** D7
Malham Gr S20 . . . . **59** D7
Malham Rd DE23. . . . . **230** F6
Malia Rd S41 . . . . **96** C6
Malin Cl DE24. . . . . **233** B5

Malinder Cl S21 . . . . 60 D6
Malinscommon La DE56. 166 C4
Malkin La DE6 . . . . 188 E2
Malkin St S41. . . . . 266 C3
Mallard Cl NG20 . . . . 119 E3
Mallard Ct
  Mansfield NG19. . . . . . . 136 A2
  6 Staveley S43. . . . . . . 78 F2
Mallard Dr S21 . . . . 60 B7
Mallard Way DE24 . . . . . . 219 D3
Mallard Wlk DE3 . . . . 230 C8
Mallatratt Pl NG19 . . . . . . 136 B4
Mallory Cl S41 . . . . 76 E3
Mall The S45 . . . . 131 C3
Malmesbury Ave DE11. . . 256 D6
Malpas Rd DE4 . . . . 143 B6
Malson Way S41 . . . . 95 F6
Maltby Cl 2 DE22. . . . . . 204 F2
Malthouse Cl
  Eastwood NG16. . . . . . . 182 F1
  Wirksworth DE4 . . . . . . 154 F3
Malthouse Ct
  4 Ashbourne DE6 . . . . . 173 C2
  Chesterfield S41 . . . . . . 266 B4
Malthouse La
  Ashover S45 . . . . 129 F3
  Boylestone DE6 . . . . 213 C4
  Froggatt S32 . . . . 72 C5
  Hatton DE65 . . . . 227 D3
  Nether Heage DE56 . . . . 168 B2
  Wingerworth S42. . . . . . 114 C3
Malthouse Rd
  Ilkeston DE7 . . . . 208 F4
  Whitwell S80 . . . . 82 A6
Maltings The
  2 Ashbourne DE6 . . . . . 173 B2
  Burton upon Trent DE15 . 248 A1
  Derby DE1 . . . . 267 B2
  Derby DE22 . . . . 218 D6
  Shardlow DE72 . . . . 235 B3
Malton Pl DE21 . . . . 205 D1
Malton Wlk S40. . . . . 114 F7
Malvern Ave DE15. . . . . . 248 A1
Malvern Cl DE3 . . . . 217 D3
Malvern Gdns
  5 Long Eaton NG10 . . . 236 A8
  Matlock DE4. . . . . 143 B6
Malvern Rd S40. . . . . 95 E4
Malvern Rise SK13 . . . . . . 10 A5
Malvern Way 3 DE21 . . . 205 D1
Manchester La DE11 . . . . 257 C5
Manchester Rd
  Buxton SK17 . . . . 65 F1
  Chapel-en-le-Frith SK23 . 46 E5
  Glossop SK13, SK14 . . . . 9 F7
  Tideswell SK17 . . . . 69 B5
Manchester St
  Derby DE22 . . . . 218 D6
  Long Eaton NG10 . . . . . 236 D6
Mandarin Way DE24. . . . . 232 F8
Manifold Ave
  Ashbourne DE6 . . . . 173 D1
  Staveley S43. . . . . 97 D8
Manifold Dr DE24 . . . . . . 233 B8
Manitoba Way NG16 . . . . 171 F7
Manknell Rd S41. . . . . 96 A8
Manners Ave DE7 . . . . . . 194 D1
Manners Cl SK23. . . . . 34 D2
Manners Ind Est DE7 . . . . 194 C1
Manners Rd DE7 . . . . 194 E1
Manners St DE7. . . . . 209 A6
Manning View DE7 . . . . . 194 F2
Mannion Cres NG10 . . . . 236 B5
Manor Adult Community Ed
  Ctr S40. . . . . 266 A3
Manor Ave
  Brimington S43 . . . . 96 F7
  Derby DE23 . . . . 218 C3
  Stapleford NG9 . . . . 223 D8
Manor Bglws 4 S18 . . . . . 56 F1
Manor Cl
  Brassington DE4 . . . . . . 153 A1
  Chesterfield S44 . . . . 80 B1
  Newton DE55 . . . . 148 A3
  Pilsley S45. . . . . 132 D1
  Swadlincote DE15 . . . . . 255 A6
Manor Court Rd S44 . . . . . 98 F3
Manor Cres
  Burton upon Trent DE15 . 255 A6
  Chesterfield S40 . . . . 95 D3
  Dronfield S18. . . . . 56 F1
Manor Croft
  Ripley DE5 . . . . 169 D3
  Tatenhill DE13 . . . . 253 A8
Manor Ct
  Barrow upon Trent DE73 . 244 B5
  Breaston DE72. . . . . 235 E8
  Breedon on the Hill DE73 . 252 F7
  Clowne S43. . . . . 80 F3
  Risley DE72 . . . . 222 D4
  Somercotes DE55 . . . . . 170 E5
  South Wingfield DE55 . . 157 E3
Manor Dr
  Brimington S43 . . . . 96 F7
  Chesterfield S40 . . . . 95 D3
  Netherseal DE12 . . . . . . 264 F6
Manor Farm S45 . . . . 132 D1
Manor Farm Barns DE21. 205 E3
Manor Farm Cotts DE45 . . 89 E4
Manor Farm Ct
  Killamarsh S21 . . . . 60 D5
  Whitwell S80 . . . . 81 F6
Manor Farm Mews
  Aston-on-Trent DE72 . . . 246 B8
  Burnaston DE65. . . . . . . 229 F5
  Long Duckmanton S44. . . 98 A3
Manor Farm Rd DE72. . . . 246 B8
Manor Fields Dr DE7 . . . . 208 D7

Manor Gr S43. . . . . 80 A6
Manor House Rd NG10 . . 236 F6
Manor La
  Fritchley DE55 . . . . 168 F8
  South Wingfield DE55 . . 157 F1
Manorleigh DE72 . . . . . . 235 E8
Manor Leigh DE72 . . . . . 235 E8
Manor Park Ct DE22. . . . . 218 B3
Manor Park Rd SK13 . . . . . 10 E1
Manor Park View SK13. . . 10 E2
Manor Park Way DE3. . . . 218 B3
Manor Pk DE72 . . . . 221 B1
Manor Rd
  Ashbourne DE6 . . . . 173 D3
  Barlborough S43 . . . . 80 A7
  Barton in Fabis NG11 . . . 237 E6
  Belper DE56. . . . . 178 F3
  Borrowash DE72 . . . . . . 221 A1
  Calow S43. . . . . 96 F6
  Chellaston DE73 . . . . . . 232 F1
  Chesterfield S40 . . . . . . 95 C3
  Derby DE23 . . . . 218 C4
  Eastwood NG16. . . . . . . 182 F1
  Harthill S26 . . . . 61 F8
  Horwich End SK23 . . . . . 45 E5
  Ilkeston DE7 . . . . 194 E1
  Killamarsh S21 . . . . 60 E5
  Mansfield Woodhouse
    NG19. . . . . 136 A4
  South Wingfield DE55 . . 157 F3
  Swadlincote DE15 . . . . . 255 B6
Manor Sch The NG19. . . . 136 C5
Manor St SK13. . . . . 10 D1
Manor View
  Hartshorne DE11. . . . . . 257 B6
  Sheffield S20 . . . . 59 E7
Manse Ave S80 . . . . 100 D8
Manse Cl S80. . . . . 100 D8
Mansfeldt Cres S41 . . . . . 95 E6
Mansfeldt Rd S41. . . . . . . 95 E6
MANSFIELD. 135 F2
Mansfield Cl DE11 . . . . . . 256 D4
Mansfield Dr S12. . . . . 44 C6
Mansfield Prep Sch
  NG19. . . . . 136 C3
Mansfield Rd
  Alfreton DE55 . . . . 159 B4
  Bramley-Vale S44 . . . . . 117 E1
  Brinsley NG16 . . . . 182 F4
  Chesterfield S41 . . . . . . 115 F6
  Clowne S43 . . . . 80 E2
  Creswell S80 . . . . 81 F1
  Derby DE1, DE21 . . . . . . 267 B4
  Eastwood NG16. . . . . . . 182 F4
  Glapwell NG19, S44. . . . 134 C8
  Heanor DE75. . . . . 182 A2
  Heath S44. . . . . 117 A3
  Holmewood S42. . . . . . . 116 C3
  Killamarsh S21 . . . . 60 F6
  Mansfield Woodhouse
    NG19. . . . . 136 C2
  Palterton S44. . . . . 118 B6
  Scarcliffe S44 . . . . 118 E5
  Selston NG16 . . . . 171 F7
  Sheffield S12 . . . . 44 B6
  Shirebrook NG20 . . . . . . 120 F3
  South Normanton DE55. . 160 D6
  Tibshelf DE55. . . . . 148 B7
  Whitwell S80 . . . . 82 F7
Mansfields Croft DE65. . . 229 B4
Mansfield St
  Derby DE1 . . . . 267 B5
  Somercotes DE55 . . . . . 170 C8
Mansfield View S12. . . . . . 44 B6
MANSFIELD
  WOODHOUSE 136 E2
Mansfield Woodhouse Sta
  NG19. . . . . 136 A3
Manton Cl
  2 Burton upon Trent
    DE13 . . . . 240 F1
  Swadlincote DE11 . . . . . 255 F6
Manvers Ave 2 DE5 . . . . 169 E1
Manvers St
  Mansfield Woodhouse
    NG19. . . . . 136 A3
  Ripley DE5 . . . . 169 E1
  Shirebrook NG20. . . . . . 120 A4
Manvers Rd S44. . . . . 97 A4
Manvers St
  Mansfield Woodhouse
    NG19. . . . . 136 A3
  Ripley DE5 . . . . 169 E1
  Shirebrook NG20. . . . . . 120 A4
Manystones La DE4 . . . . . 153 B3
Maple Ave
  Derby DE23 . . . . 231 D6
  Disley SK12 . . . . 33 A6
  Ripley DE5 . . . . 180 C8
  Sandiacre NG10. . . . . . . 223 B7
Maplebeck Ct DE1 . . . . . 267 B5
Maple Cl
  Alfreton DE55 . . . . 160 B5
  Doveridge DE6. . . . . 211 B1
  Mansfield NG19. . . . . . . 136 E1
Maple Dr
  Ashbourne DE6 . . . . 185 D7
  Aston-on-Trent DE72 . . . 246 A7
  Belper DE56. . . . . 179 B2
  Chellaston DE73 . . . . . . 233 A2
  Creswell S80 . . . . 81 E2
  Derby, Boulton DE24 . . . 233 A6
  Killamarsh S21 . . . . 60 C5
  South Normanton DE55. . 160 B4
Maple Gdns
  1 Heanor DE75 . . . . 181 D1
  Langley Mill NG16 . . . . . 182 B3
Maple Gr
  Breaston DE72. . . . . 235 F8
  Burton upon Trent DE15 . 254 E5

Maple Gr continued
  Derby DE22 . . . . 204 D5
  Glapwell S44 . . . . 134 B8
Maple Rd
  Castle Donington DE74 . 247 A5
  Swadlincote DE11 . . . . . 256 B6
Maple St S43 . . . . 97 B8
Maples The DE75 . . . . . . 194 A7
Mapletoft Ave NG19. . . . . 136 A5
MAPLETON. 172 F4
Mapleton Ave DE21 . . . . . 205 F1
Mapleton Rd
  Ashbourne DE6 . . . . 173 A2
  Draycott DE72. . . . . 235 A8
Maple View DE4 . . . . 143 C3
Maple Way
  Branston DE14. . . . . 253 F8
  Burton upon Trent DE14 . 254 A8
  Selston NG16. . . . . 171 F7
MAPPERLEY 193 E3
Mapperley CE Prim Sch
  DE7. . . . . 193 E3
Mapperley La DE7 . . . . . . 193 E2
Mapperley Rd S18 . . . . . . 56 C1
MARCHINGTON 224 E2
Marchington Cl DE22. . . . 204 E1
Marchwood Cl S40. . . . . . 95 A4
Marcie Ct DE65 . . . . 242 D2
Marcus St DE1. . . . . 219 A7
Mardale Cl S41 . . . . 76 E1
Maree Cl DE24. . . . . 231 E4
MAREHAY 180 D6
Marfleet Cl DE3. . . . . 217 D3
Margaret Ave
  Derby DE21 . . . . 219 F5
  Ilkeston DE7 . . . . 208 F8
  Long Eaton NG10 . . . . . 223 F1
  Sandiacre NG10. . . . . . . 223 B4
Margaret St DE1. . . . . 267 B5
Margery La DE6, DE65 . . . 213 C2
Margreave Rd DE21 . . . . . 219 F7
Mariana Cl DE73 . . . . 232 E2
Marigold Cl DE21 . . . . 206 B3
Marigold Pl DE11 . . . . 256 F4
Marina Dr
  Derby, Allenton DE24 . . . 232 E5
  Derby, Spondon DE21 . . 220 D5
Marina Rd DE7 . . . . 193 B8
Marine Dr S41 . . . . 96 C3
Marion Ct SK17 . . . . 85 C6
Marjorie Rd DE21 . . . . . . 219 F8
Marjory La DE6, DE65 . . . 213 C2
MARKEATON. 218 B8
Markeaton La DE22 . . . . . 218 B8
Markeaton Pk* DE22 . . . . 218 C7
Markeaton Prim Sch
  DE22. . . . . 218 E7
Markeaton St DE22 . . . . . 218 E6
Market Arc 2 SK13 . . . . . 10 C1
Market Cl
  Hope S33. . . . . 39 A4
  Shirebrook NG20. . . . . . 119 F3
  South Normanton DE55. . 160 A6
Market Head DE56 . . . . . 179 A3
Market Pl
  Alfreton DE55 . . . . 158 F4
  5 Ashbourne DE6. . . . . 173 C2
  Belper DE56. . . . . 179 A3
  Bolsover S44 . . . . 99 A1
  7 Buxton SK17 . . . . 85 B7
  Castleton S33 . . . . 38 C2
  Chapel-en-le-Frith SK23 . 47 B6
  Chesterfield S40 . . . . . . 266 B3
  Codnor DE5 . . . . 181 B8
  Compstall SK6. . . . . 15 A2
  Crich DE4. . . . . 156 F1
  Cromford DE4 . . . . 155 A6
  Derby DE1 . . . . 267 B3
  Hartington SK17 . . . . . . 137 D5
  1 Heanor DE5 . . . . 181 E1
  Ironville NG16 . . . . 170 F4
  Long Eaton NG10 . . . . . 236 E8
  Longnor SK17 . . . . 121 B6
  Mansfield Woodhouse
    NG19. . . . . 136 C3
  Melbourne DE73 . . . . . . 252 B7
  Mottram in Longdendale
    SK14 . . . . 9 A3
  Ripley DE5 . . . . 169 D1
  Somercotes DE55 . . . . . 170 C8
  Somercotes, Riddings
    DE55 . . . . 170 E6
  South Normanton DE55. . 160 A6
  Staveley S43 . . . . 78 E2
  Sutton in Ashfield NG17 . 148 F3
  Tideswell SK17 . . . . 69 C4
  Wirksworth DE4 . . . . . . 165 F8
Market Sq SK17. . . . . 69 C4
Market St
  Bakewell DE45 . . . . 109 D6
  Broadbottom SK14. . . . . 16 A8
  Buxton SK17 . . . . 85 B7
  Castle Donington DE74 . 247 B3
  Chapel-en-le-Frith SK23 . 47 C6
  Clay Cross S45. . . . . 131 D4
  Disley SK12 . . . . 32 D6
  Draycott DE72. . . . . 235 A7
  Eckington S21 . . . . 59 E3
  Glossop SK13. . . . . 10 C1
  Hayfield SK22 . . . . 25 D3
  Heanor DE75 . . . . 181 E1
  Hollingworth SK14. . . . . 9 D5
  Ilkeston DE7 . . . . 208 F8
  Ironville NG16 . . . . 170 F4
  Mottram in Longdendale
    SK14 . . . . 9 A4
  New Mills SK22 . . . . 33 B7

Market St continued
  Shirebrook NG20. . . . . . 119 F4
  South Normanton DE55. . 160 A5
  Staveley S43 . . . . 78 E2
  Sutton in Ashfield NG17 . 148 F3
  Swadlincote DE11 . . . . . 256 B4
  Whaley Bridge SK23 . . . 45 E7
Market View 15 SK17. . . . 85 B7
Markham Cres S43. . . . . . 78 F2
Markham Ct
  Derby DE21 . . . . 205 F2
  Duckmanton S44. . . . . . 98 A5
Markham La S44. . . . . 98 B4
Markham Quay S41 . . . . . 266 C2
Markham Rd
  Chesterfield S40 . . . . . . 266 B2
  Long Duckmanton S44. . . 98 B5
  Markham Ret Pk S40. . . . 266 B2
Markham Rise S45 . . . . . . 131 B4
Markland Ave S43. . . . . . . 81 A4
Markland Cres S43. . . . . . 81 A4
Markland La S80, S43. . . . 81 A2
Markland View S80 . . . . . 81 D3
Mark's Cl DE23 . . . . 231 D6
Mark St NG10. . . . . 236 D6
Marlborough Cres DE15 . 255 A8
Marlborough Dr DE56 . . . 179 C5
Marlborough Rd
  Breaston DE72. . . . . 235 D7
  Buxton SK17 . . . . 85 B8
  Derby DE24 . . . . 232 C7
  Long Eaton NG10. . . . . . 223 F1
  Mansfield NG19. . . . . . . 135 F1
Marlow Brow SK13. . . . . . 10 A4
Marlow Cres DE7 . . . . 207 D8
Marlow Dr DE14 . . . . 254 A8
Marlowe Ct DE23 . . . . . . 231 F5
Marlow St
  5 Buxton SK17 . . . . 85 C8
  5 Glossop SK13. . . . . . . 10 A5
Marlpit La
  Bolsover S44 . . . . 99 C3
  Denstone ST14 . . . . 196 D6
  Ellastone DE6 . . . . 183 A3
  Sutton on the Hill DE6 . . 228 A8
MARLPOOL. 193 F8
Marlpool Inf Sch DE75 . . 194 A8
Marlpool Jun Sch DE75 . 182 A1
MARPLE. 23 A5
MARPLERIDGE 23 A2
Marple Sta SK6. . . . . 23 A7
Marples Ave NG19 . . . . . . 136 E5
Marquis Ct DE12 . . . . 262 E5
Marquis Dr DE12. . . . . . . 262 E5
Marquis Gdns DE73 . . . . 244 E8
Marrison Dr S21 . . . . 60 C6
Marsden Cl DE56. . . . . . . 190 E3
Marsden Pl 2 S40. . . . . . . 95 D2
Marsden Row S33. . . . . . . 40 B4
Marsden St
  Chesterfield S40 . . . . . . 266 B3
  Derby DE24 . . . . 232 E7
  Glossop SK13. . . . . 10 A4
Marshall Dr 1 NG9 . . . . . 223 F8
Marshall St
  Alfreton DE55 . . . . 159 A3
  Heanor DE75 . . . . 181 F7
Marshall Way DE7 . . . . . . 208 C6
Marsham Dr SK6. . . . . 23 A5
Marsh Ave
  Dronfield S18. . . . . 57 B3
  Hope S33. . . . . 38 F4
  Ilkeston NE7 . . . . 194 E6
Marshaw Cl DE3 . . . . 217 E1
Marsh Cl S20 . . . . 59 C6
Marshes The S33 . . . . 38 E4
Marshfield Gr S43 . . . . . . 79 A2
Marshgreen Cl DE24 . . . . 233 D5
Marsh Green La S45 . . . . 129 F4
Marsh Hall La SK23 . . . . . 46 F5
Marsh Hollow DE6 . . . . . 200 F5
Marsh La
  Belper DE56. . . . . 179 B5
  Mayfield DE6 . . . . 183 D8
  New Mills SK22, SK23 . . . 33 D6
MARSH LANE 58 F3
Marsh Lane Cres DE56 . . 179 B4
Marsh Lane Prim Sch S21 58 E3
Marsh Lane Trad Est
  SK22 . . . . 33 D7
Marsh View S21 . . . . 59 B2
Marston SK17 . . . . 106 B7
Marston Cl
  Belper DE56. . . . . 179 C6
  Derby DE23 . . . . 231 D5
  Dronfield S18. . . . . 75 D8
Marstone Cres S17. . . . . . 55 F5
Marston La
  Doveridge DE6. . . . . 211 B1
  Hatton DE65 . . . . 239 D8
  Marston on Dove DE65 . . 228 B1
  Rolleston DE13 . . . . 240 A4
MARSTON
  MONTGOMERY 211 F8
Marston Montgomery Prim
  Sch DE6. . . . . 211 E8
Marston Old La DE65. . . . 239 D8
MARSTON ON DOVE . . . 240 B8
Marston Rise DE15. . . . . . 254 F8
Martin Ct S21. . . . . 59 C3
Martindale Cl S43. . . . . . . 97 C8
Martindale Ct DE56 . . . . . 179 D5
Martin Dr DE21 . . . . 220 A8
Martin Rise S21. . . . . 59 C3
MARTINSIDE 47 D3
Martins La S42 . . . . 131 B8

Martin's La DE13. . . . . . . 238 A4
Martlet Ave SK12 . . . . 32 C6
Marx Ct S45 . . . . 131 C3
Mary Ann St S41 . . . . 76 E4
Mary Devonshire Cotts
  DE45 . . . . 91 C2
Maryland Ct
  Stapleford NG9 . . . . 209 E1
  Swadlincote DE11 . . . . . 256 A7
Maryland Rd DE21 . . . . . 220 B6
Marylebone Cres DE22 . . 218 A6
Mary St
  Eckington S21 . . . . 59 D3
  Whaley Thorns NG20 . . . 101 A3
Mary Swanwick Prim Sch
  S41. . . . . 77 A3
Masefield Ave
  Derby DE23 . . . . 231 E7
  Holmewood S42. . . . . . . 116 D1
  Swadlincote DE11 . . . . . 256 C6
Masefield Rd S13 . . . . 44 C6
Mason Cres
  Sheffield S13. . . . . 44 D6
  Swadlincote DE11 . . . . . 256 E4
Mason Gr S13 . . . . 44 D7
Mason Mills Sh Village
  DE4. . . . . 155 A7
Mason Rd DE7 . . . . 194 D2
Masons Cotts S21. . . . . . . 59 A1
Masons Gr SK13 . . . . 10 A6
Masons Place Bsns Pk
  DE21. . . . . 219 D6
Mason St S80. . . . . 81 F6
Masson Cl 12 S40 . . . . 95 D5
Masson Hill View DE4 . . . 142 F7
Masson Mills (Working
  Textile Mus)* DE4. . . . . 155 A7
Masson Rd DE4 . . . . 143 A2
Masson Shopping Village
  DE4. . . . . 155 A7
Masson Terr DE4 . . . . 144 A5
Masson Wlk DE22 . . . . . . 218 E4
Mastin Ave S43 . . . . 80 D5
MASTIN MOOR 79 D4
Matcham Way SK17. . . . . 84 E5
MATHERSGRAVE 145 C3
Mather's Way S42 . . . . . . 115 D1
MATLOCK 143 A5
MATLOCK BANK 143 C5
Matlock Bank 8 SK13. . . . 9 E1
MATLOCK BATH 143 C5
Matlock Bath Aquarium*
  DE4. . . . . 143 A1
Matlock Bath Holy Trinity CE
  Prim Sch DE4 . . . . 155 A8
Matlock Bath Sta DE4. . . . 143 B1
MATLOCK BRIDGE 143 B5
Matlock Ct NG10 . . . . 235 F5
MATLOCK CLIFF 143 D4
MATLOCK DALE 143 A2
Matlock Dr S43 . . . . 97 C5
Matlock Farm Park*
  DE4. . . . . 128 D5
Matlock Gdns 5 SK13. . . . 9 E1
Matlock Gn DE4 . . . . 143 C4
MATLOCK GREEN 143 C5
Matlock Ho DE21 . . . . . . 220 E3
Matlock La 7 SK13 . . . . . . 9 E1
Matlock Parks Nature
  Reserve* DE4 . . . . 143 B3
Matlock Pl 6 SK13. . . . . . . 9 E1
Matlock Rd
  Ambergate DE56 . . . . . . 167 F4
  Ashover S42, S45 . . . . . . 113 E3
  Belper DE56. . . . . 178 F8
  Brackenfield DE55 . . . . . 145 C2
  Derby DE21 . . . . 205 L1
  Holymoorside S40, S42. . 114 B7
  Wessington DE55 . . . . . 157 E8
Matlock Riverside Sta*
  DE4. . . . . 143 A6
Matlock St DE45 . . . . 109 D5
Matlock Sta DE4 . . . . 143 B5
Mattersey Ct 4 NG19 . . . 136 B1
Matthew Cl SK13. . . . . 9 F7
Matthew Kirtley Mus*
  DE5. . . . . 170 A4
Matthews Ct NG9 . . . . . . 209 E1
Matthews Fold S8 . . . . . . 43 C1
Matthews La S8 . . . . 43 C1
Matthew St DE24 . . . . . . 232 F6
Matthew Way DE23 . . . . . 230 E7
Matt Orch S40 . . . . 160 B4
Maugerhay S8. . . . . 43 C1
Maunleigh NG19 . . . . 136 E1
Maun Valley Pk Nature
  Reserve* NG19. . . . . 136 E2
Mawfa Ave S14 . . . . 43 D2
Mawfa Cres S14 . . . . 43 D2
Mawfa Dr S14 . . . . 43 D2
Mawfa Rd S14 . . . . 43 D2
Mawfa Wlk S14 . . . . 43 D2
Mawkin La NG16 . . . . 160 F5
Maws La NG16 . . . . 195 E7
Mawstone La DE45. . . . . . 125 B3
Maxey Pl S8 . . . . 43 A6
Max Rd DE21 . . . . 219 F8
Maxwell Ave DE22 . . . . . 218 D8
Maxwell St DE72 . . . . 235 F8
May Ave S41. . . . . 77 C3
Maybank Cl SK23 . . . . 35 A1
Mayfair NG19. . . . . 255 E6
Mayfair Cres DE22 . . . . . 217 F6
Mayfair Ct DE56. . . . . 190 E4
MAYFIELD 184 C8

Mayfield Ave
Heanor DE75 . . . . **181** E1
Kilburn DE56 . . . . **192** A8
Mayfield DE6 . . . . **184** C7
Mayfield Dr
Burton upon Trent DE15 . . **255** A8
North Wingfield S42 . . . . **131** F6
Stapleford NG9 . . . . **209** F2
Mayfield Gr NG10 . . . . . **223** E1
Mayfield Rd
Burton upon Trent DE15 . . **248** A3
Chesterfield S40 . . . . **95** C2
Derby DE21 . . . . **219** E7
Marple SK6 . . . . **15** B1
Sheffield S10 . . . . **42** F7
Mayfield Terr
Hathersage S32 . . . . **53** A8
Mayfield DE6 . . . . **184** D6
Mayflower CI SK13 . . . . . **17** E8
Mayflower Ct
Sheffield S12 . . . . **44** B6
Shirebrook NG20 . . . . . . **119** E4
Mayflower Rd NG16 . . . . **195** B8
Mayhall Ave NG19 . . . . . **136** A4
Maylands DE72 . . . . **221** B1
Maylands Ave DE72 . . . . **235** E8
Maynard Rd
Chesterfield S40 . . . . **266** A1
Grindleford S32 . . . . **53** D1
Maynestone Rd SK23 . . . . **34** E5
Maypole DE11 . . . . **256** A6
Maypole La DE23 . . . . . . **230** E7
May South DE7 . . . . **194** D3
May St
Derby DE22 . . . . **218** F3
Ilkeston DE7 . . . . **194** E4
Maytree CI DE21 . . . . . . **206** C3
Mayvale Gr DE22 . . . . . . **218** C4
Mead CI DE24 . . . . **231** F4
Mead Cres DE15 . . . . . . **255** A6
Meadow Ave
Buxton SK17 . . . . **67** B5
Codnor DE5 . . . . **181** B8
Meadow Bank
Glossop SK13 . . . . **16** F7
Hollingworth SK14 . . . . **9** D6
Mansfield Woodhouse
NG19 . . . . **136** E6
South Normanton DE55 . . **160** A7
Meadowbank Rd DE21 . . . **182** D3
Meadowbank Way NG16 **182** D3
Meadow Brook DE23 . . . **230** F6
Meadowbrook Ind Est
S20 . . . . **60** A8
Meadow CI
Barlborough S43 . . . . **80** C6
Bolsover S44 . . . . **118** A8
Chesterfield S43 . . . . **77** D2
Derby DE21 . . . . **220** E4
Dove Holes SK17 . . . . **47** E1
Draycott DE72 . . . . **235** A7
Dronfield S18 . . . . **57** C4
Eastwood NG16 . . . . **182** F4
Findern DE65 . . . . **230** D2
Horsley Woodhouse DE7 . . **192** D6
Repton DE65 . . . . **242** E2
Stoney Middleton S32 . . . . **72** B3
Tibshelf DE55 . . . . **148** B7
Whaley Bridge SK23 . . . . . **45** C8
Meadow Cotts NG19 . . . **136** C3
Meadow Cres
Castle Donington DE74 . . . **247** B2
Sheffield S20 . . . . **59** B7
Meadowcroft Gdns S20 . . **59** E8
Meadow Croft S42 . . . . . **132** D8
Meadowcroft Glade S20 . . **59** E8
Meadowcroft Rise 2 S20 **59** E8
Meadow Ct
Belper DE56 . . . . **178** F4
Chesterfield S43 . . . . **77** D4
5 Derby DE3 . . . . **217** D1
Elvaston DE72 . . . . **234** D6
Kilburn DE56 . . . . **192** A7
South Normanton DE55 . . **159** F4
Meadow End DE4 . . . . . **165** E7
Meadow Farm Com Prim Sch
DE21 . . . . **220** A4
Meadowfield SK23 . . . . . . **45** D8
Meadowfield CI SK13 . . . . . **9** F3
Meadowgate Pk S21 . . . . . **60** D7
Meadow Gdns DE75 . . . **182** B1
Meadow Gr
Newton DE55 . . . . **148** A3
Sheffield S17 . . . . **55** E4
Meadowgrass CI DE23 . . **231** B6
Meadow Grove Rd S17 . . **55** D4
Meadowhead S8 . . . . **56** F8
Meadow Head Ave S8 . . . **56** F8
Meadow Head CI S8 . . . . **56** E7
Meadow Head Dr S8 . . . . **56** F8
Meadowhead Sch S8 . . . . . **57** A7
Meadowhill Rd S41 . . . . **115** D8
Meadow La
Burton upon Trent DE13 . . **248** A8
Derby, Chaddesden DE21. . **219** F5
Derby DE1 . . . . **267** D3
Disley SK12 . . . . **32** D6
Dove Holes SK17 . . . . **47** E2
Hilton DE65 . . . . **228** C1
Long Eaton NG10 . . . . . . **236** F7
Newton DE65 . . . . **159** F7
Repton DE65 . . . . **243** A4
Roston DE6 . . . . **197** C7
Shirebrook NG19, NG20 . . **119** D2

Meadow La *continued*
Swadlincote DE11 . . . . . . **256** A6
Tideswell SK17 . . . . **69** B2
Meadowlands S44 . . . . . . **99** C2
Meadow Lane Ind Est
DE55 . . . . **159** B5
Meadowlark Gr DE21. . . . **206** A1
Meadow Nook DE24. . . . **233** C5
Meadow PI DE4 . . . . **142** F7
Meadow Rd
Awsworth NG16. . . . . **195** C5
Clay Cross S45. . . . . **131** A5
Derby DE1 . . . . **267** C3
Derby, Wilmorton DE21,
DE24 . . . . **219** F1
Ripley DE5 . . . . **169** E1
Meadow Rise
Brassington DE4 . . . . **153** A1
Chesterfield S42 . . . . **94** F4
Church Broughton DE65 . . **227** B8
Glossop SK13. . . . . **16** F7
Meadows Com Sch The
S41 . . . . **77** B3
Meadows Croft DE56 . . . **190** D3
Meadows Dr S43. . . . . **97** F8
Meadowside
Disley SK12 . . . . **33** A6
Mayfield DE6 . . . . **184** D6
Whaley Bridge SK23 . . . . . **45** D8
Meadowside CI
Shirley DE6 . . . . **200** D8
Wingerworth S42. . . . . . . **115** B4
Meadows Ind Est The
DE21 . . . . **219** D5
Meadows Rd SK22 . . . . . . **25** C2
Meadows Sch The SK17 . . . **66** E8
Meadow St
Ilkeston DE7 . . . . **194** F1
Ironville NG16 . . . . **170** F5
New Mills SK22 . . . . **33** C8
Meadows The
Chesterfield S42 . . . . **95** A5
Dove Holes SK17 . . . . **47** F1
Great Longstone DE45. . . . **90** A4
3 Heanor DE75 . . . . . . **181** E1
Killamarsh S21 . . . . **60** D6
Swanwick DE55. . . . . **169** E7
Uttoxeter ST14 . . . . **210** A2
Meadow Vale SK17 . . . . . **190** D3
Meadow View
Belper DE56. . . . . **178** F3
Bolsover S43 . . . . **80** F3
Chesterfield S40 . . . . **114** A8
Darley Dale DE4 . . . . **142** F7
Doveridge DE6. . . . . **224** C8
Holmewood S42. . . . . . . **132** D8
Rolleston DE13 . . . . **240** C4
South Wingfield DE55 . . . **157** F5
Meadow View CI DE21. . . **206** B3
Meadow View Ct DE72 . . **222** E4
Meadow View Rd
Sheffield S8 . . . . **56** F8
Swadlincote DE11 . . . . . . **255** F5
Meadow Way
Chellaston DE73 . . . . **233** A1
Swadlincote DE11 . . . . . . **256** A6
Meads The S8 . . . . **57** B8
Meadway Dr S17. . . . . . . **55** D7
Meadway The S17 . . . . . . **55** D7
Mead Wlk DE15 . . . . **255** A6
Meakin St S41 . . . . **115** D8
Meal St SK22 . . . . **33** C8
Mear Dr DE72. . . . . **221** B1
Mear Greaves La DE15 . . **248** B4
Mease The DE65 . . . . . . **228** E1
Measham Rd
Appleby Magna DE12. . . . **265** F1
Donisthorpe DE12 . . . . . . **265** D6
Moira DE12 . . . . **262** F3
Meath Ave DE21 . . . . . . **220** B4
Meden Ave NG19. . . . . . . **134** F7
Meden Bank NG19 . . . . . **135** B5
Meden CI NG19. . . . . **135** B5
Meden Rd NG19. . . . . . . **136** D4
Meden Sq NG19. . . . . . . **135** B5
Medina CI DE24. . . . . . . **233** D5
Medlock CI S40 . . . . **114** B7
Medlock Rd S40 . . . . **114** C8
Medway Dr DE22 . . . . . . **205** B5
Meerbrook CI DE21. . . . . **206** A1
Meerbrook PI DE7 . . . . . **208** C5
MEERSBROOK **43** B5
MEERSBROOK BANK. . . . **43** A5
Meersbrook Park Rd S8. . **43** A5
Meersbrook Rd S8. . . . . . **43** B5
Meersbrook Works 13 S8. **43** A6
Meersdale S2 . . . . **43** C6
Megaloughton La DE21. . **220** C3
Megdale DE4 . . . . **143** A6
Melandra Castle Rd SK13. . **9** F4
Melandra Ct DE22. . . . . . **218** E4
Melandra Rd SK13 . . . . **9** E3
Melanie CI SK13 . . . . **17** A8
MELBOURNE. **252** B8
Melbourne Ave
Burton upon Trent DE15 . . **248** C3
Dronfield S18. . . . . **56** B1
Melbourne CI
Belper DE56. . . . . **179** A2
Derby DE22 . . . . **204** D2
Derby, Markeaton DE21 . . **217** F3
Melbourne CE DE24 . . . . **219** E4
Melbourne Ct
Long Eaton NG10. . . . . . . **235** F4
8 Staveley S43. . . . . **78** E2

Melbourne Hall & Gdns★
DE73 . . . . **252** C7
Melbourne Ho DE21. . . . . **220** E3
Melbourne Inf Sch DE73. **252** B8
Melbourne Jun Sch
DE73 . . . . **252** B8
Melbourne La
Breedon on the Hill
DE73 . . . . **252** E2
Ticknall DE73. . . . . **251** C5
Melbourne L Ctr DE73. . . **252** B7
Melbourne Rd NG9. . . . . **209** E1
Melbourne St
Derby DE1 . . . . **267** B1
Mansfield Woodhouse
NG19 . . . . **136** C6
Melbreak CI DE3 . . . . . . **217** E1
Melfort CI DE24 . . . . **231** F2
Melling CI S40. . . . . **114** F8
Melling Ct S40. . . . . **114** F8
Mellington CI S8. . . . . **43** C2
MELLOR. **23** D5
Mellor Dr ST14 . . . . **210** B1
Mellor La
Barlow S18 . . . . **75** E1
Chapel-en-le-Frith SK23 . . **47** A6
Mellor Prim Sch SK6. . . . . **23** C6
Mellor Rd
Burton upon Trent DE14 . . **254** B7
New Mills SK6, SK22 . . . . . **24** C3
Mellors Rd NG19 . . . . . . **135** D1
Mellor St DE24. . . . . **232** E6
Mellor Way S40. . . . . **115** A7
Melrose CI
Chesterfield S40 . . . . **95** D3
Derby DE24 . . . . **231** E2
Melrose Ct 7 S41 . . . . . . **96** A6
Meltham La S41 . . . . **96** B6
Melton Ave
Derby DE23 . . . . **231** C6
Melbourne DE73 . . . . . . **252** A8
Melton Ct
Derby DE22 . . . . **218** E6
Sandiacre NG10. . . . . **223** A5
Somercotes DE55 . . . . . . **170** C6
Melville CI DE6 . . . . **175** F3
Melville Cres S43 . . . . **96** F4
Melville Ct DE65 . . . . . . **229** B3
Melville Dr S2. . . . . **44** A8
Memorial Croft DE4. . . . . **154** F3
Memorial PI SK17 . . . . **67** C5
Memorial Rd DE22 . . . . . **204** C3
Mendip CI 1 NG10 . . . . **223** A1
Mendip Cres S40 . . . . **95** B4
Mendip Ct DE21. . . . . . . **205** E2
Menin Rd DE22 . . . . **204** C2
Mentmore CI DE55 . . . . . **170** A7
MERCASTON. **188** B3
Mercaston CI S40. . . . . . . **95** A5
MERCASTON GREEN . . . **188** B3
Mercaston La
Hulland Ward DE6 . . . . . . **188** B4
Mackworth DE6, DE22. . . **203** B8
Mercaston Rd DE21 . . . . **219** F8
Mercer Cres DE55. . . . . . **159** C3
Merchant Ave DE21 . . . . **220** D4
Merchants Cnr DE22 . . . **218** E6
Merchant St
Derby DE22 . . . . **218** E6
Shirebrook NG20 . . . . . . **120** A4
Mercia CI
Eastwood NG16. . . . . **195** A8
Hatton DE65 . . . . **239** D8
Mercia Dr
Sheffield S17 . . . . **55** E6
Willington DE65. . . . . **242** B5
Mercian CI DE7 . . . . **194** E1
Mercian Mews DE21 . . . . **220** D4
Mercian Pk DE7 . . . . **194** E1
Mere Beck DE72 . . . . . . **234** D6
Meredith Ct NG9. . . . . . . **209** E2
Mereoak La DE11, DE73 . . **257** E7
Mereside Gdns SK23 . . . . . **45** D6
Meridian CI DE7 . . . . **194** E4
Merion Gr DE23 . . . . **218** A1
Merlin Ave S44. . . . . **98** F3
Merlin CI DE56. . . . . **179** C5
Merlin Cres DE14 . . . . . . **253** F8
Merlin Gn DE24 . . . . **231** D4
Merlin Way
Burnaston DE3. . . . . **230** B7
Ilkeston DE7 . . . . **208** F4
Woodville DE11 . . . . **256** F3
Merrial CI DE45 . . . . **109** C4
Merrick CI S40. . . . . **95** D5
Merridale Rd DE23. . . . . **231** C8
Merrill Coll DE24 . . . . . . **232** E5
Merrill Way DE24 . . . . . . **232** D5
Merrybower CI DE24 . . . **231** D3
Merrydale Rd DE15. . . . . **255** A8
Mersey Bank Rd SK13 . . . . **9** F4
Merthyr Ct DE21. . . . . . . **206** B2
Merton CI 2 DE7, DE75 . **181** F1
Merton Ct NG9. . . . . **209** E1
Mervyn Rd DE15. . . . . . . **248** A3
Messiter Mews DE65 . . . **242** B5
Metcalfe Ave S21 . . . . **60** C6
Metcalfe Ct DE24 . . . . . . **233** B8
Meteor Bsns Pk DE21 . . . **205** B1
Meteor Ctr The DE21 . . . **205** C1
Methley CI S12. . . . . **43** F6
Metro Ave DE55. . . . . . . **148** A3
Mettesford DE4. . . . . . . **143** D5
Meverill Rd SK17. . . . . . . **69** D5
Mevril Rd SK23 . . . . **45** E5
Mevril Springs Way SK23. **45** E5
Mewies CI DE12. . . . . . . **253** D1

Mews Ct DE3 . . . . **217** D4
Mews The
Burton upon Trent DE14 . . **254** C8
Horsley Woodhouse DE7 . . **192** C7
Little Eaton DE56. . . . . . . **191** B2
Melbourne DE73 . . . . . . **252** B7
New Mills SK22 . . . . **33** D8
Wyaston DE6 . . . . **185** B2
Meynell CI
Burton upon Trent DE15 . . **248** B1
Chesterfield S40 . . . . **95** C2
Meynell Ct
Derby DE22 . . . . **204** C2
Kirk Langley DE6 . . . . **202** F2
Meynell Rd NG10 . . . . . . **236** D5
Meynell Rise DE6 . . . . . . **173** C4
Meynell St
Derby DE23 . . . . **218** F1
Swadlincote DE11 . . . . . . **256** A1
Meynell Way S21 . . . . **60** C6
Michael CI S42 . . . . **115** A5
Michael House Sch
DE75 . . . . **194** A6
Michael's La DE6 . . . . . . **183** C5
Michelle CI DE24. . . . . . . **231** C3
Michigan CI DE21 . . . . . . **220** C5
Michlow CI S33 . . . . **51** A8
Michlow Dr S33. . . . . **51** A8
Michlow La S33. . . . . **51** A8
Micklebring CI DE5 . . . . **169** C1
Micklecroft Gdns DE23 . . **230** E7
Mickledon CI 3 NG10 . . **236** B8
MICKLEOVER. **217** E2
Mickleover Ho DE3. . . . . **230** D4
Mickleover Prim Sch
DE3 . . . . **217** D2
Mickleross CI DE3 . . . . . **217** D4
Mickleton CI DE11 . . . . . **256** B1
MICKLEY. **56** B3
Mickley Inf Sch DE55. . . . **146** C4
Mickley La
Sheffield S17, S18. . . . . . . **55** F4
Shirland DE55 . . . . **146** C5
Middlebeck CI DE73. . . . **232** F2
Middle CI DE11 . . . . **256** B4
MIDDLECROFT. **97** C7
Middlecroft Rd S43 . . . . . **97** D7
Middlefield CI
Derby DE22 . . . . **204** D4
Sheffield S17 . . . . **55** C7
Middlefield Croft S17 . . . **55** C7
Middlegate Field Dr S80 . **82** A5
MIDDLE HANDLEY **77** F8
Middle Hay CI S14 . . . . . . **43** E4
Middle Hay PI S14 . . . . . . **43** E4
Middle Hay Rise S14 . . . . **43** E4
Middle Hay View S14. . . . **43** E4
Middle La
Clay Cross S45. . . . . **131** E3
Crich DE4 . . . . **156** D1
MIDDLE MAYFIELD **184** B6
Middle Mdw S81. . . . . **63** E7
Middle Mill 2 DE1. . . . . **267** A4
Middle Orchard St NG9. . **223** D7
Middle Ox CI S20 . . . . **59** F6
Middle Ox Gdns S20. . . . . **59** F6
Middle Pavement S40. . . **266** B3
MIDDLEPEAK. **154** E3
Middle Rd S42. . . . . **114** E1
Middle Row SK17 . . . . **89** A7
Middle Shambles S40 . . . **266** B3
Middle St
Bolsover, Hillstown S44. . . **118** C8
Bolsover S44 . . . . **99** A1
Stanton in Peak DE4 . . . . **126** C5
MIDDLETON
Wirksworth S40 . . . . **154** D4
Youlgrave **124** E3
Middleton Ave
Codnor DE5 . . . . **181** B6
Derby DE23 . . . . **218** C2
Middleton Com Prim Sch
DE4 . . . . **154** D4
Middleton Dale S32. . . . . **71** A5
Middleton Dr
Derby DE23 . . . . **218** C2
Staveley S43 . . . . **97** B5
Middleton La S32 . . . . . . **71** D3
Middleton Rd
Ilkeston DE7 . . . . **209** A5
Mansfield Woodhouse
NG19. . . . . **136** C5
Middleton St
Awsworth NG16. . . . . **195** C4
Cossall S80 . . . . **195** A1
Derby DE23 . . . . **219** A1
Middleton Top Visitor Ctr★
DE4. . . . . **154** D4
Middleton Way DE55 . . . **170** C6
Middleton Mdws S43 . . . **80** A6
Midhill Cres S2. . . . . **43** B7
Midhill Rd S2 . . . . **43** B7
Midland Ave NG9. . . . . . **223** D5
Midland Cotts
Grindleford S32. . . . . **53** D2
Pleasley NG19. . . . . **135** A6
Rowsley DE4 . . . . **110** F1
Midland Ct
Barlborough S43 . . . . **80** A5
5 Chesterfield S41. . . . . **115** B7
Midland Ind Est DE56 . . . **168** A4
Midland PI DE1 . . . . **267** D2
Midland Railway Butterley★
DE5. . . . . **169** D4
Midland Railway Ctr The★
DE5. . . . . **169** D4
Midland Rd
Chapel-en-le-Frith SK23 . . **47** A6

Midland Rd *continued*
Derby DE1 . . . . **267** D1
Eastwood NG16. . . . . **182** F2
Heanor DE75 . . . . **181** E2
Swadlincote DE11 . . . . . . **256** B4
Midland Road Ind Est
DE11 . . . . **256** B4
Midland St NG10. . . . . . . **236** E8
Midland Terr
Ambergate DE56 . . . . . . **167** F4
Barrow Hill S43. . . . . **78** B4
Blackwell DE55 . . . . **147** C1
4 Chesterfield S41. . . . . **115** B7
New Mills SK22 . . . . **33** C7
Midland View
7 Belper DE56. . . . . **178** F3
North Wingfield S42 . . . . **131** F7
Midland Way S43 . . . . **80** A5
Midway DE22 . . . . **204** E2
Midway Ctr S45. . . . . **131** D4
Midway Rd DE11 . . . . . . **256** C5
Mikado Rd NG10 . . . . . . **236** C5
Milbank CI DE22 . . . . . . **217** E6
Milburn Gdns DE21 . . . . **206** B3
Milbury CI DE21. . . . . . . **205** F2
Mile Ash La DE22 . . . . . . **204** F1
MILEHILL. **115** F5
MILFORD. **191** A7
Milford DE45 . . . . **109** D3
Milford Ave NG10 . . . . . **223** B3
Milford CI DE45 . . . . **109** D6
Milford Dr DE7 . . . . **194** D3
Milford Prim Sch DE56 . . **190** F7
Milford Rd
Duffield DE56. . . . . **190** E4
Staveley S43 . . . . **97** C5
Milford St 4 DE1 . . . . . . **218** F7
Milford The DE22 . . . . . . **218** F5
Milken La S45 . . . . **130** B4
Milking La S43. . . . . **80** B3
Mill CI DE7 . . . . **235** A1
Mill Acre CI DE7 . . . . . . **194** D2
Millash La S80. . . . . **82** B4
Millbank DE75 . . . . **194** A8
Millbank Ave DE56 . . . . **179** B2
Millbank CI DE7. . . . . . . **194** D3
Mill Bank Ct S32. . . . . **53** A8
Mill Bank Dr ST14. . . . . . **197** A3
Millbridge S33. . . . . **38** C3
Millbrook SK14 . . . . **9** D6
Millbrook Ho SK14 . . . . . . **9** E6
MILL BROW. **23** E8
Mill Brow
2 Broadbottom SK14. . . . **16** A4
Marple SK6 . . . . **23** D8
Mill Brow Rd SK6 . . . . . . **23** E8
Mill CI
Borrowash DE72 . . . . **221** C1
Findern DE65 . . . . **230** D2
Kilburn DE56 . . . . **192** A7
Newton Solney DE15 . . . . **248** E6
Swadlincote DE11 . . . . . . **256** C5
Swanwick DE55 . . . . **169** E7
Mill Cliff SK17 . . . . **85** C7
Mill Cres
Whitwell S80 . . . . **82** A6
Wingerworth S42. . . . . . . **115** C3
Mill Croft DE3 . . . . **217** D4
Millcross La S18 . . . . **75** E3
Mill Ct SK13 . . . . **10** C1
MILLDALE. **149** F2
Milldale Ave SK17. . . . . . . **84** F6
Milldale CI
Chesterfield S40 . . . . **95** C5
Ripley DE5 . . . . **180** C5
Milldale Rd
Ashbourne DE6 . . . . **185** D8
Belper DE56. . . . . **179** B3
Milldam Rd
Derby DE21 . . . . **220** F3
Long Eaton NG10. . . . . . . **236** B6
Sheffield S17 . . . . **55** F5
Milldam La DE6 . . . . **186** E7
Millennium Ave DE12 . . . **262** E6
Millennium CI DE7. . . . . **194** E3
Millennium Ct NG19. . . . **135** E2
Millennium Way
Chesterfield S41 . . . . **76** F1
Derby DE24 . . . . **219** E4
Miller Ave S43. . . . . **79** C4
Millers Ct DE1. . . . . **267** B4
MILLER'S DALE. **88** A2
Millersdale Ave DE7. . . . **194** E5
Millers Dale CI DE56 . . . **179** C5
Millers Dale CI DE15 . . . **248** B5
Millersdale Ct 3 SK13 . . **10** C1
Millers Dale Dr DE55. . . . **160** A7
Millersdale Way SK17. . . . **85** B2
Millers Gn DE4. . . . . **165** E6
MILLERS GREEN. **165** E6
Millership Way DE7 . . . . **195** A2
Millers La DE55 . . . . **145** E2
Mill Farm CI S32. . . . . **72** C1
Millfield DE72. . . . . **235** B2
Millfield CI DE7. . . . . . . **194** C3
Millfield Croft 1 DE11 . . **256** B7
Millfield Mobile Home Pk
S42. . . . . **130** F5
Millfield Rd
Ilkeston DE7 . . . . **209** A7
Kimberley NG16. . . . . **195** E7
Millfield St DE11 . . . . . . **257** A2
Mill Fleam DE65 . . . . . . **228** E1
Mill Gate DE22 . . . . **218** E6
Mill Gn
Shardlow DE72 . . . . **235** A1
Staveley S43 . . . . **78** E2
Mill Green Way S43. . . . . **80** E4

Mill Hill
Elvaston DE24. . . . . .233 C4
Long Duckmanton S44. . . .117 B6
Repton DE65 . . . . .242 E1
Mill Hill Cl DE5. . . . . .169 F1
Mill Hill La
Breaston DE72. . . . . .222 E1
Burton upon Trent DE15 . .248 B4
Derby DE1, DE23. . . . . . .267 B1
Mill Hill Rd DE23. . . . . . .267 A1
Mill Hill Sch DE5. . . . . . .180 F8
Mill Holme DE55. . . . . . .160 B4
Millhouse Ct DE72 . . . . . .235 B7
MILLINGTON GREEN 176 A4
Mill La
Ashbourne DE6 . . . . .173 F1
Ashover S45 . . . . .129 C5
Atlow DE6 . . . . .175 A7
Ault Hucknall S44 . . . . . .133 C8
Barlow S18 . . . . .75 D4
Belper DE56. . . . . .179 B3
Bolsover S44 . . . . .99 A3
Bradbourne DE6 . . . . . . .163 B6
Brailsford DE6. . . . . .201 C8
Castleton S33 . . . . .38 C3
Chesterfield S40 . . . . .95 D2
Clay Cross S42, S45 . . . .130 F5
Clay Cross S45. . . . . .131 B2
Codnor DE5 . . . . .181 B8
Cossall NG16. . . . . .195 C1
Derby DE3. . . . . .217 D4
Doveridge DE6. . . . . .211 A1
Dronfield S18. . . . . .57 B1
Ellastone DE6 . . . . .183 B2
Eyam S32. . . . . .71 E5
Grassmoor S42. . . . . .115 D3
Hartington SK17. . . . . . . .137 D5
Heath S44 . . . . .117 B1
Hilton DE65 . . . . .228 C2
Holloway DE4 . . . . .156 A5
Holmesfield S18. . . . . .74 F5
Holmewood S42. . . . . . . .116 B4
Hope Valley S33. . . . . .40 B3
Pinxton NG16. . . . . .160 D1
Renishaw S21 . . . . .60 A2
Roston DE6 . . . . .197 D7
1 Sandiacre NG10. . . . .223 C6
Scropton DE65. . . . . .226 F1
Scropton, Foston DE65 . . .226 D7
Sheffield S17. . . . . .55 F5
Shirley DE6 . . . . .200 D7
Shuttlewood S44 . . . . .98 F8
Somercotes DE55 . . . . . .170 C7
Sudbury DE6 . . . . .225 E1
Sutton in Ashfield NG17 . .148 F1
Whitwell S80 . . . . .82 A6
Mill Meadow Way DE65 . .229 B4
Mill Moor Cl DE73. . . . . .232 F2
Millom Pl DE11 . . . . .205 D1
Mill Pond Ave SK22 . . . . . .24 D1
Mill Pond Cotts DE4. . . . .155 A7
Millpool Cl DE11 . . . . . . .257 A7
Mill Rd
Cromford DE4 . . . . .155 B6
Eckington S21 . . . . .59 E4
Heanor DE75 . . . . .194 A8
Stapleford NG9. . . . . .223 D8
Mill Row DE21 . . . . .220 D5
Mills Cl DE72. . . . . .235 A4
Mills Croft DE6 . . . . .164 B1
Mills Ct DE6 . . . . .156 F1
Mill St
Alfreton DE55 . . . . .159 C1
Bakewell DE45. . . . . .109 D6
Barlow S18 . . . . .75 D3
Belper DE56. . . . . .179 A4
Chesterfield S41 . . . . .266 C3
Clowne S43 . . . . .80 E3
Coton in the Elms DE12. . .260 D3
Derby DE1 . . . . .218 E6
Glossop SK13. . . . . .10 D1
Hayfield SK22 . . . . .25 D3
Ilkeston DE7 . . . . .194 F1
Rocester ST14. . . . . .197 A3
Somercotes DE55 . . . . . .170 C8
Stoney Middleton S32 . . . .72 A3
Millstone Cl **1** S18 . . . . . .56 D2
Millstone La
Ashford in the Water
  DE45. . . . . .108 F7
Ripley DE5 . . . . .169 C8
Mill Stream Cl S40. . . . . . .95 C1
MILLTHORPE 74 F5
Millthorpe La S18. . . . . . . .75 A6
MILLTOWN 145 B8
Milltown SK13. . . . . .10 D1
Mill View DE56. . . . . .178 F5
Millway NG19. . . . . .136 D1
Millway La DE6 . . . . .149 F3
Mill Wlk
Bolsover S44 . . . . .99 A3
Whitwell S80. . . . . .82 A6
Mill Yd DE5. . . . . .170 C8
Milnbank Ave SK17. . . . . . .85 D8
Milner Ave
Codnor DE5 . . . . .181 B8
Draycott DE72. . . . . .235 A7
Milner Rd NG10. . . . . . . .236 D8
Milnhay Rd NG16. . . . . . .182 C2
MILTON 243 A1
Milton Ave
Alfreton DE55 . . . . .159 C4
Ilkeston DE7 . . . . .194 E4
Shirland DE55 . . . . .146 C4
Swadlincote DE11 . . . . . .256 C6
Milton Cl DE3. . . . . .217 C3
Milton Cres S40 . . . . .115 A7

Milton Ct **12** SK17. . . . . . .85 B7
Milton La SK23. . . . . .46 B5
Milton Pl S43 . . . . .78 F2
Milton Rd
Ilkeston DE7 . . . . .194 E4
Repton DE65 . . . . .242 D2
Milton St
Derby DE22 . . . . .218 D4
Ilkeston DE7 . . . . .194 F4
Long Eaton NG10. . . . . . .236 D7
Milton Terr NG10 . . . . . . .236 D7
Milward Rd DE75. . . . . . .181 D2
Mimosa Cres DE23 . . . . . .231 E5
Miners Hill DE4. . . . . . . .153 A1
Minimum Terr S40. . . . . . .266 A2
Minkley Dr NG16. . . . . . .182 C4
Minninglow La DE4 . . . . . .151 F8
Minster Rd DE21 . . . . . . .205 E2
Minster Way DE55 . . . . . .169 E2
Mint Gr NG10. . . . . .236 A7
Minton Rd DE74. . . . . . . .246 F4
Miracle Ct DE45. . . . . . . .109 D6
Mires La
Great Longstone DE45. . . .90 B4
Tideswell SK17 . . . . .70 A3
Mires The
Birchover DE4 . . . . .126 A1
Wetton DE6. . . . . .149 A3
Miriam Ave S40. . . . . . . .114 A8
Miry La DE65 . . . . .227 C4
Miry Mdw SK23 . . . . .47 B6
Misterton Cl DE22. . . . . . .204 E2
Misterton Ct **3** NG19. . . . .136 B1
Mistletoe Dr DE11 . . . . . .256 F2
Mitcham Wlk DE22. . . . . .218 A6
Mitchell Ave NG16 . . . . . .182 A4
Mitchells Cl DE65 . . . . . . .229 A4
Mitchell St
Clowne S43 . . . . .80 F4
Long Eaton NG10. . . . . . .236 E7
Mitchell Terr DE7. . . . . . .209 A5
Mitchell Villas S43 . . . . . . .77 E3
Mitchell Way S43 . . . . .77 E3
Mitre Dr DE65 . . . . .242 C2
Moat Bank DE15 . . . . . . .248 D2
Moat St DE11 . . . . .256 B1
Moat The DE74 . . . . .247 B4
Model Village S80 . . . . . .100 E8
Model Village Prim Sch
  NG20. . . . . .119 E3
Moffatt Rd S2 . . . . .43 B7
MOIRA 262 E3
Moira Cl DE12 . . . . .220 A7
Moira Dale DE74 . . . . . . .247 C3
Moira Furnace Mus★
  DE12. . . . . .262 E3
Moira Junc Nature Reserve★
  DE12. . . . . .262 D4
Moira Rd
Donisthorpe DE12 . . . . . .262 F1
Moira DE11 . . . . .262 D2
Overseal DE12. . . . . .262 B3
Woodville DE11 . . . . .256 C2
Moira St DE73 . . . . .252 A7
Moisty La
Marchington ST14 . . . . . .224 C3
Stoney Middleton S32 . . . .71 B3
Molineux Ave S43. . . . . . . .78 D1
Molineux St DE23 . . . . . . .219 B2
Molloy Pl **11** S8. . . . . .43 A6
Molloy St **10** S8. . . . . .43 A6
Molyneaux Bsns Pk DE4. .127 B3
Monarch Dr DE21 . . . . . .206 D3
Monarch Way DE75 . . . . .181 D2
Moncreiff Dr DE13 . . . . . .241 A1
Moncrieff Cres DE21 . . . . .220 A8
Mondello Dr DE24 . . . . . .233 C6
Monk Rd DE55 . . . . .159 B2
Monk Road Ind Est DE55 159 C2
Monks Cl
Derby DE24 . . . . .231 C3
Ilkeston DE7 . . . . .209 A8
Monksdale Cl SK17. . . . . . .69 B4
Monksdale La SK17 . . . . . .68 F2
Monk's Rd SK13 . . . . .17 A4
Monk St
Derby DE22 . . . . .267 A2
Tutbury DE13 . . . . .239 C7
Monks Way S81. . . . . .63 F7
Monkton Cl DE7 . . . . .194 D3
Monkwood Rd S41. . . . . . .95 D8
Monnies End S43 . . . . .80 D5
Monsal Ave SK17 . . . . .85 D7
Monsal Cres
Staveley S43 . . . . .97 C6
Tibshelf DE55. . . . . .147 F6
Monsaldale Cl
Burton upon Trent DE15 . .248 B4
Long Eaton NG10. . . . . . .236 B6
Monsal Dr
Derby DE21 . . . . .220 F3
South Normanton DE55. . .159 F5
Monsal Gr SK17. . . . . .85 D7
MONSAL HEAD 89 D4
Monsall Ave DE7. . . . . . . .194 E5
Monsdale La DE6 . . . . . . .151 E2
Monsom La DE65 . . . . . . .242 D3
Montague Way DE73 . . . . .232 E2
Montagu St SK6. . . . . .15 B2
Monteith Pl DE74 . . . . . . .247 B4
Montford Mews DE74. . . .247 B4
Montgomery Cl DE65. . . .228 E2
Montpelier DE22. . . . . . . .204 D7
Montpelier Cl DE14 . . . . . .254 A7
Montpelier Gdns **5** SK17. . .85 D8
Montpelier Pl SK17. . . . . . .66 D1
Montpelier Rd DE56. . . . .167 F3

Montrose Cl DE24. . . . . .231 E4
Montrose Cl NG9 . . . . . . .209 E1
Montrose Pl S18. . . . . .56 D2
Montrose Sq NG19 . . . . . .136 B6
Monument La NG16. . . . . .170 E3
MONYASH 107 C2
Monyash CE Prim Sch
  DE45. . . . . .107 C1
Monyash Cl
Derby DE21 . . . . .220 A8
Ilkeston DE7 . . . . .194 E3
Staveley S43 . . . . .97 C7
Monyash Ct **82** SK13. . . . . . .9 D1
Monyash Gr **31** SK13 . . . . . . .9 D1
Monyash Lea **33** SK13. . . . . . .9 D1
Monyash Mews **30** SK13 . . . .9 D1
Monyash Pl **29** SK13 . . . . . . .9 D1
Monyash Rd
Bakewell DE45. . . . . .109 C5
Over Haddon DE45. . . . . .109 A2
Monyash Way
Belper DE56. . . . . .179 B5
  1 Gamesley SK13. . . . . . .9 E1
Moonpenny Way S18. . . . . .57 A1
Mooracre La S44 . . . . .99 D1
Moorbridge La NG9 . . . . .209 E1
Moorbrook La S33. . . . . . .50 F7
Moor Cres S20. . . . . .59 C7
Moor Croft DE4. . . . . . . .143 E7
Moor Dr DE24 . . . . .233 B5
Moore Cl S42. . . . . .116 D1
MOOREDGE 144 C5
Mooredge Dr DE4. . . . . . .143 D6
Mooredge Rd DE4. . . . . . .157 B2
MOOREND
Bradley. 186 D8
Marple. 24 A6
Moor End DE4. . . . . .111 C3
Moor End Rd SK6. . . . . . . .24 A5
Moores Ave NG10 . . . . . .223 C7
Moore St DE23. . . . . .219 A3
Moor Farm Ave S20. . . . . .59 B8
Moor Farm Garth S20. . . . .59 C8
Moor Farm Rise S20. . . . . .59 B8
Moor Farm Road E DE6. . .185 F7
Moor Farm Road W DE6. .185 E8
Moorfield DE4. . . . . .143 C7
Moorfield Ave S41. . . . . . . .99 B1
Moorfield Cres **3** NG10 . . .223 B5
Moorfield Ct NG9 . . . . . . .209 E1
Moorfield Hts SK15. . . . . . .4 A6
Moorfield La NG20 . . . . . .100 F4
Moorfield Prec SK14. . . . . .9 D5
Moorfield Rd DE56. . . . . .191 C7
Moorfields Ave NG16. . . . .182 F3
Moorfield Sq S44. . . . . . . .99 B1
Moorfield St SK14. . . . . . . .9 D5
Moorfield Terr SK14. . . . . . .9 D5
Moor Furlong DE13 . . . . . .240 F1
Moorgate DE22 . . . . .217 E6
Moorgate Ave NG19. . . . . .134 F7
Moorgate Cres S18 . . . . . .76 B8
MOORHAIGH. 135 A3
Moorhaigh La NG19. . . . . .135 A3
MOORHALL. 74 C2
Moorhall DE45. . . . . .109 C5
Moorhay Cl S41. . . . . .95 B7
Moorhead Ave DE24. . . . .232 F5
Moorhead Prim Sch
  DE24. . . . . .232 F6
Moorings The SK12 . . . . . .32 E6
Moor La
Aston-on-Trent DE72. . . . .246 B8
Barrow upon Trent DE73. . .244 B8
Bolsover S44 . . . . .99 B1
Bonsall DE4. . . . . .142 B2
Calow S44 . . . . .116 C8
Dale Abbey DE7. . . . . . . .207 F2
Darley Dale DE4 . . . . . . .127 C4
Derby DE24 . . . . .232 C6
Elton DE4. . . . . .140 C5
Flagg SK17. . . . . .106 E4
Kirk Ireton DE6. . . . . .165 A3
Kirk Langley DE6 . . . . . . .202 F1
Little Eaton DE21. . . . . . .191 E1
Ockbrook DE72 . . . . .221 C6
Osmaston DE6 . . . . .185 F5
Scarcliffe S44 . . . . .119 A8
Taddington SK17 . . . . .87 E1
Youlgreave DE45. . . . . . . .125 B5
Moorland Ave NG9. . . . . .223 D6
Moorland Ctr The★ S33 . . .37 C8
Moorland Dr S44 . . . . . . .116 F2
Moorland Rd
Derby DE3. . . . . .217 D3
Hathersage S32. . . . . .53 A7
Moorlands Cl NG10 . . . . . .223 B2
Moorlands Dr DE6 . . . . . .184 C7
Moorlands La
Bonsall DE4. . . . . .142 B3
Froggatt S32. . . . . .72 C5
Moorlands Rd DE56. . . . . .168 B4
Moorland Terr DE4 . . . . . .144 A4
Moorland View
Apperknowle S18. . . . . . . .58 A1
Sheffield S12. . . . . .44 A2
Moorland View Rd S40. . . .95 C1
Moorlawn Ave S42. . . . . . .113 E7
Moorpark Ave S40 . . . . . .114 C4
Moorpool Cres DE56. . . . .191 C7
Moor Rd
Ashover S45 . . . . .129 F3
Breadsall DE21. . . . . .205 F5
Brinsley NG16. . . . . .182 E8
Great Longstone DE45, S32. 89 F6
Moor Rise DE56. . . . . . . .191 C8
MOORSIDE 165 A2

Moorside Cl
Cromford DE4 . . . . .155 A5
Glossop SK13. . . . . .17 B7
Sheffield S20. . . . . .59 C8
Moorside Cres DE24 . . . . .231 F4
Moorside Gdns DE72. . . . .234 C1
Moorside La DE56. . . . . . .191 C7
Moor St DE21 . . . . .220 E5
Moor The
Brinsley NG16 . . . . .182 D8
Middleton DE4. . . . . .154 C4
Moorthorpe Gn S20. . . . . .44 F2
Moorthorpe way S20. . . . . .44 F2
Moortop Rd S18, S21. . . . . .58 B1
Moor Valley S20. . . . . .44 F2
Moorview Cl
Brimington S43 . . . . .96 D7
Wingerworth S42. . . . . . . .115 B3
Moorview Ct **2** S17. . . . . . .56 B5
Moor View Rd S43 . . . . . . .79 A2
Moorway DE21. . . . . .205 E4
Moorway Croft DE23 . . . . .231 B7
Moorway La DE23 . . . . . . .231 B6
Moorways Sports Ctr
  DE24 . . . . .232 D6
Moorwinstow Croft S17 . . .55 E7
Moorwood La S17. . . . . . . .55 C1
Moorwoodmoor La
  DE55. . . . . .157 D6
Moray Cl DE11. . . . . .255 F1
Moray Ct NG16. . . . . .195 C8
Moray Pl S18 . . . . .56 D2
Moray Wlk DE21 . . . . . . .219 C8
Mordaunt Rd S2. . . . . .43 F6
Morden Gn DE22. . . . . . . .218 A6
Morden Rd NG16. . . . . . .195 C8
Morefern Dr DE21. . . . . . .205 F2
Morland Bank S14 . . . . . . .43 E3
Morland Cl S14 . . . . .43 E3
Morland Dr S14 . . . . .43 F3
Morland Pl S14 . . . . .43 F3
Morland Rd
Hayfield SK22 . . . . .25 B2
Sheffield S14. . . . . .43 F3
Morledge
Derby DE1 . . . . .267 C3
Matlock DE4. . . . . .142 F6
MORLEY 206 C6
Morley Almshouses La
  DE7. . . . . .206 B7
Morley Ave S40 . . . . .95 C4
Morley Cl
Belper DE56. . . . . .179 E6
Burton upon Trent DE15 . .248 B2
Dronfield S18. . . . . .56 C1
Morley Dr DE7. . . . . .194 D3
Morley Gdns DE21 . . . . . .220 B8
Morley Hall Prep Sch
  DE7. . . . . .206 B1
Morley Ho
Derby, Alvaston DE24 . . . .233 A7
  1 Derby, Markeaton DE3 217 D1
Morley Mews DE21. . . . . .220 A7
Morley Prim Sch DE7 . . . .206 C7
Morley Rd DE21 . . . . .220 B8
Morley St
Derby DE22 . . . . .218 C5
Glossop SK13. . . . . .17 D8
Morlich Dr DE24 . . . . .231 E5
Morningside Cl DE24 . . . . .232 D4
Mornington Cl NG10 . . . . .223 C6
Mornington Cres DE22. . . .218 B6
Mornington Rd S42 . . . . . .132 C8
Mornington Rise DE4 . . . . .143 C4
Morpeth Gdns DE21. . . . . .205 D2
Morrell Wood Dr DE56 . . .179 D5
Morris Ave S41 . . . . .95 E5
Morris Dr S41 . . . . .95 E5
Mortimer Rd S6 . . . . .31 E8
Mortimer St DE24 . . . . . . .232 C7
MORTON 146 F5
Morton Ave
Clay Cross S45. . . . . .131 B4
Ilkeston DE7 . . . . .194 F1
Morton Gdns S20 . . . . .59 F6
Morton La S18, S21. . . . . . .58 C1
Morton Mount S20. . . . . . .59 F7
Morton Prim Sch DE55. . .147 A5
Morton Rd
Pilsley S45. . . . . .147 C8
Shirland DE55 . . . . .146 D6
Morton St NG19. . . . . . . .135 E1
Morven Ave
Bolsover S44 . . . . .99 B1
Mansfield Woodhouse
  NG19. . . . . .136 B2
Morven St S80. . . . . .100 F8
MOSBOROUGH 59 D7
Mosborough Hall Dr S20. . .59 E6
Mosborough Hall Farm
  S20. . . . . .59 D6
Mosborough Moor S20 . . . .59 B8
Mosborough Prim Sch
  S20. . . . . .59 C8
Mosborough Rd S13. . . . . .44 B7
Moscow Farm Ct DE56 . . .190 F5
Mosedale Cl DE24. . . . . . .232 F8
Moseley St DE5. . . . . .169 D2
Moses La DE7 . . . . .206 E7
Moses View S81. . . . . .63 F7
Mosley Mews DE13. . . . . .240 A4
Mosley Rd SK17. . . . . .85 B6

Mossbank Cl SK13. . . . . . . .9 E4
Moss Beck Ct S21. . . . . . . .59 C2
Mossbrook Ct S21. . . . . . . .59 E4
Mossbrook Sch S8. . . . . . .57 C8
Mosscar Cl NG20. . . . . . . .120 F1
Mossdale Ave S20 . . . . . . .59 D7
Moss Dr S21. . . . . .60 D5
Moss Edge Rd HD9. . . . . . . .3 C8
Moss House Ct S20. . . . . . .59 D6
Moss La
Broadbottom SK14. . . . . . .15 F8
Hulland Ward DE6 . . . . . .175 F4
Ripley DE5. . . . . .169 D3
Moss Rd
Ilkeston DE7 . . . . .208 E7
Sheffield S17. . . . . .55 B4
Moss Rise Pl S21 . . . . .59 C3
Moss St
Derby DE22 . . . . .218 E3
Hollingworth SK14. . . . . . . .9 D5
Mossvale Dr DE23 . . . . . . .231 A6
Moss View S20. . . . . .59 C6
Moss View Rd SK23 . . . . . .47 C5
Moston Wlk S40 . . . . .114 E6
Mostyn Ave DE23 . . . . . . .218 D1
Mottistone Cl DE24 . . . . . .233 D5
Mottram CE Prim Sch
  SK14. . . . . .9 A3
Mottram Fold SK14 . . . . . . .9 A3
MOTTRAM IN
  LONGDENDALE 9 B4
Mottram Moor SK14. . . . . . .9 B4
Mottram Old Rd SK14 . . . . .15 B8
Mottram Rd SK14 . . . . .16 A8
Moulbourn Dr DE56. . . . . .190 D4
Mouldridge La DE4 . . . . . .139 F2
Moult Ave DE21. . . . . .220 E4
Moulton Cl
Belper DE56. . . . . .179 D5
Swanwick DE55. . . . . .169 F8
Mound Rd S40. . . . . .266 B1
Mountbatten Cl DE24. . . . .232 E4
Mountbatten Ct DE7 . . . . .194 F3
Mountcastle St S41 . . . . . . .95 F8
Mountcastle Wlk S41 . . . . .95 F8
Mount Carmel St DE23 . . .267 A1
Mount Cres DE55 . . . . . . .160 A3
Mountfield Ave NG10. . . . .223 A4
Mountfield Way DE24 . . . . .233 D4
Mountford Ave DE4 . . . . . .165 E7
Mountford Cl DE21. . . . . .206 B2
Mountford Croft S17 . . . . . .55 E5
MOUNT PLEASANT
Belper. 178 D6
Blackwell. 147 F2
Castle Gresley. 261 E7
Melbourne. 251 F8
Repton. 242 E1
Mount Pleasant
Ashford in the Water
  DE45. . . . . .108 F8
Castle Donington DE74 . . .247 B3
Cromford DE4. . . . . .155 B7
Ilkeston DE7 . . . . .194 E4
Ripley DE5. . . . . .169 D2
Somercotes DE55 . . . . . .170 D5
Youlgreave DE45. . . . . . . .125 C5
Mount Pleasant Ct S32. . . .72 C8
Mount Pleasant Dr
Belper DE56. . . . . .178 E5
Heage DE56. . . . . .179 E8
Mount Pleasant La DE12. 265 A8
Mount Pleasant Rd
Grindleford S32. . . . . .72 C8
Linton DE11. . . . . .261 E8
Repton DE65 . . . . .242 E1
Swadlincote DE11 . . . . . .256 D5
Mount Rd
Bretby DE15. . . . . .249 A3
Compstall SK14. . . . . .15 A6
Hartshorne DE11. . . . . . . .257 A4
Linton DE11. . . . . .261 D8
Mount St Mary's RC Coll
  S21. . . . . .60 C2
Mount St
Breaston DE72. . . . . .235 F7
Burton upon Trent DE15 . .248 A3
Derby DE1 . . . . .267 B1
Glossop SK13. . . . . .17 C8
Heanor DE75 . . . . .181 E1
Mansfield NG19 . . . . .136 A1
Stapleford NG9 . . . . .223 E7
Mount The
Chesterfield S41 . . . . .77 A3
Stapleford NG9 . . . . .223 D6
Mount View Ave S8 . . . . . .43 A3
Mount View Gdns S8. . . . . .43 A3
Mount View Lodge **2** S8. .43 A3
Mount View Rd S8 . . . . . . .43 B3
Mouselow Cl SK13. . . . . . . .9 F3
Mowbray Gdns DE24 . . . . .232 C7
Mowbray St DE24 . . . . . . .232 D8
Moy Ave DE24. . . . . .231 F2
Moyne Gdns DE73. . . . . . .245 A8
MUDD 9 A2
Mudhurst La SK12. . . . . . . .32 E3
MUGGINTON 188 F2
Mugginton CE Prim Sch
  DE6. . . . . .188 E2
MUGGINTONLANE END . . .188 E6
Muirfield Cl S41 . . . . .96 B6
Muirfield Dr DE3. . . . . . . .217 F2
Muirfield Way NG19. . . . . .136 E6
Mulberries DE22 . . . . .204 E4

Mulberry Cl
Belper DE56.............**179** B3
Wingerworth S42........**115** A4
Mulberry Croft
Brimington S43 ....**78** A1
Staveley S43 ....**78** A1
Mulberry Mews DE5......**180** C6
Mulberry Rd S21........**59** B2
Mulberry Way
Aston-on-Trent DE72...**246** A6
Hilton DE65 ....**228** E2
Killamarsh S21 ....**60** B5
Mull Ct 3 DE4........**231** D3
Mullion Pl DE24........**233** B5
Mumford Dr DE6........**185** D8
Mundella Pl S8 ....**43** A3
Mundella Prim Sch 5 S8 **43** A3
Mundy CE Jun Sch DE75 **193** F8
Mundy Cl DE1..........**218** E6
Mundy's Dr DE75 ....**193** F8
Mundy St
Derby DE1..............**218** E6
Heanor DE75 ....**181** E1
Ilkeston DE7 ....**194** E2
Munro Cl S21...........**60** D6
Munro Ct DE24.........**231** E4
Murrayfield Dr 6 S20... **59** E6
Murray Park Foundation Sch
DE3....................**217** F4
Murray Rd
Derby DE3 ....**217** F4
Killamarsh S21 ....**60** E7
Murray St DE24.........**232** F8
Musard Pl S43..........**78** D1
Musard Way S21........**60** C6
Muse La
Boylestone DE6 ....**213** A2
Church Broughton DE6 ..**226** B7
Museum of Childhood★
DE6....................**225** D5
Musgrave Ho S33 ....**40** B3
Mushroom Farm Ct
NG16...................**182** D3
Mushroom La DE11......**262** D8
Muskham Ave DE7 ......**194** F3
Muskham Ct 1 NG19...**136** B1
Mus of Industry & History
The (Silk Mill Mus)★
DE1....................**267** B4
Musters St NG20........**120** A4
Muswell Rd DE22........**217** E5
Mycock La SK17.........**106** F5
Myers Cl DE24..........**231** F4
Mynd The NG19.........**136** E6
Myrtle Ave
Long Eaton NG10........**236** C6
Stapleford NG9 ....**223** E6
Myrtle Cl
Sheffield S2..............**43** C6
Shirebrook NG20........**119** D6
Myrtle Cres S2..........**43** C7
Myrtle Dr S2............**43** C7
Myrtle Gr S43............**78** A1
Myrtle Rd S2............**43** B7
Myrtle Springs S12.......**43** F5
Myrtle Springs Dr S12....**43** F5
Mytham Bridge S33.......**40** B1
Mytholme Ct NG10.......**223** C2

N

Nabb La ST14............**196** A4
Nailers Way DE56........**179** C5
Nailor La DE4............**142** D3
Nairn Ave DE21..........**219** D7
Nairn Cl DE24...........**231** D3
Nairn Dr S18............**56** D1
Namur Cl DE22..........**218** C3
Nan Gell's Hill DE4.......**155** A3
Napier Cl
Derby DE3 ....**217** E4
Swadlincote DE11 ....**255** E2
Napier Ct S43............**80** B5
Napier St DE22..........**218** C5
Napoleon Pk DE24.......**232** E7
Narlow La DE6...........**161** F2
Narrow La
Denstone ST14 ....**196** D6
Donisthorpe DE12 ......**265** E8
Ticknall DE73...........**250** F4
Narrowleys La S45.......**129** F3
Naseby Cl DE3...........**217** C3
Naseby Dr NG10.........**236** E4
Naseby Rd DE56.........**179** D4
Nathaniel Rd NG10.......**236** F7
National Sikh Her Ctr &
Holocaust Mus★ DE23 .**219** B1
National Stone Ctr★
DE4....................**154** F3
National Tramway Mus★
DE4....................**156** E2
Navan Rd S2.............**44** A7
Navigation Home Park
DE24...................**232** E8
Neal Ct NG16............**182** A3
Neale Bank S43..........**96** D7
Neale St
Clowne S43 ....**80** F4
Long Eaton NG10........**236** E7
Near Mdw NG10.........**236** E5
Nearwell Cl SK23........**46** F6
Nearwood Dr DE21.......**205** E3
Needham St DE5.........**181** B8
Needham Terr DE4.......**143** A7

Needwood Ave DE13 ...**240** C4
Need Wood Ave NG9....**209** D2
Needwood Ct DE13.....**239** C6
Neighwood Cl NG9......**223** E2
Neilson St DE24.........**232** F7
Nelper Cres DE7 ....**209** A5
Nelson Cl DE3 ....**217** F3
Nelson Pl LE65..........**257** F3
Nelson St
Burton upon Trent DE15 ..**248** C4
Chesterfield S41 ....**96** A6
Derby DE1 ....**267** D1
Ilkeston DE7 ....**194** F3
Long Eaton NG10........**236** D6
Swadlincote DE11 ....**256** B5
Nene Cl DE13...........**240** C1
Nene Way DE65.........**240** D8
Nerissa Cl DE73.........**232** E2
Nesbit St S44............**118** B8
Nesfield Cl
Chesterfield S41 ....**95** D8
Derby DE24 ....**233** C7
Nesfield Ct DE7..........**194** E1
Nesfield Rd DE7 ....**194** E1
Ness Wlk DE22..........**204** E3
Nestor Cl DE73..........**232** D2
NETHER AVE S21........**60** C6
NETHER BIGGIN **175** F5
Nether Blindlow La
SK17...................**106** B5
NETHER BOOTH **29** A1
NETHER BURROWS **202** C3
Netherby Manor S17....**56** A7
NETHER CHANDERHILL..**94** C1
Nether Cl
Duffield DE56...........**190** E5
Eastwood NG16.........**182** F4
Swanwick DE55.........**169** F7
Wingerworth S42........**115** A2
Netherclose St DE23....**219** A1
Nether Croft Cl S43.....**96** E7
Nethercroft La S45......**131** E3
Nether Croft Rd S43....**96** E7
Netherdene Rd S18......**57** A1
Nether Farm Cl S43.....**96** F5
Netherfield Cl
Ashbourne DE6 ....**185** C8
Staveley S43 ....**79** A2
Netherfield La DE72,
DE74...................**247** F8
Netherfield Rd
Chapel-en-le-Frith SK23 ..**47** D6
Chesterfield S40 ....**114** A8
Long Eaton NG10........**236** C4
Sandiacre NG10.........**223** B4
Netherfields Cres S18...**76** A8
Nether Gdns DE4........**165** F8
NETHER GREEN **60** D7
Nethergreen Ave S21...**60** D7
Nethergreen Ct S21.....**60** D7
Nethergreen Gdns S21..**60** D7
NETHER HANDLEY **77** F7
NETHER HEAGE **168** C1
Nether La
Brassington DE4 ....**163** F8
Hazelwood DE56 ....**190** A7
Holbrook DE56..........**191** D6
Kirk Ireton DE6 ....**176** B8
NETHER LANGWITH **101** B1
Netherleigh Cl S40......**95** B3
Netherleigh Rd S40.....**95** B3
Nethermoor Ave S21....**60** D7
Nethermoor Cl S21......**60** D7
Nethermoor Cotts DE55 .**147** D5
Nethermoor Dr S21......**60** D7
Nethermoor La S21......**60** D7
Nethermoor Rd
Tupton S42..............**131** C8
Wingerworth S42........**115** A1
NETHER PADLEY **53** E1
Nether Park Dr DE22....**204** C1
NETHER PILSLEY **132** D1
NETHERSEAL **264** E7
Netherseal Rd
Chilcote DE12 ....**264** F4
Clifton Campville B79 ...**263** F2
Netherside S33 ....**51** A7
Netherside Dr DE73 ....**233** B2
Nether Springs Rd S44..**98** F3
NETHER STURSTON.....**173** F1
NETHERTHORPE **79** A2
Netherthorpe S43.......**79** A2
Netherthorpe Airfield
S80....................**63** B5
Netherthorpe Cl
Killamarsh S21 ....**60** C7
Staveley S43 ....**78** F2
Netherthorpe La S21....**60** C7
Netherthorpe Rd 3 S43..**78** F2
Nether Thorpe Rd S80 ..**63** B5
Netherthorpe Sch S43 ..**79** A2
Nether Way DE4 ....**127** C3
Nether Wheel Row S13..**44** F5
Netherwood Ct DE22....**204** C3
Nettlefold Cres DE73....**245** B1
Nettleton Cl DE23.......**231** A6
Nettleton La SK17.......**85** D3
Nettleworth Inf Sch
NG19...................**136** C4
Networkcentre Barlborough
Links **80** A5
Neville Cl DE13 ....**240** B3
Nevinson Ave DE23......**231** D7
Nevinson Dr DE23.......**231** D7
Nevis Cl
Chesterfield S40 ....**95** D4
Derby DE24 ....**231** D2
Newark 8 S20...........**59** E8

Newark Rd DE21........**205** D2
New Bank St SK13 ......**10** A5
NEW BARLBOROUGH....**80** D5
New Barlborough Cl S43 .**80** D5
Newbarn Cl NG20.......**119** D2
New Bath Rd DE4........**155** A8
New Beetwell St S40....**266** B2
Newbery Ave NG10......**236** F6
NEWBOLD...............**95** E6
Newbold Ave
Borrowash DE72.........**221** C1
Chesterfield S41 ....**95** E6
Newbold Back La S40....**95** E5
Newbold CE Prim Sch
S41....................**95** E7
Newbold Cl DE73 ....**232** F2
Newbold Com Sch S41...**95** F6
Newbold Ct 1 S41.......**95** D7
Newbold Dr
Castle Donington DE74 ...**247** B5
Chesterfield S41 ....**95** E6
NEWBOLD MOOR **95** F7
Newbold Rd S40.........**95** D6
NEW BOLSOVER **98** F2
New Bolsover Prim Sch
S44....................**98** F1
Newborough Rd DE24...**233** C6
Newbound La S45.......**134** D2
Newboundmill La NG19..**135** A4
New Breck Rd DE56.....**179** A3
Newbridge Cl DE7 ......**207** D8
Newbridge Cres DE24...**232** E4
Newbridge Ct S41.......**77** A1
Newbridge Dr S43.......**96** D8
Newbridge La
Brimington S43 ....**96** D8
Chesterfield S41 ....**77** B1
Newbridge Rd DE56.....**168** A2
Newbridge St S41.......**77** A1
NEW BRIMINGTON......**77** F1
NEW BRINSLEY **171** E1
Newburgh Terr S32.....**72** C2
Newbury Dr DE13 ....**240** C1
Newbury St DE24 ....**232** E8
Newby Cl DE15 ....**248** B1
Newby Rd S41...........**95** C8
Newcastle St
Mansfield Woodhouse
NG19...................**136** B3
Sutton in Ashfield NG17 ..**148** F3
Newchase Bsns Pk DE23 **219** C1
New Chestnut Pl DE23...**231** E7
New Church St S33 ......**51** A7
New City Park Homes
DE24...................**220** A1
New Cl S32..............**71** C6
New Cotts
Buxton SK17 ....**84** E4
Whaley Thorns NG20....**101** F3
Newcrest Cl DE23.......**218** B1
New Derby Rd NG16.....**182** D3
Newdigate St
Derby DE23 ....**232** A8
Ilkeston DE7 ....**209** A6
Kimberley NG16.........**195** F6
West Hallam DE7........**207** C8
New Eaton Rd NG9......**223** E5
Newell Way DE4 ....**127** C3
New England Way NG19 .**135** C3
New Fall St NG17 ....**148** F3
Newfield Cres S17.......**55** C7
Newfield Croft S17......**55** A8
Newfield Farm Cl S14...**43** E5
NEWFIELD GREEN **43** D6
Newfield Green Rd S2....**43** D6
Newfield La S17 ....**55** C7
Newfield Pl S17..........**55** C7
Newfield Rd DE15.......**248** B4
Newfield Sec Sch S8.....**43** C3
NEWGATE **75** D1
Newgate Cl DE73 ....**233** B2
NEWHALL **255** F6
Newhall Com Jun Sch
DE11...................**255** E6
Newhall Inf Sch DE11 ...**255** F7
Newhall Rd DE11........**256** C5
New Hall Rd S40.........**95** D2
Newham Ave DE5 ....**169** C1
Newham Cl DE75........**182** A1
NEWHAVEN.............**138** F5
Newhaven Ave NG19 ...**136** B3
Newhaven Cl S40........**95** B1
New Haven Gdns S17 ...**55** E4
Newhay DE13 ....**240** F1
New High St SK17.......**85** D8
Newholme Hospl DE45 ..**109** D7
NEW HORWICH **45** E6
New Horwich Rd SK23...**45** E7
NEW HOUGHTON **134** F7
New Houses
Chesterfield S41 ....**96** C3
Tideswell SK17 ....**88** E8
New Inn La DE21........**205** C7
New La
Bradwell S33 ....**50** E6
Hilcote DE55 ....**148** C1
Newland Dale S41.......**266** B4
Newland Gdns S41......**95** E5
NEWLANDS.............**181** F2
Newlands Ave
Chesterfield S40 ....**95** C3
Sheffield S12 ....**44** A6
Newlands Barns DE22...**189** E3
Newlands Cl
Ripley DE5 ....**169** C2
Swadlincote DE11 ....**256** A2
Newlands Cres DE55....**148** A3

Newlands Dr
Glossop SK13.............**9** F4
Heanor DE75............**181** E3
Sheffield S12 ....**44** A6
Somercotes DE55 ....**170** D5
Newlands Gr S12.........**44** B6
Newlands Ho DE55......**170** D4
Newlands Inn Sta★
DE55...................**170** C3
Newlands Rd
Sheffield S12 ....**44** A6
Somercotes DE55 ....**170** C4
Newland St DE1.........**267** A3
Newlands The S41.......**155** A7
New Lane Galleries
DE55...................**159** A4
New Lawn Rd DE7.......**208** E8
New Linden St NG20....**120** A4
New Lumford DE45......**109** C7
Newlyn Dr
3 Derby DE23 ....**231** F8
South Normanton DE55...**160** C6
Newlyn Pl S8............**43** A3
Newman Dr
Burton upon Trent DE14 ..**254** B8
Swadlincote DE11 ....**255** E2
Newmanleys Rd NG16...**194** F8
Newmanleys Rd (South)
NG16...................**182** E1
Newmanleys Road S
NG16...................**194** E8
NEWMARKET **131** A2
Newmarket Ct DE24.....**219** E1
Newmarket Dr DE24.....**232** E8
Newmarket La S45.......**130** F3
New Market St SK17.....**85** B6
Newmarket Way NG9 ...**223** F2
New Mill La NG19........**136** E3
NEW MILLS.............**33** D7
New Mills Central Sta
SK22...................**33** B7
New Mills Her Ctr★ SK22. **33** B7
New Mills L Ctr SK22.....**33** C8
New Mills Newtown Sta
SK22...................**33** B6
New Mills Prim Sch SK22.**33** B8
New Mills Rd
Broadbottom SK13.......**16** B4
Hayfield SK22 ....**25** B3
New Mills Sch Bsns & Ent
Coll 1 SK22............**33** C8
New Mount Cl DE23......**231** D5
Newness Cl DE4.........**143** C6
New Orchard Pl DE3.....**217** D2
New Park Ct SK22.......**33** D7
New Park Pl DE24.......**219** D3
Newport Cres NG19.....**135** E1
Newport Ct DE24........**233** C5
Newquay Pl DE24.......**233** C5
New Queen St S41.......**266** B4
New Rd
Alfreton DE55 ....**170** E5
Apperknowle S18.........**58** A1
Bamford S33 ....**40** B5
Barlborough S43 ....**80** B7
Barton in Fabis NG11 ...**237** F6
Belper DE56.............**178** F3
Boylestone DE6 ....**213** B4
Bradwell, Bradwell Hills S33 **51** B6
Bradwell S33 ....**51** A4
Coton in the Elms DE12...**260** D3
Crich DE4...............**168** A8
Derby DE22 ....**205** A1
Eyam S32 ....**71** F5
Flash SK17 ....**103** A3
Glossop SK13............**9** F7
Grindleford S32.........**72** B5
Heage DE56 ....**179** D8
Hilton DE65 ....**228** E2
Holmesfield S18.........**75** A5
Holymoorside S42.......**113** D7
Horwich End SK23.......**45** E6
Idridgehay DE56 ....**176** F4
Ironville NG16..........**170** F3
Middleton DE4 ....**154** B5
Ridgeway DE56 ....**168** B4
Somercotes DE55 ....**170** D2
Somercotes NG16, DE55...**170** D2
Stapleford NG9 ....**209** D1
Swadlincote DE11 ....**255** E6
Uttoxeter ST14 ....**210** A1
Weston Underwood DE6...**188** D1
Whaley Bridge, Bridgemont
SK23...................**33** F1
Whaley Bridge SK23 .....**34** A1
Wingerworth S42........**114** C3
Wirksworth DE4 ....**155** A3
Woodville DE11 ....**256** A2
Youlgreave DE45 ....**125** C5
New Rd (Baslow Rd)
DE45...................**108** F8
New Road Ind Est NG9 ...**209** D1
New Row NG16..........**171** A5
NEW SAWLEY...........**236** B5
New School Cl S20.......**59** C7
New School Ct S20.......**59** C7
New School Rd S20......**59** C7
New Scott St NG20......**101** A2
Newshaw La SK13........**9** F4
NEW SMITHY **35** A1
New Spine Rd DE11......**255** F4
New Sq S40.............**266** B3
New St
Alfreton DE55 ....**159** A4
Bakewell DE45...........**109** D6
Bolsover S44 ....**99** A3
3 Broadbottom SK14....**16** A8
Buxton SK17 ....**67** B5

New St continued
Chesterfield S40 ....**266** B2
Derby DE1...............**267** C2
Donisthorpe DE12 ......**262** E1
Draycott DE72 ....**235** A7
Grassmoor S42 ....**115** F3
Hilcote DE55 ....**160** C8
Little Eaton DE21.......**205** C8
Long Eaton NG10........**236** E8
Matlock DE4.............**143** C5
New Mills SK22 ....**33** D7
Newton DE55............**148** A4
North Wingfield S42.....**131** F6
Ockbrook DE72 ....**221** C4
Pilsley S45 ....**132** D1
Ripley DE5 ....**169** E1
Rosliston DE12 ....**260** D6
Sheffield, Holbrook S20...**60** A8
Shirland DE55 ....**146** C2
Somercotes DE55 ....**170** C8
South Normanton DE55...**160** A6
Stanley DE7 ....**207** C6
Stonebroom DE55 ......**147** A5
Sutton in Ashfield NG17...**148** F3
Swadlincote DE11 ....**256** B2
Swanwick DE55.........**169** E2
Whitwell S80 ....**81** E5
NEW STANTON **208** E3
New Station Rd S44......**99** B1
Newstead Ave
Derby DE21 ....**219** F6
Sheffield S12 ....**44** E3
Newstead Cl
Dronfield S18............**56** C1
Sheffield S12 ....**44** E2
Newstead Dr S12........**44** E3
Newstead Gr S12........**44** E3
Newstead Pl S12.........**44** E2
Newstead Rd
Long Eaton NG10........**223** C3
Sheffield S12 ....**44** F3
Newstead Rise S12......**44** F2
Newstead Road N DE7...**194** D3
Newstead Road S DE7...**194** D3
Newstead Terr 3 SK17...**85** B6
Newstead Way S12......**44** E2
New Street Bus Link S20..**60** A8
New Terr
Pleasley NG19...........**134** F5
Sandiacre NG10.........**223** B6
NEWTHORPE **195** A8
Newthorpe Comm NG16..**195** A8
NEWTHORPE COMMON..**195** A8
NEWTON...............**148** B3
Newton Cl
Belper DE56.............**179** C6
Newton Solney DE15.....**248** E8
Newton Ct 16 S41.......**95** F8
Newtondale Ave NG19...**136** E1
Newton Dr NG9 ....**223** E6
Newton Gn DE3..........**217** F2
NEWTON GREEN **148** A4
Newton La
Bretby DE15.............**249** A5
Newton Solney DE15.....**248** F7
Tibshelf DE55 ....**147** F6
Newton Leys DE15 ......**248** E8
Newton Park Cl 2 DE11..**256** A7
Newton Pk
Burton upon Trent DE15 ..**248** D7
Newton Solney DE15.....**248** D7
Newton Prim Sch DE55...**148** A3
Newton Rd
Burton upon Trent DE15 ..**248** A5
Tibshelf DE55...........**147** F6
Newtons Croft Cres S43...**80** B6
Newtons La NG16........**195** B4
NEWTON SOLNEY **248** E8
Newton Solney CE Inf Sch
DE15...................**248** E8
Newton's Wlk DE22 .....**204** E3
Newton Wonder Ct DE73 **245** B1
Newtonwood La DE55,
NG17...................**148** C5
NEW TOTLEY **55** E4
NEWTOWN.............**33** B6
Newtown Prim Sch SK22. **33** B6
New Tythe St NG10......**236** F7
New Victoria Ct DE24....**232** E5
NEW WESTWOOD **171** C4
New Westwood NG16....**171** C4
New Whittington Com Prim
Sch (Handley Rd Site)
S43....................**77** D4
New Whittington Com Prim
Sch (London St Site)
S43....................**77** D3
New Wye St SK17........**85** C8
NEW YORK **252** A7
NEW ZEALAND..........**218** C5
New Zealand La DE56....**190** C2
New Zealand Sq DE22...**218** C5
Nicholas Cl DE21........**220** E6
Nicholas St S41..........**115** D7
Nicholson Ct
9 Sheffield S8 ....**43** B6
Tideswell SK17 ....**69** C4
Nicholson Pl 7 S8........**43** B6
Nicholson Rd S8.........**43** A6
Nicholson's Row NG20..**119** F3
Nicklaus Ct DE14........**254** A7
Nicola Gdns DE23.......**231** D4
Nicolas Cl SK17.........**85** E8
Nidderdale Ct DE4.......**233** D6
Nields Way SK6..........**23** D4
Nightingale Ave NG19...**135** A4
Nightingale Bsns Pk
DE24...................**232** D8

Nightingale Cl
Chesterfield S41 . . . . . . 266 B4
Clay Cross S45. . . . . 131 E2
Holloway DE4 . . . . 155 F6
Ripley DE5 . . . . 169 D1
Nightingale Dr
Mansfield NG19. . . . . . . 135 E1
Woodville DE11 . . . . 256 F3
Nightingale Jun & Inf Schs
DE24 . . . . 232 C7
Nightingale Mews DE1 . . 267 D2
Nightingale Rd DE24 . . . 232 C8
Nikolas Rd S21 . . . . 60 B1
Nimbus Way NG16 . . . . . 195 F7
Nine Corners NG16. . . . . 195 F6
Nine Ladies Stone Circle★
DE4 . . . . 126 D3
Ninelands Rd S32. . . . . . . 53 A7
NITHEN END 84 F8
Nix's Hill DE55 . . . . 159 B2
Noble St DE1 . . . . 267 D1
Nodder Rd S13 . . . . 44 C7
Nodin Hill La DE56 . . . . 168 B3
Noe La S33 . . . . 40 A2
Noel-Baker Com Sch
DE24 . . . . 232 F4
Noel St DE22 . . . . 218 D6
No Man's Heath Rd DE12 264 F3
No Man's La DE7, DE27. . 222 D7
Nook End Rd DE75 . . . . . 181 D1
Nook La S44. . . . . 97 B3
Nook The
Barrow upon Trent DE73 . 244 A6
Heanor DE75 . . . . 181 C4
Holbrook DE56. . . . . . . 191 C7
Shirebrook NG20. . . . . . 119 C3
Stoney Middleton S32 . . 72 A4
Nooning La DE72 . . . . . . 234 E8
NORBRIGGS 79 C3
Norbriggs Prim Sch S43 . 79 B3
Norbriggs Rd S43. . . . . . 79 C3
Norburn Dr S21. . . . . . . 60 D6
NORBURY 183 D1
Norbury CE Prim Sch
DE6. . . . . 197 E7
Norbury Cl
Chesterfield S40 . . . . . . 95 B5
Derby DE22 . . . . 204 D1
Dronfield S18. . . . . 56 D1
Norbury Cres DE23 . . . . 231 C5
Norbury Ct 2 DE22 . . . . 204 D2
Norbury Hollow DE6 . . . 183 D1
Norbury Way
Belper DE56. . . . . 179 C6
Sandiacre NG10. . . . . . . 223 A6
Norfolk Ave S42 . . . . . . 115 F2
Norfolk Cl S40 . . . . 114 B8
Norfolk Com Prim Sch
S2. . . . . 43 D8
Norfolk Ct NG19 . . . . . . 136 E5
Norfolk Gdns DE22. . . . . 218 F8
Norfolk Park Ave S2 . . . . 43 D8
Norfolk Rd
Burton upon Trent DE15 . 254 D7
Long Eaton NG10 . . . . . 223 F1
Norfolk Sq 3 SK13. . . . . 10 C1
Norfolk St
Derby DE23 . . . . 219 B2
Glossop SK13. . . . . 10 D1
Norfolk Wlk NG10 . . . . . 223 B5
Norgreave Way S20. . . . . 59 E7
Norman Ave DE23. . . . . . 231 E7
Normandy Rd DE65 . . . . 228 E2
NORMANHURST PK DE4. . 127 E1
Norman Keep DE13 . . . . 239 C6
Norman Rd
Ripley DE5 . . . . 169 C1
Somercotes DE55 . . . . . 170 E7
Tutbury DE13 . . . . 239 C6
Norman St
Ilkeston DE7 . . . . 194 E3
Kimberley NG16. . . . . . . 195 F7
NORMANTON 231 F7
Normanton Ave DE55. . . 159 C3
Normanton Brook Rd
DE55 . . . . 160 D7
Normanton Gr S13. . . . . . 44 F6
Normanton Hill S13. . . . . 44 D6
Normanton Ho 3 SK17. . . 85 A7
Normanton House Prim Sch
DE23 . . . . 231 F8
Normanton La DE23. . . . 231 C8
Normanton Lodge DE23. 231 B8
Normanton Rd DE1 . . . . 267 B1
Normanton Spring Ct S13 44 F6
Normanton Spring Rd
S13. . . . . 44 F5
Northacre Rd DE21. . . . . 206 B2
Northam Dr DE5 . . . . . . 169 C2
North Ave
Ashbourne DE6 . . . . . . 173 B2
Derby, Darley Abbey DE22 205 A3
Derby DE3 . . . . 217 E2
Sandiacre NG10. . . . . . . 223 A6
North Brook Rd SK13. . . . 9 E4
North Church St DE45 . . 109 D6
North Cl
Derby DE3 . . . . 217 E3
Glossop SK13. . . . . 9 F7
South Normanton DE55 . . 159 F5
Unstone Green S18 . . . . . 76 E6
Willington DE65. . . . . . . 242 B5
Northcliffe Rd DE56 . . . . 173 B2
Northcote Ave S2. . . . . . . 43 B6
Northcote Rd S2. . . . . 43 B6
Northcote St NG10 . . . . 236 E7

North Cres
Duckmanton S44 . . . . . . 98 A5
Killamarsh S21 . . . . 60 E8
NORTHEDGE. 130 C6
Northedge La S42. . . . . . 130 B7
North End DE4. . . . . 154 F1
Northern Ave S2. . . . . 43 E7
Northern Comm S18 . . . . 56 B2
Northern Dr NG9. . . . . . 209 D3
Northern Rd DE75. . . . . . 181 D2
North Farm Cl S26 . . . . . 61 E7
Northfield
Derby DE24 . . . . 231 D3
Kilburn DE56 . . . . 179 F2
Northfield Ave
Ilkeston DE7 . . . . 194 E1
Long Eaton NG10 . . . . . 236 B3
Mansfield Woodhouse
NG19. . . . . 136 A4
Rocester ST14 . . . . 197 A4
Northfield S14. . . . . 210 A2
Northfield Cres NG9 . . . . 223 F4
Northfield Jun Sch S18 . . 57 C3
Northfield La
Mansfield Woodhouse
NG19. . . . . 135 F4
Mansfield Woodhouse
NG19. . . . . 136 B5
Palterton S44. . . . . 118 C6
Northfield Pk NG19 . . . . 136 B5
Northfield Prim Sch
NG19. . . . . 136 B5
Northfield Rd NG9 . . . . . 223 F4
Northfields
Clowne S43 . . . . 80 F3
Long Eaton NG10 . . . . . 236 B3
Northgate DE1. . . . . 267 B4
North Gate S44 . . . . 98 E3
Northgate Ho S21. . . . . . 59 D3
Northgate St 4 DE7 . . . . 194 F1
North Gr S44 . . . . 98 A6
North La
Belper DE56. . . . . 178 D2
Belper, Milford DE56 . . . 190 E7
Brailsford DE6 . . . . 187 E4
Old Brampton S42. . . . . . 94 D4
Northlands
4 Buxton SK17. . . . . 85 D8
Harthill S26 . . . . 61 E7
North Leys DE6 . . . . 173 B1
Northmead Dr DE3. . . . . 218 B3
Northmoor Cl S43 . . . . . . 96 F7
North Moor View S43 . . . 96 F7
North Par
Derby DE1 . . . . 267 B4
Matlock Bath DE4 . . . . . 143 A1
North Rd
Buxton SK17 . . . . 66 D1
Calow S44. . . . . 96 F3
Clowne S43 . . . . 80 E4
Glossop SK13. . . . . 10 C3
Hayfield SK22 . . . . 25 D3
Long Eaton NG10 . . . . . 236 C6
North Row DE22 . . . . . . 205 A1
Northside S42 . . . . 115 D1
North Side S42 . . . . 115 D1
North St
Alfreton DE55 . . . . 159 B3
Blackwell DE55 . . . . 147 F2
Bramley-Vale S44 . . . . . 117 D1
Burton upon Trent DE15 . 248 B3
Clay Cross S45. . . . . 131 B5
Cromford DE4 . . . . 155 A6
Derby DE1 . . . . 267 B5
Derby DE23 . . . . 218 C2
7 Ilkeston DE7 . . . . 194 F1
Langley Mill NG16 . . . . . 182 B3
Melbourne DE73 . . . . . . 252 A7
North Wingfield S42 . . . . 131 E6
Pinxton NG16. . . . . 160 D3
Shirebrook NG20. . . . . . 120 D4
Somercotes DE55 . . . . . 170 D6
South Normanton DE55. . 159 F5
Swadlincote DE11 . . . . . 256 B5
Whaley Thorns NG20. . . 101 A2
North Terr 1 S41. . . . . . 115 B7
Northumberland Rd
DE15 . . . . 254 D7
Northumberland St
DE23 . . . . 218 F2
North View S43. . . . . . . 218 C1
North View St S44 . . . . . . 98 F1
Northway Dr DE1 . . . . . . 218 E4
NORTH WINGFIELD 132 B8
North Wingfield Prim Sch
S42 . . . . 131 F7
North Wingfield Rd S42. . 115 C1
NORTHWOOD. 127 B5
Northwood Ave DE21. . . 219 C7
Northwood La
Ellastone DE6 . . . . 183 C5
Northwood DE4 . . . . . . 127 A6
Northwood Rise DE6 . . . 185 B8
Northwood St NG9 . . . . . 223 D8
NORTON. 57 B8
Norton Ave
Chesterfield S40 . . . . . . 114 A8
Sheffield S14. . . . . 43 E2
Shuttlewood S44 . . . . . . 98 F6
Norton Church Glebe S8 . 43 C1
Norton Church Rd S8 . . . 43 B1
Norton Free CE Prim Sch
S8 . . . . 43 C1
Norton Green Cl S8 . . . . 43 C1
Norton Hall S8 . . . . 43 B1
Norton Hall Ct S8 . . . . . . 43 B1
Norton La S8 . . . . 43 C1
Norton Lawns S8 . . . . . . 43 C1

NORTON LEES 43 A4
Norton Lees Cl S8 . . . . . . 43 A3
Norton Lees Cres S8 . . . . 43 A4
Norton Lees Glade S8. . . 43 A4
Norton Lees La S8 . . . . . . 43 A4
Norton Lees Rd S2. . . . . . 43 A4
Norton Lees Sq S8 . . . . . 43 A3
Norton Mews S8. . . . . . . 43 C1
Norton Park Ave S8. . . . . 57 B8
Norton Park Cres S8 . . . . 57 A8
Norton Park Dr S8 . . . . . 57 A8
Norton Park Rd S8 . . . . . 57 B8
Norton Park View S8. . . . 57 B8
NORTON WOODSEATS . . 43 A2
Norwell Ct 2 NG19 . . . . . 136 B1
Norwich Cl NG19. . . . . . 136 D5
Norwich St DE21 . . . . . . 219 D7
NORWOOD 60 F8
Norwood Ave S41. . . . . . 115 E6
Norwood Cl
Chesterfield S41 . . . . . . 115 E6
Derby DE22 . . . . 218 A5
Ilkeston DE7 . . . . 194 F5
Norwood Cres S21. . . . . . 60 F7
Norwood Ind Est S21. . . . 60 E8
Norwood Pl S21 . . . . 60 F7
Noskwith St DE7. . . . . . . 209 A5
Nothill Rd DE55 . . . . . . 228 E1
Nothills Cl DE73 . . . . . . 233 A1
Nottingham Canal Nature
Reserve★ DE7, NG16. . . . 195 C1
Nottingham Cl S42. . . . . 115 B3
Nottingham Dr S42 . . . . 115 B3
Nottingham La NG16 . . . 170 F5
Nottingham Rd
Alfreton DE55 . . . . 159 B2
Ashby-de-la-Zouch LE65 . 258 F1
Belper DE56 . . . . 178 F4
Borrowash DE72 . . . . . . 221 D2
Breedon on the Hill DE73 . 252 D1
Codnor DE5, NG16. . . . . 181 C3
Derby, Chaddesden DE21. . 219 E6
Derby DE1, DE21. . . . . . 267 C4
Derby, Spondon DE21 . . . 220 E3
Eastwood, Bailey Grove
NG16. . . . . 182 E2
Eastwood, Giltbrook NG16 195 C8
Ilkeston DE7 . . . . 209 A6
Long Eaton NG10 . . . . . 236 F8
Ripley DE5 . . . . 169 C2
Selston NG16. . . . . 171 F6
Stapleford NG9 . . . . 223 E7
Tansley DE4 . . . . 144 B4
Trowell NG9. . . . . 209 E5
Nowill Ct 2 S8 . . . . 43 A6
Nowill Pl 3 S8 . . . . 43 A6
Nuffield Health Derby Hospl
DE23 . . . . 230 F6
Nunbrook Gr SK17. . . . . . 85 C8
Nunn Brook Rd NG17. . . 148 E2
Nunn Brook Rise NG17 . . 148 E2
Nunn Cl NG17. . . . . 148 E1
Nunsfield Dr DE24 . . . . . 233 B7
Nunsfield Rd SK17 . . . . . 66 C1
Nun's St DE1 . . . . 218 E6
Nursery Ave
Sandiacre NG10. . . . . . . 222 F5
West Hallam DE7. . . . . . 207 E7
Nursery Cl
Borrowash DE72 . . . . . . 221 B2
4 Glossop SK13. . . . . . . 17 C8
Swadlincote DE11 . . . . . 256 B6
Nursery Croft DE4 . . . . . 165 E6
Nursery Dr
Bolsover S44 . . . . 98 F2
Buxton SK17 . . . . 66 C2
Nursery Gdns DE55. . . . . 160 C4
Nursery Hollow DE7 . . . . 208 E6
Nursery La SK17 . . . . 84 E6
Nutbrook Cres DE7 . . . . 208 D4
Nuthall Circ DE7 . . . . . . 208 C4
Nuthall Cl DE55 . . . . . . 158 F3
Nuttall St DE55 . . . . 158 F3
Nuttall Terr S44 . . . . . . 117 D1
NUTTALS PARK 169 E1
Nutwood Cl DE22 . . . . . 205 A3
Nutwood/Darley Tip Nature
Reserve★ DE56. . . . . . . 205 A2

O

Oadby Dr S41. . . . . 115 C7
Oadby Rise DE23 . . . . . . 231 E6
Oakamoor Cl S40 . . . . . . 95 A5
Oak Apple Cres DE7. . . . 208 E6
Oak Ave
Aldercar NG16. . . . . 182 B5
Disley SK12 . . . . 33 A6
Ripley DE5 . . . . 180 D7
Sandiacre NG10. . . . . . . 223 A7
Shirebrook NG20. . . . . . 119 D4
Oak Bank SK12 . . . . 33 A6
Oak Bank Ave S41 . . . . . . 77 B2
Oakbank Ct S17. . . . . 55 E5
Oak Cl
Brimington S43 . . . . 96 D7
Chapel-en-le-Frith SK23 . . 47 C5
Derby DE22 . . . . 204 E4
Duffield DE56. . . . . 190 E2
Killamarsh S21 . . . . 60 C5
Linton DE11 . . . . 261 E7
Mottram in Longdendale
SK14. . . . . 9 A4
Ockbrook DE72 . . . . 221 C5
Pinxton NG16. . . . . 160 C3
Oak Cres
Ashbourne DE6 . . . . . . 185 C7

Oak Cres continued
Derby DE23 . . . . 231 C8
Wingerworth S42. . . . . . 114 F3
Oakdale Cl S45 . . . . 131 E2
Oakdale Gdns DE21 . . . . 206 B3
Oakdale Rd DE55 . . . . . . 160 A4
Oakdell S18 . . . . 57 D3
Oak Dr
Alfreton DE55 . . . . 159 B4
Derby, Boulton DE24 . . . . 233 A6
Derby DE3 . . . . 217 E2
Doveridge DE6. . . . . 211 B1
Eastwood NG16. . . . . . . 182 E2
Hilton DE65 . . . . 228 D2
Mansfield Woodhouse
NG19. . . . . 136 E2
Oakenthorpe Nature
Reserve★ DE55 . . . . 158 C3
Oaker Terr DE4 . . . . 142 A7
OAKERTHORPE 158 C3
Oakerthorpe Rd DE4 . . . 155 B2
Oakes Cl DE55 . . . . 170 C5
Oakes Park View S14 . . . 43 D1
Oakes's Row NG16 . . . . . 170 F5
Oakes The S8. . . . . 43 D1
Oakfield Ave S40 . . . . . . 95 B1
Oakfield Ct DE7. . . . . . . 193 A2
Oakfield Dr NG10 . . . . . 223 B3
Oakfield Rd
Glossop SK13. . . . . 9 E3
Stapleford NG9 . . . . 223 D7
Oakfields DE13 . . . . 238 A4
Oakfields Gr DE21. . . . . . 220 D3
Oak Grove Gn S17 . . . . . 55 E4
Oakham Cl DE21 . . . . . . 205 D1
Oakham Way DE7. . . . . . 194 E3
Oakhill Rd S18. . . . . 57 C3
Oakhurst Cl DE56 . . . . . 178 D6
Oak La DE6 . . . . 212 D4
Oakland Ave
Long Eaton NG10 . . . . . 236 C5
Sutton in Ashfield NG17. . 148 F2
Oakland Cres DE55 . . . . 170 D5
Oakland Croft NG17 . . . . 148 F3
Oaklands S22 . . . . 25 C3
Oaklands Ave
Derby DE23 . . . . 231 C5
Heanor DE75 . . . . 182 A2
Oaklands Cl DE55 . . . . . 180 D1
Oaklands Rd DE65 . . . . . 229 C4
Oakland St DE55 . . . . . . 159 B4
Oaklands The DE55 . . . . 160 A4
Oakland Terr NG10. . . . . 236 C5
Oaklea SK17 . . . . 85 C5
Oaklea Way S42 . . . . 131 B6
Oakleigh Ave
Derby DE21 . . . . 219 F6
Mansfield Woodhouse
NG19. . . . . 136 E4
Swadlincote DE11 . . . . . 255 F5
Oakley Ave S40 . . . . 95 E4
Oakley's Rd NG10 . . . . . 236 E7
Oakley's Road W NG10 . . 236 D6
Oak Lodge Dr NG16. . . . . 195 F7
Oakmeadows DE55 . . . . 160 B4
Oakover Dr DE22. . . . . . 204 D2
Oak Rd
Denstone ST14 . . . . 196 D5
Elvaston DE72 . . . . 233 F4
Grassmoor S42 . . . . 115 F3
Matlock DE4. . . . . 143 C5
Shardlow DE72 . . . . 234 A5
Sheffield, Gleadless Townend
S12. . . . . 44 A2
Oakridge DE21. . . . . 220 B7
Oakridge Cl NG19 . . . . . 136 F1
Oakridge Pk DE74. . . . . . 247 A5
Oaks Ave
Creswell S80 . . . . 100 C8
Hayfield SK22 . . . . 25 D2
Oaks Barn DE45. . . . . . . 109 A2
Oaks Farm La S44. . . . . . 97 A2
OAKS GREEN 225 D7
Oakside Way DE21 . . . . . 206 B3
Oaks La
Ashover S45 . . . . 129 C5
Cutthorpe S18, S42. . . . . 94 A8
Oak Sq DE11. . . . . 255 F2
Oaks Rd DE65 . . . . 242 B5
Oak St
Brimington S43 . . . . 78 A1
Derby DE23 . . . . 219 A2
Glossop SK13. . . . . 10 C1
Sheffield, Heeley S8 . . . . 43 A7
Sheffield S20 . . . . 59 C8
Swadlincote DE11 . . . . . 256 A2
Oakstedge La S45. . . . . . 145 B7
Oaks The
Glossop SK13. . . . . 17 A7
Little Eaton DE21. . . . . . 205 C8
OAKTHORPE 265 F5
Oaktree Ave DE24. . . . . . 232 B7
Oak Tree Ave S44 . . . . . 134 B8
Oaktree Bsns Pk DE11. . . 255 E3
Oak Tree Cl DE72 . . . . . 221 D1
Oak Tree Cres NG19. . . . 136 B4
Oak Tree Ct DE72 . . . . . 221 D1
Oak Tree Gdns DE4 . . . . 144 A4
Oaktree Rd DE55. . . . . . 160 C8
Oak Tree Rd S43 . . . . . . 80 C2
Oakvale Ho DE23. . . . . . 219 A2
Oakwell Cres DE7. . . . . . 208 E8

Oakwell Dr
Crich DE4. . . . . 156 F1
Ilkeston DE7 . . . . 208 E8
OAKWOOD 206 A2
Oakwood SK13. . . . . 16 F8
Oakwood Cl
Derby DE65 . . . . 231 D2
Hatton DE65 . . . . 239 C8
Oakwood District Ctr
DE21 . . . . 206 A1
Oakwood Dr
Darley Dale DE4 . . . . . . 142 E8
Derby DE21 . . . . 206 B2
Oakwood Inf Sch DE24 . . 233 A6
Oakwood Jun Sch DE24 . 233 A6
Oakwood Rd SK12 . . . . . 32 D6
Oakwood Way S43 . . . . . 79 B4
Oakworth Cl 1 S20. . . . . 59 E6
Oakworth Dr S20 . . . . . . 59 D6
Oakworth Gr S20 . . . . . . 59 D6
Oakworth View S20 . . . . 59 D6
Oat Hill DE4 . . . . 165 F7
Oats Orch S20 . . . . 59 D6
Oberon Cl DE73 . . . . . . 232 E1
Oberon Ret Pk DE56 . . . 178 F3
Occupation Cl S43 . . . . . 80 A6
Occupation La
North Wingfield S42 . . . . 131 E7
Sheffield, Birley S12. . . . . 44 F3
Woodville DE11 . . . . 256 D1
Occupation Rd
Chesterfield S41 . . . . . . 95 F8
Moira DE11 . . . . 262 C8
New Houghton NG19. . . . 134 F7
Ocean Ct DE24. . . . . 219 E1
Ochbrook Ct DE7 . . . . . . 194 F3
OCKBROOK 221 D5
Ockbrook Sch DE72. . . . . 221 C5
Octavia Cl DE73 . . . . . . 232 E2
Octavia Ct S40 . . . . 266 B1
Oddfellows Cotts 16 SK17 85 B7
Oddfellows Rd S32. . . . . . 53 A7
Oddfellows Row S32. . . . . 53 A7
Oddfellows Terr S32 . . . . 53 A7
Oddfellow Terr DE45 . . . 109 D6
Oddford La DE4. . . . . . . 127 D2
Odom Ct S2 . . . . 43 B6
Odridgehay Sta★ DE56. . 176 F6
Offcote Cres 1 DE6. . . . . 173 D3
OFFERTON 52 D7
Offerton Ave DE23 . . . . . 231 F8
Offridge Cl S43 . . . . 80 F2
Off Spring Bank S22 . . . . 33 C8
Ogden St SK14. . . . . 16 B8
OGSTON 146 A4
Ogston La DE55. . . . . . . 146 B4
Ogston New Rd DE55. . . 145 E4
Okeover Ave DE6 . . . . . . 173 D1
OKER 142 D7
Oker Ave DE4. . . . . 127 B3
Oker Dr DE4. . . . . 127 B3
Oker La DE4. . . . . 142 D6
Oker Rd DE4. . . . . 142 B7
Old Bakery Cl
Chesterfield S41 . . . . 77 A2
Hognaston DE6 . . . . 164 B1
Old Bakery Way NG18 . . 136 C1
Old Bank DE6. . . . . 184 D8
Old Barn Cl DE21 . . . . . . 205 D8
OLD BRAMPTON 94 D4
Old Brick Works La S41 . . 96 C4
Oldbury Ct DE21 . . . . . . 206 A2
Old Chester Rd DE1 . . . . 219 A8
Old Church Cl DE22 . . . . 204 C5
Old Coach Rd DE4 . . . . . 143 F4
Old Coalpit La SK17 . . . . 86 F1
Old Colliery La S42. . . . . 132 E6
Old Coppice Side DE75 . . 193 E7
Old Court House Shops 4
SK17 . . . . 85 B8
Old Cross SK13 . . . . 10 E2
OLD DAM. 49 B4
Old Dam La SK17 . . . . . . 49 C4
Old Derby Rd
Ashbourne DE6 . . . . . . 173 C1
Eastwood NG16. . . . . . . 182 D3
Olde Derwent Ave DE4 . . 143 B4
Olde English Rd DE4 . . . 143 B4
Old End DE12 . . . . 265 F1
Olders Valley DE11 . . . . . 256 E4
Old Fall St NG17 . . . . . . 148 F3
Old Farm Ct NG11. . . . . . 237 E6
Old Farmhouse The
DE45 . . . . 109 D6
Oldfield Dr DE11 . . . . . . 256 C5
Oldfield La
Egginton DE65 . . . . 241 A8
Hognaston DE6 . . . . 164 B1
Kirk Ireton DE6 . . . . . . 164 F2
Snelston DE6 . . . . 184 B3
Wensley DE4 . . . . 142 A8
Old Forge Bsns Pk 5 S2. 43 A7
Old Forge Cl DE65 . . . . . 241 A5
Old Gate HD9 . . . . 2 F7
Old Gate Ave DE72. . . . . 245 C7
OLD GLOSSOP 10 E2
Old Hackney La DE4. . . . 142 F8
Old Hall Ave
Derby, Alvaston DE24 . . . 233 B7
Derby DE21 . . . . 218 B4
Duffield DE56. . . . . 190 E3
Old Hall Cl
Darley Dale DE4 . . . . . . 127 C3
Glossop SK13. . . . . 10 D2
Pilsley S45. . . . . 132 C2

Old Hall Ct DE55 . . . . **169** E7
Old Hall Dr
  Horwich End SK23 . . . . . . **45** E4
  Willington DE65 . . . . **242** B5
Old Hall Gdns
  Stoney Middleton S32 . . . . **72** A4
  Swadlincote DE11 . . . . . . **256** A2
Old Hall Jun Sch S40 . . . . . **95** C2
Old Hall La
  Church Broughton DE65 . . **227** B8
  Marple SK6 . . . . **23** C5
  Mottram in Longdendale
   SK14 . . . . **9** A5
  Whitwell S80 . . . . **81** F6
Old Hall Mews S8 . . . . **56** F7
Old Hall Mills Bsns Pk
  DE21 . . . . **205** C2
Old Hall Rd
  Chesterfield S40 . . . . **95** D3
  Derby DE23 . . . . **218** C1
Old Hall Sq **3** S13 . . . . **10** A5
Old Hartshay Hill DE5 . . . **169** C2
Oldhay Cl S17 . . . . **55** D6
Old Hay Gdns S17 . . . . **55** C6
Old Hay La S17 . . . . **55** C6
Old Hill DE6 . . . . **173** C1
Old Hillcliff La DE56 . . . . **177** A3
Old House Mus* DE45 . . **109** C6
Old House Rd S40 . . . . **95** D6
Old Houses S41 . . . . **96** C3
Oldicote La DE15 . . . . **248** E3
Oldknow Rd SK6 . . . . **23** A6
Old La
  Derby DE22 . . . . **205** A2
  Idridgehay DE56 . . . . **176** F3
  Sheffield S20 . . . . **60** A7
  Shottle DE56 . . . . **177** A5
  Wirksworth DE4 . . . . **154** F2
Old Lime Ct DE4 . . . . **143** C5
Old Lodge Cl ST14 . . . . . . **210** A1
Old Longhill Rd SK17 . . . . **65** B4
Old Manor Rd NG19 . . . . . **136** C3
Old Market Pl DE55 . . . . . **160** A6
OLD MATLOCK **143** C4
Old Mill Cl
  Duffield DE56 . . . . **190** E3
  Mansfield NG19 . . . . **136** E1
Old Mill Dr S40 . . . . **95** A8
Old Mill La
  Calver S32 . . . . **72** D2
  Mansfield NG19 . . . . **136** E1
Old Mill Lane Ind Est
  NG19 . . . . **136** C1
Old Park Ave S8 . . . . **56** D7
Old Park Rd S8 . . . . **56** D7
Old Pheasant Ct S40 . . . . . **95** A2
Old Pit La DE7 . . . . **193** A6
Old Pond The DE75 . . . . . **194** A8
Old Post Office Row S33 . **40** B4
Old Quarry Cl S43 . . . . **80** C6
Old Rd
  Branston DE14 . . . . **253** E7
  Buxton SK17, SK23 . . . . . **65** C5
  Chesterfield S40 . . . . **95** C3
  Darley Dale DE4 . . . . **127** C1
  Furness Vale SK23 . . . . . . **33** D4
  Glossop SK13 . . . . **10** A7
  Heage DE56 . . . . **179** E8
  Horwich End, New Horwich
   SK23 . . . . **45** E6
  Mottram in Longdendale
   SK14 . . . . **9** A5
Oldridge Cl S40 . . . . **95** B6
Old School Cl
  Bramley-Vale S44 . . . . . . **117** D1
  Holymoorside S42 . . . . . **113** D7
  Tideswell SK17 . . . . **69** C4
Old School Dr S36 . . . . . . **168** E1
Old School Ho The S42 . . **113** D7
Old School La
  Awsworth NG16 . . . . **195** C5
  Chesterfield S44 . . . . **96** F2
  Pleasley NG19 . . . . **135** A5
Old School Mews DE72 . . **246** B8
Old School The DE65 . . . **228** C2
Old Ship La S40 . . . . **266** B3
Old Smithy Row SK22 . . . **33** C7
Old St SK14 . . . . **16** A8
Old Station Cl
  Etwall DE65 . . . . **229** B4
  Rowsley DE4 . . . . **126** F8
Old Station Yd S43 . . . . . . **96** C8
Old Storth La DE55 . . . . . **160** B4
Old Swanwick Colliery Rd
  DE55 . . . . **158** F1
Old Tennis Courts The
  SK17 . . . . **85** B8
Old Terr NG19 . . . . **134** F4
OLD TUPTON **131** C7
Old Vicarage Cl DE23 . . . . **218** C1
Old Vicarage La DE22 . . . **204** C5
Old Vicarage Sch The
  DE22 . . . . **205** A3
Old Waterworks The
  DE73 . . . . **243** A4
Oldwell Cl S17 . . . . **55** D4
OLD WHITTINGTON **77** B1
Old Whittington La S18 . . **76** E6
Olive Ave
  Long Eaton NG10 . . . . . . **223** C1
  Shirebrook NG20 . . . . . . **119** D6
Olive Cres S12 . . . . **44** A2
Olive Gr DE21 . . . . **219** F5
Olive Grove Rd S2 . . . . **43** B4

Oliver Cl DE75 . . . . **182** B2
Olive Rd S20 . . . . **59** D7
Oliver Ho S41 . . . . **266** C3
Oliver Rd DE7 . . . . **208** C6
Olive St DE22 . . . . **218** E4
Olive Terr **1** SK14 . . . . **16** A8
Olivet St S8 . . . . **43** A3
Olivier St DE23 . . . . **219** B1
OLLERBROOK BOOTH . . . **37** D8
Ollersett Ave SK22 . . . . **33** D8
Ollersett Dr SK22 . . . . **33** D8
Ollersett La SK22 . . . . **33** D8
Olton Rd S8 . . . . **217** C4
Onslow Rd DE3 . . . . **217** E4
Onward Cotts SK17 . . . . . . **85** E8
Opal Cl DE21 . . . . **206** A2
OPENACRE **179** D3
OPENWOODGATE **179** D3
Openwoodgate DE56 . . . . **179** D3
Opera House* SK17 . . . . . . **85** B7
Orange Cl NG20 . . . . **119** E6
Orange St DE55 . . . . **159** B4
Orchard Ave
  Castle Donington DE74 . . **247** A3
  Whaley Bridge SK23 . . . . **45** D7
Orchard Bsns Pk DE7 . . . . **194** D1
Orchard Cl
  Barlborough S43 . . . . **80** A7
  Belper DE56 . . . . **191** B8
  Bolsover S44 . . . . **99** B1
  Breadsall DE21 . . . . **205** D4
  Breaston DE72 . . . . **235** F8
  Clowne S43 . . . . **80** E3
  Derby DE23 . . . . **231** C7
  Elvaston DE24 . . . . **233** D4
  Hilton DE65 . . . . **228** D1
  Melbourne DE73 . . . . . . **252** A7
  Ockbrook DE72 . . . . **221** C4
  Ripley DE5 . . . . **181** A7
  Shirebrook NG20 . . . . . . **119** E5
  Sudbury DE6 . . . . **225** E5
  1 Uttoxeter ST14 . . . . . **210** B1
  Walton-on-Trent DE12 . . **253** D1
  West Hallam DE7 . . . . . . **207** E7
  Willington DE65 . . . . **242** B6
Orchard Cotts DE56 . . . . . **190** E4
Orchard Cres
  Glapwell S44 . . . . **134** B8
  Swanwick DE55 . . . . **169** D7
Orchard Ct
  Derby DE21 . . . . **220** E5
  Doveridge DE6 . . . . **211** B1
  Langley Mill NG16 . . . . . **182** B3
  South Normanton DE55 . **159** F4
  Sutton-in-Ashfield/Nottingham
   NG17 . . . . **148** E2
Orchard Dr
  Creswell S80 . . . . **81** E2
  Gamesley SK13 . . . . **9** E1
Orchard La DE6 . . . . **185** D1
Orchard Lee S26 . . . . **61** E6
Orchard Park Ind Est
  NG10 . . . . **223** C6
Orchard Pl S21 . . . . **60** D6
Orchard Prim Sch DE74 . . **247** A3
Orchard Rd
  Compstall SK6 . . . . **15** B2
  Darley Dale DE4 . . . . **142** E8
  Matlock Bath DE4 . . . . . **143** A1
  Somercotes DE55 . . . . . . **170** C6
  Whaley Bridge SK23 . . . . **45** D7
Orchard Rise
  Alfreton DE55 . . . . **159** C3
  Heanor DE75 . . . . **181** F2
Orchard Sq S18 . . . . **56** D2
Orchard St
  Derby, Markeaton DE3 . . **217** D1
  Ilkeston DE7 . . . . **208** F7
  Kimberley NG16 . . . . **195** F6
  Langley Mill NG16 . . . . . **182** B3
  Long Eaton NG10 . . . . . . **236** E7
  Mansfield NG19 . . . . **136** B1
  Swadlincote DE11 . . . . . **255** F6
Orchards The
  Derby DE22 . . . . **204** D3
  Jacksdale NG16 . . . . **171** B4
Orchards Way S40 . . . . **95** D1
Orchard The
  Belper DE56 . . . . **179** A4
  Chesterfield S43 . . . . **80** E5
  Codnor DE5 . . . . **170** B1
  Disley SK12 . . . . **32** D6
  Horsley Woodhouse DE7 . **192** D6
  Stanton-by-Dale DE7 . . . **222** F8
  Uttoxeter ST14 . . . . **210** A4
  Youlgreave DE45 . . . . . . **125** C5
Orchard View
  Bolsover S44 . . . . **117** F8
  Mansfield Woodhouse
   NG19 . . . . **136** B3
Orchard View Rd S40 . . . . **95** C4
Orchard Way
  Chellaston DE73 . . . . . . **232** F2
  Sandiacre NG10 . . . . **223** A3
Orchid Cl
  Burton upon Trent DE15 . **255** A8
  Calow S44 . . . . **97** A3
Orchid Way NG20 . . . . . . **119** D3
Ordish Ave DE21 . . . . **219** D5
Ordley La DE6 . . . . **183** F8
Ordley Wlk DE65 . . . . **228** D1
Oregon Way DE21 . . . . . . **206** D6
Orford Ave SK12 . . . . **32** C6
Organ Way SK14 . . . . **9** D5
Oriel Cl DE1 . . . . **267** C1
Orient Way DE24 . . . . **219** E2

Orkney Cl DE24 . . . . **231** D3
Orlando Cl DE73 . . . . **232** E2
Orly Ave DE74 . . . . **247** A2
Ormesby Cl S18 . . . . **56** C1
Ormond Cl
  Chesterfield S40 . . . . **114** B7
  Sheffield S8 . . . . **57** B6
Ormond Dr S8 . . . . **57** B6
Ormonde St NG16 . . . . . . **182** B4
Ormonde Terr NG16 . . . . . **182** B4
Ormond Rd S8 . . . . **57** B7
Ormond Way S8 . . . . **57** B7
Ormsby Rd S41 . . . . **95** F7
Ormskirk Rise DE21 . . . . . **220** F4
Orpean Way NG9 . . . . **223** E2
Orpen Dr S14 . . . . **43** E2
Orpen Ho S8 . . . . **43** D2
Orpen Way S14 . . . . **43** E2
Orton Way DE56 . . . . **179** B6
Orwins Cl **5** S41 . . . . **95** D7
Osborne Cl NG10 . . . . **223** B4
Osborne Croft S26 . . . . . . **61** F6
Osborne Ct DE21 . . . . **205** D4
Osborne Pl SK13 . . . . **10** A5
Osborne Rd DE23 . . . . **219** C3
Osborne St
  Burton upon Trent DE15 . **248** A3
  Derby DE23 . . . . **267** D1
Osbourne Gdns DE15 . . . . **248** A3
Oscar Ct S43 . . . . **77** D3
Osiers Cl DE22 . . . . **204** C1
OSLESTON **215** D7
Osleston La DE6 . . . . **215** D7
OSMASTON
  Ashbourne **185** F4
  Derby **232** C8
Osmaston CE Prim Sch
  DE6 . . . . **185** F4
Osmaston Cl NG10 . . . . . . **235** F5
Osmaston Park Ind Est
  DE24 . . . . **232** E8
Osmaston Park Rd DE23,
  DE24 . . . . **232** C7
Osmaston Rd
  Derby DE23, DE24 . . . . . **219** B2
  Derby DE24 . . . . **232** D6
Osmaston St NG10 . . . . . . **223** C5
Osmaton Park Ind Est
  DE24 . . . . **219** D1
Osmund Ct S21 . . . . **59** C3
Osmund Rd S21 . . . . **59** C3
Osprey Cl
  Burton upon Trent DE15 . **248** D4
  Derby DE24 . . . . **231** E2
Osterly Gn DE22 . . . . **218** A5
Oswestry Cl DE21 . . . . **206** B3
Othello Dr DE73 . . . . **232** D2
Otterburn Dr DE22 . . . . . . **204** C2
Otterhole Cl SK17 . . . . **84** F7
Otter St
  Derby DE1 . . . . **219** A7
  Hilton DE65 . . . . **228** D1
Otter Way NG19 . . . . **135** D1
Oulton Cl DE24 . . . . **232** D4
Oundle Dr
  Ilkeston DE7 . . . . **209** B7
  Mansfield NG19 . . . . **135** D1
Ousley La DE6 . . . . **183** C5
Outfield Rd DE15 . . . . **254** F8
Outgang La
  Mansfield Woodhouse
   NG19 . . . . **136** D4
  Pleasley NG19 . . . . **135** C6
Out La S42, S44 . . . . **132** F6
Outlands Rd S33 . . . . **50** F6
Outram Cl DE72 . . . . **221** B1
Outram Ct DE5 . . . . **169** E2
Outram Dr DE11 . . . . **256** D4
Outram Rd S41 . . . . **95** F6
Outram St DE5 . . . . **169** E2
Outram Way DE24 . . . . . . **231** E2
Outseats Dr DE55 . . . . **159** B3
Oval Ct DE23 . . . . **231** C8
OVER BURROWS **202** A4
Overcroft Rise S17 . . . . **55** D4
Overdale DE6 . . . . **143** D5
Overdale Ave SK17 . . . . **85** D8
Overdale Cl NG10 . . . . **236** A6
Overdale Dr SK13 . . . . **17** B8
Overdale Gdns S17 . . . . . . **55** D6
Overdale Rd
  Derby DE23 . . . . **218** E2
  New Mills SK12 . . . . **32** F6
Overdale Rise S17 . . . . **55** C6
Overend Cl S14 . . . . **43** D4
Overend Dr S14 . . . . **43** D4
Overend Rd S14 . . . . **43** D4
Overend Way S14 . . . . **43** D4
OVERGREEN **94** B8
OVER HADDON **109** B1
Over Hill Rd SK22, SK23 . . **34** A5
Over La
  Baslow DE45 . . . . **91** E6
  Belper DE56 . . . . **179** E5
  Hazelwood DE56 . . . . . . **178** A2
Overlees S18 . . . . **75** D3
OVER LEIGH **45** F6
Overmoor View DE55 . . . . **148** B7
Over Rd DE45 . . . . **91** E6
OVERSEAL **262** A3
Overseal Prim Sch DE12 . **262** B4
OVERSETTS **255** E5
Oversetts Cl DE11 . . . . **255** F6
Oversetts Rd DE11 . . . . . . **255** E5
Overstone Cl DE56 . . . . . . **179** D4
Overton Cl S43 . . . . **78** F3
OVER WOODHOUSE **98** E3
Owen Ave NG10 . . . . **237** A6

Owen Falls Ave S41 . . . . . . **96** C3
OWEN'S BANK **239** B6
Owers Ave DE75 . . . . **193** F7
OWLCOTES **117** A4
Owlcotes View S44 . . . . . . **118** A8
OWLER BAR **55** B1
Owler Bar Rd S11 . . . . **54** B4
Owler Car La S18 . . . . **57** F5
Owlers S43 . . . . **218** C2
Owlston Cl NG16 . . . . **182** F3
Owlswick Cl DE23 . . . . . . **231** A8
OWLTHORPE **59** B8
Owlthorpe Ave S20 . . . . . . **59** B8
Owlthorpe Cl S20 . . . . **59** B8
Owlthorpe Dr S20 . . . . **59** B8
Owlthorpe Gr S20 . . . . **59** B8
Owlthorpe La S20 . . . . **59** B8
Owlthorpe Rise S20 . . . . . . **59** B8
Oxbury Rd NG16 . . . . **195** F8
Ox S45 . . . . **131** D3
Ox Close Ave S17 . . . . **56** A5
Oxclose Dr **2** S18 . . . . **56** C1
Oxclose La
  Alsop en le Dale DE6 . . . **150** C2
  Dronfield S18 . . . . **56** C1
  Mansfield NG19 . . . . **135** D3
  Mansfield Woodhouse
   NG19 . . . . **136** A3
Oxclose Park Gdns S20 . . . **59** F6
Oxclose Park Rd S20 . . . . . **59** F6
Oxclose Park Rise S20 . . . . **59** F6
Oxclose Park Road N S20 . **59** F7
Oxclose Park View S20 . . . **59** F6
Oxclose Park Way S20 . . . . **59** F6
Oxcroft Est S44 . . . . **99** D7
Oxcroft Ind Est S44 . . . . . . **99** A8
Oxcroft La
  Bolsover S44 . . . . **99** B6
  Elmton S44 . . . . **99** E8
Oxcroft View S44 . . . . **99** B8
Oxcroft Way S43 . . . . **80** B5
Oxenhope Cl DE23 . . . . . . **230** E7
Oxford Cl S43 . . . . **96** F8
Oxford Rd S43 . . . . **96** F8
Oxford St
  Blackwell DE55 . . . . **147** E1
  Bramley-Vale S44 . . . . . . **117** F1
  Derby DE1 . . . . **267** C1
  Derby, Spondon DE21 . . . **220** E5
  Eastwood NG16 . . . . **182** F2
  4 Ilkeston DE7 . . . . **208** F7
  Long Eaton NG10 . . . . . . **236** D8
  Mansfield Woodhouse
   NG19 . . . . **136** C1
  Ripley DE5 . . . . **169** D1
  Swadlincote DE11 . . . . . **256** A1
Ox Hill S20 . . . . **60** A5
Oxley Rd DE15 . . . . **248** A3
Oxmead DE6 . . . . **184** D7
Oxpasture La NG20 . . . . . **100** B5
OXTON RAKES **94** B8
Oxwich Ct DE21 . . . . **206** B2
Oyster Cl DE14 . . . . **254** B7
Ozier Holt NG10 . . . . **236** C6

P

Pacific Way DE24 . . . . **219** E2
Packenham Bvd DE65 . . . **227** A4
Packer's Row S40 . . . . **266** B3
Pack Horse Rd DE73 . . . . . **252** B8
Packman La S26, S80 . . . . . **62** C6
Paddington Ct S43 . . . . **78** B4
Paddock Cl
  Castle Donington DE74 . . **246** F4
  Wingerworth S42 . . . . . . **114** F3
Paddock Cres S2 . . . . **43** E5
Paddock Croft **9** DE21 . . **205** F2
Paddock La S33 . . . . **45** F5
Paddocks Cl NG16 . . . . . . **160** C4
Paddocks The
  Mansfield Woodhouse
   NG19 . . . . **136** C5
  Pilsley S45 . . . . **132** C2
  Ripley DE5 . . . . **180** F8
  Sandiacre NG10 . . . . **223** A5
  Staveley S43 . . . . **79** C3
  Sutton in Ashfield NG17 . **148** F2
  Swadlincote DE11 . . . . . **255** F5
Paddocks View NG10 . . . . **236** B8
Paddock The
  Alfreton DE55 . . . . **157** F3
  Blackwell DE55 . . . . **147** F1
  Bolsover S44 . . . . **99** B1
  Burton upon Trent DE15 . **248** B4
  Buxton SK17 . . . . **84** F7
  Elvaston DE24 . . . . **233** D4
  Glossop SK13 . . . . **9** E5
  Holbrook DE56 . . . . **191** C6
  Hollingworth SK14 . . . . . . **9** E5
  Horwich End SK23 . . . . . . **45** F6
  Ockbrook DE72 . . . . **221** C4
  Pleasley NG19 . . . . **135** D4
  Rolleston DE13 . . . . **240** A4
  Shirebrook NG20 . . . . . . **119** D4
Paddock Way S18 . . . . **57** B3
PADFIELD **10** C5
Padfield Gate SK13 . . . . . . **17** D7
Padfield Main Rd SK13 . . . **10** C5
Padfield Prim Sch SK13 . . **10** B5
Padley Cl
  Derby DE22 . . . . **205** A5
  Ripley DE5 . . . . **169** C3
Padley Hill S32 . . . . **53** E1
Padley Rd S32 . . . . **53** D1

Padley Way S42 . . . . **131** F5
Padley Wood La S45 . . . . . **147** B8
Padley Wood Rd S45 . . . . **132** C2
Padstow Cl **13** DE24 . . . . **231** D3
Padstow Rd DE24 . . . . **233** C5
Paget High Sch DE14 . . . . **254** A7
Paignton Ct **15** S41 . . . . . **95** F8
Painter's La DE6 . . . . **186** B5
Painters Way
  Darley Dale DE4 . . . . **127** D3
  Winster DE4 . . . . **141** C6
Paisley Cl S43 . . . . **97** C8
Palace La DE56 . . . . **166** D1
Palace Rd SK17 . . . . **85** B8
Palatine Gr DE23 . . . . **230** F7
Palerow La DE56 . . . . **166** E3
Palissy Cl DE11 . . . . **256** D4
Palladium Dr DE23 . . . . . . **231** A6
Pall Mall DE21 . . . . **205** E4
Palm Cl DE23 . . . . **218** A1
Palmer Cl DE14 . . . . **254** B8
Palmer Cres **3** S18 . . . . . . **57** B1
Palmer Dr
  Stapleford NG9 . . . . **223** D5
  Swanwick DE55 . . . . **169** E7
PALMER MOOR **224** E7
Palmersgate S40 . . . . **266** B3
Palmerston Ct DE73 . . . . . **252** B7
Palmerston Rd **4** DE7 . . . **208** F8
Palmerston St
  Derby DE23 . . . . **218** E1
  Underwood Green NG16 . **171** F2
  Westwood NG16 . . . . **171** C4
PALTERTON **118** A5
Palterton La S44 . . . . **117** D7
Palterton Prim Sch S44 . . **118** B5
Pankhurst Pl S45 . . . . **131** C3
Parade The
  4 Derby DE3 . . . . **217** D1
  Sheffield S12 . . . . **44** A4
Paradise St SK13 . . . . **10** A5
Parcel Terr DE22 . . . . **218** D5
Pares Way DE72 . . . . **221** C5
Pargate Cl DE5 . . . . **180** D6
Park Ave
  Ashbourne DE6 . . . . **173** C1
  Awsworth NG16 . . . . **195** B5
  Castle Donington DE74 . . **246** F3
  Darley Dale DE4 . . . . **127** C3
  Dronfield S18 . . . . **57** B2
  Eastwood NG16 . . . . **182** E3
  Furness Vale SK23 . . . . . . **33** D3
  Glapwell S44 . . . . **118** C1
  Holmesfield S18 . . . . **75** A8
  Ilkeston DE7 . . . . **208** F8
  Mansfield Woodhouse
   NG19 . . . . **136** C4
  Ripley DE5 . . . . **169** F1
  Scropton DE65 . . . . **227** A5
  Shirebrook NG20 . . . . . . **119** E4
  Stanley DE7 . . . . **207** C6
  Uttoxeter ST14 . . . . **210** B2
Park Cl
  Chesterfield S40 . . . . **115** A7
  Glossop SK13 . . . . **10** D2
  Kilburn DE56 . . . . **192** A8
  Linton DE12 . . . . **261** C6
  Little Eaton DE21 . . . . . . **205** B8
  Matlock DE4 . . . . **143** D4
  Pinxton NG16 . . . . **160** C2
  Shirland DE55 . . . . **146** E1
  Stanton-by-Dale DE7 . . . **222** F8
Park Cotts DE4 . . . . **127** A5
Park Cres
  Chapel-en-le-Frith SK23 . . **47** B5
  Doveridge DE6 . . . . **211** B1
  Eastwood NG16 . . . . **182** F4
  Furness Vale SK23 . . . . . . **33** D3
  Glossop SK13 . . . . **10** B3
  Heage DE56 . . . . **179** E8
  Ilkeston DE7 . . . . **209** A8
Park Ct
  Heanor DE75 . . . . **181** F1
  Swadlincote DE11 . . . . . **256** C5
Park Dene Dr SK13 . . . . . . **10** C2
Park Dr
  Chesterfield S41 . . . . **266** C1
  Derby DE23 . . . . **218** C1
  Ilkeston DE7 . . . . **208** F7
  Sandiacre NG10 . . . . **223** A3
  Swanwick DE55 . . . . **169** F6
Park Edge S32 . . . . **52** F8
Parker Ave S44 . . . . **96** F3
Parker Cl DE1 . . . . **267** A4
Parker Ctr DE21 . . . . **219** B8
Parke Rd SK17 . . . . **69** C4
Parker Gdns NG9 . . . . **223** F8
Parker Ind Est DE21 . . . . . **205** B1
Parkers Cl DE11 . . . . **257** B1
Parkers La S17 . . . . **55** D8
Parker's La NG19 . . . . **136** C3
Parker St DE1 . . . . **218** F7
Park Farm S18 . . . . **56** C2
Park Farm Ctr DE22 . . . . . **204** D2
Park Farm Dr DE22 . . . . . **204** D2
Park Farm Mews S21 . . . . . **60** D1
Parkfield Cres DE12 . . . . . **265** F1
Parkfield Ct SK17 . . . . **85** A7
Parkfield La DE6 . . . . **184** D4
Parkfield Pl S2 . . . . **43** A8
Parkfields S43 . . . . **80** E3
Parkfields Dr DE22 . . . . . . **218** E8
Parkfields View DE56 . . . . **179** E8
Parkgate
  Derby DE23 . . . . **219** B2
  Dronfield S18 . . . . **57** C2
Parkgate Cl S20 . . . . **59** A8
Parkgate Croft S20 . . . . . . **59** A8

Parkgate Dr S20 . . . . . . **59** A8
Parkgate La S21, S43 . . . . **77** E5
Park Gr DE22 . . . . **218** E7
Park Grange Croft Sta S2 **43** C8
Park Grange Ct S2 . . . . . . **43** C8
Park Grange Dr S2 . . . . . . **43** C8
Park Grange Mount S2 . . **43** C8
Park Grange Rd S2 . . . . . . **43** D7
Park Grange Rise S2 . . . . **43** C8
Park Grange View S2 . . . . **43** D8
Park Hall SK17 . . . . **85** B8
Park Hall Ave S40, S42 . . **114** B8
Park Hall Cl S40 . . . . **114** B7
Park Hall Gdns
  Chesterfield S40 . . . . **114** B7
  Mansfield Woodhouse
  NG19 . . . . **136** C5
Parkhall La S21 . . . . **60** D2
Park Hall La
  Mapperley DE7 . . . . **193** D2
  West Hallam DE7 . . . . . . **207** C8
Park Hall Rd
  Denby Village DE5 . . . . . **180** A3
  Mansfield Woodhouse
  NG19 . . . . **136** C5
Parkham Rd NG16 . . . . . **195** F7
Park Head Rd DE4 . . . . . **143** B5
Park Hill
  Awsworth NG16 . . . . **195** B5
  Eckington S21 . . . . **59** E3
Park Hill Cl SK22 . . . . . . **24** C1
Park Hill Dr DE23 . . . . . . **231** F7
Park Ho DE56 . . . . **179** A3
Parkhouse Cl S45 . . . . . . **131** B4
Parkhouse Dr DE55 . . . . **159** E5
Park House Prim Sch
  S45 . . . . **132** B4
Parkhouse Rd S42, S45 . . **132** A4
Parkin St DE55 . . . . **159** B4
Park Jun & Inf Schs The
  NG20 . . . . **119** E5
Park La
  Castle Donington DE74 . . **246** E4
  Chesterfield S41 . . . . **95** F7
  Darley Dale DE4 . . . . . . **127** D2
  Derby, Allestree DE22 . . **204** F4
  Derby, Normanton Park
  DE23 . . . . **218** C1
  Hayfield SK22 . . . . **25** D5
  Heage DE56 . . . . **179** F8
  Holbeck NG20, S80 . . . . . **101** C6
  Over Haddon DE45, DE4 . . **110** C1
  Pinxton NG16 . . . . **160** C2
  Ripley DE5 . . . . **169** A7
  Shirland DE55 . . . . **159** A8
  Shirley DE6 . . . . **200** D8
  South Wingfield DE55 . . . **157** D1
  Stanton in Peak DE4 . . . . **126** C1
  Tutbury DE13 . . . . **239** B6
  Weston-on-Trent DE72 . . **245** E4
Parkland Ave SK22 . . . . . **24** C1
Parkland Dr S42 . . . . **115** A2
Parkland Mews NG10 . . **236** D8
Parklands DE7 . . . . **245** A8
Parklands Inf Sch NG10 . **223** B1
Park Leys Ct DE21 . . . . . . **220** E4
Park Mews
  Derby DE22 . . . . **218** F8
  Mansfield Woodhouse
  NG19 . . . . **136** C4
  Somercotes DE55 . . . . . . **170** D6
Park Mill Dr DE55 . . . . . **159** D2
Park Pale The DE13 . . . . **239** C5
Park Rd
  Ashbourne DE6 . . . . **173** C2
  Bakewell DE45 . . . . **109** C5
  Belper DE56 . . . . **179** A2
  Buxton SK17 . . . . **85** A8
  Chapel-en-le-Frith SK23 . . **47** B6
  Chesterfield S40 . . . . . . **266** A2
  Derby DE3 . . . . **217** D2
  Derby, Spondon DE21 . . **220** D5
  Donisthorpe DE12 . . . . . **262** E2
  Duffield DE56 . . . . **190** D3
  Glossop SK13 . . . . **10** A4
  Heage DE56 . . . . **179** E8
  High Lane SK12 . . . . **32** A6
  Holmewood S42 . . . . **116** E1
  Horwich End SK23 . . . . . . **45** D6
  Ilkeston DE7 . . . . **208** F7
  Mansfield Woodhouse
  NG19 . . . . **136** B3
  New Mills SK22 . . . . **33** C7
  Over Haddon DE45 . . . . . **110** B2
  Overseal DE12 . . . . **262** A6
  Ripley DE5 . . . . **169** E1
  Shirebrook NG20 . . . . . . **119** C5
  Stapleford NG9 . . . . **223** F8
  Swadlincote, Church Gresley
  DE11 . . . . **256** C2
  Swadlincote DE11, DE15 . **255** D5
  Tupton S42 . . . . **131** C7
Park Rise S18 . . . . **75** A8
Park Row
  Bretby DE15 . . . . **249** B1
  Clay Cross S45 . . . . **131** D4
Parks Ave DE55 . . . . **157** F5
Parkside
  Belper DE56 . . . . **179** A3
  Buxton SK17 . . . . **85** A8
  Chesterfield S41 . . . . **96** A7
  Heage DE56 . . . . **179** E8
  Renishaw S21 . . . . **60** B1
Park Side DE55 . . . . **170** D7
Parkside Ave NG10 . . . . **236** B8
Parkside Cl NG16 . . . . . . **170** F4
Parkside Com Sch S40 . . **266** A1

Parkside Dr
  Ironville NG16 . . . . **170** F4
  Long Eaton NG10 . . . . . . **236** B8
Parkside Jun Sch DE6 . . **173** C2
Parkside La S6 . . . . **23** C6
Parkside Rd DE21 . . . . . . **220** B6
Parkside Sh Ctr S21 . . . . **60** D7
Parkside View S40 . . . . . **95** B6
Park Spring Dr S2 . . . . . . **43** C8
Park Spring Pl S2 . . . . . . **43** C8
Park Spring Way S2 . . . . **43** C8
Park St
  Alfreton DE55 . . . . **158** F3
  Barlborough S43 . . . . **80** B7
  Breaston DE72 . . . . **235** F8
  Chesterfield S40 . . . . . . **115** A7
  Derby DE1 . . . . **267** A2
  Heanor DE75 . . . . **181** D2
  Long Eaton NG10 . . . . . . **223** C1
  Mansfield Woodhouse
  NG19 . . . . **136** B3
  Ripley DE5 . . . . **169** E1
  Stapleford NG9 . . . . **223** D6
  Swadlincote DE11 . . . . . **256** A6
  Uttoxeter ST14 . . . . **210** C1
  Wessington DE55 . . . . . . **157** E8
Parkstone Ct DE3 . . . . . . **217** C2
Parkstone Delph S12 . . . **44** A2
Park Studios S40 . . . . . . **266** A2
Park Terr DE4 . . . . **127** A5
Park The
  Darley Dale DE4 . . . . . . **127** D3
  Duffield DE56 . . . . **190** E3
  Ironville NG16 . . . . **170** F4
  Mansfield Woodhouse
  NG19 . . . . **136** C1
  Mayfield DE6 . . . . **184** C8
Parkview DE21 . . . . **205** C8
Park View
  9 Ashbourne DE6 . . . . . **173** C2
  Aston-on-Trent DE72 . . **246** B6
  Bakewell DE45 . . . . **109** D5
  Barlborough S43 . . . . **80** B7
  Chesterfield S41 . . . . . . **115** D7
  Clowne S43 . . . . **80** D5
  Heanor DE75 . . . . **181** D1
  Northwood DE4 . . . . . . **127** A5
  Pleasley NG19 . . . . **135** A4
  Somercotes DE55 . . . . . . **170** D5
  Whaley Thorns NG20 . . . **100** F2
Park View S20 . . . . **59** E7
Park View Cl DE22 . . . . . **204** F4
Park View Cl S8 . . . . **43** A2
Park View Dr SK23 . . . . . **47** B6
Park View Ho DE21 . . . . . **219** C6
Parkview Prim Sch DE21 **206** A2
Park View Rise SK22 . . . . **24** C1
Parkville Cl SK17 . . . . **85** D5
Parkway
  Chellaston DE73 . . . . . . **232** E1
  New Mills SK22 . . . . **24** C1
  Whitwell S80 . . . . **82** B3
Park Way S65 . . . . **229** C4
Parkway Ct S8 . . . . **56** F7
Parkway The DE4 . . . . . **127** C3
Parkwood Sch DE55 . . . . **158** F4
Parliament Cl DE22 . . . . **218** E4
Parliament St
  Derby DE22 . . . . **218** E4
  Swadlincote DE11 . . . . . **255** F6
PARSLEY HAY **123** B4
Parsonage Cl S20 . . . . . . **59** D6
Parsonage Croft DE45 . . **109** C5
Parsonage Gdns SK6 . . . **23** A4
Parson House Outdoor
  Pursuit Ctr S11 . . . . . . **54** B6
Parsons Cl
  Hartington SK17 . . . . . . **137** D5
  Swadlincote DE11 . . . . . **256** A1
Parsons Gate S33 . . . . . . **40** A6
Parsons Gr DE5 . . . . **180** D2
Parsons La S33 . . . . **39** D3
Parson's Wlk B79 . . . . . . **263** F2
Parthenon Cl NG16 . . . . **134** F5
Partington Ct 2 SK13 . . . **10** F1
Partington Pk SK13 . . . . **10** C3
Partington Theatre ★ 7
  SK13 . . . . **10** C1
Partridge Cl S21 . . . . **59** B3
Partridge Dr DE11 . . . . . **256** F3
Partridge Way DE3 . . . . **218** A3
PARWICH **151** E1
Parwich Cl S40 . . . . **95** A5
Parwich La DE4 . . . . **151** E7
PARWICH LEES **151** A2
Parwich Prim Sch DE6 . . **151** D2
Parwich Rd S42 . . . . **131** F5
Pasteur Ave DE5 . . . . . . **169** D2
Pasture Gr S21 . . . . **59** C3
Pasture La
  Brassington DE4 . . . . . . **152** D1
  Flagg SK17 . . . . **106** D6
  Hilcote DE55 . . . . **148** C1
  Long Eaton NG10 . . . . . . **237** A5
  Stonebroom DE55 . . . . . **147** A3
Pasture Rd NG9 . . . . **209** D1
Pastures Ave DE23 . . . . **230** F7
Pastures Hill DE23 . . . . . **218** B1
Pastures The
  Duffield DE56 . . . . **190** E4
  Eastwood NG16 . . . . . . **195** B8
  Mansfield Woodhouse
  NG19 . . . . **136** E5
  Repton DE65 . . . . **242** C2
  Swadlincote DE11 . . . . . **255** F5
  Weston-on-Trent DE72 . **245** F5
Patchwork Row NG20 . . **119** F4
Paterson Ave DE21 . . . . . **220** B6

Patmore Sq DE23 . . . . . . **231** F7
Paton Gr S43 . . . . **96** D8
Patrick Cl DE12 . . . . **261** D5
Patten Ct DE24 . . . . **232** A5
Patterdale Cl 2 S18 . . . . **56** E1
Patterdale Rd DE24 . . . . **220** A1
Pattison St S44 . . . . **98** F6
Paulet High Sch DE15 . . . **254** F7
Paulet Sch DE15 . . . . . . **254** F7
Pavements The (Sh Ctr)
  S40 . . . . **266** B3
Pavilion Cl S43 . . . . **80** E2
Pavilion Ct DE7 . . . . **207** D7
Pavilion Gdns NG16 . . . . **134** F8
Pavilion Gdns The ★ SK17 . **85** B7
Pavilion Mans 3 SK17 . . . **85** B7
Pavilion Rd DE23 . . . . . . **231** C8
Pavilion Workshops S42 **116** D1
Paxton Cl
  Derby DE3 . . . . **217** C1
  Matlock DE4 . . . . **143** A6
Paxton Ct S14 . . . . **43** F4
Paxton Pl SK17 . . . . **84** E5
Paxton Rd S41 . . . . **96** C5
Payler Cl S2 . . . . **44** A8
Payne St S22 . . . . **218** D6
Peach Ave
  Selston NG16 . . . . **171** F6
  South Normanton DE55 . **160** B7
Peach St
  Derby DE22 . . . . **218** D5
  Heanor DE75 . . . . **181** D1
Peacock Cl
  Glossop SK13 . . . . **9** E4
  Killamarsh S21 . . . . **60** D6
Peacock Gr DE23 . . . . . . **231** B6
Peacock Pl DE7 . . . . **194** D4
Peacock Way DE55 . . . . **169** F8
Peacroft Ct DE65 . . . . . . **228** D2
Peacroft La DE65 . . . . . . **228** D2
Peafield La NG19 . . . . . . **136** F4
Peafield Lane Prim Sch
  NG19 . . . . **136** F3
Peak Ave DE55 . . . . **170** B6
Peak Cavern ★ S33 . . . . . **38** B2
Peak Cl
  Belper DE56 . . . . **179** A4
  Pilsley S45 . . . . **132** C1
PEAK DALE **67** B5
Peakdale Cl
  Long Eaton NG10 . . . . . . **236** A6
  Ripley DE5 . . . . **180** D6
Peakdale Cres S12 . . . . . . **44** E5
Peak Dale Prim Sch SK17 **67** B5
Peakdale Rd
  Glossop SK13 . . . . **9** E3
  Marple SK6 . . . . **23** A4
Peak District Mining Mus ★
  DE4 . . . . **143** A1
Peak Dr DE23, DE24 . . . . **232** A7
PEAK FOREST **49** B3
Peak Forest CE Prim Sch
  SK17 . . . . **49** A3
Peak Ho SK13 . . . . **10** A5
Peakland View DE4 . . . . **127** C3
PEAKLEY HILL **75** C6
Peaknaze Cl SK13 . . . . . . **17** B8
Peak Pl S43 . . . . **97** D7
Peak Railway ★ DE4 . . . . **143** A4
Peaks The NG20 . . . . . . **119** E3
Peaktor La DE4 . . . . **126** E7
Peak View
  Buxton SK17 . . . . **105** E6
  Clowne S43 . . . . **80** D5
  Glossop SK13 . . . . **9** F4
  South Normanton DE55 . **159** F5
Peak View Cl S32 . . . . . . **72** B2
Peak View Dr DE6 . . . . . **173** C1
Peak View Rd S40 . . . . . . **95** D5
Peak Village Outlet Sh Ctr
  DE4 . . . . **110** F1
Pearce La S42 . . . . **114** D3
Pearl Bank DE6 . . . . **211** F8
Pearl Cl DE21 . . . . **206** A2
Pearl Way SK14 . . . . **9** A2
Pearson Croft S41 . . . . . . **95** C6
Pearson Gdns S44 . . . . . **117** E8
Pearson Trad Est S41 . . . **96** B8
PEAR TREE **232** B8
Pear Tree Ave
  Ripley DE5 . . . . **180** D8
  Swadlincote DE11 . . . . . **255** F7
  Wingerworth S42 . . . . . . **114** E3
Pear Tree Cl
  Brimington S43 . . . . **97** A8
  Glossop SK13 . . . . **9** E4
  Hartshorne DE11 . . . . . . **257** A7
  Killamarsh S21 . . . . **60** C5
  Marple SK6 . . . . **23** B8
Pear Tree Cres DE23 . . . **232** A8
Peartree Ct
  Derby DE21 . . . . **205** D1
  Etwall DE65 . . . . **229** B4
Pear Tree Dr
  Linton DE12 . . . . **261** C6
  Shirebrook NG20 . . . . . . **119** E6
Pear Tree Inf Sch DE23 . **219** A1
Peartree La NG17 . . . . . **134** B1
Pear Tree Rd
  Derby DE23 . . . . **219** A1
  Pilsley S45 . . . . **132** C1
Peartree Sta DE23 . . . . . **232** B7
Pease Cl DE55 . . . . **159** B3
PEASEHILL **180** F8

Peasehill DE5 . . . . **180** F8
Pease Hill DE55 . . . . **159** B3
Peasehill Rd DE5 . . . . . . **180** E8
Peasunhurst La S45 . . . . **113** A1
Peatburn Ave DE75 . . . . **181** C1
Peatfield Ct NG9 . . . . . . **209** D1
Peatfield Rd
  Killamarsh S21 . . . . **60** F7
  Stapleford NG9 . . . . **209** D1
Peat La DE4, DE56 . . . . . **166** D4
Peats Cl DE6 . . . . **165** B1
Peckham Gdns DE22 . . . **218** A5
Pedley Ave 4 S20 . . . . . . **59** E8
Pedley Dr S20 . . . . **59** E8
Pedley St DE7 . . . . **208** F7
Peebles Cl DE24 . . . . **231** E2
Peel Cres NG19 . . . . **135** D2
Peel Gdns S18 . . . . **56** F1
Peel St
  Derby DE22 . . . . **218** D6
  Glossop SK13 . . . . **10** C5
  Langley Mill NG16 . . . . . **182** B3
  Long Eaton NG10 . . . . . . **236** E8
  South Normanton DE55 . **160** B6
Peers Cl DE21 . . . . **206** B2
Peet St DE22 . . . . **218** E4
Pegasus Ct S44 . . . . **99** B1
Pegasus Sch DE12 . . . . . **260** F7
Pegasus Way DE65 . . . . **228** E2
Peggars Cl S43 . . . . **80** B6
Peggs Wlk DE23 . . . . . . **231** E7
Peggy La DE55 . . . . **146** B6
Pegwell Cl DE23 . . . . . . **231** D7
Pelham Ave DE7 . . . . . . **194** C1
Pelham St
  Derby DE22 . . . . **218** F4
  Ilkeston DE7 . . . . **194** E1
Pemberton The DE55 . . . **160** B4
Pembleton Dr NG19 . . . . **135** D1
Pembrey Cl NG9 . . . . . . **209** D2
Pembroke Cl S40 . . . . . . **95** C1
Pembroke Cl S41 . . . . . . **95** F7
Pembroke Rd
  Dronfield S18 . . . . **76** A8
  Shireoaks S81 . . . . **63** F7
Pembroke St DE21 . . . . . **219** D8
Penalton Cl DE24 . . . . . . **232** E6
Pencroft Gr DE23 . . . . . . **231** C5
Pendean Cl DE55 . . . . . . **147** E1
Pendennis Cl DE24 . . . . . **233** B6
Pendine Cl DE55 . . . . . . **160** C6
Pendlebury Dr DE3 . . . . . **217** E1
Pendleside Way DE23 . . **230** E7
Pendleton La DE56 . . . . . **166** F7
Penfold Way DE55 . . . . . **147** B5
Penge Rd DE22 . . . . **218** A7
Penhaligon's Cl DE73 . . . **232** F1
Penistone Gdns S45 . . . . **131** D2
Peniston Rise S42 . . . . . . **252** A7
Penkridge Rd DE11 . . . . **256** B1
Pen La S45 . . . . **131** E3
Penmore Cl S41 . . . . **115** C8
Penmore Gdns 4 S41 . . . **96** C1
Penmore La S41 . . . . **115** C8
Penmore St S41 . . . . **115** C8
Penncroft Dr S45 . . . . . . **131** D2
Penncroft La S45 . . . . . . **131** D3
Pennie Cl NG10 . . . . **236** D4
Penniment La NG19 . . . . **135** B2
Pennine Ave DE55 . . . . . **170** C7
Pennine Cl
  Long Eaton NG10 . . . . . . **223** A1
  Mansfield Woodhouse
  NG19 . . . . **136** C4
  Newton DE55 . . . . **148** A3
  Sutton in Ashfield NG17 . **148** E4
  Tibshelf DE55 . . . . **147** F6
Pennine Dr
  Selston NG16 . . . . **171** F7
  South Normanton DE55 . **159** F5
Pennine Rd SK13 . . . . . . **17** A8
Pennine View
  Heage DE56 . . . . **179** E8
  Palterton S44 . . . . **118** A5
Pennine Way
  Chesterfield S40 . . . . **95** C5
  Grassmoor S42 . . . . **115** F3
  Swadlincote DE11 . . . . . **256** A3
Pennine Way Jun Sch
  DE11 . . . . **256** A2
Pennine Way La S42 . . . **115** F3
Penn La DE73 . . . . **252** E7
Penn Moor Cl NG10 . . . . **236** A6
Penn St DE56 . . . . **179** A4
Penny Acres Prim Sch
  S18 . . . . **74** E7
Pennycress Cl DE23 . . . . **231** A7
Pennycroft La ST14 . . . . **210** C1
Pennycroft Rd ST14 . . . . **210** A1
Penny Engine La S21 . . . . **59** E4
Pennyfields Bvd NG10 . . **236** B7
Penny Gn S80 . . . . **82** A5
Penny La S17 . . . . **55** C5
Penny Long La DE22 . . . **218** E8
Pennytown Ct DE55 . . . . **159** C1
Pennytown Ponds Nature
  Reserve ★ DE55 . . . . . . **159** D1
Pennyunk La DE45 . . . . . **89** C1
Pennywell Dr S42 . . . . . **113** D7
Penrhyn Ave DE23 . . . . . **218** C1
Penrith Pl DE21 . . . . **205** D2
Penrose Cres S44 . . . . . . **97** D3
Penryn Cl DE55 . . . . **160** C6
Pentagon The DE21 . . . . **219** C4
Pentewen Cl DE22 . . . . . **204** D2
Penthorpe Cl S12 . . . . . . **44** B6

Pentland Cl
  5 Chesterfield S40 . . . . . . **95** C5
  Derby DE21 . . . . **206** A2
Pentland Gdns NG10 . . . **223** A1
Pentland Rd S18 . . . . **56** D1
PENTRICH **169** B5
Pentrich Cl 1 S40 . . . . . . **95** D5
Pentrich Rd
  Ripley DE5 . . . . **169** D2
  Swanwick DE55 . . . . . . **169** D7
Pentridge Dr DE7 . . . . . **194** C3
Penzance Rd DE24 . . . . . **233** B5
Pepper La DE7 . . . . **208** E1
Percival Cl SK17 . . . . **138** D3
Percy St
  Derby DE22 . . . . **218** E3
  Ilkeston DE7 . . . . **208** E1
Percy Wood Cl DE65 . . . **228** C2
Peregrine Cl
  Burton upon Trent DE15 . **248** D3
  Derby DE24 . . . . **231** D4
Peregrine Way S26 . . . . . **61** E5
Perlethorpe Ave NG19 . . **136** A1
PERRYFOOT **48** C1
Pershore Dr DE14 . . . . . **254** A8
Perth Cl
  Burton upon Trent DE15 . **248** C2
  Derby DE3 . . . . **217** C4
  Mansfield Woodhouse
  NG19 . . . . **136** C5
Perth Dr NG9 . . . . **209** F1
Perth St DE21 . . . . **205** D1
Peter Baines Ind Est
  DE22 . . . . **267** A1
Peterborough St DE21 . . **219** E8
Peterdale Cl S43 . . . . **96** E8
Peterdale Rd S43 . . . . . . **96** E8
Peterhouse Terr 1
  DE23 . . . . **219** A2
Peterleas The DE12 . . . . **262** C1
Peterlee Pl DE24 . . . . . . **233** A5
Peter More Hill S80 . . . . **81** E4
Peters Ave S45 . . . . **131** B4
Peters Ct DE65 . . . . **227** D1
Petersgate NG10 . . . . . . **223** A1
Petersgate Cl NG10 . . . . **223** A2
Petersham Ct 7 NG10 . . **223** B2
Petersham Dr DE24 . . . . **233** C6
Petersham Rd NG10 . . . . **223** A1
Peter St
  Ashbourne DE6 . . . . **173** C1
  Glossop SK13 . . . . **10** A6
Peterway DE55 . . . . **170** D8
Pettifor Terr DE55 . . . . . **147** C1
Pettyclose La S41, S43 . . **96** D5
Petty Close La DE6 . . . . . **202** C1
Petworth Ave NG9 . . . . . **223** F3
Pevensey Ave S41 . . . . . . **95** E6
Pevensey Cl S41 . . . . **95** E7
Peveril Ave
  Borrowash DE72 . . . . . . **221** C2
  New Mills SK22 . . . . **24** C1
Peveril Castle ★ S33 . . . . **38** C2
Peveril Cl
  Castleton S33 . . . . **38** C2
  Darley Dale DE4 . . . . . . **127** C3
  Somercotes DE55 . . . . . . **170** C6
Peveril Cres
  Long Eaton NG10 . . . . . . **235** F5
  West Hallam DE7 . . . . . . **207** C8
Peveril Ct
  1 Glossop SK13 . . . . **17** C8
  Ripley DE5 . . . . **169** C1
Peveril Dr
  Ilkeston DE7 . . . . **194** D2
  Somercotes DE55 . . . . . . **170** C6
Peveril Gdns SK12 . . . . . **33** A6
Peveril Ho SK17 . . . . **85** A6
Peveril Mews SK12 . . . . . **33** A6
Peveril Rd
  Bolsover S44 . . . . **98** F3
  Buxton SK17 . . . . **85** C7
  Castleton S33 . . . . **38** C2
  Chesterfield S41 . . . . **95** F7
  Eckington S21 . . . . **59** E3
  Tibshelf DE55 . . . . **147** F6
Peveril St DE24 . . . . **232** D6
Pewit Cl S42 . . . . **132** D8
Pewit La DE55 . . . . **147** C6
Pewitt Carr Nature Reserve ★
  DE7 . . . . **208** F7
Pheasant Field Dr DE21 . **221** A6
Pheasant Hill NG19 . . . . **136** A1
Philip Howard Rd SK13 . . **17** C8
Philips Croft DE56 . . . . . **190** E4
Philipway DE55 . . . . **170** D8
Phoenix Cl S12 . . . . **44** E1
Phoenix Rd S12 . . . . **44** E1
Phoenix St DE1 . . . . **267** B4
Phyllis Gr NG10 . . . . **236** F7
Piccadilly La DE6 . . . . . . **172** C1
Piccadilly Rd S41 . . . . . . **96** C3
Pickard Cres S13 . . . . . . **44** D8
Pickard Dr S13 . . . . **44** D8
Pickard La DE56 . . . . . . **168** D1
Pickburns Gdns
  Belper DE56 . . . . **191** F8
  Kilburn DE56 . . . . **191** F8
Pickering Ave NG16 . . . . **182** F2
Pickering Rise DE21 . . . . **205** D1
Pickford Pl SK23 . . . . **47** B6
Pickford's House (Mus) ★
  DE1 . . . . **218** F5
Pickleys La DE6 . . . . **224** C8
Pickton Cl S40 . . . . **95** D2

Pictor Gr SK17 . . . . 85 D7
Pic Tor La DE4 . . . . 143 B4
Pictor Rd SK17 . . . . 85 D7
Piddocks Rd DE15 . . . . 255 B5
Pighills La S18 . . . . 57 B4
Pig La DE4 . . . . 111 B4
Pike Cl
  Chesterfield S40 . . . . 95 B5
  Hayfield SK22 . . . . 25 C3
PIKEHALL 139 E3
Pike's La SK13 . . . . 17 B8
Pike View Cl SK23 . . . . 34 E2
Pilgrim Ct S81 . . . . 63 F7
Pilgrims Way DE24 . . . . . . 231 C3
PILHOUGH 126 E7
Pilhough La DE4 . . . . 126 D6
Pilhough Rd DE4 . . . . 126 E5
Pillar Butts DE4 . . . . 165 E8
PILSLEY
  Baslow 91 C3
  Clay Cross 132 D1
Pilsley CE Prim Sch DE45 91 C2
Pilsley Cl DE56 . . . . 179 C6
PILSLEY GREEN 147 C8
Pilsley Prim Sch S45 . . . . 132 C1
Pilsley Rd
  Clay Cross S45 . . . . 131 E3
  Stonebroom DE55 . . . . 147 B6
Pimlico
  Derby DE22 . . . . 218 B6
  Ilkeston DE7 . . . . 208 E8
Pimm's Rd DE6 . . . . 217 A8
Pinchom's Hill Rd DE56 . 179 B3
Pinch The DE6 . . . . 150 B2
Pindale Ave S43 . . . . 97 C7
Pindale Rd S33 . . . . 38 E1
Pine Ave NG16 . . . . 182 A3
Pine Cl
  Burton upon Trent DE14 . . 254 A8
  Creswell S80 . . . . 81 F1
  Derby DE21 . . . . 220 B4
  Etwall DE65 . . . . 229 C4
  Killamarsh S21 . . . . 60 C5
  Mansfield Woodhouse
    NG19 . . . . 136 C5
  Ripley DE5 . . . . 169 D1
  Shirebrook NG20 . . . . 119 E6
  Smalley DE7 . . . . 192 F5
Pine Croft DE6 . . . . 185 D7
Pinecroft Ct DE21 . . . . . . 206 B1
Pine Gr DE11 . . . . 255 F6
Pine St S43 . . . . 97 A8
Pines The DE72 . . . . 235 B7
Pine Tree Wlk NG16 . . . . 182 E2
Pine View
  Chesterfield S40 . . . . 95 B3
  Clay Cross S45 . . . . 131 E3
Pine Wlk DE11 . . . . 261 E7
Pinewood DE5 . . . . 181 B7
Pinewood Cl DE55 . . . . . . 159 C3
Pinewood Rd
  Belper DE56 . . . . 178 E6
  Burton upon Trent DE15 . . 254 F6
  Matlock DE4 . . . . 143 B7
Pinfold SK13 . . . . 9 E4
Pinfold Cl
  Holymoorside S42 . . . . . . 113 E8
  Repton DE65 . . . . 242 D2
  Tutbury DE13 . . . . 239 C5
Pinfold Cres SK17 . . . . 69 C3
Pinfold Gdns NG19 . . . . . 136 F2
Pinfold Hill S32 . . . . 72 E2
Pinfold La
  Bradley DE6 . . . . 187 A8
  Repton DE65 . . . . 242 D2
  Stapleford NG9 . . . . 223 E7
Pinfold Rd SK17 . . . . 69 C3
Pinfold St S21 . . . . 59 D3
Pinfold The
  Belper DE56 . . . . 179 C5
  Elvaston DE72 . . . . 233 F4
  Glapwell S44 . . . . 118 B1
  Middleton DE45 . . . . 124 E3
Pinfold Trad Est NG9 . . . 223 E7
Pinfold View DE45 . . . . . . 109 C5
Pingle DE22 . . . . 204 E4
Pingle Cl S81 . . . . 63 E7
Pingle Cres DE56 . . . . 178 F5
Pingle Farm Rd DE11 . . . 255 F5
Pingle Grange S43 . . . . 96 E7
Pinglehill Way DE73 . . . . 233 B2
Pingle La
  Belper DE56 . . . . 178 F5
  Carsington DE4 . . . . 164 E7
Pingle Rd S21 . . . . 60 E7
Pingle Sch The DE11 . . . . 256 A5
Pingle The
  Derby DE21 . . . . 220 F4
  Long Eaton NG10 . . . . . . 236 D8
  Melbourne DE73 . . . . 252 A4
Pingot Rd SK22 . . . . 33 D8
Pingott La SK13 . . . . 10 A5
Pingreaves Dr DE73 . . . . . 233 A3
Pinnacle Way DE24 . . . . . 219 D3
Pintail Dr DE24 . . . . 231 D4
PINXTON 160 C2
Pinxton Gn NG16 . . . . 160 E3
Pinxton La
  Kirby-in-A NG17 . . . . 160 F6
  South Normanton DE55 . . 160 C5
Pioneer Meadows Nature
  Reserve★ 208 C4
Piper Ave S45 . . . . 131 E4
Piper La S42 . . . . 94 E3
Pipers Ct NG16 . . . . 170 F3

Pipeyard La S21 . . . . 59 C2
Pippenwell Rd SK17 . . . . . 106 A7
Pippin Gdns DE24 . . . . . . 232 F7
Pippin Hill DE5 . . . . 180 E1
Pipworth La S21 . . . . 59 F4
Pitch Cl S43 . . . . 80 E2
Pit Close La DE73 . . . . 233 A1
Pit La
  Codnor DE5 . . . . 181 A7
  Crich DE4, DE55 . . . . 157 B6
  Mansfield NG19 . . . . 135 A5
  Ripley DE5 . . . . 169 E1
  Sheffield S12 . . . . 44 A6
  Shipley DE75 . . . . 194 B6
  Shirland DE55 . . . . 158 D8
  Stonebroom DE55 . . . . . . 147 A5
Pits La DE6 . . . . 151 E1
Pittar St DE22 . . . . 267 A2
Pitt Hill Rd NG20 . . . . 100 F2
Pittlemere La SK17 . . . . 50 A1
Pitt St S21 . . . . 59 C2
Pittywood Rd DE4 . . . . . . 165 E7
Placket La DE4 . . . . 141 B6
Plackett Cl
  Breaston DE72 . . . . 235 D8
  Stapleford NG9 . . . . 223 F8
Plains La DE56 . . . . 178 B4
Plainspot Rd NG16 . . . . . . 171 E2
Plain The DE6 . . . . 201 F8
PLAISTOW 156 F6
PLAISTOW GREEN 156 F4
Plaistow Green Rd DE4 . . 156 F2
Plantain Gdns DE23 . . . . . 231 C5
Plantation Cl
  Chesterfield S40 . . . . 95 A5
  Whitwell S80 . . . . 81 E5
Plantation Rd [7] S8 . . . . . . 43 A6
Plantations The [9] NG10 236 A8
Plantin Rise S20 . . . . 59 E7
Plantin The S20 . . . . 59 E7
Plant La NG10 . . . . 236 A4
Platform Ct DE21 . . . . 220 D3
Platts Ave DE75 . . . . 181 C1
Platt St
  Glossop SK13 . . . . 10 B5
  Pinxton NG16 . . . . 160 D2
Pleasant Ave S44 . . . . 118 B7
Pleasant Cl S12 . . . . 44 B6
Pleasant Pl S40 . . . . 95 D3
Pleasant Rd S12 . . . . 44 B6
Pleasant View SK6 . . . . 15 B3
PLEASLEY 135 B6
Pleasley Colliery Mus★
  NG19 . . . . 134 F5
PLEASLEYHILL 135 C4
Pleasley Pit Country Pk★
  NG19 . . . . 134 E6
Pleasley Springs NG19 . . 135 B5
Pleasley Vale Nature
  Reserve★ NG19 . . . . 135 D7
Pleasley Vale Outdoor
  Activity Ctr NG19 . . . . . . 135 D6
Plimsoll Ct DE22 . . . . 267 A1
Plimsoll St DE22 . . . . 218 C6
Ploughfield Cl DE23 . . . . 231 B6
Plough Gate DE22 . . . . . . 204 F2
Plover Ave DE11 . . . . 256 F3
Plover Cl SK13 . . . . 17 F8
Plover Ct DE3 . . . . 230 B7
Plover Way S44 . . . . 96 F3
Plowman Ct NG9 . . . . 223 E6
Plowright Cl S14 . . . . 43 D5
Plowright Dr S14 . . . . 43 D5
Plowright Mount S14 . . . . 43 D5
Plowright Way S14 . . . . . . 43 D5
Plucksbridge Rd SK6 . . . . . 23 B3
Plumbley Hall Mews S20 . 59 C6
Plumbley Hall Rd S20 . . . . 59 C6
Plumbley La S20 . . . . 59 B6
Plumbleywood La S12,
  S20 . . . . 58 F6
Plummer Rd DE11 . . . . . . 256 A5
Plumptre Cl NG16 . . . . . . 182 F1
Plumptre Rd NG16 . . . . . 182 B5
Plumptre Way NG16 . . . . 182 F1
Plymouth Ave NG16 . . . . 160 E2
Plymouth Ct [7] S41 . . . . . . 95 F8
Pocknedge La S42 . . . . 113 D8
Podmore View ST14 . . . . 196 F3
Podnor La SK6 . . . . 24 A6
Pole's Rd DE6 . . . . 217 A8
Pollards Oaks DE72 . . . . . 221 C1
Polly Froggatt La S32 . . . . 72 B2
Polyfields La S44 . . . . 118 B8
Pomegranite Theatre★
  S41 . . . . 266 C3
Pomeroy Cotts SK17 . . . . 106 B4
Pond Cotts DE4 . . . . 143 E6
Pond End DE74 . . . . 247 B6
Pond La
  Tupton S42 . . . . 131 D8
  Wingerworth S42 . . . . 114 E4
Pond Rd DE56 . . . . 191 C7
Pond St S40 . . . . 266 B2
Pondwell Cnr S43 . . . . 96 F7
Pondwell Dr S43 . . . . 96 F7
Ponsonby Terr DE1 . . . . . 218 E5
Pontefract St DE24 . . . . . 232 D7
Pontypool Cl DE21 . . . . . 206 B2
Pool Cl
  Elvaston DE24 . . . . 233 C4
  Pinxton NG16 . . . . 160 D2
Poolclose Row NG16 . . . . 160 D2
Poole's Cavern★ SK17 . . . 85 A6
Poole St DE24 . . . . 232 E6
Pool Rd DE73 . . . . 252 D6
POOLSBROOK 98 A7
Poolsbrook Ave S43 . . . . . 98 A8

Poolsbrook Cres S43 . . . . . 98 A8
Pools Brook Ctry Pk★
  S43 . . . . 79 B1
Poolsbrook Prim Sch S43 98 A7
Poolsbrook Rd S44 . . . . . . 98 A5
Poolsbrook Sq S43 . . . . . . 98 A8
Poolsbrook View S43 . . . . 98 A8
Pool's La S21 . . . . 77 C7
Pool St DE11 . . . . 256 D2
Pope Carr Rd DE4 . . . . . . 143 C5
Poplar Ave
  Chesterfield S40 . . . . 95 B2
  Derby DE21 . . . . 220 E5
  Moira DE12 . . . . 262 E2
  New Mills SK22 . . . . 24 D1
  Ripley DE5 . . . . 180 D8
  Sandiacre NG10 . . . . 223 A7
  Swadlincote DE11 . . . . . . 256 B6
Poplar Cl
  Derby DE24 . . . . 233 B7
  Dronfield S18 . . . . 76 C7
  Killamarsh S21 . . . . 60 C5
Poplar Cres DE6 . . . . 185 D8
Poplar Dr
  Chesterfield S42 . . . . 115 C1
  Glapwell S44 . . . . 134 B8
  Pleasley NG19 . . . . 135 B4
Poplar Grange DE21 . . . . 206 C3
Poplar Nook DE22 . . . . . . 204 F4
Poplar Rd
  Breaston DE72 . . . . 235 F8
  Eckington S21 . . . . 59 C2
  South Normanton DE55 . . 160 B7
Poplar Row DE22 . . . . 205 A1
Poplar St NG19 . . . . 136 C3
Poplars The
  Derby DE22 . . . . 204 F4
  Whitwell S80 . . . . 82 A5
Poplar Terr
  Chapel-en-le-Frith SK23 . . 47 B7
  Selston NG16 . . . . 171 E6
Poplar Way
  High Lane SK6 . . . . 32 A7
  Ilkeston DE7 . . . . 208 D5
Poppy Cl NG20 . . . . 119 D3
Poppyfields DE5 . . . . 180 D7
Poppyfields Dr DE3 . . . . . 217 E2
Poppy Gdns DE55 . . . . . . 148 B7
Porlock Cl [2] NG10 . . . . . 236 A8
Porlock Ct DE21 . . . . 206 A2
Porteous Cl DE4 . . . . 127 D3
Porter Ho [9] S43 . . . . 78 E2
PORTERHOUSE 169 F1
Porterhouse Rd DE5 . . . . 169 F1
Porter La DE4 . . . . 154 E3
Porter Pl DE21 . . . . 220 D5
Porter Rd DE23 . . . . 218 F2
Porters Farm Ct ST14 . . . 224 E2
Porters La DE21 . . . . 205 F3
Porter's La
  Derby DE21 . . . . 205 F3
  Findern DE65 . . . . 230 D1
Porter St S43 . . . . 78 E2
Porthcawl Pl DE21 . . . . . . 206 C2
Portico Rd DE23 . . . . 231 A6
Portis Ct DE21 . . . . 220 D5
Portland Ave
  Bolsover S44 . . . . 99 B1
  Burton upon Trent DE14 . . 254 A7
  Creswell S80 . . . . 81 E1
Portland Cl
  Chesterfield S41 . . . . 266 B4
  Derby DE3 . . . . 217 D2
Portland Court Mews
  NG19 . . . . 136 C4
Portland Cres
  Bolsover S44 . . . . 99 B1
  Mansfield Woodhouse
    NG19 . . . . 136 D3
  Stapleford NG9 . . . . 223 E6
Portland Gr SK23 . . . . 34 E2
Portland St
  Beeston NG9 . . . . 223 F1
  Eastwood NG16 . . . . 195 B8
  Ilkeston DE7 . . . . 194 F3
  Long Eaton NG10 . . . . . . 236 B4
  New Mills SK22 . . . . 24 D1
  Shirebrook NG20 . . . . 119 F4
  Whaley Thorns NG20 . . . . 101 A3
Portland Sq DE45 . . . . . . 109 D6
Portland St
  Clowne S43 . . . . 81 A4
  Derby DE23 . . . . 232 A8
  Etwall DE65 . . . . 229 B4
  Mansfield Woodhouse
    NG19 . . . . 136 C3
  New Houghton NG19 . . . . 135 A7
  Whitwell S80 . . . . 81 F6
Portland Terr NG20 . . . . 101 A2
Portman Chase DE24 . . . . 231 D2
Portreath Dr DE22 . . . . . . 204 E3
Portsmouth Cl DE11 . . . . 255 E2
Port Way DE21, DE56 . . . 191 D5
Portway Cl DE22 . . . . 205 A4
Portway Dr DE13 . . . . 239 C5
Portway Inf Sch DE22 . . . 204 E4
Portway Jun Sch DE22 . . 204 E4
Portwood Ind Est DE11 . 256 A1
Postmans La S42 . . . . 116 C4
Post Office Row SK17 . . . . 69 E3
Post St SK13 . . . . 10 B5
Posy La DE7 . . . . 246 A7
Potato Pit La
  Dale Abbey DE7 . . . . 208 A1
  Stanton-by-Dale DE7 . . . . 222 A8
Potlocks The DE65 . . . . . . 242 C6
Potter Rd SK13 . . . . 9 E3
Potters Cl S41 . . . . 77 C2

Potters Croft
  Clifton Campville B79 . . . 263 E2
  Swadlincote DE11 . . . . . . 256 A5
Potters La DE4, DE55 . . . 157 B5
Potters Nook S81 . . . . 63 F7
POTTER SOMERSAL 212 A4
Potter St
  Derby DE21 . . . . 220 D4
  Melbourne DE73 . . . . 252 B7
Potters Way DE7 . . . . 209 A8
Potters Yd DE73 . . . . 252 B7
Pottery Cl DE56 . . . . 179 C5
Pottery La DE5 . . . . 180 C3
Pottery Lane E S41 . . . . . . 96 B8
Pottery Lane W S41 . . . . . 96 A7
Pottery Prim Sch DE56 . . 179 C4
Poulter Ctry Pk★ NG20 . 100 E2
Poulter St NG20 . . . . 100 F1
Pounder La DE4 . . . . 142 D2
Powell Dr S21 . . . . 60 C6
Powell St DE23 . . . . 218 E2
Pown St SK17 . . . . 137 A6
Powtrell Pl DE7 . . . . 209 B6
Poynter Cl DE75 . . . . 181 C1
Poynton Wood Cres S17. . 56 A6
Poynton Wood Glade S17 56 A6
Poyser Ave DE21 . . . . 220 A7
Poyser La DE6 . . . . 203 A1
Pratt Cl NG19 . . . . 135 D1
PRATTHALL 94 B7
Pratthall La DE4 . . . . 166 A6
Premier Ave DE6 . . . . 185 B8
Prescot Cl DE3 . . . . 217 C1
Press La S42 . . . . 130 D6
Prestbury Cl DE21 . . . . . . 206 B1
Preston Ave DE55 . . . . . . 159 B4
Preston St S8 . . . . 43 A7
Prestwick Way DE73 . . . . 232 E2
Prestwold Way S41 . . . . . 115 C7
Prestwood La ST14 . . . . . 196 F8
Prestwood Park Dr
  DE11 . . . . 256 D5
Pretoria St S44 . . . . 98 F6
Pride Park Stad (Derby
  County FC)★ DE24 . . . . . 219 E3
Pride Parkway DE24 . . . . 219 D3
Pride Pl DE24 . . . . 219 D3
Pride Point Dr DE24 . . . . 219 D2
PRIESTCLIFFE 87 F5
PRIESTCLIFFE DITCH . . . 87 D4
Priestcliffe Lees (Nature
  Reserve)★ SK17 . . . . 88 B7
Priestcliffe Rd SK17 . . . . . 87 F4
Priestfield Gdns S41 . . . . . 95 B7
Priestland Ave DE21 . . . . 220 D4
Priestley Ave DE55 . . . . . 146 C5
Primary Cl DE56 . . . . 179 A4
Prime Enterprise Pk
  DE1 . . . . 267 C4
Prime Ind Est DE23 . . . . . 219 C2
Prime Ind Pk DE23 . . . . . 219 C2
Prime Parkway DE1 . . . . 267 C4
Primrose Ave NG16 . . . . . 171 F2
Primrose Bank DE65 . . . . 229 C5
Primrose Bsns Pk DE55 . 147 F1
Primrose Cl
  Derby DE21 . . . . 205 F3
  Killamarsh S21 . . . . 60 E7
  South Normanton DE55 . . 160 B7
Primrose Cotts
  Hazelwood DE56 . . . . 190 C7
  Risley DE72 . . . . 222 D3
Primrose Cres [1] SK13 . . . 17 B8
Primrose Ct
  Hayfield SK22 . . . . 25 D3
  Mansfield Woodhouse
    NG19 . . . . 136 F4
Primrose Dr
  Burton upon Trent DE14 . . 254 A8
  Morley DE7 . . . . 206 C8
Primrose Hill
  Blackwell DE55 . . . . 147 F1
  Glossop SK13 . . . . 17 B8
  Ilkeston NE7 . . . . 194 E3
Primrose La
  Glossop SK13 . . . . 17 B8
  Hayfield SK22 . . . . 25 C5
  Killamarsh S21 . . . . 60 E7
  Marple SK6 . . . . 24 A4
  Tideswell SK17 . . . . 69 C3
Primrose Mdw DE11 . . . . 256 B7
Primrose Rise NG16 . . . . 195 B8
Primrose St DE7 . . . . 194 E3
Primrose Terr [2] SK13 . . . 17 B8
Primrose Vale Cotts SK22 25 C4
Primrose Way NG20 . . . . 119 F6
Primula Cl NG20 . . . . 119 D3
Primula Way DE23 . . . . . . 231 D4
Prince Charles Ave
  DE22 . . . . 218 A6
Prince Edward Prim Sch
  S12 . . . . 44 A7
Prince of Wales Rd S2 . . . 44 B7
Princes Dr DE23 . . . . 218 B2
Princes Rd SK23 . . . . 34 E2
Prince's Rd SK17 . . . . 85 D8
Princess Ave
  Linton DE12 . . . . 261 C1
  South Normanton DE55 . . 160 A5
Princess Cl
  Heanor DE75 . . . . 181 D2
  Woodville DE11 . . . . 256 F2
Princess Ct S2 . . . . 44 B8
Princess Dr
  Borrowash DE72 . . . . 221 A2
  Sandiacre NG10 . . . . 223 B4
Princess Pl S45 . . . . 131 C2

Princess Rd
  Dronfield S18 . . . . 57 B2
  Uttoxeter ST14 . . . . 210 A1
Princess St
  Brimington S43 . . . . 96 F8
  Chesterfield S40 . . . . 266 A4
  Glossop SK13 . . . . 17 C8
  Long Eaton NG10 . . . . . . 236 D8
  Swadlincote DE11 . . . . . . 261 F8
Princes St NG16 . . . . 182 F3
Prince's St DE23 . . . . 219 B1
Princess Way DE13 . . . . . 240 E1
Prince St
  Ilkeston DE7 . . . . 194 E4
  Long Eaton NG10 . . . . . . 236 D8
Printers Fold SK14 . . . . . . 9 D5
Printers Pk SK14 . . . . 9 E5
Priors Barn Cl DE72 . . . . 221 D2
Priorway Ave DE72 . . . . . 221 D2
Priorway Gdns DE72 . . . . 221 C1
Priory Cl
  Chellaston DE73 . . . . 245 A8
  Ilkeston DE7 . . . . 208 C6
  Swadlincote DE11 . . . . . . 256 A6
  Tutbury DE13 . . . . 239 B5
  Yeaveley DE6 . . . . 199 D5
Priory Ct S26 . . . . 61 E5
Priory Gdns
  Derby DE21 . . . . 205 F3
  Swanwick DE55 . . . . 170 A8
Priory Lands DE13 . . . . . 240 F2
Priory Rd
  Alfreton DE55 . . . . 159 B5
  Eastwood NG16 . . . . 182 F1
  Mansfield Woodhouse
    NG19 . . . . 136 B3
Priory Sq NG19 . . . . 136 B3
Priory Way DE5 . . . . 180 E8
Pritchard Dr NG9 . . . . . . 223 E6
Pritchett Dr DE23 . . . . . . 230 E8
Private Dr S43 . . . . 78 A1
Progress Ct DE45 . . . . . . 109 D6
Prospect Ave DE55 . . . . . 159 F5
Prospect Cotts S43 . . . . . . 80 E5
Prospect Ct
  [1] Sheffield S17 . . . . 56 B5
  Sutton in Ashfield NG17 . 148 E1
Prospect Dr
  Belper DE56 . . . . 178 F2
  Matlock DE4 . . . . 143 A6
  Sheffield S17 . . . . 55 F5
  Shirebrook NG20 . . . . 119 E3
Prospect Gdns DE55 . . . . 169 E7
Prospect Ho S43 . . . . 78 F1
Prospect Pl
  Derby DE24 . . . . 219 E4
  Sheffield S17 . . . . 56 A5
Prospect Rd
  Chesterfield S41 . . . . 76 F2
  Denby Village DE5 . . . . . 180 A1
  Dronfield S18 . . . . 57 C3
  Heanor DE75 . . . . 194 A8
  Pilsley S45 . . . . 132 C1
  Sheffield, Bradway Bank
    S17 . . . . 56 A5
  Sheffield, Lowfield S2 . . . . 43 A4
Prospect St DE55 . . . . 159 B4
Prospect Terr
  Bakewell DE45 . . . . 109 C6
  Chesterfield S40 . . . . 95 E4
  Crich DE4 . . . . 168 A4
Providence Ct DE11 . . . . 256 F2
Providence Pl
  Alfreton DE55 . . . . 158 F3
  [5] Ilkeston DE7 . . . . 194 E1
Providence St DE55 . . . . 180 E8
Provident St [4] DE23 . . . 219 A2
Pryor Mede S26 . . . . 61 E5
Pudding Bag La S45 . . . . 129 F4
Puddle Hill DE4 . . . . 142 C1
Pulborough Gdns DE23 . 231 A6
Pullman Cl S43 . . . . 78 F3
Pullman Rd DE21 . . . . . . 219 F4
Pump Cl DE4 . . . . 143 C3
Pump La DE6 . . . . 224 B8
Pump Yd DE56 . . . . 177 B2
Punch Bowl Pk SK17 . . . . 85 A8
Purbeck Ave S40 . . . . 95 D4
Purbeck Cl
  Long Eaton NG10 . . . . . . 236 A8
  Mansfield Woodhouse
    NG19 . . . . 136 C6
Purchase Ave DE75 . . . . . 181 C2
Purdy Mdw NG10 . . . . . . 235 F5
Pursglove Dr SK17 . . . . . . 69 D4
Pursglove Rd SK17 . . . . . . 69 C4
Putney Cl DE22 . . . . 217 E5
Pybus St DE22 . . . . 218 D6
PYE BRIDGE 170 F6
Pye Bridge Ind Est DE55. 170 F6
Pyegrove SK13 . . . . 10 F1
Pyegrove Rd SK13 . . . . . . 10 E1
PYE HILL 171 A5
Pye Hill Rd NG16 . . . . . . 171 A4
Pykestone Cl [6] DE21 . . . 205 F2
Pym Leys NG10 . . . . 235 F5
Pynot Rd S41 . . . . 77 B2
Pytchley Cl DE56 . . . . 179 D4

Q

Quad DE1 . . . . 267 B3
Quadrant Mews [5] SK17. . 85 B8
Quadrant The
  Buxton SK17 . . . . 85 B8
  Sheffield S17 . . . . 55 E5

Quaker Cl DE73 . . . . 252 D8
Quantock Cl DE24 . . . . . . 231 D2
Quantock Rd NG10 . . . . . . 223 A1
Quantock Way S40 . . . . . 95 B5
QUARNDON 204 D6
Quarndon Hts DE22 . . . . 204 C3
Quarndon View DE22 . . . 204 C2
Quarn Dr DE22 . . . . 204 C3
Quarn Gdns DE1 . . . . 218 F7
Quarn St DE1 . . . . 218 E6
Quarn Way DE1 . . . . 218 F6
Quarry Bank DE4 . . . . . . 143 B7
Quarry Bank Rd S41 . . . . 96 C2
Quarry Berry La DE12 . . . 264 F1
Quarry Cl SK13 . . . . 10 D1
Quarry Hill
 Eckington S21 . . . . 58 D2
 Sheffield S20 . . . . 59 A8
 Stanton-by-Dale DE7 . . . . 223 A8
Quarry Hill Ind Est DE7. 208 F5
Quarry Hill Rd DE7 . . . . . 208 F5
Quarry La
 Alton S42 . . . . 130 C5
 Brackenfield DE55 . . . . . 145 D6
 Chesterfield S40 . . . . 95 C2
 Matlock DE4 . . . . 143 E7
 Stonebroom DE55 . . . . . 146 F3
Quarry Rd
 Apperknowle S18 . . . . 58 A1
 Belper DE56 . . . . 178 F2
 Bolsover S44 . . . . 99 A3
 Hayfield SK22 . . . . 24 F2
 Killamarsh S21 . . . . 60 C7
 Morley DE7 . . . . 192 B1
 New Mills SK22 . . . . 33 D7
 Sheffield, Totley Brook S17 . 55 F5
 Somercotes DE55 . . . . . . 170 C2
Quarry Vale Gr S12 . . . . . 44 C4
Quarry Vale Rd S12 . . . . . 44 C4
Queen Anne Ct S14 . . . . . 43 E3
Queen Elizabeth Ct
 8 Ashbourne DE6 . . . . . . 173 B2
 Sheffield S14 . . . . 43 E3
Queen Elizabeth's Gram Sch
 DE6 . . . . 173 C3
Queen Elizabeth's Sch
 NG19 . . . . 136 A1
Queen Elizabeth Way
 DE7 . . . . 208 C5
Queen Mary Cl S2 . . . . . . 44 A7
Queen Mary Cres 1 S2 . . 44 A8
Queen Mary Ct
 Derby DE1 . . . . 218 F7
 Sheffield S2 . . . . 44 A8
Queen Mary Gr S2 . . . . . . 43 F7
Queen Mary Mews S2 . . . 44 A7
Queen Mary Rd
 Chesterfield S40 . . . . 95 B1
 Sheffield S2 . . . . 44 A8
Queen Mary Rise 3 S2 . . 44 A8
Queens Ave
 Heanor DE75 . . . . 181 D2
 Ilkeston DE7 . . . . 209 A5
 Stanley DE7 . . . . 207 C6
Queen's Ave SK17 . . . . . . 85 D8
Queensbury Chase DE23. 231 A6
Queens Cl S80 . . . . 82 C5
Queens Ct
 Burton upon Trent DE14 . . 254 B8
 Buxton SK17 . . . . 85 D8
 Creswell S80 . . . . 81 F2
 Derby DE22 . . . . 218 E8
 Draycott DE72 . . . . 235 A7
Queen's Ct
 Chesterfield S41 . . . . . . 266 A4
 Marple SK6 . . . . 23 A6
Queens Dr
 Brinsley NG16 . . . . 182 E7
 Derby DE23 . . . . 218 C2
 Sandiacre NG10 . . . . 223 B4
Queen's Dr
 Belper DE56 . . . . 178 E5
 Glossop SK13 . . . . 10 F1
 Ilkeston DE7 . . . . 208 E8
 Swadlincote DE11 . . . . . 256 B6
Queensferry Gdns DE24 . 232 E4
Queensgate Dr DE73 . . . 244 F8
Queens Gdns S2 . . . . 43 C8
Queensland Cl DE3 . . . . . 217 E4
Queensland Cres DE15 . . 248 C2
Queen's L Ctr DE1 . . . . . 267 B4
Queens Mews S2 . . . . 43 C8
Queen's Park Sports Ctr
 S40 . . . . 266 A2
Queens Rd
 Creswell S80 . . . . 82 C6
 Sheffield, Lowfield S2 . . . . 43 B8
Queen's Rd SK17 . . . . 85 D8
Queens Ret Pk S2 . . . . . . 43 B8
Queens Rise DE23 . . . . . 239 C6
Queens Road N NG16 . . . 182 F1
Queens Road S NG16 . . . 182 F1
Queen's Sq NG16 . . . . . . 182 F2
Queen's Stables S2 . . . . . 43 C8
Queen St
 Belper DE56 . . . . 179 A3
 Brimington S43 . . . . 77 F1
 Chesterfield S40 . . . . . . 266 A4
 Clay Cross S45 . . . . 131 C3
 Creswell S80 . . . . 81 F1
 Derby DE1 . . . . 267 B4
 Eckington S21 . . . . 59 E3
 Glossop SK13 . . . . 17 B8
 Hadfield SK13 . . . . 10 A4
 Ilkeston DE7 . . . . 208 E8
 Ironville NG16 . . . . 170 F4
 Langley Mill NG16 . . . . . 182 C3
 Long Eaton NG10 . . . . . . 236 E7

Queen St continued
 Longnor SK17 . . . . 121 B6
 Marple SK6 . . . . 23 A6
 Middleton DE4 . . . . 154 D5
 Pilsley S45 . . . . 132 D1
 Pinxton NG16 . . . . 160 D3
 Ripley DE5 . . . . 181 A7
 Sheffield, Mosborough S20 . 59 C7
 Somercotes DE55 . . . . . . 170 D8
 South Normanton DE55 . . 159 F5
 Staveley S43 . . . . 97 C3
 Swadlincote DE11 . . . . . 256 A1
 Tideswell SK17 . . . . 69 C4
Queen Street Mews S20 . 59 C7
Queen Street N S41 . . . . 96 A4
Queens View S2 . . . . 43 C8
Queensview Dr DE5 . . . . 181 A7
Queensway
 Castle Donington DE74 . . 246 F4
 Derby DE22 . . . . 204 D3
 Holmewood S42 . . . . . . 116 E1
 Melbourne DE73 . . . . . . 252 B8
 Pilsley S45 . . . . 132 C1
 Stonebroom DE55 . . . . . 146 F3
Queen's Way S42 . . . . . . 115 D1
Queens Wlk S42 . . . . 116 E1
Queen's Wlk
 Tupton S42 . . . . 115 D1
 Whaley Thorns NG20 . . . 101 A1
Queen Victoria Dr DE11 . 256 B5
Queen Victoria Rd
 Sheffield S17 . . . . 55 F5
 Tupton S42 . . . . 115 C1
Quenby La DE5 . . . . 169 E1
Quentin Rd SK23 . . . . 47 C6
Quick Cl DE73 . . . . 252 A7
Quick Hill Rd DE24 . . . . . 231 D2
Quillings Way DE72 . . . . 221 D1
Quilow La DE6 . . . . 185 E3
Quintin Rd DE24 . . . . . . 233 A8
QUIXHILL 196 E3
Quixhill Bank ST14 . . . . 196 F8
Quixhill Cl DE6 . . . . 185 E8
Quixhill La ST14 . . . . . . 196 D8
Quoit Gn S18 . . . . 57 B1
QUOIT GREEN 57 B1
Quorn Cl DE55 . . . . 148 A1
Quorndon Cres NG10 . . . 236 D5
Quorn Dr 5 S40 . . . . 95 A5
Quorn Rise DE23 . . . . . . 231 E6

R

Rabbit La SK14 . . . . 9 A6
Rabown Ave DE23 . . . . . 231 D8
Racecourse Ind Est
 DE21 . . . . 219 C8
Racecourse Mount S41. . 95 F8
Racecourse Park DE21 . . 219 C7
Racecourse Rd S41 . . . . . 76 F1
RADBOURNE 216 F5
Radbourne Comm 4 S18. 56 D1
Radbourne Gate DE3 . . . 217 D5
Radbourne La DE22 . . . . 217 E6
Radbourne St
 Derby DE22 . . . . 218 C6
 Mansfield Woodhouse
  NG19 . . . . 136 E4
Radburn Ct NG9 . . . . . . 209 E1
Radcliffe Ave DE21 . . . . 219 F7
Radcliffe Dr DE22 . . . . . 218 D3
Radford Mdw DE74 . . . . 246 F3
Radford Rd DE7 . . . . 192 F6
Radford St DE24 . . . . . . 232 F7
Radleigh Gr DE11 . . . . . 257 A2
Radleigh Grange DE11 . . 257 A2
RADMANTHWAITE 135 D3
Radmanthwaite Rd
 NG19 . . . . 135 D3
Rad Mdws NG10 . . . . . . 236 C6
Radnor Pl NG19 . . . . 135 C4
Radnor St DE21 . . . . 219 D7
Radstock Gdns DE21 . . . 205 E1
Radstone Cl DE21 . . . . . 206 B2
Raeburn Cl S14 . . . . 43 E2
Raeburn Dr
 Beeston NG9 . . . . 223 E2
 Marple SK6 . . . . 23 B8
Raeburn Pl S14 . . . . 43 E3
Raeburn Rd S14 . . . . 43 E3
Raeburn Way S14 . . . . . . 43 E2
Raglan Ave DE22 . . . . . . 218 C5
Raglan St DE55 . . . . 159 A4
Railway Ave S80 . . . . . . 100 D8
Railway Cottages S44 . . . 98 C2
Railway Cotts
 Derby DE24 . . . . 232 A6
 Derby, Stenson DE73 . . . 243 A8
 Egginton DE65 . . . . 241 B7
 Holmewood S42 . . . . . . 116 F1
 Kimberley NG16 . . . . . . 195 F6
 Temple Normanton S41 . . 116 A5
Railway Row NG16 . . . . . 170 F4
Railway Side DE11 . . . . . 256 B1
Railway St
 Glossop SK13 . . . . 10 C1
 Hadfield SK13 . . . . 10 A5
Railway Terr
 Buxton SK17 . . . . 85 C8
 3 Chesterfield S41 . . . . . 115 B7
 Derby DE1 . . . . 267 D2
 Disley SK12 . . . . 32 C6
Railway View S45 . . . . . 131 F4
Rainbow Gdns DE24 . . . . 233 A5
Rainier Dr DE21 . . . . . . 220 A6
Rain's La DE4 . . . . 154 C4
Rake Head Rd HD9 . . . . . 2 E7

Rake La DE45 . . . . 124 D3
Rakes La DE6 . . . . 162 A6
Rakes Rd DE45 . . . . 107 C1
Rake The DE45. . . . . 123 B6
Raleigh Cl DE7 . . . . 194 F3
Raleigh Rd S2 . . . . 43 B6
Raleigh St DE22 . . . . . . 218 C6
Ralley Cl S42 . . . . 132 D8
Ralph Dr DE55 . . . . 170 D7
Ralph Rd S43 . . . . 79 A2
Ralston Croft S20 . . . . . . 59 E6
Ralston Cl S20 . . . . 59 E6
Ralston Gr S20 . . . . 59 E6
Ralston Pl S20 . . . . 59 D6
Rambler Cl DE11 . . . . . . 256 A5
Ramblers Dr DE21 . . . . . 206 C3
Ramper Ave S43 . . . . 80 E2
Ramscliff Ave DE12 . . . . 265 F8
Ramsdean Cl DE21 . . . . . 219 D8
Ramsden Cl SK13 . . . . . . 10 D2
Ramsden Rd HD9 . . . . 3 B7
Ramsey Ave S40 . . . . 95 D1
Ramsey Cl NG9 . . . . 209 E2
Ramshaw Cl S41 . . . . 95 C7
Ramshaw Rd S18 . . . . . . 76 E6
Ramshaw Way DE22 . . . 218 E4
Ramsley Ct 17 S40 . . . . . 95 D5
Randal Cres SK23 . . . . . . 45 C5
Randall Dr DE11 . . . . . . 256 B4
Randall Pl 1 S2 . . . . 43 A8
Randall St S21 . . . . 59 B2
Randolph Rd DE23 . . . . . 231 F8
Ranelagh Gdns DE22 . . . 218 B7
Raneld Mount S40 . . . . . 114 C8
Rangemoor La DE6 . . . . 183 D6
Rangemore Cl DE21 . . . . 217 E4
Rangewood Rd DE55 . . . 159 F4
Ranmoor Cl S41 . . . . 115 C8
Ranmoor Hill S32 . . . . . . 52 E8
Ranmoor La S32 . . . . 52 F8
Rannoch Cl
 Derby DE22 . . . . 204 E3
 Derby, Spondon DE21 . . . 220 F5
Ranworth Cl DE24. . . . . . 232 D3
Ratcliffe Ave DE14 . . . . . 254 B8
Ratcliffe Cl S41 . . . . 115 C7
Ratcliffe La S80. . . . . 82 D6
Ratcliffe St NG16 . . . . . . 182 F2
Rauche Ct DE23 . . . . . . 267 C1
Raven Ave DE55 . . . . 147 F5
Ravencar Rd S21. . . . . . . 59 B3
Raven Cl DE55 . . . . 170 C6
Raven Ct DE75 . . . . 181 E2
Raven Oak Cl DE56 . . . . 179 A3
Ravens Cl S13 . . . . 16 F8
Ravenscourt Rd DE22 . . 218 C6
Ravenscroft Ave S13 . . . 44 E8
Ravenscroft Cl S13 . . . . . 44 E8
Ravenscroft Cres S13 . . 44 E8
Ravenscroft Ct S13 . . . . . 44 E8
Ravenscroft Dr
 Derby DE21 . . . . 219 F6
 Sheffield S13 . . . . 44 E7
Ravenscroft Oval S13 . . 44 E8
Ravenscroft Pl S13 . . . . . 44 E8
Ravenscroft Rd S13 . . . . 44 E7
Ravenscroft Way S13 . . . 44 E8
Ravensdale Ave NG10 . . 223 B2
Ravensdale Cl S43 . . . . . 97 C5
Ravensdale Cotts SK17 . . 89 A8
Ravensdale Inf & Jun Schs
 DE3 . . . . 217 E3
Ravensdale Rd
 Derby DE22 . . . . 204 C3
 Dronfield S18. . . . . 56 D1
Ravenshorn Way S21. . . 79 C8
Ravenside Ret Pk S40 . . 266 B2
RAVENSNEST 144 F7
Raven St DE22 . . . . 218 A3
Ravenstor Rd DE4 . . . . . 154 F2
Ravenstor Sta ★ DE4 . . . 154 F2
Ravenswood Rd S40 . . . . 95 A5
Ravenwood DE11 . . . . . . 256 C3
Rawdon Cl DE74 . . . . . . 247 A4
Rawdon Cl DE12 . . . . . . 262 E5
Rawdon Side DE11 . . . . . 256 D4
Rawdon St DE23 . . . . . . 218 F2
Rawlins Ct S18 . . . . 57 C4
Rawlinson Ave DE23 . . . 232 A7
Rawson Gn DE56. . . . . . 179 F1
RAWSON GREEN 179 F1
Rawson Way S43 . . . . . . 96 D8
Raynald Rd S2. . . . . 44 A8
Raynesway
 Derby, Alvaston DE21 . . . 233 B8
 Derby, Stenson DE73 . . . 220 A2
Raynesway Park Dr
 DE21 . . . . 220 B1
Ray Rushin Bsns Pk The
 DE5 . . . . 180 E7
Ray's Ave DE75 . . . . 181 E1
Ray St DE75 . . . . 181 E1
Reader St DE21 . . . . 220 E5
Realm Cl DE73 . . . . 244 E8
Rebecca Ho DE1 . . . . . . 218 E5
Recreation Cl
 Blackwell DE55 . . . . 147 E1
 Clowne S43 . . . . 80 E4
Recreation Dr NG20 . . . . 119 F2
Recreation Gd The
 (Chesterfield FC) S40 . . . 266 A4
Recreation Rd
 Calow S43 . . . . 96 F5
 New Houghton NG19. . . . 134 F7
 Sandiacre NG10 . . . . 223 B6
 Shirebrook NG20 . . . . . . 119 E6

Recreation Rd continued
 Tideswell SK17 . . . . 69 C4
 Wirksworth DE4 . . . . 165 E7
Recreation St NG10 . . . . 236 F7
Recreation Terr NG9 . . . 223 D6
Recreation View NG20 . . 119 E6
Rectory Cl
 Breedon on the Hill
  DE73 . . . . 252 E2
 Eckington S21 . . . . 59 E4
 Long Duckmanton S44 . . . 98 A3
Rectory Dr S42 . . . . 114 E4
Rectory Farm Mews
 DE72 . . . . 245 E4
Rectory Gdns
 Aston-on-Trent DE72 . . . 246 A7
 Harthill S26 . . . . 61 E6
 Killamarsh S21 . . . . 60 D6
 Long Duckmanton S44. . . . 98 A3
Rectory La
 Appleby Magna DE12. . . . 265 E1
 Breadsall DE21 . . . . 205 D5
 Kirk Ireton DE6 . . . . 165 B1
Rectory Mews DE65 . . . . 241 B4
Rectory Pl NG11 . . . . . . 237 E6
Rectory Rd
 Breaston DE72. . . . . 235 E8
 Clowne S43 . . . . 80 E4
 Killamarsh S21 . . . . 60 D5
 Long Duckmanton S44. . . 98 A4
 Staveley S43 . . . . 78 E2
Reculver Cl DE23 . . . . . . 231 D7
Redacre Cl S44 . . . . 99 C2
Red Barn Cl DE55 . . . . . 148 B3
Redbarn La DE55 . . . . . . 148 B3
Redbridge Cl
 Ilkeston DE7 . . . . 209 A7
 Shirebrook NG20 . . . . . . 119 F2
Redbrook Ave S41 . . . . . 115 B8
Redbrow Hollow SK6. . . . 15 A2
Redbury Cl DE1 . . . . 218 E4
Redcar Gdns 6 DE21 . . . 205 D1
Reddish Ave S43 . . . . 45 D6
Reddish La SK23 . . . . 45 D6
Reddish Rd SK23 . . . . 45 D6
Redens The NG10 . . . . . 236 B4
Redfern Ave DE5 . . . . . . 169 E2
Redfern Cl SK13 . . . . 10 A6
Redfern Rd ST14 . . . . . . 210 A1
Redfern St S42 . . . . 131 C7
Redgap La S45 . . . . 86 A8
Redgate SK13 . . . . 10 C4
Redgate St NG16 . . . . . . 160 D2
Redgrove Way S40 . . . . . 114 C8
Red Hill DE4 . . . . 144 C4
Redhill Ct DE56 . . . . 179 B2
Redhill La DE13 . . . . 239 B5
Red Hill La DE4 . . . . 144 D3
Redhill Lodge Rd 6
 DE11 . . . . 256 A7
Redhill Prim Sch DE72 . . 221 C5
Redhouse Cl S43. . . . . . . 77 D4
Redhouse La SK12 . . . . . 32 E7
Redhouse Stables Working
 Carriage Mus★ DE4. . . . 127 D1
Red La
 Belper DE56 . . . . 191 B6
 Brinsley NG16 . . . . 171 E1
 Chesterfield S41 . . . . 77 C1
 Disley SK12 . . . . 32 C5
 Repton DE65 . . . . 249 F6
 South Normanton DE55. . . 159 F3
Redland Cl
 Derby DE24 . . . . 231 F4
 Ilkeston DE7 . . . . 194 F3
Red Lion Hill DE4 . . . . . 153 A1
Red Lion Row S32 . . . . . 72 C8
Red Lion Sq DE75 . . . . . 181 E1
Red Lodge SK12 . . . . 32 A6
Redmires Dr DE73 . . . . . 233 A2
Redmires Rd S10 . . . . . . 42 B8
Redmoor Cl
 Burton upon Trent DE15 . 248 B3
 Codnor DE5 . . . . 170 B1
Redmoor La
 Disley SK12 . . . . 33 A4
 New Mills SK22 . . . . 33 B6
Rednall Cl S40 . . . . 95 A5
Red River Nature Reserve★
 DE75. . . . . 181 C3
Red Rose Ct DE15 . . . . . 254 E7
Redruth Pl DE24 . . . . . . 233 C5
Redshaw St DE1 . . . . . . 218 E7
Redstart Cl DE21. . . . . . 220 D7
Redthorn Rd S13 . . . . . . 44 F8
Redvers Buller Rd S40 . . 266 B1
Redway Croft 3 DE73 . . 252 A8
Redwing Croft DE23 . . . 231 D7
Redwood Ave S21 . . . . . 60 C5
Redwood Cl S43 . . . . 97 B8
Redwood Dr DE15 . . . . . 255 A8
Redwood Inf Sch DE24 . . 231 D4
Redwood Jun Sch DE24 . 231 F3
Redwood Rd DE24 . . . . . 231 E3
Reedman Rd NG10 . . . . . 236 B4
Reeves Ave S45 . . . . 132 C1
Reeves Rd DE23 . . . . . . 219 B1
Regal Gate DE73 . . . . . . 244 F8
Regency Cl
 Derby DE23 . . . . 231 D7
 4 Glossop SK13 . . . . 10 D1
Regent Cl
 Ironville NG16 . . . . 170 F4
 Swadlincote DE11 . . . . . 256 B2
Regent Gdns S41 . . . . . . 266 B4
Regents Ho 3 DE14. . . . 253 F7
Regents Park Rd DE14. . 254 B8

Regent St
 Clowne S43 . . . . 80 D4
 Derby DE1 . . . . 267 C1
 Glossop, Padfield SK13 . . . 10 B5
 Glossop SK13 . . . . 10 D1
 Ilkeston DE7 . . . . 208 F7
 Kimberley NG16 . . . . . . 195 F6
 Langley Mill NG16 . . . . . 182 B3
 Long Eaton NG10. . . . . . 236 D8
 Stapleford NG10 . . . . . . 223 C5
 Swadlincote DE11 . . . . . 256 B2
Reginald Road N DE21 . . 219 F6
Reginald Road S DE21 . . 219 F6
Reginald St DE23 . . . . . . 219 B2
Regis Cl DE21 . . . . 206 B2
Reigate Dr DE22 . . . . . . 218 A7
Reigate Prim Sch DE22. . 217 F7
Reliant Cl 2 DE11 . . . . . 256 E1
Rembrandt Dr S18 . . . . . 56 E1
Rempstone Dr S41 . . . . . 115 C7
Renals St DE23 . . . . 267 B1
Reney Ave S8. . . . . 56 D6
Reney Cres S8. . . . . 56 D6
Reney Dr S8. . . . . 56 D6
Reney Rd S8. . . . . 56 D6
Reney Wlk S8 . . . . 56 D6
Renfrew St DE21. . . . . . 219 E7
RENISHAW 79 B8
Renishaw Hall & Gdns★
 S21. . . . . 59 F2
Renishaw Prim Sch S21. . 79 B8
Renishaw Rd S43 . . . . . . 79 C4
Renshaw Dr DE11 . . . . . 255 F5
REPTON 242 E2
Repton Ave DE23 . . . . . . 218 D1
Repton Cl S40 . . . . 95 A5
Repton Ct 8 NG19 . . . . . 136 E4
Repton Dr DE7 . . . . 209 B7
Repton Pl S18 . . . . 56 C1
Repton Prep Sch DE65 . . 243 C4
Repton Prim Sch DE65 . . 242 E2
Repton Rd
 Appleby Magna DE12. . . . 265 F5
 Hartshorne DE11. . . . . . 256 F8
 Long Eaton NG10 . . . . . 235 F4
 Newton Solney DE15 . . . 248 F8
 Willington DE65 . . . . . . 242 A5
Repton Sch DE65 . . . . . . 242 C3
Reservoir Hill DE12 . . . . 262 D6
Reservoir Hos DE55 . . . . 146 A5
Reservoir Rd S43 . . . . . . 45 D7
Reservoir Terr S40 . . . . . 95 E4
Reservoir Way 6 DE11 . . 256 B5
Resthaven DE11. . . . . . . 256 B5
Retford Cl DE21 . . . . 205 D2
Revill Cl DE7. . . . . 194 C2
Revill Cres NG9 . . . . 223 F8
Revolution Ho (Mus)★
 S41 . . . . 77 A2
Reynard Cres S21. . . . . . 79 B8
Reynards La SK17. . . . . . 137 E4
Reynolds Ave DE5. . . . . 169 F1
Reynolds Cl S18 . . . . 75 E8
Reynolds Dr SK6 . . . . . . 23 B8
Rhein O' Thorns NG20. . . 120 E5
Rhodes Ave S41 . . . . 95 F5
Rhodes Cotts S43 . . . . . 80 F4
Rhodes Ho DE15 . . . . . . 248 C3
Rhodesia Rd S40. . . . . . 95 C2
Rhodes St SK13 . . . . 10 B5
Rhodes Top SK13 . . . . . . 10 B5
Rhodeswood Dr SK13 . . . 10 A6
Rhuddlan Pl SK23. . . . . . 34 D1
Ribble Cl DE65 . . . . 240 D8
Ribblesdale DE7 . . . . . . 208 C5
Ribblesdale Cl S12 . . . . . 44 C1
Ribblesdale Dr DE22 . . . 204 C2
Ribblesdale Rd NG10. . . 236 A5
RIBER. 143 E3
Riber Ave DE55 . . . . 170 D8
Riber Bank 14 SK13 . . . . 9 E1
Riber Cl
 20 Gamesley SK13 . . . . . . 9 E1
 Long Eaton NG10 . . . . . . 236 D5
 Staveley S43 . . . . 97 C5
 West Hallam DE7. . . . . . 207 E8
Riber Cres S42. . . . . 131 B5
Riber Ct 11 S41 . . . . 95 D5
Riber Fold 18 SK13 . . . . . 9 E1
Riber Gn 19 SK13 . . . . . . 9 E1
Riber Rd
 Lea DE4 . . . . 156 A8
 Matlock DE4. . . . . 143 C2
Riber Terr S40. . . . . 266 A2
Riber View Cl DE4 . . . . . 144 A5
Richard La SK17 . . . . 69 C3
Richards Ct 2 S21. . . . . . 43 B6
Richardson Dr DE7. . . . . 192 F4
Richardson Endowed Prim
 Sch DE7 . . . . 192 F6
Richardsons La DE55. . . 170 C5
Richardson St DE22 . . . . 218 D6
Richards Rd S2 . . . . 43 B6
Richard Wakefield CE Prim
 Sch DE13 . . . . 239 C6
Richmond Ave
 Derby DE23 . . . . 231 C8
 Ilkeston DE7 . . . . 194 F4
 Long Eaton DE72 . . . . . 236 A8
 Sandiacre NG10. . . . . . . 223 A4
 Sheffield S13 . . . . 44 F8
Richmond Cl
 Chesterfield S40 . . . . . . 114 E8
 Derby DE23 . . . . 231 A7
 Glossop SK13. . . . . 10 A5

Richmond CI continued
West Hallam DE7. . . . .**207** D8
Richmond Ct
5 Barrow Hill S43. . . . . . . **78** B3
Repton DE65 . . . .**242** D2
Sheffield S13. . . . . **44** D7
Richmond Dr
Duffield DE56. . . . .**190** D5
Mansfield Woodhouse
NG19. . . . .**136** D2
Richmond Farm Mews
S13. . . . . **44** D7
Richmond Gdns S41 . . . .**266** B4
Richmond Gr S13 . . . . . . **44** E8
Richmond Hall Ave S13 . . **44** D8
Richmond Hall Cres S13. . **44** D7
Richmond Hall Dr S13. . . **44** D7
Richmond Hall Rd S13 . . . **44** D8
Richmond Hall Way S13. . **44** D7
Richmond Hill Ho S13. . . . **44** D7
Richmond Hill Rd S13 . . . **44** D7
Richmond Ho DE65 . . . . .**228** C1
Richmond PI S13 . . . . **44** D7
Richmond Rd
Derby, Chaddesden
DE21. . . . .**219** F6
Derby, Rose Hill DE23 . . . .**219** A1
Sheffield S13 . . . . **44** D7
Richmond Terr SK6 . . . . . **23** B1
Richworth Rd S13. . . . . . . **44** F8
Ricroft SK6 . . . . **15** B3
RIDDINGS
Denstone **196** B4
Somercotes **170** D5
Riddings DE22 . . . .**204** E4
Riddings CI S2. . . . . **44** A7
Riddings Croft S41. . . . . . **95** C6
Riddings Inf Sch DE55. . . .**170** D6
Riddings Jun Sch DE55. . .**170** D6
Riddings La S32 . . . . **72** D4
Riddings St DE22 . . . . . .**218** F3
Riddings Sta★ NG16 . . . .**170** F5
Ridd Way S42. . . . .**115** A3
Ridge Ave SK6 . . . . **23** A4
Ridge CI SK13 . . . .**9** E3
Ridge Cres SK6 . . . . **23** A3
Ridgedale Rd S44. . . . . . .**118** A8
Ridgedale View S16 . . . . .**169** D2
Ridge End Fold SK6. . . . . **23** A2
Ridgehill Ave S12. . . . . . . **44** B5
Ridgehill Gr S12 . . . . **44** B5
Ridge La S23 . . . . **46** E1
Ridge Rd
Eckington S21 . . . . **58** E2
Marple SK6 . . . . **23** A3
Ridge The
Blackwell DE55 . . . .**147** E1
Marple SK6 . . . . **23** A3
Ridge Top La SK22 . . . . . . **25** C2
RIDGEWAY
Bullbridge **168** C4
Sheffield **58** E8
Ridgeway
Chellaston DE73 . . . .**245** A8
Clowne S44 . . . . **80** F2
Dronfield S18. . . . . **57** D3
Heanor DE75 . . . .**193** F8
Shirebrook NG20 . . . .**119** F5
Ridgeway Ave
Bolsover S44 . . . . **99** C2
Derby DE23 . . . .**231** D6
Ridgeway Craft Ctr★ S12. **58** E8
Ridgeway Cres S12. . . . . . **44** A6
Ridgeway Ct DE23. . . . . .**218** D2
Ridgeway Dr
Ilkeston DE7 . . . .**208** B5
Sheffield S12 . . . . **44** A6
Ridgeway Inf Sch DE23. . .**231** D6
Ridgeway La DE56 . . . . . .**168** C4
RIDGEWAY MOOR **58** E7
Ridgeway Moor S12. . . . . **58** E8
Ridgeway Prim Sch S12. . . **58** E8
Ridgeway Rd
Burton upon Trent DE15 . .**254** E7
Sheffield S12. . . . . **44** A5
Ridgeways The SK22 . . . . **25** D2
Ridgeway W S43. . . . . **80** E2
Ridgewood Ct DE21 . . . . .**205** E2
Ridgewood Dr DE4. . . . . .**155** C6
Ridgway The SK12 . . . . . . **32** C6
Riding Bank DE73 . . . . . .**251** F6
Riding Hill Ave NG20 . . . .**119** D3
Ridings Rd SK13 . . . .**9** F5
Ridings The
Mansfield NG19 . . . .**136** F1
Ockbrook DE72 . . . .**221** D5
Rigga La DE56 . . . .**191** B1
Riggotts Way S42. . . . . . . **94** E8
Riggs La DE6 . . . .**212** A7
Rigley Ave **10** DE7. . . . . .**194** F1
Rigsby Ct DE3 . . . .**217** C3
Riley Ave DE55. . . . .**157** D8
Riley Back La S32. . . . . . . **71** E6
Riley La DE5. . . . .**169** A6
Rimsdale CI DE24 . . . . . .**231** E3
Ringer Ct S43. . . . . **80** E3
Ringer La S43 . . . . **80** E3
Ringer Way S43. . . . . **80** E3
RINGINGLOW **42** F4
Ringinglow Rd S10, S11. . **42** E4
Ring-o-Bells La SK12 . . . . **32** D8
Ringstone Way SK23 . . . . . **45** D8
Ringwood Ave
Chesterfield S41. . . . . **95** E7
Compstall SK14 . . . . **15** A8

Ringwood Ave continued
Staveley S43 . . . . **97** C8
Ringwood CI **3** DE21. . . . **219** E8
Ringwood Rd S43. . . . . . . **96** F8
Ringwood View S43. . . . . . **96** F7
Rink Dr DE11 . . . .**256** B3
Rink Sh Ctr DE11 . . . .**256** B4
Rinkway Bsns Pk DE11 . . .**256** B3
RIPLEY. **169** C2
Ripley Ho DE21 . . . .**220** E3
Ripley Hospl DE5. . . . . . .**169** D1
Ripley Inf Sch DE5 . . . . . .**180** D8
Ripley Jun Sch DE5 . . . . .**180** D8
Ripley L Ctr DE5 . . . .**169** D1
Ripley Rd
Bullbridge DE56 . . . .**168** D5
Heage DE56. . . . .**169** A1
Ripon Cres DE21 . . . .**219** E8
Ripon Gdns SK17. . . . . . . **85** D5
Risborrow CI DE65 . . . . .**229** D4
RISE END **154** E3
Rises The SK13. . . . .**9** F5
Rise The
Derby DE22 . . . .**204** E2
Horwich End SK23 . . . . . . **45** C6
Swadlincote DE11 . . . . . .**255** F5
Risings The SK22 . . . . **24** B1
RISLEY **222** E3
Risley Ct DE7 . . . .**194** F3
Risley La DE72 . . . .**222** D2
Risley Lower Gram CE Prim
Sch DE72. . . . .**222** E4
Rivenhall CI DE23 . . . . . .**230** F7
Riverbank DE4. . . . .**110** F1
Riverbank The DE65. . . . .**242** B5
Riverbank Way SK13. . . . . **17** F7
Rivercroft ST14 . . . .**197** A3
River Ct S17. . . . . **56** A7
Riverdale S32. . . . . **72** C7
Riverdale Ct DE15. . . . . . .**248** B5
Rivermead Ho DE1. . . . . .**267** B5
Riversdale DE56 . . . .**168** B4
Riversfield Dr ST14 . . . . .**196** F3
Riverside
Baslow DE45 . . . . **91** D6
Walton-on-Trent DE12. . . .**253** C1
Riverside Bsns Pk DE45 . .**109** C7
Riverside CI
Calver S32 . . . . **72** D1
Glossop SK13. . . . . **10** D1
Riverside Cres
Bakewell DE45. . . . .**109** D6
Holymoorside S42. . . . . . .**113** E7
Riverside Ct
Ambergate DE56 . . . .**167** F3
Baslow DE45 . . . . **91** E6
Calver S32 . . . . **72** D2
Derby DE24 . . . .**219** D4
Riverside Dr
Branston DE14. . . . .**253** F7
Calver S32 . . . . **72** D1
Riverside Rd DE21 . . . . . .**219** D4
Riverside Studios S18. . . . **57** B1
Riverside Way
Bolsover S44 . . . . **98** E2
Mansfield Woodhouse
NG19. . . . .**136** D5
River St DE1 . . . .**267** B4
RIVER'S VALE **84** F7
River View
Aldercar DE55 . . . .**171** A6
Belper DE56 . . . .**190** F7
Chesterfield S40 . . . .**115** A8
Long Eaton NG10 . . . .**236** A3
Longnor SK17 . . . .**121** B6
Tideswell SK17 . . . . **88** D7
Riverview Cotts **2** SK13 . . **17** C7
Rivington Rd **3** NG9 . . . .**223** E2
Rivoli Dr **8** DE11 . . . .**256** E1
Roadmeadow CI DE6. . . .**185** D8
Robert CI S18. . . . . **76** E5
Robert Rd S8. . . . . **57** A7
Roberts Ave NG17. . . . . .**148** F2
Roberts Dr DE55 . . . .**159** B4
Robertson Rd SK17 . . . . . **85** B6
Robertson's Ave S44. . . . . **98** A4
Roberts St DE7 . . . .**209** A6
Robert St DE1. . . . .**267** C4
Robert Sutton RC Sch
DE15. . . . .**255** A7
Robey Dr NG16 . . . .**182** F3
Robian Way DE11 . . . .**256** A4
Robina Dr NG16. . . . .**195** C8
Robincroft S40. . . . .**114** F7
Robincroft Rd S42 . . . . . .**114** D4
Robin Croft Rd DE22 . . . .**204** E4
Robinettes La NG16 . . . . .**195** D1
ROBIN HOOD **92** D5
Robin Hood CI NG16 . . . .**182** F1
Robin Hood PI DE11. . . . .**256** C2
Robin Hood Prim Sch **1**
NG19. . . . .**136** B3
Robin Hood Rd DE4. . . . .**156** C2
Robinia CI DE21. . . . .**206** C3
Robinlands La S33 . . . . . . **38** B4
Robin Rd DE1. . . . .**218** F7
Robins CI DE72 . . . .**233** D5
Robinscross DE7. . . . . . .**221** B1
Robin's Cross La DE65. . .**249** F7
Robinson Ind Est DE23 . .**219** B2
Robinson Rd DE11 . . . . . .**256** A5
Robinson's Hill DE73 . . . .**251** F6
Robinson Way S21. . . . . . **60** C6
Robinwood Lodge **30** SK13 .**9** E1
Robridding Rd S45. . . . . .**129** A4
Robson Ct DE24. . . . .**233** A7
Roby Lea DE74. . . . .**246** F4
ROCESTER. **197** A3

Rocester Way S42 . . . . . .**131** F6
Roche **9** S20. . . . . **59** E8
Rochester CI
Derby DE24 . . . .**233** A5
Long Eaton NG10 . . . .**236** A7
Rochley CI DE21 . . . .**205** F2
Rock Bank
Buxton SK17 . . . . **85** C3
Horwich End SK23. . . . . . . **45** E6
Rockbourne CI DE24 . . . .**233** D6
Rockcliffe CI DE11 . . . . . .**256** B1
Rock Cres S45 . . . .**131** A5
Rockery The DE21. . . . . .**191** E4
Rockfield Rd SK17 . . . . . . **85** D8
Rockford Ct NG9 . . . .**209** E1
Rockhall Terr SK22. . . . . . **25** E2
Rock Ho DE4 . . . .**155** B6
Rock House CI DE55. . . . .**147** F5
Rockhouse Rd DE24. . . . .**233** A6
Rockingham **11** S20. . . . . . **59** E8
Rockingham CI
Chesterfield S40 . . . . **95** C3
Derby DE24 . . . .**205** A4
3 Dronfield S18. . . . . **56** C1
Rock La S44 . . . .**116** E6
Rocklands The NG20 . . . .**119** E4
Rockley CI S40. . . . .**114** F7
Rockley Way NG20 . . . . . .**119** E4
Rockmay Ho DE55 . . . . . .**170** E6
Rock Mill Bsns Pk S32 . . . . **71** E4
Rock Mill La SK22 . . . . . . **33** B7
Rock Side NG16. . . . .**195** F6
Rockside Cotts S43 . . . . . **80** E4
Rockside Hall DE4 . . . . . .**143** C6
Rockside Hydro DE4 . . . .**143** C6
Rockside Steps DE4. . . . .**143** C6
Rockside View DE4 . . . . .**143** C7
Rock Sq S32. . . . . **71** D6
Rock St SK22 . . . . **33** C7
Rocks The DE4. . . . .**144** A5
Rock Terr
Bakewell DE45. . . . .**109** D6
Buxton SK17 . . . . **85** B6
Rock Terr S45. . . . .**109** C6
Rockvale Terr DE4 . . . . . .**143** B1
Rockvale Villas DE4. . . . .**143** B1
Rock View SK17. . . . . **88** A7
Rodge Croft S41. . . . . **77** A3
Rodger's La DE55. . . . . . .**159** A5
Rodknoll La S42 . . . . **93** D2
Rod Moor Rd S17, S18 . . . **56** B4
Rodney CI DE65 . . . .**228** C2
Rodney Ho DE24 . . . .**232** E6
Rodney Way DE7. . . . . . .**194** F3
Rodney Wlk DE23 . . . . . .**230** E7
RODSLEY **200** A5
Rodsley CI S40. . . . . **95** B5
Rodsley Cres DE23 . . . . .**231** D5
Rodsley La
Rodsley DE6. . . . .**199** F7
Yeaveley DE6 . . . .**199** E5
Rodwood Ave S43. . . . . . . **80** A7
Roebuck CI SK23. . . . . **47** B6
Roecar CI S41. . . . . **77** B2
Roe Cross Ind Est SK14 . . . .**9** A5
Roe Cross Rd SK14. . . . . . .**9** A5
Roe Farm La DE21 . . . . . .**219** E7
Roe Farm Prim Sch
DE21. . . . .**219** E8
Roehampton Dr
Derby DE24 . . . .**218** A7
Stapleford NG9 . . . .**209** D2
Roe's Ct S42 . . . .**157** A2
Roe's La DE4 . . . .**157** A1
Roe Wlk DE23 . . . .**219** A1
Rogers Ave S80. . . . . **81** D1
Rogers Ct DE65 . . . .**227** D1
Rolaine CI NG19 . . . .**136** C4
ROLLESTON. **240** A4
Rolleston Cres NG16 . . . .**195** F8
Rolleston Dr NG16 . . . . . .**195** B8
ROLLESTONE **43** D5
Rolleston La DE13. . . . . . .**239** D5
ROLLESTON ON DOVE . .**240** C3
Rolleston Rd DE13 . . . . . .**240** B1
Rollins La SK6 . . . . **15** A1
Roman Bank NG19 . . . . . .**136** D3
Roman Rd DE1. . . . .**219** B7
Roman Way DE72. . . . . . .**221** C1
Romeley Cres S43 . . . . . . **80** D3
Romeley La S43. . . . . **80** B2
Romford Way **4** S43. . . . . **78** B3
Romney Dr S18 . . . . **56** E1
Romney Gdns S2 . . . . **43** B6
Romorantin PI NG10 . . . .**236** E7
Romsley Ct DE3. . . . .**217** D4
Rona CI DE24 . . . .**231** E4
Ronald CI DE23 . . . .**230** E7
Rood La
Clowne S44 . . . . **80** E3
Idridgehay DE56 . . . .**176** F6
Rookery The DE11 . . . . . .**256** F2
Roosevelt Ave
Derby DE21 . . . .**220** B6
Long Eaton NG10. . . . . . .**236** C5
Roost The S32 . . . . **53** A6
Roper Ave DE75. . . . .**193** F7
Roper Hill S10 . . . . **42** D7
Ropewalk Ind Ctr DE7. . .**195** A1
Ropewalk The
Heanor DE75 . . . .**193** F8
Ilkeston DE7 . . . .**195** A1
Stanley Common DE7 . . . .**193** B1
Rosamond Ave S17 . . . . . . **56** A6
Rosamond CI S17. . . . . . . **56** A6
Rosamond Ct S17. . . . . . . **56** A5
Rosamond Dr S17. . . . . . . **56** A6
Rosamond Glade S17 . . . . **56** A6

Rosamond PI S17. . . . . . . **56** A6
Rosamond's Ride DE23. . .**231** D8
Rose Ave
Borrowash DE72 . . . .**221** C1
Burton upon Trent DE13 . .**241** A2
Calow S44 . . . . **97** A3
Clowne S43 . . . . **81** A5
Ilkeston DE7 . . . .**194** E2
Rose Bank SK14 . . . .**9** D5
Roseberry Ct DE21. . . . . .**206** B1
Rose CI DE73. . . . .**232** E1
Rose Cottage Dr NG17. . .**148** F2
Rose Cotts
Bonsall DE4 . . . .**142** C1
Chesterfield S41 . . . . **96** C2
Rose Cres S43 . . . . **79** C4
Rosecroft Gdns DE11. . . .**256** C3
Rose Ct
Clay Cross S45. . . . .**131** A4
Long Eaton NG10 . . . .**223** D8
Rosedale Ave
Chesterfield S40 . . . .**115** B8
Derby DE24 . . . .**233** A6
Rosedale CI NG10. . . . . . .**236** B6
Rosedale View S40. . . . . .**114** B7
Rosedale Way NG19 . . . . .**136** F2
Rosedene View DE12. . . .**262** C4
Rose End Ave S44. . . . . . .**155** A6
Rose Garth CI S41 . . . . . . **96** C1
Rose Gdns S44. . . . . **97** D2
Roseheath CI DE23 . . . . .**231** E5
ROSE HILL **219** B2
Rose Hill
Chesterfield S40 . . . .**266** B3
Sheffield S20. . . . . **59** B8
Woodville DE11 . . . .**256** C5
Rose Hill Ave S20 . . . . **59** B8
Rosehill Bsns Ctr DE23 . .**219** A2
Rose Hill CI S20. . . . . **59** B8
Rosehill Ct S44 . . . . **99** A1
Rose Hill Dr S20 . . . . **59** B8
Rose Hill E S40 . . . .**266** B3
Rosehill Inf Sch DE23 . . .**219** B3
Rose Hill Mews S20 . . . . . **59** B8
Rose Hill St DE23 . . . .**219** A2
Rose Hill View S20. . . . . . **59** B8
Rose Hill W S40. . . . .**266** A3
Rose La
Mansfield Woodhouse
NG19. . . . .**136** C3
Ticknall DE73 . . . .**251** A4
Roseland La NG20. . . . . . .**119** C3
Roseleigh Cres DE11. . . .**255** F6
Rosemary CI **1** S8. . . . . . . **43** A3
Rosemary Dr DE24 . . . . . .**233** A5
ROSEMARYHILL **171** F7
Rosemoor La DE21 . . . . . .**206** B1
Rosemount Ct DE22 . . . . .**204** C3
Rosengrave St DE1. . . . . .**267** B2
Rose Tree La DE11 . . . . . .**255** F7
Rosette CI DE21 . . . .**206** C3
Rose Valley DE11 . . . .**256** A5
Rose Way S21 . . . . **60** D5
Rosewood SK14. . . . .**9** D5
Rosewood CI
Derby DE24 . . . .**233** B7
South Normanton DE55. . .**160** B7
Rose Wood S41 . . . . **95** D8
Rosewood Cres DE75. . . .**182** B2
Rosewood Rd DE15 . . . . .**254** F6
Roseybank SK23 . . . . **34** B1
Rosier Cres DE55 . . . .**170** A8
Rosling Way S44. . . . . **97** D2
ROSLISTON **260** D6
Rosliston CE Prim Sch
DE12. . . . .**260** C6
Rosliston Forestry Ctr★
DE12. . . . .**260** C8
Rosliston Rd
Burton upon Trent DE15 . .**254** D3
Walton-on-Trent DE12. . . .**259** E8
Rosliston Road S DE15 . . .**254** E5
Roslyn Cres S32. . . . . **53** A7
Roslyn Rd S32. . . . . **53** A7
Ross Ct S21 . . . . **60** D4
Rossell Dr NG9 . . . .**223** E5
Rossendale DE7 . . . .**194** E4
Rossendale CI S40 . . . . . .**114** E8
Rosser Ave S12 . . . . **43** F2
Rossington Dr DE23. . . . .**230** F6
Rosslyn Gdns DE24. . . . .**233** A6
Ross Wlk DE21. . . . .**205** E1
ROSTON. **197** E2
Roston CI **3** S18. . . . . **56** D1
Rosyth Cres DE73 . . . . . .**232** E1
Rothay CI S18 . . . . **75** E8
Rothbourne Croft DE6. . .**151** D2
Rothbury Ave NG9 . . . . . .**209** D2
Rothbury PI DE21 . . . . . .**205** E1
Rother Ave S43 . . . . **96** D8
Rother CI S40. . . . .**114** E8
Rother Croft S42 . . . .**131** D8
Rotherham CI S21. . . . . . . **60** F8
Rotherham Rd
Bolsover S44 . . . . **99** E2
Eckington S20, S21. . . . . . **59** F6
Killamarsh S21 . . . . **60** F8
New Houghton NG19. . . . .**134** F7
Scarcliffe S44 . . . .**118** D7
Shirebrook S44, NG19. . . .**118** D5
Spinkhill S43 . . . . **61** D2
Rotherham Road N S20 . . **59** F4
Rotherside Rd S21. . . . . . **59** F4
Rother St S45. . . . .**132** C2
Rothervale Rd S40 . . . . . .**115** A8
Rother Valley Ctry Pk★
S21. . . . . **60** C8
Rother Valley Way S20 . . . **60** B8

Rother Way S41 . . . . **96** B6
Rotherwood Rd S21. . . . . . **60** E7
Rothesay CI DE24 . . . . . .**231** E4
Rothey Gr S40 . . . . **94** F5
Rothwell Ho DE65. . . . . . .**228** D1
Rothwell La DE56 . . . .**179** B4
Rothwell Rd S41 . . . . **96** B6
Rough Heanor Rd DE3 . . .**218** A2
Rough La DE6 . . . .**186** E4
Roughlow La DE6. . . . . . .**183** D1
Roughpiece La DE4 . . . . .**166** D5
Roughton Cl DE3. . . . .**230** D8
Round Hill Cl SK13. . . . .**9** F3
Roundhouse Gall★ DE65 .**226** D4
Roundhouse Rd DE24 . . . .**219** C4
Round Way SK22. . . . . **33** D8
Rouse St S45 . . . .**132** C1
Rousseau Ct DE6. . . . . . .**173** D1
Routh Ave DE74. . . . .**247** B2
Rovings Dr DE21 . . . .**220** F2
Rowallan Way DE73 . . . . .**232** E1
Rowan Ave
Ripley DE5 . . . .**180** D8
Stapleford NG9 . . . .**209** E2
Rowan CI
Creswell S80 . . . . **81** C2
Darley Dale DE4 . . . .**127** B3
Denstone ST14 . . . .**196** D6
Derby, Cherrytree Hill
DE21. . . . .**220** B5
Derby, Sinfin DE24. . . . . .**231** D3
Ilkeston DE7 . . . .**208** F5
Mansfield NG19 . . . .**136** D1
Rowan Croft NG17. . . . . .**148** F4
Rowan Ct ST14 . . . .**196** F4
Rowan Dr
Kilburn DE56 . . . .**192** B8
Selston NG16. . . . .**171** D6
Shirebrook NG20 . . . .**119** D5
Shirland DE55 . . . .**146** D1
Rowan Park CI DE23 . . . .**231** D7
Rowan Prim Sch The S17. . **55** E6
Rowan Rd
Eckington S21 . . . . **59** C1
Mastin Moor S43 . . . . **79** C3
Rowan Tree CI
Ashbourne DE6 . . . .**185** D8
Killamarsh S21 . . . . **60** C5
Rowan Tree Dell S17. . . . . **55** E3
Rowan Tree Rd S21. . . . . . **60** C5
Rowan Wlk SK13. . . . .**9** E4
ROWARTH **24** E7
Rowarth Ave **13** SK13. . . . . .**9** D2
Rowarth Bank **9** SK13. . . . .**9** D2
Rowarth CI **10** SK13 . . . .**9** D2
Rowarth Fold **12** SK13 . . . . .**9** D2
Rowarth Way **11** SK13 . . . . .**9** D2
Rowbury Dr DE15 . . . .**248** B2
Rowdale Cres S12 . . . . . . **44** D5
Rowditch Ave DE22 . . . . .**218** D4
Rowditch Cotts DE1. . . . .**218** D4
Rowditch PI DE22. . . . . . .**218** D4
Rowena CI DE24 . . . .**232** F7
Rowen Ct DE56 . . . .**179** B2
ROWLAND **90** C5
Rowland Ct DE55 . . . .**158** F4
Rowland Rd **3** S2. . . . . . . **43** A8
Rowland St
Alfreton DE55 . . . .**159** A4
Derby DE24 . . . .**232** E6
Rowley CI DE11 . . . .**256** D5
Rowley Ct DE11. . . . .**256** B4
Rowley Gdns DE23 . . . . . .**231** C2
Rowley La DE23. . . . .**231** C2
Rowleys Mill **3** DE1. . . . .**218** E5
ROWSLEY **111** A1
Rowsley Ave
Derby DE23 . . . .**231** D8
Long Eaton NG10 . . . .**236** A5
Rowsley CE Prim Sch
DE4. . . . .**126** F8
Rowsley CI SK13. . . . .**9** E2
Rowsley Cres S43. . . . . . . **97** C8
Rowsley Gn SK13 . . . .**9** E2
Rowsley Gr SK13 . . . .**9** E2
Rowsley Mews SK13 . . . . . .**9** E2
Rowsley South Sta★
DE4. . . . .**127** A4
Rowsley Wlk SK13. . . . .**9** E2
Row The
Great Cubley DE6 . . . . . .**198** E1
Lea DE4 . . . .**156** B8
ROWTHORNE **134** C6
Rowthorne Ave DE55. . . .**170** A8
Rowthorne La S44. . . . . . .**134** B7
Rowthorne Trail Nature
Reserve★ NG17. . . . . . .**134** D3
Rowton Grange Rd SK23. . **47** B5
Roxburgh Ave DE21 . . . . .**219** E7
Roxton Ave **2** S8. . . . . . . **56** F8
Roxton Ct NG16. . . . .**195** F7
Royal App DE73 . . . .**244** F8
Royal Ave NG10. . . . .**223** D1
Royal CI DE72. . . . .**221** B1
Royal Court Bsns Pk S40 . .**266** B3
Royal Croft Dr DE45. . . . . **91** C6
Royal Crown Derby Visitor
Ctr★ **267** C1
Royal Derby Hospl DE23. .**218** B2
Royale CI S21. . . . . **59** E3
Royal Gate DE56 . . . .**179** D3
Royal Gr DE21 . . . .**206** D3
Royal Hill Rd DE21 . . . . . .**220** D6
Royal La DE12 . . . .**262** B4
Royal Oak Ct S43 . . . . **79** D4
Royal Oak PI DE45. . . . . .**109** D5
Royal Rd SK12 . . . . **32** D5

Royal Sch for the Deaf
(Derby) DE22 . . . . **218** D6
Royal Scot Rd DE24 . . . . **219** E2
Royal Way DE24. . . . . **219** E3
Roydon Cl DE3. . . . . **217** C3
Royle Ave SK13 . . . . **10** D1
Royle Bsns Pk DE15 . . . . **254** E3
Royston Cl
  Ashbourne DE6 . . . . **185** C8
  Chesterfield S40 . . . . . . **114** B7
Royston Dr DE56 . . . . . . **179** D5
RTC Bsns Pk DE24 . . . . . . **219** D2
Rubens Cl
  Dronfield S18. . . . . **56** F1
  Marple SK6 . . . . **23** C8
Ruby Ho S8. . . . . **43** B5
Ruby Paddocks NG16. . . . **195** F5
Rudyard Ave DE21 . . . . . . **220** E6
Rufford Cl S40 . . . . **95** E1
Rufford Rd NG19 . . . . **136** E3
Ruffstone Cl DE56. . . . . . **191** C7
Rugby Ave DE55 . . . . **159** C3
Rugby Cl DE14 . . . . **254** C8
Rugby St DE24 . . . . **219** E1
Rugeley Ave NG10 . . . . . . **237** A7
Ruislip Cl NG16 . . . . **195** E7
Rupert Rd DE21 . . . . **220** A7
Rupert St
  Ilkeston DE7 . . . . **195** A1
  Pilsley S45 . . . . **132** B3
Rushcliffe Ave DE21. . . . . **219** F6
Rushcliffe Gdns DE21 . . . **219** F6
Rushdale Ave
  Derby DE23 . . . . **231** D6
  Sheffield S8 . . . . **43** B5
Rushdale Mount **4** S8 . . . **43** A5
Rushdale Rd S8 . . . . **43** B5
Rushdale Terr **3** S8 . . . . **43** A5
Rushen Mount S40. . . . . . **114** F6
Rushes The
  Glossop SK13. . . . . **9** F4
  Mansfield Woodhouse
  NG19 . . . . **136** D5
Rushleigh Ct S17 . . . . **55** D7
Rushley Ave S17 . . . . **55** D8
Rushley Cl S17 . . . . **55** D8
Rushley Dr S17 . . . . **55** D7
Rushley Rd S17 . . . . **55** D7
Rush Leys NG10 . . . . **236** D5
Rushmere S13 . . . . **17** E8
Rushpool Ave NG19 . . . . . **136** D3
Rushpool Cl NG19. . . . . . . **136** F2
Rushton Cl DE13 . . . . **239** C6
Rushton Dr SK6. . . . . **23** A5
Rushup Cl DE22. . . . . **205** A5
Rushup La SK17, SK23. . . . **48** D8
Rushycroft SK14 . . . . **9** A4
Rushy La NG10, DE72. . . . **222** E6
Ruskin Ave NG10 . . . . **236** B5
Ruskin Rd
  Derby DE1 . . . . **218** F7
  Mansfield NG19 . . . . **135** D1
Ruskin Sq S8 . . . . **43** A6
Ruskin Way DE23 . . . . **231** B8
Rusk The S43. . . . . **80** B6
Russell Ct **1** NG10 . . . . . . **223** D1
Russell Gdns S42 . . . . **131** B6
Russell St
  Compstall SK6 . . . . **15** B3
  Derby DE24 . . . . **219** C1
  Long Eaton NG10 . . . . . . **223** D1
  Swadlincote DE11 . . . . . . **256** C3
Russet Cl
  Derby DE21 . . . . **206** B1
  Hatton DE65 . . . . **227** C1
Russet Ct DE23 . . . . **218** E2
Ruston Cl
  Chesterfield S40 . . . . **95** B6
  Swadlincote DE11 . . . . . . **256** B4
Rutherford Rise **8** DE21. **205** F2
Ruthyn Ave S43 . . . . **80** A7
Rutland Ave
  Bolsover S44 . . . . **99** A1
  Borrowash DE72 . . . . **221** C2
  Matlock DE4. . . . . **143** C6
  Ripley DE5 . . . . **181** A7
Rutland Cl DE15 . . . . **254** D6
Rutland Ct
  Ilkeston DE7 . . . . **194** D1
  Matlock DE4. . . . . **143** C6
Rutland Dr DE3 . . . . **217** C3
Rutland Gr NG10 . . . . **223** C5
Rutland Mews DE45 . . . . . **109** C6
Rutland Pl DE56 . . . . **168** B6
Rutland Rd
  Chesterfield S40 . . . . **266** A3
  Westwood NG16 . . . . **171** C4
Rutland Sports Pk DE75 . **208** D8
Rutland Sq DE45 . . . . **109** D6
Rutland St
  Chesterfield S41 . . . . **77** A2
  Derby DE23 . . . . **219** A1
  Ilkeston DE7 . . . . **194** F2
  Matlock DE4. . . . . **143** C6
Rutland Terr
  Barlow S18. . . . . **75** E3
  Ilkeston DE7 . . . . **194** F2
Rutland Way SK23 . . . . **34** D2
Ryal Cl DE72. . . . . **221** C5
Ryan Cl DE24 . . . . **231** E4
Rycroft CE Mid Sch
  ST14. . . . . **196** E4
Rycroft Rd DE24 . . . . **247** D6
Rydal Ave NG10 . . . . **223** B2
Rydal Cl
  Derby DE22 . . . . **204** E4
  Dronfield S18. . . . . **56** D1

Rydal Cres S41 . . . . **95** E8
Rydal Way S45. . . . . **131** B3
Ryde Ho DE24 . . . . **233** C7
Ryder Cl DE11 . . . . **255** C2
Rye Butts DE73 . . . . **232** E1
Rye Cl DE21 . . . . **205** E3
Rye Cres S45 . . . . **131** D3
Ryecroft DE4 . . . . **127** D2
Ryecroft Glen Rd S17 . . . . **56** A8
Ryecroft St NG9 . . . . **223** E8
Ryecroft View S17 . . . . **55** D8
Rye Ct S45 . . . . **131** D3
Ryedale Gdns DE23 . . . . . **231** C5
Ryefield Ave S40 . . . . **194** F5
Rye Flatt La S40 . . . . **95** C2
Rye Flatts La DE65 . . . . . . **227** D1
Ryegrass Cl DE56 . . . . **179** D4
Ryegrass Rd DE21 . . . . . . **206** C2
Ryehill Ave S40 . . . . **95** A2
Ryemere Cl NG16 . . . . **182** E3
Ryemere Ct NG16 . . . . **182** E2
Rykneld Cl DE23 . . . . **230** E6
Rykneld Ct S45 . . . . **131** C3
Rykneld Dr DE23 . . . . **230** F7
Rykneld Prim Sch DE14 . **253** E7
Rykneld Rise S42 . . . . **115** A3
Rykneld Sq S40 . . . . **266** B3
Rykneld Way DE23 . . . . . . **230** E6
Ryknield Hill DE5 . . . . . . **180** B2
Ryknield Rd DE56, DE7 . . **192** B8
RYLAH **117** F5
Rylah Hill S44 . . . . **118** A5
Rymill Dr DE21. . . . . **205** F1
Ryton Way DE65 . . . . **228** D1

S

Sacheveral La DE4 . . . . . . **140** F4
Sacheverall Ave NG16 . . . **160** D3
Sacheverel St DE1 . . . . . . **267** B2
Sackerville Terr S21 . . . . . . **60** B7
Sackville Cl S40 . . . . **114** B8
Sackville St DE23 . . . . **231** F8
Saddlers Cl NG19 . . . . **136** F1
Saddlers Croft S42 . . . . . . **131** F7
Saddletree View S43 . . . . . **79** B4
Saddleworth Wlk DE24 . . **232** E3
Sadler Gate DE1 . . . . **267** B3
Saffron Dr DE21 . . . . **206** A1
Saffron St NG19. . . . . **136** F2
Sage Dr DE11 . . . . **256** F4
Sage Mews S23. . . . . **47** B8
St Agnes Ave DE22 . . . . . . **204** D4
St Aidan's Ave S2 . . . . **43** D8
St Aidan's Dr S2 . . . . **43** E8
St Aidan's Pl S2 . . . . **43** E8
St Aidan's Rd S2 . . . . **43** E8
St Aidan's Rise S2 . . . . **43** E8
St Aidan's Way S2 . . . . **43** E8
St Albans Cl
  Holmewood S42. . . . . **132** E8
  Long Eaton NG10 . . . . . . **236** E5
St Alban's RC Prim Sch
  DE21. . . . . **219** F6
St Albans Rd DE22 . . . . . . **218** D3
St Albans St SK22 . . . . **33** C8
St Alkmund's Cl DE56 . . . **190** E4
St Alkmunds Way DE56 . . **190** E4
St Alkmund's Way DE1. . . **267** B4
St Andrew's CE Jun Sch
  SK13 . . . . **9** F4
St Andrew's CE Methodist
  Prim Sch **5** DE6. . . . . . . **56** D1
St Andrew's CE Prim Sch
  Clifton Campville B79 . . . **263** F2
  Stanley S7 . . . . **207** B5
St Andrews Cl DE55 . . . . . **170** A7
St Andrew's Cl B79 . . . . . . **263** F2
St Andrews Ct
  Glossop SK13. . . . . **10** A4
  Swadlincote DE11 . . . . . . **255** E2
St Andrew's Ct DE7 . . . . . **194** D1
St Andrew's Dr
  Ilkeston DE7 . . . . **208** E8
  Swanwick DE55 . . . . **169** F7
St Andrews Rise S40 . . . . . **114** C8
St Andrews Specl Sch
  DE21. . . . . **205** E1
St Andrews View DE21 . . . **205** E1
St Andrews Wlk SK22 . . . . **33** B8
St Anne's CE Prim Sch
  DE45. . . . . **91** E5
St Anne's Cl
  Baslow DE45 . . . . **91** E5
  Derby DE1 . . . . **218** E6
  Staveley S43 . . . . **97** E8
St Anne's La DE74. . . . . . . **247** B3
St Anne's RC Prim Sch
  SK17. . . . . **66** B1
St Annes St **4** SK14 . . . . . **16** A8
St Anne's Well* SK17 . . . . . **85** B8
St Ann's Cl SK23 . . . . **46** F6
St Anselm's Sch DE45 . . . **109** C6
ST AUGUSTINES **115** B7
St Augustines Ave S40 . . . **115** A8
St Augustines Cres S40 . . **115** A8
St Augustines Dr S40 . . . . **266** B1
St Augustines Mount
  S40. . . . . **266** B1
St Augustines Rd S40 . . . . **115** A8
St Augustines Rise **1**
  S40. . . . . **115** A8
St Augustine St DE23. . . . **218** F1
St Barnabas Ho **12** S2. . . . **43** A8
St Barnabas La **1** S2. . . . . **43** A8
St Barnabas Rd **5** S2 . . . . **43** A8

St Bartholomew's CE Sch
  S17. . . . . **121** B7
St Benedict RC Sch &
  Performing Arts Coll
  DE22. . . . . **204** E1
St Benedicts Ct S2 . . . . **43** D8
St Bride's Wlk DE22 . . . . . **218** B6
St Catherine's Rd DE11 . . **255** F5
St Chad's CE Inf Sch
  DE23. . . . . **218** F2
St Chad's Cl
  Denstone ST14 . . . . **196** D6
  Draycott DE72 . . . . **235** A7
St Chad's Rd DE23 . . . . . . **218** F2
St Chad's Water Nature
  Reserve* DE72 . . . . **235** A4
St Chad's Way S41 . . . . **96** A8
St Charles Cl SK13 . . . . **9** F5
St Charles's RC Prim Sch
  SK13. **9** E5
St Christopher's Way
  DE24. . . . . **219** D3
St Clare's Cl DE23 . . . . . . **218** D2
St Clare's Specl Sch DE3 **218** A2
St Cuthbert's Rd DE22 . . **218** C3
St Davids Cl NG16 . . . . . . **170** F3
St David's Ct DE23 . . . . . . **218** D3
St Davids Rd B79 . . . . **263** F2
St David's Rise S40 . . . . . . **114** D8
St Edmund's Ave NG19 . . **136** C3
St Edmund's CE Prim Sch
  NG19. . . . . **136** C3
St Edmund's Cl DE22 . . . . **204** F4
St Edward's CE Prim Sch
  DE74. . . . . **247** B3
St Edward's RC Prim Sch
  DE11. . . . . **256** B5
St Edward's Rd DE74 . . . . **247** B2
St Elizabeth Cl S2. . . . . **43** B8
St Elizabeth's RC Prim Sch
  DE56. . . . . **178** F5
St George's CE Prim Sch
  New Mills SK22 . . . . **33** C8
  Swadlincote DE11 . . . . . . **256** B1
St George's Ct DE22. . . . . **204** F3
St Georges Dr **3** NG9 . . . **223** F2
St George's Ho DE22 . . . . **204** F3
St George's Pl **1** DE56 . . **178** F4
St George's Prim Sch
  DE23. . . . . **231** C7
St Georges Rd SK22 . . . . . . **33** C8
St Giles CE Prim Sch
  Killamarsh S21 . . . . **60** C6
  Matlock DE4. . . . . **143** C3
St Giles Cl S40 . . . . **115** B8
St Giles Rd DE23 . . . . **218** F1
St Giles Specl Sch DE21 **205** C1
St Giles Wlk DE4 . . . . **143** C4
St Hardulphs CE Prim Sch
  DE73. . . . . **252** F2
St Helens Ave NG16 . . . . . **160** C4
St Helen's Cl
  Chesterfield S41 . . . . **266** B4
  Darley Dale DE4 . . . . **127** B3
  Grindleford S32 . . . . **72** D8
St Helen's Cres NG9. . . . . **209** C4
St Helen's Croft S32 . . . . . **72** D8
St Helen's Dr NG16. . . . . . **171** D7
St Helen's La DE4 . . . . **166** A7
St Helen's St
  Chesterfield S41 . . . . **266** B4
  Derby DE1 . . . . **267** A4
St Hugh's Cl DE22. . . . . . . **205** A2
St James Ave DE7. . . . . . . **209** A7
St James' CE Inf Sch
  DE23. . . . . **267** C1
St Jame's CE Jun Sch
  DE23. . . . . **219** B3
St James' CE Prim Sch **7**
  SK13. . . . . **17** B8
St James Cl
  Belper DE56. . . . . **179** D4
  Chesterfield S41. . . . . **96** C1 **2**
  Glossop SK13. . . . . **17** C7
  Willington DE65 . . . . **242** C8
St James Ct
  Ashbourne DE6 . . . . **173** D3
  Sandiacre NG10. . . . . **223** B3
St James' Dr NG16 . . . . . . **182** D8
St James Gdns NG19 . . . . **136** E6
St James' Rd DE23 . . . . . . **218** F1
St James's Ct SK17. . . . . . . **85** C3
St James Sq S40 . . . . **266** B3
St James' Sq SK22 . . . . **33** C8
St James's St **3** NG9. . . . **223** C6
St James's St
  14 Buxton SK17. . . . . **85** B7
  Derby DE1 . . . . **267** B3
  Derby, Rose Hill DE23 . . . **219** A1
St James' Terr SK17. . . . . . **85** B7
St John Fisher RC Prim Sch
  DE24. . . . . **233** C8
St John Houghton RC Sch
  DE7 . . . . **208** C6
St John's **4** SK17. . . . . **85** A7
St John's Ave DE21 . . . . . . **220** B5
St John's CE Prim Sch
  Belper DE56. . . . . **179** B5
  Ripley DE5 . . . . **169** F1
  Stapleford NG9 . . . . **223** E7
St Johns Cl
  Bamford S33 . . . . **40** B3
  Chesterfield S40 . . . . **114** B7
  Ripley DE5. . . . . **169** F2
St John's Cl
  Brinsley NG16 . . . . **171** D1
  Derby DE22 . . . . **204** D3

St John's Cres S43 . . . . **80** F3
St John's Dr
  Derby DE1 . . . . **220** B5
  Kilburn DE56 . . . . **192** A8
  Swadlincote DE11 . . . . . . **255** E5
St John's Mount S41. . . . . **95** F8
St Johns Rd S43 . . . . **78** D1
St John's Rd
  Belper DE56. . . . . **179** A4
  Buxton SK17 . . . . **85** A7
  Chesterfield S41 . . . . **95** F8
  Dronfield S18. . . . . **76** E7
  Ilkeston DE7 . . . . **209** A7
  Matlock Bath DE4 . . . . . . **143** B3
  Smalley DE7 . . . . **192** F5
  Tideswell SK17 . . . . **69** C4
St Johns Road Bsns Ctr
  S41. **95** F8
St John's St
  Long Eaton NG10 . . . . . . **236** D7
  Wirksworth DE4 . . . . **165** F8
St John St SK22 . . . . **25** D2
St John's Terr DE1 . . . . . . **218** F6
St Joseph's RC & CE Prim
  Sch S43 . . . . **97** D2
St Joseph's RC Prim Sch
  Derby DE23 . . . . **267** A1
  Matlock DE4. . . . . **143** D6
  Shirebrook NG20 . . . . . . **119** F5
St Joseph's St DE4 . . . . . . **143** C5
St Katherines Cl DE4 . . . . **110** E1
St Katherine's Ct DE22 . . **218** D6
St Laurence CE Prim Sch
  NG10. . . . . **236** E6
St Laurence Ct NG10 . . . . **236** E6
St Laurence Gdns **10**
  DE56. . . . . **178** F4
St Lawrence Ave S44. . . . . **118** C8
St Lawrence Cl DE75 . . . . **181** F2
St Lawrence Rd S42 . . . . . **131** C6
St Lawrence View S80 . . . . **81** F5
St Leonards Dr S41 . . . . . . **96** C1
St Leonards Pl DE55. . . . . **146** E1
ST LUKE'S **218** E3
St Luke's CE Prim Sch
  Glossop SK13. . . . . **10** C1
  Shireoaks S81 . . . . **63** F7
St Lukes Ct **27** S41 . . . . . . **95** F8
St Lukes View S81 . . . . **63** F7
St Margaret's Dr S40 . . . . **266** A3
St Margaret's RC Prim Sch
  SK13. . . . . **16** D8
St Marks Cl DE4 . . . . **155** A6
St Mark's Rd
  Chesterfield S40 . . . . **95** E3
  Derby DE1 . . . . **219** D6
St Martin's Cl S41. . . . . **95** D6
St Martins Dr DE55 . . . . . **158** F4
St Martin's Rd SK6. . . . . . . **23** A6
St Martin's Specl Sch
  DE24. . . . . **232** F8
St Martin's Wlk S80. . . . . . **82** C6
St Mary & All Saints Church
  (Crooked Spire)* S40. . **266** B3
St Mary's Ave DE7 . . . . . . **235** A7
St Mary's CE Fst Sch **4**
  ST14 . . . . **210** B1
St Mary's Cl
  Chinley SK23 . . . . **34** E2
  Derby DE24 . . . . **233** A6
  Newton Solney DE15 . . . **248** E8
St Mary's Cres ST14 . . . . . **210** B1
St Mary's Ct
  Derby DE1 . . . . **267** B4
  Hollingworth SK14. . . . . . . **9** C1
St Mary's Dr DE13 . . . . . . **240** F2
St Mary's Gate
  Chesterfield S41 . . . . **266** C3
  Derby DE1 . . . . **267** B3
  4 Wirksworth DE4 . . . . **165** F8
St Mary's Pl S41 . . . . **266** C3
St Mary's RC High Sch
  S41 . . . . **95** C7
St Mary's RC Prim Sch
  Chesterfield S40 . . . . **266** A4
  Derby, Darley Abbey DE22. **204** F1
  Glossop SK13. . . . . **17** D8
  Marple SK6 . . . . **23** B7
  New Mills SK22 . . . . **33** B8
St Mary's Rd
  Disley SK12 . . . . **32** D5
  Glossop SK13. . . . . **17** C8
  New Mills SK22 . . . . **33** B8
St Mary St DE7. . . . . **208** E8
St Mary's View DE4 . . . . . **142** B7
St Marys Wharf Rd DE1. . **219** B7
St Mary's Wlk NG16 . . . . . **171** B3
St Matthew's Cl S21. . . . . . **60** B1
St Matthew's St S41 . . . . . **254** C8
St Matthew's Wlk **4**
  DE22. . . . . **204** F2
St Mawes Cl DE22 . . . . . . **204** D4
St Mellion Cl DE3 . . . . **217** F1
St Michael's CE Prim Sch
  S32. **53** A8
St Michaels Cl
  Crich DE4. . . . . **156** F2
  Derby DE24 . . . . **233** C7
St Michael's Cl
  Holbrook DE56. . . . . **191** C6
  Shirley DE6 . . . . **200** D8
  Willington DE65 . . . . **242** B5
St Michael's Dr
  Appleby Magna DE12. . . . **265** F1
  South Normanton DE55. . **160** A7
St Michael's La DE1 . . . . . **267** B4

St Michaels View
  Derby DE24 . . . . **233** C7
  Selston NG16 . . . . **171** F5
St Nicholas Cl DE22 . . . . . **204** D2
St Nicholas Pl DE1 . . . . . . **267** A5
St Norbert Dr DE7 . . . . . . **208** D4
St Oswald Cres DE6 . . . . . **173** C1
St Oswald's CE Inf Sch
  DE6 . . . . **173** B1
St Oswald's Hospl DE6 . . **173** A1
St Pancras Way DE1 . . . . . **267** C5
St Pauls Ave S41. . . . . **115** D6
St Pauls Ct NG16 . . . . **195** F6
St Paul's Rd DE1 . . . . **219** A7
St Peter & St Paul Sch
  S41 . . . . **96** D3
St Peter's CE Fst Sch
  ST14 . . . . **224** F2
St Peter's CE Jun Sch
  DE23. . . . . **218** C1
St Peter's CE Prim Sch
  DE12. . . . . **264** F6
St Peter's Churchyard
  DE1 . . . . **267** B3
St Peters Cl S44 . . . . **98** A4
St Peter's Cl DE56. . . . . . . **179** A4
St Peters Croft DE56 . . . . **179** A4
St Peters Ct DE24 . . . . . . **233** A8
St Peter's Rd
  Buxton SK17 . . . . **66** D1
  Chellaston DE73 . . . . **233** A1
  Thorpe Salvin S80 . . . . . . **62** E7
St Peter's St DE1 . . . . **267** B3
St Peter's Way DE1 . . . . . **267** B2
St Philip Howard RC Sch **6**
  SK13. . . . . **17** B8
St Philip's Dr S41 . . . . **115** B8
St Quentin Cl
  Derby DE22 . . . . **218** C3
  Sheffield S17 . . . . **56** B5
St Quentin Dr S17. . . . . . . **56** B5
St Quentin Mount S17. . . . **56** B5
St Quentin Rise S17. . . . . . **56** B5
St Quentin View S17 . . . . . **56** B5
St Ronan's Ave DE56 . . . . **190** E2
St Stephens Cl DE72 . . . . **221** B1
St Stephen's Ct DE23 . . . . **231** D6
St Stephen's Ct DE11. . . . **256** E2
St Swithin's Cl DE22. . . . . **218** D3
St Swithuns Ct DE56 . . . . **179** A2
St Theresa's RC Prim Sch
  S2. . . . . **44** B7
St Thomas Cl DE55. . . . . . **147** E5
St Thomas More RC Sch
  SK17. . . . . **85** B8
St Thomas of Canterbury RC
  Prim Sch **5** S8. . . . . **56** F8
St Thomas Rd DE23 . . . . . **219** A1
St Thomas' St S40 . . . . **95** C2
St Vincent Cl NG10. . . . . . **236** E6
St Werburgh's CE Prim Sch
  Derby DE21 . . . . **220** D5
  Hanbury DE13 . . . . **238** A4
St Werburgh's View
  DE21. . . . . **220** D5
St Wilfrid's Rd
  11 Sheffield S2 . . . . **43** A8
  West Hallam DE7 . . . . **207** E8
St Wystan's Rd DE22 . . . . **218** C3
St Wystans Sch DE65. . . . **242** C2
Salcey Cl DE55. . . . . **169** F7
Salcey Dr NG9 . . . . **209** D2
Salcey Sq S40 . . . . **95** D1
Salcombe Ct **12** S41. . . . . **159** C5
Salcombe Rd DE55 . . . . . . **159** C5
Salcombe Rd Ind Units
  DE55. . . . . **159** C5
Sale & Davys CE Prim Sch
  DE73. . . . . **244** A6
Sales Ave S42 . . . . **131** C8
Sale La DE15. . . . . **248** C4
Sale St DE23 . . . . **219** B2
Salestune Mews NG16. . . **171** F6
Salford Way DE11. . . . . . . **255** E2
Salisbury Ave
  Burton upon Trent DE15 . **248** A3
  Chesterfield S41 . . . . **95** E7
  Dronfield S18. . . . . **76** A7
Salisbury Cl NG19 . . . . . . **136** D4
Salisbury Cres S41. . . . . . . **95** F7
Salisbury Dr
  Belper DE56. . . . . **179** D5
  Swadlincote DE11 . . . . . . **256** C5
Salisbury Ho SK17 . . . . **85** C7
Salisbury La DE73. . . . . . . **252** B7
Salisbury Rd S18. . . . . **76** B8
Salisbury St
  Derby DE23 . . . . **267** B1
  Glossop SK13. . . . . **10** A5
  Long Eaton NG10 . . . . . . **236** E7
Sallyfield La DE6. . . . . **183** E8
Sallywood Cl DE24 . . . . . . **231** D2
Saltburn Cl DE21. . . . . . . **205** C1
Salter Cl DE74 . . . . **246** F4
Saltergate S40. . . . . **266** B3
Saltergate La S33. . . . . **40** B2
Salters La DE4 . . . . **142** F4
Salvin Cres S43 . . . . **80** E4
Samantha Ct DE21 . . . . . **206** B1
Sampson's La NG19. . . . . . **135** B3
Sampsons Yd NG17 . . . . . . **148** F3
Samuel Cl S2. . . . . **43** D7
Samuel Ct DE5. . . . . **180** D8

Samuel Dr S2............43 D7
Samuel Pl S2............43 D7
Samuel Rd S2............43 D8
Samuel St S14...........9 C4
Sancroft Ave DE21.....220 E6
Sancroft Rd DE21......220 F6
Sanctuary Nature Reserve
The★ DE24............219 E3
Sandalwood La DE24....233 C7
Sandalwood Rd DE15...254 E6
Sandbach Cl DE21......206 A1
Sandbed La DE56.......179 C2
Sandby Croft S14........43 E2
Sandby Ct S14...........43 E2
Sandby Dr
Marple SK6............23 B8
Sheffield S14............43 E2
Sandcliffe Pk DE11.....256 D7
Sandcliffe Rd DE11.....256 D6
Sandcroft Cl DE11......256 D5
Sanderling Heath DE3...230 B7
Sanderling Way NG19...136 E2
Sanderman Ho DE11....256 E3
Sanders Cl DE7........194 C2
Sanderson Rd DE21....220 B6
Sandfield Cl DE21......220 B8
Sandfield Rd **1** NG9...223 E2
Sandford Ave NG10....236 E7
Sandford Brook DE65...228 E1
Sandgate Ave NG19....136 D4
Sandgate Cl DE24......233 A6
Sandgate Rd NG19.....136 D4
Sandhall La DE56......166 F5
Sandham La DE5.......169 C1
Sandhill La
Broadbottom SK6.......16 A2
Marple SK6............15 E1
Sandhills Rd S44........99 C1
SANDIACRE............223 A6
Sandiacre Friesland Sp Ctr
NG10................222 F5
Sandiacre Rd NG9......223 C6
Sandiway
Chesterfield S40.......114 C8
Glossop SK13..........17 F7
Sand La DE6...........211 B1
Sandlands The DE11....256 D6
Sandlands Way NG19...136 F2
Sandown Ave DE3.......217 C3
Sandown Cl
Burton upon Trent DE14..254 A7
Eckington S21..........59 B2
Sandown Rd
Beeston NG9..........223 F2
Derby DE24...........232 E8
Sandpiper La DE3......230 B6
Sandringham Ave DE15..248 A1
Sandringham Cl
Calow S44.............97 A4
5 Chesterfield S41....96 A8
Swadlincote DE11......256 B5
Sandringham Ct
13 Buxton SK17........85 B7
Mansfield Woodhouse
NG19................136 B6
Sandringham Dr
Derby DE21...........220 F5
Heanor DE75..........181 C2
Mansfield Woodhouse
NG19................136 B6
Sandringham Ho DE24..219 D1
Sandringham Pl
Ilkeston DE7..........208 D5
Sheffield S10...........42 F8
Sandringham Rd
Calow S44.............97 A4
Derby DE21...........205 E1
Mansfield Woodhouse
NG19................136 E5
Sandiacre NG10.......223 B4
Sands Cl S14............43 E4
Sandstone Ave S40....114 B8
Sandwell Cl NG10......236 A6
Sandwood Cl DE55....148 A3
Sandybank Cl SK13........9 E4
Sandybrook Cl DE6.....173 C4
Sandybrook Country Pk
DE6.................173 B5
Sandybrook Hall DE6...173 B5
Sandy Cl S80...........81 F5
Sandycliffe Cl NG19....136 F1
Sandyford La DE56.....166 F4
Sandyhill Cl DE73......233 A2
Sandy La
Broadbottom SK13......16 A4
Caldwell DE12.........261 A8
Chinley SK23...........35 B3
Crich DE4.............167 F8
Farley DE4............128 D1
Horsley DE21, DE7......192 A3
Matlock DE4...........143 D8
Whitwell S80...........81 F5
Sandypits La DE65.....229 C4
Sanforth St S41.........96 A6
Sankey Dr DE11.......256 C1
Santolina Dr DE21.....205 F1
SAPPERTON...........213 C1
Sapperton Cl DE23.....231 D5
Sapperton field La DE6,
DE65................213 D3
Sapperton La DE6......213 E1
Sapphire Dr DE5.......180 B2
Sarah Cl DE55.........170 C7
Sark Rd S2.............43 A7
Saundby Ave NG19....135 D1

Saundersfoot Way DE21.206 C2
Savage La S17...........55 D7
Save Penny La DE56....191 A5
Saville Cl NG9.........223 E8
Saville House Sch **2**
NG19................136 B3
Savoy The **2** SK17......85 B7
SAWLEY..............236 A4
Sawley Inf Sch NG10....236 A5
Sawley Jun Sch NG10...236 A5
Sawley Rd
Breaston DE72.........235 E6
Draycott DE72.........235 B7
Sawmand Cl NG10......236 C6
Sawmills Ind Pk DE75...181 D3
Saw Pit Ind Est DE55...148 C6
Sawpit La DE65.........227 C2
Saw Pit La DE55.......148 B5
Saxon Cl
Breedon on the Hill DE73..252 F2
Burton upon Trent DE15..254 F7
Saxon Croft DE65......242 D3
Saxondale Ave DE3.....217 C4
Saxon Gr DE65.........242 A5
Saxon Rd S2............43 A6
Saxon St DE15.........254 F7
Saxton Ave DE75......181 F2
Saxton Cl S41.........115 C8
Scaddows La DE73.....250 D4
Scalby Cl NG16........182 D2
Scaliot Cl SK22.........33 B8
Scalpcliffe Rd DE15....248 A2
Scarborough Ave DE7...208 E8
Scarborough Rise DE21.205 D1
SCARCLIFFE..........118 E6
Scarcliffe Cl DE24......232 E3
Scarcliffe Lanes DE21...119 C7
Scarcliffe Prim Sch S44.118 F6
Scarcliffe Terr NG20....101 A2
Scargill CE Prim Sch
DE7.................207 D7
Scargill Rd DE7........207 E8
Scargill Wlk NG16.....182 F3
Scarsdale Ave
Derby, Allestree DE22....204 D3
Derby, Littleover DE23...218 C2
Scarsdale Cl S18.........76 B8
Scarsdale Cres S43......96 D7
Scarsdale Cross **1** S18....58 B7
Scarsdale Pl **8** SK17......85 B7
Scarsdale Rd
2 Chesterfield S41.....96 A8
2 Dronfield S18........57 B1
Duffield DE56........190 E3
Scarsdale St S44.......117 E8
Scarthin DE4..........155 A6
Schofield Ct DE4.......110 F1
Sch of Nursing (Univ of
Nottingham) DE1......267 C2
School Ave S20..........59 F7
School Board La S40.....95 E3
School Cl
Blackwell DE55........147 C1
Darley Dale DE4.......127 C3
Fenny Bentley DE6.....162 A1
Glossop SK13............9 E5
Moira DE11...........256 C1
Newton DE55.........148 B3
Sheffield S20...........59 F7
Shirland DE55.........146 D2
Stonebroom DE55.....146 F4
School Croft S45.......170 D6
Schoolfield Cl S44......99 C1
School House Hill DE56.168 D1
School La
Arkwright Town S44.....97 D3
Ashbourne DE6........173 B1
Baslow DE45...........91 E5
Beeley DE4...........111 B4
Brackenfield DE55.....145 C2
Castle Donington DE74..247 A4
Chellaston DE73.......233 A2
Compstall SK6.........15 B4
Crich DE4............157 A1
Dronfield S18...........57 A1
Eckington S21..........58 E3
Hassop DE45...........91 A5
Hathersage S32.........53 A8
Heage DE56...........168 D2
Hope Valley S33........39 A3
Mansfield Woodhouse
NG19................136 C3
Old Brampton S42......93 F3
Over Haddon DE45....109 B1
Ripley DE5...........169 D1
Rolleston DE13........240 A3
Rowsley DE4..........126 F8
Sheffield, Greenhill S8...56 F7
Sheffield S8............43 C1
South Normanton DE55..160 B4
Stanton-by-Dale DE7,
NG10................222 F8
Stanton in Peak DE4....126 C5
Sudbury DE6.........225 E4
Taddington SK17........87 F3
School Lane Cl S8.......43 C1
School Piece La DE65...227 F7
School Rd
Buxton SK17...........67 B5
Chesterfield S41........96 A7
Matlock DE4...........143 D5
Uttoxeter ST14........210 A1
School Sq DE7.........207 E7
School St
Eckington S21..........59 D3
Moira DE12...........262 F2
Sheffield, Mosborough S20..59 D7
Swadlincote DE11......256 B2

School Woods Cl DE75..194 A6
School Yd The S41......267 B4
Scotches The DE56.....178 F5
Scotia Cl S2............43 F8
Scotia Dr S2............43 F8
Scotland St S80........81 F6
Scotswood Rd NG19....136 B6
Scott Cl S42..........115 C3
Scott Cres DE55.......146 F3
Scott Dr
Belper DE56..........179 E5
Marple SK6............23 B8
Somercotes DE55......170 D8
Scott St S23..........218 F1
Scotty Brook Cres SK13...17 E8
Scowerdons Cl S12......44 F5
Scowerdons Dr S12......44 F5
Scratta La S80..........63 C2
Screetham La DE4.....112 C1
SCROPTON............226 E1
Scropton Old Rd DE65..239 C8
Scropton Rd DE65......239 B8
Scropton Wlk DE24.....232 E3
Sea Breeze Terr S13......44 D8
Seaburn Rd NG9.......223 E2
Seagrave Ave S12.......44 B4
Seagrave Cl DE21......220 B8
Seagrave Cres S12......44 B4
Seagrave Dr
Chesterfield S41.......115 C7
Sheffield S12...........44 B4
Seagrave Rd S12.........44 B4
Seale St DE1..........267 B5
Sealey Cl DE65.......242 C5
Seals Rd DE12.........262 E1
Seal View DE12........261 C6
Sealwood La DE12.....261 F5
Seal Wood La DE12....261 E4
Seamer Rd NG16......195 F7
Seanor La S45.........132 B4
Searl St DE1..........218 F6
Searson Ave S44.........99 A1
Searston Ave S44......132 D8
Seascale Cl **5** DE21....205 D1
Seaton Cl DE3.........217 C3
Seaton St **9** S41........95 F8
Sebastian Cl SK6........23 B7
Second Ave
Branston DE14........253 E8
Chellaston DE73.......245 A8
Risley DE72...........222 F5
Sedbergh Cres S41......95 D8
Sedgebrook Cl **2** DE21..205 F2
Sedgebrook St NG19....136 E3
Sedgefield Gn DE3.....217 C1
Sedgefield Rd
Branston DE14........253 F7
Burton upon Trent DE14..254 A8
Sedgemoor Cl S40......95 B4
Sedgemoor Rd NG10...236 E5
Sedgemoor Way DE23..231 A5
Sedgwick Cl NG16.....160 D2
Sedgwick St
Jacksdale NG16.......171 B3
Langley Mill NG16.....182 B3
Sefton Ave NG9.......223 E8
Sefton Cl DE15........248 B1
Sefton Rd DE21.......219 F6
Sefton St S13..........17 C8
Sefton Way DE56......190 D4
Selborne St DE24......219 D2
Selby Cl
Beeston NG9..........223 E3
Chesterfield S40.......114 C8
Selhurst Rd S41.........95 F5
Selig Par S12...........44 C2
Selina Cl DE74........247 A4
Selina St DE73........252 A7
Selkirk St DE21.......219 E7
Selly Oak Gr S8.........57 C6
Selly Oak Rd S8.........57 C6
Selmer Ct S43..........96 D8
SELSTON.............171 E7
Selston Arts & Com Coll
NG16................171 F7
Selston CE Inf Sch NG16.171 E6
SELSTON GREEN.....171 D7
Selston La S12 NG16.....171 F7
Selston Rd NG16......171 B5
Selworthy Cl DE21.....206 A2
Selwyn St
Bolsover S44..........118 C8
Derby DE22...........218 C6
Senners La SK17........87 A2
Sepycoe La DE6........214 D7
Serina Ave DE23......231 D8
Serlby Dr S26...........61 F5
Serlby La S26...........61 F6
Serpentine Wlk S8.......57 B8
Setcup La S21..........59 D2
Sett Cl SK22...........33 B8
Settlement The DE72....221 C5
Setts Way S42.........115 B4
Sevenlands Dr DE24....233 C4
Sevenoaks Ave DE22...217 F6
Seven Oaks Rd DE7....209 A1
Severals NG9.........223 F7
Severale Cl DE22......205 B5
Severn Cl DE13........240 C1
Severn Cres S42.......132 A5
Severn Dr DE65.......240 D8
Severn Sq DE55.......159 A4
Severn St DE24........232 F8
Sewell Rd S20..........59 F6
Sexton St SK13..........9 F7
Seymour Cl
Derby DE22...........218 C5

Seymour Cl continued
Ilkeston DE7..........194 F5
Seymour La S43.........79 C1
Seymour Rd NG16.....182 F1
SHACKLECROSS......221 D1
Shacklecross Cl DE72...221 C1
Shady Gr DE65........228 C2
Shaef Cl DE65........228 E2
Shaftesbury Ave
Chesterfield S40........95 D3
Long Eaton NG10......236 B4
Mansfield NG19........135 E2
Sandiacre NG10.......223 A5
Shaftesbury Cres DE23..219 B1
Shaftesbury Sp Ctr DE23 219 B1
Shaftesbury St DE23....219 B2
Shaftesbury Street S
DE23................219 B1
Shafton Cl S45........131 E4
Shafton Wlk S45......131 E4
Shakespeare Ave
Creswell S80...........81 D1
Mansfield Woodhouse
NG19................136 B4
Shirland DE55........146 C4
Shakespeare Cl
Clay Cross S42........131 B6
Repton DE65.........242 D1
Swadlincote DE11......256 C6
Shakespeare Cres S18...76 C7
Shakespeare Ct **4** DE6..173 B2
Shakespeare Dr DE55..159 B4
Shakespeare Mdws
DE65................242 D1
Shakespeare Rd NG16..195 C5
Shakespeare St
Derby DE24...........232 A5
Grassmoor S42........115 E3
Holmewood S42.......116 D1
Long Eaton NG10......223 D1
Shaldon Dr DE23......218 D1
Shalfleet Dr DE24......233 C5
Shallcross Ave SK23.....45 F4
Shallcross Cres
High Peak SK23........45 E4
Horwich End SK23......45 E4
Shallcross Hall Barns
SK23................45 E4
Shallcross Mill Rd SK23..45 E5
Shallcross Rd SK23......45 E4
Shambles The S40......266 B3
Shamrock Pl S43........79 C4
Shamrock St DE23.....218 E1
Shandwick Ct **10** DE24..231 D3
Shanklin Dr NG9......223 D7
Shanklin Ho DE24......233 C7
Shannon Cl DE23......231 D6
Shannon Ho DE24......232 E5
Shannon Sq DE21......220 B4
Shap Cl **7** S40..........95 C5
SHARDLOW..........234 E2
Shardlow Bsns Pk DE72.234 D1
Shardlow Her Ctr★
DE72................235 A1
Shardlow Prim Sch
DE72................234 E2
Shardlow Rd
Aston-on-Trent DE72...246 B7
Derby DE24, DE74.....233 C6
Sharley Park Com Prim Sch
S45.................131 E3
Sharley Pk L Ctr S45...131 D4
Sharman Cl S18.........58 A1
Sharman Wlk S18.......58 A1
Sharp Cl
Ilkeston DE7..........208 C6
Long Eaton NG10......236 C6
Sharpe Ave S8..........56 E8
Sharpes Ind Est DE11...256 B4
Sharpe's Pottery Mus★
DE11................256 B4
Sharpswood Manor
DE11................256 E4
Sharrard Cl S12.........44 B5
Sharrard Dr S12.........44 B5
Sharrard Rd S12.........44 B6
SHATTON............39 F1
Shatton La
Bamford S33...........40 A1
Thornhill S32, S33......51 E7
Shawcroft **8** DE6......173 C2
Shawcroft Ave DE55...170 C5
Shawfield Rd SK13.......9 F3
Shaw La
Belper DE56..........191 B7
Glossop SK13...........9 F3
Holloway DE4.........156 C8
Marston Montgomery DE6 198 A1
Shaws Gn DE22.......218 D6
Shaws Hill DE4........156 D1
Shaw's Row S40........95 D2
Shaw St
Chesterfield S41........96 A8
Derby DE22...........218 E6
Dronfield S18..........57 C4
Glossop SK13..........17 C8
Holmewood S42.......116 D1
Shaw Street E DE7....209 A6
Shaw Street W DE7....209 A6
Shaw's Yd DE56.......191 F8
Shaw The SK13.........10 A3
Shaw Wood Cl DE55...157 F3
Shaw Wood View DE55..157 F3
Sheaf Bank S2..........43 A7

Sheaf Bank Bsns Pk S2..43 A7
Sheardhall Ave SK12....32 E5
Sheards Cl S18.........56 F1
Sheards Dr S18.........56 F1
Sheards Way S18........56 F1
Shearsby Dr NG19.....136 F2
Shearwater Cl DE23....231 D7
SHEEN...............137 A7
SHEEPBRIDGE.........76 E2
Sheepbridge Bsns Ctr
S41.................76 E2
Sheepbridge La S41.....76 E2
Sheepcote Hill S21......60 D6
Sheepcote Rd S21.......60 C6
Sheephill Rd S17.......42 F1
Sheep La DE55........158 C8
Sheeplea La S45......129 E8
Sheepwash La S45.....145 D3
Sheets Stores Ind Est
NG10................236 D5
SHEFFIELD............44 D6
Sheffield Coll (Norton Coll)
The S8...............57 B7
Sheffield Pl DE1.......267 D2
Sheffield Rd
Baslow DE45...........92 B7
Chapel-en-le-Frith SK23...47 E7
Chesterfield S41........96 A6
Creswell S80, S43......81 D3
Dronfield S18...........56 F3
Eckington S20, S21......59 C5
Glossop SK13..........10 F1
Hathersage S32.........53 A7
Killamarsh S21.........60 D7
Renishaw S21, S43......79 D8
Sheffield S20...........44 F2
Unstone S18, S41.......76 A4
Sheffield Springs Acad
S2..................43 F6
Sheffield Transport Sports
Club S8..............56 F7
Shelden Cl **4** SK13.......9 D1
Shelden Fold **3** SK13.....9 D1
Shelden Mews SK13......9 D1
Shelden Pl **5** SK13.......9 D1
SHELDON............108 A6
Shelden Cl NG10......223 B3
Sheldon Ct DE24......232 E3
Sheldon Gdns DE4....156 F1
Sheldon Rd
Buxton SK17...........85 D7
Chesterfield S40........95 B5
Heanor DE75.........181 C5
Shelford Cl DE3.......217 C3
Shelford La DE4......156 B7
Shelley Ave NG19.....136 B4
Shelley Dr
Derby DE24...........232 A5
Dronfield S18..........76 D1
Shelley Gr DE55......146 F3
Shelley Rd DE11......256 C5
Shelley St S42........116 D1
Shelmory Cl DE24.....232 E5
Shelton Cl NG19......135 E1
Shelton Dr DE24......232 F3
Shelton Gate Cl DE24..232 E4
Shelton Jun & Inf Schs
DE24................232 E4
SHELTON LOCK......232 F3
Shenington Way DE21..206 B2
Shepherd's La DE73....251 D6
Shepherd St DE23.....218 C1
Shepley St
Chesterfield S40........95 D2
Glossop SK13..........10 F2
Hadfield SK13...........9 E3
Shepley's Yd S40......266 B3
Shepton Cl DE7.......194 C3
Sheraton Way SK17.....66 B1
Sherbourne Ave S41....95 E8
Sherbourne Dr
Belper DE56..........179 B5
Burton upon Trent DE14..254 A7
Hilton DE65..........228 C1
Sherbrooke Rd SK12....32 E5
Sherbrook Gr SK17......85 C5
Sheridan Ct NG9......209 F1
Sheridan St DE24......231 F5
Sheriff Dr DE4........143 B6
Sherman Cl DE65......228 C2
Sheroside Cl DE22.....204 D4
Sherriff's Lea NG9.....223 E2
Sherroside Cl DE22....204 D4
Sherston Cl DE21......206 B2
Sherwin Rd NG9......209 F1
Sherwin St DE22......218 E8
Sherwood Ave
Borrowash DE72......221 D2
Creswell S80...........81 D1
Derby, Chaddesden DE21..219 F7
Derby, Littleover DE23...231 D5
Hope S33..............39 A3
Pinxton NG16.........160 D3
Shirebrook NG20......119 E6
Sherwood Chase S17....55 E5
Sherwood Copse SK17...69 C4
Sherwood Ct NG19....136 B2
Sherwood Dr NG20....119 E3
Sherwood Fold SK13....16 D7
Sherwood Foresters
Regiment Meml★ DE4..156 E3
Sherwood Hall L Ctr
DE4.................143 C5
Sherwood Pl **2** S18.....56 D1
Sherwood Rd
Buxton SK17...........85 C5
Dronfield S18...........56 D1
Killamarsh S21.........60 D7

Station Rd *continued*
North Wingfield S42 . . . . **131** E6
Pilsley S45 . . . . **132** D1
Renishaw S21 . . . . **60** A2
Rolleston DE13 . . . . **240** C4
Sandiacre NG10 . . . . . . **223** C5
Scarcliffe S44 . . . . **118** F6
Selston NG16 . . . . **160** E1
Sheffield S20 . . . . **59** E7
Shirebrook NG20 . . . . . **119** E6
Spinkhill S21 . . . . **60** D2
Stanley DE7 . . . . **207** C6
Stonebroom DE55 . . . . . **147** B5
Tibshelf DE55 . . . . **147** F6
West Hallam DE7 . . . . . **207** C8
Whaley Bridge SK23 . . . . **34** A1
Whitwell S80 . . . . **82** A5
Woodville DE11 . . . . . . **256** F2

Station St
Ashbourne DE6 . . . . **173** B1
Cossall DE7 . . . . **195** A1
Glossop SK13 . . . . **10** D1
Long Eaton NG10 . . . . . **236** E7
Mansfield Woodhouse
NG19 . . . . **136** B3
Swadlincote DE11 . . . . . **261** F8
Station View NG20 . . . . **119** E4
Station Wlk 🔳 SK17 . . . **85** D8
Station Yd DE73 . . . . . **252** C8
Staton La S18 . . . . **58** A1
Staunton Ave DE23 . . . . **231** E6
Staunton Cl
Castle Donington DE74 . . **247** A4
Chesterfield S40 . . . . . . **115** A6
**Staunton Harold Resr Visitor
Ctr** ★ DE73 . . . . **251** F5
Staunton La DE73 . . . . . **251** A1
STAVELEY **78** D1
Staveley Cl DE24 . . . . . **232** E3
Staveley Jun Sch S43 . . . **78** E1
Staveley La
Barrow Hill S21, S43 . . . . **78** A5
Eckington S21 . . . . **59** E2
Staveley S43 . . . . **78** E7
Staveley Rd
Chesterfield S43 . . . . **77** E3
Long Duckmanton S44 . . . **97** E4
Poolsbrook S43 . . . . **98** A8
Sheffield S8 . . . . **43** A7
Staverton Dr DE3 . . . . . **217** D4
Stead Mews S21 . . . . . . **59** D3
Stead St S21 . . . . **59** D3
Steam Mill La DE5 . . . . **170** A1
Steele Ave S43 . . . . **97** B6
Steele Ct SK17 . . . . **85** A8
Steel La S44 . . . . **99** B2
Steel's La S44 . . . . **118** B6
Steeping S7 S43 . . . . **96** E8
Steep La S42 . . . . **114** A4
Steeple Cl DE21 . . . . . . **205** E2
Steeple Dr DE5 . . . . **180** E6
Steeple End Fold SK22 . . **25** D2
Steeplegate S40 . . . . . . **266** B3
STEEPLE GRANGE **155** A3
Steeple Grange DE4 . . . . **154** F4
Steeple Grange Light Rly ★
DE4 . . . . **154** F4
Steep Turnpike DE4 . . . . **143** C5
Steetley La S80 . . . . **63** E3
STENSON **243** B8
Stenson Ave DE23 . . . . . **231** E6
Stenson Ct DE5 . . . . **169** F1
Stenson Fields Prim Sch
DE24 . . . . **231** D2
Stenson Rd DE23, DE24 . . **231** D4
Stenton Rd S8 . . . . **56** F7
Stephenson Cl S41 . . . . . **131** B4
Stephenson Ct S40 . . . . . **95** B2
Stephenson Pl S40 . . . . . **266** B3
Stephenson Rd S43 . . . . . **78** C1
Stephensons Way DE21 . . **220** A3
Stephens Rd DE14 . . . . . **254** B8
Stepping Cl DE21 . . . . . **218** E5
Stepping La DE22 . . . . . **218** E5
Sterland St S40 . . . . **95** E3
Sterling Cl DE7 . . . . **180** B2
Sterling Ct S41 . . . . **266** B4
Stirling Gr NG16 . . . . . . **195** E7

Stockbrook Rd DE22 . . . **218** D3
Stockbrook St DE22 . . . . **218** E4
Stockdove Cl DE24 . . . . **231** D4
Stocker Ave DE24 . . . . . **233** D7
Stock La ST14 . . . . **224** C1
STOCKLEY **117** E4
Stockley La S44 . . . . **117** F1
Stockley View S44 . . . . . **118** B8
Stockport Rd
Broadbottom SK14 . . . . . **15** D8
Marple SK6 . . . . **23** A6
Stocks Brow SK13 . . . . . . **10** A7
Stocks Green Ct S17 . . . . **55** D4
Stocks Green Dr S17 . . . . **55** D4
Stocks Rd NG16 . . . . . . **195** E7
Stocks The SK13 . . . . **10** A7
Stockton Dr SK23 . . . . . . **34** E1
Stockwell St S40 . . . . . . **114** F7
Stoddard Dr DE75 . . . . . **181** F2
Stodhart Flats SK23 . . . . . **47** C8
STOKE **72** C6
Stoke Cl DE56 . . . . **179** E5
Stollard St S45 . . . . **131** D4
Stone Bank Ct S18 . . . . . . **57** B1
Stonebench La SK17 . . . **106** C3
Stone Bench Way SK17 . . . **85** E8
Stonebridge La NG20 . . . **120** F4
STONEBROOM **146** F4
Stonebroom Ind Est
DE55 . . . . **147** B4
Stonebroom La DE55 . . . **147** B5
Stonebroom Prim Sch
DE55 . . . . **147** A4
Stonebroom Wlk DE24 . . **232** E3
Stonechat Cl DE3 . . . . . **218** A3
Stone Cl
Derby DE21 . . . . **220** E6
Dronfield S18 . . . . **57** D3
Stonecliff Terr SK17 . . . . **85** D8
Stone Cotts DE4 . . . . . . **184** E8
Stonecroft Rd S17 . . . . . . **55** F5
Stonedale Cl S20 . . . . **59** D7
Stone Fronts DE73 . . . . **251** A4
STONEGRAVELS **96** A5
Stonegravels Croft 🔳
S20 . . . . **96** A5
Stonegravels La S41 . . . . . **96** A5
Stonegravels Way S20 . . . **59** F6
Stoneheads SK23 . . . . . . **45** C8
Stoneheads Rise SK23 . . . **45** D8
Stonehill DE74 . . . . **247** B2
Stone Hill Rd DE23 . . . . **218** F2
Stoneholes Dr S45 . . . . . **131** E2
Stone La
Chesterfield S43 . . . . **77** D4
Sheffield S13 . . . . **44** F5
Stoneleigh Way DE55 . . . **169** F8
Stoneley Cl S12 . . . . **44** B1
Stoneley Cres S12 . . . . . . **44** B1
Stoneley Dell S12 . . . . **44** B1
Stoneley Dr S12 . . . . **44** B1
Stonelow Cres S18 . . . . . . **57** C2
Stonelow Gn S18 . . . . **57** C2
Stonelow Jun Sch S18 . . . **57** C2
Stonelow Rd S18 . . . . **57** C2
Stone Mdws NG10 . . . . . **236** E5
Stonepit La DE6 . . . . **164** A3
Stone Rd S18 . . . . **57** C1
Stoneridge SK13 . . . . **9** F5
Stone Row
Chesterfield S40 . . . . **95** D2
Marple SK6 . . . . **23** A6
Stonerows La S45 . . . . . **145** C6
Stonesby Cl DE7 . . . . . . **205** F2
Stonesdale Ct 🔳 DE24 . . **233** C6
Stones La DE4 . . . . **156** F1
Stone St S20 . . . . **59** D7
Stones The S33 . . . . **38** B2
Stonewell La SK17 . . . . . **137** D5
Stoney Cl DE45 . . . . **109** D4
Stoneycroft La S42 . . . . . **114** A5
Stoney Cross DE21 . . . . **220** E3
Stoneydale Cl DE11 . . . . **255** F3
Stoneyfield Bank DE56 . . **179** A5
Stoney Flatts Cres DE21 . . **220** A8
STONEYFORD **182** A7
Stoney Furlong Rd DE45 . . **91** E6
Stoney Gate Rd DE21 . . . **220** D3
Stoney Hill DE4 . . . . . . **155** B2
Stoney La
Appleby Magna DE12 . . . **265** F1
Ashover S42 . . . . **130** C3
Brinsley NG16 . . . . **182** D6
Derby DE21 . . . . **220** D6
Hognaston DE6 . . . . **164** A2
Selston NG16 . . . . **171** E7
Trowell NG9 . . . . **209** B5
Stoneyland Dr SK22 . . . . . **33** B8
STONEY MIDDLETON . . . **72** A4
**Stoney Middleton CE Prim
Sch** S32 . . . . **71** D1
Stoney Way DE4 . . . . . . **143** C4
**Stony Clouds Nature
Reserve** ★ NG10 . . . . . . **223** B8
STONY HOUGHTON **118** F1
Stonyhurst Ct DE24 . . . . **232** E3
Stony La DE56 . . . . **191** D6
Stony Ridge Rd S11 . . . . . **54** C5
Stoodley Pike Gdns
DE22 . . . . **204** C2
Stoops Cl S40 . . . . **95** D6
Stoppard Cl DE7 . . . . . . **194** D2
Storer La DE4 . . . . **166** B3
Stores Rd DE21 . . . . **267** D4
Storforth La S41 . . . . . . **115** B7
Storforth Lane Terr S41 . . **115** C8

Storforth Lane Trad Est
S40 . . . . **115** B8
Stormont Cl DE55 . . . . . **160** B4
Stormont Gr S43 . . . . **97** C7
Stornoway Cl 🔳 DE24 . . **231** D3
Storrs Rd S40 . . . . **95** B2
Storth Bank S13 . . . . **16** F7
Storthfield Way DE55 . . . **160** B4
Storth La DE55 . . . . **160** B4
Storth Meadow Rd SK13 . . **16** F7
Stort Sq NG19 . . . . **136** D2
Stour Cl
Brimington S43 . . . . **96** E8
Hilton DE65 . . . . **240** E8
Stourdale Cl NG10 . . . . . **236** A6
Stourport Dr DE73 . . . . . **233** A3
Stow Ct 🔳 NG19 . . . . . . **136** E3
Stowmarket Dr DE21 . . . **219** D8
Stradbroke Ave S13 . . . . . **44** D7
Stradbroke Cl S13 . . . . . . **44** E7
Stradbroke Cres S13 . . . . **44** E7
Stradbroke Dr S13 . . . . . . **44** E7
Stradbroke Pl S13 . . . . . . **44** E7
Stradbroke Prim Sch S13 **44** D7
Stradbroke Rd S13 . . . . . . **44** E6
Stradbroke Rise S40 . . . . **114** C8
Stradbroke Way S13 . . . . . **44** E7
Stradbroke Wlk S13 . . . . . **44** D7
STRAMSHALL **210** A4
Strand Arc DE1 . . . . **267** B3
Strand The DE1 . . . . **267** B3
Stranfaer Cl DE55 . . . . . . **170** A7
Stranraer Cl NG19 . . . . . **136** C6
Stratford Cl DE65 . . . . . **242** D1
Stratford Rd DE21 . . . . . **205** D2
Stratford St DE7 . . . . . . **194** D2
Strathallan Cl DE4 . . . . . **127** C4
Strathaven Cl DE21 . . . . **220** E5
Strathglen Cl NG16 . . . . **195** E7
Strathmore Ave DE24 . . . **233** A6
Stratton Rd S44 . . . . **99** A2
Strawberry Bank NG17 . . **148** E4
Strawberry La
Blackfordby DE11 . . . . . **257** B1
Rosliston DE12 . . . . **260** D5
Strawberry Lee La S17 . . . **55** B5
Straw La
Clay Cross DE55 . . . . . . **146** D8
Shirland S45 . . . . **146** D8
Streatham Rd DE22 . . . . **218** B6
Street Farm Cl S26 . . . . . . **61** E6
Streetfield Cres S20 . . . . . **59** D6
Streetfields S20 . . . . **59** E6
Street La DE5 . . . . **180** B6
Street Lane Prim Sch
DE5 . . . . **180** B5
Street The SK10, SK17 . . . **64** C5
Street The ★ SK17 . . . . . **64** E4
Strelley Ave DE5 . . . . . . **180** C8
Stretfield Rd S33 . . . . **39** B1
Strettea La DE55 . . . . . . **146** C2
STRETTON
Clay Cross **146** C7
Rolleston on Dove **240** D1
Stretton Cl DE3 . . . . **217** D1
STRETTON EN LE FIELD . **265** D4
**Stretton Handley CE Prim
Sch** DE55 . . . . **145** D7
STRETTON HILLSIDE . . . **146** B5
Stretton Rd
Clay Cross S45 . . . . **131** C1
Shirland S45 . . . . **146** C8
Stonebroom DE55 . . . . . **146** C5
Stretton View DE12 . . . . **265** F6
Striding Edge Cl 🔳
NG10 . . . . **223** B2
STRINES **23** C2
Strines Rd
Marpleridge SK6 . . . . . . **23** B3
Marple SK6 . . . . **23** A4
New Mills SK6 . . . . **32** D8
Strines Sta SK6 . . . . **23** D1
Stroma Cl DE24 . . . . **231** F4
Strutts Cl DE55 . . . . **159** F4
Strutt's North Mill ★
DE56 . . . . **178** F5
Strutt's Park Ho 🔳 DE22 **218** F7
Strutt St
Belper DE56 . . . . **178** F3
Derby DE23 . . . . **219** A2
Stuart Cl
Ashbourne DE6 . . . . **173** D1
Chesterfield S41 . . . . **96** C6
Stuart St DE1 . . . . **267** B4
Stubben Edge La S45 . . . **130** C2
Stubbing Rd S40 . . . . . . **114** F7
Stubbins La SK23 . . . . **34** D2
Stubbins Wood NG20 . . . **119** E6
Stubbins Wood La NG20 . . **119** E5
Stubbin Wood Sch NG20 **119** F6
Stubby La ST14 . . . . **224** C1
Stubley Cl S18 . . . . **56** E2
Stubley Croft S18 . . . . . . **56** D2
Stubley Dr S18 . . . . **56** E2
Stubley Hollow S18 . . . . . **56** E3
Stubley La S18 . . . . **56** D2
Stubley Pl S18 . . . . **56** E2
STUBWOOD **196** D4
Stubwood Hollow ST14 . . **196** D5
Stubwood La ST14 . . . . . **196** A4
Studbrook Cl DE74 . . . . **246** F3
Studfarm Cl DE73 . . . . . **252** D2
Studios The S40 . . . . **95** E3
Studland Cl NG19 . . . . . **136** D6
Stupenhill Post 16 Ctr
DE15 . . . . **255** A7
Sturge Croft 🔳 S2 . . . . . . **43** B6
Sturges La DE72 . . . . . . **233** F4

Sturston Rd DE6 . . . . . . **173** C1
SUDBURY **225** E4
Sudbury Ave
Ilkeston DE7 . . . . **209** B7
Sandiacre NG10 . . . . . . **223** A6
Sudbury Cl
Chesterfield S40 . . . . **95** B5
Derby DE1 . . . . **218** E5
Sudbury Ct NG10 . . . . . . **235** F4
Sudbury Dr NG17 . . . . . **148** E2
**Sudbury Hall & Mus of
Childhood** ★ DE6 . . . . . **225** D5
Sudbury Mews NG16 . . . **182** E1
Sudbury Pk DE6 . . . . . . **225** D7
Sudbury Prim Sch DE6 . . **225** E4
Sudbury St DE1 . . . . **218** E5
Sudhall Cl S41 . . . . **95** B3
Suff La NG16 . . . . **160** C3
Suffolk Ave DE21 . . . . . . **219** C3
Suffolk Rd DE15 . . . . . . **254** D7
Sugworth Rd S6 . . . . **31** F6
Sulleys Field DE22 . . . . . **204** D7
Summerbottom SK14 . . . . **16** A8
Summer Cross SK17 . . . . . **69** B4
Summer Dr DE4 . . . . **165** E7
Summerfield Cres S43 . . . **96** E8
Summerfield Rd
Chesterfield S40 . . . . . . **266** A1
Dronfield S18 . . . . **57** B3
Summerfields Way DE7 . . **194** D3
Summerfields Way S
DE7 . . . . **194** D2
Summer La
Sheffield S17 . . . . **55** D4
Wirksworth DE4 . . . . . . **165** E8
SUMMERLEY **57** F2
Summerley Lower Rd S18 **57** F2
Summerley Rd S18 . . . . . . **57** F2
Summerskill Gn S43 . . . . **97** C7
Summerville Cl DE23 . . . **231** B6
Summerwood Croft S18 . . **56** F2
Summerwood La S18 . . . . **56** F3
Summerwood Pl S18 . . . . **56** F2
Summit Dr NG20 . . . . . . **119** E4
Sumners Pl SK13 . . . . **10** B1
Sumner St SK13 . . . . **17** C8
Sunart Cl DE24 . . . . **231** F2
Sundew Cl DE21 . . . . . . **220** A1
Sundial Cl DE6 . . . . **201** E8
Sundial Wlk DE6 . . . . . . **201** E8
Sundown Ave DE23 . . . . **231** D6
Sundown Cl SK22 . . . . . . **33** A8
Sundown Pl S13 . . . . **44** F8
Sundown Rd S13 . . . . **44** F8
Sunflower Cl
Derby DE24 . . . . **220** A1
Shirebrook NG20 . . . . . **119** D3
Sun La DE4 . . . . **156** F1
Sunlaws Ct SK13 . . . . **17** C8
Sunlaws St SK13 . . . . **17** C8
Sunlea Cres NG9 . . . . . . **223** F5
Sunningdale Ave
Derby DE21 . . . . **220** D5
Heanor DE75 . . . . **193** F4
Sunningdale Cl
Burton upon Trent DE13 . . **240** C1
Chesterfield S40 . . . . . . **114** E8
Sunningdale Dr
Glossop SK13 . . . . **10** E1
Ilkeston DE7 . . . . **208** B5
Sunningdale Pk S42 . . . . **115** C1
Sunningdale Rise S40 . . . **114** C8
Sunninghill DE7 . . . . . . **207** D8
Sunnybank DE4 . . . . **110** F1
Sunny Bank
Great Longstone DE45 . . . **90** A4
Mayfield DE6 . . . . **184** C7
Tibshelf DE55 . . . . **147** B5
Sunny Bank Gdns DE56 . . **178** F2
Sunny Bank La SK17 . . . . . **69** C4
Sunny Banks 🔳 SK13 . . . . **17** B8
Sunny Brook Cl S43 . . . . . **80** E3
**Sunnydale Park Nature
Reserve** ★ DE21 . . . . . . **231** C7
Sunnyfield SK17 . . . . **85** F1
Sunny Gr DE21 . . . . **220** A5
SUNNY HILL **231** D5
Sunny Hill DE56 . . . . . . **190** F7
Sunnyhill Ave DE23 . . . . **231** E6
Sunnyside
Swadlincote DE11 . . . . . **255** E7
Whitwell S80 . . . . **82** A6
Sunnyside Cl DE11 . . . . . **255** F7
Sunnyside Rd ST14 . . . . . **210** B1
Sunnyside Terr DE4 . . . . **143** A8
Sunny Springs S41 . . . . . **266** B4
Sunnyvale Ave S17 . . . . . . **55** E4
Sunnyvale Rd S17 . . . . . . **55** D4
Sun St
Derby DE22 . . . . **267** A2
Woodville DE11 . . . . . . **256** F2
Surbiton Cl DE22 . . . . . . **218** A6
Surbiton Dr DE7 . . . . . . **207** D8
Surgery La DE4 . . . . **157** A1
Surprise Villas S32 . . . . . **53** A7
Surrey St
Derby DE22 . . . . **218** D6
Glossop SK13 . . . . **10** C1
Sussex Cir DE21 . . . . . . **219** E8
Sussex Cl NG16 . . . . **195** A8
Sussex Rd DE15 . . . . . . **254** E6
Sussex Way NG10 . . . . . **223** B5

Sutton Ct NG16 . . . . . . **182** F2
Sutton Dr DE24 . . . . **232** E4
Sutton Hall Rd S44 . . . . . **117** E8
Sutton Ho DE24 . . . . . . **233** C5
SUTTON IN ASHFIELD . . **148** C5
Sutton La
Etwall DE65 . . . . **229** B5
Hatton DE65 . . . . **227** E4
Hilton DE65 . . . . **228** D3
Long Duckmanton S44 . . . **116** F7
Sutton on the Hill DE6,
DE65 . . . . **228** B6
SUTTON ON THE HILL . . **228** B8
Sutton Rd
Church Broughton DE65 . . **227** D7
Sutton in Ashfield NG17 . . **148** D7
Suttons Ave 🔳 DE11 . . . **256** E1
Suttons Bsns Pk DE11 . . . **256** E3
Sutton Scarsdale Hall ★
S44 . . . . **117** A6
Suttons La SK6 . . . . **23** A5
**SUTTON SPRINGS
WOOD** **116** C6
Sutton View
Bolsover S44 . . . . **118** B8
Temple Normanton S42 . . **116** B4
Sutton Way S13 . . . . **10** A5
Swaddale Ave S41 . . . . . . **96** B6
Swaddale Cl S41 . . . . **96** B6
SWADLINCOTE **256** D4
Swadlincote La DE11 . . . **255** E2
Swadlincote Rd DE11 . . . **256** E3
**Swadlincote Ski &
Snowboard Ctr** DE11 . . **256** C3
Swaines Mdw DE4 . . . . . **165** D8
SWAINSPARK **262** B6
Swainspark Ind Est DE12 **262** B6
Swalebank Cl S40 . . . . . . **115** B8
Swaledale Ct 🔳 DE24 . . **233** C6
Swallow Cl DE3 . . . . **218** A3
Swallow Croft DE5 . . . . **180** D6
Swallow Ct DE5 . . . . **180** D6
Swallowdale Rd DE24 . . . **231** D4
Swallow Fold SK13 . . . . . **16** F8
Swallow Ho DE1 . . . . . . **218** E5
Swallow House Cres
SK22 . . . . **25** C3
Swallow House La SK22 . . **25** C3
Swallow Rd DE11 . . . . . . **256** F3
Swanbourne Cl 🔳 S41 . . . **96** F1
Swan Hill DE3 . . . . **230** B6
Swan La NG19 . . . . **136** B3
Swanmore Rd DE23 . . . . **231** A8
Swann Yd NG17 . . . . **148** F3
Swanson Ave NG17 . . . . **148** F3
Swans Rest DE11 . . . . . . **255** F6
SWANWICK **169** E8
Swanwick Ave NG20 . . . . **119** F3
Swanwick Gdns DE21 . . . **206** A1
Swanwick Hall Sch DE55 **169** F7
Swanwick Hill DE55 . . . . **169** E7
Swanwick Junc Sta ★
DE5 . . . . **170** A5
Swanwick Prim Sch
DE55 . . . . **169** D6
Swanwick Rd
Ilkeston DE7 . . . . **194** F5
Somercotes DE55 . . . . . **170** B7
Swanwick Sch & Sports Coll
DE55 . . . . **169** F6
Swanwick St S41 . . . . **77** A2
SWARKESTONE **244** D6
Swarkestone Dr DE23 . . . **231** C5
Swarkestone Rd
Barrow upon Trent DE73 . **244** B6
Chellaston DE73 . . . . . . **244** F8
SWATHWICK **114** D4
Swathwick Cl S42 . . . . . . **114** E4
Swathwick La S42 . . . . . **114** D4
Swayfield Cl DE3 . . . . . . **217** C3
Sweetbriar Cl DE24 . . . . **233** A5
Swift Bank SK13 . . . . **16** F8
Swift Cl
Derby DE3 . . . . **218** A3
Woodville DE11 . . . . . . **256** F3
Swift Ct NG16 . . . . **182** F2
Swinburne St DE1 . . . . . **267** B1
Swinderby Dr DE21 . . . . **206** B1
Swindon Cl NG16 . . . . . . **195** C7
Swiney Way NG9 . . . . . . **223** F2
SWINGATE **195** F5
Swinger La S45 . . . . **129** C2
Swinney Bank DE56 . . . . **179** A5
Swinney La DE56 . . . . . . **179** A5
Swinscoe Hill DE6 . . . . . **172** B2
Swinscoe Ho 🔳 DE1 . . . . **267** B2
Swinscoe Way S40 . . . . . . **95** A5
Swinson Cl ST14 . . . . . . **197** A3
Swithland Cl S41 . . . . . . **115** C7
Sycamore Ave
Chesterfield S40 . . . . **95** E2
Creswell S80 . . . . **81** E2
Derby DE22 . . . . **204** D3
Dronfield S18 . . . . **57** A3
Findern DE65 . . . . **230** E1
Glapwell S44 . . . . **134** B8
Ripley DE5 . . . . **180** D8
Swadlincote DE11 . . . . . **256** A7
Sycamore Cl
Bolsover S44 . . . . **99** C2
Burton upon Trent DE15 . **254** E5
Buxton SK17 . . . . **66** B1
Etwall DE65 . . . . **229** C4
Linton DE12 . . . . **261** D5
Mapperley DE7 . . . . **193** F3

Sycamore Cl continued
New Mills SK22 . . . . 24 E1
Pinxton NG16. . . . . 160 D3
Selston NG16. . . . . 171 D7
Shirland DE55. . . . . 146 C4
Sycamore Cotts DE6 . . . . 151 D1
Sycamore Cres NG10 . . . . 223 A7
Sycamore Croft DE56 . . . 179 B2
Sycamore Ct
Belper DE56. . . . . 179 F1
Derby DE21 . . . . 220 E5
Willington DE65 . . . . 242 B5
Sycamore Dr
Calow S44 . . . . 96 E3
Ilkeston DE7 . . . . 209 B7
Killamarsh S21 . . . . 60 C5
Sycamore La
Barlborough S43 . . . . 80 B6
Brimington S43 . . . . 78 A1
Sycamore Rd
Awsworth NG16. . . . . 195 C5
Brimington S43 . . . . 78 A1
Burton upon Trent DE15 . . 254 F6
Castle Donington DE74 . . 247 B5
Chapel-en-le-Frith SK23 . . . 47 B4
Hayfield SK22 . . . . 24 F2
Long Eaton NG10 . . . . . . 236 C5
Mansfield Woodhouse
NG19. . . . . 136 C5
Matlock DE4. . . . . 143 B6
Mayfield DE6 . . . . 184 C7
Sycamore St
Church Warsop NG20 . . . . 120 F6
Sheffield S20 . . . . 59 C8
Sycamores The
Eastwood NG16. . . . . 182 E1
Glossop SK13. . . . . 9 F3
Sheffield S13 . . . . 44 C6
South Normanton DE55. . . 160 B5
Sycamore Terr SK22 . . . . . 25 D3
Syda La S42 . . . . 93 E1
Syday La S21 . . . . 60 D1
Sydenham Rd DE22 . . . . . 218 A7
Sydney Cl
Derby DE3 . . . . 217 F3
Mansfield Woodhouse
NG19. . . . . 136 C6
Sydney Rd DE72 . . . . 235 A7
Sydney St S40 . . . . 95 E3
Sydnope Hall DE4 . . . . . . 128 A5
Sydnope Hill DE4 . . . . . . 128 A5
Syerscote La B79 . . . . 263 B2
Sylvan Cl S41 . . . . 266 C1
Sylvan Cliff SK17 . . . . 85 C7
Sylvan Dr S42 . . . . 131 A6
Sylvan Pk SK17 . . . . 85 C8
Sylvia Rd S18 . . . . 76 D5
Sywell Cl DE55. . . . . 169 F8

T

Tabley Gdns SK6. . . . . 23 A4
TADDINGTON 88 B3
Taddington Cl 2 DE21 . . 219 E8
Taddington Pl 31 SK13 . . . 9 E1
Taddington & Priestcliffe CE
Prim Sch SK17. . . . . 87 F3
Taddington Rd
Chesterfield S40 . . . . 95 B5
Derby DE21 . . . . 205 F1
Taft Ave NG10 . . . . 223 B6
Tagg La DE45. . . . . 107 A1
Taggs Knoll S33 . . . . 40 B4
Tailby Dr DE65 . . . . 242 A5
Talbot Cres S41. . . . . 115 D7
Talbot Dr NG9 . . . . 209 D2
Talbot Pl DE12. . . . . 265 E8
Talbot Rd SK13 . . . . 10 C2
Talbot Sch S8 . . . . 43 B3
Talbot St
Chesterfield S41 . . . . 115 D7
Derby DE1 . . . . 267 A4
Glossop SK13. . . . . 10 C1
Pinxton NG16. . . . . 160 C2
Swadlincote DE11 . . . . . . 256 A1
Talgarth Cl DE21 . . . . 206 C2
Tallys End S43. . . . . 80 A6
Tamar Ave DE22 . . . . 204 D4
Tamworth Rd
Appleby Magna DE12 . . . . 265 E2
Castle Donington DE72,
NG10. . . . . 235 E1
Long Eaton NG10 . . . . . . 236 C5
Tamworth Rise DE56 . . . . 190 E4
Tamworth St DE56 . . . . . 190 E3
Tamworth Terr DE56 . . . . 190 E4
Tanglewood DE56. . . . . . 179 A6
Tanner's La DE65 . . . . . . 242 C3
TANSLEY 144 B4
Tansley Ave DE7 . . . . 193 A1
Tansley Ct S41. . . . . 95 E6
Tansley Dr S40 . . . . 95 A5
Tansley House Gdns
DE4 . . . . 144 A4
TANSLEY KNOLL 144 A5
Tansley Prim Sch DE4. . . 144 A4
Tansley Rd S42 . . . . 131 F5
Tansley Rise 4 DE21 . . . 205 F1
Tansley Way S43. . . . . . . 97 C5
Tansley Wood Ho DE4. . . 143 E5
Tants Mdw DE56. . . . . . . 191 F6
Tantum Ave DE75 . . . . . . 181 C4
Tanyard Cl DE74 . . . . 247 B4

Tap La S40 . . . . 266 A3
Taplow Cl DE3 . . . . 217 C2
TAPTON. 96 C6
Tapton Bsns Ctr S41 . . . . 266 C4
Tapton La S41 . . . . 266 C3
Tapton Lock Hill S41. . . . 96 B6
Tapton Lock Visitor Ctr★
S41. . . . . 96 B6
Tapton Park Bsns Pk 11
DE11 . . . . 256 E1
Tapton Park Ind Est 10
DE11 . . . . 256 E1
Tapton Terr S41. . . . . 266 C4
Tapton Vale S41 . . . . 96 C5
Tapton View Rd S41 . . . . 95 F5
Tapton Way S44. . . . . 96 F3
Tarina Cl DE73. . . . . 233 A1
Tarn Cl NG16. . . . . 182 B4
Tarnside Fold 1 SK13. . . 17 A7
Tarquin Cl DE13 . . . . 240 E2
Tarside Fold 1 SK13. . . 17 A7
Tasman Cl DE3 . . . . 217 F3
TATENHILL 253 A8
Tatenhill La
Branston DE14. . . . . 253 D7
Tatenhill DE13 . . . . 253 A8
Tatham's La DE7. . . . . . . 194 E2
Tattersall Wlk 5 NG19 . . 136 E4
Tattle Hill DE7 . . . . 207 F2
Tatwin Ct DE73. . . . . 252 F2
Taunton Cl DE24 . . . . . . 233 C8
Taverners Cres DE23 . . . 231 C8
Tavern Rd SK13. . . . . 9 E3
Tavistock Ave DE22. . . . . 204 E3
Tavistock Cl 14 DE24 . . . 231 D3
Tavistock Ct 14 S41 . . . . 95 F8
Tavistock Sq DE55 . . . . . 159 B5
Tawney Croft DE4. . . . . . 144 A4
Tawny Way DE23. . . . . . . 231 A7
TAXAL 45 D4
Taxal & Fernilee Prim Sch
SK23 . . . . 45 D6
Taxal Moor Rd SK23. . . . . 45 C3
Tayberry Cl DE24 . . . . . . 232 E7
Tay Cl
Derby DE24 . . . . 231 D2
Dronfield S18. . . . . 56 D2
Taylor Cres
Chesterfield S41 . . . . 96 D1
Stapleford NG9 . . . . 223 F8
Taylor Ct DE6. . . . . 173 C1
Taylor La DE75. . . . . 181 D4
Taylors La ST14 . . . . 196 D4
Taylor's La
Spout DE6 . . . . 166 B4
Trusley DE6 . . . . 215 E6
Taylor St
Derby DE24 . . . . 219 E2
Hollingworth SK14. . . . . . . 9 A4
Ilkeston DE7 . . . . 194 F1
Tayside Cl DE24. . . . . 231 D3
Tay Wlk DE22. . . . . 204 E3
Teal Cl NG20. . . . . 119 D3
Tealby Wlk 10 NG19 . . . . 136 E4
Tean Cl DE15. . . . . 248 A1
Teasel Dr DE11 . . . . 256 F4
Tedder Ave SK17. . . . . . . 85 D3
Tedgness Rd S32 . . . . 53 E1
Tedworth Ave DE24 . . . . 231 D2
Teesdale Rd
Long Eaton NG10 . . . . . . 236 A6
Sheffield S12 . . . . 58 F8
Telford Cl DE3. . . . . 217 E1
Telford Cres S43. . . . . . . 78 F2
Telford Rd SK6 . . . . 23 A4
Telmah Cl DE13. . . . . 240 D1
Temperance Hill DE55 . . 145 E7
Temperance Sq SK14 . . . . 9 A8
Temperance St 5 SK14 . . 16 A8
Templar Cl DE24 . . . . 231 C3
Temple Ave SK13 . . . . . . 10 C5
Templebell Cl DE23 . . . . 231 A6
Temple Ct SK17. . . . . 85 A6
TEMPLE NORMANTON . . . 116 B3
Temple Normanton Bsns Pk
S41. . . . . 116 A4
Temple Normanton Prim Sch
S42. . . . . 116 C4
Temple Rd
Buxton SK17 . . . . 85 A6
Matlock Bath DE4 . . . . . . 143 A1
Temple St
Derby DE23 . . . . 219 A3
Glossop SK13. . . . . 10 C5
Temple View SK17. . . . . . 85 C7
Temple Wlk DE4 . . . . 143 A1
Tenant St DE1 . . . . 267 B3
Tenby Dr DE21 . . . . 206 C2
Ten Foot Cl SK13. . . . . . . 10 B2
Tennessee Rd DE21 . . . . 220 B7
Tennyson Ave
Chesterfield S40 . . . . 266 A3
Mansfield Woodhouse
NG19. . . . . 136 C2
Swadlincote DE11 . . . . . . 256 C6
Tennyson Rd S80 . . . . 81 D1
Tennyson Sq NG16 . . . . . 195 C4
Tennyson St
Derby DE24 . . . . 232 D7
Holmewood S42. . . . . 116 D1
Ilkeston DE7 . . . . 194 E3
Shirland DE55. . . . . 146 C4
Tennyson Way S42. . . . . . 115 E3
Tenter Cl NG10 . . . . 236 D5
Tenter La DE56 . . . . 168 D1
Tern Ave DE11 . . . . 256 F3
Terrace La NG19 . . . . 134 F3
Terrace Rd
Buxton SK17 . . . . 85 B7

Terrace Rd continued
Chapel-en-le-Frith SK23 . . . 47 B6
Tideswell SK17 . . . . 69 C4
Terret Gr SK17 . . . . 84 D5
Terrey Rd S17 . . . . 55 E5
Terr The DE21 . . . . 219 E7
Terry Pl DE24 . . . . 232 F6
Tetford Wlk 13 NG19 . . . 136 E4
Teversal Ave NG19 . . . . . 135 B4
Tevery Cl NG9 . . . . 223 E8
Teviot Pl DE21 . . . . 206 A2
Tewkesbury Ave NG19. . . 136 D4
Tewkesbury Cres DE21 . . 219 D8
Tewkesbury Dr NG16 . . . 195 E7
Tewkesbury Rd NG10. . . . 236 E4
Thackeray Rd DE55 . . . . 146 F3
Thackeray St DE24 . . . . . 232 A5
Thame Ct 2 S43. . . . . 96 E8
Thames Cl DE24 . . . . 217 F5
Thames Way DE65 . . . . . 228 D1
Thanet Dr DE24 . . . . 233 A6
Thanet St S45 . . . . 131 D3
Thatch Cl DE22 . . . . 204 F2
Thatchers Croft DE4 . . . . 144 A3
Thatchers La DE4 . . . . . . 144 A3
Thatchmarsh Cl NE7 . . . . 194 F6
Theatre La S41 . . . . 266 C3
Theatre Wlk DE1. . . . . . . 267 C3
Theatre Yd S40 . . . . 266 B3
Thickley Cl NG20. . . . . . . 119 F4
Thimble Hill DE6. . . . . . . 189 A2
Thirlmere Ave DE22. . . . . 204 E3
Thirlmere Cl 3 NG10 . . . 223 B2
Thirlmere Dr S18 . . . . 57 A2
Thirlmere Rd
Chesterfield S41 . . . . 95 C7
Long Eaton NG10 . . . . . . 223 B2
Thirlwell Rd S8 . . . . 43 A6
Thirsk Pl DE24 . . . . 232 D7
Thirteen Row S44. . . . . . 118 A6
Thistle Bank NG19 . . . . . 136 F4
Thistle Cl
Eastwood NG16. . . . . 195 B8
Woodville DE11 . . . . 256 F4
Thistledown Cl DE22 . . . 205 A2
Thistle Gr DE73 . . . . 232 E1
Thistlegreen Cl DE75. . . . 182 B1
Thistle Rd DE7. . . . . 209 A4
Thomas Chambers 3
SK13 . . . . 17 C7
Thomas Cl NG16. . . . . . . 170 F3
Thomas Cook Cl DE73. . . 252 A7
Thomas Ct DE1 . . . . 218 E4
Thomas St
Compstall SK6 . . . . 15 B2
Glossop SK13. . . . . 10 E1
Thompson Cl
4 Chesterfield S41. . . . . . 96 A8
Swadlincote DE11 . . . . . . 256 E4
Thompson St
Chesterfield S41 . . . . 96 A7
Langley Mill NG16 . . . . . . 182 B3
Thomson Dr DE5 . . . . . . 181 B7
Thomson Wlk DE5 . . . . . 181 A8
Thoresby Ave
Clowne S43 . . . . 81 A4
Shirebrook NG20. . . . . . . 119 E4
Thoresby Cl
Derby DE21 . . . . 206 B1
Ripley DE5 . . . . 169 E1
Thoresby Cres DE72. . . . . 234 F7
Thoresby Pl S43 . . . . 97 C6
Thoresby Rd
Long Eaton NG10 . . . . . . 236 C6
Mansfield Woodhouse
NG19. . . . . 136 A3
Thorn Ave NG19 . . . . . . 135 F1
Thornborough Cl S2 . . . . 43 C7
Thornborough Pl S2 . . . . 43 C7
Thornborough Rd S2. . . . 43 C7
Thornbridge Ave S12. . . . 44 D3
Thornbridge Cl S12 . . . . 44 D3
Thornbridge Cres
Chesterfield S40 . . . . 115 A6
Sheffield S12 . . . . 44 E3
Thornbridge Dr S12. . . . . 44 D3
Thornbridge Gr S12 . . . . 44 D3
Thornbridge La S12. . . . . 44 E3
Thornbridge Pl S12 . . . . 44 D3
Thornbridge Rd S12 . . . . 44 D3
Thornbridge Rise S12 . . . 44 E3
Thornbridge Way S12. . . . 44 E3
Thornbrook Cl SK23. . . . . 47 C5
Thornbrook Rd SK23. . . . 47 C6
Thorn Cl
Buxton SK17 . . . . 85 E8
Derby DE22 . . . . 204 D4
Thorncliffe Ave DE4. . . . . 127 A6
Thorncliffe Rd SK13. . . . . 9 F4
Thorncliffe Terr SK17 . . . 69 C3
Thorndene Cl S41. . . . . . . 96 A6
Thorndike Ave DE24. . . . 233 A7
Thorndon Cl DE3. . . . . . . 230 D8
Thorndon Way S40. . . . . 114 C8
Thorn Dr NG16. . . . . 195 B8
Thorne Cl S42 . . . . 94 F4
Thornecliffewood SK14 . . . 9 D5
Thornell Cl SK23. . . . . . . 47 C5
Thornescroft Gdns DE14. 254 B8
Thorness Cl DE24 . . . . . . 233 C5
Thornewill Dr DE13 . . . . 240 F1
Thorneywood Rd NG10 . . 236 F8
Thornfield Ave S40 . . . . . 95 B1
Thornfield Ct S41. . . . . . . 96 A5
Thornfield Sq NG10 . . . . 236 E8
THORNHILL 39 F3
Thornhill Ave DE56. . . . . 179 B2
Thornhill Dr DE55. . . . . . 160 B6

Thornhill La S33 . . . . 39 F4
Thornhill Rd DE23. . . . . . 218 C1
Thornley Pl DE6 . . . . 173 C1
THORNSETT 24 F3
Thornsett Ave SK17. . . . . 85 E8
Thornsett Cl S17 . . . . 85 E8
Thornsett Gdns S17. . . . . 55 F8
Thornsett Prim Sch SK22. 24 E3
Thornsett Trad Est SK22 . . 24 E2
Thorn St
Derby DE23 . . . . 218 F2
Woodville DE11 . . . . 256 F2
Thorn Street Mews DE11 256 F2
Thornton Pl 1 S18 . . . . . 56 C1
Thorntree Cl DE72 . . . . . 222 F1
Thorntree Cotts DE4 . . . . 154 F2
Thorntree Ct S40 . . . . . . 114 F7
Thorn Tree Gdns NG16 . . 182 F4
Thorntree La DE1. . . . . . 267 B3
Thorn Tree La DE11,
DE15 . . . . 255 F7
Thornway SK6. . . . . 32 A7
Thornwood Ct SK17. . . . . 85 A8
Thorp Cl S2 . . . . 43 A8
THORPE 161 C1
Thorpe Ave
Dronfield S18. . . . . 57 C4
Whitwell S80 . . . . 81 F5
Thorpe Cl
Burton upon Trent DE15 . . 248 C2
26 Chesterfield S41. . . . . . 95 F8
Stapleford NG9 . . . . 223 D7
Thorpe Croft DE4 . . . . . . 156 B5
Thorpe Downs Rd DE11 . 256 B1
Thorpe Dr DE3. . . . . 217 E3
Thorpe Hill Dr DE75 . . . . 193 E8
Thorpe House Ave S8 . . . 43 B4
Thorpe House Rd S8 . . . . 43 B4
Thorpe House Rise S8 . . . 43 B4
Thorpe La S80, S81 . . . . . 63 D6
Thorpelands Ave NG19 . . 136 E1
Thorpelands Dr DE22. . . . 204 E1
Thorpe Leys NG10. . . . . . 236 D5
Thorpe Rd
Eastwood NG16. . . . . 182 F4
Harthill S26 . . . . 62 A7
THORPE SALVIN. 62 F6
Thorpe's Rd
Heanor DE75 . . . . 181 D1
Shipley DE75 . . . . 193 D8
Thorpe's Rd Ind Est
DE75 . . . . 193 D8
Thorpe St
Glossop SK13. . . . . 10 E2
Ilkeston DE7 . . . . 194 E3
Thorpe View DE6 . . . . . . 185 C8
Thorpe Way DE56 . . . . . . 179 B5
Thorpleigh Rd S43. . . . . . 79 B2
Three Gates DE56 . . . . . 178 F2
Thrift Rd DE14 . . . . 254 B8
Throstle Nest Way DE6. . 201 F8
THRUMPTON 237 C3
Thrumpton Ave NG10 . . . 237 A7
Thrumpton Hall★ NG11. 237 B3
Thrushton Cl DE65 . . . . . 230 C2
Thruxton Cl DE24 . . . . . . 233 C6
THULSTON 233 F4
Thunderpit La S32 . . . . . . 71 A3
Thurgarton Ct DE6. . . . . . 173 D1
Thurgaton Way DE55. . . . 148 A3
Thurlby Ct 9 NG19 . . . . . 136 E4
Thurlow Ct DE21 . . . . . . 206 A1
Thurman St DE7 . . . . 209 A6
Thurrows Way DE73. . . . . 233 B2
Thurstan Ave S8 . . . . 56 E8
Thurston Ave DE55. . . . . 170 D8
Thurstone Furlong DE73. 232 E1
THURVASTON 215 C8
Longford 215 C8
Marston Montgomery 197 F1
Thurvaston La
Longford DE6, DE65. . . . . 214 C4
Thurvaston DE6. . . . . 215 A8
Thurvaston Rd DE6. . . . . 197 F1
Thyme Cl DE23. . . . . 231 D4
Tiber Cl DE24 . . . . 233 D5
TIBSHELF 148 A6
Tibshelf Bsns Pk DE55 . . 148 C6
Tibshelf Com Sch DE55 . 148 A7
Tibshelf Inf Sch DE55 . . . 148 A7
Tibshelf Rd
Blackwell DE55 . . . . 147 C1
Holmewood S42. . . . . 132 E7
Tibshelf Town End Jun Sch
DE55. . . . . 147 E5
TIBSHELF WHARF 148 D7
Tickham Ave DE24 . . . . . 231 C2
TICKNALL 251 A4
Ticknall La DE5, DE56. . . 180 B1
Ticknall Rd DE11. . . . . . . 257 B7
Ticknall Wlk DE23. . . . . . 231 E6
TIDESWELL 69 D4
Tideswell Bank 15 SK13 . . 9 E1
Tideswell Cl S43 . . . . 97 C8
Tideswell Ct 5 S40 . . . . . 95 D5
Tideswell Gn DE11 . . . . . 255 E5
Tideswell La S32. . . . . 71 C6
Tideswell Rd DE21 . . . . . 205 F1
Tideswell Wlk 13 SK13 . . . 9 E1
Tiger Yd 6 DE6. . . . . 173 B2
Tilbury Pl DE7. . . . . 233 A5
Tilford Gdns NG9 . . . . . . 223 F6
Tiller Cl DE23. . . . . 231 B6
Tilley Gn DE11. . . . . 255 F6
Tillotson Cl 1 S8 . . . . . . 43 A6
Tillotson Rise S8 . . . . . . 43 A6
Tilton Gr DE7 . . . . 208 C5

Timber La S45 . . . . 132 D5
Timbersbrook Cl DE21 . . 206 A1
Timor Ct DE24 . . . . 219 E2
Timsbury Ct DE21. . . . . . 205 E2
Tinderbox La DE65 . . . . . 229 F5
Tinker Croft
Ilkeston DE7 . . . . 208 E7
Ilkeston DE7 . . . . 208 E7
Tinkerley La DE6. . . . . . . 165 D1
Tinkley La S42. . . . . 130 D4
Tinsell Brook DE65 . . . . . 228 B1
Tinsley Rd DE756, NG16 . 182 D1
Tintagel Cl
Burton upon Trent DE13 . . 240 E2
2 Derby DE23 . . . . 219 B2
TINTWISTLE 10 B8
Tintwistle CE Prim Sch
SK13. . . . . 9 F6
Tipnall Rd DE74. . . . . . . 247 A3
Tipper's La DE65 . . . . . . 227 A8
Tip Tree Cl NG16. . . . . . 195 F7
Tiree Cl
Derby DE24 . . . . 231 F4
Stapleford NG9 . . . . 209 D3
Tibshelf DE55. . . . . 147 F5
TISSINGTON 162 B6
Tissington Bank 27 SK13 . . 9 D1
Tissington Cl S40 . . . . . . 95 B5
Tissington Dr DE21. . . . . 206 B3
Tissington Gn 26 SK13. . . 9 D1
Tissington Terr 28 SK13. . . 9 D1
Titchfield Ave NG19 . . . . 136 D3
Titchfield St
Creswell S80 . . . . 81 D1
Whitwell S80 . . . . 81 F6
Tithe Barn Cl SK17 . . . . . 69 C3
Tithebarn La DE6 . . . . . . 215 C5
Tiverton Cl DE3 . . . . 217 D4
Tiverton Ct 22 S41 . . . . . 95 F8
Tivoli Gdns DE1. . . . . . . 218 E7
TOADHOLE FURNANCE . . 158 C6
TOADMOOR 167 F3
Toadmoor La DE56. . . . . 167 F3
Tobermory Way DE24 . . . 231 D3
Todbrook Cl SK23. . . . . . . 45 C4
Todd St SK13 . . . . 17 D8
Toll Bar Ave S12 . . . . 43 E5
Toll Bar Cl S12. . . . . 43 E5
Toll Bar Dr S12 . . . . 43 E5
Toll Bar Rd S12. . . . . 43 E5
Tollbridge Rd S43. . . . . . 79 B2
Tollemache Cl SK14. . . . . 9 A5
Tollemache Rd SK14 . . . . 9 A5
Tollgate Cotts DE6. . . . . 184 E8
Toll House Mead S20 . . . . 59 C7
Tom Brads Croft SK23. . . 45 E8
Tom La
Chapel-en-le-Frith SK23 . . . 46 D1
Staveley S44 . . . . 97 F5
Tomlinson Bsns Pk DE65 226 F4
Tomlinson Ct DE24. . . . . 232 F7
Tomlinson Ind Est DE21 . 205 C2
Tomlinsons Cotts DE21. . 205 C2
TOMTHORN 66 E4
Tomwood Rise SK13 . . . . 16 C6
Tonbridge Dr DE24. . . . . 233 A5
Tonge La DE73. . . . . 252 F3
Tongue La SK17. . . . . 85 E7
Tongue Lane Ind Est SK17 85 E7
Tooth St 3 DE11. . . . . . . 256 E1
Top Cotts SK17 . . . . 88 F7
Top Farm Ct DE56. . . . . . 191 F8
Top Hagg La DE56. . . . . . 168 A6
Tophill La DE4 . . . . 153 D8
Tophole Rd S33. . . . . 50 F4
Top La
Crich DE4. . . . . 156 D1
Mansfield NG19. . . . . 135 A2
Old Brampton S42. . . . . . . 93 E3
Shottle DE56. . . . . 166 C1
Topley Gdns DE21. . . . . . 205 F2
Top Lons DE6. . . . . 176 B8
Top Manor Cl DE72 . . . . 221 C5
Top Mdw DE11. . . . . 256 B7
Toppham Dr S8. . . . . 56 F6
Toppham Rd S8 . . . . 56 F6
Toppham Way S8 . . . . . . 56 F6
Top Pingle Cl S43 . . . . . . 96 E7
Top Rd
Calow S44 . . . . 97 A3
Wingerworth S42. . . . . . . 114 D1
Top Row NG16. . . . . 171 A5
Topshill La DE6. . . . . 165 B2
Tor Ave DE55 . . . . 170 C6
Tor Cl DE4. . . . . 143 B2
Torfield Cotts DE4 . . . . . 127 B3
Torksey Wlk 11 NG19 . . . 136 E4
Torquay Ct 6 S41 . . . . . . 95 F8
Torrance Cl DE14 . . . . . . 254 A6
Torrani Way S42. . . . . . . 131 F7
Torridon Ct DE24 . . . . . . 231 E4
Tor Rise DE4 . . . . 143 B3
Torr St SK17 . . . . 85 B7
Torrs Valley SK22. . . . . . . 33 C7
TORR TOP. 33 C8
Torr Top St SK22. . . . . . . 33 C7
Torrvale Rd SK22 . . . . . . 33 B7
Torside Mews SK13. . . . . 10 A6
Torside Visitor Ctr★ SK13. . 6 D1
Torside Way SK13. . . . . . 10 A5
Tors Spring DE4 . . . . 168 A8
Tors The DE4 . . . . 156 F1
Tor View Rise DE4 . . . . . 155 A6
Torwood Dr S8 . . . . 56 E7
TOTLEY 55 E4
Totley All Saints CE Prim Sch
S17. . . . . 55 D4
Totley Ave 42 SK13. . . . . 9 D1

TOTLEY BROOK 55 E5
Totley Brook Cl S17. . . . . . . 55 D5
Totley Brook Croft S17. . . 55 D5
Totley Brook Glen S17 . . . 55 D5
Totley Brook Gr S17 . . . . . 55 D5
Totley Brook Rd S17 . . . . . 55 E5
Totley Brook Way S17. . . . 55 D5
Totley Cl 47 SK13. . . . . 9 D1
Totley Gdns 46 SK13 . . . . . . 9 D1
Totley Gn 23 SK13. . . . . 9 D1
Totley Grange Cl S17. . . . . 55 D4
Totley Grange Dr S17 . . . . 55 D4
Totley Grange Rd S17. . . . 55 D4
Totley Hall Croft S17. . . . . 55 D3
Totley Hall Dr S17 . . . . 55 D4
Totley Hall La S17 . . . . 55 D4
Totley Hall Mead S17 . . . . 55 D3
Totley La S17. . . . . 56 A5
Totley Lanes 43 SK13. . . . . . 9 D1
Totley Mews 20 SK13. . . . . . 9 D1
Totley Mount S43. . . . . 96 D8
Totley Pl 45 SK13. . . . . 9 D1
Totley Prim Sch S17 . . . . . 55 D4
TOTON. 223 E2
Toton Banks Road Inf Sch
  NG9. . . . . 223 F2
Toton Bispham Drive Jun
  Sch NG9. . . . . 223 E3
Toton La NG9. . . . . 223 E6
Touchstone Ct DE73. . . . 232 D2
Toulmin Dr DE11. . . . . 256 B4
Tower Bsns Pk S45. . . . . . 131 C4
Tower Cl
  Sheffield S2. . . . . 43 C8
  Somercotes DE55. . . . . 170 C8
Tower Cres S44. . . . . 118 B8
Tower Dr S2. . . . . 43 C8
Tower Ho S2 . . . . 43 C8
Tower Rd
  Burton upon Trent DE15. 248 B2
  Hartshorne DE11. . . . . . 257 A6
Towers La S32. . . . . 40 E1
Tower St S24. . . . . 232 D7
Tower View Prim Sch
  DE15. . . . . 248 C3
Towle Cl DE72. . . . . 221 C1
Towles Pastures DE74. . 247 A3
Towle St NG10. . . . . 236 A4
TOWNEND 47 C7
TOWN END
  Eyam 71 E6
  Tideswell 69 C3
Town End
  Apperknowle S18. . . . . . . 58 A1
  Bolsover S44. . . . . 99 A1
  Buxton SK17. . . . . 66 E1
  Kirk Ireton DE6. . . . . . . 165 B1
  Shirland DE55 . . . . 146 D2
Town End Rd DE72. . . . . 235 B7
Townfield La S33. . . . . 39 E1
Town Fold SK6. . . . . 23 B7
Town Gate S33. . . . . 51 A7
Town Hall Yd 3 DE6 . . . . 173 C2
TOWNHEAD 55 C7
TOWN HEAD
  Eyam 71 C6
  Tideswell 69 C5
Townhead S32. . . . . 71 C6
Town Head DE6. . . . . 173 C3
Townhead La S33. . . . . 39 F4
Townhead Rd S17. . . . . 55 C7
Town La
  Bradwell S33. . . . . 51 A7
  Broadbottom SK13. . . . . . 16 D6
  Newton DE55. . . . . 148 A3
Townscliffe La SK6. . . . . . . 23 C6
Townsend Gr DE73. . . . . . 233 A2
Townside Cl NG10. . . . . . . 236 B4
Town St
  Brassington DE4 . . . . . . 153 A1
  Duffield DE56. . . . . 190 F3
  Holbrook DE56. . . . . 191 C6
  Marple SK6. . . . . 23 B7
  Pinxton NG16. . . . . 160 E3
  Sandiacre NG10. . . . . . . 223 B5
Town The DE21. . . . . 205 C7
Town View NG16. . . . . 195 F7
Towpath Way DE21. . . . . . 220 D3
Towson Ave NG16. . . . . . . 182 C2
Trafalgar Parkway DE24. 232 B6
Trafalgar Rd NG10. . . . . . 236 D6
Trafalgar Sq NG10. . . . . . 236 E7
Trafalgar Terr NG10. . . . . 236 F7
Traffic St DE1. . . . . 267 C2
Traffic Terr
  Barrow Hill S43. . . . . 78 B4
  2 Chesterfield S41. . . . . 115 B7
Trafford Way DE23. . . . . . 231 C8
Trail View
  Alfreton DE55 . . . . 147 F6
  Glossop SK13. . . . . 10 B5
Tramway The DE11. . . . . . 255 F7
Tranmere Ave S45. . . . . . . 131 D3
Transvaal Terr S44. . . . . . 118 B5
Traso Bsns Pk S18 . . . . 57 C1
Travellers Cl S44. . . . . 98 F5
Travers Rd NG10. . . . . 223 B6
Travey Rd S2. . . . . 44 A7
Treak Cliff Cavern★ S33. 37 E3
Tredcroft St SK13. . . . . 17 B8
Tredegar Dr DE21. . . . . . . 206 B2
Treeneuk Cl S40. . . . . 95 B3
Trefoil Ct DE23. . . . . 231 A7
Tregaron Cl DE21. . . . . . . 206 C2
Tregony Way DE24. . . . . . 231 D3
Trelawney Rd S45. . . . . . . 131 D3
Trenchard Dr SK17. . . . . . . 85 D3

Trent Ave
  Buxton SK17. . . . . 85 C4
  Willington DE65. . . . . . . 242 C5
Trent Bridge Ct DE23. . . 231 C8
Trent Cl
  Derby DE24. . . . . 231 D2
  Willington DE65. . . . . . . 242 C5
Trent Coll NG10. . . . . 236 F6
Trent Dr DE23. . . . . 231 D6
Trent Gr
  Alfreton DE55 . . . . 159 A2
  Dronfield S18. . . . . 57 B3
Trent Ho NG10. . . . . 236 A4
Trent La
  Castle Donington DE74 . 247 A5
  King's Newton DE73 . . . 245 C1
  Long Eaton NG10. . . . . . 236 F5
  Newton Solney DE15. . . 248 E8
  Weston-on-Trent DE72 . 245 F4
Trent Lane Ind Est DE74. 247 B5
TRENTLOCK 236 E3
Trenton Dr NG10. . . . . . . 237 A8
Trenton Gn DE21. . . . . . . 220 B6
Trenton Green Dr DE21. 220 B6
Trent Rd DE7. . . . . 208 D4
Trent Rise DE21. . . . . 220 F4
Trent St
  Derby DE24. . . . . 233 A7
  Long Eaton NG10. . . . . . 236 E8
Trent Wlk 1 NG19. . . . . . . 136 E4
Tresillian Cl DE22. . . . . . . 204 E2
Tressall Cl DE7. . . . . 209 A8
Trevelyan Cl DE15. . . . . . . 248 C2
Treveris Cl DE21. . . . . 220 E4
Trevone Ave NG9. . . . . . . 223 E6
Trevone Ct DE24. . . . . 233 C5
Trevorrow Cres S40. . . . . 266 B1
Trevose Cl S40. . . . . 114 C7
Triangle The
  Belper DE56. . . . . 178 F4
  Ilkeston DE7. . . . . 209 A8
Trickett Cl S33. . . . . 38 C3
Trinity Cl
  Ashford in the Water
    DE45. . . . . 108 F8
  Chesterfield S40. . . . . . . 266 C6
  Ilkeston DE7. . . . . 194 E3
Trinity Ct S41. . . . . 266 A4
Trinity Gr DE11. . . . . 256 B3
Trinity Mews S41. . . . . 266 A4
Trinity View DE1. . . . . 267 C2
Trinity View NG10. . . . . . . 236 E8
Trinity Way 3 DE75. . . . . . 181 F1
Trinkey La S32. . . . . 72 A3
Tristram Gr DE13. . . . . . . 240 E2
Trocadero Ct DE23. . . . . . 267 B1
Troon Cl
  Burton upon Trent DE13. 240 C1
  Chesterfield S40. . . . . . . 114 C8
  Derby DE23. . . . . 231 A8
  Kimberley NG16. . . . . . . 195 F7
Trot La SK17. . . . . 70 A5
Troughbrook Hill S43. . . . . 97 B8
Troughbrook Rd S43. . . . . 78 B1
Trough La NG16. . . . . 195 F6
Trough Rd NG16. . . . . 195 F6
Troutbeck Gr DE23. . . . . . 231 A7
TROWAY 58 B4
Trowbridge Cl DE21. . . . . 205 C2
TROWELL 209 C5
Trowell Ave DE7. . . . . 209 A5
Trowell CE Prim Sch
  NG9. . . . . 209 D4
Trowell Gr
  Long Eaton NG10. . . . . . 223 C1
  Stapleford NG9. . . . . 209 D3
Trowell Marsh Nature
  Reserve★ DE7. . . . . 209 B4
Trowell Park Dr NG9. . . . 209 D2
Trowell Rd NG9. . . . . 209 D2
Trowels La DE22. . . . . 218 C4
Trueman St DE7. . . . . 194 F4
Truman St
  Cossall DE7 . . . . 195 A1
  Kimberley NG16. . . . . . . 195 D7
Truro Cl DE11. . . . . 256 E5
Truro Cres DE21 . . . . 219 E8
TRUSLEY 215 F4
Trusley Brook DE23. . . . . 228 D1
Trusley Gdns DE23. . . . . . 231 D5
Trusley Wlk 7 NG19. . . . . 136 E4
Trustley Cl DE14 . . . . 254 B7
Tudor Cl NG10. . . . . 223 E1
Tudor Ct
  3 Derby DE22. . . . . 204 F3
  Selston DE55. . . . . 171 D6
Tudor Falls DE75. . . . . . . 181 E2
Tudor Field Cl DE73. . . . . 233 A1
Tudor House Cl DE11. . . . 256 A7
Tudor Pl DE7. . . . . 208 C5
Tudor Rd DE21. . . . . 220 A6
Tudor Rise B79. . . . . 263 E2
Tudor St 2 S43. . . . . 78 F2
Tudor Way DE11. . . . . 256 A6
Tuffolds Cl S2. . . . . 44 A7
Tuffnell Gdns DE22. . . . . . 218 B7
Tulip Rd NG16. . . . . 195 B5
Tulla Cl DE24. . . . . 231 E2
Tumbling Hill DE56. . . . . . 168 E1
Tunicliffe Cl S41. . . . . 256 D4
Tunnel Yd 7 DE6. . . . . 173 C2
Tunstall Gn S40. . . . . 95 D1
Tunstall Way S40. . . . . 95 D1
TUNSTEAD 67 F2
TUNSTEAD MILTON. 46 C5
Tuphall Cl DE73. . . . . 233 B2
TUPTON. 131 D8

Tupton Hall Sch S42. . . . 131 D7
Tupton Moor Cl S42. . . . . 115 D1
Tupton Prim Sch S42. . . . 115 D1
Tupton Way S42. . . . . 116 D1
Turf Lea Rd SK6. . . . . 23 B1
TURLOW FIELDS 175 C7
Turlowfields La DE6. . . . . 175 C7
Turnberry Cl
  Chesterfield S40. . . . . . . 114 C8
  Ilkeston DE7. . . . . 194 C2
Turnbull Cl S40. . . . . 266 A1
Turnbury Cl DE14 . . . . . . 254 A7
Turncliffe Cl SK17. . . . . 84 F6
TURNDITCH 177 B1
Turnditch CE Prim Sch
  DE56. . . . . 177 B2
Turner Ave NG16. . . . . . . 182 A3
Turner Cl
  Dronfield S18. . . . . 56 F1
  Stapleford NG9. . . . . 223 E6
Turner Dr
  Eastwood NG16. . . . . . . 195 B7
  Staveley S43. . . . . 97 B7
Turner Rd
  Buxton SK17. . . . . 84 E5
  Long Eaton NG10. . . . . . 236 C4
Turner's Almshouses
  DE22. . . . . 218 D6
Turners La DE55. . . . . 170 A7
Turner St DE24. . . . . 232 E6
Turnlee Cl SK13. . . . . 17 C7
Turnlee Dr SK13 . . . . 17 C7
Turnlee Rd SK13. . . . . 17 C7
Turnley Rd DE55. . . . . 160 C6
Turnoak Ave NE7 . . . . 194 F5
Turnoaks Bsns Pk S40. . . 115 A6
Turnoaks La S40. . . . . 115 A6
Turnpike Bsns Pk DE55. . 158 F2
Turnpike Cl
  Alfreton DE55 . . . . 158 F2
  Matlock DE4. . . . . 143 C5
Turton Cl NG16. . . . . 182 A3
TUTBURY 239 C5
Tutbury Castle★ DE13. . 239 B7
TUTBURY, FAULD 238 C6
Tutbury & Hatton Sta
  DE65. . . . . 239 D8
Tutbury Rd DE13. . . . . 240 A1
Tuxford Cl DE21 . . . . 206 B1
Twayblade DE14 . . . . 254 B8
Tweeds Muir Cl 5 DE21. 205 F2
Twentylands DE13 . . . . . 240 D4
Twentywell Ct S17 . . . . . . 56 A7
Twentywell Dr S17 . . . . . . 56 B6
Twentywell La S17. . . . . . . 56 B6
Twentywell Rd S17. . . . . . 56 B5
Twentywell Rise S17. . . . . 56 B6
Twentywell View S17. . . . 56 B6
Twickenham Cl 11 S20. . 59 E6
Twickenham Cres S20 . . . 59 F6
Twickenham Ct 8 S20. . . 59 E6
Twickenham Dr DE22 . . . 218 A6
Twickenham Glade 10
  S20. . . . . 59 E6
Twickenham Glen S20. . . 59 F5
Twickenham Gr 9 S20. . . 59 E6
Twiggs Row DE4. . . . . 143 A7
Twin Oaks Cl DE23. . . . . . 230 F7
Twisses Bank DE6. . . . . . . 213 A2
TWO DALES 127 E3
TWYFORD 243 B6
Twyford Cl
  Heanor DE75. . . . . 193 C8
  Swadlincote DE11 . . . . . 255 F2
  West Hallam DE7. . . . . . 207 D8
  Willington DE65. . . . . . . 242 C5
Twyford Rd
  Barrow upon Trent DE73. 244 A6
  Long Eaton NG10. . . . . . 235 F4
  Willington DE65. . . . . . . 242 B6
Twyford St DE23. . . . . 267 B1
Tylney Rd S40. . . . . 114 B8
Tyndale Chase DE24 . . . . 231 C2
Tyndale Cl NG10. . . . . 236 A6
Tynefield Ct DE65. . . . . . . 229 B2
Tynefield Mews DE65. . . . 229 B2
Tynsel Parkes CE Fst Sch 4
  ST14. . . . . 210 A1
Tythe Barn La DE6. . . . . . 215 C5
Tythe The DE11. . . . . 256 B7

UFFA Magna DE3 . . . . 217 C1
Uldale Gr DE11. . . . . 256 C1
Ulley Cres S13. . . . . 44 B7
Ulley Rd S13. . . . . 44 B7
Ullswater Ave S20. . . . . . . 59 E6
Ullswater Cl
  Derby DE21. . . . . 205 D2
  Dronfield S18. . . . . 56 E2
  Sheffield S20. . . . . 59 E6
Ullswater Dr
  Derby DE21. . . . . 220 E5
  Dronfield S18. . . . . 56 E2
Ullswater Pk S18 . . . . 56 E2
Ullswater Pl S18. . . . . 56 E2
Ulverston Rd S41. . . . . 95 D7
Undercliffe DE45. . . . . . . 109 D6
Underhall Cl. 127 D2
Underhill Ave DE23. . . . . 231 E7
Underhill Cl DE23. . . . . . . 231 E6
Underhill Rd S43. . . . . 80 B6
Underpass The DE1. . . . . 267 C4
Undertown La DE6. . . . . . 197 D6
Underwood CE Prim Sch
  NG16. . . . . 171 F1

UNDERWOOD GREEN . . 171 F2
Underwood Terr
  Chelmorton SK17. . . . . . 106 A8
  Darley Dale DE4 . . . . . . 143 A7
Union Rd
  Ilkeston DE7. . . . . 208 F1
  New Mills SK22. . . . . 33 C7
  Swadlincote DE11 . . . . . 256 B5
Union St
  Ashbourne DE6. . . . . . . 173 B2
  Glossop SK13. . . . . 17 C8
  Harthill S26. . . . . 61 E6
  Long Eaton NG10. . . . . . 236 E8
  Melbourne DE73. . . . . . 252 A7
  South Normanton DE55. 159 F5
Unity Cl DE11. . . . . 256 A1
Unity Wlk SK13. . . . . 17 C7
Univ of Derby (Britannia
  Mill) DE22. . . . . 218 E6
Univ of Derby (Buxton
  Campus) SK17. . . . . . . 85 D3
Univ of Derby (Kedleston Rd)
  DE22. . . . . 204 D1
Univ of Derby (Markeaton St)
  DE22. . . . . 218 D6
Univ of Sheffield (Research
  Labs) SK17. . . . . 85 B1
UNSTONE 76 E7
Unstone Dronfield By-Pass
  S18. . . . . 56 F3
UNSTONE GREEN 76 E6
Unstone Hill S18. . . . . 76 D7
Unstone Jun Sch S18 . . . . 76 E7
Unstone Rd S41. . . . . 76 F4
Unstone St Mary's Inf Sch
  S18. . . . . 76 F7
UNTHANK 74 D5
Unthank La S18. . . . . 74 C4
Upchurch Cl DE3. . . . . . . 217 C3
Upland Dr DE4. . . . . 143 A7
Upland Rise S40. . . . . 95 D1
Uplands Ave DE23. . . . . . 231 C6
Uplands Gdns DE23 . . . . 218 E2
Uplands Rd
  Compstall SK14. . . . . 15 A6
  Glossop SK13. . . . . 17 D8
Upper Albert Rd S2. . . . . . 43 B4
Upper Bainbrigge St
  DE23. . . . . 219 A3
Upper Barn Cl DE75. . . . . 181 F2
UPPER BIGGIN 175 E4
Upper Blindlow La SK17. 106 A6
UPPER BOOTH 36 E7
Upper Boundary Rd
  DE22. . . . . 218 E4
UPPER BRADWAY 56 B5
Upper Croft
  Clay Cross S45. . . . . 131 E3
  Tupton S42. . . . . 131 D3
Upper Croft Cl S43. . . . . . 96 E7
UPPERDALE 89 B5
Upper Dale Rd DE23. . . . 218 F1
Upper Derwent Visitor Ctr★
  S33. . . . . 30 A7
Upper Dunstead Rd
  NG16. . . . . 182 B4
UPPER ELLASTONE 183 B4
UPPER END. 67 B5
Upper End Rd SK17. . . . . . 67 C4
Upper Greenhill Gdns
  DE4. . . . . 143 C6
UPPER HACKNEY 143 A8
UPPER HALL Cl DE56. . . 191 C6
UPPER HARTSHAY 169 A2
Upper Hollow DE23. . . . . 218 C1
UPPER HOLLOWAY 156 C5
Upper King St S43. . . . . . . 77 F1
UPPER LANGWITH 119 D8
Upper La DE6. . . . . 175 C4
UPPER LANGWITH 119 D8
Upper Lum Cl S41. . . . . . . 96 D2
Upper Mantle Cl S45. . . . 131 C4
UPPER MAYFIELD 172 B1
Upper Marehay Rd DE5. 180 B6
UPPER MIDWAY. 256 C7
Upper Moor Rd DE24. . . . 232 E6
Upper Moor St S40. . . . . . 95 B2
Upper Nelson St 3
  DE75. . . . . 181 D2
UPPER NEWBOLD 95 A8
Upper Newbold Cl S40. . . 95 B7
Upper Orchard St 2
  NG9. . . . . 223 E7
UPPER PADLEY 53 D2
UPPER PILSLEY 132 D2
Upper School La 5 S18. . 57 A1
UPPERTHORPE. 60 E5
Upperthorpe Rd S21. . . . . 60 D4
Upperthorpe Villas S21. . 60 D5
UPPERTOWN 129 A7
UPPER TOWN
  Birchover. 141 C8
  Bonsall. 142 C1
  Hognaston. 164 B4
Uppertown La DE4. . . . . . 142 C1
Upper Town La DE4. . . . . 126 B1
Upper Valley Rd S8. . . . . . 43 B5
Upper Wellington St
  NG10. . . . . 223 C1
UPPERWOOD 155 A8
Upperwood Rd DE4. . . . . 143 A1
Upper Yeld Rd DE45. . . . 109 C4
Upton Cl
  Castle Donington DE74. 247 B4
  Heanor DE75. . . . . 182 A1
Upton Mount NG19. . . . . 135 E1
Upwood Cl S40. . . . . 95 A5
Upwoods Rd DE6. . . . . . . 211 A1
Utah Cl DE65. . . . . 228 E2

UTTOXETER. 210 C1
Uttoxeter New Rd DE22. 218 C3
Uttoxeter Old Rd DE22. . 218 E5
Uttoxeter Rd
  Derby DE3. . . . . 217 E1
  Hatton DE65. . . . . 227 B2
  Hilton DE65. . . . . 228 C2
  Scropton DE65. . . . . 226 C4
  Scropton, Foston DE65. . 226 F3
Uxbridge St DE14 . . . . . . 254 C8

Vale Cl
  Bolsover S44. . . . . 99 A1
  Dronfield S18. . . . . 57 B1
Vale Ct NG19. . . . . 136 B3
Vale Dr NG20. . . . . 119 F2
Vale House Dr SK13. . . . . 10 A5
Vale Mills DE22. . . . . 218 F3
Valemount SK13. . . . . 10 A5
Valentine Ave NG16. . . . . 171 E7
Vale Rd
  Hartshorne DE11. . . . . . 257 A3
  Mansfield Woodhouse
    NG19. . . . . 136 B4
  Swadlincote DE11 . . . . . 256 B6
Valerian Cl SK17. . . . . 85 C7
Valerie Rd DE72. . . . . 246 A7
Vale Rise DE4. . . . . 142 F7
Vale The DE7. . . . . 194 E3
Vallance St NG19. . . . . . . 136 B4
Valley Cl S45. . . . . 132 B4
Valley Cotts S44. . . . . 117 F8
Valley Cres S41. . . . . 96 C2
Valley Gdns
  Chapel-en-le-Frith SK23. 47 C6
  Killamarsh S21. . . . . 60 D7
Valley Park Com Sch S14. 43 F2
Valley Rd
  Barlow S18. . . . . 75 D5
  Bolsover S44. . . . . 118 A8
  Broadbottom SK14. . . . . 15 E8
  Chesterfield S41. . . . . . . 96 C2
  Clay Cross S45. . . . . 131 A4
  Derby, Cherrytree Hill
    DE21. . . . . 220 B5
  Derby DE23. . . . . 218 D1
  Glossop SK13. . . . . 16 F8
  Hayfield SK22. . . . . 25 E2
  Ilkeston DE7. . . . . 208 E5
  Killamarsh S21. . . . . 60 D7
  Kimberley NG16. . . . . . . 195 D7
  Mastin Moor S43. . . . . . . 79 C4
  Overseal DE12. . . . . 262 A3
  Sheffield, Heeley S8 . . . . 43 A6
  Shirebrook NG20. . . . . . 119 E5
Valley Rise
  Barlow S18. . . . . 75 D3
  Swadlincote DE11 . . . . . 256 B5
Valley View
  Alton S42. . . . . 130 C5
  Belper DE56. . . . . 179 A2
  Ilkeston DE7. . . . . 208 E5
Valley View Cl
  Chesterfield S41. . . . . . . 115 E7
  Eckington S21. . . . . 59 C2
Valley View Dr DE7. . . . . 193 B1
Valley View Rd DE55. . . . 170 D4
Valley View Wlk ST14. . . 197 A3
Vancouver Ave DE21. . . . 220 D4
Vancouver Dr DE15. . . . . 248 C3
Vanguard Rd NG10. . . . . 236 D5
Vanguard Trad Est S40. . 115 B7
Varley Ho S41. . . . . 96 B6
Varley St DE24. . . . . 232 D6
Vaughan Pl NG20. . . . . . . 119 E6
Vaughan Rd SK23. . . . . . . 45 E5
Vauxhall Ave DE22. . . . . . 218 A7
Velvet Mill SK17. . . . . 69 B4
Venice Cl DE73. . . . . 232 E2
Ventnor Ho DE24. . . . . . . 233 C7
Ventura Ct SK22. . . . . 24 D1
Venture Cres DE55. . . . . . 159 A2
Venture Ho S41. . . . . 76 F1
Venture Way S41. . . . . 76 F1
Verbena Dr DE23. . . . . . . 231 D4
Vere Cl DE65. . . . . 242 B5
Vermont Dr DE21. . . . . . . 220 C6
Verney St NG19. . . . . 134 F7
Verney Way NG19. . . . . . 134 F7
Vernon Ct
  Bakewell DE45. . . . . 109 D5
  Shirebrook NG20. . . . . . 120 A4
Vernon Dr
  Bakewell DE45. . . . . 109 B7
  Derby DE21. . . . . 220 F4
Vernongate DE1. . . . . 218 E5
Vernon Gn DE45. . . . . 109 B7
Vernon La S45. . . . . 129 D4
Vernon Rd
  Chesterfield S40. . . . . . . 95 D3
  Sheffield S11. . . . . 55 F6
Vernon Rise S42. . . . . 115 F2
Vernon St
  Derby DE1. . . . . 218 E5
  Ilkeston DE7. . . . . 194 F4
  Shirebrook NG20. . . . . . 120 A4
Vernon Street Ind Est
  NG20. . . . . 120 A4
Verona Way DE73. . . . . . 232 E2
Veronica Dr NG16. . . . . . 195 C8

Vestry Rd DE21 . . . . 205 E3
Vetchfield Cl DE24 . . . . . 231 F2
Viadevana DE12 . . . . 262 E3
Via Gellia Rd DE4 . . . . . 154 C7
Vicarage Ave
  Derby DE23 . . . . 218 E2
  Ilkeston DE7 . . . . 194 D4
Vicarage Cl
  Belper DE56 . . . . 179 A4
  Burton upon Trent DE15 . 248 B4
  Heath S44 . . . . 117 B2
  Holmesfield S18 . . . . 75 A8
  Shirebrook NG20 . . . . . . 119 E3
  Smalley DE7 . . . . 192 F6
  Swanwick DE55 . . . . 169 E7
Vicarage Croft DE11 . . . 110 E1
Vicarage Ct DE3 . . . . . . 217 D1
Vicarage Dr
  Derby DE21 . . . . 220 A7
  Uttoxeter ST14 . . . . 210 A4
Vicarage Gdns
  Clay Cross S45 . . . . 131 C2
  Heanor DE75 . . . . 181 F1
  Swadlincote DE11 . . . . . 256 C4
Vicarage La
  Ashford in the Water
   DE45 . . . . 108 E8
  Duffield DE56 . . . . 190 E4
  Hayfield SK22 . . . . 25 D2
  Ironville NG16 . . . . 170 F4
  Little Eaton DE21 . . . . . . 205 C8
  Sheffield S17 . . . . 55 D7
Vicarage Mews DE55 . . 170 E6
Vicarage Rd
  Belper DE56 . . . . 190 F8
  Chellaston DE73 . . . . . . 232 F2
  Derby DE3 . . . . 217 C2
  Swadlincote DE11 . . . . . 256 C4
  Woodville DE11 . . . . 256 E2
Vicarage St DE7 . . . . . . 194 D4
Vicarage Wlk DE12 . . . . 260 C6
Vicar La
  Chesterfield S40 . . . . . . 266 B3
  Tibshelf DE55 . . . . 148 A6
Vicarwood Ave
  Derby DE22 . . . . 204 F1
  Holbrook DE56 . . . . 191 C7
Victor Ave DE5 . . . . 218 F8
Victor Cres NG10 . . . . . 223 C4
Victoria Ave
  Borrowash DE72 . . . . . . 221 B2
  2 Buxton SK17 . . . . 85 D8
  Draycott DE72 . . . . 235 A7
  Glossop SK13 . . . . 10 A5
  Heanor DE75 . . . . 181 D1
  Ilkeston DE7 . . . . 207 B3
  Staveley S43 . . . . 79 A3
Victoria Cl DE3 . . . . 217 E4
Victoria Cotts DE45 . . . 109 D6
Victoria Cres NG16 . . . . 170 F4
Victoria Ct
  6 Glossop SK13 . . . . . . 17 C8
  Long Eaton NG10 . . . . . 236 E7
  Matlock DE4 . . . . 143 C6
Victoria Dr
  Blackwell DE55 . . . . 147 E1
  Woodville DE11 . . . . 256 E1
Victoria Gr S43 . . . . 96 F5
Victoria Hall Gdns DE4 . 143 C6
Victoria Ho S80 . . . . 81 F1
Victoria Mews **2** SK13 . . 17 C8
Victoria Park L Ctr DE7 . 194 E1
Victoria Park Rd
  Buxton SK17 . . . . 85 D7
  Calow S43 . . . . 96 F5
Victoria Rd
  Bamford S33 . . . . 40 B3
  Draycott DE72 . . . . 235 A7
  Pinxton NG16 . . . . 160 D3
  Ripley DE5 . . . . 169 D2
  Sandiacre NG10 . . . . . . 223 B6
  Selston NG16 . . . . 171 F6
Victoria Sq **15** DE6 . . . . 173 C2
Victoria St
  Alfreton DE55 . . . . 159 B4
  Bolsover S44 . . . . 118 B8
  Brimington S43 . . . . 77 F1
  Castle Donington DE74 . . 247 B5
  Chesterfield S41 . . . . . . 266 B4
  Clay Cross S45 . . . . 131 C3
  Creswell S80 . . . . 81 F1
  Derby DE1 . . . . 267 B3
  Dronfield S18 . . . . 56 F2
  Glossop SK13 . . . . 17 C8
  Ilkeston DE7 . . . . 194 F3
  Ironville NG16 . . . . 170 F4
  Langley Mill NG16 . . . . . 182 C3
  Long Eaton NG10 . . . . . 236 B5
  Melbourne DE73 . . . . . . 252 A7
  New Mills SK22 . . . . 33 B6
  Ripley DE5 . . . . 169 F2
  Shirebrook NG20 . . . . . . 119 F4
  Somercotes DE55 . . . . . 170 C8
  South Normanton DE55 . . 160 A6
  Stapleford NG9 . . . . 223 D7
Victoria Street N S41 . . . 76 F2
Victoria Street W S40 . . . 95 C2
Victoria Terr
  Great Longstone DE45 . . . 89 F4
  Selston NG16 . . . . 160 E1
  Tibshelf DE55 . . . . 148 B7
Victoria Way DE24 . . . . 219 E3
Victoria Wlk S42 . . . . . . 115 D1
Victor Rd S17 . . . . 55 F7
Victory Ave DE5 . . . . . . 169 F1

Victory Cl NG10 . . . . . . 236 E5
Victory Dr NG19 . . . . . . 136 F1
Victory Rd DE24 . . . . . . 232 B6
Viewdales Cl DE6 . . . . . 175 F2
View Rd S2 . . . . 43 A7
Viking Bsns Ctr DE11 . . 256 F3
Vikinglea Cl S2 . . . . 44 B8
Vikinglea Dr S2 . . . . 44 B8
Village Ct DE56 . . . . 190 F3
Village Prim Sch DE23 . 231 F7
Village St DE23 . . . . 231 F8
Village The
  Dale Abbey DE7 . . . . . . 207 F2
  West Hallam DE7 . . . . . . 207 E7
Villas Rd
  Ambergate DE56 . . . . . . 167 F3
  Bolsover S44 . . . . 98 E2
Villa St DE72 . . . . 235 B7
Villas The
  Bolsover S44 . . . . 99 B2
  Whaley Thorns NG20 . . . 101 A2
Villa The SK14 . . . . 9 A5
Villiers Cl S2 . . . . 43 E6
Villiers Dr S2 . . . . 43 E6
Vincent Ave
  Derby DE21 . . . . 220 E3
  Ilkeston DE7 . . . . 208 F8
Vincent Cl DE56 . . . . 192 A8
Vincent Cres S40 . . . . 95 B2
Vincent La S40 . . . . 95 B2
Vincent St DE23 . . . . 218 F1
Vine Cl DE23 . . . . 231 B7
Vine Cres NG10 . . . . 223 B6
Vine Farm Cl DE7 . . . . . 208 D5
Vine Gr Ct S20 . . . . 59 D7
Vine Gr Gdns S20 . . . . . . 59 D7
Vineyard Terr DE4 . . . . . 127 C4
Viola Cl DE21 . . . . 206 C3
Violet Cl
  Donisthorpe DE12 . . . . . 262 E1
  Shirebrook NG20 . . . . . . 119 D3
Violet La DE15 . . . . 254 F8
Violet Lane Inf Sch DE15 254 F8
Violet St DE23 . . . . 218 F1
Violet Way DE15 . . . . . . 255 A8
Virginsalley La DE6 . . . . 184 D7
Vista The NG9 . . . . 223 E5
Vivian St
  Derby DE1 . . . . 219 B8
  Shuttlewood S44 . . . . 98 F6
Vulcan St DE23 . . . . 219 B1
Vyse Dr NG10 . . . . 236 C6

W

Wade Ave
  Derby DE23 . . . . 218 C2
  Ilkeston DE7 . . . . 209 B7
Wadebridge Gr DE24 . . . 233 C5
Wade Dr DE3 . . . . 217 E2
Wade St DE23 . . . . 218 C1
WADSHELF 93 E3
Wadsworth Ave S12 . . . . 44 D5
Wadsworth Cl S12 . . . . . . 44 D5
Wadsworth Dr S12 . . . . . 44 D5
Wadsworth Fields Prim Sch
  NG9 . . . . 223 F8
Wadsworth Rd
  Sheffield S12 . . . . 44 C5
  Stapleford NG9 . . . . 223 F8
Wagstaff La NG16 . . . . . 171 B4
Wagtail Cl DE24 . . . . 231 D4
Wain Ave
  Chesterfield S41 . . . . . . 266 C3
  North Wingfield S42 . . . . 132 A7
Wainfleet Cl DE7 . . . . . . 194 C3
WAINGROVES 181 A7
Waingroves Prim Sch
  DE5 . . . . 181 A7
Waingroves Rd
  Codnor DE5 . . . . 181 B6
  Ripley DE5 . . . . 181 A8
Wainhouse Brow SK22 . . 25 D3
Wains Cl SK17 . . . . 47 F1
Wain Way S42 . . . . 132 A7
Wainwright Ave
  Mansfield NG19 . . . . . . 135 D1
  Sheffield S13 . . . . 44 D8
Wainwright Cres S13 . . . . 44 D8
Wakami Cres DE73 . . . . . 233 A3
WAKEBRIDGE 156 D3
Wakefield Ave DE13 . . . . 239 B6
Wakefield Croft DE7 . . . 194 C3
Wakefield Ct
  Castle Donington DE74 . . 247 C4
  Derby DE74 . . . . 247 B4
Wakelyn Cl
  Hilton DE65 . . . . 228 C2
  Shardlow DE72 . . . . 234 F1
Walbrook Rd DE23 . . . . . 218 F1
Walcote Cl DE56 . . . . . . 179 D5
Waldene Dr DE24 . . . . . . 233 A6
Walden Rd S2 . . . . 43 B7
WALDLEY 211 C7
Waldley La DE6 . . . . 211 D7
Waldorf Ave DE24 . . . . . 233 A7
Waldorf Cl DE24 . . . . . . 233 A7
Walford Rd
  Killamarsh S21 . . . . 60 C6
  Rolleston DE13 . . . . 240 D3
Walgrave Cl DE56 . . . . . 179 B6
Walgrove Ave S40 . . . . . . 95 E1
Walgrove Rd S40 . . . . 95 D1
Walk Cl DE72 . . . . 235 A7
Walkdale Brow SK13 . . . . 17 B7
Walker Ave DE5 . . . . 169 E2

Walker Brow SK17 . . . . . . 47 F1
Walker Cl DE7 . . . . 209 A4
Walker Gr **2** NG9 . . . . . 223 E6
Walker La DE1 . . . . 267 A4
Walkers La S21 . . . . 60 D6
Walker St SK13 . . . . 10 A4
Walk Mill Rd SK22 . . . . . . 25 D2
Walk The DE56 . . . . 192 B8
Wallace Gdns NG9 . . . . . 223 F1
Wallace St DE22 . . . . 218 C5
WALLASH 184 C7
Wall Ditch DE6 . . . . 149 B2
Wallfields Cl DE65 . . . . . 230 D2
Wallis Cl DE72 . . . . 235 A7
Wallis Ho DE11 . . . . 256 E3
Wall Rd DE14 . . . . 254 A7
Wallsend Cl DE7 . . . . . . 194 F4
Walls La S80 . . . . 81 A8
Wall St
  Buxton SK17 . . . . 85 D8
  Ripley DE5 . . . . 169 D2
Walnut Ave
  Derby DE24 . . . . 233 B7
  Shireoaks S81 . . . . 63 F7
Walnut Cl
  Aston-on-Trent DE72 . . . 246 B8
  Barrow upon Trent DE73 . 244 A6
  Burnaston DE65 . . . . . . 229 F5
  Chellaston DE73 . . . . . . 245 A8
  Ilkeston DE7 . . . . 209 A7
  Repton DE65 . . . . 243 A2
  Swadlincote DE11 . . . . . 256 A5
Walnut Dr S21 . . . . 60 C5
Walnut Rd DE56 . . . . 179 B3
Walnut St DE24 . . . . 232 C7
Walpole St DE21 . . . . . . 219 D6
Walseker La S26 . . . . 61 C7
Walsham Ct DE21 . . . . . . 205 D1
Walter Evans CE Prim Sch
  DE22 . . . . 204 D7
Walters Ave NG16 . . . . . 182 E6
Walters Cres NG16 . . . . . 171 D6
Walter St
  Derby DE1 . . . . 218 E2
  Draycott DE72 . . . . 234 F8
Walters Wood SK23 . . . . . 45 F5
Waltham Ave DE24 . . . . 231 F4
Waltham Croft S41 . . . . 115 C7
Walthamstow Dr DE22 . . 218 B6
Waltheof Rd S2 . . . . 44 A8
WALTON 114 D8
Walton Ave DE24 . . . . . . 232 E4
Walton Back La
  Chesterfield S40 . . . . . . 114 B7
  Holymoorside S42 . . . . . 113 F7
Walton Cl
  Chesterfield S40 . . . . . . 114 B8
  Dronfield S18 . . . . 56 C2
  Swadlincote DE11 . . . . . 256 A3
Walton Cres
  Ashbourne DE6 . . . . 173 D1
  Chesterfield S40 . . . . 95 E1
Walton Ct
  Sheffield S8 . . . . 56 E8
  West Hallam DE7 . . . . . . 207 D8
Walton Dr
  Chesterfield S40 . . . . 95 E1
  Derby DE23 . . . . 231 E7
Walton Drive Ct S40 . . . . 95 E1
Walton Fields Rd S40 . . . 95 D2
Walton Hill DE74 . . . . . . 247 A4
Walton Holymoorside Prim
  Sch S42 . . . . 113 E8
Walton Hospl S40 . . . . . 114 E8
WALTON-ON-TRENT . . . 253 D1
Walton-on-Trent CE Prim
  Sch DE12 . . . . 259 D8
Walton Rd
  Burton upon Trent DE15 . 254 D5
  Chesterfield S40 . . . . 95 D1
  Derby DE21 . . . . 219 F5
Walton St NG10 . . . . 223 D1
Walton Way S42 . . . . . . 114 E4
Walton Wlk S40 . . . . 266 A2
Wansfell Cl DE3 . . . . 217 E1
Wapentake La DE6 . . . . . 165 C2
Warburton Cl S2 . . . . 43 C7
Warburton Gdns S2 . . . . . 43 C7
Warburton Rd S2 . . . . 43 C7
Ward Dr DE55 . . . . 170 D7
Wardgate Way S40 . . . . . 95 A5
Ward La
  Barlborough S43 . . . . 80 B8
  Disley SK12 . . . . 32 F4
WARDLOW 70 C2
Wardlow Ave
  Derby DE21 . . . . 220 A8
  17 Gamesley SK13 . . . . . 9 D1
Wardlow Cl S40 . . . . 114 F8
Wardlow Fold **21** SK13 . . 9 D1
Wardlow Gdns **19** SK13 . . 9 D1
Wardlow Gr **22** SK13 . . . . 9 D1
Wardlow Mews **16** SK13 . . 9 D1
WARDLOW MIRES 70 C4
Wardlow Rd
  Ilkeston DE7 . . . . 194 E3
  Sheffield S12 . . . . 44 D5
Wardlow Wlk **18** SK13 . . . 9 D1
WARDS END 143 C2
Ward's La
  Barrow upon Trent DE73 . 244 F3
  Breaston DE72 . . . . 235 D8
  King's Newton DE73 . . . 245 A2
Ward St
  Derby DE22 . . . . 218 E4
  Tupton S42 . . . . 131 D8
Wards Yd S18 . . . . 57 A1
Wardwick DE1 . . . . 267 B3

Warehouse La S33 . . . . . . 38 D4
WARHILL 9 A3
Warhurst Fold **2** SK13 . . 10 A5
WARMBROOK 165 E8
Warmbrook DE4 . . . . . . 165 F8
Warmbrook Rd SK23 . . . . 47 C6
Warminster Cl S8 . . . . 43 A4
Warminster Cres S8 . . . . . 43 B4
Warminster Dr S8 . . . . . . 43 B3
Warminster Gdns S8 . . . . 43 A3
Warminster Pl S8 . . . . 43 B2
Warminster Rd S8 . . . . . . 43 A3
Warmwells La DE5 . . . . . 180 D6
Warner St
  Chesterfield S41 . . . . . . 266 C1
  Derby DE22 . . . . 267 A1
  Derby, Markeaton DE3 . . 217 D1
Warney Rd DE4 . . . . 127 D2
Warren Ave NG9 . . . . . . 223 D7
Warren Ave Extension
  NG9 . . . . 223 D7
Warren Cl
  Burton upon Trent DE13 . 240 E1
  Pilsley S45 . . . . 132 C2
Warren Cres S21 . . . . 58 E2
Warren Ct NG9 . . . . 223 D7
Warrendale Ct DE73 . . . . 233 A2
Warren Dr DE12 . . . . 261 C6
Warren Hill **7** DE11 . . . . 255 E5
Warren La
  Branston DE14 . . . . 253 F7
  Castle Donington DE74,
   NG10 . . . . 236 B2
Warren Lea SK6 . . . . 15 B2
Warren Rise S18 . . . . 57 C3
Warren St DE24 . . . . 232 F8
Warren Wlk S21 . . . . 58 E2
Warsop Rd NG19 . . . . . . 136 D3
WARSOP VALE 120 D4
Warwick Ave DE23 . . . . . 218 D1
Warwick Cl
  Branston DE14 . . . . 253 F8
  Glossop SK13 . . . . 17 F8
  Swadlincote DE11 . . . . . 256 E5
Warwick Ct DE55 . . . . . . 170 B8
Warwick Dr DE7 . . . . 194 C3
Warwick Gdns DE56 . . . . 179 D5
Warwick Rd
  Long Eaton NG10 . . . . . 237 A7
  Somercotes DE55 . . . . . 159 C1
Warwick St
  Chesterfield S40 . . . . . . 115 B7
  Derby DE24 . . . . 219 D2
Warwick Street Ind Est
  S40 . . . . 115 B7
Wasdale Ave **5** S20 . . . . 59 E6
Wasdale Cl S20 . . . . 59 E6
WASH 35 C1
Washbrook La DE6 . . . . . 161 F4
Washford Rd DE65 . . . . . 240 E8
Wash Gn DE4 . . . . 166 B8
WASHGREEN 155 A1
Wash Hills Cl DE4 . . . . . 153 A1
Washhouse Bottom SK17 . 69 E8
Wash House La S40 . . . . . 95 C2
Washington Ave DE21 . . 220 B6
Washington Cl DE73 . . . . 252 A7
Washington Cotts DE72 . 221 D1
Washington Dr NG9 . . . . 209 F1
Washington Terr DE4 . . . 143 E7
Watburn Rd SK22 . . . . . . 24 D1
Watchorn Cl DE11 . . . . . 256 D5
Watchorn Cotts DE55 . . . 158 F3
Watchorn La DE55 . . . . . 158 F2
Watercress La S45 . . . . . 131 D2
Waterdown Cl NG19 . . . . 136 D5
Waterfoot Cotts SK14 . . . . 9 A4
Waterfoot La SK23 . . . . . . 45 D6
Waterford Dr DE21 . . . . . 220 B4
Wateringbury Gr **1** S43 . . 78 F2
Watering La DE56 . . . . . . 191 D6
Water La
  Bakewell DE45 . . . . 109 D6
  Bamford S33 . . . . 40 A3
  Bolsover S44 . . . . 117 E8
  Cromford DE4 . . . . 155 A6
  Eyam S32 . . . . 71 E6
  Hollingworth SK14 . . . . . . 9 D5
  Middleton DE4 . . . . 154 C5
  Pleasley NG19 . . . . 135 B3
  Sheffield S17 . . . . 55 F7
  Shirebrook NG19 . . . . . . 118 L1
  South Normanton DE55 . . 160 B6
  Tideswell SK17 . . . . 68 F6
  Wirksworth DE4 . . . . . . 165 F7
Water Lily Gdns S80 . . . . 81 E3
WATERLOO 132 C3
Waterloo Cl DE55 . . . . . . 160 C8
Waterloo Ct DE1 . . . . . . 267 C5
Waterloo La NG9 . . . . . . 209 F6
Waterloo Pl DE11 . . . . . . 256 B4
Waterloo Rd
  Mansfield NG19 . . . . . . 136 B2
  Matlock Bath DE4 . . . . . 143 A1
Waterloo St
  Clay Cross S45 . . . . 131 C4
  Doe Lea S44 . . . . 117 E1
Water Mdws DE73 . . . . . 244 D6
Water Meadow La S40 . . . 95 B7
Watermeadow Rd DE24 . 233 A5
Watermeadows The
  NG10 . . . . 236 A8
Watermint Cl DE23 . . . . . 231 B6
Water Orton Cl NG9 . . . . 223 E3
Waterpark Rd DE6 . . . . . 224 B8
Waters Edge SK6 . . . . 23 B8

Waters Edge La SK23 . . . . 47 C5
Waterside
  Burton upon Trent DE15 . 254 E7
  Disley SK12 . . . . 32 E7
  Furness Vale SK23 . . . . . . 33 E3
  Glossop SK13 . . . . 10 A5
  Ironville NG16 . . . . 170 F4
  Marple SK6 . . . . 23 A5
  Willington DE65 . . . . . . 242 A6
Waterside Bsns Pk SK13 . . 9 F6
Waterside Cl
  Derby DE22 . . . . 205 A2
  Sandiacre NG10 . . . . . . 223 B3
Waterside Ho DE7 . . . . . 267 B4
Waterside Jun Sch DE15 254 E7
Waterside Rd
  Burton upon Trent DE15 . 254 D7
  Disley SK12, SK22 . . . . . . 32 E7
Waterside Ret Pk DE7 . . 195 A1
Water St
  Bakewell DE45 . . . . 109 C5
  Buxton SK17 . . . . 85 D8
  Glossop SK13 . . . . 10 E2
WATER SWALLOWS 67 E3
WATERSWALLOWS
  GREEN 66 F3
Waterswallows Ind Pk
  SK17 . . . . 67 A3
Waterswallows La SK17 . . 66 F4
Waterswallows Mews
  SK17 . . . . 66 E1
Waterswallows Rd SK17 . . 66 E1
Waterthorpe Cl **4** S20 . . 59 F8
Waterthorpe Cres S20 . . . 59 F8
Waterthorpe Gdns **3** S20 59 F8
Waterthorpe Glade **5**
  S20 . . . . 59 F8
Waterthorpe Glen **2** S20 . 59 F8
Waterthorpe Rise **1** S20 . 59 F8
Waterton Cl DE13 . . . . . . 241 A1
Waterway The NG10 . . . . 223 C4
Watery La
  Bretby DE15 . . . . 249 C3
  Clifton DE6 . . . . 184 E7
  Ellastone DE6 . . . . 183 B4
  Scropton DE65 . . . . 226 E2
  Swadlincote DE11 . . . . . 255 D5
  Thurvaston DE6 . . . . . . 215 D3
Watford Bridge Ind Est
  SK22 . . . . 24 C1
Watford Bridge Rd SK22 . 24 D1
Watford La SK22 . . . . 24 C2
Watford Lodge SK22 . . . . 24 C1
Watford Rd
  Buxton SK17 . . . . 84 F8
  New Mills SK22 . . . . 24 C2
Watkin Ave SK13 . . . . 9 F4
Watkinson St DE75 . . . . . 181 D2
Watson Ave DE75 . . . . . . 181 F2
Watson La S42 . . . . 114 C3
Watson Rd DE7 . . . . 194 C2
Watson St DE1 . . . . 218 E4
Watten Cl DE24 . . . . 231 F2
Watts Gn DE45 . . . . 108 F3
Waveney Cl DE22 . . . . . . 205 B5
Waverley Ct **2** S41 . . . . . 96 A4
Waverley St
  Derby DE24 . . . . 232 F3
  Long Eaton NG10 . . . . . 236 E8
  Tibshelf DE55 . . . . 148 A7
Wayfaring Rd DE21 . . . . 206 A1
Wayford Ave S41 . . . . . . 266 C1
Wayside
  Wayside S43 . . . . 96 B8
Wayside Cl S42 . . . . 132 A7
Wayside Ct S43 . . . . 96 B8
Wayzgoose Dr DE21 . . . . 219 C6
Weaddow La DE45 . . . . . 124 F2
Weakland Cl S12 . . . . 44 F3
Weakland Cres S12 . . . . . 44 F3
Weakland Dr S12 . . . . 44 F3
Weakland Way S12 . . . . . 44 F3
Weather Hill La HD9 . . . . . 3 C1
Weathern Field DE12 . . . 261 D3
Weaver Cl
  Ashbourne DE6 . . . . 185 C8
  Crich DE4 . . . . 156 F1
Weaver Rd ST14 . . . . 210 B2
Weavers Cl
  Belper DE56 . . . . 179 C5
  Borrowash DE72 . . . . . . 221 D1
Weavers Croft DE5 . . . . . 180 E8
Weavers Ct SK14 . . . . 9 A4
Weavers Gn DE3 . . . . 217 C1
Weavers The ST14 . . . . . 196 B6
Weaving Ave S33 . . . . 38 C2
Webbs Orch SK23 . . . . . . 45 D8
Webster Ave NG16 . . . . . 182 F1
Webster Croft S41 . . . . . . 77 B2
Webster Ct S40 . . . . 95 E5
Webster St DE1 . . . . 267 A2
Webster's Terr DE4 . . . . 143 C4
Wedgewood Cl DE55 . . . 248 B1
Wednesbury Ave S12 . . . . 44 E2
Wednesbough SK14 . . . . . 9 C5
Weighbridge Rd NG20 . . 119 F2
Weightman Dr NG16 . . . 195 B7
Weir Bank DE15 . . . . 254 E6
Weirfield Rd DE22 . . . . . 205 A2
Weirside DE6 . . . . 184 D7
Welbeck Ave
  Buxton SK17 . . . . 85 C6
  Ilkeston DE7 . . . . 208 D5
Welbeck Cl
  Alfreton DE55 . . . . 170 D7
  Dronfield S18 . . . . 56 C2
  Staveley S43 . . . . 97 D6
Welbeck Ct
  1 Chesterfield S40 . . . . . 95 C2
  Clowne S43 . . . . 80 F3

Welbeck Ct continued
7 Staveley S43. . . . . 78 E2
Welbeck Dr S42 . . . . 114 E4
Welbeck Gdns
Beeston NG9 . . . . 223 F3
Bolsover S44 . . . . 99 C2
Welbeck Gr DE22 . . . . . . 204 D3
Welbeck Rd
Bolsover S44 . . . . 99 B2
Long Eaton NG10 . . . . . . 223 C3
Mansfield Woodhouse
NG19. . . . . 136 C3
Welbeck St
Creswell S80 . . . . 81 E1
Whitwell S80 . . . . 82 B6
Welburn Cl NG19 . . . . . . 136 F2
Welbury Gdns S20 . . . . . . 59 E6
Welch Ave NG9 . . . . 223 E8
Welfare Ave S40 . . . . 95 D3
Welfare Cl NG20 . . . . . . 119 E3
Welfitt Gr NG20 . . . . . . 101 B2
Welland Cl
Burton upon Trent DE15 . . 248 A5
Derby DE3 . . . . 217 D4
Welland Rd DE65 . . . . . . 228 D1
Well Banks DE6 . . . . 165 B1
Wellcarr Rd S8 . . . . 43 A2
Well Cl DE6 . . . . 175 E3
Wellcroft DE4 . . . . 126 B1
Wellcroft Grange DE6 . . 183 D8
Welldon St DE5 . . . . 181 A4
Wellesley Ave DE23 . . . . 231 D7
Wellfield DE4. . . . . 143 C6
Wellfield Cl S12 . . . . 44 E1
Wellfield Ct DE4 . . . . . . 143 C6
Well Gate SK13 . . . . 10 E2
Wellgate La DE45 . . . . . 109 B1
Wellhead Rd 4 S8 . . . . . . 43 A6
Wellington Cl DE4 . . . . . 143 D7
Wellington Cres DE1 . . . 267 D2
Wellington Ct
1 Belper DE56 . . . . 178 F3
Eastwood NG16 . . . . 182 F2
Wellington Mews DE55. . 146 D2
Wellington Pk DE55 . . . . 146 D2
Wellington Pl NG16 . . . . 182 F2
Wellington Rd DE14 . . . . 253 E8
Wellington St
Chesterfield S43 . . . . 77 D3
Derby DE1 . . . . 267 D2
Eastwood NG16 . . . . 182 F3
Heanor DE75 . . . . 181 D3
Long Eaton NG10 . . . . . . 223 C2
Matlock DE4. . . . . 143 C6
Ripley DE5 . . . . 169 E1
Stapleford NG9 . . . . 223 C6
Well La
Belper DE56. . . . . 190 F7
Blackfordby DE11 . . . . . . 257 A2
Holymoorside S42 . . . . . 112 F7
Repton DE65 . . . . 242 C1
Shirland DE55 . . . . 146 C3
Well Rd S8 . . . . 43 A6
Well Row SK14 . . . . 16 A8
Wells Cl NG19 . . . . 136 D4
Wells Ct DE23 . . . . 230 E7
Wellspring Cl
Barlborough S43 . . . . 80 B6
Wingerworth S42. . . . . . 115 B4
Well Spring Cl S43 . . . . . . 96 E7
Wellspring Dale NG9 . . . 223 E5
Wells Rd DE3 . . . . 217 E2
Wells St S44 . . . . 118 C8
Well St
Brassington DE4. . . . . . . 152 F1
Derby DE1 . . . . 267 B5
Elton DE4. . . . . 140 E7
New Mills SK22 . . . . 33 B8
Ripley DE5 . . . . 169 D1
Wellwood Rd DE11 . . . . . 256 A6
Well Yd
Belper DE56. . . . . 179 A5
Holbrook DE56 . . . . 191 C6
Welney Cl DE3 . . . . 230 E1
Welshpool Pl S40 . . . . 95 D3
Welshpool Rd DE21 . . . . 205 D1
Welton Ave DE56 . . . . . . 179 B6
Welwyn Ave
Derby, Allenton DE24. . . . 232 E4
Derby DE22 . . . . 204 D3
Mansfield Woodhouse
NG19. . . . . 136 E4
Welwyn Cl
Chesterfield S40 . . . . 95 D3
Sheffield S12 . . . . 44 A4
Welwyn Ct S12 . . . . 44 A4
Welwyn Rd S12 . . . . 44 B4
Wembley Gdns DE22 . . . 218 A6

Wenlock Cl
Chesterfield S40 . . . . 95 D4
Derby DE3 . . . . 217 E1
Eastwood NG16 . . . . 195 C8
Wenlock Cres S40 . . . . . . 95 D4
Wenlock Dr S42 . . . . . . 115 F3
Wenlock Wlk S42 . . . . . . 115 F3
WENSLEY 142 A7
WENSLEY DALE 142 B6
Wensleydale Cl NG19 . . . 136 F2
Wensleydale Rd NG10 . . 236 B6
Wensleydale Wlk DE24 . . 233 C7
Wensley Dr DE21 . . . . . . 220 F3
Wensley Rd
North Wingfield S42 . . . . 131 F5
Winster DE4 . . . . 141 D6
Wensley Way S43 . . . . 97 C8
Wentworth Ave S40 . . . . 114 E8

Wentworth Cl
Derby DE3 . . . . 217 F2
Mansfield NG19 . . . . 136 F2
Wentworth Croft DE75 . . 182 A3
Wentworth Ct NG16 . . . . 195 E6
Wentworth Dr DE13 . . . . 240 D1
Wentworth Ho 1 DE1. . . 218 E5
Wentworth Rd S18 . . . . . . 56 C1
Wentworth St DE7 . . . . . 195 A2
Werburgh Cl DE21 . . . . . 220 D4
Werburgh St DE22 . . . . . 267 A2
Werneth Low Ctry Pk★
SK14 . . . . 15 A7
Werneth Low Rd SK14. . . . 15 B6
Werneth Rd SK13 . . . . 17 A7
Wesleyan Chapel La SK17 . 88 A3
Wesleyan Chapel Wlk
NG9 . . . . 223 D7
Wesley Ct SK23 . . . . 47 C6
Wesley Ho 3 SK17 . . . . . . 85 D8
Wesley La DE72 . . . . 221 C5
Wesley Pl NG9 . . . . 223 E7
Wesley Rd
Ambergate DE56 . . . . . . 167 F3
Derby DE24 . . . . 233 B5
Stonebroom DE55 . . . . . 146 F3
Wesley St
Glossop SK13. . . . . 10 E2
Hadfield SK13 . . . . 10 A5
Ilkeston DE7 . . . . 194 E4
Langley Mill NG16 . . . . . 182 C3
Wessex Cl 5 S43 . . . . 96 F8
Wessex Dr NG16 . . . . . . 195 A8
Wessex Gdns S17 . . . . 55 D5
WESSINGTON 157 E8
Wessington Bank 9 SK13 . . 9 E2
Wessington Dr S43 . . . . . . 97 C8
Wessington Fold 12 SK13 . . 9 E2
Wessington Gn 11 SK13 . . . 9 E2
**Wessington Green Nature
Reserve★** DE55 . . . . . . 157 E8
Wessington La DE55 . . . . 158 A6
Wessington Mews
Derby DE22 . . . . 204 E1
Gamesley SK13 . . . . 9 E2
Wessington Prim Sch
DE55 . . . . 157 E8
Westacre Dr DE11 . . . . . . 255 F2
West Ave
Chellaston DE73 . . . . 232 E3
Derby DE1 . . . . 267 A4
Draycott DE72 . . . . 234 F8
Hilton DE65 . . . . 228 C2
Ripley DE5 . . . . 169 C1
Sandiacre NG10 . . . . 223 A6
Stapleford NG9 . . . . 223 E8
West Bank
Matlock Bath DE4 . . . . . 143 A1
Toadmoor DE56 . . . . . . 168 D2
Winster DE4 . . . . 141 B5
West Bank Ave
Crich DE4. . . . . 156 F1
Derby DE22 . . . . 218 F8
Mansfield NG19 . . . . 136 B1
Westbank Cl S18 . . . . 57 B4
West Bank Cl DE22 . . . . . 218 E8
Westbank Ct S18 . . . . 57 C4
West Bank Lea NG19 . . . . 136 B1
West Bank Link NG19 . . . 136 B1
West Bank Rd DE22 . . . . 204 E5
West Bars S40 . . . . 266 A3
Westbourne Ave DE55. . . 147 A4
Westbourne Ct NG19 . . . 136 E4
Westbourne St NG9 . . . . 209 F1
Westbourne Gr S40 . . . . . 95 B3
Westbourne Pk DE22 . . . 217 F7
Westbridge Rd S43 . . . . . . 80 A7
Westbrook Cl
Chapel-en-le-Frith SK23 . . 47 C5
Chesterfield S40 . . . . 94 E7
Westbrook Dr S40 . . . . . . 94 F2
WEST BROUGHTON . . . 225 A6
Westbury Ct DE22 . . . . . 218 E3
Westbury Gdns DE56 . . . 179 C5
Westbury St DE22 . . . . . 218 E4
Westby La NG16 . . . . 195 D3
West Cl DE22 . . . . 204 E2
West Cres
Duckmanton S44 . . . . 98 A5
Matlock DE4. . . . . 143 A6
West Croft Ave DE23 . . . 231 D5
West Croft Cl DE45. . . . . 125 B5
Westcroft Cres S20 . . . . . 59 E8
West Croft Ct S43 . . . . . . 97 B5
Westcroft Dr S20 . . . . . . 59 E7
West Croft Dr S43 . . . . . . 97 B5
Westcroft Gdns S20 . . . . 59 E8
Westcroft Glen

Wentworth Cl continued
Wirksworth DE4 . . . . 165 E8
West End Cl DE55 . . . . . . 159 A3
West End Cres DE7. . . . . 208 D8
West End Dr
Ilkeston DE7 . . . . 208 D8
Shardlow DE72 . . . . 234 E1
West End St NG9. . . . . . 223 C5
West End View S21 . . . . . 59 C2
Westerlands NG9 . . . . . . 223 F6
Western Ave S45 . . . . . . 169 D7
Western Dr DE75. . . . . . 193 F8
Western La SK23 . . . . 46 A8
Western Rd
Derby DE3 . . . . 217 E2
Derby, Rose Hill DE23 . . . 219 A3
Western View DE45 . . . . . 90 A4
Western Villas DE56. . . . 167 F3
WESTFIELD 59 F8
Westfield Ave
Chesterfield S40 . . . . 95 B1
5 Heanor DE75 . . . . . . 181 F1
West Field Bank S43 . . . . 80 A7
Westfield Cl
Chesterfield S40 . . . . 95 B2
Ilkeston DE7 . . . . 208 C6
Westfield Cres S20. . . . . . 59 C8
Westfield Ctr S20 . . . . . . 59 E8
Westfield Derby (Sh Ctr)
DE1. . . . . 267 C2
Westfield Dr
Blackwell DE55 . . . . 147 C1
Ilkeston DE7 . . . . 194 D2
Westfield Gdns S40 . . . . . 95 B2
Westfield Gr DE22 . . . . . 218 D4
Westfield Inf Sch S40 . . . 95 B2
Westfield La
Barlborough S43 . . . . 79 F7
Chesterfield S40 . . . . 95 B2
Staveley S43 . . . . 78 D1
Westfield Northway S20. . 59 E8
Westfield Rd
Dronfield S18. . . . . 76 C8
Killamarsh S21 . . . . 60 C5
Swadlincote DE11 . . . . . 256 B6
Westfield Southway S20 . . 59 E8
Westgate DE1 . . . . 218 E6
West Gate
Holme HD9 . . . . .3 F8
Long Eaton NG10. . . . . . 236 E7
Westgate Cl ST14 . . . . . . 196 F3
Westgreen Ave DE24 . . . 232 D5
WEST HALLAM 207 F8
**WEST HALLAM
COMMON** 207 D8
Westhall Rd DE3 . . . . 217 D8
WEST HANDLEY 77 D8
West Hill DE5 . . . . 181 B7
Westhill La S42 . . . . 115 C4
West Hill Pk NG19 . . . . . 136 B3
West Ho S18 . . . . 43 A4
West Horderns SK23 . . . . . 47 B5
Westhorpe Dr NG10 . . . . 236 C5
WESTHOUSES 159 C8
Westhouses Prim Sch
DE55. . . . . 147 C1
Westland Dr NG16 . . . . . 160 C3
Westland Gdns S20 . . . . . 59 D8
Westland Gr 3 S20 . . . . . 59 E8
Westland Rd 1 S20 . . . . . 59 E8
Westlands The ST14 . . . . 196 D6
West Lawn DE65 . . . . . . 230 D2
Westlea DE4. . . . . 143 D6
West Lea
Chesterfield S40 . . . . 95 B2
Clowne S43 . . . . 80 D4
West Lea Cotts S43 . . . . . 80 D4
Westlea View S43 . . . . . . 80 D4
Wee Lees Rd S33. . . . . . . 40 B4
Westleigh NG19. . . . . . . 136 D6
Westleigh Ave DE22 . . . . 218 C6
Westleigh Ct S40 . . . . 95 E5
Westley Cres DE21 . . . . . 191 D2
West Meadow Rise DE74 246 E4
Westminster Ave 1
NG10 . . . . 223 C5
Westminster Dr DE11 . . . 255 E1
Westminster St DE24 . . . 232 F8
Westmoor Rd S43. . . . . . . 96 F4
Westmorland Cl DE21 . . . 219 D2
Westmorland Way NG16. . 171 B3
Weston Bank DE6. . . . . . 197 F1
Weston Cl S40 . . . . 95 A5
Weston Cres NG10 . . . . . 235 F4
Weston Ct DE72. . . . . . . 245 E4
Westonhill Chalet Pk
DE72 . . . . 245 G4

West Rd
Buxton SK17 . . . . 85 B6
Derby DE21 . . . . 220 D5
West Road Ho 2 SK17 . . . 85 B6
West Row DE22 . . . . 205 A1
West Service Rd DE21. . . 220 B3
West St
Bramley-Vale S44 . . . . . . 117 D1
Burton upon Trent DE15 . . 248 B3
Chesterfield S40 . . . . . . 266 A4
Clay Cross S45. . . . . 131 A4
Clowne S43 . . . . 81 A5
Creswell S80 . . . . 81 D1
Dronfield S18. . . . . 56 F2
Eckington S21 . . . . 59 C2
Glossop SK13. . . . . 9 F7
Heanor DE75 . . . . 181 D2
Ilkeston DE7 . . . . 208 E7
Langley Mill NG16 . . . . . 182 B3
Shirebrook NG20. . . . . . 120 D4
Somercotes DE55 . . . . . 170 C6
South Normanton DE55. . 159 F5
Stonebroom DE55 . . . . . 146 F3
Swadlincote DE11 . . . . . 256 B4
Whaley Thorns NG20. . . . 101 A3
West Terr 6 DE7. . . . . . 194 F1
WESTTHORPE 60 D4
Westthorpe Fields Rd
S21. . . . . 60 C4
Westthorpe Rd S21 . . . . . 60 D5
West Towers Mews SK6. . 23 A4
West View
Barlborough S43 . . . . 80 A6
Bolsover S44 . . . . 118 B8
Hulland Village DE6. . . . . 175 E2
Mayfield DE6 . . . . 184 D6
Parwich DE6 . . . . 151 E1
Rocester ST14 . . . . 197 A3
Staveley S43 . . . . 78 D1
Tibshelf DE55. . . . . 147 F6
West View Ave DE23 . . . . 231 B7
West View Cl S17 . . . . 55 F6
West View La S17 . . . . 55 F6
West View Rd S41 . . . . . . 95 E6
Westward Cl ST14 . . . . . 210 B1
West Way S45 . . . . 159 C1
Westwell Pl S20 . . . . 59 D6
Westwick Cres S8 . . . . . . 56 D7
Westwick Gr S8 . . . . 56 E7
Westwick La S42. . . . . . . 94 D2
Westwick Pk S41 . . . . 76 D3
Westwick Rd S8 . . . . 56 E7
Westwick St DE7. . . . . . 209 B6
WESTWOOD 171 C3
Westwood Ave S43 . . . . . 97 C8
Westwood Cl S43 . . . . . . 97 C5
Westwood Dr
Derby DE22 . . . . 232 D5
Staveley S43 . . . . 97 C5
Westwood Drive Gdns
S43. . . . . 97 B5
Westwood Gdns DE55 . . . 147 B5
Westwood Inf Sch NG16 . 171 C4
Westwood La S43 . . . . . . 96 F4
Westwood Pk DE11 . . . . . 255 F5
Westwood Rd S44 . . . . . . 97 A4
Wetherby Cl DE14. . . . . . 253 F7
Wetherby Rd DE24 . . . . . 232 E7
Wetherel Rd DE15 . . . . . 248 C2
Wetlands La S43, S44. . . . 96 E4
WETTON 149 A3
Wetton La DE55. . . . . . . 148 A6
Weyacres DE7 . . . . 221 C1
Weybridge Cl DE7. . . . . . 207 D8
WHALEY 100 C4
WHALEY BRIDGE 45 D7
Whaley Bridge Prim Sch
SK23. . . . . 45 E7
Whaley Bridge Sta SK23. . 45 E8
Whaley La SK23. . . . . 45 C8
Whaley Rd NG20 . . . . . . 100 E2
WHALEY THORNS 101 A2
Whaley Thorns Her Ctr★
NG20. . . . . 101 A3
Whaley Thorns Ind Est
NG20. . . . . 100 F2
Whaley Thorns Prim Sch
NG20. . . . . 101 A3
Wharf Ct SK23 . . . . 45 E7
Wharfedale Cl DE22. . . . 205 B4
Wharfedale Rd NG10 . . . 236 A6
Wharf Hos DE13 . . . . . . 253 A1
Wharf La
Chesterfield S41 . . . . . . 266 C1
Staveley S43 . . . . 96 C7

Wheatcroft La DE4. . . . . 157 A7
Wheatcroft Way DE21 . . 205 D2
Wheatfield Cres NG19. . . 136 E5
Wheatfield Ct DE65 . . . . 242 D5
Wheatfields SK23 . . . . . . 47 C7
Wheatfield Way S42 . . . . 94 F5
Wheathill Cl
Calow S43 . . . . 96 F4
Chesterfield S42 . . . . 94 F5
Wheathill Gr DE23 . . . . . 231 A6
Wheathill La S41. . . . . . . 96 D4
Wheatland Cl DE24. . . . . 231 C2
Wheatlands DE11 . . . . . . 256 B7
Wheatlands La DE45 . . . . 91 C5
Wheatlands Rd
Burton upon Trent DE15 . . 254 E7
Wingerworth S42. . . . . . 114 E4
Wheatley Ave S45 . . . . . 159 C1
Wheatley Cl NG19. . . . . . 136 F2
Wheatley Gdns DE4 . . . . 127 C2
Wheatley La DE15 . . . . . 248 C4
Wheatley Rd DE4 . . . . . . 127 D3
Wheatsheaf Cl
Derby DE21 . . . . 206 C2
Horwich End SK23 . . . . . 45 E6
Wheatsheaf La DE4 . . . . . 156 F1
Wheatsheaf Rd SK23 . . . . 45 E6
Wheeldon Ave
Belper DE56. . . . . 179 B4
Derby DE22 . . . . 218 A4
Wheeldon Cl NE7 . . . . . . 194 F6
Wheeldon Cres S43 . . . . . 96 D7
Wheeldon Manor DE22. . 218 B4
Wheeldon Way DE6 . . . . 175 E3
Wheelwright Way DE24 . 219 D3
Whenby DE7 . . . . 217 C2
Whernside Cl DE24. . . . . 233 D6
WHESTON 68 F5
Wheston Bank SK17. . . . . 69 B4
Wheston Ct 7 S40. . . . . . 95 D5
Whetmorhurst La SK6. . . 23 E4
Whilton Cres DE7 . . . . . 207 D8
Whilton Ct DE56 . . . . . . 179 D4
Whinacre Cl S8 . . . . 57 B6
Whinacre Pl S8. . . . . 57 A6
Whinacre Wlk S8 . . . . . . 57 A6
Whinbush Ave DE24. . . . 232 E5
Whinney Bank NG19 . . . . 136 D4
Whinney Hill NG19 . . . . . 136 D4
Whisperwood Cl S44. . . . 98 A5
Whistlestop Cl DE3 . . . . 217 D4
Whiston St DE23 . . . . . . 219 A2
Whitaker Gdns DE23 . . . 218 E2
Whitaker Mews ST14. . . . 196 F3
Whitaker Rd DE23 . . . . . 218 E2
Whitaker St DE23 . . . . . . 219 A2
Whitburn Rd NG9 . . . . . 223 E3
Whitby Ave DE21. . . . . . 205 C1
Whitcombe Pl DE5 . . . . . 169 D2
Whitebank Cl S41. . . . . . 266 C1
Whitecotes Cl S40 . . . . . 114 E8
Whitecotes La S40 . . . . . 114 E8
Whitecotes Pk S40. . . . . 114 F8
Whitecotes Prim Sch
S40 . . . . 114 F8
Whitecroft Rd SK6. . . . . . 23 C1
Whitecross Ave SK17. . . . 69 C4
Whitecross Gdns DE1 . . . 218 E7
Whitecross Ho DE1 . . . . . 218 E7
Whitecross Rd SK17. . . . . 69 D5
Whitecross St DE1 . . . . . 218 E6
White Edge Cl S40 . . . . . 95 D5
White Edge Dr DE45. . . . 91 E6
Whitefield La
Ashover S45 . . . . 129 A5
Chelmorton SK17 . . . . . . 106 E8
White Gate Rd HD9 . . . . . 3 D7
Whitegates SK14. . . . . 9 A1
White Gates DE5. . . . . . . 181 B8
Whitegates Way NG17. . . 148 E3
Whitehall Terr SK23. . . . . 34 D1
White Hart Cnr S21 . . . . . 59 ?
White Hart Yd DE56 . . . . 1? ?
Whitehaven Gr DE73 . . . . ? ?
Whitehead Cl DE7. . . . . . ? D2
Whitehead Dr NG1? . . . . ?2 D8
Whitehead St . . . . ? 78 F2
White Ho? 145 D7
WHI? 46 D8
?enough Head La
SK23. . . . . 46 E8
Whitehouse Cl DE24 . . . . 232 D3
Whitehouse Rise DE56 . . 178 E6
Whitehouses S41 . . . . . . 266 C1
Whitehurst St DE24 . . . . 232 D7
White Knowle Cl SK17 . . . 85 C5
White Knowle Pk SK17 . . 85 C5
White Knowle Rd SK17 . . 85 C5
White La
Eckington S12 . . . . 44 C2
Shottle DE56 . . . . 177 D4
Whitelea La DE4 . . . . 144 B6
White Leas S40 . . . . 95 B4
White Leas Ave S42 . . . . 132 A7
Whiteleas Rd SK23 . . . . . 45 D3
WHITELEY 180 F6
Whiteley Rd DE5. . . . . . . 180 F7
White Lion Sq DE7 . . . . . 208 F7
White Lodge La DE45. . . . 91 E6
Whitelow La
Idle DE6 . . . . ? ?
Sheffield S17 . . . . 55 B7
Whitely Ave DE7 . . . . . . 194 F5

Wentworth Cl
Derby DE3 . . . . 217 F2
Mansfield NG19 . . . . 136 F2

Westcross Ave NG9 . . . . 223 E8
Westdale Cl NG10 . . . . . 236 A5
Westdale Rd
Mansfield NG19 . . . . 136 B1
Westwood NG16 . . . . . . 171 C4
Westdene Ave DE24 . . . . 232 D5
West Dr
Derby DE3 . . . . 217 D2
Doveridge DE6 . . . . 211 B1
Glossop SK13 . . . . 9 E7
West Edge Cl S45 . . . . . . 129 D4
West End
Alfreton DE55 . . . . 159 A3
Barlborough S43 . . . . 80 A7
Baslow DE45 . . . . 91 E5
Brassington DE4 . . . . 152 F1
Broadbottom SK14. . . . . . 15 F8
Elton DE4. . . . . 140 E6
Pinxton NG16. . . . . 160 C4

Weston Park Ave DE24 . . 232 E3
Weston Park Gdns DE24 232 D3
Weston Rd
Aston-on-Trent DE72 . . . . 246 A7
Weston-on-Trent DE72 . . 245 F6
Weston Rise DE73. . . . . . 245 A8
Weston Spot Cl DE5. . . . 180 D7
Weston St
Heanor DE75 . . . . 194 A8
Swadlincote DE11 . . . . . 256 B3
WESTON UNDERWOOD . 189 A2
West Park Ct NG10 . . . . . 236 D7
West Park L Ctr NG10 . . . 236 B7
**West Park Mdw Nature
Reserve★** DE7. . . . . . . 220 C5
West Park Rd DE22. . . . . 218 E8
West Park Sch DE21 . . . . 220 D5

DE72 . . . . 245 F5
Weston Park Ave DE24 . . 232 E3

Wharf Road Ind Est
NG16. . . . . 160 D2
Wharf Road Ind Est
NG16. . . . . 160 D2
Wharf Road Ind Est
. . . . 160 D2
Whaley Bridge SK23 . . . . 45 E7
Wharf Road Ind Est
NG16. . . . . 160 D2
WHARF THE 210 C1
Wharf The DE72 . . . . . . 235 A2
Wharmby Ave NG19 . . . . 135 D3
Wharncliffe Cl SK13. . . . . 9 E2
Wharncliffe Rd DE7. . . . 208 E8
Wharton Dr S41 . . . . . . 266 C3
WHATSTANDWELL 156 C1
Whatstandwell Sta DE4 . 156 C1
Wheal La SK17. . . . . 107 D7
Wheatbridge Rd S40 . . . 266 A3
Wheatbridge Ret Pk S40 266 A3
WHEATCROFT 157 A7
Wheatcroft SK13. . . . . 9 E2
Wheatcroft Cl
Clay Cross S45. . . . . 131 D2
Wingerworth S42. . . . . . 115 A4

Whitely Cl **3** NG9......223 E8
WHITE MOOR......179 C5
Whitemoor Hall DE56...179 D5
Whitemoor La DE56......179 D5
White Rd
  New Mills SK22......24 C2
  Staveley S43......79 A3
Whites Cl DE55......159 A2
Whites Croft View S43...80 B6
Whites La DE55......147 F1
Whitesmead Cl SK12.....32 D5
White St DE22......218 E7
White Thorns Cl S8......57 B5
White Thorns Dr S8......57 B6
White Thorns View S8...57 B5
White Tor Rd DE4......143 C2
Whiteway DE22......204 E2
Whitewell Gdns DE24....233 C5
Whitewells La DE56......178 C8
Whitewells Rd DE56......167 C2
Whitewood Way DE4.....143 B3
WHITFIELD......17 D8
Whitfield Ave SK13......17 C7
Whitfield Cross SK13.....17 D7
Whitfield La DE45......124 E2
Whitfield Pk SK13......17 C7
Whitfield Wells SK13....17 D7
Whiting Ave **2** NG9.....223 F2
Whiting St **8** S8......43 A6
Whitle Bank Rd SK22.....24 B2
Whitle Rd SK22......24 C1
Whitley Way DE6......185 E8
Whitley Wlk SK13......16 F8
Whitmore Ave S42......115 E2
Whitmore Rd DE21......219 F6
Whitstable Cl DE23......231 D7
Whittaker La DE21......191 C1
Whitt Cl DE72......221 C1
Whitting Mews S41......76 F2
Whittington Hill S41......77 A2
Whittington La S18......76 F5
WHITTINGTON MOOR.....96 A7
Whittington Rd S43......77 F4
Whittington St DE24......232 D6
Whittington Way S41......77 A1
Whitting Valley Rd S41...77 B1
Whittlebury Dr DE23......230 F7
WHITWELL......81 E6
Whitwell S80......82 A5
Whitwell Bank **5** SK13...9 D2
Whitwell Cl
  4 Gameslery SK13......9 D2
  Ilkeston NE7......194 E6
Whitwell Fold **1** SK13....9 D2
Whitwell Gn **2** SK13......9 D2
Whitwell Lea **3** SK13......9 D2
Whitwell Prim Sch S80...82 A5
Whitwell Rd S80......63 A4
Whitwell Sta S80......82 A5
Whitworth Ave DE4......127 C3
Whitworth Cl DE12......262 E4
Whitworth Hospl DE4....142 F8
Whitworth Rd
  1 Chesterfield S41......96 A6
  Darley Dale DE4......127 B4
  Ilkeston DE7......208 F7
Wholey Pl S45......131 C3
Whysall Rd NG10......236 B7
Whysall St DE75......181 E2
Whyteleafe Gr DE21......206 B1
Wichal Farm Cl S45......180 D7
Wickenlow La SK17......103 D1
Wickersley Cl **1** DE22...206 B1
Wickets The DE15......254 F8
Wickfield Cl S12......44 F5
Wickfield Dr S12......44 F5
Wickfield Gr S12......44 E4
Wickfield Pl S12......44 F5
Wickfield Rd S12......44 F5
Wickins Pl S43......79 B3
Wicksteed Cl DE56......179 D5
Widdop Cl S13......44 D8
Widdop Croft S13......44 D8
Widdowson Rd **2** NG10..236 B5
Widdybank Cl DE22......204 C2
Widecombe Ct **24** S41...95 F8
Wideshaft DE11......256 C4
Widmerpool St NG16......160 C2
WIGLEY......93 F4
Wigley Prim Sch S42......93 E4
Wigley Rd S43......97 C6
Wigmore Cl DE3......217 C3
Wikeley Way S43......96 D7
Wilberforce Rd NG19.....135 D2
Wilcock Ho DE21......219 C6
Wilcox Ave NG19......136 B5
WILDAY GREEN......75 A2
Wildaygreen La S18......75 B2
Wilden Croft S43......96 C8
Wilderbrook La DE56......178 A8
Wilders Lea Ct DE56......179 A2
Wildersley Rd DE56......179 A1
Wildhay Brook DE65......228 C1
Wildhay La DE6......183 C7
Wild Hill NG17......148 E7
Wild La DE4, DE55......157 B4
Wildpark La DE6......202 D6
Wildsmith St DE24......233 A8
Wild St DE22......218 D5
Wilfred St DE23......219 B2
Wilhallow La NG16......171 E2
Wilkin Hill S18......75 E2
Wilkins Dr DE24......232 E7
Wilkinson Cl
  Chesterfield S40......115 A6

Wilkinson Cl continued
  Pleasley NG19......135 A5
Wilkinson Dr S43......97 B7
Willbury Dr S12......44 A6
Willcock Rd DE14......254 A7
Willersley Castle ★ DE4..155 B7
Willersley Ct **3** S41......95 D7
Willersley Ho NG10......236 A5
Willersley La
  Matlock Bath DE4......155 C8
  Matlock DE4......143 C1
Willesden Ave DE22......218 A7
Willetts Rd DE21......220 A7
William Allitt Sch DE11...255 E7
William Ave NG16......182 F2
William Cl
  Duffield DE56......190 D4
  Sheffield S20......59 D6
William Cres S20......59 D6
William Gilbert Endowed
  Prim Sch DE56......190 E4
William Gregg VC L Ctr
  DE75......181 F1
William Holmes Almshouses
  DE5......169 F2
William Levick Prim Sch
  S18......56 C2
William Lilley Inf Sch
  NG9......223 D6
William Nadin Way DE11 255 F4
William Newton Cl DE65..241 B5
William Rd NG9......223 D7
William Rhodes Prim Sch
  S40......266 A2
Williams Cl DE55......170 D6
William Shrewsbury Prim
  Sch DE13......240 E1
Williamson Ave SK17.....66 C1
Williamson Cres SK23....45 D8
Williamson Rd SK23......45 D8
William St
  Belper DE56......178 F4
  Chesterfield S41......96 A6
  Derby DE1......218 E6
  Eckington S21......59 D3
  Long Eaton NG10......223 C2
William Street N S41......76 F2
WILLIAMTHORPE......132 C8
Williamthorpe Cl S42.....132 A7
Williamthorpe Ind Pk
  S42......116 D2
Williamthorpe Ponds ★
  S42......116 E2
Williamthorpe Rd S42....132 B7
William Wood La NG20...120 C5
WILLINGTON......242 A6
Willington Prim Sch
  DE65......242 B5
Willington Rd
  Etwall DE65......229 D3
  Findern DE65......242 D8
  Repton DE65......242 B4
  Willington Sta DE65......242 A6
Willn St DE7......218 F1
Willoughby Almshouses
  NG16......195 C1
Willoughby Ave NG10.....223 C3
Willoughby Cl DE72......235 F8
Willoughby Ct DE72......222 D4
Willoughby Ho DE11......256 C4
Willow Ave
  Long Eaton NG10......223 D1
  Ripley DE5......180 D3
  Shirebrook NG20......119 D5
  Stapleford NG9......223 D6
Willowbath La DE4......165 F7
Willowbrook Cl DE55......228 C2
Willowbrook Grange
  DE73......233 A1
Willow Cl
  Aldercar NG16......182 B4
  Alfreton DE55......159 B5
  Aston-on-Trent DE72......246 B7
  Creswell S80......81 F1
  Derby DE72......204 F2
  Pilsley S45......132 C1
  South Normanton DE55...160 B5
  Stanley Common DE7......193 A2
Willow Croft DE24......233 C4
Willowcroft Rd DE21......220 E4
Willow Ct
  Ashbourne DE6......185 D7
  Calow S44......97 A3
  Swadlincote DE11......256 C4
Willow Dr
  Chapel-en-le-Frith SK23...47 B5
  Mastin Moor S43......79 C4
  Swadlincote DE11......255 F7
Willow Farm Bsns Pk
  DE74......247 B6
Willow Farm Ct DE65.....230 D2
Willowfields DE65......228 D2
Willow Garth Rd S41......95 C8
Willow Gr
  Belper DE56......179 A2
  Willington DE65......242 A6
Willowherb Cl DE24......231 F2
Willow Ho DE21......219 C6
Willow Meadow Rd DE65 185 D7
Willow Park Way DE72...246 A7
Willowpit La DE65......228 E5
Willow Pl DE15......254 E7
Willow Rd
  Castle Donington DE74...247 B5
  Killamarsh S21......60 C5
Willow Rise NG10......223 B5
Willow Row DE1......267 A4
Willows Ave DE55......159 B5

Willows Ct DE5......169 C1
Willowsend Cl DE65......230 D1
Willowside Gn DE21......220 D3
Willow Sq S42......115 C1
Willows Sports Ctr DE1..267 A4
Willow St DE55......146 C1
Willows The
  Hulland Ward DE6......175 F3
  Pleasley NG19......135 A5
Willow Stream SK22......33 D8
Willowtree Dr DE21......220 B7
Willow Tree Dr S43......80 F2
Willow Way DE4......127 B3
Willridding La DE6......183 C7
Will Shore's La DE4......142 D6
Willson Ave DE23......231 D8
Willson Dr DE55......170 C7
Willson Rd DE23......231 C8
Wilmans Wlk SK13......10 A6
Wilmington Ave DE24.....233 B5
Wilmore Rd DE24......232 B5
WILMORTON......219 E2
Wilmot Ave
  Derby DE21......219 F5
  Weston-on-Trent DE72.....245 E5
Wilmot Dr DE7......192 F6
Wilmot Rd
  Belper DE56......179 A4
  Swadlincote DE11......256 B3
Wilmot St
  Derby DE1......267 B2
  Heanor DE75......181 E1
  Ilkeston DE7......194 E1
  Long Eaton NG10......236 A5
  Matlock DE4......143 B6
Wilmslow Dr DE21......206 B1
Wilne Ave NG10......236 A4
Wilne Cl NG10......235 F4
Wilne La
  Breaston DE72......235 D4
  Shardlow DE72......235 B2
Wilne Rd
  Draycott DE72......235 B5
  Long Eaton NG10......235 F4
Wilshaw Cl SK23......47 C5
WILSON......252 F6
Wilson Ave
  Blackwell DE55......147 E1
  Clowne S43......80 F5
  Heanor DE75......181 B4
Wilson Cl
  Burnaston DE3......230 C8
  Clay Cross S45......131 D2
Wilson La S44......117 B2
Wilson Pl **6** S8......43 A7
Wilson Rd
  Derby DE21......219 F8
  Dronfield S18......57 C4
  Eastwood NG16......182 F1
Wilson Rise DE73......252 E6
Wilson St
  Alfreton DE55......159 B4
  Derby DE1......267 B2
  Dronfield S18......76 B8
  Mansfield NG19......135 D2
  Pinxton NG16......160 D3
Wilson's Terr SK13......17 B8
WILSTHORPE......236 B7
Wilsthorpe Bsns & Enterprise
  Coll NG10......223 B1
Wilsthorpe Rd
  Breaston DE72......235 E8
  Derby DE21......220 A7
  Long Eaton NG10......236 B7
Wilton Cl DE24......231 C2
Wilton Pl DE7......194 F1
Wilton St **5** DE7......194 F1
Wiltra Gr DE56......190 F3
Wiltshire Ave NG16......171 B4
Wiltshire Dr SK13......17 F8
Wiltshire Rd DE21......219 E7
Wimbledon Rd DE22......218 A7
Wimborne Cres S41......95 F7
Wimbourne Cl DE73......233 A2
Wimpole Gdns DE22......218 B6
Wimsey Way DE55......159 B2
Wincanton Cl DE24......219 D1
Winchcombe Dr DE15....248 B1
Winchcombe Way DE21..206 B2
Winchester Cl S42......131 F6
Winchester Cres DE7.....209 A8
Winchester Dr
  Burton upon Trent DE14..254 C8
  Linton DE12......261 D5
  Mansfield Woodhouse
    NG19......136 D4
  Swadlincote DE11......256 D6
Winchester Rd S41......95 E7
Windermere Ave
  Dronfield S18......56 E1
  Ilkeston DE7......208 D5
Windermere Cl NG19......136 E3
Windermere Cres DE22...204 E3
Windermere Dr DE21......220 E5
Windermere Gdns NG10..223 B2
Windermere Rd
  Chesterfield S41......95 D7
  Clay Cross S45......131 B3
  Long Eaton NG10......223 B2
Winders Cnr S43......80 B5
Winding Wheel The ★
  S41......266 C3
Windlea Rd DE55......170 C6
WINDLEY......189 D7
Windley Cres DE22......204 F1
Windley Dr DE7......194 D3
Windley La
  Idridgehay DE56......176 E5

Windley La continued
  Turnditch DE56......177 A1
  Windley DE56......189 E7
WINDMILL......69 F8
Windmill Ave DE56......192 A8
Windmill Cl
  Bolsover S44......99 A3
  Castle Donington DE74...247 B2
  Elvaston DE24......233 D4
  Ockbrook DE72......221 C5
  3 Uttoxeter ST14......210 B1
Windmill Dr ST14......224 E3
Windmill Greenway S20..59 E5
Windmill Hill La DE22....218 C6
Windmill La
  Alderwasley DE56......166 F6
  Ashbourne DE6......173 C4
  Belper DE56......179 A4
  Eyam S32......71 C6
  Snelston DE6......184 E2
  Unstone S18......77 A6
Windmill Mdw DE21......220 D5
Windmill Rd DE65......229 B3
Windmill Rise
  Belper DE56......179 A5
  Somercotes DE55......170 D7
  South Normanton DE55...159 F5
Windmill St DE11......256 A1
Windmill View DE56......179 E8
Windmill Way S43......96 C8
Windrush Cl DE22......205 B5
Windrush Ct **4** S43......96 E8
Windrush Rd DE65......240 D8
Windses Est S32......53 D2
Windsmoor Rd NG16......182 D8
Windsor Ave
  Derby DE23......231 B8
  Melbourne DE73......252 A8
Windsor Cl
  6 Ashbourne DE6......173 D3
  Borrowash DE72......221 C1
  Chesterfield S40......95 C1
  Heanor DE75......181 E3
  Swadlincote DE11......256 A6
  Swanwick DE55......170 A7
  Trowell NG9......209 B5
Windsor Cres
  Ilkeston DE7......208 E4
  Stapleford NG9......223 E7
Windsor Ct
  Derby DE3......217 D3
  Long Eaton NG10......236 E7
  Sandiacre NG10......223 B4
  West Hallam DE7......207 D8
Windsor Dr
  Derby DE21......221 A6
  Dronfield S18......56 C1
  Wingerworth S42......114 E4
Windsor Park SK17......85 D8
Windsor Rd
  Buxton SK17......85 C8
  Linton DE12......261 D5
  Uttoxeter ST14......210 A1
Windsor St NG9......223 E7
Windsor Wlk **7** S41......96 C1
Windy Fields Rd S42......113 D7
Windy House La S2......44 A8
Windy Knowle SK22......25 A3
Windy La DE21......191 C1
Windyridge SK17......121 B6
Winfield Gr SK6......15 B1
WINGERWORTH......114 F4
Wingerworth Ave S8......56 E4
Wingerworth Cotts S42..115 E3
Wingerworth Park Rd
  DE21......220 E5
Wingerworth St S42......115 E3
Wingerworth Way S40....114 F7
Wingfield Cl **6** S18......56 C1
Wingfield Cres S12......44 C5
Wingfield Dr
  Derby DE21......205 F1
  Ilkeston DE7......194 D3
Wingfield Gr SK13......17 F7
Wingfield Hall DE55......157 F3
Wingfield Manor House ★
  DE55......157 E2
Wingfield Rd
  Alfreton DE55......158 E3
  Tupton S42......131 D8
Wingfield View S45......131 E4
Winhill Rd SK22......24 C1
Winkpenny La DE55......147 F5
Winnat Pl S43......97 C7
Winnats Cl
  Chesterfield S40......95 D5
  Glossop SK13......17 F8
Winnats Rd S33......37 E2
Winney Hill S26......61 E5
Winney La S26......61 E3
Winnings The S80......101 E8
Winnington Rd SK6......23 A7
Winn La DE6......174 F7
WINSHILL......248 B3
Winshill Village Prim Sch
  DE15......248 C3
WINSICK......115 E6
Winslow Ave SK14......9 A2
Winslow Gn DE21......220 C6
WINSTER......141 C5
Winster CE Prim Sch
  DE4......141 D6
Winster Cl
  Belper DE56......179 B5
  Clay Cross S42......131 A5
Winster Ct S41......96 A5
Winster Gn **3** DE11......255 E5
Winster Gr SK17......85 E7

Winster La DE4......140 F7
Winster Market House ★
  DE4......141 C6
Winster Mews SK13......9 E2
Winster Rd
  Derby DE21......205 E1
  Staveley S43......97 C8
Winster Sq SK17......85 E7
Winster Way NG10......235 F5
Winston Cl NG9......223 E8
Winterbourne Dr NG9....209 E1
Winter Closes NG16......171 F1
Wintercroft La DE6......161 E1
Wintergreen Dr DE23.....230 F6
Winyard Ct **9** S40......95 D5
Wire La DE55......148 B3
Wirestone La S45......129 A3
Wirksmoor Rd SK22......33 B7
WIRKSWORTH......165 E8
Wirksworth CE Inf Sch
  DE4......154 F1
Wirksworth Hall Gdns
  DE4......165 F8
Wirksworth Heritage Ctr ★
  DE4......154 F1
Wirksworth Ind Ctr DE4..154 E8
Wirksworth Inf Sch DE4..154 F1
Wirksworth Jun Sch
  DE4......155 A1
Wirksworth L Ctr DE4....165 F8
Wirksworth Rd
  Duffield DE56......190 B4
  Holloway DE4......156 B2
  Idridgehay DE56......176 F3
  Ilkeston DE7......208 C4
  Kirk Ireton DE6......165 B2
  Shottle DE56......177 C3
Wirksworth Sta ★ DE4...155 A1
Wisbech Cl S40......114 E8
Wisgreaves Rd DE24......232 F8
Wishing Stone Way DE4..143 E6
Wiston Way S41......115 C2
Witham Cl
  Chesterfield S41......96 C6
  Hilton DE65......228 C2
Witham Ct S40......95 C3
Witham Dr DE23......231 B5
Witney Cl DE24......232 C8
Witney St S8......43 A8
Wittering Cl NG10......236 E5
Witton Ct DE24......231 D4
Woburn Cl
  Blackwell DE55......147 E1
  Swanwick DE55......169 F7
Woburn Cotts DE4......143 B7
Woburn Croft NG10......223 A4
Woburn Ho DE55......147 E1
Woburn La NG19......135 C4
Woburn Pl
  Derby DE22......218 B5
  Pleasley NG19......135 C4
Woburn Rd NG19......135 C4
Wolds Rd DE4......143 D7
Wolds Rise DE4......143 C4
Wolfa St DE22......267 A2
Wolfcote Cl S45......131 D1
Wolfe Cl S40......95 D1
Wolfscote Dale DE11......255 F2
Wollaton Ave S17......56 A5
Wollaton Dr S17......56 A5
Wollaton Rd
  Derby DE21......219 F8
  Sheffield S17......56 A5
Wollaton Road N **5**
  DE21......205 F1
Wollen Cl S80......81 F1
Wolseley Rd **2** S8......43 A7
Wolverley Grange DE24..233 C8
Woodale Cl DE23......230 F6
WOODALL......61 C6
Woodall La S26......61 D6
Woodall Rd S21......60 F5
Wood Ave
  Creswell S80......81 D1
  Sandiacre NG10......223 A6
Woodbank Ct S17......56 A7
Woodbeck Ct DE21......206 B2
Woodbine Cl DE14......253 E6
Woodbine Terr SK23......47 A6
Woodborough Rd NG19..135 E1
Woodbourne Rd SK22.....33 A5
Woodbridge Cl
  Chellaston DE73......232 F1
  Heanor DE75......182 B1
Woodbridge Jun Sch
  DE55......159 A3
Woodbridge Rise S40.....114 B8
Woodbrook SK23......45 E8
Woodbrook Ct SK23......45 E7
Woodchester Dr DE24....233 D6
Wood Cl S42......114 D4
Woodcock Gr SK13......10 E1
Woodcock Rd SK13......11 A1
Woodcock Sq DE3......230 C8
Woodcote Way DE23......231 A7
WOODEND
  Disley......32 E8
  Hanbury......238 A1
Wood End DE4......156 B6
Wood End La DE73......244 D1
Wood End Rd DE75......181 E2
Woodfall La
  Duffield DE56......190 A1
  Windley DE22......189 E3
Wood Farm Ct NG11......237 D2
Wood Farm La DE11......256 E4
Woodfield Cl SK13......9 F5

Woodfield Dr
Ripley DE5 . . . .**170** A1
Swadlincote DE11 . . . .**256** C5
Woodfield Rd
Pinxton NG16 . . . .**160** D4
South Normanton DE55 . . .**159** F4
Woodford Rd DE22 . . . . . .**218** A7
Woodford Way S43 . . . .**78** B4
Woodgate Dr DE73 . . . .**233** A1
Wood Gdns SK22 . . . .**25** C3
Woodhall Dr DE23 . . . . . .**230** E8
Woodhall House Farm
S26 . . . .**61** C6
WOODHEAD
Crowden **7** C4
Littlemoor **130** E2
Woodhead La S45 . . . .**130** D1
Woodhead Rd
Glossop SK13 . . . .**10** D5
Holme HD9 . . . .**2** E6
Sheffield, Highfield S2 . . . .**43** A8
Tintwistle SK13 . . . .**10** B8
Woodhouse Ct NG19 . . . .**136** C2
Woodhouse La
Barlborough S43 . . . .**79** E5
Bolsover S44 . . . .**98** E3
Mastin Moor S43 . . . .**79** C5
Scropton DE65 . . . .**226** F7
South Normanton DE55 . . .**159** E5
Winster DE4 . . . .**141** C6
Woodhouse Rd
Kilburn DE56, DE7 . . . . . .**192** A7
6 Mansfield NG19 . . . . .**136** B1
Rowsley DE4 . . . .**126** F7
Sheffield S12 . . . .**44** B6
WOODHOUSES **252** A5
Woodhouse St DE11 . . . .**256** D3
Woodhouse Station Ent Ctr
NG19 . . . .**136** B3
Woodhurst Cl DE21 . . . .**219** D8
Wood La
Belper DE56 . . . .**190** F7
Church Warsop NG20 . . . .**120** F7
Creswell S80 . . . .**100** C8
Crich DE4 . . . .**157** B3
Hanbury DE13 . . . .**238** A4
Hayfield SK22 . . . .**25** C3
Holloway DE4 . . . .**144** A1
Horsley Woodhouse DE7 . .**192** D5
Ible DE4 . . . .**153** E6
Idridgehay DE6, DE56 . . . .**176** E8
Kniveton DE6 . . . .**163** A1
Pleasley NG19 . . . .**119** D1
Ripley DE5 . . . .**169** A4
Scarcliffe S44 . . . .**118** F6
Shirebrook NG19 . . . .**119** E1
Swadlincote DE11 . . . .**256** A7
Woodland Ave
Borrowash DE72 . . . .**221** C2
Breaston DE72 . . . .**235** F8
Ilkeston DE7 . . . .**194** D4
Sutton in Ashfield NG17 . .**148** E4
Woodland Dr
Rocester ST14 . . . .**196** F3
Scropton DE6 . . . .**226** A4
Sheffield S12 . . . .**44** B2
Woodland Gr
Barlborough S43 . . . .**80** A6
Clay Cross S42 . . . .**131** B6
Clowne S43 . . . .**81** A4
Mansfield Woodhouse
NG19 . . . .**136** C4
Woodland Pl S17 . . . .**55** F5
Woodland Rd
Derby DE22 . . . .**218** E8
Mansfield NG19 . . . .**136** F1
Sheffield S8 . . . .**43** B3
Swadlincote DE15 . . . .**255** B4
Woodlands
Brimington S43 . . . .**96** D7
Great Longstone DE45 . . . .**89** F3
Nottingham NG16 . . . .**160** E3
Wirksworth DE4 . . . .**165** E8
Woodlands Ave
Breaston DE72 . . . .**235** F8
Derby DE24 . . . .**232** E4
Woodlands Brow DE6 . .**173** D4
Woodlands Cl
Glossop SK13 . . . .**9** F6
Little Eaton DE21 . . . .**205** B8
Melbourne DE73 . . . .**252** A8
Thorpe DE6 . . . .**161** D1
Woodlands Cres DE12 . .**262** B4

Woodlands La
Chellaston DE73 . . . .**245** A8
Quarndon DE22 . . . .**204** D6
Woodlands Rd
Chapel-en-le-Frith SK23 . . .**47** B4
Derby DE22 . . . .**204** E5
High Lane SK12 . . . .**32** A6
New Mills SK22 . . . .**33** A8
Overseal DE12 . . . .**262** B4
Woodlands Sch DE22 . . . .**204** D4
Woodlands The
5 Mansfield NG19 . . . . .**136** B1
Melbourne DE73 . . . .**252** B8
Tatenhill DE13 . . . .**253** A8
Whaley Thorns NG20 . . . .**101** A3
Woodlands View DE7 . . .**193** A2
Woodlands Way DE73 . . .**252** B8
Woodlands Yd DE73 . . . .**245** A8
Woodland View
Buxton SK17 . . . .**85** C8
Chilcote DE12 . . . .**264** F3
Crich DE4 . . . .**167** E8
Hathersage S32 . . . .**53** A7
Horwich End SK23 . . . .**45** F2
Sheffield, Abbeydale Park
S17 . . . .**56** A7
Sheffield, Charnock Hill S12 **44** B2
Whaley Thorns NG20 . . . .**101** A3
Woodland Views ST14 . .**224** E2
Woodland Way
Clay Cross S42 . . . .**131** B6
Eastwood NG16 . . . .**182** E2
Woodland Wlk S40 . . . . . .**94** F5
Woodlea Gr DE21 . . . . . .**205** C8
Woodlea Rd SK13 . . . .**17** B7
Woodleigh Cl S40 . . . .**94** F5
WOODLINKIN **181** E6
Woodmans Croft DE65 . .**227** C1
Woodmere Dr S41 . . . .**77** C4
Woodminton Dr DE73 . . .**232** F3
WOODNOOK **94** E5
Woodnook Cl S42 . . . .**95** A4
Wood Nook Cl NG16 . . . .**171** F6
Woodnook Gr S21 . . . .**58** E2
Woodnook La S42 . . . .**94** F5
Woodnook Way S42 . . . . . .**94** F4
Woodpecker Hill DE7 . . .**208** A2
Wood Rd
Derby, Chaddesden
DE21 . . . .**220** A8
Derby, Oakwood DE21 . . . .**205** F1
Derby, Spondon DE7 . . . . .**221** A6
Woodridge The DE56 . . .**190** F6
Woodrising Cl DE21 . . . .**206** B3
Woodroffe Wlk DE23 . . .**231** E7
Woodrove Ave S13 . . . .**44** B7
Woodrove Cl S13 . . . .**44** B7
Woodseat Gr ST14 . . . . . .**197** A4
WOODSEATS **16** A6
Woodseats La SK13 . . . . . .**16** B6
Woodshop La DE73 . . . . . .**244** D6
Wood's Hospl SK13 . . . . . .**10** C3
WOODSIDE **192** D4
Woodside
Buxton SK17 . . . .**85** C7
Carsington DE4 . . . .**164** E7
Eastwood NG16 . . . .**182** E3
Horsley DE7 . . . .**192** D3
Woodside Ave
Holmesfield S18 . . . .**75** A8
Killamarsh S21 . . . .**60** F7
Ripley DE5 . . . .**180** D8
Woodside Cl
Bakewell DE45 . . . .**109** D5
Chesterfield S40 . . . .**95** B4
Woodside Cres
Ilkeston DE7 . . . .**194** D5
Long Eaton NG10 . . . .**236** B8
Woodside Dr
Bakewell DE45 . . . .**109** D5
Derby DE22 . . . .**205** A4
Woodside Pl S45 . . . .**131** B4
Woodside Rd
Sandiacre NG10 . . . .**223** B5
Shirebrook NG20 . . . .**119** C5
Shireoaks S81 . . . .**63** F7
Woodside St SK22 . . . .**33** B6
Woodside View S18 . . . . . .**75** A8
Woods La
Burton upon Trent, Stapenhill
DE15 . . . .**254** F8
Derby DE22 . . . .**267** A1
Woods Mdw DE72 . . . . . .**233** D5
Woodsome Pk S42 . . . . . .**116** D1

Woodsorrel Dr DE21 . . . .**206** B3
Wood St
Alfreton DE55 . . . .**159** C5
Codnor DE5 . . . .**181** B8
Derby DE1 . . . .**267** C4
Eastwood NG16 . . . .**182** F3
Glossop SK13 . . . .**17** C8
Hollingworth SK14 . . . .**9** D5
Holmewood S42 . . . .**116** E1
Ilkeston DE7 . . . .**194** F1
New Mills SK22 . . . .**33** B7
Ripley DE5 . . . .**169** D2
Somercotes DE55 . . . .**170** C8
Swadlincote DE11 . . . .**256** B2
Wirksworth DE4 . . . .**165** F8
Woodstock Cl DE22 . . . .**204** D4
Woodstock Ct **5** S41 . . . .**96** A6
Woodstock Dr S41 . . . . . .**115** C8
Woodstock Rd NG9 . . . . .**223** F3
Woodstock Rise S41 . . . .**115** C8
Wood Street N DE55 . . . .**159** C5
Woodthorne Ave DE24 . .**232** E4
WOODTHORPE **79** C2
Woodthorpe Ave
Clay Cross S45 . . . .**131** A4
Derby, Chaddesden DE21 . .**219** F6
Woodthorpe CE Prim Sch
S43 . . . .**79** C1
Woodthorpe Cl S44 . . . . . .**98** F7
Woodthorpe Com Prim Sch
S13 . . . .**44** C7
Woodthorpe Cres S13 . . .**44** C8
Woodthorpe Rd
Sheffield S13 . . . .**44** C7
Shuttlewood S44 . . . .**98** F8
Staveley S43 . . . .**79** C2
Woodvale Cl S40 . . . .**114** A8
Wood View S21 . . . .**79** A8
Woodview Cl S42 . . . .**114** F2
Woodview Gdns DE22 . . .**218** F8
Wood View Ho S21 . . . .**59** C3
Woodview Rd DE11 . . . . .**255** E5
WOODVILLE **256** E3
Woodville CE Jun Sch
DE11 . . . .**256** F2
Woodville Inf Sch DE11 . .**256** F2
Woodville Rd
Hartshorne DE11 . . . .**257** A5
Overseal DE12 . . . .**262** B4
Woodwards Cl DE72 . . . .**221** D1
Woodward's Pl DE11 . . . .**256** C3
Woodward Way DE11 . . .**256** D4
Woodyard Cl DE11 . . . . . .**255** F1
Woodyard La DE65 . . . . .**226** F5
Wooley Cl S42 . . . .**131** B7
Wooliscroft Wy DE7 . . . .**194** C2
Woollaton La SK17 . . . . . .**138** D2
WOOLLEY **145** E5
Woolley Bridge Rd
Glossop SK13 . . . .**9** F5
Hadfield SK13 . . . .**9** F5
Woolley Cl SK14 . . . .**9** D4
Woolley La SK14 . . . .**9** D4
Woolley Mill La SK13 . . . .**9** E7
WOOLLEY MOOR **145** D7
Woolley Rd DE4 . . . .**143** B6
Woolley's Yd DE4 . . . .**141** C6
Woolrych St DE23 . . . . . .**218** F8
Woolsthorpe Cres DE7 . .**208** D4
Woolstitch Pk DE12 . . . .**264** E7
Woosnam Cl DE14 . . . . . .**254** A6
Worcester Ave NG19 . . . .**136** C6
Worcester Cl S45 . . . .**131** E4
Worcester Cres DE21 . . .**219** E8
Worcester Gr SK13 . . . . . .**17** F8
Worcester Mews NG19 . .**136** C6
Worcester Rd DE15 . . . . .**254** E6
Wordsworth Ave
Derby DE24 . . . .**231** F5
Mansfield Woodhouse
NG19 . . . .**136** B4
Swadlincote DE11 . . . .**256** C6
Wordsworth Dr DE24 . . .**232** A5
Wordsworth Pl S18 . . . . . .**76** C7
Wordsworth Rd
Awsworth NG16 . . . .**195** C5
Chesterfield S41 . . . .**95** F8
Works La S44 . . . .**97** B3
Worksop Rd
Mastin Moor S43 . . . .**79** D4
Thorpe Salvin S80 . . . .**62** E7
Whitwell S80 . . . .**81** F6
Works Rd S43 . . . .**78** B2
WORMHILL **68** C1

Worrall Ave NG10 . . . . . .**223** E1
Worthington La DE73 . . .**252** F1
Wortley Ave NG9 . . . .**209** D3
Wortley Cl DE7 . . . .**209** A8
Wortley Ct S33 . . . .**51** B7
Wragley Way DE24 . . . . . .**231** D2
Wreakes La S18 . . . .**56** F2
Wren Cl DE11 . . . .**256** F3
Wren Ct NG10 . . . .**236** A3
Wren Nest Cl SK13 . . . . . .**17** B8
Wren Nest Rd SK13 . . . . . .**10** B1
Wren Nest Ret Pk SK13 . .**10** B1
Wren Nest Terr SK13 . . . .**10** C1
Wren Park Cl
Belper DE56 . . . .**178** E5
Chesterfield S40 . . . .**114** F7
Eckington S12 . . . .**58** E8
Findern DE65 . . . .**230** D1
Wren Park Prim Sch
DE3 . . . .**218** A2
Wrenpark Rd S42 . . . .**114** D4
Wren Way DE3 . . . .**230** B7
Wretham Cl DE3 . . . .**230** D8
Wright Ave DE5 . . . .**169** F1
Wright Cres DE6 . . . .**185** D8
Wright St DE5 . . . .**181** B8
Wroxham Cl DE24 . . . . . .**232** D4
Wulfic Cl S2 . . . .**43** F8
Wulfric Pl S2 . . . .**43** F8
Wulfric Rd
Eckington S21 . . . .**59** C3
Sheffield S2 . . . .**44** A8
WYASTON **185** D2
Wyaston Cl DE22 . . . .**204** E1
Wyaston Ct DE6 . . . .**185** D1
Wyaston Gdns DE6 . . . . .**185** D7
Wyaston Rd DE6 . . . .**185** C6
Wyatts Way DE5 . . . .**169** F3
Wyatville Ave SK17 . . . . . .**84** E5
Wybersley Rd SK6 . . . .**32** A8
Wychwood Dr NG9 . . . . .**209** D2
Wycliffe Rd DE55 . . . .**159** A4
Wycombe Grange NG19 .**136** F2
Wye Bank DE45 . . . .**109** E5
Wye Bank Gr DE45 . . . . . .**109** E4
Wye Cl DE65 . . . .**240** D8
Wye Croft Ct DE45 . . . . . .**109** D5
Wye Dale DE11 . . . .**255** F2
Wyedale Cl
Bakewell DE45 . . . .**109** E4
Buxton SK17 . . . .**85** B6
Wyedale Cres DE45 . . . . .**109** E4
Wyedale Ct **5** S41 . . . . . .**95** E7
Wyedale Dr DE45 . . . .**109** E4
Wyedale View DE45 . . . . .**109** E4
Wye Gr SK17 . . . .**85** A7
Wye Head Cl SK17 . . . .**84** F7
Wye Ho SK17 . . . .**66** B1
Wyelands Cl SK17 . . . .**84** F7
Wye Mill SK17 . . . .**89** A6
Wye St
Buxton SK17 . . . .**85** C8
Derby DE24 . . . .**233** A8
Wye Terr DE4 . . . .**126** F8
Wylam Cl S45 . . . .**131** D5
Wyming Brook Dr S10 . . .**42** B8
Wyndale Dr DE7 . . . .**208** C6
Wyndham Cres DE15 . . . .**248** C3
Wyndham St DE24 . . . . . .**233** A7
Wynd The S21 . . . .**79** C7
Wynton Ave DE24 . . . . . .**232** F8
Wyntor Ave DE4 . . . .**141** C6
Wynyard Cl DE7 . . . .**194** C3
Wysall Cl NG19 . . . .**135** E1
Wystan Ct DE65 . . . .**242** D2
Wyston Brook DE65 . . . .**228** D1
Wythburn Rd S41 . . . .**95** C7
Wyver La DE56 . . . .**178** F6
Wyvern Ave NG10 . . . . . .**236** D5
Wyvern Bsns Pk DE21 . . . .**220** A4
Wyvern Cl
Eastwood NG16 . . . .**195** A8
Matlock DE4 . . . .**143** A6
Wyvern Gdns S17 . . . .**55** E6
Wyvernside DE21 . . . .**219** F4
Wyvern Way DE21 . . . . . .**220** A4

Y

Yard Cl DE11 . . . .**256** B4
Yardley Cl DE55 . . . .**169** F8
Yardley Way DE56 . . . . . .**179** D4
Yard The **4** SK13 . . . .**10** C1

Yarmouth Ho DE24 . . . . .**233** C7
Yarncliff Cl S40 . . . .**95** D5
Yarrow Cl
Burton upon Trent DE15 . .**248** B2
Derby DE21 . . . .**231** E2
Yarwell Cl DE21 . . . .**205** D1
Yates Ave DE72 . . . .**246** A7
Yates Rd SK22 . . . .**33** C7
Yates St DE23 . . . .**219** A1
Yeardsley Ave SK23 . . . . .**33** D3
Yeardsley Gn SK23 . . . . . .**45** D8
Yeardsley La SK23 . . . . . .**33** D3
YEAVELEY **199** D5
Yeld Cl DE45 . . . .**109** C4
YELDERSLEY CI S40 . . . . .**95** B5
YELDERSLEY HOLLIES . . .**186** F4
Yeldersley La
Brailsford DE6 . . . .**187** B2
Osmaston DE6 . . . .**186** E6
Yeld Rd DE45 . . . .**109** D5
Yeld The DE45 . . . .**109** C5
Yelt La DE6 . . . .**224** D8
Yeoman Park Sch NG19 . .**136** C4
Yeoman St DE4 . . . .**142** D1
Yeovil Cl DE24 . . . .**233** C7
Yerley Hill DE6 . . . .**172** C6
Yewdale Gr DE21 . . . .**206** C3
Yews Cl DE73 . . . .**233** A1
Yew Tree Ave DE72 . . . . .**221** D5
Yew Tree Cl
Ashover S45 . . . .**129** F3
Darley Dale DE4 . . . .**127** B3
Derby DE24 . . . .**233** C7
Yew Tree Cotts DE72 . . .**222** E3
Yewtree Cres DE15 . . . . .**254** F7
Yew Tree Ct DE65 . . . . . .**227** C2
Yew Tree Dr
Chesterfield S40 . . . .**114** A8
Clay Cross S42 . . . .**131** B6
Killamarsh S21 . . . .**60** C5
Shirebrook NG20 . . . .**119** D5
Sutton in Ashfield NG17 . .**148** F2
Yew Tree Gdns DE12 . . . .**260** C6
Yew Tree Hill DE4 . . . . . .**156** B5
Yew Tree La
Bradley DE6 . . . .**186** E8
Elvaston DE72 . . . .**233** F4
Yewtree Rd DE11 . . . .**255** F7
Yew Tree Rd
Hatton DE65 . . . .**227** D1
Rosliston DE12 . . . .**260** C6
Yokecliffe Ave DE4 . . . . .**165** E8
Yokecliffe Cres DE4 . . . .**165** E8
Yokecliffe Dr DE4 . . . . . .**165** E8
Yokecliffe Hill DE4 . . . . .**165** E8
Yokecliffe La DE4 . . . . . .**165** E8
York Ave
Jacksdale NG16 . . . .**171** B4
Sandiacre NG10 . . . .**223** A5
York Cl DE11 . . . .**256** D6
York Cres DE4 . . . .**117** E1
Yorke St NG19 . . . .**136** B2
York Pl
North Wingfield S42 . . . . .**132** B7
Shireoaks S81 . . . .**63** F7
York Rd
Derby DE21 . . . .**219** F7
Long Eaton NG10 . . . .**223** C1
Shirebrook NG20 . . . .**119** E3
Swadlincote DE11 . . . .**256** B2
Yorkshire Way SK13 . . . . .**17** F8
York St
Chesterfield S41 . . . .**115** C7
Derby DE1 . . . .**218** E5
Glossop SK13 . . . .**10** E1
York Terr SK13 . . . .**17** C8
YOULGREAVE **125** B5
Youlgreave Cl DE21 . . . .**205** F1
Youlgreave Cres SK13 . . . .**9** D1
Youlgreave Dr S12 . . . . . .**44** D5
Young St DE23 . . . .**218** F1
Yoxall Dr DE22 . . . .**218** C4
Ypres Rd DE22 . . . .**204** C2

Z

Zetland Cres DE24 . . . . .**231** C2
Zion Ho DE11 . . . .**256** C1